Praise for Volker Ullrich's

Hitler

A *Time* Top Ten Nonfiction Book of the Year

An *Air Mail* Best Book of the Year

"The impulsiveness and grandiosity, the bullying and vulgarity, were obvious from the beginning; if anything, they accounted for Adolf Hitler's anti-establishment appeal. . . . Ullrich argues that the very qualities that accounted for the dictator's astonishing rise were also what brought about his ultimate ruin." —*The New York Times*

"Ullrich's work is much more than just a biography. It is a work of synthesis, certainly, but a thorough and thoroughly readable one nonetheless, which stands muster alongside Hitler's most significant earlier biographers: Bullock, Toland, Fest and Kershaw." —*BBC History*

"Ullrich's work is a remarkable treatise on the malevolence of power in modern times. Take care, lest we fall into the trap of autocracy." —*New York Journal of Books*

"The reader who plunges in is rewarded with insight, understanding, fine judgements and read-me narrative drive." —*Daily Mail* (London)

"Magisterial. . . . Lucidly formulated for a new generation of readers and scholars." —*Library Journal*

"An endlessly revealing look at the Nazi regime that touches on large issues and small details alike." —*Kirkus Reviews* (starred review)

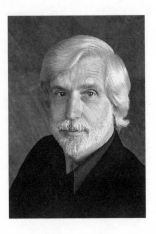

Volker Ullrich

Hitler

Volker Ullrich is a historian and journalist whose previous books in German include biographies of Bismarck and Napoleon, as well as a major study of Imperial Germany, *Die nervöse Grossmacht 1871–1918* (The Nervous Superpower). From 1990 to 2009, Ullrich was the editor of the political book review section of the influential weekly newspaper *Die Zeit*. He lives in Germany.

ALSO BY VOLKER ULLRICH

Hitler: Ascent 1889–1939

Hitler

Hitler

Downfall 1939–1945

VOLKER ULLRICH

TRANSLATED FROM THE GERMAN BY

Jefferson Chase

VINTAGE BOOKS

A Division of Penguin Random House LLC

New York

FIRST VINTAGE BOOKS EDITION, SEPTEMBER 2021

Translation copyright © 2020 by Jefferson Chase

All rights reserved. Published in the United States
by Vintage Books, a division of Penguin Random House LLC, New York,
and distributed in Canada by Penguin Random House Canada Ltd., Toronto.
Originally published in Germany as *Adolf Hitler: Die Jahre des Untergangs* by S. Fisher
Verlag GmbH, Frankfurt am Main, in 2018. Copyright © 2018 by Volker Ullrich.
This translation originally published in hardcover in Great Britain by The Bodley
Head, an imprint of the Random House Group Limited, London, and subsequently
in hardcover in the United States by Alfred A. Knopf, a division of Penguin Random
House LLC, New York, in 2020. Published by arrangement with The Bodley
Head, a division of the Random House Group Ltd., London.

Vintage and colophon are registered trademarks
of Penguin Random House LLC.

The Library of Congress has cataloged the Knopf edition as follows:
Names: Ullrich, Volker, author. | Chase, Jefferson S., translator.
Title: Hitler: downfall, 1939–1945 / Volker Ullrich ; translated from
the German by Jefferson Chase.
Other titles: Adolf Hitler: die Jahre des Untergangs 1939–1945. English.
Downfall 1939–1945.
Description: London : The Bodley Head, 2020. |
Includes bibliographical references and index.
Identifiers: LCCN 2019053386 (print) | LCCN 2019053387 (ebook)
Subjects: LCSH: Hitler, Adolf, 1889–1945—Political and social views. | Hitler, Adolf,
1889–1945—Influence. | Germany—Politics and government—1933–1945. |
National socialism. | Heads of state—Germany—Biography. |
World War, 1939–1945—Campaigns.
Classification: LCC DD247.H5 U45413 2020 | DDC 943.086092 B—dc23
LC record available at https://lccn.loc.gov/2019053386
LC ebook record available at https://lccn.loc.gov/2019053387

Vintage Books Trade Paperback ISBN: 978-1-101-87206-2
eBook ISBN: 978-1-101-87401-1

Author photograph © Roswitha Hecke

www.vintagebooks.com

Printed in the United States of America
10 9 8 7 6 5 4 3 2 1

Contents

CONTENTS

Illustrations

Hitler with Ribbentrop in Poland, 13 September 1939 (*Bayerische Staatsbibliothek München/Bildarchiv*).

Georg Elser after his arrest (*Bayerische Staatsbibliothek München/Bildarchiv*).

The triumphant Hitler in his Wolf's Ravine headquarters, 17 June 1940 (*ullstein bild/Walter Frentz*).

Reception for Hitler and Mussolini in Munich, 18 June 1940 (*Bayerische Staatsbibliothek München/Bildarchiv*).

Hitler promoting his generals, 14 August 1940 (*ullstein bild/Süddeutsche Zeitung*).

Hitler's order for Operation Barbarossa, 18 December 1940 (*Bundesarchiv RM 7/962, Bl. 209*).

Hitler and his court in the Wolf's Lair headquarters, 24 June 1941.

German troops invading the Soviet Union (*Bildarchiv Preussischer Kulturbesitz*).

Holding camp for Soviet POWs in the early stages of Operation Barbarossa (*Bundesarchiv 183-B21845/Wahner*).

Team of horses struggling through the mud at Kursk, March 1942 (*Bundesarchiv 101 I-289-1091-26/Dinstühler*).

Hitler and Eva Braun with the daughter of Braun's friend Herta Schneider, 1 May 1942.

Hitler and Himmler on the Obersalzberg, 3 April 1944 (*ullstein bild/ Walter Frentz*).

Hitler with Stauffenberg in the Wolf's Lair, 15 July 1944 (*ullstein bild*).

Hitler with Mussolini in the destroyed situation room, 20 July 1944 (*Bundesarchiv 146-1969-071A-03*).

Hitler delivering his radio address after the assassination attempt, 20 July 1944 (*ullstein bild*).

Hitler's final New Year's reception in his Eagle's Nest headquarters, 1 January 1945 (*SZ Bildarchiv, Sammlung Megele/Süddeutsche Zeitung Photo*).

The aged dictator with magnifying glass (*ullstein bild/Heinrich Hoffmann*).

East Prussian refugees crossing the frozen Vistula Lagoon, early January 1945 (*ullstein bild*).

Hitler poring over a model of his hometown of Linz, February 1945 (*ullstein bild*).

Situation meeting in Harnekop Palace, 3 March 1945 (*ullstein bild*).

Hitler's final public appearance, receiving Hitler Youth members in the Chancellery garden, 20 March 1945 (*Bayerische Staatsbibliothek München/Bildarchiv*).

Hitler inspecting the damage to the New Reich Chancellery, late March 1945 (*Bayerische Staatsbibliothek München/Bildarchiv*).

Every effort has been made to trace and contact copyright holders. The publishers will be pleased to correct any mistakes or omissions in future editions.

Hitler

Introduction

The first volume of this biography concerned Hitler's time of "ascent." It described how an obscure private in the First World War worked his way up in the 1920s to become the undisputed leader, the Führer, of the racist and nationalist right in Germany; how he got hold of the levers of power thanks to an alliance with conservative elites in January 1933; and how after establishing his dictatorship, he dismantled the Treaty of Versailles piece by piece, gradually moving from a politics of revision to a politics of expansion. That part of Hitler's story concluded with his fiftieth birthday celebrations, replete with enormous pomp, on 20 April 1939. At the time, his meteoric rise seemed unstoppable. Yet, as a number of acute contemporary observers recognised, his fall had already begun. Nemesis was knocking at his door.

The second volume of this biography covers Hitler's "years of downfall." It encompasses the relatively brief period from his unleashing of the Second World War in the summer of 1939 to his suicide in the air-raid bunker of the Reich Chancellery in the spring of 1945. It has been said, correctly, that Hitler and National Socialism "found themselves" in the war.[1] As a magnifying glass does with sunlight, armed conflict focused the criminal dynamics of the Nazi regime and the man at its head. War gave Hitler the opportunity to act on his ideological obsessions and realise his homicidal aims: the conquering of "living space in the east" as a basis for German domination of first Europe, then the world; and the removal of Jews from Germany and, if possible, the whole European continent. On the other hand, as we will see, Hitler would never have been able to realise these goals as much as he did without willing helpers in almost all the institutions of the Nazi state and broad parts of German society.

In war, we see Hitler in a new role, that of a military commander. After Germany's unexpectedly swift victory over France in May and June 1940 at the very least, Hitler was not just nominally, but also practically Germany's commander-in-chief. He increasingly reserved the right to make final decisions about the planning and execution of military operations, thereby reducing the influence of the professional officers in the general staff. From that point on, he devoted the lion's share of his time and energy to discussing the military situation in his ever-changing series of headquarters. In a sense, he only served "part time" as Nazi Party leader and German chancellor.[2] In keeping with this, a considerable part of this book will be dedicated to the military history of the Second World War.[3]

In their post-1945 memoirs, Germany's generals rejected any responsibility for the country's military defeat. The war could have been won, they argued, had the "dilettante" Hitler not got involved and botched things. One star witness for this point of view was a former head of the general staff, Franz Halder. By the summer of 1946, the Americans had already engaged him to work for the German department of the Historical Division in the US Army Center of Military History, in the hope that the expertise of Wehrmacht commanders would be useful in the incipient Cold War with the Soviet Union. In a pamphlet published in 1949, Halder denied that Hitler had any military talent whatsoever, dismissing him as "not a military leader in the German sense" and "by no means a field commander." Unable to temper his demonic determination, Halder added, Hitler had repeatedly disregarded the limits of what was possible militarily and caused the German catastrophe.[4] One obvious function of that narrative of the strategically incompetent Führer, divorced from all reality, was to exonerate people like Halder himself. Blaming Hitler alone for all mistakes removed the need to discuss one's own shortcomings. Yet Hitler was not at all as incompetent in military matters as the German military leadership claimed after 1945.

The course of the Second World War directly reflected the man who started it. Hitler's hostile personality and conviction that Germany needed additional "living space" made war inevitable, and at the start of the conflict, his tendency to go for broke and act in surprising and outrageous ways worked astonishingly well on the battlefield. Those same qualities, however, also proved his undoing because they led him to overstretch himself—there is no way to understand the key moments in the conflict, Operation Barbarossa and declaring war on the United States, except as consequences of Hitler's personality. Meanwhile, his role as field commander gradually overwhelmed him so that he could no longer call upon useful traits such as strategic flexibility or ruthless realism. And once things began going wrong, they rapidly spiraled out of control, as Hitler's alternately hot-headed and intransigent responses—constantly dismissing his military professionals, ruling out tactical retreats—only made the situation worse. By the conclusion of the war, the catastrophe he wreaked on Germany, with the support of the German people, was mirrored by the physical and psychological catastrophe he wreaked on himself. Germany ended up in ruins, just as its Führer ended his life as a complete wreck.

In no way does this make Hitler or a small group of Nazi "elites" exclusively responsible for German atrocities between 1939 and 1945. Like most high-ranking Nazi functionaries, German generals styled themselves as victims of Hitler who had not been able to override his commands; and they laid the blame for crimes against humanity in Poland and the Soviet Union squarely at the feet of Himmler and Heydrich's SS death squads, the Einsatzgruppen. The Wehrmacht leadership and the units under their command, it was claimed, knew nothing of the atrocities. It was not until two widely visited historical exhibitions staged by the Hamburg Institute for Social Research in 1995 and 2001 that the myth of the Wehrmacht's "clean hands," tenaciously maintained for decades, was finally discredited.[5] In the wake of the fierce debates that followed, in particular after the first exhibition, historians published a series of studies proving beyond doubt that numerous Wehrmacht units were involved in Nazi crimes against humanity.[6] Today, there is no longer any debate among historians about the character of Nazi Germany's campaign against the Soviet Union, Operation Barbarossa, as a historically unprecedented, racially motivated war of conquest and annihilation.

This all means that, by necessity, this volume will pay special attention to the relationship between Hitler and the Wehrmacht elites. How did the commander-in-chief exercise his role as supreme leader, and in what ways was the general staff involved in his strategic decisions? To what extent did Germany's generals support Hitler's criminal aims, and what efforts did they make to either promote or hinder them? Did relations between the Führer and his military leaders change over the course of the war and, if so, what caused that change?

At the centre of this book is also what the National Socialists called the "final solution to the Jewish question"—the genocide of European Jews. This atrocity was unique in human history because, as Eberhard Jäckel put it in 1986 amid a highly publicised debate among West German historians, "never before had a state, authorised by its leader, decided and announced that it was going to wipe out a certain group of people, including the elderly, women, children and infants, and then used all imaginable instruments of power to carry out that decision."[7]

For decades after the end of the Second World War, Holocaust research remained a relatively neglected area of history, and it is no accident that in his celebrated Hitler biography of 1973 Joachim Fest devoted only scant attention to the topic.[8] It was only in the 1990s, with the belated reception of Raul Hilberg's *The Destruction of the European Jews*, originally published in 1961, that Holocaust studies established itself as a major branch of German history. Since then, remembrance of this unique crime against humanity has been at the core of both the German and the international culture of memory.[9]

Today, the literature on the Holocaust is almost impossible to survey. The year 2008 saw the beginning of a sixteen-volume edition of documents on the persecution and murder of Europe's Jews by Nazi Germany that aims to take a comprehensive look at all European countries involved in the Shoah.[10] In particular, recent research has yielded two main insights. First, the circle of direct German and Austrian perpetrators was much larger than was long assumed: historians now put their number at between 200,000 and 250,000 people. In addition, millions of others directly profited from the destruction of the Jews. Second, Hitler never issued a written order to commence the genocide. The Holocaust developed from the complex interaction between, on the one hand, the central authority in Berlin and, on the other, SS, German police and Wehrmacht units operating on the periphery of the area under German control in the east. At the same time, more attention is also being paid to collaborators, particularly in the occupied countries of eastern Europe.

Yet while it is important not to restrict our perspective to Hitler and the direct executioners of his insane and genocidal ideas, Himmler and Heydrich, we should not downplay the role of the dictator at the centre of the decision-making process in pushing forward and legitimising the Holocaust. The present book seeks to define Hitler's specific contribution to the Holocaust as precisely as possible by showing when, how and with what results he intervened and accelerated the genocide.

To that end, this book retains the approach employed in the first volume. The focus will be on Hitler's person and the fateful role he played, without which neither the course of the war nor Germany's road to the Holocaust can be adequately described and understood. For that reason, it is crucial to trace the depths of his character—those complexes, obsessions and homicidal urges that determined how he thought and behaved.

Just as research into the perpetrators of Nazi crimes draws on the history of various European societies during the Second World War, so a biography of Hitler must also link his life to the social history of the Third Reich. Especially during the war, the National Socialists depended on the heightened mobilisation of all sections of society. Considerable attention, therefore, needs to be paid to social context. This book will continually ask how the German populace reacted to the course of the war and what effects it had on the levels of acceptance and popularity of the Führer.

One important source of that sort of information is the SS Security Service's secret reports about the popular mood, the "Meldungen aus den Reich." They remained surprisingly true to their stated aim of providing the leadership of the Nazi Party and the state with an unvarnished picture of what ordinary Germans were thinking and feeling.[11] In addition, like the previous volume, this book will seek to include as broad a spectrum as possible of contemporary voices. They include admirers and followers of Hitler, first and foremost Propaganda Minister Joseph Goebbels, whose extensive diaries represent a key document not just for Hitler's biography but for the entire history of the Third Reich.[12] But we will also not neglect the "little people," such as Lore Walb, a young student of German literature who like millions of other Germans believed in "her Führer" to the bitter end.[13] Conversely, we also hear amply from Hitler detractors like the writer Thomas Mann, who followed and commented on events in Germany from exile in the United States; the Jewish former university lecturer Victor Klemperer, who survived the nightmare years of the Third Reich in Dresden thanks to his marriage to a Gentile woman; and a former general director of the Krupp company, Wilhelm Muehlon, who had emigrated to Switzerland during the First World War out of disgust for the jingoistic nationalism of Wilhelmine Germany.[14]

A truly excellent source is the wartime diaries of Friedrich Kellner, which were first published in 2011.[15] Kellner was a court official in the western German town of Laubach and attentively monitored the National Socialist press while recording things he overheard or was told by friends. His diaries show that it was entirely possible for normal people in small-town Germany to see through the lies of Nazi propaganda and learn of things like the "euthanasia" murders of patients in psychiatric institutions and the mass executions carried out in occupied parts of eastern Europe.

A recently published collection of diplomatic correspondence contains a wealth of important material on the views of foreign observers[16] and this volume also makes use of the insightful notes of Ivan Maisky's, the Soviet ambassador in London, which were discovered in Russian archives.[17] Taken together, these sources provide a kaleidoscope of ideas and attitudes, interpretations and misapprehensions—and astonishingly accurate estimations of what would happen in Hitler's dictatorship during the war.

This biography will continue to proceed more or less chronologically with the occasional analytic interruptions. Thus, the chapter "Total War and Ethnic-Popular Community," for example, examines how successful Hitler and his paladins were in mobilising the loyalty of the masses even as defeat became more and more inevitable, air raids on German cities were stepped up and all manner of necessities grew ever scarcer.

The chapter "Decline of a Dictator" summarises the changes in Hitler's personality over the course of the war. It proceeds from the assumption that the decisive turn of Germany's military fortunes came not, as often asserted, with the capitulation of the 6th Army in Stalingrad in late January/early February 1943, but much earlier with the failure of Operation Barbarossa to bring about a quick defeat of the Soviet Union in the autumn and winter of 1941. How did military setbacks affect the self-image and physical and mental constitution of a dictator so accustomed to success? How did he manage to preserve his rule and prevent the rise of rivals while he increasingly avoided appearing in public and became virtually invisible for the vast majority of his "ethnic-popular comrades"?

The chapter on "The Berghof during the War" continues a theme I explored in the first volume. Notwithstanding arguments that, given the monstrous dimensions of Hitler's crimes, any attempt to depict the "private Hitler" is superfluous or even inappropriate, it is impossible to cleanly distinguish the dictator's private life from the political and military sphere. On the contrary, both arenas were interwoven to an unusual degree, and this was most vividly apparent in Hitler's Alpine retreat, the Berghof. It was here, among circles of intimates, that the dictator sought to preserve the vestige of a private sphere even as the war took its course. On the other hand, the Berghof was also the site of numerous discussions of military strategy, of decisions about how to wage the war and advance his genocidal obsessions. By looking at Hitler's Alpine world, we can see how fluid the boundary was between idyllic pretence and criminal reality.

The final chapters are devoted to the apocalyptic last days of the Third Reich. They seek to show how Hitler consciously staged his own downfall and what mythical images and models he called upon. In so doing, we will draw connections between developments at the front and the domestic situation in the final months of Hitler's life. How was the Nazi regime able to pursue a hopeless war down to the bitter end? And why did large segments of the German populace remain willing to follow their leadership?

From Hugh Trevor-Roper to Joachim Fest, the insane world of the subterranean bunker under the Chancellery in the war's final days has been often described.[18] Indeed, the drama of events in that phase carries a special appeal for all biographers. But we must separate what really happened from the numerous mythical post-war embellishments. The concluding chapter will attempt to generally evaluate the "case of Hitler" and describe its place in history.

"Resist it as we might, but we must always return to think about Adolf Hitler," Friedrich Kellner noted in his diary in December 1942.[19] Little has changed in the more than seven decades since the dictator's suicide. Hitler is considered the epitome of evil, and the monstrous crimes committed under his regime constantly demand new explanations. The procession of new books on the subject is continuous, and for each new biographer, it is increasingly difficult to maintain an overview.[20]

For the second volume of this biography too, published source material was augmented with extensive research at the Federal German Archive in Koblenz, the Federal Military Archive in Freiburg, the Federal Archive in Berlin-Lichterfelde and the Institute for Contemporary History in Munich. I was especially interested in the estates of major protagonists in the Nazi regime and leading military officers with whom Hitler spent the most time in the final six years of his life. Since the dictator destroyed all his personal documents shortly before committing suicide, the papers left by the men around him are most likely to yield new insights.

In total, I have devoted eight years to what the historian Golo Mann rightfully called a "repulsive subject." It was an enterprise that took a definite psychological toll. My relief at now being able to pursue other, happier topics is mixed with the hope that the second volume of this biography, like the first, will find an interested readership.

I

Unleashing the War

"I have overcome the chaos in Germany, restored order and hugely increased productivity in all areas of our national economy," Hitler proclaimed to the Reichstag when he looked back on his first six years of rule on 28 April 1939, a few days after his fiftieth birthday. "To ward off the threats by another world, I have not only politically united the German people but armed them militarily, and I have tried to eradicate, page for page, that treaty whose 448 articles contained the most dastardly rape ever perpetrated on peoples and human beings. I have given back to the Reich those provinces that were taken away from us in 1919 . . . I have restored the 1,000-year-old territorial integrity of the German living space, and I have . . . endeavoured to do all of this without shedding blood or inflicting the pain of war on my people or others. I have done this . . . solely on the back of my own strength as someone who was an unknown worker and soldier for my people twenty-one years ago. I can thus claim before history a place among those human beings who achieve the maximum of what can be fairly and justly demanded of an individual."[1]

What the German dictator did not mention, of course, was the dark side of his seemingly perfect record of success. Hitler had indeed reimposed "order"—but only with the help of a finely honed system of repression and terror that targeted his former political opponents, the communists and Social Democrats; dissident Catholic priests and Protestant pastors; various marginal groups stigmatised as "anti-social"; and above all Germany's Jewish minority, which had been harassed, pressured and stripped of all civil rights. With the pogrom in November 1938, ordered by Hitler, the Third Reich had departed the community of civilised nations for good. Mass unemployment had indeed been taken care of unexpectedly quickly, and Germany rearmed at a furious pace, but only at the cost of recklessly shaky finance politics which in the long term could only end in disaster. The terms of the Treaty of Versailles had been revised one after another, but only because the Western powers had allowed themselves to be fooled repeatedly by Hitler's assurances about his peaceful intentions and felt too weak to offer decisive resistance. With the annexation of the remainder of the Czech part of Czechoslovakia in March 1939, in breach of the Munich Agreement, the German dictator had irrevocably crossed a line and forfeited any claim to be trustworthy in future.

When Hitler crowed about having "restored the 1,000-year-old territorial integrity of the German living space," he conveniently forgot to mention that his ultimate, non-negotiable goal was to conquer "living space" that extended well beyond the Greater German Reich deep into eastern Europe, and that this was to be achieved by a racist and ideological war of annihilation against the Soviet Union. Moreover, what he considered to be his achievements were by no means down to his own strength alone, as he claimed. In all his endeavours, he had received help from all German institutions and all social classes, which had not only done his bidding, but often acted in anticipation of his wishes on their own initiative.

In his 1978 book *Defying Hitler*, Sebastian Haffner argued that in 1938, at the height of Germany's general faith in the Führer, "probably more than 90 per cent of Germans" were behind Hitler.[2] That is no doubt an exaggeration, but it can scarcely be denied that the Führer enjoyed the overwhelming support of the German populace, particularly after the *Anschluss* of Austria. If Hitler had been assassinated at that point, Joachim Fest once wrote, hardly anyone would have hesitated to call him "one of the German people's greatest statesmen and perhaps the man who completed their historical destiny."[3] We can extend this counter-factual game of imagination by asking: what would have happened if in the spring of 1939, after his latest foreign policy coup, the absorption of the rest of the Czech state and the Lithuanian Memel (Klaipėda) region, he had changed his course and been satisfied with what he had achieved.

Yet such speculations are completely futile. As we saw in the first volume of this biography, stopping or reversing the course leading to war would have run contrary not only to the massive momentum of his regime but also to Hitler's own personality. "A high-tension electrical condenser that slowly recharges after every powerful discharge, only to release another jolt when a certain ignition point has been reached—that is what Hitler reminded me of in the fateful year of 1939," the head of the Reich Press Office, Otto Dietrich, would later recall. "He was like a roulette player who refuses to quit while he has a winning streak because he believes he has a system that can recoup all his losses and break the bank."[4] And indeed, immediately after the Munich conference of 29–30 September 1938, whose result he interpreted as a defeat because it averted the war he wanted with Czechoslovakia and prevented him from annexing the entire country, Hitler had already set his eyes on the next victim of his aggression: the country with which he had, to the astonishment of many, concluded a non-aggression pact in January 1934.

Hardly had British prime minister Neville Chamberlain left Hitler's private apartment on Munich's Prinzregentenstrasse on the morning of 30 September 1938, to fly back to London with their joint pledge to settle all future disagreements peacefully, than the German dictator told his military adjutants Rudolf Schmundt and Gerhard Engel that he did not feel bound by his word. "There is no rush to resolve the controversial issues with Poland," he remarked, but when the time was ripe he was going to soften up Poland with "tried-and-tested methods" to prepare for the final assault.[5] By that Hitler meant a combination of seduction, deception and blackmail—everything up to and including the threat of declaring war.

Initially, the regime tried diplomatic means to make Poland receptive to German wishes. On 24 October 1938, German foreign minister Joachim von Ribbentrop invited the Polish ambassador, Józef Lipski, to the Grand Hotel in Berchtesgaden and suggested a "general clearing up" of all sources of friction between their two countries. Specifically, he demanded the return of the Free City of Danzig (Gdańsk) to the German Reich and Warsaw's assent to the construction of an extraterritorial German rail line and motorway to East Prussia through the Polish "corridor." In addition, Ribbentrop wanted Poland to join the 1936 Anti-Comintern Pact between Germany, Italy and Japan. In return, Germany would guarantee the borders of the Polish state and extend the 1934 non-aggression pact for "ten to twenty-five years."[6]

Although the three-hour discussion had been friendly in tone, the Polish government was not fooled. In Warsaw it was only too apparent that the German proposals were the start of an offensive aimed at making Poland dependent on the Third Reich and forcing it into a common front against the Soviet Union. In his official answer to Ribbentrop's suggestions on 19 November, the Polish foreign minister, Józef Beck, rejected the reincorporation of Danzig into the Reich, although he agreed to consider replacing the League of Nations statute with a German-Polish treaty as long as Danzig continued to be a Free City and the customs union with Poland was maintained. Beck did not comment on the idea of an extraterritorial connection with East Prussia, although when he delivered the answer to Ribbentrop, Lipski made it known that he believed a compromise could be found on this score.[7] In an unmistakable demonstration of its intent to stake out an independent position between its powerful neighbours to the east and west, on 27 November Poland extended the non-aggression pact it had concluded with the Soviet Union in July 1932.

Hitler was angered by the unexpected rejection of his offer and on 24 November ordered the Wehrmacht Supreme Command to prepare for a "surprise occupation of Danzig." Nevertheless, at that point he did not want to start a war with Poland: he was only going to exploit the "politically favourable situation" for a lightning-quick strike.[8] On 5 January 1939, Hitler received Beck at the Berghof for lengthy consultations, confronting him again with the list of German demands from the previous October. While declaring that Germany viewed "a strong Poland . . . simply as a necessity," Hitler reiterated German claims on Danzig, telling Beck that "Danzig is German, will always be German and will join Germany sooner or later." The Polish foreign minister reacted evasively, saying that he was going to take time to think things over, but cited public opinion in Poland, which was very sensitive on the issue and did not give him much room to manoeuvre. In conversation with Ribbentrop in Munich the following day, Beck stuck to his formally cordial, but resolutely negative position. Ribbentrop also returned empty-handed from a reciprocal visit to Warsaw at the end of the month.[9]

Nonetheless, in his speech to the Reichstag on 30 January 1939, Hitler avoided an aggressive tone towards Poland. On the contrary, he characterised the non-aggression pact signed five years previously as a "truly relieving agreement" and praised German-Polish friendship as "one of the calming phenomena of European political life."[10] What was foremost on Hitler's mind in the first months of 1939 was not the coming conflict with Germany's eastern neighbour, but the question of how he could take over the rest of Czechoslovakia. After lunch in the Chancellery in early February, Goebbels noted: "Almost all the Führer talks about now is foreign policy. He is mulling over new plans again. A Napoleonic personality!"[11] But it was clear to keen observers that the German dictator would turn his attention to Poland after landing his coup in Prague on 15 March. It was generally assumed, the Polish consul general in Dresden reported to Lipski, that as soon as the Memel region had been incorporated, Hitler "would have to move on to the demands on Poland, first and foremost a takeover of Danzig and the 'corridor.'" In his attempts to resolve these issues, he could count on the "understanding and acceptance" of the German people.[12]

On 21 March, Ribbentrop summoned Lipski to the Foreign Ministry and reiterated, this time in the form of a near ultimatum, the German demands of October 1938 and January 1939. Hitler was "baffled" by the Polish government's position, Ribbentrop said, adding that it was imperative to "avoid the impression that Poland was simply refusing to play ball."[13] For Warsaw it was now clear that Poland faced the same fate as Czechoslovakia. If the Polish government acceded to the German demands, Berlin would simply make more, and the case of Prague amply illustrated what a guarantee of territorial integrity from Hitler was worth. On 24 March, Beck told his staff that Germany had "lost its predictability." There was no giving in to Hitler, he added. The German dictator should be met with decisiveness and clear signals that Poland was prepared to fight if necessary.[14] As Count Jan Szembek, state secretary in the Polish Foreign Ministry, noted in his diary: "In my opinion, we must now bare our teeth at the Germans."[15]

On 26 March, Lipski returned to Berlin and presented Ribbentrop with a memorandum from the Polish government that flatly rejected the German proposals. Politely but unmistakably, Beck also made it known that while he would like to accept Ribbentrop's invitation to visit Berlin, such a visit would have to be subject to careful diplomatic planning. The Polish foreign minister was not about to expose himself to the same brutal strong-arming experienced by Austrian chancellor

Schuschnigg in February 1938 and Czech president Hácha earlier in March. Ribbentrop reacted in extremely brusque fashion. If things continued to develop the way they were going, the German foreign minister growled, "a serious situation could arise in the near future." Ribbentrop threatened outright that Germany would regard "a violation of Danzig's sovereign territory by Polish troops" as an attack on the Reich and react accordingly.[16] In response, on the evening of 28 March, Beck summoned Germany's ambassador in Warsaw, Hans-Adolf von Moltke, to the Polish Foreign Ministry and informed him that Poland would see it as a *casus belli* if Germany "unilaterally tried to alter the statute governing the Free City." Poland continued to be interested in negotiations, Beck said, but was increasingly getting the impression that they had reached "a turning point in German-Polish relations."[17]

At that juncture, Hitler was still unsure how to react to Poland's wait-and-see position. On the evening of 24 March, after returning from the German-annexed Memel district, he discussed his future plans with Goebbels, who wrote: "The Führer is mulling over how to solve the Danzig question. He wants to put some pressure on Poland and hopes it will cause a reaction." In this vein, Hitler said over lunch at the Chancellery the following day: "Poland has yet to make up its mind concerning Danzig, but our pressure will be increased. We hope we can achieve our goal."[18] To the commander of the army, Walther von Brauchitsch, Hitler revealed that he did not intend at that point to try to solve the "Danzig question" with violence because he did not want to drive Poland "into England's arms." Nonetheless, he added, in the "near future," under "particularly favourable political circumstances," a situation could arise in which a solution to the "Polish question" would become a necessity. The Wehrmacht general staff should begin preparing for this eventuality. If it became a reality, Hitler declared, "Poland must be defeated so thoroughly that it will no longer be regarded as a political factor in the coming decades."[19]

In the late evening of 25 March, Hitler travelled to Munich and Berchtesgaden to relax for a few days. Thus he was not in Berlin when Ambassador Lipski delivered Poland's ultimate refusal of the German proposal, although Ribbentrop no doubt swiftly informed him of it. Goebbels described Hitler's reaction after a telephone call with the Führer, noting in his diary on 27 March: "Poland is creating major difficulties. The Poles will always be our enemies, even if for selfish reasons they have done us several favours in the past."[20]

On 30 March, Hitler returned to Berlin and immediately met with his foreign minister. "There was a certain tension in the air," Hitler's adjutant Nicolaus von Below remembered.[21] The next day events took a turn the dictator had not anticipated, when Chamberlain guaranteed Polish independence before the House of Commons. If Polish sovereignty came under serious threat, Chamberlain declared, the British government would offer all forms of assistance in its power. The French government also endorsed this guarantee. With that, it became clear that a German attack on Poland would mean war with the Western powers. (Similar guarantees were issued for Romania and Greece on 13 April.) After Hitler's crass violation of the Munich Agreement, London finally understood that the German dictator could not be appeased. As Foreign Office under-secretary Alexander Cadogan explained the change of direction, the main objective of Britain's guarantee to Poland was to deter Germany from further acts of aggression.[22] In early April, Polish foreign minister Beck paid a visit to London, at the end of which it was announced that the two countries had signed a mutual assistance pact. An American correspondent in Berlin, William Shirer, was confident that "this will halt Hitler for the time being, since force is something he understands and respects and there is no doubt in my mind after a week here that the Poles will fight and that if Britain and France fight too, he is in a hole."[23]

Hitler learned of the British guarantee on the evening of 31 March on his special train, which was taking him to the North Sea port of Wilhelmshaven. There, on the morning of 1 April, he attended the launching of the MS *Tirpitz*, Germany's second-largest warship after the MS *Bismarck*. In his speech at a mass rally in the town square that afternoon, Hitler talked about this latest development. Britain, he fumed, was engaging in a "policy of encirclement" against the German Reich similar to the one it had pursued before 1914. He threatened to cancel the naval agreement of 1935 in retaliation and fired off a warning to "satellite states"—by which, of course, he meant Poland. Those who were happy to "take the chestnuts out of the fire" for the Western powers, Hitler said, should be prepared to get their "fingers burned."[24] Goebbels immediately picked up on the term "encirclement," making it the centre of his anti-British propaganda in the weeks that followed.

Just as had happened before 1914, the idea was to trigger public fears and direct the blame for an eventual war in advance onto the British government.[25]

That very evening, Hitler boarded the cruise ship MS *Robert Ley*, built to take people on state-sponsored "Strength through Joy" holidays, before it set off for its maiden voyage. He made a relaxed impression on the holidaymakers, letting people take his picture and bathing in the enthusiasm and respect with which he was universally greeted. At noon on 4 April, the ship docked in Hamburg. Hitler had himself driven to Dammtor station and proceeded via special train back to Berlin, where he only paused for a couple of hours before leaving for an extended stay on the Obersalzberg.[26]

The day before, while still aboard ship, he had instructed the Wehrmacht Supreme Command to begin preparing an attack on Poland under the code name "Case White." The attack was to be carried out "at any time from 1 September 1939."[27] On 11 April, the day after Easter, at the Berghof, Hitler signed the "Instruction for Unified War Preparations of the Wehrmacht for 1939–40." The section concerning Case White began with the statement that Germany would continue trying to avoid "disturbances" in its relationship with Poland. Nonetheless, and notwithstanding the still-valid German-Polish non-aggression pact, if Germany's eastern neighbour should adopt a "posture threatening the Reich," a "final reckoning" would become necessary: "The goal is then to destroy the Polish military capacity and to create a situation in the east favourable to the needs of defending our country. At the outbreak of the conflict at the latest, the Free City of Danzig will be declared territory of the German Reich. The political leadership regards it as its task to isolate Poland, that is to restrict the war to Poland, in this case." The Wehrmacht was charged with annihilating the Polish army. To that end, it was crucial to "set and prepare a date for a surprise attack."[28] It appears that Hitler wanted to invade Poland without formally declaring war.

The scepticism with which the military leadership had regarded Hitler's plans for war on Czechoslovakia the previous year had by now disappeared completely. On the contrary, in a speech to senior officers in the latter half of April, Franz Halder, the chief of the army general staff, backed without reservation the "excellent . . . instinctively correct policies of the Führer." Because of the technological backwardness of its armed forces and the poor training of its soldiers, Poland was "not a serious adversary," and the Wehrmacht would ensure that it was completely defeated by the "quickest possible route." "We have to dispatch Poland within three weeks and, if possible, fourteen days," Halder added. In that case, he believed that Germany could even afford to risk British and French intervention.[29] Here, the traditional anti-Polish sentiment of Germany's nationalist military elite was again making itself felt. In the eyes of the generals, war against Germany's hated neighbour to the east was an ideal scenario. Hitler had no reason to fear any resistance from his army commanders.

Hitler returned to Berlin on 18 April, as preparations to celebrate his fiftieth birthday were in full swing. The following evening, despite a full schedule of appointments, he received the Romanian foreign minister, Grigore Gafencu, for a two-hour audience during which he vented his anger at Britain's guarantee of Polish sovereignty. If Britain wanted war, Hitler told his visitor, it could have it. "But it will not be the easy war that [Britain] imagines it to be," Hitler raged. "It will be a war of destruction that is beyond anyone's imagination."[30]

The Führer spent the days after the birthday celebrations working on a speech to the Reichstag in which he was going to respond to a message from US president Franklin D. Roosevelt.[31] Washington was alarmed at Germany's "grab for Prague" on 15 March and Italy's occupation of Albania three weeks later. On 14 April, Roosevelt appealed to Hitler and Mussolini to return to policies of peace and resume negotiations over arms reduction. The president listed thirty-one states in both Europe and the Middle East by name and demanded assurances from the German and Italian regimes that they did not intend to attack any of them.[32] Hitler considered this an affront, characterising it to Goebbels as "an impertinently stupid new Wilson-style swindle."[33] He then used his 2½-hour speech to the Reichstag on 28 April to pour scorn and contempt upon the US president. He had enquired of each of the states named whether they felt threatened by Germany, Hitler claimed, and the answer had always been "a thoroughly negative and sometimes brusquely dismissive one." Some of the states, Hitler added, could not be approached "because, like for example Syria, they are not currently in possession of their freedom, being occupied and denied their rights by the military forces of democratic states."[34]

Marianne von Weizsäcker, the wife of the state secretary in the Foreign Ministry, Ernst von Weizsäcker, came away impressed, particularly by the passages of the speech dealing with the Treaty of Versailles. Hitler had "spoken from her heart," she wrote in a letter, adding: "What was felt back then was said today."[35] William Shirer, who had followed the speech from the Reichstag press gallery, had to admit that "Hitler was a superb actor today—he drew every last drop of irony." Reichstag deputies had rewarded Hitler's words with shouts of approval.[36] But Hitler had done more than just make fun of Roosevelt. He had also announced the cancellation, with immediate effect, of the 1935 naval treaty with Britain and the German-Polish non-aggression pact. Twisting the facts as was his wont, the German dictator blamed his adversaries. Thanks to its "policy of encirclement" against Germany, Britain had destroyed the basis for mutual trust, and by agreeing to support Britain, Poland had violated the 1934 pact. Warsaw reacted cautiously to this latest provocation from Berlin. In a major speech to the Polish parliament, Foreign Minister Beck stressed his government's determination not to bend to German strong-arming. "We Poles do not know the idea of peace at all costs," he said. "In the lives of human beings, peoples and states there is only one commodity that has no price: honour!"[37]

Germany's withdrawal from its agreements with Britain and Poland immediately raised tensions in Europe. "The obligatory crisis is now commencing," Goebbels noted. "We will, of course, win out sooner or later. But this time, the Western powers have no easy way of backing off."[38] In the meantime, Hitler had abandoned his original intention of using negotiations to make Poland receptive to German wishes and reduce it to the status of a satellite. He was now placing all his bets on the military option. "The Poles need to get socked in the face at the next possible opportunity," Goebbels quoted Hitler as saying. "Warsaw will end up where Prague ended up."[39] To buttress the attack planned for the late summer, Germany sought to deepen its relationship with Italy. Although Hitler was enraged at Mussolini for not consulting him about Italy's attack on Albania on 7 April, calling it an "aping" of his own coup against Prague, he also expressed understanding of the Duce's position, admitting that he had not asked for Mussolini's advice either. "If you confide in those talkative Italians, you may as well speak to the newspapers," he remarked.[40]

Such denigrating opinions notwithstanding, Berlin now pressed for the political Axis to be expanded into a military alliance, and Göring visited Rome on 15–16 April for talks to that end. In his first conversation with Mussolini and the Italian foreign minister, Galeazzo Ciano, he adopted such an aggressive tone towards England and Poland that the Italians came away with the impression that Germany was about to declare war. The next day, Göring backed off somewhat, stressing that Hitler had told him that "he was not planning anything against Poland." Still, Mussolini found it necessary to point out that the Axis powers would need two to three years to "enter into a general conflict well-armed enough to have prospects of victory."[41] Italy's ambassador in Berlin, Bernardo Attolico, was also worried about German intentions. Hitler, he warned on 18 April, had after the Polish refusals of the German suggestions "gone into that Sphinx-like state . . . which precedes all of his attacks." Given the fact that an attack on Poland could bring about Anglo-French intervention, he added, Rome should take care not to be presented with a *fait accompli*.[42]

During talks with Ciano on 6 May in Milan, Ribbentrop tried to dispel the Italian fears. He was certain that if in several months the "Polish question" came to a head, no Englishman or Frenchman would march to war to defend Poland. Ciano once again said for the record that Italy needed three more years of peace. But that evening, to the surprise of the German delegation, Mussolini came out in favour of a military alliance with Nazi Germany.[43] Consequently, on 22 May, Ciano and Ribbentrop signed the German-Italian Friendship and Alliance Agreement, soon to be known as the "Pact of Steel," in the reception hall of the New Chancellery building. It was initially limited to ten years and required the signatories not just to consult closely, but to defend one another in case one of the parties "became embroiled in hostilities with another power or powers."[44] Hitler attended the signing ceremony, and Ciano found that he had "aged somewhat." He had dark circles under his eyes, and from Hitler's entourage Ciano heard that the Führer was sleeping "less and less."[45]

The sumptuous party Ribbentrop hosted in his Berlin villa for the Italian delegation could not conceal the fact that the two Axis partners were deeply mistrustful of one another's intentions. Whereas for Ciano the military pact contained "true dynamite" because the mutual defence promise applied to cases of German aggression and not just self-defence, Goebbels was laconically sceptical about the value of the treaty. "Hopefully, the Italians will keep their end of it," he remarked.[46] As would soon become apparent, such doubts were entirely justified.

Mussolini, too, had every reason to be concerned about Hitler's next moves. Hardly had Ciano departed Berlin on the morning of 23 May than the German dictator called a meeting in his Chancellery office of the commanders of the army, navy and air force and their chiefs of staff to brief them on the overall political situation as he saw it. There, Hitler reaffirmed his decision, and the subsequent instruction of 11 April, "to attack Poland on the first suitable occasion" and left no doubt that this war was to be only the beginning of the realisation of his wider plans. The minutes of the meeting, taken by Wehrmacht adjutant Schmundt, read: "Danzig is not the true object of all this. For us, the point is to expand our living space in the east and to secure food as well as to resolve the Baltic problem." Hitler said that it was necessary to "isolate" Poland so that things "did not come to a simultaneous conflict with the West." Nonetheless, he conceded that depending on circumstances, it might not be possible to localise the German-Polish conflict and that England and France could intervene. In that case, it would be better "to attack the West and take care of Poland at the same time." Fundamentally, Hitler doubted that there could be a peaceful reconciliation with Britain. "England sees our development as the establishment of a hegemony that would weaken England," he said. "England is thus our enemy, and the conflict with England is one of life and death."

Hitler told the leaders of the Wehrmacht to get ready for a long struggle. If Schmundt's notes are correct, he even spoke of a "war of ten to fifteen years' duration." The key to success, he said, was secrecy: "Our goals must be kept secret even from Italy and Japan." Thus, the ink on the Pact of Steel, which had been signed only hours before, was hardly dry before Hitler declared that he did not feel bound to share information or consult with his ally. The only person who spoke at the meeting apart from Hitler was Göring, who wanted to know when the three branches of Germany's armed forces should expect major hostilities. Hitler's answer that the armaments programmes were to be "completed by 1943 or 1944" probably came as a relief to the military commanders. After all, Hitler had named the same time frame in their meeting on 5 November 1937, and a lot could happen between now and then. On the other hand, anyone who had believed Hitler was not serious about going to war with Poland now knew better. The Führer had made it abundantly clear that with Poland he did not expect a "Czech repeat" of an act of aggression not leading to war. "Further successes cannot be achieved without shedding blood," Hitler predicted.[47]

As operational preparations went on behind the scenes for Case White, Hitler tried to assure the public that nothing out of the ordinary was going on. He spent most of the summer months on the Obersalzberg and was only spotted a few times in the German capital, for instance during a state visit by the prince regent of Yugoslavia from 1 to 4 June or for the reception of the Legion Condor, when it returned from the Spanish Civil War on 6 June.[48] After that, he travelled extensively. On 7 June, he informed himself about the progress of the construction of the Volkswagen factory near Fallersleben. Three days later he arrived in Vienna to take part in "Reich Theatre Week," attending the performance of a Richard Strauss opera with the portentous title *Day of Peace* and receiving the musicians afterwards. The following day, he went to the Burgtheater. "Here was where he once had his major theatrical experiences," noted Goebbels. "And now the entire city is cheering him."[49] Before leaving for Linz on 12 June to discuss his plans for developing the city with the local Gauleiter, August Eigruber, he visited the grave of his niece Geli Raubal. *En route* from Linz to Berchtesgaden, Hitler stopped off in two places of his childhood: Hafeld, where his father had moved after his retirement in 1895, and Fischlham, where his tiny one-room former schoolhouse had remained unchanged.[50] To those around him, it seemed as though he were living in his past.

But that impression was mistaken. Even at the Berghof, along with making plans for monumental construction projects, he was constantly thinking about the imminent war with Poland. When Goebbels visited Hitler in his Alpine residence on 20 June, the dictator immediately came to the point, predicting that "Poland will first offer resistance and then pathetically collapse after its first defeat." The campaign could be over and done with in a fortnight, Hitler assured Goebbels, and England would never keep its pledge to guarantee Polish sovereignty. "London will leave Warsaw in the lurch," he said. "They are just bluffing.

They have too many other concerns."[51] It is difficult to say whether Hitler truly believed his "bluff theory" or whether he just wanted to act optimistic in front of his propaganda minister. In the meeting with his highest military commanders on 23 May, he had refused to rule out an intervention by the Western powers, but had said that it was improbable.

On 3 July, Hitler visited the Luftwaffe's test base in Rechlin am Müritzsee and inspected the latest technological innovations in German aviation. The following evening, he once again sounded a confident note to his entourage in the Chancellery: "Our fortifications are fantastic. Our potential for war grows day by day. Above all, our defensive weapons are much better than those of our adversaries. This is a pleasant result of Versailles. In any case, everything is going as well as it can."[52] The day after hosting a reception for Bulgarian prime minister Georgi Ivanov Kyoseivanov on 5 July, Hitler flew to Munich in a new four-motor Condor plane that was not only far more spacious but also 100 kilometres an hour faster than the Ju-52. During his subsequent week-long stay on the Obersalzberg, he devoted himself to the details of the Wehrmacht's planned campaign against Poland.[53] To conceal what he was doing from the German and international public, he announced on 10 July that the annual Nuremberg Rally would go ahead in September as usual. The event was given the cynical title of "Reich Rally for Peace." Preparations also continued for a planned act of state on 27 August at the Tannenberg Memorial in East Prussia to commemorate the twenty-fifth anniversary of the First World War battle that had been fought there.[54]

As he had the previous two years, Hitler also participated in events related to the "Day of German Art" in Munich. On the evening of 14 July, he hosted a large-scale reception for artists in the Führerbau, which was attended by representatives from the Nazi Party, the government and the Wehrmacht as well as an Italian delegation led by the minister for popular education, Dino Alfieri. "A festive, intoxicating scene!" gushed Goebbels. "It was very nice and lively. The Führer is in a splendid mood."[55] The dictator even took time the next day for the annual meeting of the Reich Chamber of Fine Arts in the ballroom of the Deutsches Museum, and at the opening of the Third Great German Art Exhibition on 16 July in the Haus der Deutschen Kunst he held a speech in which he praised the "purification" of German culture from the corrosive influence of modernism. "The whole swindle of a decadent, sickly, mendacious, fashionable art has been swept away," the Führer proclaimed.[56] But fate was not on the side of the festival parade that afternoon. Rain came down in buckets, which significantly dampened the atmosphere. "Hitler was in a very poor mood—he had sent his raincoat over to his 'friend,' Miss Braun," the former German ambassador to Italy Ulrich von Hassell learned from the Bruckmanns, Hitler's early patrons, whose enthusiasm for the dictator had noticeably cooled.[57]

On the morning of 17 July, Hitler had breakfast with Alfieri in his private apartment in Munich and then withdrew to the Obersalzberg. A week later, he set off for his annual visit to the Wagner festival in Bayreuth. At the opening performance on 25 July, he did not wear the customary tuxedo or dinner jacket but rather his party uniform. For alert observers this was a sign that unusual things were afoot. And indeed, Bayreuth was not exempt from politics. At the invitation of press chief Otto Dietrich, Lord Kemsley, the publisher of the *Sunday Times*, had travelled to the Bavarian city to discuss the modalities of an exchange of articles between German and English newspapers. At a meeting in the Villa Siegfried, Hitler was noticeably reserved, repeating in a monotone voice that the preservation of peace in Europe was up to England alone. He declined even to receive the British ambassador, Sir Nevile Henderson, who arrived in Bayreuth on 29 July.[58] By contrast, he paid considerable attention during the festival to Unity Mitford and her sister Diana, the wife of British fascist leader Sir Oswald Mosley. During a meal with Winifred Wagner, Lady Mosley asserted with great conviction that because of its insufficient armaments programme, England was completely incapable of waging war. According to his adjutant Engel, that was music to the Führer's ears.[59] It was entirely possible that Hitler saw this as confirmation of his belief that the British government was only bluffing and would back off declaring war at the last minute.

Hitler spent the next three weeks without interruption on the Obersalzberg. While the Führer was demonstrably displaying normality and pursuing a "tactic of silence" towards the Western powers, Goebbels' propaganda ensured that the conflict with Poland was kept on the boil.[60] The German press constantly reported on alleged Polish offences against the country's German minority. As in the Sudeten crisis the previous year, incidents were staged to incite Polish reactions which could then be exploited for publicity. "In Poland we already have our first casualty," Goebbels reported gleefully in mid-May 1939. "Everything is taking its preordained path."[61] On 7 August, Hitler summoned the Gauleiter of Danzig, Albert Forster, to the Obersalzberg and told him he was "at the limit of his patience" with Poland. Upon returning home on 10 August, Forster stoked the mood of agitation with an event on Langer Markt (Długi Targ). Poland, he told the crowd, needed to be aware that Danzig was "not alone and abandoned" and that "the Greater German Reich, our motherland and our Führer Adolf Hitler" were standing firmly by the city.[62]

On 11 August, Hitler had one of his private airplanes fly the high commissioner of the League of Nations in Danzig, Carl Jacob Burckhardt, to Salzburg. He received the Swiss diplomat and historian in the Adlershorst, a large teahouse above the Berghof, and with no further ado revealed that at "the slightest incident" he would "destroy Poland without warning." When Burckhardt objected that this would bring a "general war," Hitler exclaimed: "Then so be it!" If he had to wage war, the Führer added, then "better today than tomorrow." At the end of the conversation, as the high commissioner recalled in his memoirs twenty years later, Hitler reiterated: "I am not bluffing. If anything at all happens in Danzig or happens to our minorities, I will strike a hard blow."[63] Again Hitler showed how good he was at fooling his conversation partners, since no matter how things developed in Danzig, he was determined to go to war against Poland in any case. The same day he received Burckhardt, he ordered the anti-Polish campaign to be ratcheted up to "80 per cent volume," causing Goebbels to note, correctly: "It is coming down to the final sprint."[64]

On 12 August, Hitler authorised the Wehrmacht to prepare the invasion of Poland and set 26 August as the day it would commence. Two days later, he called Brauchitsch and Halder to the Berghof and told them that it was impossible to obtain further political or military victories without risk. Nevertheless, he said his conviction that the war could be localised was growing "from day to day." Everything indicated that "England and France will not join the war since they are under no obligation."[65] Afterwards, Hitler told a small group of listeners that he had summoned the two military leaders to "give them a shot in the arm."[66] Not that they needed one. The prospect of soon being able to strike against Poland put wind in the military commanders' sails and gave them great satisfaction. Like Hitler, they were certain that, given German military superiority, they could conclude the Polish campaign in a couple of weeks.

Meanwhile, fears were growing in Rome that despite the consultation clause of the Pact of Steel, Italy's ally was going to present Mussolini with a *fait accompli*. In early July 1939, Foreign Minister Ciano ordered Ambassador Attolico to find out precisely what Germany intended to do on the Polish issue. While Ribbentrop offered assurances on 6 July that Hitler had no concrete war plans and would not let himself be lured into "any heedless gestures,"[67] the Italian military attaché in Berlin, General Efisio Marras, passed along reliable information to the ambassador dispelling any doubts that the German leadership intended to attack Poland. In what was perhaps an attempt to apply the brakes, Attolico suggested reviving the German suggestion of a meeting between Hitler and Mussolini. The Duce and Ciano agreed, and 4 August was set as a date. The Italians were hoping to use the meeting, as they had in Munich the previous September, to gain German support for the idea of an international conference. But Berlin was not forthcoming. Ribbentrop summarily rejected the conference proposal—and no doubt he was of one mind with Hitler on this score. For the Führer a diplomatic solution to the crisis was out of the question: he was set for war against Poland. In late July, the meeting of the two dictators was postponed indefinitely.[68]

Instead, on 11 August, Ciano travelled to see Ribbentrop on his country estate, Fuschl Castle, near Salzburg. Before he left, Mussolini had insisted that he "make the Germans clearly see that war with Poland must be avoided since it will be impossible to localise and a larger war would be disastrous for everyone."[69] But right from the outset, Ribbentrop informed his Italian colleague in no uncertain terms that Hitler had decided to attack Poland and that his decision was final. "The will to war is unbending," Ciano summarised in his diary. "He rejects any solution that would satisfy Germany and avoid war."[70] Ribbentrop brushed aside Ciano's objections that the Western powers would inevitably intervene. The German foreign minister, observed the translator Paul Schmidt, "was already in a state of feverish excitement, like a hunting dog that cannot wait for its masters to turn it loose on its prey."[71] The atmosphere during the foreign ministers' ten-hour meeting was icy. Over dinner, the two did not exchange a word.

The following day, Hitler received Ciano at the Berghof. He treated his guest with emphatic cordiality but was as unyielding as Ribbentrop on the Polish question. "He has decided to strike, and he will," Ciano noted. "Our objections will not deter him in the slightest. He kept repeating that he would localise the war with Poland, but his contention that the great war would have to be waged while he and the Duce are still young only strengthens my suspicion that he is duplicitous."[72] Whereas Ciano had energetically contradicted the German foreign minister on 12 August, the following day he seems to have simply capitulated to the Führer's monologue, folding, as Schmidt remembered, "like a pocket knife." Schmidt quoted Ciano as saying: "You have been proven right so often that I consider it possible that this time, too, you see things more correctly than we do."[73] From that point on, the Italians could be under no more illusions about the German determination to start a war. Their only options were either to break the pledge of military assistance made in the Pact of Steel or to be sucked by Hitler into a military adventure whose outcome was completely unclear. "I am returning to Rome, disgusted by Germany, its leaders and their behaviour," Ciano entrusted to his diary. "They have deceived and swindled us."[74]

Ribbentrop and Hitler had also concealed from their ally one of the main reasons why they had so candidly blurted out the truth: Nazi Germany was about to reach a deal with its mortal enemy Bolshevik Russia. Since the spring of 1939, Moscow had been sending signals to Berlin indicating that the Soviet Union was ready to change its policies towards Germany. In his report to the Eighteenth Party Congress on 10 March 1939, Stalin had declared that he would not allow the country to be "dragged into conflicts by war-mongers" who were only interested in "getting others to take the chestnuts out of the fire for them."[75] The jibe was aimed at the Western powers, which the Soviet dictator suspected of trying to embroil his country in war with Germany as a way of taking themselves out of the firing line. Stalin had no illusions about Hitler's long-term aims or the inevitability of war between the Soviet Union and Nazi Germany. But he wanted to delay the conflict for as long as possible so that he could build up the Soviet military. An arrangement with the Third Reich to Poland's detriment not only allowed him to play for time but gave him a portion of the spoils—those territories that revolutionary Russia had been forced to surrender to Poland, the Baltic states and Finland between 1917 and 1920.[76]

On 3 May, the people's commissar of foreign affairs, Maksim Litvinov, an advocate of collective security and Russian cooperation with the West, was replaced by the Stalin loyalist Vyacheslav Molotov. "Much scratching of heads about Litvinov's resignation," commented Goebbels. "In London and Paris they think Moscow wants to orientate itself more strongly towards us."[77] It was precisely this impression which the chargé d'affaires of the Soviet embassy in Berlin, Georgy Astakhov, sought to reinforce in conversation with Legation Counsellor Karl Julius Schnurre, the director of the eastern Europe division in the economic department of the German Foreign Ministry. According to Schnurre, Astakhov raised the question of "whether this event would change our position towards the Soviet Union."[78]

Initially, Berlin was sceptical about the Soviet advances. After all, since the early 1920s, Hitler had constantly railed against "Jewish Bolshevism," depicting it as the greatest threat to Germany and the ideological mortal enemy of National Socialism. A sudden deviation from this principle would confuse Hitler's supporters and the German public as a whole. On the other hand, Hitler was enough of a *Realpolitiker* to recognise the advantages of temporarily making common cause with Stalin. It would keep his back free in the east in case war broke out with the Western powers while he was subjugating Poland. Berlin had looked on with concern as London and Paris extended feelers towards Moscow to entice Stalin into a mutual defence pact. The Soviet dictator was in the enviable position of being courted by both sides.

In late May 1939, as State Secretary Weizsäcker informed Germany's ambassador in Moscow, Count Friedrich Werner von der Schulenburg, Hitler gave the green light to "sound out" the Russians.[79] "We are making advances," Weizsäcker told Astakhov in early July on Hitler's instructions. "You can be our friends or our enemies, as you wish."[80] Nonetheless, Berlin was not sure what Moscow wanted. Soviet policy was "for the time being non-transparent to the Führer," Goebbels noted. It was "difficult to comprehend."[81] The German Foreign Ministry feared that the Soviet leadership might only be using talks with Germany to increase the price for an alliance in its negotiations with the Western powers. But a month later, after talks between Molotov and Schulenburg, the misgivings appear to have been cleared up. On 8 July, when Goebbels visited the Obersalzberg, Hitler confided in him. "He no longer believes that London and Moscow will reach an agreement," Goebbels noted. "The path is clear for us."[82]

In mid-July 1939, the deputy director of the Soviet trade mission in Berlin, Yevgeny Babarin, returned from Moscow with instructions to resume negotiations over a German-Soviet trade pact. On 26 July, on orders from Ribbentrop, Schnurre invited Astakhov and Babarin to dinner at a Berlin restaurant and broached the question of whether they could go beyond the economic negotiations to reconstruct German-Soviet relations by "taking into account our mutual vital political interests." From the German perspective, Schnurre said, there were no fundamental obstacles since despite all their differences in world view, the two sides had "one thing in common . . . opposition to the capitalist democracies."[83] A few days later, on 2 August, Ribbentrop summoned Astakhov to the German Foreign Office and told him that "from the Baltic to the Black Sea there is no problem that cannot be solved to our mutual satisfaction." That was a loaded choice of words: an implicit offer that Germany and the Soviet Union could divide up Poland.[84]

For the Soviet leadership, this was an unmistakable sign that the Germans were seriously interested in reaching an agreement and that the desire to successfully conclude negotiations as quickly as possible meant that war with Poland was imminent. On 12 August, Astakhov issued an invitation for negotiations in Moscow, although Molotov initially dragged his feet on Ribbentrop's offer two days later to travel to the Russian capital for "immediate talks" with Stalin.[85] The Soviets knew that time was on their side. On 16 August, Ribbentrop repeated his offer. He declared himself ready "at any time" from 18 August onwards to fly to Moscow "with the complete authorisation of the Führer to negotiate over the entire constellation of German-Russian issues and to sign any resulting treaties."[86] Once again, Molotov was evasive, saying that a visit by the German foreign minister would require careful preparation. The matter went back and forth, with the

German side becoming increasingly nervous. The planned date for attacking Poland was only a few days away.[87]

"The great crisis of nerves has begun," Goebbels noted on 17 August. ". . . The air is full of tension and pressure." Two days later, the propaganda minister got a call from the Obersalzberg. He was told to turn up the campaign of hatred against Poland to "full volume." "So we can begin," Goebbels noted. From the chief of the Wehrmacht Supreme Command, Wilhelm Keitel, he learned about the state of play. "Everything is ready for an attack on Poland. Almost 2.5 million men under arms. Everyone is waiting for the Führer to give the signal to start . . . It would take a miracle to avoid war."[88] On 20 August, the German-Soviet Credit and Trade Agreement was signed in Berlin, but the two sides were still far apart with regard to Poland. Then Hitler decided to make an unusual gesture. That very day, he sent a telegram to Stalin asking him to receive Ribbentrop on 22 August or at the latest on 23 August. The German foreign minister would bring with him the "most comprehensive general authorisation" to sign a non-aggression treaty and the "additional protocol" that the Soviets had requested to delineate the two sides' spheres of influence in eastern Europe.[89] Hitler assured Stalin that the conclusion of the non-aggression pact represented a "commitment of German policy in the long term"—a bare-faced lie that would have hardly deceived Stalin as to Hitler's future intentions. The telegram was delivered at 12:45 a.m. in Moscow but only relayed by Schulenburg to Molotov in the afternoon of 21 August.

On the Obersalzberg, Hitler waited with visible agitation for Stalin's answer. Finally, during dinner, a servant brought a note. "He scanned it, stared straight ahead for a moment, his face turning red, then pounded the table so that the glasses clinked and cried out with his voice breaking, 'I have them! I have them!'" recalled Albert Speer. "Seconds later he had already regained control of himself. No one dared ask any questions, and the meal continued."[90] In his telegram, which arrived at the Berghof at 9:45 p.m., Stalin agreed to "the arrival of Mr. Ribbentrop in Moscow on 23 August." The Soviet leader also expressed his hope that the non-aggression pact would create "the basis for the liquidation of political tension and for the creation of peace and cooperation between our two countries."[91] Later that evening, German radio interrupted its regular music broadcast to announce the sensational news that Germany and the Soviet Union had agreed to a non-aggression pact. "This produces a whole new situation," Goebbels commented. "We are on top again."[92]

On 22 August, Hitler called the leaders of the three branches of the Wehrmacht to the Obersalzberg to run through the reasons for the imminent war one more time. The fifty or so high-ranking officers travelled to Hitler's Alpine retreat in civilian clothing to avoid attracting scrutiny. Only Göring stood out in his imaginative hunting outfit. In the great hall of the Berghof, several rows of chairs had been set up for the military men. At noon, Hitler, as usual wearing his simple party uniform, began a two-hour speech. He spoke extemporaneously, only casting the odd glance at the notes he held in his left hand. Since the spring, he said, it had become clear to him that "it will come to conflict with Poland sooner or later." Originally, he had wanted first to "turn against the West" in a few years' time, and only afterwards go after "the East," but he had been forced to reverse that sequence. Germany's relations with Poland had become "intolerable" and the time to strike was auspicious. "At present the probability is high that the West will not intervene," Hitler said. "We need to take this chance with ruthless decisiveness." England and France may have assured Poland of their assistance, but because of their insufficient military preparations they were incapable of providing it. "Our adversaries are little worms," Hitler sneered. "I observed them in Munich."

Another great advantage for Germany at that juncture was the Führer himself: "In the future there will never be a man who holds more authority than I do . . . But I can be killed at any time by a criminal or an idiot." While Germany's highest military leaders were used to hearing their commander-in-chief speak like this, they would have been surprised at the emphasis Hitler put on the economic necessity to go to war now. "We have nothing to lose and everything to gain," he proclaimed. "Because of the restrictions our economic situation imposes on us we can only hold out for a few years . . . We have no choice. We must act." With that, the dictator admitted that its gigantic military expenditures had indeed brought Germany to the verge of economic collapse, just as a former president of the Reichsbank, Hjalmar Schacht, who had been fired in January, had predicted. It was already clear from Hitler's words that the planned war would transfer the costs of this financial crisis to the peoples that Germany was going to subjugate.

Hitler withheld his big surprise until the end of his speech: the imminent signing of the German-Soviet non-aggression pact. This was a true bombshell. "Now I have got Poland right where I want it," Hitler crowed, adding that Germany no longer needed to fear a British blockade. "The east will provide us with grain, livestock, coal, lead and zinc." His only remaining concern was that, as in the autumn of 1938, "some swine will present a last-minute plan for mediation." At 3 p.m., after a snack on the Berghof terrace, Hitler resumed his lecture and sharpened his tone, possibly because he thought his generals were not showing sufficient enthusiasm for the planned operation. "We must show steely determination," a summary of Hitler's words read. "Shy away from nothing. No one should be in any doubt that we were determined right from the start to fight the Western powers. A struggle for life and death." Hitler promised to spark the conflict with an operation disguised as a Polish provocation. It did not matter how believable the pretence was. "Eighty million people must be given what is rightfully theirs," Hitler asserted. "Their existence must be secured . . . What matters is to give the German people sufficient living space."[93]

That evening, Hitler expressed his satisfaction with his speech even if he could not be entirely certain how it had been received. He was a "very good popular psychologist," he boasted, and in larger groups he always knew how his words came across. "With the older officers, it is different," the dictator admitted. "They always maintain a rigid, mask-like face that is impossible to read. That's how it was today."[94] Hitler's fear that his plans could be thwarted by a last-minute mediation proposal seemed to come true when that very evening the British ambassador, Sir Nevile Henderson, contacted Hitler with an urgent request that he be allowed to communicate a personal message from Prime Minister Chamberlain. In it, Chamberlain asserted unmistakably that his country would honour its commitments to Poland no matter what sort of deal Nazi Germany signed with the Soviet Union. War between Germany and England, Chamberlain added, would be a "great catastrophe." "I cannot see," the prime minister wrote, "that there is anything in the questions arising between Germany and Poland which could not and should not be resolved without the use of force."[95]

At noon the following day, Henderson arrived at the Berghof accompanied by Weizsäcker and the liaison between the Foreign Ministry and the Chancellery, Walther Hewel. Hitler was agitated when he received the British diplomat, subjecting him to tirades about purported Polish violence against the German minority in the country. "Hundreds of thousands of ethnic Germans are being mistreated, put in concentration camps and displaced in Poland today," he claimed, adding that England had issued Poland a "blank cheque," which it was now required to cover.[96] After a break, during a second audience, Hitler had calmed down somewhat but still rejected any compromise. In his reply to Chamberlain, which he handed to the ambassador, he accused the British government of rebuffing years of friendly overtures on the part of Nazi Germany. British guarantees of Polish security, he fumed, had unleashed a "wave of horrible terror" against ethnic Germans in Poland, and his regime could no longer tolerate it. If England were to stand by its ally and attack Germany, Hitler promised, he was prepared for a "long war" and determined to fight it.[97] Henderson must have come away from this conversation with the impression that Hitler was a man ruled by his emotions who was hardly capable of rational calculations. But in fact Hitler had been putting on a show. "Hardly had he closed the door behind the ambassador," Weizsäcker recalled, "than Hitler slapped his thighs with a laugh and told me: 'Chamberlain will not survive this conversation. His cabinet will fall by this evening.'"[98]

Yet in reality Hitler was not quite so confident about the British reaction. In the afternoon of 23 August, having gained "a comprehensive overview of the situation," he spoke to Goebbels, who had been summoned to the Berghof the day before, and was far more careful in his predictions. It was impossible to say whether the West would intervene. That would depend on the circumstances. "London is more committed than in September 1938," Hitler said. "We must go about it very cleverly. At the moment, England does not want war. But it has to save face. London is leaving no trick untried. In any case, we have to be prepared for an attack in the west." Meanwhile "nothing definitive" could be ascertained about France's position, either. In Italy, people were "not enthusiastic" about Germany's actions, but they would "probably have to go along with it." Japan, after refusing to join the German-Italian military alliance, had "missed its hour." Hitler left no doubt that the 1936 Anti-Comintern Pact had become obsolete for him: "The question of Bolshevism is at the moment of secondary importance . . . We face an emergency, and needs must."[99]

The previous evening, Ribbentrop had flown to Moscow in a new four-motor Condor. As per Hitler's express wish, the photographer Heinrich Hoffmann travelled with him. Hoffmann was charged with conveying the Führer's personal greetings to Stalin and attempting to form an exact picture of the latter's personality.[100] After a stop in Königsberg (Kaliningrad), the plane landed late in the morning of 23 August in the Soviet capital. At the airport, the German delegation was treated to the unusual sight of the swastika and hammer-and-sickle flags flapping cordially in the breeze.[101] After a quick breakfast in the German embassy, Ribbentrop went to the Kremlin to meet Molotov and Stalin. Time was of the essence, and negotiations progressed quickly. Back in the German embassy for dinner, Ribbentrop was certain: "We will definitely reach agreement tonight."[102]

Meanwhile at the Berghof, Hitler was waiting impatiently for news from Moscow. After dinner, he paced the terrace, collaring first one member of his entourage and then the next for conversations. Suddenly everybody's attention was grabbed by a rare natural spectacle. The sky darkened and bathed the legendary Unterberg mountain opposite the Berghof in a deep red. The adjutant Nicolaus von Below later claimed to have whispered to Hitler that this was a sign of a "bloody war," whereupon the Führer supposedly responded: "If it has to be, then better sooner than later."[103] Soon afterwards, Ribbentrop called from Moscow with the news that talks were making progress, although Stalin was demanding that the Latvian ports of Liepāja and Ventspils be made part of Russia's sphere of influence. Hitler quickly consulted a map and gave his approval.[104] Hours passed. "We tried to pass the crawling time by watching a film," Goebbels noted. "But that was hardly successful."[105] Eva Braun took a series of photographs showing Hitler and his paladins anxiously awaiting the result of Ribbentrop's mission.[106] Then, one hour after midnight, the German foreign minister called again and announced that the negotiations had been successfully concluded. "Finally, at one o'clock in the morning, receipt of the communiqué: complete agreement," recorded Goebbels, who stayed up with Hitler until 4 a.m. "A treaty with a long future and effective immediately. A world-historical event of unforeseeable consequences. The Führer and all of us are very happy."[107]

According to the pact, which was valid for ten years, the signatories agreed to refrain from "every act of violence, every aggressive action and every attack against one another" and not to join any political alliances that were "directly or indirectly against the other side." In the opaque diplomatic language of Article 2, Stalin gave Hitler *de facto* a free hand for his imminent war against Poland: "In the event that one of the parties concluding this treaty should become the object of war-like actions on the part of a third power, the other party concluding this treaty will not support this power in any form." A "top secret" additional protocol laid out the "delineation of the respective spheres of influence in eastern Europe." Finland, Estonia and Latvia would be part of the Soviet Union's sphere; Lithuania, part of Germany's. Poland was to be partitioned, with the border running along the Narew, Vistula and San rivers. And finally, Germany recognised Russia's interest in the Romanian province of Bessarabia.[108]

Although it did not come as a complete shock, the news of the German-Soviet non-aggression pact caused considerable surprise. "Russia in his bag!" wrote Shirer of Hitler's diplomatic coup. "What a *turn* events have taken in the last forty-eight hours. Bolshevik Russia and Nazi Germany, the arch-enemies of this earth, suddenly turning the other cheek and becoming friends and concluding what, to one's consternation, looks like an alliance."[109] Even those with "less tender sensibilities," wrote the court official Friedrich Kellner in his diary, were "thrown off balance for several days" by the sudden about-face.[110] Older National Socialists were particularly shocked by the pact. Several hundred members of the NSDAP, Baldur von Schirach was told, had discarded their party emblems in front of the "Brown House," the Nazi Party headquarters in Munich.[111]

The Nazi leadership disagreed as to how useful the pact was. For Goebbels, it was beyond question that Hitler had once again pulled off a "brilliant chess move."[112] On the other hand, Alfred Rosenberg, a defender of the anti-Bolshevist faith, was anything but pleased. "This Moscow pact will come back to haunt National Socialism at some point," he confided to his diary. "How can we talk about saving and re-forming Europe, if we have to ask the destroyers of Europe for help?"[113] Within his inner circle, however, Hitler made it clear that the pact with Stalin was but a temporary tactical measure and that he had by no means given up his goal of conquering "living space" in the east. "Everything I undertake is directed against Russia," he is supposed to have told Carl Jacob Burckhardt on 11 August. "If the West is too stupid and blind to realise this, I will be compelled to reach an understanding with the Russians to defeat the West, in order to turn, after it has been beaten, all my strength against the Soviet Union."[114] And a few days after the signing of the pact, he explicitly spoke out against those critics who had mistaken his manoeuvres for a fundamental ideological *volte-face*. In reality, Hitler explained, the deal was "a pact with Satan to drive out the devil."[115]

Over lunch at the Berghof on 24 August, Hitler acted disappointed at the scant echo the "world sensation" of the German-Soviet pact had attracted in the West. Chamberlain had not resigned as he had expected. On the contrary, the prime minister's determination to stand up to Germany's threats, which Chamberlain once again emphasised in a speech to Parliament, enjoyed the complete support of the British people.[116] "The war of nerves is approaching its high point," Goebbels concluded. ". . . There is once more a lot at stake on the next throw of the dice."[117] There were now only two days to go before the planned attack on Poland, and after his long absence, Hitler decided to return to the German capital.

In the afternoon of 24 August, the Führer's motorcade drove from the Obersalzberg to Reichenhall-Berchtesgaden airport. "The populace remained unusually silent as Hitler drove by—hardly anyone waved," recalled Albert Speer.[118] This was a first indication that the dictator's political preparations to take Germany to war were not popular. In Berlin as well, after Hitler's plane had landed at Tempelhof Airport shortly after 6 p.m., the calm was almost spooky. Even in front of the Chancellery, he was not greeted by the usual cheering crowds.[119]

An hour after Hitler had returned, Ribbentrop reported on his Moscow trip in the presence of Weizsäcker and Göring. Euphoric, "like a conquering hero," the German foreign minister had stridden through Hitler's apartment and been "very warmly greeted" by Hitler, Below reported.[120] Ribbentrop was still impressed from meeting Stalin and Molotov and had felt "somewhat like among old party comrades" in Moscow.[121] Hoffmann, whom Hitler invited to join them for dinner, chimed in with a positive estimation of the Soviet dictator. Stalin, the photographer said, had played the role of the "congenial host without any posing and in sovereign fashion." Hitler, who listened to this while inspecting the photos Hoffmann had taken, expressed his satisfaction. This was precisely how he had imagined his treaty partner, he said. And when Hoffmann praised the Crimean sparkling wine that had flowed in abundance in the Kremlin, Hitler joked that he was glad he had sent a representative who could "hold his alcohol just as well as Stalin."[122] In the days that followed, much to the surprise of his lunch guests, Hitler continued to express his regard for Stalin. The Soviet dictator's life resembled his own, he told them: the Georgian, too, had worked his way up from "an unknown man to the leader of a state."[123]

The following morning, Hitler sent a personal message to Mussolini. That was overdue, for Germany's Axis partner was visibly disgruntled at being kept in the dark about the negotiations with the Soviet Union. Hitler made up some transparent excuses for the lack of communication and sought to impress on the Duce the result he had achieved in Moscow. The German-Soviet non-aggression pact, Hitler wrote, had created a "completely new global political situation," which had to be seen "as a major victory for the Axis." At the same time, Hitler let it be known that an attack on Poland was imminent and that he expected Italy to honour their alliance.[124]

At 12:45 p.m., British ambassador Henderson received word that Hitler wanted to talk to him in fifteen minutes' time at the Chancellery. Unlike two days earlier at the Berghof, this time Hitler did not play the wild man, but rather treated the diplomat with studied politeness. He had "thought things over again," Hitler said, and wanted to take a step towards England "that would be just as decisive as the step towards Russia that had led to the most recent agreement." While Hitler left no doubt that he intended to solve the "German-Polish problem" by using violence—he said he could no longer tolerate such "Macedonian conditions on his eastern border"—he intimated that he would make Britain a "large, comprehensive offer" if he was allowed to have his way. Hitler was prepared to guarantee the continued existence of the British Empire "no matter the circumstances" and assist the British "wherever such assistance might become necessary." In addition, Hitler promised that he would no longer turn a deaf ear to "reasonable limits on armaments" and acknowledge Germany's western border as perma-nent. This was his "final offer," he stressed in conclusion, suggesting that Henderson immediately fly back to London to present these proposals to the British government.[125] Hitler's seeming generosity was nothing more than a ham-fisted attempt to get Britain to renege on its promises to Poland. Even Goebbels, never one to demur from praising his Führer's every feint as an inspired move, was sceptical about the prospects of success this time around. "England is not going to believe us any more," he noted.[126]

Hardly had Henderson left the Chancellery than, shortly after 3 p.m., Hitler summoned Keitel and issued orders to attack Poland.[127] The invasion was to commence at 4:30 the following morning. Goebbels was charged with drafting two statements, one to the German people and the other to the members of the NSDAP. The subject: "Clarification of the necessity of an armed conflict with Poland. Preparation of entire people for war which, if necessary, could last for months and years. Everything is to start that night."[128] At 5:30 p.m., Hitler received the French ambassador, Robert Coulondre, to inform him, as he had Henderson, that the German Reich was no longer prepared to accept the alleged Polish provocations. He harboured "no hostile feelings for France," Hitler said, and would regret it if their two countries came to war over Poland. Coulondre gave his "word of honour as an officer" that France would "send its forces to stand alongside Poland" in case of an attack.[129] A short time later, news arrived that Britain and France had formally concluded the mutual defence pact with Poland that had been agreed in principle on 6 April. This piece of news, a member of the German embassy in London told the British the next day, hit Berlin like a "bombshell."[130]

At 6 p.m., Italian ambassador Attolico had an appointment to deliver Mussolini's anxiously awaited reply to Hitler's missive from that morning. Considering how the Germans had treated the Italians in the preceding months, the response should not have come as a surprise. On 23 August in Rome, Ciano had already told the German finance minister, Count Lutz Schwerin von Krosigk, that England and France were prepared to go to war. He had been assured of that, Ciano said, "with unambiguous clarity" by the two countries' ambassadors to Italy. His country, Ciano added, was neither financially nor militarily prepared for a major war.[131] In unusually frank language, the Duce now informed the Führer that Italy was not ready to go to war and its ally could not expect any military assistance. The agreement had been for war in 1942, when Italy would have finished rearming; at present, an Italian intervention could only be considered if Germany delivered the hardware and raw materials that Italy needed to defend itself against an Anglo-French attack.[132] Hitler was "extraordinarily downcast" at Mussolini's answer, his adjutant Engel recorded, and "seemed to be at a loss."[133] Once again, in the eyes of the German leadership, Italy had gone back on its word. "The Italians are behaving just as they did in 1914," Hitler exploded after he had coolly dismissed Attolico.[134] Goebbels saw his worst fears confirmed: "So there we have it . . . Italy is not joining in . . . That changes the whole situation . . . The Führer broods and ponders. It is a heavy blow for him."[135]

It seems to have been this spate of bad news that made Hitler rescind the attack order around 7:30 p.m., after Keitel and Brauchitsch had assured him that it was still possible to halt the German war machine.[136] Although many troop commanders reacted with disbelief, the order to stand down got through almost everywhere. In Zossen, 50 kilometres south of Berlin, where the German Army High Command now had its headquarters, Hitler's countermand added to the already prevailing chaos. "At 10:10 p.m. the withdrawal order became known," noted Helmuth Groscurth, the liaison officer between the German military intelligence, the Abwehr, and the Army High Command. "Everyone was running around, their nerves frayed, even bearers of the Blood Order," the decoration given to Nazi Party veterans.[137]

Hitler detractors around Admiral Wilhelm Canaris, the chief of the Abwehr, believed that the Führer's prestige had been badly damaged and would not recover.[138] But that conclusion was mistaken. Even if the order to attack had been suspended, mobilisation continued. Still, some people close to the dictator hoped that he might change his mind at the last minute. "The door is not yet closed, but the crack is already quite small," Marianne von Weizsäcker reported on 25 August, adding that her husband was working "day and night" trying "everything humanly possible" to find a peaceful way out of the crisis.[139]

The chances for that were "somewhat better," Ernst von Weizsäcker told Hassell on the morning of 26 August, speculating that Hitler might be ready to moderate his demands.[140] The American broadcaster

William Shirer also told his listeners that day that people at the German Foreign Office were more optimistic about the prospects for peace.[141] But Hitler was not considering a change of course for a moment. When Göring asked him whether the postponement of the attack meant the cancellation of war, he was told: "No. I will have to see whether we can eliminate England's intervention."[142] And that was precisely the focus of his efforts in the final days of August, even though London had sent clear signals that he should not hope for any change in the British position. Still, Hitler called upon the mediation of a Göring confidant, the Swedish industrialist Birger Dahlerus, who conducted a secret shuttle diplomacy between Berlin and London in parallel to the countries' official contacts. The initiative yielded no results.[143]

"Another fantastic and exciting day," Goebbels concluded, looking back at the events of Saturday, 26 August. "The craziest rumours are circulating in Berlin."[144] That day the Nazi government announced it would be rationing food and raw materials important to the war effort.[145] Public transport was restricted, and called-up army reservists crowded the platforms at Berlin's major train stations. Anti-aircraft guns were installed on rooftops. It was evident just how serious the situation was when it was announced that the Tannenberg celebrations, which were going to take place the following day, and the Nuremberg party rally planned for September had both been cancelled.[146]

On the morning of the 26th, Henderson flew to London with Hitler's offer. The dictator had recovered somewhat from the shock of the previous day, remarking to a small group of listeners that England "would not declare war even if there was war with Poland." But when Walther Hewel contradicted him, saying, "My Führer, don't underestimate the British," an irritated Hitler abruptly terminated the conversation.[147] That afternoon, Attolico delivered the list of raw materials and other military necessities that Hitler had requested from Mussolini the night before. The Italian demands were intentionally made so high that there was no way Germany could fulfil them. "Again there were harsh words for Italy, although not for Mussolini," recalled the translator Paul Schmidt.[148] Hitler had no other choice than to ask his ally to at least support the German war efforts with "active propaganda and appropriate shows of military force." The Führer also reiterated his determination to "solve the question in the East . . . even at the risk of involving the West."[149]

In the evening, Coulondre appeared at the Chancellery and presented Hitler with a letter from French prime minister Édouard Daladier, confirming that France would stand by Poland. The decision over whether there would be war or peace now rested entirely in Hitler's hands, Daladier wrote, and no one would understand if he failed to seek a peaceful solution. Mincing no words, the prime minister invoked the consequences of a new world war, which would surely be even more devastating for the peoples of Europe than the war of 1914–18.[150] Coulondre could tell from Hitler's reaction that Daladier's appeal had been in vain. Things had proceeded too far, he was told. Poland was not going to hand over Danzig, but Hitler had set his mind on the city "returning to the Reich."[151]

On Sunday, 27 August, there was calm before the storm. "Developments have stagnated somewhat," wrote Goebbels, who met with Hitler that noon. "No one knows what is coming." The dictator did not conceal his disappointment over his rejection by Mussolini, which he demanded be kept top secret. "The death penalty for any betrayal," Hitler announced.[152] At 4 p.m., Ribbentrop delivered Hitler's response to the French ambassador. It confirmed Coulondre's impression from the day before. It may have requited Daladier's personal tone—"as a former frontline soldier I know as you do the horrors of war"—but on the issue itself, Hitler remained unbending. Indeed, he even upped the ante, demanding not just Danzig and a corridor to the city but control of the entire territory of the corridor. He did not see any possibility, he wrote, "of moving Poland, which with its guarantees now feels invulnerable, to reach a peaceful solution."[153] Hitler of course had long since ceased to be interested in any sort of "peaceful solution." He was merely trying to divert blame onto the Polish government. By this point, at the latest, Paris would have known where it stood with the German dictator.

Hitler had called a session of the Reichstag for 26 August, the original date for launching the attack on Poland, and the deputies had arrived in Berlin. To avoid their journey having been in vain, Hitler invited them to an informal gathering at 5 p.m. on 27 August in the New Chancellery. There, the Führer appeared with Reichsführer-SS Heinrich Himmler, Security Police chief Reinhard Heydrich,

SS-Obergruppenführer Karl Wolff, Reichsleiter Martin Bormann and Propaganda Minister Joseph Goebbels. Halder sketched the topics of Hitler's brief speech in his diary: "Situation very serious. Determined to solve the eastern question one way or another. Minimum demand: return of Danzig, solution to the corridor question. Maximum demand: 'depends on military situation.' If minimum demand not met, then war: brutal! He himself leading the way . . . War very difficult, perhaps hopeless. 'As long as I live, there will be no talk of capitulation!'" Halder also recorded his personal impression of the Führer as "in need of sleep, hunched, cracking voice, distracted."[154] The constant tension of the preceding days seems to have taken its toll on the German dictator. His adjutants found him "irritable as never before, grim and harsh."[155] At lunch on 28 August, Goebbels also perceived his Führer as "very serious and somewhat exhausted." "It is no wonder considering the stress on his nerves," wrote the propaganda minister. Goebbels was not at all happy that Hitler continued to speak positively of Italy and Mussolini. "Military alliances have no point," he complained to his diary, "if they can be cancelled twenty-four hours before a war."[156]

On 28 August Hitler set 1 September as the new date for the attack on Poland, although he did not rule out a further postponement.[157] William Shirer, in any case, reported that tension had got so acute that no one thought it could continue for very long. Germany already seemed to be at war: "Housewives stood in lines beginning early this morning to get their ration cards. It was the first time since the World War that these cards had made their appearance and the people, who had hardly believed a couple of days ago that war was possible, certainly looked grimmer as they stood patiently waiting for their cards."[158] More and more military personnel could be seen on Berlin's streets. "Cars with high army officers sped up and down the Wilhelmstrasse, or down the Tiergartenstrasse to the War Ministry in the Bendlerstrasse. Many cars and motorcycles were requisitioned . . . Squadrons of big bombers have also been roaring low over the city in formation."[159] Everyone was waiting for Nevile Henderson to return from London. What answer would he bring back from Whitehall?

Henderson arrived in the German capital at 5 p.m. but was not received at the Chancellery until 10:30 p.m. "Hitler was once again friendly and reasonable," Henderson recalled, "and appeared not dissatisfied with the answer which I had brought to him."[160] But that impression was mistaken. After scanning the memorandum, Hitler recognised that the British government had reacted to his "final offer" with a clever move. London had received assurances from Poland, the letter said, that it would resume the talks with Berlin that had been suspended in March. Therefore, Britain insisted that any understanding between Britain and Germany be preceded by a resolution of the differences between Germany and Poland. The Polish government was prepared to enter into direct negotiations, so it was up to Germany to agree to talk. In this fashion, London hoped to "open the way to world peace." The British government politely but firmly rejected Hitler's offer of guarantees for the empire in return for neutrality. It could not, the British letter stated, "for any advantage offered to Great Britain, acquiesce in a settlement which put in jeopardy the independence of a State to whom they have given their guarantee."[161]

That put Hitler on the spot. He could not reject negotiations with Poland out of hand without putting himself in the wrong in front of the German public and the international community. So he played for time. Shortly before midnight he took his leave of Henderson, telling the ambassador he would study the British letter carefully and answer it the following day. Afterwards, he conferred for quite some time with his closest advisers. Göring, who had been informed in advance of the British response via his mediator Dahlerus, seems to have pressed Hitler to proceed down the path of a peaceful resolution to the German-Polish conflict. "We do not want to go for broke," Weizsäcker quoted the field marshal as saying, to which Hitler replied "I have gone for broke all my life."[162]

If Weizsäcker accurately relayed Hitler's words, it was one of the rare moments in which the Führer was telling the truth. As a politician, Hitler had indeed always gone for broke—from the putsch of November 1923, through the last days of the Weimar Republic when his all-or-nothing approach had almost blocked his path to power, to his foreign-policy "weekend coups" in 1935 and 1936, when military intervention by the Western powers could have prematurely ended his rule. It was no accident that in August 1939, as he was about to embark on his final, fatal gambit, Hitler repeatedly invoked his great role model. "He said that like Friedrich the Great he was willing to bet everything on a single card," Groscurth noted in his diary.[163]

Like many others, Goebbels was deceiving himself when he wrote, following Hitler's conversation with Henderson, that "everything was up in the air."[164] There was no doubt that the German dictator was bent on going to war. On 29 August, his doubts—this time unfounded—that his generals would follow him without reserve caused Hitler to explode in a tirade. "One thing was clear," recorded Engel: "He was never going to let himself be told by military officers whether there should be peace or war. He simply did not understand the Germans soldiers who feared taking up arms. Friedrich the Great would turn in his grave, if he saw today's generals." Hitler believed he was following in the footsteps of the great Prussian king in the First Silesian War of 1740: just as Friedrich had annexed the Austrian province of Silesia, now he was going to take Poland. If the Western powers were "dumb enough" to stand by Poland, it was "their own fault, and they would have to be destroyed."[165]

Hitler pondered how to respond to Henderson all day on 29 August, finally deciding to act as though he were accepting the British invitation to resume direct negotiations with Poland while insisting on so many conditions that the Poles would find them unacceptable. At 7:15 p.m., when the British ambassador was once more summoned to the Chancellery, Hitler received him in a completely different mood than the previous evening. While the two men were still standing, Hitler handed Henderson his reply. The note began with the familiar litany of complaints about Polish intransigency and the persecution of the German minority in Poland, and reiterated the demands for a return of Danzig and the cessation of the corridor, before accepting the British suggestion of re-engaging in direct negotiations with Poland. The catch, however, was Hitler's demand that "a Polish personage with complete negotiating authority" be sent to Berlin by 30 August— the very next day.[166] That sounded like an ultimatum, Henderson protested. Hitler disagreed, and the conversation turned heated. When Hitler, simulating outrage, proclaimed that Britain clearly did not care how many Germans were "butchered" every day in Poland, Henderson raised his voice and even pounded his fist on the table, saying that he would not tolerate hearing any more such allegations. As always when he noticed that his bullying was not having the desired effect, Hitler switched roles. In a measured tone of voice, he expressed his hope that Germany could have cordial relations with Britain.[167]

A short time after Henderson had left the Chancellery, Attolico appeared with a personal message from Mussolini, in which the Duce offered to assist British efforts to negotiate a settlement. It seemed as though what Hitler had feared most was about to happen: namely, that some "swine" would wreck his designs for war with a last-minute mediation plan. As interpreter Schmidt recalled, Hitler dismissed the Italian ambassador with pronounced coolness: "He said that he was already in direct contact with the English and had already declared himself willing to receive a Polish negotiator."[168] What he failed to mention, of course, was that this was just a trick and he was not seriously considering holding talks with Poland.

The politicians in London saw through Hitler's games. Even before Whitehall officially responded on 30 August, it was made known through various channels that Hitler's final demand that Poland send an authorised representative that very day was unacceptable.[169] The morning editions of the newspapers reported that the Polish government had ordered a general mobilisation for 2:30 p.m. "That changes nothing about the military, but perhaps alters the psychological situation," Goebbels noted with satisfaction.[170] That evening, Hitler called Brauchitsch and Keitel to him and decreed that the attack was now definitively to begin on 1 September. He also signed an edict ordering the formation of a Ministerial Council for the Defence of the Reich, chaired by Göring, whose members included Keitel, Rudolf Hess as deputy Führer, Interior Minister Wilhelm Frick, Economics Minister Walther Funk and Chancellery chief Hans Heinrich Lammers.[171]

Hitler spent 30 August drawing up a list of sixteen points to be presented to Polish negotiators. They encompassed, among other things, the return of Danzig to the German Reich, an internationally monitored referendum in the territory of the corridor within a year, the creation of an intermediate transit corridor and the setting up of an investigatory committee to evaluate the treatment of Poland's German minority.[172] Because no one counted on the Poles actually sending a negotiator by such a tight deadline, these relatively moderately formulated demands served to provide an official pretence that Germany was willing to negotiate. "I need an alibi, particularly in front of the German people, to show that I have done everything I can to preserve peace," Hitler said a couple of days later. "For that reason, I made this generous suggestion about how to resolve the Danzig and corridor question."[173]

Around midnight, Henderson appeared under orders of his government at the German Foreign Ministry. What he told Ribbentrop could have come as no surprise after the clear signals earlier in the day. The British government declared that it could not recommend that the Polish government immediately send an authorised negotiator to Berlin and suggested that the German regime "get things rolling in the normal diplomatic manner by presenting its proposals to the Polish ambassador."[174] Ribbentrop nonetheless reacted with considerable irritation, repeatedly jumping up and yelling at Henderson, causing the Englishman to gradually lose his composure and raise his voice as well. Both breathing heavily, with "sparks in their eyes," according to interpreter Schmidt, the two diplomats faced one another like fighting roosters, almost coming to blows. When the pair had finally calmed down, Ribbentrop read out Hitler's sixteen-point list, but refused to give it to his British colleague as would have been standard diplomatic procedure. The list, Ribbentrop said, was "obsolete anyway since the Polish negotiator had failed to turn up."[175] There could have been no clearer demonstration that Hitler's putative "generous offer" was nothing more than a feint. Henderson left the Foreign Ministry "convinced that the last hope for peace had vanished."[176]

Ribbentrop immediately went to the Chancellery, where he was awaited by Hitler and Göring. The entire evening, those in his company had found the dictator "withdrawn, serious and at times apathetic." But after Ribbentrop's briefing he revived and hurled invectives at the British government, accusing it precisely of what he was guilty of himself. London was not playing fair, Hitler complained, and he tried—just as the Reich leadership had done in 1914—to shift the blame for the war onto others. He declared that he had no faith in any further talks, whether they were mediated via Dahlerus or anyone else. All of his efforts to drive a wedge between Poland and England had come to naught. Even he no longer thought it probable that Britain would abandon its commitments. In response to Göring's remark that he still could not believe that England would go to war,

Hitler is supposed to have answered, "When the Englishman ratifies a treaty, he does not break it twenty-four hours later."[177]

On 31 August, the tension began to simmer. As had been the case in all previous crises, people hectically scurried in and out of the Chancellery. When Hitler was not talking behind closed doors with ministers and generals, he was seen surrounded by his paladins. "Everyone wanted to hear the latest, and it was not hard to tell from Hitler's words that he was determined to solve the problem one way or another," wrote Below.[178] That afternoon, the dictator signed "Order No. 1 for Waging War," which decreed that the attack on Poland would begin at 4:45 the following morning.[179] "It seems that the die has finally been cast," commented Goebbels.[180] Throughout the day, Polish ambassador Lipski desperately tried to talk to Ribbentrop, but his German colleague kept him waiting until 6 p.m., and when Lipski answered in the negative to the question of whether he carried full authorisation to negotiate over the German proposals, Ribbentrop immediately cancelled the audience.[181] At 9 p.m., Goebbels ordered radio stations to report that the Nazi government had waited in vain for two days for a Polish negotiator and now considered its proposals "practically rejected." Hitler's sixteen points were read out as "evidence" that the Führer had extended the hand of peace until the very last.[182]

Around the same time, SS commandos staged a series of border incidents, including an attack on the German radio station in Gleiwitz (Gliwice) to give Germany a pretext to attack its neighbour. At the scene of the fake attack, they deposited the bodies of murdered concentration camp inmates dressed in Polish uniforms. "Polish attack on the Gleiwitz station—we will be making this really big," wrote Goebbels, even though he knew the truth behind the "attack." In the same diary entry, the propaganda minister noted: "The SS has special orders tonight."[183]

Hitler stayed up until midnight with his paladins in the Chancellery studying maps of the future theatre of war. He then dictated the speech he intended to give to the Reichstag the next morning.[184] At 4:45 a.m. on 1 September 1939, the battleship *Schleswig-Holstein*, anchored in Danzig harbour, opened fire on the Polish garrison on the Westerplatte Peninsula. In Danzig, police and SA and SS men swarmed out and arrested Polish civil servants, teachers and priests whose names were on lists that had been prepared. A fierce battle ensued for the city's main post office, which the Germans took after fierce resistance from Polish defenders. Shortly after the start of hostilities, Gauleiter Albert Forster, who had proclaimed himself the leader of the Free City on 23 August, announced that Danzig had been annexed by the Third Reich. Everywhere along the German-Polish border, Wehrmacht troops tore down barriers and crossed into Poland, as the Luftwaffe bombarded military bases as well as cities. The first target to be bombed as dawn was breaking was the militarily insignificant town of Wieluń.[185]

Shortly after 10 a.m., Hitler went to the Kroll Opera House after having received an energy-boosting injection from his doctor, Theodor Morell. The Reichstag had only been convened the day before, so not all the deputies had managed to travel back to Berlin in time. But in his role as president of the Reichstag, Göring arranged for the empty seats to be filled with SS men and party functionaries.[186] In a calculated symbolic gesture, Hitler wore a field-grey uniform. He was greeted in silence by the entire house. "He is very serious and looks worn, pale and thin," noted Rudolf Buttmann, a long-term party comrade from Hitler's Munich days. "His hair sticks up and looks like he has just raised his head from his pillows. His red eyelids also indicate sleepless nights."[187]

As was evident to all, Hitler was not on his best form. He seemed tired and occasionally had to search for words, something his listeners had never previously experienced. He began his speech by complaining about how Britain had disdainfully rejected his proposals. He claimed that Poland had provoked fourteen border incidents the previous night and had for the first time sent "regular army soldiers" to invade German territory. Using these lies, Hitler sought to portray the German attack as a defensive reaction, although, struggling for concentration, he mistakenly claimed hostilities had commenced an hour later than they actually had. "As of 5:45 a.m., we are firing back!" he exclaimed. "And from now on bomb will be met by bomb." Theatrically, Hitler declared that he wanted "nothing else now than to be the first soldier of the German Reich," promising that he would wear his grey uniform until Germany had won victory—or else "he would not live to see the end." He reiterated what he had told deputies on 27 August: "There is one word I have never known: capitulation!" Again he cited the example of Friedrich the Great, who "confronted a great coalition with a laughably small state and in the end triumphed in three struggles because he always kept heart, which we too need to do right now."[188] With that Hitler indicated that the war would not be limited to Poland and that the intervention of the Western powers was inevitable. Hitler's words were greeted with noticeably less applause than on earlier occasions.[189]

Sitting in the gallery, unnoticed by Hitler's audience, was Eva Braun. On 24 August, she had travelled with Hitler's entourage from the Obersalzberg to Berlin and had spent the final week of the month in an apartment furnished especially for her next to Hitler's in the Old Chancellery building. If something should happen to the Führer, she confided to her older sister, she wanted to die too.[190]

At the press conference following Hitler's speech, Goebbels instructed journalists to avoid the word "war" in all their reports and editorials. They were to take the line that Germany was repulsing a Polish attack.[191] Nonetheless, the German public did not react as the Nazi leadership hoped. As Shirer observed, the mood on the streets of Berlin that morning was sombre to apathetic. "None of the men bought the Extras which the newsboys were shouting," Shirer wrote in his diary.[192] In general, people had believed that despite his aggressive rhetoric, Hitler would solve the issue of Danzig and the corridor without war, as he had all previous crises.[193] Now they were unpleasantly surprised that their optimism was unfounded. "It is a given" that the war "was not greeted with enthusiasm," the Danish ambassador to Germany reported from Berlin on 1 September.[194] Even Goebbels had to admit that the mood was "serious," if "composed."[195]

Late in the afternoon, air-raid sirens sounded for the first time in Berlin, and everyone ran to their basements. But by the evening, something approaching normality seemed to have returned. Cafés, restaurants and beer taverns were as full as usual.[196] It seems most likely that many people still hoped that France and England would not enter the war. In Dresden, Victor Klemperer overheard a young man reading a newspaper in a display case say: "The English are much too cowardly to do anything." Variations of that, Klemperer wrote, summed up the general mood. The scholar himself doubted whether Britain would come to Poland's aid: "There still has been no declaration of war from them. Is it coming, or are they giving up their opposition and only issue weak protestations?"[197]

That morning, having been informed that Germany had attacked Poland, Chamberlain and Daladier ordered the general mobilisation of their respective countries. In the evening, Henderson and Coulondre gave Ribbentrop notes from their governments demanding that Germany immediately cease its aggression and withdraw its troops from Polish territory. Otherwise, Britain and France would not hesitate to honour their commitments to Poland.[198] Hitler's valet Heinz Linge claimed he heard the Führer remark that evening, "We will see whether they help Poland. They will back down again." Below concluded from the way the dictator behaved "that in his heart of hearts he still hoped the English would relent."[199] But this could only have been a vague hope, if indeed it existed. It was very probable that the Western powers would declare war on Germany, and Hitler knew it.

On 2 September, Mussolini tried again to mediate, suggesting that Germany and Poland should be pressured into an immediate cease-fire and that an international conference be convened to resolve the German-Polish quarrels. "The Führer would not be disinclined to agree if he had a bargaining chip," Goebbels wrote. "For that reason, all military efforts are directed at sealing off the corridor."[200] That evening, the British government rejected Mussolini's suggestion, arguing that Germany would first have to withdraw its troops from Poland before there could be any talk of negotiations.[201]

At 10:30 p.m., the British cabinet met, and a final decision was made. Henderson was to issue an ultimatum at 9:00 the following morning. If the German government had not agreed by 11 a.m.—noon in Germany—to desist from all hostilities and withdraw its troops, Britain would declare itself to be in a state of war.[202] Following his instructions, Henderson appeared at the appointed hour at the German Foreign Ministry and presented the ultimatum to the translator Paul Schmidt, since Ribbentrop refused to receive him. Schmidt hastened to the Chancellery, where he slowly translated the note, word for word. "When I was done, there was complete silence," he recalled. ". . . As if turned to stone, Hitler sat there staring. He was not dumbfounded, as some later claimed, nor did he burst out in a rage, as others have asserted. He sat there, completely still, not twitching a muscle. After what seemed to me to be an eternity, he turned to Ribbentrop, who had remained frozen at the window. 'What now?' Hitler asked his foreign minister with an enraged look in his eyes." Göring, who had remained with a group of others in the antechamber, is said to have remarked: "If we lose this war, heaven have mercy upon us!"[203] Historians have concluded from Schmidt's account that Hitler had comforted himself until the final moment with the illusion that England would not make good on its commitments. But there was no real conviction that Britain would remain neutral. The English declaration of war, which Chamberlain announced on the radio fifteen minutes after the ultimatum had expired, came as no surprise to the Führer, even if he may have secretly hoped right up to the final minute that the British would be put off by the risk of war and back away from their position.[204]

At 12:20 p.m., Coulondre passed along the French ultimatum, which ran out at 5 p.m.[205] A short time later, Hitler, pacing his conservatory, dictated a "Proclamation to the German People" to Below. He once again accused Great Britain, and particularly its "Jewish-plutocratic class of masters," of war-mongering. But the British government, he raged, should not deceive itself: "The Germany of the year 1939 is no longer the Germany of 1914! And the chancellor of the Reich today is no longer named Bethmann Hollweg."[206]

William Shirer was on Wilhelmplatz, where some 250 people heard the announcement via loudspeakers that England had declared war. "They just stood there as they were before," he wrote. "Stunned. The people cannot realise yet that Hitler has led them into a world war." Afterwards Shirer walked the streets of Berlin, where, in contrast to 1914, there was "no excitement, no hurrahs, no cheering, no throwing of flowers, no war fever, no war hysteria."[207] Shirer's observations are borne out by many German contemporaries who also registered a mood of, if anything, depression rather than enthusiasm for war.[208] The anti-Polish and anti-English propaganda had clearly not had the desired effect. It seems that only a small number of Germans, Nazi true believers, placed any stock in the official narrative that Germany was defending itself against an act of foreign aggression. "The atmosphere here is terrible—a mix of hopelessness and sadness," wrote Helmuth James von Moltke, later the head of the Kreisau Circle of resistance, to his wife on 3 September. "This war has something spectral and unreal. People do not support or want to bear it."[209]

Yet if there was widespread incomprehension at the Chancellery around noon that day, by the evening Hitler, at least, had recovered his usual self-confidence. The dictator sought to cheer up his entourage by asserting that England and France had "only made a pretence of declaring war so as not to lose face in front of the world." He was convinced that there would be "no fighting despite the declarations of war."[210] In private conservation with Goebbels, Hitler also dismissed the West's wait-and-see war. But in the meantime it had been announced that Chamberlain had appointed First Lord of the Admiralty Winston Churchill to his cabinet, leading the propaganda minister to doubt whether the Führer's prophecy would be proven right this time. "No one can say whether this will be a long and difficult war," Goebbels confided to his diary.[211] At 9 p.m., Hitler boarded a special train bound for Bad Polzin (Połczyn-Zdrój) in eastern Pomerania near the German-Polish border. A new chapter in his career had begun: the political leader was going to prove himself as the German people's "first soldier" and commander on the field of battle.

Ever since the 1960s and the controversy surrounding the historian Fritz Fischer's book *Germany's Aims in the First World War*, the consensus among German and international scholars has been that Imperial Germany bore the main responsibility for the First World War; even Christopher Clark's enormously popular *The Sleepwalkers* has not changed that view, as much as there may still be debate about the relative complicity of the other European powers.[212] There has never been any doubt about which side unleashed the Second World War. Germany alone bears absolute and sole guilt for that conflict, which, to quote Hans-Ulrich Wehler, "revealed the true nature of National Socialism and the goals of its charismatic Führer."[213] That much was clear to Thomas Mann on 28 August 1939, four days before Germany attacked Poland, when he noted that it would be a "blessing" if Hitler "were no longer allowed to engage in this repulsive business of blackmail and were to prove that his regime carried catastrophe within it right from the beginning."[214] Friedrich Kellner reached the same conclusion in December 1944 when he wrote that the war "did not suddenly break out overnight" but had been "prepared for years and intentionally unleashed." Kellner added: "There is no need to prove Germany's guilt for the war. It is clearly evident to the eyes of the world."[215]

Hitler wanted the war. It was the logical end to the path which he had taken since being appointed chancellor on 30 January 1933, and upon which conservative elites—generals, diplomats and industrial arms manufacturers—with few exceptions had willingly followed him.

As the dictator himself emphasised in a speech to his commanders a few weeks after the conclusion of the Polish campaign in the autumn of 1939, he would never have undertaken to "educate the people, build up the Wehrmacht and rearm" if he had not had the will to use force "right from the beginning."[216] There was no room for the idea of lasting peace in Hitler's social-Darwinist world view. Peace, Hitler often reiterated privately, would only "lead humanity into a quagmire." Every generation, he believed, had to "steel itself anew and collect new experiences."[217]

The only fault that can be attributed to the Western powers is that they failed to stay Hitler's arm while that was still possible. They had tried everything they could, to the point of self-abnegation, to tame his drive for expansion in the interests of preserving peace in Europe. It was not until the policy of appeasement had definitively failed in the spring of 1939 that the Western powers decided to confront Germany's Führer—too late to undermine Hitler's determination to wage war, if indeed that drive could have been checked under any circumstances. By contrast, in order to buy time for a conflict it knew was coming, the Soviet Union temporarily allied itself with its mortal enemy and became complicit, in the short term, in Hitler's policies of aggression.

None of that changes by one iota Nazi Germany's sole responsibility for the catastrophe that was set in motion with the invasion of Poland. None other than the industrialist Fritz Thyssen—the early patron of the Nazi movement who had distanced himself from the regime soon after 1933 and emigrated to Switzerland at the start of the war—expressed the fact clearly in a letter to Hitler in late December 1939. "I condemn the politics of the last years," Thyssen wrote, "and I raise my voice against this war, into which you have unscrupulously plunged the German people and for which you and your advisers must bear responsibility . . . Ultimately, your policies will amount to *finis Germaniae*."[218]

2

Poland 1939–1940: Prelude to a War of Annihilation

"Annihilation of Poland in the foreground. Goal the eradication of vital forces, not the reaching of a certain line," read a bullet-point summary of Hitler's speech at the Berghof on 22 August 1939, when he described to his commanders how he envisioned the coming war. ". . . Hearts closed to pity. Brutal action . . . The stronger is in the right. Maximum severity."[1] Already on 3 February 1933, in Hitler's first appearance in front of Germany's assembled commanding officers, the newly appointed chancellor had talked of the "ruthless Germanisation" of territories to be conquered in the east. In later speeches too—most recently in an address to army troop commanders in the Kroll Opera House on 10 February 1939—Hitler had left no doubt he would "never shy back from the extreme" to solve "the German problem of space." Now the dictator sharpened his tone and made it unmistakably clear to his commanders that the Polish campaign would not be restrained by the limits of conventional warfare. For Hitler and those who executed his ideological obsessions, Germany's invasion of Poland was from the very outset a war of racial extermination. Poland was to be turned into an experiment for creating a "new order" in central eastern Europe. Here the Germans would demonstrate, for the first time, what the "conquest of living space" meant in practice.[2]

In the early hours of 1 September, fifty-four German divisions, encompassing 1.5 million men, launched the attack on Poland. The German plan of operation aimed at a swift military decision. Two army groups—one in the north under Colonel-General Fedor von Bock and the other in the south under Colonel-General Gerd von

Rundstedt—were to entrap and destroy Polish forces in several pincer attacks following in quick succession. Within the first few days, the German armies had already breached Polish lines and penetrated deep into the country. Krakow fell on 6 September and two days later, German tanks had reached the outlying districts of Warsaw. "Militarily, Poland is about to collapse completely," Hitler told Goebbels. "They are sitting in a cauldron. Their situation is hopeless. Our tanks are advancing unstoppably."[3] Within a fortnight, the conflict was decided, although parts of the Polish army continued to put up desperate resistance.[4]

The reasons why German forces achieved such a strikingly quick victory are obvious. Polish troops were hopelessly inferior to the Wehrmacht, particularly in terms of warplanes and tanks. It had only been a matter of hours before German Stukas had taken out the Polish air force and established absolute domination of the skies. "The Poles had no defence against it; no way of moving their troops without subjecting them to decimation from the air. It was one-sided warfare," reported William Shirer.[5] For the first time, German commanders had closely coordinated their motorised units with the activities of the Luftwaffe. It was a prelude of the Blitzkrieg to come.[6]

Polish hopes that France and England would launch an offensive in the west and provide some relief for their own badly damaged troops were disappointed. Hitler's prophecy proved true: the Western powers remained inactive. "Not a single shot fired in the west," noted a baffled Goebbels on 7 September, and that would not change in the days that followed.[7] "If France and Germany are at war . . . it's strange kind of war," noted Shirer. Most of his fellow foreign correspondents were depressed by what seemed to be the seemingly unstoppable German advance. "It begins to look as though in Hitler we have a new Napoleon who may sweep Europe and conquer it," Shirer confided to his diary.[8]

On 17 September, the Polish government fled to Romania. That same day, Stalin ordered the Red Army to invade Poland from the east and take possession of the territory east of the Narew–Vistula–San line that the Soviet Union had been promised under the non-aggression pact. Vanguard German units, however, had already advanced as much as 200 kilometres past the agreed demarcation line and had to be ordered back, much to the disgruntlement of the

German army leadership. Halder spoke of a "day of shame for the German political leadership," when Brauchitsch informed him about the Nazi-Soviet agreement.[9]

On 25 September, the Luftwaffe bombarded Warsaw. Thousands of civilians fell victim to the air raid, the worst of the campaign thus far, and broad sections of the old city lay in ruins. Two days later, Warsaw capitulated, and on 6 October, the remnants of the Polish armed forces surrendered. Casualty figures show how uneven the fighting had been: 70,000 Poles were killed and 133,000 wounded, compared with 11,000 dead and 30,000 wounded Germans; 700,000 Polish soldiers became prisoners of war.[10] With victory over Poland, the "toughest task has been completed," wrote Colonel-General Walter von Reichenau, commander of the 10th German Army, on 7 October to the Reich protector of Bohemia and Moravia, Konstantin von Neurath. "It would not have been good if things had started up on both fronts."[11]

Hitler spent most of the three weeks of the Polish campaign in the mobile headquarters of his special train. It moved around several times. On 5 September, it travelled 30 kilometres from Bad Polzin to a troop exercise ground in Gross Born (Borne Sulinowo) near Neustettin (Szczecinek). From there, it pushed forward to Ilnau (Jełowa), northeast of Oppeln (Opole) in Upper Silesia, and then, three days later, to Gogolin, 22 kilometres further to the south. Each of these locations was declared a restricted military zone and sealed off from the outside world by a range of security measures, directed by the commandant of the Führer's main headquarters, Major-General Erwin Rommel.[12] The special train, which was pulled by two locomotives, was protected from aerial attack by special armed carriages at the front and back equipped with anti-aircraft guns. Behind Hitler's salon car was his command carriage with its "situation room" and intelligence centre, which remained in constant contact with the Army High Command and the frontline command posts. Hitler was accompanied by his closest staff members: his personal adjutants, Wilhelm Brückner and Julius Schaub; his secretaries, Christa Schroeder and Gerda Daranowski; his doctor, Karl Brandt or sometimes, as a replacement, Hanskarl von Hasselbach; his valets, Heinz Linge and Karl Krause; and his four military adjutants, Rudolf Schmundt, Karl-Jesko von Puttkamer, Gerhard Engel and Nicolaus von Below. Hitler's permanent entourage also included Martin Bormann, the staff director in the Office of the Deputy of the Führer, who had begun to make himself indispensable well before 1939; press chief Otto Dietrich, who kept his boss informed about the news; and the photographer Heinrich Hoffmann, who followed the Polish campaign as a "pictorial reporter." One carriage was reserved for the top military leaders, including Keitel, head of the Wehrmacht Supreme Command, Alfred Jodl, and the liaison officers to the army, navy and air force.[13]

The proximity of the Führer's special train to the theatre of war allowed Hitler to form his own impression of running operations. After Jodl's situation reports, the dictator usually set off for the front with his military advisers and members of his entourage, only returning in the late evening. "The boss drives off with his gentlemen in a car, and we are condemned to wait and wait," wrote Christa Schroeder to a friend on 11 September 1939.[14] When visiting the headquarters of his armies, Hitler would take briefings about the progress of the campaign but rarely got involved in operational decisions. Even towards Brauchitsch, with whom he met several times, Hitler held back.[15] Hoffmann took photos of the Führer in the role of "first soldier of the Reich," which were then published in magazine articles about "the Führer on the Front." They depicted Hitler sitting with his military subordinates in front of his special train and studying maps, or palling around with soldiers at the front and taking mess with them. "The commander-in-chief shares the food of the front-line soldier" ran the caption. With his book of photographs *Hitler in Poland*, which was published in late 1939 and enjoyed healthy sales, Hoffmann helped established the propagandistic image of the "caring Führer," who looked after soldiers' well-being at the front.[16] By contrast, Dietrich's belated attempt in his book *On the Road to Victory* to attribute the Wehrmacht's military triumph to Hitler's strategic genius rang hollow, given that the campaign had still been prosecuted entirely by the professional military commanders.[17]

On 18 September, Hitler left Upper Silesia for East Prussia. A day later, travelling via Danzig-Oliva (Oliwa), he reached the sea resort of Zoppot (Sopot), where he stayed in the luxurious Casino Hotel, the first time on his trip that he had quartered himself in a building. That afternoon, to cheers from crowds, he had himself driven to the Artushof on Langer Markt in Danzig. "It was a victory parade," recalled Hitler's army liaison officer Nikolaus von Vormann. ". . . Everyone who could crawl had turned out. Cheering, waving and yelling, the crowd broke through the barriers and pressed up against our car to get a close look at the Führer or to shake someone's hand."[18] After being greeted by Gauleiter Albert Forster, Hitler addressed the crowd. In his address, broadcast on all German radio stations, he once again blamed Poland for the war and declared the fighting over after only eighteen days. "Never before in history has the couplet 'With horses, carts and men, /God has defeated them' been more fitting," Hitler boasted. Addressing England and France, he reiterated his determination to persevere in a long war—"Germany never capitulates"—but also signalled his willingness to negotiate peace with the Western powers, albeit on his terms.[19] Listening to the speech on the radio in Princeton, Thomas Mann noted: "The expected peace offensive is full of calculated lies and invokes God. A most repulsive impression."[20] Twice, on 22 and 25 September, Hitler flew to an airstrip on the margins of the besieged Warsaw and inspected through a scissors telescope the havoc wreaked by the Luftwaffe and artillery bombardments. In the afternoon of 26 September, almost unnoticed by the public, Hitler's special train pulled into Berlin's Stettin Station.[21]

That morning, Colonel-General Werner von Fritsch, whom Hitler had unceremoniously removed from his position as army high commander in early 1938, was buried in Berlin's Invalidenhof Cemetery. He had been mortally wounded four days previously by a ricocheted bullet in the Warsaw suburb of Praga. "We are all stunned by this tragedy," wrote General Günther von Kluge, the commander of the 4th Army. ". . . His death has reopened old wounds and causes pain, suffering and bitterness."[22] Hitler, who had happened to be not far away the day Fritsch was shot, received the news of the incident without emotion, ordering a state funeral. Originally, he had intended to take part in the ceremony but his plane could not take off in time due to bad weather—perhaps a welcome excuse to skip the proceedings.[23]

On 1 October, Italian foreign minister Ciano arrived in Berlin on a mission to improve Mussolini's relations with his German ally, which had deteriorated since late August. He found Hitler "very cheerful" and "relaxed." For almost two hours, the dictator regaled the diplomat with anecdotes about the military campaign, reciting endless figures concerning prisoners of war and captured military hardware. "I was most impressed by his confidence in victory," Ciano wrote in his diary.[24] On 5 October,

Hitler flew to Warsaw to inspect the victory parade of the 8th Army—
it was to be the only time the Führer took part in an event of this sort.
Before the flight back to Berlin, Brauchitsch had prepared a breakfast in
Hitler's honour on the airstrip. But the Führer refused to take his seat
at the lavishly set table, remarking that he "only ate standing up at the
field mess with the soldiers," before turning his back brusquely on the
table. Thus Hitler played the role of the simple soldier in his grey
uniform, who considered himself duty bound to refuse every comfort,
even if it was offered by the Wehrmacht's top brass.[25]

How did the German people react to the triumphs of the Polish
campaign? On 8 September, Shirer noted a "strange indifference of
the people to the big news" and over the following days registered
his surprise that life in the German capital seemed to go on unchanged,
with opera houses, theatres and cinemas open for business and packed.
Shirer saw "no wild rejoicing." Instead he wrote in his diary of hearing
"considerable grumbling about the war" from women on the metro.[26]
Nor was there any visible enthusiasm for the war in the German
provinces. "Subdued mood," noted the diarist Friedrich Kellner on
16 September. People's spirits were particularly lowered by the strictly
enforced nighttime blackout. "In the evenings, whole towns are as still
as cemeteries," Kellner wrote. "Old people hardly dare to go out on
the street because it is so dark."[27]

In late September, however, as a quick German victory became
certain, the mood changed. "I have still to find a German, even among
those who don't like the regime, who sees anything wrong in the
German destruction of Poland," confided Shirer to his diary. " . . . As
long as the Germans are successful and do not have to pull in their
belts too much, this will not be an unpopular war."[28] Victor Klemperer
witnessed similar scenes in Dresden: "Everywhere things are dominated
by absolute confidence and the intoxication of victory . . . This
monstrous victory has caused all internal dissatisfaction to recede."[29]
The change in mood derived not least from the expectation that a peace
agreement with the West would follow the end of military operations.
Everyone believed that "the Führer would soon succeed in making
peace," Goebbels summarised the prevailing sentiment in the capital.[30]

Hitler was initially unsure about whether he should make a peace
offering after the end of the Polish campaign or launch a military

offensive in the west. In conversation with Goebbels, who visited him on 14 September in his quarters in Upper Silesia, he emphasised his intention to "clear things up in the west" once "things had been settled in the east." He did not want a long war: "Any war must be short and complete."[31] By contrast, Dietrich, who was already back in Berlin by 23 September, reported that in the face of the imminent fall of Warsaw, Hitler was "not disinclined to make peace" and did not want to "proceed aggressively in the west," preferring to give diplomacy a chance.[32] It seems that the German dictator was pursuing a double strategy of courting the West with false prospects of peace while pushing forward with preparations for military conflict on the western front.

In the afternoon of 27 September, just one day after returning to the German capital, Hitler ordered the heads of the Wehrmacht to the Chancellery and told them, in the presence of Keitel, that they should "get their heads around" the thought of the war continuing. Time was not on Germany's side, he said, since the Western powers would use any pause in the hostilities to close the military gap, particularly in terms of tanks and warplanes. "For that reason, we must not wait until the enemy attacks, but strike the West, if a peaceful resolution is impossible," Hitler said. "The sooner, the better." Hitler gave the three top military commanders no opportunity to express their views of the situation.[33]

It would seem that from the start Hitler had little faith in the possibility of a "peaceful resolution" with the Western powers, although he did put some stock in the propagandistic value of a peace initiative, particularly among the German people. On 30 September, he informed Goebbels that he planned to convene the Reichstag after the end of the Polish campaign and make a "major peace offer" that would confront England and France with an "either–or situation."[34] Hitler began working on his speech intensively at the beginning of October. On the fifth of the month, before setting out to inspect the German victory parade in Warsaw, he gave his draft to Goebbels to read. "A masterpiece of diplomacy," the propaganda minister commented, gushing that the speech would build London and Paris "every golden bridge" and make "an enormous impression on the whole world."[35] But Hitler and Goebbels were fundamentally deceiving themselves.

At noon on 6 October, Hitler approached the lectern in the Kroll Opera House to address the Reichstag. He spoke more calmly than usual, although at times he was reading from his script so quickly that some of the deputies had trouble following his words.[36] What he said was ill-suited to encourage any desire for peace in so far as the prospect actually existed. Most of the speech consisted of clichéd remarks about his willingness to reach an understanding that would have had no resonance with the Western powers after their experience of the German dictator in 1939. Hitler's address contained few concrete proposals, but the Führer did make it abundantly clear that the state of Poland had ceased to exist in its previous form. Germany and the Soviet Union alone would determine the new borders in eastern Europe, with the rest of Europe being allowed no say in the matter. The audience must have been correspondingly sceptical about Hitler's suggestion that a conference of the great nations of Europe should be called. What purpose could that possibly serve, especially when the dictator followed up his conciliatory-sounding remarks with naked threats to "Churchill and comrades," whom he characterised as henchmen of "Jewish-international capitalism"? Should his outstretched hand be rebuffed, Hitler warned, there would be no further offer forthcoming from his side. "We will fight," he snarled. "Neither the power of arms nor time will put down Germany."[37]

"This dirty charlatan wants to be released from war to win time and enslave everyone using tried-and-tested 'peaceful' means," Thomas Mann commented. "There is nothing at all to be gained by the democracies in terms of an honourable peace. The war must continue undeterred."[38] Still, Hitler's speech did encourage the belief among the German public that a peace agreement was at hand. On the morning of 10 October, a rumour spread like wildfire that the English king had abdicated his throne, Chamberlain had resigned and an armistice had been agreed. "On Berlin's streets and squares there were joyous celebrations by people who believed the news," reported the SS Security Service. The denial issued via radio that afternoon as part of the "News from the Reich" caused "profound despair" everywhere— a sign of how much the German people hoped for peace.[39]

Two days later, on 12 October, Chamberlain emphatically rejected Hitler's overtures in a speech to the House of Commons. The Reich chancellor's vague proposals were no basis for negotiations, the prime minister said, and if Germany wanted peace, it would have to prove it by deeds, not words.[40] For his part, in a conversation with the Soviet ambassador to London, Ivan Maisky, First Lord of the Admiralty Winston Churchill called Hitler's offer "absolutely unacceptable," adding that the dictator was setting out the terms of a conqueror, even though the British people had yet to be conquered.[41]

Hitler was by no means surprised by this rejection. Already on 10 October, he had drawn Brauchitsch's and Halder's attention to a lengthy memorandum he had written in which he once again argued for the necessity of an offensive in the west, ideally in the autumn of 1939. The goal consisted of "taking care militarily once and for all" of the Western powers, which meant stripping them of the "power and capability to once again oppose the German people's state consolidation and further development in Europe."[42] The basic idea behind the memorandum had flowed into "Order No. 6 for Waging War" of 9 October, in which Hitler re-emphasised his determination to "act actively and offensively" in the near future if England and France were unwilling to end hostilities. A "lengthy waiting period" would only increase the military strength of the enemy, Hitler argued.[43] Over lunch at the Chancellery on 13 October the dictator seemed positively relieved at Chamberlain's rejection, saying that he was "glad" that the war against England "could now start." The English would have "to learn from their mistakes."[44] In the days that followed, German propaganda stepped up its attacks on the British leadership. The hardest shots were reserved for Churchill. "We will not let him get away," wrote Goebbels. "We will not rest until he has been swept aside."[45]

On 21 October, Hitler invited his Gauleiters to the Chancellery to inform them about his plans. There was no more talk of peace. In the not too distant future, Hitler said, he would "sock the English on the jaw," which would knock them out. While he might announce officially that he was willing to abide by international agreements concerning the conduct of war, in reality he was not going to spare anyone, including civilian populations. Once England and France had been subdued, he would "turn his attention back to the east and clear things up there." Whereas in his Reichstag speech of 6 October he had still spoken of the "common interest with Russia" as the beginning of a "positive, lasting cooperation,"[46] Hitler now admitted with extraordinary openness to his paladins that he had by no means lost sight of his long-term project: waging a war for "living space" against the Soviet Union. The meeting between German troops and the Red Army had revealed how little the "Russian army" with its "badly trained and equipped" soldiers was worth. The end result, in Goebbels' summary of the two-hour speech, would be "the greater, all-encompassing German people's Reich," which would completely revise the balance of power in Europe established after the Peace of Westphalia of 1648. The Führer announced that it would also "incorporate" Belgium and Switzerland.[47]

Hitler had had no concrete plans for the future destiny of Poland at the beginning of Germany's military campaign. According to the secret additional protocol to the German-Soviet non-aggression pact of 23 August, it was down to later agreement to decide "whether it was in the [signatories'] joint interest to preserve an independent Polish state and what its borders were to be."[48] It seems that, to start with, Hitler was inclined to support the creation of an independent Polish rump state. On 12 September, Ribbentrop declared that this was the "solution to which the Führer was most amenable because he could then negotiate a settlement for peace in the east with a Polish government."[49] In his speech in Danzig on 19 September, however, Hitler confined himself to stating that the "ultimate shaping" of the occupied Polish territories depended primarily on Germany and the Soviet Union, "which both had vital national interests there."[50]

On 27 September, Ribbentrop flew back to Moscow to sign the German-Soviet Boundary and Friendship Treaty. It revised the demarcation line running through the middle of Poland. Stalin forwent the *voivodship* of Lublin and the eastern part of the *voivodship* of Warsaw, i.e., the central Polish territory between the Vistula and Bug Rivers, as well as the Suwałki Gap. In return, the Third Reich recognised Lithuania as part of the Soviet sphere of influence. By this point, there was clearly no longer any interest in forming a rump Polish state from territory conquered by either of the two powers.[51]

In his Reichstag speech on 6 October, Hitler announced a "new order of ethnographic relations," by which he meant large-scale population resettlements in occupied Poland.[52] The impressions he had gathered on his travels to the front line had strengthened his fantastic belief in a "master race." "The cities were caked in filth," he told Alfred Rosenberg in late September. "If Poland had ruled for another couple of decades over the old parts of the Reich, everything would have been infested and dilapidated. Only an unerring masterly hand can rule here."[53] He expressed even greater contempt in conversations with Goebbels in early October. "The Führer's verdict on the Poles is devastating," the propaganda minister wrote. "More animal than human, completely coarse and undistinguished . . . They should be squeezed into their own little state and left to their own devices."[54] By now Hitler was no longer entertaining the notion of a rump Polish state with its own government, but rather a residual territory under German rule—a kind of reservation for Poles.[55]

In a series of edicts in October 1939, Hitler defined the contours of this "new order." Large parts of western Polish territory were annexed by the Reich and divided into two new *Gau* districts: Danzig–West Prussia under Albert Forster and Posen—or, as it was known from 1940, the Wartheland—under Arthur Greiser, the former president of the Danzig Senate. Other parts of Poland were added to the existing *Gaue* of East Prussia and Silesia. With that the border of the Third Reich had been moved 200 kilometres to the east. Some 7.8 million Poles lived in the annexed territories, making up 80 per cent of their population.[56] The rest of central Poland, including the districts of Warsaw, Lublin, Radom and Krakow, formed the "General Government of Poland," which was treated as an "ancillary country" of the Reich, a category unknown under international law. The Third Reich's leading lawyer, Hans Frank, was appointed governor-general, reporting directly to Hitler. From November 1939, he resided like a landed aristocrat in Krakow's Wawel Royal Castle.[57]

On 25 October, the military administration in occupied Poland was replaced by a civilian administration. Hitler had already laid out with brutal clarity the methods by which administrators were to operate at a meeting on 17 October in the Chancellery that was attended by Frank, Himmler, Hess, Bormann, Lammers, Keitel, Frick and Frick's state secretary Wilhelm Stuckart. A "bitter ethnic struggle" would have to be waged that would "know no legal bounds." It was not the administration's task to economically develop or make a "model province" of the occupied territories. On the contrary, the standard of living was to be kept low. "All we want to harvest there is labour," Hitler stated, and every effort had to be made to prevent a Polish intelligentsia from emerging as a leadership elite. He summarised his core message as: "Any traces of a consolidation of conditions in Poland must be swept aside. A worthless 'Polish economy' should be allowed to blossom. Governing the territory must enable us also to cleanse the Reich of Jews and Polacks."[58] At the same time, on 17 October Hitler decreed that the SS and the police were no longer subject to either military or civilian law. In future, in view of their "special deployment," they were to be subject to a "special liability in criminal affairs."[59] With that, the conditions were in place to unleash an unlimited rule of violence, guided by the ideological and racist imperatives of the regime and its Führer.

In the first days of the war, regular Wehrmacht units were followed by first five, later seven, SS Einsatzgruppen, which had been formed the previous July on the orders of Heydrich as the head of the Security Police. Their members, around 2,700 men in total, were primarily recruited from SS and police departments in the eastern parts of Germany where the German armies had assembled to invade Poland. The commanders of these mobile commandos, among them the head of the Hamburg Gestapo, Bruno Streckenbach, had been selected by Heydrich personally. According to the "Guidelines for the Foreign Deployment of the Security Police and the Security Service," which had been agreed with the military High Command, they were responsible for "fighting all elements hostile to Germany and the Reich in enemy territory behind the lines of the fighting forces."[60] This was an elastic job description that gave the Einsatzgruppen remarkable leeway. Formally, they were under the command of the respective armies to which they were attached, but practically they operated on their own authority in what was in effect an extralegal space, serving as the eager executioners of the "bitter ethnic struggle" ordered by the leadership of the Reich.

On 3 September, Himmler, doubtlessly with Hitler's approval, ordered "Polish insurgents apprehended in the act [of rebellion] or in possession of weapons" to be shot on the spot. Four days later, at a meeting with the administrative directors of the Gestapo, the Criminal Police and the Security Service, Heydrich announced that "the leading segments of the Polish population . . . were to be rendered as non-harmful as possible."[61] A special wanted list with the names of those belonging to the Polish intelligentsia, the Catholic clergy, the aristocracy and Poland's Jewish communities had been prepared by Heydrich's henchmen the previous spring.

Following these orders, the Einsatzgruppen unleashed a terror that overshadowed everything following the *Anschluss* of Austria in March

1938 or the invasion of the rump of Czechoslovakia in March 1939. In September 1939 alone, 12,000 Poles were shot to death.[62] At a further meeting of the administrative directors on 21 September, Heydrich reported that by now "at most 3 per cent . . . of the Polish leadership" were still alive in the occupied territory and that these people too needed to be made "non-harmful."[63] The murders continued after the end of the fighting. Between September and December 1939, at least 40,000 Poles fell victim to this campaign of terror.[64]

The Einsatzgruppen were assisted in their bloody work by the Volksdeutscher Selbstschutz (Ethnic German Self-Protection) organisation, a militia formed primarily from members of the German minority in Poland. In the months prior to the start of the war, Goebbels' hateful and ever-intensifying propaganda had dramatically bolstered tensions between Poles and ethnic Germans. These had been vented in reprisals against Germans after the beginning of the German attack. The worst incident occurred on 3 September in the city of Bydgoszcz (Bromberg in German), where Polish civilians killed over a hundred Germans.[65] Himmler and Heydrich used the "Bloody Sunday of Bromberg" as a welcome pretext to portray the cruelty of the Einsatzgruppen and the militias as a retribution for Polish "atrocities" and to order the executioners in the field to be even more ruthless. Selbstschutz paramilitaries in Western Prussia under the command of Himmler's former adjutant Ludolf von Alvensleben were particularly brutal. "You are the master race," Alvensleben told his underlings in October 1939. "Do not be soft. Be pitiless and clear away everything that is not German and that could slow us down in our efforts to rebuild."[66] In the initial months of the occupation, Alvensleben's death squads murdered more than 4,000 civilians. In early November, Himmler dissolved the Selbstschutz and incorporated its men into the SS. By the end of that month, Heydrich's deputy, Werner Best, ordered the Einsatzgruppen to disband too. Their members were assigned to offices of the Security Police and the Security Service in Krakow, Lublin, Radom and Warsaw, where they continued their murderous mission.[67]

Right from the start, not just the Einsatzgruppen and ethnic German militias but regular soldiers in the Wehrmacht were involved in this orgy of violence. Many of them had invaded Poland with racist preconceptions of "the Slavs" and "the Jews" in their heads. A long-fostered sense of cultural superiority was mixed with deep-seated anti-Polish and anti-Semitic resentment that had been reinforced by propaganda. The letters German soldiers sent home from Poland provide ample evidence of this. They are full of references to "Polacks" and "repulsive Jewish characters."

But stereotypical images of the enemy and prejudice are not sufficient to explain the depth of the German brutality; it required, in addition, impressions gathered on the field of battle. When Germany invaded Belgium in 1914, fear of *franc-tireurs*, or partisans, had led to massacres of Belgian civilians, and in 1939, too, many German soldiers and officers believed that the enemy was devious and would gladly resort to ambushes. "The Poles are treacherous," wrote General Erich Hoepner. "They fire at military columns and individual soldiers behind the lines."[68] Such fears may have barely reflected reality; in most instances, the reported incidents were mere figments of soldiers' imagination. But they had very real and devastating consequences, reducing their scruples about attacking Polish civilians.[69] As early as 5 September, Quartermaster General Eduard Wagner noted that "the difficulties in backward Poland are getting ever greater. Terrible fighting with bands and *franc-tireurs*, uncertainty everywhere. The troops are taking vigorous measures."[70]

In many cases Wehrmacht units cooperated closely with SS and police units. German soldiers were involved in the arbitrary executions of civilians and prisoners of war, helped burn down towns and made fun of Orthodox Jews by shaving off their beards and making them perform humiliating tasks. In the eyes of ordinary German soldiers, it was open season on Jews, and they were treated accordingly.[71] All of this offered a taste of the far greater and more extreme violence that would be meted out in the occupied parts of the Soviet Union from the summer of 1941.[72]

The army command was kept informed by regular reports about the mass murder. On 10 September, Chief of the General Staff Halder noted in his diary: "Disgusting scenes behind the frontline."[73] Although the Wehrmacht and the Einsatzgruppen cooperated in many places, some military commanders were outraged at the excessive violence, not least because they worried it would damage the morale and discipline of their men. Among higher officers, there was also a noticeable reluctance to simply override the traditional restrictions on warfare in international law in favour of an ideological campaign of annihilation. On 8 September, Heydrich complained to the head of the Abwehr, Wilhelm Canaris, about the lack of understanding among the Wehrmacht leadership. Courts-martial "worked much too slowly" in sentencing Polish partisans, a witness to the two men's discussion recorded. Heydrich "was going to change that. These people had to be immediately shot or hanged without a trial." When informed of Heydrich's plans, Halder shrugged and referred to "the intention of the Führer and Göring to destroy and root out the Polish people."[74] Keitel had the same reaction when Canaris told him about the mass executions on board Hitler's special train in Ilnau on 12 September: "The matter has already been decided by the Führer . . . If the Wehrmacht does not want to have anything to do with it, it will still have to accept that the SS and the Gestapo will operate alongside it."[75]

By this point no one in the Wehrmacht leadership could have doubted that the "ethnic cleansing measures" were not autonomous actions of individual SS and police forces but a concerted programme ordered by Hitler and carried out by Himmler and Heydrich. But none of the military leaders was prepared to speak out against it and risk a direct confrontation with the political leadership. They were more concerned with evading responsibility by ensuring that the "ethnic reallocation of land" only took place after a civilian administration had taken over from the military. On 21 September, Brauchitsch informed the army group and army commanders that Hitler had charged the Einsatzgruppen with "ethnic-political tasks," whose execution was "outside the responsibility of military commanders."[76]

Nonetheless, criticism of the actions of the Einsatzgruppen refused to die down even after the Polish campaign was over. "I am ashamed to be a German!" wrote general staff officer Hellmuth Stieff to his wife in November 1939. "This minority that is besmirching us by murder, looting and arson will be the misfortune of the entire German people, if we do not stop what they are doing."[77] The most explicit expression of disgust came from Colonel-General Johannes Blaskowitz, the commander of German troops in Poland after the military administration had been dissolved. In a report to Brauchitsch on 27 November, he insisted that the army refuse "to be identified with the atrocities of the Security Police . . . and to cooperate with the Einsatzgruppen that are working almost exclusively as execution commandos." The latter, Blaskowitz continued, had done nothing but "spread terror among the populace" and represented an "intolerable burden" for the Wehrmacht. In the following months, Blaskowitz kept on protesting in reports and memorandums about the "excessive brutality and moral turpitude" evident in the actions of the Einsatzgruppen. "Every soldier feels disgusted and repulsed by these crimes, which are being committed in Poland by members of the Reich and representatives of its state authority."[78]

Hitler reacted with anger to criticism from army circles. The Führer is "very upset," his adjutant Engel noted in his diary on 15 October. The officers should desist from "every form of emotional silliness" and the Wehrmacht should "keep its nose out of things it does not understand." A month later, when he was shown a memorandum by Blaskowitz in which the general expressed his "greatest concern at the illegal executions, arrests and confiscations," Hitler threw an angry fit, levelling "grave accusations at the 'childish mentality' in the army leadership." The "methods of the Salvation Army" were of no use in war. He had "never trusted" Blaskowitz and was now pondering "removing him from his position since he is obviously unfit for it."[79] In early May 1940, Blaskowitz was relieved of his command and transferred to the western front.

On 4 October 1939, Hitler had already issued a blanket amnesty and cancelled courts-martial for all crimes committed by German soldiers out of "bitterness at the atrocities perpetrated by the Poles" since 1 September.[80] On 7 October, Himmler was appointed "Reich Commissar for the Consolidation of German Nationhood." That appointment placed the "ethnic reordering" of the German-conquered parts of central eastern Europe in the hands of the SS and police leadership, and their central institution, the Reich Security Main Office, which had only been created on 27 September.[81] The new task Hitler had given them massively expanded Himmler's and Heydrich's scope of activity. On the one hand, they were responsible for ethnically cleansing the areas of western Poland that had been amalgamated into the Reich—in other words, to drive Poles, in so far as they could not be "Germanified," and Jews into the General Government. On the other, they were thereby to create space for the "ethnic Germans" from the regions that were now under Stalin's control. Late that September, Hitler had made no bones about "how the former eastern provinces of Posen and West

Prussia were to be integrated." Those Poles considered "racially valuable" could be "Germanised," while the rest were to be deported to the Polish rump territory of the General Government. In thirty years at the latest, the annexed territories were to be so completely "Germanified" that a traveller would not know that they had ever been disputed by Poles and Germans.[82] "These eastern provinces will become a core German area," Hitler told Goebbels. "We will create farms of up to 200 acres and populate them with German soldier-farmers. Our settlement is proceeding according to plan and is calculated for the long term . . . In any case, German history has taken a new turn, and the German nation has work to do for the next two generations."[83]

The planned resettlement of hundreds of thousands of people required an extensive bureaucratic apparatus, and the first steps in creating it were made in October and November 1939.[84] In December, Heydrich ordered the first large-scale transfer of populations to make room for 40,000 Baltic Germans. Around 88,000 Poles were rounded up in the *Reichgau* of Posen and deported in freight trains to the General Government.[85] There nothing had been prepared to house them. Wilm Hosenfeld, one of the few German officers who rejected Germany's homicidal occupation policies from the very start, described the arrival of these unfortunate people: "Why rip these people from their places of residence if we do not know where to accommodate them? They stand around in the cold all day, or squat on their pathetic bundles of belongings, and no one gives them anything to eat. There is a system to this. These people are to be made sick, miserable and helpless. They are supposed to die."[86] The food and shelter situation in the General Government, which also received large numbers of refugees from the Soviet-occupied Polish territories, was already critical and the mass deportations from the German-annexed western Polish provinces exacerbated the problem. Governor-general Hans Frank, who had initially supported the resettlement project, now resisted the idea of his "Reich ancillary land" being used, in his words, as a "human rubbish dump." In negotiations with the Reich Security Main Office, he succeeded in slowing the pace of the compulsory resettlements. By the end of 1940, over 300,000 Poles had been relocated from the Warthegau, Danzig–West Prussia and parts of Upper Silesia into the General Government—far fewer than Himmler's ambitious plans had originally foreseen.[87]

Frank established a brutal form of occupation rule in the General Government. In early October 1939, even before he was officially appointed, he described the task he had been given by Hitler as follows: "Exploitation of the land by ruthless asset-stripping . . . Reduction of Poland's entire economy to the minimum necessary to maintain a most basic standard of living for the population. Closure of all educational institutions, especially technical schools and universities, to prevent the development of a Polish intellectual class . . . Poland is to be treated like a colony, the Poles will become the slaves of a Greater German world empire."[88] After moving into Wawel Royal Castle on 7 November, Frank issued a spate of edicts all designed to exploit the territory and its resources, make Polish lives as difficult as possible and take away any possibility of resistance. Even the smallest misdemeanours were punishable by death. Poles were to be worked until they "do not know whether they are coming or going" and "have no time to carry out acts of sabotage," Frank proclaimed in January 1940. His cynicism knew no limit: "My relationship to the Poles is that of the ant to the aphid," he once remarked.[89]

The German civil administration of the General Government was split into three levels, with the government headquarters in Krakow at the top; the four districts of Krakow, Warsaw, Radom and Lublin in the middle, to which Galicia with the city of Lwów (Lviv) was added after Nazi Germany attacked the Soviet Union in 1941; and a lower level consisting of district and city administrators (Kreis- and Stadthauptleute). It was the local officials in particular who played a key role in implementing the German policies of exploitation and extermination. Most of them were trained lawyers who had already gained administrative experience in the "Old Reich" and who had been promoted into their new jobs. Like Frank himself, they behaved like tin-pot dictators in their fiefdoms and led lives of luxury to the detriment of the local population. Corruption and embezzlement were the order of the day. This small group of extremely ideological functionaries, all in all around 130 civil servants, possessed a large amount of discretionary authority, which Frank was constantly encouraging them to put to use. With "iron determination," he demanded on 25 November 1939, district and city officials in and around Radom should ensure "that Poles would never again dare to see Germans as anything but masters."[90]

From the first day of the occupation, the 1.7 million Polish Jews now under German rule were subject to unfettered acts of terror. Here too, after the end of the military administration it was regional officials, given secure backing by the governor-general, who kept pushing forward with new initiatives. At the same conference in Radom in late November, Frank issued them a blank cheque: "Make quick work of the Jews. A joy to finally be able to go after the Jewish race physically. The more that die, the better . . . Jews must feel that we have arrived."[91] Frank and others who carried out anti-Semitic policies in the General Government were convinced that they were acting entirely in the interest of Hitler and his "bitter ethnic struggle" when they pressured Jews, stole their property, confiscated their homes and began moving them out of the countryside and into the bigger cities. Indeed, local officials were instrumental in the establishment of the first unofficial, "wild" ghettos from the autumn of 1939. Here they created a *fait accompli* before large-scale ghettoisation began to be carried out. It was a preliminary stage in what would become systematic extermination.[92]

When recruiting and sending Polish labourers to the Reich, district officials worked together closely with the General Government's employment offices. They were following a directive of Hitler, from 17 October that the occupied territories should provide cheap labour. While at first these efforts focused on finding volunteers, when such recruitment disappointed expectations, the transition was made to rigorous conscription from the spring of 1940. Young Poles were picked up on the street or apprehended in nighttime raids and transported to Germany. By July 1940, 311,000 people had been "recruited" mainly to work in agriculture.[93] Talking to Frank on 2 October 1940, Hitler re-emphasised the principles of the occupation policy he had set the previous year, calling the General Government "our reservoir of labour for low forms of work." The minutes of the meeting, taken by Bormann, continue: "Once again the Führer underlined that Poles could only have one master, and that was the German. There cannot and should not be two masters. For that reason, all members of the Polish intelligentsia were to be killed. That sounded harsh, but it was a law of life."[94]

Not only did the army leadership allow the Polish campaign, from the very start, to violate the boundaries of international law and take on characteristics of a war of extermination: it also did nothing to rein in the occupation authorities. On the contrary, in early 1940, Halder assured Colonel-General Wilhelm Ritter von Leeb, the commander of Army Group C, in the west, that reports of abuses were "exaggerated or false" and that the "cruelty in Poland is diminishing."[95] In a letter to all army and army group commanders on 7 February 1940, Brauchitsch wrote that while there had been "regrettable mistakes" here and there, the "resolution of ethnic-political tasks necessary for the securement of German living space as ordered by the Führer" had unavoidably led to "unusual, severe measures towards the Polish population of the occupied territory." Indeed, the "accelerated execution" of these tasks, "made necessary by the imminent decisive battle of the German people," would bring a "further intensification of these measures."[96]

Nonetheless, Brauchitsch had an interest in easing the outrage felt in segments of the officer corps at SS atrocities. To this end, he invited Himmler to present his views of the situation to the army leadership in Koblenz in March 1940. The SS leader's talk, of which only the main points have been preserved, left no doubt that everything that had happened and was still happening in Poland was part of a project to create a "Greater Germanic Empire" that was ordered by Hitler himself and not just the result of subordinate authorities exceeding their bounds. Himmler's main points were recorded as: "Execution of the leading minds of the opposition movement. Very harsh but necessary. Was there myself—no wild activities by subordinate leaders nor by me. Know exactly what is going on."[97] One of the officers present, General Wilhelm Ulex, remembered Himmler declaring: "In this group of the highest officers of the army, I can be frank: I do nothing without the Führer's knowledge."[98]

We have no record that the military leadership ever responded to what Himmler had told them. Some of those present might still have had private concerns, but there was no open protest. With that a dangerous precedent was created: the military leadership accepted Hitler's racist and ideological aims as facts and thus became complicit in his criminal policies.[99] In this regard too, Poland was a laboratory for experiments that were already casting a dark shadow on the future and presaged the behaviour of the Wehrmacht in the coming war of annihilation against the Soviet Union.

3

Decision in the West?

"The way things stand, time is most probably the Western powers' ally and not ours," Hitler had written in his memorandum of 9 October 1939, in which he justified his decision to attack the West as soon as possible. Hitler also cited uncertainty about how the Soviet Union would behave in future. "There is no treaty or agreement that can guarantee the lasting neutrality of Soviet Russia," he wrote. "At the moment everything speaks against it abandoning its neutrality. In eight months, a year or even several years, that can be different. The scant importance attached to the value of written agreements has been demonstrated on all sides in recent years."[1] That was particularly rich coming from a dictator who had never abided by treaties and contractual agreements. Nonetheless, developments in the United States were also reason for a rapid attack in the west. "The attempts of certain circles in the US to turn things in an anti-German direction" may not yet have been successful, but that could change. "Here, too, time has to be seen as working against Germany," the Führer opined.[2] Over lunch in the Chancellery in the second half of October, Hitler left no doubt that he was serious about a western offensive. The Führer was "no longer thinking about peace," Goebbels wrote in his diary. "He wants to beat England to the punch."[3]

While the military leadership had more or less accepted without objection Hitler's brutal racist and ethnic policies in Poland, there was resistance to his plans for war in the west. Most military commanders were dismayed that Hitler already wanted to attack in the autumn of 1939. The troops were insufficiently equipped for another campaign, they complained. The generals still needed time to replace the casualties sustained in Poland. Older high-ranking Wehrmacht officers in particular were still much affected by the trauma of the First World

War, with its years of intransigent trench warfare that had caused horrendous loss of life. They considered France a formidable adversary and were convinced that England would be very difficult to defeat.[4] "The tenacity above all of the English, and that of the French when in England's wake, together with how they fought in the Great War, tell us that they will hold out to the last if attacked," warned Colonel-General Wilhelm Ritter von Leeb, commander of Army Group C, in a memorandum of 11 October to his supreme commander, Walther von Brauchitsch. The proclaimed goal of "subjugating England and France so that they would sue for peace" was "not attainable." On the contrary, as in the First World War, there was the threat of a long war of attrition in which German capabilities would be gradually exhausted. It would be much more advantageous, Leeb believed, for "the German army to stand with their rifles at the ready" and maintain a position of strategic defence.[5]

Yet when Brauchitsch tried to convince Hitler to change his plans on 16 October, he was rebuffed. Only after "blows" were struck would England be forced to give in, Hitler argued, so it was imperative to attack "as quickly as possible." He did not set a date for the offensive but specified as the earliest point in time the days between 15 and 20 November.[6] Hitler's announcement caused nothing short of panic among the army command. Abwehr chief Wilhelm Canaris returned "very shaken" from a briefing with Halder. "A complete nervous breakdown" is how he described the chief of staff's psychological condition. "Brauchitsch also dumbfounded. Führer demands an attack. Refuses to listen to any practical objection. Only bloodlust."[7] Even Keitel, the head of the Wehrmacht Supreme Command, ever ready to do Hitler's bidding, seems to have doubted for a time that the planned attack in the west had a chance of succeeding. When he voiced his concerns in the Chancellery after conferring with Brauchitsch and Halder in Zossen, Hitler accused him of conspiring with the generals against his plans instead of adopting and promoting them without reservation. Keitel later claimed to have tendered his resignation, which Hitler had refused to accept, saying he was the one who would determine whether he wanted to replace someone or not.[8]

On 27 October, Brauchitsch and Halder tried again to convince Hitler to postpone the western campaign. The dictator awarded them and some other officers a newly created medal, the Knight's Cross of the Iron Cross, for their performance in Poland but refused to budge on the issue of attacking in the west, setting 12 November as the date for what was code-named "Case Yellow."[9] "Attack seems to have been ordered once and for all," Leeb wrote in his diary in late October. "The Führer does not listen to anyone . . . Brauchitsch hardly gets a word out, collapses in front of the Führer . . . Keitel is a mere ordnance officer without any influence."[10] The army leadership saw itself as facing a choice between preparing for an offensive it considered irresponsibly risky or staying the dictator's arm at the last minute, which would have meant a test of strength and quite possibly a change at the top of the regime. On 14 October, Halder held an "in-depth meeting" with Brauchitsch to weigh three options: "attack, wait-and-see, fundamental changes." But none of the three alternatives promised complete success, Halder concluded, especially not the third one, because it was "fundamentally negative and created moments of weakness."[11] Germany's highest-ranking military leaders could not make up their minds. Their fear of the possible consequences of a military putsch was greater than the potential nightmare of the imminent offensive.

However, "fundamental changes" in the regime leadership were the goal of those opposition circles that had formed a network of contacts in September 1938 and now, in late October and early November 1939, saw the chance to make amends for previous failures to strip Hitler of power. At the start of the war, the Wehrmacht officer Hans Oster, enjoying Canaris' protection, had brought the lawyer Hans von Dohnanyi, a former employee of Justice Minister Franz Gürtner, to his department in the Abwehr.[12] The group they formed, which also included Dohnanyi's fellow lawyer and friend Justus Delbrück, established connections with officers in the army command, including Colonel Helmuth Groscurth, a former close associate of Canaris, who had become the director of the new department for special tasks at the Army High Command in mid-September 1939. Groscurth played a key role in bringing together the opposition groups in the Abwehr and at the Army High Command's headquarters in Zossen with opponents of the regime in the Foreign Ministry, led by Erich Kordt and legation secretary Hasso von Etzdorf, as well as with individuals in the civilian resistance such as former Leipzig mayor Carl Goerdeler, former German ambassador to Italy Ulrich von Hassell and former chief of the general staff Ludwig Beck.[13] Notwithstanding great differences in temperament and political background these men all agreed, as Hassell put it in his diary in mid-October, that it was "high time . . . to put the brakes on the wagon rolling down the hill and put a stop to the policies of an adventurer." Every attempt had to be made to "bring about a turn" before the planned western offensive.[14] The question was how this could be done and, above all, which high-ranking military commanders could be won over for a *coup d'état*.

Any conspiracy was doomed to failure if no general was prepared to take the bull by the horns. Yet this "central point," as Hassell repeatedly noted with disappointment in his diary, was precisely the problem.[15] The conspirators had little faith in Brauchitsch, so they focused on Halder, who, just as he had done in September 1938, avoided taking a stand.[16] In late October, however, he seemed to be warming to the idea of a coup. In a confidential conversation with Groscurth, he suggested "arranging accidents" for leading representatives of the Third Reich, including Ribbentrop and Göring. With tears in his eyes, much to the astonishment of Groscurth, Halder said that "for weeks he had taken a pistol when he met Emil [Hitler] in order to have the option of blowing him away."[17] Was Halder really contemplating doing away with Hitler? It seems that the anti-Hitler circles assumed he was. With feverish haste, preparations were made for a coup, but on closer examination, in the words of historian and Beck biographer Klaus-Jürgen Müller, it was "more a wild drawing up of plans, a hectic establishing of contacts and a host of well-intentioned conversations than a coherent, realistic plot."[18]

On 2–3 November, Halder and Brauchitsch went on an inspection tour of the western front. Rundstedt and Bock, the commanders of Army Groups A and B, continued to voice their reservations about the planned offensive but also made it clear that they would "do their duty to the best of their ability" if an attack were ordered.[19] Only Leeb, the commander of Army Group C, signalled a willingness to take part in some kind of action against Hitler. In a letter of 31 October, he assured Brauchitsch that "I will stand behind you with my life in the days to come and will draw all desired and necessary consequences."[20]

Bolstered by this support, on 5 November the Wehrmacht commanders made one final attempt to talk Hitler out of an offensive in the west. While Halder waited in the antechamber, Brauchitsch read out a memorandum he had put together and which once again listed all the arguments that from his point of view spoke against going on the attack. Initially, Hitler kept his temper, but when he heard that German troops in Poland had been "less than happy about attacking" and that there had been breaches of discipline similar to those in 1917 and 1918, the dictator jumped out of his chair. Keitel, who had joined the meeting, described the scene as follows: "It was fully incomprehensible to him, Hitler said, that . . . a high commander would insult and denigrate his own army. No frontline commander had ever spoken to him about a lack of willingness to attack in the infantry. And now he was hearing this after a unique military triumph in Poland." Seething with rage, Hitler said that he recognised "the spirit of Zossen" and would eradicate it. Then he stormed out of the room and slammed the door behind him.[21] That evening, Hitler was "extremely agitated," spoke of "army sabotage" against his plans and dictated to his secretary Christa Schroeder a lengthy summary of the meeting, which he put with his personal documents in his safe in the Chancellery. He changed his mind about firing Brauchitsch the next day on the advice of Keitel, who pointed out that there was no successor in sight.[22]

Brauchitsch was apparently very shaken by the dictator's tantrum. "White as chalk" and "with a pained expression," he had returned to Halder, recalled Hitler's adjutant Engel.[23] In a state of high alarm, the two military commanders returned to their Zossen headquarters. They had every reason to fear that Hitler had got wind of the conspiratorial ruminations of the opposition. Halder immediately ordered the destruction of all possible incriminating documents.[24] Afterwards he summoned Groscurth and revealed that "all military means" had been exhausted and the offensive could no longer be stopped. "With that the forces that have been counting on us are no longer bound," Halder told Groscurth. "You understand my meaning." "A very depressing impression," Groscurth commented in response to the chief of staff's implicit rejection of any coup. A day later he noted: "These indecisive leaders disgust me—horrendous."[25] The civilian conspirators had to bury all hopes that the military leadership would involve itself in an action against Hitler. Their second attempt to launch a coup had failed.

Immediately after his meeting with Brauchitsch, Hitler confirmed 12 November as the start date for the attack. Two days later it was postponed, however, because of poor weather forecasts. It would not be the last time that the operation was put back. "The final hope is that perhaps reason might prevail in the end. All soldiers share my hopes," General Erich Hoepner wrote on 7 November.[26] But Hitler had by no means abandoned his military plans. On the contrary, over lunch in the Chancellery, he spoke extremely disparagingly about the military leadership's hesitancy: "The generals say they are not ready, but an army is never ready. And anyway, that is not the point. The main thing is to be readier than the others." Goebbels, who recorded Hitler's monologue, had no doubt that "the strike against the Western powers will not wait very much longer . . . Everyone is waiting with bated breath for the Führer's coming decisions."[27]

On 8 November, Hitler flew with his entourage to Munich to give his annual speech to the "old fighters" in the Bürgerbräukeller on the anniversary of the 1923 putsch attempt. Usually his speech on that occasion lasted from 8:30 to 10 p.m. But this time he arrived in the Bürgerbräukeller shortly after 8 p.m. and spoke for barely an hour. His pilot, Hans Baur, had warned him that because of expected fog, it probably would not be possible to fly back to Berlin the next day. His only option to return to the capital was to take his special train that was scheduled to depart at 9:31 from Munich's main station that evening.[28]

"The Führer was received with unimaginable cheering," gushed Goebbels. "In his speech, he cuttingly dispensed with England."[29] In fact, the dictator confined his words more or less to his familiar polemic against British politicians like Churchill who, he alleged, begrudged Germany its return to world-power status and had "incited" their country to war. "Everything is conceivable but never a German capitulation!" he declared, once again invoking the power of "providence," which had thus far "visibly blessed" his plans and which guaranteed that the war would end happily: "Only one side can emerge victorious, and that is us."[30] After his adjutant Julius Schaub had repeatedly put notes on his lectern, to remind him that time was running out, Hitler ended his speech at 9:07 p.m. and left shortly afterwards with his entourage for the train station.[31] Only a few minutes later, at 9:20, a large package of explosives in the pillar behind the lectern blew up. Parts of the building's roof caved in. Three people were killed immediately, and five died later from their injuries. More than sixty people were injured, including Eva Braun's father, Friedrich, and had to be treated in nearby hospitals.[32]

Shortly before midnight, at 11:57 p.m., the duty station master in the small town of Roth was startled by a priority call, which ordered him to halt the Führer's special train, scheduled to arrive in a couple of minutes, and instruct press chief Otto Dietrich to contact Berlin "in the fastest way possible." The station master found these instructions curious and refused, pointing out that the train was scheduled to stop shortly afterwards in nearby Nuremberg anyway.[33] Thus it was that Hitler first learned of the bomb blast when his train halted briefly in Nuremberg. At first he thought the news of the explosion was a bad joke, but after telephone calls with Munich police president Baron Friedrich Karl von Eberstein and Gauleiter Adolf Wagner, there was no doubt that an assassination had been attempted. "The Führer and all of us have miraculously escaped death," Goebbels noted in his diary. "Had the ceremony been conducted as it had all the years before, none of us would be alive any more. But the Führer . . . stands under the protection of the Almighty. He will only die when his mission has been fulfilled." Not only the propaganda minister but Hitler himself was convinced that "providence" had been at work. On the question of who had been behind the assassination attempt, everyone soon reached agreement: it was "no doubt conceived in London and probably carried out by a Bavarian royalist."[34]

The next morning, Hitler arrived at Berlin's Anhalter Station, where he was awaited by Göring and State Secretary Hans Heinrich Lammers. Hitler received congratulations from all sides for the "miracle" of his rescue "calmly and composedly," his adjutant Below noted. At the same time, it was noticeable that he was "deeply preoccupied internally" with what had happened.[35] Goebbels immediately called a press conference and instructed journalists on how to report about the failed assassination. The *Berliner Lokalanzeiger*, for example, ran a headline reading "All of Germany Echoes with This Damnable Crime."[36] On 11 November, Hitler flew back to Munich to take part in a theatrically staged state ceremony in front of the Feldherrnhalle in honour of the victims of the assassination attempt. He did not speak himself and just stared silently at the coffins on display. Afterwards, he visited the wounded in hospital and inspected the half-destroyed ballroom in the Bürgerbräukeller.[37]

Already in the early morning of 9 November, Hitler had ordered Himmler to form a "special Bürgerbräu commission," which took up its work the following day in Munich's Gestapo headquarters. The investigation was led by Arthur Nebe, the chief of the Reich Criminal Police Office (Office V in the Reich Security Main Office). Initially, the investigators were completely in the dark. There was no evidence at all for the immediate suspicions that the British secret service had been behind the attack and that a group of Bavarian monarchists had carried it out. "There is no trace of the perpetrators," Goebbels had to admit on 11 November. Three days later, Hitler also remarked over lunch in the Chancellery that the investigation had "thus far produced no result." It was likely that the assassins had "already long gone abroad."[38] But precisely at this juncture the special commission made a decisive breakthrough. All the evidence now pointed to a lone assassin, Georg Elser, from the town of Königsbronn near Heidenheim in southwestern Germany. In the autumn of 1939, the 36-year-old had dared to try what the generals lacked the courage for. Acting entirely by himself, he had sought to remove Hitler, and he came closer to doing so than all members of the military and civilian opposition prior to the Stauffenberg assassination attempt of 20 July 1944.

Elser had received some basic schooling for seven years before doing an apprenticeship as a carpenter. He was a fierce individualist who was proud of his skill working with his hands. In Konstanz, where he lived between 1925 and 1932, he was loosely affiliated with socialist and communist circles. He joined the traditionally left-wing wood-workers' union and was even briefly a member of the communist paramilitary Rotfrontkämpferbund (Alliance of Red Front-Fighters). Before 1933, he voted for the German Communist Party (KPD) but never joined it. He had felt a deep antipathy for the Nazis right from the start. In 1932, he told colleagues at work that you only had to take one look at Hitler's "criminal face" to know what he was really like. Unlike many of his ideological comrades, however, who switched sides or adapted to the new circumstances after 1933, he remained uncompromising in his rejection of the Nazi regime. In the autumn of 1938, he had decided after careful consideration to kill Hitler. Later, under interrogation, he said he had been motivated by his desire "to improve the conditions of the working class and to avoid a war." A fundamental change to the system, he was convinced, could only be reached "by eradicating the current leadership." Elser procured explosives, a detonator and other components, and cleverly and dexterously assembled them into a powerful bomb. In early August 1939, he moved to Munich, hiding out for more than thirty nights in the Bürgerbräukeller, where he worked painstakingly to conceal his bomb in a pillar above the gallery.

During the night of 5–6 November, he placed the explosives there and installed the detonator. On the evening of 7 November, he returned a final time to the Bürgerbräukeller to check both of the clocks attached to his bomb. Everything seemed perfectly planned. The bomb would explode at 9:20 p.m., the time Hitler was expected to be halfway through his speech, and Elser would slip across the German border with Switzerland at Konstanz. He knew the area well but had the bad fortune to be apprehended by a customs patrol. In his bag, officers discovered parts of a detonator and a postcard depicting the Bürgerbräukeller. That raised their suspicions when the news of the assassination attempt arrived by telephone around 11 p.m. On 9 November, the Konstanz Gestapo brought him to Munich by car to face the special commission. Employees of the Bürgerbräukeller recognised him, as did a Munich shopkeeper from whom he had ordered an insulating plate to dampen the ticking of the clocks. After days of interrogation and torture, Elser confessed in the night of 14–15 November.[39]

The Nazi leadership did not want to believe that a lone person, born in humble circumstances to boot, could have been behind such a well-planned enterprise. "Himmler has found the first assassin," Goebbels noted on 16 November. "A technician from Württemberg. But the men behind the scenes are still missing." The following day, Goebbels believed the background to the assassination attempt was now "extremely clear": "The assassin himself is a creature of Otto Strasser, who was in Switzerland on the days in question. After the attack, he immediately left for England, obviously crawling back to those who paid him and told him what to do. The work of the Secret Service."[40] Otto Strasser, the former leader of the left wing of the Nazi Party, had broken with Hitler in 1930. He had founded a "Fighting Association of Revolutionary National Socialists" but had never really represented serious competition to Hitler. After 1933, he had continued to fight against the Führer in Austria and then Czechoslovakia. He fled to Switzerland in the spring of 1939 before moving on to Paris that November.[41] Hitler too was convinced that his old enemy Strasser had put Elser up to his "monstrously sophisticated" deed. "He too must soon pay the price," Hitler said over lunch at the Chancellery on 21 November. "We are going to get him. The whole plan originated in England of course."[42]

On 18 November, Elser was taken to the Reich Security Main Office at Prinz-Albrecht-Strasse 8 and in the days that followed was interrogated constantly. Gestapo officers were determined to use all the means at their disposal to force him to name the people who had been behind the assassination attempt. But Elser disappointed them and was able to prove convincingly that he had acted alone.[43] Nonetheless, on 22 November, at Hitler's behest, Himmler published a communiqué that named Elser as the would-be assassin but also claimed: "Those that gave Elser the orders and the money are the British secret service. The attack was organised by Otto Strasser."[44] To make this lie seem more believable, Himmler connected Elser's arrest with an incident that had taken place on 9 November, the day after the assassination attempt, on the German-Dutch border. In the Dutch city of Venlo, SS men who had been passing themselves off as members of an anti-Hitler resistance group had lured two British spies—the section chief of the Intelligence Service for western Europe, Major Richard Henry Stevens, and Captain Sigismund Payne Best— into a café and then spirited them away to Germany.[45] Himmler's announcement encouraged the conclusion that the two agents had pulled the strings of the assassination attempt, and Goebbels publicised this version of events in a mass-produced brochure with the title "Murder! Espionage!! Assassination!!! The Bloody Trail of the English Secret Service Leading to the Munich Bomb Attack."[46]

Although all the evidence clearly indicated that Elser had acted alone, Hitler and Goebbels stubbornly clung to their conspiracy theories. As late as April 1941, a few months before Germany launched its war against the Soviet Union, the propaganda minister noted: "We talk about the Bürgerbräu assassination attempt. The man behind the scenes still not found. The assassin keeps his silence. The Führer thinks it is Otto Strasser."[47] At this point, Elser had already been taken to

Sachsenhausen concentration camp, where he was interned as a "special prisoner" of Hitler. The plan was to stage a show trial with him and the two British intelligence agents after the war. In early February 1945, he was transferred to Dachau, where he was murdered, a few days before the war ended, on 9 April 1945.[48] It took a long time for Georg Elser to be given the public recognition in Germany that he deserved as one of the most determined and courageous opponents of Hitler. Even in the mid-1950s, Gerhard Ritter, the doyen of West German historians, could still write, despite the lack of any evidence, that Elser was a "foreign communist spy" who may have been used by the Gestapo. Although any traces of a connection had been carefully covered up, Ritter wrote, "whether Himmler was behind this must remain an open question."[49]

The news of the assassination attempt caused ripples throughout Germany. "The agitation is positively massive," a Social Democratic Party (SPD) informant in Germany reported to the party executive-in-exile in Paris. "The wildest rumours are going round."[50] Supporters of the regime tended to believe the official version that the British had planned the attack. But there were also sceptical voices that asked how the British intelligence service could have "slipped through the ranks of the omnipotent German police" to deposit a bomb of such destructive power in the Bürgerbräukeller without anyone noticing.[51] The attempt on the Führer's life was "devilishly conceived," the tank regiment commander Lieutenant Hermann Balck noted, adding that it indicated "a major failing of all security organs—that is the saddest and most shameful part of it."[52]

Opponents of Hitler were inclined to believe that the Nazis themselves had staged the assassination attempt, just as they were thought to have organised the Reichstag fire in February 1933, to whip up anti-British sentiment among the German people. The "mentally more active segment of the population," the diarist Friedrich Kellner wrote, were forming "their own opinions" and did not believe in "a real assassination attempt, but rather in a kind of Reichstag farce."[53] Within Helmuth Groscurth's circle, people surmised that the perpetrators might have been "disgruntled old party comrades" or "the Gestapo itself, perhaps in conjunction with Göring."[54] Opponents of Hitler too, therefore, could not imagine that a lone individual had taken such a decision and put into action such a carefully conceived plan.

In the main, so the Security Service observed, ordinary Germans were glad that the attempt on Hitler's life had failed: "Love for the Führer has grown even stronger, and attitudes towards the war have become more positive among many circles as a result of the assassination attempt. There is a pronounced hatred for Great Britain."[55] But the public reaction was anything but homogeneous. Ulrich von Hassell witnessed little of the "fanatical outrage" claimed by official propaganda. Instead, he registered an "astonishing indifference," with people occasionally expressing regret that the bomb had exploded "too late."[56] Such sentiments were, of course, never uttered in public, only in the presence of the like-minded, where people believed they were safe from informers.[57]

In his dispatches to the government in Copenhagen, the Danish emissary Herluf Zahle wrote of a "certain fermentation" within the German population, caused in particular "by the various effects of the war on everyday life." But as he had since the early days of the Third Reich, Zahle also warned against assuming that "the system in charge now faced a rapid fall." Only a "military-political crisis" would create a situation that brought the possibility of "regime change."[58] In the wake of Germany's unexpectedly easy victory over Poland, however, that seemed like a very distant eventuality. Nonetheless, relief that the assassination attempt had failed was mixed with concerns about how the war would progress. "Naturally many people believe that 'providence' saved Hitler's life," wrote an SPD observer in western Germany. "But everyone is still dominated by the feeling that something is in the offing. The adventure of war will lead to fresh surprises at home."[59]

At noon on 23 November, Hitler convened the entire leadership of the Wehrmacht, two hundred generals and staff officers, in the grand ballroom of the New Reich Chancellery to fire them up for the imminent western offensive. After his clash with Brauchitsch on 5 November, Hitler was aware that the army leadership had considerable reservations against the planned campaign, and his two-hour speech was aimed at dispelling them. He began by looking back at his "political work" since 1919, which had continually confronted him with difficult decisions and required a prolonged struggle. With unusual openness, Hitler expressed his faith in his social-Darwinist creed: "Struggle and more struggle. I see struggle as the lot of all living beings. No one can avoid struggle, if he does not want to be defeated." Equally directly, he drew a connection to the project to which he had committed himself in the mid-1920s and which he had started to realise in 1937 when expansionist policies had begun to replace his earlier revisionism: the conquest of "living space" in the east. "It is an eternal problem: how to bring the numbers of Germans into accordance with their territory," Hitler proclaimed. "We need to secure necessary space. No sophisticated cleverness will help here. It can only be resolved with the sword. A people that cannot summon the strength to fight must abdicate [its place in the world]."

After the victory over Poland, Hitler claimed, Germany's strategic situation was better than ever before. But while there was no need to fear a two-front war, no one could say how long this situation would last. At the moment, Russia was "not dangerous" and was also bound to Germany through the non-aggression pact. Yet Stalin would only abide by the agreement for as long as he saw fit. Hitler left no doubt that after achieving victory over the Western powers, he would order an attack on the Soviet Union: "We can only confront Russia if our hands are free in the west." Italy, he added, would only join the war in the west once Germany had launched an offensive against France— although everything depended on Mussolini. If the Duce were to die suddenly, the situation would change entirely. "I myself have recently experienced how easily death can take away a statesman," Hitler explained, referring to the assassination attempt in the Bürgerbräukeller. Suffused with a sense of his own uniqueness, Hitler told his officers that no one, "neither a military man nor a civilian," could replace him. That was another reason why Germany had to seize the day: time favoured its enemies. At the moment, the United States did not present a danger and its support for Britain was not yet decisive. "The present constellation of power cannot get better but only worse for us . . . The fate of the Reich depends on me alone . . . Today we are superior to the enemy, also in terms of numbers in the west. The army is backed by the mightiest arms industry in the world."

Hitler had plenty of barbs left over for the army leadership, particularly Brauchitsch. It had "offended him most deeply," he said, "that the German army did not measure up" and that the infantry had failed in Poland. Everything rested with the officers. They had to provide an example of "fanatical determination." "I can do anything with the German soldier as long as he is well led," Hitler boasted, adding that his mind was "irrevocably" made up: "I am going to attack France and England at the next best opportunity. It does not matter if the neutrality of Belgium and Holland is violated. No one will remember that if we are victorious." As was his wont, by the end of his speech, Hitler had worked himself into a seeming frenzy while nonetheless coolly calculating the effect of his words: "If we survive this battle—and we will survive it—our epoch will go down in the history of our people. I will either stand or fall in this battle. I will not survive a defeat of my people. No capitulation without, no revolution within."[60]

The response to Hitler's speech seems to have been mixed. Average listeners, Hassell wrote, were deeply affected by Hitler's "wild, partisan torrent of words" while more sophisticated ones were reminded of a "temperamental Genghis Khan."[61] Groscurth, who was in attendance, simply noted: "Shattering impression of an insane criminal." But such reactions were the exception. There was now less opposition to Hitler than ever before within the military leadership. "Everyone is agitated and fighting among themselves," a resigned Groscurth wrote. "But no one takes a decision to act. We are soldiers, bound by our oath of loyalty to the Führer etc. . . . but above all, we all remained glued to our posts."[62]

That afternoon, Hitler received the army group and army commanders for a separate meeting. He told this smaller circle of officers again that he was "convinced of victory." He continued: "No one could have predicted that Poland would be subjugated in eighteen days. Perhaps we are confronted with decisions whose consequences no one can anticipate. The military leaders must believe in victory and communicate that belief to their subordinates."[63] Still, Hitler remained convinced that, of all people, his two highest military commanders, Brauchitsch and Halder, lacked this faith. "Repeatedly there were jibes against the army," noted Engel.[64] On the evening of 23 November, Hitler called Brauchitsch and Halder to a further meeting. When the Führer again levelled accusations of defeatism at the army leadership, referring to the "spirit of Zossen," Brauchitsch offered to resign. But Hitler refused the offer, telling the commander that he would "have to do his duty like every other soldier."[65]

With the weather remaining poor, Hitler had put off the launch of the attack in the west until early December.[66] But conditions in the weeks before Christmas continued to be unfavourable, so the operation was further postponed until early January. "With this fog and mud, there is nothing you can do," a regretful Goebbels noted.[67] Nevertheless, Hitler never stopped thinking about the western offensive. "I want to defeat England, cost what it may," he said over lunch in the Chancellery on 11 December. "That is the goal of all my thoughts and actions."[68] The news that the armoured German warship MS *Admiral Graf Spee* had been scuttled after a battle with English cruisers off Montevideo on 17 December only intensified his hatred of Britain. "The English will pay heavily for this someday," he vowed.[69]

On 20 December, Hitler paid his annual pre-Christmas visit to the publishers Elsa and Hugo Bruckmann, his early patrons in Munich. Physically, the Führer made "a fresh impression, not tense, but rather in a good mood and optimistic," Elsa Bruckmann told Hassell two days later. Hitler had declared that he would "force England to its knees in eight months, and the majestic reconstruction of the Reich, far beyond the current boundaries of Germany, would begin."[70] In the couple's guestbook he noted that his visit had taken place "in the year of the struggle for the construction of a Greater German Empire." During Christmas itself, the dictator inspected troops on the Siegfried Line. As Germany's "first soldier," Goebbels' propaganda tried to suggest, Hitler was a "comrade among comrades." Upon returning to Berlin on 26 December, the Führer said he had been impressed by the confidence he had encountered among the troops. As soon as the weather allowed, he was determined to launch his "great offensive."[71]

The winter of 1939–40 was very cold, and the first snow came in December. By early January, temperatures had plummeted to minus 20 degrees Celsius. "Half the population freezing in their homes and offices and workshops because there's no coal," wrote Shirer. "Everyone is grumbling. Nothing like continual cold to lower your morale."[72] Even Goebbels worried about the "very serious coal situation in Berlin and the entire Reich" and called for "draconian measures" since people's misery was "weighing heavily on the general mood."[73] The reports of the Security Service also spoke of "serious uneasiness in the populace." Rumours began to circulate in Berlin that there had been "coal demonstrations" in various districts, and that police had been forced to fire shots.[74] Although the dissatisfaction was primarily directed at individual government departments and party function- aries, it also tarnished Hitler's prestige. "Enthusiasm for the Führer has markedly receded," Berlin police president Count Wolf Heinrich von Helldorff told Groscurth in confidence. ". . . Doubts are being cast on all radio and press reports. People do not even believe in genuine success stories."[75]

Hitler spent the New Year on the Obersalzberg, as always, only returning to Berlin on 6 January.[76] Four days later, he called the commanders of the army, navy and Luftwaffe to the Chancellery. Weather reports were predicting a "high-pressure system of rare dura- tion and strength," so despite the continuous frost, Hitler ordered the western offensive to commence on 17 January.[77] But during the night of 10–11 January, the Army High Command received a report that caused considerable concern in Berlin. A German courier plane carrying the latest plans for military operations had got lost and been forced to land near Mechelen in Belgium. It had to be assumed that at least some of these plans had fallen into Belgian hands and that the information would be shared with the British and the French.[78] Hitler was enraged by the foolishness of his Luftwaffe officers and immediately issued "Führer Directive No. 1," according to which no military office or officer was to be told more about "matters of secrecy" than was "absolutely necessary for them to carry out their task."[79] This order also expressed Hitler's growing scepticism about the loyalty of his underlings. The longer he ruled the more he tended to keep the circle of those who were in the know about his plans as small as possible. It was a practice born of caution, but one which also allowed him to play his paladins against one another according to his cherished "divide and conquer" principle of rule.

On 16 January, the incident in Mechelen, together with weather forecasts that were suddenly unfavourable again, made Hitler put back the offensive in the west until the spring.[80] It was Goebbels with whom he shared what he was thinking most frankly during that time. If faced with "very difficult decisions," the dictator said, you had to "courageously destroy the bridges behind you." He continued, "You are only truly daring when there is no turning back . . . Otherwise it is easy to become cowardly in hours of great stress." The fact that the Führer referred to the German "policies in Poland" in this context shows that he was well aware that his ethnic "housecleaning" had irreversibly crossed a moral line. Goebbels agreed: "We simply cannot lose the war."[81]

On the evening of 22 January, a "most cheerful" Hitler told a small social gathering in his Chancellery apartment how he envisaged the state of Europe after the expected German victory in the west. "England must be swept out of Europe, and France lose its status of a major power," he declared. "Then Germany will have hegemony, and Europe peace." Hitler announced that after his victory, he only wanted to stay in office "for a couple of years" to see through his "social reforms and construction projects." Then he would withdraw and "merely hover over politics like a benevolent ghost." Hitler was once more displaying his play-acting skills. It is of course completely out of the question that he was seriously thinking of retirement. After all, next up after his expected victory in the west was his war for "living space" in the east. Nonetheless, Goebbels, who hung on his Führer's every word, believed both this seemingly noble sentiment and Hitler's grandiose announcement that, as his legacy, he would "write down everything that was on his mind—as the gospel of National Socialism, so to speak."[82]

When he appeared in public, Hitler tried to elevate the mood and spread confidence in German victory. In an address to seven thousand officer candidates in the Sportpalast on 24 January, he stressed that "the German giant" was better armed than at any previous time in its history. Six days later in his annual speech to mark the anniversary of his "seizure of power," he told his audience that in the past five months a "massive amount had been achieved." The Wehrmacht was "the leader of the world" and was supported domestically by a committed community of eighty million people "inspired by a single, glowing faith and suffused with a fanatic will."[83] In this way Hitler tried to fire up his listeners for the inevitable military confrontation with the Western powers, all the while giving them no indication of when the fighting was actually to begin.

So where precisely was the attack in the west to commence? The Army High Command's original plan of operation of 19 October 1939 emphasised the right flank. Army Group B under Fedor von Bock was to advance quickly through Belgium to the English Channel coast, destroying as many enemy troops as possible.[84] But Hitler was worried that this was nothing but "the old Schlieffen plan of the strong right arm": he believed there was no way to carry out the same operation twice "without getting punished."[85] This early intervention reveals that, unlike during the Polish campaign, Hitler now sought to get directly involved in the operational military planning and develop alternatives to the ideas of the Army High Command. Hitler had a relief map of the entire western front installed in a hall of the Chancellery where daily situation meetings were to take place. According to Below, he often stood for hours in front of the map, studying its every detail.[86] On 25 October, in a meeting with Brauchitsch and Halder, Hitler first suggested transferring the main thrust of the attack further south to Army Group A under Gerd von Rundstedt and then ordering troops to the northwest to surround the enemy as they gathered in Belgium. The surprised army leadership registered its objections.[87] But he was certain that Germany's western offensive would be "the greatest victory in world history," Hitler boasted in late November in the Chancellery map room.[88]

Yet independently of Hitler, Lieutenant-General Erich von Manstein, the chief of the general staff of Army Group A, had developed a similar operational approach. In a series of memorandums starting in late October 1939, he demanded that the main thrust of the attack be shifted from Army Group B in the north to Army Group A in the centre. Powerful tank formations were to advance where an attack was least expected: through the difficult terrain of the Ardennes forests. Troops were then to cross the river Maas near Sedan, overrun French fortifications and penetrate to the mouth of the Somme on the English Channel coast. The basic idea of this plan was to trap the French armies and the British Expeditionary Force in northern France and Belgium in a gigantic pocket.[89] Initially the army leadership refused even to consider Manstein's operational drafts, considering them an "egotistical" attempt to bolster Army Group A at the expense of the other army groups and increase its size. In late January 1940, the unwanted strategist Manstein was appointed the commanding general of a new army corps being raised in Stettin (Szczecin) and thus taken out of the frame.[90]

After the "Mechelen incident," however, the previous operational plans could no longer be used, and Halder slowly began to warm to Manstein's proposal. Nonetheless, the decisive initiative came from

Hitler's main adjutant, Colonel Rudolf Schmundt. During a visit to the Army Group A headquarters in Koblenz, Manstein had showed him his alternative plan, and Schmundt had not failed to notice that its basic idea was more or less the same as the thoughts Hitler had expressed over the previous months.[91] On returning to Berlin, he informed Hitler about what he had been shown, and the dictator agreed to receive Manstein. That meeting, called a "working breakfast" and held behind Brauchitsch's and Halder's backs, took place on 17 February in the Chancellery. Unusually, Hitler allowed Manstein to lecture him without interruption. In the end, he came away impressed, remarking: "Personally, he is not my type, but he has talent."[92] He immediately ordered the army leadership to adopt his preferred strategic idea, which he saw confirmed by Manstein. By 24 February, the Army High Command had drawn up a new plan of operations. "Finally there has been an unequivocal decision, even if it comes at the expense of my army group," concluded Bock, although he feared that the advance through the Ardennes would get "bogged down, if the French have not completely lost their minds."[93] As it happened, the Manstein plan was the recipe for success that delivered the Wehrmacht's astonishingly quick victory in 1940.[94]

On 24 February, Hitler went to Munich for an afternoon speech at the Hofbräuhaus, where twenty years before he had announced the NSDAP party manifesto. With no further ado, he slipped into the role of the beer hall demagogue of the 1920s who still knew how to bring an auditorium to the boil with hatred-inciting tirades. Hitler poured scorn and contempt not just on his adversaries of yore but on the Western statesmen of the present: "At home and abroad, I was unlucky enough always to have to battle against a bunch of zeroes." He let his anti-Semitism flow with equal licence. "When the Jews, all that rabble that used to run around in Germany in those days, insulted me, how often did I tell you in this hall that it was my greatest honour?" The National Socialists, Hitler continued, had "gone after the international financial hyenas in Germany" and would now break "the organised terror of an abominable global plutocratic clique." Naturally, he also did not neglect to underscore his own significance in this great battle. Just as he "followed through" on everything in his life and did nothing "by half measures," he had given the Wehrmacht "the most modern arms in the world" and mobilised "enormous energies." "I am nothing but a magnet that continually passes over the German nation and extracts the steel from the people," Hitler crowed. That being so, there was no way Germany could be defeated: "It cannot turn out any other way: we must be victorious, and therefore we will be victorious!"[95] On 29 February, in the Chancellery, he promised his Reichsleiters and Gauleiters that after this victory "the new peace will be dictated in Münster."[96] Referring to the city where the treaty had been signed that ended the Thirty Years War and established France's subsequent predominance on the European continent, Hitler was thereby signalling that he was aiming for a revision of the power balance in Europe. At the same time he was laying claim to the legacy of the Holy Roman Empire for the German nation. "The old holy empire was the greatest state creation of post-Roman times," Hitler declared in private conversation. The "imperial character" that the old empire had taken over from the Romans would have to be adopted in turn by the new Greater German Reich. "Thanks to our organisation and excellent selection, the mastery of the world will necessarily fall into our laps."[97] "Mastery of the world"—that was the long-term goal intoxicating the German dictator. For that reason, too, Berlin was to expand into "the capital of the world, Germania," the construction work for which had been suspended with the start of the war, but which was to be resumed as soon as possible.[98]

In early March 1940, US Under Secretary of State Sumner Welles announced that he would visit Berlin. President Roosevelt was sending him to the European capitals as a special envoy to explore the possibility of starting peace talks. The American diplomatic initiative could not have come at a worse time for the Nazi leadership, which was chomping at the bit to launch the western offensive. "We have to watch out not to get ourselves on thin ice," Goebbels remarked.[99] He instructed the German press to ignore Welles' visit, and Hitler ordered Ribbentrop, Hess and Göring to exercise reserve when talking to the American diplomat. They were to let him speak his piece and then recite, quickly and concisely, the Nazi government's position that "a new and truly peaceful Europe" could only be established "if the Anglo-French will to destruction is broken."[100] But when Hitler himself received Welles on 2 March, he practised none of the reserve he had demanded of his paladins. After a couple of minutes, the Führer monopolised the conversation and began attacking England and France: "The German goal for the war, 'peace,' stands in direct contrast to the others' goal for the war, which is 'extermination.' The German people, which has learned its lessons from the terrible experience of 1918, stands as one behind me. If anyone wants to make peace, he has to induce Germany's adversaries to give up their war aims of annihilation."[101] He "had not minced words" with Welles, Hitler said afterwards, adding that he had made it unmistakably clear how hopeless peace negotiations were at present. "The plutocracy is now reaping what it sowed," he bragged.[102]

German leaders were also unhappy about Welles' mission because they feared that Roosevelt's envoy would get a warmer reception in Rome. Relations between the two Axis partners had been strained for some time. On 3 January, Mussolini had sent a long letter to Hitler advising against a western offensive and recommending instead a campaign against the Soviet Union. "The solution to the question of your living space lies in Russia and nowhere else!" the Duce had told the Führer. Mussolini failed to understand that the pact with Stalin did not mean Hitler had given up his goal of conquering living space in the east. Defeating England and France was a necessary precursory stage. And Mussolini completely misunderstood the German plans when he suggested that Italy could help arrange a "restoration of the Polish state" to pave the way for a possible understanding with the Western powers.[103]

Hitler was visibly irritated by Mussolini's letter and did not answer for two months. It was not until 10 March that Ribbentrop travelled to Rome, bearing a response. The tone was conspicuously friendly. Berlin had a vested interest in keeping Italy on side with the start of the western offensive approaching. Roosevelt's intervention via his envoy, Hitler claimed, had been solely aimed "at buying time for the Allies" and "paralysing Germany's offensive intentions." But the Führer would make his decisions based "exclusively on aspects of military functionality" and "sooner or later" Italy would have to fight side by side with Germany.[104] In their second meeting, Mussolini assured Ribbentrop that Italy "stood by Germany steadfastly and unalterably" and would enter the war at an appropriate time. It was agreed that the German and Italian dictators should meet soon.[105]

That meeting took place on 18 March at the Brenner Pass. It was snowing when Hitler's train arrived at the small Italian border station where Mussolini and Ciano were already waiting. The conversation in the Duce's salon car lasted for two and a half hours, and Hitler did almost all the talking, treating his host to extensive descriptions of his military triumphs during the Poland campaign and his preparations for the western offensive. But he said nothing about when the attack in the west was to take place. Apparently he did not trust the Italians to keep a secret. Mussolini was left with only a few minutes at the end of the meeting to renew his promise to enter the war on Germany's side, although he reserved the right to determine when that would be.[106] With hearty declarations of friendship, the two dictators went their separate ways, but Mussolini was left with a bad taste in his mouth. Hitler's behaviour made it clear that he did not at all consider the Duce an equal, but rather a junior partner. How their roles had changed since the first time they met in Venice in 1934! What annoyed Mussolini, Ciano wrote in his diary, was that "Hitler had been talking the entire time. Even though [the Duce] had a lot he wanted to say, he had no choice but to listen and stay silent."[107] By contrast Hitler returned to Berlin "beaming with joy and extremely satisfied."[108] Mussolini had shown himself to be a "true man," there was no doubting his commitment to the alliance, and the Italian dictator would "come along at the decisive moment."[109] One result of the meeting was that Ambassador Attolico, whose critical views had long made him a thorn in the side of the Nazi leadership, was recalled and replaced by the Hitler-friendly director of the Ministry for Popular Enlightenment, Dino Alfieri.[110]

On 17 March, the day before he left to meet Mussolini, Hitler had taken a major personnel decision and named Fritz Todt the head of the new Ministry for Armament and Munitions. The engineer had distinguished himself with his considerable practical energy during the construction of the Siegfried Line and was now charged with dramatically increasing arms production, particularly of ammunition for the army. Hitler's generals were horrified by the choice of a non-military man for the job and viewed his appointment, correctly, as further evidence of the Führer's distrust of the military leadership. Even as he praised the Wehrmacht as the best-equipped army in the world, Hitler was unhappy with the performance of the German arms industry and blamed the "paper-pushers" in the Army Procurement Office for all difficulties that arose. The office's director, General Karl Becker, was so insulted by the criticism that he committed suicide.[111]

Everyone within the Nazi leadership was convinced that Todt would "get things going on that score,"[112] and indeed, the new minister succeeded relatively quickly in installing a centrally controlled system of specialist committees to give arms production a more efficient foundation. The rapid rise in munitions-making in the first half of 1940, however, was also due to better supplies of raw materials like copper and steel, for which the Military Economy and Armaments Office in the Army High Command under General Georg Thomas was responsible. Still, Todt mainly got the credit for the improvement.[113]

It was for economic as well as strategic reasons that Hitler decided to open another front before striking in the west. In late November 1939, the Soviet Union attacked Finland. Berlin now feared that Britain might occupy Norway and cut Germany off from its essential supply of Swedish iron ore, which travelled through the year-round port of Narvik and was crucial to German armaments. Grand Admiral Raeder, the commander of the navy, in particular, had long warned Hitler of the danger, without failing to point out the usefulness of bases on the Norwegian coast for the U-boat war against Britain. On 15 and 17 December 1939, Hitler had received Vidkun Quisling, the leader of the National Rally, Norway's fascist party, in the Chancellery to discuss the situation. Following those meetings, he ordered the Army High Command to start thinking about how Germany could take possession of Norway.[114]

On 24 January 1940, a "Special Staff North" was established in the Army High Command to work out the operational details under the code name "Weserübung." Those preparations were accelerated by an incident that took place on 16 February in the Jössingfjord, in Norwegian waters. Here a British destroyer captured the MS *Altmark*—a supply ship of the armoured warship *Admiral Graf Spee*, which had been sunk the previous December—and freed three hundred British prisoners of war. This action, during which several German seamen lost their lives, was a clear violation of Norwegian neutrality, and

Goebbels' propaganda ran the gamut in an attempt to unleash a "storm of outrage." Hitler was beside himself with fury. "The ruling caste in London will one day pay dearly for their prank with the *Altmark*," he fumed over lunch in the Chancellery.[115]

On 21 February, he assigned Nikolaus von Falkenhorst, the commanding general of an army corps stationed in Koblenz, with directing the planned operation in northern Europe. In 1918, Falkenhorst had served as an officer in Finland, making him in Hitler's and Keitel's eyes an expert on conditions in Scandinavia. On 1 March, Operation Weserübung was authorised. The occupation of Denmark and Norway, it was claimed, was intended to "prevent English attacks on Scandinavia, secure our ore supply from Sweden and expand starting positions for the German navy and the Luftwaffe against England." The whole operation was to take on the "character of a peaceful occupation," aiming to provide "armed protection to secure the neutrality of the Nordic states." Still, any resistance was to be broken "using all military means."[116]

Operation Weserübung was a novelty. For the first time, Hitler had charged the Wehrmacht Supreme Command with operational planning, bypassing the army general staff, which was actually responsible. "Not a word was exchanged concerning this matter between the Führer and the army's supreme commander," wrote an outraged Halder in his diary. "That has to be recorded for posterity."[117] Hitler knew that the army leadership would be upset, and he didn't care. Part of his style of rule was to blur areas of responsibility and encourage rivalries to remind everyone concerned of his position as the sole ultimate arbiter. Because of their proximity to the Führer, the supreme commander of the Wehrmacht, Keitel, and his closest associate, the head of the Wehrmacht general staff, Jodl, were better positioned than the leaders of the army. After the Poland campaign, Keitel and Jodl moved into offices on the first floor of the Old Chancellery building and from now, together with their adjutants, formed part of the *maison militaire*, Hitler's most intimate military entourage. Jodl always gave a briefing at the daily situation meetings, and before long, he had become Hitler's most important adviser on the conduct of the war.[118]

On 22 March, Hitler flew from Tempelhof to Ainring Airport, near Salzburg, and spent the Easter holidays at the Berghof.[119] After his return to the capital, he pressed for a start to the Scandinavian operation because he feared the British could beat him to the punch. On 2 April, after General von Falkenhorst and the commanders of the Luftwaffe and the German navy, Göring and Raeder, confirmed that preparations were complete, Hitler ordered Operation Weserübung to commence on 9 April.[120] The following day, transport ships full of well-camouflaged troops and military hardware set sail for Norway. The British were completely in the dark as to what the Germans were up to. On 8 April, they informed the government in Oslo in a note that they had starting mining Norwegian waters. With that, they gave the German military a pretext for hostilities that were in fact already well underway.

On the afternoon of 8 April, Hitler informed Goebbels during a walk through the Chancellery garden about the imminent occupation of Denmark and Norway. "With their mine dispatch, the English have pushed a jumping board in our direction," Hitler said. "Everything down to the last detail has been prepared. Some 250,000 men will carry out the operation. Most of the infantrymen and ammunition have already been transported there camouflaged in steam ships. It is inconceivable that there will be any resistance at all." Hitler was not unduly concerned about the reaction of the United States. It would be a year and a half before its support of the Western Allies would have any effect. By that time Germany must have achieved victory. "Otherwise the material superiority of the other side would be too great," Hitler admitted. "A long-term war would also be difficult to bear psychologically." The dictator made no bones about what he intended to do with Norway and Denmark. "If the kings behave honestly, they can stay. But we are never going to give back these countries."[121] Both were to be incorporated into Germany's sphere of dominance and become parts of the planned "Greater Germanic Reich."[122]

Operation Weserübung counted on surprise, and again the German military's plans seemed to work. By the evening of 9 April, Hitler was already talking about one of the "greatest triumphs of our policies and waging of war."[123] But the operation by no means ran as smoothly everywhere as Berlin had expected. Whereas the Danish government capitulated on the very day the country was invaded, the Norwegian king called on his subjects to resist and refused to recognise the puppet

Quisling government that Germany tried to install. With Quisling enjoying little support among the population, Hitler dropped him and installed the Gauleiter of Essen, Josef Terboven, as Reich commissar. German troops were able to swiftly seize the most important ports and airstrips, but the Norwegians fought bravely, and British ships inflicted heavy losses on the German navy.[124] The situation was most critical near Narvik, where mountain troops under General Eduard Dietl found themselves confronted by superior Allied forces. "Our position in Narvik is somewhat touch-and-go," Goebbels wrote on 14 April. "The English seem to be concentrating all their forces on this point."[125]

It seems that Hitler's nerves could not take the tension, and he reacted hysterically to the unfavourable news from Narvik. He had Keitel order Dietl to withdraw his troops to Sweden and allow themselves to be interned there. For the general staff officer Colonel Bernhard von Lossberg the decision to give up Narvik was a "crisis of nerves like in the blackest days of the Battle of the Marne."[126] The "agitation is terrible," Jodl noted, but, with Lossberg's support, he managed to get Hitler to retract the order. "One should only give up something when it is lost," Jodl remarked.[127] For a time, the dictator calmed down, but the news that the English had succeeded in landing large units north and south of Trondheim put him back in a state of panic. Hitler wanted to send immediate reinforcements to Trondheim, but the Army High Command declared itself unable to provide additional forces with the western offensive imminent. There were again heated scenes in the Chancellery. Even Jodl, otherwise an absolute loyalist, spoke of "leadership chaos" and Hitler's impulsive interventions "ruining all the orderly work of the responsible military leadership."[128]

In contrast to the previous year's pomp, Hitler barely celebrated his fifty-first birthday on 20 April, cancelling all appointments.[129] Nonetheless, Goebbels noted, "the people stood from early morning onwards on Wilhelmsplatz, showering the Führer with ovations." Shirer observed a somewhat different picture when he passed the Chancellery on the eve of Hitler's birthday. Only around seventy-five people had turned out to see the Führer, compared to several thousand in the years before.[130]

In late April, the military situation in Norway improved. Dietl was able to hold his position at Narvik, and German troops established a land connection between Oslo and Trondheim. Hitler was "beside himself with glee" and invited Jodl to sit next to him at lunch—a special gesture of favouritism that demonstrated a new level of appreciation.[131] In early May the Allied troops which had landed near Trondheim shipped out again, although fighting around Narvik continued until June. But by then Hitler had lost interest in the Scandinavian theatre. His eyes were firmly trained westwards, where the first period of clement weather was on its way.[132] By contrast, the army leadership looked to the coming weeks with trepidation. Their commander-in-chief had demonstrated a significant lack of self-control the first time his nerves had been tested. What would happen during the western offensive, Brauchitsch fretted, "if Hitler lost his nerve and wanted to give up on a situation like that in Narvik?"[133]

Hitler set 5 May as the new date for launching the German attack in the west, but Göring succeeded in getting it postponed by several days after fog threatened the Luftwaffe's effectiveness. "Everyone is waiting for the great offensive," Goebbels noted on 7 May. "The tension is slowly becoming unbearable."[134] Two days later, with an improving weather forecast, the final decision was made to commence Case Yellow on 10 May. "The army will embark upon a different path tomorrow," Quartermaster General Eduard Wagner prophesied. "It will cost a lot of blood and cause pain, but everyone is ready to go . . . There has probably never been an offensive that has been prepared so well and so thoroughly."[135] Hitler made a confident impression in the days before the attack. In only a few weeks, he predicted, France would be conquered, and England too would no longer be able to continue the fight.[136] Hitler's biggest fear was that the attack plan would leak out at the last minute and deprive him of the element of surprise he was again counting on.

For that reason, the Führer's journey to the front was kept top secret. On 9 May, his personal train was readied at the tiny station of Finkenkrug near Berlin, west of the Staaken airstrip. Even the members of his entourage, with the exception of his military adjutants, did not know where they were headed. Hitler's secretaries speculated that "the boss" wanted to inspect the troops in Scandinavia, and the Führer declined to clear up their misconception, joking: "If you behave well, you can take home a seal skin as a trophy." And the train did indeed start out in the direction of Hamburg. But that evening, just past Hanover, it suddenly veered southwest. There could be no doubt as to the ultimate destination. In the early hours of 10 May, the train arrived at the small station of Euskirchen, where a Mercedes motorcade was waiting to take the dictator and his retinue to a specially prepared headquarters near Münstereifel. A few minutes after they arrived there, at 5:35 a.m., the German attack in the west began.[137]

The "Cliff's Nest," as Hitler's first field headquarters was called, was well concealed on a mountaintop covered with forest. The facility was deliberately kept simple so as to underscore Hitler's putatively simple tastes. The subterranean bunker, artificially ventilated, consisted of a combination office and bedroom, kitchen and bathroom as well as three further rooms, where Hitler's adjutant Julius Schaub and his valet Heinz Linge as well as Keitel were accommodated. Such proximity to the Führer was both an honour and a source of irritation for the head of the Wehrmacht. The concrete walls conducted sound and Keitel believed he could even hear the rustle of the pages every time Hitler read a newspaper. A second bunker accommodated Jodl, Hitler's military adjutants, his physician Karl Brandt and one of Keitel's assistants. Alongside the bunkers for living and sleeping, there was also an "eating bunker," with a map of France on the wall, and further down the slope a wooden barracks for meetings. The rest of the staff members and the press office were quartered in a nearby village. The Army High Command set up shop in a barracks camp about half an hour's drive from the Führer's headquarters.[138] Hitler would later describe the Cliff's Nest as his "nicest quarters."[139] It was located in a charming landscape, with birdsong filling the air. The idyllic setting could almost make people forget that the Germans were once again about to bring death and destruction upon their neighbours.

On the morning of 10 May, Ribbentrop summoned the Belgian and Dutch ambassadors and informed them that the Reich would be violating their countries' neutrality. At the same time, in a "Proclamation to the Soldiers on the Western Front," Hitler announced that the ensuing battle would determine "the fate of the German nation for the next thousand years."[140] Disgusted by such megalomania, the court official Friedrich Kellner entrusted to his diary the hope that it was "probably high time someone rapped these gentlemen on their criminal knuckles."[141] Like Kellner, many foreign observers were convinced that Hitler had gone too far and was doomed to defeat. "Now there will be bloody battles," noted Wilhelm Muehlon, a former Krupp director who had become a committed opponent of Wilhelmine hegemonic policies during the First World War and had been living in Swiss exile ever since. "But the world is breathing a sigh of relief that the stultifying wait is over and a decision will follow swiftly."[142]

The attack in the west had come as a surprise, Marianne von Weizsäcker wrote to her mother. She had believed to the last minute that it would miraculously be headed off. Nonetheless "the calm and confidence among the people" was "admirable," and first reports from the new theatre of war sounded favourable. "Everyone you talk to thinks that the war will not last long."[143]

The relative military strength of the combatants, however, at least on paper, spoke for the Western powers. Including Belgium and the Netherlands, they had 144 divisions compared to 141 German ones. With 13,974 pieces of artillery and 3,383 tanks, the Allies enjoyed clear superiority over the Wehrmacht, where the respective numbers stood at 7,378 and 2,445. The only area in which the German side had a numerical advantage was in warplanes: here 5,446 aircraft faced 3,099 Allied machines.[144] Hitler was well aware of the risk he was taking, and the tension of the first days of the offensive had been "almost unbearable," he admitted to Goebbels several weeks later.[145] But everything happened much more quickly than the dictator and his generals had dared hope. German troops broke through Dutch and Belgian lines on the north flank, and paratroopers and special units captured important bridges and fortifications. By 15 May, Dutch forces had already surrendered, and the government and Queen Wilhelmina fled to London. The previous day, a German bomber squadron had bombarded central Rotterdam, killing 800 civilians. After Warsaw, this was the second big city that had been subjected to such a ruthless aerial attack. The violence unleashed in such bombardments would rebound against German cities over the course of the war.[146]

What decided the western offensive was the German operational plan and Germany's success in deceiving the Allies about where the main thrust of the attack would take place. Since the Allies expected the primary advance of the invading German army to come in the north, through Belgium, and concentrated their best units there, the tank divisions and motorised units of Army Group A were able to pass through the Ardennes unimpeded. On 13 May, they broke through the defensive line on the river Maas near Sedan, opening up the opportunity for wide-ranging mobile warfare. The wedge of the break-through was "developing in nearly classical form," noted Halder. "West of the Maas everything is progressing swiftly."[147] On the evening of 14 May, Hitler called Goebbels from his headquarters and was, in the words of the propaganda minister, "in utter bliss after his grandiose triumphs."[148] French defensive forces were no match for German tanks, which received effective support from the Luftwaffe. Panic was spreading. In Berlin Shirer registered "very long, stunned faces among the foreign correspondents and diplomats today."[149]

In the French campaign, Hitler decided right from the start to serve not just as the nominal but as the factual commander-in-chief of the Wehrmacht. During the daily situation meetings, which took place early in the afternoon and again around midnight, he did not simply listen. He asked questions and issued orders. Having inten-sively studied the operational plans in the preceding months, on more than one occasion he surprised his military commanders with his detailed knowledge.[150] At the same time, as had been the case during Operation Weserübung, he was very much at the mercy of his mood swings. Hitler's euphoria at German troops crossing the Maas on 13 May was followed a few days later by a bout of nerves caused by the exposed southern flank of Army Group A, which seemed to invite an enemy counter-attack. For the first time, he made a major intervention in running operations, pressuring the Army High Command to halt the rapidly advancing tank column under Ewald von Kleist until infantry divisions could catch up and secure its flanks. "A truly unhappy day," Halder noted in his diary on 17 May. "The Führer is unbelievably nervous. He is scared by his own success and is unwilling to take any risks and would rather stop us." The following day, Halder wrote: "The Führer is incomprehen-sibly worried about the southern flank. He raves and yells that we are on our way to ruining the operation and running the risk of defeat." It was not until the afternoon of 18 May that the chief of the general staff succeeded in changing Hitler's mind and received the "all-clear to continue to advance."[151]

The very next day, Hitler was a different man. "Mood of the Führer is grand," his press chief Otto Dietrich reported from the Führer's headquarters. "Historical victory right on our doorstep."[152] On 20 May, vanguard German tanks reached the mouth of the Somme at Abbeville, completing the encirclement of Allied troops. The majority of English, French and Belgian forces, more than 400,000 men, were now trapped between Army Groups A and B. "Führer beside himself with joy," Jodl noted. "Speaks in terms of the highest respect of the German army and its leadership."[153] Goebbels concurred, drawing an analogy with Rome and Carthage: "A new Battle of Cannae is at hand . . . We have succeeded in the greatest encirclement in military history."[154] Quartermaster General Wagner was no less euphoric: "Who would have thought that we would ever experience anything like this after 1918? . . . The way this campaign has gone militarily is so fantastic it is like a dream."[155] For those who opposed Hitler, of course, the military catastrophe the Allies were facing came as a shock. In the Swiss canton of Graubünden, after hearing the terrible news in the evening of 21 May, Wilhelm Muehlon decided to stop listening to the radio.[156]

What happened next would go down in history as the "Miracle of Dunkirk." On 24 May, with German forces a mere 15 kilometres from the Allies' last remaining port on the Channel coast, Hitler issued orders to stop the advance. "The tanks and motorised units are standing still, as if nailed to the spot on the hills between Béthune and Saint-Omer, after a command from the highest level and are not allowed to attack," Halder complained to his diary after Hitler had once again intervened in running operations. "As things stand, it will take weeks to clear out the pocket. It greatly damages our prestige and our further ambitions."[157] There has been much speculation about what led Hitler to take this fateful decision. What is certain is that his order to halt the advance was not his decision alone, but rather came after an intensive discussion with Colonel-General von Rundstedt. During the morning of 24 May, the dictator met with the commander of Army Group A in his headquarters in Charleville to discuss how to proceed. There, he learned that Rundstedt had already ordered German troops to halt so that motorised units and infantry divisions could catch up with the battle-worn tank groups.

Hitler agreed with Rundstedt about the situation. The dictator was already looking ahead to the next phase of the campaign and wanted to conserve his tank force for coming operations. To this end, he explicitly left it up to Rundstedt when the advance would continue.[158] Thus Hitler's actions were guided by military considerations. A few days later, however, when it became clear that he had made a serious error, he cited an *ex post facto* political reason, claiming that he had purposely let the British expeditionary corps escape so as to preserve the possibility of a peace settlement with Britain. "The army is the backbone of England and the Empire," Hitler said. "If we destroy the invasion corps, the Empire would fall apart. Since we are neither willing nor able to take on its inheritance, we have to give the Empire a chance. My generals failed to understand this."[159] But there is no truth in the idea that Hitler wanted to take it easy on the British. On the contrary, the Führer trusted Göring's assurances that the Luftwaffe would easily be able to stop an evacuation of the British Expeditionary Force by sea. Hitler probably also wanted to demonstrate his superiority to Brauchitsch and Halder and make it clear once and for all that it was he alone who made fundamental operational decisions.[160]

On 26 May, Rundstedt lifted the order for the troops to halt, but the forty-eight-hour pause in their forward momentum proved decisive since the British had already started evacuating their troops under the code name "Operation Dynamo." By the time German forces took Dunkirk on 4 June, hundreds of ships had saved the British expeditionary corps together with some French troops, around 370,000 men in total. "The supreme command's halting of the tank formations turns out to be a serious mistake," Fedor von Bock wrote on 30 May.[161] He was right. It was only thanks to the "Miracle of Dunkirk" that Britain was able to continue fighting in the summer of 1940. "It was without doubt a turning point of the European war whose importance cannot be estimated highly enough," the military historian Rolf-Dieter Müller has concluded.[162]

Belgium surrendered on 28 May. King Leopold III stayed behind in the country, but the government went into exile in London. A few days later, Hitler moved his headquarters to Brûly-de-Pesche, a small village in southern Belgium, 25 kilometres south of Charleroi, that consisted of a few farms, a school and a church. Here, at lightning speed, the Organisation Todt had built Hitler a concrete bunker. His staff and security guard were quartered in barracks and buildings vacated by villagers, while the Army High Command set up camp several kilometres away in Chimay. Hitler named this base the "Wolf's Ravine."[163] "Wolf" was the name he had used the first time he stayed at the Obersalzberg in the summer of 1923, and he allowed certain close female friends, like Winifred Wagner, to call him by it. But Hitler found his new forest headquarters less to his liking than his previous ones, complaining about the "horrible multitude of mosquitoes" and claiming, even months later, that the wood stain used on the newly built barracks had affected his eyes and left him unable to see properly.[164] Situation meetings largely took place in the schoolhouse or out in the open.

The fifth of June marked the start of the second phase of the campaign, "Case Red," which saw German troops thrust into the heart of France. The previous day, Hitler had expressed the hope that everything would be "done in four to six weeks,"[165] but again progress was faster than anticipated. By 9 June, German troops had already breached French lines on the Somme and the lower Aisne. Two days later, they crossed the Marne, and a few days after that Army Group C attacked the Maginot Line. French defences were collapsing. "It is truly a beaten army," wrote Quartermaster General Wagner. "Incomprehensible how the troops completely broke down physically and mentally, threw all their weapons into the trenches, left everything behind and fled in panic."[166] On 14 June, the Wehrmacht marched into Paris, and a day later it took Verdun, the site of the bloodiest battle of the First World War. There were scenes of indescribable misery on France's roads as millions of refugees tried to flee to the south of the country ahead of the German troops. The French capital itself resembled a ghost town. "First shock; the streets are utterly deserted, the stores closed, the shutters down tight over all the windows," wrote Shirer in his diary after arriving in Paris on 17 June. "It was the emptiness that got you."[167]

On 16 June, French prime minister Paul Reynaud, who had succeeded Daladier in March, resigned. He named as his successor the 84-year-old Marshal Philippe Pétain, the popular army commander from the First World War. The following day, the French government, which had fled to Bordeaux, asked for a cease-fire. When Hitler learned of this in his headquarters in Brûly-de-Pesche, he immediately struck a pose and stamped his right foot on the ground. Cameraman Walter Frentz captured this scene, which showed the dictator suffused by triumph, for the weekly newsreels.[168] In a hastily improvised speech,

Keitel praised Hitler as the "greatest military commander of all time"—
the German acronym for the title, *"Gröfaz,"* would later be used with
bitter irony when the fortunes of war turned against Hitler.[169]

Ex-Kaiser Wilhelm II sent Hitler a gushing telegram from his Dutch
exile in Doorn, congratulating the dictator on forcing France to
surrender. Referring to Friedrich the Great's victory over Austria in
the Seven Years War, he wrote: "All German hearts sound with the
chorale of Leuthen, which the singers of Leuthen, soldiers of the
great king, took up: Now Thank We All Our God."[170] Crown Prince
Wilhelm, the Kaiser's eldest son, was not about to be outdone. "From
today, the weapons are silent in the west, and the path is clear for a
showdown with perfidious Albion," he wrote. "In this hour of the
greatest historical significance, I would like as an old soldier and an
admiring German to shake your hand." The younger Wilhelm signed
off his telegram with the words *"Sieg Heil!"*[171] Viktoria von Dirksen,
who had helped introduce aristocrats to the Nazi movement before
1933, telegrammed: "A hundred-thousandfold *Sieg Heil, Sieg Heil* to our
most beloved Führer"; while Grand Duke Friedrich Franz von
Mecklenburg-Schwerin, who had been a member of both the NSDAP
and the SS since 1931, told Hitler that he was "deeply moved by the
news that Paris has been occupied." He wished the Führer and the
"incomparable Wehrmacht . . . God's blessing."

Congratulatory telegrams also arrived from Gottfried Feder, who
had not played much of a role in the Nazi Party since his disloyal
behaviour in the Strasser crisis of December 1932, and from the former
press baron and chairman of the German National People's Party
(DNVP), Alfred Hugenberg, whom Hitler had manoeuvred into political insignificance within a few months following January 1933. Equally
enthusiastic about the "unparalleled victory" was Daimler-Benz executive Jakob Werlin, who had serviced Hitler's early passion for the latest
car models. "Not many Germans know how great your prior worries
and efforts, how unshakable your faith and will always were, as they
all now result in the crowning moment of your life," he telegrammed.
"With heartfelt affection, I think of this greatest historical moment."[172]

On the evening of 17 June, Hitler called Goebbels to tell him that
France had surrendered. The dictator was "very emotional and moved
to the core," the propaganda minister noted.[173] In his headquarters,
people had never seen the Führer in such a cheerful mood, and his

euphoria was contagious among his entire entourage. Hitler was also in fine shape physically. His personal physician Morell admitted in a letter to his wife that he had "hardly anything to do." The only thing Hitler complained about was having "much too large an appetite." Morell concluded: "He is in fantastic health. He is fresh and full of energy."[174]

The following day Hitler travelled to Munich for talks with Mussolini. The Italian dictator, who had hesitated joining Germany in the war, had been feeling nervous after the Wehrmacht's swift victory and worried that he would arrive too late to get his share of the spoils. In late May he had ordered Italy's new ambassador to Germany, Dino Alfieri, to communicate the news that his country would declare war on the Allies on 5 June. Hitler had been anything but thrilled by this announcement, as he wanted to take all the credit for what he believed would be certain victory. He asked the Duce to delay his declaration by five days. Mussolini obliged, formally declaring war from the balcony of the Palazzo Venezia on 10 June.[175] In his headquarters, Hitler had taken to mocking his Axis partner, and diplomats in Berlin had nothing but scorn for their Italian "harvest helpers."[176]

During the two dictators' talks in the Führerbau on Königsplatz, Hitler surprised the Italian delegation with his unexpectedly moderate peace demands. Mussolini, who had come to Munich in the hope of gaining Nice, Corsica and Tunisia, had to renounce all of his territorial ambitions because Hitler wanted to make it as easy as possible for France to sign an armistice. The German dictator feared that if conditions were too harsh, France could decide to fight on in northern Africa and make its still-intact fleet of warships join with the British navy. Ciano was impressed by Hitler's seeming "moderation and foresight," writing: "I can hardly be suspected of having many tender feelings for him, but in that moment I truly did admire him."[177] In Munich, Mussolini was once again confronted with the fact that he was clearly the junior partner in the alliance. Politely but firmly, Hitler rejected the Italian request for a seat at the table when peace was negotiated. The fact that the Italian offensive against French troops in the Alps, which Mussolini ordered immediately after returning home, would stall after only a couple of days reinforced the German military leadership in their view that Italy's fighting forces were of little value.

On the evening of 20 June, Paul Schmidt was summoned to Hitler's headquarters to translate the German terms of peace into French. In the village church in Brûly-de-Pesche, by candlelight, Schmidt went to work, with Hitler and Keitel stopping by from time to time to check on his progress.[178] As the site for the signing of the armistice agreement, Hitler had chosen the very clearing in the forest of Compiègne where the German delegation led by Matthias Erzberger had formally ended hostilities in the First World War on 11 November 1918. To that end, the salon carriage in which the signing ceremony had taken place back then was located and brought to the precise spot in which it had stood in 1918.[179] Every detail of the signing event was staged. The symbolically charged location was viewed as the perfect setting for Hitler to make a grand appearance. The message was unmistakable: the ceremony of 21 June 1940 was an act of revenge for the lost war of 1914–18 and the "humiliation" of the Treaty of Versailles.[180]

That afternoon, at around 3:15, Hitler's motorcade arrived at Compiègne. He was accompanied by Göring, Raeder, Brauchitsch, Keitel, Ribbentrop and Hess. They paused for a moment before a memorial stone bearing the inscription: HERE ON THE ELEVENTH OF NOVEMBER 1918 SUCCUMBED THE CRIMINAL PRIDE OF THE GERMAN REICH. VANQUISHED BY THE FREE PEOPLES WHICH IT TRIED TO ENSLAVE.[181] William Shirer, who had been sent by CBS to broadcast live on the signing ceremony, watched the scene through a telescope. "I have seen that face many times at the great moments of his life," Shirer said. "But today! It is afire with scorn, anger, hate, revenge, triumph. He steps off the monument and contrives to make even this gesture a masterpiece of contempt. He glances back at it, contemptuous, angry . . . Suddenly, as though his face were not giving quite complete expression to his feelings, he throws his whole body into harmony with his mood. He swiftly snaps his hands on his hips, arches his shoulders, plants his feet wide apart. It is a magnificent gesture of defiance, of burning contempt for this place now and all that it has stood for in the twenty-two years since it witnessed the humbling of the German Empire."[182]

A short time later, Hitler and his retinue took their seats in the train carriage, with the German dictator occupying the very chair where Marshal Foch had sat in 1918. Then the French delegation, led by General Charles Huntziger, arrived. The Germans stood up in greeting, whereupon Keitel read out the preamble of the cease-fire agreement, drafted by Hitler himself. It described the choice of location as an "act of restorative justice . . . to extinguish a memory that held no historical glory for France and that was considered by the German people as the deepest humiliation of all time."[183] Schmidt, who translated this into French, would later describe both sides as sitting there with "stony faces," like "figures in a wax museum."[184] Afterwards, Hitler got up and left the carriage with his entourage. Only Keitel and Schmidt remained to communicate Germany's conditions for a cease-fire. The entire ceremony lasted a mere quarter of an hour, and that very day, Hitler returned to his headquarters. In the evening, he described events to Goebbels by phone and said that he wanted to have the train carriage taken to Berlin. "Our humiliation has now been erased," he crowed. The propaganda minister's worship no longer knew any bounds. "The Führer . . . is the greatest genius we have ever possessed in all our history. It is an honour to serve him."[185] In a letter to his friend Rudolf Hess, the geographer Karl Haushofer too praised the ceremony staged at Compiègne as a world-historical event "comparable to the crowning of Charlemagne," during which "the mantle of immortality passes through the historical moment and you can almost physically feel the beating of its wings."[186]

At 6:50 p.m. on 22 June, the German-French cease-fire was signed by Keitel and Huntziger. For State Secretary Weizsäcker, the conditions imposed on vanquished France bore signs of "the Führer's masterly hand," being "elastic" and permitting "complete room to manoeuvre towards a devastating peace."[187] Germany would occupy the north and west of France, including its entire Atlantic and English Channel coastline. Parts of central and all of southern France remained unoccupied and were to be ruled by a French government under Marshal Pétain with its centre in Vichy. The regime was required to cooperate closely with the German military administration and follow its instructions. The armistice took effect in the night of 24–25 June, after Italy and France had also signed a cease-fire. In his headquarters, Hitler and his entourage listened to radio reports about the event. Even amid such a small group, Hitler could not cease playing the conquering hero, ordering the lights turned off and the windows opened. "We sat there silently in the dark," recalled Albert Speer, "bowled over by the knowledge that we were experiencing a historical moment in the proximity of the man who created it."[188]

The previous day, 23 June, Hitler had flown to Paris–Le Bourget Airport in the early hours of the morning. He was accompanied by Speer and his fellow architect Hermann Giesler as well as the sculptor Arno Breker. It was the first and only time the German dictator visited the French capital, and he travelled there solely for the purpose of sightseeing. Hitler later said he had come early in the morning to "create as little a stir as possible among the people."[189] The streets were almost empty as three large Mercedes sped from the airport to the Opéra Garnier. In his younger years, Hitler had studied the construction of this neo-Baroque landmark, and as he and his entourage were given an impromptu tour of the building by an usher, he was able to show off what he knew. From there, Hitler and his retinue proceeded down the Champs-Elysées, past the Arc de Triomphe with the Tomb of the Unknown Soldier, to the Eiffel Tower, where Hitler ordered the vehicles to stop. In the Dôme des Invalides, Hitler stood for a long time in front of Napoleon's sarcophagus, remarking that he wished to have the body of Napoleon's son, the Duke of Reichstadt, moved from Vienna to Paris. The tour concluded with a look at the Sacré-Coeur de Montmartre, after which Hitler slipped out of the city as unnoticed as he had arrived in it. All told, he spent three hours in Paris.[190]

"Was Paris not lovely?" Hitler remarked to Speer that evening. "Berlin has to become much lovelier!" The dictator ordered the architect to immediately resume work on the major building projects that had been put on ice. "Through new construction Berlin is to be given, within a short time, the expression of the greatness of our victory as the capital of a powerful new empire," Hitler wrote in a decree he dated 25 June, the first day of the cease-fire. It was with the realisation of his megalomaniacal architectural plans, which he ordered completed by 1950, that Hitler intended to crown his life's work. He believed the campaign in the west was over, assuming that England would soon capitulate, and his thoughts were already turning to the next stage: his war for "living space" with the Soviet Union. As Speer was taking his leave, he heard a cheerful Führer tell the head of the Wehrmacht Supreme Command: "Now we have shown what we are capable of. Believe me, Keitel, a campaign against Russia would be child's play in comparison."[191] In late June, Halder learned from Weizsäcker that Hitler's eyes were "firmly set on the east" but that in the Führer's assessment Britain "would probably require another demonstration of our military might before it gives in and frees up our hands for the east."[192]

Before Hitler left the Wolf's Ravine on 27 June for his new "Tannenberg" headquarters on the Kniebis Ridge in the Black Forest, he permitted himself a special indulgence. Together with his former wartime comrades Sergeant Max Amann and runner Ernst Schmidt he visited the old German positions on the battlefields of Flanders. Once again, the former army private demonstrated his prodigious memory, recalling many places and events his companions had long forgotten.[193] Then, from his new headquarters, Hitler drove through Alsace to the battlefields in the Vosges, visited Strasbourg Cathedral and inspected parts of the Maginot Line. He summoned Goebbels to discuss his impending reception in Berlin, telling his confidant that he was planning to deliver a major speech to the Reichstag and "give England one last chance." Britain would have the opportunity to accept a peace settlement on the same terms Hitler had presented in October 1939. He had no interest in destroying the British Empire, the dictator claimed, since it would not benefit Germany but rather "major foreign powers," by which he presumably meant the United States and Japan. If London once again refused his offers, he warned, it "would have only itself to blame for the consequences."[194]

On 6 July, Hitler returned to the Reich capital he had surreptitiously slipped out of two months previously. Goebbels had had ample time to prepare a suitably pompous welcome. Hundreds of thousands of people lined the streets, which were strewn with flowers, from Anhalter Station to the Chancellery. Standing up in his limousine, Hitler drank in the acknowledgement of the masses. "The storm of celebrations by a completely happy people was beyond description," Goebbels noted, once again intoxicated by an event he had staged himself.[195] But the popular enthusiasm was more than just a product of propaganda. It also expressed people's genuine relief that the war against France had been neither as long nor as bloody as they had feared. Most Germans were "feeling pretty elated at the victory," reported Shirer: "They also believe that the decisive battle has been won and that the war will certainly be over by the end of the summer. That also makes them feel good."[196]

While there had been significant dissatisfaction during the winter of 1939–40, now confidence was brimming. The whole nation was "filled with a faithful trust in the Führer that had perhaps never before existed to this extent," an NSDAP regional director from Augsburg noted in an official report. "If an increase in feeling for Adolf Hitler was still possible, it had became reality with the day of the return to Berlin."[197] The aura of military genius now ascribed to him added a powerful new dimension to the mythology of the Führer. "How magnificent that at this hour the German people have such a brilliant person at their head," the twenty-one-year-old German literature student Lore Walb enthused. "With the Führer, the war can only end in victory for us! Everyone is convinced of that."[198] In a speech on 20 May, Göring had already compared Hitler with Germany's greatest historical leader. "It is rare in German history that the wisdom of a statesman and the genius of a field commander come together in one person," Göring gushed. "In Friedrich the Great, Germany had such an individual, and in Adolf Hitler we have been blessed with another genius."[199] The victory over France did indeed represent the apex of Hitler's popularity. "The profound and noble way in which the Führer erased the humiliation of 1918 once and for all from history is being met with boundless admiration," concluded a Security Service report on the mood of the German people.[200]

Even those who were sceptical about Hitler's policies and the way he conducted the war shared this enthusiasm. The psychologist and doctor Willy Hellpach, who had run in the Reich presidential election of 1925 for the liberal German Democratic Party (DDP), celebrated in a letter to Karl Haushofer "a tremendous world-historical transformation whose rhythm is truly breathtaking."[201] The historian Friedrich Meinecke wrote to his student and colleague Siegfried Kaehler: "The tremendous things we have experienced seem ever more tremendous by the day . . . Joy, admiration and pride in this army outweigh everything else within me. And the recapturing of Strasbourg! How can anyone's heart not skip a beat?"[202] Weizsäcker described the cease-fire signing at Compiègne in a letter to his mother: "I wish Papa could have witnessed today. He would have surely asked you to play the *Hakkapeliitta [Finnländischer Reitermarsch]* on the piano."[203]

Hitler was now also held in far more esteem among Germany's military commanders. Those "who had not completely trusted" him at first, the dictator told Goebbels, were "now completely enthusiastic."[204] Despite all of the experts' reservations, Hitler had been correct in his estimation of France's fighting capabilities, and the plan he had developed with Manstein had been a resounding success. "The glory is entirely down to the Führer," Eduard Wagner proclaimed, "for without his will it would have never been put into action."[205] The quartermaster general was hardly alone in this view. Infantry General Gotthard Heinrici too was full of "admiration for a state leadership that had known how to deliver all of our enemies, one by one, in front of our sword."[206] It seems that all the tensions and conflicts Hitler had caused by involving himself in running operations were forgotten, as were the dictator's mood swings, which had tried the nerves of the military leadership.

The rapturous praise heaped upon him from all sides had a clear effect on the dictator's ego. In Hitler's own mind, his triumph in the west was confirmation of his abilities as a military commander. Just as he had been convinced shortly after coming to power in 1933 that he had to remove foreign policy from the incompetent hands of the Foreign Ministry's career diplomats, he was now certain of his own superiority in every respect over the skittish worriers in the Wehrmacht general staff. Hitler's tendency to overestimate himself blinded him to his own dependency on professional advice where military decisions were concerned. A year later, in October 1941, when victory in his war against the Soviet Union seemed but a matter of days, he boasted in his headquarters: "I am a commander against my will. I have only got involved in military affairs because there is no one better at it right now. If we had a Moltke today, I would let him get on with it."[207]

Among those who opposed Hitler, the mood ranged from despair and resignation to determination in the face of adversity. There was no disputing "the greatness of the victory Hitler had achieved," remarked Hassell, but that changed "nothing about the essential character of his deeds and the horrible threat posed to all higher values."[208] For Helmuth James von Moltke, who had been plunged into a deep depression after France's collapse, the new situation motivated him to do even more to combat the criminal regime. He who reminds himself every day "of what good and evil are and does not get distracted by the triumph of evil, no matter how great, has already laid the first stone in the overcoming of evil," Moltke wrote to his wife in early June 1940.[209] The Kreisau Circle, which was coalescing from the summer of 1940 around Moltke and Peter Yorck von Wartenburg, would go on to play a central role in the resistance to Hitler. "The shame, aggrievement and hatred of these days will never be forgotten: they are scarcely tolerable," Thomas Mann wrote about Germany's military successes in his diary in late May 1940. For Mann as well as for many others throughout the world who opposed Hitler, Britain represented a last hope. "If England stays on its feet, holds firm and gives the war a positive turn," wrote Mann, "then the English are the greatest people on earth."[210]

But what would England do? That was the big question of the summer of 1940. On 10 May, the day Nazi Germany's western offensive commenced, Neville Chamberlain stepped down. His successor, First Lord of the Admiralty Winston Churchill, formed an all-party government. Churchill had warned early on about the danger Germany represented and had been a fierce critic of the policy of appeasement. Now he became Hitler's main foe—a "man of destiny," in Sebastian Haffner's words—who never left any doubt as to his determination to continue the war until the barbarism of Nazism had been defeated.[211] On 13 May, in his inaugural address to Parliament, Churchill delivered his famous "blood, sweat and tears" speech to rally his compatriots for the severity of the war against Germany. Britain, he said, was committed "to wage war against a monstrous tyranny never surpassed in the dark and lamentable catalogue of human crime."[212] During the critical days at the end of May, when the British Expeditionary Force looked in danger of being destroyed at Dunkirk and Lord Halifax suggested approaching Mussolini about the possibility of suing for peace, Churchill was able to prevail in cabinet with his uncompromising position. It was always preferable to go down fighting, he argued, than to bend to the enemy's dictated terms. And if Britain continued to face bravely up to Germany, he believed, it would awaken sympathies in the United States, which had thus far stayed out of the war.[213]

A partnership between Britain and America was precisely what Hitler tried to prevent. On 13 June, he granted an interview in his headquarters to Karl Wiegand, the chief correspondent for the Hearst press group. Published two days later, it seemed to show Hitler as a moderate. He avoided his usual polemics against Roosevelt and praised the Monroe Doctrine and US policy of non-interference in European affairs. "America for the Americans, and Europe for the Europeans—that is my motto," Hitler told Wiegand. And he reiterated that it had never been his intention to destroy the British Empire.[214] Churchill was decidedly unimpressed. On 4 June, he had used the slogan "Never surrender" in his "We shall fight on the beaches" speech. Two weeks later, after France had capitulated, he restated his absolute determination to continue the war, telling the House of Commons that should the British Empire and Commonwealth still exist in a thousand years' time, people would say: "That was their finest hour."[215] As the Soviet ambassador in London, Ivan Maisky, described the effect of this speech: "The initial shock and confusion have dissipated. Now a storm front of cold, persistent, truly British fury is brewing. Everything indicates that the English will defend themselves to the very end."[216] If further evidence were needed that the British were serious about their decision to fight on, they delivered it on 3 July, when the Royal Navy sank the greater part of the French fleet, anchored off Mers-el-Kébir, near Oran in Algeria, so that it would not fall into German hands; it cost the lives of 1,250 French sailors.[217]

Hitler was indecisive about whether he should even make a further overture to Britain under the circumstances and postponed his Reichstag speech, which he had almost finished writing.[218] Weizsäcker believed that the German leadership would now grow more willing "to go all in and destroy the British Empire and its ruling class."[219] Ciano, after visiting Berlin on 7 July, also had the impression that the Führer was inclined to continue the battle against Britain with all the means at his disposal. "He intends to unleash a storm of fire and iron against the English," the Italian foreign minister wrote. "But a definitive decision has not yet been made."[220]

As was so often the case when he needed to make up his mind about something important, Hitler retreated to the Obersalzberg to ponder his next move. On 11 July, he received Raeder to discuss the possibility of an invasion of Britain. The navy commander warned of the dangers of trying to cross the English Channel, saying that it could only be attempted if Germany had established air superiority over southern England. The following day, Jodl shared his thoughts on "the continuation of the war against England," which he had laid out in a memorandum on 30 June. He too described the attempt to land German troops in England as a last resort. On 13 July, Hitler consulted with the chief of the general staff. "Hitler is most concerned about the question of why England does not want to pursue the route of peace," Halder noted in his diary. England, Hitler believed, was hoping for a change of policy in the Soviet Union. Therefore, it would have to be "forced by violence to make peace." Hitler was, however, reluctant to embark on such a move because English defeat would spell the end of the British Empire, something in which he had no interest. "By spilling German blood, we would achieve something whose sole beneficiaries would be Japan, America and other nations," he remarked.[221]

By 16 July, Hitler had made up his mind. His "Führer Directive No. 16" began with these words: "Since England, despite its hopeless military situation, still shows no signs of being willing to reach an agreement, I have decided to prepare and, if necessary, carry out a landing operation against England. The purpose of this operation is to disable the English motherland as a base for the continuing war against Germany and, should it prove necessary, to completely occupy it." The operation was given the code-name "Sea Lion," and preparations were to be completed by mid-August 1940.[222] The phrase "if necessary" indicated that Hitler still intended to make Britain a final offer before launching military operations. He confirmed this on 16 July during a visit to the Obersalzberg by Franz von Papen, the former chancellor and later vice-chancellor in the Hitler-led Cabinet of National Concentration who had been Germany's ambassador to Turkey since April 1939.[223] Hitler's speech to the Reichstag was scheduled for 19 July, and it was not until that very morning that the Führer returned to Berlin. Over lunch in the Chancellery, he sketched out the contents of the speech. He was going to make a "short, terse offer" to England "without making any precise proposals but clearly indicating that this would be the final offer." It would then be "up to London" to make a choice.[224]

The Kroll Opera House was a strange sight on the evening of 19 July 1940. The picture was dominated by men in uniforms from all branches of the Wehrmacht. In the front rows were the leaders of the army, the navy and the Luftwaffe.[225] Hitler, who was greeted with frenetic applause from Reichstag deputies, spoke for more than two hours and was, in Shirer's estimation, in top form. "His voice was lower tonight; he rarely shouted as he usually does; and he did not once cry out hysterically as I've seen him do so often from this rostrum. His oratorical form was at its best." Once again, Shirer was struck by what a good actor Hitler was and how skilfully he used his hands, "which are somewhat feminine and quite artistic."[226] Happily striking the pose of the victorious conqueror, Hitler devoted the majority of his speech to his military triumphs of recent months, doling out credit to all parts of his armed forces and taking the opportunity to promote no fewer than twelve army commanders, including Bock, Leeb and Rundstedt, to the rank of field marshal. Göring, who already held that title, was named "Reich marshal." The promotions came with a sizeable tax-free monetary award. Following his role model Friedrich the Great, Hitler hoped that his generosity would buy the loyalty of the military leadership and bind them to their oath. He did not demand that his generals be National Socialists, he told his military adjutants around this time, but "politically they had to submit completely to the leadership of state and blindly obey whatever that leadership demanded of them."[227]

Hitler praised Italy for its friendship, although he had more than once privately expressed his dissatisfaction with his main ally. He also stressed that German-Russian relations had been "secured once and for all" with the delineation of the two countries' respective spheres of influence, despite the fact that Hitler had never given up on his goal of procuring "living space" in the east and was already beginning to contemplate attacking the Soviet Union. It was not until the final minutes of his speech that he got round to delivering his core message. He wanted, Hitler said, "to address once again an appeal to reason in England" before continuing the war. As planned, he made no concrete suggestions for how to end the conflict. Instead he lashed out at "blood-spattered Jewish-capitalist war-mongers" and Churchill personally.[228]

If Hitler's intention was to strengthen the hand of those in Britain who favoured peace and to drive a wedge between the prime minister and his critics, he could hardly have gone about it in a more ham-fisted fashion. Late that very evening, the first sharply worded reactions arrived from London. "At the moment, the Führer does not wish to acknowledge England's answer," wrote Goebbels, who had never had much hope that Churchill would give in. "He plans to wait for a bit."[229] In a radio address on 22 July, Lord Halifax categorically ruled out any chance of a negotiated peace. That finally convinced Hitler that England had "definitively rejected" his overtures. "The die is cast," a pleased Goebbels noted. "We will not have to wait long for the large-scale attack on England . . . The drama must be played out to its conclusion."[230]

4

Strategic Stalemate

"It is unclear what will happen in England. Preparations for an armed decision must be taken as soon as possible," Hitler declared at a meeting on 21 July in the Chancellery with commanders of the three branches of the Wehrmacht, Raeder, Brauchitsch and Göring's deputy Hans Jeschonnek, adding that he did not want to "lose the military-political initiative."[1] That was a precise description of the dilemma into which the German dictator had manoeuvred himself in the summer of 1940. The surprisingly swift success of the western offensive had removed France from the anti-Hitler coalition, but it had failed to convince Britain to sue for peace. On the contrary, all indications suggested that British resistance was stiffening under Churchill and that there was no reason to hope for a diplomatic solution. As an explanation for the unexpected stalemate, Hitler blamed London's hope that America would "come around." The Führer was under no illusions that the longer the war in the west lasted, the greater the chance that the United States would begin openly to support Britain. On 19 July, a few days after announcing that he would run for a third term as president, Roosevelt gave a speech at the Democratic National Convention which Hans-Heinrich Dieckhoff, the German Foreign Ministry's America expert and a former ambassador to Washington, called a "clear declaration of hostility towards Germany." "With fanatical hatred," Dieckhoff wrote, "the president declared the totalitarian states 'the enemy' . . . England was to be prevented from giving in. English resistance should be strengthened, and the war continued."[2]

The question for Hitler was how he could break such resistance before the economic and military might of the United States came into play. A landing operation of the sort foreseen in Führer Directive No. 16 entailed, as he freely admitted to his military commanders, "a great risk." Therefore, troops would be crossing the English Channel only when "no other way of reaching a conclusion with England is left open." Hitler declared he would make a final decision in early August whether submarine and aerial warfare "in the most severe form" would commence. "If we attack, England must be taken care of by mid-September," he cautioned. Hitler was unsure about whether the precondition for Operation Sea Lion, complete air superiority, could even be achieved. But if not, how was he supposed to continue the war and bring it to a victorious conclusion?

In this context, Hitler's thinking became increasingly dominated by the idea of solving his strategic dilemma by bringing forward the war for "living space" that he intended to wage against the Soviet Union, thereby cementing Germany's dominance over the European continent and forcing Britain to give in. In July 1940, Churchill had sent Stafford Cripps to Moscow as Britain's new ambassador, and Berlin feared that the Soviet Union, all denials to the contrary, might be open to British advances after Germany's unexpectedly quick victory over France. "Stalin is flirting with England," Hitler told his military commanders on 21 July, adding that the Soviet leader wanted Britain to continue the war and tie Germany down in the west "in order to have time to take whatever he wanted and what can no longer be taken if peace breaks out." Hitler now ordered the military to "tackle the Russian problem." The goal, as Brauchitsch relayed it to Halder the following day, was "to defeat the Russian army or at least to capture enough Russian territory to prevent air raids on Berlin and the industrial areas of Silesia." Brauchitsch estimated that between eighty and a hundred divisions would be needed for the operation, which, apparently following Hitler's express wish, was to commence that autumn.[3]

Halder was hardly surprised by the news. Back at the start of July, he had instructed the chief of the operations department, Colonel Hans von Greiffenberg, to scrutinise "how a military strike against Russia could be carried out . . . in order to force that country to recognise Germany's dominant role in Europe."[4] But Halder had assumed that before launching such an attack Germany would have already dealt with Britain—something that was no longer in the cards in late July. The two-front war the military leadership had always sought to avoid had become a realistic possibility. Hitler had never made any bones to his generals that the non-aggression pact with the Soviet Union was only an interim, tactical measure so that he could destroy Poland and keep his hands free for a decisive battle in the west. More than once, he had admitted with surprising frankness to groups of officers, large and small, that he would never give up his project of conquering "living space" in the east. Now, in the stalemate situation of the summer and autumn of 1940, Hitler began to see a Blitzkrieg against the Soviets as the best way to realise that ultimate goal and at the same time make Britain realise that its own situation was hopeless. In Hitler's restlessly meandering thoughts, racist dogma and strategic military calculations were by no means incompatible. On the contrary, they were interwoven with one another.[5]

Hitler remained in Berlin for only a few days, and on 21 July, he headed south again. Originally, he had not planned on attending the Bayreuth Wagner Festival,[6] but on 23 July, he made a surprise appearance at a performance of *Götterdämmerung* ("Twilight of the Gods"). In April he had decreed that the Wagner festival was to go on despite the war. Organised by the Kraft durch Freude ("Strength through Joy") association, part of the German Labour Front, tickets were given primarily to wounded soldiers, nurses and armament workers. As "guests of the Führer" they had the opportunity to spend three days in the hallowed musical ground that during peacetime had been reserved for a bourgeois audience and Nazi functionaries.[7] Hitler's relationship with Winifred Wagner, who directed the festival, had cooled considerably after her second daughter Friedelind had turned her back on Nazi Germany and her family of Hitler admirers. Having spent significant time abroad, she had refused to return to Bayreuth at the start of the war, travelling via Switzerland to London, where in a series of articles for the *Daily Sketch* she laid into the man she had once worshipped as a god.[8] Goebbels was outraged: "The fat Wagner daughter has written her first article against the Führer in the London press: how lowdown . . . The fat pig is committing nothing short of treason. A product of the worst sort of upbringing. To hell with her!"[9]

Hitler told Goebbels that he was "shaken by the baseness of Friedelind Wagner" but concealed those feelings from Winifred.[10] Over afternoon tea in the Villa Wahnfried, he talked about his jaunt to

Paris and made some optimistic remarks about Germany's military prospects, remarking: "I hear the wings of the goddess of victory beating."[11] Who among the Wagner clan could have suspected that the *Götterdämmerung* of Hitler's own regime was about to commence? This was to be the dictator's final visit to the Bayreuth festival. In future, he would have no further personal contact with his old friend Winifred, although he remained grateful to her. As he remarked in his military headquarters in the spring of 1942: "Mrs. Wagner brought Bayreuth and National Socialism together—that is her great historical legacy."[12]

On 24 July, Hitler returned to Berlin for two days, and spoke of his impressions in Bayreuth over lunch at the Chancellery. He was happy, he said, "to have heard some music again after such a long time." "And that audience of ordinary people!" he added. "Tactful, enthusiastic and full of understanding. In comparison, our better circles are unbearable, dull-witted and inflexible." Goebbels relished the Führer's remarks. "He spoke with contempt for the higher circles of society," the propaganda minister noted. "They are of no great use to us. We must always stay close to the people."[13] Even after Berlin had given him a triumphant welcome in early July, and he seemed to be at the apex of his popularity, Hitler still had the inferiority complex of a parvenu. His resentment of social elites, in particular people considered educated, would increasingly resurface in direct proportion to the approaching downward turn in Germany's military fortunes.

On 29 July, having returned once more to the Obersalzberg, Hitler held his regular noontime situation meeting and then asked Jodl, who had been promoted to the rank of general, whether there was any chance that Germany could attack the Soviet Union that autumn. Jodl considered an offensive within such a short time impossible, and the two men agreed that the earliest conceivable date for an invasion would be May 1941. Following that conversation, Jodl informed his closest associates on his staff, who were waiting aboard a special train at Bad Reichenhall, of what the Führer had in mind. As General Walter Warlimont remembered it, some in the group reacted with incomprehension, asking: "Does that mean we would intentionally start the two-front war that we have previously been lucky enough to avoid?" Jodl reportedly answered that the "confrontation with Bolshevism" was "unavoidable" and that it was better to launch the campaign at the height of Germany's military power than at a later point in time.[14] It seems that Hitler's closest military adviser had by now adopted one of the dictator's central ideological fixations—his utter enmity towards Bolshevism.

On the final day of July, Hitler summoned the heads of the Wehrmacht to the Berghof for a crucial meeting. It started with Raeder giving an overview of Operation Sea Lion's chances of success. The admiral stressed that the navy's preparations "were proceeding full steam ahead" and that the earliest possible date for an attempt to land troops in England was 15 September. But he also cited a series of difficulties, not least the unpredictable weather, which had convinced him that the operation should be postponed until the spring of 1941. Hitler made no secret of his scepticism about whether a landing operation would be technically possible. It was imperative, he declared, to avoid taking unnecessary risks. "The decision about whether to carry out the invasion in September or postpone it until May 1941 will be taken once the Luftwaffe has carried out enhanced raids on southern England for eight days," Raeder wrote in his notes from the meeting. "If the enemy air force, ports, naval forces etc. have been badly damaged by these raids, Sea Lion will proceed. Otherwise it will be postponed until May 1941."[15]

After Raeder had departed, Hitler got down to the actual point of the meeting: preparing the army leadership for the coming conflict with the Soviet Union. The previous day, Brauchitsch and Halder had agreed that it was better to maintain Germany's "friendship with Russia" than to incur the risk of a two-front war.[16] But Hitler now reiterated what he had already stated on 21 July: "England's great hope is Russia and America. If the hope in Russia is gone, the same will be true of America because the Russian disappearance will lead to a tremendous bolstering of Japan's status in the Far East." Hitler was speculating that the United States would be so bound up with the Pacific realm that it would not be able to effectively support Britain. This made him conclude that Germany should attack Russia to deprive Britain of its "Continental sword." "Once Russia has been destroyed, England's last hope has disappeared," Halder cited Hitler in his diary as saying, "Germany will then be the master of Europe and the Balkans. Decision: as part of this conflict, Russia has to be dispatched with." Because not enough time remained until the autumn, the Wehrmacht was to prepare for May 1941 as a possible date for the attack. The goal of the operation, Hitler said, was "the destruction of Russia's strength to exist."[17]

There is no indication that the military commanders raised any objections to Hitler's plans. That was no doubt partly down to the fact that they, like Hitler, did not have much regard for the Red Army as a fighting force. A large section of its experienced officer corps had fallen victim to Stalin's purges, and in the Winter War against Finland in 1939–40, the weakened Soviet army had encountered unexpected difficulties putting down the Finns' determined resistance. Hitler had repeatedly watched films of the fighting on the Finnish border.[18] This material, together with tank commander Heinz Guderian's report of encountering the Red Army in Brest-Litovsk in September and October 1939, reinforced Hitler's conviction that no serious military resistance was to be expected from the Soviet Union. "If you get a firm grip on this colossus, it will collapse more quickly than the entire world suspects," Hitler told his adjutants in early August 1940.[19] Major-General Erich Marcks, who presented the first "Operational Draft for the East" on 5 August, reached much the same conclusion. "The Russians will soon succumb to the superiority of German troops and leadership," Marcks wrote, if the enemy's might could be broken quickly in major battles at the border. Marcks estimated the campaign could be over in nine weeks, or in seventeen weeks at the worst.[20] Here the arrogance and self-overestimation of the German military leadership after the triumph in the west mixed with traditional German feelings of superiority towards the Slavic peoples.

Hitler's "determined decision" of 31 July 1940 did not mean that he had committed once and for all to launching an eastern campaign to the exclusion of all other options. But it was a signal to the army leadership to start preparing more intensely for this eventuality. Operations were referred to as the "eastern build-up."[21] Trainload after trainload of German troops now arrived in the General Government and East Prussia. One of those transferred east with his unit was Walter Frick, the son of Interior Minister Wilhelm Frick. He was quartered in "a truly poor, dirty village," Walter wrote to his father in a letter that displayed the typical racist prejudices German soldiers held against Poles. "Being forced to sit here, you cannot help but wish that we hand the General Government over to the Polacks."[22] In late

September, Fedor von Bock of Army Group B assumed command in the east. Yet Brauchitsch failed to inform him about the full extent of Hitler's intentions. "There are no orders for the east," Bock noted after a meeting with the army's supreme commander.[23]

In the meantime, German-Soviet relations had noticeably chilled. Hitler had sent a congratulatory telegram to Stalin on his sixtieth birthday in December 1939, and a major commercial treaty was signed in February 1940.[24] But Berlin watched with displeasure as the Soviet dictator rigorously used the time in which Germany had its hands full with the western campaign to incorporate the territories promised him under the secret protocol of the non-aggression pact into his realm of rule. Under the Moscow Peace Treaty of 12 March 1940, Finland had to hand over parts of Karelia, and in late July 1940 the Baltic states of Estonia, Latvia and Lithuania, which had already been forced to accommodate Soviet military bases in late September and early October 1939, were declared Soviet republics and formally annexed by Moscow. One month earlier, Stalin had demanded that Romania cede Bessarabia and North Bukovina and had sent in Red Army troops.[25] "This is anything but pleasant for us," Goebbels commented. "The Russians are exploiting the situation."[26] The propaganda minister admitted that Russia was more than meeting its commitments in the commercial treaty, writing that "Stalin is trying his best to please us." But he remained convinced that "Bolshevism . . . is our global enemy number one." "At some point we will need to meet it head on, and the Führer thinks so too," he noted after a lunchtime conversation in the Chancellery on 8 August.[27] Nonetheless, Hitler kept his decision to attack Russia in the spring of 1941 secret from his propaganda minister and confidant.

He was more forthcoming with his newly appointed field marshals, who received their marshal's staffs on 14 August in the Chancellery. While at present Russia was behaving "loyally," Hitler told them, there were two potential scenarios that could make it necessary for Germany to intervene: "1. Russia grabs all of Finland. Then Germany would lose its dominance of the Baltic Sea and it would be more difficult to attack Russia. 2. Further Russian aggression against Romania. That is intolerable because of Romanian petrol supplies to Germany. Therefore Germany needs to stay prepared: by spring, 180 divisions."[28] Although Hitler was keen to conceal his own aggressive intentions by portraying his policies as reactions to Soviet incursions, he left his military commanders in no doubt as to the strategic rationale behind his order of 31 July. "England hopes to play Russia against Germany," he explained. "But Germany is far superior to Russia. The film footage of the Russian war against Finland is laughable."[29] A campaign against the Soviet Union, the confident dictator told his field marshals, would be child's play.

Hitler was not exaggerating when he expressed his concerns about Romanian oil. The mobility of the German army, navy and Luftwaffe greatly depended on Germany's ability to import oil from that country.[30] Thus he was very keen to de-escalate any conflict in southeastern Europe.[31] In August 1940, when quarrelling intensified between Hungary and Romania and the two countries seemed to be on the brink of war, Hitler summoned Ribbentrop and Ciano to the Berghof. "Under all circumstances, I need to secure our oil supply from Romania to further fight my wars," he told them.[32] In the Second Vienna Award of 30 August, Romania was forced to cede a large part of Transylvania to Hungary. In return, Germany and Italy guaranteed "the integrity and inviolability of Romanian state territory," an agreement that was to block off any further Russian encroachment in the Balkans.[33] The reaction in Romania to the agreement was outrage, and King Carol II had to abdicate his throne in favour of his son Mihal. The new Romanian prime minister and strongman, General Ion Antonescu, immediately sent Hitler a letter promising his submissiveness on 7 September.[34]

While Hitler was working behind the scenes to lay the groundwork for a war against the Soviet Union, the German people anticipated with increasing tension the beginning of the offensive against England. "From day to day, the population is growing more impatient," a Security Service report stated on 11 July.[35] Many Germans hoped that an invasion of Britain in the autumn would end the hostilities and spare them the hardship of another winter of war. Most Berliners, William Shirer reported on 27 July, were "deadly certain that the war will be over before the winter sets in."[36] German soldiers shared this conviction. In mid-July 1940, Walter Frick wrote to his father: "I think that by the end of the month enough materiel will finally have been brought up to the coast to beat England to a pulp."[37] Yet the longer they had to wait for the invasion, the more nervous people got. Even Goebbels expressed his disappointment in late July that Hitler "has not truly tackled England." The decision "to give the signal for a major offensive" was clearly difficult to make, wrote the propaganda minister: "We are waiting and waiting. When is the Führer finally going to proceed against England?"[38]

Finally, on 1 August 1940, Hitler signed "Führer Directive No. 17." "In order to create the conditions for subduing England once and for all," it read, "I intend to prosecute the air and naval war against the English motherland in more severe form than previously." Göring's Luftwaffe was ordered to "beat down the Royal Air Force" with all means at its disposal.[39] The intensification of the war in the air was to commence on 5 August, but bad weather led to the date being postponed twice. Then, on 13 August, the time had come. "The great offensive against England has begun," wrote a happy Goebbels. "Everything is at stake now. There will be no quarter given."[40] That day Hitler received Raeder, who once again stressed that because of the "limitations on our means of naval war and transport" an invasion "could only be a last resort in case England cannot be forced to make peace in another way." Hitler agreed with the grand admiral's assessment. If Sea Lion were to fail, it would greatly increase Britain's prestige. There was no choice but to wait and see "what effect the enhanced aerial warfare will have."[41] When he received the newly appointed field marshals on 14 August, Hitler also tried to dampen expectations. "It cannot be predicted whether the army will need to be used," he told them. "In any case, this will only happen if it is necessary and secure conditions have been created through air superiority and naval protection. It is questionable whether the Luftwaffe will have achieved the required success before the onset of the stormy season. If not, the decision will have to be made in the spring (May)."[42]

The Battle of Britain showed that Hitler was right to be sceptical. The British used the two months between the evacuation of their troops from Dunkirk and the beginning of stepped-up German air attacks to create an effective air defence system. Fifty-two radar stations along the coastline were able to locate incoming Luftwaffe squadrons early in their missions, and that information was relayed to Fighter Command headquarters near Stanmore, to the north of London. As of April 1940, British specialists were also able to decipher German radio messages using Enigma code machines.[43] And while the Luftwaffe had a numerical advantage in terms of aircraft, in the Spitfire and the Hurricane the RAF had two fighters that performed markedly better than their German equivalent, the Messerschmitt Me-109. Last but not least, the British were able to redeploy pilots shot down over southern England if they had managed to parachute to safety, while every German pilot shot down was lost to the Luftwaffe.[44]

In the first days of the Battle of Britain German propaganda was optimistic. The official figures of aircraft shot down made it seem as though the RAF was on the brink of total destruction. On 17 August, Shirer, who was reporting from the Channel coast, was told by a Luftwaffe officer: "It's a matter of another couple of weeks, you know, until we finish with the RAF. In a fortnight the British won't have any more planes."[45] In reality, German losses were greater than British ones, and only a week later, on 24 August, Shirer reported from Berlin that the German air campaign had come to a dead end.[46] That same day, Goebbels confided to his diary that "little by little the German people will have to get used to a second winter of war."[47]

On 24 August, a German bomber formation attacked London. The RAF answered with its first attacks on Berlin in the night of 25–26 August, followed by further raids in the days to come. Although no significant damage was done, the attacks did have a psychological effect. "The Berliners are stunned," wrote Shirer. "They did not think it could happen." "For the first time the war has been brought home to them," he noted a few days later.[48] Throughout the Reich, the attacks on the capital caused a "considerable stir because people had been convinced that no enemy would be able to reach the city centre," the SS Security Service reported.[49] On 29 August, Hitler returned to Berlin from a two-week stay on the Obersalzberg "very perturbed," as Goebbels noted: "The Führer wants to be in Berlin while the city is being bombed."[50] On 4 September, Hitler used the launch of the second wartime winter relief campaign in the Sportpalast to announce that he would exact "vengeance" on the British. "If they tell us they are going to launch large-scale attacks on our cities, let us proclaim that we will wipe theirs off the map!" he thundered. "We are going to put a stop to these pirates of the night, as God is my witness." The dictator also sought to dispel fears that he might have given up on the invasion of Britain: "People in England today may be very curious and ask, 'Why does he not come?' Rest assured—he is coming. You should not always be so curious!"[51] When speaking these words, Shirer noted, Hitler "squeezed every ounce of humour and sarcasm out of his voice." The speech was greeted by "hysterical applause."[52]

The Security Service reported that Hitler's appearance in the Sportpalast had made an "extraordinarily deep impression" and had reinforced the German people's belief that they would triumph in the end. "Rest assured—he is coming" became "a popular saying."[53] But the truth was that the dictator recognised sooner than most that the air offensive was not achieving its intended goal of establishing German air superiority, and as early as late August he began backing away from his half-baked notions of invading Britain. On 30 August, Jodl quoted Hitler as remarking that "given the current state of the air war against England, the preconditions for Operation Sea Lion . . . have yet to be fulfilled." He was going to wait until 10 September before deciding whether to launch an invasion.[54] When that date arrived, however, he again postponed the decision because the "results of the enhanced air war on England are not fully clear."[55] Four days later he summoned the commanders of the three branches of the Wehrmacht and their chiefs of staff. He praised the work of the Luftwaffe, whose attacks had had "tremendous effects," but admitted that the precondition for a "felicitous landing"—the "complete destruction of the enemy's fighter force"—had not been met. Nonetheless, Hitler did not want to publicly cancel Operation Sea Lion, in order to keep up the psychological pressure on Britain: "The idea of the threat of an invasion should not be taken away . . . It would lead to the relaxation of the enemy's nervous tension and should therefore be avoided."[56] On 17 September, however, two days after German bomber units had suffered more serious losses in a major air raid over London, the invasion was postponed indefinitely. On 12 October, the Wehrmacht Supreme Command officially put it off until the following spring. In fact, this meant that Hitler no longer believed it would ever become reality.[57]

The possibility of a German invasion of Britain was nonetheless maintained as a threat. Not only did it allow Hitler to disguise the redeployment of German divisions to the east, but he also still hoped he could break the British people's morale. Nighttime air raids were stepped up on London and extended to central English cities. The British were engaged in a "hopeless battle" and would "one day collapse," the dictator predicted in late September, comparing the war to a prize fight: "Sometimes a fight goes through many rounds, and it is hardly noticeable that one of the fighters is hurt. And then suddenly, he is on the floor. That is how it is with England." But Hitler also added that "no one knows today when it will be over. The important thing is that we are determined to fight until we achieve victory."[58]

One of the worst Luftwaffe air raids was carried out on Coventry on the night of 14–15 November 1940. The entire city centre, including the city's medieval cathedral, was destroyed, and five hundred people were killed.[59] "People now speak of 'coventrying' a city to refer to its total destruction," wrote the Berlin journalist Ruth Andreas-Friedrich. "People are proud of this neologism, ignoring the possibility that this may someday rebound terribly against us."[60] But few Germans thought as she did. Most clung to the hope, as Walter Frick put it in early December, "that the war in Europe will be over in a couple of months and England will be forced to capitulate without us having to invade. Soon there will be little left of its industrial cities."[61]

In reality British morale remained unbroken. If anything, the determination of the British people to fight on was stronger than ever. In that respect, as Shirer presciently noted, the Battle of Britain was a real "turning point" in the war.[62] Even if he did not admit it, Hitler had suffered his first defeat, one which, to quote the historian Hans-Ulrich Wehler, "can only be compared in its historical significance to the lost Battle of the Marne at the start of the First World War."[63] Goebbels' diary entries reveal how seriously the Nazi leadership took the situation after Operation Sea Lion had been put on ice. In mid-October 1940, he drew parallels with the crisis the NSDAP had faced in 1932: "It is like October and November 1932. Back then, our right attitude was key, and because we had that, we won out in the end."[64]

The German "Blitz" of Britain also began to change popular opinion in the United States. In particular the live reporting from London of Edward R. Murrow, CBS's lead European correspondent, allowed Americans to imagine the horrors of modern bombing war.[65] The sympathies thus mobilised for the British people boosted Roosevelt's policy of actively supporting Britain and allowed him to better combat the strong isolationist tendencies in America. The first clear step was the Destroyers for Bases Agreement of 2 September 1940, which saw the US give the Royal Navy fifty warships from the First World War in return for permission to station troops in the western Atlantic and the Caribbean.[66] Germany saw the agreement as a hostile act and an indication of the increasingly close cooperation between America and Britain. "If the war lasts beyond the winter, we are almost dead certain to see America enter the war," wrote an enraged Goebbels. "Roosevelt is a Jewish underling."[67]

In Germany too the authorities registered a marked change in the public mood. After the euphoria of the summer, indifference and resignation began to grow. "Only a very few ethnic-popular comrades [*Volksgenossen*] believe that the war will soon be over," read a Security Service report from mid-October.[68] Goebbels was alarmed and demanded that "the nation rigorously prepare itself for its second winter of war." To this end, he announced a large-scale propaganda campaign: "We must do more to keep up morale."[69] Those around him found Hitler strangely vacillating and indecisive in these weeks. His military adjutants had the feeling that he did not know "how things should continue."[70] Goebbels encountered him in the pensive mood that often came over the Führer ahead of major decisions and predicted: "He is about to hatch something again."[71] If Britain could not be defeated by massive air warfare, perhaps there was some other way of making the enemy receptive to peace, particularly ahead of the war planned for the spring against the Soviet Union. In this situation, ideas Jodl had formulated in his 30 June memorandum began to gain currency, namely of hurting England by "extending the war to the periphery." Jodl was primarily thinking of the Mediterranean. By supporting an Italian attack from Libya on Egypt and the Suez Canal, on the one hand, and by teaming up with Spain to take Gibraltar, on the other, so ran the logic, England's strategic predominance in the Mediterranean could be undermined.[72]

Raeder tried to win Hitler over for similar ideas in two briefings in September 1940. From the admiral's perspective as well, controlling the Mediterranean was of "decisive importance" since it would create a favourable position for further operations against the British Empire.[73] Initially Hitler did not take to the proposals for a "periphery strategy," but his interest grew the longer his strategic air war on Britain failed to yield the desired results. In early September, he spoke for the first time about the "Azores, the Canary and the Cape Verde Islands being taken by German-Italian forces in time to prevent the English or the

Americans from gaining a foothold."[74] But whereas Raeder's proposals were aimed at convincing Hitler to abandon his plan to attack the Soviet Union, the dictator never saw them as an alternative to his eastern campaign, only as a way of forcing England to give in and thus of avoiding a two-front war.[75]

Parallel to the "periphery strategy," increasing importance was also placed on a project Ribbentrop had proposed for some time: the creation of a Euro-Asian "Continental Bloc," which would oppose Britain and deter American involvement in the war. The German foreign minister conceived this alliance, built around the Germany-Italy-Japan axis, to be potentially open to Vichy France, Spain and even the Soviet Union.[76] On 27 September, Ribbentrop, Ciano and Japan's ambassador to Germany, Saburo Kurusu, signed the Tripartite Pact in the reception hall of the New Reich Chancellery. In its first two articles, Japan recognised the "leadership of Germany and Italy in creating a new order in Europe," while Germany and Italy acknowledged "Japan's leadership in creating a new order in the greater Asian realm." Article 3 obliged the three signatories "to assist one another with all political, economic and military means if one of the signatories were attacked by a power not currently engaged in the European war or the Sino-Japanese conflict."[77] This passage was clearly aimed at deterring US intervention. "The purpose of the pact, in our eyes, is to warn the Americans," Weizsäcker remarked.[78]

Hitler attended the ceremony and hosted a state reception for all participants immediately afterwards. German propaganda celebrated the pact as a historic event. "We have won a great diplomatic victory," Goebbels enthused. "The Führer has once again cut through the Gordian knot."[79] Ciano was far more sober, not believing that the pact would do much to impress the Americans. "Only one thing is certain," he remarked: "The war will last a long time." Ciano also noted the depressed mood among Berliners: "People spend four to five hours a night in basements seeking shelter from air raids. Lack of sleep, cold and being cramped together with other people—none of it improves the mood . . . The damage from bombs is slight, but the toll on the nerves is enormous."[80]

Including Vichy France and Spain in the anti-British coalition while at the same time serving the interests of Germany's ally Italy was a task tantamount to squaring a circle. The three countries all wanted profoundly different things. In June 1940, Mussolini put his territorial demands against France on ice—but only temporarily. After the French capitulation, General Franco had signalled his willingness to enter the war on the side of the Axis but had in return also made broad territorial demands. In addition to Gibraltar, he claimed large stretches of the French colonial empire in northern and western Africa, including Morocco and Oran. Hitler had declined to take up the Spanish offer. But after his hopes for an "arrangement" with Britain had been dashed and Operation Sea Lion abandoned, Spain's entry into the war became increasingly desirable.[81] The problem was that if Germany granted Franco's demands, it ran the risk that the French colonies currently loyal to the Vichy regime would go over to the Free France movement, which General Charles de Gaulle had begun to organise from London.

Still, Hitler was prepared to go some distance to accommodate Spain and, as he told the army leadership, "to promise them everything they want, even if we cannot deliver it."[82] On 16 September, Spanish interior minister Ramón Serrano Suñer—Franco's brother-in-law and future foreign minister—met with Ribbentrop in Berlin for two days of meetings. He brought with him the familiar list of Franco's territorial wishes. Ribbentrop gave him hope that Germany might take Morocco away from France in a peace treaty and "hand it over" to Spain, but in return he demanded naval bases on Mogador Island and in Agadir and its environs as well as "a share of Moroccan raw materials (phosphate and manganese)." Serrano refused those terms as well as Ribbentrop's additional demands that Spain cede the Canaries to Germany and allow Spanish Guinea (Equatorial Guinea) and the island of Fernando Pó (Bioko) to be incorporated into a German imperial realm in central Africa.[83]

Hitler received Franco's emissary on 17 September. The dictator had swapped roles as need be, Serrano reported, going from being occasionally "accommodating" to "hard as steel, like a predator ready to pounce, fully concentrated on his passion and fanaticism."[84] As always, Hitler was confident of achieving ultimate victory. The war with England, he told Serrano, was "already decided . . . on the Continent." Without directly addressing controversial territorial issues, Hitler launched into a digression about how he envisioned the conquest of Gibraltar, which the Wehrmacht High Command was preparing under the code name "Felix." Hitler promised to do everything in his power to assist Spain in this endeavour, for "if Spain were to join the war, Germany would have every interest in Spain's success."[85] Hitler also suggested a meeting between himself and the "Caudillo" on the Spanish-French border to "feel out" the matter, a wish that was welcomed by Franco. But during a second round of negotiations with Serrano in Berlin a week later, it became clear how far from an agreement the two sides really were.[86] In a conversation with Ciano on 28 September, the day after the signing of the Tripartite Pact, Hitler complained that the Spanish did not display "the same intensity of desire in giving as in receiving."[87]

On 4 October, Hitler met with Mussolini for a second time at the Brenner Pass to discuss the question of how "France and Spain could be brought into line and create a Continental coalition against Britain." The two dictators agreed that Franco would have to considerably lessen his demands for French territory as a condition for Spain's entry into the war, if a deal was ever to come about. At most, Hitler said, they could give Spain a part of Morocco if France were compensated with British Nigeria. Mussolini was prepared to back down from some of his own original claims to French territory, but he insisted on the redrawing of the Franco-Italian border near Nice and the ceding of Corsica, Tunis and French Somaliland (Djibouti). Hitler assured his ally that he would never conclude a peace treaty with France without taking Italian interests into account. His own demands towards France consisted of military bases on the Moroccan coast in Agadir or Casablanca, the fleshing out of a future German colonial empire in Africa, and the re-Germanification of Alsace-Lorraine with strategically improved borders, as well as the ceding of the mineral region of Longwy and Briey and a strip of land south of Belfort. It again showed how difficult it would have been to balance all the various interests, even if Mussolini had fully agreed to the "creation of a Continental coalition including France and Spain."[88]

On the face of it, the meeting at the Brenner Pass had gone "very harmoniously,"[89] but in reality, the relationship between the two Axis partners had long been one of mistrust. Hitler allowed Mussolini to believe that he was still planning to invade Britain and was just waiting for good weather before launching his "major strike." Conversely, Mussolini was at pains to emphasise the success of the Italian offensive against Egypt, which had commenced on 13 September, even though it had ground to a halt after only a couple of days 90 kilometres behind the Libyan-Egyptian border.[90]

After his meeting with Mussolini, Hitler rested on the Obersalzberg for several days. Between 10 and 15 October he was in Berlin before returning to his Alpine residence for five days. On 20 October, he took his special train to France for personal talks with Franco and the leaders of Vichy France in an attempt to get the Continental Bloc project off the ground. Two days later he arrived at the small train station at Montoire, 50 kilometres north of Tours, where Ribbentrop was waiting for him. There the Führer held an initial meeting with French deputy prime minister Pierre Laval, who was known to be receptive to German wishes. Right from the start, Laval assured Hitler that in his view "an honest and full cooperation with Germany" was "France's only salvation" and that he would take every opportunity to push President Pétain in this direction. Hitler stressed that he was going to "mobilise every conceivable resource against England." He added that whether French interests would be taken into consideration in the future peace treaty would largely depend on whether France was prepared to take part in the "general expansion of the front" against Britain.[91]

That very night, Hitler and his entourage travelled on to Hendaye on the Franco-Spanish border, where the Führer was to meet with Franco the following afternoon. The Spanish dictator's train was late, as the Germans noted with displeasure, and Hitler became even more irritated by the course of their talks. Although he used all the persuasiveness at his disposal, his Spanish counterpart remained aloof. "Small and portly, dark-skinned and with lively dark eyes," noted the interpreter Paul Schmidt, Franco sat in an armchair in Hitler's salon carriage with an "inscrutable face," letting the Führer's torrent of words spill over him.[92] As he had with Serrano Suñer, Hitler painted Germany's military situation in the rosiest of colours before cutting to the chase. "If an entire front against England could be formed," Hitler said, "the battle could be waged more easily and be more quickly completed for everyone concerned." But "Spanish wishes and French hopes stood in the way" of realising these ends.[93] With that Hitler put the brakes on any further territorial wishes on Franco's part, holding out only the vague prospect that Spain could receive French colonial territories, if France were compensated with British ones. In the end, Hitler came to the main point. He suggested that Spain ally itself with Germany and called upon Franco to enter the war in January. If that happened, the German special forces who had taken the Belgian fortifications in Liège would conquer Gibraltar and hand it over to Spain that same month.

Franco reacted evasively, pointing out the difficult food situation in his country and calling for significant German shipments of grain as well as modern arms, including large numbers of heavy artillery and flak guns. Spanish national pride, he said, ruled out accepting Gibraltar as a foreign-conquered gift. Franco clearly mistrusted Hitler's optimistic description of the situation, interjecting that even if England were occupied by German troops, the British government and the British fleet would surely flee to Canada and continue to fight with American help. Hitler grew more and more agitated. At one point he even jumped up from his chair, exclaiming that further talks were pointless. But he immediately calmed down and sought to win over his stubborn guest. His efforts were in vain. In the end, after the two dictators had departed, Ribbentrop and Serrano wrote up a joint "secret protocol" that alluded in non-committal fashion to Spain possibly joining the war.

Hitler did not try to conceal his disappointment. "He is just as grabby as many of our own people," Hitler complained to his adjutants after the meeting.[94] Even days later, Hitler was still cursing the "Jesuit swine," remarking he would "rather get three or four teeth pulled than go through that again."[95] The Spanish side was unimpressed too. "These people are unbearable," Franco allegedly told his foreign minister. "They want Spain to enter the war without offering anything substantial in return."[96] Thus the Hendaye meeting was a total fiasco. Goebbels was either misinformed or deluding himself when he noted: "Everything went well. We can now be sure of Spain. Churchill is in for some dark hours."[97]

Hitler's irritation still had not passed when, the following afternoon, he met Pétain and Laval at the station in Montoire. The German dictator paid his respects to the aged French field marshal by approaching and guiding him into his salon carriage.[98] Although their talks were far less frosty than the previous day's, the result would again fall short of Hitler's expectations. As he had to Laval, Hitler once again stressed Germany's splendid military position and his intention to continue the war "until the insular centre of the British Empire is destroyed." To this end, he was "about to organise a partly European and partly extra-European alliance against the British Continental enemy" and had come to Montoire "to determine to what extent France would be inclined to join this community and work with it." Pétain declared his willingness in principle to cooperate but cautioned that he "could not conclude any ties without consulting the French government." Laval supported this argument, adding that France could cooperate effectively with Germany even without a formal declaration of war against England. The modalities, a summary of the talks recorded, were to be "determined and decided individually and case by case."[99]

After the meeting Hitler praised Pétain effusively, remarking that he was impressed by "his dignified performance as French head of state and his clear, military nature."[100] But Hitler's positive impression did not conceal the fact that he had not made an inch of progress towards his goal. "There is no need for the world to get excited about what was negotiated yesterday with the French and the day before with the Spanish," remarked Ernst von Weizsäcker. "Everyone who reads the newspaper will guess that no date was set for Spain to enter the war and nothing concrete was agreed at all with the French."[101]

On the journey back to Berlin in his special train, news reached Hitler that Mussolini was about to attack Greece. Hitler was beside himself with rage. Not only did he doubt that Italy would be any more successful than during its previous military campaigns, he also feared that the conflict "could affect all of the Balkans."[102] He ordered the train to head south immediately and that a meeting with the Duce be arranged. Yet Mussolini's surprise announcement was a direct response to how Germany had proceeded with Romania. On 12 October, again without informing his ally, Hitler had sent a military mission to that country—officially to help Romania reorganise its army but in reality to bring the oil reserves so vital to the German war effort under German control. The Italian dictator considered this an affront. "Hitler is always presenting me with *faits accomplis*," Mussolini complained. "This time, I am going to pay him back in kind. He will only learn from the newspapers that I have marched into Greece."[103]

By the time Hitler and his entourage arrived in Florence in the morning of 28 October, Italian troops had already crossed the Albanian-Greek border, and a cheerful Mussolini received his visitor with the words: "Führer, we are on the march!"[104] Again the German dictator demonstrated his extraordinary self-control, concealing his anger and avoiding any recriminations of his host after his cavalier action. During the two men's talks in the Palazzo Vecchio, he focused on bringing Mussolini up to speed on his efforts to forge a Continental Bloc, talking up the fruitless meetings at Hendaye and Montoire. Unlike at their meeting at the Brenner Pass, however, Hitler made no mention of invading Britain. Instead, he talked in detail about his relationship with the Soviet Union. Taking up Mussolini's fears about Germany getting too close to Moscow, Hitler stressed that Italy and Germany were "natural allies" whereas "the cooperation with Russia only arose from considerations of usefulness." Hitler then informed Mussolini about the upcoming visit of the Soviet commissar for foreign affairs, Vyacheslav Molotov, to Berlin. Perhaps it would be possible to win over the Soviet Union for the anti-British coalition, Hitler said, and divert its attention to India. Advisedly, Hitler kept his initial preparations for an invasion of the Soviet Union to himself.[105]

The two dictators took leave of one another with their usual assurances of mutual friendship, but Hitler remained angry at Mussolini for going it alone, telling Jodl on 1 November that he had "lost any inclination for close military cooperation with Italy." Ten days later, while visiting Field Marshal Fedor von Bock at his sick bed, he was still "beside himself at the Italian escapade in Greece."[106] Hitler's scepticism about the prospect of the Greek campaign proved entirely justified. After a week, the Italian offensive stalled, and by mid-November 1940 Greek forces counter-attacked, pushing the Italians back into Albanian territory. On 11 November, the Italian navy lost half of its battleships anchored in the port of Taranto to a British air raid. And as if that were not bad enough, the Italian offensive against Egypt also came to a standstill when the British counter-attacked in December.[107]

These military setbacks had immediate consequences for the Axis partners' relations. "The Greeks are already fighting on Albanian soil," Goebbels noted on 16 November. "The Italians have been routed. It is an embarrassment for us all." In the weeks to come, hardly a day went by without Goebbels complaining about the military weakness of Nazi Germany's main ally.[108] At a meeting with Hitler and Ribbentrop at the Berghof on 18 November, Ciano got a taste of the new climate. "Hitler is pessimistic and considers the situation in the Balkans to be extremely dangerous," the Italian foreign minister wrote.[109] Hitler also vented his spleen for the first time at Mussolini personally in a letter two days later. Italy's misbegotten Greece campaign had played directly into the hands of the British, Hitler fumed, allowing them to occupy crucial air and naval bases like Crete, from where they could threaten the Romanian oil fields.[110] Mussolini was not happy about being lectured in this form, complaining that Hitler had "rapped his knuckles with a ruler."[111] But given the ongoing fiascos in Greece and North Africa, he had no choice but to give up his ambitions of waging a "parallel war," independent of Germany, and to ask his ally for military assistance.

While the Nazi leadership was perturbed at Italy's loss of face, Berlin was relatively sanguine about Franklin D. Roosevelt's landslide re-election on 5 November 1940 over his Republican opponent, Wendell Willkie. Since Roosevelt "was already supporting London with all means" at his disposal, "that will not cause any more damage," Goebbels concluded. Moreover, Roosevelt had campaigned on a promise not to lead America into the war on Britain's side, and there was little chance that he could take back this pledge. "The thing now is to wait and see," wrote the propaganda minister.[112] Weizsäcker found that the only difference between Roosevelt and Woodrow Wilson was that the former was more explicitly anti-German. "I am not going to praise everything about us," he wrote in a private letter. "But the United States' war-mongering and incitement are intolerable. In this case, the word 'Jewry' is definitely appropriate."[113] On the other hand, Roosevelt's re-election provided a boost to Hitler's opponents all over the world. "It is the first occasion for joy, the first victory in seven years that have brought nothing but disappointment and dismay," Thomas Mann wrote in his diary. "This event could decide the war."[114]

On 4 November 1940, during a *tour d'horizon* of the latest military situation, Hitler assured Wehrmacht leaders that an American intervention in the war would not happen before 1942. The Soviet Union, on the other hand, remained "the great problem of Europe," requiring that "everything must be done to be ready for the great showdown."[115] The dictator reminded his military commanders of his order of 31 July. In the meantime, German-Soviet relations had deteriorated. Germany had fallen behind with the deliveries it had promised under the commercial treaty, and Moscow regarded the conclusion of the Tripartite Pact and the deployment of a military mission to Romania as hostile acts.[116] In a letter of 13 October, Ribbentrop had invited Molotov to Berlin. It was going to be a test of the two countries' relations. Ribbentrop had written of the "historic task" of coordinating the policies of the Soviet Union, Italy, Japan and Germany and "steering the future development of their peoples by defining their interests in the long term."[117] But it seems that Ribbentrop was here presenting his own vision rather than the Führer's view. Hitler had always been sceptical about the possibility and indeed the desirability of including the Soviet Union in the Continental Bloc. Ribbentrop's state secretary, Weizsäcker, agreed.[118] Still, the dictator had not yet set his mind on another offensive. "It remains an open question what will happen in the east," Hitler told Bock on 11 November, although he added that circumstances there could compel Germany to intervene "to head off a more dangerous development."[119] In his "Führer Directive No. 18" the following day, when Molotov arrived in Berlin, Hitler decreed that, regardless of the outcome of the German-Soviet talks, "all orally issued preparations for the east" were to be continued.[120]

The Soviet delegation was given a decidedly cool reception. Goebbels had rejected the Foreign Ministry's suggestion of hiring people to cheer the Soviets as they arrived,[121] and the two sides' differing positions were painfully obvious when Hitler and Molotov met on the afternoon of 12 November. The German dictator initially tried to deflate Molotov's complaints about German policy in the preceding months by pointing out that Germany was at war, whereas the Soviet Union was not, and that much of what he had done had been made necessary by the military conflict. Germany, Hitler claimed, had "no political interests whatsoever" in the Balkans, but was only acting "under the compulsion of securing certain natural resources." First and foremost, the Führer meant the Romanian oil fields, which "were to be defended at all costs." Beyond all current disagreements in German-Soviet relations, Hitler added, it was important to agree the "major lines" of the two countries' future cooperation.

Molotov responded that he would welcome Nazi Germany and the Soviet Union "working together and not fighting one another." He also asked a series of precise questions that made Hitler visibly uncomfortable. Did Germany stand behind the treaty of August 1939, which made Finland part of the Soviet sphere of influence? What was the significance of the Tripartite Pact, and would the Soviet Union be involved in it? What was the German government's position concerning Soviet interests in the Balkans and the Black Sea? Such questioning was unusual for the man who already saw himself as the master of Europe and the future director of world events. But unlike in Hendaye, Hitler did not lose his composure for a second. On the contrary, he became solicitous, emphasising that the Tripartite Pact was by no means an attempt to confront the Soviet Union with a *fait accompli* and that Moscow would have the opportunity to "say its piece in those areas where it had interests." But Molotov was not prepared to content himself with such generalised answers. While Soviet participation in the Tripartite Pact seemed to be acceptable provided that Moscow was an "active partner and not just an object," the goal and significance of the pact would have to be more clearly defined, in particular when it came to the "borders of the greater Asian realm." Hitler was glad when their talks were interrupted by an air-raid alert and he could put off his insistent questioner until the following day.[122]

At noon the next day, Hitler hosted a small lunch for the Soviet delegation. Goebbels found Molotov to be "clever" and "sly" but also "very secretive," so that it was difficult to get "much of anything out of him." At the same time, the propaganda minister regarded the Soviet commissar's team as "more than mediocre," containing "not a single clever mind." Goebbels added that "fear of one another and inferiority complexes" were written all over their faces.[123] Weizsäcker was even more condescending, dismissing Molotov as a "schoolteacher type" and remarking that his retinue would make good "underworld gangsters in a movie." "If only some true peasants had come instead of this unresponsive, coarse bunch," Weizsäcker groaned.[124] The elitist arrogance of the German career diplomat combined here with racist feelings of superiority towards the allegedly primitive Russians.

In the two sides' second meeting on the afternoon of November 13, the atmosphere was even frostier than the day before, as bitter verbal blows were exchanged behind the façade of diplomatic niceties.

The Soviet Union must understand, Hitler reiterated, that his country was engaged in a "life-or-death struggle." Germany continued to recognise that Finland was part of the Soviet sphere of influence, but at the same time Berlin depended on Finnish nickel and wood. Moreover, Germany did not want to see any further hostilities between the Soviets and Finland because it would draw Sweden into the conflict and threaten the German position in the Baltic. If there was "good understanding" between the Soviet Union and Germany, countered Molotov, the Finnish question could be "solved without war." The precondition was that "there were neither German troops in Finland nor anti-Soviet demonstrations in the country." Hitler shot back that his regime had nothing to do with any anti-Soviet protests, and he had no intention of stationing any German troops in Finland in the long term, adding that the Wehrmacht units that were there at present were only in transit to northern Norway.

Hitler then turned to the "wider perspective," once again suggesting the idea of a "community of interest stretching from North Africa to the Far East" and consisting of the Tripartite Pact states, the Soviet Union, Spain and France. This "global coalition," Hitler proposed, would divide up the assets of the bankrupt British Empire among themselves. But Molotov did not rise to the bait, responding that the two sides should talk over present problems rather than racking their brains over an uncertain future. The Soviet Union regarded German and Italian guarantees of Romanian sovereignty as hostile to its own interests as a Black Sea power. What would Germany say, he challenged Hitler, "if Russia issued Bulgaria a guarantee under similar conditions," referring to Germany's military mission in Romania. The question took Hitler by surprise. He would have to consult with Mussolini, he replied, turning evasive. Again he broke off the meeting by using a possible British air raid as an excuse.[125]

There was an actual air-raid alarm that evening, and the banquet Molotov was holding for Ribbentrop in the Soviet embassy on Unter den Linden had to be abruptly terminated. Ribbentrop invited his colleague to join him in his air-raid shelter on Wilhelmstrasse. Here the two men had an extended conversation in which Molotov apparently named the long-term goals of Soviet foreign policy much more clearly than he had in his talks with Hitler. As the "most important Black Sea power," the Soviet Union not only had interests in Turkey and Bulgaria: it was "by no means indifferent" to the fate of Romania and Hungary. Molotov also wanted to know what the Axis powers intended to do with Yugoslavia and Greece, how they imagined Poland's future, and whether Berlin was still interested in maintaining Swedish neutrality. Last but not least, Molotov stated, his country had a vested interest in controlling the egresses from the Baltic Sea. Ribbentrop refused to discuss any details but said that all these questions would take care of themselves if the Soviet Union and Germany "stood back to back and not chest to chest, mutually supporting one another in achieving their aspirations."[126]

Hitler was not at all dissatisfied with the results of the Molotov visit. On the contrary, his adjutants found him "genuinely relieved" the day after the Soviet delegation had departed Berlin. He had "put no stock in it anyway," he said, and was glad that Molotov had "let the cat out of the bag." "Letting the Russians into Europe would spell the end of central Europe," he added. "Finland and the Balkans would be dangerous flanks."[127] By this time, Hitler had clearly decided to break with the Soviet Union and embark on the war he had envisaged for the spring of 1941. As early as 15 November, he instructed his military adjutants Schmundt and Engel to join the minister for armaments and munition, Fritz Todt, in looking for a "permanent headquarters in East Prussia." Returning from the region, they suggested establishing a new main Führer headquarters in a stretch of forest 8 kilometres east of Rastenburg (Kętrzyn). Hitler agreed and ordered the facility to be completed by April 1941.[128] Everyone around the dictator was flushed with confidence. There was every reason to be satisfied with what had already been achieved and "to look forward to the future with reassurance," the navy adjutant Karl-Jesko von Puttkamer noted on 21 November. The Führer would "get the job done . . . he had clearly shown that before."[129] At lunch in the Chancellery on 23 November, Weizsäcker found Hitler "looking good, calm and active as always."[130]

The second half of November 1940 was dominated by attempts to bring the nations of southeastern Europe closer to the Axis. On the 18th, Hitler received Bulgaria's King Boris III for what was declared a private visit, but his guest was noticeably reserved when Hitler urged him to join the German-Italian-Japanese alliance. By contrast, Hungary, Romania and Slovakia eagerly joined the Axis on 20, 23 and 24 November, respectively. On the day before the alliance-signing ceremony with Romania in Berlin, Hitler met with General Antonescu for the first time. This encounter would determine the two men's relationship. The Führer was deeply impressed by the personality of the "Conducător" and regarded him as a reliable ally in the coming battle with the Soviet Union.[131] Hitler even assured him that the Second Vienna Award, which had transferred northern Transylvania from Romania to Hungary, was not the final word on the matter—even though Hungary had joined the Axis two days previously.[132]

Later that month, when it was obvious that Hitler had failed to tie the Soviet Union to his Eurasian Continental Bloc, the Führer began to push for faster plans for the eastern offensive. "The eastern question is becoming acute," he declared on 3 December, when he visited Bock to congratulate him on his sixtieth birthday. "Ties are said to have been made between Russia and America, and with that a Russian-English connection is also probable." It would be dangerous to sit back and do nothing about such a development, Hitler asserted, returning to the central strategic idea with which he had justified his order of 31 July: "If the Russians are eliminated, England will have no more hope of defeating us on the Continent, especially as America will be prevented from intervening effectively by Japan, which will protect our backs."[133]

On the afternoon of 5 December, Hitler summoned Brauchitsch and Halder to the Chancellery and ordered them, in front of Keitel and Jodl, to put "in full motion" their preparations for the eastern campaign. "Hegemony in Europe will be decided in the battle against Russia," he told them. Late May was set as a tentative date for the invasion. "In the spring, we will have an obvious maximum level in leadership, materiel and troops while the Russians have a conspicuous ebb. Once the Russian army has been beaten, the disaster will take its course." Once again, Hitler's ideologically nourished underestimation of Soviet fighting ability came to the fore. "The Russians are inferior. Their army is without leadership." The basic operational idea for the invasion followed the Blitzkrieg concept employed in Germany's two previous offensives. Russia's armies were to be "prised apart" in large-scale battles of encirclement and then "strangled" individually. In the territories Germany would conquer, new "buffer states"—Ukraine, Belarus, Lithuania, Latvia—were to be created, and territory ceded to enlarge Romania, the General Government and Finland.[134] On 13 December, Halder briefed the chiefs of staff of the army groups and armies about Germany's military and political position, as he had understood it from his meeting with Hitler. Halder told them to get used to the idea that they would "face off against Russia" in the spring of 1941, "if the political situation made it necessary."[135]

Five days later, on 18 December, Hitler signed "Führer Directive No. 21" for "Operation Barbarossa." Its opening sentence summarised the considerations that had crystallised in the months since June 1940 to lead to an irrevocable decision: "The German Wehrmacht must be prepared even before the end of the war against England to subjugate the Soviet Union in a swift campaign." The main parts of the Red Army stationed in western Russia were to be "destroyed in bold forays led by wedges formed by tanks" and enemy troops still capable of fighting "prevented from withdrawing into the vastness of Russian territory." The "final destination of the operation" was defined as the Volga–Archangelsk line. From there air raids would be carried out against whatever Soviet arms production was still operational in the foothills of the Urals. Hitler stressed that the entire operation was to be kept top secret. The number of officers assigned to its preparation was to be kept as small as possible, and further participants were to be initiated "as late as possible and only in so far as needed to perform their individual functions."[136]

Brauchitsch was still uncertain as to whether Hitler was really serious about this order or was just "bluffing." He asked Engel to sound out the Führer.[137] Hitler again insisted that he "reserved the right to make all decisions" but that he had indeed made up his mind. Leaving aside the fact that he had never lost sight of conquering "living space in the east," he was now convinced that attacking the Soviet Union was the way out of the strategic dilemma in which he had been trapped since the previous summer. In his eyes, all previously considered tactical alternatives had proven insufficient or impossible to realise.

Hitler had experienced a further disappointment on 8 December, when Franco told Canaris, who had been sent to Madrid, that Spain would be unable to enter the war by the German deadline. With that, Hitler abandoned his plan to take over Gibraltar. Operation Felix disappeared from the agenda as silently as Operation Sea Lion.[138] Instead, in "Führer Directive No. 19," issued on 10 December, Hitler decreed that preparations be made for "Operation Attila" to "swiftly occupy the still-unoccupied parts of the French motherland" in case the parts of the French Empire ruled by General Maxime Weygand ended their loyalty to the Vichy government.[139]

Hitler had also had to scale back his hopes that Vichy France would cooperate more closely with Germany as part of an anti-British alliance. On 13 December, Pétain had dismissed his deputy Laval, a notorious *collaborateur*, and appointed Pierre-Étienne Flandin as his successor. Hitler regarded this as a personal affront, and the Nazi government tried in vain via its ambassador in Paris, Otto Abetz, to get Laval reinstated.[140] Hitler was even more enraged that Pétain had declined the German invitation to attend the 15 December ceremony at which the remains of Napoleon's son, the Duke of Reichstadt, were brought to the Dôme des Invalides. Among those close to Pétain rumours circulated that the Germans were trying to lure him to Paris to have him kidnapped. On 25 December, during his Christmas trip to the Channel coast, Hitler made a scene in front of Pétain's envoy, Admiral Jean-François Darlan. It was an "unheard-of infamy," Hitler complained, that he had been accused of such base motives after making such a generous gesture. He threatened that if French policy continued in the direction taken with Laval's dismissal, France would be taught "a far more terrible lesson."[141]

In early December, radio audiences in the United States heard William Shirer's words "This is Berlin" for the final time. The correspondent left the capital of the Third Reich, worn down by his battles with German censors, who made any sort of open reporting impossible. In his diary, he wrote on 1 December that the Germans were "disappointed, depressed, disillusioned that peace did not come this fall," but added that "these people, ground down and cheated though they may be by the most unscrupulous gang of rulers modern Europe has yet seen, will go a long, long way in this war." Shirer sought to explain this apparent contradiction with the extraordinary popularity of Adolf Hitler. For many Germans, he concluded, the Führer had become "a myth, a legend, almost a god . . . a figure remote, unreal, hardly human. For them he has become infallible."[142]

The dictator himself knew that his aura of infallibility would eventually suffer if he failed to deliver further military triumphs and, ultimately, the long-promised "final victory." When appearing in public, he sought to dispel fears that the war could carry on for an unforeseeable duration, projecting confidence in victory instead. Germany and its allies, he promised, were "strong enough for any combination [of enemies] in this world." At the annual memorial ceremony on 8 November 1940, which had been moved from the traditional Bürgerbräukeller, the site of Elser's assassination attempt, to the Löwenbräukeller, he boasted that "there is no coalition of forces that is a match for us in military terms."[143] Two days later, he told armaments workers at the Borsig factory in Berlin: "There will be no German defeat . . . Whatever may happen, Germany will emerge victorious from this struggle!"[144] The following day, he assured a Gauleiter meeting: "We have got victory in our pocket if we do not forfeit it through our own folly."[145] And finally, on 18 December, he proclaimed to 5,000 officer candidates in the Sportpalast that the German people formed "the best core on earth by a wide margin" so that "victory cannot fall to any other nation but ours."[146]

In his New Year's address, Goebbels continued in the same vein. In rhapsodic terms, the propaganda minister celebrated the Führer, behind whom the entire German nation had united with a "passionate feeling of gratitude." "Long may he live," Goebbels gushed. "Long may he stand above the people as the defender and protector of the Reich, as the first warrior for a genuine, true peace and for the happiness, honour and glory of his people. The world admires him, but we are lucky enough to be allowed to love him. Let us join hands and unite around him, solid and indivisible."[147]

How many Germans remained clear-eyed after such proclamations of absolute faith in Hitler? One of them, Friedrich Kellner, wrote in his diary on New Year's Eve: "The year 1940 is being carried to its grave. Has it not brought unspeakably great suffering to an enslaved world? And what awaits? We can only guess. No one knows."[148]

5

Operation Barbarossa

"The year 1941 will bring the completion of the greatest victory in our history," announced Hitler in his New Year's address to the Wehrmacht.[1] This statement by the Führer was at the centre of "political considerations everywhere" and bolstered the "general confidence in victory," the SS Security Service reported.[2] Foreign observers understandably painted a different picture. Only the gullible parts of the population, who took Hitler's every word as gospel, had been impressed in any serious way, the American consul in Frankfurt relayed back home. Lots of other Germans had found themselves anything but reassured. The consul cited a young soldier complaining that "he said the same things last year."[3]

Reality would quickly and radically give the lie to the dictator's prediction. The year 1941 would not bring the greatest victory in German history: it would ring in the beginning of the end of the Third Reich. Operation Barbarossa, which Hitler had decided on in December 1940, was predicated on the notion that the Soviet Union could be defeated in a military campaign lasting only a few months. Afterwards, Hitler expected, Germany would assume a position of hegemony over continental Europe and, having gained control of a massive, economically autarchic territory immune to blockades, it would possess the resources to take up the "final battle" against Britain and, if necessary, the United States. As he had so often in his career, Hitler was betting everything on a single card. If he failed to defeat the Red Army quickly and decisively, his entire strategic concept would come crashing down around him.

With a few brief interruptions, Hitler spent the first three months of 1941 on the Obersalzberg preparing for the coming operations with his military advisers.[4] On 8–9 January, he summoned the Wehrmacht and army High Commands to again run through his reasons for launching Barbarossa. Stalin, he said, was "a clever mind," who, while "unwilling to publicly oppose Germany" in the short term, was "driven to push westwards" and would "cause increasing difficulties." Meanwhile, only the prospect of Soviet intervention was keeping up the spirit of the British. "They will only quit the race once this last Continental hope has been dashed," Hitler proclaimed. Thus the Soviet Union had to be "demolished," after which Britain would either give in or Germany would be able to resume the fight under more favourable conditions. Moreover, the "demolition of Russia" would enable Japan to "concentrate all its strength against the United States" and possibly prevent it from entering the war against Germany.

Timing was important, Hitler stressed to his commanders. The Red Army was still "a clay colossus without a head," but its future development could not be "predicted with certainty." It was crucial, therefore, to undertake the military operation at a point when this strategic window of opportunity was still open—and in Hitler's logic that was yet another reason for a rapid invasion. After the expected victory, the Germans would have "the gigantic Russian territory" with its "immeasurable riches" at their disposal. This would be Germany's great trump card, which would allow it "to wage war against whole continents since it could no longer be defeated." The Führer ended his monologue with theatrical bathos, boasting that once Operation Barbarossa was underway, "all of Europe would hold its breath."[5]

The military commanders in attendance, recalled Hitler's adjutant Below, listened to the Führer's soliloquy "silently and without contradicting him."[6] But they did share their doubts and worries with one another. After a meeting with Brauchitsch on 28 January, Halder jotted in his diary: "Barbarossa. The point is unclear. We will not hit the English. Our economic basis would not improve dramatically. Risk in the west should not be underestimated."[7] Over in the Foreign Ministry, Weizsäcker was likewise sceptical. He was unable to see, he remarked over the New Year, "the actual point of the spring offensive against Russia": the "urgent priority" was to defeat Britain. As long as that had not been achieved, Weizsäcker cautioned, Germany was better advised "not to lock horns with Russia."[8]

On 31 January, Brauchitsch and Halder met with the supreme commanders of the three army groups—Bock, Leeb and Rundstedt—

and discussed the basics of the planned operation. When asked whether
he had good reason to believe that the Red Army would take up positions in front of the Daugava–Dnieper line, the chief of the general
staff had to admit that things "could turn out quite differently"—an
astonishing admission of the shaky planning for the campaign.[9] But
Bock was the only one who directly raised this topic with Hitler the
following day. While speaking confidently about the operation's chance
for success, he expressed doubts about whether Germany could make
the Soviets sue for peace. If occupying Ukraine and taking Leningrad
(St. Petersburg) and Moscow were not sufficient, Hitler shot back, the
Wehrmacht would have to advance quickly on Sverdlovsk (Yekaterinburg).
In any case, he was ready for a "swordfight" and convinced that the
German attack would blow aside the Red Army "like a hailstorm."[10]

Unlike before the western offensive in the autumn and winter of
1939–40, there was no real resistance on the part of the military leadership to Hitler's plan of war. That was partly down to the fact that
most commanders, like the Führer himself, were convinced that the
Red Army would not be able to put up much resistance and believed
they could defeat the Soviets within a matter of weeks. "Three weeks
after our attack, the whole house of cards will have collapsed," Jodl
was quoted as saying.[11] Moreover, after Germany's triumph over
France, Hitler's military prestige had risen so enormously that it did
not appear advisable to openly criticise his decisions. Until now, the
Führer had always been right in his estimation of risk. Why should
that not be the case this time round?

On 3 February 1941, Halder presented Hitler with the completed
"Mobilisation Plan East." It contained not a word of doubt about the
operation's feasibility. The mission of the three army groups—North
under Leeb, Centre under Bock and South under Rundstedt—was to
"shatter the frontlines of the expected masses of the Russian army
with a sudden and deep penetration of strongly equipped and highly
mobile units north and south of the Pripet Marshes and to exploit
the breakthrough by annihilating the isolated groups of enemy troops."
It was of the utmost importance to prevent significant enemy forces
"from taking early evasive action and escaping destruction west of
the Dnieper–Daugava line."[12]

Hitler declared himself "basically satisfied" with this plan of operations but stressed again that "the desired encirclement of large portions

of the Russian army . . . would only be successful if it could be carried out across the board."[13] The question of what should be the focus of the operation after the initial German breakthrough and the battles of annihilation remained unanswered, however; this uncertainty would prove the source of immense conflict between the dictator and the army command over the course of the campaign.[14] For the time being, the underlying disagreements were bridged by the mutual certainty that the first military blows would suffice to make the Bolshevik system collapse. Tellingly, during these weeks Hitler already began to ponder the future after the Soviet Union had been defeated. On 17 February, he ordered Jodl to carry out a study on a possible "invasion of Afghanistan and conflict with India after the conclusion of Operation Barbarossa."[15] Such absurd pipe dreams, which recalled the conquests of Alexander the Great, focused directly on the heart of the British Empire. If he could become the absolute ruler of a continental empire stretching from the Atlantic to the Urals, Hitler believed his strategic position would be unassailable. He could then deal Britain a mortal blow before challenging the United States to a war for global domination.

In the meantime, the situation of Italian troops in North Africa had dramatically deteriorated. In January 1941, the British took the port of Bardia, capturing thousands of Italian soldiers. Without German help, warned Italy's military attaché in Berlin, Efisio Marras, Cyrenaica could not be held, and all of Italian North Africa might be lost.[16] "Our friends have got us into a complete jam," Goebbels complained.[17] At a meeting at the Berghof on 9 January, Germany's future stance towards its Axis partner followed Operation Barbarossa as the second item on the agenda. Hitler favoured coming to Italy's assistance militarily, as he was concerned about the psychological effect that the loss of Libya would have on Germany's other allies. The Italians, he sneered, were apparently incapable of standing up to the English "on their own," so enough help had to be offered that "they could hold out for the coming months."[18] Two days later, Hitler signed "Führer Directive No. 22," which declared: "The situation in the Mediterranean, where England is deploying superior forces against our allies, requires German assistance for strategic, political and psychological reasons." The first of the planned aid measures was to send a tank force to the North African theatre to block the British advance.[19]

Following his military setbacks, Mussolini had avoided another meeting with Hitler for several weeks. Finally, on 5 January, he agreed to an encounter, although he insisted that it should receive as little publicity as possible. In two days of consultations at the Berghof on 19 and 20 January, Hitler played the tactful host keen to avoid anything that could offend his Italian friend's sensibilities.[20] The Führer did not say a word about his plans to invade the Soviet Union that year, describing the concentration of German troops in the east as a precautionary measure. "As long as Stalin, who is clever and cautious, is alive, Russia definitely will not start anything against Germany," Hitler said. "But it is not clear who his successor will be, so Germany needs to be strong." Hitler devoted most of the conversation to the deployment of German troops in Romania and for Operation Marita, the German attack on Greece that had been prepared since December 1940, before the Führer had decided on Barbarossa. It was important, Hitler advised, that their "cards not be revealed too early." He then proceeded to describe the technical aspects of the operation with such expertise and knowledge of detail that the Italian military delegation accompanying Mussolini came away highly impressed.[21]

Mussolini agreed to the deployment of a German tank force to shore up his troops in Libya, thereby once and for all ending Italian attempts to wage a "parallel war" independent of Germany. "A good result overall," noted Ciano of the visit. "The solidarity between the two Axis partners is complete, and we will march together in the Balkans."[22] But the relationship between the two allies was hardly all that harmonious. On 22 January, Tobruk fell to the British. "The spoils of the English . . . are enormous," commented Goebbels. "Italy is being stripped bare in Africa. The mask is being ripped off, and if it continues, it will destroy all the prestige of fascism in general."[23] In Germany, the perennial lack of regard for the Italian ally expressed itself in condescending remarks. Italian military bulletins were jokingly nicknamed "spaghetti reports" because they were so long and thin, the Security Service noted.[24]

Publicly, Hitler repeatedly emphasised that the Italian need for prestige had to be respected. In February, in a directive concerning the "Behaviour of German Soldiers in the Italian Theatre of War,"

he instructed German officers and men to avoid "any injurious arrogance despite their justified pride, feelings of worth and past achievements."[25] In private, however, Hitler did not bother to conceal his
increasing irritation with his military ally. "The crazy thing is that on
the one hand the Italians cry for help and never tire of describing how
poor their arms and equipment are," the Führer complained. "And on
the other, they are so jealous and childish that they do not really want
German soldiers and German help."[26]

Despite all this, on 3 February, Hitler reaffirmed his decision to
hurry to the Italians' aid in Libya. He now called for the holding force
to be bolstered by a strong tank division. When the British "encounter
fresh, well-equipped German forces," he boasted, "the balance of
power will soon swing in our favour."[27] In a letter to Mussolini two
days later, he announced that he was putting the mission in the hands
of the "most daring tank commander we have in the German army,"
Lieutenant-General Erwin Rommel.[28] After earning Hitler's favour in
1939 as the commander of the Führer's headquarters, the swashbuck-
ling Rommel had reinforced his reputation by commanding a tank
division in the French campaign. He was an unreserved admirer of
Hitler and convinced of the latter's military genius. "What would we
do without the Führer?" he had written in April 1940. "I doubt whether
any other German man would be able to master the art of military
and political leadership with equal brilliance."[29] On 6 February,
Rommel received the orders for his new mission personally from
Hitler. Six days later, the first Afrikakorps troops arrived in Tripoli.
Nominally they were subordinated to the local Italian commander,
but Rommel had been sure to insist that they be allowed to operate
as a unit under his own leadership. By the end of the month, he was
able to report that the situation in North Africa was becoming more
stable by the day. By building mobile replica tanks made of wood,
he succeeded in deceiving the British about the true size of the
Afrikakorps.[30] At the same time, to secure the sea route to North
Africa, the Luftwaffe launched heavy air raids on Malta, Britain's
crown colony.[31]

On 20 March in the Chancellery, Hitler awarded Rommel with the
Oak Leaf of the Knight's Cross and conferred with him about his
plans for reconquering Cyrenaica. "A fabulous officer," opined Goebbels.
"He told us about the difficulties of desert fighting. Our motors are

holding up wonderfully. The Italians only get in the way. Not a people of war. They should be happy we are there. Just like the Führer, who is very happy that we got our motorised troops there safely. The Führer does not want to give up Africa under any circumstances."[32] In late March, Rommel launched his counter-offensive. Over the course of April, he retook Bardia, surrounded Tobruk and drove the British out of Cyrenaica. It was not until June that his tempestuous march forward was halted on the Egyptian border. While the Army High Command observed the triumphs of Hitler's favourite general with mistrust and sought to rein him in, Nazi propaganda celebrated the "Desert Fox" as a hero. "Rommel has become a legendary figure for both our troops and the Italian soldiers," noted Goebbels in June 1941.[33]

At their meeting in January, Hitler had asked Mussolini to try and make General Franco change his position by pointing out the assistance he had received in the Spanish Civil War.[34] But a conversation between the Duce and the Caudillo on 12 February in Bordighera produced no results. In return for Spain joining the war Franco made such exaggerated demands that there was no way the Axis would fulfil them. Hitler gave up all hope of winning over the Spanish dictator. "The Führer is dropping Spain," noted Walther Hewel, Ribbentrop's attaché with Hitler. "They will go to the dogs."[35] Operation Felix, the conquest of Gibraltar, was cancelled once and for all, dashing any Axis hopes of forcing the British fleet from its positions in the western Mediterranean.

Nor did Germany's relations with Japan develop the way Hitler had hoped. In early February 1941, at the leaving ceremony for Japan's ambassador to Berlin, Saburo Kurusu, the Führer crowed about "the definitive sealing of German-Japanese cooperation" in the Tripartite Pact of September 1940, saying that such cooperation "would in future be particularly close since the two countries . . . are not competitors and do not have any competing territorial interests."[36] On 28 February, Japan's new ambassador, Hiroshi Oshima, who was known as a great advocate of Germany, presented his credentials to Hitler at the Berghof. That gave the Führer an opportunity to reiterate the two countries' common interests. Germany, Hitler said, "has no territorial claims in the Far East and has no intention to reach out for colonies there . . . For Germany, it is sufficient to restructure Europe and establish colonies in Africa."[37] Hitler's Führer Directive No. 24 of 5 March left no doubt about what he hoped to achieve from the partnership: "Japan must be forced into action as soon as possible in the Far East. That will tie down powerful English forces, and the focus of US interests will be diverted to the Pacific." The directive explicitly stated that "no indications whatsoever" should be made to Japanese diplomats about Operation Barbarossa.[38]

On 26 March, the Japanese foreign minister, Yosuke Matsuoka, visited Berlin. Goebbels had pulled out all the stops to give him a regal reception. "Hundreds of thousands on the streets," the propaganda minister noted. "My instructions were largely followed . . . The reception by the people was very thunderous."[39] Critics of the Nazis like Friedrich Kellner were left scratching their heads at the enormous energy expended for the occasion. Kellner witnessed none of the spontaneous popular enthusiasm that the newspapers reported. "The stagehands are responsible for the political façade and the 'enthusiastic' reception," he noted in his diary. "In the last war, the Japanese were slant-eyed bandits who stole the Kiaochow Bay [Jiaozhou Bay] territory from us. Today they are 'friends.' How changeable is your soul, O German newspaperman!"[40]

In his meeting with Matsuoka the following day, Hitler got straight to the point. Japan, he advised, should not pass up the opportunity to strike against British positions in the Far East, declaring that rarely "has the risk been smaller, with war dominating Europe, England being tied down there, America only beginning to rearm, Japan representing the strongest force in eastern Asia, and Russia unable to act because 150 [German] divisions are waiting on its western border." But Matsuoka was evasive, saying that while he too was convinced that his country should attack Singapore as soon as possible, it was a view not supported in cabinet. At this point in time, therefore, he could not "make any pledges that Japan would act." Hitler was scarcely able to conceal his disappointment. His mood did not improve when Matsuoka later showered him with flattery, remarking that a people could boast such a leader "only once every 1,000 years."[41]

Hitler neglected to mention that he had already decided to invade Russia. At a lunch he hosted for his Japanese guest on 28 March, he promised that, if the Soviet Union attacked Japan, Germany would not hesitate to support its ally "with the force of weapons."[42] Hitler reiterated this guarantee with regard to the United States on 4 April, when Matsuoka, stopping again in Berlin after visiting Italy, had a further meeting with the German dictator. If Japan should come into conflict with the United States, Hitler pledged, Germany "would immediately draw the consequences."[43] It is striking that Hitler did nothing to secure Japanese support in the event that Germany went to war with the Soviet Union, which suggests that the Führer was confident he could defeat Russia without any outside assistance. Nevertheless, Berlin was unpleasantly surprised to learn on 13 April that during Matsuoka's return trip to Japan, the foreign minister had concluded a "neutrality pact" with Moscow.[44] The Japanese government wanted to rule out getting dragged against its will into a war between Nazi Germany and the Soviet Union. From conversations with Ribbentrop and Weizsäcker, Oshima had gleaned that Germany was preparing intensively for an eastern invasion.[45]

As Matsuoka was about to leave from the Moscow rail station, Stalin made an unusual gesture. Before the eyes of the assembled diplomatic corps, he demonstratively put his arms around the shoulders of Germany's ambassador to the Soviet Union, Count Friedrich Werner von der Schulenburg, declaring: "We have to remain friends, and you must now do everything you can to see we do."[46] The Soviet dictator was clearly doing everything *he* could to pacify Hitler. As late as January 1941, Moscow signed a new trade agreement with Germany, and the Soviets were extremely assiduous about meeting their agreed deliveries of goods. The idea was to avoid anything that could provoke Hitler and give him a pretext for war. "Russia is completely docile, but only because it feels surrounded," noted Goebbels, whom Hitler had only told about Operation Barbarossa in late March.[47]

Hitler scrupulously avoided mentioning the Soviet Union in public appearances like his Reichstag speech of 30 January—a fact which some Germans registered with amazement.[48] But on the inside he pressed for preparations for Barbarossa to be speeded up. At the same time, his ideological motivation emerged ever clearer. On 3 March, he told Jodl that the coming campaign would be "more than just a battle with weapons": it would have to be waged as a "conflict of two world views." The "Jewish-Bolshevik intelligentsia" needed to be swept away "as the enslaver of the people" and Russia divided up into a number of smaller states dependent on Germany.[49] Hitler's instructions were reflected in Keitel's "Guidelines for Special Areas of Order No. 21," issued on 13 March, which set out the general framework for a war of annihilation. It specified that in the German army's theatre of operations Himmler would be given "special tasks at the behest of the Führer," which would arise from the "decisive battle of two opposing political systems." The SS leader was explicitly assured that he would be able to act "independently and on his own authority." This was a reaction by Hitler and the Wehrmacht Supreme Command to their experiences during the Polish campaign, when conflicts had arisen between the SS and some army leaders over the homicidal butchery of the Einsatzgruppen. As far as the fighting allowed, occupied parts of Russia would be removed from the operational theatre of the army and "subsumed in states with their own governments." The idea was to set up three "Reich commissariats" in the Baltic states, Belarus and Ukraine, reflecting the territories of operation of Army Groups North, Centre and South. The political administration was to be handed over to Reich commissars, who would receive their orders directly from Hitler.[50]

On 17 March, in a meeting with Halder and the head of the army's operations division, Colonel Adolf Heusinger, Hitler once again spelled out his expectations for Barbarossa. "We have to create Stalin-free republics," he announced. "The intelligentsia deployed by Stalin must be destroyed. The leadership machinery of the Russian empire must be shattered. In the greater Russian area, the most brutal violence must be used. Ideological ties do not hold the Russian people together firmly enough. When the functionaries are done away with, the people will split apart."[51] Ten days later, on 27 March, Brauchitsch summoned the commanders of the army groups, armies and tank groups to Zossen to inform them about the nature of the projected eastern offensive. He told them that German troops "had to realise that the battle would be carried out race against race and they would have to act with the necessary severity."[52] These meetings were a prelude to the crucial speech Hitler gave to his officers on 30 March 1941—a date which the historian Johannes Hürter rightly calls "an extraordinary day in German military history."[53] On that Sunday, Hitler sought to enlist the entire German military elite on behalf of a racist war of conquest and annihilation unparalleled in human history.

The speech was delivered in the cabinet room of the New Chancellery. Here, the commanders of the three branches of the military (Brauchitsch, Göring and Raeder), representatives of the Wehrmacht Supreme Command (led by Keitel and Jodl) and the commanders of the army, Luftwaffe and navy groups earmarked for Barbarossa—around one hundred officers—assembled in the morning.[54] At 11 a.m., Hitler commenced his 2½-hour-long speech.[55] In the first part of his address, he repeated the strategic arguments he had been advancing since the Berghof meeting on 31 July 1940 to justify the envisioned "eastern war." He sought to allay his officers' fears of a two-front war by telling them that the "western battle" was practically over and that the situation was thus completely different from that in the First World War. He did, however, concede that the situation in northern Africa was unclear and that it had yet to be determined whether anti-British policies would prevail in Vichy France.[56] He had strong words of criticism for the Italian military, whose setbacks had had a "catastrophic effect abroad" and improved Britain's strategic position in the Mediterranean.[57] Hitler reiterated that Britain's best hope was the United States, recapitulating arguments already familiar to his audience. "If England survives for a year to eighteen months," he said, "American assistance will have an effect." The focus of the German war economy would then have to be switched to the Luftwaffe and the navy, and equipping the army throttled back. "But first Russia must be subdued," he continued, adding that the prospects of getting rid of the "Russian-Asian threat for all time" were still favourable. Only this would give Germany the necessary "freedom of action" to prevail in the conflict with the Anglo-Saxon powers.[58] "It would be a crime against the future of the German people, if I did not seize this opportunity!" Hitler proclaimed.[59] He defined the goals of the invasion as the destruction of the Red Army and the dissolution of the Russian state. Once again, he reaffirmed his conviction that despite the "endless territorial space" and Soviet numerical superiority, the Wehrmacht would succeed in quickly deciding the campaign by "focusing on crucial points" and combining "massive deployments of the Luftwaffe and tanks."[60]

It was not until the second half of his speech that Hitler turned to the ideological motivation that would give Operation Barbarossa its special character. Halder noted the following bullet points: "Battle of two world views. Ultimate condemnation of Bolshevism as anti-social crime. Communism as an immense danger for the future. We need to dispense with ideas of solidarity among soldiers [on both sides]. The communist is not a fellow soldier before or after. This is a battle of annihilation. If we do not realise this, we will defeat the enemy but will be confronted with the communist enemy again thirty years down the road. We are not waging war to preserve the enemy." There was no doubt as to what Hitler meant when he spoke of "the annihilation of the Bolshevik commissars and the communist intelligentsia": this was "not a question for courts-martial"—troops would have to take the matter into their own hands. "Commissars and the members of the State Political Directorate are criminals and must be treated as such," Hitler demanded. He appealed to his commanders to discard any moral scruples: "The battle will be very different to the battle in the west. In the east, severity [now] is a form of mildness towards the future."[61] His decision had not been an easy one, and he had "wrestled with himself for a long time," the Führer claimed. Once again he invoked his role model Friedrich the Great and his "insoluble" task: "How much easier we have it today!"[62]

Never before had Hitler revealed his criminal intentions so unmistakably to leading representatives of the Wehrmacht. "No one moved, and there were no words other than his own to hear," recalled Walter Warlimont, deputy chief of the Wehrmacht general staff.[63] After 1945, Halder spread the legend that the front commanders had been "completely outraged" at Hitler's "presumption" and told Brauchitsch and Halder: "We are not going along with that."[64] But there is not a shred of evidence to back up that claim. Bock concluded his diary entry that day with a remark that did not indicate the slightest distance from the monstrous things he had just heard: "All in all, plans and tasks the Führer himself described as gigantic."[65] Over the joint lunch and during the reports of the army group leaders that followed Hitler's speech, no one was prepared to voice any objections or even merely demand that these matters be discussed.

This failing was not just a reflection of the officers' cowardice when confronted with the imposing authority of a Führer who was, in the eyes of many commanders, infallible. There was significant consensus between Hitler and his military leadership. Both were of the same mind concerning the fighting power of the Red Army and Barbarossa's chance of success, and there also does not seem to have been any fundamental disagreement about the goals of the eastern campaign and the methods to be employed. "Jewish Bolshevism" was the *bête noire* of the German officer corps, and the idea that Germany needed to counter a "peril from the east" was a well-worn anti-Russian cliché of the Prussian/German military elite.[66] Thus, in a briefing of division commanders on 25 April, Colonel-General Georg von Küchler, the commander of the 18th Army, proclaimed that Russia was "thanks to the sheer mass of its territory an Asian state" which was separated by a "deep abyss . . . of ideology and race" from Germany, and whose aggressive urge to expand westwards represented an ever-present threat. "The favourable hour" had to be seized, Küchler said, to eradicate this danger for all time, and to "destroy European Russia and dissolve the Russian European state."[67] General Erich Hoepner, the commander of Tank Group 4 and later a figure in the anti-Hitler resistance, referred in his daily orders in early May to the war against the Soviet Union as a "fundamental chapter in the struggle for the existence of the German people": "It is the age-old struggle of the Germanic tribes against the Slavs, the defence of European culture against Muscovite-Asiatic inundation and the repulsion of Jewish Bolshevism."[68] Anti-Bolshevism, anti-Slavism, anti-Semitism, social Darwinism—these were the basic prerequisites with which many Wehrmacht generals embarked on war with the Soviet Union. Hitler was extremely adept at sounding these themes in his speech on 30 March, as he sought to win over his military leaders for his idea of a massive campaign of annihilation.

For a short time in the spring of 1941, however, the spotlight turned to the Balkans. Before embarking on Barbarossa, Hitler wanted to draw as many states as possible into the German sphere of power. "Now we are supposed to create order in the Balkans," complained Weizsäcker.[69] After Romania, Hungary and Slovakia had signed on to the Tripartite Pact in November 1940, Germany set its sights on Bulgaria and Yugoslavia. At a meeting with Hitler on the Obersalzberg in early January 1941, Bulgarian prime minister Bogdan Filov still resisted the German overtures. He was afraid of complicating his relationship with the Soviet Union, which, as had been made clear by Molotov in Berlin, still considered Bulgaria to be part of its sphere of influence. Hitler sought to reassure his guest that there was no need to fear a Russian intervention "because the Russians must know that the conflict would spread along the entire length of the German-Russian border."[70] On 1 March, Bulgaria joined the Tripartite Pact. Hitler travelled to Vienna where the official signing ceremony was held in Belvedere Palace. The following day, German troops crossed from Romania into Bulgaria. "A huge success for the Führer," noted Goebbels. ". . . The march into Bulgaria came off without a hitch."[71] Moscow reacted with remarkable reserve to this affront, in line with Stalin's orders not to give the Germans a pretext for aggression. In a letter to the Turkish president, İsmet İnönü, Hitler assured him that the entry of German troops into Bulgaria was not directed at Turkey and that these forces would stay far enough away from the Bulgarian-Turkish border so that "no false conclusions can be drawn about the purpose of them being there."[72]

It was far harder to get Yugoslavia on board. Here the traditionally close ties of the Serbs, in particular, with their Slavic brothers in Russia discouraged an alliance with Germany. On 14 February 1941, Hitler received Yugoslavia's prime minister, Dragiša Cvetković, and the foreign minister, Aleksandar Cincar-Marković, for a 2½-hour meeting at the Berghof in an attempt to persuade them to join the Tripartite Pact. It was a "unique historical opportunity for Yugoslavia," Hitler argued, ". . . to determine its place in Europe once and for all." It was thus in Yugoslavia's deepest interest to play a part in the "new order" Germany and Italy were trying to create.[73] But initially, Hitler's overtures got the cold shoulder. "The Yugoslavs do not want to fully play along," Hewel noted.[74] The breakthrough only came with a secret visit by Prince Pavle, the Yugoslav prince regent, to the Obersalzberg on 4 March. There it was agreed that Yugoslavia would not have to provide any military assistance to Germany or grant Axis troops any transit rights. In addition, Yugoslavia would have the prospect of acquiring the Greek port of Thessaloniki with its access to the Aegean Sea. Under these conditions, and despite the opposition of some government ministers, the royal council in Belgrade approved the country joining the Tripartite Pact. An agreement was signed on 25 March, also in Vienna and with Hitler again in attendance. "We have got that done as well," wrote a relieved Goebbels. "It was a difficult birth."[75]

But the relief was premature. Only two days later, during the night of 26–27 March, Serbian officers staged a coup, deposing both Pavle and Cvetković and installing the seventeen-year-old Petar II as the country's new king. When Hewel broke the news to Hitler in the early hours, the Führer began quivering with rage, immediately summoning Keitel and Jodl to the Chancellery. He was not going to take this lying down, he told his paladins. He would clean things up in the Balkans. They would find out who they were dealing with.[76] But before long, his initial anger gave way to a mood of positive excitement as Hitler realised that the coup in Belgrade was the perfect excuse to combine Operation Marita against Greece with punitive measures against Yugoslavia into one major offensive. By 1 p.m., Jodl informed his staff by telephone that Hitler had decided to "shatter Yugoslavia"; Brauchitsch and Göring were already at the Führer's side.[77] "If the gods want to damn someone into perdition, they strike him blind," Hitler told the Hungarian ambassador at a noon-time reception, adding that the developments in Yugoslavia were "not a difficulty but a relief" for Germany.[78] A short time later, he told the Bulgarian ambassador that a "terrible thunderstorm" was about to break over Yugoslavia "with a velocity that will knock them sideways."[79]

In the afternoon of 27 March, before receiving Japanese foreign minister Matsuoka, Hitler summoned the heads of the Army and Wehrmacht High Commands to the Chancellery and demanded that a "strike against Yugoslavia" of "remorseless severity" be carried out in a "lightning operation"—even though this would probably delay the planned start of Operation Barbarossa by four weeks.[80] That very evening, Hitler signed "Führer Directive No. 25": "The military coup in Yugoslavia has changed the political situation in the Balkans. Even if it issues declarations of loyalty, Yugoslavia has to be considered an enemy and must be broken up immediately."[81] Halder got down to work without delay and three days later had finished a plan for a combined campaign against Greece and Yugoslavia.[82] In the night of 5–6 April, Hitler summoned Goebbels and informed him that the attack would begin at 5:20 a.m. "He estimated the entire operation will take around two months," Goebbels noted. "I think it will be shorter." Hitler did not mince words, showing himself to be a vehement Serb-hater whose animosity stemmed from the times of the Austrian-Hungarian and Wilhelmine empires. "The Balkans have always been a powder keg," Hitler proclaimed. "We need to deprive London of the possibility of tossing a torch in there whenever it wants. The entire Serbian clique of conspirators must fall." For Hitler, the fact that the Soviet Union had only hours earlier signed a friendship and non-aggression pact with Yugoslavia was not a reason to cancel the operation. On the contrary, Hitler declared: "If we do not act now the entire Balkans including Turkey would begin to slide, and we must prevent that."[83]

In the early hours of 6 April 1941, Germany commenced the military campaign with a massive bombardment of Belgrade. Large parts of the Yugoslav capital were reduced to rubble, and thousands of civilians killed. It was clear right from the start that neither Yugoslav nor Greek troops, despite their spirited resistance, were a match for the concentrated assault by the Wehrmacht. Vanguard German tanks, supported by the Luftwaffe, breached enemy defensive lines everywhere. "A grand mood," Hewel noted on 9 April when news arrived that Thessaloniki had fallen.[84] But the euphoria was dented that night when British bombers attacked Berlin, causing serious damage in the centre, particularly to the boulevard of Unter den Linden. The Prussian state opera house burned to the ground, and the university, the state library and the Crown Prince's Palace were all badly hit. German propaganda made a meal of this "attack on Berlin's cultural district" to divert attention away from the Wehrmacht's barbaric destruction of Belgrade.[85]

On the evening of 10 April, Hitler left Berlin on his special train, arriving—after a brief stop in Munich—on the morning of 12 April in Mönichkirchen, 35 kilometres south of Wiener Neustadt. Here, on a loop of the Vienna–Graz railway line, near a tunnel that would provide shelter in case of an air raid, the train stopped. This was the Führer's headquarters, sarcastically named "Spring Storm," where Hitler would follow the operations in southern Europe for the next two weeks.[86] Once again, they were concluded far more swiftly than Hitler himself had estimated in his most optimistic calculations. Yugoslavia capitulated on 17 April, Greece four days later. By 27 April, the swastika was flying atop the Acropolis. Most of the British Expeditionary Force, deployed in previous months to support Greek troops in the Peloponnese, had been able to avoid being captured by the Wehrmacht. But that was only a slight dent in the German triumph.[87]

Far more annoying was the grotesque tug-of-war that ensued between the Germans and Italians over the conditions of the Greek surrender. Mussolini was anything but thrilled that the Wehrmacht had succeeded in a few days at something his troops had been trying, in vain, to achieve since the previous October. He also felt slighted that the Greeks had intentionally only surrendered to the German commander, Field Marshal Wilhelm List. Now the Italian dictator refused to agree to the cease-fire until the Greek military command had surrendered to his generals as well, and the signing of the armistice was repeated with Italian representatives present. In Hitler's headquarters, there was outrage. "General anger—from the Führer as well," Hewel noted on 21 April.[88]

The day before, Hitler had celebrated his fifty-second birthday. In contrast to the overblown ceremonies of past years, the congratulations, broadcast live on radio, lasted for only two hours. It was suggested that the Führer was busy with urgent matters in his role as Germany's commander-in-chief.[89] On the morning of 26 April, Hitler's special train left Mönichkirchen and returned to Berlin via Klagenfurt, where Hitler visited his old history teacher from his days in Linz, Leopold Pötsch.[90] Once back in the German capital on 28 April, he immediately summoned Goebbels, who found the Führer in a "beaming mood after his triumph." The propaganda minister crowed: "The expected two months turned out to be three weeks. Our soldiers have once again put us to shame."[91] But if Security Service reports are accurate, popular enthusiasm was muted. Satisfaction at Germany's triumph in the Balkans was mixed with fears that a German-Soviet war had become more likely since many people believed that Stalin would not sit back and allow the "annihilation of Yugoslavia."[92]

It took only a few hours after his return to Berlin for Hitler to resume thinking about Operation Barbarossa. On the evening of 28 April, he received Ambassador Schulenburg, who had heard rumours about Germany's preparations for invasion. Schulenburg tried to convince the Führer of the advantages of continuing cooperation with the Soviet Union, but his entreaties were brusquely rejected. Hitler complained about the Soviet-Yugoslav friendship and non-aggression pact 5 April, which he interpreted as evidence of Moscow's hostile intentions. When Schulenburg pointed out that Stalin was prepared to make "further-reaching concessions" and was willing to exceed the deliveries of supplies agreed to in the commercial treaty, Hitler terminated the conversation with the words: "And one more thing, Count Schulenburg: I am not planning a war on Russia!"[93] It was precisely this assurance that confirmed the mistrustful ambassador's worst fears. The decision to go to war had been taken a long time ago, he told a circle of intimates that evening.[94]

Equally fruitless was a memorandum Weizsäcker sent that same day to Ribbentrop in which the state secretary confessed that he too considered a war against the Soviet Union a "misfortune" that would only give the British "new moral momentum": "We would not only confirm that the war will continue for a long time," Weizsäcker wrote. "We would ourselves lengthen rather than shorten it."[95] But Ribbentrop had gone over completely to Hitler's line of reasoning and accused his deputy of once again "turning negative on the occasion of this big decision."[96] Unfazed by objections from professional diplomats and bolstered by the compliant attitude of his leading military commanders, on 30 April Hitler set the date for the start of Operation Barbarossa as 22 June.[97] He did not consider the delay caused by the Balkan campaign a serious factor. On the contrary, Hitler's most recent triumph had reaffirmed his belief that defeating the Red Army would be child's play.

"Nothing is impossible for the German soldier"—that was the main message of Hitler's address to the Reichstag on 4 May, in which he offered an account of the Balkan campaign that had just been ended. He combined his hymn to the performance of the Wehrmacht with repeated insults aimed at Churchill, whom he blamed for Germany getting mixed up in the Balkans. Yet the public reacted with unease to his appeal to German women to volunteer in greater numbers for work details and his concluding remark that the German soldier, who "already had the best weapons in the world," would be "getting even better ones this year and in the ones to follow."[98] Had the Führer not announced in his New Year's address that the war would be over in 1941, many people wondered? Even the devoted Goebbels was less than thrilled by Hitler's words. "A certain depression has come over us because we thought the war would be over this year," the propaganda minister wrote. "We have to prepare ourselves for certain psychological difficulties."[99]

Hitler followed through on his threat to break up Yugoslavia to reduce Serbian influence. "The Serbs have always stirred up trouble," he had declared on 7 April, one day after the start of the campaign. "It is now up to us to stop them."[100] The first step in that process was to recognise an independent state of Croatia on 15 April, which would also include Bosnia-Herzegovina. Ante Pavelić, the leader of the clerical-fascist Ustaše movement, was installed as head of state. To satisfy the competing demands not only of Germany's ally Italy but also of Hungary and Bulgaria for a portion of the spoils of war, lengthy negotiations were necessary. The Third Reich effectively annexed a large part of Slovenia, including Styria and Carniola, and placed the Serbian heartland under military administration. Italy received the rest of Slovenia, including the capital, Ljubljana, as well as most of Dalmatia and the majority of the Adriatic islands. Italy's satellite state Albania got most of Kosovo and western Macedonia. Bulgaria absorbed the rest of Macedonia proper, while Hungary had to be content with the return of Bačka and other territories it had been forced to cede after the First World War.[101] But the region was by no means "pacified." The continuing rivalries between nationalities, the resettlement and displacement of minorities in the annexed territories, the Ustaše's terrorising of Serbs, the brutality of the German occupiers—who were responsible for numerous massacres, including the murder of Jews in Serbia—and growing partisan resistance under Josip Broz Tito all ensured that the Balkans remained a source of instability and a "permanent ancillary theatre of war" that tied down significant Axis forces.[102]

On 9 May, Hitler returned to the Obersalzberg. Here, on the morning of 11 May, he received news that horrified the entire Nazi leadership: the day before, Rudolf Hess had flown to Britain on his own initiative to try to broker a peace settlement. There has been great speculation about his motives ever since. What is certain is that since the mid-1930s, despite the large number of offices he had secured in the struggles for power within the Third Reich, Hess had increasingly lost authority and influence. The former fellow inmate in

Landsberg Prison and private secretary of Hitler had been largely elbowed aside by his ambitious and scheming chief of staff, Martin Bormann. Although Hitler had honoured Hess in his Reichstag speech of 1 September 1939 by naming him second in line after Göring to succeed him, that did not prevent the deputy Führer, who was of a brooding disposition and fond of astrology and homeopathic medicine, from becoming ever more the outsider. "When I speak with Göring, it is like bathing in steel, and I feel refreshed," Speer quoted Hitler as saying in 1940. "With Hess every conversation turns into an intolerably torturous effort. He always arrives with unpleasant things and refuses to relent."[103] It is entirely possible that by flying to Britain, Hess was trying to reclaim lost ground and get back into Hitler's good books, acting in what he believed to be the Führer's interests.

Hess had conceived the idea of a peace initiative in the summer of 1940, after London had rebuffed Hitler's overtures and preparations for Operation Sea Lion had commenced. In late August he consulted with his old mentor and father figure Karl Haushofer about whether it would be possible to extend feelers to circles in Britain working for peace in order to "stave off something utterly ominous."[104] For a time, Haushofer's son Albrecht was engaged as a mediator since he had good connections in Britain that included the Duke of Hamilton in Scotland, with whom Hess was also acquainted. But attempts to establish contact bore no fruit.[105] Thus from November 1940, the Führer's deputy gradually became convinced to go all-in and fly to Britain on a personal mission. As an experienced pilot, who had continued to pursue his love of flying as Hitler's private secretary despite the Führer's disapproval, Hess considered himself able to carry out such a risky enterprise.[106] In preparation, he undertook some trial flights in a Messerschmitt two-engine fighter, the Me-110. In the spring of 1941, when Hess got wind of the planned attack on the Soviet Union, he concluded he had no time left to lose.[107]

Hess failed to show up at a conference for Gauleiters and Reichsleiters on 5 May; nobody could explain his absence.[108] On the evening of 10 May, the deputy Führer appeared at the Haunstetten airstrip near Augsburg, got into a fighter plane, flew down the Rhine, crossed the North Sea and reached the west coast of Scotland at around 10 p.m. One hour later, he parachuted to the ground near the Hamiltons' estate in Dungavel, spraining his foot in the process. The plane crashed and was destroyed. Members of the Scottish Home Guard took the pilot, who told them his name was Captain Alfred Horn, into custody. Hess insisted that he had to see the Duke of Hamilton, for whom he had an important message. The letter he carried with him had been translated into English by the head of the Nazi Foreign Organisation, Ernst Wilhelm Bohle, who had no idea that Hess intended to deliver it to Britain himself.[109]

It was not until the following afternoon that Hamilton was convinced the strange prisoner was in fact the deputy Führer of Nazi Germany. He called the Foreign Office and also communicated the news that evening to Churchill, who was staying at Ditchley Park in Oxfordshire. "Hess or no Hess, I am going to watch the Marx Brothers," the indignant prime minister is said to have responded.[110] After some back and forth, it was decided to send Sir Ivone Kirkpatrick, the former secretary with the British embassy in Berlin, to Scotland to investigate the mysterious mission of the Führer's deputy. In three interrogations on 13–15 May, it emerged that Hess had not brought any offers that went beyond those made by Hitler in October 1939 and July 1940. "He had come here without the knowledge of Hitler," Kirkpatrick reported, "in order to convince responsible persons that since England could not win the war, the wisest course was to make peace now. From a long and intimate knowledge of the Führer . . . he could give his word of honour that the Führer had never entertained any designs against the British Empire. Nor had he ever aspired to world domination. He believed that Germany's sphere of interest was in Europe and that any dissipation of Germany's strength beyond Europe's frontiers would be a weakness and would carry with it the seeds of Germany's destruction."[111] All Hess was offering, therefore, was the familiar deal of a free hand for Germany on the European continent in return for a free hand for Britain in its empire. It was a sign of how blind Hitler's deputy was that he thought this would impress the British leadership.

How did Hitler and those around him react to Hess's mission? On the morning of 11 May, a Sunday, the atmosphere at the Berghof was deceptively calm, when Karlheinz Pintsch, one of Hess's two adjutants, announced that he needed to speak with Hitler about a matter of urgency. The dictator, who was still asleep, was awakened by his valet

Linge and went from his private quarters to the Berghof's Great Hall. There Pintsch handed him an envelope with the words: "My Führer, I have been charged by Mr. Hess to deliver this letter."[112] Hitler read the letter and was immediately overcome with an "enormous agitation" that quickly spread to his entire entourage.[113] Speer, who had been summoned to the Obersalzberg with some architectural blueprints, recalled hearing an "inarticulate, almost animalistic cry" followed by the dictator shouting: "Get me Bormann immediately! Where is Bormann?"[114] Turning to Göring's representative General Karl Bodenschatz, Hitler bellowed: "How is it possible, General, that the Luftwaffe allowed Hess to fly an aeroplane after I expressly forbade that?"[115]

Hess's letter has never been found,[116] but we know what it contained from a summary by Nazi press spokesman Otto Dietrich, who was given it to read several days later. Hess tried in verbose fashion to explain his motivations to the Führer. He claimed that he had not embarked on this "most daring flight" out of "cowardice or weakness" but rather out of his conviction that he was responding to Hitler's deepest wish for an Anglo-German understanding. Hess characterised the goal of his mission as "the establishment of contact between England and Germany by extending personal feelers towards English acquaintances of his, which he considered necessary in the interest of both peoples, in order to make a serious effort to end the war through negotiations." He had been forced to conceal his plan, Hess added, because he knew that Hitler would have forbidden him to fly to England.[117] The tenor of the letter, in Dietrich's recapitulation, is consistent with the farewell letter Hess would address to Hitler on 14 June, the day before his first suicide attempt in Britain. In that letter, Hess thanked Hitler profusely for "everything you have given and meant to me." He continued: "I die in the conviction that even if my last act ends in death it will bear fruit somehow. Perhaps despite or precisely because of my death, my flight will bring about peace and understanding with England."[118]

In one fell swoop, the Berghof was ripped from its Sunday torpor and became a hive of activity. While the private guests were asked to withdraw to the upper floor, Hitler and Bormann pondered what to do next. At 2 p.m., Hitler called Göring, who was staying in Veldenstein Castle near Nuremberg, which he had acquired two years earlier, and ordered him to come to Berchtesgaden immediately. "Something terrible has happened," Hitler told him. Ribbentrop was also summoned from Fuschl Castle near Salzburg.[119] By the afternoon Hitler had sufficiently recovered his composure that he could receive Admiral Darlan—since February the deputy French president and designated successor to Pétain—for a discussion about the prospects of closer Franco-German cooperation. But all the participants at the meeting had the impression that he was "not concentrating on the matter at hand."[120] Hitler could not stop thinking about Hess and the potential consequences of his flight. He was particularly unsettled by the idea that the British might now have a trump card in the propaganda war. "Imagine—Churchill now has Hess in his hand," Hitler's adjutant Julius Schaub recalled the Führer's remarks. "They will give Hess medication and make him go on the radio and say whatever Churchill wants him to say. I will not be able to deny that it is Hess's voice. Everyone knows it."[121]

There was no way of knowing whether Hess had actually arrived in Scotland or whether his plane might have crashed somewhere along the way. Hitler debated this question with Göring, who arrived at the Berghof at 9 p.m., and Luftwaffe general Ernst Udet until deep into the night and the following day. Hewel noted that "Göring and Udet are of the opinion that Hess could not have made the difficult flight to Glasgow because flying the latest aircraft requires a maximum of skill. But the Führer believes in Hess's abilities."[122] Despite the uncertainty as to the fate of the deputy Führer, Hitler decided on the afternoon of 12 May to release a public statement and dictated a message to be read out on all German radio stations at 8 p.m. Although the Führer had explicitly forbidden him any "flying activities," the message read, Hess had commandeered an aircraft and set off on a flight on 10 May, from which he had yet to return. It had to be assumed that he had "crashed or suffered an accident somewhere." The message did not specify the destination or the motivation of Hess's flight. Instead the deputy Führer was declared to have lost his mind. A letter he had left behind, it was claimed, showed "in its confused nature the unfortunate signs of a mental breakdown, giving rise to fears that Party Comrade Hess has become the victim of delusions."[123] In Berlin, Goebbels, who had only a little earlier received the news about Hess, together with orders to have Hitler's statements broadcast immediately, was appalled. "It is a major, almost unbearable blow," he noted. "What a spectacle for the world: the second man in line to the Führer mentally unstable. Horrifying and unimaginable. All we can do now is grit our teeth."[124]

On the morning of 13 May, the propaganda minister arrived at the Berghof, where Hitler was waiting to brief him on the details of the affair. "Nobody will believe us that Hess acted on his own initiative," Goebbels noted. "It was a crazy breach of discipline. He is done as far as the Führer is concerned. Hitler is utterly shocked. He is spared nothing. Hitler speaks of Hess in the harshest terms although he concedes [Hess possessed] a certain idealism."[125] In the meantime, the BBC had reported that the Führer's deputy had parachuted into Scotland and had been arrested and positively identified by the Home Guard.[126] In response, Hitler and Goebbels drew up a second statement that appeared in the German press on 14 May. It referred to the BBC report and admitted that Hess's "personal step" had been motivated by the assumption that he could arrange a truce between Germany and England. That statement too advanced the theory that Hess had lost his mind. He had suffered from health problems for quite some time, it was claimed, and had increasingly consulted "magnetists, astrologers etc." who were partially responsible for his mental confusion. People within the Nazi Party expressed their regrets that "this idealist has fallen victim to such a terrible delusion."[127]

Security Service reports agreed that the official announcements had caused "grave concern" in the populace and "deep depression" in party circles.[128] Immediately after the broadcast of the first statement on the evening of 12 May, Goebbels was flooded by calls from Gauleiters and Reichsleiters. "No one wants to believe this insanity," the propaganda minister noted. "It sounds so absurd that people are completely mystified."[129] Without doubt, the affair had led to a "painful loss of prestige abroad and domestically," reported a Danish diplomat from Berlin.[130]

Hitler's opponents interpreted Hess's flight as an early sign of disagreements at the top of the Third Reich. "The first man to jump off the government carriage is Rudolf Hess," Friedrich Kellner noted with satisfaction. "This is an unusually heavy blow for the system. Will the entire structure begin to quiver? What is going on?"[131] People did not believe the official version of a mental breakdown. "The physical and technical demands [of the flight] alone prove that Hess cannot be deemed crazy," Ullrich von Hassel wrote, voicing a common opinion.[132] The German press and German radio merely passed along the two government statements. Otherwise they were under orders to say nothing about the affair, and that opened the door to rumour and speculation. Jokes circulated and doggerel verse was composed. "There is a song throughout the land, / We're going to go to Eng-el-land. / But when someone makes the journey, / They tell everyone he's crazy," people recited in Berlin.[133] In Dresden, they quipped: "A brown budgie has escaped its cage. If captured, please return to the Chancellery."[134]

But for one person, Hess's misadventure was a stroke of good fortune. On 12 May, Hitler decreed that the Office of the Führer's Deputy was to be renamed the Party Chancellery and would be subordinated to himself personally. Martin Bormann was put in charge, and he was soon given the authority of a Reich minister and a member of the Reich Defence Council. The ever-willing vassal of the Führer had climbed up another rung of the career ladder that would eventually make him one of the most powerful and feared functionaries in the Third Reich.[135] Thus it was no wonder that he was the only one who remained "relaxed and cheerful" during those heady days at the Berghof. Hitler's adjutants agreed that Bormann believed "his hour had finally come."[136] Goebbels tracked Bormann's rise enviously, writing that he had "cheated his way into his position more than earned it" and "acted disloyally" towards Hess. "Hess was short-sighted but honest," Goebbels noted. "By contrast, what can we expect from Bormann?"[137]

In alliance with Himmler, Bormann immediately went after subordinates, relatives and friends of his former boss. Hess's adjutants Pintsch and Alfred Leitgen were arrested and brought to the Sachsenhausen concentration camp. After talking with Bohle, Heydrich, the head of the Reich Security Main Office, believed that Hess had been heavily influenced by the two Haushofers.[138] Karl Haushofer was interrogated for days by the Gestapo and then placed under house arrest while his son Albrecht was jailed for several months. Hess's brother Alfred, the deputy head of the Nazi Party Foreign Organisation, was stripped of his office and thrown out of the party. Ernst Schulte-Strathaus, the man responsible for cultural matters on Hess's staff and who had provided his boss with astrological predictions, was also arrested and taken to Sachsenhausen. In addition, Bormann did everything he could to spread libellous rumours about his former patron and isolate the Hess family.[139] Elsa Bruckmann, wife of a Munich publisher, was one of the few Hitler intimates who did not break off all relations with the family. In a letter of gratitude to her, Hess's wife Ilse rejected the official version of events, writing that her husband had "certainly not been trapped by a delusional idea" but had calculated the effects of his mission "clearly and soberly in the interests of the Führer and of Germany."[140] Ilse Hess never wavered from this account. Months later, in a letter to the nationalist novelist Hans Grimm, she insisted that both she and her husband had been "obviously defamed" but would "remain faithful to the law according to which we volunteered in 1920 to serve under the flag of the Führer."[141]

On the evening of 12 May, Bormann summoned the Reichsleiters and Gauleiters to the Obersalzberg for the following afternoon.[142] The point of the meeting was to brief the restive party leadership about the mysterious events surrounding Hess and to get them to renew their loyalty to the Führer. Bormann started by reading out Hess's letter of farewell. Then, around 5 p.m., Hitler himself appeared. Baldur von Schirach, who had been the Gauleiter and Reich governor in Vienna since late June 1940, was shocked at how exhausted he looked: "Three days after his deputy absconded, he still seemed shocked by the blow. His eyes were bloodshot. He spoke softly, his voice quaking with agitation."[143] Hitler laid into Hess, accusing his deputy of "acting without his knowledge" and of putting him in an "impossible position, particularly *vis-à-vis* Italy." He had sent Ribbentrop to Rome, Hitler continued, to "reassure the Duce, who would have assumed that Germany had sent Hess to Britain to negotiate behind his back." Hess had always been "rather idiosyncratic," Hitler complained, and associated with the "strangest of people," most notably astrologers. He had defied Hitler's express prohibition on flying planes, had had a Messerschmitt specially equipped for his purposes, had been regularly procuring weather reports and had managed to make it solo to Scotland in four hours, "which was, in any case, a good performance for a pilot."[144] Amid all the turmoil, it seems that Hitler did not notice that his acknowledgement of that achievement to some extent contradicted his depiction of Hess as mentally unstable.

Hitler's appeal to the loyalty of his paladins had the desired effect. At the end of the meeting, the Reichsleiters and Gauleiters gathered around him in a silent semi-circle. "A very moving event," Hewel noted before repeating a phrase of Goebbels'. "A feeling of pity: the Führer is never spared anything."[145] Goebbels wrote that after the "initial surprise," "boundless outrage" had set in. "Everyone is now tightly bound with the Führer," he added. "Now our task is to stick together and stay strong."[146]

There has been speculation ever since that Hitler knew about—and perhaps even encouraged—Hess's plans. But both his spontaneous reaction on the morning of 11 May as well as his behaviour in the days that followed clearly suggest that the Führer was utterly shocked and had not the slightest understanding for the actions of his deputy. Why would he have approved of a mission that he believed, after all his rejected overtures towards Britain, was doomed to fail? Why would he have run the risk of the British government learning from the uninvited peacemaker what had been kept a strict secret: that Germany was about to attack the Soviet Union? And why would he voluntarily have put himself in a situation that reflected badly on him in relation to his Axis allies? Rome was extremely alarmed by the Hess affair, and Ribbentrop had difficulty convincing Mussolini that the German government was not behind it.[147] All in all, it is almost certain that Hess set out on his journey without Hitler's knowledge or approval—albeit in the mistaken belief that he was serving his Führer.[148]

The Nazi leadership followed a double strategy in its attempt to reassure the agitated German public. Firstly, Goebbels instructed newspapers and radio broadcasters to focus "energetically" on other topics and pretend that nothing had happened. "The affair must be systematically buried in silence," the propaganda minister decreed.[149] Secondly, on the Obersalzberg on 13 May, the Reichsleiters and Gauleiters received orders to convince party members by word of mouth that Hess was a traitor who had divorced himself from Hitler's inner circle and whose departure was no cause for regret.[150] This strategy worked. After only a few days, Goebbels noted that interest in the Hess case had diminished and the public was turning its attention to other issues. "That is how quick things move in these lively times," the propaganda minister concluded. "Hess should have known that himself."[151] Hitler too seems to have swiftly got over the shock at the news of 11 May. "Führer once again fresh and relaxed," Hewel noted on 19 May.[152]

Nonetheless, one uncertainty remained. How would the British government treat its famous captive? What political and propagandistic capital would it be able to derive from him? Above all, the Nazi leadership feared that the British would be able to force Hess to reveal compromising details about Hitler and his inner circle. "I tremble at the thought that this could happen," Goebbels admitted. "But it seems that once again a guardian angel is watching over us. We are dealing with stupid dilettantes over there."[153] The British government was, however, by no means dilettantish in its handling of Hess. On the contrary, it used the affair in a series of sophisticated diplomatic manoeuvres to improve its own difficult position in the fight against the Third Reich. Thus, British diplomats signalled to the Soviet Union that Hess's mission had been a serious peace offer and that certain circles in Britain were inclined to accept it. The nightmare scenario of Anglo-German rapprochement was supposed to motivate Stalin to distance himself from Hitler and make him more receptive to Britain. London also used the Hess imbroglio to spread rumours about a possible Anglo-German cease-fire in Washington. It was hoped that this would lead the United States to increase its support for the British war effort.[154]

On 11 March, Roosevelt had signed the Lend-Lease Act, which allowed the US president to place all sorts of arms at the disposal of "the government of any country whose defense the President deems vital to the defense of the United States."[155] The act was passed specifically with Britain in mind and moved America one step closer to joining the conflict, even if its assistance had yet to have any real effect. The Germans took this measure very seriously, interpreting it as tantamount to a declaration of war.[156] Roosevelt had finally "let the cat out of the bag," Hitler spat, adding that if he had been looking for a pretext for waging war on the United States, the Americans had obliged. Hitler believed that a direct confrontation with the US would come "one way or another" but felt that it did not suit him at the moment.[157] After all, the Führer intended to defeat the Soviet Union before turning his attention to his Anglo-Saxon foes.

Roosevelt, too, shied away from all-out war because of the continuing strength of isolationist tendencies in America. He deflected

Churchill's idea of the US Navy protecting English commercial vessels against German submarine attacks in the North Atlantic and was unwilling to go further than expanding a "security zone" for navy patrols to the 25th Parallel.[158] Hitler had no interest in ramping up a confrontation with the United States so close to the start of Operation Barbarossa, and he instructed the German naval command to avoid incidents with American ships at all costs.[159] After a meeting between Hitler, Keitel and Raeder on 22 May, Hewel noted: "Führer still vacillating in his stance towards America. 'It is impossible to see into Roosevelt's soul.' . . . Without the US, war will be over this year. With the US, it will last many years."[160] The next day, Hitler received the former US ambassador to Belgium and *Life* magazine correspondent John Cudahy for an interview. The Führer began by insisting that "convoys mean war." He also sought to convince Cudahy that rumours about German plans for an invasion in the western hemisphere were nonsense. The idea, Hitler claimed, was as "fantastic as an invasion of the moon." German armed forces, he argued, were concentrating on short-distance expeditions such as the 100 kilometres to Crete or the "40 kilometres of open water" to England, not the 4,000-plus kilometres to America.[161]

Yet Washington was in no doubt that if Britain were to drop out of the war, Hitler would set his sights on the United States. Uneasy at the rumours of Britain concluding a separate peace with Nazi Germany, Roosevelt decided to send an unmistakable signal. In a radio broadcast on the evening of 27 May, one of the series that became known as "fireside chats," he declared an "unlimited national emergency" that required "the strengthening of our defense to the absolute limits of our national power and authority."[162] But he did not specify what that meant in practical terms. "Roosevelt has spoken," noted Goebbels. "Proclaimed a national emergency. But drew no consequences. We will have to wait and see what he will do. In any case, there was no talk of war in the short term."[163]

However, Hitler and his inner circle had been shocked that very morning by the news of the sinking of the MS *Bismarck*. The battleship, which had been sailing in the North Atlantic, had sunk Britain's largest warship, HMS *Hood*, three days before but had been hit in the rudder by a torpedo and been left unable to manoeuvre. A Royal Navy squadron had then destroyed it and 2,300 German sailors had gone down with the ship. The mood at the Berghof was "very depressed."[164] Hitler had sent a late-night telegram to the captain of the *Bismarck*, Admiral Günther Lütjens, encouraging him to hold out and telling him that "all of Germany is with you." Now the Führer flew into a rage, ordering that in future no German battleship or cruiser would be allowed to set sail into the Atlantic without his express approval.[165]

Operation Mercury—the occupation of Crete, which Hitler had ordered on 25 April after the end of the Balkan campaign—was also proving a costly endeavour.[166] The invasion had begun on 20 May with the landing of German paratroopers and paragliders but would not be completed until 2 June. By then, 15,000 British, Australian and New Zealand troops had been evacuated from the island, while more than 12,000 Allied soldiers had been captured and almost 1,700 lost their lives. In addition, 1,800 British sailors had been killed. But German casualties were also high. The paratrooper units had recorded 1,600 men killed and 1,400 missing in action—more men than the Wehrmacht had lost in the Yugoslav and Greek campaigns combined. The majority of German transport planes had also been destroyed. At the Berghof on 31 May, Göring spoke of the Luftwaffe's "bloodletting."[167] In response Hitler issued a ban on any such future landings, for example in Malta or Cyprus.

Undivided attention now returned to the campaign against the Soviet Union. In an edict on 23 May, Hitler approved support for the Axis-friendly Iraqi government of General Rashid al-Gailani, who had seized power in a coup, but also stressed: "Whether and how we will topple the English positions between the Mediterranean and the Persian Gulf . . . will only be decided after Barbarossa."[168]

By now officials at the Army and Wehrmacht High Commands were busy translating Hitler's ideological order of 30 March to prepare a war of annihilation against the Soviet Union into practical instructions for German troops. On 28 April, after negotiations between the army's Quartermaster General Wagner and Heydrich, Brauchitsch signed an order instructing the army to cooperate with the Security Police and Security Service. It specified that in the theatre of operations special Security Police and Security Service commandos would be deployed "to undertake specific security tasks beyond those of the troops." The commandos were empowered to carry out executive measures against civilians "on their own authority," falling under army command only with regard to "travel, quarters and provisions."[169] On 13 May, in Hitler's name, Keitel issued the final "Edict on the Exercise of Martial Law in the Barbarossa Territory and Special Measures." The first part of the edict was concerned with "the treatment of crimes by enemy civilians," who were to be "removed until further notice" from the authority of courts-martial. Partisans were to be "done away with remorselessly whether they fight or flee," and all other hostilities by enemy civilians were to be "put down . . . by extreme means including physical annihilation." Troop leaders were ordered to use "collective physical punishment" in places where German soldiers were attacked "from behind or treacherously" in so far as "the circumstances do not allow for quick apprehension of individual perpetrators." The second part of the order determined that members of the Wehrmacht were not to be held accountable for their actions against civilians, "even if their deeds qualify as military crimes and transgressions."[170] These orders removed the final remnants of conventional military legal responsibility. Murderous soldiers could essentially do whatever they wanted to the civilian population.

Brauchitsch seems to have had second thoughts, however, when he passed on the Wehrmacht Supreme Command's order to the army groups and armies. In a supplemental order on 24 May, he sought to water down the instructions. "The more severe interventions," he told his subordinates, should only be considered in "serious cases of rebellion," while "infractions of a lesser nature" should be punished less harshly. The task of commanding officers was to "prevent excesses by individual members of the army" and "ward off rampant behaviour among the troops in timely fashion."[171] Nonetheless, these qualifications did nothing to rescind the earlier order freeing soldiers from legal responsibility. If anything, the former reaffirmed the core of the latter. Bock was highly critical of the Wehrmacht Supreme Command's order, writing in his diary that it "gives every soldier a *de facto* right . . . to shoot, from the front or the back, every Russian he thinks or pretends to think might be a partisan . . . [This is] intolerable and incompatible with manly discipline."[172] As had been the case in the Polish campaign, the German military leadership's reservations were not primarily of a legal or humanitarian nature: the generals were

mostly concerned with a potential loss of control. Brauchitsch had
little difficulty convincing Bock that his supplementary order had
addressed this concern.[173]

Closely connected to the Wehrmacht Supreme Command's order
were its "Guidelines for the Treatment of Political Commissars," issued
to the army leadership on 6 June. Commanders did not need to read
further than the preamble to receive an ideological justification for
systematic murder, as it accused the other side of practising what the
Germans now intended to do themselves: "In the fight against
Bolshevism, there is no reason to assume the enemy will behave in
accordance with the principles of humanity or international law.
Hateful, terrible and inhumane treatment of our prisoners is to be
expected particularly from political commissars of all types, who will
be the ones leading the resistance." For that reason there was no place
for "mildness and recourse to international law [when dealing with]
these elements." As they were the "ones who introduced barbaric,
Asian fighting methods," if captured "in battle or resistance" they
were to be separated from the rest of the prisoners and liquidated
immediately. Non-military commissars not suspected of partisan activities—that is, civilian Soviet functionaries—were to be "initially
spared." Only later in the campaign would it be decided whether they
should be "left as they were or handed over to the special commandos."[174]
The fates of these people thus rested with the arbitrary decisions of
commanding officers.

Thirty copies of the commissar order were handed out to the
commanders of the army groups, armies and tank forces in the east and
passed down the line of command—from army corps and divisions to
regiments, battalions and companies—in the final two weeks before
Germany attacked the Soviet Union. As Felix Römer has shown after
painstaking research in the archives, orders were handed down "mostly
without friction and with an impressive routine."[175] On 20 June, for
example, two days before the start of the invasion, the commander of
the 27th Infantry Regiment (of the 16th Army of Army Group North)
acquainted his officers with the commissar order and told them that "a
war of world views" was at hand. "The mood is excellent," noted company
commander Theodor Habicht, a former Nazi Party official in Austria.[176]

After 1945, most German troop commanders claimed that in the
run-up to the invasion they had rejected the commissar order and

then done everything they could to see that it was not enforced. But that simply is not true. Whereas the order granting SS troops and others immunity had caused concern among some military leaders, the commissar guidelines enjoyed broad popularity. Commanders had no doubt largely internalised the demonised image of the Soviet political commissar upon which the order was based and thus had no scruples about helping Hitler realise his criminal goals. They acted not because they were under orders, as many later tried to claim, but because they agreed ideologically with the Führer. There were only isolated cases of resistance from low-level leaders. Several officers expressed unease and sought to qualify the guidelines somewhat. But to follow Römer, such modifications usually concerned the execution but not the goal of the order: "Ultimately, they did not alter at all the fate of the commissars who were taken prisoner. At most, all they meant was a short-term, insignificant delay."[177]

Alongside the immunity and commissar orders, "Guidelines for the Conduct of Troops in Russia" completed the complex of commands that would turn the eastern campaign into a unique racist war of ideology and annihilation. The opening sentences left no doubt as to the ultimate purpose of the campaign: "Bolshevism is the mortal enemy of the National Socialist, German people. Germany's battle is directed against this corrosive world view and those who maintain it. This struggle demands remorseless, energetic action against Bolshevist rabble-rousers, partisans, saboteurs and Jews, and the complete erad- ication of any active or passive resistance."[178] The guidelines were supplemented by the "Regulations about Prisoners of War during Operation Barbarossa" of 16 June, which required German soldiers to maintain "cautious distance and extreme vigilance" towards Red Army captives since "treacherous behaviour" was to be expected, "particu- larly from prisoners of war from Asian backgrounds." One sentence ominously foreshadowed the later murder of millions of Soviet captives whom the German army starved to death: "A special order will be issued about how to provide for prisoners of war."[179]

In early April 1941, in a private conversation, Hitler had assured the chief Nazi Party ideologue and fanatical anti-Bolshevist Alfred Rosenberg, who had been somewhat sidelined since the non-aggression pact: "Rosenberg, your hour is at hand!"[180] Hitler told him to set up an office for "eastern tasks" and appointed him his commissioner for the central administration of eastern European affairs. In a number of memorandums, Rosenberg developed his thoughts about the future civil administration of the conquered territories, the responsibilities of the planned "Reich commissionerships," and the filling of these new positions with fanatical National Socialists.[181]

But Operation Barbarossa was conceived not just as a pitiless battle of opposing world views, but also as a colonial war of plunder. It was not only about breaking up the Soviet Union and annihilating Bolshevism, but about maximising the economic exploitation of food and raw materials from the occupied territories. Under the auspices of the Office for the War Economy and Armaments, an "Economic Staff East" was created to coordinate the ruthless plundering of eastern Europe.[182] The plans accepted that millions of Soviet citizens would starve to death. On 2 May, the state secretaries of all the larger ministries, including Herbert Backe from the Ministry of Food and Agriculture, met with the head of the War Economy and Armaments Office, General Georg Thomas. Notes taken at that meeting read: "1. The war can only continue in its third year if the entire Wehrmacht is fed by Russia. 2. Without doubt untold millions of people will starve if what is necessary for our survival is extracted from the land."[183] The plans for Germany's eastern campaign were without parallel in their contempt for human life. Civilian and military experts were certain that they were fulfilling the "will of the Führer" as they now competed to put directives from on high into action.

In the final weeks before the start of Operation Barbarossa, rumours spread throughout Germany that the attack on the Soviet Union was imminent. There was no way to keep people from noticing the fact that troops continued to be transferred to the Third Reich's eastern border. "Day and night giant convoys roll towards the east, and the columns of marching soldiers stretch for 30 to 50 kilometres," the infantry general and army corps commander Gotthard Heinrici wrote to his wife. "The streets are humming, and everything is wrapped in impenetrable clouds of dust."[184] A Security Service report of early May singled out letters sent home from soldiers stationed on the Russian border as the main source of the increasing rumours.[185] The general uncertainty was evident in a letter Walter Frick sent to his father: "The month of June has to bring some clarity about what is going on. We will be able to breathe easily if we finally know 'whether we will' or 'whether we won't' . . . Rumours of all sorts are flying around, and to amuse ourselves we sometimes swap the sensationalist stories we have picked up."[186]

The confusion was the result of a conscious strategy from on high. The Wehrmacht leadership and the Propaganda Ministry worked hand in hand to conceal Germany's preparations for the invasion. "Fantastic rumours about Russia," Goebbels noted on 2 May. "People are gradually figuring us out. There are so many lies that truth and swindle can scarcely be distinguished. That is best for us at the moment."[187] To distract public attention away from the Soviet Union, Goebbels spread reports in the Swiss press that Germany was about to invade Britain.[188] Thus it was all the more embarrassing for Goebbels when one of his subordinates, foreign press chief Karl Bömer, openly referred to Operation Barbarossa in a drunken conversation with Bulgarian journalists. Hitler was so incensed that, over Goebbels' objections, he called in the Gestapo and had Bömer brought up before the People's Court, which sentenced him to two years in prison.[189]

In late May, Goebbels intensified his efforts to muddy the waters with false reports. In conjunction with the Wehrmacht Supreme Command, and with Hitler's approval, he came up with a particularly impertinent deception. On 13 June, only a few days before the invasion, he published an article headed "Crete as an Example" in the *Völkischer Beobachter*. The piece was written to make it seem as though the author had unintentionally revealed an imminent invasion of Britain. To reinforce that impression, German police then confiscated most of that edition of the newspaper. "Everything is set up to conceal the mission in the east," Goebbels boasted: "a masterpiece of deception!"[190] And the ruse seems to have worked. "English radio explains that our build-up against Russia was a bluff behind which we were trying to conceal our invasion plans," a satisfied Goebbels wrote. "And that was the whole point of the exercise."[191]

As part of this strategy of concealment, Hitler had resided on the Obersalzberg without interruption since early May. There he seemed to be enjoying a relatively normal life, spending his evenings with his close associates and taxing their patience with endless monologues. But the closer the date for the invasion, the more nervous he became. In early June, he had a long conversation with Hewel about the Soviet campaign's prospects for success. "Difficult enterprise but has trust in the Wehrmacht," Hewel summarised the conversation. "Greatest build-up in history. If it fails, everything is lost anyway."[192] Such statements were all too typical of Hitler the political gambler and his all-or-nothing approach.

At a meeting with Mussolini at the Brenner Pass on 2 June, Hitler still did not say a word about the impending invasion. Instead he talked vaguely about the struggle "remaining difficult" but the worst being over for the Axis partners. The only danger, Hitler said, would be the loss of French North Africa, but that could be averted by "skilful diplomacy."[193] Afterwards, Mussolini told his foreign minister that Hitler had spent most of their conversation talking about Hess and that the Führer had wept.[194] Turning on the waterworks had long been part of Hitler's acting repertoire. In reality, he had long since got over the affair. After all, the political damage he had feared Hess's flight would bring had been limited.

Hitler was more forthright towards the Japanese ambassador, Hiroshi Oshima, whom he received the following day. German-Soviet relations, he said, had worsened and a war "perhaps could no longer be avoided." Finland and Romania would take part, Hitler continued, and he was convinced that the main operations would be concluded "within quite a short span of time." Hitler said it was entirely up to the government in Tokyo what position Japan took in a German-Soviet war, although Oshima came away with the impression that Japanese participation would be welcomed.[195] At a meeting with Oshima on 4 June, Ribbentrop reaffirmed what Hitler had said, but was careful to add that not many people were in the know on the matter, which was among "Germany's most important secrets." He therefore asked the Japanese government to be "extremely scrupulous" about maintaining confidentiality.[196]

As far as Romania's participation was concerned, Hitler had no need to employ his powers of persuasion when he let Antonescu in on his plans on 12 June in the Führerbau in Munich. Hardly had he begun to speak before the Romanian head of state declared that "the Slavic peril that had made itself felt over the centuries" had to be defeated "once and for all." Antonescu assured the Führer of Romania's unconditional support for his "most serious step in the east."[197]

★

On the morning of 13 June, after five weeks away from the capital, Hitler returned to Berlin.[198] The following day, he summoned the commanders of the army groups, armies and tank groups, together with the comparable ranks in the Luftwaffe and navy, to the Chancellery for a final meeting before the start of Barbarossa. To avoid attracting attention, the military commanders had to arrive at different times and use separate entrances to the building.[199] In the morning, the army leaders held briefings about the state of preparations. Contrary to his habit, Hitler only rarely interrupted them, "listening attentively and silently."[200]

After lunch, the dictator gave a "comprehensive political speech," in which he again laid out the strategic reasons for his decision to attack the Soviet Union.[201] "Russia is a major threat to Germany's rear, and we have to keep our backs free," he explained. "Once Russia has been subdued, England will have no more potential allies on the Continent, and only on the Continent can Germany be defeated." The British would give up their "hopeless continuation of the war," especially since assistance from the United States would "only become really felt in the summer of 1942 at the earliest."[202] The generals were abundantly familiar with Hitler's litany. What was new was the Führer's exhortation not to underestimate the Red Army. The Russians, Hitler suddenly opined, would "fight hard and put up stiff resistance."[203]

Did Hitler with his sense for coming dangers suspect that this campaign might take a different course than the one he and his generals anticipated? Those around the Führer were struck by how disquieted, even depressed, he seemed in the final days preceding Barbarossa. Russia seemed "uncanny" to him, he told his secretaries over their usual afternoon coffee in the Chancellery, "like the ghost ship in *The Flying Dutchman*." "Nothing at all can be known about Russia," he continued. ". . . It could be a gigantic soap bubble, but it could also be completely different."[204] If only they were already "ten weeks further on." Hitler admitted that he was well aware of the "great risk" entailed by his decision. It was like standing in front of a "closed door," he told Hewel, who recorded in his diary that Hitler had to take sleeping pills to get any peace at night.[205]

"The Führer is existing in a tension that is beyond description," Goebbels noted after a long private conversation in the Chancellery on the afternoon of 15 June, even though Hitler had been optimistic in front of his propaganda minister. "It will be a mass attack in the grandest style. No doubt the most enormous that history has ever seen . . . The Führer estimates the operation will take four months, while I think it will be less. Bolshevism will collapse like a house of cards. We are standing on the verge of an unprecedented victory." Goebbels felt "deep satisfaction" at the fact that the old National Socialists would be able to experience this triumph. The pact with Russia, he wrote, had been a "blemish on our crest of honour" that would now be washed off. "What we have fought against all our lives, we will now destroy," Goebbels crowed. Hitler agreed with these sentiments and revived arguments he had used in January 1940 in view of the atrocities committed in Poland: "Once we have achieved victory, no one will ask about our methods. We have already pushed things so far that we must achieve victory. Otherwise our entire people, with us at the top and everything we hold dear, will be wiped out."[206] Hitler was entirely aware of the unprecedented criminal nature of the impending war. Once begun, there would be no going back.

On 18 June, the Führer dictated an appeal to the "Soldiers on the Eastern Front!" For more than two decades, he said, "the Jewish-Bolshevist string-pullers in Moscow have tried to inflame not just Germany but all of Europe." In the months just past, the Soviet Union had constantly strengthened its troops on Germany's eastern border. To watch helplessly in the face of this threat would be "not just a sin of omission but a crime towards the German people and indeed Europe as a whole." Therefore the time had come to "resist this conspiracy of Jewish-Anglo-Saxon war-mongers and the equally Jewish powers in the Bolshevik headquarters in Moscow." Remarkably, Hitler characterised the impending campaign not only as a preventive war in anticipation of a Russian attack but as a battle to save "the entirety of European civilisation and culture."[207] In light of the criminal orders under which Operation Barbarossa was launched, this was the height of cynicism.

Hitler's appeal was printed on hundreds of thousands of flyers on 19 and 20 June, which were taken under the tightest security to the eastern front, where they were to be distributed to troops on Day X. As a precautionary measure, Goebbels had the workers who had produced the flyers locked up inside the printing building. "This whole procedure is very awkward, but it is the only way to guarantee secrecy," Goebbels noted.[208] In the night of 20–21 June, on Hitler's command, the Wehrmacht Supreme Command transmitted the code word "Dortmund," signalling that the attack was to commence in the early hours of 22 June.[209] Hitler decided that it was now time to inform Mussolini. On 21 June, he wrote the Duce a long letter, which Germany's chargé d'affaires in Rome delivered at 3:00 the next morning, only a quarter of an hour before the start of the invasion. Whatever might happen, Hitler wrote, the situation of the Axis "could only get better, not worse" by taking this step. Hitler added that he now felt "liberated inside" and that the cooperation with Russia had "often weighed upon him" since it had entailed a break with his earlier beliefs and all the ideas he had maintained since he was a young man.[210]

Of course, the build-up of a million-strong army on the Soviet Union's western border could hardly remain concealed from the government in Moscow, but Stalin was convinced that Hitler would never run the risk of a two-front war. So he ignored all the warnings reaching him from various sides. On 13 May, he had the Soviet news agency TASS denounce all the rumours of an impending German attack as "completely baseless."[211] Goebbels could hardly believe it. "Russia has issued a formal denial," he noted. "It says it knows nothing about any intentions by the Reich to attack. We are redeploying our troops for some other reason. In any case, Moscow is doing nothing about our alleged intention to attack. Fantastic!"[212] To deceive the public even further, the propaganda minister spread the rumour that Stalin would visit Berlin shortly and red flags were being frantically stitched together for the occasion.[213] Spreading like wildfire through Germany, it seems that these stories were believed by many people.[214]

Even when the Soviet minister of state security, Vsevolod Merkulov, presented reliable reports that Germany had completed its invasion preparations on 16 June, Stalin dismissed them as misinformation. And when Defence Minister Semyon Timoshenko and the chief of the general staff, Georgy Zhukov, demanded that Russian forces be put on alert, the Soviet dictator persisted in his deluded estimation of the situation. Germany, he insisted, would "never fight Russia alone."[215] Thus the Red Army was largely unprepared for the German attack.

Still, the Nazi leadership was worried that the Soviet government would find out at the last minute what they were up to. When on 18 June the Soviet ambassador in Berlin, Vladimir Dekanozov, asked for a meeting with Weizsäcker, German diplomats were alarmed. "What will he be bringing?" Hewel wondered. "Is Stalin about to land another coup? A major offer etc.? Long conversation between the foreign minister, Engel and myself, weighing up all alternatives. The Führer and foreign minister have to disappear—must be unreachable."[216] That evening, however, Ribbentrop had good news. Dekanozov had only spoken with Weizsäcker "in a relaxed, cheerful mood about minor ongoing matters."[217] On 21 June, Dekanozov again announced himself to the Foreign Ministry, bringing a note from his government in which the Kremlin complained about repeated violations of Soviet airspace by German reconnaissance planes. Ribbentrop pretended to be unavailable. Weizsäcker only accepted the note in the evening, at 9:30, but refused to discuss the matter before an official statement by the German government had been issued. Instead he drew Dekanozov's attention to alleged Russian border violations.[218]

At 3:15 a.m. on 22 June, 160 divisions with more than three million soldiers and over three thousand tanks attacked the Soviet Union. A quarter of an hour later, Ribbentrop informed the visibly shocked Soviet ambassador that the Third Reich saw itself compelled in light of the threat on its eastern border to take "military counter-measures." The term "declaration of war" did not occur in the memorandum Ribbentrop read out.[219] At 5:30 a.m., Franz Liszt's "Les Préludes" sounded on all German radio stations: after much deliberation, Goebbels had settled on that work as a new fanfare of war. The propaganda minister then read out Hitler's proclamation to the German people, which aside from a few minor deviations was identical to the dictator's appeal to the "Soldiers on the Eastern Front."[220] At 6 a.m., Ribbentrop called a press conference in the Foreign Ministry to announce the news of the German military offensive to a crowd of sleepy-eyed German and international journalists. Ribbentrop justified the action, following Hitler's terminology, as a preventative answer to aggression planned by the Soviet Union.[221]

The idea, put out into the world by German propaganda, that Germany was engaging in a pre-emptive war has had an astonishing longevity and has been revived perennially by ultra-conservative Russophobic historians.[222] In reality, there is no evidence whatever that the Soviet Union had any intention of attacking Nazi Germany in June 1941. On the contrary, Stalin's entire policy was focused on not giving Hitler a pretext to attack. The redeployment of strong Red Army forces to the Soviet Union's western border was a precautionary measure for the worst-case scenario, nothing more. Indeed, the German side did not view them as a threat, but rather a factor that favoured their own plans for a Blitzkrieg-style strike. "The Russians are massing on the border," wrote Goebbels on 16 June. "It is the best thing that can possibly happen for us."[223] The leadership in Berlin was only concerned that Stalin could "ruin our concept with a gesture of compromise at the last hour."[224] Shortly before the start of Operation Barbarossa, Hitler appeared relieved, as though a "mountain of pressure" had been lifted from him. "This cancerous tumour must be burned out," he told Goebbels before retiring to his private apartment in the Chancellery at 2:30 a.m. on the fateful day. "Stalin will fall."[225]

In the German population, news of the attack on the Soviet Union caused "great surprise" and a "certain dismay," since people had assumed the signs pointed to a relaxation in German-Soviet relations after the rumours that Stalin was about to visit Berlin.[226] The realisation that they had been misled by German propaganda was mixed with concerns that the war could be prolonged indefinitely. "We are all very despondent," wrote a military doctor from Gummersbach in his diary. "Hitler is a madman! What will come of this?"[227] There was less enthusiasm than ever before for this latest military campaign. Even Goebbels had to admit that the populace was in a "slightly depressed mood."[228] But after the initial shock, most people returned to their usual Sunday routines. "Even this Berlin Sunday seemed to pass like all the others in the summer months—with strolls down Unter den Linden and rowing boats on the lakes," the press attaché of the Italian embassy, Cristiano Ridomi, marvelled.[229] That evening, Victor Klemperer wrote in Dresden: "General public cheerfulness . . . To the people, the Russian war means new hullabaloo, a prospect of new sensations and new pride."[230]

At 12:30 p.m. on 23 June, Hitler's special train left Anhalter Station in Berlin. In the early hours of the following day it arrived at his new headquarters, called the "Wolf's Lair," near Rastenburg in East Prussia. From there, the dictator intended to direct military operations over the coming months. To his closest circle he appeared to be in the "best of all moods," as the first news of German military successes began to come in.[231] "The unfolding of all measures of force is tremendous," General Heinrici wrote to his wife. "Everyone is hoping for a quick outcome."[232]

6

The War Turns, 1941–1942

"It will be a mass attack in the grandest style," Hitler and Goebbels agreed. "No doubt the most enormous that history has ever seen. The example of Napoleon will not be repeated."[1] The dictator and his propaganda minister did not find it at all ominous that the start of Operation Barbarossa fell on the same day that the French emperor had crossed the river Neman with the Grande Armée 129 years earlier. After his first visit to the Wolf's Lair on 8 July 1941, Goebbels declared that a "repetition of the case of Napoleon" was out of the question—if for no other reason than that it would be "infinitely easier" for the German Wehrmacht with its highly mobile tank divisions "to master the enormous spaces in the east."[2]

In fact, it became clear after only a few weeks that Hitler and his generals had drastically underestimated the Red Army's capacity for resistance. The expectation that the Soviet Union would come apart at the seams after the first decisive blows was revealed as a gigantic miscalculation.[3] As early as mid-July 1941, Field Marshal Günther von Kluge admitted in a letter sent from Barysau in Belarus: "The Russians are fighting extremely well, reinforced by ever new forces, including tank divisions deployed to an extent we did not suspect."[4] When the German advance got bogged down before Moscow and the Russians launched a counter-offensive in early December, the fate of the French emperor did indeed seem to be repeating itself. "Our situation bears a horrible resemblance to that of Napoleon in 1812," the tank group commander Colonel-General Erich Hoepner wrote on 12 December. "The Russians were right that the winter would put a halt to us."[5]

With a great deal of difficulty, the Germans succeeded in stabilising the eastern front and averting a catastrophe of Napoleonic proportions, but for the military leadership it was a disaster none the less.

The Wehrmacht's aura of invincibility was broken. The Blitzkrieg against the Soviet Union had failed, rendering moot the entire strategy of continuing the conflict with the Anglo-Saxon powers after a quick victory in the east. Instead of keeping its back free, once Hitler declared war on the United States on 11 December 1941, the Third Reich found itself fighting without sufficient resources against not one, but two global powers. Now Germany's defeat was as good as assured, even though the war would drag on for another three and a half years, costing millions of lives, particularly Soviet ones. Helmuth James von Moltke was more prescient than most when he wrote in January 1942 that a new period had begun "with the battle that commenced around Christmas . . . a period that would represent a greater turnaround than the Battle of Valmy," in which a French volunteer army had won a historic victory over Prussian troops sent to quell the revolution.[6]

When on 24 June 1941 Hitler arrived at his new headquarters in East Prussia, he could not have suspected that this was where he would spend most of his few remaining years. The facility, which the Organisation Todt had constructed in record time, was located in a plot of forest several kilometres east of Rastenburg. It was perfectly camouflaged from view from the air and protected from the outside world by a series of cordoned-off zones. Security was tightest in Zone I, which housed Hitler, his close retinue and a telephone switchboard centre equipped with the latest technology. The Wehrmacht leadership staff and the Führer's headquarters command centre with its various staffs were accommodated in Zone II. Some 20 kilometres to the northeast in a thick forest on Lake Mauer (Lake Mamry) near Angerburg (Węgorzewo), the Army High Command set up its "Mauerwald" field quarters. Surrounding the Wolf's Lair at various distances was a network of further command posts for Göring and the Luftwaffe High Command, SS leader Heinrich Himmler, head of the Reich Chancellery Hans Heinrich Lammers and the foreign branch of Wehrmacht intelligence, the Abwehr. Whenever he was in the area, Ribbentrop resided in Steinort Castle, the seat of the aristocratic Lehndorff family. The Führer's headquarters complex also included a small train station at Görlitz (Gierłoż) in Zone III, where Hitler's special train was kept at the ready on a side track, and the Wilhelmsdorf (Wilamowo) airstrip 5 kilometres away from the Wolf's Lair, where the Führer's flying squadron under the command of his chief pilot, Hans Baur, was stationed.[7]

During his visit in July, Goebbels found the Wolf's Lair to be more of a "summer holiday camp" than a "command centre for the German war leadership."[8] But those who spent any time there found the atmosphere dark and depressing. Hardly any sunlight penetrated the crowns of the trees or the camouflage that hung over the paths and buildings. Inside it was permanently damp, attracting swarms of mosquitoes. After only five days, Hitler's secretary Christa Schroeder, who with her colleague Gerda Daranowski shared a small bunker in Zone I, complained in a letter to a friend about the "damn mosquito plague": "My legs have been bitten all over and are swollen. Unfortunately, the mosquito repellent we have been given only works for a little while. With their high leather boots and thick uniforms, the men are better protected against the infernal stings than we are. Their only vulnerable places are their necks. Some of them run around constantly in mosquito netting." Hitler also complained on occasion that "the swampiest, most mosquito-infested and most inhospitable area had been picked out for him."[9]

The Führer's entourage also felt increasingly isolated. Zone I was surrounded by a two-metre-high security fence, and the area was patrolled by members of the Security Service and the SS. In addition, Hitler's bunker, located off to one side in the north of the facility, was cordoned off by barbed wire.[10] There were guards everywhere and people were constantly being required to show their identification. Remaining in the same discrete circle inside the fence, one was "permanently closed off from the world" and ran the danger of "losing contact with real life," Schroeder complained in late August.[11]

As he had before the war, Hitler maintained a daily routine. After waking up at 10 a.m. and taking a stroll around an area reserved specially for him, he listened to a daily situation report and then ate breakfast, most of the time consisting of just a glass of milk and a grated apple. Around noon, there was a major briefing in Keitel's bunker. It usually lasted until 2 p.m. but could go on longer if important decisions had to be taken. That was followed by lunch in the mess of Casino I. The food, typically served in three courses, was simple; occasionally there was just a stew. Hitler himself ate vegetarian meals prepared by his personal nutritionist. Afternoons were reserved for consultations with non-military officials, and sometimes Hitler invited people for coffee and cake with his secretaries. Dinner was served at 8 p.m. The company in the evenings was usually the same as at lunch: Keitel, Jodl, Bormann and his adjutant Ministerial Counsel Heinrich Heim, press chief Otto Dietrich, Hewel, Göring's deputy Karl Bodenschatz and Hitler's military adjutants Schmundt, Engel, Below and Puttkamer. In addition there were guests from the Nazi Party, the government and the military whom the dictator had received earlier and whom he wished to honour with a dinner invitation.

Late in the evening, after a second situation briefing, Hitler would invite a small circle of intimates to the office in his bunker to relax after the day's exertions. This group usually included Bormann, Heim, Hewel, his personal physician, Theodor Morell, and his personal adjutant, Julius Schaub. Hitler's head adjutant, Wilhelm Brückner, had fallen from grace after quarrels with the Führer's household manager, Arthur Kannenberg, and had been dismissed in October 1940.[12] Hitler's two secretaries were also often present, at the Führer's express wish, because he felt their presence underscored the casual nature of the company. These nighttime "teas," during which Hitler could indulge his tendency to hold long monologues, sometimes lasted past midnight and demanded a great amount of self-discipline and stamina from all the participants. "The night before last, it was already light outside when we left the boss," Schroeder wrote in mid-July 1941. "Surely never again will there be the sort of strange job that Daranowski and I have: eat, drink, sleep, occasionally write something and provide hours of company in the intervals."[13]

In the initial phase of Operation Barbarossa, Hitler's entourage found "the boss" almost invariably in a bright mood and inclined to joke.[14] The dark premonitions from the eve of the campaign had disappeared. The Wehrmacht had succeeded in surprising the enemy, and the Red Army had been unprepared for the German attack. On the very first day of the offensive, Göring's Luftwaffe had been able to destroy the majority of Soviet aircraft before they could even engage in battle. Tank units from all three army groups breached enemy lines and penetrated 400 kilometres into the Soviet Union. The greatest triumphs belonged to Army Group Centre, which surrounded and annihilated twenty Soviet divisions in the joint battles of Białystok and Minsk. The Red Army lost an immense amount of manpower and materiel.[15] "Here the opinion prevails that half of the Russian air force has been destroyed," reported Weizsäcker from Berlin on 29 June. "The triumphs against the Russian army are great. There are rumours that the Russian house is beginning to creak internally."[16] The victories were "once again like something from a fairy-tale," Adolf Heusinger, the head of the operational division in the general staff, wrote to his wife in late June. If things continued that way, everything might be over much quicker than anyone had dared hope.[17] At the beginning of the campaign, the German population had been dismayed, but the mood soon shifted. Russia was "generally not highly regarded as a military foe," read the Security Service's report on 26 June. People believed that the war would be over within six weeks.[18]

On Sunday, 29 June, German radio broadcast at hourly intervals twelve special bulletins from the Wehrmacht Supreme Command, each one introduced by the fanfare from Liszt's "Les Préludes." Even Goebbels found that "a bit rich," noting that radio listeners had been left feeling "slightly exhausted."[19] But the propaganda minister's warning about overdoing it went unheard: the victory announcements were Hitler's own idea. When Dietrich also cautiously expressed reservations, he was curtly told off. He knew "the mentality and sensibilities of the masses far better" than Dietrich and "all the other intellectuals," Hitler told him.[20] Opponents of Nazism like the journalist Ruth Andreas-Friedrich compared the Sunday radio barrage to the hysterical screaming of a funfair: "We shut our ears to it. We do not want to hear a word. It is tasteless to dress up the spilled blood and deaths of countless people as Sunday entertainment."[21] The Security Service reported that the special bulletins had made an "extraordinary impression," although there was also "a certain disappointment" because rumours had suggested that German troops were making far more progress on Russian soil than they actually had.[22] Indeed, Goebbels' propaganda was soon faced with the dilemma of how to reduce people's exaggerated expectations to halfway realistic proportions. "The delusion of victory is ruling the nation," Friedrich Kellner noted in his diary in early July. Even reasonable people, he reported, were "convinced of the invincibility of our weapons" and "refused to be convinced that if Russia collapsed, it would not change anything about our situation as a whole."[23]

The "delusion of victory" being at hand extended from the home front to the Führer's headquarters. It would "not be saying too much," Halder noted on 3 July, to assert that the "campaign against Russia can be won within fourteen days." At the same time, Halder conceded that the war was "not yet over" and that "the vastness of the territory and the stubborn resistance pursued by all means possible will continue to occupy us for many weeks."[24] Hitler was more optimistic. Everything was turning out "much better than thought," he told his secretaries in late June. Pointing at a map he proclaimed: "In four weeks we will be in Moscow. Moscow will be razed to the ground."[25] With Army Group Centre continuing its march forward in the first half of July, and about to close a large circle around Smolensk, the Führer thought he was about to achieve his goals. He always tried to "put himself in the enemy's place," Hitler remarked at the military briefing on 4 July. "But in practical terms he has already lost this war. It is good that we destroyed Russia's tank and air forces right at the beginning. The Russians will not be able to replace them."[26]

When the two men met again at the Wolf's Lair on 8 July, Goebbels encountered a positively euphoric Hitler. The war in the east, the Führer said, "was fundamentally already won," with two-thirds of Soviet forces having been destroyed or badly impaired. There would still be a series of battles to fight, but the Red Army could never recover from the defeats it had already suffered. In the days and weeks to come, German tanks would advance to the Volga and, if necessary, to the Urals. There could be no doubt that "the Kremlin will fall— sooner or later."[27] At his late-night tea on 11 July, Hitler appeared supremely confident of victory. Germany would emerge from this struggle as "the greatest power on earth," he proclaimed, and after the eastern campaign, his most determined enemy, Churchill, would "also fall very suddenly."[28] Four days later, Hitler received Japanese ambassador Oshima at the Wolf's Lair and assured him that "the resistance in European Russia will not last longer than six weeks." The Bolshevik regime would experience "a terrible collapse."

Confidence in victory had produced a rare consensus between the dictator and his generals. He had "commanders of historic stature and an officer corps that is one of a kind," Hitler told Oshima.[29] On 13 July, Weizsäcker wrote that his friends in the general staff were "unconcerned" about the further progress of operations. Russia was considered incapable of "organised, disciplined resistance." People were already packing their bags in Moscow and looking for places to take refuge in the Urals. "Most likely, the second chapter, the administration of Russia, will be the more difficult task," the state secretary predicted.[30]

Convinced that victory over the Soviet Union had already been secured, in mid-July Hitler began to address military plans for the period after Barbarossa. In an edict of 14 July, he announced that he would "soon significantly reduce the size of the army" and shift the emphasis of arms production to the Luftwaffe to prepare it for the final battle with Britain.[31] The following day, notes for a presentation by the operational division of the Army High Command contained some initial thoughts about the "restructuring of the army after the conclusion of Barbarossa." It was anticipated that infantry troops could begin returning to Germany in early August. A mere fifty-six divisions were foreseen for the "occupation and securing of conquered Russian territory."[32]

With the collapse of the Soviet Union seemingly within his grasp, Hitler was astonishingly open in these days and weeks about how he envisioned the future of the German-occupied eastern territories. We have Bormann to thank for preserving these thoughts. In early July 1941, he ordered his adjutant Heim to write down everything the Führer said over lunch and dinner. Heim made some discreet notes at the table, then dictated a summary to Bormann's secretary the following day. By contrast, it was impossible to take notes during the "tea conversations" late at night, for which Heim had to rely on memory alone. Bormann reviewed these minutes and passed them on to the Party Chancellery in Munich in October 1941, with the instruction to "take special care of these records," since they would undoubtedly prove "extremely valuable in the future."[33] It seems that Hitler had no idea that his words were being recorded,[34] which makes the transcripts such a unique historical source. They allow us an authentic look, beyond deceptions and disguises, at Hitler's thoughts about all the political and artistic questions that interested him. Above all, they provide access to the monstrous ideas that guided Hitler as he set out to realise his long-held ambition of conquering "living space in the east" and annihilating "Jewish Bolshevism." In this regard, a useful supplement is provided by the reports drawn up by Werner Koeppen, Rosenberg's liaison at Hitler's headquarters, between early September and early November 1941. These reports were composed from memory when, unbeknown to Hitler, Koeppen wrote down what he recalled from conversations over lunch and dinner.[35]

Heim's and Koeppen's notes reveal Hitler to be a brutal, hateful bully who, in anticipation of his imminent triumph, saw himself as the omnipotent ruler of Europe and no longer felt a need to tolerate any constraints. "Bolshevism must be eradicated" was one of his fundamental demands. As the "seat of this doctrine," Moscow would have to be "wiped off the face of the earth," and the borders of German-controlled Europe would have to be extended to at least the Urals. "To the west of that no organised Russian state can be allowed to exist!" Hitler declared.[36] In the occupied territories, the Slavic population that had managed to survive elimination by the Germans would be reduced to the status of slave labourers without any rights: their sole purpose would be to serve and obey the Germanic "master race." The children born to such people would not receive any education— it would be enough if they could distinguish between German traffic signs. Southern Ukraine and Crimea were to be populated exclusively with German settlers. These would be soldier-farmers: veterans of military service who were to be given large farms on which they could start big families and who would be prepared to take up arms at any time to defend their stolen land.[37]

According to Heim, for three days in early August, Hitler regaled his guests with a shining vision for the future: "The 'Reich farmer' is to live in stupendously beautiful settlements, German offices and authorities are to have wonderful buildings; the governors will have palaces . . . At a distance of 30–40 kilometres, every city will be surrounded by a ring of lovely villages connected by the best of roads. Beyond will be another world where we will let the Russians live as they see fit, with the proviso that we shall rule over them. In case there is a revolution, we will only need to drop a few bombs on their cities, and that will be that."[38]

By conquering and subjugating the European parts of the Soviet Union, Hitler believed he would take a major step towards accomplishing his goal of creating a vast economically self-sufficient area that would be practically invulnerable. "The battle for world hegemony will be decided in Europe's favour through the possession of the expanses of Russia," Hitler declared. "It will turn Europe into the part of the world most resistant to blockades." The Soviet Union's rich reserves of raw materials—coal, iron ore and oil—would be plundered, and Ukraine and the Volga delta turned into "Europe's granary." In return the local populations were to be given cheap consumer products—"headscarves, glass-bead necklaces and everything else colonial peoples like." As Hitler once again emphasised: "Our fellow Germans will live inside a closed community that will be like a fortress. Within it, the lowliest stable hand will stand taller than any of the natives without."[39]

Hitler claimed that he had been inspired by the British Empire. "The Russian realm is our India," he explained. "Just as the English rule over India with a handful of people, we will govern our colonial realm."[40] But in their extreme criminality, Hitler's plans went far beyond classical colonial rule. His obsession with "living space," his racism and his social Darwinism created a murderous mixture that cancelled all norms of civilisation. If somebody were to ask him where he derived the right to "expand the Germanic realm to the east," Hitler said, there was a simple answer: "We have to create a situation that allows our people to multiply and that restricts the breeding of the Russians . . . The stronger prevails: that is the law of nature. The world does not change. Such laws remain."[41]

On 16 July, Hitler invited Göring, Lammers, Keitel, Rosenberg and Bormann to his office in the Wolf's Lair for a five-hour meeting about future occupation policies in the east. Right at the start, he told the participants that the true intentions must not be revealed to the outside world. Instead, the official line was to be that the Wehrmacht had to temporarily retain control of the conquered territory to ensure calm and security. "It should not become evident that these arrangements will be final!" Hitler stressed. "But we will carry out all necessary measures—executions, expulsions etc.—and continue to do so." Summarising his main goal, Hitler said that the idea was to "correctly slice the giant cake so that we can firstly rule, secondly administer and thirdly exploit it." The Baltic states, Crimea with its "considerable hinterlands," the settlements of the Volga Germans and the region around the oil fields of Baku were to become "territories of the German Reich." No foreign military presence was to be tolerated west of the Urals. "Nobody must ever be allowed to bear arms except the

Germans," Hitler demanded. And at the slightest resistance, Germans would make ample use of their weapons. "This gigantic expanse must of course be pacified as quickly as possible, and this can be best achieved by shooting everyone who even looks at us the wrong way."[42]

The following day, Hitler signed a decree naming Rosenberg the Reich commissioner for the occupied eastern territories. Initially not made public, the appointment gave the chief Nazi ideologue authority over the civilian administration in all areas occupied by Germany, which would be divided into two Reich commissariats: Ukraine and "Ostland," the latter consisting of the Baltic states and Belarus.[43] But in Göring, who was responsible for the Four-Year Plan, and Himmler as the head of the SS and the German police, Rosenberg had two powerful adversaries who were by no means prepared to accept restrictions on their own power on behalf of the newly created ministry. The Führer's decree of 29 June had already confirmed that Göring alone was authorised to take any measures aimed at "optimising the exploitation of existing supplies and economic capacities" in the occupied territories. At the same time, Himmler was charged, also by a decree from Hitler dated 17 July, with "policing and securing the newly occupied Eastern Territories," which entitled him to issue orders to Reich commissars.[44] It was typical of Hitler's style of rule to create such conflicts of authority, and right from the start it was clear that Rosenberg had been handed the short straw. His idea of granting Ukrainians a measure of independence was difficult to reconcile with Hitler's and Himmler's vision of remorselessly subjugating, enslaving and decimating millions of people.[45]

The blueprint for the future was the so-called General Plan East, which Himmler in his authority as the Reich commissar for the reinforcement of German nationhood had commissioned from professor of agriculture Konrad Meyer. The plan, which was agreed with the Reich Security Main Office, foresaw the forced displacement of thirty-one million Slavs to Siberia, where they would be abandoned to the cruelties of fate. The historian Richard Evans has described these plans as prosposing "destruction on a scale never before contemplated in human history."[46]

The Reich commissar for Ukraine, East Prussia's Gauleiter, Erich Koch, also rejected any notion of Ukrainian independence. Supported by Hitler, he declared over lunch on 18 September that the occupiers would have to be "brutal and harsh right from the start." As Koeppen summarised: "The mood at the Führer's headquarters is very favourable for Koch. Everyone considers him the right man for the job and a 'second Stalin' who will fulfil his appointed tasks."[47]

All these territorial plans for a German empire in the east presupposed that the Red Army would be incapable of large-scale resistance and that Stalin's regime was close to collapse. But by the second half of July 1941, it was already becoming apparent that neither was the case. Immediately after the German attack began, chaos and confusion had prevailed not only in the Soviet leadership but among frontline commanders. Stalin, who had refused to the very end to believe warnings about Nazi Germany's intentions, was paralysed for days, leaving it to Molotov to inform the Soviet populace at noon on 22 June about the German invasion and to call upon the people to resist. "We are fighting for a just cause," he declared in his radio address. "The enemy will be defeated, and victory will be ours!"[48] Initially, of course, it looked as though it was the Soviet armies and not the German ones that were headed for defeat. By 3 July, however, Stalin had recovered from his shock and addressed the Soviet public in a radio broadcast for the first time since the German attack. His initial words revealed a significant change of tone, addressing his listeners not as "comrades" but as "citizens" and "brothers and sisters." Stalin freely admitted that the Red Army had been caught off guard by the attack and that Hitler's Wehrmacht had already conquered large parts of the Baltic states, Belarus and western Ukraine. In this "life-and-death fight" against the fascist aggressors, Stalin said, "the entire Soviet people" had to rise up to "defend its homeland." It marked the beginning of the dictator's efforts to cast the conflict as the "Great Patriotic War." It explicitly invoked the mythology of Russia's war of liberation against Napoleon, which now resonated with unusual power.[49]

One of the main reasons for the success of Stalin's appeal to the patriotism of his countrymen and -women was the German conduct of the war. From the first day, it was apparent that the Soviet campaign was an unparalleled orgy of excessive violence, unlike the war waged in the west in the spring of 1940. The tone was set by the criminal commands the Wehrmacht leadership had formulated on Hitler's orders in the months prior to Operation Barbarossa. They included the commissar order of 6 June 1941, which, despite what German military leaders claimed after the war, was by no means tacitly sabotaged. In fact, almost all German units in the east followed it to the letter, killing thousands of people.[50] On 27 June, a Foreign Ministry representative with Army Supreme Command 9 reported: "The question of the political commissars is being addressed comprehensively. All captured political commissars are being immediately executed."[51]

Not only the commissars but ordinary Soviet POWs would experience for themselves that norms of international law had been suspended in this "war of world views." Many of them were shot immediately upon being captured. Sometimes, these acts of murder were justified as retribution for alleged violations of the international law of war by the Soviet side. "The Russians have behaved bestially towards our wounded," General Heinrici told his wife in early July. "Now our people are beating and shooting dead everybody running around in a brown uniform."[52] Other commanders justified mass executions as responses to purported "treacherous" Soviet tactics. On 30 June, Field Marshal von Bock noted: "Troop commanders report that the treachery of the Russians, who pretend to surrender only to resume fire, has so enraged our men that they kill anything that crosses their path."[53] The army edict guaranteeing soldiers immunity had given many German soldiers an additional licence, significantly lowering their scruples about killing defenceless prisoners.

Many of the captured Red Army soldiers died on lengthy death marches from the front lines to holding camps back in the German-occupied rear. Anyone who was too exhausted and could not continue was shot. In British captivity Lieutenant-General Baron Friedrich von Broich later recalled one such march of 6,000 emaciated men: "Every 100 or 200 metres, one, two or three men fell to the ground. Some of our soldiers rode on bicycles beside the column, armed with pistols. Everyone who fell down was shot in the back of the head and tossed into the ditch."[54] In the first encirclement battles in June and July 1941, the Wehrmacht had already taken several hundred thousand prisoners. No provisions had been made to feed and accommodate them. The holding camps consisted of little more than open spaces surrounded by barbed wire, in which prisoners were left to cower on the bare ground or in little depressions in the earth without anything like enough food. In one of these horrific camps near Minsk, 100,000 POWs and 40,000 civilian prisoners were crammed into the space of roughly the size of one Berlin city square, Wilhelmsplatz, reported Xaver Dorsch from the Organisation Todt to Rosenberg on 10 July 1941: "The prisoners . . . are hardly able to move and are forced to defecate wherever they are standing. These men have not eaten in six to eight days, and hunger has driven them into a state of bestial apathy. All they are interested in is finding something edible . . . The only possible language of the understaffed guard commando, which is on duty day and night, is the firearm, which they use ruthlessly."[55]

Most of the Soviet prisoners died in the temporary or regular camps, be it of starvation, cold, disease, arbitrary acts of cruelty or targeted murder by guards. Three million of the 5.7 million Red Army soldiers captured by the Germans in the war perished. The historian Ulrich Herbert has described the mass deaths of Soviet POWs, which reached their peak in the autumn of 1941, as the "greatest and most terrible crime of the Germans in the Second World War" after the genocide of European Jews.[56] Racial prejudice played a major role in the murders of both Red Army members and civilians. In the eyes of Hitler and his generals, the Slavs were an inferior race, and for many German officers and soldiers, too, they were primitive, uncultured and dirty. Instances of cannibalism in the holding camps were seen not as a desperate response to the German policy of starvation, but as evidence of the "bestial" character of the Russians.[57]

Even in places like western Ukraine and the Baltic states, where Wehrmacht soldiers were originally greeted as liberators from Bolshevik domination, the brutal German occupation turned initial sympathies into disappointment and hatred. No regard whatsoever was paid to the needs of the civilian population. Hitler's armies exploited the places they occupied to feed themselves, plundering the countryside and stealing all the food farmers had. Many regions were "eaten bare," so that urban areas could not be supplied and starvation also spread to the cities.[58] Under such circumstances, it was no wonder that Stalin's call on 3 July for people to form partisan units soon found an echo. The Germans responded with ever more brutal reprisals. Red Army soldiers who had lost their units and civilians were executed on the slightest suspicion of being partisans.[59] On 16 July, Hitler coldbloodedly remarked that Stalin's call to arms now allowed Germans to "exterminate everyone who opposes us." In a supplemental edict on 23 July, he ordered the occupying forces to spread "the sort of terror capable alone of removing every desire to rebel from the populace."[60]

News of the Wehrmacht's inhumane treatment of prisoners, the mass executions and the brutal rule of the occupation forces spread swiftly throughout the Soviet Union, convincing people that the German aggressors were waging a pitiless war of conquest and annihilation. That existential threat repressed people's memories of Stalin's terror in the 1930s and lent the Soviet Union new legitimacy. With every village German soldiers burned down, new fighters joined the ranks of the partisans. Every Red Army soldier knew what awaited him in German captivity, and that made him fight even more tenaciously. "I wonder how much further east we will have to march," Walter Frick wrote to his father on 17 July 1941. "You can only tip your cap to the bravery of the Russian soldiers. The tank crews are telling us that here on the Dnieper almost all of them had to be killed in hand-to-hand combat, because no one surrendered." Twelve days after writing these lines, Walter Frick was himself killed in battle.[61]

From mid-July, the resistance of the Red Army stiffened and the Wehrmacht's forward progress was halted for the first time. German troops were showing initial signs of exhaustion. "We are now in the fourth week of fighting without a day of respite in the searing heat," reported Colonel-General Erich Hoepner, commander of the 4th Tank Army, which was advancing on Leningrad. "The men are getting tired, losses are mounting and more and more vehicles are breaking down."[62] Euphoric faith in certain victory was yielding to disillusionment. The German people should "no longer be promised so much," Goebbels warned. Instead, they needed to be "informed about the harshness of the battle taking place in the east." Like most others, Goebbels had been contemptuous of the enemy's fighting strength before the start of Barbarossa, but he now realised that the campaign would be no "stroll to Moscow." Goebbels conceded that "the Bolsheviks are putting up fiercer resistance than we imagined, and above all the materiel at their disposal is greater than we assumed."[63] In the absence of further special bulletins about German victories, the Security Service noted a "decline in the hopeful mood." Rumours of heavy German casualties were constantly nourished by increasing numbers of death notices in German newspapers.[64]

The army leadership also began to realise that the "lightning victory" they had expected was a pipe dream and that the campaign would drag on for a long period of time. The Red Army may have suffered horrific losses, but it was constantly able to regroup. "The Russians are unbelievably tough," conceded Field Marshal von Bock, the commander of Army Group Centre, in late July. Meanwhile, General Heinrici was forced to admit: "All the previous campaigns were child's play compared to the fighting at the moment . . . The enemy facing us is an astonishingly active and tenacious fellow . . . Everyone underestimated the Russians . . . It is possible that the front will become stationary deep inside Russia this winter."[65] Even Chief of the General Staff Halder could not ignore the reality before his eyes. It was becoming "ever clearer," he wrote on 11 August, that "we have underestimated . . . the Russian colossus," especially in terms of its "purely military capabilities." Halder added: "At the start of the war, we anticipated around 200 enemy divisions. But we have already counted 360 . . . and when a dozen are destroyed, the Russians bring forth another dozen."[66] Hellmuth Stieff, a member of the operational division of the general staff, discerned an "unfamiliar irritability and nervousness" at the Army High Command's Mauerwald headquarters. There was a gloomy feeling of being in a "serious crisis," although it was of course carefully concealed from outsiders.[67]

At the daily lunches in the Wolf's Lair, the Führer suddenly turned taciturn and pensive.[68] It was perhaps no accident that the first time Hitler fell ill during the war was in early August 1941, when he realised that his plans for a Blitzkrieg campaign in the east had failed. The dictator told his personal physician that he had never felt worse in his life, complaining of dizziness and nausea and declaring himself unable for several days to take part in situation meetings. Morell, who had never experienced Hitler in "such a bad mood," did what he could, giving the dictator a series of injections to get him back on his feet. He also recommended that Hitler take more exercise outside, saying that the damp air of his bunker was detrimental to his health.[69] Hitler's adjutants were ordered to maintain "the strictest silence" about the Führer's indisposition.[70] On returning to the Wolf's Lair on 18 August, Goebbels was confidentially told by Schaub that Hitler had suffered an "attack of dysentery" and that the last few weeks had "taken a toll on him" and made him "very irritable." At Goebbels' first meeting with the dictator that noon, Schaub's description was confirmed. "He was extraordinarily cordial, but looked somewhat worse for wear and sick," the propaganda minister noted. Hitler came right out and admitted that he and his generals had "completely underestimated the might and especially the equipment of the Soviet armies." The military situation, he added, "had sometimes been very critical" in the past weeks. The priority now was to "bring the eastern campaign to a satisfactory result for our needs, and for further military operations, by the onset of winter." This was a major confession. Hitler no longer believed that the campaign could be concluded in 1941, and it spoke volumes that he invoked the vague hope that "perhaps the moment will come when Stalin asks us for peace."[71]

If there had been consensus between Hitler and his military commanders during the initial phase of the campaign, open conflicts now arose. The seeds had been planted back in Hitler's Barbarossa edict of 18 December 1940, which had not answered the question of how the campaign was to continue after the early battles waged to encircle the enemy had been won. Whereas Halder had pleaded for all available troops to be concentrated in Army Group Centre to force the Soviet armies into a decisive battle outside Moscow, Hitler wanted to transfer tank units from the centre to launch an attack by Army Group North on Leningrad and enable Army Group South to take the industrial regions around Kharkov (Kharkiv) and the Donets basin and cut off Russian access to oil supplies in the Caucasus. During a meeting at Army Group Centre's headquarters on 4 August 1941, the dictator reaffirmed his intention to "take away the areas the Russian enemy needs to survive." His priority was to cut off Leningrad, followed by occupying the Donets region. "The entire basis for the Russian economy is there," Hitler proclaimed. "Taking away this area would lead to the certain collapse of the enemy's entire economy." An operation targeting Moscow was of lesser importance to the Führer, although he reserved the right to change his mind before making a final decision.[72]

By 8 August at the latest, Hitler seems to have made that decision. His adjutant Engel recorded the dictator's thoughts after the evening situation briefing: "Definitely Leningrad: for political and ideological reasons . . . In the centre: transition to defence. Everything mobile towards the south: Ukraine, Donets basin, Rostov. Führer sees the economic subjugation of the Russians as the most important goal at the moment."[73] But Halder refused to give up. In a memorandum of 18 August, he once again pointed out that the enemy was massing its troops before Army Group Centre and consequently he regarded an attack on Moscow to be the greatest danger. "If we could succeed in decisively defeating these enemy forces," Halder argued, "the Russians would no longer be able to maintain a joined-up defensive front."[74] Hitler's answer amounted to a slap in the face for the chief of staff: "The army's suggestion for continuing operations in the east does not conform to my intentions." Three days later, without admitting any further discussions, Hitler issued the following orders: "The most important goal to be achieved before the onset of winter is not the conquest of Moscow, but the taking of Crimea, the industrial and coal-producing areas on the Donets, the cutting off of Russia's oil supplies from the Caucasus, the encirclement of Leningrad in the north and joining up with the Finns."[75] As if that were not clear enough, in an extensive "study" on 22 August, Hitler once again justified why he attached the highest priority to taking Russia's most important bases for raw materials and why the "Moscow problem" was of secondary importance.[76]

Adjutant Engel wrote of a "black day for the army" and felt himself reminded of the major conflict of early November 1939. Stieff felt that if Brauchitsch and Halder accepted this "unheard-of" treatment, Hitler would believe he could "do anything he wanted."[77] But once again, the army leadership failed to mount any effective opposition. In his diary, Halder described the situation after Hitler's intervention in military strategy as "intolerable," but he abandoned any thought of quitting his post, after Brauchitsch refused to resign in solidarity.[78] Instead he sent General Heinz Guderian as a proxy since Hitler was known to have high regard for the tank group commander. But even this officer, with his vast experience of frontline fighting, failed to sway the dictator. "My generals do not understand anything about wartime economies," Hitler complained, to the dutiful nods of Keitel and Jodl. In the end, even Guderian seemed persuaded. Much to Halder's disappointment, he withdrew his objections and assured Hitler that he would support a southern advance as much as he could with his tank group.[79] Hitler had prevailed. The army leadership had bent to his authority as commander-in-chief—another step along the road towards its total subjugation.

On the morning of 25 August 1941, Mussolini arrived for a visit. Hitler picked him up from the small train station in Görlitz and brought him to the Wolf's Lair. The Führer's headquarters made a claustrophobic impression on the Italian delegation. "Here reality stops," one of the Italians noted, "and an isolated, lonely world begins, where concealed beneath the trees of a dark forest, protected by barriers and barbed-wire fences stretching for kilometres, the master of war and his commanders reside."[80] As had been the case in previous encounters with Hitler, in their meetings Mussolini's role was reduced to that of a listener rarely allowed to interrupt the digressive monologues in which the Führer talked up Germany's allegedly sparkling prospects for victory.[81] The following day, the two dictators inspected the fortifications at Brest-Litovsk, which German heavy artillery had reduced to rubble. On 28 August, Hitler and his guest flew to Field Marshal Rundstedt's headquarters in Uman, Ukraine, to inspect the Italian expeditionary force stationed there. It was one of the contingents of soldiers that its allies had placed at Germany's disposal. Along with Finnish and Romanian troops, Hungarian, Croatian and Slovenian units also fought on the eastern front, together with volunteers from almost all other European countries. At the beginning of Barbarossa, Nazi propaganda had used their presence to suggest the campaign was a European crusade against Bolshevism. The communiqué Hitler and Mussolini released on 29 August also spoke of a "new European order" that would emerge from German victory and lead to lasting peace and cooperation between all peoples on the continent.[82]

Equally mendacious was the communiqué released after a visit by the Hungarian regent, Admiral Miklós Horthy, on 8–10 September. It touted the "spirit of traditional comradeship in arms of the two peoples, which is now being tested in the joint battle against Bolshevism."[83] In reality, Hitler had a very poor opinion of Hungarian military capabilities. But to bolster German interests in the Balkans, it was important to maintain good relations with Hungary as well as with fellow Tripartite Pact members Romania and Bulgaria—"alliances of convenience," as Hitler termed them over dinner on 8 September to Hewel. Germany's partnership with Italy too, he added, was based not on the mutual affection of the two peoples but on the personal connections between himself and Mussolini. "We Germans only have affection for Finland," Hitler declared.[84]

As the war entered its third year in September 1941, the Security Service reported a "certain unease" among the German people. What had previously been the rare opinion that "the German advance in the east was only progressing very slowly" was becoming more widespread. That impression was supported by letters from soldiers who wrote of increasing difficulties and declining morale.[85] "The general question is whether things will be decided in Russia before the wet season in the autumn," wrote Victor Klemperer in Dresden on 2 September. "It does not look like it . . . One is counting how many people in the shops say 'Heil Hitler' and how many 'Good day.' 'Good day' is apparently increasing."[86] Goebbels was especially sensitive to such symptoms of crisis, warning that in the coming winter the Nazis would encounter problems "whose scope we probably cannot imagine right now." It was therefore imperative to cease giving people "illusions," he concluded.[87] The protracted Russian campaign was also lowering spirits among those closest to Hitler. "Our residence in these quarters drags on and on," complained his secretary Christa Schroeder in a letter to a friend on 30 August. "At first we thought we would be back in Berlin by the end of July. Then they talked about mid-October. And now people are saying we will not get out of here until the end of October or even later."[88]

Still, the offensive ordered by Hitler in the southern sector of the eastern front proved a surprise success. On 19 September Kiev fell, and seven days later the battle around the surrounded Ukrainian capital, the largest so far in the campaign, came to an end. Five Soviet armies had been destroyed, and 665,000 soldiers taken prisoner. The path to the Donets basin was clear.[89] Hitler celebrated another triumph. Once again, he seemed to have been proven right over the reservations of the army leadership.[90] Extensive special news bulletins brought about a quick turnaround in public opinion. "The depression of the past weeks is forgotten," Goebbels noted in late September. "The German people once again look towards their future with courage and confidence in victory."[91]

German troops were also making progress to the north. By 9 September, they had almost completely encircled Leningrad, cutting the city off from its hinterland. Tank commander Colonel-General Hans-Georg Reinhardt had already started plotting out routes to invade the city on a Leningrad map, when the order came for the troops to halt.[92] Hitler did not want to take but rather to starve the city on the Neva with its three million inhabitants and then raze it to the ground— the same fate he envisioned for Moscow. "An example should be made here, and the city will disappear from the face of the earth," the dictator told his lunch guests on 10 September.[93]

The consequences for the people of Leningrad were horrific. By January 1944, when the Red Army finally broke the blockade around the city, nearly a million people had died of starvation or illnesses associated with malnutrition. In September 1941, Goebbels had predicted: "This will be the biggest drama of a city in human history." It was a prediction that would prove correct.[94] Once again, the Wehrmacht played the role of accessory and executioner in the National Socialists' homicidal "strategy of starvation." German artillery destroyed not only factories and shipping docks but grain silos, bakeries and slaughterhouses. Leningrad residents who tried to escape this hell were driven back by gunfire. Like the treatment of Soviet POWs, the blockade of Leningrad was part of a war of annihilation that not only accepted but cold-bloodedly intended to cause the deaths of millions of civilians.[95]

When Goebbels was summoned to the Wolf's Lair on 23 September for private consultations with Hitler, he found the Führer in a completely different disposition than the previous month. "He looks . . . healthy, is in an excellent mood and sees the current situation extremely optimistically," the propaganda minister noted. Hitler claimed the success of the most recent military operations was largely his own doing, for which he had been forced to defy the advice of the specialists in the general staff. After the cauldron around Leningrad had been cleaned up, he told Goebbels, the advance would quickly continue to Kharkov and then on to Stalingrad (Volgograd). Further great victories could be expected. "The spell is broken," Hitler crowed. He reiterated his demand that Leningrad be completely liquidated. "This is the city where Bolshevism started, and in this city, Bolshevism will be utterly destroyed. This is the nemesis of history—harsh perhaps, but just." Hitler also informed Goebbels that he had given the go-ahead for the operation towards Moscow, which the Army High Command was demanding; he expected that the Soviet capital would be surrounded by 15 October. At that point, Stalin would either capitulate or offer a separate peace which Hitler would "of course accept." The Führer added: "The military power of Bolshevism will be broken, and it will no longer present a threat. It will be driven back into Asia." Goebbels, who had demanded only a few weeks previously that the military situation be acknowledged without illusion, himself now succumbed to Hitler's power of suggestion and left the Wolf's Lair "filled to the brim with optimism and energy."[96]

In his "Führer Directive No. 35" of 6 September, Hitler commanded that by the end of the month an attack on Moscow be prepared. Army Group Centre was charged with destroying the armies of Marshal Timoshenko ahead of them and then advancing on the Soviet capital.[97] Operation Typhoon, as it was named, was to definitively break the Soviet Union's fighting capability and decide the campaign. Not without considerable effort, the German army leadership managed to raise an additional seventy-eight divisions of almost two million men. "Today my men have set off for the great offensive against Moscow, an assault across 500 kilometres," wrote Halder on 2 October. "Kiev was only an arm we chopped off. This operation is intended to sever the spine."[98] That same day, Hitler called upon the "Soldiers of the Eastern Front!" to summon "one final mighty blow . . . that will destroy the enemy before the onset of winter."[99] Goebbels hastily had 200,000 copies of Hitler's proclamation printed for distribution at the front. "Our soldiers know what is at stake and how the fate of the Reich has been placed in their hands," the propaganda minister wrote. "Let us hope to God that the Soviet Union will be felled by this numbing blow."[100]

Late on the evening of 2 October, Hitler's special train left for Berlin, arriving in the capital at 1 p.m. the following day.[101] Goebbels had been pressuring Hitler for quite some time to speak in public again. His last appearance, after the end of the Balkan campaign, was now six months old. The dictator had agreed to address the opening of the winter relief campaign on 9 September in the Sportpalast, but in view of the uncertain military situation on the eastern front, his trip back to the German capital had been repeatedly postponed.[102] Now that Operation Typhoon had got off to a successful start, he thought the right time had come to address the German people. Immediately after arriving in Berlin, he called Goebbels to the Chancellery and announced his conviction that "if the weather stays halfway favourable, Soviet defences will be essentially shattered within fourteen days."[103]

That afternoon in the Sportpalast, Hitler was greeted by frenetic ovations. Goebbels was somewhat concerned about whether "the boss" could recapture his old rhetorical form after such a long period of abstinence, but Hitler did not disappoint, running through all the tried-and-tested registers of uninhibited demagoguery. He lashed out at "the conspiracy of democrats, Jews and freemasons" which he claimed had plunged Europe into war; repeated the lie of the pre-emptive war against the Soviet Union, which had been necessary to prevent a "second Mongolian storm from a second Genghis Khan"; and asserted that the "greatest battle in world history," which had been raging since 22 June, was "going to plan." Hitler received the biggest applause when he stated: "I tell you this today because I can reveal that the enemy is already broken and will never again rise up."[104] Hitler returned to the Wolf's Lair that very evening.

Over lunch the next day, he expressed his satisfaction with how well the Sportpalast speech had been received: "The mood was the same as at the best meetings during the 'time of struggle' . . . The engagement and applause of Berliners on the streets on the way there were greater and more genuine than had been the case for a long time."[105] It is difficult to assess how much of the celebration of the dictator was genuine and how much of it was staged. But Hitler was no doubt correct in his belief that his popularity would remain high as long as there was the prospect of a successful conclusion to the eastern campaign. Domestically, Hitler's speech had "worked almost like a miracle," Goebbels noted, adding: "All criticism, pessimism and worry have disappeared completely."[106]

The progress made by Operation Typhoon seemed to justify the boldest hopes. In the dual battles of Vyazma and Bryansk, eight of Timoshenko's armies were obliterated and 673,000 Soviet soldiers captured. As early as 7 October, when Vyazma was surrounded and the noose around Bryansk was drawing tighter, Jodl was talking about the "day of decision in the Russia war," comparing it with the Battle of Königgrätz, which sealed Prussia's victory over Austria in 1866.[107] Even the usually cautious Heinrici believed that "the enemy is now beaten" and that "by the end of the month, he will be without a capital and without the famous industrial area of the Donets basin."[108] Guderian shared this prognosis although he cautioned that the Germans "should not get ahead of themselves" since war often brought "unpleasant surprises."[109]

There was no sign of such scepticism back in the Wolf's Lair. Here the first three weeks of October were dominated by euphoria comparable to that at the start of the campaign. "With the Führer this evening," Hewel noted on 10 October. "Wonderfully relaxed and in a great mood. Free of all worries."[110] At the Army High Command, the leadership assumed that the enemy "no longer had any reserves worthy of the name" and ordered Army Group Centre to "seize the area around Moscow and encircle the city tightly."[111] On 12 October, Hitler decreed that a capitulation, should the city offer it, be rejected. Moscow was to be subjected to the same fate as Leningrad.[112]

Hitler was once more intoxicated by his monstrous vision of an "eastern realm" ruled over and settled by a Germanic "master race." At dinner on 17 October, with Todt in attendance, he proclaimed: "This territory must lose the character of the Asian steppes and be Europeanised!" To that end, gigantic motorways would have to be built not only to the southern tip of the Crimea but all the way to the Caucasus. "German cities will line them like a necklace of pearls, and German settlements will surround them," Hitler fantasised. In twenty years, the territory would accommodate twenty million Germans, and in 300 it would have been turned into "a blossoming park landscape of unusual beauty." Other northern and western European peoples would be allowed to participate in this massive project, albeit under German dominance. As far as the brutal treatment of the native population was concerned, there was no need to suffer any pangs of conscience. "I am approaching this matter ice-coldly," Hitler proclaimed. "I feel myself to be but the executioner of the will of history."[113] There is no record that any of the other dinner guests interrupted the Führer or expressed even the slightest of doubts. On the contrary, they hung on his every megalomaniacal, inhumane word, as he promised them a golden future: "Once we are the lords of Europe, we will hold the dominant position in the world."[114]

One remarkable incident on 9 October illustrated just how certain of victory Hitler and his minions were at the time. At noon, Dietrich, who had just arrived from Hitler's headquarters, invited German and international journalists to a special press conference at the Propaganda Ministry in Berlin. The day before, Hitler had dictated what Dietrich now told reporters in a triumphant tone of voice. After Germany's latest victories, he announced, "the entire Soviet front has been smashed" and the campaign in fact decided. "With this last mighty blow we have meted out," Dietrich bragged, "the Soviet Union is finished."[115] This was a sensational statement, and it was interpreted to mean that the eastern campaign was over. As the American correspondent Howard K. Smith recalled the following year: "When Dietrich had finished, there was a tense excitement. Uniformed men pushed up to him and shook his hand without interruption. They were congratulating themselves on German victory. Agency stringers rushed down the hall to the telephones and phoned in short breaking-news reports to their offices. The correspondents from the Axis and Balkan states applauded and celebrated. They stood up and took their leave of Dietrich by extending their arms in the Hitler salute."[116]

The following day the newspapers published special editions. The headline of the *Völkischer Beobachter* read "Campaign in the East Decided."[117] Goebbels found the situation unsettling and thought that Dietrich had gone too far. It was wrong, the propaganda minister fretted, to make the people look forward to an event "without being able to say in the meantime when it would arrive." Goebbels thus spent the following days trying to "dampen the far too widely spreading optimistic mood somewhat."[118] On 15 October, at an inspection of SA leaders, he remarked that the war against the Soviet Union "may have been decided but it is not over." This caused Friedrich Kellner to note perceptively in his diary: "Once again, they have opened their mouths too far, and a reaction has come."[119] And indeed, in the wake of the illusory expectations, the public mood plummeted all the more dramatically after it emerged that German advances had slowed and the fighting was by no means coming to an end. The "exaggerated optimism" unleashed by Dietrich's announcement began to give way to a "certain disappointment" and worries about the imminent Russian winter, the Security Service reported.[120] And the more the German military situation on the eastern front took a turn for the worse in December, the more harshly Goebbels criticised Dietrich's press conference, which he believed had done inestimable damage to German propaganda. On January 1942, he called it "probably the greatest psychological mistake of the entire war."[121]

Since mid-October 1941, the weather had shifted on the eastern front, with constant rains turning roads into bottomless morasses. The German advance literally got stuck in the mud. "We have given up all hope," Heinrici wrote to his wife in late October. "We are trapped in the mud and on the impassable roads with all of our replacement supplies. The vehicles have no fuel, the men no bread, the horses no feed. What a demonic twist of fate that we are coming to a halt so close to the gates of Moscow. The closest divisions are only 60 kilometres, three short days' march, away from the city. Our hand is already reaching for the bastion of communism, so to speak."[122] The stagnation of the German offensive gave the Red Army time to reorganise and receive fresh reinforcements from Siberia and the Far East. Under the direction of the new supreme commander of the Soviet western front, General Georgy Zhukov, effective defensive positions were established before Moscow. A fundamental turnaround was about to take place in the Soviet theatre of war.

For the time being, Hitler refused to acknowledge the changed realities. During a visit by Ciano to the Wolf's Lair on 25 October, he reassured the Italian foreign minister that "the great goal of annihilating the enemy forces in the east has to a large extent been realised and the rest is just a matter of exploiting victory in all directions." The winter would bring a "repetition of Napoleon's fate—but for Russia, not for Germany and its allies." The dictator said that he had seen reports by the Turkish ambassador to Moscow that suggested a "collapse of order and discipline."[123]

It was true that panic had broken out in Moscow in mid-October as the seemingly unstoppable Wehrmacht tanks had approached the city, and that Stalin ordered the evacuation of the diplomatic corps and the Soviet ministries. Party functionaries and civil servants had fled, and many Muscovites joined them. But Stalin himself, conscious of the psychological effect of his presence, had chosen to remain behind. When the traditional military parade to celebrate the anniversary of the Russian Revolution was held on Red Square on 7 November, it sent a further signal that the leadership of state was determined to continue the fight under all circumstances.[124]

Hitler with Foreign Minister Joachim von Ribbentrop in front of the Führer's train in Poland on 13 September 1939. Before his first field headquarters became operational in May 1940, Hitler used specially equipped trains as mobile headquarters. From there, the Führer and his subordinates inspected various front lines and theatres of war.

After his arrest, Georg Elser used a drawing to explain the bomb he had made. On 8 November 1939, he almost succeeded in killing Hitler in Munich's Bürgerbräukeller.

Hitler suffused with the feeling
of triumph: on 17 June 1940 in his
Wolf's Ravine headquarters in
Brûly-de-Pesche, he learned that
France was suing for peace. The
cameraman Walter Frentz caught
this scene on film. To Hitler's left
is Walther Hewel, the Führer's
liaison in the Foreign Ministry;
to his right, Hitler's personal
physician, Theo Morell.

On 18 June 1940, ahead of the armistice in Compiègne,
the people of Munich gave Hitler and Mussolini a rousing reception.

On 14 August 1940, after Germany's victory over France, Hitler promoted ten generals
to the rank of field marshal. Left to right: Wilhelm Keitel, Gerd von Rundstedt, Fedor
von Bock, Hermann Göring, Hitler, Walther von Brauchitsch, Wilhelm Ritter von Leeb,
Wilhelm List, Hans Günther von Kluge, Erwin von Witzleben and Walter von Reichenau.

"Order Number 21" of 18 December 1940 authorising Operation Barbarossa, in which Hitler decreed that the Soviet Union be "subjugated in a swift campaign."

On 24 June 1941, two days after the start of Operation Barbarossa, Hitler and his court moved into the Wolf's Lair. In the foreground, from left to right: Hewel, Ribbentrop, Martin Bormann, Hitler and Admiral Erich Raeder.

The German invasion of the Soviet Union began on 22 June 1941. From its very inception it was a war of plunder and annihilation unprecedented in human history.

In the first months of Operation Barbarossa, the Wehrmacht took hundreds of thousands of Soviet POWs. They were crammed into open-air holding camps and left to starve.

Even the motorised war in the east could not make do without horses.
This photograph from March 1942 shows a team struggling through the mud near Kursk.

BERLIN, den 1.Sept.1939.

ADOLF HITLER

Reichsleiter B o u h l e r und
Dr. med. B r a n d t

sind unter Verantwortung beauftragt, die Befug -
nisse namentlich zu bestimmender Ärzte so zu er -
weitern, dass nach menschlichem Ermessen unheilbar
Kranken bei kritischster Beurteilung ihres Krank -
heitszustandes der Gnadentod gewährt werden kann.

Hitler's "euthanasia" order to
Philipp Bouhler and Karl Brandt,
backdated to 1 September 1939.
Around 200,000 ill and disabled
people fell victim to various sorts
of murder.

In the ravine of Babi Yar
near Kiev, a German special
commando of Security Police
and Security Service forces shot
dead 33,771 Jews on 29 and 30
September 1941. This photo was
taken in early October, when
trees were planted in an attempt
to cover up the massacre.

War souvenirs:
German soldiers
take photographs
of an execution of
"partisans" in the
Soviet Union.

One of many mass deportations from Germany: on 25 April 1942, 852 Jewish men and women were loaded with their belongings on trains at a freight yard in Würzburg and "sent east."

Within fifty-six days, starting in May 1944, 430,000 Hungarian Jews were deported by train to Auschwitz-Birkenau. This campaign of murder was directed by a small staff led by Adolf Eichmann and relied on the cooperation of Hungarian collaborators.

On 26 April 1942, the Reichstag convened for the last time in Berlin's Kroll Opera House. The authorisation Hitler received allowed him to act until the end of the war unbound by any legal strictures. Every German who did not perform their "duties" could be prosecuted without regard to their "so-called vested rights."

Hitler at a situation meeting on 1 June 1942, in the main headquarters of Army Group South at Poltava. From left to right: Lieutenant-General Ernst, Colonel-General Maximilian von Weichs (rear, wearing glasses), Hitler, General Friedrich Paulus, General Eberhard von Mackensen and Field Marshal Fedor von Bock.

On that same 7 November, Hitler boarded his special train to attend the annual memorial ceremonies for the failed Munich putsch of 1923.[125] The following afternoon, in front of the "old fighters" in the Löwenbräukeller, he gave a speech designed to dispel any doubts as to a victorious conclusion to the war. Untruthfully, he claimed "never to have used the word 'Blitzkrieg,'" although if anything it was applicable to the eastern campaign: "Never before has a gigantic empire been so quickly smashed and defeated as Soviet Russia."[126] On Hitler's express orders, this speech was not broadcast on the radio as his addresses had been in previous years: perhaps Hitler was not completely sure of himself. The following day, in an address to the Reichsleiters and Gauleiters, Hitler chose his words much more cautiously. While in essence the Red Army may have been "defeated already," no one could predict how long it would continue to put up resistance. "In four weeks he hoped to achieve those goals that could be reached before the onset of winter," the minutes of the meeting read, "and then the troops were to take to their winter quarters . . . The attack would resume the following spring." This was in effect an admission that he had been wrong in his arrogant announcement of victory the previous month. But before the Reichsleiters and Gauleiters too, he left no doubt as to his intentions in the occupied eastern territories. "This land . . . will never be given back again," Hitler promised. "In the future, millions of German farming families will be settled here, thereby extending the Reich far to the east."[127]

By the afternoon of 11 November, Hitler was already back at the Wolf's Lair and intervened in the military discussions about how to continue the offensive. Halder, who took the lead at the meetings, clung to the hope that he could somehow push through his original operational goal. Army Group Centre was to surround Moscow as widely as possible, while Army Groups North and South pushed forward to achieve a "favourable final position before winter arrived in full." But his idea of issuing an appeal to the troops for a final "summoning of strength" encountered unexpected opposition at a meeting of the chiefs of staff of the army groups and armies in Orsha, near Smolensk, on 13 November. The troop commanders considered Halder's plan unrealistic. Many German divisions were exhausted after months of constant fighting and no longer capable of carrying out major operations. "Our units are so burned out it makes your heart bleed," Hellmuth Stieff, now chief of staff of Army Supreme Command 4 of Army Group Centre, had written two days earlier. "We can still attack once more in a limited fashion, and that is what the troops are willing to do. But they do not feel up to more than that. Their physical limit will soon be reached."[128] In the end, the military leadership agreed on such a limited attack on Moscow.

On 15 November, the offensive was resumed. German tank units again made some advances, reaching the periphery of the Soviet capital. But the time when Wehrmacht troops could easily encircle the enemy's forces was over. German soldiers were only able to fight their way forward in frontal assaults that brought enormous casualties, and although the frost that had set in since the start of November rendered roads passable again, the cold and icy wind took their toll on the German infantrymen. By the end of November, Bock was beseeching the Army High Command "for God's sake" not to over-estimate the strength of his army group. It was "five minutes to midnight," Bock complained. If his men did not succeed in breaching the northwestern front before Moscow in the next few days, the offensive should be halted, and the troops should concentrate on defending the ground they had taken.[129]

On 21 November, Hitler travelled to Berlin to take part in the state funeral for Luftwaffe director general of equipment Ernst Udet, whose dismay at the insufficient equipping of the German air force had led him to commit suicide four days before.[130] During a three-hour meeting with Goebbels at the Chancellery, the dictator did not seem particularly worried about the situation at the eastern front. If the weather held, Hitler said, the attempt should still be made to "encircle Moscow and subject it to starvation and complete destruction." The operation would have to be discontinued by mid-December because snowfall would restrict the mobility of the armoured units. "Then the soldiers should withdraw to their winter quarters," Goebbels summarised. "He hopes that by then they will have reached a line that enables them to do so."[131] But Hitler seems to have been less confident than his propaganda minister recognised. Four days later, he told his adjutants that he had "grave concerns about the Russian winter and weather," adding that the assault on Moscow had "begun a month too late."[132]

At the end of November, in a massive propaganda effort, the Nazi regime staged an extensive celebration of the fifth anniversary of the signing of the Anti-Comintern Pact. A host of other nations, including Finland and Denmark, now joined the pact, which was extended for a further five years, and Hitler returned to Berlin for the occasion on 27 November to hold talks with the foreign ministers and diplomats in attendance. Here too he displayed a forced optimism. The operations in the east were going to plan, he suggested. German troops were working their way towards Moscow, and although they had yet to reach their goal, that was only down to the bad weather, not the Red Army, which was incapable of recovering from the blows it had already received. "The big picture," Hitler bragged, was that the war was "already won."[133] He also put a far too positive spin on things at noon on 29 November when he consulted with Goebbels about the military situation. Since with the occupation of the European parts of the Soviet Union Germany would have "food in great abundance and almost all the natural resources" it needed, Hitler claimed, victory was "no longer in doubt at all."[134]

But when Hitler returned to the Wolf's Lair on the evening of 29 November, he came face to face with reality. Alarming news had come in from the southern part of the front. The day before, Ewald von Kleist's tank group had been pushed out of Rostov, which had just been conquered, by a Red Army counter-offensive. The supreme commander of Army Group South, Field Marshal von Rundstedt, had defied Hitler's orders and approved the tank group's retreat to a pre-agreed line. He was dismissed from his post on 1 December and replaced by Field Marshal Walter von Reichenau, the commander of the 6th Army (although he would die soon after, of a stroke on 17 January 1942). The next day, Hitler flew to the headquarters of Army Group South in Mariupol' to get a picture of the situation. He was grudgingly forced to admit that Rundstedt had made the right decision, although the field marshal was not restored to his command.[135] By way of consolation, however, Rundstedt received a generous severance bonus of 250,000 reichsmarks for his services.[136]

"For the first time in the war, the Army High Command has had to report disadvantageous news," wrote Friedrich Kellner after the retreat from Rostov. ". . . November 1941 will go down as a black month in German military history."[137] In fact, the setback in the south was but a mild prelude to what would happen in the centre of the front in the days to come. In early December temperatures fell to minus 40 degrees Celsius, and heavy snowfall set in. The German soldiers were completely unprepared for the extreme cold, with many still wearing their ragged summer uniforms. "Why have we been sent with such inadequate clothing into a winter battle with its superhuman demands?" Heinrici asked his diary on 4–5 December. "In little groups the troops stand pathetically frozen around a tiny fire . . . I think to myself: when the Russians see these troops, they will not think much of us. That is how miserable they appear."[138] More and more field commanders reported that their companies were at the limits of their strength. On 3 December, tank groups under Generals Reinhardt and Hoepner, who had advanced to within 30 kilometres of central Moscow, had to halt their attack.[139] Two days later General Guderian followed suit with his tank army on the southern flank. The offensive capabilities of Germany's eastern forces had been exhausted. The war had reached a dramatic turning point.[140]

The moment it was clear that the Wehrmacht's assault on Moscow had failed, the Red Army went on the counter-attack, catching Army Group Centre utterly off guard and immediately breaking through German positions that had hardly been prepared for defence. On 8 December Guderian wrote to his wife of the "sad fact that the top leadership has taken things too far." He would have never thought it possible that "such an excellent position in war could have been squandered in two months through stubbornness." If the decision to suspend the offensive had been taken in time and the troops withdrawn to defensive positions appropriate to the winter conditions, nothing would have been lost. But now Germany's eastern forces were standing on the edge of a "terrible abyss."[141] In a private letter of 7 December, Stieff also wrote of a "very grave crisis." Some members of his staff had already begun to consider withdrawing the whole army 250 to 300 kilometres: that, argued Stieff, would be a disaster. "The Russians are constantly receiving fresh forces optimally equipped for the winter and are now experiencing a surge of superiority," Stieff wrote. "We are balanced on a knife-edge every day. That is why we feel so betrayed."[142]

Initially Hitler refused to see the impending danger. He did not believe in "fresh Russian forces," he snapped at Jodl during the situation briefing on 8 December. It was all just a "bluff." In reality Moscow was throwing its "final reserves" into battle. "He went on and on like this," Engel recounted. "But you could tell from all of it how nervous and uncertain he was."[143] In Hitler's "Führer Directive No. 39," issued that very day, the dictator decreed that all offensive operations were to be suspended and the transition to defence be prepared. He justified this order not by acknowledging the new situation created by the massive Russian counter-offensive but by blaming the "surprisingly early harsh winter" and the "accompanying supply difficulties."[144]

A few hours previously, late in the evening of 7 December, news had arrived in the Wolf's Lair that immediately dispelled the depressive atmosphere. Japanese warplanes had attacked the US Pacific Fleet in Pearl Harbor, causing massive damage. The assault amounted to a declaration of war by Japan on the United States and Britain. When Dietrich reported this, Hitler first reacted with amazed disbelief. Then he sprang up, snatched the telegram and hurried to Keitel's bunker. The Führer felt as though he had been "freed from a nightmare," the head of the Wehrmacht Supreme Command later recalled.[145] But the glee was not confined to Hitler. The news unleashed a "delirium of joy" throughout the Wolf's Lair, and the bad news from the eastern front momentarily faded into the background.[146] The consensus was that with Japan's entry into the war, Germany's prospects for victory had significantly improved. "With things not having gone as we imagined, this is an extraordinarily favourable turn of events for us," wrote Goebbels.[147]

That night, Hitler phoned his propaganda minister and told him he intended to call the Reichstag to session in the coming days so that he could clarify Germany's position. "Because of the Tripartite Pact, we probably cannot get around declaring war on the United States," Hitler told Goebbels. "But that is not so bad. We are protected on that flank." Hitler was confident that the US would no longer supply Britain with as much wartime materiel as previously since it would now be needed for America's own war against Japan.[148] In a small circle on 8 December, the beaming dictator proclaimed that Germany could no longer lose the war: "We now have an ally that has not been defeated in 3,000 years."[149]

German-American relations had continuously declined since the start of Operation Barbarossa. On 7 July 1941, American troops landed on Iceland in a further step towards actively joining the war on Britain's side. But Hitler rebuffed Grand Admiral Raeder's request to expand German submarine warfare in the Atlantic to include American ships. Hitler declared he did not want to get involved in a war with the United States before the Russian campaign was victoriously concluded. Therefore, his previous orders to "avoid any incidents" still applied.[150] Hitler stuck to this line, although he was convinced that war with the US was inevitable, sooner or later. In his anti-Semitic fantasy world, Roosevelt was a representative of the "Jewish plutocracy" that intended to destroy Germany.[151]

The Nazi regime had also reacted hesitantly to the Atlantic Charter, signed by Roosevelt and Churchill on 14 August 1941 after a historic meeting in Placentia Bay on the eastern tip of Newfoundland, even though its sixth point called for the "final destruction of the Nazi tyranny." Although Goebbels interpreted the document to mean that the United States had "unequivocally positioned itself on the British side," he still dismissed it as a "clumsily stupid propaganda manoeuvre."[152] Hitler too thought the charter had no practical significance since it would not do Germany "any harm at all." In Hitler's view, Roosevelt had wanted to throw Churchill a bone because domestic pressure in America precluded the US from entering the war, as the prime minister wished.[153]

In September 1941, tensions increased after an engagement between an American destroyer, the USS *Greer*, and a German submarine, with Roosevelt announcing that in future the US Navy would be allowed to fire without warning on all Axis warships in the expanded zone of neutrality in the Atlantic.[154] "So he is starting to fire from his side without issuing an official declaration of war," wrote an outraged Goebbels. "We will not allow ourselves to be provoked . . . The longer a formal declaration of war is delayed, the better it is for us. Once . . . we have successfully concluded the eastern campaign, it will not be able to hurt us much."[155] In his speech in the Löwenbräukeller on 8 November, Hitler reaffirmed his order to German submarines in the Atlantic not to attack American vessels, although he did allow them to defend themselves if attacked. "I will put any German officer who does not defend himself up before a court-martial," Hitler promised.[156]

The longer the fighting continued on the eastern front and the more likely it looked that the US would enter the war, the more significance Japan took on in the Nazi leadership's considerations. The initial expectation that Tokyo would enter the war against Russia on Germany's side had been disappointed. Now people in the Wolf's Lair and in Berlin hoped all the more that tensions between Japan and the US would increase and lead to a war in the Pacific.[157] A change of government in Tokyo on 14 October, which brought in a cabinet led by the hawkish war minister, General Hideki Tojo, fuelled those hopes. But for some time, Germany remained in the dark as to the Japanese government's intentions. "In Tokyo, they are vacillating between intervention and conciliation," Goebbels noted on 16 November. "There is no way at present of getting absolute clarity on the Japanese position." Two days later, the propaganda minister was still convinced that "at the moment there can be no talk of the Japanese intending to intervene in the war."[158]

In fact, by that point, things were already in motion. On 5 November, the Japanese leadership had reached a basic agreement to attack the US in early December, if a diplomatic solution to all outstanding disputes had not been reached. The final decision in favour of war would be made on 1 December.[159] In the meantime, Tokyo enquired whether Berlin would support Japan and not seek a separate peace with the US. Germany was under no obligations under the Tripartite Pact since it only applied in case one of the signatories was attacked by a third party. But back in early April 1941, Hitler had given a positive signal to the then Japanese foreign minister, Matsuoka, and Ribbentrop had affirmed at a meeting with Japanese ambassador Oshima on 28 November that, "should Japan become involved in a war with the United States, Germany would of course immediately get on board. Under such circumstances it would be completely impossible for Germany to conclude a separate peace with the United States. The Führer is completely decided on this score."[160]

The Japanese now sought a written agreement to bolster these oral assurances, and Ribbentrop declared that he needed Hitler's permission. It was given on 4 December, after the dictator returned to the Wolf's Lair from his visit to Army Group South headquarters. An agreement that essentially superseded the Tripartite Pact was quickly drafted, and Mussolini's consent was swiftly procured.[161] Thus even before Pearl Harbor, the Axis powers had agreed to go to war with the United States. Still, Germany and Italy were not informed in advance of the Japanese attack on the US Pacific Fleet. The news hit Berlin "like a bolt from the blue."[162]

Historians have long racked their brains to explain why Hitler decided to declare war on the US, but his decision was not as puzzling as it appeared at first glance. The Führer was convinced that the Americans were already waging an "undeclared war" on Germany and that he would not be able to avoid open conflict for long. Another major factor was that Hitler seriously underestimated the United States' industrial and military potential. American entry into the war posed "no acute threat," he told Goebbels on 21 November. "They cannot change anything about the situation on the Continent. We are sitting secure in Europe, and we are not going to let the reins be taken from our hands."[163] Hitler thought that Japan would tie down the US in the Pacific and weaken Britain's bastions in the Far East, giving him the time he needed to break Soviet resistance in the coming year and bring the eastern campaign to a favourable conclusion. He would also be free to accede to his naval leadership's demands for unlimited submarine warfare in the Atlantic. He already issued orders to that effect on the night of 8–9 December, before war had officially been declared.[164]

Hitler's decision, taken alone, did not meet with universal approval. Weizsäcker would have preferred Germany not to go ahead with a declaration of war but to wait for an American declaration, from which propagandistic capital could have been made.[165] But Hitler was of a diametrically opposed mind. He thought that for propaganda reasons it was better to anticipate the Americans. "A major power does not wait for the enemy to declare war on it," Ribbentrop told Weizsäcker, no doubt parroting the Führer's words. "It declares war itself."[166] Particularly in a situation in which the Wehrmacht had been forced to accept its first setbacks, Hitler wanted to show the world that he was still the master of his own decisions. But in reality he was more the prey than the predator, increasingly losing his ability to steer the course of the war. In this light, his declaration of war on the United States appears like a desperate act of attack as the best form of defence. It also continued Hitler's habit of betting everything on a single card—only this time the odds were much longer than ever before.[167]

On the morning of 9 December, Hitler arrived in Berlin. Among the first people he met was Goebbels, whom he informed of his decision to use the planned Reichstag session to announce his declaration of war on the United States. With great satisfaction, he told Goebbels that Japan had decided to dispense with preliminaries and had already "launched the first devastating blow." It was possible, Hitler claimed, that the US Pacific Fleet had been so badly damaged that it would not be able to strike back. By contrast, the dictator downplayed the German crisis on the eastern front. Events there were "no great tragedy," he said: the troops were simply taking a "desperately needed rest." Next spring they could start a new offensive, which "would lead to victory in only a few blows." "The Führer once more exuded a wave of optimism and confidence in victory," Goebbels noted.[168]

The Reichstag session originally planned for 10 December had to be postponed for a day because Hitler had not completed his speech and finishing touches were still being applied to the agreement with Italy and Japan. Ribbentrop, Oshima and Italian ambassador Dino Alfieri only signed the joint declaration of war the following day. Shortly after 2 p.m. on 11 December, Ribbentrop then presented it to the American ambassador in Berlin in his office on Wilhelmstrasse. The justification for the declaration of hostilities was the usual one-sided accusation that the US government had finally gone from "initial violations of neutrality to open acts of war against Germany," thereby "creating the practical conditions of war."[169]

One hour later the Reichstag convened. Hitler's speech lasted for an hour and a half and he began by talking about the progress of the war, bragging that it would "decisively shape not just Germany but European and world history for the next 500 to 1,000 years." It was not until the second half of his address that he talked about declaring war on the United States. His remarks consisted of a flood of crude insults against Roosevelt, who now took Churchill's place as the "main culprit." Once again, Hitler vented his anti-Semitic bile: "It is the Jews in all their satanic treachery who flocked to this man and to whom this man is also reaching out." Hitler's personal attacks on the US president culminated in the remark that he considered him "just as mentally ill as Woodrow Wilson." In conclusion he read out the declaration agreed with Italy and Japan, in which the allies pledged to "jointly wage this war forced upon us with all means available until its victorious conclusion" and "not to conclude without mutual agreement a ceasefire or peace with the United States or England."[170]

According to the reports of the Security Service, the German people received Hitler's speech with "great inner approval." Only in a few isolated cases had there been "voices of surprise or some concern about the addition of a new enemy."[171] German propaganda did all it could to stress Japan's early triumphs in the Pacific and to distract from the setbacks on the eastern front. But it is doubtful that this influenced the public mood much.[172] After the public relations disaster of Dietrich's press conference in early October, people had grown far more sceptical about proclamations of victory.

During the afternoon of 12 December, Hitler summoned his Gauleiters to the Chancellery to brief them about the situation, as he had the previous month in Munich. Japan's entry into the war, he told them, had fallen into Germany's lap "like a gift," lifting "a huge weight of burden" from his own heart. Concerning the situation in the east, Hitler tried to obscure the true dimensions of the reversal of fortune, as he had at his meeting with Goebbels. The Wehrmacht, as the propaganda minister now summarised his speech, was in the process of "performing a clean-up of the eastern front" and withdrawing the assault wedge back to winter positions, so that "next year Soviet Russia at least as far as the Urals could be taken care of."[173] Hitler himself said much the same thing the following day to Oshima, specifying that the first advance would be carried out in the Caucasus to seize the oil fields there. He sought to flatter the Japanese ambassador, saying that his "heart had leaped" when he heard about the initial Japanese operations. "It was a great achievement of the Japanese that they destroyed the aura of American invincibility right from the start," he added.[174] In gratitude for the services he had provided to German-Japanese friendship, Hitler presented Oshima with the highest German medal, the Large Golden Cross of the Order of the German Eagle. Afterwards the Führer amused his entourage by telling them that he had temporarily forgotten what the medal was called when he was presenting it to the ambassador.[175]

When Hitler returned to the Wolf's Lair on the morning of 16 December, he found that the situation in the east had turned critical:[176] the Red Army's counter-offensive had punched wide holes in the German defences. Army Group Centre was threatening to collapse, which would have ushered in a catastrophe of Napoleonic dimensions for the entire eastern forces. "One is scared to answer the telephone, which never stops ringing," Hoepner reported. "Our men are so fatigued they fall asleep on their feet. They have been so dulled that they no longer throw themselves to the ground when the shooting starts. Death by freezing is almost more common than by bloodshed."[177] It spoke volumes that in the commanders' conversations and diary entries these days parallels were repeatedly drawn with the demise of the Grande Armée almost 130 years earlier. "If there is no miracle, another 1812 awaits us," Stieff wrote on 9 December.[178] The same day Guderian reported to Bock that he no longer knew how he was supposed to repel the enemy's attacks and wrote of a severe "crisis of confidence" among his men.[179] On 15 December, army supreme commander Brauchitsch returned from a tour of the front to Army Group Centre and discussed the situation with his general staff. "He was very depressed and no longer saw any way of rescuing the army from this difficult situation," Halder wrote in his diary.[180] Via his adjutant Schmundt, who had accompanied Brauchitsch on his trip, Hitler received a frank report on the situation.

It was only then that the dictator seems to have realised how much was at stake, and as was his wont in crisis situations, he reacted promptly. Before leaving Berlin on the night of 15 December, he summoned Colonel-General Friedrich Fromm, the commander of the Replacement Army, to the Chancellery and consulted with him about the necessity of providing reserves for the eastern front.[181] Hitler was clear that the shaky front lines had to be held at all costs since a retreat during the Russian winter could quickly turn into a disorderly flight. On his way back to the Wolf's Lair, he dictated his first "holding order," writing that "a broad withdrawal of large parts of the army in the middle of winter, with only limited mobility and winter equipment and without prepared fallback positions, would have the gravest of consequences."[182] During the night of 17 December, Hitler called Bock and reaffirmed his command "not to go back a single step, to fill the gaps and hold positions."[183] On 18 December, a second holding order, sharper in tone, instructed commanders to "force their troops to put up fanatical resistance in their positions without regard to enemy breakthroughs on their flanks and to their rear."[184]

At the same time, Hitler took another decision of far-reaching significance: he relieved Brauchitsch of his command and installed himself as the supreme commander of the army. This step was hardly a surprise. It had been evident for some time that Brauchitsch did not have the nerves for confrontations with the Führer. He literally got the shakes before every situation briefing and avoided coming face to face with Hitler. "The man simply repulsed him as a human being," Halder recalled after 1945. "The same Brauchitsch with whom I could verbally joust for thirty minutes at a time would stand in front of Hitler without getting a single word out."[185] In early November, Brauchitsch had suffered a "severe heart attack" that had laid him up for several weeks.[186] On 6 December, he had asked Hitler to relieve him of his position in consideration of his poor health. The dictator refused. It seemed inopportune to replace the top-ranked officer in the army just as the Soviets were launching their counter-offensive. Nonetheless it was clear to all in the know that Hitler intended to get rid of the supreme commander. Brauchitsch was regarded as nothing more than a "letter-carrier," Halder wrote, with Hitler communicating directly "over his head" with the commanders of the army groups.[187] When Goebbels arrived at the Wolf's Lair on 17 December, Hitler told him that Brauchitsch would soon be replaced and that he himself intended to assume command.[188] With his characteristic instinct for power, Hitler recognised that he could thereby transfer responsibility for the failed eastern campaign and use the luckless field marshal as a scapegoat. Even months later, Hitler still fumed about how Brauchitsch had ruined his beautiful plans, calling the officer "a vain, cowardly little runt who was unable even to comprehend the situation—to say nothing of mastering it."[189]

The transition was officially announced on 19 December. Hitler's total usurpation of military command elicited a mixed reaction from his generals. Guderian hoped that Hitler would "intervene with his usual energy in the overly bureaucratic gear work" of the army command. Heinrici, on the other hand, opined that even the Führer "will not be able to turn things around."[190] Halder, who retained his post as chief of the general staff, issued an appeal to the troops that stressed his loyalty to Hitler: "We can and must be proud that from now on the Führer himself is standing at the head of the army."[191] But of course, by taking on command of the army, Hitler had burdened himself with an additional amount of work. The familiar rhythm in the Wolf's Lair began to change. The daily situation meetings, which Halder was also now required to attend, lasted even longer. In a private letter to a friend in January 1942, Christa Schroeder reported: "Lunch is supposed to be served at 2 p.m., but is increasingly postponed to times of the day when normal people eat dinner . . . Dinner is correspondingly delayed, and our evening teas in the Führer's bunker, which used to start at 10 p.m., now often start after midnight (the record is 2 a.m.). That means we all go to bed between 4 and 5 in the morning."[192]

In the days after Brauchitsch's dismissal, Hitler again stressed to field commanders that they were "not to retreat a single step voluntarily" but "were to fight with their last reserves of strength for every foot of ground."[193] With that, commanders were unable to react flexibly in emergencies and to take evasive action to reduce losses of men and materiel. Nonetheless, most of them obeyed this rigid doctrine. The only one who rebelled was Guderian. On 20 December, he flew to the Wolf's Lair to try to persuade Hitler that the order was counterproductive and that he should be allowed to gradually withdraw his tank group. In a heated, five-hour meeting, the dictator insisted on his order to hold out at all costs, accusing Guderian of showing "too much sympathy" for his men. "Do you think Friedrich the Great's grenadiers died gladly?" Hitler asked him. "They would have liked to stay alive as well, yet the king had every right to demand that they sacrifice their lives. And I think I equally have every right to demand from the German soldier that he sacrifice his life."[194] On 26 December, after Guderian had returned to the front and kept allowing his army to evade the enemy, the tank commander was relieved of his post and transferred to the Führer's Reserve of the Army High Command in Berlin. His demotion set a decisive precedent.[195] Anyone who defied Hitler's orders and questioned his authority as a field commander could expect to lose his job, no matter how many medals he had won during previous campaigns.

The Führer wanted to finally make the Wehrmacht into an obedient instrument of his absolute dictatorial will. In conversation with

Goebbels on 17 December, Hitler had announced that there would be further personnel changes. He needed men, he said, "with strong nerves who do not topple over at the first sign of crisis." Whereas Hitler himself had behaved hysterically during the Norwegian operation and at the start of the campaign in France, he now wanted to project to his general staff officers the image of the unyielding field commander with nerves of steel. His generals were too old, he sneered, and most came from the Blomberg era, which had never been completely overcome.[196] On 16 December, Bock had asked to be relieved of his command, as he no longer felt equal to its demands. Hitler approved his sick leave and named Field Marshal Günther von Kluge, previously commander of the 4th Army, to replace him at the head of Army Group Centre. On 13 January 1942, Field Marshal Wilhelm Ritter von Leeb, the supreme commander of Army Group North, resigned after failing to gain operational freedom. Hitler appointed Colonel-General Georg von Küchler to succeed him. All three powerful army group commanders—Rundstedt, Bock and Leeb—were thus replaced. Hitler also made a negative example of Hoepner. In early January 1942, an army corps from the tank group under his command had retreated without the express permission of Hitler and Kluge, whereupon Hoepner was immediately removed from his post and discharged from the Wehrmacht.[197]

In the meantime word had spread throughout Germany how serious the situation was on the eastern front. Even those who preferred to stick their heads in the sand were confronted with the grim reality when on 20 December Hitler called on the German people to donate winter clothing for the soldiers in the east. To open the clothing drive, Goebbels delivered an address on all German radio stations.[198] In the weeks that followed, newspapers and radio stations reported constantly on the initiative. In the eyes of the propaganda minister, it provided a chance to "get through that tiresome Christmas and New Year season" and to strengthen feelings of solidarity between home and the front.[199] Among ordinary Germans Hitler's appeal caused some confusion, however, since in the preceding months it had been reported that soldiers at the front had enough winter clothing.[200]

"Depressing Christmas," noted Hewel on 24 December. "Führer's thoughts are elsewhere. No candles lit."[201] And indeed, in contrast to the festivities at the Berghof of the pre-war years, the Wolf's Lair on

New Year's Eve was a study in melancholy. One piece of bad news after another arrived from the front. Thirty minutes before midnight, when the members of Hitler's entourage assembled to wish "the boss" a happy New Year, Kluge phoned. For three hours, he beseeched Hitler to approve a partial retreat of his men. But despite the army commander's desperate appeals, Hitler remained adamant that every metre of territory had to be held at all costs; in the end the field marshal gave up.[202] Hitler's closest circle whiled away the time in the officers' mess. It was not until 2:30 a.m. that they were asked to take the customary tea. "It has always been the case that extremely difficult times preceded very great events," Hitler remarked, trying to cheer up the group. Hewel was reminded of the time the two of them had spent together at Landsberg Prison in 1924. While Bruckner's Seventh Symphony was playing on the gramophone, the exhausted dictator eventually fell asleep.[203]

In his New Year's address to the German people, Hitler did not say a word about the difficulties on the eastern front. Instead, with characteristic hyperbole, he celebrated the past year as "one of the greatest triumphs in human history." His concluding words were: "Let us all ask God our Lord that 1942 brings the decision that rescues our people and our nation's allies."[204] That sounded less boastful than Hitler's speech the year before, but Goebbels still thought it went too far by awakening a "very powerful hope" that might prove "exceedingly difficult" to fulfil.[205] Those who had learned not to be overwhelmed by the constant drone of the regime's propaganda were under no illusions that the situation had fundamentally changed. "In the cold light of day, I have come to the conclusion that it is impossible for Germany to win this war," wrote Kellner as 1942 dawned.[206]

The situation on the eastern front remained extremely critical in January. It seemed only a matter of days until large parts of Army Group Centre would be surrounded. "Everywhere the first signs of defeat are appearing," Heinrici told his wife on 11 January. "Tomorrow our main supply road will be blocked off. In a few days, rail connections will be cut as well. What then?"[207] But Hitler was not prepared to budge from his rigid prohibition of tactical retreats. In situation meetings there were "furious scenes," as Hitler accused his generals of lacking the spine to take "tough decisions."[208] Raging like a berserker, the dictator refused to accept the impending catastrophe. Even late at night, when he was with those closest to him, he refused to show a single moment's vulnerability. "Every crisis has an end," he assured the others. "The main thing is not to bend under any circumstances!" He had mastered a great number of crises in his own life, Hitler boasted, and he would ensure that this one ended well, too. "No matter how threatening the winter, spring inevitably arrives!"[209]

Hitler refused to acknowledge that the Wehrmacht's failure to take Moscow had scuttled the entire strategic concept of Operation Barbarossa. He even saw a positive side to how things had developed. It was lucky winter had come so soon, he claimed; otherwise vanguard German units would have advanced 200 to 300 kilometres further into the Soviet Union and been hopelessly cut off. "Providence intervened," Hitler asserted, "and saved us from a catastrophe."[210]

It was not until 15 January that Hitler allowed Kluge to move his troops some 150 kilometres back. "It is the first time in this war that I have issued a command to withdraw a larger part of the front," he growled. "I expect that the soldiers will retreat in a manner worthy of the German army."[211] With that, Army Group Centre finally got what it wanted and was now better able to mount a flexible defence. On 19 January, when Goebbels met with Hitler at the Wolf's Lair, the dictator was already feeling confident about his ability to "gradually stabilise the eastern front." He had "three weeks of the most barbaric work behind him," Hitler said, and for many days "he had stood from early in the morning until late at night in the map room, so that his feet had swollen up." Again and again, he had been forced to raise the "sinking morale" of his generals. Sometimes he thought of himself as someone "whose main job it was to blow air back into deflated rubber men."[212]

Hitler claimed full and sole credit for averting a catastrophe on the eastern front, and his faithful vassal Goebbels was only too eager to believe his version of events. "In the past four weeks, the Führer has once again saved the nation," wrote the propaganda minister.[213] Puttkamer concurred that Hitler was "the sole person . . . who could have persevered in this situation."[214] Opinion among military leaders was divided on this score. In his cell at the Nuremberg trials in 1946, Keitel would remain convinced that "only the Führer's iron energy" had spared the German army "the fate of 1812."[215] By contrast, after

the war, Halder was highly critical of Hitler's "holding doctrine."
A "serviceable basic idea" had been taken much too far and become
a "grave mistake" that had cost the eastern forces irreplaceable men
and materiel.[216] Whichever way one looks at it, Hitler most likely had
no other option in the face of Army Group Centre's imminent collapse.
After the fact, Hitler tried to sell the army leadership on his policies
by claiming that only "the standpoint of absolutely holding territory"
had allowed him to "counteract panic."[217]

What averted a major catastrophe more than anything, though, were
the mistakes made by Stalin. Instead of concentrating on a few important goals, the Soviet leader ordered the Red Army to attack across the
entire expanse of the front in January 1942, thereby sacrificing its
reserves. By the end of the month, it was evident that the Soviet advance
had played itself out.[218] Thus Hitler saw no reason to cancel his traditional address on the anniversary of his taking power in 1933. On 29
January, freshly arrived in Berlin, he described the situation in the east
as "more or less . . . absolutely consolidated." Alarming reports from
the front had dwindled to a minimum, and the "Bolsheviks" had not
been smart enough to exploit their advantages operationally. "If they
do not achieve anything in winter, what can they hope for in the coming
spring and summer, when we will regroup at greater strength and push
them on to the defensive?"[219] Hitler still tended to underestimate the
Soviet regime's ability to mobilise people and resources, although the
failure of Operation Barbarossa should have taught him better.

For Hitler's speech the following afternoon in the Sportpalast,
Goebbels had assembled a handpicked audience of workers at Berlin's
arms manufacturers, military nurses and wounded soldiers.[220] Right
from the start, there was an emotional charge in the air, and Hitler
did everything he could to raise the tension. In the coarsest terms, he
insulted Western political leaders, dismissing Churchill as a "drunkard,"
a "layabout of the first order" and "one of the most infamously
Herostratian personalities in world history," and labelling Roosevelt
"his crony in the White House" and a "poor lunatic." Non–National
Socialists listening to this speech on the radio may well have asked
themselves whether the Führer of the Greater German Empire was
himself in possession of his senses. But as was always the case with
his major speeches, Hitler kept himself under control. He knew exactly
what he was saying and how he could bring his audience to the boil.

There was no way for him to conceal the fact that the Wehrmacht had gone onto the defensive, but he tried to downplay the amount of territory the Red Army had recaptured. Soviet forces had "only advanced a few kilometres in isolated places," Hitler claimed, and the German soldier had not lost his "sense of towering superiority over the Russian." The worst was over, and the front had been stabilised, Hitler pledged, adding that come spring the Wehrmacht, the "mightiest army in the world," would again go on the attack and defeat the enemy. But for that to happen, the home front had to stand behind the troops without reservation.[221]

That very evening, Hitler returned to the Wolf's Lair. "I have rarely seen him as fresh, lithe and above all optimistic about things to come as now," noted Goebbels. "He has charged up the entire people like an accumulator."[222] Indeed, Hitler's speech seems to have made a strong impression on the German people and reinforced their faith in the "final victory."[223] One reason may have been the explicit references Hitler had made to Friedrich the Great: "A man with an iron will held the banner high through all setbacks and never forsook his people. Even if he sometimes felt like forsaking them, he pulled himself back together again and again to take up the banner in his strong hand."[224]

This was precisely the image depicted in the historical film *The Great King*, with actor Otto Gebühr in the role of Friedrich, which, in Goebbels' estimation, contained "surprising parallels with the present."[225] It was a work by the German UFA studio's star director, Veit Harlan. Originally, its premiere was planned for 30 January to accompany Hitler's speech, but a few last-minute changes meant that it first hit cinemas in March 1942. The film's message was obvious: just as the great Prussian king had persevered in his battle against a mighty coalition in the Seven Years War, Hitler too would overcome all crises and ultimately triumph.[226] After Germany's defeat at Stalingrad in 1943, a Wehrmacht major would draw a pithy analogy of victory following defeat in a letter to General Friedrich Hossbach: "Friedrich the Great too experienced a Kunersdorf and followed it with a Leuthen."[227] The more the Third Reich's military situation deteriorated, the more the mythology of the Prussian king was enlisted to lend Hitler and the Nazi elites crucial legitimation.[228]

★

On 7 February 1942, Fritz Todt travelled to the Wolf's Lair for a meeting with Hitler about Germany's armaments programme. The minister for armaments and munitions had already urged the Führer to seek a political end to the war in late November 1941, as the debacle before Moscow was taking shape, since from an armaments perspective there was almost no way Germany could emerge victorious. Hitler had brusquely rejected the suggestion.[229] No details about the two men's meeting on 7 February are known, but apparently there was another difference of opinion that left both the dictator and his minister in poor humour.[230] The following morning, Todt boarded his plane back to Berlin, but the aircraft exploded shortly after take-off, killing everyone on board. The cause of the explosion was never determined. The immediate suspicion was that Todt had been assassinated, but there never has been any proof of this.[231]

According to his adjutant Below, Hitler was "very shaken" by the news of Todt's death and sat staring silently for quite some time.[232] But the dictator soon recovered his composure, summoning Albert Speer, who was at the Wolf's Lair after a trip to Dnepropetrovsk (Dnipro), and without any discussion appointing him Todt's successor.[233] The personnel decision raised eyebrows since the Führer's favourite architect was an absolute layman when it came to the armaments economy. But in the eyes of Hitler, with his distrust of experts, that seems to have been a positive. Before 1939, Speer had proven a skilled organiser and a loyal helper in realising some of the Führer's megalomaniacal architectural plans. "What Hitler especially liked was that he always performed his tasks with a small apparatus and a casual nonchalance that signalled his enjoyment of a sporting challenge," recalled Rudolf Wolters, who from 1937 had worked for Speer in his role as general building inspector for the Reich capital.[234] Hitler had faith in Speer's unorthodox, non-bureaucratic ability to inject new momentum into the wartime economy and increase arms production to record levels. In this regard, the new arms minister would not disappoint his master even if the increases in productivity fell short of the "arms miracle" that Nazi propaganda later touted.[235] At Todt's memorial service in the mosaic hall of the New Chancellery building on 12 February, which was attended by all the leading figures of state, party and Wehrmacht, Hitler himself delivered the key address. There is no definitive way of telling whether he was play-acting or felt genuine grief, but he was described as having been "so shaken that at times he was hardly capable of speaking."[236]

By mid-February 1942, the acute crisis on the eastern front was over. On 12 February, the Army High Command wrote that the phase of defensive battles had "passed its zenith" and the time had come to "finally solidify the front and improve it in places."[237] Hitler too declared that there would be no catastrophe. The situation had been secured, and the military could now take its time and prepare for the new offensive.[238] Hitler confessed to those closest to him that he had been "deadly afraid" in the weeks past and that a repeat of 1812 had been "hanging by a thread."[239] In a speech to officer candidates in the Sportpalast on 14 February, he once again demonstrated unbroken confidence. Germany's previous campaigns, he crowed, were just "stages of a victory streak the world had never seen before." Soviet forces were "to a large extent either paralysed or already smashed," and he doffed his cap to the "German musketeers who had done their duty at the front in the icy cold." He appealed to the candidates to "always live up to these heroic deeds," telling them: "You have the honour of being leaders of the best of German manhood."[240]

Several positive reports from the North African and Pacific theatres of war helped buoy the mood. In January, Rommel's Afrikakorps had gone on the offensive and retaken most of the territory the British had captured the year before. By early February, he was at the gates of Tobruk. On 1 February, in a major blow to the British Empire, the Japanese captured Singapore. Twelve days later the battleships *Scharnhorst* and *Gneisenau* and the cruiser *Prinz Eugen* succeeded in passing through the English Channel from Brest and returning home largely undamaged. German propaganda hailed this naval manoeuvre as a massive victory. Waging war was "a lot more fun again" than it had been in December, Goebbels mused in mid-February. He added: "Our chances have visibly improved, and the German people are registering the successes of the Axis powers with great joy and profound emotion. We are once again standing solidly on our own two feet."[241]

Self-deception did not come any bigger than this. While the "winter crisis" may have been overcome, its consequences for the German forces had been grave. According to the Army High Command, 1,073,066 men had been killed or wounded or had gone missing from the beginning of Operation Barbarossa to 20 March 1942. That was roughly one-third of Germany's eastern forces.[242] In addition, a huge number of tanks, warplanes, vehicles and technical equipment had been destroyed. The Wehrmacht had been battered and would never regain its original strength.[243]

The dramatic turn of Germany's fortunes in 1941–42 had also taken a heavy toll on Hitler himself. After the exhaustion of the winter months, he was losing strength. "The boss" was "always very tired," his secretary noted in late February, but he could never go to bed early. The nighttime teas were increasingly becoming a chore with conversation being "rather lukewarm and difficult" and always revolving around the same topics.[244] On 19 March, Hitler made a very different, "shattering" impression on Goebbels than he had in late January. The propaganda minister found his master "very grey" and "heavily aged." Hitler was also complaining about health problems, remarking that he occasionally had to fight against "the strongest attacks of vertigo." But if he had "shown weakness even for a moment the front would have begun to slip," Goebbels quoted Hitler as saying, "and a catastrophe that would have far overshadowed Napoleon's would have been at hand."[245]

It was only his determination that had prevented this nightmare scenario, and once again his will had triumphed over all adversity—of that Hitler was convinced. The myth of the saviour that he had so successfully exploited in the dying days of the Weimar Republic once again came into play. "When everyone else loses their nerve, it is I alone who stands his ground," he bragged during one of his nightly teas in the Wolf's Lair.[246] That was another barb directed at his military commanders, whom he repeatedly accused of lacking courage in critical situations. "He does not think as highly of the generals as he used to," Goebbels registered. "For many of them he has nothing but contempt."[247] Thus, whereas Hitler may have emerged physically weakened from the winter crisis, his ego was stronger than ever, and he was even less inclined to listen to advice from military experts. From now on, his relationship with his generals was one of the deepest mistrust.

Did the dictator truly believe he could turn things around again? A few days after Germany's surrender in May 1945, Jodl would testify that following the winter catastrophe of 1941–42 Hitler realised that the "culmination point" of the war had passed and "no victory" could be achieved.[248] But it is highly questionable whether Hitler thought any such thing. At least outwardly, he projected optimism. "After the most difficult winter of my life, at the start of a great new year," Hitler wrote in Elsa Bruckmann's guestbook in the spring of 1942.[249] In front of his closest associates, the Führer continued to be the picture of unshakable faith in victory. Of course, that does not preclude the possibility that he harboured occasional doubts about how the war would end. After all, he had had dark premonitions on the eve of Barbarossa, and they returned briefly at critical junctures during the campaign. One very revealing statement was a seemingly off-the-cuff remark Hitler made to Danish foreign minister Erik Scavenius in late November 1941: "If the German people prove not strong or willing enough to make sacrifices and shed their blood for the sake of their existence, they deserve to die out and be destroyed by another stronger force."[250]

7

The Road to the Holocaust

"I already told the German Reichstag on 1 September 1939—and I take care not to make any prophecies out of turn—that this war will not end the way the Jews imagine, namely with the extermination of the European-Aryan peoples. The result of this war will be the destruction of Jewry. Now, for the first time, the true ancient Jewish law will be applied: 'An eye for an eye, a tooth for a tooth.'"[1] With these words from his Reichstag speech on 30 January 1942, which was broadcast live on radio, Hitler recalled the threat he had issued to "international financial Jewry" before the German parliament exactly three years previously.[2] Conspicuously, the dictator moved the date of his prophecy to 1 September 1939, the day Germany attacked Poland. Since Hitler possessed an excellent memory, we have to assume that this was not a mistake and that he consciously changed the date in an attempt to suggest a direct connection between the beginning of the war and his intended "final solution to the Jewish question."[3]

These two things had in fact always been connected in Hitler's mind. Since the mid-1920s, his obsession with "removing the Jews in their entirety" had been bound up with his racist vision of conquering "living space." But it was only with the war of annihilation against the Soviet Union and the explosion of violence it entailed that it became possible to realise both of these long-term goals. By eradicating "Jewish Bolshevism," Hitler could proceed with his programme of murdering all the European Jews who lived under German domination. The road to the "final solution" did not run in a straight line, but consisted of several bursts of what the historian Hans Mommsen has called "cumulative radicalisation."[4] What is certain, however, is that without Hitler and his eliminatory anti-Semitism, the genocide of European Jews would not have happened. "If, in a counterfactual experiment, we take

Hitler out of the decision-making process, the crucial figure would be lacking for the planning, execution and, especially, the legitimation of the mass murder," the historian Hans-Ulrich Wehler has written. "Without authority and approval from the Führer, Himmler, Heydrich and their ilk would not have been able to organise, execute and justify the Holocaust as a Europe-wide project of homicide."[5] We should add that without hundreds of thousands of assistants and accessories who willingly helped the executioners, this epochal crime against humanity would not have happened either.

On the eve of the Second World War, around 200,000 mostly older Jews lived in the Greater German Empire. They were an impoverished, terrified, socially isolated minority helplessly exposed to repression by the organs of the Nazi state. In the first days and weeks of the war, a constant flood of new ordinances increasingly restricted their already severely constrained lives. Jews were prohibited from leaving their homes after 8 p.m., they were forced to hand over their radios, their food rations were cut, and they were only allowed to shop at certain hours in certain stores. Many merchants refused to sell anything to Jews. In November 1939, the diarist Friedrich Kellner observed the following scene in a shop in his hometown of Laubach: "It was an old woman's turn. 'What's your name?' she was asked. 'Katz,' she said. 'Are you a Jew?' 'Yes.' 'Then you're not getting anything from me. As a National Socialist I do not sell to Jews.'" Kellner wrote: "Why have we become such a horrid people? This is the inhumane fruit of all this miserable incitement. How unbearably sad of someone to take his inculcated hatred out on a defenceless old woman."[6]

Little by little Jews were forced to leave their homes and live in so-called Jew houses—for many people a painful caesura entailing a loss of their private sphere. "Our entire style of life has been transformed," wrote Victor Klemperer, who together with his Gentile wife was compelled in May 1940 to move from their home in the Dölzschen district of Dresden into the "Jew house" on Caspar-David-Friedrich-Strasse.[7] From the spring of 1940, Jewish men and women were also increasingly made to perform forced labour, usually in armaments factories. This was a lucrative business for entrepreneurs who could extract a maximum of labour for minimal pay. Local administrations and police departments were extraordinarily imaginative in thinking up ways to harass and repress Jews. "It is a total war against us," wrote the former university lecturer Willy Cohn, who considered himself a patriotic German. "And it will have a huge number of victims." Faced with the bewildering plethora of prohibitions and rules, Klemperer complained: "No one knows what exactly is allowed. You feel threatened everywhere. Any animal is freer and more legally secure."[8]

With the start of the war, it became considerably harder for Jews to emigrate. Most European countries were off limits because, like England and France, they were at war with the Reich or, like Switzerland, they had tightened immigration restrictions when the fighting began. Overseas countries like the United States and the Latin American nations were also accepting fewer and fewer immigrants. In July 1940, the leader of the regional government of Upper and Middle Franconia, the northern part of Bavaria, reported: "Because Jewish emigration overseas (to America) is now the only possibility, and people can no longer board ships for the passage across in central and western European harbours, emigration has to take place via the Baltic countries, Russia and Japan. The routes are significantly longer and more difficult than previous ones, and older people are unable to make the trip."[9] Many of those Jews who had stayed behind came to realise with paralysing certainty that they had delayed fleeing their home country for too long and were now trapped there. "Our plans too are now ruined, and my premonition that I would suffer the fate of Moses seems to be coming true," Cohn noted on 4 September 1939. "We were no longer able to make the *aliyah* in time."[10] From the beginning of the war until October 1941, when Jewish emigration was officially prohibited, only 23,000 Jews succeeded in leaving Germany.[11]

Increasing repression went hand in hand with an intensification of anti-Semitic propaganda. In the first months of the war, Hitler rarely missed an opportunity to scapegoat "the Jews" as those pulling the strings behind the conflict. "Our Jewish-democratic global enemy has succeeded in putting the English people in a state of war with Germany" was how Hitler began his proclamation to the Nazi Party on 3 September 1939.[12] The immediate result of this incitement was a rapid rise in anti-Semitic sentiment among the German population. Already on 6 September, an informer to the Security Service in the Münster area reported a "great bitterness," which expressed itself in people talking about "locking Jews up or lining them against the wall and shooting ten Jews for every fallen German."[13] In his 1940 New Year's address, Hitler repeated his attacks on the "Jewish-capitalist world enemy," whose sole goal was to "destroy Germany and the German people." In his speech to mark the twentieth anniversary of the Nazi Party programme on 24 February 1940 in Munich, he promised to break the "organised terror of a treacherous global plutocratic clique." "We have driven off these international financial hyenas in Germany," Hitler railed, "and we are not going to let anyone tell us what to do from abroad."[14]

Whereas right up until the signing of the German-Soviet non-aggression pact in August 1939 "Jewish Bolshevism" had been the Nazis' number one enemy, it was now replaced by the "Jewish plutocracy"—an anti-Western variation of anti-Semitism. Klemperer, a keen observer of the use of language in the official communications of the Third Reich, noticed that the expression "Bolshevism" had disappeared completely from Nazi propaganda. Instead people heard "only of plutocracy."[15] That was an accurate understanding of the general thrust of the anti-Semitic campaigns at the start of the war. "The concept of plutocracy must be better elucidated," noted Goebbels in early February 1940. "Under it we can be victorious." Hitler valued the work of his propaganda minister. "The Führer has praised our battle against the plutocracy," Goebbels wrote after a lunch in the Chancellery in late March 1940. "It must be repeated endlessly, never losing intensity. That is the key to propaganda in any case."[16] It was only with the start of Operation Barbarossa that the old enemy "Jewish Bolshevism" was reactivated. "We are slowly redeploying the heavy anti-Bolshevist steamroller," noted Goebbels on 24 June 1941. "But gradually, so that the transition is not too abrupt."[17]

Goebbels consulted closely with Hitler about producing anti-Semitic films. In early October 1939, the propaganda minister charged Fritz Hippler, the head of the ministry's film division, with the biggest project to date: a documentary to be titled *The Eternal Jew*. Material for what the Nazi leadership alternately called "the ghetto film" or "the Jew film" was shot in Poland. "It has to be the most incisive anti-Semitic propaganda imaginable," Goebbels declared.[18] Hitler took an interest in the project right from the start. In late October, he asked to watch the first trial footage, and in the months that followed, he repeatedly demanded changes to the rough cut.[19] By April 1940, the film was finished. "It is now good and can be shown to the Führer," Goebbels wrote.[20] But Hitler seems to have been less than fully satisfied. Goebbels had to make a number of alterations before the film finally premiered in October 1940. "The time has come for it to be released," Goebbels noted. "We have worked on it long enough."[21]

Goebbels had an easier time with his second major work of anti-Semitic cinema, the feature film *Jew Süss*. This historical drama was based on the (falsified) life of Joseph Süss Oppenheimer, an eighteenth-century financial adviser to Duke Karl Alexander of Württemberg.[22] The first trial footage was shot in November 1939. To direct the picture, Goebbels hired Veit Harlan, and the cast included several well-known actors, including Ferdinand Marian as Süss and Werner Krauss as both Süss's secretary Levy and a rabbi named Loew. The propaganda minister was delighted with the finished product: "A work of great genius," Goebbels gushed. "The sort of anti-Semitic film we were hoping for."[23] In early September 1940, the picture opened at the Venice Film Festival, and on 24 September the German premiere took place in Berlin's UFA-Palast cinema. "A very large audience included almost the entire Reich cabinet," noted Goebbels. "The film was a smash success. All you heard were words of enthusiasm. The cinema was crackling. Just what I wished." Hitler was also "very pleased" by the film's success and praised it "to the stars" over lunch at the Chancellery, as did everyone at the table.[24]

If Security Service reports are to be believed, *Jew Süss* was given a "lasting, extremely approving reception" throughout Germany. Rarely was the public opinion about a film "so united." It may have taken its "realistic portrayal of a horrific episode unusually far, but it was completely convincing artistically and full of tension that 'doesn't let you go.' "[25] Already in mid-October 1940, cinemas in Bielefeld reported that the film had exceeded expectations at the box office. "Even ethnic-popular comrades who rarely or never go to the movies do not want to miss this picture," one Security Service report read.[26] By 1943, twenty million Germans were said to have watched the film.

By contrast, *The Eternal Jew*, which premiered on 29 October 1940, was a commercial flop. Even the Security Service admitted that "only the politically more active part of the population wants to see this documentary, while the typical film audience avoids it and word on the street objects to the picture's all-too-realistic depiction of Jews."

The graphic nature of some of the scenes, including one depiction of a ritual slaughter, turned off parts of the potential audience. There were frequent remarks to the effect that *"Jew Süss* already depicted Jewry so convincingly that there is no need for . . . this new, even crasser, bit of evidence."²⁷

Both films helped reinforce anti-Semitic stereotypes, but it is possible that the images from *The Eternal Jew* were burned more indelibly in people's memories. One particularly repugnant scene featured hordes of rats and a voice over: "Where rats turn up, they spread diseases and carry extermination into the land. They are cunning, cowardly and cruel; they mostly move in large packs, exactly as the Jews among the people."²⁸ Comparisons like this had no purpose other than to deny Jews any sort of human dignity, to encourage hatred and revulsion and to propagate their complete "removal" from the "ethnic-popular community" as an urgent necessity. It was no accident that *The Eternal Jew* concluded with a clip from Hitler's speech on 30 January 1939 in which he had threatened Jews with destruction should another war break out. After this scene, a Security Service report from Munich noted, the audience "applauded . . . freely and enthusiastically."²⁹ There can be no doubt: murder was in the air in Germany.

The first victims, however, were not the Jews, but the ill and disabled. Here, too, the exceptional situation of war made it possible for the Nazi leadership to realise a horrific idea: what pre-war doctors had previously discussed under the labels "euthanasia" and "the eradication of unfit life," and which in fact had already been put into partial practice in the form of compulsory sterilisation. According to his former adjutant Fritz Wiedemann, who had been sent off in January 1939 to become consul general in San Francisco, Hitler repeatedly expressed his intention over lunch and dinner to "eradicate the incurably ill, and not just the mentally ill, if there was a war."³⁰ The start was the decision to kill physically deformed newborns and small children. In the spring of 1939, the father of a severely disabled child from Leipzig sent a request via the Chancellery to the Führer to allow a "mercy killing." The dictator assigned his personal physician Karl Brandt to the case and allowed him to have the child killed after consulting with local paediatricians.³¹ Soon Hitler empowered Brandt and the head of the Chancellery of the Führer, Philipp Bouhler, to take comparable action in similar cases. At their initiative, a group of experts was formed, operating under the obfuscating name "Reich Committee for the Scientific Registration of Major Genetic and Congenital Suffering," to put together a child "euthanasia" programme.

On 18 August 1939, just days before the start of the Second World War, an Interior Ministry edict ordered doctors and midwives to report all cases of physical deformity in newborns and children under the age of three to the committee. These reports were then sent on to evaluators who would decide over the life and death of the children concerned. If a negative judgement was rendered, the victims were taken to special clinical facilities known as "child specialist departments," where they would be murdered, usually with an overdose of the sleeping agent Luminal or some other medication.[32] It only took a few months for child "euthanasia" to be expanded into a comprehensive programme for murdering adult patients at medical institutions. Here too it was Hitler who pushed developments forward. At some point in the late summer of 1939, the exact date being unknown, he summoned Lammers, Bormann and Reich health leader Leonardo Conti and told them he thought the "lives of severely mentally ill people unfit for life should be eradicated through interventions bringing about their death."[33] Originally the dictator had intended to make Conti responsible for carrying out his wishes, but Bouhler and Brandt made sure that they were given responsibility for the expanded "euthanasia" programme.[34]

On 21 September 1939, the Interior Ministry ordered a list to be drawn up by all hospitals and care facilities "in which the mentally ill, epileptics and the retarded resided on a more than temporary basis." On 9 October, the bureaucrats began to collect the names of individuals. Questionnaires were sent out to the institutions, and doctors were required to fill them in immediately and return them to the ministry's medical division.[35] That day a meeting was held in Berlin between Viktor Brack, Bouhler's deputy in the Chancellery of the Führer, Interior Ministry officials, members of the Reich criminal police and two professors of psychiatry and nervous diseases, Werner Heyde and Paul Nitsche. The meeting was about not only how the residents of the medical facilities would be killed but who would be included in this homicide programme. On the first score, the expertise of pharmacologists and officials at the Criminal-Technical Institute of the Security Police had already been enlisted: the recommendation was to use carbon monoxide gas as a means of killing. When it came to the number of patients to be killed, carefully calculated statistics arrived at a figure of 65,000–70,000 people.[36]

Probably over the course of October 1939, Hitler authorised Bouhler and Brandt to "expand the powers of specifically named doctors, so that they can carry out mercy killings of ill people deemed incurable after critical evaluation of the extent of their illness."[37] This instruction was typed up on Hitler's personal letterhead and back-dated to 1 September 1939. Here, too, the dictator wanted to insinuate a connection between the start of the war and a programme that was a death sentence for tens of thousands of people. It was one of the rare cases when Hitler dropped his guard and put something like this in writing. It seems that Bouhler and Brandt had insisted that they needed an unambiguous statement of the Führer's will before they set about realising a criminal undertaking such as the planned systematic murder of hospital patients. At the same time, Hitler's order of empowerment was left deliberately vague. That was in keeping with his leadership style, which was to encourage the organisational ambition of his paladins and set no limits on their efforts to achieve his aims.[38]

While the preparations for the "euthanasia" programme were underway in the older parts of the Reich, the murder of both Polish and German patients was already going on in the annexed Polish territories that made up the *Gaue* of Danzig–West Prussia and the Wartheland. They were carried out by members of the *Wachsturmbann Eimann* commando stationed in Danzig, which had already participated in the murder of Polish intellectuals. Among the victims were patients at hospitals in Pomerania who on the initiative of Pomeranian Gauleiter Franz Schwede-Coburg were transported to West Prussia in November and December 1939. There they were shot. Soon a special commando headed by criminal police commissar and SS-Untersturmführer Herbert Lange began killing patients with carbon monoxide. The first "trial gassing" took place in December 1939 in Fort VII on the edge of Posen (Poznań), where the SS had converted a bunker into a gas chamber. In early 1940, the facility was replaced by a truck with a mounted air-tight chamber into which the deadly gas was pumped. In total, the murder commandos in West Prussia and the Warthegau killed more than ten thousand patients between September 1939 and the spring of 1940.[39]

To introduce "euthanasia" across the Reich, a bureaucratic apparatus had to be built up at the same time as its purpose was kept carefully concealed from the outside world. The entire operation was carried out under the code name "T4," named after the central office's address in a luxurious villa at Berlin's Tiergartenstrasse 4. The umbrella organisation was known as the "Reich Working Association of Hospitals and Care Facilities," and its main administrative department, which was responsible for paying about 500 employees, went under the name of the "Charitable Foundation for Facility Maintenance." Patients were transferred to the killing centres by the "Charitable Patient Transport PLC." It is hard to imagine a more cynical cover for a criminal endeavour of this sort. Patients were murdered at six locations: Grafeneck near Reutlingen, Brandenburg an der Havel, Sonnenstein near Pirna, Hartheim near Linz, Bernburg on the Saale and Hadamar near Limburg. From the start of the operation until August 1941, more than 70,000 sick and disabled people were murdered in gas chambers disguised as showering facilities.[40]

Despite all the secrecy, rumours about mass murder of hospital patients began to circulate among the general population, causing concern within the Nazi leadership. On 1 May 1940, Goebbels noted: "With the Führer. Bouhler reported about the liquidation procedure for the insane, which is so necessary and is now being put into practice. Still secret. It is creating great difficulties."[41] On 19 September, when a lone English warplane mistakenly bombed the Bodelschwingh care facilities for disabled children in Bethel, near Bielefeld, killing several of them, it was a welcome pretext for Nazi propaganda to divert attention away from the "euthanasia" crimes. "The Bethel case provides a big story," Goebbels noted. "We can conceal everything unpleasant behind it." The following day the headline in the *Völkischer Beobachter* read: "British Massacre of the Innocents. Bombs Dropped on Bethel Hospital."[42]

In late September 1940, William Shirer was told by a source that ill and disabled people were being murdered, and he decided to investigate. On 25 November, only a few days before he left Nazi Germany, he noted what he had been able to find out in his diary. "The Gestapo," Shirer wrote, "with the knowledge and approval of the

German government, is systematically putting to death the mentally deficient population of the Reich." There were already thousands of victims, and their numbers were climbing every day. Using death notices taken out in local papers by the victims' relatives, Shirer was able to name three of the killing centres, Grafeneck, Hartheim and Sonnenstein. He also received copies of the standard letter that was sent to victims' families. "It's a Nazi, messy business," Shirer wrote.[43]

The murder of ill and disabled people had great significance for the radicalisation of National Socialist racial policies. For the first time, an efficient technique was developed and used to exterminate tens of thousands of defenceless men, women and children. It was no accident that the majority of the personnel recruited for the T4 operation would be involved in establishing the death camps in the General Government in late 1941.[44] There they could apply their experience in operating gas chambers in far more monstrous dimensions. In that regard, "euthanasia" was an intermediary step on the road to the systematic extermination of the Jews. It was, as Raul Hilberg has written, "a conceptual, technological and administrative precursor to the 'final solution' in the death camps."[45]

With the conquest of Poland in September and October 1939, more than two million Polish Jews fell into German hands. After some 300,000 fled or were deported across the demarcation line to the Soviet-occupied territory, around 1.7 million remained under German rule. Occupied Poland now became a laboratory for new strategies to "solve the Jewish question." In the eyes of Hitler and the executioners of his ideological obsessions, it had the advantage that here far more ruthless ideas could be tried out, away from the world's attention, than in the Reich itself.[46]

One early idea was to resettle all these Jews in a yet-to-be-designated "reservation" in Poland. In a priority letter to the leaders of the Einsatzgruppen on 21 September 1939, Heydrich advocated this idea. The head of the newly created Reich Security Main Office distinguished between a "final goal," the deportation of Jews from the Reich and the annexed Polish territories, which it would take a long time to achieve, and preparatory measures such as the "concentration of Jews from the countryside in larger cities" and the formation of councils of elders in all Jewish communities. On 29 September, at a meeting of the office heads of the Reich Security Main Office, Heydrich provided more concrete details of his plan. The territory between the rivers Vistula and Bug, in the Lublin district which, Germany had just received in the German-Soviet agreement signed the day before, would be used for a "Reich ghetto" containing "Polish and Jewish elements that will have to be resettled from the future German *Gaue*."[47]

Apparently Heydrich had discussed his plan with Hitler. That very day, the dictator described very similar ideas to Goebbels and Rosenberg. Conquered Polish territory was to be divided into three zones, to the easternmost of which, "the land gained beyond the Vistula, bad Polish elements and Jews, also from the Reich," were to be deported.[48] The systematic destruction of Jews was not yet under discussion, but Hitler left no doubt that their fate would not be a happy one. The "Jewish problem" would likely be "a difficult one to solve," he declared over lunch at the Chancellery on 6 October 1939. He added: "The Jews are no longer human beings. They are predators equipped with a cold intellect that need to be rendered harmless."[49] Two days later, speaking to the closest members of his entourage, he expressed regret that he had been so "humane and generous" in formulating the Nuremberg Laws. The "Jewish question," he said, was "not a religious but a racial problem" and required a solution "not just in Germany but in all countries under German rule." In Poland, he continued, work had already begun on ghettos, but "they would not suffice." Together with Himmler and Heydrich, he considered how the "greatest part of the Jewish population" could be deported to territory in Poland.[50]

Goebbels, constantly trying to elicit expressions of his Führer's favour, did everything in his power to appear a fanatic hater of Jews and to push for a further radicalisation of anti-Jewish policies. In late October 1939, he undertook a trip to Poland and, together with Governor-General Frank, visited the Łódź ghetto. Afterwards he noted with repugnance: "These are not human beings any more. They are animals . . . We have to make surgical cuts here, very radical ones. Otherwise Europe will perish from the Jewish disease." On returning to Berlin, he shared his impressions with Hitler. "My account of the Jewish problem in particular met with his full approval," Goebbels noted afterwards. "Jewry is a waste product. More a hygienic than a social issue."[51] After a further trip to Danzig–West Prussia and the

Wartheland in late November 1939, the propaganda minister again extensively reported back to the Führer. And once again, the two men were in complete agreement. "We must expunge the Jewish danger," Goebbels noted. "Although it will reappear in several generations. There is no cure-all for it."[52] This remark illustrates how far removed the Nazi leadership, despite its readiness to make "radical surgical cuts," still was from the physical extermination of European Jews as a "final solution to the Jewish question." The Nazi leadership's initial, rather vague plans focused on a territorial solution: to find a "reservation" outside the Reich into which Jews could be "packed."

Within this general context falls the so-called Nisko Project, prepared under Adolf Eichmann's leadership. In July, the SS-Sturmbahnführer had become the director of Prague's Central Office for Jewish Migration, which was based on the Viennese model. On 8 October 1939 he was ordered by the head of the Gestapo, Heinrich Müller, to prepare the deportation of Jews from Katowice in eastern Silesia and Ostrava in the Protectorate of Bohemia and Moravia to somewhere east of the Vistula. The operation was to be a trial, and based on the experience collected, a comprehensive "resettlement programme" was to be devised.[53] Eichmann set about this task with characteristic energy. He immediately travelled to Vienna to ensure that Jews still living there would be part of the first wave of deportations. On 12 October, together with the head of the Security Police in the Protectorate, Franz Walter Stahlecker, he then went to Poland to search for a suitable location. Near the small railway station at Nisko on the river San, on the western border of the Lublin district, he found what he was looking for. There a "transit camp" could be built, from which the flow of deportees would be channelled into the "Jewish reservation." On 18 October, the first train with almost 1,000 Jews departed from Ostrava. In the following days, further transports rolled out of Vienna and Katowice. All told 4,700 Jews were taken to Nisko. There nothing had been prepared to accommodate them. A small number of Jews were conscripted to build barracks, while the rest were driven by SS and policemen over the demarcation line into Soviet-occupied territory.[54]

The Nisko Project had been started hastily, and it ended just as abruptly. On 20 October, Eichmann was ordered to stop the deportations. The plans for a "Jewish reservation" in the district of Lublin were never officially scrapped, but the idea was put on ice for the time being. The operation, however, had not gone unnoticed by the German people. In Bad Kissingen, there were rumours that "the Jews are all being taken, down to the last man, to the territory between the San and the Bug rivers. It is said to be an area of 300 square kilometres. Jews from Austria and the Czech region have already arrived there."[55] The improvised camp at Nisko was not closed until April 1940, when several hundred remaining inmates were allowed to return to the Protectorate and Austria. The project's failure would not prove a stumbling block to Eichmann's career. On the contrary, he had again demonstrated that he possessed the necessary measure of brutality combined with personal initiative and organisational talent. In December 1939, Heydrich made him his special expert in Office IV of the Reich Security Main Office, responsible for the "central supervision of security matters during the execution of the evacuations in the east."[56]

The cessation of the Nisko Project was the direct result of the treaty concluded with the Soviet Union on 28 September 1939, in which it was agreed that German minorities would be resettled from Soviet-controlled areas. It meant that space had to be found immediately in the German-annexed sections of Poland for these "ethnic Germans" from the Baltic and other parts of eastern Europe. The plan was therefore to expel hundreds of thousands of Poles and Jews into the General Government. This gigantic "resettlement programme," which was put under the authority of Himmler's Reich Commissariat for the Consolidation of German Nationhood, was given top priority. In comparison, the deportation of Jews from the Reich and the Protectorate was considered less urgent.[57]

The realisation of these plans ran into unexpected difficulties. "At the moment, Himmler is moving people around," Goebbels remarked in January 1940. "Not always with success."[58] Governor-General Frank in particular resisted accepting constant transports of people into his territory, and he could count on the support of Göring. At a meeting at the field marshal's Carinhall estate on 12 February 1940, Himmler was forced to agree that further deportations would only be carried out with Frank's prior permission. The same day, more than 1,000 Jews from Stettin, whose homes were to be freed up for resettled Baltic Germans, were taken to Lublin. A transport with 160 Jews from

Schneidemühl (Piła) followed on 12 March. On 23 March, after Frank complained, Göring as chairman of the Ministerial Council for the Defence of the Reich ruled out all further "evacuations" into the General Government, unless they were approved personally by himself and Frank. With that, the idea of a "Jewish reservation" in the Lublin district was shelved.[59]

By the spring of 1940, it had become unmistakably clear that because of conflicting interests and self-created constraints, German "Jewish policy" had gone down a dead end. In a conversation with the travel writer Colin Ross in March of that year, Hitler asserted that "the Jewish question is a question of space" that was especially difficult to solve since he did not have "any space at his disposal."[60] The failure of the resettlement plans meant that the ghettoisation of Jews in certain cities gained speed. The first large-scale ghetto was established in Łódź, which was part of the Warthegau and had been renamed Litzmannstadt after a German First World War general. In late April 1940, the Jewish neighbourhood in the north of the city was cordoned off. It marked the start of a desperate struggle for survival for the more than 160,000 people that were crammed into the ghetto.[61] The plan to establish a similar ghetto in Warsaw was initially postponed because in the early summer another idea for a territorial solution of the "Jewish question" emerged: the resettlement of Jews from German-controlled areas to the French colony of Madagascar, off the eastern coast of Africa.

The idea was not new. On the contrary, it had been part of the repertoire of racist and anti-Semitic pamphlets since the end of the nineteenth century; Hitler himself had brought it up in April 1938 in conversation with Goebbels.[62] But as long as there was no way of getting France to cede the island to Germany, any plans in that direction necessarily had to remain abstract. That situation changed with the rapid success of Germany's western campaign in May and June 1940. Suddenly, the idea seemed a realistic option that offered a way out of the impasse in which German plans had got stuck after the demise of the "reservation" solution in the General Government. The revival of the idea began with a memorandum entitled "On the Treatment of Foreign Ethnic Groups in the East" that Himmler had composed during the campaign in France. In it he expressed his hope "to see the concept 'Jew' completely erased through the possibility of emigration by all Jews to Africa or some other colony."[63] On 25 May, with France's defeat imminent, the SS leader presented the memorandum to Hitler at the Cliff's Nest. As Himmler noted in his pocket calendar, the Führer seemed "very much in agreement."[64]

The Madagascar project also had supporters in the Foreign Ministry, most prominently the head of the Department for Jewish Matters and Racial Policy, Franz Rademacher. "The question must be addressed: where to with the Jews?" he wrote on 3 June 1940 to his departmental director, Martin Luther. As alternatives, he proposed either removing all Jews from Europe or keeping eastern European Jews in German hands as "bargaining chips to paralyse the Jews of America in their fight against Germany." The career diplomat Rademacher, like the ideological fanatics in the NSDAP, saw the US government as beholden to the Jewish lobby, and the idea was to use eastern European Jews as hostages to prevent Washington from entering the war against the Third Reich. The Jews of western Europe, however, were definitely to be sent elsewhere, "for example, to Madagascar."[65] In two other memorandums from early July, Rademacher became more precise, suggesting that in the armistice treaty France should be forced to cede the island as a mandate. Jews brought there were to be allowed a certain amount of self-determination but would be subject to strict supervision from a "police governor" accountable to Himmler. "From the German perspective, the Madagascar solution means the creation of a large-scale ghetto," Rademacher wrote. "Only the Security Police have the necessary experience in this area. They have the means to prevent people from fleeing the island."[66]

The idea of a "resettlement" of the Jews of Europe to the French island colony quickly captured the imagination of the Nazi leadership. Both Hitler and Ribbentrop supported it when they met Mussolini and Ciano on 18 June 1940 in Munich.[67] Two days later, Hitler also brought it up in a conversation with Admiral Raeder,[68] and in early July, he promised Frank that "no more Jewish transports to the General Government would take place." The plans were, Frank told his subordinates after returning to Krakow, "to transport the whole Jewish clan in the German Reich, the General Government and the Protectorate to an African or American colony as swiftly as conceivable after the conclusion of peace—Madagascar is under consideration."[69] By that point, Goebbels had also got wind of the idea. "By the way, Jews in Europe in their entirety are to be deported to Madagascar," he noted on 26 July. "It will become a German protectorate under a German police governor."[70] On 16 August, Hitler confirmed to him in the Chancellery that the idea was being considered: "We intend to ship the Jews to Madagascar in the future. There they can establish their own state."[71] Like the plans for the "Jewish reservation" in Poland, the Madagascar project did not remain a secret. News of it spread like wildfire. On 1 July, the chairman of Warsaw's Jewish Council, Adam Czerniaków, was told by the head of the Jewish department of the Gestapo, SS-Oberscharführer Gerhard Mende, that "the war will be over in a month, and we will be travelling to Madagascar."[72] The same story was passed around in early July among the Jews of Dresden, together with rumours that the British government was about to step down. "Now they make peace, and we will be sent to Madagascar," Victor Klemperer noted.[73]

Heydrich was anything but pleased about this Foreign Ministry initiative. In a letter to Ribbentrop on 2 June 1940, he reminded the foreign minister that Göring had named him the director of the Reich Central Office for Jewish Emigration, giving him authority for all matters pertaining to this issue. By this point, Heydrich wrote, the "overall problem" of 3.25 million Jews living in German-controlled areas could no longer be solved by emigration alone. "A territorial solution will thus be necessary," Heydrich concluded, no doubt refer-ring to the Madagascar project. He demanded in no uncertain terms that the Foreign Ministry include him in all meetings on this topic.[74] The "Jew experts" in the Reich Security Main Office, Adolf Eichmann and his colleague Theodor Dannecker, were not sitting around on their hands, either. By mid-August they had drawn up proposals of their own for the Madagascar project. Dannecker sent the Foreign Ministry the results of their labours, in the form of a voluminous memorandum. Its core sentence read: "To avoid other peoples' constantly coming in contact with Jews, an overseas solution of an insular nature is preferable to all others." By now there were four million European Jews under German rule, and it was proposed that as many as 3,000 per day be shipped to Madagascar. In this way, the Reich Main Security Office calculated that it could solve the "Jewish problem" within four years.[75]

But all these plans remained mere hot air as long as one crucial condition was not fulfilled: the end of Germany's war with England. After his victory over France, Hitler had assumed that this would be a matter of course, but Churchill's unexpected determination to continue the fight under all circumstances put paid to that idea. As long as Britain had not surrendered, there was no way Germany could think of transporting millions of Jews by sea to Africa. In the autumn of 1940, after Germany had failed to bring Britain to its knees through aerial warfare and Hitler decided to put off invading the island, the Madagascar plan was essentially mothballed. The fact that the dictator returned to it occasionally in the months that followed does not mean that he seriously thought it could be realised.[76]

If only he knew "what to do with the few million Jews," Hitler complained to his adjutant Engel in early February 1941, adding that he would demand of France that it "put space for resettlement on the island of Madagascar up for disposal." In response to Bormann's question about how the Jews were to get there, Hitler declared that he would prefer to use the entire "Strength through Joy" cruise-ship flotilla, but that was difficult in wartime because of the danger presented by enemy submarine attacks. Ominously he went on to say that he now thought "very differently," and not in a more amiable sense, about some things.[77] At his meeting with Mussolini at the Brenner Pass on 2 June 1941, Hitler seemed not to have completely given up on the earlier idea, though, saying that "all Jews will have to leave Europe after the war . . . perhaps they can be resettled in Madagascar." The word "perhaps" indicates that by then, shortly before the start of Operation Barbarossa, Hitler was already considering other options. The Madagascar idea was finally laid to rest in early 1942, by which point the murder of Jews in the Soviet Union had already been going on for six months.[78]

As fantastical as the Madagascar plan might seem today, in the summer of 1940, at the height of German euphoria at France's capitulation, it was seriously discussed by the entire leadership of the Third Reich. The fact that Heydrich was still using the phrase "territorial final solution" in this context indicated that the decision to physically eliminate Europe's Jews had not yet been taken. Instead, the idea was to send Jews overseas, to the extreme periphery of Germany's sphere of influence. This concept was by no means the product of human-itarian considerations. On the contrary, it too contained a genocidal component since it was safe to assume that many European Jews would not survive the climate of a remote, primitive tropical island.[79]

Once hopes for a swift end of the war—and with them the prospect of a "Madagascar solution"—had been disappointed, plans were revived to confine Jews to the ghettos in the General Government. On 2 October 1940, Ludwig Fischer, the governor of the Warsaw district, ordered the creation of a closed ghetto in the city, specifying the neighbourhood into which all of its Jews were to be crammed. By mid-November, construction work had been completed, and the ghetto was cordoned off by a three-metre-high wall. Somewhere between 380,000 and 465,000 Jews were trapped there. The numbers vary because, on the one hand, the mortality rate rose from month to month due to the catastrophic living conditions while, on the other, Jews were constantly arriving from smaller cities and from the Warthegau. "Conversation about the noose around our neck," recorded Czerniaków on 25 October 1940, a brief note that says every-thing about the desperation of the ghetto's inhabitants.[80]

"The Jews have been brought together in a ghetto," wrote General Heinrici in a letter from Siedlce to his family in May 1941. "They are identified by a white armband with a blue star. In the smaller cities the ghettos are not separated from the populace. You only have that in Warsaw, where a three-metre-high wall, fortified with barbed wire and glass, hermetically seals it off. In smaller cities, Jews run around freely and are frequently conscripted into work; often they are indis-pensable as artisans . . . In our city, the bread ration for Poles is 75 grams and for Jews 65 grams . . . It is amazing that these people are still alive."[81]

Before 1939, German "Jewish policies" had been radicalised by the interplay between acts of violence "from below" and administrative measures "from above," with Hitler as the supreme authority deter-mining the rules of action.[82] This dynamic was replicated during the war. In the autumn of 1940, radical provincial potentates sought to exploit the favourable situation by deporting, on their own initiative, more than 6,500 Jews from Baden and the Saarpfalz region by train to the non-occupied part of France, where they were interned in several camps. The driving forces behind what at that point had been the largest deportation from the Reich itself were the Gauleiters Robert Wagner and Josef Bürckel. They were competing with one another to make their jurisdictions "free of Jews," after Hitler had given them the green light. The news spread quickly. "No one can tell whether a similar fate awaits us here," Willy Cohn wrote in Breslau (Wrocław). He packed several small suitcases for himself and his family "to be prepared with the basic necessities for the worst case that we are forced to leave."[83]

The Gauleiter of Vienna, Baldur von Schirach, now demanded a resumption of deportations to the General Government. On 2 October 1940, he made his request to Hitler in the presence of Frank and the Gauleiter of East Prussia, Erich Koch. Fifty thousand Jews still lived in Vienna, Schirach said, and the governor-general would have to take them off his hands. "Dr. Frank characterised this as impossible!" Bormann wrote in his minutes of the meeting.[84] Hitler initially refused to make a decision, but in early December, he had Lammers inform Schirach that the deportations would be "accelerated while the war is still on."[85] In reality, only around five thousand Viennese Jews were deported, far fewer than Schirach had demanded. The reason was that most of Germany's means of transportation were required for the troop build-up in the General Government in the months prior to Operation Barbarossa. In mid-March deportations were temporarily suspended.

The planned attack on the Soviet Union seemed to open up another possibility for a territorial "final solution." After the expected swift victory and the collapse of the Bolshevik system, so the thinking ran, space would be found in the vast reaches of conquered Soviet territory where Jews could be deported and abandoned to their fate. In sketchy form, this idea occurred in the notes Eichmann made on 4 December 1940 for a speech Himmler was scheduled to give several days later to the Reichsleiters and Gauleiters. Here, under the heading "The Final Solution to the Jewish Question," was talk of the "resettlement of Jews from the European economic space of the German people to a yet-to-be-determined territory." As vague as this formulation was, it is obvious that the Reich Security Main Office had given up on the Madagascar project. According to Eichmann's calculations, there were no longer 4 million but 5.8 million Jews who were candidates for resettlement. The difference probably indicated the inclusion of the Jewish populations in the southeastern European states allied with the Third Reich.[86]

On 21 January 1941, Dannecker, who had been made the Gestapo's Jewish affairs expert in Paris the preceding September, noted: "In line with the will of the Führer, after the war, the Jewish question within the part of Europe ruled or dominated by Germany will be given a final solution." Heydrich, he revealed, had already received orders from Hitler to draw up a "proposal for the final solution project." Dannecker described this as a "gigantic piece of work" that would also have to encompass "the planning of a settlement operation, worked out to the final detail, in the territory yet to be determined."[87] On 26 March, Heydrich presented Göring with his proposals for the "solution of the Jewish question." The field marshal approved them "with a single change concerning Rosenberg's responsibilities." Since at this point Rosenberg was earmarked for a major role in the civilian administration of the territories to be conquered in the Soviet Union, we can conclude that the "territory yet to be determined" could only be an area to the east of the General Government.[88] A few days earlier, on 17 March, Hitler had assured Frank that the General Government would be "the first area to be made Jew-free." He repeated this pledge on 19 June, three days before Germany attacked the Soviet Union. Jews, Hitler said, would "in the foreseeable future be removed from the General Government," which would then only be a kind of "transit camp."[89] The dictator left it open where Jews would be deported to, but the context in which he made his statement allows us to infer that as a possible destination he favoured territory that would have previously belonged to the defeated Soviet Union.

In the spring of 1941, the consensus among the leadership of the Third Reich was that the comprehensive "final solution project" Heydrich had been charged with preparing would only be undertaken *after* the war. But with the planning of Operation Barbarossa, a new problem presented itself. What should be done with the more than three million Jews that would fall into German hands in the conquered Soviet territories? From the very beginning, this question was closely connected with general considerations about the character of the war against the Soviet Union, defined by Hitler and his generals as an ideological battle and an unprecedented war of conquest and annihilation. As we have seen, the Reich Security Main Office was eager to avoid the sorts of conflict between the Wehrmacht and the SS that had broken out during the Polish campaign. It meant that the SS needed to secure maximum freedom to act on its own. For its part, the Wehrmacht leadership was interested in relieving its units of rearguard "security operations." By late March 1941, in several rounds of negotiations, Heydrich and Army Quartermaster General Wagner had drawn up an agreement concerning "the deployment of the Security Police and the Security Service in conjunction with the army." Signed by Brauchitsch on 28 April, it allowed SS Einsatzgruppen in the theatre of operations to "carry out executive measures towards the civilian population on their own authority." It was left relatively vague who would be especially affected by this mandate. There was talk of "leading emigrants, saboteurs, terrorists etc." There was no direct mention of Jews, but based on the Polish campaign there could be no doubt that the destructive fury of the SS would be primarily directed against them.[90]

In addition to the Wagner-Heydrich agreement, Himmler announced on 21 May that, after consultations with Brauchitsch "on the implementation of the special commands given to me by the Führer for the area of political administration," he would be deploying high-ranking SS and police officers in the three rearguard zones of the army. They were to take charge not only of the Security Police and Security Service Einsatzgruppen but also of further units of the Order Police and the Waffen-SS. With that, having secured Hitler's approval, the head of the SS had created an instrument of power he could use to counteract competition from the Ministry for the Occupied Eastern Territories, which was still being formed under Rosenberg.[91]

Over the course of the spring, four Einsatzgruppen with some 3,000 men in total were put together. Each was assigned to follow an army group as it invaded the Soviet Union. Einsatzgruppe A was paired with Army Group North, Einsatzgruppe B with Army Group Centre, Einsatzgruppe C with Army Group South, and Einsatzgruppe D with the 11th Army, which would be invading the south of the Soviet Union together with the allied Romanian armies. Each Einsatzgruppe was made up of two Sonderkommandos (SK) operating directly behind the front and two Einsatzkommandos (EK) that were active further to the rear.[92] In choosing his leadership personnel, Heydrich drew upon long-term members of the SS and the police apparatus that he could rely on to behave unscrupulously and be highly motivated about their assigned tasks. Two of the four Einsatzgruppe leaders had occupied high-level positions in the Reich Security Main Office: Arthur Nebe, head of Office V and responsible for the Criminal Police, took over Einsatzgruppe B, while Otto Ohlendorf, head of Office III (Domestic Affairs), assumed responsibility for Einsatzgruppe D. Command of Einsatzgruppe A was given to Franz Walter Stahlecker, the former leader of the Security Police and Security Service in Prague. The head of Einsatzgruppe C was the inspector of the Security Police and the Security Service in Königsberg, Otto Rasch, who had already led an Einsatzgruppe in Poland. Three of these men—Stahlecker, Rasch and Ohlendorf—held doctorates. Moreover, with only a few exceptions, the leaders of the SKs and EKs had studied law, and many had received PhDs. They were therefore by no means the criminal dregs of German society. On the contrary, they were highly educated, relatively young and ambitious representatives of a class of elite functionaries, who had practical experience within the SS and police apparatus and whose behaviour was a homicidal mixture of cold empiricism and ideological fanaticism.[93]

On 17 June 1941 in the Prince Karl Palace in Berlin, Heydrich issued detailed instructions to the Einsatzkommando leaders, and shortly before the start of the invasion of the Soviet Union, he summoned them to the border police academy in Pretzsch on the Elbe to send them off. No documentation has survived from these two meetings, so it is impossible to say precisely what instructions were given. For a long time, it was assumed that orders were issued to kill all Jews in occupied Soviet territories. Such assumptions were based primarily on Ohlendorf's testimony to the Nuremberg Military Tribunal in 1946–47, in which he claimed that the head of the personnel division of the Security Main Office, Bruno Streckenbach, had delivered a "Führer order" to that effect a few days before the invasion. But historians now believe that Ohlendorf was lying to his interrogators to back up his claim that he and the other Einsatzgruppe leaders had no choice but to follow orders. As far as we can tell, no comprehensive order to destroy Soviet Jews was issued *before* the start of Operation Barbarossa.[94]

However, indications about what the Einsatzgruppen were charged with are provided by the written instructions Heydrich drew up *after* the invasion of the Soviet Union had begun. On 29 June, he told the Einsatzgruppe heads not to intervene against "self-cleansing measures among anti-communist and anti-Jewish groups" in the occupied territories. In other words, they were to encourage pogroms and purges without taking a role that would be noticeable from the outside. In a memorandum to higher SS and police officers on 2 July, he listed as people to be "executed" communist functionaries, other "radical elements" and "Jews who occupy party and state positions."[95] The definition of these groups of victims was intentionally left rather vague. That gave the heads of the Einsatzkommandos broad leeway so that they could act as they saw fit on the ground. It was largely left up to them how to interpret their instructions and translate them into action. This soon resulted in a competition over who could murder the greatest number of people.[96]

The mass shootings of Soviet Jews represented a quantum leap on the road to the systematic genocide of European Jews.[97] Right from the start, the homicidal actions of the Einsatzgruppen and police battalions were not restricted to just "Jews in party and state positions" but targeted all Jewish men capable of taking up arms. Without doubt, the extreme climate of violence surrounding the Wehrmacht's advance encouraged the breakdown of moral limits. Furthermore, Einsatzkommando leaders knew that they had no reason to fear potential sanctions. On the contrary, they were confident they were acting in the interests of their superiors in the Reich Security Main Office, if they interpreted their licence to kill as broadly as possible and threw all scruples overboard. From the onset, Einsatzgruppe A distinguished itself through its excessive cruelty in the Baltic. In keeping with Heydrich's directive, it unleashed pogroms against the Jewish populations in Kaunas, Vilnius and other Lithuanian cities. Soon Stahlecker's men embarked on mass shootings. By late July 1941, far more than ten thousand people, mainly Jewish men, had fallen victim to this first wave of murder alone.[98]

The fact that the Soviet secret police had executed political prisoners before it had evacuated the western territories served as a pretext for killing Jews in "reprisal" for the NKVD murders. In Lwów, even before the arrival of German troops on 29 June, Ukrainian militias had already begun hunting down Jews. The next day, when the commandos from Einsatzgruppe C followed, this impromptu pogrom was superseded by the systematic murder of Jewish men. Similar butchery occurred in Tarnopol (Ternopil) and other places in eastern Galicia. There too thousands of civilians were killed in the first weeks of Operation Barbarossa.[99] The true extent to which Lithuanian, Latvian and Ukrainian nationalists collaborated with the German occupiers only became known with the opening of eastern European archives after 1989. Without their cooperation, the relatively small Einsatzgruppen, who constantly travelled from one place to the next, could not have carried out their homicidal work nearly as effectively.[100]

Goebbels exploited the NKVD murders in Lwów and elsewhere to renew his campaign against "Jewish Bolshevism." "Tendency: the veil is dropping, Moscow unmasked," he noted. "In addition, all the horrific material from Lwów, where I am now sending twenty journalists and radio men." The weekly cinema newsreel in Germany featured repulsive images of the NKVD's victims, and in a nighttime phone call from the Wolf's Lair, Hitler expressed his enthusiasm for the propaganda initiative. "He said it was the best weekly newsreel we have ever made," Goebbels wrote.[101] "Bolshevik atrocities" became a frequent topic of conversation among the German people. According to the Security Service, most thought that "these images showed the true nature of Bolshevism and Jewry . . . and should be repeatedly shown so that every single ethnic-popular comrade can be convinced by this sobering material of the threat of Jewish Bolshevism and be reminded in concrete form of the ultimate significance of the German struggle."[102]

Not meant for public German consumption were the "Operational Situation Reports—USSR," regular dispatches sent by Einsatzgruppen and their commandos to Berlin and collected by the Reich Security Main Office. They made no effort to conceal German atrocities. On the contrary, in pedantic statistical detail, they recorded the number of people killed in various massacres. The reports were circulated to Nazi government ministries, including the Foreign Ministry.[103] After an order by Gestapo head Heinrich Müller on 1 August 1941, they were also presented to Hitler, although it is uncertain whether he actually read them. In the spring, he had established the general principle; he was not interested in the details of homicidal actions.[104] He left that up to Himmler, who he rightly assumed would be able to correctly interpret his wishes and translate them into concrete actions.

Only a few days after the start of Operation Barbarossa, Himmler, Heydrich and other SS leaders set off for the first inspections of the occupied territories to see for themselves what the Einsatzgruppen were doing. On 30 June, Himmler heard reports of the executions that had taken place in the Polish town of Augustów. He approved "entirely" of what had gone on there.[105] On 8 July, he headed for Białystok, where on 27 June members of a police battalion had carried out a particularly gruesome massacre, herding five hundred men, women and children into the city's main synagogue, setting it on fire and shooting those who tried to escape the inferno.[106] Here too Himmler and the head of the Order Police, Kurt Daluege, who accompanied him, made it clear that they not only approved of the operation but expected the same degree of personal initiative in the future. By visiting the sites of massacres and encouraging commando leaders to intensify the persecution of victims, Himmler and other high-ranking SS officials helped revoke limits on violence and accelerate the dynamics of murder.[107]

From August and September 1941, Einsatzgruppen and police battalions, supported by two SS brigades, started indiscriminately gunning down Jewish men, women and children. Entire Jewish communities in the occupied parts of the Soviet Union became targets for the death squads. Massacres of thousands of victims were an everyday occurrence. The worst of them all took place on 29 and 30 September 1941 in the Babi Yar ravine near Kiev. There, Einsatzgruppe C's Sonderkommando 4a, under the command of SS-Standartenführer Paul Blobel, murdered 33,771 Jews. "The action itself proceeded smoothly with no disruptions," the corresponding operational report for early October read. "It has not become widely known that the Jews were liquidated, but according to previous experiences, it would scarcely be rejected in any case. The Wehrmacht too welcomed the measures."[108]

Whereas atrocities committed by the Einsatzgruppen had caused tension between the Wehrmacht and the SS in occupied Poland in 1939, the two bodies worked together without any friction in the war of annihilation against the Soviet Union. "Cooperation with the Army High Command excellent," reported Stahlecker in early July 1941.[109]

After some initial difficulties, Nebe confirmed on 14 July, the activities of his Einsatzgruppe B were being "recognised and supported by all Wehrmacht offices."[110] Nothing changed about that in the months that followed. In late August, Einsatzgruppe C reported with satisfaction: "The relationship with the Wehrmacht is without problem. Above all, Wehrmacht circles are showing a growing interest and understanding for security tasks and concerns. This could be particularly observed at executions."[111]

Military commanders were not just informed early on about the mass executions carried out by SS and police forces. They also assisted them in a variety of ways that amounted to a division of labour. Indeed Wehrmacht field and local commanders led the way in registering and identifying Jews with armbands and badges as well as in sending them to ghettos and commandeering them for forced labour. It was this preliminary work that allowed the death squads to get hold of their victims so easily. Moreover, local military offices offered logistical help by providing trucks and ammunition or cordoning off the areas where mass executions took place. Occasionally Wehrmacht soldiers participated directly in the shootings. Without Wehrmacht assistance, as historians Johannes Hürter, Dieter Pohl and Christian Hartmann have conclusively demonstrated, the mass murder of Jews in occupied Soviet territory would hardly have been possible.[112]

The most intense cooperation took place between the Wehrmacht and SS and police units in the jurisdiction of Army Group C, and it was therefore no accident that it was here that the destruction of the Jewish populace took on its most monstrous dimensions. One of the main culprits was the commander of the 6th Army, Walter von Reichenau, a fanatical follower of Hitler known for his radicalism. In his daily order of 10 October 1941, a few days after the Babi Yar massacre, he called upon his men to show "full understanding for the necessity of this severe but just retribution for Jewish bestiality." In this "crusade against the Jewish-Bolshevik system," Reichenau continued, soldiers were not just "fighters according to the rules of warfare" but "bearers of an unrelenting ethnic idea" whose "historical task" it was to "liberate the German people once and for all from this Asiatic-Jewish peril."[113]

Army group commander Rundstedt declared himself in "complete agreement" with Reichenau's order and passed it on to his army and rearguard commanders. It was not long before the order came to Hitler's attention. The dictator found it "excellent" and instructed the Army High Command to use it as a "model order" for all troop commanders in the east.[114] Several of them were inspired to issue daily orders that were even more radical than Reichenau's. Thus Colonel-General Hermann Hoth, the commander of the 17th Army, characterised the "extermination of the Jewish class of people" as an "imperative for self-preservation," adding: "Any soldier who criticises these measures does not remember the earlier years of corrosive and treasonous activity by Jewish-Marxist elements within our own people."[115]

But there was no need to remind German soldiers of their purported "ethnic duty." As their letters amply attest, many soldiers had thoroughly internalised anti-Semitic stereotypes and were convinced that no limits applied in the fight against "Jewish Bolshevism." "The deeper we advanced into Russia, the more Jews we encountered," one private wrote in mid-August 1941. ". . . We should stand more of these deformed monsters up against the wall than we have so far." Another wrote of how happy he was that "the Jewish question is being resolved with impressive thoroughness" and recalled Hitler's prophecy of 30 January 1939: "The Jews must have known that the Führer meant what he said, and now they must bear the consequences. They are unrelentingly severe but necessary, if peace and quiet is to return among peoples." In early November 1941, referring to a destroyed synagogue, one infantryman wrote that the Jews "soon would need no more houses of worship." "For these horrible creatures, it is the only proper solution," the soldier added.[116]

In the early phase of the Soviet campaign, when German victory seemed to be a matter of weeks, not much energy was expended in cordoning off the areas where mass executions took place. Thus many soldiers involuntarily witnessed them, although a considerable number decided to join the ranks of the onlookers and even photograph the horrific scenes. In some regions there was a kind of "execution tourism." Individual army commanders prohibited rubbernecking and photography, but the bans do not seem to have been particularly effective.[117] It was easy for Wehrmacht soldiers to take part in the murders as they were often carried out under the pretext of combating partisans. "Where there's a partisan, there's a Jew, and where there's a Jew, there's a partisan"—Army Group Centre officers and SS and police commanders agreed on this formula when they met to compare their experiences in Mogilev in late September 1941.[118] A special case was Serbia, which was under German military administration and where it was exclusively Wehrmacht soldiers under the command of General Franz Böhme that took "retribution," murdering thousands of Serbian civilians, primarily Jewish men and "gypsies."[119]

By the end of 1941, the number of Jewish civilians killed by Einsatzgruppen, police battalions, SS brigades and Wehrmacht units ran to at least half a million.[120] In his final dispatch of the year, SS-Standartenführer Karl Jäger, the head of Einsatzkommando 3 in the field of operations of Einsatzgruppe A, reported that his men had executed 137,346 Jews between 4 July and 1 December. With pride, he concluded that "the goal of solving the Jewish problem for Lithuania" had been achieved, since there were "no more Jews here except those drafted for work and their families."[121]

As monstrous as the extent of the mass executions was, the Reich Security Main Office knew that they would not suffice to bring a "solution to the Jewish problem," as one operational report put it on 3 November 1941.[122] Thus at an early juncture SS leaders began to consider alternative ways of killing large numbers of people. As far back as 16 July 1941, in response to the catastrophic food shortages in the Łódź ghetto, the head of the Security Service main office in Poznań, Rolf-Heinz Höppner, had asked whether the "most humane solution" would not be to dispatch Jews unfit to work "with some quick-acting means" rather than "allowing them to starve."[123] Here the SS-Sturmbahnführer was thinking about the murder of the incurably ill with poisonous gas that had been carried out by the Sonderkommando Lange in the Warthegau in 1939 and 1940.

In mid-August, Himmler attended an "execution of partisans and Jews" near Minsk.[124] There are some indications that Hitler's cameraman Walter Frentz may have filmed it, although there is no hard evidence that the Führer ever watched the footage, which would in any case have run contrary to his preference for keeping at a distance the reality of the genocide he had set in motion.[125] After the executions, Himmler gave a speech justifying the killings as a severe but necessary step in the fight against "Jewish Bolshevism." He also charged

Arthur Nebe with finding a method of execution that could be carried out in secrecy and would be less "psychologically burdensome" for the men of his commando. Nebe, the head of Einsatzgruppe B, summoned to Minsk a leading member of the Criminal Technical Institute, the chemist Albert Widmann, who had already prepared bottles of carbon monoxide for use in murdering the ill and disabled.[126] It marked the beginning of the transfer of German "euthanasia" techniques to occupied eastern Europe.

Over the course of the spring and summer of 1941, rumours about the mass murder of hospital patients had continued to spread and created significant unease within the German public. "Hospitals and care facilities have become murder centres," Friedrich Kellner noted in his diary in late July.[127] But then, on 3 August, something happened that was unprecedented in the Third Reich. In a sermon, the Bishop of Münster, Count Clemens August von Galen, broke the silence about what was going on, condemning the killings of thousands of innocent people in the harshest of terms. He sketched out the consequences for German society as a whole: "If it is accepted that people have the right to kill 'unproductive' fellow human beings— and even if the first victims are only poor, defenceless, mentally ill people—then it essentially allows for the murder of all unproductive people: the incurably sick, those rendered invalids from work and war, and all of us when we become old, weak and unproductive."[128] The sermon created quite a stir, and the text of it was swiftly disseminated both inside and outside Germany. The courageous bishop was, in Kellner's words, "a gleaming star in Germany's deepest darkness" and would serve as "an illuminating example to coming generations."[129]

The Nazi leadership were initially uncertain about how they should react to Galen's provocation. Goebbels called it "a stab in the back of the fighting front" and a "crime ripe for the prosecutor's office," adding: "If it were up to me, I would make an example here." But after a few days, the propaganda minister came round to thinking that, given the unexpected difficulties Germany was encountering on the eastern front, it might be better to avoid drawing attention to the affair and further depressing the mood. "That would be extremely unproductive in a critical period of the war," Goebbels concluded. "We should keep everything explosive away from the people at the moment." When the propaganda minister visited the Wolf's Lair on 18 August, Hitler agreed that "we do not have to bring things to a head in the church question." The final reckoning could be postponed until after the war.[130] Six days later, the dictator ordered a halt to the "euthanasia" operations, although the murder of hospital patients did not cease completely. The killings would go on, albeit not in centrally directed gassing facilities but in less conspicuous, decentralised fashion, with doctors giving sick people deadly doses of medication.[131]

The T4 personnel freed up by the cessation of the "euthanasia" programme quickly found new employment in the east. In September 1941, Bouhler and Brack travelled to Lublin for a meeting with SS and police chief Odilo Globocnik to explore possibilities for cooperation.[132] In Mogilev, Widmann was already experimenting with killing disabled people by piping toxic combustion-engine fumes into a sealed space. These experiments yielded a new generation of gassing trucks in which victims were no longer killed by carbon monoxide from bottles but by exhaust fumes diverted into the airtight compartment on the truck bed. The central figure pushing forward this innovation was the director of the "technology group" in the Reich Security Main Office, SS-Standartenführer Walther Rauff.[133] In early November 1941, the new killing technique was tested out on Soviet prisoners in the Sachsenhausen concentration camp. A short time later, the first gassing trucks were delivered to the Einsatzgruppen. At the same time in Chełmno in the Warthegau, Jews from the Łódź ghetto were also being gassed to death in trucks.[134]

From this point, it was but a short step to building stationary gas chambers that used the same technique to kill Jews. At a meeting with Globocnik in Berlin in mid-October 1941, Himmler had given the green light to construct a death camp in Belzec, near the border of the Lublin district with eastern Galicia. Building work began at the start of November, and one by one the experts from the T4 programme arrived there, led by SS-Hauptsturmführer Christian Wirth, who became Belzec's first camp commandant.[135] The transition to systematic, factory-like genocide was underway.

But did this mean that the Nazi leadership had already decided to murder all Jews in areas under German control? This question has been fiercely debated by historians. Christopher Browning has most forcefully advanced the thesis that at the height of the euphoria over German military victories in July 1941, Hitler "inaugurated the decision-making process that led to the extension of the Final Solution to European Jewry."[136] His central piece of evidence is Göring's memorandum to Heydrich of 31 July, authorising him to make "all necessary preparations" for a "total solution of the Jewish question" in the European territories under German influence. Heydrich was also charged with submitting a "comprehensive draft" of "initial measures for the implementation of the desired final solution of the Jewish question."[137] In fact this mandate, prepared by Eichmann and signed by Göring, did not represent a qualitatively new element but rather was merely written confirmation of Göring's verbal instruction given to Heydrich the previous March. At the point when victory seemed within Germany's grasp, it appears that Heydrich's main concern was to cover his back formally before following up on the plan he had been considering since the end of 1940, namely to deport the Jews of Europe to some remote part of the occupied Soviet Union. In other words, a decision in favour of genocide on a huge scale had not yet been taken. The "Jewish experts" in the Reich Security Main Office were still contemplating some sort of vaguely conceived "territorial solution."[138]

At a meeting with the Croatian defence minister, Slavko Kvaternik, on 22 July, Hitler once again underlined his intention to remove all Jews from German-controlled territories. "If there were no more Jews in Europe, the unity of the European states would no longer be disrupted," he asserted. "It does not matter whether the Jews are sent to Siberia or Madagascar."[139] The Madagascar scheme was already dead—it appears that Hitler used the name as a mere cypher for some faraway place—and the idea of deporting Jews somewhere "to the east" would also soon be revealed as nothing more than a chimera. In August 1941, Hitler and the Wehrmacht leadership were forced to recognise that the Blitzkrieg against the Soviet Union had failed. By the end of October at the latest, they knew that the campaign would not be over by the onset of winter. Once again the "territorial solution to the Jewish question" had to be postponed indefinitely.[140] Decision-makers in the Wolf's Lair and in Berlin were confronted once more with the urgent question of what to do with the Jews under their control.

★

Since the start of Operation Barbarossa, the situation of Jews in Germany had further deteriorated. Propaganda was constantly inciting popular anti-Semitism. "Verbal abuse of Jews more extreme, repulsive than ever," Klemperer noted.[141] In early July 1941, after consulting with Hitler, Goebbels issued a general guideline that "the cooperation between Bolshevism and the plutocracy should be laid bare and the Jewish character on this score exposed."[142] In this context, it was a boon to the propaganda minister that a book entitled *Germany Must Perish* was published in the United States. It demanded that all German men be sterilised and German territory divided up between its European neighbours. The author, a thirty-one-year-old American Jew named Theodore N. Kaufman, had self-published his screed, and it attracted almost no attention. But German propaganda turned it into a major scandal, contending that Kaufman's proposals had been inspired by Roosevelt himself. The headline of the *Völkischer Beobachter* on 24 July read: "The War Aim of Roosevelt and the Jews: Complete Extermination of the German People."[143]

Goebbels decided to publish a translation of the pamphlet in a "popular edition" of millions of copies. "It will be extraordinarily edifying for every German man and woman to learn what will be done to the German people if they show weakness as they did in November 1918," the propaganda minister noted in his diary.[144] Hitler approved the idea, and Wolfgang Diewerge, a Goebbels underling, produced an abbreviated and annotated German edition, of which five million copies were distributed.[145] "Even dyed-in-the-wool complainers" were "shaken to the core" by the book, concluded a Security Service report. It showed that "this war is a matter of life and death."[146]

In August, the incendiary mood resulted in demands, primarily from party members, that Jews within Germany itself should be required to wear a means of identification like those used in the General Government.[147] Goebbels, who had already advocated such a measure in the spring, now saw his chance. "I too consider it necessary that Jews be given a badge," he wrote. "After all, they do their best to criticise everything and ruin the mood in queues, on public transport and elsewhere in public."[148] On his visit to the Wolf's Lair on 18 August, he had no trouble in getting Hitler to approve his proposal to introduce "a large visible badge of identification for all Jews in the Reich." The dictator, who had become aware in the preceding days that his plans for the Soviet campaign had failed, lashed out with ominous threats about the Jews' future. Once again, he recalled his prophecy of 30 January 1939, which, Goebbels noted, "would be fulfilled in the coming weeks and months with an almost eerie certainty": "In the east, Jews will have to pay the cost. In Germany they have already paid it in part and will be forced to pay even more in future . . . In any case, Jews will not have much reason to laugh in the world to come."[149] These statements came at a time when the Einsatzgruppen were beginning to expand their murder sprees in the occupied parts of the Soviet Union, and they show that Hitler not only knew, but approved, of this escalation of anti-Jewish violence.

The "Police Decree on the Identification of Jews" was issued on 1 September. From 15 September, all Jews over the age of six had to wear a yellow star with the word "Jew" clearly visible on their left breast when out in public. They were also prohibited from leaving their "area of residence" without permission.[150] On top of all the other harassments Jews had been forced to endure, this new ordinance was considered especially humiliating: Klemperer called it the "worst blow yet." On 19 September, when his wife sewed the Yellow Star on his overcoat, he experienced a "fit of desperate rage."[151] Willy Cohn complained: "This is worse than the Middle Ages!" But he tried to keep his spirits up: "We will not let this get us down, even if life is getting increasingly difficult."[152]

According to the observations of the Security Service, the introduction of the Yellow Star was welcomed with "true satisfaction" by the German people, since it removed "every possibility" for Jews to "disguise themselves." The local Security Service office in Bielefeld reported that "generally the hope is that soon the last Jew will have left the German fatherland."[153] But in reality the positive resonance was not as universal as the Security Service suggested. Some Germans expressed unease and sympathy with the victims. "The majority of the people are not happy about the new ordinance," the journalist and Hitler opponent Ruth Andreas-Friedrich wrote in her diary about the reaction in Berlin.[154] In Breslau, Cohn, who like all Jews had to summon his courage every time he went out on the street to buy something, wrote that the Yellow Star was "more of an embarrassment to the ethnic-popular comrades than to us."[155] Ulrich von Hassell observed a scene that does not seem to have been unique: "On the train, a humongous labourer said to a poor old Jewish woman, 'Come on, my little shooting star, have a seat.' When someone complained, he growled, 'I can do whatever I like with my behind!' "[156]

Yet we should not overestimate such gestures of human solidarity. Clearly, only a small minority of Germans maintained a sense of decency and humanity. The shame many Germans felt when they saw someone wearing the Yellow Star was not born of empathy but was the unpleasant realisation of witnessing an injustice of the sort they had closed their eyes to for many years. No doubt, some people were surprised at how many Jews still lived among them. After initially being taken aback somewhat, most Germans soon accepted their regime's latest shameful action and became uninterested and apathetic towards the fate suffered by their Jewish neighbours.[157]

Nonetheless, the partly negative reactions were enough to make Goebbels uneasy. "The Jews only need to send a little old lady with a Yellow Star across the Kurfürstendamm boulevard, and the typical German is inclined to forget everything the Jews have done to us in years and decades past," he complained to his diary.[158] Press and radio should do more to combat such "sentimental humanitarianism," he fumed. At the same time, in conjunction with the Reich Security Main Office, the propaganda minister stepped up the pressure on Hitler to approve the resumption of deportations from the Reich. In late July, the dictator had rejected a request by Heydrich to that effect, and at their meeting of 18 August, Goebbels was only able to get Hitler to agree to "deport Jews from Berlin to eastern Europe immediately after the completion of the eastern campaign."[159]

In mid-September 1941, Hitler changed his mind and decided that Jews should be deported "to the east" even as the war continued. There were apparently several reasons for the shift. Evidence suggests that Hitler was reacting to Stalin's deportation of the Volga Germans to Siberia, which had become known in Germany earlier that month, stirring up considerable dust among the Nazi leadership.[160] In retribution, Rosenberg demanded that "the Jews of central Europe be taken to the territories under German administration further to the east." Via his ministry's liaison officer with the Army High Command, Otto Bräutigam, he brought up the subject with Hitler on 14 September.[161]

But the United States also played a role in the dictator's thinking. On 11 September, Roosevelt had decreed that the US Navy was allowed to fire on Axis warships in the neutral zone in the North Atlantic. It was looking increasingly likely that America would join the war. Correspondingly, there was a growing inclination among the Nazi leadership to try to use Jews as bargaining chips to prevent this.[162] Finally, the beginning of Allied air raids on Germany may also have influenced Hitler. That September, the Gauleiter of Hamburg, Karl Kaufmann, had asked him "to evacuate the Jews so that at least some of the bombed-out residents of the city can be given new places to live."[163] Measures like this were thought to limit the psychological effects of the bombing war on the urban population.

We cannot be sure precisely when Hitler made up his mind. On 16 September, Himmler visited the Wolf's Lair, and the following day Hitler discussed Rosenberg's proposal with Ribbentrop, before the foreign minister conferred with Himmler that evening.[164] The decision to deport German Jews seems to have been taken on one of these two days, since by 18 September Himmler was already communicating to the Gauleiter of the Wartheland, Arthur Greiser, the Führer's wish that "the old Reich and Protectorate be emptied of and liberated from Jews." As a "first stage," they were to be transported to German-annexed Polish territories and then "deported further east" in the coming spring. Himmler said he wanted to send a further 60,000 Jews to the already drastically overpopulated Łódz' ghetto that winter.[165] On a visit to the Wolf's Lair on 23 September, Goebbels received long-awaited permission from Hitler to gradually remove Jews from Germany. "The first cities to be made Jew-free are Berlin, Vienna and Prague," Goebbels wrote. "Berlin will be the start, and I hope that over the course of the year we will succeed in transporting a large portion of the city's Jews to the east."[166]

The deportations began on 15 October. In the first wave, which continued until 5 November, almost 20,000 people were taken in twenty transports from Vienna, Prague, Berlin, Frankfurt, Hamburg, Cologne and other cities to the Łódź ghetto. In a second wave from 8 November to 21 February 1942, 33,000 people were deported in thirty-four transports to Minsk, Kaunas and Riga.[167] But Goebbels was dissatisfied with what he considered the faltering start to the deportations. "We should not just deport some Jews from all our cities, because then the problem remains acute," he wrote. "We should be completely evacuating one city after another. Berlin of course is first in line. The capital of the Reich must be Jew-free, as much as circumstances allow."[168] Nonetheless, after consulting with Heydrich on 17 November, Goebbels had to admit that deporting Jews from the Reich was more difficult than had been anticipated. He wrote: "15,000 Jews will have to remain in Berlin one way or another because they are employed performing important and extremely perilous tasks that are vital to the war."[169] Four days later, Hitler approved Goebbels' suggestion to proceed city by city, but he avoided specifying any dates for the Reich capital. "It is thus uncertain when Berlin's turn will be," noted Goebbels. "But when it comes, the evacuation is to be carried out as quickly as possible."[170]

The deportations followed a set procedure. Several days in advance of the transports, the heads of Jewish communities were summoned by the Gestapo and informed about the upcoming "resettlement." Officials decided who was a candidate for deportation with the help of lists of names that had been compiled. Those selected were made to fill out a questionnaire indicating all their valuables. The complete expropriation of these people was made legal by the 11th Supplementary Ordinance to the Reich Citizenship Law of 25 November 1941, which revoked the citizenship of deported Jews and transferred all their assets to the Reich. On 23 October, the Reich Security Main Office had already issued a blanket ban on emigration, thus closing the final escape route for Germany's Jews. The Gestapo specified exactly what the deportees were allowed to take with them. They were then ordered to report to a collection point on the date in question. From there they were herded, often in broad daylight, towards goods yards where trains stood waiting.[171]

"Increasingly devastating news about the Jewish transports to Poland," Klemperer noted in late October 1941. "They are being forced to leave literally naked and empty-handed."[172] More than a few Jews suspected what their ultimate fate would be and took their own lives: the number of suicides shot up in the final quarter of 1941.[173] On 13 November, the head of the Kreisau anti-Hitler resistance circle, Helmuth James von Moltke, wrote from Berlin to his wife: "Yesterday I took my leave of a formerly famous Jewish attorney, a holder of the Iron Cross First and Second Class, the House Order of Hohenzollern and the Golden Badge of the War Wounded, who intends to commit suicide with his wife today because they are scheduled to be picked up tonight." Moltke asked himself a question every German should have been asking in light of such horrific news: "Is it permissible for me to learn of such things and still sit in my heated apartment drinking tea? Am I not making myself complicit by doing this?"[174]

But unlike the introduction of the Yellow Star, the deportation of German Jews did little to unsettle the population as a whole. Many Germans even seemed relieved that Jews disappeared from view so they no longer felt pangs of conscience when they saw them.[175] Moreover, the homes and households left behind by the deported were highly coveted. Nonetheless, the Security Service did register isolated expressions of sympathy. A report from Minden in mid-December 1941 about views in pious Christian circles read: "[They say] it is beyond comprehension that human beings could be treated so brutally. Whether they are Jews or Aryans, all are ultimately human beings created by God."[176]

The decision to deport German Jews did not initially mean that they were to be liquidated wherever they were sent, or indeed that an overarching plan for the eradication of European Jews existed. This is evident in the different treatments to which various deportees were subjected. Whereas those deported in the first wave were all sent to Łódź and crammed into the city's ghetto, the first five transports originally scheduled for Riga between 25 and 29 November were diverted to Kaunas, where the deportees were immediately executed by Karl Jäger's Einsatzkommando 3. Among the 5,000 people murdered there were most likely Willy Cohn, his wife and two daughters, who had been deported from Breslau on 25 November.[177] It is unlikely that the massacre was personally ordered by Himmler, since a short time later, when a further transport of more than 1,000 Jews set off for Riga, Himmler phoned Heydrich and noted in his work calendar on 30 November: "Transport of Jews from Berlin. No liquidation."[178] But it was too late. In the early morning hours, SS and Police Commander Friedrich Jeckeln had ordered the Jews to be executed in a forest near Riga. That earned him an admonition from Himmler: "The Jews resettled in eastern regions are to be treated solely in accordance with the guidelines issued by me or the Reich Security Main Office at my behest. I will punish any autonomous actions and defiance."[179] After this rebuke, Jews deported to Riga were no longer murdered but put into the city's ghetto or taken to concentration camps in Lithuania. The same was true of transports to Minsk, although there, to make room for German Jews, the Security Police and the Security Service shot almost 12,000 Soviet Jews that November.[180]

While there may not yet have been any blanket authorisation to murder German Jews in the autumn of 1941, the point was rapidly approaching at which they and all Jews in German-dominated Europe had to fear for their lives. The more the war turned against Germany, the more hateful Hitler's tirades against "global Jewry" became—Saul Friedländer writes of an "explosion of the vilest anti-Jewish invectives and threats."[181] In his "Proclamation to the Soldiers on the Eastern Front" on 2 October, Hitler described the conditions in the Soviet Union as the result of "a 25-year Jewish rule of Bolshevism that was at its root the basest form of capitalism." Hitler went on: "In both cases, the bearers of the system are one and the same: Jews and Jews alone!"[182] Once it became clear that Operation Typhoon would not decide the war, Hitler ratcheted up his verbal abuse of Jews even further. "If we eradicate this plague, we will do a good deed for humanity of whose significance our men out there can have no idea," he declared over lunch at the Wolf's Lair on 21 October, a few days after the first deportation trains had left the Reich for the east.[183] Over dinner on 25 October, in the presence of Heydrich and Himmler, he recalled his "prophecy" of January 1939 and proceeded to say: "This criminal race has two million dead in the world war on its conscience, and now hundreds of thousands more. No one can tell me that we cannot send them out into a swamp. Who cares about our own people? It is good if the fear precedes us that we will exterminate the Jews."[184]

In the evening of 5 November, Hitler delivered another poisonous monologue about Jews' alleged lack of culture. "I have always said that the Jews are the stupidest devils there are," he ranted. "They do not have a single true musician or thinker. They have no art, nothing, nothing at all. They are liars, counterfeiters, swindlers . . . We can live without the Jews, but they cannot live without us." Hitler had begun his outburst with the ominous words: "The end of the war will be a fall from grace: a fall for the Jews."[185] Three days later, when he addressed the "old fighters" in Munich, he devoted much of his speech to attacks upon "international Jews" as "global arsonists." For Hitler the "driving force in the global coalition against the German people" was no longer the Anglo-Saxon "plutocracy," but rather Stalin's dictatorship, which he excoriated as "Jewry's biggest servant." The "slave state" of the Soviet Union was ruled by a "regime of commissars, 90 per cent of whom have Jewish roots." And Hitler justified Germany's campaign of annihilation as an unavoidable epochal conflict with the "all-mighty Jewry" and a "battle for existence."[186]

Goebbels mined much the same territory on 16 November in an editorial in the weekly newspaper *Das Reich*, which bore the headline "The Jews Are to Blame!" He too directed his readers' attention back to Hitler's "prophecy" of 30 January 1939 before openly declaring: "We are experiencing the fulfilment of this prophecy, and with it a destiny, a hard but just destiny, is being visited upon the Jews. Sympathy or regret have no place here. Global Jewry . . . is undergoing a gradual process of destruction, which it had wanted to inflict upon us and which it would have enacted without scruple, if it had possessed the power. Now its demise is taking place according to its own law 'An eye for an eye, a tooth for a tooth'!"[187] The article was read out on radio and widely disseminated as a special pamphlet. It had been "extensively cited in the world press," noted Goebbels, and "attracted significant applause above all among party members."[188]

Rosenberg spoke even more frankly at a press reception on 18 November, one day after his appointment as the new minister for the eastern territories was officially announced. His remarks were made off the record and were never intended to become public. What he said must have sounded extreme even to the ears of true-believing Nazi journalists: "There are some six million Jews living in the east, and this question can only be solved by the biological eradication of the entirety of Jewry in Europe. The Jewish question is only resolved for Germany when the last Jew has left German soil—and for Europe when no Jew remains on the continent all the way to the Ural Mountains. That is the task with which destiny has presented us . . . And that makes it necessary to force them over the Urals or otherwise somehow eliminate them."[189] Three days earlier Rosenberg had had a long meeting with Hitler during which the "Jewish problem" had also been discussed, and on 16 November, he had had dinner with Hitler and Himmler.[190] Thus there is no reason to assume that Rosenberg would be so blunt before the press unless he was certain that he was speaking in the name of Hitler and Himmler. Since for the foreseeable future, the military situation would preclude deporting Jews to a territory beyond the Urals, the only remaining option was the second one named by Rosenberg—"somehow eliminating them." Following this logic, the question was no longer *whether* but *how* to kill the Jews. We must remember that Rosenberg's speech came at a time when the T4 experts were busily establishing a network of annihilation in the General Government that aimed to replace mass shootings with murder by poisonous gas.

On 28 November, Hitler received the Grand Mufti of Jerusalem, Mohammed Amin al-Husseini, and declared his determination "to force the European nations step by step to solve the Jewish problem and to appeal to the non-European peoples to do the same at an appropriate juncture." Germany, he promised, would not pursue any imperialist aims in the Middle East, but would support the liberation of the Arab people. He did, however, have one goal for the region: "the destruction of the Jewry that lives in the Arab realm under the protection of British power."[191] In his public tirades, Hitler avoided directly alluding to the concrete measures of destruction. He preferred to adopt a strangely ambivalent way of speaking that both revealed and concealed the horrors that were unfolding. But his eliminatory anti-Semitic rhetoric, eagerly seized upon by Goebbels and other high-level functionaries, was doubtless aimed at radicalising Germany's anti-Jewish policies. It was crucial in creating the climate of murderous violence that made the Holocaust possible in the first place. There was no need for a written order to exterminate the Jews. It was enough if the dictator made his wishes known verbally and signalled to his eager mass executioners, above all Himmler and Heydrich, that they could cite the "Führer's will" as justification for anything and everything they did.

On 29 November, Heydrich invited representatives of government ministries and departments as well as SS and Nazi Party offices to a conference at which they might arrive at "a consistent approach among the central organs involved" towards all the questions connected with the "final solution." He underscored the "extraordinary importance" of the meeting by referring to the deportation of Jews from the Reich and the Protectorate, which had commenced on 15 October. To bolster this message, he included with the invitation a copy of Göring's memorandum of 31 July 1941 charging Heydrich with preparing "a comprehensive solution to the Jewish question."[192] The conference was originally scheduled for 9 December, but it was postponed on the eve of that date. In a second letter on 8 January 1942, Heydrich blamed the delay on "events that were suddenly announced" and "the demands placed by them on some of the gentlemen invited." A new date was set for 20 January 1942.[193]

The unexpected events Heydrich was referring to were clearly the Soviet counter-offensive, which had begun in earnest on 5 December, and the Japanese attack on Pearl Harbor two days later, which led to Germany's declaration of war against the United States. This dramatic turn in the war had direct effects on Hitler's stance on the "Jewish question." Any calculations that Jews could be used as bargaining chips to keep America out of the war were now obsolete. A European war for continental hegemony had become a global conflict, fulfilling the conditions Hitler had laid out in his "prophecy" of January 1939 and reiterated many times since. It was no accident, therefore, that when he spoke to the Reichsleiters and Gauleiters in Berlin on 12 December 1941, he began with precisely this topic. Goebbels recorded the key points of that address in his diary: "Concerning the Jewish question, the Führer has decided on a total clean-up. He prophesied to the Jews that if they started a world war, they would experience their own destruction. This was not just a turn of phrase. The world war is now here, and the destruction of Jewry must necessarily be the result. This question is to be addressed without sentimentality. We are not here to have pity on the Jews, but to have pity on our own people. If the German people have again sacrificed 160,000 men in the eastern campaign, then those who caused this bloody conflict will have to pay for that with their lives."[194]

On 17 December, having returned to the Wolf's Lair, Hitler reiterated in conversation with Goebbels his determination to "continue to proceed stringently and not be restrained by bourgeois sentimentality" on the "Jewish question." "The Jews are all to be deported to the east—what becomes of them there can be of no interest to us," Hitler told Goebbels. The propaganda minister was satisfied that despite being occupied with the military crisis on the eastern front, the Führer had taken the time to discuss the "Jewish problem" with him. "He alone is capable of solving this problem once and for all with the necessary severity," Goebbels concluded.[195] The following day, Hitler also received Himmler at the Wolf's Lair. After their meeting, Himmler noted in his work calendar: "Jewish question. To be exterminated as partisans."[196] Ever since executions had been expanded in the occupied eastern territories, the SS and the Wehrmacht had begun to use "partisans" and "Jews" as synonyms, and this equivalence entailed nothing less than mass murder. The occupied eastern territories were to be made "Jew-free," Himmler later recalled. "The Führer placed the execution of this very difficult order on my shoulders."[197]

The historian Christian Gerlach has interpreted Hitler's statements between 12 and 18 December as proof that he took a "fundamental decision" at that time to murder Europe's Jews.[198] This thesis has been as hotly debated as Browning's, although it seems more plausible. While Hitler had already repeatedly threatened to wipe out Europe's Jews in previous weeks, it was only in the context of the "winter crisis" on the eastern front and America's entry into the war that he seems to have decided to turn those threats into action and no longer postpone the "final solution" until after Germany had defeated the Soviet Union. Saul Friedländer has correctly concluded that "crossing the line from local murder operations to overall extermination required a go-ahead signal from the supreme authority."[199] Hitler seems to have first given this sort of signal in his address to the Reichsleiters and Gauleiters on 12 December. At least that was how the functionaries present understood him, as is revealed in a speech Hans Frank gave to officials in the General Government when he returned to Krakow four days later. "I want to tell you openly that, one way or another, an end must be put to the Jews," Frank announced. Recapitulating Hitler, he called upon his listeners to free themselves of all pangs of human sympathy: "As a rule, we want to have sympathy only with the German people and no one else in the world . . . As a long-time National Socialist I must say: if the Jewish clan were to survive the war in Europe, and we had sacrificed our best blood to preserve Europe, then this war would only be a partial success. As far as the Jews are concerned, I proceed from the fundamental expectation that they will disappear. They have to go."

Frank's words made it clear that Jews in the General Government were also to be eliminated. But where and how was that to happen?

The original idea of deporting them to some unspecified part of the conquered Soviet Union was now obsolete. As a result, Frank tried to prepare his government officials for mass murders being carried out in his region of authority. "We were told in Berlin: why create all these problems? We do not know what to do with them in the Ostland or the Reich Commissariat [Ukraine] either. Liquidate them yourselves! . . . Wherever we find them and wherever it is possible we have to eliminate the Jews in order to preserve the overarching structure of the Reich." Frank was not yet certain about the method to be used in this elimination, but he said he hoped that would become clear at the conference Heydrich had called for mid-January in Berlin. "In the General Government," he continued, "we have an estimated 2.5 million Jews, perhaps 3.5 million if we include all sorts of relatives. We cannot shoot these 3.5 million Jews. We cannot poison them either. But we will be able to make interventions that lead in some way to their successful destruction. This will happen in the context of large-scale measures to be discussed by the Reich. The General Government must become as free of the Jews as the Reich itself."[200]

By December 1941 senior civil servants in Berlin had learned that Jews were now to be physically eliminated, as is revealed in a conversation between the state secretary in the Interior Ministry, Wilhelm Stuckart, and his expert on "race questions," Bernhard Lösener, on 19 December. Horrified by the murder of the Berlin Jews in Riga, Lösener had tendered his resignation. But Stuckart told him: "The procedure against the evacuated Jews is based on a decision from on high. You will have to learn to live with it!" Significantly, the state secretary completely adopted Hitler's justification for the change in policy: "If we are striking back with severity, it must be realised that this severity is a world-historical necessity. We cannot ask timidly whether this or that Jew who has been evacuated and now faces his fate is personally culpable."[201]

On the morning of 20 January 1942, fifteen high-ranking representatives of the Nazi regime assembled on Berlin's Wannsee in a lakeside villa that had been seized from Friedrich Minoux, an industrialist convicted of embezzlement, and had served as an SS guest house since 1940. One-third of those present were ministerial leaders: Stuckart; State Secretary Roland Freisler from the Justice Ministry, later the head of the infamous People's Court; Foreign Ministry under-

secretary Martin Luther; the deputy head of the Office for the Four-
Year Plan, Erich Neumann; and the ministerial director of the Reich
Chancellery, Friedrich Kritzinger. The German civilian administration
in the occupied eastern territories was represented by Frank's deputy
Josef Bühler, Gauleiter Alfred Meyer and Reich Office director Georg
Leibbrandt from Rosenberg's Eastern Ministry. Representing the SS
and Nazi Party offices concerned with "race questions" were
SS-Oberführer Gerhard Klopfer from Bormann's Party Chancellery
and SS-Gruppenführer Otto Hofmann, the director of the SS Race
and Settlement Main Office. Heydrich had of course also invited high-
ranking members of his own office: Gestapo head Heinrich Müller;
Adolf Eichmann, director of the "Jewish department" (IV B4) in the
Reich Security Main Office; the head of the Security Police and Security
Service in the General Government, Karl Georg Schöngarth; and
SS-Sturmbannführer Rudolf Lange, director of Einsatzkommando 2
and commander of the Security Police and Security Service in the
General District of Latvia.[202]

Eichmann produced the minutes of the conference from stenographic notes taken by a secretary. Heydrich edited the text, which
was classified as a "confidential Reich matter," and had thirty copies
of it made for circulation. The minutes would be discovered in March
1947 in the files of the German Foreign Ministry by employees of US
prosecutor Robert Kempner in their preparations for the Nuremberg
trials. Since then, they have been rightly regarded as the key document
in the history of the genocide of European Jews.[203]

In his introductory remarks, Heydrich reminded the conference that
Göring had appointed him as "delegate for the preparations for the final
solution of the Jewish question in Europe." The purpose of the meeting
was to clarify "fundamental questions" and to coordinate the actions
of "all central offices immediately concerned with these questions."
After once more insisting that the leadership of this enterprise rested
with Himmler and himself, Heydrich proceeded to give an overview of
the measures already taken. Between 1933 and October 1941, he told the
conference, 537,000 Jews had been convinced to emigrate from Germany,
Austria and the Protectorate. "After relevant prior approval by the
Führer," Heydrich continued, "the evacuation of Jews to the east has
replaced emigration as a further possible solution." Somewhat cryptic-
ally, he characterised these "actions" as "mere alternative possibilities,"

although the "practical experiences" gained from them would be of "great significance with regard to the coming final solution of the Jewish question." Without doubt, Heydrich was referring to the deportations to Łódź, Minsk, Kaunas and Riga.

According to a detailed list of calculations, prepared by Eichmann, eleven million Jews in total would be affected by the "final solution." That number included not just Jews in the Reich and in German-controlled territories but also in neutral countries like Ireland, Sweden, Switzerland and Turkey and even in still-to-be-conquered Britain. This was an indication that the Holocaust was conceived as a long-term project that would continue after the conclusion of the war. When it came to short-term plans, Heydrich explained: "Under proper guidance, in the course of the final solution the Jews are to be allocated to appropriate labour in the east. Able-bodied Jews, separated according to sex, will be taken in large work columns to these areas for work on roads, in the course of which action a large portion will without doubt be eliminated by natural causes. The possible final remnant will, since it will undoubtedly consist of the most resistant portion, have to be treated accordingly, because it is the product of natural selection and would, if released, act as a seed of a new Jewish revival."[204]

Behind the carefully chosen, camouflaging words, the idea was that Jews would be worked to death. The minutes do not mention Jews who were unable to work, above all women and children. But within the context of what was said, there can be no doubt as to what fate was envisaged for them. Frank's representative Bühler insisted that the "Jewish question" be resolved in the General Government as "quickly as possible," arguing that the majority of the 2.5 million Jews there were "unfit for work" and could be immediately liquidated. By contrast, Heydrich's plan was to send Jews from the Reich and the Protectorate "group by group to so-called transit ghettos, from which they will be transported to the east." The language does not conceal the genocidal implications: even if the Jews could have been deported to some faraway territory in the Soviet Union, something that Germany's military setbacks had made very unlikely, there can be no doubt that most of them would not have survived the trip. In the language of the planners of the "final solution," the phrase "evacuation to the east" was a euphemism that concealed their murderous intentions.

Heydrich announced that there were no plans to "evacuate" Jews over the age of sixty-five and Jewish veterans of the First World War. They were instead to be put in the "old people's ghetto" of Theresienstadt. With this expedient solution, many interventions on their behalf would be prevented "in one fell swoop," he claimed. What Heydrich left unsaid but must have been clear to the conference was that such a model ghetto would be ideal for deceiving the public about the fate of other deported Jews.

The final part of the conference was devoted to the problem of Jewish partners in "mixed marriages" and "persons of mixed blood." Heydrich made detailed suggestions about how these categories of people would be incorporated into the deportation programme and where exceptions would be made. But on this score, ministerial representatives had some qualms. Stuckart, for instance, objected that Heydrich's proposal would create "endless administrative work." No agreement was reached, and neither did the subsequent conferences that took place over the course of 1942 resolve the issue.[205]

Nonetheless, Heydrich had reason to be satisfied with what had come out of Wannsee. He had achieved basically everything he had set out to accomplish. All the participants had accepted the leading role of the Reich Security Main Office in the planning and execution of the "final solution," and he had succeeded in getting representatives of the highest Reich offices to commit to a joint deportation programme. All this meant that the systematic mass murder of European Jews would now commence during wartime. No one had objected. On the contrary, there had been remarkable agreement among the men around the conference table. Heydrich's elation continued after the ninety-minute meeting was over. He asked Gestapo head Müller and Eichmann to stay behind after the others left. Together they sat around a cosy fireplace, drinking cognac and enjoying the feeling that they had taken a giant step forward.[206]

On 31 January 1942, Eichmann sent to all directing offices of the state police a memorandum in which he drew the first consequences from the Wannsee Conference. "The recent evacuations in individual areas of Jews to the east," he wrote, "represent the beginning of the final solution of the Jewish question in the old Reich, the Ostmark and the Protectorate of Bohemia and Moravia." He added that "new possibilities for accepting" Jews were being sought with the goal of "deporting further contingents," for which it was necessary to make a "conscientious record of Jews still residing in Reich territories."[207] On 6 March, Eichmann called Gestapo representatives to Berlin to discuss the details of a new "evacuation" programme, in which 55,000 people were to be deported, this time chiefly from Prague (20,000) and Vienna (18,000). The percentage of Jews from other cities would "depend on the number of Jews still present in each state police district."[208] The second wave of deportations began in mid-March, with the destination this time being a series of ghettos in Lublin.[209] "Jews are again being evacuated from Berlin on a large scale," noted Goebbels. "We are talking about around a thousand who will be shipped east every week. The percentage of suicides among these Jews to be evacuated is extraordinarily high. But that does not bother me. The Jews deserve no other destiny than the one they are suffering today."[210]

Hitler seems to have been informed of the results of the Wannsee Conference straight away,[211] and in the weeks and months that followed, he further sharpened his tone. "This has to be done quickly . . . The Jews must leave Europe," he declared over lunch on 25 January in the Wolf's Lair in the presence of Himmler and Lammers. "Otherwise we will never reach a European understanding. They incite [discord] everywhere . . . I can only say they have to go. If they are destroyed in the process, I cannot help that. I see only one option: complete extermination, if they do not go voluntarily. Why should I look at the Jews with other eyes than at Russian prisoners?"[212] Since as of October 1941 Jews were prohibited from leaving Germany voluntarily, everyone at the table must have understood what the dictator was planning, and the reference to Soviet POWs, hundreds of thousands of whom had already died, underscored his homicidal intentions. As we have already seen, in his Reichstag speech of 30 January 1942 Hitler threatened to annihilate Europe's Jews. The Security Service reported that the phrase "an eye for an eye, a tooth for a tooth" was widely interpreted to mean "that the Führer's battle against Jewry will be pursued to the end with unrelenting stringency and that soon the last Jew will be driven from European soil."[213]

He was "determined to ruthlessly clean up the Jews in Europe," Hitler re-emphasised in conversation with Goebbels on 14 February 1942. "No sentimental feelings" could be permitted: "The Jews deserve

the catastrophe they are now experiencing. Together with the destruction of our enemies, they will experience their own destruction. We
must accelerate this process with unemotional ruthlessness, and in
doing so we will perform an inestimable service to humanity, which
has suffered under and been tormented by Jewry for thousands of
years."[214] At the end of a long conversation with Goebbels on 19 March
in the Wolf's Lair, the dictator repeated his pronouncement: "The
Jews must be made to leave Europe, if necessary by using the most
brutal of means."[215]

Two days earlier the gassing of people had begun in Belzec. The
first victims were the inhabitants of the Lublin ghetto. Every day,
trains rolled into the death camp. Within the first four weeks of
operations alone, more than 70,000 people were murdered in the gas
chambers, 43,000 from the district of Lublin and more than 27,000
from neighbouring Galicia.[216] This "action" was directed by Odilo
Globocnik, who had been given instructions by Himmler when the
latter visited Lublin on 14 March.[217] The Nazi leadership was well
informed about the start of the factory-like mass killings. On 27 March,
Goebbels noted: "Beginning in Lublin Jews are now starting to be
deported to the east from the General Government. An extremely
barbaric procedure that I do not want to describe more closely is being
used, and not much is left of the Jews themselves. Generally, we have
to conclude that 60 per cent of them have to be liquidated, while only
40 per cent can be deployed for work. The former Gauleiter of Vienna,
who is carrying out the action, is doing this with great discretion and
with a procedure that is not too conspicuous. Jews are subjected to a
punishment which is barbaric but which they have completely
deserved." Goebbels not only knew the name of the former Viennese
Gauleiter, Globocnik, responsible for the "action"—he was also clearly
familiar with the new "inconspicuous" method for killing victims by
diverting engine exhaust fumes into stationary gas chambers. Moreover, he was fully aware that deported German Jews were facing the
same fate as Polish Jews. "The cities of the General Government that
have been freed up will be filled with Jews deported from the Reich,"
he wrote, "and after a certain time, the process will be renewed."[218]

In February 1942, work commenced on a second death camp near
Sobibor (Sobibór) on the eastern border of the Lublin district. It was
put into operation in early May. Two weeks before, on 17 April, after

inspecting the Warsaw ghetto, Himmler commissioned a third death camp near Treblinka, to the northeast of that city. Construction began in May and was finished in July. The contours of a gigantic murder complex were beginning to emerge.[219] At the same time, preparations began, with the German Foreign Ministry and the Reich Security Main Office working hand in hand, to subject other European states to the programme of genocide.[220] As of 1942, Jews from the puppet state of Slovakia were deported to the Lublin district. In June they began to be sent directly to Sobibor. Meanwhile increasing pressure was being put on states allied with or dominated by Germany to give up "their" Jews.[221] A Europe-wide genocide had begun.

On 26 April, after a large percentage of Lublin's ghetto population had already been gassed to death, Goebbels once again spoke to Hitler at length about the "Jewish question." "His standpoint towards this problem is unyielding," the propaganda minister noted afterwards. "He absolutely wants to push the Jews out of Europe. And that is the proper thing to do. The Jews have inflicted so much suffering on our part of the earth that the most severe punishment to which they can be condemned is still too mild."[222] On 18 May, members of a communist-Jewish resistance group tried to set fire to the anti-communist exhibition "The Soviet Paradise" in Berlin's Lustgarten Park.[223] Little damage was done, and it only took the Gestapo a couple of days to round up everyone involved. The attack was welcome fodder for Goebbels. "Typical," he wrote on 24 May, after five Jews and three half-Jews were among those arrested. The incident, he claimed, showed "how correct our Jewish policies are and how necessary it seems to continue our course most radically and ensure that the 40,000 Jews still present in Berlin . . . are either concentrated or liquidated as quickly as possible—of course liquidation would be best." Hitler was most receptive to such proposals, but Speer objected. As long as no replacements had been found for Jews working in arms production, Speer argued, they should not be deported.[224]

On 27 May, acting on behalf of the Czech government-in-exile, two Czech agents carried out a bomb attack on Heydrich in his car as he was on his way to Prague Castle. In late September 1941, not trusting Konstantin von Neurath to break the growing Czech resistance, Hitler had given the head of the Reich Security Main Office the additional office of deputy Reich protector of Bohemia and Moravia; Neurath remained nominally in charge but was stripped of all real power. Heydrich more than fulfilled Hitler's expectations, ruling according to the carrot-and-stick principle. On the one hand, he had hundreds of Czechs executed, while on the other, he increased food rations for workers in arms factories and augmented the Czech social insurance system, bringing it up to Reich levels.[225] At first it appeared that Heydrich would survive the attack, but on 4 June, he died from his injuries. The National Socialists exacted a terrible revenge. On Hitler's personal orders, 199 men from the village of Lidice, mistakenly believed to be the assassins' home and base, were taken out and shot. The women were all sent to the Ravensbrück concentration camp and most of the village's ninety-eight children were murdered in Chełmno. The village itself was razed to the ground. All in all, five thousand people lost their lives in the German orgy of vengeance.[226]

On 9 June, Heydrich was buried after a pompous state ceremony in Berlin. The entire leadership of the Third Reich assembled for the memorial service in the mosaic hall of the New Reich Chancellery. Himmler gave the main speech, but Hitler also spoke briefly, praising Heydrich as "one of the best National Socialists" who had "fallen as a martyr . . . for the preservation and security of the Reich." He also posthumously bestowed upon Heydrich the highest class of the German Order, a distinction that had only ever been previously given to Todt after his fatal plane crash.[227] The death of the man who was every bit Himmler's equal in his cold-blooded executioner's mentality did nothing to halt the machinery of genocide. On the contrary, it accelerated the campaign of murder since in their irrational conspiracy theories, the Nazi leadership blamed the assassination on Jews. The very evening of Heydrich's funeral, Himmler spoke to SS leaders in Berlin, telling them that the time had come "to get serious, without pity or weakness, about destroying the enemies of our people." The Reichsleiter-SS added: "We will have definitely concluded the migration of the Jews within a year; then there will be nobody left to deport. It is time to clear up the matter."[228] It was no accident that Himmler chose the same phrase Hitler had used in his speech to the Reichsleiters and Gauleiters on 12 December 1941.

In early June 1942, in a letter to his mother, Heinz Doering, a former Bavarian district administrator who had become an official in Frank's regime, spoke entirely openly about what was happening in the General Government. "Krakow is now almost Jew-free, and Lublin, earlier the stronghold of world Jewry, is entirely Jew-free," Doering wrote. "The Jews themselves have been 'resettled.' More to come when we speak . . . Now Jews from the Reich are being transported here. They will be treated similarly. The Führer once said that the next world war would mean the end of Jewry in Europe. They probably did not take this as literally as he meant it. At present there are still some skilled Jewish workers we cannot do without here. The rest of them are now wheeling and dealing with Abraham."[229]

On 19 July, Himmler ordered the SS and police chief in Krakow, Friedrich Wilhelm Krüger, to ensure that "the resettlement of the entire Jewish population" in the General Government was completed by the end of the year.[230] Four days later, on 23 July, the first transport trains travelled from the Warsaw ghetto to Treblinka. That same day, the head of the Warsaw Jewish Council, Adam Czerniaków, took his own life in despair at his inability, despite all his efforts, to protect his fellow Jews from the worst. On his desk, he left behind a brief farewell letter to his wife. It read: "They are demanding that I kill the children of my people with my own hands. There is nothing left for me but to die."[231]

The mass deportation from the Warsaw ghetto marked the start of the most murderous phase of the "final solution": the systematic annihilation of Polish Jews. In internal SS correspondence, it was referred to as the "Reinhardt Action," after Heydrich's (misspelled) first name.[232] Step by step, the large ghettos were emptied and Jews were taken by train to the nearest death camps, where they were herded into the gas chambers by SS men and Ukrainian auxiliaries. By the end of 1942, around 1.25 million Jews had been murdered in Belzec, Sobibor and Treblinka, the three camps that were part of the "Reinhardt Action." By the autumn of 1943, after the removal of the last Jews from forced-labour camps, the number had risen to 1.7 million.[233] That was more people than were killed in the Auschwitz-Birkenau death camp, the place which has become synonymous with the genocide of European Jews.[234]

The Polish border town of Auschwitz (Oświęcim), 70 kilometres southwest of Krakow, had been added to the *Gau* of Eastern Upper Silesia when Germany annexed western Poland and was therefore part of the Reich. In early 1940, Himmler decided to build another concentration camp there. The location suggested itself primarily because it was a railway hub and thus had good transport connections. A complex of former military barracks made up the core of the main camp, where in the beginning almost exclusively Polish prisoners were kept. In May 1940, Himmler appointed Rudolf Höss camp commandant, an experienced former block leader in Dachau and previously in charge of those taken into protective custody in the Sachsenhausen camp. By November 1943, when Höss was transferred to one of the top positions in the Main Economic and Administrative Office of the SS in Berlin, Auschwitz had become the biggest death camp of all. Whereas primarily Polish Jews were killed in Belzec, Sobibor and Treblinka, Auschwitz was supposed to be the final destination for Jews from the rest of Europe. It was here, too, that a more efficient method of killing was employed. In early September 1941, the first experimental killing of Soviet POWs with the prussic acid compound Zyklon B was carried out in a basement of Auschwitz's Block 11. In the eyes of Himmler's henchmen, the experiment was a success.[235]

In October, construction began on a second camp in Birkenau (Brzezinka), some 3 kilometres away from the main camp. Originally conceived as a way of housing Soviet POWs after the conclusion of the "Reinhardt Action" in 1943, it became the actual centre of genocide. In the spring of 1942, the first trains with Jews from Upper Silesia, Slovakia and France arrived, and soon Jews from all parts of occupied Europe would be brought there. The newly arrived were subject to a "selection" process on the train station ramp. Those who were considered "unfit for work" were forced into two bunkers on the edge of the camp, where provisional gas chambers had been installed. On 17 and 18 July 1942, Himmler inspected the camp complex and witnessed the entire killing process, from "selection" to gassing. The head of the SS had watched "in complete silence . . . without objecting to anything," Höss would write in the memoirs he composed before his own execution in 1947. Afterwards, over dinner, Himmler had been in "the finest, radiant mood."[236]

At Himmler's behest, Höss, who found himself immediately promoted to the rank of SS-Obersturmbannführer, energetically pushed forward the expansion of the camp's deadly capacities. After Himmler's visit, four new, extremely effective killing facilities were constructed, with combination gas chamber–crematoria, in which as many as 10,000 people could be murdered every day. The genocide would reach one final tragic zenith between May and July 1944, when 430,000 Hungarian Jews were deported to Birkenau; 320,000 of them were gassed to death immediately upon arrival. All told at least 1.1 million people were murdered in the Auschwitz complex, including 960,000 Jews (90 per cent), 70,000–75,000 Gentile Poles, 21,000 Sinti and Roma, 15,000 Soviet POWs, and 10,000–15,000 people of other nationalities. The final number of murdered Jews is estimated to be between 5.3 and 6.1 million. Most of them, as many as 3 million, were killed in the death camps, 700,000 died in mobile gas trucks, 1.3 million were shot to death in mass executions, and as many as 1 million died in the ghettos and concentration camps of various causes.[237]

The Holocaust, a crime unique in human history, was the result of a finely worked-out division of labour. Along with the SS and the Nazi Party apparatus, a multitude of institutions, offices, organisations and social groups were involved. Without the Wehrmacht's assistance and cooperation, the Einsatzgruppen and police battalions would not have been able to operate. Local authorities and police administrations did their bit by issuing deportation orders and guarding the transports as they took place. Others who were complicit included German railway employees who drew up timetables and dispatched trains;[238] Foreign Ministry diplomats who prepared the deportations in other countries;[239] collaborators who served the German occupiers; and the commercial providers of the technology of annihilation, such as Topf & Sons of Erfurt, which built the death-camp crematoria, and Tesch & Stabenow of Hamburg, which supplied Zyklon B.[240] The chemical company IG Farben built a factory at Monowitz (Monowice), only a few kilometres away from the main camp in Auschwitz, to produce Buna, a synthetic form of rubber, drawing upon the giant reservoir of camp inmates for labour.[241] Doctors like SS-Hauptsturmführer Josef Mengele carried out the "selections" on the station ramp and used the unlimited "human material" at their disposal for monstrous medical experiments.[242] Experts at the German Finance and Economics Ministry confiscated Jewish assets in a Europe-wide act of grand larceny. Finally, untold numbers of "ethnic-popular comrades," men and women, bought up the household items and other belongings of deported and murdered Jews at bargain prices.[243]

If we look at this complex system of the perpetrators, henchmen and profiteers of mass murder, it is easy to lose sight of the driving force and ultimately decisive figure: Adolf Hitler. Particularly when it comes to the beginnings of the Holocaust, we should recall the statement Richard Walther Darré made in his testimony at Nuremberg about the general law that governed the development of National Socialism: "When one looks at the basics of things, the force driving this rotating stage is always Hitler himself. He causes . . . the motion that is transferred to figures whose dynamics release other dynamics, but the central figure Hitler with his surprising impetuses always remains the actual motor of the rotating stage."[244]

The sheer fact of an all-mighty dictator with well-known anti-Semitic obsessions provided a powerful impetus for the careerists around him to try to advance themselves by making suggestions and showing initiative of their own on "Jewish policy." Indeed, very often they tried to outdo one another. As he had before 1939, Hitler exercised a constant influence, both direct and indirect, on the decisions being made from the beginning of the war. Indirectly, he verbally informed his underlings of his wishes while simultaneously encouraging them to show imagination and to come up with their own plans. "The Führer tends to express his wishes not in the form of commands but precisely as wishes," Goebbels once noted. "It has always been the custom of the party that a wish of the Führer is a command."[245] And the propaganda minister was not the only one who possessed a fine sense for wishes that sometimes were uttered as mere asides. Bormann and Himmler were keenly attuned to such remarks and ever ready to translate them into concrete instructions.[246] As his hateful anti-Semitic tirades grew ever more extreme in tone and language, particularly with the constant reminders of his "prophecy" of 30 January 1939, the dictator provided a rhetorical umbrella under which the most radical proponents of a "final solution to the Jewish question" considered themselves covered and legitimated.

On the other hand, Hitler repeatedly intervened directly in specific key decisions and set the direction developments were to follow. It was he who decreed that Operation Barbarossa was to be a crusade against "Jewish Bolshevism" and demanded his military commanders commit to that idea. Himmler, Heydrich and the leaders of the Einsatzgruppen could be absolutely confident that they were acting in accordance with Hitler when they expanded the targets of mass executions to include the entire Jewish population of the occupied Soviet territories. There was never a formal order to do so, but that was not necessary anyway. As was typical for Hitler's rule, the genocide developed in an "interaction between the centre and the periphery," in which subordinate SS authorities and death squads extensively exploited the considerable leeway they had been granted.[247]

Hitler did not always provide the initial impetus. For example, it was the Gauleiters, led by Goebbels, who pressed for requiring Jews to wear Yellow Stars as identification and for deporting them from the territory of the Reich. But in both cases a decision to pursue a certain course was only taken after Hitler had granted his approval, in August and September 1941, respectively. This approval also did not take the form of a written order, but rather of an announcement of the dictator's will in conversation, which Hitler's paladins correctly interpreted as authorisation to take action.[248]

Ultimately, the final quantum leap to the systematic annihilation of Jews in the spring and summer of 1942 would have been unthinkable if Hitler had not previously made it known what he wanted. He presumably did this at the secret meeting with the Reichsleiters and Gauleiters in his private apartment in Berlin on 12 December 1941. If so, it was the logical extension of both the reversal of Germany's military fortune on the eastern front, which had revealed the utter unfeasibility of the "territorial solution" of deporting Jews to some remote part of the Soviet Union, and the entry of the United States into the war, making the conflict a truly global one and realising the scenario in which Hitler had always threatened Jews with total destruction. Once again, Hitler did not issue his decision as a precisely formulated order. He found it enough to give an unmistakable hint that the time had come for the great confrontation he had always predicted. Only after this had been made clear could the executioners of the "final solution" commence with their Europe-wide campaign of annihilation against Jews.

Hitler's role was thus ultimately decisive. Goebbels was not at all wrong when he pointed out in March 1942: "Here too the Führer is the unrelenting vanguard warrior and spokesman for a radical solution that is required by the way things stand and that consequently seems unavoidable."[249] One year later, when Goebbels found himself able to report to Hitler that the Jews of Berlin had been almost completely "evacuated"—that is to say, sent to their deaths—the dictator noted with satisfaction that it had taken the war to give him the possibility of "solving a series of problems that he would never have been able to solve in normal times." First and foremost, this was the "final solution of the Jewish question," Hitler boasted. "One way or another, the Jews will be the losers of this war."[250] The following year, in early March 1944, a satisfied Hitler told his propaganda minister that he had pursued "such radical policies" of destruction over the "Jewish question" that "the Jews will not be able to do us any further harm."[251]

How much did ordinary Germans know about the Holocaust? For a long time, German historians considered this question taboo. Only with the turn of the millennium did a number of studies confirm what Raul Hilberg had concluded in his groundbreaking book *The Destruction of the European Jews* in 1961: despite all the attempts of the perpetrators to conceal their monstrous crimes, the Holocaust was an "open secret."[252] This fact can hardly be surprising. As surveillance recordings of conversations among German POWs show, knowledge of the annihilation of European Jews was widespread among Wehrmacht soldiers, many of whom had themselves witnessed mass executions or heard from comrades about them.[253] Thus, in a letter to his girlfriend Sophie Scholl in Munich in June 1942, Lieutenant Fritz Hartnagel, who was deployed in the southern section of the eastern front, wrote: "It is revolting how cynically and hard-heartedly my commander talks about the butchering of all Jews in occupied Russia. He remains completely convinced of the justice of this action."[254] In the summer of 1942, knowledge that Polish Jews were being murdered spread rapidly and became a common topic of conversation among occupying German soldiers. On 25 July, Wilm Hosenfeld, who was stationed in Warsaw, noted in his diary: "If what is being said in the city is true, and the people who say it are believable, it is no honour to be a German officer . . . This week, 30,000 Jews have reportedly been led out of the ghetto and sent somewhere east. Despite all the secrecy, it is also common knowledge what is done to them there."[255] Even if Hosenfeld may not have known the details about how Jews were being murdered in Treblinka, he knew all too well that thousands of Jews were being killed there every day. Displaying far less human sympathy, a German tank commander who travelled through Galicia for two days in February 1944 wrote in his personal journal: "A difference of day and night when you cross the old Russian border, and there is Galicia without Jews! . . . Our administration has made much of this place and, above all else, has worked very cleverly."[256]

News of mass murder made its way into the "old Reich" via letters and soldiers and officers on home leave. In late October 1941, Friedrich Kellner noted: "A soldier on leave who was an eyewitness told of terrible atrocities in the occupied part of Poland. He said he had seen naked Jewish men and women lined up in front of a long deep ditch and, on the order of the SS, shot in the back of the head by Ukrainians, so that they fell into that ditch."[257] The mass shootings in the occupied Soviet territories were already well known when German Jews began to be deported in the autumn of 1941. The deportations were not kept secret but were carried out in broad daylight. Many Germans may have comforted themselves with the official narrative that these people were being "resettled in the east," where they would be "deployed for work." But more than a few knew or at least suspected that the deportees faced death. A schoolteacher from Hamburg wrote on 15 December 1941: "The few remaining Jews in Germany are being taken away, to the east, people claim. And that now, in winter! . . . It is crystal clear that this means their destruction."[258] The rumours about the terrible fate awaiting deportees in "the east" multiplied over the course of 1942 and congealed into certainty. Kellner wrote that September: "In the last few days, the Jews of our district have been transported away . . . From a well-informed source, I heard that all Jews are being brought to Poland where they are shot by SS formations . . . Such shameful crimes will never be erased from the book of human history. Our homicidal regime has stained the name of Germany for all eternity! For an upstanding German, it is incomprehensible that no one puts a stop to the doings of these Hitler bandits."[259]

But not many Germans thought the way Kellner did. For most of them, the "Jewish problem" was resolved as soon as Jews were deported. They did not give a second thought to the fate of the deportees. In most cases, the ubiquitous claim after 1945 not to have known anything was meant to conceal the fact that Germans did not *want* to know:

that they refused to investigate what they observed, ask questions and draw conclusions.[260] An indication of what average Germans could have known if they wanted to can be found in the diary kept by Karl Dürkefälden, an engineer in a machine factory in the city of Celle. Dürkefälden learned about the mass murder of Jews for the first time from the BBC in the autumn of 1942 and connected that report with other information. His brother-in-law, who had worked as a construction foreman in Kiev, had told him about mass executions. From a former employee of his company, who was stationed in Vilnius as a soldier, he learned in January 1943 that "the Jews from France and other occupied countries were brought to Poland and sometimes shot, sometimes gassed to death there." All these pieces of information, combined with a critical reading of the Nazi press, allowed Dürkefälden to form an extremely accurate picture of the genocide of Jews. He never found out any specifics, however, about how they were murdered in the death camps.[261]

Unsurprisingly, concealment was never perfect, especially at the epicentre of the genocide. Auschwitz was not only a transport hub: it also served as a new home for numerous Germans from the Reich, including tens of thousands of SS men and their families. Rumours soon began to circulate among the city's civilian population about what was going on behind the barbed-wire fences of the camp. The fiery glow from the crematoria at Auschwitz-Birkenau could be seen at a distance of 15–20 kilometres, and the sickly sweet smell of burning human flesh indicated what was happening at the death camp to the immediate environs. It was an ongoing topic of conversation at the construction site for the IG Farben factory that those deemed unfit for work were being gassed.[262] But you did not have to live in or around Auschwitz to know about the monstrous crimes being committed. Soldiers on leave frequently stopped off there. In a letter to his family in December 1942, one soldier wrote: "Around 7,000–8,000 Jews arrive here in Auschwitz every week, and after a short while, they die a 'hero's death.'"[263]

Information was also passed among Jews who had not yet been deported. In Klemperer's diary, the word "Auschwitz" occurs for the first time in an entry for 16 March 1942: "Recently I have heard Auschwitz (or something similar) near Königshütte [Chorzów] in Upper Silesia named as the most terrible concentration camp." By the autumn of that year, Klemperer was aware that Auschwitz was a "rapidly working slaughterhouse" although he did not know how the people deported there were killed. He did not connect the place with the rumours about gassings he was hearing from all sides. "By the way, it has long been said that many of those evacuated do not arrive in Poland alive," Klemperer wrote. "They are gassed to death in cattle cars during the journey, and the wagon stops *en route* in front of a prepared mass grave." Klemperer never unravelled the complete secret of this killing complex, but Auschwitz still serves in his diary as a cypher for mass murder. By late 1944, he was certain that "we will never see any of the six to seven million Jews . . . who have been butchered or, to be more precise, shot or gassed."[264]

Thus, while it is true that few Germans knew *everything* about the "final solution," very few knew *nothing* about it. Their knowledge may have been confined to individual aspects of the genocide, for instance reports about ghetto massacres or rumours about gassings. Partial pieces of information, individual observations and rumours did not automatically connect to form an overall picture. For that, people had to be prepared to see details as indications of the whole, as was the case with Erich Kuby. In early March 1942 near Warsaw, while on his way to the eastern front, the private witnessed a deportation train and wrote to his wife: "You could not see anything but a crowd of people with Yellow Stars on their breasts and shoulders, all crammed together, but that was an image compatible with everything I knew."[265] In other words, you did not need to know the name Auschwitz to know that Jews were being killed. But the "normal" German reaction was to try to deny the unprecedented horror, the truth about a crime unique in human history. People preferred to keep it at a distance or repress it.

"Must I believe this horrific report?" the Berlin journalist Ursula von Kardorff asked her diary on 27 December 1944, after reading in a Swiss newspaper that Jews were being "systematically gassed" in Auschwitz. "That exceeds even my worst intimations. It simply cannot be true. Even the most brutal fanatic cannot possibly be that bestial."[266] More than any official policy of secrecy, it was the sheer monstrosity of the truth itself that kept it from becoming more widely acknowledged. The murder of millions, planned with bureaucratic thoroughness and carried out in partly factory-like fashion—the singular dimensions of the crime taxed the imagination of even those who otherwise believed Hitler and his henchmen capable of all sorts of evil. A psychological self-defence mechanism worked against people thinking the unthinkable and believing that Auschwitz was real. No one described the barrier to intolerable knowledge any more precisely than the Hanover psychologist Peter Brückner in his autobiography. "Among people with otherwise keen ears, there was a tangible resistance to admitting certain news about the horrors of the Nazi state," he recalled. "People were shocked, but stayed silent, became recalcitrant and forgot. I wanted to find things out, and 'forgetting' seemed unworthy to us. But I remember feeling the occasional impulse to close myself off like an Indian monkey who does not want to see or hear anything. Why? . . . I wanted to live and not just to survive—and that meant I wanted to laugh, fall in love, enjoy a glass of tea and write poems . . . How is one supposed to not love life? And how could one do that knowing all too well what was happening in those places under the power of the Nazi state and its armies?"

8

Stalingrad and the Battle for Oil

"The soldiers on the eastern front have a winter behind them the like of which has not been seen for 140 years in eastern and central Europe," Hitler told listeners in his speech to mark Heroes' Commemoration Day in Berlin on 12 March 1942. Nonetheless, the Führer continued, the leaders in the Kremlin had not succeeded in inflicting upon the Wehrmacht the "destiny of Napoleon in 1812." This gave Hitler the confidence to promise that "the Bolshevist hordes who were unable to defeat German and allied soldiers last winter will be vanquished, indeed destroyed, by us this summer."[1] The shock of the "winter crisis" had passed, and the eastern front had been stabilised. Cautious optimism was spreading. Hitler boasted to his intimates that during his "time of struggle," especially in the days before his assumption of power in January 1933, he had stared into "very different abysses" and "more than once" faced the choice between life and death. Since then, he claimed, no difficulties could shake him.[2]

In the spring of 1942, Hitler refused to entertain any talk of German forces merely consolidating their positions in the east. On the contrary, he pinned all his hopes on the troops' ability to deal the Red Army a decisive blow. Time was of the essence. Hitler was aware that he had to bring the war in the east to some sort of conclusion before the Anglo-American alliance was able to throw the full weight of its economic and military resources into the war in the west. On this score, Halder and Hitler were in complete agreement. "If we allow the Russians to catch their breath, and the threat from America increases, we will cede the initiative to our enemies and never regain it," Halder stated. "Thus we have no choice but to make another attempt despite all reservations."[3] Hitler and his military commanders figured that if they could defeat the Soviet Union in time, there was reason to believe that they could secure "Fortress Europe" against an Allied invasion and compel Churchill and Roosevelt to give up. Goebbels shared this conviction: "If we succeed in bringing the situation in the east to a satisfactory conclusion this summer, we will be on our way . . . Once the Soviet system has been brought to its knees, we will have practically won the war."[4]

But the Wehrmacht had been extraordinarily weakened in the previous nine months. Of the 3.2 million soldiers available at the start of Operation Barbarossa on 22 June 1941, more than 1 million were dead, wounded, missing in action or held captive in the Soviet Union. "My God, how the troops have melted away," exclaimed General Heinrici on 12 March 1942 in his diary, "and how bad things look for officers and munitions."[5] No matter what they did, there was no way for German military commanders to compensate for such losses. In preparation for a meeting with Hitler on 21 April, Halder determined that the eastern army needed 625,000 more men. He noted in bullet points: "Battle-readiness diminished by lack of seasoned officers and lower-level commanders. Lack of experienced specialists. Fatigue of men, horses and materiel."[6] Such attrition ruled out any thoughts of an offensive along the entire front from Leningrad to the Black Sea. Instead, the new German attack would concentrate on one section of the line, that held by Army Group South. "The Führer does not intend to go on the offensive on the entire front, but rather push forward and break through in one section in order to advance in ways that are significant," Goebbels wrote in late March, summarising Hitler's strategic plans.[7]

Although he should have known better, Hitler still overestimated his own possibilities and undervalued the Soviet Union's capacity for resistance. While he occasionally expressed grudging admiration for Stalin at table in the Wolf's Lair—calling him "an inspired fellow in his own way," and an "overwhelming personality" who had "forged together a gigantic empire with an iron fist"—Hitler continued to look down on the Red Army's fighting capabilities.[8] The enemy, he proposed, had "used up its last strength" with the winter offensive of 1941–42, and it was now just a question of "pushing over what is already falling."[9] Hitler's military advisers reinforced him in these erroneous convictions. In the spring of 1942, Halder asserted that the Russian divisions were "no longer worth much" and that he could make out symptoms of "disorganisation" in the Russian hinterland.[10] In reality, Stalin's dictatorship had by no means reached its limits in manpower resources and industrial output. On the contrary, in 1942 the Soviet Union succeeded in surpassing the Third Reich in almost all categories of arms production. As Adam Tooze has shown, the true "armaments miracle" of 1942 took place not in Germany but in the weapons factories in the Urals.[11] And the Soviet Union achieved this basically on its own since the American Lend-Lease Act would only begin to have a major effect in 1943.

The astonishing mobilisation of resources achieved by the Soviet Union enabled it not just to survive the second major German offensive, but to launch a carefully prepared counter-offensive in November 1942. With that, Hitler and his military commanders' hopes of forcing a decision in the east were dashed once and for all. "This will be the German army's grave," the military attaché at the Italian embassy in Berlin, Efisio Marras, exclaimed in March 1942, pointing on a map at the lower reaches of the river Volga.[12] Marras' prophecy came true when the German 6th Army was encircled in Stalingrad and had to capitulate. Moreover, with their joint landing in French North Africa in November 1942, British and American forces created a springboard for attacking the soft underbelly of the Axis. By early 1943, the anti-Hitler coalition was on the front foot. At their meeting in Casablanca in January, Roosevelt and Churchill reaffirmed their intention to prosecute the war until they had forced Nazi Germany and Imperial Japan into unconditional surrender.

In a meeting at the Wolf's Lair on 28 March 1942, Halder presented the army's marching orders for the summer offensive. Hitler gave his approval but left no doubt that the coming attack would be carried out in accordance with his wishes as commander-in-chief. The Wehrmacht Supreme Command Order No. 41 of 5 April was essentially the Führer's handiwork: for the first time he had made extensive corrections and revisions to the draft Jodl had prepared.[13] The introduction to the order stated that the Soviet Union had used up most of its reserves in the winter battle. Consequently, as soon as the weather and terrain conditions allowed, "German military commanders and troops, in their superiority, must seize back the initiative." The goal of what was called Operation Blue was to "destroy once and for all the remaining Soviet defences and strip the Soviets as much as possible of the most important sources of strength for their war economy." Army Group Centre was to hold its position, while to the north Leningrad was to be taken and a land bridge with Finland created, and to the south troops were to break through to the Volga and the Caucasus. But since the forces at the Wehrmacht's disposal were not sufficient to achieve both goals simultaneously, the initial focus of the operation would be on the southern front. Its intent was to "destroy the enemy in front of the river Don and then to capture the Caucasian oil fields and pass through the Caucasus itself." In preparation for the main operation, the Kerch Peninsula and the stronghold of Sevastopol in Crimea were to be taken, and an enemy-held bulge in the front on both sides of Izyum, which threatened Kharkov, the jumping-off point for the German assault, was to be "cleaned up."[14]

Hitler's plans were thus primarily motivated by concerns about the war economy. He believed that he could deal the Soviet Union a mortal blow by cutting the Caucasian oil fields off from the rest of the country. By taking them, the Wehrmacht would be able to cover its own immense oil needs and become able to survive a protracted war with the Anglo-Saxon powers. "If I do not get the oil of Maikop and Grozny, I will have to liquidate this entire war," Hitler was quoted as saying during a visit to Poltava before the beginning of the campaign.[15] That was a deliberate exaggeration in the interest of winning over his military commanders to his strategic ideas, but once again Germany's highest generals did not dare contradict their commander-in-chief. Halder told the German navy's liaison officer that he too considered the Caucasus campaign an "urgent necessity" since this region had "roughly the same importance as the province of Silesia has for Prussia." Halder explained: "Only when it possesses this territory will the German empire of war be able to survive in the long term."[16]

But as the German preparations for the summer offensive were going full swing, the Royal Air Force stepped up its bombing war. In 1940 and 1941, British bombing raids on Germany had remained limited, causing scant damage. But in part to assist the Soviet Union in its battles against Hitler, the British war cabinet decided in the spring of 1942 to embark on a new strategy of carpet bombing. The main idea was not to hit targets producing armaments or major transport hubs but to weaken the morale of the German people, especially that of the industrial labour force. The strategy was the brainchild of Air Marshal Arthur Harris, who took over Bomber Command on 22 February 1942.[17] The city selected for a trial of this type of air warfare was Lübeck in northern Germany, whose densely built-up medieval centre made it an ideal target for incendiary bombs. In the night of 28–29 March, British bombers carried out three raids, reducing large parts of central Lübeck to rubble. Three hundred and twelve people were killed, and more than 700 wounded in the attack. It was the largest number of casualties caused by an aerial bombardment in Germany to date.[18]

Hitler appeared "very downcast" after the Lübeck catastrophe.[19] When he received word of what had happened on 29 March, he called Goebbels from the Wolf's Lair and ripped into Interior Ministry officials "with extraordinary rage," accusing them of not showing initiative in responding to the raid. "The Führer has stripped them of responsibility for taking care of areas damaged in air attacks and has given me unlimited authority in this matter," noted Goebbels, who was delighted at yet another sign of his Führer's trust.[20] In early April, Goebbels viewed film footage of the destruction in Lübeck's old town centre and came away "chilled to the bone." If the British attacks "continued in this style for a number of weeks," the propaganda minister conceded, it could "certainly have a demoralising effect on the German population."[21] Indeed, between 23 and 27 April there followed a series of air raids on Rostock that destroyed 60 per cent of the centre of the city and killed 216 people.[22] On 31 May, more than 1,000 RAF bombers carried out the largest air raid to date, on Cologne, causing widespread devastation. Four hundred and eighty-six people were killed, more than 5,000 wounded and 59,000 made homeless.[23]

Hitler was furious and called for retribution, exclaiming that "terror must be met with terror, and the attempt to destroy German sites of culture must be answered by levelling English sites of culture."[24] Of course, Hitler conveniently ignored the fact that the carpet-bombing strategy was by no means an RAF invention, having been practised numerous times by the Luftwaffe. Friedrich Kellner recalled this in his diary after the British raid on Cologne: "Who devastated Warsaw and Rotterdam? Who reduced London to rubble? . . . Who wanted to wipe English cities off the map? Was it not the Führer? Did not all of Germany celebrate the 'heroic deeds' of the fighter pilots? And now these swindlers turn things around and talk about 'terror'?"[25] Thomas Mann sounded the same themes from his California exile in a radio address to German listeners after the attack on Lübeck. The Nobel laureate expressed his pain at the destruction of his home city, but added: "I think back to Coventry and can have no objections to the lesson that what goes around comes around."[26] In April and May, the Luftwaffe carried out air raids on Exeter, Bath, Norwich, York and Canterbury, but the German air force did not have anything approximating the strength of Harris's Bomber Command. The attacks became known in Britain as "Baedeker raids" because they supposedly targeted buildings with three stars in the famous travel guide.[27] But although they caused serious damage to the buildings in question, they did nothing to diminish the British war effort.

The Nazi leadership had every reason to be concerned about the psychological effects of Britain's stepped-up bombing campaign. Security Service reports registered expressions of "great dismay" throughout the population, as ordinary Germans asked themselves how attacks like the one on Lübeck could have been possible and where Germany's defences had been.[28] After the bombardment of Cologne, Swiss consul Franz-Rudolf von Weiss characterised the mood in the city as a mix of "indifference, apathy, complete lack of spirit and desperation." Notes had been put up on many of the destroyed buildings reading: "We have you to thank for this, my Führer."[29] Along with the air raids, reductions in food rations created discontent in the spring of 1942. The mood among workers had reached a "previously unseen low," the Security Service reported in late March. "With great bitterness . . . there is talk that the so-called privileged classes are procuring scarce items in addition to their appointed rations thanks to their connections and their fatter wallets."[30]

Goebbels believed that the time had come to "consolidate and strengthen the home front."[31] To combat the decline in morale, he favoured radical measures to suppress the black market. On 19 March 1942, while visiting the Wolf's Lair, he suggested to Hitler that a law be passed to punish with imprisonment, or even death for severe cases, anyone who violated the "well-known basic principles of the National Socialist conduct of the people." Such a law, Goebbels argued, would give the waging of the war at home an entirely "new basis." He also criticised the behaviour of judicial officials whose "judgments are foreign to the people and to reality" and who failed to understand the signs of the times. Hitler listened eagerly to these suggestions, declaring that he would convene the Reichstag and have himself issued "blanket authority" to proceed against judges and other officials who were not doing their duty.[32] In front of his entourage, Hitler repeatedly vented his rage at the judiciary. The "entirety of German jurisprudence" would have to be "turned inside out" after the war, he demanded, and the principle that judges be appointed for life abolished. "Only he who knows the ideology and the tasks of his people is able to judge in the name of that people," Hitler declared.[33]

The Reichstag session was called for 26 April and Hitler arrived in Berlin the day before. "He looks to be in excellent health and is in top physical and mental form," a pleased Goebbels noted. The dictator was optimistic about the prospects of the coming offensive. Goebbels, however, had been made less sanguine by the experiences of the past year and was more reserved in his predictions. "No one can say right now whether we will succeed in striking a blow that will destroy the Bolsheviks this summer," the propaganda minister wrote.[34]

The Reichstag convened in the Kroll Opera House on the afternoon of 26 April. "Lots of uniforms and some wounded among the deputies," Goebbels observed. "The atmosphere was extraordinarily charged." Hitler began his speech with uncharacteristic hesitancy, later admitting to feeling "somewhat numb."[35] But he collected himself and quickly recaptured his old rhetorical form. It was only at the end of his address, after all the usual tirades against the purported Jewish string-pullers behind the global war and glorifying descriptions of the winter battles outside Moscow, that he got to his actual point and demanded absolute authority to do whatever he considered necessary for prosecuting the war without having to abide by any legal regulations. The resolution to that effect, which Göring presented to the Reichstag, enabled Hitler to require of every German—whether officer, government official, judge or party functionary—to "fulfil his duties with all means deemed appropriate." It also empowered the Führer to "mete out a commensurate punishment if, after conscientious evaluation and without regard to any vested rights, those duties are found to have been violated."[36] The Reichstag unanimously passed the resolution, removing the final pathetic remnants of the rule of law and elevating Hitler's will to the highest principle in the land. The Reichstag would never convene again.

On the way back to the Chancellery from the Kroll Opera House, Hitler basked in the adulation of the masses. "You can tell from the entire mood of the people that the Führer has spoken from the heart of the nation," Goebbels opined.[37] But in fact Hitler's speech had an ambiguous echo. A good number of Germans were puzzled why Hitler had demanded "yet another special enablement" when as chancellor and Führer he already personally held all the power there was. In "more ordinary circles," however, reported the Security Service, Hitler's words met with approval because people expected that "from now on all ethnic-popular comrades, no matter who they were or what position they occupied, would be ruthlessly targeted if they did not fulfil their duties to the ethnic-popular community." Government officials, on the other hand, were "deeply distressed," and judges in particular felt that Hitler's criticism of the judicial system insulted their professional honour.[38] Kellner noted with satisfaction: "Yes, you collaborators and imitators, you have heard correctly. The slave mentality is getting its just deserts! The whore 'justice' is being treated exactly as she deserves for her previous behaviour. In 1933, they all crawled along with everything. Today, they are getting kicked. For me it is a delicious time. Carry on, Adolf Hitler!"[39]

In fact, Hitler was not as energetic as Goebbels initially thought. That very evening, Hitler left Berlin for the Obersalzberg to rest for a few days, having confessed to his propaganda minister that he was feeling "pretty worn down at the moment."[40] But the trip was anything but relaxing. On 29 and 30 April, talks were scheduled with the Italians in Klessheim Castle, a Nazi government guesthouse near Salzburg. Hitler had not seen Mussolini since the latter's visit to the Wolf's Lair in late August 1941, and the strategic situation had fundamentally changed with the failure of Operation Barbarossa. The main point of the meeting was for Nazi Germany to try to reassure its ally about military prospects in the east and to dispel any doubts that the war might not be brought to a successful conclusion. Hitler welcomed his guest with his usual expansiveness, although he made an exhausted impression on Ciano. "The months of the Russian winter have severely weighed upon him," the Italian foreign minister remarked. "It was the first time I noticed how much grey there is in his hair."[41]

The war, declared the Führer, could only be ended with a victory; a "peace of compromise" was out of the question. "The huge sacrifices that have been made by the Axis must be rewarded," Hitler told his visitors. Britain would give in, he continued, when it recognised it had no more chance of winning the war. "This moment will come—with absolute certainty," Hitler predicted.[42] Ribbentrop too projected confidence in front of Ciano concerning the coming summer offensive: "Once its sources of oil have been sealed off, Russia will be brought to its knees. Then, the Tories and even Churchill, who is after all a rational man, will do everything to salvage what they can of their decaying empire."[43] The meeting ended without any concrete results, however. Although Hitler did not completely dismiss the Italian desire to take Malta from the British, he asked for more time given the dramatic losses that the occupation of Crete had caused. Instead, every attempt should be made to strengthen Rommel's Afrikakorps so that it would be able to "continue to exert energetic pressure on England." As the translator Paul Schmidt noted: "Concrete plans for action against Egypt were not discussed. It was only agreed that advancing to the Suez Canal would be a worthwhile goal for the future."[44]

In the subsequent talks, Hitler again could not suppress his tendency to hold monologues. "Hitler talked and talked and talked, and Mussolini, who is accustomed to talking himself and had to just listen the entire time, suffered," wrote Ciano, before going on to express sympathy for the Führer's underlings: "They have to swallow this every day, and I am sure that there is not a word, a gesture or a pause that they do not know by heart. After a heroic battle to stay awake, General Jodl fell asleep on the divan. Keitel was also nodding off, but he succeeded in keeping his head upright. He was seated too closely to Hitler to give in to his impulses as he no doubt would have liked to."[45] Goebbels was wrong when he wrote in his diary that there was no sign of tension between the two allies, whose relationship, in the eyes of the propaganda minister, was "loyal and heartfelt" as never before.[46] Mussolini was visibly upset that Hitler had once again shunted him into the role of junior partner, and the Italians suspected that the Germans had deliberately painted the prospects for success in rosy colours.

Hitler had originally intended to spend a few days at the Berghof, but when it began to snow he declared that, after the severe winter just past, he could not bear to see any more snow.[47] On 2 May, he abruptly left the Obersalzberg. He arrived back in the Wolf's Lair the following day.

On 8 May, preparatory measures for Operation Blue began. The 11th Army under Colonel-General von Manstein succeeded in retaking the Kerch Peninsula eleven days later. In the process, three Soviet armies were destroyed and 170,000 Red Army soldiers taken prisoner. "The first great victory against the Soviet armies this year!" celebrated Goebbels. "Everyone is breathing a sigh of relief."[48] In early June, the assault on Sevastopol commenced, and the city was recaptured after fierce fighting on 1 July. With that, all of Crimea was in German hands. Hitler promoted Manstein to field marshal and painted the rosiest of pictures of the Crimean future in his mealtime monologues. South Tyroleans could be resettled there into what he envisioned as a new Reich *Gau* named "Gotenland," and "the old object of quarrels with Italy" thus buried once and for all. "No power on earth will dislodge us from there again," Hitler proclaimed.[49]

The second prerequisite for Operation Blue, according to Hitler's instruction of 5 April, was the destruction of the 100-kilometre-deep Soviet bridgehead on the western bank of the Donets near Izyum. Here, too, Army Group South under the command of Field Marshal von Bock, who had taken over from Reichenau after the latter's death in January 1942, had more success than anticipated. Unexpectedly, the Soviet armies under Marshal Timoshenko had launched an attack on Kharkov from a vanguard position on 12 May, which gave the German tank formations the opportunity for a major pincer operation. On 22–23 May, Kharkov was surrounded, and five days later, Soviet resistance collapsed. The Red Army had suffered further massive losses, and some 290,000 soldiers were captured.[50] Hitler awarded Friedrich Paulus, commander of the 6th Army since January, the Knight's Cross of the Iron Cross, and the previously largely unknown military commander clearly enjoyed the recognition he now received from all sides.[51]

News of German victories in the east temporarily suppressed popular dissatisfaction back home with air raids and reduced food rations. "At the moment it can be observed that faith in victory has got new momentum," noted Kellner in late May 1942. "The exaggerated army reports about the battles on the Kerch Peninsula and at Kharkov have bucked up those who were hanging their heads. The hope barometer is rising."[52] The Security Service also reported a noticeable improvement in mood among the German people. The latest victories were seen as evidence of the "continuing unbroken might of the German forces," and it was hoped that the war in the east would be decided that year after all.[53] In the Wolf's Lair, the gloomy atmosphere of the early months of 1942 had given way to a "generally brilliant mood."[54] Hitler concluded from the large numbers of prisoners taken that the Red Army had exhausted its reserves and that the summer offensive would achieve its aims more quickly than previously assumed.[55]

On 15 May 1942, the Gauleiter of Weser-Ems, Carl Röver, died in the northern German city of Oldenburg. Hitler ordered that a state funeral be held in the New Chancellery building and travelled to Berlin on 22 May. He had summoned the Reichsleiters and Gauleiters for the following afternoon to brief them and reassure himself once more of their loyalty. Hitler had not spoken to these functionaries for almost six months, and he was concerned that some might have come to doubt Germany's ultimate victory. He began his two-hour speech with an appeal for solidarity among the "old guard" before devoting most of it to a look back at the winter crisis. Hitler made no bones of the extreme danger Germany's soldiers had faced on the eastern front from mid-December to mid-January. If he had given in to his generals' wish for a retreat, Hitler bragged, the result would have been "doubtless a complete catastrophe and a Napoleonic debacle." As Goebbels later noted: "If the Führer has been hard and unrelenting and has brutally insisted on his way, the German people will one day fall to their knees in gratitude."

Hitler told his minions that German divisions would soon go on the attack on the southern sector of the front. The goal of the operation was to cut off the Soviet Union from its oil supplies, so that Stalin would be unable to continue the fight. He was determined to put the enemy "out of his misery" that summer. But even if the fighting should last into the winter, Hitler reassured his underlings, every preparation had been made to prevent another crisis like the one the troops had just got through. At the end of his speech, Hitler again discussed his ambitious plans for the future of conquered eastern

Europe. "Once we have possession of the territory we want and need for consolidating Europe, we will construct a gigantic wall separating Asia from Europe," he declared. Germany, he added, would never again tolerate a consolidated state on its eastern border. Moreover, if "calculated population policies" were instituted, the German people could grow to 250 million within seventy or eighty years, and those additional Germans would enjoy the fruits of the National Socialist drive for expansion. By gaining control over the vast territories and raw materials of the east, Hitler concluded, Germany would be "freed from all threats in the future." After his speech, Hitler sat talking with his Reichsleiters and Gauleiters, swapping recollections of the "time of struggle," and the dictator visibly relaxed. "He still feels most comfortable in these circles," Goebbels remarked.[56]

That evening, Hitler travelled to his East Prussian headquarters, but returned to Berlin on 29 May to speak before some 10,000 officer candidates in the Sportpalast. This time he avoided talking about the current situation at the front and Germany's prospects for the war. Instead, he engaged in a general lecture on his social-Darwinist and racist-expansionist dogmata. War was the "father of all things," he told his audience. A natural law of "eternal selection," in which the strong prevailed and the weak fell by the wayside, meant that Germany, because of its geographically central location, was fated to "fight for its existence" and needed to conquer "living space" commensurate with its population in order to escape destruction.[57] In conversation with Goebbels before and after his speech, Hitler drew quite optimistic conclusions from the battles on the Kerch Peninsula and at Kharkov. He was sure that the Soviets would not be able to replace the tanks they had lost, and the enemy was now in "roughly the same situation" the Wehrmacht had been in the previous winter, yet "without the same possibilities for further resistance." With the planned offensive in the Caucasus, Hitler boasted, German troops would "punch the Soviet Union's Adam's apple in." But Hitler expressed regrets that he had been forced to put his construction projects, particularly the remaking of Berlin, on ice. "Everything now has to serve the war and the cause of victory," he explained. "Once victory is in our grasp, we will make up for lost time as quickly as possible."[58]

★

On 4 June 1942, Hitler flew to Finland. The official occasion was the seventy-fifth birthday of the supreme commander of the Finnish armed forces, Field Marshal Carl Gustaf Emil Mannerheim. With the exception of his trip to Italy, it was the only time that Hitler would ever travel to a country not under German control—a fact that underscored the importance he attached to the Finnish "fraternity of arms." Indeed, his visit was intended to bind Finland even more closely to the Axis. But Hitler's talks with Mannerheim in the latter's personal train are also of historical interest because the Finns secretly recorded them. These recordings are one of the few audio documents of Hitler speaking not as an orator but as an astonishingly smooth diplomat.[59] Afterwards, Hitler raved about his trip. "The Finns have won the Führer's heart," Goebbels noted. "They are steadfast, courageous and humble and do not need much to get by. Without doubt they will continue to be of great service to us in waging the war."[60]

After Heydrich's state funeral on 9 June, Hitler returned to the Obersalzberg for some peace and quiet before the start of the summer offensive. On 20 June, he visited the Hermann Göring armaments factory in Linz and informed himself about the state of Germany's tank production. The following day he travelled to Munich, where he took part in the memorial service for the leader of the National Socialist Drivers' Corps, Adolf Hühnlein.[61] While *en route* back to Berlin in his special train on the night of 22 June, Hitler received word that the Afrikakorps had captured Tobruk, taking 33,000 British soldiers prisoner. Hitler immediately made Rommel a field marshal, and the commander expressed his gratitude to the Führer with these words: "The tank army in Africa will continue to put the sword to the enemy according to the maxim: Forward to victory for the Führer, the people and the Reich!"[62] Nazi propaganda celebrated "Rommel's majestic triumph" in enthusiastic tones.[63] The "Desert Fox" was, in Goebbels' words, "the hero of the day" and the "most popular army leader we have at present."[64] At lunch the following day, Hitler was "over the moon" at Rommel's "stroke of genius." Goebbels wrote that the Führer "sees the situation in northern Africa as completely settled and consolidated and thinks it possible that we could now press on towards Egypt."[65] That very day, Hitler wrote to Mussolini expressing these sentiments. Instead of trying to conquer Malta as the Duce had suggested, Rommel's triumph should be exploited to the full and the offensive extended to the Suez Canal. "The goddess of luck in battle only visits a commander once," Hitler proclaimed to his ally. "He who fails to seize such a moment will often never get a second chance!"[66]

What Hitler especially liked about Rommel was his ability to improvise and his willingness to take risks—qualities he found lacking in the other officers of the general staff. "[Rommel's] way of working pleases the Führer very much," remarked Goebbels. "Rommel is an improviser. He does not allow himself to be pressed into any system. He is not a general staff intellectual. He is a man of practice, and it was as such that he earned his greatest victories."[67] Reports of further triumphs soon arrived from North Africa. On 24 June, Rommel's vanguard units reached Sidi Barrani in Egypt, and three days later they took the Egyptian port of Mersa Matruh. Hitler was convinced he had all of Egypt in his hands, and on 28 June, during a visit by Göring to the Wolf's Lair, he ordered that Rommel be given "whatever reinforcements he wishes."[68] But only a few days later, German dreams of seizing the Suez Canal were rudely dispelled. Near El Alamein, only around 100 kilometres from Alexandria, British tank divisions, backed by superior air cover, halted Rommel's advance. The German public's lofty expectations had been hugely disappointed.[69] Hopes now shifted to the offensive on the southern sector of the eastern front.

Before returning to the Wolf's Lair on 24 June 1942, Hitler made it clear that responsibility for directing the offensive would not be left solely up to the general staff, but that he himself would keep his generals on a "short leash." If the operations went to plan, he predicted, Stalin would be "beyond salvation," and the Germans could begin to "develop the eastern territory and fortify Europe" to make Germany immune to British military strategy. "Then we will have more leverage and can hold out for as long as we want."[70]

In the early morning of 28 June, the German offensive began with attacks by the corps under the command of Colonel-General Maximilian von Weichs on the northern wing of Army Group South. Two days later, the 6th Army under Paulus advanced from Kharkov. Although the plans for Operation Blue had fallen into Soviet hands after a German courier plane was shot down behind enemy lines, Stalin, who still expected the main thrust to be directed at Moscow, thought they were a feint.[71] Thus the Wehrmacht command once again succeeded in surprising their adversaries, and vanguard German tanks made swift progress. On 3 July, they reached the river Don. On 6 July, the important transport and arms-manufacturing centre of Voronezh fell. Euphoria once more took hold in German headquarters. In a conversation with the departing Turkish ambassador to Germany on 13 July, Hitler compared the Soviet Union to a bone "that resisted being bitten through on the first chew but was now gradually yielding."[72] It was obvious, as the Soviet ambassador to Britain, Ivan Maisky, noted in his diary on 19 July, that the Germans were trying to get to Stalingrad, to penetrate the Volga line and to separate the Caucasus from the rest of the Soviet Union. "If they are successful," Maisky added, "the situation will be critical."[73]

But the longer the campaign went on, the clearer it became that the German plans were built on sand. The Red Army had learned from its past mistakes. Instead of allowing the enemy to engage them in large-scale battles of encirclement, Soviet troops flexibly avoided them, even if it meant ceding territory. Germany's pincer attacks grabbed at thin air. "There is no longer the old stubbornness when they are about to be surrounded," Halder noted on 3 July, describing the new tactics of the Soviet High Command.[74] As a result, German troops captured far fewer prisoners than in previous operations. By mid-July it was obvious that the operational goal of encirclement and destruction could no longer be attained. Hitler held the leader of Army Group South, Field Marshal von Bock, responsible and stripped him of his command on 13 July. Weichs was appointed his successor,[75] and although the general claimed in his unpublished memoirs to have been outraged that such a decorated commander as Bock could simply be sent home, he had no scruples about taking the job.[76]

On 16 July, Hitler moved his headquarters to Ukraine to be closer to the fighting and to better direct operations. In a stretch of forest 10 kilometres north of Vinnitsa (Vinnytsya), Organisation Todt workers and Soviet slave labourers had built a complex consisting of block houses, barracks and three small bunkers. The "Werewolf," as Hitler called it, was, like the Wolf's Lair, secured by two off-limits zones and camouflaged so as to be invisible from the air. Parts of the Army High Command were quartered directly in Vinnitsa, but most officers now had to commute between East Prussia and Ukraine.[77] Although the quarters in the Werewolf were more spacious than in the Wolf's Lair and the whole atmosphere seemed friendlier to visitors, Hitler did not like his new headquarters.[78] He was suffering from severe headaches, and he particularly hated the stifling, humid heat that made being outside torturous. "It is a veritable greenhouse here: 50 degrees, downpours and then more heat," he lamented.[79] On top of that, the mosquitos were even worse than in East Prussia. "On hot days, a wild battle is fought against those beasts that have got inside despite the gauze-covered windows," reported Christa Schroeder, who along with Johanna Wolf was part of Hitler's Werewolf entourage. "They get through every crack and buzz around you as you try to sleep. They keep at it until you get out of bed cursing." In order to ward off malaria, which was transmitted by anopheles mosquitos, everyone attached to the Werewolf, including Hitler, had to swallow bitter-tasting medicine every evening.[80]

Such nuisances only increased Hitler's irritability, as the dictator realised that prospects for deciding the war with a few major strikes against the enemy were disappearing.[81] Tension was growing between him and Halder by the day. As General Walter Warlimont remembered, there was a "thunderstorm atmosphere, palpable in the room" at every situation meeting.[82] On 23 July, the tension discharged itself when Hitler threw a "tantrum." As Halder wrote in his diary: "The constant underestimations of enemy capabilities are gradually becoming grotesque and dangerous. It is increasingly intolerable. There is no chance of working seriously any more. Pathological reactions to momentary impressions and an absolute lack of judgement concerning the military leadership apparatus and its abilities are the defining characteristics of this 'leadership.'"[83]

Hitler's proclivity to overestimate his own strengths and undervalue those of his adversaries made itself felt that day in "Führer Directive No. 45," which concerned the continuation of the summer offensive. It began: "In a campaign of a little more than three weeks, the broad goals I set the southern wing of the eastern front have essentially been achieved. Only some weak enemy forces from Timoshenko's armies succeeded in escaping encirclement and reaching the southern bank of the Don." That was an extremely positive estimation of the situation, but nevertheless Hitler used it as the basis for a fateful decision. According to the original plan outlined in "Führer Directive No. 41" of 5 April, the attack on the Caucasus was supposed to take place only once Stalingrad had been taken and disabled as an arms-producing metropolis. But now Hitler divided Army Group South into a northern Army Group B under Weichs and a southern Army Group A under Field Marshal Wilhelm List. The weaker units of Army Group B were to occupy Stalingrad, block all traffic on the Volga and then press forward to Astrakhan, while Army Group A was to capture the eastern coast of the Black Sea and conquer the entire Caucasus, including the oil fields of Maikop, Grozny and Baku.[84] Once again, Hitler was going all in. Instead of proceeding in stages, the dictator chose to ignore Halder's counsel and launched two parallel partial offensives, a fateful decision that could only overstretch the already weakened German forces.[85]

After 1945, in an effort to downplay or entirely cover up their own part in Germany's military and moral catastrophe, Germany's generals cited Hitler's order of July 1942 as a prime example of his dilettantism as a field commander. As Halder would put it, it was the expression of "a volatile personality following momentary impulses, refusing to accept the limits of what was possible and acting on wishful thinking."[86] Nonetheless, although he was taking an enormous risk, there was a rational basis for Hitler's decision. The Führer was under time pressure. He knew he had to end the war in the east before the Allies opened a second front in the west. In the days immediately before Operation Blue, he had expressed "major concerns about enemy attempts to land in the west" and worried that German forces stationed there would be too weak to mount an effective defence.[87] In an order of 9 July, he talked of the "high probability" of an impending invasion in the area under the supreme commander west since Germany's initial successes in the summer offensive in the east might leave England "facing the choice between launching a major landing to establish a second front or risk losing Soviet Russia as a political and military factor."[88] In fact, Stalin had been pushing for a second front for quite some time, hoping that it would provide the Soviet war effort with a much-needed respite. During a visit to Moscow in August 1942 Churchill had been forced to declare that there was no chance of the Allies landing on the French Channel coast that year. He did, however, promise to expand air raids on Germany to aid Britain's inconvenient ally.[89]

Nonetheless, Hitler remained extremely nervous about a possible Allied invasion in the west. He thought his fears had come true when on 19 August 1942 two British-Canadian brigades, in a trial operation, made land at Dieppe, although they were forced to retreat back out to sea after only a few hours, having suffered heavy casualties. Still, Hitler declared in late September that Germany would have to reckon with "an attempted landing on a grand scale." In response, he ordered several battle-ready SS divisions to be transferred to the west and decreed that the Channel and Atlantic coasts would have to be turned into an impregnable fortress.[90]

In the east, the now separately operating army groups continued to make significant territorial gains in the second phase of the summer offensive. On 6 August, the armies of Army Group A crossed the river Kuban and three days later reached the Maikop oil fields. But before retreating, Soviet forces had so badly damaged the oil wells that a swift restoration of production was out of the question.[91] Nevertheless, Hitler was once again feeling confident when Goebbels visited him at the Werewolf on 19 August. Operations in the Caucasus, he boasted, were going "extraordinarily well" and after Maikop, Grozny and Baku would be captured as well. Then, Hitler promised, "not only will our oil supply be secured, but all the Bolshevik sources of oil will be smashed." Without oil, so Hitler's not entirely irrational reasoning went, the "Soviet system will not be able to wage war as it has to date." But Hitler went further. In vivid language, he described a "gigantic plan" that would have had German forces pressing forward to the Middle East. After crossing the Soviet border, they would occupy all of Asia Minor, steamroll Iraq, Iran and Palestine and cut off Britain from its "last oil reserves."[92]

After his talk with the Führer, Goebbels felt "refreshed as though after a bath." And that was clearly the whole point of Hitler's remarks.[93] To a large extent, his optimism was play-acted, concealing great uncertainty about how the campaign would proceed. That became apparent on 21 August, as reports came in that a group of mountain infantrymen had raised the Third Reich's flag of war on Mount Elbrus, the highest peak in the Caucasus, without Hitler's prior approval. He threw a fit of rage at such a militarily senseless "joyride." "I often saw Hitler furious," reported Albert Speer later, "but seldom did his anger erupt from him as it did when this report came in." He raved for hours as though this little enterprise had ruined his entire plan for the campaign.

Even days later, he was still constantly cursing to anyone who would listen about "those crazy mountain-climbers," who "belong before a court-martial."⁹⁴ At the end of August, however, Army Group A's advances slowed in the northern inclines of the Caucasus, and by early September things had come to a standstill. German forces would never reach Grozny or Baku.⁹⁵

Army Group B was initially able to continue its offensive, with Paulus' 6th Army marching forward, seemingly unstoppable. "Kharkov is now 500 kilometres to our rear, and we hope that we can deal the Russians further decisive blows," Paulus wrote on 5 August.⁹⁶ In a tank battle at Kalush, lasting from 7 to 10 August, his men were able to achieve another spectacular victory before the supply problems began to make themselves felt. Lack of petrol in particular meant that the troops were repeatedly forced to halt their advance.⁹⁷ But when Weichs described his problems over the phone to Hitler, he was taken aback at the Führer's reaction: "In contrast to his otherwise swiftly flowing speech, he stumbled over his words and repeatedly fell silent so that at times you did not know whether he was still on the line."⁹⁸

The closer the Germans got to Stalingrad, the stiffer Soviet resistance became. On 28 July, Stalin had issued his famous Order No. 227, which decreed that the time had come to end the strategic retreat. "Not one step back!" was Stalin's slogan now, and draconian punishments underlined how seriously he meant this appeal to his troops.⁹⁹ The hard-bitten Soviet defence of the city that bore his name would prove how effective Stalin's order had been. At the same time, the Wehrmacht also had to deal with setbacks on other parts of the front. To the north, the plan to take Leningrad had to be abandoned after the Red Army launched a counter-offensive south of Lake Ladoga in late August. And as of late July Army Group Centre too found itself confronted with a counter-offensive near Rzhev, which for a time looked as though it could result in a major Soviet break-through.¹⁰⁰

As always Hitler sought to divert blame from himself onto others. In conversation with Goebbels on 19 August, he complained that he was "only getting very incomplete support" when it came to leading the army and that "nothing has changed or got substantially better" since Brauchitsch's departure. "The old Father Christmases have remained," Goebbels noted. ". . . He is forced to endure nerve-racking battles with almost every single major order. It is nothing short of insulting that such incompetents and dilettantes create difficulties for a genius like the Führer."[101] Five days later, the extremely tense atmosphere in the Werewolf ignited in another bitter quarrel between Hitler and Halder. The army chief of staff had suggested during the noon situation briefing that the severely pressured 9th Army at Rzhev be allowed to retreat to a shortened line. Hitler recoiled as if stung by a tarantula. "You always suggest retreats," he snarled. ". . . We need to remain strong to set an example to the troops. I demand the same severity from my leadership as I do from the men at the front." For the first time, Halder lost his cool and shot back. "I possess severity, my Führer. But out there countless thousands of riflemen and lieutenants are falling as useless casualties in a hopeless situation—and all because the military leadership's hands are tied and they are unable to take the only tenable decision." Hitler puffed himself up in front of Halder, mustering him from head to toe before screaming: "Colonel-General Halder, how dare you talk to me like that? You want to tell me how men feel at the front? What do you even know of the front? Where were you in the First World War? And you accuse me of not understanding the front? I will not put up with it! This is unheard of!"[102]

There was no turning back from this falling out and Halder knew it. "It is all over," he was supposed to have said to the head of the operations division of the Army High Command, Adolf Heusinger, on the way back to their quarters.[103] While Hitler tried to brush aside the embarrassment by being exaggeratedly friendly to his military commanders over dinner, it was only an act.[104] He had already begun to look for a replacement for the army chief of staff. On 30 August, Halder noted: "The meetings with the Führer were again today accompanied by serious accusations against the military leadership of the highest ranks. Intellectual arrogance, unwillingness to learn and inability to recognise the essentials were the charges levelled."[105]

The following day, Field Marshal List arrived at the Werewolf together with his first general staff officer in an attempt to convince Hitler that the divisions of his army group would not be able to resume the offensive against stiff Soviet resistance. The dictator, already upset by the stagnation of the Caucasus front, ordered the 4th Mountain Division to attempt a breakthrough on the coast near

Gudauta, north of Sukhumi. Hitler had not given up his hopes of getting his hands on the oil fields of Grozny and advancing on to Astrakhan and the Caspian Sea. The taking of Baku "could be postponed until next year if necessary."[106]

Hardly had he returned to Army Group A's headquarters in Stalino (Donetsk) than List had more doubts about the feasibility of an assault on Gudauta and asked for Jodl to be sent, so that he could see the difficulty of the German situation for himself. After a visit on 7 September, Jodl agreed with List. Upon returning to the Werewolf that evening, he reported as much, sending Hitler into an "unbelievable explosion of rage." The Führer berated Jodl: "I did not send you off so that you could tell me about your concerns. No sooner are my gentlemen somewhere else than they come under foreign influences." For the first time, Jodl was unable to maintain his carefully practised reserve, barking back that he was not just a messenger of commands and slamming the door behind him when he left the room.[107]

Jodl's trip to Stalino triggered the most serious crisis between Hitler and his military advisers since August 1941. The Führer was "filled with hatred," recorded his adjutant Engel after witnessing the quarrel. "The mood is gruesome here."[108] The first victim of the rancour was List. On 9 September, Keitel flew to Stalino to tell him he was fired. Hitler himself temporarily assumed command of Army Group A, only passing on this authority to the commander of the 1st Tank Army, Ewald von Kleist, in November. "It feels damn lonely to be the only survivor of the whole field marshal guard," remarked the commander of Army Group Centre, Günther von Kluge.[109] At the same time, Hitler had Keitel tell Halder that he was thinking of removing him from his post since the chief of staff no longer seemed "up to the psychological burdens of his position."[110]

As if that were not enough, Hitler was also mulling over a change at the top of the Wehrmacht Supreme Command. On 18 September, he told Keitel that he could no longer work with Jodl. "I demand from an associate that he stands behind me absolutely blindly when the knives are out," Hitler said. "And if I give a command, he has no right to disobey that command and to represent a different view. His task is to press on and represent my view with absolute tenacity."[111] Hitler initially wanted to make Paulus Jodl's successor but deferred because he did not want to remove the commander of the 6th Army from his

position before Stalingrad had been taken.[112] Nonetheless, the leadership of the Wehrmacht was abuzz with rumours of a major personnel
cull similar to the one Hitler had carried out during the Blomberg-
Fritsch crisis in February 1938. In front of his adjutants, Hitler's
contempt for his generals knew no bounds. "He says that he cannot
talk with any one of them politically," Engel noted. ". . . Sometimes
he wonders whether there is not something to the Russian principle
of political commissars."[113]

The atmosphere in Hitler's headquarters had been rendered permanently toxic, and the dictator restricted his contact with his military
commanders to a bare minimum, no longer taking lunch or dinner
with them.[114] For a time, his seat at the officers' mess remained empty,
before Bormann took it over. Hitler withdrew completely to his block-
house, refusing to leave it during daytime. It was here, and no longer
in the building that accommodated the Wehrmacht main staff, that
situation meetings were now held. The mood was "icy," Halder
noted.[115] Contrary to his previous habit, Hitler no longer shook hands
with anyone and, as Warlimont recorded, behaved towards representatives of the Wehrmacht Supreme Command like someone "filled
with hatred."[116] At the same time, he ordered several stenographers
from the Reichstag to be brought to the Werewolf to record every
word spoken in the twice-daily situation meetings. The dictator wanted
not only to ensure that his instructions were being faithfully carried
out, but also to document for future generations of military historians
his marvellous achievements as Führer-meets-field-commander. With
Bormann as a witness, he made the stenographers swear an oath of
absolute secrecy about what was contained in the roughly 100 typed
pages that were generated every day.[117]

Hitler's explosions of rage and hatred cannot be explained solely
by differences of opinion about how operations in the Caucasus should
proceed. The hostility ran deeper. In September 1942, it must have
become clear to him that he had lost his bet that he would be able
to bring the Soviet Union to its knees on his second attempt. The
threatening spectre of a two-front war was approaching fast. "The
Führer sees no end in Russia after none of the goals of the summer
of 1942 were attained," Engel noted on the night of 8 September. "He
said himself how great his fear of the coming winter was. On the
other hand, he never wants to retreat."[118] For the first time, it must

have dawned on Hitler that the war was unwinnable. It is probably no accident that in these days he repeatedly articulated the wish that he could "cast off" his grey military uniform.[119] His refusal to take meals with his staff officers may well have been not just an expression of his displeasure with them. It could also have been related to his inability to pose any longer as the genius field commander. That thought suddenly occurred to Warlimont, the deputy chief of the Wehrmacht leadership staff, after Hitler gave him "not a greeting but a long, hateful glare" at a situation meeting. "The man has lost face," Warlimont wrote. "He has realised that his deadly game is coming to an end . . . For that reason he cannot bear the presence of the generals who all too often have been witness to his mistakes and errors, his illusions and fantasies. That is why he wants to get rid of them so suddenly and surround himself with other minions whose faith in him is as unburdened as it is unshakable."[120]

On 24 September, Hitler made good on his threats and dismissed Halder. Considering that the chief of the general staff had served for four years, his dismissal was embarrassingly undignified. The general's nerves were gone, the dictator curtly declared, and his own nerves were also frayed by the constant confrontations. There was no choice but to part ways. At the same time, Hitler made it known to Halder that as an old-school general staff member he had not met the profile and demands of a National Socialist officer. He needed men, Hitler said, who had been raised to "fanatically believe in an idea."[121]

Hitler thought that he had found one such man in Kurt Zeitzler, the chief of staff with the supreme commander west, Field Marshal von Rundstedt, since April 1942. This short, bald and corpulent officer, whose nickname was "Lightning Ball," had attracted attention to himself as a particularly daring officer, most recently in repulsing the British-Canadian landing near Dieppe. At forty-seven, he was relatively young and fresh, and most importantly, he was considered a loyal follower of Hitler. When he was brought by plane from Rundstedt's headquarters in Saint-Germain to Vinnitsa, he had no idea what was in store for him. Hitler received the new arrival late at night, mustered him with a penetrating gaze and talked to him for an hour. He ended his monologue with the words: "That is why I have decided . . . that Colonel-General Halder will be replaced and you will become chief of the army general staff."[122]

In his inauguration address, Zeitzler wasted no time demanding that every general staff officer should not only believe in "the Führer and his leadership" but "radiate his belief to his subordinates and surroundings." Anyone who could not meet that requirement had no place on the general staff.[123] Under these auspices, the working relationship between the Führer and the new man, who was promoted on the spot to infantry general, was relatively harmonious. "The Führer has complete trust in Zeitzler," wrote Karl-Jesko von Puttkamer. "He is happy and relieved to finally have as his chief of the general staff a man who will follow him without exception."[124] Hitler repeatedly praised Zeitzler in front of everyone and treated him, in contrast to other members of his military court, with demonstrative politeness.[125]

Along with replacing Halder with Zeitzler, Hitler took another major decision, transferring responsibility for all personnel matters concerning staff officers from the chief of the general staff to the army personnel department. As of 2 October, the latter was put under the directorship of the absolutely loyal chief adjutant of the Wehrmacht, Major-General Schmundt.[126] That accelerated the restructuring of the officer corps. In future, years of service would no longer be the decisive factor in promotions but rather proof of abilities at the front together with complete and utter alliance with the National Socialist world view. The general staff had mutated into a "study circle which served no purpose other than its own . . . and whose weapon was the feather and not the sword," Hitler scoffed in September 1942. "Young frontline officers must now be brought into the general staff and give it a new face."[127]

In the meantime, not only the offensive on the Caucasus front had come to a standstill. The conquest of Stalingrad was proving not as easy as Hitler had envisaged. On 21 August, Paulus ordered his 6th Army, a force of nearly 300,000 men, to attack. Two days later, the tank corps under General Alfred von Wietersheim reached the Volga north of the city, and the Luftwaffe began a series of massive air raids. Large parts of the city centre were destroyed and thousands of civilians killed.[128] In early September, Hitler issued a cold-blooded decree that the "entire male population" of the city was to be exterminated because "Stalingrad with its population of one million adherents of communism is especially dangerous."[129] But when it seemed only a matter of days until it would be taken, Red Army resistance stiffened. "The battle for the city is extraordinarily difficult," Goebbels admitted on 9 September. "What is transpiring here is truly a struggle of giants."[130]

On 12 September, Paulus flew to Vinnitsa to brief Hitler at the Werewolf. The previous evening Weichs had assured the Führer that it would only take ten more days to conquer Stalingrad.[131] But Paulus now pointed out the 6th Army's vulnerability to Soviet counter-attacks from the north and south. Hitler dismissed those warnings. The Russians, he declared flatly, were "at the end of their strength" and no longer capable of strategic operations dangerous to German troops. He therefore ordered not only that the entirety of Stalingrad be taken but also that an advance on Astrakhan be prepared in line with Führer Directive No. 45 of 23 July.[132] The assault on the city commenced on 13 September. But what Hitler envisaged as a lightning-quick strike turned into a costly static battle in which every street and block was bitterly fought over. "A building was first ours, then the enemy's, then ours again so that you could not really say where the front was," recalled the commander of a Soviet guards rifle division.[133] Soviet soldiers were able to take cover everywhere in the ruins of the bombed-out city, and despite their losses, they remained able to bring in reinforcements across the Volga. By the end of September, the city centre was in German hands, but the 62nd Army under Vasily Chuikov maintained control of several bridgeheads on the western bank of the river. Paulus was losing so many men that he had to suspend attacks aimed at completely taking the city.[134]

People around the world took an increasing interest in the struggle over Stalingrad, which had developed into a duel for prestige between Hitler and Stalin. "This is truly a question of life or death, and our reputation as well as that of the Soviet Union depends heavily on how it ends," Goebbels wrote on 23 September.[135] Ordinary Germans were waiting "with increasing, nervous impatience" for the report that the city had been taken, the Security Service reported at the end of that month.[136] In the town of Klosters in the Swiss canton of Graubünden, Wilhelm Muehlon was highly impressed with the heroic defence put up by the Red Army. Every day Stalingrad held out, he wrote, was "another nail in Hitler's coffin": "The Russians and only they have saved England and its allies until now, allowing them to get prepared for the clash with Germany."[137]

★

Hitler recognised that it was time to appear in public again. In August he had agreed to inaugurate the Winter Aid Campaign in Berlin, although the exact date had been left open.[138] On 27 September, he flew to the capital, where the following morning he spoke to officer candidates in the Sportpalast. Goebbels, who visited him in the Chancellery immediately afterwards, found him in "the best of moods," fresh and energetic, even though the first Allied air raid on Munich had just taken place and the Führer's private apartment on Prinzregentenstrasse had been damaged. The dictator tried to accentuate the positive, claiming that it was "a moral boon for the capital of the Nazi movement" if the city now also felt some of the hardship of the war. With regard to Stalingrad, Hitler was optimistic. "In a short time," he assured Goebbels, German troops would succeed in "bringing the entire city into our possession." The offensive in the Caucasus could then be resumed and, exploiting the milder climate there, continued even during the winter months.[139]

But Hitler's forced optimism was not shared by Colonel-General Friedrich Fromm, the head of army procurement and the commander of the Replacement Army. He had become convinced that military victory was no longer possible and that Hitler had to be enlightened as to how serious the situation was. To this end, he wrote an extended memorandum demanding that the war be "liquidated" as soon as possible—the implication being that peace talks should be initiated. On 29 September, when Fromm presented his main points in the Chancellery, he was rewarded with "icy silence." Hitler ordered Speer no longer to include Fromm in meetings concerning armaments. The general remained in his post because there was no one available to replace him, but he had become a *persona non grata*.[140] Yet Fromm had not only overestimated his influence on Hitler: he was also labouring under the fundamental delusion that the war could be settled by peace talks. That option no longer existed, as would become apparent at the Allies' conference in Casablanca in January 1943 at the latest. On that score, Hitler saw things more realistically.

On the afternoon of 30 September, Hitler spoke at the opening of the Winter Aid Campaign in a packed Sportpalast. "You could tell from the enthusiasm with which he was received how necessary it was for him to be among the people again," noted Goebbels, who kicked off the event.[141] But the dictator did not have much new to tell his fanatical admirers other than to assure them that the German people had survived "the most portentous test" in the winter of 1941–42. "Nothing worse can or will occur," he promised. Once again, he heaped sarcasm and scorn on the Allied leaders. It was time for Churchill to come and open up a second front, he scoffed, as though trying to steady himself in the face of his worst fear. "No matter what location he chooses, he will count himself lucky if he manages to stay on land for nine hours," Hitler bragged. At two junctures in his speech, however, the Führer revealed more than he probably intended to. On the one hand, he made direct reference to the destruction of the European Jews, which had entered its final and most terrible phase the previous spring. "The Jews once laughed at my prophecies in Germany as well," he sneered. "I do not know whether they are still laughing or whether they have already choked on their laughter. I can assure you that they will choke on their laughter everywhere." On the other hand, he dismissed any doubts that the fall of Stalingrad was imminent, telling his listeners "that no one will ever again drive us away from that place."[142]

With that, Hitler had publicly defined the complete conquest of Stalingrad as a goal and a mark of his personal prestige. There was now no way for him to back down without losing face. When Zeitzler and Jodl pointed out the losses German troops were absorbing in house-to-house fighting and suggested subordinating Stalingrad as a goal to free up forces, Hitler brusquely rejected the idea, asserting that the taking of the city was "urgently necessary not only for operational reasons but also psychologically."[143] At a meeting with the Reichsleiters and Gauleiters on the afternoon of 1 October, he led them to believe that Stalingrad would fall with absolute certainty, claiming that "it can only be a matter of time—the fact of the matter can no longer be changed." As he had in conversation with Goebbels on 19 August in the Chancellery, Hitler announced his intention to advance as far as the plains of Mesopotamia to cut off Britain's oil supplies. "At the moment these are still abstract plans, but they are thoroughly within the realm of possibility," he asserted. He ended his three-hour monologue with the surprising conclusion that "the war is practically lost for the other side no matter how long they remain capable of waging it." Only Germany's "internal collapse" could help the enemy to victory, and the Reichsleiters and Gauleiters all had to ensure that this remained impossible. In Goebbels' estimation, the Führer's speech worked "like a miracle."[144] The whole point of the meeting was to boost the morale of Hitler's minions and dispel any doubts in Germany's ultimate victory.

On 4 October, Hitler flew back to Vinnitsa, and two days later he ordered that the "complete capture" of Stalingrad be made the "highest priority" of Army Group B. "All other issues are to be put aside for this necessity," he commanded.[145] The following day, he received the secretary of the Fascist Party in Italy, Aldo Vidussoni, at the Werewolf and instructed him to tell Mussolini that he was "absolutely optimistic in his assessment of the situation." There was still "a severe and heavy battle" ahead in Stalingrad, but there was no question that the city would fall in the "foreseeable future."[146] Reality would quickly belie this forced optimism. The attack that resumed on 8 October brought only minor gains in territory. On 17 October, German troops took the Red Barricade munitions factory and the following day the Red October smelting works, which had been fought over with particular ferocity. Those gains, however, had come at a heavy price. One German division after another was being bled dry in the ruins of the city. On 26 October, Paulus had no choice but to report that because of tenacious Soviet resistance the fighting "was likely to lead to the total conquest of the city only around 10 November."[147] This prediction, too, would prove false.

The longer the wait became for the news that Stalingrad had fallen, the greater the concerns grew among the German population. People began comparing the fighting in the city to the Battle of Verdun in the First World War, worrying that, like then, Germany "would be put on the defensive and ultimately be defeated in the arms race by the unified forces of the enemy."[148] Rumours about negotiations and a separate peace with the Soviet Union circulated widely and were sometimes met with enthusiasm. From the town of Freiberg in Saxony came reports of "scenes of fraternisation on the street" between people "overjoyed with glee" at such a prospect.[149] Goebbels' propaganda could do little to stem the tide of these rumours since many Germans no longer believed anything of what they heard on the radio or read in the state-controlled press.

★

The Axis powers were also forced onto the back foot in other theatres of war. Back in June 1942, the US military had inflicted a heavy defeat on Japan in the Battle of Midway, and when marines landed on Guadalcanal in August, it ushered in a new phase of island-hopping, amphibious operations that would slowly but surely push the Japanese back from the parts of the Pacific they had conquered.[150] In North Africa, too, the course of the war was about to be reversed. On 30 September, while still on recuperative leave in Germany, and having spent several days at the Goebbelses' residence, Rommel had been received by Hitler, who presented him with his field marshal's baton. At the event at the Sportpalast that day, the crowd applauded him just as rapturously as they did the Führer. "That shows you just what a people's general he is," noted Goebbels.[151] He predicted that Rommel would be the future supreme commander of the army[152] and got Hitler to allow the "Desert Fox" to appear before the domestic and international press on 3 October. No leading military commander had ever been shown that sort of favour before, and the man so honoured did not disappoint the expectations of his patrons. "Today we stand 100 kilometres from Alexandria and Cairo and have the gateway to Egypt in our hands," Rommel told reporters. "And we intend to use it. We did not go all the way there to be pushed out again sooner or later. You can count on one thing: we will keep what we have taken."[153] It was the sort of boastful language Hitler himself employed in his speeches.

But only a few weeks later the seemingly invincible "Desert Fox" had lost his magic. On 23 October, the British 8th Army under General Bernard Montgomery launched a counter-offensive at El Alamein. On 2 November, Sherman tanks supported by the RAF broke through German lines. Rommel, whom Hitler had ordered to curtail his leave, telegraphed for help that afternoon. After ten days of the most vicious fighting, he wrote, his army was exhausted and faced "gradual destruction."[154] That sent the Werewolf into turmoil. "While everyone still hopes that Rommel will succeed again in getting himself out of such an extraordinarily precarious situation, that hope is not particularly great," Hitler's chief adjutant Schmundt reported in a telephone call to Berlin.[155] The bad news from North Africa even temporarily pushed Stalingrad into the background. Before midnight on 2 November, Hitler sent Rommel a telegram commanding him to "hold out" and "not to retreat a single step" while promising that everything possible would be done to send reinforcements. The dictator closed with the bathetic words: "It would not be the first time in history that the stronger will triumphed over the stronger battalions of the enemy. You must show your troops no other path than that leading to victory or death."[156]

But before he received that telegram, Rommel had already ordered his men to fall back, and a report to that effect arrived at Jodl's Wehrmacht staff in the early hours of 3 November. The major on duty did not immediately pass it on to Hitler: the news only reached him at 9 a.m. together with the other usual reports. Hitler was incensed, believing that the Wehrmacht Supreme Command had intentionally held back Rommel's report in order to present him with a *fait accompli*. He promptly summoned the major, threatening him: "If you do not tell me the whole truth, in ten minutes you will be a dead man." The unfortunate duty officer was immediately demoted to the ranks. Hitler had Keitel tell Warlimont, the deputy head of the Wehrmacht staff, that he too was dismissed from his post. However, after Schmundt put in a good word for Warlimont, Hitler rescinded his decision a few days later.[157]

On 1 November, after three and a half months in the Werewolf, Hitler moved his headquarters back to the Wolf's Lair, where the Organisation Todt had made several alterations. Barrack extensions had been added to the concrete bunker, making the accommodation for the Führer's entourage somewhat more pleasant. An additional large wooden barracks had been built for the stenographic service. Here the stenographers transcribed the notes taken during the situation meetings and deposited them in a safe for security reasons.[158] Hitler did not resume his habit of taking meals with the military, instead remaining absent from the lunch and dinner table. He did, however, continue his evening tea with his closest associates.

On the afternoon of 7 November, Hitler travelled via Berlin to Munich, where the following day he was set to give his traditional speech to the "old fighters." His retinue was in a stir. For days, reports had come in that the British and Americans had assembled an armada of transport vessels and warships off Gibraltar and were about to attempt a landing somewhere in the Mediterranean after passing through the strait. In the night of 7–8 November, Hitler's train was halted in Thuringia, where the Foreign Ministry informed him that an American expeditionary force had begun making land in Algiers, Oran and Casablanca.[159] Hitler immediately realised the significance of the Allied landing in North Africa: it was there, and not on the French coast, that the enemy was trying to open a second front. "This is the greatest collection of ships in world history," the Führer told his minions.[160] He ranted and raved about the Luftwaffe's failure to develop long-range bombers that could have been used to attack the landing parties and he immediately ordered Jodl to mobilise all available Wehrmacht forces to defend Tunis. French-administered North Africa was controlled by the Vichy government, and now, according to Engel, Hitler's biggest worry was whether the French collaborators would "stay the course." Hitler admitted that perhaps he could have offered them "better incentives" for their loyalty, but the fact remained that only Pétain and Laval could be trusted. All of the others, including Darlan, the supreme commander of the French armed forces, were playing "both sides against the other."[161]

At 4 p.m. on 8 November, Hitler arrived at the Nazi Party headquarters in Munich, where he held some frantic consultations with Goebbels, Ribbentrop, Himmler, Keitel and Jodl. The dictator was unsure of how he should behave towards the Vichy government: he could not be certain whether the resistance the French had put up to the Allied landing troops was real or fake.[162] Then, a few days later, reports arrived that on the orders of Darlan, who was in Algiers at the time, the defenders of French North Africa had laid down their arms.

Goebbels had been forced to delay the start of Hitler's speech to the "old fighters" in the Löwenbräukeller by an hour, putting it back to 6 p.m. A few minutes before that, Hitler withdrew to collect his thoughts and make some notes. As a well-versed actor, he succeeded in concealing his concerns about the latest developments and projected confidence into the auditorium. Goebbels wondered from where his Führer derived the strength "to be equal to such tests." Although Hitler had hardly slept for two days, he spoke "as clearly, directly and fluently as if he had been pondering his speech for weeks and had polished it word for word."[163] That was how Goebbels saw things. Wilhelm Muehlon, listening on the radio, came away with a very different impression: "It was a blabbering, faintly shrieking, confusedly murmuring Hitler . . . The man is over and done. As soon as his series of victories stops, even his oldest followers will laugh and abandon him like a spent fool."[164]

Hitler's core message was that in this "battle for existence" no compromises of any sort could be made, and there would be no further peace offers from the German side. He compared the situation of the Third Reich with that of Wilhelmine Germany in 1918. But in contrast to Wilhelm II, Germany's enemies were now forced to deal with a man "who refuses to even think of the word capitulation." Even as a boy he was always able to "get the final word in," Hitler boasted. The enemy could be assured of one thing: "Then Germany laid down its arms at quarter to twelve—as a matter of principle I only stop at five past twelve." The terrible implications of this assertion do not seem to have occurred to the frenetically applauding crowd. Hitler wasted few words on the Allied landing in French North Africa and the setbacks suffered by Rommel's Afrikakorps. They did not represent a danger to Axis positions, Hitler claimed. The decisive factor would be "who could land the decisive blow"—and that would be Germany. When it came to Stalingrad the dictator claimed that here the battle had already been won. With the exception of a "few small areas," Hitler lied, the city was under German control, and if people asked why quicker progress was not being made, the answer was: "Because I do not want a second Verdun there . . . Time does not matter. There are no ships sailing up the Volga any more. That is what matters."[165]

Hitler's speech had the desired effect on his old party comrades, however "horrified" his adjutants were about the rosy picture the dictator had once again painted of the military situation at Stalingrad.[166] Yet Hitler's appearance at Munich did not make much of a lasting impression on the public at large. The Security Service reported that the fresh news of the Allied landings in North Africa had "created a tremendous stir and in part came as a shock."[167] The fact that Hitler had barely referred to these events did little to calm the mood. In the weeks and months to come, the Nazi leadership would have more and more difficulty deceiving the German people about the true seriousness of the situation by glossing over it with rhetorical formulas.

By the evening of 9 November, when he was receiving Italian foreign minister Ciano in the Führerbau, Hitler had made a decision. The

Wehrmacht would be sent into the non-occupied part of France, Germany's Italian ally would occupy Corsica, and together the Axis powers would create a bridgehead in Tunis. "Hitler was neither nervous nor jittery," Ciano noted, "but he does not underestimate the American initiative and wants to counter it with everything at his disposal."[168] The French chief of state, Pierre Laval, who met Hitler and Ciano on the afternoon of 10 November, was presented with a *fait accompli*. By then it had become widely known that Darlan had ordered French defences to stand down in North Africa, and Hitler, suspicious of an insidious plot between the Vichy regime and the Allies, treated his French guest with cold arrogance. There were only two paths open to France, the Führer said: "either a definitive and clear alliance with the Axis or the loss of its entire colonial empire."[169]

The following morning German troops marched into the previously unoccupied part of France, the operation coming off without a hitch. In a letter to Pétain, Hitler described it as a necessary step to head off a British-American invasion of southern France. He promised that the German action was not directed at either Pétain himself, "the honourable leader of brave French soldiers in the world war," or French forces, with whom he hoped one day to defend France's colonial African possessions against the "larcenous Anglo-Saxon coalition."[170] But only two weeks later, little was left of this promise. Troops in Vichy France were disarmed, and the military port of Toulon occupied. The only reason the French fleet did not fall into German hands was because sailors scuttled it on 27 November.

While work continued on the Tunisian bridgehead, the situation for Rommel's Afrikakorps was coming to a head. Step by step, it was being forced back by Montgomery's troops. On 13 November, the British retook Tobruk, whose capture by the Germans in July had been celebrated as a turning point in the war. Seven days later, Benghazi fell. "The German people are beginning to have their doubts about Rommel," Goebbels fretted. "The evacuation of Benghazi has caused a fresh shock here."[171] On 28 November, Rommel suddenly appeared at the Wolf's Lair in an attempt to convince Hitler to withdraw his men from the North African theatre. Hitler rejected the idea out of hand. Not least for the sake of the Italians, the dictator believed, he could not abandon the North African bridgehead without a fight. "The Führer is against relinquishing the African theatre of war," Rommel noted. "It has to be held, whatever the cost."[172] The field marshal, who as recently as early October had bathed in the favour of the Nazi leadership, was henceforth an unwelcome guest at Hitler's court. There was no way of getting rid of him, though, because his aura as the cunning field commander still had a lot of reach and continued to be useful for propaganda purposes.

With news of setbacks in northern Africa pouring in, the Nazi leadership waited anxiously for the report that Stalingrad had fallen. "It would be time to present a larger victory to restore our somewhat dented image," Goebbels remarked.[173] But the news from the Soviet theatre was anything but good. After his meetings with Ciano and Laval, Hitler had withdrawn to the Berghof, perhaps a sign that he did not consider the situation on the eastern front all that dramatic. But on 19 November his newly promoted chief of the general staff, Zeitzler, called from the Wolf's Lair and breathlessly reported that the Soviets had launched a counter-offensive on the Don front north of Stalingrad and immediately breached the lines held by Romanian troops.[174] The Red Army's attack had been prepared for a long time. The Soviet High Command had noticed the overstretched German flanks on the Don and the Volga, which practically cried out for a large-scale encircling manoeuvre. Marshal Zhukov and his staff had put together a top-secret plan of operation, code-named "Uranus," which Stalin had approved. More than a million soldiers were assembled for the offensive and equipped with 13,500 pieces of artillery and 900 tanks.[175]

On 19 November, the day after the Romanian lines had been breached, another Soviet attack was launched to the south. Red Army troops again achieved major breakthroughs. Three days later, the vanguards of the Soviet tank divisions linked up at Kalach. The noose had been closed. The 6th Army, parts of the 4th Tank Army and the remnants of the Romanian 3rd Army—all told 22 divisions of around 260,000 men—were now surrounded.[176] "With that, an extraordinarily threatening situation has been created," an alarmed Goebbels realised. "If we do not succeed in freeing ourselves from this encirclement, our entire Stalingrad and Volga front is in huge danger."[177] Hitler, too, was aware of the severity of the situation. On 20 November, he ordered that the Army High Command 11 under Field Marshal von Manstein be moved from Vitebsk in the north, and Manstein given command of the newly formed Army Group Don. The following afternoon, before the ring around Stalingrad had closed completely, Hitler ordered the 6th Army to maintain its position "despite the danger of being temporarily encircled." He reconfirmed that order the next day. "No matter what happens, we have to hold out at all costs," Hitler's adjutants heard the Führer say again and again.[178]

The dictator could no longer put off his return to the Wolf's Lair. Late in the evening on 22 November, his personal train departed from Berchtesgaden. The journey took over twenty hours because every three or four hours a stop had to be made to establish contact with the Army High Command.[179] Immediately upon arriving in Rastenburg in the evening of 23 November, Hitler conferred with Zeitzler. The chief of staff agreed with the commander of Army Group B, Weichs, that the 6th Army would have to be given permission to attempt to break out of the cauldron, but in a highly dramatic discussion, he failed to persuade the Führer. "I am not leaving the Volga! I am not leaving the Volga!" Hitler screamed, pounding the table with his fist.[180] He refused to budge an inch from his conviction that Stalingrad must not be given up under any circumstances. Paulus was unable to change his mind, in a radio communication in which the commander of the 6th Army asked for permission to break out towards the southwest, warning that otherwise his men "would soon be staring destruction in the face."[181] In the early hours of 24 November, after Göring had assured Hitler that the surrounded troops could be completely supplied from the air, a "Führer directive" was issued: the 6th Army was to hold out in its present position—relief would be forthcoming. With his cavalier assurance, Göring, whose reputation had been badly damaged by the Luftwaffe's failure to defend Germany against Allied bombing raids, briefly regained Hitler's favour. The Reich marshal would get the job done "just like in the old days," Hitler enthused, remarking that the leadership of the Luftwaffe was not ruled "by the same timidity that holds in many parts of the army."[182]

The only senior military commander who supported Hitler's position was Manstein. On 24 November, the field marshal arrived in Starobelsk (Starobilsk), the main headquarters of what had been Army Group B, to take command of the new Army Group Don, of which the 6th Army was also now part. In contrast to Zeitzler, Weichs and

Paulus, in his first situation assessment for the Army High Command, Manstein opposed the idea of attempting a break-out as long as there was the prospect of effectively supplying the troops from the air. What really mattered, he contended, was to raise enough divisions for a relief operation. Only when that had failed could a break-out be considered, as the last resort.[183] On 26 November, Hitler once again stressed to Manstein that the "goal had to be to hold Stalingrad with any and all resources at our disposal" since giving up the city would mean "relinquishing the fundamental gains of this year's offensive."[184] Paulus, who confessed in a handwritten note to Manstein how conflicted he was between what he believed was the necessity of a break-out and the duty to remain loyal to Hitler, was told by the new commander of Army Group Don on 27 November: "What happens after the army has fulfilled the command of the Führer and fired its final bullet is not your responsibility!"[185] The same day Paulus appealed to the men of the 6th Army: "Stand your ground—the Führer will get us out."[186] Letters from Stalingrad show that in late November and early December many German soldiers did indeed trust that promise and believed that relief would be coming soon. This was no doubt a reflection of both the men's faith in Hitler and their desire not to unduly worry their families.[187]

In the first days of December, Hitler had wanted to return to the Obersalzberg for an extended stay in order to "clear his head for new decisions," but Zeitzler was able to convince him to change his plans in light of the critical situation of the 6th Army.[188] On the morning of 12 December, two tank divisions under General Hermann Hoth, the commander of the 4th Tank Army, launched an offensive intended to establish a German supply line from the south into the cauldron. Initially, they made the expected progress, but soon ran into strong Soviet resistance. By 20 December, Hoth's staff had to acknowledge that they would not be able to achieve their goal. Two days later, the relief offensive ground to a halt around 50 kilometres south of the cauldron.[189] Realising the dramatically worsening supply situation of the encircled German troops, Manstein now also began to lobby Hitler to allow the 6th Army to launch a break-out. But supported by Göring, who downplayed the supply problems, Hitler categorically refused.[190] The fate of the 6th Army was sealed. "Deepest depression here," wrote Engel on 22 December. "Almost everyone had hoped that Paulus would take the risk and order a break-out on his own . . . No one has any idea what is going to happen in Stalingrad. The Führer is very silent and almost never seen outside the situation meetings and briefings."[191]

When Ciano visited the Wolf's Lair on 18 December, he found the entire atmosphere there deeply oppressive.[192] In three days of talks, Hitler's main objective was to reassure his Italian ally. He did not discuss the critical situation of the 6th Army in any detail, speaking merely of "difficult situations" that tend to arise in warfare. He blamed Soviet successes on the "poor cooperation between the Axis armies on the eastern front." In future they would have to "stay in the closest of contact," with Germany "called to lead them." This was a first attempt to transfer blame for the catastrophe in Stalingrad to Germany's allies Romania and Italy. For his part, Ciano asked on behalf of Mussolini "whether it would not be better to find a political solution with Russia to avoid a two-front war." The Duce envisaged as an "ideal solution" something like the peace of Brest-Litovsk of March 1918. Hitler rejected the idea out of hand. No compromise could be reached between the two sides "with regard to their respective needs for food and raw materials," Hitler asserted. An armistice, even if the Soviets would agree to one, would only give them the chance to regroup. And there was no way of knowing whether the enemy would abide by a cease-fire. "To expect fidelity to treaties from Russians is like expecting holy deeds from the devil," Hitler remarked.[193] It was the height of hypocrisy from a politician who himself had no respect for treaties. The talks with Ciano ended without any concrete results. "Shadow games in the dark forest near Rastenburg" was how the translator Paul Schmidt described them.[194]

By Christmas, German troops inside the cauldron at Stalingrad knew that the relief attempt by Hoth's tank army had failed. They clung to the hope that things might turn round, and to boost their spirits sang the chorus of a hit by Lale Andersen: "Everything does pass, / Everything goes its way, / On the back of every December / There always comes a May."[195] Yet they gradually realised that they had been abandoned by their own leadership. The supply situation was worsening by the day. Only a fraction of the food needed and promised by the Luftwaffe was getting into the cauldron. "We often have to go hungry," reported one armoured infantryman in a letter home on 21 December. "In the mornings and evenings we only get a slice of bread, and at noon there is watery soup." A private wrote on New Year's Eve that it "almost broke his heart" when he thought about home: "How demoralising and hopeless everything here is. For four days, I have not had any bread. I am getting by on a ladle of soup at mid-day . . . Hunger, hunger, hunger, and on top of that, lice and filth. Day and night we are attacked from the air, and the artillery fire rarely stops . . . You are reduced to a bundle of jittery nerves. Your heart and your brain are overtaxed, and you tremble as though you have a fever . . . I have no hope, and I ask you not to cry too much when the news comes that I am gone."[196]

Soldiers sent thousands of letters like this, and at home they strengthened the general impression of Stalingrad as an incipient tragedy. "There are rumours in many parts of the Reich that the German troops in Stalingrad . . . are completely surrounded, causing renewed fears that Stalingrad could turn into a 'second Verdun' after all," the Security Service reported on 17 December.[197] Official news sources adopted a strategy of silence. In the aftermath of Hitler's proclamation of 8 November that the city on the Volga was as good as conquered, there had been no news about the Soviet counter-offensive or anything else. Wehrmacht reports refused to explicitly acknowledge that the 6th Army had been surrounded.[198] The only way family members could find out what was going on was from soldiers' letters.[199] Even Goebbels was "not very happy" about the official news policy. "We talk about difficult defensive battles, but we tell the people hardly anything about the seriousness of the entire situation," he noted. "Right now a gargantuan military drama is playing itself out in the east, whose outcome remains at the moment utterly uncertain."[200]

Hitler again avoided telling the German populace the truth about the military situation in his 1943 New Year's address. Instead he took refuge in propaganda clichés about Germany being forced into a war that was truly about "life or death" but that would inevitably end with Germany "being the last one standing on the battlefield." In his "Daily Order to the Soldiers of the German Wehrmacht," the dictator promised new weapons that would lead to victory and, using a familiar image of the enemy, cast the war as a crusade to defend Europe: "May

God have mercy on Europe if the Jewish-capitalist-Bolshevik plot succeeds. Europe would be lost for good, but within it, my dear soldiers, lies the homeland for which you are fighting."[201] In his personal New Year's greetings to Paulus, Hitler again promised to do everything he could to get relief to the "defenders of Stalingrad"—even though he knew full well that by this point he did not have the forces needed for that. Paulus was probably not fooled. Nonetheless he telegraphed back: "My Führer, your confident words for the new year have been received here with great enthusiasm . . . You can rest assured that, from the oldest general to the youngest infantryman, we are all suffused with a fanatical will to hold out and will do our part for the final victory."[202]

In the meantime, the Red Army had made its final preparations to attack the cauldron. On 8 January 1943, it sent a radio message to the command of the 6th Army demanding that it lay down its arms. The following day, Soviet planes dropped a large number of leaflets on the city calling for German surrender.[203] After consulting with Hitler, Paulus refused. "We are determined to fight to the last bullet," Paulus wrote in his army order on 9 January. "Negotiations are to be rejected, to go unanswered, and peace envoys are to be driven off with gunfire."[204] Thus, on 10 January, the Soviets began an artillery barrage that marked the start of their efforts to destroy the cauldron. There were immediately deep breaches of the German lines, and after three days the cauldron had shrunk to only a third of its original size. The Germans lost the airstrips of Basargino and Pitomnik, further hindering delivery of supplies.[205] But when Marshal Antonescu visited the Wolf's Lair on 10–11 January, Hitler still projected optimism that the situation would improve if the encircled army held its position "under all circumstances."[206] He had the same message for Captain Winrich Behr, whom Paulus had sent to the Führer's headquarters on 14 January to give Hitler a frank assessment of the condition of the troops in the cauldron.[207] After the war, Zeitzler wrote of Hitler "showing his Janus face" in these days. To the outside world, he radiated "courage and confidence" and the "firm belief in a happy ending in Stalingrad." Yet, Zeitzler added, "he concealed what was going on inside him. Only those who knew him very well, had been around him a lot and had experienced all of his moods, had an inkling of that."[208]

On 16 January, for the first time, the Wehrmacht Supreme Command published a report that, if only indirectly, acknowledged the encirclement of the 6th Army. "Yesterday in the region around Stalingrad, our troops, who have been engaged in a heroic defensive battle against enemy attacks from all sides for weeks, again repulsed fierce attacks by enemy infantry and tank units, causing major losses to the Bolsheviks."[209] The German public read the report as confirmation of its worst fears and concluded that Stalingrad "must already be considered lost."[210] Goebbels now wanted to prepare for that case, arguing that it was essential to "come out with the truth on our part so that we will have the necessary moral backing to accept this terrible news." Stalingrad, he argued, had to become "what Alcazar is for the Spanish Civil War: a heroic epic of German soldiery more moving and tragic than anybody could have previously imagined."[211]

With that a propaganda strategy was put in place, and Goebbels got Hitler to agree to it when he visited the Wolf's Lair on 22 January. The dictator left no doubt that he had already written off the 6th Army. There was, he admitted, "not the slightest hope of us relieving it." In Stalingrad, he added, "a great heroic drama of German history was playing itself out, unprecedented in its tragic and shattering form." While Hitler and Goebbels were conferring, a young major arrived from Stalingrad and reported: "The troops have nothing left to eat, no more ammunition and no more firewood. They sit in their bunkers in large numbers, starving and freezing to death." A cynical and duplicitous Goebbels commented: "A scene of truly Classical proportions. I lack the words to describe this heroic drama."[212] Henceforth the Nazi leadership directed all their efforts towards transforming the imminent military catastrophe into a heroic sacrifice of mythic dimensions to cushion the shock that it would cause among the German people.

Yet such mythologising was only possible if the 6th Army held out to the bitter end. On 16 January, Paulus wrote a letter of farewell to his wife: "I stand where I now stand as a soldier following orders. I do not know what my destiny will be. I will have to accept whatever God doles out to me."[213] On 22 January, after the loss of the final German-held airstrip at Gumrak, Paulus reported to the Army High Command that any further resistance would be futile and beseeched the leadership to allow him to end the fighting. Hitler refused. A capitulation by the 6th Army, he said, "was impossible from the standpoint of honour alone." Paulus again obeyed orders. That evening, he called upon his remaining men to defend "every foot of territory" and mobilise their "last reserves of strength . . . until the Russians relent and victory swings back to our side. Hold out!"[214] Such appeals to persevere could only have sounded cynical in the ears of the soldiers. On 26 January, Soviet forces succeeded in splitting the cauldron in two. A coordinated defence was now no longer possible, but Paulus still refused to stop the senseless carnage. On 30 January, he sent Hitler an obsequious telegram of congratulations on the tenth anniversary of the dictator's coming to power. "The flag still flies over Stalingrad," it read. "May our struggle serve as an example to living and coming generations never to capitulate, even in the most hopeless situation. Then Germany will be victorious. Hail to my Führer!"[215]

This anniversary could hardly have come at a more inopportune moment for the Nazi leadership. "This is not the time for glittering parties, not even within a scope appropriate to wartime," Goebbels noted soberly. He developed an alternative programme, which Hitler agreed to on 22 January and in which the Führer abstained from his customary speech. Instinctively, Hitler knew better than to appear in public in a situation when news of the demise of the 6th Army could arrive at any minute. Instead, Goebbels would open the proceedings in the Sportpalast and read out a proclamation from the Führer.[216] The propaganda minister did so with practised professionalism, whipping up passions in the auditorium by invoking an unshakable faith in Hitler that could "move mountains."[217] Hitler's proclamation consisted of nothing more than a tedious list of purported achievements of the Reich in its ten-year history. He only devoted a single sentence to the "heroic struggle of our soldiers on the Volga," which should remind everyone "to go to the limit in the battle for Germany's freedom and the future of our people."[218] It was left to Göring, in a speech in the Aviation Ministry that evening, to focus on the myth of the heroes of Stalingrad, establishing it as a "master narrative" in the canon of National Socialist legend. He described the battle for the Volga metropolis as the "greatest heroic battle of our history," comparing it with the legendary sacrifice of the Spartans in the Battle of Thermopylae and that of the Nibelungs in the court of Attila the Hun.[219] "Germany is one army poorer and one heroic saga richer," commented the company leader Theodor Habicht.[220] Those soldiers in Stalingrad who followed Göring's speech on the radio, however, received this "conse-cration of the painful death" of an entire army with "outrage, indeed with nausea."[221]

On 31 January, Hitler promoted Paulus, who had only become a colonel-general the previous November, to the rank of field marshal. The Führer expected no doubt that the commander of the 6th Army would die a hero's death and shoot himself.[222] But he was wrong. That very evening, the southern part of the cauldron surrendered, and Paulus, who had withdrawn to the basement of the Univermag depart-ment store, allowed himself and his staff to be taken prisoner without a fight.[223] Two days later, the northern part of the cauldron surren-dered. After seventy-two days, the battle for Stalingrad was over. Some 110,000 German and Romanian survivors went into captivity. Only around 5,000 of them would eventually return home.[224]

Hitler was beside himself when he heard that Paulus had allowed himself to be taken captive. "So many men had to die, and then this fellow goes and tarnishes in the last minute the heroism of so many others," he yelled in the situation meeting on the afternoon of 1 February. "He could have freed himself from all pain and gone down for eternity in national immortality. But he prefers to go to Moscow. How can there be a choice? That really is insane!"[225] During his rise to political power, Hitler had repeatedly threatened to kill himself, convincing those around him that he would find such a decision not at all difficult. On 1 February, he proclaimed: "How easy it is! To use a pistol—that is child's play. How much of a coward do you have to be to shy back from that?"[226]

On the afternoon of 3 February 1943, German radio transmitted a special report about the end of the fighting in Stalingrad: "Loyal to their last breath to their oath to defend the flag, under the exemplary leadership of Field Marshal Paulus, the 6th Army has succumbed to the superior power of the enemy and the misfortune of circumstances." To make the propaganda about heroic sacrifice more plausible, a bald-faced lie was unrolled: "Generals, officers, junior officers and troops battled shoulder to shoulder until the final bullet was fired. They died so that Germany will live."[227] Goebbels had worked out every detail and procured Hitler's approval for the "heroic ceremony" that would frame this announcement. Funeral marches were played, followed by muted drum rolls and three verses of the song "I Once Had a Comrade." After three minutes of silence, it was announced that all cinemas, theatres and places of amusement would remain closed for three days. The broadcast ended with a passage from Beethoven's Fifth Symphony.[228]

But even Goebbels could not conceal that this special report unleashed a "kind of shock wave" among the German people. "It was expected, but now that it is here, it is more painful than anticipated," he wrote.[229] The university student Lore Walb noted in her diary on 3 February: "Today is the darkest day for Germany in the history of our war . . . A previously unexperienced mourning weighs upon us all."[230] The Security Service reports talked about "deep distress." The general belief was that "Stalingrad marks a turning point in the war." One report added that "more unstable ethnic-popular comrades even tend to see in Stalingrad the beginning of the end."[231] Reports about the popular mood from various *Gaue* described "probably the hardest test of faith since the beginning of the war." The population, it was concluded, had never considered such a setback possible. There was particular criticism of the radio and the press, which had kept people in the dark for too long about the situation in and around Stalingrad.[232]

The man at the top was now coming in for some criticism as well. People remembered Hitler's speech on 8 November, when he had announced that Stalingrad was about to be taken.[233] "For the first time, Hitler is not able to pass the buck," Hassell remarked in mid-February. "For the first time, the critical murmuring is focused directly on him."[234] Needless to say, the shift did not remain concealed from the propaganda minister with his acute sensibility for changes in the popular mood. It was "extraordinarily perilous," Goebbels noted, "that the Führer is now being criticised to a greater extent." Although such criticism was still confined to "certain segments of the people," everything possible had to be done to ensure it did not spread.[235] If Speer's memoirs are accurate, Goebbels even spoke at the time not of a "crisis of leadership" but a "crisis of the leader," the Führer himself.[236] Stalingrad severely dented Hitler's popularity and his aura as a "genius field commander." Jokes began to circulate: "What's the difference between the sun and Hitler?"—"The sun rises in the east, Hitler goes down in the east."[237]

Opponents of Hitler all over the world began to gain hope. Wilhelm Muehlon was seized with a "shock of a good kind," when he heard about what had happened in Stalingrad.[238] Thomas Mann even dictated words of congratulations to the Red Army on 5 February, praising it for performing "services of a truly epic, powerful kind; services benefiting humanity and its freedom; acts of defence that will remain unforgotten for all time."[239] The few remaining persecuted Jews living in the Reich also took heart. "The debacle in Russia is supposed to be genuine and decisive," Victor Klemperer wrote on 5 February. The Dresden academic did not believe that the Nazi regime was in any danger of falling soon, but "in any case, a bit of hope alone perks you up."[240]

In the night of 3–4 February, the members of the White Rose, a student resistance group that had formed around the siblings Hans and Sophie Scholl and Alexander Schmorell, daubed the slogans "Down with Hitler" and "Freedom!" on walls at twenty locations around Munich. The sixth and final leaflet distributed by the group explicitly referred to the German defeat: "Our people stand shaken at the defeat in Stalingrad. The genius strategy of the Great War private has senselessly and irresponsibly driven 330,000 German men into death and ruination. Führer, we thank you!" On 18 February, as the Scholls were distributing their flyers in the hallways and staircases of Munich University, throwing the remaining ones out of a second-storey window into the courtyard, they were discovered by the caretaker. The dean, SS-Standartenführer Walter Wüst, who had a chair in "Aryan philology," informed the Gestapo. Only four days later, after a brief trial presided over by the president of the People's Court, Roland Freisler, the Scholls and their friend Christoph Probst were sentenced to death and beheaded in Munich's Stadelheim Prison. The same fate was meted out several months later upon three further members of the circle: Munich University professor of philosophy Kurt Huber, Schmorell and Willi Graf.[241] Such murderous retribution was aimed to quash any form of resistance. But the deeds of the White Rose quickly became widely known. The "capital of the movement," people said, was becoming the "capital of the countermovement." Some even speculated that revolution would break out in Munich "before long."[242]

Nonetheless we should not overestimate the significance of signs of a change in public sentiment and growing distance to the state leadership. The foundations of the Nazi regime had not been shaken, nor had the mythology around Hitler lost its power. The Swiss consul general in Munich, Hans Zurlinden, warned against false interpretations, diagnosing an "unstable and moody mentality that changes like the weather with the ups and downs of war." It could not be ruled out, he added, that after fresh victories "the Germans almost down to a man would once again enthusiastically bellow 'Heil Hitler!' "[243] Friedrich Kellner also sounded a cautious note in his diary, writing that while the number of people "who are beginning to think" had increased after Stalingrad, propaganda ensured that the truth "continued to be suppressed just like before" and the German defeat given a positive spin. "The people, spoiled by victories, are doubtless somewhat shaken," Kellner wrote, "but it will take several impressive defeats to deal the popular faith a mortal blow."[244]

On 7 February, Hitler summoned the Reichsleiters and Gauleiters to the Wolf's Lair. He had last spoken to this group in early October, but the difference between the two occasions could hardly have been starker. Instead of the promised glorious victory, a catastrophic defeat had taken place. The dictator was under pressure to justify himself in front of his closest minions, and again he demonstrated his continuing powers of persuasion and acting skills. "I believe today more than ever in victory," he began his two-hour address, "and do not intend and will not let this faith be shaken by any event." It was entirely untrue, he continued, that the Reich was "on its last gasp." Although it had suffered a "serious setback," compared with the crises the party had overcome prior to 1933 and the difficulties Friedrich the Great had mastered, the current situation was harmless. As he had insinuated in his talks with Ciano and Antonescu, Hitler blamed the Stalingrad debacle on the "complete failure" of Germany's allies, now stating that Italian and Romanian units had behaved with "total cowardice"— statements that seemed to belie Hitler's assurance that he, of course, would assume "undivided responsibility for all events this winter." In conclusion, the dictator expressed the hope that German forces would "recover their operational freedom" over the course of the spring. "Then we will soon be back on top," he promised. At the same time, he repeated the grim threat that would become part of his standard repertoire in the final years of the war: "If the German people should at some point become weak, it would deserve nothing else than to be obliterated by a stronger people, and no one should have any pity with it."[245]

Hitler's paladins returned home strengthened with new conviction.[246] But the dictator had kept them in the dark about how truly dire the military situation was on the southern sector of the eastern front. For a time, the entire Caucasus front had been in danger of collapse. In late December, after a long struggle, Zeitzler had succeeded in gaining Hitler's approval to shorten the lines of Army Group A.[247] The subsequent retreat was basically complete by the end of January. That not only spelled the end of Hitler's megalomaniacal daydreams of pushing forward into Mesopotamia to the heart of Britain's positions in the Middle East; it also meant that Hitler had definitively failed to seize the Caucasian oil fields, which had been the main goal of the summer offensive.[248] The situation of Army Group B too was, in the words of its commander, Weichs, "critical in the extreme." The Italian and Romanian units had largely disbanded, and the weakened German forces were unable to plug the resulting holes. After some back and forth, Hitler approved a partial retreat here too, while demanding that Kharkov and Kursk be held at all costs.[249] In the north, the Red Army had succeeded in breaking the blockade of Leningrad on its 506th day in January and in re-establishing overland supply lines to the encircled city.[250] Still, it would not be until 27 January 1944 that, after long and costly battles, the siege would be finally ended.

On 6 February, Hitler received Manstein for a long meeting in the Wolf's Lair. The field marshal had an ambitious agenda for the talk, hoping to convince the dictator to alter the military command structure that had crystallised since Brauchitsch's dismissal in December 1941. The main idea was to create a new position of general chief of staff for all parts of the Wehrmacht to ensure the war was conducted in unified fashion. This would not only have meant the abolition of the dual structure of Wehrmacht and army high commands; it would have weakened Hitler's status as supreme commander of the army. The Führer reacted with astonishing calm to this suggestion. Instead of openly rebuffing Manstein, he replied that there was no way Reich Marshal Göring would be subordinate to a Wehrmacht general. In truth, Hitler was not prepared to give up an ounce of his authority, not least because of his fundamental distrust of his generals' motives, which had only increased since the failure of the 1942 summer offensive.

Manstein did, however, get Hitler to approve the withdrawal of his severely pressured Army Group Don beyond the river Mius, thereby vacating the eastern part of the Donets basin.[251]

Meanwhile, the Red Army was continuing to advance in the south, recapturing vast swathes of territory. On 8 February, Kursk was liberated, and a week later, Kharkov followed.[252] On the German home front, this further spate of bad news sent fresh ripples of shock through the populace. "It seems as though things are beginning to fall apart" was the prevailing opinion.[253] In the face of the severity of the situation, Zeitzler was able to persuade Hitler to fly to Zaporozhye (Zaporizhzhya) to visit the headquarters of Army Group South, as Army Group Don had been renamed on 14 February.[254] Here the atmosphere was extremely tense. Only after lengthy argument did Hitler approve Manstein's plans for a more mobile strategy that would combine offensive and defensive actions. But the attempt to get Hitler "to think operationally in the long term" failed precisely because the Führer refused to commit himself long-term. During the two days of consultations, the Red Army advanced to within 60 kilometres of Manstein's headquarters. There were fears that Soviet tanks could take the airstrip to the east of Zaporozhye, and relief abounded when Hitler and his retinue hastily left at noon on 19 February. As the Führer's plane took off, Soviet artillery could already be heard in the distance.[255]

Hitler did not immediately return to the Wolf's Lair, choosing instead to stay in his Ukrainian headquarters, the Werewolf, until 13 March.[256] From there, he could follow Army Group South's counter-offensive, which began on 19–20 February. Reinforced by battle-ready divisions brought in from the west, it quickly gained momentum. After pushing westwards hundreds of kilometres, for the time being the Red Army had reached the end of its attacking strength. German tank armies repelled advancing Soviet vanguards and now pushed forward themselves. On 14 March, Kharkov was recaptured—a prestigious victory. "Thank God the worst is behind us now," Goebbels noted. "The past winter was terrible, but in the end we overcame it."[257] In late March, the fighting ground to a halt. Manstein had succeeded in stabilising the southern section of the front. By and large, it ran along the same lines as when the 1942 summer offensive had commenced.[258]

★

The fighting in the winter of 1942–43 had been disastrous for Germany. The Battle of Stalingrad may not have been the decisive turning point of the war—that had already occurred in December 1941—but many Germans saw it as such. "There is a very strange, apathetic, grim mood these days," wrote Mathilde Wolff-Mönckeberg from Hamburg in early March 1943. "You can see desperation in so many faces and feel the impatience, breathless fatigue and irritability everywhere—on the tram, in the post office, in the shops. How different it is from the first year of the war, when swastika flags would be waved at the most minor occasion, powerful drum rolls announced victories on the radio, and everyone was shooting their mouth off. Now, since Stalingrad has capitulated, everything is grey and we have total war."[259] For people in the Soviet Union, too, the defence of the Volga metropolis and the destruction of an entire German army were of great psychological significance. They strengthened people's confidence, raised their morale and gave them hope that at the end of all their efforts and sacrifices there would be victory over the hated fascist aggressor. "I'm in an exceptional mood," wrote one Red Army soldier to his wife after the Soviet victory at Stalingrad. "If you only knew, then you'd be as happy as I am. Imagine it—the Fritzes are running away from us!"[260]

Hitler and the German army command stood before a shambles. Their attempt to force a decision in the east before the Western Allies could bring their overwhelming power to bear had failed. None of the goals of the summer offensive had been attained. The attempt to seize the oil in the Caucasus had come to nothing. The important transport route of the Volga and parts of the Donets basin were once more under Soviet control. By spreading his forces throughout the southern sector of the eastern front and strictly forbidding the 6th Army to break out of the Stalingrad cauldron, Hitler had played a major part in this disaster. The strategic initiative had passed over to the anti-Hitler coalition, and it would never return.[261] Germany's dramatic defeat in Stalingrad also ushered in a caesura in its relations with its allies. Hitler's attempts to blame them exclusively for the debacle left behind a lot of bitterness. The more the prospects for victory disappeared, the more intensively Hitler's allies began to consider if it might not be advisable to distance themselves from the "Greater German Reich" and its leader, who was growing increasingly divorced from reality. "If only our allies don't give up!"—this fear would henceforth play a dominant role within the Nazi leadership.[262]

Hitler was not in the best of health. In a one-to-one conversation with Goebbels, he repeatedly complained that he "no longer felt up to the severe demands" and did not know whether he would "survive the war physically intact."[263] Above all, he was plagued by insomnia and nervous stomach cramps. His personal physician Morell had his hands full with administering injections of stimulants to keep Hitler able to work. Since the end of 1942, the trembling in his left arm had got worse, and when he walked he dragged his left leg behind him.[264] General Guderian, whom Hitler had brought back from banishment, naming him general inspector of the German tank force on 17 February 1943, was stunned when he saw the Führer for the first time again. "His left hand trembled, his posture was stooped, his gaze was empty, and his eyes bulged out a little and were without gleam," Guderian wrote. "There were red spots on his cheeks, and he was far more short-tempered. When overcome with fury, he would easily lose composure and was unpredictable in his words and decisions."[265] Göring too told Goebbels in early March 1943 that he thought Hitler had "aged fifteen years in the three and a half years of war." The two men agreed: "It is tragic that the Führer cuts himself off so much from life and leads such an inordinately unhealthy existence. He never gets any fresh air and never relaxes. He just sits in his bunker, does this and that and broods."[266]

The symptoms of physical decline were indeed accompanied by increasing self-isolation, combined with a renunciation of all diversion and entertainment. In the past, Hitler had always played records of his favourite music during his nighttime teas. After Stalingrad, if Christa Schroeder is to be believed, he could no longer bear listening to music.[267] Whereas he had once drawn energy from his interactions with the masses, he now reduced his public appearances to a minimum. He even refused to allow the weekly newsreels to show footage of him on occasions such as his Sportpalast speech on 30 September 1942. Goebbels was unhappy. "I am in something of a bind," he wrote. "The people want to see him. The Führer does not want to be shown on the news. What am I supposed to do?"[268] Was Hitler afraid that news-reel footage of him would elicit expressions of disapproval rather than the earlier storms of enthusiasm? The dictator had tied his personal destiny to ultimate military victory, and the more the prospect of success receded, the more internally insecure he became and the more he tended to close his eyes to reality. Unlike Goebbels and the other Nazi "dignitaries," Hitler never visited a bombed-out German city. It seems as though he shied back from contact with the people.[269]

One episode recorded by Speer in his memoirs illustrates the point. It took place on 7 November 1942 on the train journey to Munich that was interrupted several times by reports about the Allied landing in French North Africa. "In earlier years, Hitler had the habit of presenting himself at the window of his special train at every stop," Speer recalled. "Now these encounters with the outside world seemed undesirable to him; instead the shades on the station side of the train would be lowered. The table was elegantly set with silver flatware, cut glass, good china, and flower arrangements. As we began our ample meal, none of us at first saw that a goods train was stopped on the adjacent track. From the cattle car, bedraggled, starved and in some cases wounded, German soldiers just returning from the east stared at the diners. With a start, Hitler noticed the sombre scene two yards from his window. Without as much as a gesture of greeting in their direction, he peremptorily ordered his servant to draw the shades."[270]

Hitler's withdrawal from the public eye nourished rumours that he was seriously ill. In part to counteract them, he decided to hold a speech on Heroes' Commemoration Day, although he asked Goebbels to postpone it from 15 to 21 March to allow for the situation on the southern sector of the eastern front to stabilise.[271] "It is good that he is speaking and that the German people can hear his voice again and can derive a sense of strength and faith in victory from what he says," a pleased Goebbels noted.[272] But Hitler disappointed expectations. At ten minutes his speech was not only unusually short. He also read so hastily and monotonously from a piece of paper that many people could not follow him. Thomas Mann, who had listened to the broadcast in California, characterised it in his radio address to German listeners on 28 March as follows: "You notice from the speech with how little desire it was held. You notice that the only reason it was given was because it seemed necessary for the commander-in-chief in war to give a sign of life after months of depressive silence. Yet it failed precisely as an expression of life. It was evidence of a fatigued, if not broken, temperament."[273] Many Germans did indeed find the speech depressing, and speculation abounded that it was not Hitler himself but a double who had spoken, because the Führer had suffered a nervous breakdown after Stalingrad and was now being kept under observation on the Obersalzberg.[274] The weekly newsreel in late March, the first one in a while to show footage of Hitler, dispelled such rumours, but the Security Service nonetheless reported a great amount of dismay at how "exhausted," "tense" and "aged" the Führer looked.[275] If we consider that Hitler owed his political rise first and foremost to his unusual speaking talent, his uninspired, listless appearance on 21 March 1943 symbolised his inexorable decline not just as a public orator, but as a leader of state.

9

Total War and Ethnic-Popular Community

"We can only resolve in the coming year to work with all our energy to wage war totally and radically in all areas," noted Goebbels on 1 January 1943. "The main tenet of my philosophy of war remains the same: the most radical and total war is the shortest war and brings the most decisive victory."[1] The propaganda minister had lobbied for quite some time to intensify the war effort on the home front. The methods used thus far were inadequate, Goebbels determined in late September 1942, as the failure of the summer offensive could no longer be concealed and another winter of war approached. The conflict had now entered a phase in which "sentimentalities of public opinion" could no longer be taken into consideration. "The time for blowing kisses is over," Goebbels wrote. "Now we have to get out the whistles." In the months that followed, he repeatedly proclaimed that there were still plenty of unused reserves in the Reich that could be mobilised for the war effort. If women replaced men at work and government bureaucracies were "combed through," then "the Führer would doubtless have hundreds of thousands, if not a million, fresh soldiers at his disposal." Although Goebbels never tired of warning in public about the perils of Bolshevism, privately he admitted that Germany could learn a thing or two from the Soviet Union about the "energy and totality" of government measures. In Germany, endless talk about "waging total war" was never followed through. "But what has not been the case soon will be," Goebbels noted in his diary.[2]

In the spring of 1942, Hitler had taken the first step in the direction Goebbels was proposing, when he named infantry general Walter von

Unruh as his special envoy to the Reich commissariats of Ostland and Ukraine, instructing him to round up reserves of personnel from all military and civilian offices. On 22 November 1942, the day the 6th Army was surrounded in Stalingrad, the dictator expanded Unruh's authority. Henceforth he was also to examine whether in the Greater German Reich "all forces were being used sensibly and to their fullest to meet the demands of war."[3] All in all, though, the "Unruh Action" proved to be a failure. The efforts to reduce bureaucracy and free up men in the ministries in Berlin met with obstructionism and delaying tactics. For quite some time, Goebbels would joke about the failure of the "hero-snatching general." "He would go to a Reich department in Berlin, reduce personnel and head to the next department," Goebbels wrote. "But no sooner had he turned his back than the department expanded again. Everyone was laughing. When he arrived, everything was set up to trick and deceive him, and the entire Unruh Action, though well intentioned and undertaken with colossal *élan* . . . simply petered out."[4]

To combat the resistance, the propaganda minister went in search of allies. Since the autumn of 1942, he had made it a habit to invite leading personalities for an exchange of opinions to his official apartment or his villa on the island of Schwanenwerder, near Berlin. They included his former deputy Walther Funk, now economics minister, Reich organisational director Robert Ley and Albert Speer. In Speer, particularly, Goebbels found a strong supporter. "He is one of the few men who entirely take in my suggestions and offer me valuable help," Goebbels wrote.[5] Over Christmas 1942, as the Stalingrad catastrophe was taking shape, Hitler too arrived at the conclusion that more radical measures were needed to offset the enormous losses on the eastern front. On 28 December, he sent the director of the Party Chancellery, Martin Bormann, to Berlin to discuss the "total deployment of the German people to increase the war potential" with Goebbels and the head of the Reich Chancellery, Hans Heinrich Lammers.[6] The propaganda minister did not conceal his glee. Everything he had thought and hoped for had now "all at once been translated into reality."[7] He immediately asked the ministerial director of the Propaganda Ministry, Werner Naumann, to draw up a proposal for "total war deployment of the home front," which he passed on to Lammers on 2 January 1943. Along with the introduction of mandatory work for women, it included the "ruthless closure of all businesses not essential to the war effort."[8] "With this," Goebbels commented, "civilian life will be heavily curtailed. But that is the point of the whole exercise."[9]

On 4 January, Goebbels met with Lammers, leaving with the impression that the previously reserved head of the Reich Chancellery had "come round entirely to my thinking."[10] The decisive "top meeting" took place on 8 January in the Chancellery. Taking part along with Lammers, Goebbels, Bormann, Speer and Funk were Keitel and Fritz Sauckel, the general representative for labour deployment. Keitel painted a dire picture of the reinforcements situation. In many places, he said, the front was "so thinly manned" that it threatened to be "torn apart." New soldiers would have to be placed at the Führer's disposal "in great dimensions" so that he could not only master the present difficulties but go back on the offensive the next summer. Goebbels demanded that, as soon as possible, 700,000 men previously deemed essential to the war effort should be freed up to be sent to the front. To fill the resulting gaps, all possibilities for mobilising previously unused personnel would have to be exhausted. Lammers was charged with drawing up a "Führer proclamation" to that effect. Hitler was "very interested" in the results of the meeting. Several times over the course of the evening, he had calls made from the Wolf's Lair to track the progress of the negotiations.[11]

On 13 January, the dictator signed a proclamation "on the comprehensive deployment of men and women for Reich defence tasks" that gave Goebbels most of what he had demanded. All men aged sixteen to sixty-five and women between the ages of seventeen and fifty were now required to register with the state, if they had not already done so. Moreover, trade, artisan and commercial activities not essential to the war were to be discontinued. On 27 January, registration was instituted, followed by regulation about shutting down non-essential businesses two days later.[12] To ensure that these ordinances were enforced, Hitler named a so-called Committee of Three consisting of Bormann, Lammers and Keitel. Goebbels, who had been the driving force behind the initiative in the past months, felt slighted and could not conceal his disappointment. Lammers sought to mollify him by promising that all measures would be taken in close consultation with him. For the time being, the propaganda minister was satisfied by this pledge, believing that he had the necessary influence to "give this matter the right appearance."[13]

Passing over Goebbels was a carefully calculated move by Hitler, who tended to encourage rivalries among his paladins as a way of preventing any one of them from growing too powerful and threatening his own position. This consideration no doubt inspired him to leave Goebbels off the committee. He seems to have feared that this body, if it were to include the crafty propaganda minister and perhaps other heads of ministries, would develop into a kind of "war cabinet" that could one day form the nucleus of an alternative centre of power to his own and call his absolute authority into question.[14] Of course, Hitler avoided giving Goebbels any inkling of such fears. When the two men met on 22 January 1943 for lengthy consultations in the Wolf's Lair, Hitler tried to sell Goebbels on his decision by claiming he did not want his propaganda minister weighed down with "administrative tasks." Instead he was to take over "the role of the continuously running motor in this matter." In other words, Goebbels' job was to keep stoking the propaganda campaign for total war.[15]

And indeed, Goebbels left no stone unturned in his efforts to intensify his propaganda. In an agenda-setting article entitled "Total War" in *Das Reich* on 17 January, he repeated his core message: "The more radically and totally we wage war, the more quickly we will arrive at a victorious conclusion." One week later in the same newspaper, he expounded about the decisive "psychology of waging war": "The visual appearance of our civilian life should not represent a provocative contradiction to the actual war but must be in tight harmony with it." Bars, taverns and luxury restaurants would have to be closed.[16] When Goebbels explained his concept of total war at the annual commemoration of Hitler's assumption of power on 30 January in the Sportpalast, he was interrupted by shouts of "It's high time!" As the propaganda minister concluded: "Not only am I not too radical for the people in my demands: I am not radical enough. We cannot press this thing hard enough right now."[17]

Goebbels certainly did drive home the point in another, more notorious, Sportpalast speech on the afternoon of 18 February 1943. He had prepared for that appearance for days, polishing his address right down to the last minute in the hope that it would be a "masterpiece of oratory" and surpass in radicalism "everything that has ever come before."[18] When he took to the lectern shortly after 5 p.m., a huge banner proclaiming "Total War—Shortest War" hung above the stage, and the roughly 14,000-strong audience were already full of feverish excitement. The propaganda minister had once again ensured that the auditorium was full of "good old party comrades" as well as numerous celebrities, including the beloved actor Heinrich George, almost all of the Reich cabinet and many of the Reichsleiters and Gauleiters.[19]

Goebbels began his speech, a recording of which was broadcast on all German radio stations at 8 p.m., by promising to give an "unvarnished picture of the situation." He called the demise of the 6th Army at Stalingrad "providence's greatest wake-up call to the German nation" and conjured up the immense peril of Bolshevism. The force behind the "storm from the steppe," he claimed, was "international Jewry, the infernal fermenting agent of decomposition," which had set its sights on liquidating the entire intellectual elite and leadership class of the Reich and subjecting the working masses to "Bolshevik-Jewish slavery." Once again, he accused the Soviets of doing precisely the things the Nazi leadership had themselves long practised, together with the SS and the Wehrmacht. Germany had no intention of bowing to this threat, Goebbels exclaimed. On the contrary, it would be "promptly countered, if necessary with the complete and most radical eradication—I mean, the disabling of Jewry." This was anything but a slip of the tongue: It was a calculated reference to the mass murder of Jews that now turned his audience into knowing accomplices. And the crowd reaction captured on the recording of the speech—"loud applause, wild cries and laughter"—suggests that the audience approved of what they were hearing.

Having painted a horror scenario, Goebbels went on to demand "rapid and fundamental action." "Total war is the order of the hour!" he proclaimed. "There must be an end to bourgeois sensitivity, which even in this fateful battle follows the principle 'Give me a bath but don't get me wet'!" Goebbels pledged that the leadership of state would ensure that the burdens of war were fairly shared. "Rich and poor and high and low must be called upon in equal measure." After enumerating the measures the government had already taken or planned to take to mobilise the Reich in its entirety, Goebbels moved on to the finale of his address. He posed a series of ten questions to those assembled, who, he declared, represented a "cross-section" of the German population, implying that the reaction he awaited from them was the equivalent of a plebiscite of the entire nation. Every one of the questions was greeted with thunderous applause, especially the fourth one: "I ask you: do you want total war? If necessary, do you want it to be more total and radical than we can even imagine today?" The icing on the cake was a citation from the military poet Theodor Körner from the time of the Napoleonic Wars: "Now, people, stand up—and storm, break out!"[20]

The speech had a gigantic effect. "The end of the event got lost in the turmoil of a heart-racing atmosphere," Goebbels wrote afterwards. "I think that not even in the battle days had the Sportpalast experienced anything like it." Even days later, Goebbels was still glowing about the international echo of his speech: "It is a first-rate sensation and has commanded the headlines and the front pages of all the world's newspapers . . . There has probably never been a speech held in Germany over the whole course of the war that has been so much cited and commented on around the globe."[21] Hitler, who was in Vinnitsa at the time, had been unable to listen to the broadcast, but he asked for the manuscript and praised the event as a "psychological and propagandistic masterpiece of the highest class."[22] There may have been an undertone of envy in these words since for quite some time Hitler had not been able to celebrate any comparable rhetorical triumph. Continuing to avoid public appearances, on 24 February 1943 he declined to attend the traditional celebrations of the anniversary of the founding of the Nazi Party, instead having his old comrade-in-arms Hermann Esser read out a proclamation.[23]

Hitler had no reason to doubt Goebbels' loyalty, but he still followed the propaganda minister's ceaseless activity with mixed feelings. In fact, the dictator's ever-wakeful mistrust was not entirely unfounded. On the evening of 18 February, in his function as Gauleiter of Berlin, Goebbels invited a number of important figures of state and party, including Speer, Ley, Stuckart, Luftwaffe general inspector Erhard Milch and Justice Minister Otto Georg Thierack, for a gathering at his villa near the Brandenburg Gate. "Much was discussed that evening," the host wrote portentously, adding that he intended to stage further such meetings "to establish a certain leading role for the Gauleiters." This was necessary as, in Goebbels' eyes, "in the Führer's absence from

Berlin a central political leadership was missing."[24] On 26 February, Speer, Funk and Ley met again with the propaganda minister to consider how to solve the persistent leadership crisis. They agreed to reactivate the Ministerial Council for the Defence of the Reich and use it as a lever to "neutralise" the influence of the Committee of Three on Hitler. The ministerial council had been formed shortly before the war, but under Göring's leadership it had remained largely inactive. The idea was now to install a "suitable deputy" at Göring's side, a position for which Goebbels volunteered: "I would form a circle of ten men, all capital fellows, with whom I would govern, that is to say: establish a domestic leadership."[25] Rarely had the propaganda minister articulated his designs on power so openly, even in his diary.

Two days later, on 28 February, Speer went to see Göring, who had withdrawn to his holiday home on the Obersalzberg. Goebbels had given Speer clear instructions before he set off on his journey. First and foremost, Göring would have to be convinced "that we want to work with him most loyally and intend to create a forum for him to get more involved in domestic policy." Speer's mission proved successful. Despite being initially "somewhat irritated and distrustful," Göring said he wished to speak with Goebbels as soon as possible. "If I succeed in winning over Göring 100 per cent for the new war policy, it would be a hugely positive factor in our entire prosecution of the war," a confident Goebbels wrote.[26] He arrived on the Obersalzberg the very next day. Göring received his guest with the "greatest amiability," and Goebbels took care not to mention the "minor disagreements" that had weighed upon the two men's relationship in the past. Goebbels even found the "rather baroque outfits" Göring wore, which he had always mocked, "positively charming" this time round.

After five hours of discussions, the two men agreed completely on what Germany's fate would be in case it was defeated. "Above all on the Jewish question, we are so committed that there is no escape any more," Goebbels noted. "And that is a good thing. Experience teaches us that a movement and a people that have burned many bridges behind them fight much more unreservedly than those who have the possibility of backing off." Göring did not require much persuading to support Goebbels' plan of "transferring the tasks of the Reich political leadership from the Committee of Three to the ministerial council." The Reich marshal also talked scornfully about the "three wise men." Lammers, he scoffed, was "an arch-bureaucrat," Bormann a careerist and Keitel an "absolute zero." Göring also liked the suggestion of adding to the council several "men of strength" who would have the energy "to bring this war to a victorious conclusion." Goebbels made no bones of the fact that he primarily had himself in mind, but he studiously avoided giving any impression of questioning Hitler's authority or wanting to limit his power. On the contrary: "The men who have come together in an alliance of loyalty to the Führer have no other ambition than to support each other and create a solid defensive wall around him," Goebbels declared. He and Göring agreed to meet again in Berlin to push things forward. Before that, Goebbels and Speer were to visit the Werewolf to make the idea palatable to Hitler. Goebbels departed from the Obersalzberg convinced that he had established a "truly friendly basis of trust" with Göring.[27]

On 5 March, Speer flew to Vinnitsa to get the lay of the land. He was followed three days later by Goebbels. Immediately on the propaganda minister's arrival, Speer warned him that Hitler did not have much good to say about Göring.[28] The night of 2–3 March had seen the heaviest air raid yet on Berlin, and Hitler held the Reich marshal as the head of the Luftwaffe directly responsible for Germany's poor air defences. In conversation with the dictator, it was apparent that "Göring's reputation with Hitler has suffered colossally." Hitler did not hold back with sharp criticism of the Luftwaffe's shortcomings, even hinting that he was going to fire Göring. As a result, Goebbels decided not to broach the subject of the revival of the ministerial council for the moment. "The time is not right at present," he conceded. "We will have to postpone this matter until a little later." Following dinner with Hitler, after which the men repaired to the fireplace in a casual atmosphere, Goebbels and Speer decided that they would make an attempt nonetheless. But before they could do so news arrived that Nuremberg, the host city of the Reich party days, had also been the target of a major air raid. Hitler flew into a rage, summoning Göring's main adjutant, General Karl Bodenschatz, out of bed and raining down on him recriminations about the "incompetent Reich marshal." Goebbels and Speer were able to gradually calm down the Führer, but they had made no progress in advancing their agenda. Afterwards, Speer would come to suspect that Hitler had intentionally staged a scene because he had got wind of his paladins' intentions and wanted to prevent them from making their pitch.[29]

On 17 March, Goebbels, Ley and Funk went to see Göring at his villa near Berlin's Leipziger Platz to consult about how to proceed. The Reich marshal went on and on about the "psychology of the Führer." The trick, he said, was to "approach him correctly and make one's case with the right arguments at the right time." Göring still seemed confident of achieving this, even though he could hardly have remained unaware how far he had fallen in the Führer's favour. He promised to get the ball rolling the next time he met with Hitler. "Göring made a somewhat more solid impression than on the Obersalzberg," noted Goebbels. "It seems that he was deeply impressed that I appealed to his honour."[30] But the propaganda minister was wrong. Göring in fact did nothing and soon lapsed back into his previous lethargy. The plan to undermine the Committee of Three using the ministerial council proved to be dead on arrival.

Instead Hitler sent an unmistakable signal when on 12 April he named Bormann "secretary of the Führer."[31] With that, the head of the Party Chancellery had finally been given a key job. Because of his proximity to Hitler, Bormann had the advantage of knowing his master's views and wishes before anyone else, and he exploited his exclusive position of trust to go beyond party matters and meddle in all areas of German domestic policy. What was more, he controlled who got access to the Führer. No minister, Reichsleiter or Gauleiter could set up a meeting with Hitler without Bormann's consent. In August 1943, for example, Ley tried in vain to get an appointment with the dictator.[32] Even Lammers, the head of the Chancellery, had to ask Bormann when he wanted to inform the Führer about something, with Bormann making him feel that he was now clearly playing second fiddle.[33]

Goebbels was forced to acknowledge that he had bet on the wrong horse with Göring and began to reorient himself. In early May, following the funeral of the head of the SA, Viktor Lutze, who had died in a car accident, the propaganda minister had a chance to discuss personnel issues with Hitler and his new secretary. He came out of that meeting with a revised opinion of Bormann, who had behaved "extremely loyally." Goebbels noted: "If you compare the promises he has kept to those made by Göring, Göring without question draws the short straw. There is no relying on Göring any more. He is tired and worn out."[34] In the weeks that followed the propaganda minister's diary was filled with lamentations about Göring's passivity.[35] And the more the propaganda minister wrote off the Reich marshal as a potential ally, the more he sought to curry Bormann's favour. Goebbels was, of course, only too aware of Hitler's growing opinion of his equally diligent and unconditionally subservient secretary.[36]

Goebbels' failure to instrumentalise the ministerial council to combat the Committee of Three was not his only setback. Unexpected resistance also emerged to his drive to "totalise" the waging of the war. "Some ethnic-popular comrades are disappointed at how various actions have developed," the Security Service reported in mid-March. "The momentum with which the public was initially seized has begun to ebb into apathy and scepticism. There is no noticeable sign of the storm, to cite the final words of Dr. Goebbels' Sportpalast speech, that was to break out among the people."[37] Goebbels encountered the greatest resistance when it came to introducing a comprehensive requirement for women to work. This, among other things, ran against Hitler's idea of women's "natural" role as child-bearers to increase the German population. At the Führer's behest, the age limit in Sauckel's ordinance was lowered from fifty to forty-five, and numerous exceptions meant that upper- and middle-class women were largely able to avoid registration.[38] Repeatedly Hitler warned that women were not to be subjected to "petty harassment." They should not be antagonised, he warned. "It is nothing to be despised when women try to look beautiful for their men," Hitler also proclaimed, "and the National Socialist outlook prohibits neither make-up nor hair dyes."[39]

The campaign against commercial activities deemed non-essential to the war effort also proved unpopular. The initiative mainly affected smaller, middle-class businesses, and as it was handled differently from *Gau* to *Gau*, rules were enforced arbitrarily, and businessmen's connections to Nazi functionaries often played an important role. Much to Goebbels' irritation, Göring himself intervened to prevent the closure of Berlin's gourmet restaurant Horcher.[40] In its final report of July–August 1943, the Committee of Three determined that only 150,000 men had been freed up, many of whom were of no use for arms manufacturing.[41] Goebbels' "combing-out" measures attracted more and more criticism and dissatisfaction. The Security Service reported that workers who had initially welcomed the propaganda minister's announcement began to question whether "the circles that had previously been able to 'shirk all labour deployment' were now really being called on." For working-class people, the enforcement of the requirement to register "truly without exceptions" was "nothing less than a litmus test of whether an ethnic-popular community really did exist."[42] As enforcement was anything but complete, that only strengthened the impression that the burdens of "total war" were distributed inequitably.

Among the middle classes, on the other hand, people feared that the businesses and shops that had closed would not open again after the war. Many even suspected that "in practice National Socialism was increasingly coming to resemble Bolshevism," and that the regime was consciously pursuing the "'demise of the middle class' on behalf of a state-capitalist concentration of the economy, in which a thin stratum at the top would derive all the benefits."[43] Opinions like this were all the more worrisome to the Nazi leadership because they were voiced from the ranks of those who had previously been their most loyal supporters. In late summer 1943, the business closure initiative was discontinued.[44]

On the whole, the measures aimed at a total mobilisation of the German home front largely failed to fulfil their purpose. Instead of giving the Nazi regime new legitimacy, they aggravated the latent crisis of trust between people and government in the wake of Stalingrad, and the results yielded lagged far behind expectations. In response, the regime decided to utilise foreign labour, above all from the occupied parts of eastern Europe, to a greater degree.[45] In the summer of 1941, some three million foreigners had already been working in the Reich, mostly in agriculture. They included 1.2 million French POWs and 700,000 Polish civilian labourers. But with the failure of the Blitzkrieg against the Soviet Union and the war turning in the winter of 1941–42, the German arms industry's labour needs increased dramatically. Hitler now overcame his previous ideological reservations and approved the use of Soviet POWs as workers, although most of the Red Army soldiers captured had already been allowed to starve to death.

On 21 March 1942, the dictator named Thuringian Gauleiter Fritz Sauckel his "general representative for labour deployment." Sauckel's task was to bring as many foreign workers as possible into the Greater German Reich in as little time as possible, and Hitler's long-term minion set about it with great energy and brutality. In the occupied Soviet territories, press gangs hunted down young and able-bodied men and women. "They are catching people now like the knacker used to catch dogs in the old days," one Ukrainian farmer complained in the autumn of 1942.[46] Between April and November 1942 alone, 1.4 million civilian labourers were brought against their will to Germany. That amounted to around 40,000 per week and an impressed Goebbels wrote: "Here again it can be seen that if you put a task, no matter how difficult, in the hands of a true, energetic and focused National Socialist, it is as good as done."[47] By the summer of 1943, the army of foreign workers had grown to 6.5 million, and by September 1944 it would swell to 7.6 million, including 5.7 million civilians and almost 2 million POWs. Every fourth person working in German industry and agriculture was from abroad, and in some arms factories, foreigners made up 80 per cent of the workforce. It was only the massive exploitation of slave labourers that allowed Nazi Germany to keep waging war for another two years after the catastrophe at Stalingrad.

In the final years of the war, the gigantic nexus of slave labour became an established part of everyday German life. Big cities all had networks of camps and other facilities for accommodating foreign labourers. There were four hundred in Munich alone, spread out all over the city. "In late afternoons you can hear in Munich's streets every language of Europe save German since the citizens of the Reich have apparently grown quieter," reported the Swiss consul there in April 1943.[48] No inhabitant of the city could avoid seeing foreign workers and concentration camp inmates on labour duty being herded to their places of work or being forced to clear damage from air raids. At table, Hitler contemptuously dismissed these people in blanket fashion as "riff-raff."[49] But there were stark contrasts in the living conditions of various types of foreign workers. Separate guidelines for how to treat every single group of foreigners were issued, and they were open to differing interpretations from place to place and

from enterprise to enterprise. At the bottom end of the racist hier-
archy were Poles and "Eastern workers" who had been forcibly
deported from the occupied Soviet Union. They were governed by
special edicts subjecting them to comprehensive discrimination and
social control. They had to wear special badges reading "P" or "East,"
were confined to camps of barracks surrounded by barbed wire, and
faced the death penalty if caught being intimate with German women.
"Sex crimes" was how the perverse language of the Nazi "master
race" termed the phenomenon.

After the shock of Stalingrad, the rations for "Eastern workers"
were increased slightly, and the conditions in which they were held
improved somewhat. But these changes were made in the interest of
increasing economic productivity, not for any humanitarian reasons.
Even a fanatic like Goebbels recognised that arms production could
not be improved with half-starved and completely exhausted people.
"We should not regard or treat them as slaves," he wrote. "We have
to accord them a treatment that does not turn their stay in the Reich
into hell."[50] Many companies that derived additional profits from forced
labourers also began to realise that it might be advantageous after the
end of Nazi rule if they did not treat their foreign workers in the
worst of fashions.

"No contact with the German population and above all no solidarity," Göring had ordained. "It is a general principle that the German
worker is the Russian's superior."[51] Nonetheless there were signs of
solidarity and tacit consensus between Germans and foreigners, for
instance, when both sides agreed to work go-slows. On the other hand,
the rise of many German workers to positions of command undermined any such solidarity. The sense of community within the prole-
tarian milieu, which had already been dramatically lessened after labour
organisations had been destroyed in 1933, was weakened still further.[52]
Just as they had been indifferent to the fate of deported Jews, most
Germans took little interest in the fortunes of foreign labourers beyond
their daily contact at work. And as air raids grew more and more
frequent, concerns for one's own survival increasingly took centre
stage. "The drama of the destruction of whole cities and the steadily
growing number of victims are creating a more intense state of alarm
and continual fear," reported the Italian consul in Cologne in July
1943.[53] Discrimination against Poles and Russians in particular seemed

like a natural fact of life. For the Nazi deployment of forced labour to function, racism had to have become a habit and a reality experienced and accepted every day.

Memories of the First World War played an important role in everything the Nazi regime did—or did not do—in the Second World War. They included the experiences of hunger, inflation, defeat and the November Revolution, which inspired the propaganda legend that frontline soldiers had been "stabbed in the back" by traitors on the home front. "Hitler and the majority of his political followers came from the generation that experienced the revolution of November 1918 as soldiers and had never got over it," recalled Speer. "In private conversation, Hitler often suggested that one could not be careful enough after the experience of 1918."[54] A repeat of the "trauma of 1918" was to be prevented at all costs.[55] Consequently, any measures that could negatively impact the public mood had to be avoided. That meant above all that the burden on the masses had to be kept as light as possible. Hitler never tired of stressing that it was not the German people who had come up short in the First World War; it was their leadership. The mistakes that had been made in the past needed to be rectified now. Then, Hitler promised, "it will be possible to make a proud victory out of the defeat of 1918 and the countless victims and suffering it caused."[56]

In line with this, the regime was very cautious in its taxation and finance policies. The War Economy Directive of 4 September 1939 levied a war supplement of 50 per cent on wage and income taxes from the beginning of 1940, but only on people who earned more than 2,400 reichsmarks a year. Moreover, generous allowances meant that, according to the official statistics for 1943, around 70 per cent of employed people paid no supplemental tax at all and a further 26 per cent with annual incomes up to 6,000 reichsmarks were required to contribute relatively little. Thus it was only the wealthiest 4 per cent who had to pay the full surcharge.[57] The directive had also stipulated that additional pay for working nights, Sundays and holidays was to be abolished, which would have meant painful income losses for large segments of the working class. But in a letter to Göring on 18 September 1939, Rudolf Hess protested against the new rules, writing: "The Führer and all of us have not fought to win the trust of the working class for two decades so that this can be threatened in the most critical moment for the sake of more or less theoretical considerations."[58] That part of the War Economy Directive was consequently rescinded in November 1939, and as of December 1940, all supplemental pay was exempted from taxes and social contributions.[59] In 1941, when the regime was confident that Germany would achieve a quick victory over Russia, it even cut taxes and significantly raised pensions.[60]

All in all, people's real income rose despite the ban on wage increases ordered at the start of the war;[61] the downside was the reduced availability of consumer goods. Excess consumer spending power thus led to fears of rampant inflation, which the regime tried to combat by creating incentives to save. To this end, in late 1941 the "Iron Saving" initiative was launched. This was a state-supported savings plan in which a monthly sum was withheld from people's wage packets in return for lower taxes and social contributions. The drawback was that savers could only access their money after the final victory the Nazi leadership promised. Working-class people were evidently quite sceptical about the Iron Saving plan whereas it proved rather popular among better-earning, white-collar employees.[62] Unlike during the First World War, the government did not issue any bonds: instead it secretly availed itself of people's savings to finance some of the exploding costs of war. Over the course of 1943, however, there was a significant decline in people's inclination to save for the future. The number of newly concluded savings plans fell by almost 90 per cent compared to the previous year—a sign that popular trust in the regime's promises was diminishing.[63]

While indirect taxes on tobacco, beer, spirits and sparkling wine were raised incrementally, Hitler refused to increase income tax even during the second half of the war. When Finance Minister Schwerin von Krosigk drew up plans to do so, in the interest of curbing exploding state debt, the dictator put his foot down. "If we make a grab for small incomes, it will undoubtedly create a huge psychological burden," wrote Goebbels, who was of one mind with Hitler on the issue. "The people cannot be subjected to additional burdens . . . if they are not necessary to win the war."[64]

The fear of a collapse in public optimism and a decline in mass loyalty also affected how the regime took care of the families of soldiers drafted into the war. The fundamental principle for measuring family support payments was the "preservation of property." Unlike in the First World

War, when the German government had failed to provide adequately for soldiers' families so that many had suffered through bitter privation, the soldiers in the Second World War were to have no concerns about the welfare of their loved ones. The Family Support Law of July 1940 defined such provisions as "a duty of honour to be fulfilled by the state." Assistance was so generous that soldiers' wives commonly received more than 85 per cent of what their husbands had earned in civilian life. Considering that the state paid the soldiers' wages too, and fed and housed them, many families were better off than before the war. Under these circumstances, the soldiers' wives often had no incentive to work in arms factories, for instance, since whatever they were paid was deducted from their state support. A comparison with other countries illustrates how good German soldiers' families had it: they retained on average almost 73 per cent of their peacetime income compared to 38.1 per cent in Britain and 36.7 per cent in the United States.[65]

In addition, the regime devoted special attention to taking care of the relatives of those killed. "All our affection, love and care go out to them," Hitler declared in a speech on 30 January 1941.[66] Local Nazi Party leaders were instructed to personally break the news of the death of a husband or son to the wife or mother and to support the bereaved in their grief. As was the case with family support payments, compensation for the victims of war was generous and doled out in non-bureaucratic fashion. After the reform of the Wehrmacht Care and Provision Law in 1942, pensions paid to the bereaved were no longer calculated according to military rank alone, but also on the basis of the deceased's civilian employment. That meant that war widows had decidedly more money in their pockets.[67]

The state and party took care of those bombed out of their homes equally intensively. Special offices of the National Socialist Welfare organisation, local party chapters and care workers offered "immediate help."[68] Bombing victims were first given something to eat. "If after the terrors of the night, those who have been bombed out have a piece of bread with butter and a thick slice of ham in their hand, along with a cup of coffee or a bowl of pea soup, the world starts to look a bit brighter straight away," remarked Hamburg's mayor, Carl Vincent Krogmann, at a meeting of municipal politicians in February 1944, six months after devastating air raids had destroyed that northern German city.[69] The immediate assistance measures included payments or vouchers with which those affected could buy clothing and household effects to get them through the first weeks.

After the air raid on Lübeck in March 1942, Hitler had charged Goebbels with organising the relief efforts. At the start of 1943, the dictator also gave him responsibility for the newly created Inter-Ministerial Air War Damage Committee, which was supposed to coordinate all measures in bomb-ravaged areas.[70] The main point was to compensate those who had lost everything in air raids quickly and effectively. Goebbels saw this as an excellent psychological measure to win back lost trust. "The party has gained enormous prestige because it takes care of the people most generously," he wrote in June 1943.[71] To replace homes, furniture and household items, local authorities distributed the property left behind by emigrated or deported Jews. In late December 1941, Hitler had allowed the so-called Deployment Staff of Reich Director Rosenberg, which was responsible for the organised looting of art in occupied Europe, to extend its activities to the seizure and confiscation of Jewish property in France, Belgium and the Netherlands. Between March 1942 and July 1943, forty-five shiploads with more than 27,000 tonnes of furniture, household effects and clothing stolen from Dutch Jews arrived in Hamburg alone. Those who had been bombed out were not the only ones to profit. The historian Frank Bajohr has estimated that at least 100,000 households in Hamburg acquired items looted from Jews. "Simple housewives . . . suddenly wore fur coats, bartered with coffee and jewellery, and possessed antique furniture and rugs from the port, from Holland and from France," remembered one resident of the northern German city.[72]

Hitler promised that after the war all cities affected by air raids would be rapidly rebuilt, and an edict by the Führer of 11 October 1943 ordered Speer to start making preparations to that end. The architect was facing a "task of truly historical proportions," opined Goebbels.[73] In private, the dictator repeatedly stated that "from a larger perspective," the destruction was not "all that bad" since most German industrial cities were "badly laid out, musty and often miserably built." Here the destruction wrought by the bombing war would create space for a splendid reconstruction of places like the industrial Ruhr Valley, which would "blossom anew from the ruins."[74]

*

The biggest factor affecting the mood of the German population was food supplies. Memories were still fresh of the First World War, in particular the "turnip winter" of 1916–17, when Germans had had little to eat except the universally unpopular vegetable. When food was rationed and made available only in return for government-issued vouchers at the start of the Second World War, it immediately brought back unpleasant memories. Still, in the first two and a half years of war, most Germans did not have to seriously tighten their belts. The first dramatic reductions only came in April 1942, when rations of bread, meat and fat were reduced by up to 25 per cent.[75] This caused dissatisfaction among working-class people in particular. "In the firms a mood is growing ever stronger which is reminiscent of that in 1918," warned the Security Service in the Ruhr Valley.[76] It was no surprise that Goebbels kept a particularly close eye on the tense food situation. "Most people can no longer eat their fill, and a hungry belly always tends towards rebellion," he noted, adding that if the "stomach of the people" could no longer be filled, the situation would turn serious.[77]

In August 1942, Hitler declared his intention to restore former levels of bread rations by October while simultaneously increasing meat allowances. He made no bones about how this was to be achieved: by stripping the occupied territories bare. This was no time for "false sentimentality," he declared.[78] Consequently the ration cuts were rescinded in the autumn of 1942. In his harvest festival speech on 4 October, in which Hitler's decision was announced, Göring invoked the "terrible turnip winter" of the First World War to highlight the differences "between then and now." The food crisis of the spring had been solved, Göring said, because the Wehrmacht had conquered "the most fertile areas known anywhere in Europe" in the east. Eggs, butter, flour—everything was present there in "amounts you cannot even imagine," the Reich marshal boasted. In his speech, broadcast on all German radio stations, Göring followed Hitler in frankly admitting that Germans would be better supplied at the cost of people in the occupied territories. "If there has to be hunger, then not in Germany!" was Göring's guiding principle.[79] His boastful promises, which also included bonus rations for the Christmas holidays, blunted public dissatisfaction. On 12 October, the Security Service reported that "the mood among women has become significantly better."[80] "Is this a bluff?"

Victor Klemperer asked after the increase in rations. "A desperate measure? Whatever the case, it has shut people up for a while. The war continues, and the time necessary to exterminate us has been won."[81]

Hitler and the Nazi leadership were not the only ones who wanted to extract everything they could from occupied Europe. Many common German foot soldiers emulated their leaders. In October 1940 Göring had issued the so-called schlepp edict that essentially lifted all restrictions on what members of the Wehrmacht could purchase abroad. It read: "The soldier is allowed to take with him whatever he can carry and is intended for his own personal use or that of his family."[82] That was the opening signal for an unprecedented campaign of private looting across Europe. An army of bargain-hunters stormed department stores, combed through whole stretches of territory and snapped up whatever there was to buy. "The stores were of course bought out by soldiers, especially the things no longer available in Germany," wrote Private Heinrich Böll, the later author and Nobel laureate, in September 1940 from France. Initially he had scruples about participating because, "although everything is paid for, it is almost like stripping a corpse." Böll soon overcame his reservations, however, and began sending coffee, butter, cosmetics, shoes and many other articles back to his family in Cologne. In fact, he soon asked them to send more money so that he would "not have to let the splendours of the 'black market' pass him by."[83]

Millions of packages were sent by post back home where they supplemented the rations of "ethnic-popular comrades" while people in the occupied countries, particularly in eastern Europe, went hungry. Hitler rejected all attempts by military and customs officials to limit the "schlepp edict." In the Werewolf in August 1942, he scoffed: "What is there to take in the East? Art treasures? There are none! So a bit of grub is all there is! And there is nothing better to do with it than make it benefit a soldier's family at home."[84] In October 1942, Hitler himself sent Goebbels a large package of food from Ukraine as a forty-fifth birthday present. "There was something in it for every member of the family," the appreciative propaganda minister noted.[85]

Nonetheless, this does not quite amount to what the historian Götz Aly calls a "prosperity sweetened by wartime socialism."[86] Despite the many packages sent back home in the second half of the war, the situation of the vast majority of the population remained precarious, and it grew worse the more the Red Army reconquered occupied parts of the Soviet Union. The loss of these territories was, "in terms of food, the start of another 1917," complained Herbert Backe, state secretary in the Ministry of Food and Agriculture.[87] In May 1943, meat rations had to be reduced again—a measure that caused considerable dismay because it gave the lie to Göring's premature promise of the preceding October.[88] In November 1943, when potatoes became scarce, Goebbels feared that Germany would have to use turnips as a "substitute food source," which would surely awaken "an unpleasant memory" in the populace.[89]

The more difficult it became to supply Germans with the necessities, the greater was their inclination to obtain scarce commodities on the black market. "It must be admitted that food supply is working much better in this war than that of 1914–18," conceded the diarist Friedrich Kellner in July 1943. "But there is at least as much if not more back-alley dealing . . . Barter is king. If you give me this, I will give you that."[90] The response of the regime to the emerging black-market economy was highly contradictory. On the one hand, it pledged to go after such dealing and bartering because it ran contrary to the propagandistic notion that all "ethnic-popular comrades" were equal. On the other hand, when combating the black market, the regime had to take care not to further fuel popular dissatisfaction. A system needed to be found, proclaimed Hitler in June 1942, "of treating misdemeanours as misdemeanours while punishing truly severe violations of wartime law with lengthy incarceration, if not with the death penalty." The justice system was doing the exact opposite, the Führer complained: "Often the large-scale fences get off scot free while the small ones are hanged." The "little people," Hitler ordained, were not to be harassed "if here and there they obtain a little bit extra for their households from relatives and acquaintances."[91] In a memorandum of July 1943, Bormann issued corresponding instructions to the police not to pursue people illicitly procuring small amounts of fruit and vegetables from the countryside. The effect of such petty searches, he told them, was by no means worth the public disgruntlement they caused.[92] This policy too was informed by the experience of the First World War, when police rigorously went after small-time "hamsters," who had managed to acquire the odd backpack full of black-market food, while ignoring the commercial-scale profiteers—a perceived injustice that had caused huge popular outrage.

Yet despite the regime's policy, food was by no means equitably distributed in the German wartime economy. Working-class people complained with "great bitterness," the Security Service reported, that "most of the so-called better-situated classes use their connections and their fatter wallets to acquire scarce goods in addition to the food to which they are entitled."[93] In the second half of the war, public ire was directed in particular at Nazi Party bigwigs, often known as "golden pheasants" in reference to their ostentatious uniforms. In his "Proclamation on the Lifestyles of Leading Personalities" of 21 March 1942, Hitler required all his underlings to demonstrate "exemplary behaviour" and abide by all restrictions "down to the letter and as a matter of course."[94] He also repeatedly cautioned his Gauleiters against adopting the "false allures of potentates" and called upon them to adapt their "personal lifestyles" to the "seriousness of the situation."[95] But such appeals rarely had any effect.[96]

Above all in occupied Poland and the occupied Soviet Union, Hitler's underlings led lives of luxury. Leading the way in pomp and shameless profiteering were Governor-General Hans Frank and his wife.[97] But the Gauleiters within the Reich too, despite propagating "total war," were rarely subject to any visible privations. "The consumption of alcohol especially sometimes takes on abnormally large dimensions, which at the moment of course, from a purely psychological stand-point, brings with it extraordinary disadvantages," fretted Goebbels in early February 1943.[98] On Hitler's orders, Bormann read the riot act to the Reichsleiters and Gauleiters. This was not the time for receptions or banquets, he warned. The people had "no understanding for many leaders' peacetime levels of amusement or extensive drinking sessions."[99] Nonetheless, that did not prevent Bormann himself from opening up his own house on Obersalzberg to nighttime revelries in 1943.[100]

Despite his appeals to his paladins, Hitler was inclined to ignore their transgressions in this regard. After all, he too generously handed out gifts and bonus payments to ministers, generals and Gauleiters to make the recipients beholden to him, thereby shoring up his power.[101] Not surprisingly, therefore, he tended to be correspondingly mild in his judgements about nepotism and corruption. "There used to be ten thousand times as much corruption and cronyism as there is today," he told his entourage in the Wolf's Lair. "If someone is found guilty of corruption, we should not say 'Look what state we are in!' Those are just isolated cases!"[102] Hitler even felt loyal to the thoroughly corrupt former Gauleiter of Franconia, Julius Streicher, who had been stripped of his post by a party court back in February 1940. He kept asking himself right up until the end of the war whether he could not find some other use for the man who had won over Nuremberg to the Nazi Party.[103]

A typical example of the dictator's behaviour was his treatment of the Berlin delicatessen supplier August Nöthling. In July 1942, Nöthling's company was fined 5,000 reichsmarks for providing large amounts of food to people without ration coupons. Nöthling filed an appeal claiming that his customers included "important men from the party, the state, the Wehrmacht and the diplomatic corps." When questioned in investigative custody in late January 1943, he named names, and the list included a series of prominent figures: Frick, Bernhard Rust, Ribbentrop, Darré, Reich Labour Service leader Konstantin Hierl, Raeder and Brauchitsch had all heavily availed themselves of Nöthling's services. Others who had illicitly procured food, albeit in lesser dimensions, were Lammers, Funk, Reich radio programming director Eugen Hadamovsky, Keitel, the head of the Luftwaffe general staff, Hans Jeschonnek, and a number of state secretaries and ministerial directors.[104] In mid-March, Berlin police president Count von Helldorff sent Goebbels a report covering the results of his investigations.

The propaganda minister was shocked by the extent of the corruption. "It is scandalous that prominent people in the state, the party and the Wehrmacht have behaved in a fashion that sabotages the war like this," Goebbels wrote. "Under no circumstances will I tolerate the spread of a form of corruption that over the long term would undermine the war effort."[105] On 21 March 1943, after Hitler's speech on Heroes' Commemoration Day, Goebbels brought up the Nöthling case. In Goebbels' account, the dictator was very "taken aback" but immediately decreed that in the "interests of state" it was not advisable to make a "national case" out of the affair. Instead, he instructed Goebbels to consult with Justice Minister Thierack to find an elegant way to sweep the whole matter under the carpet.[106] Predictably,

Thierack came to the conclusion that "given the large circle of prominent figures" involved, it was politically impossible to put the wrong-
doers on trial. Hitler followed his recommendation and decided on 2
April 1943 that a court case was "out of the question."[107] Nöthling
hanged himself in his cell in early May—a convenient end to an affair
that had stirred up considerable resentment. "We want to hear that
the bigwigs are being treated like any old common Müller or Schulz—
otherwise there will be hell to pay" was how the head of the Security
Police and the Security Service, Ernst Kaltenbrunner, summarised
feelings in working-class circles.[108]

The more the pressure mounted because of the air raids and the
economy of scarcity, the harder the regime tried to distract the population from the everyday hardships of war and offer people relaxation.
"It is also crucial to the war to keep people in a good mood," Goebbels
had written in February 1942. "We failed to do that during the [First]
World War and were rewarded with a terrible catastrophe. That
example must not be repeated under any circumstances."[109] In line
with this sentiment, the propaganda minister ordered radio broadcasts
to be made more relaxed, with entertainment, not political education,
in the foreground. The "Request Concert for the Wehrmacht" was
particularly beloved, as were popular-music ditties like Lale Andersen's
"Lili Marleen." The standard fare in cinemas was not expensively
produced propaganda films, but rather light entertainment such as
The Great Love from 1942, which would become the highest grossing
movie of the war years. The film's popularity was down to, among
other things, a pair of morale-boosting songs sung by the sultry-voiced
Swedish actress Zarah Leander: "I Know Someday a Miracle Will
Happen" and "This Isn't the End of the World." Most theatres also
catered to people's need for light-hearted relief, performing more and
more comedies, farces and operettas.[110] In February 1943, when several
thousand previously "indispensable" people from the culture industry
were about to be sent to the Wehrmacht and into arms production,
Hitler issued "strict orders" to leave theatre, film and orchestral music
"entirely untouched." At a time in which the populace was being
called upon to do more and more, Hitler explained, cultural life should
not be constricted. That, the Führer said, would only make people
"fall into grey hopelessness."[111]

But cultural offerings were not the only means by which the regime tried to maintain public morale. It also promised further social benefits after the end of the war. As early as February 1940, Hitler had charged Robert Ley to come up with suggestions for the "implementation of a comprehensive and generous old-age pension system for the German people."[112] The Labour Studies Institute of the German Labour Front put together a social-benefits programme called the Social Works of German People that was intended to offer the population a rosy vista for the time after Germany's "final victory." The core of the programme was a newly regulated pension and health system that was supposed to guarantee an adequate existence to all pensioners, provided of course that they were of "German or related blood." "In return for the sacrifices of war, the German people are to be rewarded with a carefree old age," Ley declared in September 1940.[113] At a reception for arms industry workers in the Chancellery on 14 November, Hitler reaffirmed his intention to "expand the German social-welfare state into a shining example for the world after our victory."[114] Over the course of the war, the dictator would repeat over and over his promise to create a true "people's state." In conversation with Goebbels on 21 May 1943, Hitler proclaimed: "In this people's state, not only will economic and social equity prevail. It will also create a certain equality, not of rights and duties but of opportunities. It is our task after the war to realise this elevated goal of National Socialist politics."[115]

That was all in the future, of course. In the meantime, the Nazi state tried to show "the gratitude of the nation" to the working classes in a series of carefully staged propaganda displays.[116] One of them was the symbolic elevation of the status of arms industry work. In May 1942, after consulting with Speer, Hitler decided to award the Knight's Cross of the War Merit Cross to Franz Hahne, an especially productive foreman at the Berlin metalworking company Rheinmetall-Altmärkische Kettenwerke. At the same time, hundreds of War Merit Crosses First Class and thousands of War Merit Crosses Second Class were given to arms workers throughout the Reich. Goebbels noted that Hitler pinned extraordinarily high hopes on "such symbolic action for the preservation of morale in the entire German arms-manufacturing workforce." These prestigious awards would "help bolster the internal sense of community."[117] Reports from arms factories seemed to confirm that this was indeed the case. "Scenes such as those recorded in 1917–18 have not occurred anywhere," a pleased Goebbels noted in October 1943 in reference to the industrial unrest in Germany during the First World War.[118]

Yet despite all the efforts of the Nazi leadership, exhaustion and war fatigue were clearly taking hold of the German people. On the third anniversary of the start of the war in early September 1942, Security Service reports recorded an alarming phenomenon: "The increasing shortages of necessities; three years of constraints in all areas of daily life; more and more fierce, large-scale enemy attacks from the air; and fear for the lives of relatives at the front . . . are all factors exerting an increasing influence on the mood of broad sections of the population and causing increasingly frequent wishes that the war would end."[119]

After the Stalingrad catastrophe at the latest, fewer and fewer Germans believed in slogans about imminent "final victory." A great many "ethnic-popular comrades . . . cannot really imagine how the war will end," the Security Service reported in early April 1943.[120] In June that year, the court official Friedrich Kellner compared the behaviour of the people around him with that of "defendants when the court has adjourned for deliberations . . . They are waiting morosely to see how things will turn out, of which they have dark premonitions."[121]

Such reactions seem to show some awareness of guilt or at least a vague feeling of complicity in an ongoing injustice. Indeed, in many places, Allied air raids were interpreted as punishment for the deportation and murder of the Jews. People commonly made remarks to the effect that if the Jews had not been treated so badly, Germans would not be being made to suffer under "these terror attacks."[122] It was, as we have seen, part of the leadership's strategy to implicate ordinary people by making targeted reference of the crimes against humanity being committed. The idea was to convince them that there was no way out and that it was thus in their own interest to wage a "total war." In March 1943, one German journalist characterised the Nazi leadership's strategy as "strength through fear."[123]

Nonetheless, as of 1943, the regime's popularity was noticeably diminishing. In July of that year, the Security Service registered "evidence of corrosion in the attitude of the population," noting that political jokes aimed at the state were increasing, people had grown "conspicuously less likely in recent months" to use the Hitler salute, and party members tended not to wear party insignia any more.[124] The less effective their efforts to appeal to the populace became, the more the Nazi leadership fell back on repression.[125] Over the course of the war, the criminal code was significantly expanded and sharpened. A host of new crimes were introduced, including listening to foreign radio broadcasts, "undermining defensive strength" and various crimes of "backstabbing." Making scornful remarks about representatives of the Nazi Party or critical comments about the state of the war were considered major infractions and could be punishable by death. The Gestapo could count on help from civilians who reported such crimes, and in the second half of the war, the number of denunciations dramatically increased. The informants were by no means always party members. Often they were ordinary people taking the chance to settle private scores.[126]

Such terror on the inside was intended to nip rebellion in the bud. Here too the Nazi leadership was haunted by the ghosts of 1918. If only back then all the criminals had been shot instead of "turned loose on the German people," Hitler told the Reichsleiters and Gauleiters on 23 May 1942, there would have been no revolution. The situation first became dangerous, he claimed, "when the prisons were opened."[127] In his monologues in his headquarters, he confirmed his determination to put down any attempt at an insurrection "with the most barbaric of means." If a "mutiny" were to break out anywhere in the Reich, he would have not just its leaders but all the inmates of the country's prisons and concentration camps shot. The rebellion, Hitler declared, would then "collapse on its own from a lack of mutinying elements and followers."[128]

On 20 August 1942, Hitler dismissed the acting justice minister, Franz Schlegelberger, and replaced him with Otto Thierack, the president of the People's Court. Thierack had been a member of the NSDAP prior to 1933, and the dictator expected his appointment would transform the judicial system once and for all into an instrument of the regime. Hitler would not be disappointed. The number of death sentences shot up dramatically, from 926 in 1940 to 5,336 in 1943. For the first time, under its new president, Roland Freisler, the People's Court sentenced more people to death than to prison terms in 1943. Like Hitler, Goebbels was extremely satisfied: "The never-ending complaining has diminished significantly since we made defeatism a capital offence, enforced the law and published the names of the offenders. That has had a sobering and deterrent effect on the defeatists."[129]

The increasing terror exercised by the justice system was not the only sign of how fractured the much celebrated *Volksgemeinschaft*, or "ethnic-popular community," had become. Both before and after 1933, the promise to overcome the differences between parties and social classes, and to create a stable political and social order with a minimum of conflict, had been one of National Socialism's most appealing policies and had done much to increase Hitler's popularity.[130] There is evidence that in the first two years of the war, when victory seemed at hand, slogans about national solidarity had lost none of their appeal. But after the downturn in the Wehrmacht's fortunes in 1941-42 and its defeat at Stalingrad at the latest, such slogans lost their effectiveness.[131] Hitler still took every opportunity during his less and less frequent public appearances to invoke the ordering social and political ideals of National Socialism. In his Sportpalast speech of 30 September 1942 he proclaimed: "What our party aspired to in peacetime—to forge an ethnic-popular community out of the experience of the First World War—is now being consolidated."[132] But such promises stood in stark contrast to reality. It was blatantly obvious that the burdens of war were by no means evenly distributed and that, alongside old inequities, new factors of inequality determined the daily life of many German people.[133] Workers and their families in industrialised regions were much more severely affected by air raids and food shortages than people who lived in the countryside or in smaller cities. The chances of survival were far slimmer on the eastern front than in the west. And thanks to privileges and connections, Nazi functionaries could avoid wartime privations in ways that the oft-invoked "little people" could not.

As social inequalities continued and worsened, people began taking offence at slogans about the "ethnic-popular community" and increasingly scoffed at the idea. The result was not public rebellion, but a retreat into the private sphere, a kind of "silent turning away" from the regime.[134] This development proceeded slowly, and Hitler was less affected by it than other leading representatives of the party and the state. Even though the Führer was no longer considered sacrosanct after Stalingrad, and his personal prestige had taken a major hit, many Germans evidently still believed that he could reverse the nation's fortunes and tended to exempt him from criticism. "Despite numerous voices of doubt after Stalingrad and a plethora of rumours, the general faith in the Führer among the broad masses of the populace remains unshaken," the Security Service reported on 20 April 1943, Hitler's fifty-fourth birthday.[135] Amid the crisis of legitimacy that began for the regime in 1942–43, the continuing connection between the people and their Führer would prove to be one of its strongest stabilising forces.

IO

On the Defensive

"For all my life I have never been a man of the defensive. We will now go from the defensive back on the attack," Hitler remarked as late as March 1945 in a situation meeting.[1] So it is perhaps not surprising that this was also his philosophy in the spring of 1943, after Manstein had succeeded with great difficulty in restabilising the southern sector of the eastern front. Given the circumstances, a transition to a defensive approach to the war seemed to be the only sensible option. But Hitler was not prepared to consider that for a minute. Despite all the Wehrmacht's setbacks, he wanted to seize the initiative again, and in early February 1943, scant days after the 6th Army had surrendered at Stalingrad, he expressed hopes of being able to win back "operational freedom" by the end of the spring. Once that happened, Germany would soon be "on top again."[2]

Nonetheless, even the Führer acknowledged that his forces were no longer sufficient to launch a large-scale offensive as they had in the summer of 1942. In mid-February 1943, when he visited Army Group South's headquarters in Zaporozhye, he indicated that the Wehrmacht could not mount any more large operations that year, even if it was able to attack swiftly in limited offensives.[3] In the eyes of Manstein and Kluge, the commanders of Army Groups South and Centre, the obvious target of such manoeuvres was the salient held by the enemy in the front near Kursk, which was some 200 kilometres wide and extended 120 kilometres into German lines. There, at the seam between Army Groups South and Centre, German troops could launch a pincer attack to surround and destroy the Soviet armies in the bulge. Hitler, who had initially favoured a counter-attack south of Kharkov, in the end agreed to the commanders' idea[4] and largely left responsibility for the operational planning in Zeitzler's hands. He had been able to work with the new army chief of staff without most of the conflicts that had marred his relationship with Halder. On 13 March, Hitler signed the "Order for the Waging of War on the Eastern Front in the Coming Months," drafted by Zeitzler. It stated that after the end of the winter and the muddy season the objective would be to pre-empt fresh attacks by the enemy and "dictate the action to him on at least one section of the front."[5] In his Operational Order No. 6 of 15 April, Hitler committed himself to what was code-named "Operation Citadel," which was supposed to restore initiative to the Wehrmacht on the eastern front. As one central passage read: "Every leader and every man must be suffused with the decisive significance of this attack. Our victory in Kursk has to send a signal to the world."[6]

Compared with the campaigns of 1941 and 1942, the operational planning for the year 1943 was modest. The aim was no longer to bring about a strategically decisive battle but to launch an action whose goals were limited right from the start, even though the German side did hope to deal the Red Army such a severe blow that it would no longer be capable of further offensives of its own.[7] At some point, Hitler figured, the enormous losses of men and materiel would exhaust the enemy's strength. Although the Nazi leadership had no way of knowing how long the Soviet military would be able to hold out, as Hitler told Goebbels on 19 March, "once this colossus starts to wobble, we will experience an epochal collapse . . . We just have to keep fighting tenaciously and stubbornly until the enemy hits the ground."[8] Hitler's reasoning was shaped not just by military but also by political and psychological considerations. He needed a military triumph to keep his allies on board and to dispel the contagious doubts about Germany's ultimate victory on the home front. According to his order of 15 April, Operation Citadel was scheduled to commence in early May, but it had to be delayed for two months until early July. This undermined its chances for success right from the start, since it was predicated on the notion that it would come as a surprise and the enemy would not have time to take counter-measures.[9]

On 21 March 1943, Hitler's special train left Berlin, arriving in Munich the following day. There the Führer met with Gerdy Troost, the widow of his first architect, Paul Troost, who had died in 1934, and with her he visited an exhibition in the House of German Art. After dinner in his favourite restaurant, Osteria Bavaria, he travelled on to the Obersalzberg.[10] Hitler wanted to both recover from the tribulations of the preceding weeks and receive representatives from allied countries so that he could "calm them back down."[11] Stalingrad had severely disrupted Nazi Germany's relations with Romania, Hungary and Italy, all the more so because Hitler had blamed those countries for the catastrophe. Finland and Bulgaria were also distressed at the extent of the debacle and had begun looking for ways to escape German domination. In mid-February 1943, Goebbels recorded his unease at Germany's allies "becoming somewhat shaky." Above all, the Finns seemed to him to have "no true desire any more to continue the war." He added: "If they could extract themselves from it with only a black eye, they would certainly do so."[12]

The meetings, for which the Baroque Klessheim Castle near Salzburg was again chosen as the location, were supposed to halt the erosion of solidarity within the Axis. The consultations kicked off on 31 March with Bulgaria's King Boris III. On 7 April, Mussolini arrived. Romania's Marshal Antonescu followed on 12 April, four days before the Hungarian regent, Admiral Horthy. On 19 April, the eve of Hitler's fifty-fourth birthday, Hitler received Norway's prime minister Quisling, followed several days later by Slovakian president Jozef Tiso, Croatian leader Ante Pavelić and finally, on 29 April, the restored French president, Pierre Laval.[13] The communiqués issued after these meetings all talked up the unbreakable friendship of the Axis partners. In reality, their relations were clouded by mutual mistrust.[14]

The consultations with Mussolini were most important to Hitler since it had become manifest that the Fascist regime in Italy was stuck in deep crisis. In the spring of 1943, a wave of strikes rocked the north of the country. Food shortages combined with increasingly severe Allied air raids, and military setbacks on the eastern front and in North Africa had made Italians weary of war and eager for peace. The Duce's authority had been undermined, and among traditional Italian elites— the royal court, the diplomatic corps and the general staff—some were beginning to ponder how they could end his rule.[15] In early February, Mussolini had attempted to stage a domestic coup by firing his entire cabinet and replacing them with men loyal to him. One of those affected was his son-in-law Galeazzo Ciano, who was demoted from foreign minister to ambassador to the Vatican.[16] Concerned by the news from Italy, Hitler sent Ribbentrop to Rome in late February with a message in which the Führer again stressed that there was no way he would negotiate with Stalin, as Mussolini had urged, until the military situation on the eastern front had conclusively turned in Germany's favour.[17] Upon returning to Germany, Ribbentrop assured his master: "The Duce is truly our only entirely trustworthy ally in Italy. As long as he is at the helm, we have nothing to fear."[18]

Because he wanted to strengthen Mussolini's position, Hitler refused to abandon the Axis bridgehead in North Africa, even though it had become obvious by late March that the worn-out German and Italian forces would not be able to hold Tunis for long.[19] At this point, Rommel, whose health was poor, had already departed the North African theatre of war and had handed over command to Colonel-General Hans-Jürgen von Arnim. On 11 March in the Werewolf, Hitler awarded the "Desert Fox" Germany's highest military distinction, the Oak Cluster of the Knight's Cross with Swords and Diamonds.[20] The German public was kept in the dark about Rommel's withdrawal so as not to damage his nimbus as a reliably triumphant field commander.[21]

On the eve of Mussolini's visit, Hitler was in high spirits. In front of the evening fireplace at the Berghof, he entertained those present with anecdotes about his visit to Italy in May 1938, making fun of the diminutive Italian king and praising Mussolini as an extraordinary statesman while at the same time cursing the Italians generally as a "a dishonourable band of thieves."[22] This time round, Mussolini had promised his associates before leaving for the Reich that he would stand up to the Führer and insist on a political solution to the conflict in the east. He intended to present Hitler with a corresponding memo-randum, prepared by Italy's new foreign minister, Giuseppe Bastianini. But during his four days of meetings with the German dictator, from 7 to 10 April, the roles from earlier consultations were repeated: Hitler talked and Mussolini listened. The Italian delegation returned home empty-handed. Hitler, by contrast, was quite satisfied. He had succeeded by "applying his entire strength of nerve" in "getting Mussolini back in form," he boasted several weeks later. The Duce, Hitler added, had undergone a complete metamorphosis in those four days: "When he alighted from his train . . . he had looked like a broken old man; and when he returned, he was an energetic human being with his head held high."[23]

In the meantime, the situation in North Africa had further deteri-orated, as Axis troops were pushed back into a weak defensive belt around Tunis and Bizerta. Their positions there were "almost hope-less," Goebbels noted in mid-April. "Our soldiers and officers are doing what they can, but the [enemy's] superiority is just too great."[24] With the Americans and British enjoying absolute air and naval dominance and receiving constant reinforcements, it was an uneven fight. By the end of April it was apparent that Tunis would fall within days. By the time Hitler left the Berghof for Munich on 2 May, he too had written off North Africa. A meeting with Germany's most senior military leaders had been called for 4 May in the Bavarian capital, to decide the best time to launch Operation Citadel. Whereas Zeitzler, Kluge and Manstein favoured an early date, preferably in late May or early June, Hitler was inclined towards a further postponement. He was supported by one of his favourite military commanders, Colonel-General Walter Model, who had demanded that troops on the eastern front be first provided with a sufficient number of the latest Tiger and Panther tanks to establish German superiority over the Soviet T-34 model. A few days later, Hitler ordered the start of the operation to be put off until mid-June, a date that would also not be kept.[25]

On the evening of 6 May, Hitler met with Goebbels in Berlin. The propaganda minister, who hastened to welcome back the Führer, found him "somewhat fatigued." He had not been able to relax on the Obersalzberg, Hitler explained, because there had been "work and more work and negotiations upon negotiations." The dictator was now convinced that the situation in North Africa was "quite hopeless." Goebbels commented: "If one pauses to consider that 150,000 of our best men are still in Tunis one can get an idea of the catastrophe we are facing there." The propaganda minister feared a defeat "of a scale similar to Stalingrad" and made some initial suggestions as to how the new shock could be cushioned for the German people.[26]

On the afternoon of 7 May, after the state funeral of SA leader Viktor Lutze, Hitler received the Reichsleiters and Gauleiters. He did not say a word about the critical situation in North Africa or about the Allied bombing raids on Germany. Instead, he devoted his entire speech to the conflict with the Soviet Union, calling it a battle of two "ideological states." Still, he found some grudgingly complimentary words for Stalin. With his purges in the 1930s, Hitler said, the Soviet leader had strengthened rather than weakened the fighting capacity of the Red Army because he had taken care of potential opposition within the officer corps. The introduction of political commissars was "some stroke of genius" because it had put "extraordinarily active and energetic men from the party" in positions of command. Hitler's message to his minions was clear. Unlike Stalin, he constantly had to deal with incompetent generals who did not even stand firmly on the solid ground of the National Socialist world view.

Hitler announced that it would not be long before a fresh offensive was launched in the east. Even if it was not on the scale of earlier operations, he hoped it would result in "significant successes." After Germany's Axis partners had proven unreliable, only German troops would be fighting this time. When it came to the future of Europe, Hitler did not mince words. The whole "jumble of numerous small states" would have to be "liquidated" as soon as possible and German hegemony secured for all time. This was, in practical terms, "the path towards global domination" since "he who controlled Europe would be able to seize the leadership of the world." By contrast, Hitler sketched out in harsh terms what was in store for the German people should they be defeated, which did not bear thinking about. Therefore, the Führer asserted, "never should the slightest doubt in victory come over us."[27] Since the September crisis of 1942, Hitler had been forced to acknowledge that the war was hardly winnable any more, but he had to repress this knowledge in order to make credible appearances in front of his underlings. To that end, he always projected optimism and invoked faith in a victory in which he secretly no longer believed himself. This tension between his own growing suspicions that the war could not be won and his constant assurances to the contrary put the dictator under extraordinary psychological stress.[28] That was probably a major reason why he was increasingly prone to losing his temper.

In the days that followed, Goebbels had several opportunities to speak with Hitler at length, and the dictator talked with extreme contempt about his generals. He "could no longer bear the sight of them," the Führer said, explaining that this was the reason why he no longer took his meals in their company in his headquarters. "All the generals lie," Hitler told Goebbels. "All the generals are disloyal, all the generals are against National Socialism and all the generals are reactionaries."

Goebbels found this opinion somewhat "prejudiced" but basically took his master's side. "They have done too much that is bitter to him," Goebbels noted. "They lack intellectual and cultural class and accordingly cannot arrive at the basis of an understanding with the Führer." Although the propaganda minister may also have harboured doubts about the outcome of the war, he was still under the sway of Hitler's aura. "As long as he lives and leads," Goebbels wrote, "no irremediable harm can be visited on the German people."[29]

On the evening of 12 May, Hitler flew back to the Wolf's Lair,[30] where the following day news arrived that the Axis forces in North Africa had surrendered. More than a quarter of a million battle-hardened German and Italian soldiers allowed themselves to be taken captive, making the defeat a worse debacle than Stalingrad.[31] Before the German public was informed, Hitler had ordered the Wehrmacht Supreme Command to let it be known that Field Marshal Rommel had been in Germany on recuperative leave for the last two months. Hitler did not want Rommel's name besmirched by the defeat at Tunis because, as Goebbels recorded the Führer's logic, "a military authority like Rommel's cannot be created and then wiped away at will."[32]

The German people had followed developments in the North African theatre of war with growing concern. They had begun to speak of a "second Stalingrad" and a "German Dunkirk."[33] After the capitulation at Tunis on 13 May, the public mood sank to a new low. Therefore, Goebbels opined, "strong and solid propaganda" was now needed "to keep the people playing along and put down the resignation popping up in places."[34] But no one was convinced by Goebbels' attempts to portray the defeat in Tunis as a victory because the persistence of the Axis bridgehead had tied down Allied forces for months. The Anglo-American victory there, Friedrich Kellner recognised, was of "decisive importance for the situation as a whole," since Allied control of North Africa represented "a massive threat to Italy and indeed the entire southern front."[35]

In Hitler's headquarters preparations were now being made for the scenario of Italy quitting the Axis, and initial plans to occupy the country were drawn up under the code names "Operation Alarich" and "Operation Konstantin." Hitler was even prepared to withdraw battle-ready units from the eastern front to that end, since he believed he had at all costs to prevent the Allies from establishing themselves on his southern periphery. Europe had to be defended "at a distance," he declared at a situation meeting on 15 May: "No front must be allowed to exist on the borders of the Reich."[36] Five days later, Hitler received Ribbentrop's liaison to the Afrikakorps, Konstantin Alexander von Neurath, the son of the Reich protector of Bohemia and Moravia and former German foreign minister. Neurath had just returned from Sicily and reported that Italian troops displayed little enthusiasm for defending the island against an Allied invasion. The population of southern Italy, Neurath added, was thoroughly Anglophile. Hitler saw his worst fears confirmed and heaped wild insults upon the Italian royal family and military, which he claimed had "sabotaged" the war right from the start. The question was, he remarked, whether the sickly Mussolini would prevail against these hostile circles. In any case, a sudden collapse of Mussolini's reign could no longer be ruled out, and Germany had to be prepared to "intervene with a helping hand"—a euphemism for subjecting yet another country to German occupation.[37]

The defeat in Tunis was not the only setback the Axis powers were being forced to swallow. The course of the submarine war in the Atlantic was also beginning to turn against the Reich, after the British had succeeded in breaking the German code, allowing them to monitor all radio communications between German submarines. What was more, the Americans were increasingly deploying long-range B-24 Liberator bombers to protect supply convoys. Germany was losing more and more submarines every week: forty-one U-boats were sunk in May 1943 alone. Admiral Karl Dönitz, the Hitler loyalist who had succeeded Raeder as the supreme commander of the German navy at the end of January, had no choice but to order his submarine fleet to refrain from attacking convoys in the North Atlantic and leave its waters. From that point on, Germany was no longer able to seriously disrupt the Allies' transatlantic supply lines.[38] In mid-May 1943, the Swiss newspaper *Baseler Nationalzeitung* published an article arguing that the situation of the Axis had taken a serious turn for the worse over the course of half a year. Even Goebbels had to admit the truth in that assertion. "We have been pursued by extraordinarily bad luck in the last six months," the propaganda minister wrote. "One misfortune has followed another."[39]

★

Around this time, however, an unexpected accident gifted the Nazi leadership an opportunity to go on the propaganda offensive. In early April, Polish slave labourers assigned to the Organisation Todt had discovered mass graves in a forest near Katyn, 20 kilometres west of Smolensk. Here 4,400 Polish officers had fallen victim to executioners from the Soviet secret service in the spring of 1940.[40] German radio broadcast its first report about the horrific discovery on 13 April 1943. By the following day, it was the top story in all news bulletins.

From the start, Goebbels was determined to use the discovery as fuel for incitement in his crusade against "Jewish Bolshevism": "I issued instructions to exploit this propaganda material to the greatest of extents. We can live off it for several weeks."[41] And indeed, for weeks, German press and radio fed readers and listeners with every fresh detail of the "Jewish mass murder," as the massacre was called, fulfilling the propaganda minister's promise to "fan the flames."[42] Hitler encouraged Goebbels to make Katyn a *cause célèbre* and insisted that the "Jewish question be put at the centre of subsequent explanations."[43] As a result a new wave of anti-Semitic propaganda flooded the country.

The Nazi leadership was pursuing two objectives with the Katyn propaganda campaign. On the one hand, it wanted to drive a wedge between the Western Allies and the Soviet Union. On the other, it hoped to illustrate to Germans what sort of horrific destiny awaited them from their arch-enemies, "the Jews," should the war be lost. But the campaign failed to achieve either of these goals. Moscow might have broken off relations with the Polish government-in-exile in London, much to Berlin's satisfaction, but the Western Allies were careful not to alienate Stalin and kept quiet. "Even if the German allegations were to prove true my attitude towards you would not change," Churchill told the Soviet ambassador to Britain, Ivan Maisky. "You are a brave people, Stalin is a great warrior." The British prime minister added that at the moment he saw everything primarily as a soldier who wanted to defeat a common enemy as quickly as possible.[44]

Among the German people, on the other hand, the news about the Katyn massacre elicited unexpected reactions. "We have no right to be outraged by these actions of the Soviets because the Germans have done away with far greater numbers of Poles and Jews," the Security Service quoted one person as saying.[45] That was not the only such remark in the reports filed by the Security Service in April and May

1943—another indication of how widespread knowledge of the SS and Wehrmacht crimes was at that point. Nearly simultaneously with the Katyn campaign, SS units brutally put down a major rebellion in the Warsaw ghetto, killing almost 14,000 of the 56,000 people who still lived there. On 16 May, SS-Brigadegeneral Jürgen Stroop proudly announced: "There is no longer a Jewish residential neighbourhood in Warsaw!"[46]

Hitler had originally wanted to leave the Wolf's Lair for the Werewolf, but feeling in poor health, he changed his mind on 21 May and headed back to the Obersalzberg for several weeks. "At the moment it is the best thing he can do," wrote Goebbels. ". . . If he regains his former vitality thanks to a stay at the Berghof, it can be considered the most important positive factor for Germany's prosecution of the war."[47] While the dictator and his entourage were enjoying the peaceful spring days in his Alpine retreat, the Ruhr Valley was rocked by a series of heavy aerial bombardments. In mid-May, British Lancasters destroyed the Möhne and Edertal dams, killing more than 1,200 people in the resulting floods. Major air raids followed on Dortmund, Essen, Wuppertal-Barmen, Düsseldorf, Bochum, Krefeld, Duisburg and Mülheim. "There is only one thing to say about the air war: we are almost helplessly overpowered and have to absorb the British and American blows with determined fury," noted Goebbels on 24 May after a nighttime bombardment of Dortmund had destroyed large parts of the city.[48] The bombing left ordinary Germans feeling increasingly fearful and on edge. People were beginning to ask what would come next, reported party representatives from the various *Gaue*. The "retribution" the regime had been promising must start soon, they demanded, before "the west [of Germany] was reduced to a field of rubble."[49]

On 18 June, Goebbels set off on a tour of bombed-out cities along the Rhine and in the Ruhr Valley, holding a speech that evening in the crammed Westfalenhalle arena in Dortmund in which he announced the build-up of a "new air armada of revenge."[50] When Goebbels visited Hitler on the Obersalzberg five days later, the Führer promised to visit the bombed-out cities himself.[51] But he reneged on this promise, most likely because he feared it would dent his prestige. "Thus far, the Führer has not yet honoured any of the cities affected by the air war with a visit," a resigned Goebbels would write several months later. "That cannot be sustained in the long term."[52]

On the Obersalzberg in the final weeks of May and the first weeks of June, Hitler was preoccupied above all with preparations for Operation Citadel. In the meantime, the conflict about whether the operation made any sense had intensified. In mid-June, Zeitzler and Jodl suggested scrapping it entirely and concentrating instead on deploying a powerful operational reserve in the east to repel the expected Soviet summer offensive.[53] Guderian also communicated his concerns to Hitler that the technology of the new German tanks was still not completely foolproof and the men who would operate them had not yet received adequate training. The dictator admitted to having "butterflies in his stomach" when he thought about the offensive, but finally decided on 18 June to go ahead with the operation. A few days later, he decreed that the attack would start in early July.[54] "The die has been cast," read the entry for 20 June in the war journal of the Army Supreme Commando 9.[55] In front of his intimates, Hitler was more confident. After the enormous losses during the winter crisis of 1942–43, he declared, the eastern front was now "almost opulently furnished with men and materiel." With the Tiger and the Panther, German troops had at their disposal "the finest tanks there are in the world right now." The coming offensive, Hitler promised, would be "very well prepared and appear like a bolt from the blue."[56]

On 29 June, Hitler left his Alpine retreat and returned to the bunker landscape of the Wolf's Lair in East Prussia. He had summoned the supreme commanders and commanding generals involved in Operation Citadel for a meeting on 1 July, at which he justified the operation as necessary to head off a possible enemy attack. He also told them that a significant triumph would be desirable to shore up support among Germany's allies and morale on the home front.[57] In a call to the "Comrades on the Eastern Front" on the eve of the offensive, the dictator announced: "The blow that German forces will deliver must be of decisive significance and bring about a turning point in the war."[58] In fact, even if everything went to plan, Hitler did not expect a decisive turning point, and he might have been less effusive about the prospects for the operation had he been privy to what the head of the Foreign Armies East division (Abteilung Fremde Heere Ost), Reinhard Gehlen, told Zeitzler on 4 July. The Red Army had been expecting a German offensive for weeks, Gehlen revealed, and had made the necessary preparations. It was thus "not very likely that the German attack will achieve any breakthrough." Gehlen concluded his warning with the words: "I consider the intended operation a definitive mistake that will rebound heavily against us."[59]

Gehlen's prediction was accurate. Stalin and his general staff had received word about the German plans early on and had begun careful preparations, constructing a deeply layered defensive system with anti-tank obstacles, minefields and trenches in the Kursk salient. Almost two million Soviet soldiers, equipped with the most modern weaponry, had been assembled. And the Soviets knew not only where but when the assault would take place. Before German troops even began their attack on the morning of 5 July, Soviet artillery batteries had already opened the battle with a massive barrage.[60] Thus a central precondition for the success of Operation Citadel was never fulfilled—it came as no surprise. The relative strength of the two sides also did not augur well for the German forces: 625,000 Wehrmacht soldiers were confronting 1.9 million Soviet troops. The attackers had 2,700 tanks at their disposal; the defenders more than 8,000. The balance of artillery firepower was even more lop-sided: fewer than 10,000 pieces for the Wehrmacht versus 47,000 guns for the Red Army. If that were not enough, the Soviet air force also enjoyed a huge advantage, with almost 6,000 planes at its disposal compared to only around 1,400 machines available to the Luftwaffe.[61]

Nevertheless, at least initially, the largest tank battle of the Second World War seemed to go well for the Germans. On 5 July, Model's 9th Tank Army succeeded in driving an 8-kilometre-deep wedge into Red Army positions in the north. But territorial gains in the ensuing days were scant. "The battle has taken on the sort of dimension experienced during the heaviest defensive battles of the west in 1914–18," General Friedrich Hossbach, Hitler's former Wehrmacht adjutant, wrote to his wife on 11 July. "There is enormous materiel on both sides. The Russians are fighting with a tenacity I have never experienced."[62] The next day, the Soviets launched their feared counteroffensive to the rear of the 9th Tank Army. Model had to halt his attack.

The German pincer manoeuvre to the south was able to generate more momentum. On the second day of the offensive, vanguards of the tank armies advanced 25 kilometres through Soviet minefields and anti-tank obstacles. While the new German armour proved generally superior to the Red Army's T-34 tanks, technical flaws rendered most of the brand-new German Panthers inoperable from the very start. Still, on 11 July, the German side achieved its greatest success, with the tank corps ripping deep holes into the Soviet lines of defence. The high point of the battle came the following day as powerful Red Army tank units tried to halt the German advance at Prokhorovka. In Soviet history books 12 July would be celebrated as a decisive day, marking the turning point of the war as a whole. But the reality was rather less heroic. Russian losses were several times larger than those of the Germans. The "myth of Prokhorovka" was intended to obscure how ruthlessly the Soviet leadership dealt with the lives of their own people.[63]

Hitler spent the first days of the battle "as though with fever," calling Zeitzler on an hourly basis to check how operations were going.[64] "The Führer is very satisfied with the initial successes of the offensive," Goebbels noted on 7 July. But soon the news relayed by Hitler's head-quarters was less promising. The fighting at Kursk was "extraordinarily heavy," and a "battle of materiel of unimaginable dimensions" had developed.[65] Then, on 13 July, Hitler summoned Kluge and Manstein to inform them that he had decided to break off Operation Citadel. Forcing the Führer to change his plans was the Soviet offensive against Army Group Centre near Oryol, which had begun the day before and was threatening to destroy Model's 9th Army. "The Russians are able to do whatever they want, and we cannot even cut off the Kursk salient," Hitler raved. Manstein countered that the battle was nearing its "decisive point" and victory might well be "within grasp." But this time, it was the dictator who had a more sober view of German prospects. He only allowed Manstein to launch a limited operation against Soviet units south of Kursk, and that too was soon halted.[66]

Such was the end of the final German offensive on the eastern front. Once again, Germany's military commanders had underesti-mated the enemy's strength and potential to keep its armies supplied. It was the first time that an operation begun in summer had to be broken off after only a few days. The initiative had passed over to the Soviets once and for all. In the months to come, the Wehrmacht was driven little by little from the territory it had conquered in a series of fierce and bloody battles. "The Germans are retreating," wrote a Russian tank soldier after the Battle of Kursk. "The moment to settle our account with them has come."[67]

Further bad news arrived at the Wolf's Lair while the Battle of Kursk was still raging. On 9–10 July, American and British forces landed on Sicily. The invasion was no great surprise, although Hitler had expected the target to be Sardinia. As expected, Italian troops barely put up any resistance, and German forces under the command of General Hans Hube were too weak to defend the island. By 23 July, the Allies controlled all of western Sicily.[68] It was obvious that from there they would try to cross over to the Italian mainland. "We must realise that we are increasingly sliding into a two-front war—what we were lucky to avoid . . . is slowly becoming a fact," Goebbels noted about this dramatic development.[69] Hitler's nightmare seemed to be coming true: that Italy would be driven from the war. He decided to meet Mussolini once more for a last attempt to bolster Italian morale.

Before he left, in the early hours of 18 July, Hitler summoned Morell, complaining of abdominal pain. For the first time, the doctor gave his patient Eukodal, an anaesthetic that both dulled pain and created feelings of euphoria. It seems to have worked since Hitler was in fine form for the next two days.[70] That afternoon his pilot Baur flew him in a four-engine Condor to Salzburg, from where he made a brief stop at the Obersalzberg. The next morning, he and his staff set off for Italy, landing at a military airstrip near Treviso, north of Venice, after a ninety-minute flight. There Hitler was welcomed by Mussolini and the supreme commander of the German troops in southern Italy, Albert Kesselring. He was then taken by special train and car to a remote country estate in Feltre. Hitler complained vociferously about the discomforts of the trip. Compared with previous meetings with Mussolini, the atmosphere was noticeably cool.[71]

For two hours, Hitler talked at the Duce. Even the news of the Allies' first-ever bombardment of Rome hardly interrupted his monologue, which painted the Axis' military situation in the rosiest of colours. There was no need to worry, the Führer assured Mussolini, about shortages of natural resources or food. Although there had been some ups and downs, as was common in war, he who demonstrated his "iron will to victory" would harvest the laurels in the end. Hitler did not neglect to underline his own historic role in this process, freely admitting his "immodest standpoint that after himself, there would be no greater master of things." For that reason, he was making the greatest of personal sacrifices to "force a decision within his own lifetime." Moving on to the situation in Sicily, Hitler was of two minds. If Italy was truly prepared to fight for the island and "fanatically draw all the consequences," he too would support such a defensive action. If not, it would be a "waste of every man sent to Sicily."[72] It is doubtful that such appeals even reached the fatigued and apparently uninterested Mussolini. The translator Schmidt called the meeting one of the "most depressing encounters" to which he had ever been witness.[73] Another participant, Field Marshal Baron Wolfram von Richthofen, wrote in his diary: "Probably less has come of all this than you could carry away under the nail of your little finger."[74]

It was not long before Richthofen's assessment was confirmed. On the evening of 24 July, the Fascist Grand Council convened in Rome for the first time since December 1939. The marathon session lasted ten hours, after which a large majority of deputies expressed their lack of confidence in Mussolini and demanded that he hand back control of the country's armed forces to the king, Vittorio Emanuele III. The following afternoon the monarch summoned Mussolini to his Roman residence and told him he intended to appoint Marshal Pietro Badoglio, the former chief of the general staff of the Italian army, the country's prime minister. Upon leaving the Quirinal, the deposed Duce was arrested by *carabinieri* and taken to a military barracks in an ambulance. The Mussolini era, which had begun in October 1922 with the March on Rome, had seemingly come to an end.[75] News of his fall led to Italians spontaneously expressing their joy in the streets. Across the country, people tore down symbols of the Mussolini regime from public buildings and burned Fascist uniforms and decorations. Ernst von Weizsäcker, who after a reshuffle in the Foreign Ministry in April 1943 had been forced to swap his post as deputy foreign minister for that of ambassador to the Vatican, remarked on 26 July: "Today you can see Italian flags and individual groups of people. Most are quite happy, presumably because they assume that Mussolini's downfall means the end of the war . . . Fascism has been simply extinguished without any sensation."[76]

On the evening of 25 July, word of the revolution in Italy reached Hitler's headquarters. Even though he had long steeled himself for the worst, Hitler was still shocked by Mussolini's fate. "Badoglio, our most determined enemy, has taken over the government," Hitler fumed at the evening situation meeting. "They will naturally declare that they are staying the course, that much is clear. But it is a betrayal. They will never stay the course." Hitler's first thought was to occupy Rome with a division of paratroopers and tanks to "catch the whole rabble." He did not even want to spare the Vatican. "Do you think I care about the Vatican?" he raved. "The whole pack of swine is there, and we will get them out."[77] Late that night he ordered his closest advisers—Göring, Goebbels, Himmler, Speer, Ribbentrop, Rommel, Guderian and Dönitz—to his headquarters for a crisis meeting.

Hitler's paladins arrived at the Wolf's Lair over the course of the following morning. In the meantime, Hitler had regained his cool and projected, if Goebbels is to be believed, "calm confidence" and "sovereign superiority."[78] The biggest question to be discussed was whether to wait for further developments in Italy or act as quickly as possible to control the situation. Hitler was initially in favour of "striking lightning quick," as Germany had done in Yugoslavia in April 1941. The new Italian government, a "typical putsch regime," would not offer any resistance, he argued. In a meeting that afternoon, over the objections of Kluge, the Führer announced that he would transfer SS tank divisions from the eastern front to that end. "Only first-class units with a strong affinity with fascism" are of use down there, Hitler said.[79] At that evening's situation meeting, he pressed again for quick action but encountered resistance from Rommel, who had recently been made supreme commander of the German forces in northern Italy. The whole action had to be carefully considered and meticulously planned, the field marshal argued.[80] No final decision was reached, and in the days to come Hitler continued to put off making up his mind. Nonetheless, under the code name "Case Axis," plans were drawn up for an invasion of Italy and a disarming of Italian forces.[81]

The news of Mussolini's fall reverberated throughout Germany. Even though the press were initially instructed to hold back in their reports about it, the wildest of rumours began to circulate.[82] Ardent Nazis, in particular, asked worriedly how "a system of government that had, after all, lasted for twenty years could have been brought down within a few hours."[83] Many others also feared that the potential loss of Italy to the Axis would hand "an enormous boost" to Germany's enemies. "The number of ethnic-popular comrades who remain optimistic and high-spirited is small," concluded the Security Service.[84]

The mood was also depressed because just as Mussolini was being deposed, the heaviest air raid yet on a German city was in process. Between 25 July and 3 August, in Operation Gomorrah, British and American bombers laid waste to broad stretches of Hamburg. Fanned by the summer heat, the attack created a huge firestorm in the northern German city. According to conservative estimates, some thirty-four thousand people were killed, and tens of thousands fled Hamburg. In his initial report, the city's Gauleiter, Karl Kaufmann, spoke of a "catastrophe of unimaginable proportions."[85] The authority of the state and the Nazi Party was badly damaged, as ordinary Hamburgers began to harshly criticise the Nazi leadership. "Party emblems were torn off people's clothing, and a cry went up: 'Give us the murderer!'" wrote Mathilde Wolff-Mönckeberg. "The police did not intervene." Security Service reports spoke of a "November mood," an atmosphere akin to the one that had sparked revolution and brought down Imperial Germany at the end of the First World War.[86]

The Nazi leadership was growing increasingly worried that what had happened in Italy could serve as a model for Germany. On 26 July, Bormann warned the Gauleiters "to be as soothing as possible towards all those nervous and agitated souls," and the same day Hitler ordered Himmler to meet "possible dangers with police measures of the most vigorous sort."[87] One month later, on 24 August, he made Himmler interior minister. The dictator had long been dissatisfied with Himmler's predecessor, Wilhelm Frick, who was considered "too old and used up" to enforce a hard line on the home front.[88] With Himmler, Hitler had turned to the "most radical, the notorious bloodhound of the party," commented Victor Klemperer. "How bad have things become in Germany that the hangman . . . has been made minister of the interior!"[89]

Himmler's appointment to yet another post heightened the power struggles among the leadership of the Third Reich. Although Goebbels approved of the move, calling Himmler "the most suitable man for guaranteeing internal security under all circumstances,"[90] he also jealously monitored the situation to ensure Himmler did not get too powerful and position himself as Hitler's presumptive successor, a role Göring had not been able to fill for quite some time now. In this respect, Goebbels had an ally in Bormann, who also feared that Himmler was being given too many responsibilities. Goebbels noted: "It is not good if one individual in the National Socialist leadership gets too big. The others have to take care that he is brought back into line."[91] But keeping rivalries among his underlings simmering was precisely what Hitler intended, so he could sit back and watch and relax, as they wrestled for power and influence.

The extreme tension in Hitler's headquarters lasted all of August. The Führer did not believe a word of Badoglio's assurances that Italy would honour its alliance, and Germany's military presence on the Apennine Peninsula was successively increased. For the time being he could not create a *"tabula rasa"* of Italy, Hitler declared on 9 August, because the new Italian government had been at pains to meet all of Germany's demands. But should the Italians show any signs of changing sides, he would "strike immediately and very forcefully." There was no way he was giving up Italy as a battleground and letting the British and Americans advance to the north of the country.[92] On 11 August, Kesselring began to evacuate Sicily, and 40,000 German and 62,000 Italian men shipped out with their equipment to the mainland across the Strait of Messina.[93] In the days that followed, rumours spread that the Badoglio government was conducting secret negotiations with the Allies to take Italy out of the war.

A BBC broadcast on 8 September left no further doubts. The Badoglio government had surrendered unconditionally and concluded a cease-fire with the Allies. "And this after Germany has sacrificed so much for Italy!" exclaimed an outraged Hermann Balck, commander of the 11th Tank Division. "The average German simply did not think that this level of Roman treachery was possible."[94] At the same time, British and American troops landed near Reggio and Salerno, south of Naples, and were able to establish bridgeheads despite fierce German resistance. As threatened, Hitler reacted promptly, using the code word "Axis" at 8 p.m. that day to order military commanders to commence the German occupation of Italy.[95] Again, Goebbels was summoned to the Wolf's Lair for a crisis meeting. Although Hitler had flown to Zaporozhye to consult with Manstein that morning and had got little sleep,[96] he made a surprisingly fresh impression on the propaganda minister. "You can always observe that the Führer goes beyond his limits physically, emotionally and intellectually in times of crisis," Goebbels noted. ". . . He sees the Italian matter as a complete mess and knows that we are going to have to summon all our strength to master it." Sixteen divisions had been assembled for the invasion of Italy, and Hitler was convinced they would encounter only light resistance: "The Italians simply do not want to fight and are happy if they can . . . hand over their weapons."[97]

Indeed, the occupation came off without a hitch. On 10 September, German troops marched into Rome, a day after the king and Badoglio had fled to the American-controlled south. From the very onset, Operation Axis was something of a hateful, punitive enterprise. Within a few days, one million Italian soldiers had been disarmed, and more than 600,000 were taken in cattle trucks to Germany for forced labour. They were not considered formal POWs, but rather "military internees," a status that exposed them to particularly ruthless treatment. Speer insisted that the Italians be quickly assigned to German arms production.[98] What is more, Speer's underlings were quick to employ the industrial resources of northern Italy to bolster German armaments output. Wherever Italian troops refused to surrender without a fight, there were massacres. One of the worst took place on the Ionian island of Cephalonia, where Wehrmacht units shot some 5,000 Italian officers and soldiers. The brutality continued when the Italian *resistenza* formed to combat the occupation. Partisan attacks usually brought on horrific acts of retribution that cost thousands of innocent civilians—men, women and children—their lives.[99]

For weeks now, Goebbels had been pressuring Hitler to speak to the German people. His last appearance had been on Heroes' Commemoration Day in March 1943 and Hitler had "disappeared somewhat in the clouds," lamented the propaganda minister. Only "a word from the Führer" could settle the unease in the German population and "restore clarity." The dictator continued to refuse, saying that he could only speak when the situation in Italy was clear.[100] But on 9 September, during his visit to the Wolf's Lair, Goebbels finally got what he wanted: Hitler agreed to a radio address, and it was recorded the following afternoon in the Wolf's Lair and broadcast that evening.[101] Hitler confined his remarks almost entirely to current developments in Italy, which, he insisted, he had long foreseen and had now countered with the necessary measures. He praised his friendship with Mussolini, "the greatest son of Italian soil since the collapse of the Classical world," in fulsome terms only to immediately condemn the overthrow of the Duce and Italy's departure from the Axis as an unprecedented "break in loyalty." But Hitler also sought to reassure listeners that the loss of Italy as a military partner would have little impact since it was German troops doing the main fighting on the southern front. Enemy hopes that a "25 July" could be replicated in Germany were in vain, he asserted. The "ring of steel" binding the home front and the military front would never be broken. In closing, the dictator promised that Allied air raids would soon be "avenged with other more effective means"—a clear suggestion that new "miracle weapons" were being developed.[102]

If Security Service reports are to be believed, Hitler's radio address hit its mark: "The self-confidence with which the speech was delivered shored up belief in victory by itself."[103] But more important than Hitler's words for the rapid improvement in the public mood was the news that Italy had been swiftly occupied, which was interpreted as evidence of the "unimpeded fighting power" of the Wehrmacht: "The most reassuring recent message for the population is that, just as at the start of the war, Germany is capable of acting with lightning quickness when the moment requires it."[104] Nonetheless, Goebbels was deluding himself when he wrote of a "fundamental change of mood" in which "almost no pessimism and defeatism can be felt any longer."[105] It would not be long before new reports about the critical situation on the eastern front would darken the horizon.

At noon on 12 September, a German special unit commanded by SS-Hauptsturmführer Otto Skorzeny succeeded in freeing Mussolini from a hotel on Gran Sasso Mountain, where he had been held prisoner for the past few weeks. The operation caused a sensation. That evening Hitler received word that the Duce had arrived safe and sound in Vienna, and around midnight the Führer called Goebbels to express his happiness at the spectacular coup. In his plans for a restoration of the Fascist regime in Italy, Mussolini was to play a central role. Goebbels was more sceptical, doubting whether Mussolini was capable of "a major political action."[106] Indeed, when the Duce landed on 14 September at the airstrip near Rastenburg to Hitler's warm greetings, he made a battered impression. "He looked pale and wan," commented one eyewitness. "It cost him effort to go down the stairs."[107] Hitler and Mussolini held talks, mostly by themselves, for four days, and in the end, the Duce agreed to head a Fascist government in the German-occupied part of Italy. Nevertheless Hitler was not satisfied. Stripped of power, the Duce had not seemed as strong as he had in earlier encounters, he remarked. Above all, he was disappointed by Mussolini's refusal as his first act to stage a "large-scale tribunal to prosecute those who had betrayed him." It was an indication of his "limitations," Hitler added, showing that he was "no revolutionary."[108]

The reconstituted Fascist government, which called itself the Italian Social Republic, established its seat in Salò on Lake Garda, but from the very beginning, it was nothing more than a German puppet regime. Mussolini, once so proud, had become Hitler's marionette. It was not he but the Reich envoy in Italy, career diplomat Rudolf Rahn, who held the actual power in the occupied parts of the country. The Social Republic actively assisted the Nazi attempt to annihilate the Jews by deporting thousands of Italian Jews to Auschwitz, where they were murdered. And the tribunal Hitler had demanded also took place. After a show trial in Verona in January 1944, five of the six defendants were shot, including Mussolini's son-in-law Ciano.[109] Prior to his execution, the former Italian foreign minister had revealed that the day before the German western offensive on 10 May 1940, the Duce had received the Belgian ambassador to Italy and told him about the imminent attack. "That was the last straw for the Führer," Goebbels noted. "For all intents and purposes Mussolini is now finished for him."[110]

While the Western Allies slowly fought their way forward in southern Italy, the Red Army was sprinting from one victory to another.[111] On 5 August 1943, Soviet troops captured Oryol. On 23 August, Kharkov fell, reversing again the German reoccupation that had been trumpeted as a huge triumph in March. Yet that seems not to have changed Hitler's outlook. "He has never had any doubts of victory," wrote Goebbels, "and he does so even less today."[112] But the Soviets pressed ahead with their offensives on all fronts. Over the course of September, they forced German troops to abandon the Donets basin and the Kuban bridgehead, a fallback position on the Taman Peninsula—and an object of prestige to which Hitler had tenaciously clung in order to keep open the possibility of launching a Caucasus offensive. On 25 September, Smolensk, the scene of the great cauldron battle of the summer of 1941, was liberated. The Red Army constantly pursued retreating German divisions, ensuring that they could not establish stable lines of defence. As they withdrew, Wehrmacht troops employed a scorched-earth strategy, destroying anything that could have been used by the enemy. "I've had to drive round a good many of the settlements that the Germans have abandoned in the recent past," a Soviet engineer wrote home to his family. "You cannot imagine what these places, that used so recently to be blossoming centres of population, look like; not one dwelling without damage, everything burned, and what they didn't manage to burn has been destroyed by aerial bombing."[113]

By early October, the Wehrmacht had pulled back to beyond the Dnieper, a line Hitler believed would be "easy to defend."[114] But the Red Army had already succeeded in establishing several bridgeheads on the western bank of the river. On 23 October, Soviet troops liberated Melitopol. "The Russians are doing everything to force a decision or at least weaken us to the extent that the definitive final act, as far as they are concerned, can follow in winter," General Hossbach wrote around this time to his wife. He added: "They must have a huge arms industry and be getting significant support from the Anglo-Saxons. We lack such a wealthy ally."[115]

On 6 November, Soviet troops marched into the Ukrainian capital, Kiev. The following day, Manstein travelled to Hitler's headquarters and demanded that the Führer evacuate Crimea after a Soviet offensive had cut off the land bridge to the peninsula and isolated German and Romanian troops stationed there. Hitler refused. He was afraid of the political effects a loss of Crimea might have on neutral Turkey and the loyalty of Axis partners Romania and Bulgaria. He also worried that the Soviet air force would be able to attack the Romanian oil fields so crucial to the German war effort. Hitler demanded that German troops defend the bridgehead of Nikopol on the Dnieper, whose reserves of manganese ore were deemed essential to the war effort. "My generals only ever think about military considerations, never economic ones," he complained to Zeitzler. "If we lose the ore mines at Nikopol, our arms production will decline while that of the Russians increases. We cannot afford that."[116]

Despite all the setbacks, Hitler maintained an iron façade of confidence. In evening conversations, he directed the talk back to the "years of struggle" from 1930 to 1933. Just like then, he preached to his entourage, the important thing was "to keep our nerve and be steadfast." In the end, "the enemy would bend to the stronger morale."[117] Disregarding the tense situation on the eastern front, he made a snap decision to speak to the "old fighters" on the twentieth anniversary of the Beer Hall Putsch of 8–9 November 1923. It would be the final time he addressed this group. His special train arrived in Munich at 4 p.m., and one hour later the commemoration began in the Löwenbräukeller.[118] "The mood among the old marchers was brilliant," noted Goebbels. "Here we are in fact dealing with the original fighters of National Socialism, even if many of them have grown old and somewhat frail."[119]

Hitler had written out the first part of his speech but held the second section fully extemporaneously. He only briefly discussed the situation in Italy, which, he assured his listeners, was completely under control with the occupation of the country and the freeing of Mussolini. The "storm on the Brenner Pass" announced by the Allies, he scoffed, had become a "snail-paced offensive far south of Rome." Germany would likewise repel any attempt by the Allies to land in western Europe. Hitler devoted the main part of his speech to the fighting on the eastern front and the Allied bombing war, and his words were aimed at reassuring his audience. All attempts by the "Bolshevist-Asian colossus" to collapse the German front would fail, he pledged, contending that it was no big deal if here and there a few hundred kilometres of territory had to be given up, as long as the fighting took place far away from Germany's borders. He again promised to rebuild bombed-out German cities to be "more beautiful than ever before and in the shortest of time" and threatened that the "hour of vengeance" was rapidly approaching. He reiterated his mantra of holding out: "The war can go on for as long as it wants but Germany will never capitulate. We will never repeat the mistake of 1918 and lay down our arms at a quarter to twelve."[120] The speech was broadcast on German radio at 8:15 p.m., after Goebbels, with Hitler's approval, had cut out a few "somewhat clumsy phrases."[121]

In the short term, Hitler's speech seems to have "animated the will to hold out," in the words of the Security Service, and his remarks about retribution in particular were met with "keen attention and joyous approval."[122] But the surge in mood did not last. Only a week later, against the backdrop of the bad news from the eastern front, Security Service reports struck a more sombre tone: "After the great successes of the Wehrmacht of the past years, ethnic-popular comrades simply do not understand why we are continually falling back and seem unable to put up resistance to the Soviets."[123] German propaganda dismissed the constant retreats as a mere "straightening of the front." The journalist Ruth Andreas-Friedrich noted: "If you open an atlas, these surreptitious retreats actually lengthen the front. I believe we will still be straightening our lines when they are 10 kilometres from Berlin—as an act of successful defence and victorious resistance."[124]

Buoyed by the reception of his Munich speech, Hitler seems to have temporarily regained his taste for public appearances. On 20 November 1943, he held a speech before 10,000 young army, navy and Luftwaffe officers. Because Berlin had been deemed unsafe on account of possible air raids, the event was moved to the Jahrhunderthalle auditorium in Breslau. This time, Hitler's speech was only summarised, not broadcast on the radio. In the face of "plans of destruction dictated by Jewish hatred," the radio commentator proclaimed, the Führer had emphasised "the unshakable determination of the people to emerge victorious in this epochal struggle thanks to their most extreme tenacity and the application of all their strength."[125] This was the last time Hitler would speak before an audience of this size.

Since the failure of the German operation at Kursk and the success of the Soviet counter-offensive, there were increasing rumours that Germany and Russia would conclude a separate peace. Ulrich von Hassell wrote that all indications were that the Nazi leadership was "flirting more and more with a special Russian peace," which for Hitler would be the "only way out."[126] Not only Mussolini, but the Japanese government too had repeatedly if unsuccessfully encouraged Berlin to test the chances for an agreement with the Soviet Union.[127] In early September 1943, Goebbels made an exploratory attempt to sound Hitler out as to whether "something could be done with Stalin sooner or later," but the Führer summarily rejected the idea.[128] In late September, the dictator qualified his answer, remarking there was no possibility for negotiation at the moment. England was not sufficiently "softened up and tired of war" and would interpret any overtures as "signs of weakness." It was more conceivable to extend feelers towards the Soviet Union, but here Hitler did not believe he could achieve a positive result because Stalin had the military advantage and would not agree to cede the territories Hitler would demand of him. "We have to get through the present crisis no matter the cost," Hitler proclaimed. Still, Goebbels insisted that the German Reich had "never won a two-front war" and that they would have to look for ways to "get out of this somehow."[129]

In late October, when Goebbels again raised the subject, Hitler was less virulently opposed. He indicated that he might be willing to reach an arrangement with the Soviet Union, "for instance on the basis of 1939, after the Polish campaign." But he interjected that the precondition for even the "loosest arrangement" would be Germany winning back the initiative on the eastern front and achieving some victories: "We cannot negotiate now . . . when things are going so badly for us."[130] The dictator categorically refused to try to do a deal from a position of weakness. In practice, this meant that the door to a political settlement would remain closed. Hitler knew better than many of his underlings that Operation Barbarossa, conceived as a war of annihilation, had burned Germany's bridges and that with the failure of the winter offensive of 1941–42 there was no longer any possibility of retreating into diplomacy.[131] Thus, all the feelers for peace extended by Ribbentrop's Foreign Ministry and the Abwehr via the German embassy in Stockholm were consigned to the realm of obscure, utterly unrealistic, speculation.[132]

The rumours about a separate peace spread by the German side were primarily aimed at sowing mistrust between the Western powers and the Soviet Union. In the last two years of the war, hopes that the anti-Hitler alliance would collapse became a straw at which the Nazi leadership could clutch. Conversely, the rumours helped Stalin increase pressure on the Western Allies to finally agree to open up the "second front" that he had long demanded. After preparatory conferences in Quebec, Moscow and Cairo, the "big three"—Roosevelt, Churchill and Stalin—met from 28 November to 1 December 1943 in Tehran. There the Soviet leader promised to help subdue Japan after victory over Germany, and Roosevelt and Churchill agreed to launch Operation Overlord, a landing in northern France, in May 1944. The three men also worked out the basics of a division of Germany after the country's defeat. There was no longer any talk, however, of restoring the former borders of Poland, which Britain had guaranteed in 1939. Stalin was now in a strong position and succeeded in getting the others to agree to shift the Soviet-Polish border westwards, along the lines of the 1939 non-aggression pact he had signed with Hitler. Poland would be compensated for its losses with German territory east of the Oder–Neisse line.[133]

In Berlin, the leadership was left scratching its head as to what had been agreed at the Tehran conference. The communiqué that was issued to the press from the meeting was remarkably nebulous. "We can publish it almost word for word in the German press," wrote Goebbels after conferring with Hitler. "There is nothing dangerous for us in it."[134] But an informer at the British embassy in Ankara—code-named "Cicero"—gradually fed the Nazi leadership with detailed information, including the fact that the Allied leaders had discussed Operation Overlord, although no concrete dates for the planned landing were passed on. The German Foreign Ministry and the Wehrmacht Supreme Command were not even sure that the documents provided by "Cicero" were not fake material prepared by the British secret service to steer the Wehrmacht in the wrong direction.[135]

In late November 1943, Berlin was hit by a series of major air raids that destroyed most of the government ministry buildings. Hitler's living quarters in the Old Reich Chancellery were also damaged, and the luxury Kaiserhof hotel, a favourite of Hitler's in the days before 1933, burned to the ground.[136] "Berlin makes a horrific sight late in the evening," noted Goebbels after the first wave of bombing on 22 November. "You would think the entire government district was on fire. On Wilhelmplatz it is almost as bright as day . . . In the Reich capital, we are now living in the middle of a war zone."[137] The propaganda minister and Gauleiter of Berlin recognised the opportunity to demonstrate his abilities as a crisis manager. From his bunker on Wilhelmplatz he coordinated assistance for the various parts of the city affected. Visiting the sites of destruction himself and talking to those who had been bombed out, his diary entries are full of praise for what he described as the Berliners' unbroken morale.[138]

But the German people were now demanding that Hitler make good on the "retribution" he had so often promised. And the longer they were kept waiting, the more disappointed they grew. "More than a few ethnic-popular comrades have even come to fully doubt retribution," the Security Service reported in December 1943. "They think it is nothing but a grand propaganda manoeuvre by the German leadership aimed at scaring the population in England and making the Anglo-American leadership prematurely commence with an incompletely planned invasion."[139] Goebbels ordered the German press not to use the term "retribution" until further notice.[140]

When Goebbels paid a brief visit to the Wolf's Lair on 19 December, Hitler congratulated him on how quickly public life had been restored in Berlin and characterised the fortitude of the capital's populace as "truly admirable." But he was of no mind to follow Goebbels' example to view the destroyed parts of the city with his own eyes. As far as "retribution" was concerned, the Führer intended to resume massive air attacks on London after Christmas. He was more optimistic, however, about the potential effect of Germany's new flying bombs and missiles, which would first be deployed in February and March 1944. After a certain time, he vowed, life in London would "no longer be possible."[141] But the German V-1 and V-2 rockets would take several months longer than that to be deployable, and when they were ready, they would not have anywhere near the destructive power the Nazi leadership had hoped.

In mid-December, the Red Army began its winter offensive. The main thrust was directed in the centre against Vitebsk and in the south against Zhitomir (Zhytomyr) and Vinnitsa, where Manstein had set up his new headquarters after losing Zaporozhye. "We are mired in one of the most serious crises of the war," wrote tank commander Hermann Balck. "Hopefully the Führer will finally make up his mind on some decisive sacrifices—that is: to give up territory that can no longer be held."[142] Once again, the entire Wolf's Lair was alarmed, and once again Hitler sought to downplay the danger. There was no reason to assume, he told a situation meeting on 27 December, that the enemy was like a "giant of Antiquity that grows stronger every time he falls to the ground." At some point, Hitler promised, "he will run out of breath." But it was a mark of how modest Hitler's expectations on the eastern front had become that he added, as an aside, that "struggling through victoriously" now meant "to bring the whole thing to a halt somewhere." Zeitzler dutifully agreed that it would be a triumph just to halt the enemy's progress. "We cannot defeat him," the chief of staff admitted.[143] On 30 December, Hitler ordered Field Marshal Georg von Küchler, by then the supreme commander of Army Group North, to send further units to the struggling Army Groups Centre and South.[144] As a result, Army Group North could no longer hold its overstretched lines. On 20 January 1944, Soviet troops retook Novgorod, and a week later, the blockade of Leningrad was finally ended after nearly 900 days. Küchler was stripped of his command and replaced by Colonel-General Model, the commander of the 9th Tank Army, whom Hitler considered a particular strategist of hard-bitten defence.[145]

The Führer spent New Year's Eve with his secretary Bormann in his bunker in the Wolf's Lair.[146] Shortly after midnight, he called Goebbels and expressed his "firm conviction" that Germany would "master the crisis and deal the enemy the heaviest of blows" in the new year.[147] That was also the message of his New Year's greetings to the German people and the soldiers of the Wehrmacht. Both addresses projected confidence that Germany would ultimately emerge victorious from the "life-or-death" struggle. Hitler proclaimed: "The fighting in the east may have been heavy and will still be so, but Bolshevism has not achieved its goal. The plutocratic world in the west may undertake its threatened landing attempt wherever it wants, but it will fail!"[148] But such forced optimism could no longer quell the growing doubts about Germany's final victory, particularly among army officers who knew what was really happening at the front. As acknowledgement spread that the war was lost, so did the tendency not to follow orders from the Führer without question.

Conversely, Hitler sensed the reservations which parts of his officer corps maintained towards him and saw them as confirmation that his hostility towards the old military caste was justified. Although as recently as September 1943 he had dismissed the possibility that his generals could "betray" him as the Italian military leadership had Mussolini, he remained deeply mistrustful.[149] This attitude was strengthened by the activities of the League of German Officers, which had been founded in mid-September in a POW camp near Moscow and had joined forces with the National Committee for a Free Germany, which had been established two months prior to that largely by German communists. Through radio broadcasts and flyers, the league called on German soldiers to rise up against the Nazi regime and rebel against their supreme commander. Hitler was incensed by such insurrection, saying that he regretted that, unlike Stalin, he had not freed himself from "every form of military opposition." In Goebbels' presence, he raged: "Deep inside, the generals on the southern front and a large number of the army generals altogether do not believe in our cause. They are either, in the best case, special-ists and craftsmen or, in the worst, dilettante politicians who, protected by their officers' uniforms, approach the war politically in defeatist fashion."[150]

The leader of the League of German Officers was a highly decor-ated troop commander from a venerable Prussian aristocratic family, artillery general Walther von Seydlitz. In Hitler's eyes, Seydlitz personi-fied the nationalist-conservative military elites whom he so loathed and who he unfairly thought had always put obstacles in his way. "It speaks strongly against the German officer class," Goebbels and Hitler agreed, "that such men had once had a place in its ranks."[151] Seydlitz and his fellow rebels' appeals had little effect on the Wehrmacht, however, where they were considered treasonous.[152] Nonetheless, Hitler took the dangers that came from them seriously and now considered intensifying the indoctrination of soldiers into Nazi ideology. On 22 December 1943, he created a new Nazi leadership staff in the Wehrmacht Supreme Command, with infantry general Hermann Reinecke at its head. On 7 January in the Wolf's Lair, the general discussed with Hitler what his new role would entail. "National Socialist leadership officers" were to be appointed for all troop formations. They would exclusively consist of men suffused with boundless faith in the Führer and a fanatical will to wage war until victory. Hitler stressed that he considered the inculcation of Nazi ideas into the entire Wehrmacht "the most important thing there is," but he feared that there would be "great resistance" among the officer corps.[153]

Field Marshal von Manstein in particular now attracted Hitler's ire. He was "extraordinarily tactically gifted and flexible, a clever expert, but without any ideological attitude and any inner fortitude of character," Hitler complained in late October 1943. By that point, he was already considering firing Manstein and giving Model command of Army Group South.[154] On 4 January 1944, Manstein flew to Hitler's headquarters in an attempt to convince him to allow the southern wing of his forces to fall back, thereby abandoning the Nikopol bridgehead and evacuating Crimea. Again his entreaties fell on deaf ears. "The loss of Crimea would cause Turkey to fall, followed by Romania and Bulgaria," he was told.[155] In a conversation after the situation meeting, Manstein tried again to win Hitler over for his idea of reforming the Wehrmacht's top brass. The critical situation on the eastern front, he argued, was down not just to the enemy's material superiority but to shortcomings in the military leadership. In his memoirs, Manstein would describe Hitler's reaction as follows: "He stared at me with a look that made me feel as if he was trying to subdue my will to keep speaking . . . Suddenly I could not help but think of an Indian snake charmer. You could say that a wordless struggle played itself out between us within a few seconds."

But this time the field marshal refused to be cowed, demanding the appointment of a chief of the general staff responsible for the entire conduct of war, so as to get rid of the parallel and sometimes opposing activities of the Wehrmacht leadership, the Army High Command, the Luftwaffe, the German navy and the Waffen-SS. Part of the new order would involve a supreme commander for the entire eastern front, who would be given "complete autonomy for the total conduct of war." Hitler understood at once not only that this would limit his own authority but that Manstein was hoping to become the man who had the final say in the east. His response was commensurately cutting: "The field marshals do not even obey *me*! Do you think they would be, for example, more obedient with *you*?" That was the end of the conversation.[156] But his irritation at Manstein's proposals was still evident when he spoke with Goebbels on 24 January about his poor relations with his generals. "He does not trust Manstein in the slightest," noted the propaganda minister. "But he has no replacement. There is apparently no one who could succeed him. He calls him a [Hjalmar] Schacht among the generals."[157]

On 27 January, Hitler assembled the more than one hundred commanders on the eastern front in the Wolf's Lair. The purpose of the meeting was to convince the generals that greater Nazi indoctrination was needed in the Wehrmacht. But Hitler's speech ended on an unforeseen note as he was trying to convince his listeners of the value of unquestioning obedience. "If in the end, I as the supreme leader should find myself abandoned by everyone else, then I expect my entire officer corps to stand around me with daggers drawn, just as every field marshal, every colonel, every commanding general, every divisional and every regimental commander must expect his subordinates to stand by him in a critical hour," Hitler declared. When he took a rhetorical pause, Manstein called out: "That is the way it will be, my Führer!" Never before had a military commander interjected when Hitler was speaking. For a brief moment, the Führer lost his train of thought, but then replied sharply: "That is just lovely! If that is the case, then we can never lose this war . . . I greatly appreciate it, Field Marshal von Manstein."[158]

Manstein, who must have sensed the mistrust of the military implicit in Hitler's speech, apparently wanted to publicly announce his loyalty in the name of all present. But Hitler interpreted the incident very differently. Against the backdrop of his recent exchange with Manstein, he saw it as a further attempt to challenge his authority.[159] After his speech, he called Manstein over to him and made a scene, saying that he did not allow himself to be interrupted. "You would not put up with that from a subordinate yourself," Hitler told him.[160] The dictator "yelled and raved in a fashion that was hard to put up with," General Walter Scherff, Hitler's "special representative for military history," noted afterwards. Hitler had called Scherff over too to record for posterity how the Führer had dressed down a highly decorated field marshal.[161] But Hitler was not only concerned with his historical legacy. He also wanted to intimidate a military commander who was too self-assured for his own liking.

As he had the previous year, Hitler spent 30 January 1944, the eleventh anniversary of his becoming chancellor, in the Wolf's Lair. However, he had promised Goebbels he would address the German people on the radio.[162] His speech, broadcast that day at noon, avoided any reference to the critical situation on the eastern front, and it did not include any of the usual promises of retribution against Britain. Instead, Hitler merely regurgitated some propaganda clichés that must have been overly familiar to his audience, such as the claim that

Bolshevism aimed to "completely exterminate" the German people and that this was also the "the openly acknowledged goal of international Jewry."[163] For the first time, the ensuing Security Service reports informed the government that Hitler's words had had no effect on the "grave and depressed mood of the population."[164] Even Goebbels thought little of the speech. It had been "too little concerned with current problems to give the German people something powerful to hold on to," the propaganda minister criticised.[165] That evening, Berlin was subject to more heavy bombing. The Sportpalast, the site of so many mass Nazi Party events, burned to the ground. "The fact that this happened on 30 January is surely not a good omen for the party," Goebbels thought.[166]

Even more ominous was the news coming from the eastern front. On 8 February 1944, the Wehrmacht was forced to vacate the Nikopol bridgehead, which Hitler had deemed essential to the German war effort. Two weeks later, the Red Army occupied the important industrial city of Krivoi Rog (Kryvyi Rih), and German troops encircled near Cherkassy (Cherkasy) only barely succeeded in breaking out and fighting their way west. But Hitler still clung to his doctrine of holding conquered territory for as long as possible. He ordered the creation of so-called strongholds, exposed positions where German troops were to allow themselves to be surrounded and put up fierce resistance so as to tie down the enemy's strength and halt its forward progress. The pointlessness of this idea would soon become apparent. "Strongholds" did nothing to weaken the Red Army. On the contrary, it was easy for the enemy to surround the cities so designated and take time capturing them, while the vanguard of Soviet tank units pressed forward ever further.[167]

By the latter half of February, Hitler was becoming increasingly worried that the Allies might launch a massive air strike on his East Prussian headquarters. "They know where we are, and they will destroy everything with targeted bombings," he fretted. "I expect them to attack any day."[168] For that reason, he decided to leave the Wolf's Lair for a while. During his absence, the bunkers in Restricted Zone I were to be given massive concrete reinforcements.[169] On the evening of 22 February, Hitler's special train left for Berchtesgaden, stopping off in Munich on 24 February so that Hitler could give his traditional speech to the Nazi old guard in the Hofbräuhaus in celebration of the anniversary of the founding of the party. The Führer had been battling an intestinal problem for some weeks, and Morell was keeping him on his feet with a variety of pills and energy-boosting injections.[170] Still, Goebbels found that he gave "a very lively speech—at least livelier than we have heard in quite some time." Unusually, however, the speech was neither broadcast on radio nor covered in the press. Indeed, no reference was made to it anywhere. Hitler had insisted upon this, and Goebbels had no choice but to accede to the Führer's wishes. The speech had contained a "series of psychological swerves . . . which the old guard is happy to overlook but which could have a negative impact on the population at large under certain circumstances," wrote Goebbels, referring primarily to remarks about the military situation.[171] Hitler may have continued to prattle on about the victory to come, seemingly unmoved by reality, but the German people were feeling increasing dread in the face of the rapid advances made by the Red Army. It was a commonly held view that only a "major miracle" could turn the situation around.[172]

After his speech, Hitler immediately travelled on to the Obersalzberg, where he would remain for over four months, until mid-July 1944. On 26 February, he received Marshal Antonescu in Klessheim Castle for two days of talks. He assured the Romanian leader that once the Allied invasion in the west had failed, as he was sure it would, Germany would go back on the offensive in the east. Concerning the fate of Crimea, the two dictators agreed that, in view of expected political reprisals, the peninsula would have to be held for as long as possible. At the same time, all necessary preparations were to be made for a smooth evacuation if a crisis developed. Hitler also repeated what he had tried to hammer home to his Romanian ally in talks the preceding April: "In the battle between Europe and the Soviets, only one of the two can emerge the victor. If Germany proves too weak, Europe is done for . . . The Jews are behind all of this since they hope for a victory of Bolshevism over European culture."[173]

In the meantime, Goebbels had taken the initiative in an attempt to improve the poisonous climate between Hitler and his military commanders. Over dinner with Hitler's main adjutant, Rudolf Schmundt, in late February, the propaganda minister suggested drawing up a declaration in which the army leadership would distance itself "in the brusquest manner" from the activities of General von Seydlitz. "This declaration will have to represent a passionate avowal of loyalty to the Führer and is to be signed by all of the army's field marshals," Goebbels proposed.[174] Schmundt welcomed the idea and set off on a tour of the fronts with the propaganda minister's declaration in hand. Eleven days later, he could report to Goebbels that his mission had been a success. Not only had the field marshals all signed the document; they had also agreed to come to the Obersalzberg to present it to the Führer personally.[175] The ceremony took place on 19 March. The most senior of the field marshals, Rundstedt—supreme commander of the German forces in western Europe since March 1942—read out the declaration: "In this hour above all others, we pledge to you, our Führer, with our deepest comradeship and unwavering loyalty, to stand true to you and your cause. More than ever, it will be our task to anchor your ideas, filled with high ideals, in the army, so that every soldier will be an even more fanatical fighter for the National Socialist future."[176] Hitler seemed to be deeply moved by the oath, but he was a skilled enough actor to conceal his real feelings. The same was true for Manstein's subsequent report about the state of Army Group South, with which the dictator acted impressed.[177]

In any case, if the military leaders thought this spectacle had laid to rest Hitler's suspicions, they quickly learned better. On 30 March, Manstein and Ewald von Kleist, the commander of Army Group A, were summoned to the Berghof. With no further ado, Hitler informed them that he had decided on a change of leadership in their army groups. "In the east the time of larger-scale operations is . . . over," Hitler declared. "The main thing now is to stubbornly hold on." To that end, he needed new men in charge. Hitler sought to sugar-coat the two commanders' dismissal by awarding them Germany's highest military honour. No sooner had they left the Berghof than their successors were presented: Colonel-General Walter Model and General Ferdinand Schörner. In them, Hitler believed he had found what he thought Manstein lacked: blind faith in victory and uncompromising severity.[178] Army Group South and Army Group A were renamed Army Group Northern Ukraine and Army Group Southern Ukraine, even though by that point Germany only controlled a small corner of western Ukraine. The new names were clearly intended to suggest that the two regions, so crucial to the German war effort, were to be reconquered. Chief of Staff Zeitzler was so incensed by the dismissal of the two experienced army commanders that he asked Hitler to relieve him too of his duties. "A general is to remain at his post," he was told.[179]

On 19 March, the same day that Hitler received the leaders of the military on the Obersalzberg, German troops marched into Hungary. The invasion had been coming for some time. After the departure of Italy in September 1943, Hitler feared losing his allies Hungary and Romania and had ordered his strategists to draw up plans to invade both countries; the plans were known as "Margaret I" and "Margaret II." After his talks with Antonescu, Hitler believed he could rely on Romanian loyalty, but he was deeply distrustful of the Horthy regime in Hungary. It had not escaped his notice that the Hungarians had extended feelers to the West concerning a separate peace settlement. In the spring of 1944, with Soviet troops bearing down on the Hungarian border, Hitler decided it was time to act. "The Hungarians are committing constant acts of betrayal," he complained early in March, adding that he was determined to overthrow the Hungarian regime, detain Horthy and install a puppet government in Budapest.[180] On 11 March, he ordered Operation Margaret I to commence. "This action is designed to occupy Hungarian territory in a set of drastic strikes," Hitler told Goebbels before revealing another motivation for the invasion. "Hungary has 700,000 Jews. We will make sure that they do not slip through our hands."[181]

Hitler summoned the Hungarian regent to Klessheim on 18 March and tried to strong-arm Horthy as he had Austrian chancellor Schuschnigg in February 1938 and Czech president Hácha in March 1939.[182] He demanded that his guest agree to the occupation of his country and name a new, pro-German government. Horthy was dumbfounded and threatened to stop the talks, telling Hitler: "If everything has already been decided here, there is no point in me staying any further." To prevent Horthy from leaving, Hitler's underlings simulated an air raid, sounding sirens and enveloping Klessheim Castle in clouds of smoke. The talks resumed that afternoon, and eventually Horthy gave in.[183] He returned to Budapest that evening a beaten man.

He was accompanied on the train journey by Ribbentrop's envoy, SS-Brigadeführer Edmund Veesenmayer, whom Hitler had named Reich commissioner for Hungary, with the authority to do whatever was needed to ruthlessly subordinate the country to German interests. The new Hungarian government was headed by the former Hungarian ambassador to Germany, Döme Sztójay, who had the backing of the Nazi leadership.[184]

The occupation of Hungary proceeded with no complications. The Wehrmacht entered the country first, followed by eight SS and Security Service Einsatzkommandos, with the Reich Security Main Office's genocide specialist, Adolf Eichmann, at the helm. Within only eight weeks, 430,000 Hungarian Jews were deported to Auschwitz-Birkenau. The majority of them were gassed to death immediately upon arrival. Around one-quarter of these people were assigned to perform slave labour in the German arms industry, and many of them would lose their lives on death marches in the final weeks of the war. Without the cooperation of Hungary's puppet government, the German occupiers would never have been able to realise this genocidal campaign, especially not within so short a time.[185]

When he met with Antonescu again at Klessheim Castle on 23 March, Hitler justified his actions in Hungary. He could not tolerate a repeat of what had happened with Italy, the Führer explained. He added that he would continue to "ruthlessly confront every threat to the joint conduct of war"—a clear warning that Romania would face a similar fate if it were to contemplate switching sides. Hitler once more categorically ruled out ending the war by compromising: "If you have destroyed the last bridges behind you, you go more lightly into battle and have better chances of achieving victory." Turning to the southern part of the eastern front, Hitler announced that he would be "seizing the initiative again."[186] But this was a hollow promise. On 10 April, Soviet troops took Odessa and advanced quickly towards Crimea. Hitler still could not bring himself to abandon the peninsula. When Zeitzler warned that thousands of German soldiers were being needlessly sacrificed, Hitler replied coldly: "A thousand more or less no longer makes any difference."[187] On 9 May, however, Hitler was forced to issue orders for a hasty retreat, and by 13 May, Soviet troops had been able to retake Crimea— or what was left of it. The retreating Germans had smashed the peninsula's entire infrastructure, destroyed livestock and grain stores, and left behind "dead zones."[188]

Elsewhere on the eastern front, the fighting subsided somewhat in the spring of 1944. "The situation here is calm, but it is no doubt the calm before the storm," tank commander Hermann Balck noted.[189] The Red Army was regrouping. In mid-July, it would launch a major offensive and inflict a devastating defeat on the Wehrmacht at the heart of the front.

II

Operations Overlord and Bagration

"The danger in the east has remained, but a greater one is approaching in the west: the Anglo-Saxon landing," Hitler stressed in his "Führer Directive No. 51" of 3 November 1943. "In the east the vastness of the space means large amounts of territory can be lost without the German vital nerve being hit." In the west that was not the case: "If the enemy succeeds in broadly breaching our front here, the short-term conse-quences are unforeseeable." In Hitler's mind, all signs indicated that the Western Allies would begin their invasion in the spring of 1944 or perhaps earlier. For that reason, urgent measures were to be taken to allow German defenders to prevent a landing "by counter-attacking with the greatest of fury" and "driving the enemy back into the sea."[1]

Whatever the outcome, Hitler was convinced it would be of crucial significance. "If they attack in the west, that attack will decide the war," he declared in a situation meeting on 20 December, adding that the moment such an attack started would come as a "relief" to him.[2] As conscious as the dictator was of the danger of a successful Allied invasion, he also greatly valued the opportunities that would become available to him if the landing failed. In that case, he would be able to transfer significant German forces from the western front and go on the offensive in the east to reverse the course of the war there. It was a hope he shared with many of his military commanders. "If we can hold out on the eastern front until the attempted English invasion has happened and, God willing, been repulsed," wrote infantry general Friedrich Hossbach, "the situation could fundamentally take on a face far more in our favour."[3]

But all of these hopes presupposed that the German armies in the east could in fact withstand another Soviet counter-attack. Even if the Allied invasion in the west could be promptly beaten back, it would still be weeks until the divisions thus freed up could be transferred east. In the interval a "window of vulnerability" would open up, and that gave Wehrmacht commanders nightmares.[4] On 7 November 1943, four days after Hitler had issued Directive No. 51, his most trusted military adviser, Alfred Jodl, presented a frank assessment of the situation to the Reichsleiters and Gauleiters in Munich. Jodl admitted that the defensive lines in the east were thinly manned, and "further major crises" were possible at any time. Nonetheless, strength could not be siphoned off from the well-equipped operational reserves in the west since if Germany allowed the opening of another front, it would lose all control of the situation. Typical of the compliant mentality that prevailed within the Wehrmacht Supreme Command, Jodl followed up this relatively sober judgement with a passionate declaration of faith in Hitler, who was "destined in his entire development, will and ambition to lead our people to a better future." The Wehrmacht chief of staff concluded his remarks with a sentiment that, coming from a professional military man, was pretty close to lunacy. "We will be victorious because we must be victorious," Jodl told his listeners. "Otherwise, world history would lose all its sense."[5]

In the first months of 1944, Hitler occupied himself with the expansion of the Atlantic Wall to include a dense network of fortifications along the northwestern French coast. They were intended to prevent the Allies from establishing bridgeheads and advancing into the interior of the country. The dictator himself drew sketches for various types of bunkers, and with typical immodesty, he characterised himself as the "greatest fortification builder of all time."[6] In early November 1943, Hitler had dispatched Field Marshal Rommel to the west to supervise the construction work and fix any shortcomings. The popular commander was one of the few senior officers who still enjoyed the Führer's trust, and despite his defeat in Africa, he still carried a considerable aura for ordinary Germans. That too no doubt motivated Hitler in January 1944 to name Rommel commander of Army Group B, the more northern of the two army groups in France subordinate to the supreme commander west, Field Marshal von Rundstedt. Every morning, Rommel would set off from his headquarters in the La Roche–Guyon Castle on the Seine, 60 kilometres downstream from Paris, to carry out inspections on the Atlantic and Channel coasts. He was firmly convinced, he wrote to his wife, "that we will win the defensive battle in the west if we are given a little more time to set ourselves up."[7]

But the German commanders on the western front disagreed about how best to combat the impending invasion. Rommel believed that the initial hours would decide whether such an operation succeeded or failed and he wanted to station tank divisions near suspected landing locations. Rundstedt and the commander of Tank Group West, General Baron Leo Geyr von Schweppenburg, thought it was a mistake to disperse armoured forces along the coast, where they would be vulnerable to barrages from enemy warships. They wanted to lure the Allies into establishing a bridgehead and then attack and destroy enemy forces from the hinterland. Hitler decided the quarrel with a compromise typical of his style of rule. Army Group B under Rommel was given four tank divisions, as was Army Group G under General Johannes Blaskowitz, which was tasked with defending the coast from the Bay of Biscay to the Mediterranean. Four additional tank divisions were kept as a mobile reserve to take orders directly from the Wehrmacht Supreme Command. As a result, right from the start, German forces were fragmented.[8]

If Hitler had any doubts that his Atlantic Wall would be able to fulfil his expectations, he did not betray them to those around him. When Goebbels visited him in the Wolf's Lair in late January 1944, he described the preparations being taken as "impressive and far-sighted," adding: "We have not overlooked a thing, and unless a miracle of destiny helps the enemy, he will not have any success."[9] During another visit by Goebbels to the Obersalzberg in early March, the dictator told him he was "absolutely sure" that the Allied landing troops would be pushed back into the sea. The German forces stationed in the west were of "the best quality" and were immaculately prepared for the task at hand. Goebbels was less sanguine. "We have been disappointed so often recently," he noted in his diary, "that a certain internal scepticism arises."[10]

Still, despite all of his demonstrative confidence, Hitler was by no means certain whether the Allies would dare to launch an invasion at all and were merely seeking to give that impression in order to tie battle-ready German forces down at the western front. In mid-March, he briefly toyed with the idea of pretending to withdraw a number of divisions from the west "in order to tempt the British and Americans and to strike back brutally when they arrived." Goebbels did not think London and Washington would fall for such a trick, pointing out that Allied intelligence was "so sophisticated that it would easily see through such a manoeuvre."[11] Indeed, it was the Allies who deceived the Germans, and not vice versa, in terms of both the timing and the location of the invasion.

On 17 April 1944, Hitler travelled from the Obersalzberg to Munich to participate in the funeral for the city's deceased Gauleiter, Adolf Wagner. Reports that an invasion in the west would definitely take place had become more frequent, but the Nazi leadership were left scratching their heads over where and when. Once more, in private conversation with Goebbels, Hitler displayed his confidence that the Allied operation was bound to fail. Admiringly, he praised Rommel for having "performed in exemplary fashion in the west" and being ready to "resume the conflict with his old foes." While in Munich, Hitler took the opportunity to assemble the Reichsleiters and Gauleiters. He had last spoken to this circle of men in early May 1943 and in the meantime, the failure of the Kursk offensive, the loss of Italy as an ally and the seemingly unstoppable advance of the Red Army had dramatically worsened Germany's situation. Even the most fanatical of his underlings could hardly have been blind to the fact that the war was probably no longer winnable. In an extemporaneous speech, the dictator used all of his persuasive tricks to convince them of the opposite. Once again, he invoked the "battle years" in which victory had been achieved by stubborn persistence, not in one fell swoop. In a jibe at his generals, Hitler said that while so many men had turned weak, he, the Führer, was the only one with "the necessary energy and brutal strength of will" to take "calm and self-assured decisions." After the invasion in the west had been repulsed, Hitler promised, Germany would go back on the offensive in the east and retake Ukraine.[12]

On 20 April 1944, as Hitler celebrated his fifty-fifth birthday at the Berghof with the closest members of his entourage, Goebbels ordered Nazi flags to be flown throughout Berlin. While driving through the badly damaged Reich capital, the propaganda minister was satisfied to note: "The city is covered in banners reading 'Our walls may break, but our hearts will not.' Swastika flags are flying atop even the last pile of rubble."[13] On 19 April, Goebbels had held his traditional speech honouring the Führer in the Berlin State Opera House. It had been a difficult address to write since, as the propaganda minister admitted, it was "very hard to find the right words in these times."[14] His attempt to bridge the gap between Hitler worship and the dismal state of the war turned out less than convincing. Thomas Mann, who listened to the speech on the radio, noted succinctly and incisively: "The sound of a dinner plate breaking."[15]

On the afternoon of his birthday, Hitler received General Hans Hube, who had rescued his tank army from Russian encirclement at Kamenets-Podolsky (Kamianets-Podilskyi) and whom Hitler personally awarded Germany's highest military honour, the Knight's Cross with Golden Oak Leaves, Swords and Diamonds. But early the following morning, Hube's plane crashed shortly after taking off from the Ainring airstrip near Salzburg and the general was killed instantly. Walter Hewel, Ribbentrop's liaison with Hitler, was badly injured. Hitler was "very shaken" by this event. For him, Hube had personified his idea of the dashing Nazi officer, and he had considered him a candidate for his next army chief of staff.[16] Some two months later, on 23 June, a plane carrying General Eduard Dietl, a fanatical Hitler disciple, also crashed on a return flight from the Obersalzberg to Norway. Everyone on board was killed.[17] This unusual cluster of plane crashes gave rise to all kinds of rumours, but they seem to have been nothing more than bad luck.

Hitler himself flew to Berlin for Hube's memorial service in the Mosaic Hall of the New Reich Chancellery—something Goebbels considered a "bottomless foolishness," as Allied bomber squadrons by now controlled the skies over Germany. From his plane window, Hitler saw for the first time the dimensions of the damage that had been done to the Reich capital. He would "rebuild Berlin from the ground up without regard for . . . what was still standing," he declared after the state funeral, conferring with his propaganda minister until the early hours in the quarters that had been provisionally arranged for him in the Old Chancellery building. Hitler still projected demonstrative optimism about the military situation. Stalin, he said, would once again "bet everything on a single card," but Germany's forces in the east would withstand the attack, and preparations to meet the Allied invasion in the west had been completed. Rommel had put "the final touches to the fortifications," and the British and Americans were welcome to try their luck. Hitler again gave free rein to his anti-Semitism: "The Jews must be punished for their crimes against the European peoples and indeed the whole civilised world. Wherever we can get hold of them, they should not escape retribution." He expressed his satisfaction that Hungary's Jews, the last large remaining group of European Jews, had come under German control and could now be sent to their destruction.[18]

After their meeting in the Wolf's Lair in September the previous year, Hitler had avoided any direct contact with Mussolini, who had been restored as Duce. But in late April 1944, he received him for two days of talks in Klessheim Castle. Mussolini was a shadow of his former self and came as a petitioner. His new Italian government, he argued, had to be given greater autonomy to counter the impression that it was only being "maintained by German bayonets." He also asked Hitler to improve the conditions of Italians being held prisoner in Germany since their fate weighed heavily upon the mood in his country. Hitler turned a deaf ear to these entreaties, joking afterwards that he had acted "like a kind of squid." Goebbels recorded him saying: "All unpleasant topics were pushed to one side as quickly as possible so that the Duce never really got his turn."[19] Instead, Hitler treated his guest to a verbal deluge about Badoglio's "treachery," the new "miracle weapons" that would "reduce London to rubble," and the gigantic defensive fortifications in the west against which all enemy landing attempts would smash themselves to smithereens. The only thing that mattered was "to stubbornly hold out since the enemy front was bound to break not only militarily but politically." Here Hitler again referred to the example of his great hero Friedrich the Great in the Seven Years War.[20]

It is doubtful that the Italian delegation was very impressed by this historical parallel. The situation had again worsened in the Italian theatre of war. In January, American and British troops had landed at Nettuno and Anzio, 50 kilometres south of Rome, and German troops had been unable to drive them back. On the night of 11–12 May, the Allies began a major offensive on the main front at Monte Cassino, breaking through German lines and linking with troops advancing from the Anzio bridgehead. On 4 June, they entered Rome with little resistance. It was the first European capital to be liberated.[21] But the news did not cause any drastic downturn in the mood in Germany. There everyone's attention was directed towards the imminent events in the west.

Not only the Nazi leadership, but the German population at large feverishly anticipated the Allied landing in the spring of 1944. "It is not just expected; it is longed for," wrote Goebbels.[22] The Security Service confirmed this impression, writing on 4 May that most "ethnic-popular comrades" were approaching the invasion with "great hopes" and viewing it as "the last chance to turn things around." It was rare for people to express doubts that the Atlantic Wall would hold or concerns that Germany would be in dire peril if the Red Army were to launch a new major offensive at the same time as the invasion was taking place in the west. The majority did not share such fears. "The worst thing that could happen," one Security Service report stated, "was that contrary to expectations the invasion might not come at all."[23]

That outlook was shared by the Wehrmacht leadership. If all the signs were not deceiving, Jodl announced to the Reich cabinet on 5 May, the "great landing of the Western powers" was at hand. He was looking forward to the imminent battle "with complete confidence." A defensive victory would "fundamentally change the military and political situation," since there would be no way that the Allies could stage such an enormous and time-intensive landing a second time around.[24] Rommel was likewise optimistic. "In the west, we are quite confident of getting the job done," he wrote to his wife in mid-May. "We get stronger day by day." He added proudly that Hitler had lavished him with praise for how the expansion of Germany's fortifications had proceeded.[25]

Hitler himself showed no doubts that Germany's defensive action would be a resounding success. He hoped the invasion would come "as soon as possible," he told Slovak president Jozef Tiso at a meeting at Klessheim Castle on 12 May, boasting that the Atlantic Wall was "the most grandiose achievement ever in the history of the human building of fortifications." Churchill's time as prime minister would be up, he predicted, when the invasion failed and people in Britain came to see that the war could not be won.[26] Hitler made similar remarks two weeks later to the Japanese ambassador, Hiroshi Oshima, whom he received again after a long interval at the Berghof. But his words revealed that the German leadership remained unsure not just as to the precise date but the location of the invasion. Hitler speculated that it would come along the coasts of Brittany and Normandy, but was not ruling out the narrowest point of the English Channel, at the Strait of Dover, either.[27]

On 26 May 1944, a large circle of generals and officers assembled on the Obersalzberg. They had taken part in an ideological training course at a special elite Nazi facility, the SS-Ordensburg Sonthofen, and in culmination were now sworn in by their commander-in-chief to follow the dictates of his philosophy. The ceremony took place at the Platterhof Hotel, which had been built near the Berghof in 1940. It had primarily been used by Nazi bigwigs, although since 1943 it had also partly served as a hospital.[28] In his speech Hitler did not mention the expected invasion. Instead, as so often, he began with a long-winded recapitulation of the course he had followed since 1918. It was an attempt to convince his audience that someone like him, who had come through so many crises, could not be shaken by any setbacks. Only later did he get to his actual topic: why he had gone after Jews "so brutally and ruthlessly." The dictator left no doubt that his 1939 prediction had been fulfilled—the elimination of European Jews was largely complete. Hitler told his listeners: "Of course, one might say to me, 'Could you have dealt with this more simply? No, not more simply, since everything else would have been more complicated—but more humanely?' My dear officers, we stand here in a fight for life or death. If our enemies triumph in this battle, the German people will be exterminated . . . Here as elsewhere, 'humanity' would be the greatest possible betrayal of my own people. Although I have attracted the hatred of the Jews, I for one do not want to do without the advantages that hatred brings. Our advantage is that we possess a clean, organised body politic, with which nobody else is allowed to interfere."[29] As had been the case with Himmler's notorious Poznań speech the preceding October, Hitler's intent here was to make his higher officers, in so far as they were not already in the know, accessories to his crimes against humanity and thereby collectively culpable for them.

In early June 1944, nothing indicated that the great Allied landing was imminent. A deceptive calm hovered over the Berghof when

Goebbels arrived there on 5 June to consult with Hitler about the overall situation. The dictator had visibly recovered in the previous weeks and was in a splendid mood amid his entourage. He dismissed the recent fall of Rome as insignificant. He could not say how things would develop in Italy, he explained, but the real decision would take place in the west anyway, when, as he hoped, the Allies finally commenced their invasion. During an afternoon walk to the teahouse, the Führer continued his conversation with his propaganda minister. Once again, he dismissed any thoughts of reaching an arrangement with the British "plutocracy." "He considers England a lost cause," Goebbels recorded, "and is therefore determined to deal it a fatal blow if he has even the slightest chance of doing so." That evening, the assembled company stayed up late in front of the fireplace reminiscing about the good old days. When Goebbels returned to Berchtesgaden at dawn the following day, the first reports were beginning to arrive of the start of the invasion. "With that the decisive day of the war has begun," he noted in his diary.[30]

The Allies had spent over a year preparing Operation Overlord. In April 1943, a joint staff under the command of the British general Frederick Morgan had begun drawing up initial plans. There were two options for the landing: Pas-de-Calais and Normandy. Pas-de-Calais had the seeming advantage of offering the shortest route across the Channel and therefore easier logistics. On the other hand, for precisely that reason, it was there that German fortifications were particularly strong. Thus Morgan's staff decided on Normandy, especially the area between the mouth of the Seine and the Cotentin Peninsula. Resistance was likely to be less fierce, and the area offered the port of Cherbourg, which would be essential for receiving supplies. General Dwight D. Eisenhower, who had distinguished himself as the commander of Operation Torch, the Allied landing in North Africa, was named supreme commander of the entire operation. The other key positions were occupied by British officers: Admiral Bertram Ramsey commanded the naval forces, Air Marshal Trafford Leigh-Mallory the air forces, and General Bernard Montgomery, the hero of El Alamein, the ground troops. Montgomery, in particular, was a headstrong commander who more than once would test Eisenhower's diplomatic skills.[31]

The Allies realised that Operation Overlord could only succeed once absolute air supremacy had been established. To that end, Bomber Command had stepped up the aerial offensive against the Reich in the first half of 1944, targeting not only German aircraft production, but hydrogenation plants in an attempt to hit the German arms complex at a particularly weak spot: its production of synthetic fuel. The refineries near the Romanian oil fields of Ploeşti, crucial to German fuel supplies, also came in for increased bombardment.[32] Additionally, the Allies systematically bombed French infrastructure—railway lines, switching stations and bridges—to deprive the Germans of the ability to move reinforcements quickly to the invasion site. Such attacks came at the cost of heavy French civilian casualties and dampened the pro-Allied mood in France.[33] The British and Americans also spent considerable energy deceiving the enemy as to the exact date and place of the invasion. Fake tanks and trucks went on display throughout Kent to suggest that the attack would come at Pas-de-Calais. With the help of German spies who had been uncovered and flipped, Allied intelligence baited the other side with false information. German intelligence never found out that most of the landing troops were massing in southwestern England.[34]

Originally, the invasion was scheduled to begin on 5 June, but the weather turned bad two days earlier. An Atlantic low-pressure system brought storms and rain, and Eisenhower was forced to delay the assault by a day. Operation Overlord commenced with three airborne landing divisions capturing important strategic points to the rear of the German lines shortly after midnight. Then, in the dawn hours of 6 June, a gigantic armada of warships and landing boats moved in on the Normandy coast. Allied warplanes dropped their payloads on the strip of coastline and battleships, cruisers and destroyers subjected German coastal batteries and fortified bunkers to precision fire. Five divisions made land on five separate beaches: British and Canadian troops on the three eastern ones, code-named "Gold," "Juno" and "Sword," and the Americans on "Utah" and "Omaha" to the west. Before noon, the Allies had succeeded in overcoming German defences everywhere but on Omaha Beach, where the enemy put up fierce resistance and inflicted heavy casualties on the Americans. But by the end of day one, invading troops had gained a foothold and established bridgeheads on all five landing locations.

The Atlantic Wall had utterly disappointed Hitler and the army leadership's expectations.[35]

The Allies had been able to exploit the element of surprise. Because of the bad weather, Rommel did not think the invasion was imminent and had headed to the southern German town of Herrlingen to celebrate his wife's fiftieth birthday on 4 June. By the time he arrived back at his headquarters in La Roche–Guyon on 6 June, the initial successes of the Allied landing were already becoming apparent.[36] The supreme commander west, Colonel-General von Rundstedt, on the other hand, still suspected that the Normandy operation might be a diversion and that the main attack would come at Pas-de-Calais. He hesitated, losing valuable hours, before ordering any counter-measures.[37]

Hitler was still asleep when the initial reports sounding the alarm arrived on the Obersalzberg on 6 June. At first his entourage assumed that the Allies were launching a feint and did not bother to wake him up.[38] It was only at the situation meeting in the Berghof's Great Hall at noon that Jodl told him the specifics about what was going on. Hitler did not conceal his relief. As artillery general Walter Warlimont would recall: "With a completely carefree smile and the bearing of a man who has finally found the long-awaited opportunity to settle a score with a foe, he approached the maps, remarking in with what was even for him an unusually strong Austrian accent: 'So it has started up.'"[39] As the hours progressed, Hitler became positively euphoric. "The Führer is extraordinarily excited," observed Goebbels. "The invasion is taking place precisely where we expected it and with exactly the means and methods we prepared for. We will be damned if we are not up to the task."[40] Early that evening, Hitler ordered two additional tank divisions to be deployed—too late for them to join the fighting that day. It was a sign of how unconcerned Hitler was about developments in the west that he spent almost two hours in a meeting with the new Hungarian prime minister, Döme Sztójay, at Klessheim Castle on the day that was ostensibly to decide between victory and defeat. Here his obsessions with the "Jewish question" again dominated the conversation. Germany's occupation of Hungary had its positive side, he told his guest, since it would allow that country too to undergo a "thorough cleansing" and "finally put a stop to the Jews' nefarious activities."[41]

"Last night the enemy began his long-prepared, long-expected attack in western Europe," the Wehrmacht radio bulletin told the German people on 6 June.[42] A short time later, the Security Service reported that the news had been like a "purifying thunderstorm" and had been "generally received as relief from an unbearable tension and oppressive uncertainty."[43] If we credit this report, then the German people and their Führer had rarely been more in agreement than on 6 June 1944. But the public mood was by no means as united as the Security Service suggested since the expression "At last!," with which people greeted the news of the invasion, meant a variety of things. The great masses of Hitler supporters no doubt harboured hopes that final victory was still within reach, while the far smaller numbers of Hitler opponents may have thought that the death knell was beginning to toll for the regime.[44] And between these two groups were many Germans who simply expected that the invasion would decide things one way or another and that an end to the war was finally approaching.

But even where people had vocally celebrated the news, disillusionment soon set in. After only a few days it had already become clear that the quick German defensive victory touted by the leadership was nowhere to be seen. On the contrary, British and American forces were able to expand their bridgeheads, using artificial ports—so-called Mulberry harbours—to bring in steady supplies of reinforcements and materiel. On 7 June, they liberated Bayeux, and five days later they succeeded in linking their bridgeheads. While the Americans pushed up the Cotentin Peninsula to the west, Montgomery initially failed in his attempt to storm the city of Caen.[45] Nonetheless, on 8 June, the journalist Ruth Andreas-Friedrich wrote in her diary: "There is no doubt that the invasion has succeeded . . . And with every [Allied] success, the party comrades' faces are getting longer, and one swastika pin after another is disappearing from the buttonholes of Hitler's followers."[46]

The decisive disadvantage for the German defenders was the Allies' absolute air supremacy, which made it difficult to bring up reserves. Tank units could only move by night, arriving sporadically and late at the front. Increasing shortages in fuel and transport capacities also made themselves felt. Moreover, Hitler and the German military leadership, still unsure whether the main landing might not yet come at Pas-de-Calais, ordered most of the forces stationed there to stay put.[47]

Hitler's first trump card, the Atlantic Wall, had not won the day, but he believed he had a second one up his sleeve: a new rocket that could be launched from firing ramps in Pas-de-Calais at Britain. Technical hitches had repeatedly delayed its deployment, but on 16 May 1944, Hitler had ordered the "long-distance barrage against England" to commence by mid-June. The main target was to be London.[48] In his monologues, he talked himself into raptures when speaking about his supposed "miracle weapon": "Panic will break out everywhere in England. The effect of this weapon places such strain on the nerves that no one can withstand it for long."[49] On 5 June, Hitler told Goebbels that preparations were finished, and that 300–400 rockets would rain down on London in the next few days.[50] But the weapon's first deployment on the night of 12–13 June did not live up to the promise. Only ten rockets could be launched, of which four crashed immediately after take-off, one disappeared over the English Channel and just five reached Britain. A second attempt on 15 June was more successful, when 244 rockets were fired, with the majority reaching their target. From that point on, the Germans kept up a steady barrage of the British capital.[51]

On 16 June, the Wehrmacht Supreme Command released its first report about the use of a "novel kind of explosive" over Britain. The news spread like wildfire. Germany's oft-invoked and always postponed "retribution" finally seemed to be becoming a reality. "True enthusiasm," reported the Security Service, gripped circles of "open-minded, positive ethnic-popular comrades," leading to "a certain strengthening of trust in the leadership."[52] At Goebbels' suggestion, Hitler named the rocket the V-1, which suggested that further top-secret weapons would follow.[53] But the propaganda minister was also worried that triumphant newspaper reports would stir false hopes, which would rebound as disappointment when they did not come true. He thus ordered newspapers and radio to adopt a reserved tone in their reporting.[54]

And indeed, the V-1 did not have anywhere near the destructive power that the German side had hoped for, even if this new threat from the air did burden the nerves of Londoners. In relative terms, the number of casualties was limited: 5,842 people were killed and 15,900 injured during June, July and August.[55] Germany's secret weapon "had not changed anything," Andreas-Friedrich wrote on 18 June, and went on to speculate that perhaps it had "only been invented to preserve

German war morale" since "its propaganda effect in Germany far exceeds its destructive effect in England."[56]

By mid-June, any remaining German hopes of pushing the Allied invasion "back into the sea" had been well and truly dashed. Since the Allies dominated the skies, Rundstedt warned, "all major troop movements have become impossible in daylight." Without being hindered in any real way by the Luftwaffe, the enemy was constantly able to move up reinforcements and now threatened to break through to the French interior.[57] At a meeting at the Berghof on 16 June, Keitel and Jodl described the situation as "very serious." If the enemy was able to use his bridgeheads to establish "operational freedom for mobile warfare," they cautioned, all of France would be lost.[58] Hitler's entourage was growing increasingly nervous. The Führer's secretary Traudl Junge recalled feeling like she was "sitting on a powder keg."[59] On the evening of 16 June, Hitler summoned Rundstedt, Rommel and their chiefs of staff for a meeting the following day in the town of Margival, northeast of Soissons. Here the Organisation Todt had constructed the "Wolf's Ravine 2" headquarters, a gigantic collection of bomb-proof bunkers from which Hitler had originally planned to supervise Operation Sea Lion.[60] The facility would only ever be used that day, 17 June 1944, when the dictator arrived there in the early hours from Metz. "He looked pale and sleepless," Rommel's chief of staff, Hans Speidel, recalled five years later in his memoirs. "He played nervously with his glasses and various coloured pencils he held between his fingers. He alone was seated, bent over on a stool, while the field marshals remained standing."[61]

After a few frosty words of greeting, Hitler exploded with rage over the Allied landing, placing the blame for the disaster not on himself and the Wehrmacht Supreme Command, but on local commanders. Rundstedt and Rommel rejected this view, arguing that commanding officers and troops had put in "superhuman performances but had been helpless against the enemy's crushing superiority in the air and on the sea." Both stressed the danger that the invading army could break out of the Caen-Bayeux area and the Cotentin Peninsula and advance in the direction of Paris. They demanded more freedom to manoeuvre and suggested shortening German lines by withdrawing beyond the river Orne. Hitler would not hear of any such retreat, ordering his two commanders to hold the port of Cherbourg, which had been declared a "fortress," and launching into lengthy digressions about how the V-1 rockets would decide the war. Speidel recalled that Rommel tried one final time, with urgency, to warn Hitler that German forces in the west could collapse, encouraging him to seek a negotiated settlement to the war. Hitler snarled back: "Don't you worry about how the war will continue: take care of your front against the invasion."[62]

Yet the confrontation was clearly not as dramatic as Speidel described it, since on the evening of 17 June, after returning to his headquarters, Rommel told his navy liaison officer, Vice-Admiral Friedrich Ruge, that he was satisfied with how the meeting had gone. Hitler had once again proved his powers of persuasion in winning over a sceptic. "He must possess true magnetism," an admiring Ruge remarked.[63] For his part Rommel wrote to his wife that he was "now far less worried than a week ago. The V-1 attack was a huge relief. It is hardly possible that the enemy will achieve a quick breakthrough to Paris. We now receive lots of supplies and reinforcements. The Führer was very nice and in a good mood. He thoroughly recognised the gravity of the situation."[64]

On 18 June, the Americans advanced westwards on the Cotentin Peninsula, cutting off Cherbourg. Hitler ordered the commander of the city, Lieutenant-General Karl-Wilhelm von Schlieben, to hold it at all costs: "I expect you to wage the battle like Gneisenau once did in defending Kolberg [Kołobrzeg]."[65] It was no accident that Hitler chose a comparison with this act of Prussian defiance against long odds during the Napoleonic Wars. In June 1943, four months after the German defeat at Stalingrad, Goebbels had commissioned film director Veit Harlan to make a movie in colour about Prussian resistance to the French at Kolberg Castle in 1807. This mammoth epic, starring Horst Caspar in the role of Major August von Gneisenau and Heinrich George as the militia leader Joachim Nettelbeck, would eventually premiere in Berlin in late January 1945, a few months before the demise of the Third Reich.[66]

Cherbourg would be defended "down to the last bullet," Hitler vowed when he met with Goebbels on 21 June for three hours to discuss the general situation. In the interim, he had ordered two SS tank divisions to be transferred from the east to bolster German forces in the west. This "massive concentration of armoured strength," the Führer thought, would make it possible to "clean out" the Allied bridgehead. With the V-1 having disappointed expectations, the dictator now pinned his hopes to the A-4 rocket, later renamed the V-2, which had been developed at Germany's Peenemünde testing facility and which would first be deployed in early September. While it would not be enough to finish the war directly, Hitler believed it would go "a long way towards deciding [it]."

He could hardly have been more deluded. Even the reverent Goebbels thought that Hitler was viewing the situation "too optimistically," although he kept such doubts to himself. In his diary, he noted that he had not wanted to contradict the Führer, who "has more of an overview and greater expertise." The propaganda minister was in fact all too aware that open contradiction in this critical phase of the war would run the risk of losing him the dictator's favour. He did, however, again try to make his case for radical changes, particularly a "top-to-bottom reform of the Wehrmacht," only to register with disappointment that Hitler did not think the crisis was bad enough to require this most drastic of measures.[67]

The day after his meeting with Goebbels, Hitler addressed a group of generals and officers in the Platterhof Hotel. Once again he launched into an extended screed about war as the expression of an iron law of natural selection and the inevitable triumph of the strong over the weak. He downplayed the critical situation in Cherbourg: there could be no talk of a reconquest of France. The coming months would place great demands on German troops' resilience, the Führer said, but all these dangers could be mastered if officers led their men by example as "true National Socialists."[68] In Hitler's mind, the decisive factor was no longer professional military ability but ideological fanaticism, with which all energies should be rallied for the "final battle."

On 27 June, Allied intelligence services reported the taking of Cherbourg. Hitler flew into a rage that Schlieben, like Paulus in Stalingrad, had allowed himself to be taken prisoner instead of fighting to the last bullet. Officers like Schlieben, he fumed, were "dishonourable swine" who took it for granted that others would sacrifice themselves while thinking only of how to save their own skin.[69] With Cherbourg under their control, the Allies now had a location for coordinating supplies and reinforcements, even if German demolition crews had so badly damaged port facilities that they took weeks to repair. After conquering the Cotentin Peninsula and liberating Cherbourg, however, American progress slowed. It was not until 22 July that US troops would achieve their next major objective, the taking of the city of Saint-Lô. That same day, the British decided the battle for Caen in their favour.[70]

On 29 June, Hitler ordered Rundstedt and Rommel to the Berghof. In a clear sign of disrespect, he kept them waiting for hours, before finally receiving them in the evening. The dictator had by now given up all hope of "clearing out" the Allied bridgehead. His new orders were to "pin down the enemy by establishing a 'containing front' and . . . to wear him down and hem him in through small engagements."[71] By this point, the Red Army had commenced its long-feared major offensive in the east. Much more so than at Margival, things got tetchy when Rommel demanded that Hitler draw the political consequences and try to negotiate a settlement to end the war in the west so as to hold the front in the east. This time Hitler's reaction was more brusque: he told his field marshal that he was only to speak on military matters. When Rommel pressed the point, the Führer banished him from the room.[72]

A few days later, on 3 July, Hitler did indeed draw some consequences, stripping Rundstedt of his command and replacing him with Field Marshal Günther von Kluge, the former commander of Army Group Centre on the eastern front who had recovered from a serious car accident in October 1943. Also relieved of their command were the leader of the Tank Group West, Geyr von Schweppenburg, and Field Marshal Hugo Sperrle, who was responsible for Germany's western air defences. Rommel escaped demotion for the moment, but his reputation within the innermost circles of power in the Third Reich had been badly damaged. The Africa campaign, carped Goebbels, seemed to have "taken such a toll on him that he no longer possesses that flexibility and inner vitality necessary to lead responsibly in such a decisive phase of the war."[73] But Hitler feared a demotion of the "people's general" would be tantamount to a public admission that the situation in the west could no longer be mastered.

Nevertheless, the public mood had hit a new low in late June and early July. "The general elation of the first days after the invasion and our retribution has greatly ebbed," various Security Service reports concluded. Initial hopes that the course of the war could be decisively altered had "given way to much sobriety and scepticism."[74] The German people's greatest concern, however, was the Soviet summer offensive, which had commenced on 22 June and quickly achieved deep breakthroughs in the centre of the eastern front. Psychologically, the unexpectedly rapid advances of the Red Army had created a new situation, Reich propaganda offices reported: "For the first time, the population is seeing the war, which aside from the air raids has played out far away from their homeland, coming perilously close to German borders."[75]

During the first phase of Operation Overlord, all was quiet on the eastern front, causing great bafflement among the German leadership. "Stalin is still standing with his rifle by his side—I wonder why?" Goebbels noted on 20 June.[76] A day later, however, Hitler told him that the Soviet Union was likely to launch its offensive on the symbolic day of 22 June, the third anniversary of Nazi Germany's attack on the USSR.[77] The Führer's prediction would prove correct.

Since March the Soviet general staff had been preparing Operation Bagration, named after Pyotr Bagration, one of the leaders of the Russian army in its war against Napoleon in 1812. After a feint against Finnish troops in Karelia to distract the enemy, the plan was to launch a main assault against German Army Group Centre, with further advances targeting Army Groups Northern and Southern Ukraine. The Red Army amassed an unprecedented concentration of troops in the centre of the front: some 2.5 million soldiers, more than 6,000 tanks and assault guns, and 7,000 warplanes took part in the operation.[78]

The German military leadership expected the main assault to come to the south against Army Group Northern Ukraine and had deployed Wehrmacht reserves there.[79] The three armies of Army Group Centre were thus left with only 34 divisions, numbering around 850,000 men, to defend a front line of 1,100 kilometres. When it came to equipment, the Soviet advantage was even greater. Red Army units had nine times the amount of artillery, ten times as many warplanes and twenty-three times as many tanks as their German foes. Moreover, numerous partisan groups were operating behind German lines, hindering reinforcements and supplies. As Colonel-General Hans-Georg Reinhardt characterised it in June, the weakened Army Group Centre resembled "a house of cards ready to fall."[80]

It was therefore no wonder that in the first days of the offensive the Red Army quickly succeeded in creating deep breaches in German lines. To the north, the 3rd Belorussian Front broke through the positions of the 3rd German Tank Army near Vitebsk on 22 June, surrounding five German divisions. In a reference to the Battle of Amiens on 8 August 1918, which had ushered in the military defeat of Wilhelmine Germany in the First World War, Reinhardt described 22 June 1944 as a "Black Friday."[81] Soviet tank units poured westwards almost unimpeded through holes ripped in the German lines. On 23 and 24 June, the inferno descended upon the German 4th and 9th Armies further to the south. In a series of graded, concentrated attacks, the 1st and 2nd Belorussian Fronts also broke through German positions and surrounded most of the 9th Army near Bobruisk.[82] "How is it possible that the situation on the eastern front, which only a week ago our generals told us had been consolidated, has suddenly become so critical?" Goebbels asked himself.[83] He was not the only one to pose that question.

On 26 June, the commander of Army Group Centre, Field Marshal Ernst Busch, flew to Berchtesgaden to brief Hitler on the gravity of the situation. Still the dictator stubbornly stuck to his strategy of defending the "strongholds" of Vitebsk, Orsha, Mogilev and Bobruisk as long as possible. Yet his orders to hold out were obsolete before they even reached the troops. Two days later, Busch, who had always blindly followed Hitler, was relieved of his command. Once again, a high-ranking military commander was made a scapegoat after a defeat. Busch had "failed to bring the necessary flexibility to the leadership of Army Group Centre" was how Hitler justified his decision.[84] Busch's replacement was Hitler's favourite military commander, Field Marshal Walter Model, who took up the task in addition to his command of Army Group Northern Ukraine. "Model will certainly do everything that must be done to stop the fall backwards," wrote Goebbels, agreeing with his master.[85]

But the situation could hardly have been more desperate. Four hundred kilometres of the German front had been ripped open, and in places, the Red Army had advanced 150 kilometres westwards. Around Minsk the pincers were beginning to close. Now it was the

Red Army that successfully waged the battles of encirclement with which the Wehrmacht had achieved their greatest triumphs in the summer of 1941. The Soviets were aided by Hitler's doctrine of holding out at all costs. In his Operational Directive No. 8 of 28 June 1944, the Führer had arbitrarily drawn another line on the map, behind which "no territory shall be given up without a fight."[86] The 4th Army suffered most from this strategic blunder. Caught in a system of "wandering cauldrons," it tried to fight its way west. Before the river Berezina, where Napoleon's Grande Armée had also met its match in 1812, the situation descended into chaos as German troops were exposed, nearly defence-less, to Soviet aerial attacks.[87] On 3 July, the Belorussian capital, Minsk, was liberated. "The Red Army passed by like a typhoon. The enemy has scuttled off in disarray . . . ," a Soviet communications engineer noted the following day, almost at a loss for words at the tempo of his army's advance. "Even the Germans did not manage this in 1941."[88]

In late June, Zeitzler had drafted an operational plan to save Army Group Centre from certain destruction. It had Army Group North, which was also at risk of being surrounded, evacuate the northern Baltic territory and retreat to the lower Dvina River. The troops freed up by shortening the front would be assigned to reinforce the embat-tled Army Group Centre. On 30 June, Zeitzler passionately sought Hitler's approval for the plan. When he failed he asked to be relieved of his post: "My Führer, you have forced me to act against my convic-tion twice—once at Stalingrad and again with regard to Crimea. I am not going to allow myself to be forced a third time."[89] Shortly after-wards, Zeitzler suffered a complete breakdown. He was temporarily replaced by the head of the Operations Division, Adolf Heusinger, before Guderian was given the post on 21 July. The more hopeless Germany's situation became, the quicker Hitler wore out his top military personnel.

On 8 July, Soviet troops surrounded Vilnius. Hitler had declared that city too a "fortress," but Heusinger succeeded in getting his approval for German troops to attempt a breakout.[90] The Red Army was now advancing closer and closer towards East Prussia. Goebbels was under no illusions about what this meant. "We are experiencing an extraordinary crisis of our Reich and people, one that may prove under certain circumstances to be fatal," he confided to his diary.[91] Hitler had nowhere near such a clear-eyed view of the situation. On

9 July, he flew to Rastenburg to meet with Model and the new commander of Army Group North, Colonel-General Johannes Friessner. Both generals expressed confidence that they could bring the situation under control if they were given fresh new divisions quickly, and a somewhat mollified Hitler returned that same day to his Alpine retreat.[92] Model did in fact succeed in temporarily stabilising the front along the Kaunas–Brest-Litovsk line. But on 13 July, the 1st Ukrainian Front launched an attack on the Army Group Northern Ukraine, smashing German positions within a few days and advancing deep into Galicia. On 18 July, the left wing of the 1st Belarussian Front launched an assault on the German salient at Kovel, ripping open a 100-kilometre-wide gap between Army Group Northern Ukraine and Army Group Centre, which allowed the Soviet armies to push westwards. On 24 July, they took Lublin and liberated the Majdanek death camp. The following day, the Soviet vanguard reached the Vistula. Warsaw was in their sights.[93]

By mid-July, the Red Army had advanced almost 400 kilometres. Twenty-eight divisions of Army Group Centre had been destroyed or so badly weakened that they could no longer operate. German casualties were enormous. According to the latest estimates, 250,000 Wehrmacht soldiers fell in the first three weeks of Operation Bagration, 130,000 from the 4th Army alone. "This is the greatest military defeat we have experienced in the course of this war," a shocked Goebbels noted. "Even Stalingrad has been overshadowed."[94]

Hitler was no longer content to follow the action from the Obersalzberg. On the evening of 14 July, he returned to his East Prussian headquarters, where workers from the Organisation Todt were still occupied with securing Restricted Zone I of the Wolf's Lair. The old bunkers had been given a seven-metre-thick shell of concrete so that they loomed up like camouflaged Egyptian pyramids through the treetops. Since the interior reconstruction of Hitler's bunker was not yet finished, he temporarily moved into the bunker reserved for guests. Situation meetings were held in a nearby barracks that was only provisionally protected against shrapnel from bombs.[95]

Several days after his arrival, Hitler received a telegram from Rommel of a sort to which the dictator was not accustomed. The situation in Normandy, the field marshal wrote, was getting "more difficult by the day" and was approaching a "serious crisis." It was likely that the Allies would succeed in the near future in breaking through the thin German front and "advancing into the breadth of French territory." Rommel concluded his missive with an appeal: "The troops are fighting heroically everywhere, but this uneven battle is nearing its end. I must ask you to draw immediate consequences from this situation."[96] That sounded like an ultimatum, but Rommel was never to learn how Hitler responded. On 17 July, while he was on an inspection tour in Normandy, his car was strafed by Allied warplanes. Rommel's driver was killed, and he himself seriously wounded, putting him out of commission for weeks.[97]

That very day, a symbolic parade was held in Moscow as fifty thousand German POWs were made to march through the city centre. Muscovites turned out to watch the spectacle with satisfaction. So this was what Hitler's victory-spoiled warriors looked like, who thought they could conquer the entire expanse of land to the Urals, enslaving and destroying local populations. The pathetic procession was showered in curses and oaths.[98]

12

The Berghof during the War

"The Führer intends to transfer his working base from the Obersalzberg to the Wolf's Lair," noted Goebbels on 14 July 1944. "From there, he wants to direct the entire defence of East Prussia, not just militarily, but also politically. I think this is an excellent idea."[1] Hitler had put off returning to his East Prussian headquarters for quite some time, but the catastrophic collapse of Army Group Centre now left him no other choice. On the evening before his departure, in the Berghof's Great Hall, he walked past all the paintings of which he was so proud, studying them for quite some time. After that he took wordless leave from the female members of his entourage. He probably suspected that he was saying goodbye for ever.[2]

For Hitler, the Berghof had always been both a refuge, where he could live a private life undisturbed by curious onlookers, and a second centre of government rivalling the Chancellery in Berlin. Yet during the war, his Alpine residence also became the "Führer's military head-quarters" whenever Germany's commander-in-chief spent a stretch of time on the Obersalzberg. On these occasions the Wehrmacht Supreme Command under Keitel and Jodl took over the branch office that the Reich Chancellery had opened near Berchtesgaden in 1937. Until late 1942, the Wehrmacht general staff worked on a special train at Salzburg station and then resided in a riflemen's barracks in Bischofswiesen. As a rule the army chief of staff arrived once a week from the Führer's field headquarters to give a report.[3]

The more Hitler took over the direction of military operations, the more he was needed in those field headquarters, especially when something unforeseen happened. On the other hand, his deteriorating health repeatedly forced him to take breaks of various length to recuperate. Thus, over the course of the war, in accordance with Germany's fortunes his visits to the Berghof became not only rarer but more irregular.

After visiting the western front, Hitler ushered in the New Year 1940 on the Obersalzberg, as he had before the war.[4] In the months that followed, which were devoted to preparing the western offensive, he mostly stayed in Berlin, only returning to his Alpine residence in late March for Easter. "Those were four pleasant and restorative days," Nicolaus von Below recalled. Hitler had given up his favourite form of entertainment, nightly film screenings, because he felt they were inappropriate during the war, but otherwise his life in the mountains followed his normal routines.[5]

In the second half of 1940, after Germany's victory over France and his triumphant reception in Berlin in early July, Hitler shuttled constantly between Berlin, Munich and the Obersalzberg.[6] During this time, as we have seen, he distanced himself from the plan to invade Britain and became determined to attack the Soviet Union. That Christmas, he visited German troops on the western front, as he had the previous year, and then celebrated the New Year on the Obersalzberg. On New Year's Eve he toasted Germany's "final victory" with his guests, all of whom believed that it was now assured.[7] With only one brief interruption, Hitler stayed at his Alpine residence until mid-March 1941, drawing up operational plans with his generals for his war with the Soviet Union. Before the start of Operation Barbarossa, he returned to the Berghof for another month—not least to spread confusion about his intent to launch his eastern attack. "Calm before the storm," Goebbels wrote about Hitler's trip south. "It will not last long."[8]

The unexpected failure of Germany's Soviet campaign and the turning point in the war that came in the winter of 1941–42 kept Hitler in his headquarters near Rastenburg, and the traditional New Year's celebrations at the Berghof were cancelled. It was only in late April 1942, after an absence of more than ten months, that Hitler returned to his mountain residence for several days, during which he met Mussolini. There was little sense in the Bavarian Alps that a war was on and Munich had yet to suffer any air raids. But the Obersalzberg was hardly the idyll it had once been. There was constant building work. On the express orders of Göring in his function as the head of the Four-Year Plan, construction at the Berghof was classified as essential to the war effort, and even as raw materials grew scarce, the companies charged with carrying out the work were given whatever they needed.[9] Martin Bormann, who supervised the construction projects, insisted that they be finished as soon as possible. In 1936, the architect Roderick Fick had taken over responsibility for the building sites from Alois Degano, but he had to cede it in late 1941, at Bormann's behest, to the general building inspector of Munich, Hermann Giesler, who three years later was also put in charge of remaking Linz. At its height, some six thousand men worked in construction on the Obersalzberg, including increasing numbers of slave labourers.[10]

In June 1942, before the beginning of the summer offensive in the east, Hitler spent nine days of calm in his Alpine residence. He returned in November for what he planned to be an extended stay. "Being cooped up for long periods in his field headquarters with the same people was torturous for him," his navy liaison Karl-Jesko von Puttkamer wrote.[11] But the dramatically worsening situation at Stalingrad forced the Führer to depart in his special train for the Wolf's Lair after only ten days.[12] It would not be until March 1943 that Hitler issued orders to his entourage to head for Bavaria. Traudl Humps, a young woman who had been hired as a secretary in December 1942, described Hitler's hectic departure: "Everything had to happen secretly and quickly. People were constantly talking on the telephone. The Berghof management had to be informed about our arrival, the Führer's apartment in Munich had to be ready to receive him, and the special train, which always stood ready close by, had to be equipped for a long journey and many guests."[13]

This time round, the dictator spent almost three months on the Obersalzberg, until early July 1943, just before German troops launched their Kursk offensive.[14] But the hopes of Hitler's retinue, above all Goebbels, that the Führer would be revived by the fresh mountain air and regain his previous vigour were largely disappointed.[15] Hitler had spent almost all of April receiving the leaders of Germany's allies and had rarely found the chance to relax in the months that followed.

The general mood at the Berghof was no longer as carefree as it had been in previous years. "Hitler would sit quietly before the giant fireplace, as he often did now, staring for hours into the flames" was how Albert Speer recalled a visit in late November 1942.[16] The preceding

September Munich had been hit for the first time by a major air raid, the first of thirty-one aerial bombardments over the course of the war.[17] When Goebbels travelled from Salzburg to the Obersalzberg on 24 June 1943, he might not have noticed much of a change: "The region is suffused with a peace that almost seems unreal . . . In Berchtesgaden, spa guests stroll around as if they were trying not to pay any heed to the war."[18] But Hitler thought it was only a matter of time before Allied bombers targeted the Obersalzberg. For him, as he remarked, it was "almost a given" that his Alpine retreat would be destroyed.[19]

The summer of 1943 saw another flurry of activity. Flak guns were positioned on the heights surrounding the Obersalzberg, and machinery installed to cover the entire area in artificial fog as soon as the air-raid sirens sounded. By Christmas, the first section of a 130-metre-long series of subterranean bunkers had been completed. It was only a few steps from the back of the main house to the bunker entrance, and sixty-six steps further down there were living spaces and bedrooms for Hitler and Eva Braun, personnel quarters and a kitchen, well-stocked pantries and safe storage for valuable art works, files and books. Tunnels were also carved out of solid rock beneath Bormann's and Göring's nearby country homes and the Platterhof Hotel. They and other tunnels were connected by narrow passageways so that "the entire Obersalzberg was undermined like a gigantic molehill."[20]

Thus when Hitler arrived back at the Berghof at the end of February 1944, after an absence of seven months since his one-day stopover on his way to meeting Mussolini in Feltre on 19 July 1943, his security was assured. His last stay at his Alpine residence would also be his longest: he remained there for almost five months.[21] From the time of his arrival until April, it snowed almost constantly. Metres of snow piled up, and it took a lot of effort to clear a narrow path up to the teahouse on the Mooslahnerkopf Hill.[22] Hitler again received a number of state visitors during these months, including Romania's Marshal Ion Antonescu, Slovakian president Jozef Tiso, Hungarian prime minister Döme Sztójay and Japanese ambassador Hiroshi Oshima. Here he also gave his final speeches to large audiences of generals and business leaders. However, what had been his great strength, extemporaneous speaking, was becoming more and more difficult. His address to about one hundred representatives of the armaments industry at the Platterhof Hotel on 26 June 1944, for example, was a fiasco. As Speer, who had encouraged the Führer to accept this engagement, remembered: "He misspoke often, stammered, failed to finish sentences or connect his thoughts and sometimes got confused. His speech was proof that he was terribly exhausted . . . None of us could believe it."[23] By this point, it could no longer be denied that the Allied invasion in the west had succeeded and that the Wehrmacht had little to counter the suffocating superiority of the Red Army. On the Obersalzberg a mood of despair and demise was spreading throughout Hitler's entourage.[24]

All told Hitler spent nearly 400 days, over a year, of the war at the Berghof, and just like in peacetime, a certain daily rhythm was established during his stays there.[25] The Führer would rise late, awakened by a valet, between 11 a.m. and noon, whereupon his personal physician would often administer a pick-me-up injection. The Führer would then eat breakfast alone in his office on the first floor. Around 1 p.m., cars brought the military leaders from Berchtesgaden, and the officers, orderlies and stenographers would make their way to the Great Hall for the day's first situation briefing. It usually lasted for two hours, but could take longer. Meanwhile, Hitler's guests would pass the time in their rooms or on the terrace if the weather was nice. Occasionally Eva Braun would impatiently ask one of Hitler's adjutants if the meeting looked as though it would be short or long.

As soon as Hitler emerged from the Great Hall and greeted his hungry entourage, his bearing would suddenly alter. "I noticed with admiration that the man who had just come from a situation briefing left all of his grave work thoughts behind the heavy drapes that separated the hall from the living room," recalled one of Hitler's secretaries. "His face was that of a cheerful host entertaining company in his country home."[26] His chameleon-like ability to change roles from one moment to the next was a mark of Hitler's skill at transforming and disguising himself. It allowed him at table to play the role of the charming, congenial host seemingly unconcerned with the urgent problems of the day.

Lunch rarely took more than an hour and was usually followed by a walk to the small teahouse, which provided Hitler with an opportunity to engage in a confidential chat with the lucky guest at his side.[27] After returning to the Berghof, the dictator would repair to his office for an hour or two to read the newspapers and study the news wire reports. The rest of the company would prepare for dinner, which was usually served between 8:00 and 8:30 p.m. No sooner had the evening meal ended than the military men would reappear for a second situation briefing. When that was over, Hitler would review the coming weekly newsreel in the Great Hall, sometimes ordering changes not only to the footage but to the accompanying script as well.[28] The day concluded with nighttime conversation before the fireplace which, as was also the case in the Wolf's Lair, often extended into the early hours. Here too Hitler dominated the proceedings, condemning his guests to the role of passive listeners. Still, Otto Dietrich, the Reich press chief, frequently felt that the dictator's thoughts were somewhere else: "Every now and then, when the conversation faltered, Hitler demanded to be brought reports from the Wehrmacht Supreme Command, the Foreign Ministry and the press, and went off to a neighbouring room with his on-duty adjutants, if he thought important instructions needed to be issued."[29] Before taking final leave of his guests and withdrawing to his upstairs quarters, he would ring the bell for his valet Heinz Linge and ask if there had been any reports of Allied bombers having crossed the Reich's borders.

During Hitler's stay at the Berghof in the spring and summer of 1944, however, this rhythm began to change. Air-raid sirens now sounded nearly every day, frequently in the early morning hours. The fog machines sprang into action, and Hitler's sleepy-eyed guests would seek refuge with their luggage in the underground caverns. The Führer was woken up at even the most preliminary of alarms, and he got dressed quickly. Surrounded by his adjutants, he would inspect the effectiveness of the fog machines from the Berghof terrace. He rarely took cover in the bunkers, and when he did it was only after the flak guns had opened fire on the bomber squadrons far overhead. It is possible that he was unable to climb down to safety. In early March 1944, Goebbels observed to his dismay that Hitler found it "very difficult" to descend or ascend the sixty-six steps and had to "walk very slowly."[30] At the same time, Hitler insisted that no member of his court leave the bunkers before the all-clear was sounded. At table, he admonished his guests that it was "a sign not of bravery, but rather stupidity," if they did not get themselves to safety.[31]

Yet not a single bomb fell on the Obersalzberg until the final days of the war. In a proclamation on 24 February 1945, Hitler even expressed regret that the Berghof had been spared for so long, saying that he did not want to have it any better than his "ethnic-popular comrades."[32] But the inequity would eventually be redressed. On 25 April, only a few days before Hitler's suicide in Berlin, British Lancaster bombers launched a major attack on the Obersalzberg, inflicting heavy damage. The Berghof was hit directly, and SS men burned down the ruins when they withdrew from the site.[33] Thomas Mann's son Klaus, then a reporter for the US Army newspaper *Stars and Stripes*, arrived at the Berghof together with American GIs on 8 May, the day the Wehrmacht surrendered. "After the bombs had terribly cleared out this place, plunderers had dutifully gone about their work," he later remembered. "Broken walls and charred beams, deep craters full of rubble and ash, smashed furniture, shards and filth, a pile of ruin."[34] What remained of Hitler's Alpine residence was demolished in late April 1952.

The society that frequented the Berghof during the Second World War hardly differed from Hitler's regular company before 1939. First and foremost it consisted of the Führer's consort Eva Braun, her sister Gretl and friends Herta Schneider and Marion Schönmann. Reichsleiter Martin Bormann, who as of April 1943 was also the Führer's secretary, was always at Hitler's side, ready and willing to fulfil his every wish. Other favourite guests were Albert and Margarete Speer, the physicians Karl Brandt and Theodor Morell, and Walther Hewel, although Ribbentrop's liaison officer was badly injured in the plane crash that killed General Hans Hube in April 1944 and only able to return to his position at the end of that year.[35] Other individuals who were constantly present included Hitler's personal staff: Reich press chief Otto Dietrich and his deputy Heinz Lorenz; the head of the Führer's SS bodyguard, Leibstandarte *Adolf Hitler*, Sepp Dietrich; and military adjutants Rudolf Schmundt (head adjutant), Karl-Jesko von Puttkamer (navy), Gerhard Engel and (as of 1943) Heinrich Borgmann (army), and Nicolaus von Below (Luftwaffe) with his wife Maria. Then there were the Führer's personal adjutants Friedrich Darges, Otto Günsche and Martin Bormann's brother Albert (the two mutually detested one another).

Hitler's chief personal adjutant, Wilhelm Brückner, had fallen from grace in October 1940, after Arthur Kannenberg, the manager of Hitler's household at the Reich Chancellery, began scheming against him.[36] Brückner was replaced by Julius Schaub, whom Speer once called "Hitler's most loyal follower."[37] During Germany's campaign against Poland in 1939, Hitler had fired his long-time valet Karl Krause because of a minor infraction.[38] As of 1940, Heinz Linge and Hans Junge took care of Hitler's domestic affairs. Junge married the Führer's secretary Traudl Humps in June 1943 and fell in battle in August 1944 after he had asked to be sent to the front.[39] He was replaced by Wilhelm Arndt, who had learned his trade at hotel school in Munich's Pasing district. Along with the valets, Hitler's secretaries—Johanna Wolf, Christa Schroeder and Traudl Junge—were on constant call at the Berghof. Hitler's fourth secretary, Gerda Daranowski, married Luftwaffe major and Wehrmacht staff officer Eckhard Christian in November 1942 and only returned to Hitler's service at the end of the following year. Hitler's wedding present was a cheque for 10,000 reichs-marks, and he also paid for the renovation of a flat confiscated from a deported Berlin Jew, which Speer in his capacity as Reich general building inspector had signed over to her as Hitler's secretary.[40]

Heinrich Hoffmann remained another frequent Berghof guest, although Hitler grew increasingly irritated with his former confidant's alcoholism. "Hoffmann, your nose looks like a rotten pumpkin," he once told his "court photographer" when he turned up inebriated. "I bet you would explode if someone held a match to your mouth when you exhaled. Before long red wine will flow in your veins instead of blood."[41] Goebbels, by contrast, was always welcome since he was a good entertainer and always cheered Hitler up. No one in the Führer's company could match the propaganda minister's sharp wit, which he usually exercised at others' cost. When Otto Dietrich once remarked that he often got his best ideas in the bathtub, Goebbels shot back: "Then you should bathe far more frequently, Doctor Dietrich!"[42]

New to Berghof society during the war was cameraman Walter Frentz, who had worked with Leni Riefenstahl and from 1939 was the "film reporter" responsible for the footage of Hitler used in the weekly newsreels. He used his stays on the Obersalzberg to take hundreds of images of the life and goings-on at the Berghof, including not just arrivals and departures of official state visitors, but private shots of the guests. At the behest of Eva Braun, he took a series of photographs of her together with Hitler and her friend Herta Schneider's children— staged images simulating a family. Other Frentz pictures show guests relaxing together on the terrace and in front of the Great Hall fireplace in the evening, or Hitler strolling to the teahouse accompanied by Goebbels, Himmler or Hewel.[43] Frentz obviously enjoyed the particular trust of Braun, who was a passionate amateur photographer and film-maker herself,[44] and both tried to capture the private Hitler without any of his Führer poses.

Nonetheless, as the war went on, it became increasingly difficult to maintain this seeming idyll. Neither Frentz's photographic portraits nor Braun's home movies could conceal the fact that Hitler had aged dramatically. In March 1944, Braun put on a private screening of some colour film footage she had taken in 1939 and 1942 for a select handful of guests. Afterwards Goebbels noted that you could see "how much the Führer has changed during the war. Back then he was a young man, and now he has grown older and older and walks with a pronounced hunch."[45] Hitler's Munich housekeeper, Anni Winter, was also struck by the changes in Hitler when she visited the Berghof for a final time in June 1944: "He seemed to have deteriorated terribly. His vision had declined to the point that a typewriter with letters three times the normal size was needed to produce the notes he had dictated, which he then read out loud."[46]

By contrast, Eva Braun—Hoffmann's shy, reserved former darkroom assistant—had grown more confident. She no longer had to fight for her position within Hitler's court but was generally accepted and respected by company as the first lady of the Berghof.[47] Traudl Junge was surprised when she first saw Braun on the Obersalzberg in late March 1943: "She was very well dressed and turned out, and I was impressed by how natural and at ease she was. She did not look at all like the ideal of young German womanhood you saw in League of German Girls ads and fashion magazines. Her well-groomed hair was dyed blond, and her pretty face had been made up with a fair amount of cosmetics, but also very tastefully."[48] The domestic personnel at the Berghof addressed her respectfully as "Dear Miss" or "Ma'am," and the guests simply called her "Miss Braun."[49] Her relationship with Hitler had grown noticeably more intimate. Within the trusted circle of invited guests, they addressed one another informally, and in the evening in front of the fireplace, they held hands—something they had never previously done in front of other people.[50]

Braun took liberties towards Hitler that were unthinkable for others. At table, she dared to openly disagree with him and would pointedly ask the time when the dictator had launched into one of his endless monologues. As Schroeder recalled: "Hitler would then stop talking and excuse the company from the table."[51] Once, at the teahouse, Braun criticised him for his hunched posture. Hitler took this with astonishing aplomb, joking that the reason was "the heavy keys in his front pocket" and the "whole sack of worries" he carried with him.[52] During the long months Hitler spent at the Wolf's Lair, Braun occasionally wrote him letters in which she complained about petty bureaucratic disruptions to her daily life. They spoke far more often on the phone, however. After Stalingrad, it was said that Hitler called Braun almost every day.[53] Whenever an air raid was reported on Munich, Hitler would pace around "like a lion in a cage" until he had made contact with his lover, Junge recalled.[54] Braun by no means lapsed into melancholy when Hitler was not around. On the contrary, she threw festive parties at the Berghof or in her Munich villa, went swimming with visitors in the Königssee on hot summer days and travelled to Italy once a year with her mother and friends, the last time in the summer of 1942.[55]

Goebbels was well aware of Braun's increased status in Hitler's court. For many years, he did not mention the existence of the Führer's lover in his diary—no doubt out of discretion but also because he felt she did not have much influence on the dictator. That changed in the second half of the war. During a visit to the Obersalzberg in late June 1943, Goebbels engaged Braun in an extended conversation for the first time. "She made the finest impression on me," he noted in his diary. "She is extraordinarily well read and extraordinarily clear and mature in her judgements on artistic questions, and she will certainly be a worthwhile source of support for the Führer."[56] On a trip to the Wolf's Lair the following August, the attentive Goebbels also registered that Hitler had spoken with the greatest respect for his consort, emphasising "in the most complimentary terms . . . her calm, clever and matter-of-fact manner." The propaganda minister added: "Eva Braun is a clever girl who means a great deal to the Führer."[57] Goebbels was well aware that if he was to continue to enjoy Hitler's favour, he could no longer ignore Braun. For that reason, he began paying considerable attention to her whenever they met on the Obersalzberg. At dinner in early June 1944, for instance, he talked to her at length about film and theatre, writing afterwards: "Here, too, Miss Braun is developing an extraordinarily accurate, critical ability to differentiate."[58] It is difficult to say, however, whether this was Goebbels' true opinion or whether he wrote these lines in the belief his diaries would be published one day.[59]

What Hitler seems to have valued about Braun in particular was her absolute loyalty. On various occasions, he said that she was the only person who would "stay true down to the final decisive hour."[60] In the end, Hitler's feelings would not be disappointed. As Germany's coming defeat was becoming increasingly clear in the spring and summer of 1944, in her unself-conscious way Braun entertained and distracted her guests from the grim reality.[61] In April of that year, she even hired the magician Helmut Schreiber, alias "Kalanag." Assisted by his wife, for two weeks he put on magic shows almost every evening in the Great Hall. Hitler is said to have perked up noticeably during the performances, frequently laughing and applauding.

The eerie juxtaposition of Berghof society enjoying themselves in such seemingly harmless fashion and the horrific reality of war and genocide was only possible because Hitler's entourage repressed and refused to discuss what was going on. It was an iron-clad rule that there was to be no talk about the increasingly dire military situation at meals. Hitler's guests mostly conversed about anodyne topics like the latest fashion, films and theatrical productions. Hitler would tell stories about the pranks he played as a schoolboy and the amusing things that happened during his "battle years," not caring how many times his guests had already heard these tales. He enjoyed holding forth on the health risks of eating meat, although he does not seem to have spoiled the appetite of his guests. When Maria von Below, Anni Brandt or Margarete Speer were present at table, he played the concerned host who took an interest in how their children were doing.[62]

Hitler's final stay at the Berghof from late February to mid-July 1944 coincided with the last chapter of the Holocaust: the deportation and murder of Hungarian Jews. It is likely that Hitler discussed this act of genocide with Himmler when the latter came to visit in early April.[63] In an address to Wehrmacht officers in the Platterhof Hotel on 26 May 1944, he left no doubt as to the fate he had in mind for the Jews of Hungary. "I have intervened here, and this problem, too, will now be solved," he told his audience.[64] There is no doubt that the members of Hitler's entourage knew about these crimes against humanity, but even in private conversations, they seem to have kept silent about them.[65]

Only once was this taboo subject broached. After the war, Henriette von Schirach claimed that she had told Hitler one evening in April 1943, during their usual get-together in the Great Hall, about watching from an Amsterdam hotel window as Jewish women were herded together and deported. Hitler at first listened calmly to this story, but then all of a sudden he jumped up and shouted at her: "You are being sentimental! What concern of yours are Jewesses from Holland?"[66] However, it is doubtful that this scene unfolded as Henriette and Baldur von Schirach later claimed: no witnesses ever corroborated their story. Hitler's secretary Christa Schroeder only heard it from Henriette von Schirach herself in 1978, and it was related secondhand to Traudl Humps by Hans Junge.[67]

There was definitely a confrontation between Hitler and the Schirachs at the Berghof in late June 1943, although it was not about inhumanity towards Jews but about Baldur von Schirach's post as Reich representative in Vienna. Goebbels was present and described this episode extensively in his diaries. It seems that Hitler had displayed his old antipathy towards the people of Vienna, which he expressed in effusively praising the behaviour of Berliners during the war over that of the Viennese. For that reason, he announced, he would one day make Berlin into the "most beautiful city in the world," while neglecting the Austrian capital. When the Schirachs countered that "Vienna is also a city enthusiastic about National Socialism," Hitler did not tolerate any contradiction and responded extremely aggressively. "Mrs. von Schirach was very taken aback by what the Führer said to her and had tears in her eyes," Goebbels noted. "But the Führer refused to budge . . . He answered her with a severity that was truly extraordinary. [Baldur von] Schirach seemed to shrink and held his tongue . . . Afterwards, Mrs. von Schirach expressed her unhappiness by asking to be allowed to return with her husband to Munich . . . The Führer categorically refused, saying that Schirach had a responsibility to carry out his assignment from the party and the Reich in Vienna."[68] As of this evening, the Schirachs had fallen from grace and were never again invited to the Berghof. Weeks after the incident, Hitler still took umbrage at Henriette von Schirach's behaviour, remarking that it had enraged him down to the last bone in his body.[69]

The estrangement between Hitler and the Schirachs indicated that behind the harmonious Berghof façade, tensions were growing within the Führer's entourage. As long as the war was going well, conflicts could be bridged by the prospects that would open up for each individual member of this closed society in a German-dominated Europe. But the more "final victory" was revealed as a chimera, the more jealousy and rivalries made themselves felt.[70] In late June 1943, after learning from Alfred Bormann and Julius Schaub about the backstabbing that had arisen at the Berghof, Goebbels noted angrily in his diary: "This entire retinue of court jesters and irresponsible agitators should go to hell."[71]

Even the occasional parties were only temporarily able to paper over the cracks in Berghof society. Hitler deliberately chose to celebrate his fifty-fourth and fifty-fifth birthdays in 1943 and 1944 in the isolation of his mountain residence, and as in previous years, gifts and good wishes piled up everywhere, Hitler's entourage and personnel lined up to congratulate him at midnight, and the Speer and Bormann children, carrying bouquets of flowers and dressed up in fancy clothes, recited a happy birthday wish. But on both occasions the mood was decidedly non-festive, and already by the afternoon the military situation had taken over again. On the day of his fifty-fifth birthday Hitler inspected new tank and assault gun models on a stretch of motorway near Salzburg.[72]

On 3 June 1944, only three days before D-Day, there was another lavish party at the Obersalzberg, as Eva Braun's sister Gretl married SS-Gruppenführer Hermann Fegelein. In 1943, the then thirty-seven-year-old former director of the SS Cavalry Academy in Munich had commanded the 8th SS Cavalry Division during its actions against "partisans" in the Pripet Marshes and had been responsible for some of the worst German crimes committed against Soviet civilians. He was wounded and after his recovery, in early 1944, he became the

Waffen-SS liaison to Hitler. Eva Braun apparently liked this highly decorated SS officer, who was known as a lady's man and something of a braggart, and saw to it that he was regularly invited to dine at the Berghof. She also arranged for him to marry her sister.

The two were wed at Salzburg town hall, and the witnesses were Himmler and Bormann. Afterwards, Hitler invited the young couple and their wedding guests to lunch at the Berghof. Following that, the group—without Hitler—ascended to the Kehlstein teahouse. "Celebrations went on in all the rooms," Hitler's valets Linge and Günsche later recalled. "A band played dance music. Waiters served champagne, liqueurs and the most elegant treats. Eva Braun was all aglow . . . She danced, flirted and enjoyed the party the most of all." The celebrations carried on until the early hours in Bormann's villa.[73] It was the final party to be held on the Obersalzberg. The revellers were dancing on the edge of the abyss.

13

The Stauffenberg Assassination Attempt and Its Aftermath

"I suspected all the time that something like this was coming," Hitler told his secretary Christa Schroeder shortly after 20 July 1944, when a bomb placed by Count Claus Schenk von Stauffenberg detonated in the Wolf's Lair barracks where the situation meetings were held.[1] The dictator had feared being assassinated ever since he became German chancellor in January 1933, and over the years the measures to protect him had been tightened again and again. Every trip Hitler made in his special train, for instance, was kept top secret,[2] and in the autumn of 1943, a special Restricted Zone A, to which only Hitler's closest circle had access, was set up within what was already the heavily fortified Restricted Zone 1.[3] The more Hitler withdrew from public life and retreated into the bunkers of his field headquarters, the safer he seemed. He and his entourage were less afraid of an assassination than an aerial attack. In September 1943, Goebbels again posed the question of whether the Wolf's Lair was adequately guarded against an assault by paratroopers.[4] Those around the Führer also ensured that his vegetarian food was thoroughly checked to prevent any possibility of him being poisoned.[5]

Nonetheless, in February 1944, rumours began to spread that an assassination plot was underfoot. While reading through his daily press briefing, Hitler stumbled across a report from Stockholm, according to which an army staff officer had been chosen to shoot him dead with a pistol. Hitler's adjutant Nicolaus von Below immediately consulted with SS-Gruppenführer Hans Rattenhuber, who was responsible for the Führer's security. Together, they decided that in future all visitors to the Wolf's Lair would have to be thoroughly searched for weapons.[6]

Hitler himself initially thought such enhanced checks superfluous. He knew there was no such thing as total security, and perhaps he believed that his ability to sniff out danger would not desert him if things got critical. He often had premonitions of peril, he confessed to Mussolini immediately after the assassination attempt on the afternoon of 20 July. During the First World War, Hitler boasted, he had frequently leaped from his foxhole just in the nick of time because he was certain a shell would explode there.[7] The dictator would repeat this claim over and over again in the weeks that followed. In late August, he still talked of the premonition that something was going to happen to him, which had weighed upon him "like an Alpine mountain" even before his departure from the Obersalzberg. He had given Eva Braun instructions about what to do in case of his death, he added. As Goebbels, always Hitler's most loyal disciple, commented: "The prophetic vision the Führer possesses is truly astonishing. He has secret powers we cannot explain."[8]

Plans to get rid of Hitler or at least to strip him of power had been discussed since the autumn of 1938. Back then, a group of regime opponents from the Wehrmacht, the diplomatic corps and the Abwehr (the military intelligence division of the Wehrmacht Supreme Command) had come together with the goal of preventing Hitler's aggression towards Czechoslovakia, which they feared would lead to war with the Western powers. But the Munich Agreement had undermined this vaguely conceived "September conspiracy." The following year, plans were again discussed to prevent the German attack Hitler had ordered in the west immediately after the Polish campaign. This second attempt at offering resistance also failed, in part because no military leaders could bring themselves to take decisive action.[9] They could of course have followed the example of the southern German carpenter Georg Elser, who had displayed such great courage and skill installing explosives in Munich's Bürgerbräukeller. As we have seen, it was only luck, and not some innate ability to read the future, that had allowed the dictator to cheat death on 8 November 1939.[10]

Germany's military successes in the spring and summer of 1940 paralysed the small group of Hitler opponents within the army. The scepticism of the military leadership towards Hitler seemed to have been refuted. The Führer's go-for-broke strategy had not led to catastrophe, as they had predicted, but to barely imaginable Wehrmacht triumphs. The Führer was at the apex of his popularity, and any hopes of regime change by toppling him had disappeared for the time being. But the civilian and military opposition to Hitler gained new impetus when the tide of war turned in 1941–42. Leading minds of the nationalist-conservative opposition came together around former Leipzig mayor Carl Goerdeler. They included Ludwig Beck, who had resigned his post as chief of the general staff in August 1938 to protest against Hitler's belligerence; the diplomat Ulrich von Hassell, who had been Germany's ambassador in Rome until he was fired in early 1938; and Johannes Popitz, who had served as Prussian finance minister under Göring since 1933. The political outlook of this circle was heavily conditioned by the authoritarian, obedience-driven traditions of Wilhelmine Germany; indeed, Goerdeler and his allies flirted with a restoration of the Hohenzollern dynasty. Moreover, they believed that if they toppled Hitler in time, they could negotiate a peace settlement that would preserve German dominance in Europe.[11]

Goerdeler took an ambivalent stance towards the regime's "Jewish policy," condemning the injustice being done to Jews while sharing the anti-Semitic prejudices that had been endemic among the nationalist-conservative bourgeoisie since the Wilhelmine era. In the autumn of 1941, in his pamphlet "The Goal," he wrote: "The question of whether races should mix must always be left up to the healthy common sense of the people." And in an essay written from prison in September 1944, the section entitled "Jewish Question" read: "We should not try to cover up what has happened. But we must also emphasise the great culpability of the Jews, who intruded into our public life in forms that lacked every bit of respectable modesty."[12]

Such absurd ideas were quite foreign to the Kreisau Circle, which had coalesced at the start of the war around the Silesian landowners and lawyers Helmuth James von Moltke and Peter Yorck von Wartenburg. It encompassed people of very diverse social and political backgrounds: Social Democrats Carlo Mierendorff, Theo Haubach, Julius Leber and Adolf Reichwein; Jesuit fathers Augustin Rösch and Alfred Delp; Protestant clergymen Eugen Gerstenmaier and Harald Poelchau; and diplomats Adam von Trott zu Solz and Hans Bernd von Haeften. Unlike the conservative nationalists around Goerdeler, most members of the Kreisau Circle had been committed opponents of National Socialism right from the start, and many had lost their jobs and positions soon after 1933. Some had even been interned in prisons and concentration camps. During intense discussions on three separate occasions at Moltke's Silesian estate in 1942 and 1943, members agreed on a joint agenda that aimed at a thorough political and intellectual renewal in Germany. Starting from the idea of "small communities"—that is, grass-roots democratic initiatives—they ultimately advocated a united Europe, into which Germany would peacefully integrate, having renounced all hegemonic ambitions. The circle was equally progressive in its economic and social policies. Members sought to find a third way between socialist economic planning and laissez-faire capitalism that would reconcile individual liberty and the benefits of competition with social security and a sense of responsibility among the propertied classes.[13]

Alongside the group that had formed in 1938 and 1939 in opposition to Hitler's plans to take Germany to war, and which was led by Hans Oster and Hans von Dohnanyi in the Abwehr, a second hub of military opposition crystallised in Army Group Centre on the eastern front in the latter half of 1941. Here the driving force was Colonel Henning von Tresckow, the army group's first general staff officer. Little by little he engaged a series of trusted comrades to work with him, including lawyer and reserve lieutenant Fabian von Schlabrendorff and Major Count Rudolf-Christoph von Gersdorff. These three officers had learned early on about the mass murder of Soviet Jews by Einsatzgruppe B, and the massacre at Borisov on 20–21 October 1941, in which Security Police and Security Service troops shot more than 7,000 men, women and children, dispelled any remaining illusions about what was going on. The trio's outrage at such terrible crimes was combined with a realisation that the Blitzkrieg in the east had failed and Germany's military defeat could no longer be ruled out.[14] Tresckow sought to win over Field Marshal von Kluge, the supreme commander of Army Group Centre, who was incensed by Hitler's constant interference in his operational decisions, remarking that it took "the patience of an angel to put up with it."[15] But Kluge could never bring himself to join the active resistance. Every time Tresckow thought he had convinced the field marshal, the commander would retreat into non-committal generalities. The conspirators would never succeed in getting a prominent army leader to join their cause.[16]

★

Over the course of 1942, the various resistance circles began to network with one another. At Tresckow's bidding, Schlabrendorff went to Berlin that July to liaise directly with Goerdeler and Beck. Via Oster, the military and civilian opposition also succeeded in linking up with General Friedrich Olbricht, the head of the General Army Office and deputy to Replacement Army commander Friedrich Fromm. He was to play a major role in operational preparations for the coup d'état that was to follow Hitler's assassination. These were based on the Replacement Army's plans in case of internal unrest, which were code-named "Operation Valkyrie."

Preparations for the assassination itself gained momentum as Germany's military catastrophe at Stalingrad approached. In late January 1943, Tresckow travelled to Berlin and urged that action be taken soon. Time was of the essence, he argued, and since Germany's field marshals could not be expected to "light the initial fuse," the conspirators would have to take matters into their own hands.[17] Field Marshal Erwin von Witzleben, who had been relieved of his command as supreme commander west in Paris in March 1942 and been replaced by Rundstedt, declared himself willing to assume command of the Wehrmacht after Hitler had been killed. But it remained uncertain how Fromm would act. In early March 1943, he was contacted by the former Berlin police vice-president and reserve lieutenant Count Fritz-Dietlof von der Schulenburg. Once a fervent National Socialist, Schulenburg had broken with the regime after some painful deliberation during the war. After the debacle at Stalingrad, he joined the opposition without reservation, becoming a key liaison between the various conspiratorial groups. But he had little success in winning over Fromm. Although the commander of the Replacement Army did not categorically rule out supporting a coup d'état, he played his cards close to the chest.[18]

Notwithstanding Fromm's reticence, Tresckow and his fellow conspirators decided that the time for action had come. As Schlabrendorff remembered it, on 13 March 1943, while Hitler was visiting Army Group Centre's main headquarters at Smolensk, they succeeded in smuggling a bomb disguised as a gift onto his airplane. It was set to go off during the Führer's return flight to Germany, but the detonator failed, probably because of the cold in the aircraft's cargo hold. After hours of anxious waiting, the depressing news arrived that Hitler and his retinue had arrived safely back in Rastenburg.[19] A few days later another assassination attempt seems to have been made. Gersdorff later recounted that he had volunteered to carry out a suicide bombing attack on Hitler immediately after the latter's speech on 21 March, Heroes' Commemoration Day, when the dictator was scheduled to inspect an exhibition of captured Soviet weaponry. But as though sensing danger, Hitler had rushed so quickly through the display that Gersdorff had no opportunity to carry out his mission.[20] It is uncertain, however, whether these two assassination attempts were actually undertaken. The only witnesses we have are the two protagonists themselves.

In the months that followed, the resistance suffered a series of setbacks. In March, Beck fell seriously ill with bowel cancer, undergoing several operations and being put out of commission as a central figure in the Berlin opposition.[21] In April, Dohnanyi and his co-conspirator Dietrich Bonhoeffer, a pastor of the Confessing Church who had also been working for the Abwehr under Admiral Wilhelm Canaris since July 1940, were arrested and Oster was placed under house arrest. Investigating suspected currency dealing on the black market, the Gestapo had uncovered the conspiratorial nature of Dohnanyi and Bonhoeffer's foreign connections. The secret police saw the revelations as their chance to triumph in their long-standing rivalry with the Abwehr for dominance in domestic intelligence. Canaris himself was initially unaffected, but the smashing of the Oster group deprived the resistance of an important conspiratorial control centre.[22] It was further weakened in October, when Tresckow was transferred to Army Group South, where he was named chief of staff of the 2nd Army. With that, the opponents of the regime in Army Group Centre had lost their leading figure.[23]

Since the blow dealt to the Abwehr, other resistance figures began to be subjected to enhanced surveillance. In November, Himmler told Goebbels about the existence of a "circle of enemies of the state," which included Johannes Popitz.[24] The Prussian finance minister had attracted the Gestapo's attention in late August when he succumbed to the absurd idea of sounding out none other than Himmler, head of the SS and newly appointed Reich interior minister, about where he stood on changing the domestic power situation. Himmler informed Hitler and, having secured the Führer's approval, pretended to be interested in further discussing this eventuality in order to learn more about conspiratorial circles.[25] In September 1943, Hitler told Goebbels that he was "absolutely clear that Popitz is our enemy." The Führer added that he was keeping him under observation so as to "have suitable material against him."[26] Two weeks after the assassination attempt of 20 July 1944, Himmler would brag to the Reichsleiters and Gauleiters that he had "long been on the trail of all the reactionary conspiracies," specifically naming Popitz.[27] Still, the truth was that the Gestapo failed to uncover the 20 July plot and hinder its preparations for the assassination and coup attempt.

Yet despite that failure, the noose was drawing ever tighter around the conspirators' necks. On 19 January 1944, Moltke was arrested and thrown in a cell in the notorious basement of the Reich Security Main Office headquarters at Prinz-Albert-Strasse 8. Ironically, his arrest had nothing to do with the conspiratorial activities of the Kreisau Circle, of which Himmler's henchmen at this point knew nothing. Instead Moltke was taken into custody for the relatively harmless offence of warning a colleague in the Abwehr, Otto Carl Kiep, that he was being watched by the Gestapo. Coming on the heels of the death of Carlo Mierendorff at the start of the previous month in an air raid on Leipzig, Moltke's arrest was another heavy blow to the Kreisau plotters.[28] On 11 February, Canaris was suspended from service and held prisoner in Lauenstein Castle in northern Bavaria. The Reich Security Main Office had reached its goal: the Abwehr was broken up, and the entire intelligence service placed under Himmler's control.[29]

The constant danger of being discovered increased the psychological strain on opponents of the regime and the already present tension and animosity between the various conspiratorial groups. People joining the anti-Hitler resistance knew full well that they were risking not only their lives but those of their families too. "We must constantly remind ourselves that we are heading for extremely grey days, whose worries and suffering we cannot yet begin to imagine," Moltke had written to his wife, Freya, back in 1941.[30] The conspirators also knew that they did not enjoy the support of the public at large, which would not at all welcome an assassination of Hitler. More than a few members of the resistance feared that getting rid of the dictator would create a new stab-in-the-back legend, so that Hitler's opponents and not the Führer and his lackeys would be held responsible for Germany losing the war. For this reason, Moltke was among those arguing against an assassination attempt.[31]

Another factor that hindered the anti-Hitler resistance was the bitter knowledge that they could not count on any concessions from the Western Allies should their attempt at regime change succeed. The demand for unconditional surrender that had been formalised at Casablanca in January 1943 precluded any negotiated peace settlement. Not without reason, the Allies regarded men like Goerdeler, Hassell and Beck as representatives of the old, nationalist-conservative elite that had helped bring Hitler to power. Cutting any sort of deal with them seemed increasingly inappropriate the more the military situation after Stalingrad turned in favour of the anti-Hitler coalition.[32]

The resistance was bolstered by one man who combined repulsion at Hitler's criminal regime with the will to act: Lieutenant Colonel Count Claus Schenk von Stauffenberg. It had been a long journey for him too, from his initial enthusiasm for the "national renewal" of 1933 to his ever-greater disillusionment with National Socialism. Stauffenberg had taken part in the campaigns against Poland and France and like many young officers had felt intoxicated by Germany's victories. He experienced the war against the Soviet Union as a member of the organisational division of the army general staff. Even after the course of the war had turned against the Wehrmacht in 1941–42, he still believed that Germany would ultimately triumph and had welcomed Hitler's assumption of supreme command. Before the 1942 summer offensive, he visited the 6th Army under General Paulus. Afterwards, he told the general in a letter that the visit had made him realise again what he had been "missing so far away from the troops," and how "refreshing" the air was "where people dare to give their all without hesitation and sacrifice their lives without complaint." Stauffenberg had added: "General, you are again in the midst of an operation, and we are following your every step with a passionate heart."[33]

It was over the course of 1942 that Stauffenberg, appalled by the mass deaths of Soviet POWs, the genocide against the Jews and the brutal treatment of the populace in German-occupied territories, turned against Hitler and decided that the dictator had to be got rid of. After sounding out Field Marshal von Manstein in January 1943 at the latest, he was under no illusion that he could count on Germany's top military leaders. "Those guys are either the kind who shit their pants or have rocks in their head," Stauffenberg was said to have remarked after the Manstein meeting. "They simply do not want to do anything."[34] In early April 1943, Stauffenberg was badly wounded as German troops retreated in Tunisia, losing his right eye and hand while two fingers of his left hand had to be amputated. While still recovering in a Munich hospital, he learned that infantry general Friedrich Olbricht had named him his chief of staff at the General Army Office. Before assuming that position, on his arrival in Berlin Stauffenberg was informed by Olbricht and Tresckow about the state of preparations for a coup. From that point on, he was part of the inner circle of the conspiracy.

Together with Tresckow, Stauffenberg now further tailored Operation Valkyrie, so it could be used for the planned coup. The two men drafted a secret order that was to be issued directly after the assassination. It began: "The Führer, Adolf Hitler, is dead! An unscrupulous clique of party leaders who have never served at the front has tried to exploit this situation and attack the fiercely fighting front from behind and seize power." Furthermore, in order to maintain "calm and order," the new Reich government was to declare a "state of military emergency." Thus the plotters sought to mask the actual purpose of Operation Valkyrie: instead of protecting the regime against internal unrest it would be used to remove the regime entirely. The orders also dictated what was to be done in the greater Berlin area and the Reich's other twenty-seven military districts and stipulated that the headquarters of Hitler, Himmler, Göring and Ribbentrop in East Prussia were to be occupied.[35]

But who would carry out the assassination? The search for a suitable individual proved difficult. The first candidate was Colonel Hellmuth Stieff, who as the head of the organisational division of the Army High Command had access to Hitler's situation briefings. But when Stauffenberg approached him in October 1943, Stieff declared himself unfit for such decisive action. A series of further attempts to get younger, physically more vigorous frontline officers to kill Hitler also came to nothing.[36] Slowly but surely, the conspirators were running out of time, as the war turned irrevocably against Germany. With the Allied landing in Normandy on 6 June 1944 and the immediate successes of the Soviet offensive of 22 June, it became increasingly obvious that the Third Reich was headed for disaster, and it seemed more and more questionable whether a coup even made any sense under the circumstances. Stauffenberg articulated such doubts, but in response Tresckow argued that the plotters' ethical and moral motivation would be their lasting legacy: "The assassination has to take place regardless of the cost. Even if it fails, action must still be taken in Berlin. This is not a matter of practicality but of demonstrating before the world and before history that the German resistance movement dared to make a decisive attempt. In view of that, everything else is irrelevant."[37]

If they were going to act, the conspirators would have to do so immediately. The danger of being discovered was growing every day. In early July 1944, two members of the Kreisau Circle, Julius Leber and Adolf Reichwein, were arrested for contacting representatives of the banned German Communist Party to sound out the possibility of cooperation. On 17 July, the Gestapo issued an arrest warrant for Goerdeler. The signs were that these detentions would be just the beginning of a major wave of arrests. All sorts of rumours circulated in Berlin. A friend of Schulenburg, the journalist Ursula von Kardorff, wrote that "Fritzi" reminded her of a "hounded animal": "If only something would happen. The tension is hardly bearable."[38]

Since no one else had volunteered, Stauffenberg decided to assassinate Hitler himself. On 1 July 1944, he had been named chief of staff to the commander of the Replacement Army and promoted to colonel. His successor in Olbricht's General Army Office was his friend and fellow conspirator Colonel Albrecht Mertz von Quirnheim. His new position gave Stauffenberg direct access to Hitler, one of the prerequisites for the assassination. But his decision to serve as the assassin entailed a big problem: he could not be allowed to risk his own life in carrying out the attack because he was irreplaceable as an organiser of the coup in Berlin. This double role would prove to be a major flaw in the plan.[39]

Stauffenberg made several attempts. On 6 and 11 July, he took part for the first times as Fromm's chief of staff in meetings with Hitler on the Obersalzberg. On both days, he had a briefcase full of explosives with him but decided not to detonate them—probably because the conspirators had agreed that the assassination was only to proceed if Himmler and Göring were also present at the meeting.[40] On 15 July, Fromm and Stauffenberg were summoned to the Wolf's Lair, in East Prussia, where Hitler had just returned. This time, Stauffenberg was determined to act whether Himmler was present or not, but for unknown reasons he again postponed the assassination attempt. That morning, preliminary orders for Operation Valkyrie had already been issued, and upon learning that Hitler had not been assassinated, Olbricht only just succeeded in halting things and declaring them to be a practice drill. This meant it was no longer possible for the conspirators to trigger the initial stages of Operation Valkyrie again without attracting suspicion: the next time it had to be completed—and succeed.[41] But the repeated postponements of the assassination had also dampened spirits among the plotters in Berlin. Hardly anyone believed any more that the coup would succeed. "The whole enterprise seems to be subjected to the curse of 'too late,'" complained the diplomat Hans Bernd von Haeften.[42] But success or failure was no longer the decisive criterion. What mattered to Stauffenberg, Tresckow and Beck was to make an attempt and thereby send a signal that could not be ignored. Then, a few days later, another opportunity to carry out their plan presented itself.

The twentieth of July 1944 was a hot, humid summer day. That morning, Stauffenberg drove to the Rangsdorf airstrip south of Berlin, where a Heinkel He-111 was waiting for him and his adjutant Werner von Haeften. At 10:15 a.m., the plane landed at Rastenburg. After breakfast with the commandant of the Führer's headquarters in the officers' mess in Restricted Zone 2, Stauffenberg headed to Restricted Zone 1, where he took part in preparatory meetings with General Walther Buhle, head of army staff at the Wehrmacht Supreme Command, and Field Marshal Keitel in the latter's bunker. Only then did he learn that the situation briefing with Hitler had been brought forward to 12:30 p.m. because of an imminent visit by Mussolini. There was little time. Excusing themselves to freshen up and put on clean shirts, something hardly outlandish given the sweltering heat, Stauffenberg and Haeften withdrew to a room near the entrance of the bunker to prepare the detonator for the two packages of explosives they had brought with them. However, their preparations were interrupted by a staff sergeant who told them in the name of Keitel's adjutant, Major Ernst John von Freyend, that they needed to hurry up. As a result, Stauffenberg could only activate one of the bombs and transfer it to his briefcase, while Haeften took care of the other. The haste with which Stauffenberg had to work explains why it did not occur to him to bring along the second parcel of explosives, which, even if not activated, would have significantly increased the force of the blast.[43]

Major-General Adolf Heusinger had already started his report on the situation at the eastern front when at 12:37 p.m. Keitel and Stauffenberg entered the barracks, whose windows were open wide to combat the heat. Keitel announced Stauffenberg to the group. Hitler, who was sitting in the centre of the heavy oak table's long side with his back to the room's entrance, turned around, briefly mustered the late arrivals and wordlessly acknowledged their greeting. Stauffenberg had asked to be seated near the dictator. The briefcase with the bomb, which Keitel's adjutant had brought in, was placed against the right table base. A few minutes later, Stauffenberg whispered to Keitel that he needed to make an urgent phone call and left the meeting. To avoid attracting suspicion, Stauffenberg left his sword belt and cap behind in the antechamber.[44]

Shortly after 12:40 p.m., a tremendous explosion rocked the situation room. Spurts of flame licked over the edges of the tabletop, and everyone sitting at it was hurled to the floor. Shards of glass, wood and scraps of paper swirled. The air was full of impenetrable smoke and the cries of the injured. At the moment the bomb went off, Hitler had been bent over the table studying a map. That spared him the full force of the blast.[45] He checked whether he could still move, the dictator said a few days later, and once the initial shock had subsided, he sought to get out into the open since the room had been engulfed in flames. Keitel had thrown his arms around him in violation of normal protocol, Hitler added, and exclaimed: "My Führer, you are alive, you are alive!"[46] Supported by Keitel and his adjutant Günsche, Hitler went back to his bunker. "He walked firmly and upright," recalled Below. "His jacket and trousers were ripped, but otherwise he did not seem to have suffered any serious injuries."[47] Once again, good fortune had been on Hitler's side. Most of the other twenty-four people at the meeting were far more gravely hurt. Eleven had been injured so badly that they had to be taken to hospital in Rastenburg. Three died a few hours later. Hitler's head adjutant, Schmundt, lost an eye and a leg and succumbed to his injuries several weeks later. By contrast, Puttkamer and Below were able to resume their duties in the Wolf's Lair after being given recuperative leave.[48]

Stauffenberg had hastened to the nearby adjutants' building, where he met Haeften. While they waited for their car, they heard the explosion. Convinced that there was no way Hitler could have survived, they made their way to the Rastenburg airstrip. They passed the guards in Restricted Zone 1 without incident, but in the meantime, the alarm had been sounded and the sergeant on duty in the external restricted zone stopped the two conspirators. A call was placed to the command centre, before they were given permission to proceed, with Stauffenberg telling his driver: "Right now every minute counts!"[49] On their way to the airstrip, Haeften tossed the second parcel of explosives out of the car window. At 1:15 p.m., their airplane took off for Berlin.

By that point, Hitler had returned to his bunker, and a doctor, Hanskarl von Hasselbach, was summoned. He administered first aid until Hitler's personal physician, Theodor Morell, arrived to take over treatment of the Führer, who by now had overcome his initial shock and whose blood pressure had almost returned to normal. An examination revealed that both his eardrums had been perforated, and his right forearm was quite swollen and dangled limply. The dictator had burns on his hands and legs, and dozens of wooden splinters from the massive table base against which Stauffenberg had rested the briefcase with the bomb had to be extracted from his lower legs. Most of the hair on the back of his head had been singed and his forehead carried a graze from a fallen ceiling beam. Had that wooden beam struck him directly, it might well have smashed his skull, Hitler remarked.[50] The Führer made an astonishingly composed, almost euphoric impression on those around him. "Well, ladies, once again everything turned out well" was how he greeted his secretaries with a smile. "More proof that Providence has chosen me for my mission— otherwise I would not still be alive."[51] He displayed his ripped black trousers like a trophy, telling Christa Schroeder to send them to Eva Braun at the Berghof with instructions that they be preserved for posterity.[52]

In the hours after the assassination the entire Wolf's Lair was in a state of feverish agitation. All conversations centred around who could have planted the bomb. Initially suspicion fell on construction workers from the Organisation Todt, which was still expanding Hitler's field headquarters.[53] But soon Stauffenberg became the focus of investigations. A guard who had been on duty at the barracks' telephone switchboard during the assassination attempt reported that instead of placing a call after he left the situation room, the colonel had rushed off with a strange expression on his face. Hitler ordered Stauffenberg's whereabouts to be determined, but he was nowhere to be found. The initial suspicions were firmed up that afternoon when Reich Security Main Office investigators arrived and discovered the remnants of Stauffenberg's briefcase in the ruins of the building. They also found the second bomb parcel Haeften had thrown away. Hitler and his paladins did not suspect at this point that the assassination was intended to spark a *coup d'état*, which was to begin once Stauffenberg had returned to Berlin. In retrospect, Goebbels described it as a stroke of luck that Stauffenberg had not been apprehended at the Rastenburg airstrip. If he had been arrested, the propaganda minister surmised, the coup attempt in Berlin would not have been "rolled out," and the would-be putschists would have remained undiscovered and would "probably still enjoy the privileges of their offices."[54]

At 3 p.m., half an hour later than expected, Mussolini arrived at Görlitz's small train station. Hitler had insisted upon welcoming his guest personally to dispel any rumours that he had been seriously injured. There was no sign anything unusual had taken place other than the fact that Hitler's right arm was in a sling, which meant that he had to greet Mussolini by extending his left hand. On the way back to the Wolf's Lair, Hitler described what had happened. "He did so in a conspicuously calm, almost monotone voice," recalled the interpreter Paul Schmidt, "while Mussolini's face betrayed the horror he felt that someone could attempt an assassination of the German dictator in the middle of his headquarters." Hitler took his visitor to see the devastated scene of the explosion. "Here, right in front of my feet, the bomb exploded," he explained. After his "miraculous rescue," the Führer said, he was more convinced than ever that he was predestined to bring "their great joint cause to a successful conclusion." Mussolini agreed excitedly that his survival was "a sign from the heavens." At 7 p.m., Hitler took his leave of his guest. It would be the last time the two men saw one another.[55]

At Fromm's offices on Bendlerstrasse, the conspirators had been waiting since noon for news from the Wolf's Lair. A short time after the assassination attempt, presumably around 1 p.m., one of the plotters, the head of communications at the Wehrmacht Supreme Command, General Erich Fellgiebel, called Lieutenant-General Fritz Thiele, the chief of staff of army communications, and told him that Stauffenberg had detonated his bomb but that Hitler had survived. Thiele initially decided to keep this news to himself. Given that only five days previously the signal to start Operation Valkyrie had been given prematurely, Fromm's deputy Olbricht now thought it advisable to wait until reliable information came in. At 3:45 p.m. Stauffenberg's plane landed at Rangsdorf. From the airstrip, Haeften called Bendlerstrasse and reported that Hitler was dead. No car awaited him and Stauffenberg, so it was not until three-quarters of an hour later that the two men arrived in downtown Berlin.[56]

In the meantime, on his own authority, Mertz von Quirnheim had given the first signal to commence Operation Valkyrie, and at around 4 p.m. Olbricht had taken the preliminary orders to Fromm for his signature. But the commander of the Replacement Army was suspicious and phoned the Wolf's Lair, speaking first with Keitel's adjutant, Freyend, and then Keitel himself. Both confirmed that there had been an assassination attempt but that Hitler had survived. At the end of the call, Keitel asked where Fromm's chief of staff was. Fromm answered, truthfully, that Stauffenberg had not yet returned from East Prussia.

Fromm was in a quandary. He knew that the assassination, the decisive prerequisite for a successful coup, had failed. Under those circumstances it seemed senseless to trigger Operation Valkyrie and he refused to sign the orders Olbricht brought him. From that point on, his major concern was to cover up any evidence that suggested he had known about the plot.[57] Yet hardly had Olbricht returned to his office than Mertz von Quirnheim informed Fromm that he had issued further orders to go ahead with Valkyrie. When Fromm learned of this, he had Mertz von Quirnheim detained. A short time later,

Stauffenberg and Haeften arrived, and for a time it looked as if the course of events in Bendlerstrasse would swing around. Stauffenberg succeeded in persuading his fellow conspirators that, despite rumours to the contrary, the assassination had succeeded and that the coup must now go ahead despite the delay. But a final attempt to get Fromm on board proved fruitless. Instead Fromm called upon Stauffenberg to shoot himself, and when the latter refused, he placed Olbricht and Mertz von Quirnheim formally under arrest. Stauffenberg responded coolly: "You are deceiving yourself about the true relations of power. If anyone is to be taken into protective custody, it is you, General." After a brief struggle, Fromm submitted to his fate and was confined to his adjutant's office. That evening he was allowed, under guard, to return to his apartment in the Bendlerstrasse complex. His duties as "supreme commander on the home front" were assumed by Colonel-General Erich Hoepner, whom Hitler had relieved of his command of the 4th Tank Army in January 1942 and forced out of the Wehrmacht.[58]

Between 4:30 and 5 p.m., Ludwig Beck, the designated head of state in the post-Hitler government, arrived at Bendlerstrasse, where he learned to his dismay that Operation Valkyrie had only just commenced. At the same time, more and more reports were coming in that Hitler had survived the assassination attempt. Yet Beck refused to be dissuaded: "For me, this man is dead . . . We cannot afford to waver from that line; otherwise we will sow confusion among our own ranks. Proof positive that Hitler, and not some doppelgänger, is still alive will take hours to come from his headquarters. By then, the Berlin mission must be concluded." At that point, Hoepner called together the department heads in Bendlerstrasse and informed them that Hitler was dead, Colonel-General Beck had assumed leadership of the Reich, and Field Marshal von Witzleben had taken over the command of the Wehrmacht, but most of the officers were not convinced. When one of them asked how reliable this information was, Hoepner became evasive.[59] But soon there could be no more doubts. At 6:28 p.m., German radio reported that a bomb attack had been carried out against Hitler but that the Führer had suffered only minor injuries and had "immediately resumed work." The fact that the conspirators had neglected to seize control of Germany's radio stations was now coming back to haunt them.[60]

In the Wolf's Lair, meanwhile, measures to put down the insurrection were in full swing. Here too one of the biggest mistakes of the plotters was Fellgiebel's failure to cut the telephone lines. Members of Hitler's staff were able to phone government offices in Berlin without any problems.[61] Thus, it soon became clear that the bomb was not the work of a lone assassin but part of a conspiracy aiming to depose the regime. Immediately, Hitler named Himmler head of the Replacement Army, dismissing Fromm, whom he suspected of having known about the plot all along. Keitel sent telexes to the commanders of Germany's defence districts informing them of this change and instructing them to accept no orders from Fromm, Witzleben or Hoepner. At the same time, Bormann telegrammed the Gauleiters, describing what had happened and ordering them to arrest anyone and everyone connected with the "reactionary, criminal rabble."[62]

Goebbels' role in all this was initially rather nebulous: there is a conspicuous hole in his diary from 17 to 22 July. Did he perhaps wait to see how things developed and keep his options open in case Hitler was in fact assassinated?[63] In any case, it seems strange that on the afternoon of 20 July he hesitated to approve a brief news item that Hitler had survived the bomb attack, which he had been handed by press head Dietrich. The propaganda minister explained that he needed to work out an accompanying commentary piece. A displeased Hitler snapped: "I did not order any commentary piece. I want the news to be spread, and I want it to be spread immediately." Hitler got his wish.[64]

Ninety minutes earlier, the commander of the Guard Battalion *Grossdeutschland*, Major Otto Remer, had been summoned by the commandant of Berlin, Lieutenant-General Paul von Hase. Something had happened to Hitler, he was told, and the executive power of the government had been transferred to the army. The battalion was charged with hermetically sealing off the government district.[65] Speer, whom Goebbels had asked to come to his villa at 5 p.m., where he was informed that a "military putsch was underway throughout the Reich," watched from a window as soldiers in full battle dress, with hand grenades in their belts and submachine guns in their hands, advanced in small groups towards the Brandenburg Gate.[66]

By 6:30 p.m. the government district had been completely cordoned off. But the Nazi liaison with the battalion, Captain Hans Hagen, in his civilian job a consultant within the Propaganda Ministry, had become suspicious. He contacted Goebbels and persuaded the propaganda minister to receive Remer.[67] At 7 p.m., the major entered Goebbels' apartment. The propaganda minister, who had procured cyanide capsules to be prepared for the very worst, was visibly nervous. Goebbels reminded Remer of the oath of loyalty he had sworn to Hitler, and the officer replied that he was "100 per cent behind the Führer" but had been told he was dead. He was therefore following the instructions of his commanding officer, Hase. "The Führer is alive!" Goebbels assured him, saying that he had got off the phone with him just beforehand. Remer's amazed disbelief gave way to joyous excitement when Goebbels offered to let him call Hitler. A line was established to the Wolf's Lair within seconds. Hitler asked Remer whether he recognised his voice, which the major said he did, and the dictator then ordered him to put down the putsch by all means necessary. The lock-down of the governmental district was lifted.[68] Remer's troops assembled in the "Ministerial Garden" between the Brandenburg Gate and the central Potsdamer Platz, where Goebbels got them to renew their oath of loyalty to Hitler.[69] The battalion changing sides disrupted a decisive element of Operation Valkyrie. The attempted coup was now doomed to failure.

At the centre of the conspiracy, in the Bendlerstrasse complex, desperation was growing as the certainty that Hitler had survived now devastated the plotters' morale. Yet Stauffenberg was still not prepared to give up. He constantly placed calls to command centres in various parts of the Reich, issued orders and sought to prop up those conspirators who were beginning to waver.[70] At 8 p.m., Witzleben, the designated new supreme commander of the Wehrmacht, arrived with his marshal's staff in his hand. He knew by now that the assassination attempt had failed. "What a bloody mess," he hissed at Stauffenberg when the colonel reported to him, declaring that "everything you are doing here is senseless." Forty-five minutes later, Witzleben left Bendlerstrasse and withdrew to his country estate.[71]

Later that evening, a counter-rebellion was formed in Bendlerstrasse by officers loyal to the regime. After German radio announced at around 10:15 p.m. that Hitler would address the German people shortly, they went to Olbricht and demanded to know whether Operation Valkyrie was directed against the Führer. They let it be known that they had no intention of allowing themselves at the last minute to get drawn into a putsch that was on the verge of collapsing. After Olbricht failed to give them a precise answer, they demanded to speak with Fromm, their commanding officer, who was still being kept under house arrest.[72]

Shortly after 11 p.m., accompanied by armed troops, Fromm entered his office, where Beck, Hoepner, Olbricht, Stauffenberg, Mertz von Quirnheim and Haeften had gathered. The last act of the drama now commenced. "So, gentlemen, now I am going to do with you what you did with me this noon," Fromm is said to have exclaimed, announcing that the six conspirators were under arrest and demanding that they surrender their weapons. Only Beck was allowed to retain his pistol for "private purposes," so that the former chief of the general staff could commit suicide. Beck indeed tried to shoot himself twice but only succeeded in inflicting serious head wounds. While he lay in his death throes, Fromm left the room, only to return after a short time with the news that a court-martial he had convened had sentenced Olbricht, Stauffenberg, Mertz von Quirnheim and Haeften to death. But if he thought that he could wriggle out of the noose around his own neck by executing all those who knew of his role in the plot, he was sadly mistaken. His independent decision to execute the leading conspirators before they could be interrogated by Himmler's henchmen only attracted suspicion.

At 12:30 a.m. on 21 July, Fromm had the condemned officers marched into the Bendlerstrasse courtyard and executed, one by one, by members of the Guard Battalion *Grossdeutschland*. An officer was ordered to put Beck out of his misery. The five bodies were taken in a truck to the cemetery of the St. Matthaeus congregation in the Schöneberg district and buried there. Still, the regime felt it needed to take revenge on the dead. The following day, on Himmler's orders, the conspirators' remains were dug up and burned in a crematorium. The ashes were scattered over a Berlin landfill site.[73]

Hitler's initial euphoria at the "miraculous" rescue had already dissipated by the evening of 20 July. In blunt language he vented his anger at the conspirators: "What cowards they are! If only they had fired shots at me, I could respect them! But they do not dare to risk their own lives . . . The blockheads have no idea what chaos will result if they release the strings from my hand. I am going to make such an example of them that no one will ever feel the slightest desire to commit a similar betrayal of the German people!"[74] A radio truck had arrived in the meantime, and in the officers' mess in Restricted Zone 1, a broadcast connection with Berlin was established. At around 11:30 p.m., Hitler's entourage assembled there, among them officers who had been lightly wounded in the assassination attempt. The dictator insisted on recording his radio address in front of a small circle of trusted people because it would make him feel less inhibited.[75] Shortly after midnight, Germans could hear on all radio stations the familiar, trusted voice of their Führer, who told them that "a tiny clique of ambitious, unscrupulous, criminal, stupid officers" had hatched a plot to do away with him and the entire Wehrmacht leadership. Hitler considered the fact that he had "no injuries other than some small abrasions, bruises and burns" as "a sign from Providence" to continue his life's work. Once again, the dictator invoked the German trauma of 1918, portraying the events of the day as a similar "stab in the back" of the troops at the front. But this time, he assured his listeners, the conspirators had miscalculated and would now "be paid back in the fashion National Socialists are accustomed to."[76]

After his address, Hitler returned to his bunker, where Morell re-examined him and administered painkillers. During this time, a telegram from Fromm arrived: "Attempted putsch by irresponsible generals put down by force. All leaders executed." Fromm reported that he had taken back command of the Replacement Army after being "temporarily detained by armed captors." This fooled no one in the Nazi leadership. At 1 a.m., when Fromm appeared at Goebbels' apartment and requested to speak to the Führer on the telephone, the propaganda minister had him arrested at Hitler's behest.[77] Fellgiebel was also taken into custody that night after spending all afternoon in the Wolf's Lair and congratulating Hitler on surviving the attempted assassination. The dictator wondered why the head of army communications had not simply shot him, scoffing: "And then this ass calmly walks to and fro, as if he was completely uninvolved in the attack."[78] At 3:40 a.m. on 21 July, Bormann told the Gauleiters that the coup attempt had been put down and Himmler had assumed command of the Replacement Army.[79] Herbert Backe, who had succeeded Darré a few months earlier as minister for food and agriculture, was ecstatic at Himmler's further promotion: "Now I no longer need to force myself to believe in victory."[80]

At first, Operation Valkyrie was more successful in Paris than in Berlin. There, the leading figures were General Carl-Heinrich von Stülpnagel, the German military commander in France, and a staff officer, First Lieutenant Cäsar von Hofacker, a cousin of Stauffenberg. Although Field Marshal Kluge, now the Wehrmacht's supreme commander west, still could not be persuaded to support the rebellion, these two officers went ahead with the operation and succeeded by 11 p.m. in arresting over 1,000 SS and Security Service men, including SS-Obergruppenführer Carl Albrecht Oberg. But when the conspirators heard Hitler's midnight radio address, they gave up and released their prisoners. Over a few bottles of champagne, the two sides agreed to declare the whole affair a "misunderstanding." Yet Stülpnagel knew that there was no escape for him. On his way back to Germany, near Verdun, he tried unsuccessfully to take his own life. Badly wounded and blinded, he was captured and placed under arrest.[81]

A variety of factors contributed to the failure of the attempted coup of 20 July. Almost from the very start, even among enemies of Hitler the conspirators were accused of "dilettantism."[82] Certainly, they were accountable for several serious mistakes, including the delayed initiation of the first Operation Valkyrie measures and the fact that they did not block lines of communication with the Wolf's Lair or occupy the radio stations. But far more key to the demise of the whole enterprise, of course, was the failure to kill Hitler. That was partly down to an unlucky sequence of accidents—for instance, that Stauffenberg was interrupted before he could arm the second bomb or the fact that the situation briefing had taken place in a wooden barracks with the windows open rather than a sealed bunker, which would have magnified the impact of the explosion. Yet Hitler's death was crucial: the entire operation was predicated on his demise. For senior officers like Fromm or Kluge, whose loyalty to the Führer was wavering, a successful assassination was a *sine qua non* for supporting the coup. As soon as it became known that Hitler had survived, that support began to falter.

Yet even if the assassination attempt had been successful, it is by no means certain that the conspirators would have been able to topple the regime. There were many military commanders who still felt bound by their oath and considered the putsch an act of high treason.

Perhaps there would have been armed confrontations between units that had joined the rebellion and those Wehrmacht and SS forces that remained loyal to the regime. We can only speculate about who would have come out on top of that conflict.[83]

In any case, one of the resistance's biggest handicaps would have been its lack of broad support among the German people. From the very onset, the conspirators were under no illusions about their lack of popularity. Before departing on the morning of 21 July for the front, where he would blow himself up with a hand grenade, Henning von Tresckow told his friend Fabian von Schlabrendorff: "Now the entire world will attack and curse us. I consider Hitler not only the arch-enemy of Germany but the arch-enemy of the world. In a few hours, when I appear before God's judgment to justify what I have and have not done, I will be able in good conscience to defend what I have done in the fight against Hitler . . . The moral value of a person only begins when he is prepared to give his life for his convictions."[84]

How did the German people react to the assassination attempt? The first Security Service reports spoke of the attack on Hitler "unleashing, like a shock wave, the strongest dismay, disbelief, deep anger and rage among the entire population." Women were described weeping in the streets, whereas the news of Hitler's survival had allowed people to "catch their breath" and exclaim "Thank God, the Führer is alive!"[85] Indeed, the great majority of Germans seem to have disapproved of the assassination attempt. Even among those critical of National Socialism, the view appears to have been widespread that Hitler's death would have only made the situation worse and possibly led to civil war. Images of the scene of the attack published in the news-papers made people realise the destructive force of the bomb and agree with the propagandistic assertion that the Führer was blessed by Providence and had only survived the assassination attempt thanks to a "great miracle."[86] Relief that Hitler had been saved was mixed with outrage at the "aristocratic clique of officers" that was held responsible for the attack. Robert Ley, the head of the German Labour Front, sought to further incite such animosity by demanding in a radio speech on 22 July, and in a newspaper article the following day, that "this scum be exterminated and annihilated from the roots on up."[87] That went too far even for Hitler, and he got Bormann to instruct

On 18 February 1943, Joseph Goebbels spoke in front of a fanatical audience in Berlin's Sportpalast. His speech culminated in a question that was greeted with thunderous applause: "Do you want total war?"

In his "schlepp edict" of October 1940, Hermann Göring decreed: "The soldier is allowed to take with him whatever he can carry and is intended for his own personal use or that of his family." It was the start of an unprecedented campaign of private looting across Europe. This photo of a German soldier embarking on home leave was taken in December 1941.

Hitler and Goebbels on the Obersalzberg in late June 1943, a few days before the start of Operation Citadel.

Situation meeting in Klessheim Castle on the day of the Allied landing in Normandy, 6 June 1944. From left to right, standing: Ribbentrop, Luftwaffe General Günther Korten, Artillery General Walter Warlimont, Göring, Colonel-General Alfred Jodl, Hungarian Chief of the General Staff János Vörös, Keitel; sitting: Hungarian Prime Minister Döme Sztójay and Hitler.

The Red Army's Operation Bagration led to the complete defeat of Army Group Centre and the loss of twenty-eight Wehrmacht divisions in July 1944. This picture shows war materiel left behind by the German 9th Army on a road near Babruysk in Belarus.

On 17 July 1944, 50,000 German POWs were paraded through Moscow.

Evening society in the Berghof's Great Hall in May 1944. In this idyllically located residence on the Obersalzberg, Hitler and Eva Braun (left on the rear sofa) tried to lead private lives even in wartime.

Hitler and Eva Braun with the daughter of Braun's friend Herta Schneider on 1 May 1942. Braun had asked cameraman Walter Frentz to produce such images, which were intended to communicate familial intimacy.

Hitler and his guest Heinrich Himmler on a stroll to the Mooslahnerkopf tea house on 3 April 1944. Along the way, they may have discussed the deportation of Hungarian Jews to the death camps.

In the Wolf's Lair on 15 July 1944, from left to right: Count Claus Schenk von Stauffenberg, Admiral Karl-Jesko von Puttkamer, General Karl Heinrich von Bodenschatz, Hitler, Keitel.

20 July 1944: having just survived the assassination attempt, Hitler showed his guest Mussolini the destroyed situation room in the Wolf's Lair.

At midnight on 20 July 1944, Hitler gave a radio address in the officers' mess of the Wolf's Lair. Sitting in the first row, with his head bandaged, is Wehrmacht Chief of Staff Alfred Jodl. To the left of the radio engineer (standing) is Hitler's personal adjutant Julius Schaub. Sitting in the second row are Hitler's secretaries, Traudl Junge and Christa Schroeder.

Hitler's final New Year's reception in the Eagle's Nest near Bad Nauheim on 1 January 1945. Congratulating the Führer were (left to right) Albert Speer, Jodl, Keitel and Ribbentrop.

In the final years of the war, the visibly aged dictator increasingly made use of a magnifying glass so as not to have to wear glasses.

In early January 1945, hundreds of thousands of people fled west from East Prussia on foot or in horse-drawn wagons. Here a column of refugees makes its way across the frozen Vistula Lagoon.

In February 1945 Hitler still pored over plans for remaking his home city of Linz. In the cellar of the New Reich Chancellery, architect Hermann Giesler repeatedly set up a model of the city for the Führer's diversion.

Situation meeting concerning the Oder front on 3 March 1945 in Harnekop Palace near Wriezen: (from left to right) Lieutenant-General Wilhelm Berlin, Luftwaffe Field Marshal Robert Ritter von Greim, Luftwaffe Major-General Franz Reuss, Artillery Major-General Job Odebrecht and Lieutenant-General Theodor Busse, the commander of the 9th Army at the Oder.

Hitler's final public appearance: on 20 March 1945, accompanied by Reich Youth Leader Arthur Axmann, the dictator received twenty Hitler Youths in the chancellery garden. They had distinguished themselves on the eastern front and were awarded Iron Crosses for bravery.

One of the last photos of Hitler, presumably from late March 1945: accompanied by his long-time personal adjutant Julius Schaub, the Führer inspected damage to the New Reich Chancellery building.

the Reichsleiters and Gauleiters that no one was allowed to get carried away and "attack or insult the officer corps, the military leadership, the aristocracy or parts of the Wehrmacht *in corpore.*" Instead, Hitler ordered, it was crucial to stress that the conspirators represented a "certain, relatively small clique of officers."[88]

Meanwhile, on Hitler's orders, Goebbels organised events throughout the Reich, and they were well attended. Even if these were not, as Nazi propaganda claimed, spontaneous gatherings of the German people, the attack had undoubtedly boosted Hitler's popularity. "Almost universally, people's connection to the Führer has grown more profound and trust in the government has increased," the Security Service reported.[89] Goebbels wrote that "loyalty to the Führer" was being "expressed in previously unknown ways" and that it felt as though "a great victory" had been won.[90] We must bear in mind, of course, that people were not at liberty to express all their opinions about the assassination attempt, especially as state repression was stepped up afterwards. In her diary, the journalist Ursula von Kardorff noted on 23 July that the editor-in-chief of her newspaper, the *Deutsche Allgemeine Zeitung*, had warned reporters to exercise "the greatest caution" in whatever they wrote: "There are going to be arrests in the thousands."[91] Regret that Hitler had survived the assassination attempt could only be expressed in small circles of like-minded people or in private journals, such as the diary of a sixteen-year-old Hamburg schoolboy, who wrote on 21 July: "A bomb attack was carried out . . . yesterday against Hitler. Unfortunately, the bastard miraculously survived uninjured."[92]

Soldiers at the front would also have been wary of expressing their true feelings in letters home since these might fall into the hands of military censors. Nonetheless, in the main, ordinary soldiers too seem to have rejected the assassination attempt. In August 1944, for example, the postal censor for a tank unit within Army Group Centre reported a "large number of joyous, emotional sentiments that the Führer had been saved." This was "not just proof of the love for and loyalty to the Führer," the report continued, but also served as evidence for "solid determination . . . to fight and achieve victory on his behalf."[93] Reading the letters from the front compiled by the historians Ortwin Buchbender and Reinhold Sterz, even if their selection may not be representative, it is easy to get the same impression. "What do you say to this nasty trick played on the Führer?" one private wrote. ". . . Thank God, everything turned out to be all right. It is hard to believe anything this low. Here everyone is deeply outraged at this crime. Hopefully, those behind it will all be punished as severely as they deserve." Another soldier reported: "The members of my company and myself were all speech-less after this shameful, contemptible act became known. Thank God, Providence preserved our Führer so that he might save Europe. It is now our most sacred duty to hold on to him all the more tightly, to make up for what a few criminals, who were probably paid by our enemies, have done without consideration for our people as a whole."[94] A poll carried out by the Allies among German POWs found that trust in Hitler's leadership had risen from 57 per cent in the first half of July to 68 per cent in August.[95]

Among officers loyal to the regime there was great outrage about the assassination attempt. "What were these people thinking?" the tank general Hermann Balck asked. "You can only be shocked by such political stupidity . . . There can be no mercy here. Anyone who conspired with them must be laid low."[96] Colonel-General Hans-Georg Reinhardt was likewise appalled, calling it in a letter to his wife "a deed that can only have been born of insanity." "What was supposed to happen if the assassination had succeeded?" Reinhardt asked. "There is no one who would have enjoyed comparable trust as the new leader of Germany and who could have claimed similar achievements and successes as the Führer."[97] And in his diary he noted on 21 July: "Completely broken up. Incomprehensible! What damage has this deed done to our officer class! We can only be deeply ashamed."[98]

Surveillance reports on German generals in British captivity, however, reveal how diverse the reactions were among high-ranking officers. Some regretted the failure of the assassination attempt while criticising the lack of professionalism with which it had been carried out. "I do not understand how Stauffenberg could take such a small bomb," one captured general remarked. "He is otherwise such a reli-able man." Others expressed doubt that the attempt to kill Hitler had been genuine, speculating that it could have been a fake designed to "get rid of all inconvenient people in one fell swoop." Others still, perhaps most of the officers, condemned the attack, invoking the oath of loyalty German soldiers had sworn to the Führer. "I have always believed that a soldier is to obey his supreme commander under all circumstances," one man opined.[99]

Some opponents of Hitler, like the court official Friedrich Kellner, were also convinced that the attempted assassination had been staged by the regime to bolster Hitler's damaged prestige. "The bomb allegedly placed by Colonel von Stauffenberg supposedly fizzled out two metres in front of the Führer," Kellner noted in his diary. "The Führer remained unharmed. That is the core of the whole story. Who can doubt any longer that the Führer enjoys the protection of Providence? A tangible miracle has occurred. That was the whole point." If the attack really had happened as the Nazi-controlled media depicted it, Kellner continued, it would have been "a very clumsy enterprise," since an officers' revolt without popular support would have been "dead on arrival." Under these circumstances, Kellner even welcomed Hitler's survival since it meant the Führer would have to experience everything up to the "bitter end"—that is, Germany's total defeat—and the political right in Germany would not be able to invent another stab-in-the-back legend akin to 1918. "Future eras must not have any excuses," Kellner wrote.[100]

"It is the beginning of the end," noted Thomas Mann on hearing of the attempted assassination.[101] Victor Klemperer, who was by then living in perpetual fear in a "Jew house" in Dresden, was less confident: "Even now it is not obvious whether this is the beginning of the end—how often have we had such beginnings, only to remain at the starting point!" After all, Klemperer pointed out, the Nazis remained in power, and the failed assassination attempt would give their propaganda a powerful impetus: "Millions will once again believe in final victory."[102] Yet as it turned out, the failure of the bomb attack only temporarily put wind in the regime's sails. By early August 1944, the Security Service in Stuttgart reported that "most national comrades . . . have now lost all faith in the Führer."[103] At the end of the month, Goebbels was forced to acknowledge that in view of the critical situation on all fronts, "a certain feeling of desperation" prevailed. One could "barely imagine how the current crisis can be overcome," he wrote.[104]

Hitler's injuries proved more serious than had originally been assumed. On 21 July, he suffered intense pain and began bleeding from his right ear. The following day, attending physician Karl Brandt summoned the head staff physician and ear, nose and throat specialist at the

Karlshof reserve field hospital, Dr. Erwin Giesing, to the Wolf's Lair. The dictator complained about being almost totally deaf in his right ear and half-deaf in his left one and said he was suffering from bouts of vertigo. Giesing examined Hitler and found that his right inner ear had been badly damaged and his sense of balance disrupted. During the examination, Giesing had the chance to take a closer look at the dictator: "His face was pale and slightly puffy . . . His eyes did not make that entrancing impression on me that was so often described in the press and by people. I particularly noticed his pronounced nasolabial lines (running on both sides of his nose down to the corners of his mouth) and his dry, chapped lips. His hair had begun to turn grey and was not very neatly combed . . . His face was clean shaven, but his skin sagged, which I attributed at that moment to exhaustion."[105] On 23 July, Professor Carl von Eicken, the director of the ear, nose and throat department at Berlin's Charité Hospital, who had removed a polyp from Hitler's vocal cords back in 1935, was brought in for consultations. He confirmed Giesing's diagnosis and told Hitler's entourage to take it easy on the dictator in light of his health problems.[106] Guderian, who had been named Zeitzler's successor as chief of the general staff on the evening of 20 July, found Hitler "very much the worse for wear" the following day.[107] And Bernd Freytag von Loringhoven, Guderian's personal adjutant, was positively taken aback when he saw Hitler two days after that: "This was not the Führer of the Greater German Reich, but a 55-year-old with the posture of a geriatric, bent, limping, his head retracted between his shoulder blades, with a pale face, a dull gaze and wan, grey skin. He took tiny steps when he walked, dragging his left leg behind him and wearing a sling around his right arm, which had been slightly injured in the attack . . . I saw to my horror that the Reich was being led by a human wreck."[108]

Hitler's health would remain precarious for weeks after the failed assassination. In a situation meeting on the night of 31 July–1 August, the Führer himself conceded that he no longer dared speak in front of a large audience for fear of "suddenly being beset by vertigo and fainting."[109] At first, a side-effect of the bomb blast was that the trembling in his left arm and leg subsided somewhat, but it soon returned stronger than ever.[110] Hitler was still bleeding from his right ear in August, when he made a "somewhat fragile impression" on those around him, with one eyewitness writing: "Gradually it is being revealed that the Führer suffered a severe physical shock from the attack."[111] Werner Kreipe, named Luftwaffe chief of staff in late July to replace Günther Korten, who had died in the attack, noted on 11 August: "The Führer has become very hunched. Wears cotton wool in his ears. Often he trembles severely. You can only shake his hand very gently."[112]

Hitler's irritability discharged itself in bursts of rage at the conspirators and the general staff as a whole. "Now I have finally got the swine who have been sabotaging my work for years," the Führer snarled on one occasion. ". . . Now I have proof that the whole general staff is contaminated."[113] His distrust of the military leadership, already strong, was transformed into boundless hatred. It was clear why all of his military plans of the past few years had failed, he proclaimed, as more and more details of the conspirators and the background of their plot emerged. "Betrayal" had been at work everywhere.[114] Hitler's outbreaks were a mix of rage and satisfaction since the dictator also felt that he had all at once been proven right: that Germany's military setbacks were the result not of his own failings, but rather of ongoing sabotage by the officer corps. Over lunch on 23 July, he called the assassination attempt a "disgrace for the German army of epochal proportions."[115] In the situation meeting the following day, he asserted that the conspiracy had been planned and launched in close collaboration with the British, who would now be forced to realise that they had backed the wrong horse and the "whole thing had collapsed." Hitler added that despite everything it was "a stroke of luck" that the assassination attempt had come when it did. A higher power had brought Stauffenberg with his bomb to the Wolf's Lair at precisely the "most advantageous" psychological moment. "By the way, the fellow had also gone through the Berghof and inspected my dining room," Hitler added.[116] The Führer would return again and again to the events of 20 July in the coming weeks and months. Indeed, it became his favourite topic for conversation: a date that represented, in his eyes, not only "the deepest point in our wartime crisis" but the "inaugural day of our re-ascent."[117]

One consequence of the failed assassination attempt was that security in the Wolf's Lair was drastically tightened. It was now "very difficult to get into the main headquarters," Goebbels noted when he visited Hitler on 22 July. "The attack has also had an effect on how the Führer is guarded. Thank God. What transpired during the treacherous betrayal of Count Stauffenberg must never be repeated."[118] The propaganda minister found the atmosphere in the Wolf's Lair on the whole quite oppressive, writing that he "constantly felt as though a general staff officer were standing in the shadows with a drawn pistol or a parcel of dynamite at the ready."[119] From now on, everyone who took part in situation briefings would be physically searched for weapons or explosives.[120] Officers invited to the headquarters to be decorated by the Führer had to undergo the same procedure. Major Remer was appointed "battle commandant" of the Wolf's Lair as a reward for his actions on 20 July.[121] One further consequence, in the immediate aftermath of the attack, was that the Hitler salute was made mandatory for the Wehrmacht. Göring had suggested this on 23 July, and Hitler approved the change "entirely without emotion."[122]

Driven by his limitless thirst for revenge, Hitler was determined to set a "bloody example" and "eradicate from the roots up the whole clan of generals that opposes us." "The judgement to be carried out will have to be of historical dimensions," the dictator ordered.[123] At Hitler's command, a "court of honour" that included Keitel, Guderian and Rundstedt was convened to expel all the officers involved in the conspiracy from the Wehrmacht and put them up before the People's Court for trial and conviction. "They should be hanged like common traitors," Hitler demanded. "And they should not be allowed at any time to hold long speeches [in their defence]." Hitler believed that the People's Court chief judge, Roland Freisler, "will get the job done." "He is our Vyshinsky," the Führer remarked in reference to Stalin's chief prosecutor in the show trials of the 1930s.[124]

On 7 August, the first trial began. In the dock were eight conspirators, including Witzleben, Hoepner, Stieff and Yorck von Wartenburg. Freisler more than fulfilled Hitler's expectations, intervening in the proceedings in ways that made a mockery of normal legal procedure. He left no opportunity unused to heap ridicule and scorn on the defendants and deprive them of their dignity, interrupting their testimony whenever they sought to explain themselves, or simply shouting them down.[125] On 8 August, all eight defendants were sentenced to death and hanged that evening in Berlin's Plötzensee Prison. A camera recorded every last twitch of the condemned men during their strangulation. The film footage was sent with photos of the hanged men to the Wolf's Lair. It is uncertain whether Hitler ever watched the film or looked at the images.[126]

After 20 July, the regime did all it could to apprehend everyone involved in any way with the conspiracy. The head of the Reich Security Main Office, Ernst Kaltenbrunner, was put in charge of the investigations. The day after the attack, he formed the "Special 20 July Commission," and the results of this body's activities were summarised in reports Kaltenbrunner sent to Bormann.[127] It soon became clear that, contrary to initial assumptions, the attack had not been the deed of a "small clique" of officers, but had extended far more widely. More and more people were being arrested. "I think we are on the trail of the biggest military plot that Prussian-German history has ever known," Goebbels remarked on 25 July.[128] The propaganda minister was particularly outraged when he learned that even Count Wolf Heinrich von Helldorff, the former Berlin police president, had been involved in the attempted putsch. Hitler ordered that Helldorff, who was sentenced to death in mid-August, be forced to watch the hanging of three other condemned men before he himself was executed.[129]

Those who were arrested were made to suffer before they were put up before the People's Court. The Gestapo brutally tortured them during interrogations in the hopes they would give up the names of other putative conspirators and those who had known about the plot. Gradually, a broad network was uncovered and hardly anyone involved escaped the clutches of the persecuting authorities. In early February 1945, when Freisler was killed in an air raid on Berlin, the Nazi judicial system continued the trials. All told, more than a hundred death sentences were handed down, and numerous other people received terms of imprisonment.[130] Family members of conspirators were also held accountable, with women being sent to jail or concentration camps, and children to foster homes under false names. On top of that, in August 1944, Himmler initiated Operation Thunderstorm, which saw the arrests of around five thousand former parliamentary deputies and functionaries of the Weimar Republic, above all of the Social Democratic Party (SPD) and the German Communist Party

(KPD). As part of this operation, on 18 August the SS leader also obtained Hitler's permission to murder former KPD chairman Ernst Thälmann, who had been in prison since 1933, in the Buchenwald concentration camp.[131]

Among those who fell victim to the regime's vengeance was Hitler's one-time favourite military commander, Erwin Rommel. The field marshal, who had been severely wounded on 17 July, learned about the assassination attempt in hospital. "We can thank God that it turned out so well," he wrote to his wife on 24 July.[132] Was Rommel trying to conceal the fact that he had known in advance about the attempt on Hitler's life? On 9 July, the reserve Luftwaffe officer Cäsar von Hofacker had gone to see Rommel and tried to win him over to the resistance. It is uncertain to what extent the field marshal went along with the idea, but in any case, Hofacker was convinced that Rommel had changed sides and seriously incriminated him in Gestapo interrogations after the attack. In early August, Hitler was informed about the suspicions concerning Rommel. "The Führer got me to read out the report Kaltenbrunner composed about the statements of First Lieutenant Hofacker regarding his meeting with Rommel," Jodl noted. "He wants to question R. once he has recovered and then discharge him without any further testimony."[133]

By that point, as he told Goebbels, Hitler was quite certain that "while Rommel had not taken part in the planned assassination, he did know about it."[134] Such suspicions were fed by statements by other officers accused of being involved in the plot, including Stülpnagel and Rommel's chief of staff, Hans Speidel, who had been arrested on 7 September. Rommel was further implicated by the testimony of an informant who said the field marshal had expressed himself "very pessimistically" about the military situation to the Nazi district leader of Ulm, Rudolf Meier, when the latter visited him during his convalescence at his home in Herrlingen. The field marshal had also criticised Hitler, saying that the dictator was surrounded by men "with no experience of the front" and had, unlike Churchill, never shown his face in Normandy, which soldiers there had taken amiss. A party comrade of Meier in Ulm heard about these statements and sent an account of them to Bormann, who immediately not only informed Himmler but passed on the report to Hitler.[135] In a file note of 28 September, Bormann summarised the conclusion of the investigation by saying that Rommel had been "in the frame" and "had declared his willingness to participate in a new government after a successful assassination."[136]

At the latest after Speidel's arrest, Rommel knew that storm clouds were brewing up against him. In a handwritten letter to Hitler on 1 October, he vouched for his chief of staff and assured the dictator of his unreserved loyalty: "You, my Führer, know how I have given all my strength and ability, whether it be during the western offensive in 1940 or in Africa in 1941–3 or in Italy in 1943 or again in the west in 1944. I am completely consumed by the thought of fighting and achieving victory for your new Germany."[137] He signed the letter "Hail my Führer." Hitler was not fooled and summoned Rommel to Berlin a few days later. The field marshal suspected what was up and refused to follow the order, claiming that his health did not permit him to leave home for any length of time. The dictator interpreted Rommel's refusal as an admission of guilt. On 14 October, the commander was paid a visit in Herrlingen by General Wilhelm Burgdorf, Schmundt's successor as Hitler's chief adjutant, and General Ernst Maisel, who was in charge of "matters of honour" in the army's personnel office. In Hitler's name, they presented Rommel with the incriminating inter-rogation testimony and gave him a choice of committing suicide or appearing before the People's Court. The Nazis must have been extremely sure of what Rommel would choose since it would have been a huge risk to haul up the still very popular field marshal in front of the People's Court. In part to protect his wife and son from perse-cution, Rommel decided to end his life. He took leave of his family, got into the car with Hitler's messengers and swallowed a cyanide capsule just outside the Herrlingen town boundary. Officially, his death was attributed to the injuries he had sustained in July. Hitler arranged for a pompous state funeral in Ulm, and Rundstedt topped off this hypocritical performance by concluding his memorial address with the words "His heart belonged to the Führer."[138]

The failure of the conspiracy led to a further radicalisation of the home front of the sort Goebbels had demanded in June 1944. On 22 July, leaders of the Wehrmacht, the state and the Nazi Party, including Keitel, Bormann, Goebbels, Speer, Funk and plenipotentiary for labour deployment Fritz Sauckel, came together in the East Prussian field quarters of the head of the Reich Chancellery, Hans Heinrich Lammers, to discuss how to master the current crisis. Lammers declared that the Committee of Three, which had been formed in early 1943, had not been able to fulfil its function as a leadership instrument because of the resistance of the heads of various departments. He now suggested that Goebbels be equipped with broad-ranging powers to mobilise the entire civilian sector. Himmler, whom Hitler had already appointed head of the Replacement Army, would also be given special authority to reorganise the Wehrmacht.[139] These proposals were aimed at creating an "internal wartime dictatorship," Goebbels noted, adding that he felt "equal to the task and strong enough to use his powers to achieve the greatest possible effect for the war effort."[140]

In a meeting at the Wolf's Lair on 23 July, Hitler declared himself in basic agreement with the proposed measures. Goebbels was elated to see that the dictator had adopted in their entirety the arguments he had previously put forward in a memorandum. "Something fundamental must be done or else we will not win the war," the propaganda minister wrote, summarising Hitler's reasoning. "We still have enormous reserves at our disposal, but they are not being utilised. In view of the situation at the front, this is practically irresponsible . . . The standpoint represented by the Führer is quite radical and decisive . . . What has happened particularly on the day of the assassination attempt and on the eastern front has lent clarity to the decisions." To avoid offending Göring, Lammers formulated the "Edict of the Führer on the Total Commitment to War" in such a way that the Reich marshal did not feel as if he had been bypassed. "In order to adapt public life in all its aspects to the demands of waging total war," Göring was to appoint a "Reich plenipotentiary for the total war effort" who would ensure that a "maximum of strength was freed up for the Wehrmacht and arms production." Everyone involved understood that Goebbels was the only candidate for this post. The propaganda minister left the Wolf's Lair feeling he had achieved "probably the greatest success of [my] life."[141] Hitler signed the directive on 25 July, and Goebbels ordered the German press to give "the most extensive coverage" to his appointment to the new post.[142]

Along with Himmler and Goebbels, the other great winner coming out of the events of 20 July was Bormann, nicknamed the "Führer's Mephisto."[143] He now restricted access to the dictator even more rigidly than before and exploited the atmosphere of crisis to strengthen the Gauleiters at the expense of the state bureaucracy, thereby expanding his own sphere of influence.[144] In the wake of the attack on Hitler, he told the Reichsleiters and Gauleiters, the leading men of the regime would have to conduct themselves in exemplary fashion in every respect. It was "more necessary than ever" to show "the deepest connection with the people." For that reason, Nazi leaders should steer clear of parties and amusements. "These are no longer times for partying but for working tirelessly and constantly," Bormann puffed.[145]

The fourth figure to benefit from the radicalisation of domestic policy was Speer. Ever since he had restructured Germany's arms production, achieving impressive increases in output in all sectors, he had risen in Hitler's estimation and accrued more and more power. In September, Hitler personally promoted him from minister of arms and munitions to minister of armaments and wartime production. He seemed to be well on his way towards supplanting Göring as the second-highest functionary in the Nazi state.[146] Speer made no bones about his drive for power in his memoirs, about which his long-term associate Rudolf Wolters effused in 1969: "Descriptions flow with particular ease from your pen about how you avoided all the traps set by your powerful competitors and got those who set the traps to stumble into them, how you as a 'master in diplomatic intrigue' ultimately pushed your adversaries to one side, how to the amazement of everyone involved you expanded your office to a previously unknown scope, and finally how easily you got your armaments machine up and running at top speed within the shortest span of time."[147]

In January 1944, Speer had suffered a breakdown and had been checked into the Hohenlychen Clinic, north of Berlin. In the constant tug of war for Hitler's favour, it was a great disadvantage for an underling to disappear from the Führer's radar for even a short period.[148] Speer was gone for months, and his enemies in the party— first and foremost Bormann and ambitious competitors within his ministry such as Technical Office head Karl-Otto Saur and Organisation Todt director Xaver Dorsch—exploited his absence and tried to undermine his standing with Hitler. But after clearing the air at the Berghof in April, Speer was back in good graces as a member of Hitler's court, and in early May, he returned to his position, where he was able to consolidate and even expand his power. On 1 August, Göring was forced to cede responsibility for air force armaments. From that point on, Speer and his ministry were in charge of all significant production of weapons.[149]

The radicalisation of the regime after 20 July had produced a four-man leadership team consisting of the most efficient and unscrupulous of Hitler's underlings. In the final year of war, this quadrumvirate controlled the lion's share of the Nazi apparatus of rule, but their power was mediated, not autonomous. Hitler remained the decisive force, and everything Himmler, Goebbels, Bormann and Speer embarked on took place within the framework set by the Führer. "I lived in constant 'fear of my master,'" Speer confessed in 1975. "It was not easy to deal with him and keep or, if possible, intensify his favour."[150] The three other Nazi leaders must have felt likewise. Until the final days of the war, none of them even thought of challenging Hitler's authority. Their long-term personal connection to the Führer continued intact, even as they competed among themselves to extend their authority at the expense of the others.[151]

The Reichsleiters and Gauleiters were introduced to this new constellation at a conference in Posen on 3 and 4 August 1944. Goebbels lectured them about the measures he intended to take as the Reich plenipotentiary for total war, Speer presented impressive arms production figures, and Himmler discussed the prehistory of the 20 July plot and the consequences that would be drawn in terms of reforming the Wehrmacht.[152] Following the conference, Hitler summoned the Reichsleiter and Gauleiter to the Wolf's Lair to reassure himself of their loyalty. Still visibly shaken by the assassination attempt, the dictator repeated the claim he had made in front of smaller circles that the attack was the act of a conspiracy of officers and the culmination of years of betrayal, which had been aimed solely at sabotaging his will. Hitler told his minions that it was "a sign from Providence and a personal relief that the domestic resistance, which has never been apprehensible, has now been uncovered and the clique of criminals got rid of." The putsch's failure, he added, had given him a conviction more profound than any he had known before: that "in the end we will . . . come through this war victorious."[153]

Goebbels threw himself into his new responsibility with élan. In a memo to all government offices, he wrote that he was determined "to carry out the total waging of war so that the nation yields the absolute peak performance." Germans would be more willing to make the necessary sacrifices, he continued, "if they could see the leadership setting a positive example and knew that the burdens of war were being fairly distributed."[154] But the propaganda minister was mistaken in his belief that his new office conferred upon him near-dictatorial powers. Although he could issue instructions to high-level government offices, he needed the support of Bormann and the Gauleiters. In fact, he soon encountered great obstacles. Although the previous year the two men had been pulling in the same direction, the propaganda minister's attempt to divert large numbers of labourers deemed essential to arms production to the Wehrmacht now foundered on determined opposition by Speer. As a result Goebbels sought to ally himself with Bormann against the armaments minister. "I think we have allowed this young man to get a bit big," Goebbels complained in late September after Speer had threatened to resign.[155] As usual Hitler avoided taking sides in the struggle between his paladins, but everyone concerned could see that Speer was in danger of losing his role as the Führer's favourite as quickly as he had regained it.[156]

On the other hand, by no means did Hitler automatically agree with all of Goebbels' radical suggestions. Hitler was even keener at calculating the psychological effects of each individual measure than his propaganda minister. Thus, in August 1944, Bormann told Goebbels that the Führer had stressed that "fundamentally, in every case, it must be considered whether an end result justified the disruption it entailed in the short or long term." In line with this principle, Hitler ruled out any cutbacks to the post office and the cancellation of magazines for the front,[157] and he needed considerable persuading to shut theatres and entertainment venues. He also vetoed the discontinuation of the production of sweets and beer. Soldiers "depended on lozenges during marches," he reasoned, and he feared "severe psychological setbacks, particularly in Bavaria," if brewing beer was forbidden. "The Führer views this question more from a Bavarian mentality, which is quite alien to me," complained Goebbels, who found it difficult to give up "these plans, which have grown close to my heart."[158] However, the newly named plenipotentiary did succeed by the end of 1944 in mobilising around a million men for deployment in the Wehrmacht, although many were hardly battle-ready and overall the numbers did not compensate for Germany's severe losses on all fronts.[159] It was becoming increasingly clear that the Third Reich faced military defeat, and after the attempt to get rid of the regime from within had failed, for its opponents the only alternative now was Germany's total demise. "The most terrible thing about this year was having to bury the hope of a turnaround from within," Ursula von Kardorff wrote at the end of 1944. "To witness and experience the demise and be unable to change anything."[160]

I4

Final Rally

"We will fight, if necessary, on the banks of the Rhine," Hitler proclaimed in a situation meeting in late August 1944. "Regardless of the circumstances, we will continue this battle until . . . one of our damned enemies will be too tired to fight, and until we obtain a peace that secures the life of the German nation for the next fifty or hundred years." If he had been killed in the 20 July assassination attempt, he added, it would have brought "liberation" from his daily cares: "It lasts only a fraction of a second, and then you are freed from everything, and you have calm and eternal peace." Nonetheless, he was "grateful to Providence" for keeping him alive since only an "iron-willed personality" such as his own could master the current crisis.[1]

Having failed to "push the Allies back into the sea" as planned, Hitler now pinned all his hopes on the prospect of the anti-German coalition falling apart. At some point the tensions between the Western powers and the Soviet Union would grow to the point that the alliance would break apart, he speculated. All Germany had to do was "watch for this moment"—under no circumstances could it afford to "lose its nerve."[2] The dictator who had once proclaimed, before and after the start of the war in 1939, that he had no time to lose was now playing a waiting game. "It must be in our interest to gain time and ensure that the moment things have ripened on the other side we are still standing in full strength on the battlefield," Hitler trumpeted in early September 1944.[3] He constantly referred back to the example of Friedrich the Great in the Seven Years War, arguing that the Prussian king had not got demoralised by military setbacks and had triumphed in the end when Empress Yelizaveta died suddenly, taking Russia out of the war and reversing what seemed to be a hopeless situation for Prussia. The more the myth of the Führer crumbled as Germany's defeat approached, the more Hitler resorted to invoking the "miracle of the House of Brandenburg" and the myth of Friedrich the Great as a source of legitimation. "As of 1944, comparisons with Friedrich's crisis-management techniques were part of Hitler's daily historical and political diet," the historian Wolfram Pyta has written.[4] Comparisons with Prussia's miraculous salvation became the Nazi Party's preferred means of keeping alive hopes that the war would end well. "Whoever talks to me about a peace without victory will lose his head, no matter who he is and where he stands" was something Hitler repeatedly said in situation meetings after 20 July.[5]

Of course, considerable distance from reality was required to turn a blind eye to Germany's precarious situation on both the western and eastern fronts. On 25 July, American troops west of Saint-Lô began Operation Cobra, a massive campaign of air bombardments of German positions that led to the Allies' decisive breakthrough in Normandy. Six days later, US troops took Avranches, clearing the way for a mobile offensive into the heart of France. While a corps of the US 3rd Army under George Patton advanced west to take the ports of Brittany, three other corps pushed south to the Loire and east towards Paris. "We are facing an enemy with massive superiority in materiel and manpower who is gradually wearing down my bravely fighting soldiers," Field Marshal Günther von Kluge, Germany's supreme commander west, confessed in a private letter. "I could tear myself to shreds, but it would probably have no effect on the dark cloud descending that will soon reach us."[6] Hitler was well aware of the danger in the west. "If we lose France as a theatre of war, we will lose the basis for our submarine warfare," he declared at a meeting with Jodl on the night of 31 July–1 August. While conceding that, given the Allies' air superiority, there was no way to fundamentally turn things around, Hitler believed that by manoeuvring cleverly, German troops could make it "colossally more difficult" for the enemy to "operate in the depth of space."[7]

That was precisely the focus of the German counter-offensive, code-named "Operation Lüttich," which Hitler ordered a few days later. It was supposed to burst through the left flank of Patton's army, cutting its supply lines. But the offensive, for which four German tank divisions were mobilised and which commenced during the night of

6–7 August, bogged down after a single day. Instead of inflicting heavy casualties on the enemy, German units, who had pressed forward 10 kilometres, now ran the risk of being encircled near Falaise. To salvage what he could, Kluge himself travelled to the headquarters of the embattled German 5th Tank Army on 15 August. When he could not be reached for twenty-four hours, however, Hitler suspected the field marshal had secretly established contact with the Allies to negotiate an armistice. On 17 August, he stripped Kluge of his command and replaced him with Field Marshal Walter Model, who was expected to do in the west what he had partially achieved in the east: stabilise a hopeless-looking front.

Kluge was stung by his failure to achieve his mission and beset with worries that he could be hauled up in front of the People's Court because of his connections to the 20 July conspirators. On his way back to Germany on 19 August, he committed suicide near Metz; a Reich Security Main Office investigation revealed that he had taken cyanide.[8] In a farewell note to Hitler, Kluge called on the Führer to end the war. At the same time, he praised his supreme commander for having "fought an honourable and great battle." Kluge concluded his note with these apparently heartfelt words: "I depart from you, my Führer, as someone who in the knowledge of having done his duty to the very limit was closer to you than you perhaps realise."[9]

The day Kluge took his life, his troops were surrounded in Falaise. Between 35,000 and 40,000 German soldiers, including the majority of staff members and higher-ranking officers, had been able to escape encirclement, but 50,000 others were taken captive. In addition, the troops had lost most of their tanks and assault guns. By now the Allies were racking up impressive triumphs not just in Normandy but in southern France as well. The fifteenth of August saw the start of Operation Dragoon, in which US forces landed on the Mediterranean coast on either side of Saint-Tropez, quickly expanding their bridge-head and pressing north. With the situation hopeless, Hitler had no choice but to order a general German retreat from southern France. Absorbing heavy casualties, Army Group G under Colonel-General Johannes Blaskowitz succeeded in battling its way through the Rhône Valley towards Alsace-Lorraine.[10] The German retreat meant that the days of the Vichy regime were numbered. On 20 August, the Security Service brought Marshal Pétain and his underlings first to Belfort and then to Sigmaringen, near Lake Constance. There they formed a French "government-in-exile" that would exist until late April 1945.[11]

Hitler would not hear of vacating Paris without a fight. In early August 1944, he named Lieutenant-General Dietrich von Choltitz commander of the Wehrmacht in Greater Paris and ordered him to defend the city with all the means at his disposal. The French metropolis, the Führer stressed again on 23 August, would only be handed over to the enemy as a "field of rubble."[12] But Choltitz did not carry out Hitler's orders. After the Résistance had begun an uprising against the German occupiers, Allied troops entered Paris on 25 August, with a French tank division at the vanguard. General Charles de Gaulle, the leader of the Free France movement, was celebrated with indescribable joy as he made his way down the Champs-Élysées. But in many *départements*, the German occupation ended with the executions of prisoners, mostly members of the Résistance, and Waffen-SS and Wehrmacht units massacred French civilians as they beat their retreat.

In late August and early September, a catastrophe seemed to be brewing for Germany in the west. There was no longer any cohesive front, and the Wehrmacht was more fleeing than retreating. One soldier reported that all the troops he encountered, with very few exceptions, had given up hope and tried to move backwards any way they could.[13] Among the remains of units pouring back towards Germany were bureaucrats and officials who had heretofore led a comfortable existence in France. "The swine behind the front who filled their gullets and stuffed their bellies were of course the first to leave the French capital," an outraged Goebbels wrote. "Now they show up in ragged caravans in Lorraine . . . and offer a pitiable spectacle of German decline."[14]

At a meeting with his propaganda minister on 2 September, Hitler as usual blamed the collapse of the western front on "sheer betrayal." Ignoring the truth, he insisted that Kluge had intended to "go over to the enemy" and had purposely sabotaged the German counteroffensive in Avranches. In blunt language, Hitler regretted having awarded Kluge a generous bonus and honouring him in front of other officers.[15] On this score, not even Goebbels could resist remarking critically in his diary: "I always considered the Führer's accommodation of the army generals entirely misguided. The commanders do not understand generosity. They have to be kept on a short leash;

otherwise they get above their station." At their meeting, the dictator expressed his hope that dispersed German troops could be reassembled and a solid front re-established in the west. The border with the Reich had to be defended at all costs, he stressed, and therefore all forces at Germany's disposal must be thrown at the Siegfried Line.[16] But initially at least, the chances of stopping the enemy advance did not look good. On 3 September, Allied troops liberated Brussels, and the following day Antwerp, with the city's vital port facilities falling into their hands undamaged. Nonetheless, it was two months before they could be used for resupply purposes since German forces still controlled the mouth of the river Scheldt.[17]

On 11 September, American troops crossed the German border for the first time near Aachen, although it would not be until 21 October that they took the badly damaged city.[18] On 5 September, Hitler had reinstated Rundstedt as supreme commander west, with Model taking over command of Army Group B. Nine days later, Rundstedt ordered the Siegfried Line to be held "until the final bullet or the complete destruction" of the enemy. This command was followed two days later by instructions from Hitler that anticipated the extremity of his infamous "Nero decree" of March 1945: "Every bunker, every block of houses in a German town, every German village, must become a fortification in which the enemy bleeds to death or the occupiers are entombed in man-to-man fighting."[19] As had been the case during the German retreats from the Soviet Union and France, in Germany too nothing potentially useful for waging war was to be left intact to fall into enemy hands. Goebbels echoed Hitler when he wrote: "This is the ultimate extreme, and if a nation is fighting for its life, we cannot shy away from the ultimate extreme." Yet Goebbels was contradicted by Speer, who informed the propaganda minister that strictly applying the scorched-earth principle to the industry and infrastructure of the Ruhr Valley, for instance, would leave it so devastated that reconstruction would take years, and there would be no sense in retaking it. If Germany's industrial heartland and the centre of its arms production were lost, Speer added, the Reich would not be able to continue the war for long.[20]

In the second half of September, American and British advances slowed as the Allies struggled to resupply their troops. At the same time, German resistance stiffened. General Montgomery's Operation

Market Garden, the airlifting of paratroopers into the Netherlands at Arnhem, proved a disaster, marking the failure of the plan to cross the Rhine, skirt the Siegfried Line to the north and then penetrate the Ruhr Valley.[21] All Allied talk of an "easy stroll through the heart of the Reich" had ceased, a relieved Goebbels noted.[22] In fact, US and British forces would face months of fierce fighting and heavy casualties. A quick end to the war in the west was nowhere in sight.

Over the course of the summer of 1944, the Red Army retook the rest of the Soviet territory that had been occupied since 1941 and pushed through eastern Poland to the Vistula. In the second half of July, Model had managed to stabilise the front occupied by Army Group Centre, which Hitler had described as a "hole."[23] But by the end of the month a new crisis had arisen. Soviet troops achieved a breakthrough on the seam between Army Groups North and Centre and advanced to the Gulf of Riga near Tukums, trapping Army Group North on the Baltic. At the same time, the situation for Army Group Centre was again growing critical. A gap had been created on their southern flank with Army Group Northern Ukraine, which vanguard Soviet tank units were able to exploit. After reaching the Vistula in the Puławy region, they turned north and began to attack Warsaw on 27 July. It seemed only a matter of time until the city would fall, but then there occurred what the German side would later call "the second miracle on the Vistula"—the first being Marshal Józef Piłsudski's victory over the Red Army before the gates of Warsaw in 1920. Catching the Soviets by surprise, four German tank divisions, which Model had transferred from other parts of the front, attacked leading Red Army units east of Warsaw, inflicting a costly defeat. Army Group Centre's front, which had threatened to collapse like a house of cards, had been saved again.[24] "We think we have survived the worst of it and that things will soon be looking up in a major way," Governor-General Hans Frank wrote confidently to his wife.[25]

This surprising turnaround had catastrophic effects for the Polish capital. Trusting that the Red Army was about to enter the city and German troops were no longer capable of mounting any effective defence, the Polish resistance under General Tadeusz Bór-Komorowski had launched an uprising in Warsaw on 1 August. They hoped to send a signal that they were able to liberate the city on their own. At the same time, they wanted to demonstrate their independence from the Lublin Committee, the puppet regime installed by Stalin after he had become estranged from the Polish government-in-exile following the revelations about the Katyn massacre in 1943. Having lost the tank battle before Warsaw, Soviet troops could hardly have rushed to the Polish insurgents' rescue even if they had wanted to, but even later, when they were able to help their nominal allies, Red Army soldiers stayed on the Vistula and did nothing. It was evidently part of Stalin's plans for a reordering of central Europe after the war to weaken the non-communist forces fighting for Polish independence. Thus the Germans were given a free hand to crush the Polish resistance, and they went about that task with extreme brutality.[26] SS units not only killed thousands of insurgents, but arbitrarily massacred civilians. On 2 October, the Polish underground army surrendered, and Warsaw was levelled.[27]

Field Marshal Model had been transferred to the western front on 16 August, and Colonel-General Hans-Georg Reinhardt had assumed command of Army Group Centre. Operation Doppelkopf commenced that very day. It saw two tank corps push northeast through the so-called Baltic gap in an attempt to re-establish a connection with Army Group North. At the last minute, just as the operation seemed doomed, German troops achieved a breakthrough. On 20 August, a force led by Major-General Court Hyazinth Strachwitz reached Army Group North's lines. That led to an extended period of calm along the northern front.[28]

By contrast, the southern sector of the front was in flux again. In the early hours of 20 August, the long-feared major Soviet offensive commenced, and by the second day, it was clear that German and Romanian troops would not be able to hold their defensive positions in Moldavia and on the Dniester. It looked as though Army Group Southern Ukraine, which had been under the command of Colonel-General Johannes Friessner since 23 July, was headed for a debacle.[29] But at stake also was Romania's participation in the Axis. "The Romanians are not holding their ground, and it is likely that they will jump ranks politically as well," prophesied Goebbels.[30]

The German leadership had long had its doubts about Romania's reliability as an ally. The Romanian people were clearly tired of the war, and opposition groups were forming in both the army and Romanian politics that wanted to get the country out of the conflict as quickly as possible. To this end, opposition leaders sought to contact both the Western Allies and the Soviet Union. At a meeting in the Wolf's Lair on 5 August, Marshal Antonescu responded evasively when Hitler asked him "if he was willing to endure the battle to the end." The marshal reassured his ally that Romania would loyally do its duty, but he also brought up the "serious unease that had seized himself, the Romanian army and the Romanian people over events on the eastern front." He added that Romania had suffered disproportionately from enemy air raids, which, if they continued, would soon cause "a social, military and economic catastrophe."[31] By this point, Hitler must have recognised how unstable the situation in Romania was. On 23 August, he remarked that Antonescu would go "through thick and thin" with Germany but that he was likely to be deposed in the very near future.[32]

The Führer's prophecy came true even sooner than he expected. That very afternoon, Romania's King Mihal I had Antonescu arrested and installed a cross-party government under Colonel-General Constantin Sănătescu. In a radio address that evening, the king told his subjects that Romania would immediately cease all hostilities and conclude an armistice with the Allies. Hitler wasted no time in ordering the coup to be put down by German troops stationed in the Bucharest area. But this hasty operation, supported by massive Luftwaffe air strikes on the Romanian capital, was a pathetic failure. On 25 August, Romania declared war on Germany, and within a few days, Soviet troops had taken almost all of its territory. On 28 August, they occupied Bucharest and two days later the oil fields of Ploeşti that were so critical to the German war effort. Within two weeks, some 286,000 Wehrmacht soldiers had been killed or captured, and Friessner retreated back over the Carpathian mountain passes with the remnants of his army group.[33]

Romania's change of side put pressure on its southern neighbour, Bulgaria, whose government had successfully avoided getting drawn into the Axis' war on the Soviet Union and from 1943 onwards had gradually distanced itself from Nazi Germany. By late August 1944, the Bulgarians demanded that the German regime immediately with-draw its military commission and all its troops. Nonetheless, on 5

September, the Soviet Union declared war on Bulgaria, and three days later the Red Army marched into the country. That same day, 8 September, Bulgaria declared war on Germany.[34] The loss of Romania and Bulgaria, and the Soviet Union's swift occupation of both countries, shattered Germany's position in southeastern Europe. Now Army Group E, stationed on the Greek mainland and islands, faced being isolated. In early September, German forces began retreating from the Balkan Peninsula. On 12 October, the final German units left Athens, and two days later British troops entered the Greek capital.[35] Hungary remained loyal to the Axis, but Admiral Horthy was by now also considered an unreliable ally and Germany's leadership began to prepare for a variety of eventualities. "There is a danger that the Hungarians will turn on us just like the Romanians and Bulgarians," noted Goebbels in late September. "There is no counting on Horthy. For that reason, the Führer intends to take energetic political measures here."[36]

Hitler's empire was wobbling not only in the southeast of Europe but in the north as well. In the spring of 1944, the Finnish government held secret peace talks with the Soviet Union. Initially Moscow's terms were so harsh that Helsinki put the negotiations on ice. But the major setbacks suffered by Army Group North that summer convinced the Finns to resume the peace discussions. On 1 August, the government under President Risto Ryti stepped down, just five days after assuring Hitler that Finland would only reach a settlement with the Soviet Union if given Germany's prior approval. Ryti's successor, Marshal Carl Gustaf Emil Mannerheim, did not feel bound by this promise, and Hitler's attempt on 17 August to bind him to their alliance by having Keitel award him the Oak Cluster of the Knight's Cross of the Iron Cross did nothing to change Mannerheim's mind. On 2 September, he informed Hitler that Finland could no longer continue the war on Germany's side. Seventeen days later, after some difficult negotiations, the Finnish-Soviet armistice was signed. Around 200,000 German troops retreated to Norway via Lapland, leaving "scorched earth" in their wake.[37] "Politically the loss of Finland is of course very regrettable," remarked Goebbels. "It will also contribute to worsening our prospects in the war."[38] The German war economy had a hard time compensating for the loss of the Petsamo nickel mines.

With Germany suffering defeat everywhere, states that had vacillated between the two sides in the war began to reorient themselves. On 2 August, Turkey broke off diplomatic relations with the Third Reich, a serious blow above all to the German arms industry's supply of chrome. The previous year, in July 1943, neutral Sweden had cancelled the transit treaty with Germany that allowed German military transports access to its territory, and in September 1944 it closed its waters to all belligerents—a move that was primarily directed against Germany since it prevented iron exports.[39] It was obvious that the German war economy would have difficulty maintaining high levels of production in the long term. Moreover, there was increased resistance in all countries collaborating with Germany. A rebellion broke out in Slovakia in late August 1944, and German troops were forced to occupy the country to prop up Jozef Tiso's puppet government. As they had in Warsaw, the occupiers put down the rebellion with extreme brutality.[40]

"Naturally we only get unpleasant news from the occupied areas," Goebbels wrote in mid-September 1944. "No one believes in a German victory any more. Our stock has hit rock bottom."[41] By that point, the mood in the Reich itself had reached an "unprecedented low." The Propaganda Ministry's reports spoke of increasingly widespread concern that "the war can no longer be won" and of more and more "ethnic-popular comrades" contemplating suicide. The desertion of Germany's allies drew remarks like "The rats are leaving the sinking ship."[42] Goebbels himself was having increasing difficulty writing his weekly editorials in the newspaper Das Reich. "One hardly knows what to write," he sighed.[43]

Against this grim backdrop, an article in the Völkischer Beobachter in late August attracted much attention. The author, war correspondent Joachim Fernau, cited an uncompleted sentence supposedly uttered by Winston Churchill: "We have to end the war by autumn or else . . ." Fernau commented: "By autumn . . . so we know why we are expending one final great burst of effort. This is not beyond our strength. We have never given up in a critical situation in this war. We will pay the final price we have to pay. With all means available and with all our strength. Victory truly is quite near!"[44] Goebbels was incensed when he read the article, which he saw as raising the false hope among the population that a "complete turnaround in the war could happen in no time."[45] In fact, Fernau had been speculating about a German miracle weapon that, it was rumoured, was to be deployed in the autumn and decide the war. The article was "the maddest thing" the Nazis had ever come up with on the propaganda front, thought Victor Klemperer. Yet he too was unsure whether it might not contain a kernel of truth. "Germany is playing poker," he wrote. "Is it bluffing or does it have a few trumps left?"[46]

One such trump card would have been an atomic bomb whose power would have overshadowed anything previously known. Back in late March 1942, Goebbels had been briefed about the results of Germany's nuclear research. As the propaganda minister had commented: "Modern technology gives human beings means of destruction that are inconceivable. In this regard, German science is at the pinnacle, and it is necessary too that we lead the way, since he who introduces a revolutionary novelty into the war is more likely to win it."[47] At his meeting with Antonescu on 5 August 1944, Hitler made oblique references to a new super-weapon whose effects were so great that "all human life would be destroyed in a radius of 3–4 kilometres around the site of impact."[48] Yet by that point, Germany had already lost the race to build the atomic bomb.

In the summer of 1942, the fundamental decision had been taken to pursue Germany's nuclear programme only in modest fashion. At the time, the Nazi leadership had expected to subdue the Soviet Union on the second attempt, thereby deciding the war, while the nuclear physicists around Werner Heisenberg had insisted that, even with huge amounts of money and resources, it would take years to build an atomic bomb. Speer and Hitler therefore concluded that this new weapon would have no decisive significance for the war. By contrast, the United States had decided in June 1942 to push ahead with the development of the atomic bomb on an industrial scale. As a result, enormous effort was put into the Manhattan Project. While the Americans were carrying out the first successful test of an atomic weapon in the desert of New Mexico in July 1945, even at the end of the war, Germany was still a long way from a nuclear bomb. The American historian Mark Walker has disproved as legend German scientists' post-war claims that they purposely sabotaged Germany's nuclear programme to keep Hitler from getting the bomb. If they had been given sufficient resources, they would no doubt have built an atomic weapon, and Hitler would surely have had no scruples about using it.[49]

In the summer and autumn of 1944, rumours again surfaced of Germany concluding a separate peace with the Soviet Union. The initiative again came from Japan. Germany's east Asian ally had been forced to swallow one defeat after another in the Pacific War. In June and July 1944, American GIs had conquered the Mariana Islands, where they set up bases for bombarding Japan. On 18 July, the Tojo regime stepped down, although the new government announced that it would continue the war by all means necessary.[50] Ambassador Oshima in Berlin was instructed to press the German government to reach an understanding with the Soviet Union. The Japanese believed that the Wehrmacht would then be in a position to concentrate all of its forces in the battle with the Western Allies, providing relief for Japanese troops in the Pacific. On 4 September, Oshima presented his government's request in the Wolf's Lair. Hitler was reserved, saying he had heard nothing about any willingness on Stalin's part to enter into talks with Germany. When asked whether Tokyo had put out any feelers in that regard, Oshima answered in the negative.[51]

But the Japanese ambassador refused to relent. On 19 September, he announced to Goebbels' deputy in the Propaganda Ministry, Werner Naumann, that a separate peace between Germany and the Soviet Union was in Japan's "vital interest." Stalin, he argued, was "a realist" and would not turn a deaf ear to the wish for such an arrangement. Germany would, it was true, have to make a sacrifice and scale back its war aims in the east. But in return it would regain a "free hand towards the west." Naumann immediately briefed Goebbels about this conversation.[52] Oshima's initiative came at an opportune time for the propaganda minister, who had himself intensively pondered in previous days "how the war could be turned around by political means."[53] Goebbels had keenly followed the news about the conference between Roosevelt and Churchill in Quebec from 11 to 16 September and had concluded that the differences between the Western Allies and the Soviet Union were growing.[54] German diplomacy, he reasoned, would have to exploit this situation, even though he considered Foreign Minister Joachim von Ribbentrop uniquely ill suited to bring about a political resolution. "Foreign policy now belongs in the hands of a man who possesses intelligence, vigour and the necessary flexibility," Goebbels wrote.[55] The man the propaganda minister had in mind was most probably himself.

So Goebbels decided to take an unusual step. On 20 September, he composed a long memorandum in which he not only tried to convince Hitler that he needed to reach an understanding with Stalin but also demanded Ribbentrop be replaced as foreign minister. The propaganda minister was so pleased with his words that he included them in their entirety in his diary. "We are currently facing what we sought to avoid under any circumstances at the start of the war: the worst sort of a two-front battle," he wrote, adding that Germany had never won such a war in its history and would not be able to do so now. For that reason, Germany had to try to derive political capital from the conflicts in the enemy coalition that had emerged at the Quebec conference. Playing adeptly to Hitler's self-image, he drew a comparison to the situation the Nazis had found themselves in in late 1932 and early 1933. Back then, the party leadership had "operated cleverly" to exploit differences in the opposing political camp, thus achieving victory on 30 January 1933. The propaganda minister reiterated Oshima's arguments for a separate peace with the Soviet Union: "The German people would welcome such a turn in the war with the deepest satisfaction. We would become able to catch our breath in the west, and given the force of such an event, the English and Americans would hardly be able to continue fighting indefinitely." That, Goebbels admitted, would not be "the victory we dreamed of in 1941, but it would still be the greatest victory in German history."

Goebbels made no bones of the fact that he considered Ribbentrop unfit for taking the necessary steps in this scenario, and he went on to badmouth the foreign minister: "For him, prestige is more important than everything else. He refuses to accept good advice because he is too arrogant to listen to it. He alienates everyone, and in his stubbornness, for which he has so often been praised, he lacks the required intellectual elasticity. He treats foreign policy as some dark art he alone has mastered, and whenever he does deign to lift the veil somewhat, the only result is a poorly written editorial." To combat suspicions that he was angling for Ribbentrop's job, Goebbels concluded with assurances that he was not pursuing any "selfish ends" and that his memorandum had arisen from the "purest of intentions."[56] But given how familiar he was with the intrigues and machinations of his paladins, Hitler would hardly have been fooled.

Eagerly, Goebbels awaited Hitler's response from the Wolf's Lair. Several days passed before he learned that Hitler "had read through [the memorandum] attentively," but had not said anything about the points raised in it.[57] Much to Goebbels' renewed disappointment,[58] the Führer not only stuck with Ribbentrop, but never mentioned his propaganda minister's proposals in later conversations. Nothing had changed about his attitude towards a separate peace with the Soviet Union since the autumn of 1943. Hitler realised far more clearly than Goebbels that peace negotiations had no prospect with any of the Allies while the Third Reich was militarily on the defensive. If an opportunity for a political solution presented itself, he would not let it pass by, he declared at a situation meeting on 31 August 1944. But in times of heavy military defeats, Hitler explained, it was "of course childish" to hope for such a moment.[59]

Hitler was still dealing with the after-effects of the attempt on his life on 20 July. On 28 September, he collapsed, complaining of stomach and intestinal cramps, as his skin turned yellow. Morell prescribed strict bed rest and tried to ease the symptoms by administering castor oil and chamomile enemas. For days, Hitler lay apathetically on his bed in his bunker. For his entourage, this was an unaccustomed sight. "It seemed to me as though his body had realised the senselessness of all his mental efforts and his powerful will and gone on strike," his secretary Traudl Junge later recalled.[60] It was not until 2 October that Hitler could leave his bed and get dressed again, but he still felt weak for days. It took another nine days before he was able to walk from his bunker, and he was forced to sit down after only a few steps. Over the course of two weeks, he had lost eight kilograms.[61]

One of the consequences of Hitler's long infirmity was a vicious quarrel between his doctors. It was sparked by a seemingly explosive discovery made by the ear, nose and throat specialist Erwin Giesing. One day while examining the dictator, he noticed that among the many daily medications his patient was taking were little black pills against flatulence. Dr. Köster's Anti-Gas Pills contained strychnine, and when Giesing asked, Hitler's valet Heinz Linge confirmed that his master ingested two to four of them with every meal, far more than the usual dosage. Giesing informed Hanskarl von Hasselbach about what he had learned, and Hasselbach in turn told Karl Brandt. All three physicians concluded that thanks to Morell's negligence, the Führer was slowly being poisoned, and that strychnine was the true cause of his health complaints.[62]

Brandt saw this as a chance to discredit Morell, whom he had always considered a quack, and drive him from Hitler's court. Several weeks earlier, the unscrupulous Brandt, who had jointly organised the Nazi's "euthanasia" programme, had managed to get himself put in charge of general health care in the Third Reich—much to the ire of Bormann and Goebbels, who had jealously followed the rise of this Hitler favourite and member of Berghof society. "Brandt is a very ambitious young man who has no scruples and has largely realised his wide-ranging plans by constantly working on the Führer," Goebbels snarled.[63] In late August, Hitler appointed Brandt his Reich commissioner for medical services and health affairs. His office was categorised as a "Supreme Reich Authority." Equipped with this level of power, Brandt believed he would have an easy time engineering Morell's downfall. On 3 October, he informed his rival that he had evidence Hitler's illness was the result of "simple strychnine poisoning."[64] Morell responded that he had not prescribed the excessive dosage and complained to Hitler that evening about Brandt's attack. The dictator was extremely irritated, snapping: "Then these gentlemen should come to me—what do these stupid people want?"[65]

Brandt had underestimated Morell's influence while overestimating his own. Hitler's faith in his personal physician's abilities remained unbroken. "Without Morell, I could very well be long dead or unable to work," he was wont to say. "He was and is the only one who can help me."[66] On 8 October, he informed Morell that he intended to fire Brandt and Hasselbach as attending physicians, and the following day the two men were officially dismissed. Hitler's new attending surgeon was SS-Obersturmbannführer Ludwig Stumpfegger, a young doctor close to Himmler.[67] Goebbels could barely conceal his delight at how the "battle of the doctors" had turned out. Hitler had put his "unbridled faith" in Morell, Goebbels wrote, while Brandt would "soon realise how difficult it is when he can no longer lean on the Führer."[68] And indeed, Brandt shared the fate of other individuals who had been banned from Hitler's court. Without proximity to Hitler and the dictator's favour, his influence suddenly evaporated. Meanwhile, his hated rival Morell was still bathing in the Führer's good graces. "'My dear doctor, I am overjoyed that I have you,'" Morell recorded Hitler saying to him in early November 1944. "As he said that, he took my hand, squeezed it emotionally and gazed at me with a long, grateful look."[69]

Hardly had the dictator left his sick bed than he saw himself confronted with new threats on the eastern front. On 5 October, the Red Army started its major offensive against Army Group North, breaking through the 3rd Tank Army's positions and reaching the Baltic Sea north of Memel five days later. Most of Army Group North's thirty-three divisions were surrounded in Courland in western Latvia. Hitler and Guderian were soon at each other's throats. The chief of staff wanted to withdraw the army group and deploy it to defend East Prussia, while the dictator ruled out evacuating the cauldron. Courland, he insisted, was needed for testing out new submarines at the navy bases there. Moreover, battling the cauldron would tie down Soviet forces. The fighting in the area would continue up until the end of the war.[70]

Yet the roughly 250,000 frontline soldiers ordered to hold out in Courland were badly needed when the Red Army turned to attack East Prussia, where panic had already broken out in the summer as Soviet troops were drawing perilously close to the Reich borders. The Gauleiter of East Prussia, Erich Koch, ordered hundreds of thousands of civilians, women and men, to dig trenches and erect fortifications— a bulwark of exceedingly dubious military value.[71] On 16 October, the Red Army commenced its assault on German positions with unusually heavy artillery barrages. Two days later it succeeded in crossing the Reich border. Red Army tank units advanced 60 kilometres through Goldap (Gołdap) and Gumbinnen (Gusev), reaching the village of Nemmersdorf (Mayakovskoye) on 21 October. The Wolf's Lair near Rastenburg was less than 100 kilometres away. But the 4th Army under General Friedrich Hossbach, Hitler's former Wehrmacht adjutant, managed to hold the Soviet advance with a surprise counter-offensive, driving Red Army troops back out of all but a narrow strip of borderland in East Prussia. The Soviets discontinued their offensive in the centre of the front, and there was no more heavy fighting there until January 1945.[72]

Nonetheless, this episode in October 1944 gave the civilian German population in the east a taste of what was coming. Red Army soldiers had fought their way forward hundreds of kilometres towards the west, and wherever they advanced they encountered the aftermath of destructive German rage on the Soviet territory they had occupied. Hatred for the invaders and the desire for revenge, nourished by Soviet propaganda, discharged themselves in furious violence when Red Army soldiers reached German soil.[73] Nemmersdorf, the westernmost point which Soviet troops reached, became the scene of a bloodbath, with only a small number of the 637 villagers able to escape being slaughtered. After inspecting the sight of the fighting on 23 October, General Werner Kreipe noted: "In and around Nemmersdorf, executed women and children nailed to a barn door."[74] Yet a report by the Secret Field Police, which carried out investigations of their own on 25 October, did not note such horrific detail. It confirmed that the corpses of twenty-six civilians had been discovered, mostly elderly men and women, who had been killed with shots to the head. Executions, rapes and plundering were also reported from other places.[75]

Such atrocities were perfect propaganda fodder for Goebbels, who wrote on 26 October that he intended to use them as an "opportunity for a major press educational campaign." The idea was to make it clear to "even the most guileless of observers" what the German people could expect "if Bolshevism were in fact to take possession of the Reich."[76] Goebbels released images of corpses in Nemmersdorf for use by both the weekly newsreel and German newspapers. "The Raving of the Soviet Beasts" was the headline in the *Völkischer Beobachter*.[77] But the sensationalist reporting provoked in parts of the population a reaction Goebbels had not intended. The Security Service office in Stuttgart reported that people were wondering what the Nazi leadership was trying to achieve by publishing such images: "It should ask itself whether every thinking person who sees these bloody pictures of victims would not immediately think of the atrocities we have committed abroad and even in Germany. Did we not ourselves butcher Jews by the thousands? Do soldiers not repeatedly tell of Jews in Poland having to dig their own graves?"[78] In the wake of such reports,

Goebbels decided to discontinue the campaign in early November. "I do not find it opportune at the moment to go further into this subject," he noted.[79]

When Hitler saw the images from Nemmersdorf, he swore revenge. "These are not human beings: they are beasts from the Asiatic steppes, and the battle I am leading against them is the battle for the dignity of the people of Europe," he fumed to his secretaries.[80] Naturally no one in his entourage was going to suggest, even mildly, that the German "master race" was being paid back in kind, however modestly, for what it had inflicted on others in the Soviet Union.

In October 1944, Hungary once again became an acute problem. In late August, after Romania had left the Axis and Army Group Southern Ukraine (soon to be renamed Army Group South) had been almost completely obliterated, the Red Army occupied the country and pushed on to Romania's border with Hungary in northern Transylvania. Horthy had been convinced for quite some time that Germany could no longer win the war. On 29 August, he dismissed Prime Minister Döme Sztójay and appointed his ally Géza Lakatos to the post. This set alarm bells ringing in the Nazi leadership that Horthy was "on the verge of leaving . . . and going over to the enemy camp."[81] In fact, the Hungarian regent had already made diplomatic contact with the Western Allies, although they had told him to negotiate with the Soviet Union. On 11 October, Horthy accepted the terms Moscow dictated for a cease-fire, including an immediate declaration of war by Hungary against Germany. But the German leadership had learned early on about the details of the negotiations and prepared measures to combat Hungary's change of course. After losing the Ploeşti oil fields in Romania, Hitler was by no means prepared to forgo the Hungarian oil fields at Zala and Zistersdorf. Under the leadership of Waffen-SS colonel Otto Skorzeny plans were drawn up under the code name "Operation Panzerfaust" ("Bazooka") to depose Horthy and transfer power to Ferenc Szálasi, the head of the radical fascist Arrow Cross Party.

Skorzeny's first move on the morning of 15 October was to kidnap, on Hitler's orders, Horthy's son Miklós. That noon, when the regent announced on the radio his intention to conclude a cease-fire with the Soviet Union, Arrow Cross paramilitaries led by the SS staged a putsch, seizing Buda Castle the following day. After some initial resistance, Horthy was forced to revoke his proclamation. That evening, having received assurances from Hitler's plenipotentiary in Hungary, Edmund Veesenmayer, that nothing would happen to his son, Horthy stepped down and named Szálasi prime minister.[82] The new Arrow Cross regime not only continued fighting on Hitler's side but also tried to fulfil Germany's wishes to annihilate Hungary's Jews, sending thousands of Jews from Budapest to work as slave labourers in the Third Reich. Many of them died on death marches to the west.[83]

On 18 October, while Horthy and his family were being brought by special train to a castle in Upper Bavaria, where they would stay until the end of the war, Himmler took to the radio to read out Hitler's edict of 25 September about the formation of a national militia to be called the Volkssturm (People's Storm). The eighteenth of October was the anniversary of the Battle of Leipzig of 1813. Prussia's great triumph in the wars of liberation against Napoleon had been mythologised into the rebellion of an entire people against an enemy power, a national uprising that was also the subject of the last major film Goebbels had commissioned, about the defence of Kolberg Castle. Hitler's edict contrasted the "total will to destruction of our Jewish-international enemies" with the "total deployment of all German people." The dictator decreed that all German males between the ages of sixteen and sixty were to register to serve in the Volkssturm and receive battle training. The Gauleiters were put in charge of mustering these irregular troops. Himmler, as the commander of the Replacement Army, was responsible for training, equipping and deploying them.[84] The Volkssturm was intended to compensate for the Wehrmacht's enormous losses, but it was scraping the bottom of the barrel. Hastily trained and badly equipped, its members were hardly serious soldiers. More often than not, in the final months of the war, they were used as cannon fodder in an attempt to slow the Allies' advance into the Reich and keep the Nazi regime alive for a little longer.[85] The German public interpreted the call to form the Volkssturm as further evidence of the enemy's superiority. "A growing chorus of voices say that we are being forced into a hopeless act of defence," reported Reich propaganda offices.[86]

By the autumn of 1944, there was no ignoring the harbingers of Germany's total defeat. Although Allied advances through France had been halted in late September, the British and Americans had stepped up their air offensive. Three times as many bombs were dropped on Germany between September 1944 and May 1945 as in all previous years of the war.[87] Air raids focused on hydrogenation plants and transport hubs, and they severely disrupted not only the Wehrmacht's ability to produce synthetic fuel but also supplies for Germany's arms production. Major raids against German cities were also intensified. On the night of 10–11 September, the Royal Air Force unleashed a firestorm in Darmstadt, killing 8,500 people. On 30 October, Cologne was again subjected to a massive bombardment that effectively dealt a death blow to the city. "For the time being, we will have to write off this beautiful Rhenish metropolis," bemoaned Goebbels. "Restoring public life would consume resources that are no longer at our disposal."[88] Duisburg, Essen and Bochum were also battered. And it was not just such industrial centres as the Ruhr Valley that were subjected to an unprecedented inferno in the autumn and winter of 1944, but many other cities in Germany that had previously been spared. Heilbronn, for instance, was almost completely destroyed on the night of 4–5 December, with more than 5,000 civilians being killed.[89]

No one in the Nazi leadership was under any illusions about the psychological effects of the bombing war. People were asking themselves "where this will all end," wrote Goebbels, "sometimes desperately." So many cities were being attacked every day that they were no longer listed in Wehrmacht Supreme Command reports because "it would be too depressing." The aerial war hung "like a sword of Damocles over the Reich," Goebbels complained, adding that if Germany did not succeed in developing an effective defence, the future would be "very dark."[90] In the Wolf's Lair, Hitler once again blamed Göring and the Luftwaffe and seems to have toyed with the idea of replacing Göring with Colonel-General Robert Ritter von Greim, but he did not follow through on this idea because he believed that, owing to his previous services, Göring could not simply be dropped.[91] In any case, the Third Reich was incapable of breaking the Allies' air superiority, despite the high hopes that were placed in the Messerschmitt Me-262, the first jet-engined warplane. But the aircraft had not reached a stage of development suitable for mass production in 1944, and that process was further slowed by Hitler's insistence that it be built as a bomber and not a fighter.[92]

★

In the final days of October, as Soviet tanks were rolling towards Königsberg, and the thunder of artillery could be heard on clear days in the Wolf's Lair, Hitler came under pressure to move his headquarters to Berlin or the Obersalzberg. There was concern about the Führer's security. As Bormann told his wife, Soviet tanks could quickly advance sixty to eighty kilometres, and in any case, more comfortable quarters would be preferable. But the dictator declared that he would leave the Wolf's Lair only if he were in immediate danger. His presence there was necessary, he argued, to maintain morale in East Prussia and motivate German divisions to give their all.[93] In secret, however, Bormann and Schaub made arrangements for the evacuation of the compound. All files that were not deemed crucial to daily business were packed up and sent off, and the personnel was reduced to a level that allowed everyone in the Wolf's Lair to pull up stakes at short notice.[94]

Unlike the previous year, Hitler did not travel to Munich for the anniversary of the 1923 putsch attempt, abruptly changing the date of commemorations from 8 to 12 November and sending Himmler in his stead to read out a proclamation. It repeated previous statements, identifying the Jews' "Satanic will to persecution and destruction" as the "driving force" behind the attempt to obliterate the German people. Hitler made no direct reference to American treasury secretary Henry Morgenthau's plan to de-industrialise Germany, although he did invoke it obliquely. He blamed German setbacks at the front on the "betrayal" of Germany's former allies and the "ignominious, desperate conspirators" of 20 July. As long as he lived, the dictator vowed, "Germany would never experience the fate of those European nations that have been flooded by Bolshevism." But he made no promises other than the vague prospect that "the moment will come in which success will crown our endeavours."[95] Goebbels expressed regret that the Führer had not delivered his speech himself: "Himmler's voice is a little too cold to tease the entire effect from such a proclamation."[96] Hitler's failure to speak on the most important Nazi Party holiday astonished outside observers. "Why is this man, who previously could not use his voice often enough, suddenly silent?" the diarist Friedrich Kellner asked himself. "A strange matter!"[97]

For months, Goebbels had tried to persuade Hitler to speak to the German people again on the radio. It was "not right for the Führer to fall into silence during such acute crises," he complained repeatedly in his diary.[98] But although Hitler promised to sit down and write a speech as soon as he could, he continually found excuses not to, for instance by claiming that he needed to wait for the Hungarian situation to be settled. Goebbels remained unconvinced: "I fail to see what developments in Hungary have to do with the Führer addressing the German people."[99] Hitler's absence from the public sphere gave rise to numerous rumours, and the fact that he had charged Himmler with reading out his proclamation on 12 November caused rampant speculation that he had suffered a nervous breakdown and had been forced to hand over power to Himmler and Goebbels.[100] Not only in Germany, but abroad too people wondered about Hitler's physical and mental condition and a possible shake-up at the top of the Third Reich. "Wild rumours about Hitler's illness, madness, disappearance," noted Thomas Mann on 15 November. "Himmler sole ruler."[101]

Stories like this refused to dissipate in the weeks that followed. People whispered that Hitler was no longer alive but that those who now wielded power in Germany were keeping the news from the public. "The craziest rumours are being spread about the Führer," Goebbels fretted in early December. "It is payback for the Führer's months of silence."[102] The extent of the speculation that Hitler was seriously ill or even dead was a clear indication that for most Germans, the dictator had become an otherworldly, shadowy figure. Although the mythic status of the Führer had briefly revived after 20 July, by the autumn of 1944, his reputation was rapidly disintegrating in the face of Germany's catastrophe at the fronts and the inferno of the bombing war. The Security Service cited a remark people seemed to have made frequently under their breath in these fateful months: "The Führer was sent to us from God, though not in order to save Germany, but to ruin it."[103]

Hitler, however, was by no means ready to admit defeat. On the contrary, he clung to the hope that the fortunes of war might again turn his way. It was clear to him that if the Wehrmacht remained on the defensive, it would only delay the end of the conflict but would not avert defeat. Thus he had no choice but to place all his bets on a final offensive in an attempt to regain the initiative on at least one of the fronts. He believed that he had better chances in the west, not only because the distances were shorter and the supply problems commensurately fewer, but also because he considered the British and Americans less determined adversaries than the Soviets.[104] On 19 August, he shared his thinking with Jodl, demanding that the chief of staff "adjust to it."[105] On 2 September, he informed Goebbels of his intention to "go on the offensive again" that autumn in the west. The propaganda minister summarised the Führer's reasoning: "Even if we do not have the means to carry out in-depth operations, he believes he can deal some heavy blows to the English and the Americans, especially when the weather renders it impossible for them to deploy their air forces for operational purposes."[106] Hitler believed that the acute threat on the eastern front had passed, assuming, wrongly, that instead of training its sights on Berlin, the Red Army would pursue Russia's traditional imperial goal of securing the Turkish straits. "On the whole, the Führer figures that the Russians will head for Constantinople and is basing everything upon that," noted tank general Hermann Balck after a meeting with Hitler on 10 September.[107]

In the weeks that followed, Hitler intensively pondered on which section of the front the offensive should be launched. On 16 September, after the regular noontime situation briefing, he announced his decision to a small circle of intimates at a special meeting: "Counter-offensive from the Ardennes, goal Antwerp." Hitler was thus envisioning a repeat of the operation from the summer of 1940, which would have had German tanks thrust forward through the Ardennes Forest to the river Maas and then press on to retake Antwerp. The idea was not just to deprive the Allies of a major port for resupplying their troops but to drive a wedge between the American and British armies, with the intention of surrounding and destroying the latter. "Rip open the seam between the English and the Americans, new Dunkirk" was how the Luftwaffe chief of staff, Werner Kreipe, summed up Hitler's ideas. The Führer brushed aside Guderian's fear that if Germany's last reserves were thrown at the western front, the Wehrmacht would be unable to resist a Soviet offensive in the east. He also countered Jodl's warnings about Allied air superiority with the argument that if the German offensive was carried out in a "period of bad weather, then the enemy will not be able to fly." In conclusion, Hitler stressed to his military commanders the need for absolute secrecy. Only a handful of utterly reliable men were to be initiated into the German plans.[108]

In late September Hitler ordered Keitel and Jodl to prepare the operation. It was not until 22 October that he summoned the chiefs of staff of the supreme commander west and Army Group B, Colonel-General Siegfried Westphal and General Hans Krebs, to the Wolf's Lair and informed them of his intentions, ordering them to keep their knowledge completely confidential. Upon returning to the western front, they reported back to their commanders-in-chief. Both Rundstedt and Model were sceptical about whether their forces would be sufficient to achieve such ambitious operational goals, but they put aside their doubts. On 10 November, Hitler signed the orders for the Ardennes offensive—code-named "Operation Watch on the Rhine"— which became known among the Allies as the Battle of the Bulge. The Führer defined the mission's goal as "bringing about a decisive turn in the western campaign and perhaps the war as a whole by destroying enemy forces north of the Antwerp–Brussels–Luxembourg line." Under the supreme command of Army Group B led by Model, the German armies were to attack along a 170-kilometre stretch of front between Monschau in western Germany and Echternach in Luxembourg. The 7th Army under General Erich Brandenberger was charged with covering the southern flank, in the centre General Hasso von Manteuffel was ordered to advance across the Maas, and the main strike was to be carried out by the 6th SS Tank Army under SS-Oberstgruppenführer Sepp Dietrich on the northern flank.[109] The preparations were supposed to be completed by 27 November, but later that month the launch of the offensive was pushed back, first to 10 December, then to 16 December.

Hitler was aware of the risks this operation entailed, but in the autumn of 1944 he was again determined to go all-in. In early November, he confided to Morell that he was about to make "the biggest decisions of his life" and was therefore under "constantly increasing strain."[110] He boasted to Speer that "this will be the big blow, which simply must succeed." If it did not, Hitler saw "no chance any more for a favourable end to the war."[111] Nonetheless, there were huge obstacles to German success. One was Allied air supremacy, which only allowed German troops to attack in bad weather. Another was the fuel shortages German troops had endured since losing the Ploeşti oil fields and once Allied bombers had begun targeting German hydrogenation plants. Germany's tank armies only had enough fuel to advance 60 kilometres, which meant that in order to reach Antwerp they would have to capture some enemy supplies.[112] It would have required "enormous luck" and a tactical miracle for the Ardennes offensive to succeed, Jodl admitted from his Nuremberg prison cell in 1946: "It was a desperate gambit born of a desperate situation."[113]

On 20 November, Hitler left his East Prussian headquarters for what would be the last time. The reason was not the imminent offensive in the west, but the severe hoarseness he had suffered for weeks—one of the reasons he was reluctant to approach the radio microphone and address the German people.[114] On 18 November, he was examined by Professor Carl Otto von Eicken, the director of the ear, nose and throat clinic at Berlin's Charité Hospital, who discovered a polyp on Hitler's right vocal cord. As he had in 1935, Hitler decided to undergo an operation.[115] The Führer's special train left Görlitz at 3:15 p.m. and arrived in Berlin at 5:30 the following morning.[116]

In late June 1941, the dictator had moved into the Wolf's Lair as a seemingly invincible conqueror in the best of spirits. He returned to the Reich capital in November 1944 a depressive, ill man. His secretary Traudl Junge would later recall that she had "never seen [Hitler] so crestfallen and absent": "His voice rarely exceeded a loud whisper, and his eyes remained fixed upon his plate or stared vacantly at a spot on the white tablecloth. An oppressive atmosphere weighed upon the confined, swaying cage we had boarded together, and we were all overcome by unease."[117] Between 23 and 25 January 1945, as the Red Army approached, Hitler's eastern command centre, which had been constructed at such effort in the forest near Rastenburg, would be demolished. The explosions were so powerful that they shattered windows in the city eight kilometres away. Also destroyed was the Tannenberg memorial near Hohenstein (Olsztynek), which commemorated Germany's victories over the Russian armies in August 1914. The coffins containing the remains of German war hero Field Marshal Paul von Hindenburg and his wife were transported to the west.[118]

Hitler remained in Berlin for three weeks, staying in his still-intact private apartment on the first floor of the Old Chancellery. The day after his arrival, Eicken removed the small growth on his vocal cord, which turned out to be benign.[119] Despite Hitler's fears that something would go wrong, the operation proceeded without complications, although the dictator was forbidden from using his voice and had to communicate by means of written notes at the situation briefings in the pompous offices of the New Chancellery.[120] Days passed without his secretaries and adjutants laying eyes on him. When he reappeared one morning, he was only able to whisper. Before long, Hitler's entire entourage took to whispering themselves, prompting the Führer to remark that the problem was his voice, not his hearing.[121]

Eva Braun kept Hitler company. The Führer's lover had been alarmed by reports of his illness and the Red Army's initial advances into East Prussia.[122] She seems to have reckoned with the chance of Hitler dying and in response made preparations to take her own life, drawing up her last will and testament on 26 October. In it, she left everything she owned—jewellery, clothing, paintings, furniture and cash—to family members and friends. Her older sister, Ilse Fucke-Michels, who lived in Breslau, was to inherit her house on Munich's Wasserburgerstrasse, while her younger sister, Gretl Fegelein, was to receive all of her films, photo albums and correspondence with Hitler.[123] On 21 November, Braun travelled to Berlin and settled into rooms adjacent to Hitler's apartment. Almost every day, they had lunch and dinner alone together, often eating the latter well after midnight.[124] In early December they were joined by Gretl Fegelein. Officers like Guderian's adjutant Freytag von Loringhoven, who had not been part of Berghof society and did not know that Hitler had a mistress, were astonished when the two elegantly dressed young women appeared in the Chancellery.[125]

It was not until 1 December that Hitler had sufficiently recovered to summon Goebbels for a meeting. The propaganda minister was glad to see that, other than a slight hand tremor, the dictator was in good health. "When I think back to a few weeks ago when I saw him so ill and weak in bed . . . I can only say that it is a miracle," Goebbels noted. The two men's conversation went on from the afternoon into the early hours of the following day, with a break only around midnight. Hitler was extremely optimistic about the prospects of the imminent offensive. "It should be a blow of great proportions," Goebbels recorded. Within ten days, German tank units would have advanced to Antwerp, surrounding enemy forces and inflicting upon them a battle of annihilation of "unimaginable dimensions." The key to success would be to keep the enemy from learning of Germany's plan, which was thus to be "cloaked in the veil of the deepest secrecy." Hitler believed the operation would yield "not only a military but a political victory," perhaps even serving as "the Lippe of the war." This was a reference to the local election in Lippe-Detmold in mid-January 1933, in which the Nazis had achieved a victory following their national electoral losses the preceding November; it had opened the door to Hitler becoming German chancellor two weeks later. Initially, Goebbels seems to have been sceptical, but by the end of their meeting, "one of the most interesting and reassuring" he had ever enjoyed with the Führer, Hitler had mesmerised him. "He is once again on top of the situation and offers an inspiring model of National Socialist fighting spirit," Goebbels effused.[126]

Two days later, on the afternoon of 3 December, Hitler took time to pay his first private visit to the Goebbels family in almost four years. "He was received as one of the family, and the girls wore long dresses to welcome him," the propaganda minister wrote. Hitler spent two hours playing with the children and reminiscing with their parents while betraying none of the stress he was under in the run-up to the Ardennes offensive. The atmosphere had been "wonderfully relaxed," and the time had "flown by," Goebbels confided to his diary.[127] Hitler promised to come and see the family again soon, but this was to be his final visit.

The following day was the last time he received a foreign guest of state, the head of Hungary's puppet Arrow Cross regime, Ferenc Szálasi. Hitler revealed nothing about his plans to attack Allied forces in the west, although he did voice the expectation that "the enemy coalition . . . would one day collapse with a gigantic crash." The minutes of the meeting quote Hitler as saying: "As is so often the case in world history, the main thing is that a man determinedly stays his course with the power of his heart and his faith in the future of his people. [The Führer] was firmly convinced that triumph could be compelled in the end."[128] Szálasi's visit provided a welcome opportunity for German propaganda to publish the first images of Hitler for a long time and to silence the rumours that he had died.[129]

On 7 December, Hitler invited Wieland and Verena Wagner and their spouses for dinner at the Chancellery. Having not seen him for a while, these young people were shocked by the sight of the Führer, who had visibly aged and who was barely able to conceal the tremor in his hands. Hitler had reminded him "strangely enough of Friedrich the Great," Wieland Wagner later recalled, adding: "His hair had not gone any greyer but his eyes bulged . . . and his frame was quite hunched." The dictator was still capable of projecting optimism, speaking of an imminent turn in the fortunes of war and saying that Bayreuth would have to prepare for a "festival of peace" in 1945. Nonetheless, the Wagner progeny came away from the evening feeling that Hitler had taken his leave. Wieland's wife later recalled their host being in a "gentle mood" and sighed: "Everything so profoundly moving and mysterious!"[130]

Before Hitler's departure for the western front, Morell gave the Führer a pick-me-up injection. "The most exciting days of a lifetime," the physician noted. "A great victory must be achieved."[131] At 5 p.m. on 10 December, Hitler's special train pulled out of Berlin, reaching a small station in Hesse in western Germany at 3:00 the following morning. There, Hitler and his retinue got into cars that took them to his Eagle's Nest headquarters near Ziegenberg, west of Bad Nauheim, where they arrived at 7:30 p.m.[132] These headquarters had been built between September 1939 and August 1940 in a stretch of forest and consisted of seven buildings, camouflaged as log cabins, with air-raid bunkers underneath. Supreme Commander West Rundstedt and his staff installed themselves in nearby Ziegenberg Castle.[133] Hitler's daily routine was essentially the same as it had been in the Wolf's Lair. After being woken around midday, he would read the latest reports and receive his first visitors. He took lunch at 2 p.m. and dinner at 8 p.m. with his secretaries Christa Schroeder and Gerda Christian. (They were relieved on 12 January by Johanna Wolf and Traudl Junge.) Situation briefings were held between 4 and 5 p.m. and at midnight or sometimes half an hour later. Hitler's day ended in the early hours with his customary tea.[134] But unlike in the Wolf's Lair, where he had hardly left his bunker, Hitler took long walks in the woods and fields of the Taunus Valley, which seemed to benefit his health.[135]

On the afternoon of 11 December and again the following day, Hitler summoned twenty-one generals and division commanders to his new headquarters to instruct them about the imminent large-scale offensive. They were required to hand over their personal firearms and briefcases before being led to a room in a bunker, where Hitler was seated at a table. After a lengthy digression looking back at all the battles for predominance in Europe since the Peace of Westphalia of 1648, Hitler informed them of his reasoning for going back on the attack. Wars, he said, were not won by staying on the defensive, but by showing the enemy "with ruthless blows from time to time" that he had nothing to win and could "never count on a surrender." Teaching the enemy coalition this lesson, he continued, was the "most important task" of what had now been code-named "Operation Autumn Mist." Once again the dictator invoked the example of Friedrich the Great in the Seven Years War, whose "steadfastness" had made it possible for "a miracle of reversal to intervene in the end." On this score, Hitler emphasised what he saw as the differences between the Western powers and the Soviet Union, differences which he believed were "increasing by the hour." He concluded: "If a couple of major blows are landed here, this artificially maintained common front could at any moment suddenly collapse with a gigantic clap of thunder." We have no way of knowing whether the dictator's optimistic outlook convinced his military commanders. In any case, if they had any reservations, they kept them to themselves.[136]

On 15 December, Hitler once more ordered Model, the commander of Army Group B, who was charged with directing the whole operation, "to carry out all commands from the uppermost leadership unconditionally and to enforce discipline down through the lowest of the ranks." If this could be ensured, a "great victory would be certain."[137] In his order of the day, Supreme Commander West Rundstedt wrote that "everything was at stake" and now commanded his soldiers to "give their all and make superhuman sacrifices for our fatherland and our Führer."[138]

Early in the morning on 16 December, after an hour-long artillery barrage, twenty-four German divisions, comprising 200,000 soldiers and 600 tanks, went on the attack. They succeeded in surprising their adversaries: the Allies were no longer expecting a German counter-offensive, and bad weather prevented their air forces from intervening. But already the very next day, the German 6th Tank Army under Sepp Dietrich encountered fierce resistance from the Americans. Demolished bridges and rain-soaked streets also made it difficult for German troops to advance quickly. Disappointed and angry, they committed a series of war crimes, the worst of which took place near Malmedy on 17

December, where soldiers of the 1st SS Tank Division murdered seventy-two American POWs.[139]

While the 7th Army under General Brandenberger also failed to take significant territory on the southern front, the 5th Tank Army under General Hasso von Manteuffel made significant progress in the centre, breaking through the American defences and advancing west. Nonetheless, it failed to take the major transport hub of Bastogne. German supplies therefore had to be diverted around the besieged city, delaying their arrival. Moreover, as the days stretched on, fuel shortages increasingly took their toll. The Wehrmacht's hope of seizing Allied fuel supplies never materialised. By 23 December, vanguard German tank units had advanced to within 7 kilometres of the Maas near Dinant, but that was to be the end of their progress. The ultimate goal of reaching Antwerp, which was subjected to constant bombardment by V-2 rockets, receded into the distance.[140]

Hitler was euphoric during the first days of the attack. In the night of 19–20 December, he called Goebbels from the Eagle's Nest. "You immediately noticed from his voice that the triumphs already achieved had fundamentally changed his entire mentality," the propaganda minister noted. Hitler himself characterised the effects of the German offensive as "colossal." The US 1st Army, he bragged, was as good as "completely destroyed," Germany's booty was already enormous, and the enemy remained in the dark as to the goal of the German operation. For that reason, he ordered, German reporting about the offensive was to continue to exercise "extreme reserve."[141]

At the start of the attack, Hitler and Goebbels had agreed that German newspapers and radio would play down the operation so as not to raise unrealistic expectations.[142] It was not until 18 December that the offensive was mentioned in Wehrmacht Supreme Command reports, and German newspapers passed on the news the following day. If Propaganda Ministry reports are accurate, the news was greeted less with celebrations than with general amazement that the Wehrmacht "was even capable of such an operation." "What a nice Christmas present!" seems to have been the general response.[143] In Berlin, the city's entire holiday supply of schnapps was "consumed in a single night," Goebbels noted. The surprise was all the greater because, aside from a select few initiates, no one had suspected that Germany was going to attack in the west.[144] But if here and there hopes re-emerged that the war might end well for Germany after all, they were quickly dampened.

On Christmas Eve, the skies over Europe cleared, and the Allies could once again exploit their air superiority. British and American planes relentlessly pounded German tank units, artillery positions and supply lines. The Wehrmacht was only able to move supplies and reinforcements at night. On 26 December, the US 3rd Army was able to break up the siege at Bastogne.[145] It was now obvious to any clear-headed person that Operation Autumn Mist had failed. "At the moment, there is no hope that we can pursue our offensive any further," a disappointed Goebbels admitted. "We shall be happy if we can hold the territory we have captured."[146]

On 24 December, Chief of the General Staff Guderian had travelled to the Eagle's Nest to convince Hitler to break off the offensive and move troops from the west to the east. Intelligence collected by the Foreign Armies East division suggested the Red Army was preparing an imminent large-scale offensive. Hitler turned a deaf ear to any talk of impending peril. "This is the greatest bluff since Genghis Khan," he raged. Jodl too rebuffed Guderian, telling him that Germany could not "relinquish the initiative that has just been regained." The Wehrmacht could afford to make territorial concessions in the east, but not in the west, Jodl added. With his mission unaccomplished, Guderian returned to Zossen, where his staff was again based after leaving its East Prussian headquarters.[147]

Only a few days after the Ardennes offensive had ground to a halt, Hitler and the Wehrmacht Supreme Command ordered Army Group G under Colonel-General Blaskowitz to launch an attack to relieve pressure on Model's troops. Operation North Wind envisioned eight German divisions advancing from the Saarbrücken area into northern Alsace to surround the US 7th Army and the French 1st Army.[148] On 28 December, Hitler summoned the troop commanders responsible for the attack to his headquarters. He admitted that the Ardennes offensive had "unfortunately not led to the comprehensive victory that could have been expected." But he insisted that it had achieved "massive relief" and turned the operational plans of the Allies "completely on their heads." The "overall situation" had begun to change in a way that "would surely have been unimaginable fourteen days ago." Hitler no longer mentioned the original goal of the operation: to take Antwerp.

Army Group B's mission now consisted solely of holding the territory that had been won and tying down as many American divisions as possible.[149]

On New Year's Day 1945, Hitler fulfilled his promise to Goebbels and spoke for the first time since 20 July to the German people. Five minutes after midnight, after bells had rung and the final notes of the "Badenweiler March" faded, Hitler's voice came over the radio.[150] His address contained nothing new. Once again, he complained about the "global Jewish-international conspiracy" plotting to enslave and "exterminate" the German people. He stressed again that there would "never be a repeat of 9 November in the German Reich" and underscored his "rock-solid certainty" that Germany would emerge victorious. Significantly, he did not mention the German offensive in the west; and neither did he even allude to "miracle weapons" capable of turning the tide of the war.[151] Nonetheless, Hitler's speech seems to have had the intended effect, at least among his most fervent admirers. It was not what he said but the fact that he had spoken in public again after such a long time that made the biggest impression. Propaganda offices reported that many Germans had "tears in their eyes" when they once again heard the voice of their Führer and that numerous rumours about Hitler's health had been "swept aside with a single blow."[152]

In an editorial for Das Reich, Goebbels heaped praise upon the Führer, who had "turned his back completely on the everyday joys and ordinary comforts of life" in order to "remake the face of the continent." The propaganda minister gushed: "You only need to be in his presence for a while to physically sense his power and appreciate how strong he is." A Security Service report from Stuttgart found that never before had an article by the propaganda minister attracted so much attention—albeit much of it critical. Only a "minority of ethnic-popular comrades and of course the loyal old fighters" had read the article positively. It was a sign of how much power the original cult of the Führer had lost by now.[153]

After Hitler's speech, at around 2 a.m., Albert Speer, who had travelled from the western front, arrived at the Eagle's Nest, where he found Hitler surrounded by his entourage. Champagne was flowing, and the originally rather sombre mood improved the longer the euphoric dictator went on about Germany's purportedly bright prospects in the war. In the end, everyone in attendance was in a strangely carefree, drunken condition. In Speer's recollection of this spectral occasion, Hitler was still in possession of his "magical abilities."[154]

Sobriety quickly followed. Launched on 1 January 1945, Operation North Wind had little effect other than achieving some minor territorial gains. The Allies retained Strasbourg, and Operation Baseplate, a parallel initiative by the Luftwaffe aimed at destroying Allied airstrips in Belgium and northern France, ended in disaster. A third of the nine hundred German warplanes involved were destroyed, some shot down in error by German flak gunners.[155]

On 3 January, in a major meeting also attended by Goebbels to discuss the Wehrmacht's fallback positions, Hitler once again spoke "extremely indignantly" about the failings of the Luftwaffe and the lethargy of Göring, who was allowing himself to be "lied to and deceived by those who worked with him." Speer and Albert Ganzenmüller, state secretary of the Reich Transport Ministry, voiced opposition to the suggestion by Goebbels, as Reich plenipotentiary for total war, that drastic personnel cuts should be made in the areas of transport and armaments to compensate for the losses of the Wehrmacht, but this time Hitler backed the propaganda minister. The Führer also stated that he was convinced that the war would be "largely decided" in the summer of 1945. By then, fifty new divisions of seventeen-year-olds, born in 1928, were to be raised and readied for battle. "Experience teaches that major offensive actions can only be carried out by enthusiastic young people," Hitler proclaimed. In a confidential discussion following the meeting, the dictator made no bones about the fact that the Ardennes offensive had fallen far short of expectations, but called it a triumph that Germany had forced its enemies to "regroup" its forces. The main thing, Hitler continued, was to "keep the initiative in our own hands and never release it for a moment."[156]

That was nothing more than wishful thinking. The failure of the Ardennes offensive had irrevocably transferred the initiative back to the Allies. Hitler's final trump card had not worked, and the game was almost up for the man who had always risked everything. All he had achieved was to postpone the American and British invasion of Germany by several weeks, and in so doing he had sacrificed most of his final reserves, who would be sorely missed elsewhere. All told 80,000 German and 70,000 US soldiers had been killed or wounded or were missing, and both sides had lost around 700 tanks and armoured vehicles.[157] On 8 January, Hitler acceded to a request by the supreme commander west and allowed the 6th SS Tank Army to retreat. It was a tacit acknowledgement that Operation Autumn Mist had been a mistake. Step by step, the units of Army Group B pulled back from the Ardennes to the Siegfried Line.[158]

On 12 January, Guderian's repeated warnings became reality. The Red Army launched their winter offensive, achieving a major break-through after only two days.[159] With the situation in the east critical, Hitler decided to leave the Eagle's Nest and return to Berlin. At 6 p.m. on 15 January, he and his retinue were driven to the train station. Around 10 a.m. the following day, his special train arrived in the Reich capital. From the station in Berlin's Grunewald district, Hitler's motorcade proceeded to the Chancellery, passing mountains of rubble and burned-out buildings. No one spoke a word along the way.[160] The final act of his downfall had begun, and Hitler no doubt knew it.

15

Decline of a Dictator

The Hitler of 1939 was not the same man who had become German chancellor in 1933, remarked Germany's long-time finance minister, Count Lutz Schwerin von Krosigk, shortly after the end of the Second World War. Six years of absolute power had had a pernicious influence on the dictator's personality—and this trend continued during the war itself so that the Hitler of 1945 was no longer the same man he had been in 1939.[1] While he had by no means turned into an entirely different person, several of his character traits had become even more pronounced: his egocentrism, his inability to self-criticise and his commensurate tendency to overestimate himself, his lack of scruples when choosing means to his ends, his habit of betting everything on a single card, his contempt for others and his lack of empathy. The more hopeless the war became and the more Hitler withdrew from the company of others, the more dominantly the hatred and vengefulness of the pig-headed fanatic emerged. Joachim Fest rightly described the final phase of Hitler's life as a "rapid process of reduction" in which his "true nature emerged without disguise."[2]

That view is supported by an incisive observation made in late January 1943, after the turning point of Stalingrad, by the exiled German journalist Sebastian Haffner in the London *Observer* about a photograph of Hitler. Now that the dictator was a clear failure and had blocked off his ways back or out, Haffner wrote, the mask of the imperator he had assumed in his years of triumph slipped, and his face once more wore the features of the crude beer-cellar rabble-rouser of the early 1920s, that "loser stewing in his hatred for the entire world."[3]

One of Hitler's most prominent traits had been his constant mistrust of others. Towards the end of the war it turned into paranoia, especially in his relationships with his military commanders. At the start of the hostilities, the dictator still tried to treat his generals without acrimony, rewarding them after Germany's initial triumphs with rapid promotions, high honours and generous bonuses. Hitler awarded their medals personally and gave the honourees the feeling that he valued and appreciated their work. As Lieutenant-General Hans-Georg Reinhardt, one of the officers awarded the Knight's Cross of the Iron Cross in October 1939, reported: "We assembled in the beautiful office of the Führer, and at exactly 1 p.m. he appeared, accompanied by Brauchitsch. He walked before us and spoke, briefly but extremely impressively and warmly, as if the handful of us deserved the main credit for victory thanks to our personal efforts and those of our men. Then he approached each one of us, personally presenting us our medals with a lengthy handshake." Afterwards, Hitler invited the newly decorated commanders to a lunch of "white beans with potatoes and speck—just like in the field but finely served." After the meal, the dictator talked with the officers extensively about their experiences in the war: "We told many stories and were always surprised how much the Führer already knew about everything, including our wishes and concerns. Only a genius such as the Führer can have such comprehensive knowledge."[4]

In fact, Hitler assiduously read up on weapons technology and military history, acquiring a knowledge of facts with which he delighted in impressing military experts. His head for figures in particular was feared by all around him. The initial scepticism of the general staff towards the dilettante gave way to admiration after Germany's unexpectedly quick victory over France. It was now widely accepted that Hitler was not just an exceptional politician and leader of state but also an extraordinary field commander. "With this war and what is sure to be the equally great peace with which he will end this most enormous of conflicts, Hitler will go down as the greatest man in three millennia," effused Major-General Walther von Seydlitz to his wife in late May 1940—the same Seydlitz who would turn his back on Hitler after the defeat at Stalingrad and lead the League of German Officers.[5] For his part, the dictator was completely satisfied with the performance of his armed forces in the western offensive of 1940 and praised the general staff in the highest terms to Jodl.[6] During the first weeks of Operation Barbarossa too, when the collapse of the

Soviet Union seemed to be but a matter of days away, Hitler and his generals got along splendidly. Despite occasional differences of opinion, Germany's highest military men were eminently willing to submit to the leadership of their supreme commander.

Hitler's trust in his generals was first dented in the winter crisis of 1941–42. The Führer became convinced that only his steadfastness had prevented a German collapse on the eastern front and that if he had listened to his military commanders, Germany would have suffered a debacle of Napoleonic proportions. In conversations with Goebbels and Speer, Hitler now spoke extremely disrespectfully about the "old men" on the general staff who had lost their nerve as soon as things got rough.[7] From that point on, the dictator was determined to ruthlessly enforce his military authority and had no scruples about dismissing decorated veteran army leaders. His desire for control became an addiction, with Hitler demanding to be kept informed about all movements and changes at the front and reserving the right to make even the smallest tactical decisions.[8]

Still, it was not until September 1942 and the failure of the summer offensive in the east that Hitler's relationship with Germany's military elite was irreparably damaged. The external manifestation of the estrangement was the fact that he no longer joined the officers at meals, where he had previously enjoyed conversing with them.[9] The newly appointed army chief of staff, Kurt Zeitzler, found the atmosphere at Hitler's headquarters in Vinnitsa, where "mistrust and resentment" were omnipresent, indescribably oppressive. "No one seemed to trust anyone else, and Hitler mistrusted everyone!" Zeitzler recalled. "Many of the officers were depressed because they believed they had fallen out of favour."[10] Nothing expressed the poisoned atmosphere more clearly than the fact that from this point on Hitler had every word uttered in the situation meetings minuted. The stenographers employed to this end directly experienced a dismal reality utterly unlike their idealised image of Hitler. In his memoirs, Speer wrote that he could still picture them "scribbling along with their pale faces and wandering about the headquarters, cowed, in their free time."[11]

The dictator reduced his interactions with his military leaders to only what was absolutely necessary and increasingly withdrew to his bunker. This is where he poured out his heart to the architect Hermann Giesler in October 1942. "I live and work in the oppressive certainty of being surrounded by betrayal!" he complained. "Who can I trust completely, and how can I make decisions, issue orders and lead credibly when mistrust arises because of deceptions, false reports and obvious betrayal . . . if I already feel mistrust right from the start?"[12]

The German defeat at Stalingrad was more food for this distrust. Just as Hitler had dismissed Brauchitsch and assumed command of the army himself in December 1941, he now sought to blame others for his own mistakes. His utter lack of self-criticism and his need to find a scapegoat for any failure would determine his behaviour until the end of his days. As a result, the Führer burned his way through the top military personnel. After the dismissal of List in September 1942, Field Marshal von Kluge wrote that Rundstedt was "the only one left of the old guard" among the supreme commanders of the army groups. "Where will this lead?" Kluge asked.[13] The more critical things got on the eastern front, the more rapidly the commanding generals were replaced. Under these circumstances, hardly anyone dared to voice opposition and give the dictator a frank assessment of the situation. In his conversations with Goebbels, Hitler may have complained that his generals were forever "swindling" him, for example by providing false statistics, but he studiously ignored the fact that his own style of leadership elicited this sort of behaviour.[14]

One of the few people who spoke his mind to Hitler was Zeitzler. After an unusually harmonious first few weeks of working together, a massive fight erupted. The cause of the conflict was Zeitzler's insistence that Hitler make up his mind in a relatively minor matter because otherwise the "men on the frontlines" would lose their trust in the leadership. In response, Hitler pitched a fit like the one he had thrown in front of Halder several weeks before. "That is something you know nothing about," Hitler shouted. "You are just a general staff officer sitting at a desk. I was a frontline soldier in the First World War, and I know how men at the front feel." Those present, particularly Göring, beamed, hardly able to conceal their delight that the new man was being dressed down. Zeitzler composed himself and responded calmly: "My Führer, may I point out that as an ensign I was a junior officer in an active infantry regiment and went into the field with a gun on my shoulder and a knapsack on my back in August 1914; that I was promoted to lieutenant that year . . . after displaying bravery in the face of the enemy; and that I led a company for two and a half years and was wounded twice. I believe, my Führer, I have the same front-line experience as you do." The room suddenly got "very, very still," Zeitzler recalled. "Everyone was waiting for Hitler to explode with anger. I myself figured that he would throw me out. Hitler had grown very pale. His hands were shaking, but he did not say a word. After a short time of breathtaking tension, he just said, 'Let's move on!'" The dictator never again tried to attack him personally, Zeitzler wrote, adding that the Führer knew "just how far he could go with every single individual."[15]

This incident suggests that Hitler could in fact treat people with respect if they showed backbone and refused to be intimidated. Those who approached him with anxious submissiveness, as was the case with most Wehrmacht Supreme Command officers aside from Keitel, often came in for derogatory remarks.[16] Nothing could persuade Hitler to curb his tongue, Speer testified during his initial interrogation in the summer of 1945. On the contrary, his tone of voice grew ever more contemptuous. Hitler repeatedly made statements to the effect that all generals were "dishonourable, stupid and mendacious" in the presence of officers, Speer recalled, and everyone had borne such insults without a word of protest.[17]

Whereas at the start of the war Hitler had enjoyed handing out medals and field marshals' staffs in the interest of personally binding military commanders to him, in the summer of 1943, before a circle of confidants, he mocked this whole "circus," for which he had "no understanding at all."[18] The more the generals lost credibility in his eyes, the more the Reichsleiters and Gauleiters rose in his estimation. The Führer felt "most comfortable" in their company, noted Goebbels: "He knows all these men—you could say from his youth onwards. He knows their flaws, but also their virtues, and above all he is clear about which tasks he can assign to them and which he cannot."[19]

Hitler's smouldering resentment was not pacified by the oath of loyalty his officers swore in March 1944. On the contrary, after 20 July 1944, it turned into full-blown paranoia. The Führer interpreted the fact that a wide circle of officers was involved in the plot to kill him as confirmation for his bottomless mistrust.[20] More than ever, he felt surrounded by betrayal and sabotage, and more than ever he gave free rein to his hatred and desire for revenge. If he had previously been remarkably adept at preserving his demeanour in crises, he now blew his cool with increasing frequency, lapsing back into the coarse jargon of his "street-fighting days."[21] With every passing month, meetings increasingly became "torture," remembered Guderian, who succeeded Zeitzler as chief of the general staff.[22]

The death of Hitler's conciliatory chief adjutant Rudolf Schmundt in early October 1944 from injuries suffered in the assassination attempt, and his replacement by the uncouth General Wilhelm Burgdorf, removed the final moderating influence within Hitler's entourage. The atmosphere in situation meetings was henceforth ruled by general distrust. Afraid of attracting the Führer's ire, more than ever the generals kept any criticism to themselves. Wilhelm Heinrich Scheidt—the replacement for the injured plenipotentiary for military history, General Walter Scherff, in Hitler's headquarters after the assassination attempt—noted with astonishment: "How pale these gentlemen become as soon as they stand before the Führer! Submissive cowards one and all! Not one stands out as a personality. The whole scene is unmistakably dominated by Hitler."[23] For his part, in early December 1944, the Führer expressed his satisfaction to Goebbels that he had "finally silenced his enemies in the general staff," adding: "They are afraid of getting the noose."[24]

At the start of the war, Hitler made numerous trips to the front, where, wearing his field-grey uniform, he posed as the "first soldier of the Reich" and had himself celebrated as a benevolent supreme commander caring for his men. In January 1946, from a Nuremberg jail cell, Jodl remembered the "boundless enthusiasm among the troops" wherever Hitler showed up in the theatre of war.[25] After the first defeats, however, the dictator began to avoid the battlefield. Even visits to the staff quarters behind the front lines became more and more infrequent, with the last one, to Army Group South, taking place in early September 1943. Instead, Hitler directed Germany's war effort with the help of maps in headquarters located far away from the fighting. Measuring 2.5 by 1.5 metres, the maps serviced Hitler's obsession with detail, and even the smallest movement of troops, right down to battalion and company level, was marked with little flags. The dictator was "completely enthralled with the magic of these markers" and loved moving entire divisions back and forth.[26] But every initiate knew that in the final phase of the war these maps represented only a virtual reality: the strengths of the divisions they indicated had long since ceased to be accurate. Thus the maps only encouraged Hitler's tendency towards self-deception and helped him escape into a dreamworld.[27]

Just as he avoided the front, the dictator also refused to visit places badly damaged by air raids, such as the devastated cities of the Ruhr Valley. He seems to have shied back from confronting the misery he had brought upon Germany. Accompanying him on drives from the Stettin train station to the Chancellery in Berlin or to his apartment on Prinzregentenstrasse in Munich, Speer observed "how emotionless and disengaged Hitler was when the trip unavoidably took him past a gigantic landscape of rubble."[28] Guderian's adjutant Freytag von Loringhoven recalled never hearing a word of sympathy from Hitler's mouth concerning the soldiers at the front or those who had been made homeless or become refugees. "The suffering of other human beings did not interest him," Freytag concluded.[29] In 1943, when press spokesman Otto Dietrich tried to tell Hitler about a visit to his heavily bombed home city of Essen, the dictator immediately changed the subject, complaining about some minor press report. Dietrich got the impression that Hitler did not want to be enlightened about the terrible consequences of the air raids.[30] Heinrich Hoffmann experienced something similar when he advised Hitler to inspect cities that had been bombarded, as Churchill did in Britain. "You are only suggesting that in order to take pictures!" Hitler responded.[31] In late November 1944, in one of his monologues at the Chancellery, Hitler even tried to see the positive side in all the destruction. "We are going to rebuild our cities to be lovelier than they were," he announced. "I give my word on that. With more monumental buildings than ever existed before."[32]

The more the war dragged on and victory refused to materialise, the more the dictator, who before 1939 had hardly missed an opportunity to make a public impression and bathe in mass adulation, avoided appearing in front of the German people. In December 1940, after a speech to armaments workers at the Borsig factory in Berlin, he had been "quite buoyed" by the enthusiastic reaction. "He intends to speak more frequently," a satisfied Goebbels noted. "The people are his true audience, as he knows them best."[33] Yet Hitler's public appearances dwindled. In 1941, he gave seven speeches before live audiences; in

1942, five; and in 1943, a mere three: on Heroes' Commemoration Day on 21 March, on the anniversary of the 1923 Beer Hall Putsch on 8 November in Munich, and on 20 November before young soldiers in Breslau. In addition he gave a radio address on 10 September. Goebbels was not at all happy about Hitler's reticence. The Führer had "somehow disappeared into the clouds," he complained in early August 1943. "This is not good for the practical conduct of war. Considering how constantly the Führer spoke up in front of the German people in good times, it is surely all the more necessary now that times are tough!"[34]

Goebbels doggedly nagged the dictator to show himself and address his subjects more often, but to no avail. Hitler made no public appearance whatever in 1944 aside from his speech in the Hofbräuhaus on 24 February to commemorate the founding of the Nazi Party; and even then his performance was considered so poor that it could not be broadcast on radio. His only other public words were two radio addresses: the first on 30 January, on the anniversary of his assumption of power in 1933; the second late at night on 21 July after the unsuccessful assassination attempt against him. The once omnipresent Führer had become a spectral, otherworldly figure.[35] His visits to Berlin were kept secret, and whenever he travelled in his special train from the Reich capital or Munich, great care was taken to prevent Hitler from having any contact with the outside world. Even during daytime, the windows of Hitler's train were blacked out, and the carriages artificially lit.[36] The days of the mass pilgrimages to the Obersalzberg in the hope of getting a glimpse of the man that people believed would save Germany were long gone.

Hitler's disappearance from the public eye was symptomatic of the crisis of the regime, which first became apparent after Stalingrad and continually worsened afterwards. Since the whole system of Nazi rule was conceived around the figure of the Führer and dependent on the popular support he alone could mobilise, his absence necessarily had serious consequences. Goebbels tried to fill the gap left behind, for example with his "total war" speech of February 1943, and he enjoyed the praise he received as the "dynamo of the people" who knew how to lift the popular mood whatever the circumstances.[37] But he knew too well that he could never replace Hitler as an orator. "Only the Führer possesses the authority to restore the people's courage and confidence in the current situation," the propaganda minister admitted in late August 1944.[38]

The Führer's public silence was a caesura for Hitler personally as well as for the Nazi system as a whole. The dictator had always drawn strength from his speeches to mass audiences and the intoxicating enthusiasm they elicited. They were a source of energy not just for his faithful believers but for himself. In November 1943, Goebbels alluded to this phenomenon in a note about Hitler's Breslau speech: "It is very good for the Führer once again to speak in front of a large gathering. He not only communicates strength. He derives it too."[39] But this speech would be Hitler's last live appearance before thousands of people. In the second half of the war, he was no longer able to exploit one of his great strengths: the constant exchange of energy between himself and the masses. Hitler's decline as a popular orator was the beginning of the end of his rule.

As he disappeared from public view, Hitler increasingly isolated himself in his East Prussian headquarters. At the start of the war, the dictator continued his peacetime habit of regularly visiting the Goebbels family on Schwanenwerder Island, near Berlin, where he would play with the children and reminisce about the old days. In November 1940, for instance, on the eve of receiving Soviet foreign minister Molotov, Hitler personally congratulated Magda Goebbels on her birthday, staying with the family until the early hours of the morning. "He is completely sure of himself and relaxed just like in the old days of peace," noted the propaganda minister. "We are very lucky to have had the Führer as our guest for such a long time."[40]

But once Operation Barbarossa had begun, Hitler ceased socialising with the Goebbels family. From then on, military officers in his head-quarters were his main source of company. And after the crisis of September 1942, he withdrew from them too, taking meals alone in his bunker and rarely receiving visitors. Conversations with the Führer over lunch grew more difficult, indeed torturous, from month to month, Albert Speer complained, with Hitler often lapsing into brooding silence. "I had the impression that this was a person who was gradually being extinguished," Speer recalled.[41] Heinrich Hoffmann also found that Hitler was becoming "increasingly withdrawn from others": "He was short-tempered whenever contradicted and refused to speak so that uncomfortable pauses interrupted the conversation."[42] Towards the end of his life, Hitler's secretaries kept him company at meals: two ate lunch with him, and two joined him for dinner. But whereas previously after situation meetings he had been able to switch effortlessly to the role of the charming host at table, he increasingly seemed obsessed with dark thoughts and spent more time talking to himself than to his companions.[43]

Like everything else he did and did not do, Hitler's withdrawal was partially staged for effect. Thus, once the war was underway, he gave up his nightly habit of watching a film or two because he ostensibly wanted to focus completely on his new role as field commander. He stopped his regular visits to the Bayreuth Festival after the summer of 1940. Following the German debacle at Stalingrad, he ceased playing records in the evening, refusing to listen even to the symphonies of his compatriot Anton Bruckner, his other favourite composer after Wagner. The Führer had no time any more for "amusement and diversion," Goebbels noted in late January 1943. "That has all been discontinued. The Führer's entire life is devoted to the war and to serving the people."[44]

The dictator also tried to give the military men around him the impression that he was sacrificing his private pleasures for the duration of the war. There was "nothing pleasant" for him about conducting the war, he declared in late August 1944 in his headquarters. He had lived "for five years here divorced from the rest of the world" and had "visited no theatre, attended no concert and seen no film."[45] This complaint contained an element of criticism for the members of the general staff, whom Hitler accused of being exclusively concerned with the handiwork of war and entirely uninterested in artistic matters. He was "fed up" with consorting with them, he carped to Goebbels, adding that they had "no intellect or culture." For that reason, there was "no common ground" between them and he approached the officers as "a completely foreign class of people."[46]

Goebbels worried about Hitler's lack of human contact, remarking that it was "tragic that the Führer has cut himself off from life like this . . . He does not get to relax any more and just sits in his bunker, working and brooding. If only he could be transplanted to a different environment for a change!"[47] Goebbels did not seem to comprehend that Hitler felt quite at home in the role of the lonely, self-denying military leader. It was part of his strategy to reinforce his pretence, particularly in trying situations, of being a superlative military commander. In so doing he styled himself on his Prussian idol. "Do not worry," he told Zeitzler after the 6th Army was surrounded at Stalingrad. "It is in misfortune that you first get the chance to show how great you are. Friedrich the Great did this as well."[48]

Typical of the gloomy unapproachability Hitler maintained during the last two years of the war was the fact that the only living thing he intensely cared about was his dog. He had been given a young German shepherd in 1942 by his admirer Gerdy Troost, the widow of his first favourite architect, Paul Troost. Hitler named the dog Blondi and spent many an hour teaching her tricks. "It is almost moving to watch him play with this young German shepherd," noted Goebbels. "The animal has got so accustomed to him that it hardly takes a step without him . . . At the moment, the dog is the only living thing constantly at his side."[49] Blondi accompanied Hitler on his short morning walks in the close vicinity of his bunker. The dictator was very proud of his clever pet and got annoyed if she sniffed any of his guests.[50] The affection he displayed for his dog went hand in hand with his resentful contempt for his fellow human beings. "Speer, I will only ever have two friends, Miss Braun and my dog," he kept telling his armaments minister from the autumn of 1943, in anticipation of the end of his life.[51]

The war dramatically changed how Hitler lived and worked. Before 1939, phases of hectic activity alternated with periods of relaxation, in which the dictator would recover and calmly consider his next plans. By contrast, in the Wolf's Lair he was subjected to a work regime that corseted him in daily duties and required self-discipline. That changed little when he was on the Obersalzberg. There too the lengthy daily situation meetings and the constant stream of visitors allowed him few opportunities for regeneration. The only times for relaxation were his nighttime teas in the Wolf's Lair or chats in front of the fire at the Berghof. On those occasions, surrounded by people he trusted, Hitler tried to distract himself from the hard reality of the war, often losing himself in memories of days gone by.[52]

By 1943 at the latest, Hitler was showing clear signs of being over-worked. "You see, I have to do everything myself," he complained to Speer on his fifty-fourth birthday. ". . . I am surrounded by highly decorated generals, specialists and armaments experts, but everything, large and small, rests on my shoulders!"[53] Once again the dictator overlooked the fact that his problems were self-inflicted. His obsession with detail and control did not allow him to delegate decisions. On the contrary, he believed that he had to take responsibility for everything. For that reason, in January 1942 he refused to sign an edict, drawn up by the head of the Reich Chancellery, Hans Heinrich Lammers, that would have temporarily relieved him of the burden of running government and administrative matters.[54] The constant demands ultimately exhausted Hitler. When armaments manager Hans Kehrl listened to him speak to a group of industrialists at the Platterhof Hotel in June 1944, he wrote: "Once he was a master of words and speeches. Now he faltered, not finishing his sentences and becoming entangled in his thoughts. In short he was the picture of a person suffering from severe exhaustion and losing his concentration for a time. He was obviously not in control of himself."[55]

More and more frequently, Hitler articulated the wish to hang up his uniform and withdraw from all military matters. "He said that he looked forward to nothing more than to trade his grey [military] tunic for his brown [party] jacket and be able again to go to the theatre and cinema . . . and mix with people," Goebbels wrote after a private conversation.[56] Such dreams of escape were centred on Linz. Despite halting all major construction plans in Berlin and other cities for the duration of the war, he allowed Hermann Giesler to continue work on expanding his home city on the Danube. Hitler's vision was to elevate Linz into a counterweight to Vienna and an "industrial and cultural city of the greatest sort."[57] For his pet project, the planned "Führer Museum," the dictator had a special plenipotentiary, the director of Dresden's Old Masters Gallery, Hans Posse, steal works of art from around occupied Europe. After Posse's death in December 1942, his successors, Wiesbaden's museum director, Hermann Voss, and the Dresden art dealer Hildebrand Gurlitt, continued the plundering.[58] Hitler dreamed of withdrawing to Linz when the war was over and living out his final years there. "As an old man, I will write my memoirs, surrounded by clever, cultured young people," he told his secretaries. "I will not want to see any officers—they are nothing but block-headed ignoramuses, one-dimensional and obstinate."[59]

★

At what point did Hitler know that Germany would be defeated? The question is not easy to answer since the dictator maintained an "impenetrable silence" on this issue.[60] In his Nuremberg jail cell, Jodl reached the conclusion that Hitler had come to "suspect and know" that the war was lost "before anyone else in the world."[61] The Wehrmacht chief of staff did not specify an exact point in time for this realisation. There is considerable indication that it would have dawned on Hitler that victory was no longer possible after the debacle at Stalingrad at the latest.[62] But admitting defeat would have been incompatible with his self-image as a military genius. Outwardly he continued to project confidence, playing the role of the indomitable supreme commander.

Such demonstrative optimism allowed Hitler to counter the increasing general scepticism about Germany's chances for ultimate victory. In October 1943, Goebbels wrote of his amazement that in all their conversations, "even in the most critical and unhappy hours of the war," Hitler showed a "firm and confident attitude." The propaganda minister predicted: "A man who refuses to be knocked off his feet by the hardest setbacks will achieve victory for his country and his people in the end."[63] On 6 June 1944, the day the Allies landed in Normandy, Goebbels commented again: "It is impressive how sure the Führer is of his historical mission."[64] Hitler's faithful propaganda minister was not the only one to be infected by the dictator's seemingly unassailable confidence. Many of the military commanders who came to the Wolf's Lair burdened with serious worries and doubts returned full of faith after meeting with the Führer. "When they emerged from his office at his headquarters, they almost invariably had the expressions and bearing of completely different people from before," recalled Otto Dietrich.[65] Like so many others, the military leaders usually succumbed to the suggestive powers of persuasion Hitler was still capable of exerting in conversation.

It seems that Hitler's ceaseless invocation of "final victory" also convinced the man himself, allowing him to hope, despite his better judgement, that the war would have a positive end. In any case, the more he was forced into the defensive, the more emphatically he called upon "Providence," which he believed had always been on his side in his many endeavours. In this process of auto-suggestive self-assurance, reminiscences of the Nazi Party's "battle years" were a welcome source of consolation and strength. "What crises and struggles we have gone through in our party!" Hitler and Goebbels agreed at the apex of the winter crisis of 1941–42. "How minor they appear today, now that we have put them behind us. That is the way it will be with this struggle."[66] Again and again in the months that followed, the dictator returned to the situation in late 1932 and early 1933, when all hopes of achieving power seemed lost, only for Hitler to move into the Chancellery a few weeks later. "In 1932, we only achieved victory by being stubborn to a point that resembled madness, and that will be the case again today," Goebbels noted in May 1943.[67]

Of course, it required a considerable amount of willpower for Hitler to betray no signs of weakness and maintain a façade of faith in victory in the face of the increasingly hopeless situation. This was almost certainly one cause of the nervous irritability he displayed. "Every fly on the wall can make him fly into a rage," Hitler's valet Heinz Linge wrote about his master in the autumn of 1942.[68] Hitler's more and more frequent temper tantrums may well have been a way of discharging the internal tension he felt, of proving to himself and others that his "happy star" would guarantee a favourable outcome this time as well, even though the initiative was now with his enemies.

In the first two years of war, Hitler enjoyed robust good health. He had no trouble meeting physical demands, and his personal doctor, Morell, had little to do.[69] The Führer first fell ill in early August 1941, the point at which his hopes for a lightning quick victory over the Soviet Union were revealed as a chimera. In the years that followed, the physical and mental condition of Germany's supreme commander would fluctuate depending on the military situation. Spells of vertigo and symptoms of exhaustion became increasingly frequent the more the tide turned against the Third Reich and its allies. It took a considerable physical toll on Hitler to get through the winter crisis of 1941–42. "If you only look at him superficially, you may think that he is in the best of health," Goebbels remarked, but appearances were deceiving. Hitler himself had admitted in an "intimate conversation" that he was "struggling with severe bouts of dizziness."[70]

On a visit to Vinnitsa in early September, after Operation Blue had proven a failure, Field Marshal von Kluge got "a true shock" from how "miserable" Hitler looked. It was no wonder Hitler was in such bad shape, Kluge opined, given the burdens he put upon himself, which "not even a man of will like him can bear."[71] The definitive turn in the war in 1942–43 accelerated Hitler's physical deterioration. "You can see how much recent times have gnawed at him," Goebbels conceded after a visit to the Obersalzberg in June 1943. "Only some of the physical vigour we always admired in him remains."[72] Anyone seeing the dictator for the first time in a while was struck by his changed appearance and demeanour. "My general impression of the Führer was of a man who had aged severely since 1938 and was almost exhausted," General Friedrich Hossbach, Hitler's former Wehrmacht adjutant, recalled about visiting the Wolf's Lair in November 1943 to receive the Oak Cluster of the Knight's Cross of the Iron Cross.[73]

The signs of age could no longer be overlooked. Hitler's hair had gone grey, there were bags under his clouded eyes, he stooped when he walked and his left hand trembled. The tremor appeared for the first time in August 1941 and had become increasingly noticeable after the German defeat at Stalingrad. Following the failed assassination attempt of 20 July, it suddenly disappeared, but it would soon return, even more pronounced, spreading to his left arm and leg as well. Today most medical historians agree that Hitler suffered from Parkinson's syndrome. That did not, however, affect his mental capabilities.[74]

Morell was confounded by this illness[75] and prescribed a plethora of medications to combat chronic intestinal complaints and increasingly frequent symptoms of exhaustion. They included laxatives, sedatives, sleeping pills, painkillers, heart and circulatory medicine and stimulants. Most of these were readily available, over-the-counter medications, and some came from Morell's own pharmaceutical empire. In July 1943 and increasingly in 1944, Morell administered injections of the painkiller and anti-cramp medication Eukodal, which seemed to have fuelled Hitler's tendency towards auto-suggestive flights from reality.[76] Morell was going to "great lengths to keep the Führer fit for the war," Goebbels remarked in early June 1944. That was of the essence, the propaganda minister added, because Germany's prospects depended entirely on Hitler staying healthy: "If something happened to the Führer's health, I would in fact no longer know what could be done."[77]

In a recent sensationalist book that mixed fact and fiction, the writer Norman Ohler sought to revive the old idea that Morell had got Hitler hooked on drugs.[78] The Führer paid for his devotion to his personal physician with the "continuing destruction of his health," Ohler contended, and he claimed that Hitler experienced "hardly a sober day" in the second half of 1944, becoming a "junkie" who demanded greater and greater dosages "until his inevitable collapse."[79] But there is no proof that Hitler was an addict, as the former president of Berlin's Charité Hospital, Hans-Joachim Neumann, and the historian Henrik Eberle showed in 2009. They found that Morell's injections had no effect on the dictator's decision-making capacity: "Hitler always knew what he was doing."[80]

The Führer's physical deterioration had less to do with his consumption of medications than with his permanent overexertion and his unhealthy lifestyle, particularly his lack of exercise. Hitler spent most of his days in the artificial light and sticky air of his bunker.[81] His architect Giesler provided a vivid description of a sickly Führer in late September 1944 in the Wolf's Lair: "Adolf Hitler lay on a camp bed in a windowless cell in his bunker. There was a low table at the head of this bed covered with reports, dispatches, maps, several books and a telephone. Overhead glowed an adjustable wall lamp, and the light grey walls reflected its light, giving the small room the unreal pallor of a burial chamber. The fresh air provided by a quietly humming fan struggled to combat the smell of concrete typical of a bunker."[82] Prior to and during the first phase of Germany's Ardennes offensive in December 1944, the dictator physically revived one last time. But once this final attempt to regain the initiative had failed Hitler's reserves of energy were very nearly used up.

16

Staged Exit

"I know the war is lost," admitted a deeply depressed Hitler in early January 1945. "The [enemies'] superiority is too great . . . I would like to put a bullet in my head." But he immediately pulled himself together: "We will not surrender, never ever. We may go down but we will take a world with us."[1] It was a rare moment of candour in which the dictator revealed the thinking that in the final months of his life would increasingly shape his thoughts and actions. If Germany's demise was inevitable, it was to be made into a heroic example for future generations. On the evening of 28 January, Hitler declared that he wanted to prove himself "worthy of the great role models of history."[2]

It was no contradiction that, while engaging in such calculations, Hitler continued to project unbroken confidence to the outside world. "Never does the Führer allow the slightest doubt in our coming victory to emerge," Goebbels wrote on 1 February.[3] If the battle was to be fought to the bitter end, there could be no public acknowledgement of the growing hopelessness of the situation. Even within Hitler's closest entourage, the myth of Germany's "final victory" had to be preserved.

Hitler devoted most of his remaining energy in the spring of 1945 to staging Germany's "heroic demise." In so doing he could call upon myths anchored in the collective German psyche. First and foremost among these was *The Song of the Nibelungs*, which after its rediscovery in the eighteenth century had become a German national epic.[4] Göring had already invoked the final battle of the Nibelungs in his speech of 30 January 1943, in which he sought to interpret the 6th Army's destruction at Stalingrad as a grand gesture of self-sacrifice. It was no accident that, in his final letter to his wife from the Reich Chancellery bunker in early April 1945, Martin Bormann also cited this myth. If destiny had chosen them "to fall like the ancient Nibelungs in King Etzel's hall," Bormann wrote, they would "meet their deaths proudly and with heads held high."[5] The trope would take a central place in Hitler's vision of Germany's downfall and his own. When the dictator spoke of taking an entire world down with him, it is likely he was thinking of *Twilight of the Gods*, the final part of Wagner's Ring cycle.[6]

Hitler was also influenced by the maxims of the Prussian philosopher of war Carl von Clausewitz, whose works he had studied intensely. In *The Campaign of 1812*, published a year before the war to liberate Europe from Napoleonic domination began, Clausewitz declared that there was no value higher for a people than to defend the "dignity and freedom of their existence . . . to the last drop of blood." Whereas "the shame of cowardly submission can never be erased . . . even the loss of freedom after an honourable and bloody battle secures the rebirth of the people."[7] In his "political will," written on 29 April, the day before his suicide, Hitler harkened back to Clausewitz's words, declaring: "From the sacrifice of our soldiers and my own solidarity with them until death, the seeds will be planted in German history for the radiant rebirth of the National Socialist movement and, with it, the creation of a true ethnic-popular community."[8] Thus Hitler was concerned not only with his own place in history, but with ensuring the future revival of his ideology. No one cut through the pathos of this rhetoric of heroic downfall better than Thomas Mann, who had told his radio listeners on 1 January 1945 that "every gesture of external heroism that Nazi Germany acts out" is "only a grimace: the terrible expression of criminals who have long been brought down by justice."[9]

The Soviet winter offensive in 1945 ushered in the downfall of the Third Reich. Little remained with which the Wehrmacht could counter the overwhelming superiority of the Red Army. On 12 January, the 1st Ukrainian Front under Marshal Ivan Konev launched an attack from the Vistula bridgehead at Baranów, around 200 kilometres south of Warsaw. By that evening they had opened a 45-kilometre-wide breach of the German lines. "Understandably everything is now very tense," wrote Governor-General Hans Frank to his wife from Krakow that day. The defensive fortifications it had taken months of intense labour to construct would now have to prove that they could halt the Soviet advance. "I myself am completely calm and relaxed and sit here in my castle like a venerable patriarch," Frank added.[10] Krakow had so far been spared any fighting, but on the night of 18–19 January, Soviet forces arrived outside the city. By that time, Frank had already fled west.[11] Little more than a week later, on 27 January, Soviet troops captured the Auschwitz death camp and liberated seven thousand sick and exhausted inmates left behind when the SS commando had hastily withdrawn. By the end of the month, most of the Upper Silesian industrial areas, so crucial to the German war effort, had fallen intact into the hands of the Red Army. Only the Lower Silesian capital, Breslau, would be held until the end of the war, thanks to the fanaticism of the Wehrmacht units that defended it.

On 13 January, the 2nd Belorussian Front under Marshal Konstantin Rokossovsky and the 3rd Belorussian Front under General Ivan Chernyakhovsky, supported by the 1st Baltic Front, advanced on East Prussia, achieving an operational breakthrough on the third day of the offensive. Tilsit (Sovetsk) fell on 20 January. Soviet units progressed via Goldap and Gumbinnen towards the Baltic coast. On 26 January, they reached the Vistula Lagoon near Tolkemit (Tolkmicko), east of Elbing (Elbląg), thereby cutting off East Prussia from the rest of the Reich. Although suffering heavy losses, the besieged German troops managed to hold on to Königsberg and the surrounding area, as well as the port of Pillau (Baltiisk).

On 14 January, the 1st Belorussian Front under Marshal Georgy Zhukov commenced the primary Soviet offensive from the Vistula bridgehead at Warka, south of Warsaw, breaking through German defensive lines the following day. On 17 January, Soviet and Polish troops entered the Polish capital, which had been completely destroyed. Two days later, they took Łódź, and on 21 January they encircled Posen, the governmental seat of the Wartheland *Gau*. Gauleiter Arthur Greiser too had promptly fled the approaching enemy. Zhukov's men made quick progress to the river Oder. On 31 January, they were able to establish a first bridgehead on the western riverbank. Berlin was now only 80 kilometres away, but the Red Army stopped to catch its breath before launching its final assault on the German capital. Soviet troops had advanced 500 kilometres west, liberated occupied Poland

and captured most of eastern Germany in only three weeks. Like a gigantic wedge, the front on the Oder cleaved the territory of the Third Reich.[12]

The Red Army's rapid advance produced huge numbers of refugees. In icy temperatures, hundreds of thousands of people from the eastern German provinces sought to make their way west or to the Baltic ports on foot or with horse and cart. Rumours about outrages committed by the Soviets fuelled their panic, and indeed the atrocities committed when Red Army soldiers first set foot in East Prussia the previous October continued and intensified. The pitiless campaign of annihilation that the Wehrmacht and the SS had waged against the Soviet Union was coming home to the civilian German population. Feelings of hatred and the desire for revenge discharged themselves in waves of violence. "May the German mother curse the day she bore a son!" wrote one Red Army soldier from Tiraspol in western Ukraine to his family on 30 January 1945. "May German women now feel the terrors of war! May they now experience what they have wanted to inflict on other peoples!"[13]

From 23 January there were no more train services between Königsberg and the rest of Germany, so refugees only had two options. Those from the northeast of the region tried to reach Königsberg and the Samland Peninsula to the north in the hope of fleeing by ship from Pillau. Everyone else had to trudge across the frozen Vistula Lagoon to reach the narrow Vistula Spit and from there continue to Danzig and Gotenhafen (Gdynia). By the end of January, almost a million refugees packed these places, hoping to board one of the ships the government had assigned to bring East Prussians to safety. On 30 January, a Soviet submarine torpedoed the MS *Wilhelm Gustloff*, a former cruise ship used by the Nazi Strength through Joy organisation. Most recent estimates put the number of people killed at more than 9,000.[14] The sinking of the *Wilhelm Gustloff* would become central in the collective German memory of wartime atrocities. But few Germans chose to remember that SS men murdered around 3,000 prisoners, mostly Jewish women from the Stutthof concentration camp and its ancillary camps, in the Baltic seaside town of Palmnicken (Yantarny) on the following night, 31 January–1 February.

News of what was happening in the east spread quickly and caused shockwaves throughout Germany. No one had reckoned with the possibility of the Red Army reaching the borders of the Reich so soon. People anxiously followed the fate of the refugees, and that only worsened their fears of being directly threatened themselves.[15] Thousands of displaced persons arrived every day in Berlin alone. "There are throngs of refugees in all parts of the city," noted the journalist Ruth Andreas-Friedrich. "They curse the godforsaken times loudly and quietly. No one holds their tongue. Those who have lost everything have nothing left to fear. And they do not care where the end comes. The police turn a deaf ear to this."[16] Initially Goebbels, concerned about further stoking panic among the columns of refugees and the population at large, hesitated to exploit Soviet atrocities for propaganda purposes. But in early February he changed his mind. After obtaining Hitler's permission, he released waves of anti-Bolshevist "horror propaganda" throughout the Reich. The Nazi leadership hoped that it would have a "positive and motivating influence on the fighting troops." "What else can we produce to get the nation to hold out, if this material no longer has an impact and the German people and the Wehrmacht react negatively to it?" the propaganda minister asked.[17] And indeed, the fear of becoming the victims of an orgy of vengeance by the Red Army does seem to have significantly increased Germans' willingness to fight on in the east.[18]

In late January, those around Hitler still assumed that the Red Army would advance directly on Berlin from its bridgehead on the Oder. "*Stalin ante portas!*" noted Goebbels' press chief, Wilfred von Oven, on 31 January. "This horrified cry spread like the wind through the Reich capital this morning when news came that the Russians have succeeded in crossing the Oder."[19] As Gauleiter of Berlin, Goebbels worked feverishly to prepare the defence of the capital, with anti-tank barricades and fortifications being set up, tanks and assault guns massed and Volkssturm militia equipped with bazookas deployed all over the city. The propaganda minister vowed that he was "determined to create a masterpiece in the defence of the city," perhaps trying to summon courage.[20] But in the first days of February, it became clear that Zhukov's armies were halting at the Oder and that Berlin was not yet in immediate danger. By the middle of the month, after conferring with Bormann, Lammers decreed that it was a "matter of honour" for all Reich government offices to remain in the capital. Any officials ordering an evacuation on their own authority would be considered guilty of desertion and sentenced to death.[21]

Hitler reacted to the catastrophe unfolding on the eastern front in typical fashion: by blaming the generals for failing to follow his strict orders to hold out. On 17 January, on learning of the German evacuation from Warsaw, which had been declared a "fortress," the Führer once again saw himself the victim of betrayal. The head of the operations division of the Army High Command, Colonel Bogislaw von Bonin, and two of his subordinates were arrested and subjected to hours of Gestapo interrogations. Bonin was sent to Dachau, where he would be held prisoner until the concentration camp was liberated.[22] One after another, leading generals were stripped of their commands. In mid-January, the supreme commander of Army Group A, Colonel-General Josef Harpe, whom Hitler held responsible for the collapse of the Vistula front, was replaced by Colonel-General Ferdinand Schörner, a dyed-in-the-wool Nazi. On 26 January, the supreme commander of Army Group Centre, Colonel-General Hans-Georg Reinhardt, was likewise demoted in favour of the Austrian Colonel-General Lothar Rendulic, who was also considered impeccably loyal to Hitler. Not even Hitler's former Wehrmacht adjutant General Friedrich Hossbach, who had distinguished himself as the commander of the 4th Army in the defence of East Prussia the previous autumn, was spared the axe. He was dismissed after authorising his troops to fall back towards the west to escape being surrounded.[23]

As Hitler was firing his generals, the army groups between the Baltic Sea and the Carpathian Mountains were being renamed. Army Group A now became Army Group Centre, while the old army group of that name was rechristened Army Group North; that group in turn was now called Army Group Courland. On 21 January, Army Group Vistula was formed and charged with filling the gap between the new Army Groups North and Centre and defending West Prussia and Pomerania.[24] Hitler entrusted command of this new group to a military dilettante, Reich Leader–SS Himmler, whom he considered best able to stabilise the unsteady front by utilising all available forces. The decision, wrote Goebbels, "mainly reflects the fact that troops retreating from the Soviet advance have dispersed and a firm hand is needed to turn them again into solid fighting units."[25] To the first general staff officer of his new army group, Hans-Georg Eismann, Himmler boasted that he would "stop the Russians in their tracks, pound them and throw them back." In the same breath, very much in the manner of Hitler himself, the SS leader vented his contempt for the officers of the general staff, who "only ever worried" and were "incapable of improvising." He would put an end to that, Himmler promised, and "tackle matters with ruthless energy."[26]

One order by Hitler expressed more than any other his bottomless mistrust of his military commanders. Issued only a few days into the Soviet offensive, it required all commanders from division leaders upwards to report any intended evacuation and retreat promptly enough so that it would be possible for the Führer to "intervene in the decision-making, and if necessary, a counter-command could reach the forwardmost troops in time." Moreover, the dictator deemed it necessary to stipulate that all reports to him should contain "the unvarnished truth." In the future, he vowed, he would "punish in draconian form any attempt at concealment, be it intentional or negligent or caused by a slip in concentration."[27] With this order, Hitler was tightening his reins of control. Any attempt by military commanders to take decisions of their own in the face of pressure from the enemy was to be curtailed in advance.

Under these circumstances, it was no wonder the relationship between Hitler and Guderian increasingly deteriorated. The chief of the general staff had demanded that the 6th SS Tank Army under Sepp Dietrich, which had been withdrawn from the Ardennes, be transferred to the Vistula front to halt the Red Army advance. But Hitler decided otherwise and ordered these troops to mass in Hungary. His reasoning was that he needed to secure the Hungarian oil fields, which, given the loss of Romanian oil supplies and stepped-up Allied air raids on German hydrogenation plants, were considered crucial to the war effort. "If you do not receive any more fuel, your tanks will not be able to roll and our airplanes cannot fly," Hitler told Guderian. "That should be clear to you. But my generals understand nothing about the economy of war."[28] The dictator also stressed the necessity of "securing our supply of oil" to Goebbels, with whom he met on 23 January, after returning from his headquarters in the west.[29] Three days later, with Sepp Dietrich in attendance, Hitler gave the propaganda minister a deeper insight into his strategic thinking.

"The Führer continues to energetically pursue the goal of taking back the Hungarian oil fields because that is the precondition for the successful continuation of the war," Goebbels noted. "If we regain possession of oil, we can go on a moderate offensive again . . . The Führer intends to inflict a devastating defeat on the enemy in the Hungarian theatre. He hopes that he will be able to free up twelve divisions, which can then be deployed to liberate our own eastern territories." Goebbels considered this plan "somewhat too optimistic," indeed calling it "wishful thinking," but he kept his reservations to himself.[30]

Most German military leaders too followed the commands of the dictator, even though they could see all too clearly that Germany was hurtling towards defeat. One participant at situation meetings described the atmosphere as a "miasma of servility, nervousness and dishonesty" that occasionally made him even "feel physically unwell." The officer continued: "There was nothing there but fear: fear in all of its shades, from the anxiety of attracting the Führer's displeasure or angering him with some ill-considered remark to the naked terror about how to survive the imminent end of the drama."[31]

The only one with enough nerve to speak his mind was Guderian, and quarrels between him and Hitler became an almost daily occurrence. The chief of the general staff particularly raised Hitler's hackles in early February when he reiterated his demand that the Courland cauldron be evacuated and the troops thereby freed up be assigned to defend Berlin.[32] But the worst argument erupted during a situation meeting on 13 February. Guderian, who considered Himmler utterly unfit to be a military commander, insisted that one of his most capable subordinates, General Walther Wenck, be promoted to the general staff of the new Army Group Vistula. This was an unmistakable challenge to Hitler, and the dictator responded commensurately. "Cheeks flushed with rage, with fists raised and his whole body trembling, the man stood before me, beside himself with fury and fully out of control," Guderian would recall. "After every outburst of anger, Hitler would pace along the edge of the carpet, then stop directly in front of me and hurl the next recrimination. He yelled himself hoarse, his eyes bulged from their sockets and the veins in his forehead swelled up . . . I had never experienced a scene like this. I had never seen Hitler rage with such lack of control."

It is difficult to know whether this tantrum was staged or real. Suddenly, as quickly as he had blown up, Hitler calmed down and gave in, ordering Wenck to report immediately to Himmler's head-quarters. At that point, sitting down on a chair and putting on "his most charming smile," he told Guderian: "Please continue with what you were saying. The general staff has won a battle today."[33] Only a few days later, however, Wenck was seriously injured in a car accident while returning to his quarters from a situation meeting and was laid up for several weeks. Hitler never forgave Guderian for taking more liberties than other officers. The Führer had already decided to relieve him of his post back in late January, telling Goebbels in confidence that the chief of the general staff had "failed to live up to his hopes" and calling him "a tired man."[34]

At 10 p.m. on 30 January 1945, Hitler addressed the German people over the radio for the last time. Goebbels had overcome the Führer's initial scruples about speaking by assuring him that the new Magnetophon reel-to-reel tape-recording technology would allow him to repeat any passages with which he was unhappy.[35] But the dictator seems to have been able to read out his twenty-minute speech without any glitches. There was little new about what Hitler said aside from his conspicuously frequent references to the "Almighty One," who had protected him on 20 July 1944 and who would also not desert him in future. Hitler only briefly touched upon "the horrible fate unfolding today in the east" before launching into his familiar litany of complaints about the "Jewish-international world conspiracy." He concluded his address with an appeal to the German people to "gird themselves with an even mightier, harder spirit of resistance," for then the "dead of this massive war will be buried with a wreath and bow reading 'And you triumphed in the end after all!'"[36] Goebbels registered with relief that Hitler had sounded "very firm and masculine," betraying "not the slightest sign of weakness." He predicted that the Führer's words would "make a deep impression on the German and world public."[37]

He could have hardly deceived himself any more greatly. Hitler's address had no effect whatsoever. A report by a Wehrmacht propaganda officer on 1 February described the mood in Berlin as "downcast." People had "hardly any more hope for a positive outcome to the war," and "major doubts and worries" were now being "expressed without constraint."[38] Even Goebbels had to admit that nearly all of the letters he received contained "only hopelessness" and that extensive "criticism is being levelled at the leadership and indeed partly at the Führer himself."[39] Hitler's popularity, which had been the glue binding the people to the regime for so long, was dissolving. Only a small minority of the most fanatical National Socialists clung to their faith in the Führer and their unshakable conviction that Germany would triumph in the end. One of them was a twenty-four-year-old League of German Girls leader from Stettin. "If we maintain a strong heart, we can never be defeated," she wrote to her mother in February. "For our faith can only die with us and it stays alive as long as we live." A few days later she reaffirmed her belief: "The decisive thing is that we will emerge victorious. Not only because the Führer says so but because it is the law of our lives."[40]

On 3 February, American bombers carried out their heaviest air raid yet on the Reich capital, reducing large parts of the city centre to rubble. Almost 3,000 Berliners were killed and 120,000 bombed out of their homes.[41] Many households had to do without water and electricity for days. Only slowly did the traffic start moving again. The Old Reich Chancellery building took a direct hit, and the wing housing Hitler's private quarters was completely destroyed, forcing the dictator to move into the bunker in the Chancellery garden.[42]

Only a few months after becoming chancellor, Hitler had ordered the construction of an underground bunker when the building was being renovated in 1933. The New Reich Chancellery on Vossstrasse, built by Speer in 1938–39, also contained a subterranean complex, which was connected with the bunker in the Old Reich Chancellery by an eighty-metre tunnel. After the course of the war had turned against Germany in 1941–42 and the Allies stepped up their air raids, Hitler no longer found these catacombs safe enough, and in 1942 he charged Speer's office with building an even deeper bunker. It was largely completed by the autumn of 1944, although minor work continued until the spring of 1945.[43]

The protective space under the Old Reich Chancellery now became the "ante-bunker," giving onto a flight of stairs leading down to the Führer's bunker. It encompassed eighteen small and sparsely furnished rooms. With its close quarters, artificial light, smell of concrete and sticky air, visitors found the atmosphere oppressive. To the right of the corridor was the machine room with the ventilation equipment, which was followed by telephone switchboards, a servants' room, a first-aid room and bedrooms for Linge and Morell. At the back end of the corridor, which also served as a waiting room for people attending meetings, one door on the left led to a situation room, another to Hitler's private office, bedroom and bathroom. A greater contrast to the expansive, splendid chambers of the Old and New Reich Chancelleries was hard to imagine. Hitler's office, measuring just three metres by four, was dominated by Anton Graff's portrait of Friedrich the Great over the Führer's desk. The dictator often used to say that he would stand in front of this image to get "renewed strength," whenever bad news threatened to bring him down. In his bedroom, at the foot end of his bed, was the safe in which Hitler kept his personal papers and a bottle of oxygen in case the diesel-powered ventilators supplying the bunker with fresh air were to fail.[44]

The bathroom led to a small dressing room and then on to Eva Braun's living room and bathroom. Together with her sister Gretl, Hitler's mistress had returned to Berlin on the afternoon of 19 January.[45] Nothing had changed the decision she had made the previous October to share Hitler's fate until the very end, and the dictator made no effort to prevent her from doing so. On the contrary, when Goebbels announced in late January 1945 that his wife had decided to remain in the capital with their six children, Hitler declared that Braun too "did not want to leave Berlin, particularly in the present critical situation." That drew words of the "highest acknowledgement and admiration" from the dictator, Goebbels noted, adding: "She deserves them too."[46]

As he had done when they were together in December, Hitler took lunch and dinner in Braun's company.[47] On 5 February, only two days after the devastating air raid on Berlin, Braun celebrated her thirty-third birthday in her small apartment in the Old Reich Chancellery, which had remained undamaged. Among the guests were Hitler, her sister, her brother-in-law Hermann Fegelein, Bormann, Speer and, rather surprisingly, Anni and Karl Brandt—evidence that Hitler's former attending physician had not been completely banned from the Führer's entourage after being dismissed in the autumn of 1944.[48] That would only happen in mid-April 1945, when Brandt was accused among other things of sending his wife and son towards the safety of advancing American troops. He was sentenced to death but escaped with his life thanks to a fortuitous series of coincidences.[49]

On 9 February, Braun left Berlin with her sister to say goodbye to family and friends in Munich and on the Obersalzberg and put a few final things in order. On 7 March, she returned to the Reich capital—this time for good.[50] It is a myth that Hitler tried to send her away. This legend was the invention of photographer Heinrich Hoffmann, who paid a final visit to Hitler in early April 1945 and who later claimed that Hitler had asked him to try to convince Braun to flee.[51]

The Führer's physical deterioration visibly accelerated. He hardly ever left his bunker, and when he did, it was usually only for short walks in the Chancellery garden.[52] "It chokes me up to see the Führer in his bunker in such a withered condition," noted Goebbels.[53] Other observers also noticed the dictator's frailty. His face looked paler and more like a mask than usual, his physical tremor had worsened, his movements were lamer, and he stooped more. Cavalry captain Gerhard Boldt, whom Guderian brought along to a situation meeting in Hitler's office in February, recalled his first meeting with the dictator: "His handshake was limp and soft, without any strength and making no impression. His head bobbled slightly . . . His left arm dangled lamely, and his left hand shook badly. In his eyes was an indescribable, flickering glow, which was quite frightful and completely unnatural. His face and particularly the skin around his eyes looked completely slack and worn out. All his movements were those of an ill, senile man. He reminded me of a burned-out piece of iron."[54]

Another staff officer was shocked when seeing Hitler for the first time in a long while that March: "He dragged himself around arduously and heavily, hurling his upper body forward and dragging his legs behind, from his living room to the meeting room in the bunker. He had lost his sense of balance. When he was stopped by someone along this short stretch of 20–30 metres, he had to sit down on one of the benches along the walls or hold on to whomever he was talking to . . . His eyes were bloodshot, and although all documents for his perusal were typed in letters three times the normal size, he could only read them with powerful glasses. Spittle often dangled from his mouth—it was an image of misery and horror."[55] Hitler's handwriting had changed as well. In Speer's eyes it revealed the "frailty of an old man" and was barely legible.[56]

Hitler's secretary Christa Schroeder recalled her boss being "almost permanently irritated" during his last months alive. Conversations were torturous since they consisted only of "monotone repetitions of the same stories," and the dictator's preferred topics were "dog-training, nutrition, and the stupidity and badness of the world."[57] On the other hand, there were no indications that Hitler's mental faculties had gone into a parallel decline. His prodigious memory continued to function astonishingly well, and he never lost his capacity to sugges-tively entrance and persuade others. On 19 February, General Otto Wöhler, who had replaced Johannes Friessner as supreme commander of Army Group South in December, came away revitalised from a meeting in Hitler's bunker. The Führer had been "fresh and confident," Wöhler reported, as though possessing a trick up his sleeve. For that reason, the general concluded, it was correct to continue carrying out his orders. "From the mouth of Wöhler, who is by no means a follower of the Führer, such a statement has objective value," commented General Hermann Balck.[58] Gauleiter Albert Forster, who travelled to Berlin in March to report on the desperate situation in Danzig, also emerged from a meeting transformed and returned home full of hope.[59]

In the unreal atmosphere of Hitler's subterranean refuge, the border between day and night became blurry, and the Führer's daily rhythm was pushed back even further. Now Linge would first wake him at 1 or 1:30 p.m., unless he had been driven from bed prior to that by an air-raid siren. The first situation meeting, which due to the almost daily bombardments now also took place in the bunker's tiny confer-ence space, usually began at 4 p.m. and went on until 6 or 7 p.m. The second situation meeting tended to be held long after midnight and lasted until the early hours. Despite the time shift, however, Hitler refused to forgo his teas at the end of the day. It meant that two of his four secretaries had to stay awake until five or six in the morning. Most of the time, an exhausted Hitler lay on the small sofa in his office, Schroeder recalled. "At least he still had the strength to get up to return our greetings," she wrote. "After a while he would lie down on the sofa again, where his valet would prop up his feet."[60]

The gloomy monotony of Hitler's days was interrupted only by visits to the gigantic model of his home city of Linz, which the architect Hermann Giesler had set up in the basement of the New Reich Chancellery. Hitler first inspected it on 9 February 1945, and cameraman Walter Frentz photographed the scene. The pictures show the dictator hunched over, seemingly lost in the act of viewing. Never had he seen Hitler "so grave, so absent and so moved at the same time," Giesler remarked.[61] In the days that followed, Hitler repeatedly went to look at the model of the city where he had determined that he would retire. It seems that these moments offered some welcome diversion from the dire reality of the war. His enthusiasm recalled his rapture at Speer's models of the "world capital Germania." On 12 February, Hitler told Goebbels that he had spent his few free hours the preceding night with Giesler's sketches. "The plans have . . . turned out splendidly," Goebbels recorded. "While the Führer does not believe they can be realised at present, they provide him with a certain relaxation amid his severe and pitiless work rhythm, which is to be thoroughly welcomed."[62] The dictator enjoyed showing visitors the model and explaining all the details of the planned reconstruction to make Linz the most beautiful city on the Danube. That was in keeping with his strategy of make-believe, of projecting optimism and clinging to the chimera of ultimate German victory.[63] Anyone planning in such obsessive detail for the future—at least, that was the impression he wished to communicate—could hardly consider the war already lost.

One of the few larger German cities to have been spared aerial bombardment was Dresden. But between 13 and 15 February, British and American bombers levelled parts of the city centre. Some 25,000 people were killed, including many refugees from Upper Silesia. The high numbers of casualties were the result of Dresden's false sense of security that the beautiful Baroque city—it was often referred to as "Florence on the Elbe"—would not be destroyed. Not enough air-raid shelters had been built, and air defences were woefully inadequate. Most of the flak guns had been taken down and transported to the front. Not a single fighter took off at night to oppose the enemy bombers. Goebbels' Propaganda Ministry added a zero to the end of the death toll to amplify the dimension of the catastrophe—the deception was intended to mobilise foreign public opinion against the Allies.[64] As terrible as the bombardment was, for Victor Klemperer it meant salvation. In the general chaos, he removed the yellow star from his clothing and set off with his wife on a veritable odyssey that ended in the Bavarian village of Unterbernbach, where the couple remained until the war ended.[65] Dresden would not be the last city to fall victim to the Allies' unfettered bombing offensive. On 16–17 March, Würzburg was destroyed; on 22 March, Hildesheim; on 8 April, Halberstadt; on 10–11 April, Plauen; and finally, on 14–15 April, Potsdam.[66]

Hitler received the news of Dresden's destruction with a "stony face," his hands "clenched into fists."[67] As a reprisal, Goebbels demanded that 10,000 British and American POWs be executed. That would have meant a serious violation of the Geneva Convention towards the Western Allies—Hitler and his generals had never observed the convention in the east—and might have resulted in Allied retaliation against German POWs. This possibility made the idea attractive to Hitler, who assumed that German troops in the west would fight as doggedly as those in the east if they were robbed of the prospect of humane treatment by the enemy. But Jodl, Ribbentrop and others threw their weight against disregarding the Geneva Convention, and in the end the dictator decided not to take that step.[68]

On 24 February 1945, the twenty-fifth anniversary of the publication of the Nazi Party programme, it was again Hermann Esser, Hitler's old Munich comrade, who read out a proclamation by the Führer over German radio. As he had in his speech on 30 January, the dictator raged against the "unholy alliance between exploitative capitalism and Bolshevism, which destroys human beings." He also called on Germans to "give their last ounce of strength with extreme fanaticism and embittered tenacity." The proclamation concluded with the words: "Twenty-five years ago I predicted victory for the movement. Today, suffused as always by faith in our people, I prophesy victory in the end for the German Reich!"[69] But the SS Security Service reported that the message had no effect on "broad segments of the population," eliciting remarks like "The Führer is making prophecies again" and "It sounds like a broken record." The Security Service in Berchtesgaden even concluded that "the content of the proclamation blew past the majority of ethnic-popular comrades like the wind through leafless branches."[70]

Rather than travelling to Munich, on 24 February Hitler received the Reichsleiters and Gauleiters in Berlin for the final time. Not all of them had been able to accept Hitler's invitation. Two of the most brutal ones—Erich Koch, the Gauleiter of East Prussia, and Karl Hanke, the Gauleiter of Lower Silesia, who had taken charge of the defence of "Fortress Breslau"—were absent.[71] At 2 p.m., when the doors of the mosaic hall of the New Chancellery were opened and Hitler entered accompanied by Bormann, the dictator's minions, who had not seen him since the previous August, were confronted with a devastating sight. "Laboriously, his shoulders sagging, he approached us," recalled Baldur von Schirach. "One of his legs . . . dragged across the marble floor. His face was ashen. With a trembling hand, he greeted each of us. At times he held his left hand in his right to conceal the tremor. Standing before us was no longer the Führer with the persuasive aura of old, but rather a ghost who called upon us to hold out to the last in order to extend his days for a short while."[72]

After the greeting, Hitler and the Nazi functionaries repaired to the adjacent cabinet chamber. Hitler sat down at a small table and began to speak, slowly and hesitantly. During the dictator's ninety-minute address, Karl Wahl, the Gauleiter of Swabia, had the chance to get a close-up look at Hitler: "His left hand—in fact, his entire left arm—trembled so violently and constantly that it made his whole body vibrate. This was no longer a tremble. It was a powerful, rhythmic shaking that made me very uneasy the whole time he spoke. No matter how Hitler tried to suppress or conceal this shaking, which he obviously found quite embarrassing, he never succeeded." The sight of the frail dictator had brought tears to his eyes, recalled Wahl, writing that for him it had been tantamount to the "end of the world."[73]

Hitler seemed to sense how horrified the Reichsleiters and Gauleiters were and himself touched on his poor health at the end of his speech. Only now, he said, did he truly understand Friedrich the Great, who had returned home from his military campaigns "a sick, broken man." Just as the Prussian king had been forced to spend the final years of his life "with a bent frame, plagued by gout and a whole gamut of other afflictions," Hitler explained, the war had left "deep marks" on him.[74] After trying and failing to raise a glass of water to his lips, he assured his listeners: "Today my hand trembles, and maybe my head will as well someday, but my heart will never tremble!"[75]

This half-joking remark shows that Hitler was now using even his own physical frailty as a prop. More and more, he played the part of his great role model. "In his posture and mannerisms, he involuntarily recalls the aged Friedrich the Great," Field Marshal Ewald von Kleist had already noted after a meeting in Zaporozhye in February 1943.[76] This was Hitler's final role, one with which this public chameleon, in the words of the historian Wolfram Pyta, could "identify whole-heartedly."[77] Goebbels' diaries reveal what an enormous impression Hitler's identification with the Prussian king made on those around him. On 24 January, in what was something of a trial run for his appearance in front of the Reichsleiters and Gauleiters, he told his propaganda minister that "while the trials of war sometimes made his hands shake, his heart remained unbroken." Goebbels immediately drew the intended parallel: "He can only be compared with Friedrich the Great in the severe crises of the Seven Years War."[78] Three days later, Hitler complained about the "bitter irony" that he as an "artis-tically inclined person" had been forced to lead "the gravest of all wars for the Reich." Here was another parallel with Friedrich: "He too was cut out not for the Seven Years War, but for dalliance, philosophy and flute-playing, yet he still had to live up to his histor-ical mission."[79] Part of Hitler's imitation of his hero was his neglect for his physical appearance. Once, when she discovered stains on his grey military uniform, Eva Braun scolded him in front of his secre-taries: "You do not have to emulate everything about 'Old Fritz' and run around so disgustingly."[80]

Goebbels, however, was delighted by Hitler in the role of the Prussian king and sought to bolster such pretensions. In late February, when he told Hitler that he had read Thomas Carlyle's mid-nineteenth-century biography of Friedrich and shared some of his impressions from it, he discovered that Hitler knew the work very well. The two men agreed: "We have to be like Friedrich the Great and act accordingly." Their main concern was how they would go down in history. As Goebbels noted: "The Führer completely agreed with me when I said it should be our ambition that, if Germany should face another great crisis in 150 years' time, our descendants will invoke us as a heroic example of steadfastness."[81] In March, Goebbels gave Hitler a copy of Carlyle's biography. That presented the dictator with another opportunity to proclaim that it was the "great role models" of history that had to be "lived up to" and that Friedrich the Great represented "the most exceptional personality."[82]

Goebbels also frequently consulted Carlyle's work in these weeks. He was particularly interested in the sudden turn of fate in 1762 when Prussia was rescued by the death of Yelizaveta of Russia. "Why should we not be able to hope for a similar miraculous turn of events?" the propaganda minister wondered.[83] On occasion, he read out loud to Hitler from this part of Carlyle's book, bringing "tears to [the Führer's] eyes," as he later told Finance Minister Schwerin von Krosigk.[84]

Indeed, despite acknowledging, realistically, that the war was lost, Hitler never gave up hope for a miracle. At several points in the spring of 1945, he proclaimed that the enemy coalition would crumble under its internal disagreements. Germany had to be prepared for this moment, he claimed. Until then, it was essential to hold out and defend as much territory as possible.[85] But the meeting of the Big Three—Stalin, Roosevelt and Churchill—in Yalta from 4 to 11 February gave little reason for such hopes. The conference in the Crimea reaffirmed the decisions made in Tehran in late November 1943. Germany would be divided up into occupation zones, and Stalin reluctantly agreed that France would be offered the chance to take responsibility for one zone and become a member of the Allied Control Commission, headquartered in Berlin. With only minor deviations, the future eastern boundary of Poland was to run along the Curzon Line, with Poland gaining large swathes of former German territory to the north and west, although the exact borders would only be finally set at a post-war peace conference. In their final communiqué, the three powers reaffirmed their intention to "ensure that Germany will never again be able to disturb the peace of the world." To this end, the country's military potential was to be smashed, its industry placed under foreign control, its war criminals swiftly tried and convicted, and the NSDAP and all its institutions banned. In addition, Germany would be made to pay reparations for the damage it had caused.[86]

Hitler received the reports coming out of Yalta "strangely unmoved . . . as if none of this affected him," wrote one of his adjutants.[87] This lack of reaction would seem to suggest that the dictator no longer reckoned with a splintering of the alliance against him any time soon, even if he did occasionally clutch at that particular straw. By contrast, in his diary Goebbels made no bones about his general dismay, even though it remained to be seen how things would turn out since "the final word has yet to be spoken" on that score. "Although the communiqué has more substance than we originally assumed," he wrote, "it still does not represent a resolution to the latent conflicts among the enemy powers."[88]

Given the demonstrative Allied determination in Yalta to carry on the war until Germany's unconditional surrender, Ribbentrop's attempts in January and February to extend feelers for peace in Stockholm had no chance of success.[89] Hitler was kept informed about these efforts but seems to have considered them meaningless. Goebbels may have written in February that the dictator was "much more open to political considerations" than the previous autumn,[90] but Hitler's attitude remained fundamentally unchanged. He knew that without military success, every attempt to engage the enemy in dialogue would be fruitless. If anything, he considered a separate peace with Stalin more likely than with the Western Allies, but only if Germany succeeded in "driving the Soviets back in the east and inflicting extraordinarily heavy losses of men and materiel on them." Such a separate peace would not achieve the goals of 1941, the Führer admitted to Goebbels on 11 March, but he still hoped that it could help to "arrive at a partition of Poland, subject Hungary and Croatia to German authority and gain operational leeway in the west."[91]

Germany, however, no longer had the slightest chance of turning the tide in the east. A limited counter-offensive by the newly formed Army Group Vistula went nowhere, and in response, Soviet tanks were able to break through in Pomerania, reaching the Baltic Sea town of Köslin (Koszalin) on 7 March. A few days later, they surrounded Kolberg, a symbolic location ever since the film of the same name that had tried to encourage Germans to hold out through hardship. Completely overwhelmed by his new role as supreme commander of an army group, Himmler fell ill and withdrew to the SS Hohenlychen sanatorium.[92] Hitler held the SS leader accountable for the loss of Pomerania, criticising him harshly in his absence. Goebbels, who as recently as January had recommended that Himmler succeed Guderian as chief of the general staff, dutifully took the Führer's side: "I considered it absolutely wrong of Himmler to accept responsibility for leading an army group . . . The Führer is very displeased with him."[93] The man who had once been the second most powerful figure in the Third Reich was now learning what it meant to fall from Hitler's grace. Himmler's diminished stature was evident to all, and his competitors for the Führer's favour, above all Martin Bormann, could scarcely conceal their satisfaction.

On 3 March, Hitler left the grounds of the Chancellery, pockmarked with bomb craters, for the last time to inspect the front line on the Oder. That morning, six all-terrain vehicles picked up the Führer and his entourage. Hitler needed help from his valet Linge to get into his transport. The trip was kept top secret, with one of Hitler's adjutants having travelled the route the previous day to rule out any surprises. "The roof of the vehicle was covered," Linge later recalled in a Russian POW camp. "The days when Hitler would triumphantly stand in an open car driving through Berlin before the eyes of the people were long gone. Now, he turned up the collar of his insulated leather coat . . . He fidgeted back and forth in his seat. His facial muscles quivered. Deathly silence descended over the vehicle."[94] Once he had arrived at the staff headquarters of the commander of the 9th Army, General Theodor Busse, Hitler collected himself and sought to project as energetic an impression as possible, but he seems to have failed. "His physical condition caused considerable dismay," Goebbels recorded several days later.[95]

Hitler was accompanied by Heinrich Hoffmann's colleague, the photographer Franz Gayk, and cameraman Walter Frentz, for whom Hitler posed one final time. The resulting images were published in the German press and broadcast in the weekly newsreels under the headline "Adolf Hitler at the Front in the East." But the German media dated them 11 March to explain why Hitler had not participated in the Heroes' Commemoration Day ceremonies. In his stead, Göring placed a wreath at the monument on Berlin's Unter den Linden and inspected the accompanying parade.[96]

The sixth of March saw the beginning of Operation Springtime Awakening, the final German offensive in Hungary, which Goebbels as well as Hitler hoped would bring a "true breakthrough success." "If this is the case, our prospects in the war would improve considerably, and we could possibly start over again," Goebbels wrote.[97] But the operation was doomed. Thawing ground and rain hampered the German advance, and many tanks and heavy vehicles got stuck in the mud. "It is a curse of fate how the weather has turned against us," complained tank general Hermann Balck to his diary.[98] By 12 March, having sustained heavy losses, German soldiers had succeeded in battling their way as much as 40 kilometres forward, but then the offensive stalled. On 16 March, the Red Army counter-attacked. Once again, Hitler, with the support of the supreme commander of Army Group South, General Otto Wöhler, ordered that not a metre of territory was to be given up without a fight. But even Sepp Dietrich's 6th SS Tank Army ignored this senseless command and retreated to Austria. With that the Hungarian oil fields were lost. By late March vanguard Soviet troops had reached Wiener Neustadt in Austria.[99]

Hitler flew into a rage and ordered the men of the SS divisions concerned, which included his own honour guard, to be stripped of their insignia. The order upset many SS generals, but Hitler justified this disciplinary measure by invoking Friedrich the Great, who had also not shied away from punishing regiments for displaying cowardice during the Seven Years War.[100] Himmler's days as the commander of Army Group Vistula were now also numbered. On 20 March, a few days after giving him what Goebbels called an "extraordinarily energetic dressing down," Hitler relieved Himmler of his command. The SS leader, noted a satisfied Goebbels, had "unfortunately allowed himself to grasp for military laurels and has of course failed miserably."[101] Himmler's successor was General Gotthard Heinrici, the commander of the 1st Tank Army in the Carpathians since the preceding August. Guderian told him that he had successfully insisted on his promotion. Any future cooperation with Himmler was out of the question. "Military thinking is completely alien to the man," Guderian scoffed.[102]

That same day, a ghostly ceremony took place in the garden of the Chancellery. Here Hitler received twenty members of the Hitler Youth, one as young as twelve, who had distinguished themselves fighting on the eastern front. Newsreel footage shows the Führer, accompanied by Reich youth leader Artur Axmann, moving as if in slow motion down the line of boys, shaking their hands, slapping their backs and occasionally tweaking their ears. It is the last film footage of Hitler.[103]

Meanwhile, all hope was lost on the western front as well. On 8 February, British, American and Canadian forces had launched an assault on the Reich proper, and by early March, they had succeeded in pushing the Wehrmacht back beyond the Rhine, taking Cologne on 7 March and Bonn the following day. Hitler and Goebbels continued to delude themselves that they could "hold the Rhine as a defensive line,"[104] but on 7 March, GIs from the US 1st Army under General Courtney H. Hodges seized the Ludendorff Bridge near Remagen before German demolition crews could destroy it. Within twenty-four hours, the Americans had established a bridgehead on the eastern bank of the Rhine. On receiving word of this, Hitler was incensed and ordered those purportedly responsible to be severely punished.[105] A "flying court-martial" was convened under General Rudolf Hübner, and five officers were sentenced to death. Over the objections of his general staff, Hitler insisted that the men's sentences be published in the Wehrmacht Supreme Command's report as a deterrent.[106]

The Remagen debacle was the final straw in Hitler's relationship with Supreme Commander West Rundstedt, who was now fired. "Rundstedt has got too old and operates too much with ideas from the [First] World War to master a development like that which has commenced in the west," Hitler sneered about the commander who had once been his favourite.[107] Taking over from Rundstedt was Field Marshal Albert Kesselring, who had distinguished himself as a defensive strategist in northern Italy. The priority, Hitler informed the new commander, was to "bridge the time" until a decisive battle could be waged against the Red Army and fresh troops could be redeployed to the west.[108] But there was nothing the new man in charge could do. By mid-March, US forces had crossed the Moselle in several locations and taken the iron- and steel-producing Saarland region. Koblenz, Kaiserslautern, Worms and Mainz fell, and on 22 March, GIs established a second Rhine bridgehead near Oppenheim. "Even the most vivid imagination would not have considered the cities named in the latest Wehrmacht Supreme Command report vulnerable fourteen days ago," wrote Goebbels on 23 March. "It is a measure of how critical the situation in the west has become for us."[109] The following day, after British and Canadian troops under Montgomery had also crossed the Rhine, the propaganda minister was forced to admit: "The military situation in the west has entered into an extraordinarily critical stage that seems almost fatal."[110]

Whereas Goebbels chose to keep such insights to himself, Albert Speer decided to act. By late January 1945, with the loss of industrial Upper

Silesia, the unscrupulous armaments minister, who had achieved record levels of armaments production the preceding autumn, had concluded that the war could not be continued for much longer economically. While he still did everything in his power to ensure that the Wehrmacht could continue to wage its hopeless battle, at the same time, he began to prepare for a time after Hitler. With a view towards the Reich's precarious financial situation he suggested to Finance Minister Schwerin von Krosigk that all private wealth acquired since 1933 be confiscated by the state and himself offered to donate all the money he had earned as an architect during these years.[111] Together with industrialists from the Rhine and Ruhr regions, he also began pondering how a large portion of Germany's economic potential could be salvaged for the post-war period. That meant abrogating the scorched-earth strategy Hitler had mandated in his directive of 16 September 1944.[112]

On 13–14 March 1945, after returning from the west, Speer told Goebbels that "economically speaking, the war is lost" and argued that the "task of war policy cannot be to lead the people into their heroic demise."[113] The armaments minister elaborated this perspective in an extensive memorandum to Hitler on 15 March, in which he predicted the "final collapse of the German economy" within four to eight weeks. For the scenario that "the fight continues to be waged on Reich territory," he demanded that, rather than being destroyed, industrial plants, mines and electrical and transport facilities be merely rendered temporarily inoperable. "We have a duty," Speer wrote, "to preserve for the people all possibilities for ensuring a quick reconstruction in the distant future."[114] Speer knew the memorandum was a challenge to Hitler's authority, and he entrusted it to the Führer's adjutant Nicolaus von Below, instructing him to pass it on to Hitler at an appropriate moment.[115]

In the night of 18–19 March, when Speer visited the bunker in the Chancellery, he brought a second memorandum designed to pacify the dictator's expected rage and assure himself of Hitler's continued favour. In order to defuse any suspicions that he was making common cause with "defeatist" circles, Speer bluntly demanded "drastic measures to defend the Reich on the Oder and the Rhine." For this purpose, all available Wehrmacht formations, including divisions from Norway and northern Italy, as well as the

Replacement Army and Volkssturm units, were to be concentrated along both rivers. "Several weeks of tenacious resistance on the current frontlines can earn the enemy's respect and perhaps improve our prospects at the end of the war," Speer wrote.[116] The armaments minister never intended to persuade Hitler to end the senseless fighting as soon as possible. On the contrary, like the other members of Hitler's court, he was under the illusion that a defensive victory could avert Germany's complete defeat.

Despite all this, Hitler was in a foul mood at their meeting. This was less because Speer had predicted Germany's imminent economic collapse than because the armaments minister was undermining his plan of staging Germany's approaching defeat as a "heroic downfall" aimed at taking the entire country down with him into the abyss. If the war was lost, Hitler declared, the German people "will also be lost," and there was no reason to consider "the basics which the people need for their continued existence" since they would have proven themselves to be "weaker" than their opponents. "Only the inferior ones will be left anyway," Hitler raged. "The good ones will have fallen!"[117] Speer found himself brusquely dismissed, and Hitler promised that, this time, he would receive a written answer to his memorandum. That very night, Hitler signed the so-called Nero Decree, which required the party and the Wehrmacht to carry out his scorched-earth policy. It stipulated: "All military transport and communication facilities, industrial establishments and supply depots, as well as anything else of value within Reich territory which could in any way be used by the enemy immediately or within the foreseeable future for the prosecution of the war, will be destroyed." Hitler assigned responsibility for carrying out this command to the military command offices and the Gauleiters in their function as Reich defence commissioners.[118]

For Speer, the decree was proof that Hitler was prepared to trample all over his own people, and from that point on he tried to distance himself from the dictator and prevent the execution of his order.[119] He returned to western Germany to convince military leaders and the Gauleiters that it was senseless to completely destroy German industry and infrastructure.[120] Time was of the essence since Allied troops were now pressuring the industrial Ruhr Valley from their bridgeheads on the eastern bank of the Rhine. Speer's activities did not remain hidden from Hitler, however, and on 27 March, the Führer vented his anger to Goebbels. Speer was "more of an artistic nature," the dictator fumed, and although he possessed "great organisational talent," he was "too inexperienced and unschooled politically to be absolutely reliable in these critical times." The armaments minister was allowing himself to be too heavily influenced by the industrialists and for that reason was "not helping . . . to cut off the German people's thread of life." Hitler announced that he would summon Speer and present him with a clear choice. "Either he will have to obey the principles of the current prosecution of the war, or the Führer will do without his services," Goebbels noted. The propaganda minister was delighted that after Himmler, Speer too was now about to fall from Hitler's grace. "I think Speer will not have an easy game of it in the days to come," he crowed.[121]

Indeed, Hitler treated his former favourite to a frosty reception when Speer returned to Berlin in late March, demanding an unequivocal declaration that the armaments minister did not consider the war a lost cause. Otherwise, Hitler threatened, he could not continue in office. Unusually, Speer was given twenty-four hours to consider his answer.[122] The armaments minister later claimed to have sat down immediately to write a letter in which he tried to meet Hitler halfway while seeking nonetheless to change the dictator's mind. Until their meeting of 18 March, Speer wrote, his "faith in a positive turn of our fate" had been unbroken, but Hitler's statements that day had been "deeply unsettling." He could not "continue to believe in our cause," Speer argued, "if we are at the same time systematically destroying the basis of our people's existence in these decisive months." The letter continued: "This is such a great injustice to our people that fate will no longer be on our side. We are not permitted to destroy that which generations have built up." However, if the dictator decided to revoke his decree of 19 March, Speer would "once again have the faith and courage to continue his work with the greatest of energy."[123]

In Speer's telling, Hitler refused to accept the letter and ordered the armaments minister to report back to his bunker on the night of 29–30 March. Their conversation this time was less dramatic than it had been the previous day, with Speer immediately pledging his unreserved loyalty and acceding to Hitler's demand by declaring: "My

Führer, I stand behind you unconditionally."[124] That same day, Goebbels learned that Speer had given in.[125] In return, the dictator agreed to moderate his decree. In a new proclamation on 30 March, Hitler ordered that, instead of complete destruction, a temporary "paralysis" of industrial establishments and transport facilities was allowed under certain circumstances. Responsibility for executing this order was placed in Speer's hands, and the armaments minister immediately reinstituted his original instructions, which Hitler had declared null and void on 19 March.[126]

During the trial at Nuremberg in 1945 and 1946 and in the memoirs he published in 1969 after being released from Spandau Prison, Speer sought to stylise himself into a *spiritus rector* of the resistance against Hitler's scorched-earth policy. According to the legend, it was only thanks to his own tireless efforts that Hitler's insane drive for complete destruction had been stopped and the worst prevented. But this self-depiction, which many biographers, particularly Joachim Fest, have been willing to follow, is just another piece of the myth which Hitler's former favourite architect and armaments minister invented about his role in the Third Reich after 1945 and which helped him avoid the gallows at Nuremberg. In fact, given how rapidly the Allies were advancing, it would have been impossible to completely execute Hitler's Nero Decree. Moreover, as the historian Klaus-Dietmar Henke has shown, in many places there already operated at the local and regional level an "alliance of the reasonable"—encompassing representatives from companies, the Wehrmacht and even the Nazi Party—who opposed the senseless destruction of the material basis for Germany's existence. As Henke concluded: "The opposition to the policy of ruination and self-destruction . . . was so strong on the ground that it did not need Speer."[127]

Hitler was careful to avoid a break with Speer because he believed he could not do without him. The same was not true of Guderian, with whom he had been constantly at odds since January. Hitler relieved him of his post on 28 March with the words: "Please see to it that you regain your health since in six weeks the situation will be very critical and I will urgently need you then."[128] His successor was General Hans Krebs, whom Hitler expected to be more malleable. In the final days of March, the Führer also parted ways with his long-time press spokesman and member of Berghof society, Otto Dietrich.

Goebbels had been trying to undermine him for quite some time, remarking that "Dr. Dietrich is a decided weakling who is not equal to the current crisis."[129] Hitler was swayed by his propaganda minister's malicious whispering and abruptly fired the man who had worked for him since 1931. "You are too soft," Dietrich was told. "Right now I can only use hard men. I am dismissing you. Leave Berlin by this evening!"[130]

From late March, it was only a matter of time until German forces collapsed in the west. On 1 April, the noose closed around the Ruhr Valley, trapping the more than 321,000 men of Model's Army Group B. While British and Canadian troops under Montgomery continued their march through the Münster region towards northern Germany, the US 3rd Army under Patton pushed forward via Darmstadt, Frankfurt and Aschaffenburg to Thuringia, encountering only light resistance.[131] Everywhere there were signs of German morale disintegrating. Entire Wehrmacht units dissolved, allowed themselves to be captured or fell back in chaotic fashion. "It was pathetic to see these worn-out, tattered remnants of the German army, mostly without weapons, taking flight," wrote a police sergeant from the town of Friedberg in western Germany. "There was not a trace of an orderly military retreat any more."[132] The court official Friedrich Kellner made a similar observation on 27 March in the western German town of Laubach: "The final remnants of the Hitlerian 'army' passed through this morning. Looking like wild hordes, or a band of robbers, a bunch of the worst sort, a desolate, animal-like mass of Huns and barbarians . . . Here . . . was a part of that German army which had set out as highwaymen to rob and plunder other countries, commit outrageous crime after outrageous crime and bring shame upon the German name for all times."[133]

Before the Americans and British arrived, portraits of Hitler disappeared from offices and private homes, copies of *Mein Kampf* were removed from bookshelves, and uniforms, party insignia and swastika banners were burned.[134] In many places, Allied soldiers were greeted with white flags waving. Nazi propaganda about the genocidal intentions of the enemy had apparently not taken hold widely in the west. "Some women go so far as to humiliate themselves by greeting and hugging the Americans," an outraged Goebbels recorded.[135] The propaganda minister found it "positively shameful" that white flags were also flown in his hometown of Rheydt. After consulting with Hitler, he decided to have a special commando murder the mayor, Heinrich Vogelsang, who had been installed by the Americans, but he was unable to carry out the plan.[136]

Many Wehrmacht soldiers deserted their units and, as government officials reported with concern, were spreading "a corrosive and defeatist mood." One soldier was recorded saying on a train: "What? You are still obeying Hitler? I'm going home to my old lady, where they can look for me. By the time they find me, the war will be over."[137] The regime resorted to draconian measures to combat the incipient disintegration. SS commandos hunted down deserters, with "flying courts-martial" sentencing thousands of people to death in the final months of the war. Seeing soldiers strung up with signs around their necks reading "I am a deserting coward" was no rare sight in the dying days of the Third Reich in the spring of 1945. Those who uttered doubts about Germany's ultimate victory, who hung a white flag from their window, who opposed senseless acts of destruction or who tried to get their hometown to surrender without a fight had to fear for their life if they fell into the clutches of the SS, the Gestapo or fanatical Nazi supporters. The terror the regime had exported to the occupied countries of Europe was now being turned against the German populace.[138]

Hitler's secretary Martin Bormann sent one memorandum after another to the Reichsleiters and Gauleiters urging them to hold on and reminding them that the populace, particularly in areas under immediate threat by the enemy, needed "firm leadership by the party." On 17 March, he demanded: "Everyone wielding authority must feel the duty to embody as a role model our unbending will to fight." A few days later he threatened: "It is a dirty bastard who leaves his Gau, when besieged by the enemy, without an express order from the Führer and without fighting until his final breath . . . The only slogan that counts now is victory or death."[139] But most high-ranking Nazi functionaries, derided by ordinary Germans as "golden pheasants," had no time for such slogans and no intention whatever of following their Führer into a "heroic downfall." As a rule, they were the first to flee when Allied troops approached and usually took care to transfer their personal wealth somewhere safe. "The behaviour of our Gauleiters and district leaders in the west has caused a serious erosion of trust among the population," Goebbels noted. "The people thought they could expect our Gauleiters to fight and, if necessary, to fall. But that has not been the case anywhere. As a result the party is largely played out in the west."[140]

Public regard for Nazi functionaries was not the only thing taking a beating. Hitler's authority too was no longer beyond question, although the concentration of power in the Führer still prevented any cabal at the top of the regime from challenging his authority. Hitler continued to provide the legitimation for power within the regime, and even the most influential of his paladins depended on his favour. Of the four members of the quadrumvirate, two— Himmler and Speer—had fallen from grace. Only Bormann and Goebbels still enjoyed Hitler's complete trust, and both were wary about risking that valuable privilege. In his diary, the propaganda minister increasingly articulated doubts about Hitler's ability to master the crisis. Instead of holding "long speeches" in front of his military advisers, Goebbels complained in mid-March, Hitler should issue them "short orders . . . and then ensure with all necessary, brutal energy that those orders were obeyed."[141] Later that month, Goebbels took exception to Hitler's decision to evacuate the population from western areas. "We issue commands in Berlin which in practice never arrive on the ground—to say nothing of them being carried out," the propaganda minister complained. "I see the danger of an extraordinary loss of authority."[142] But Goebbels did not criticise Hitler directly for fear that he would lose his privileged position within the dictator's court.

He did, however, press Hitler to give another radio address. Both the Wehrmacht and the German people, he argued, longed for some "slogan to spark and elevate men and women," and that was something only the Führer could deliver. Again, after some initial hesitation, Hitler agreed to Goebbels' request, although he never intended to keep his promise. "At present, the Führer has a fear of the microphone I find incomprehensible," registered a resigned Goebbels.[143] But Hitler's refusal to speak in public was hardly baffling. He decided to keep silent because after Germany's final offensive had failed in Hungary, he had no positive news to pass on.

Whether Hitler spoke or not, the mood among the German population had hit an all-time low. No one believed in victory any more, the SS Security Service reported in late March. The people had "no more trust in the leadership" and were voicing "sharp criticism of the party, certain leading personalities and German propaganda." Even Hitler, who had been "the final support and last hope for millions," was being "increasingly included in the daily criticism and was losing trust."[144] Reports by the Wehrmacht's propaganda officer in Berlin spoke of a "growing irritability" that "expressed itself at the slightest opportunity." "People see no way out and no ray of light," the officer wrote. "Our propaganda is like an orchestra on a ship that diligently keeps playing while the vessel sinks." Increasingly, people could be heard remarking that "an end should be put to this" since all "further sacrifice is senseless." "Better a horrible end than no end to the horror" was a widespread sentiment.[145]

Even Goebbels could not conceal the fact that public criticism was being directed "more and more" against the Führer, and that many party comrades were "starting to waver" and ask themselves "how they could shed this terrible life in the best, most honourable fashion."[146] Indeed, the number of suicides shot up from early April 1945. This was another consequence of Goebbels' propaganda, which impressed upon Germans that they had no prospects at all for the future if they were defeated. In the east in particular, it was fear of falling into the hands of the Red Army that drove people to kill themselves.[147]

Yet despite the internal deterioration of the Nazi regime's power, the terror apparatus of the police and the courts functioned well into the final days of the war. In fact, it got more radical the closer German defeat approached. It targeted not just Germans who opposed the senseless continuation of the war but increasingly foreign labourers. The mere presence of millions of slave labourers from the formerly occupied countries of Europe, who had every reason to take revenge on Germans for their suffering, nourished nebulous fears to which the Nazi organs of state responded with bursts of excessive violence. As a result, between the end of March and the middle of April 1945, hundreds of foreign labourers were killed by Gestapo murder commandos in all the major Ruhr Valley cities.[148]

An especially horrific chapter in the bloody final days of the collapsing Nazi regime were the death marches which thousands of emaciated prisoners from Ravensbrück, Sachsenhausen, Buchenwald, Flossenbürg and other evacuated concentration camps were forced to undertake over country roads and through villages. Those who collapsed or tried to flee were shot by the guards. The civilian population in the parts of the Reich not yet occupied by the Allies now witnessed this act of mass murder right on their doorsteps. More than a few members of the Volkssturm and the Hitler Youth as well as ordinary people took part in hunting down prisoners who sought to escape. Of the 700,000 concentration camp inmates in January 1945, it is estimated that at least 250,000 died during the death marches.[149] On 11 April, American troops liberated Buchenwald; three days later British troops reached Bergen-Belsen. The liberators found thousands of unburied corpses and prisoners who had been starved down to skin and bones. These images of horror were shown around the world.

On Easter Sunday, 1 April 1945, German radio listeners were surprised to hear something new coming over their "people's receivers." A new station, Radio Werewolf, had begun broadcasting. In the name of a "movement of National Socialist freedom fighters," a call to partisan warfare was issued: "Hate is our prayer, and revenge our battle cry!"[150] The initiative had originated with Goebbels, who had approved every detail and who had written the script that was now being read.[151] By late March the propaganda minister believed that "the hour has come to discard the final bourgeois trappings. Now is the time for revolutionary thought and above all revolutionary action . . . Half-measures are of no use any more."[152] Among the "revolutionary" proposals were plans for forming a guerrilla organisation to spread terror and fear among the Allies. Preparations for such a group had been underway since the autumn of 1944 under Himmler's direction, and the propaganda minister now wanted matters to be accelerated. The guerrilla struggle was meant to hark back to the Nazi Party's mythological "time of struggle" at the end of the Weimar Republic. "The Werewolf operation," Goebbels proclaimed, "should be to the current war situation what the [Berlin Nazi newspaper] *Attack* was in our battle days not just for Berlin, but for the entire Reich—an umbrella for all activists who disagree with any idea of compromise." In conversation with Hitler on 30 March, Goebbels promised to "boost partisan activities to a peak in the Allied-occupied western regions within the shortest span of time."[153]

Once again, Goebbels had bitten off more than he could chew. The surprisingly rapid Allied advance into the heart of the Reich scuppered all his plans. The few weeks that remained for the regime were insufficient to call to life a guerrilla movement, and the initiative lacked the basic prerequisite: the support of the German people in the occupied areas in the west. The few fanatical Hitler Youths who mostly made up the Werewolf never formed a pack, remaining basically isolated. Nonetheless, their activities should not be completely discounted. They did carry out attacks on Allied soldiers and Germans suspected of collaboration, most spectacularly on 25 March 1945 when they murdered the mayor of Aachen, Franz Oppenhoff, who had been installed by American liberators.[154]

On 12 April 1945, US president Franklin D. Roosevelt died of a stroke. "A great man has passed away, a statesman and hero, a friend to and leader of men who elevated his country to a new level of social education and made it ready to harness its strength for the community of peoples and the organisation of peace to which his own life and struggle were dedicated," eulogised Thomas Mann in a radio address to German listeners.[155] Goebbels received the news of Roosevelt's death on the night of 12–13 April, on his way back from a visit to General Busse's 9th Army on the Oder front. He immediately phoned Hitler with words of congratulations: "It is written in the stars that the second half of April will be the turning point for us. This is Friday, April the 13th. It is the turning point!"[156] The news also seems to have momentarily elated Hitler. If we can believe Speer's memoirs, the Führer proclaimed: "Here we have the great miracle I always predicted. Who is laughing now? The war is not lost."[157] Hitler was not the only one who may have believed that the "miracle of the house of Brandenburg" from 1762 was repeating itself, as if the passing of Roosevelt, like the death of Yelizaveta of Russia towards the end of the Seven Years War, made it possible that the enemy coalition would disintegrate. "It is not only divine justice—it is a divine gift," Schwerin von Krosigk believed, adding that Germany should seize the opportunity to negotiate with the Americans.[158]

But the euphoria did not last. It soon became clear that the death of the American president had no effect at all on Allied operations.

On 13 April, the Red Army took Vienna. Four days later, the cauldron battle of the Ruhr Valley was over, with more than 300,000 German soldiers and thirty generals taken prisoner. Model, the supreme commander of the defeated Army Group B, stole away from his staff and committed suicide in a forest near Duisburg.[159]

"If you consult the map, you see that today the Reich is a small tube from Norway to the Valli di Comacchio," commented Goebbels in one of his final diary entries. "Our most important regions for food production and armaments potential have been lost."[160] In case the Western Allies and the Red Army were able to connect in central Germany and split the Reich in half, Hitler issued a "fundamental decree" on 15 April. It stipulated that wherever the Führer should find himself, Admiral Dönitz was to assume supreme command in the northern half, and Field Marshal Kesselring in the south.[161] This order notwithstanding, Hitler had decided to make his final stand in Berlin and not, as many people advised him, on the Obersalzberg. "The Führer is adamant about not moving his headquarters from Berlin," Goebbels had written back in February, and nothing had happened to alter Hitler's resolve.[162] If he wanted to stage his demise amid an apocalyptic "world inferno," then staying in the rubble of the Reich capital was infinitely more effective than relocating to the remote idyll in the Bavarian Alps.

Since the start of April, Berliners had awoken every day expecting a fresh Soviet offensive at the Oder. Repeatedly General Heinrici, the new commander of Army Group Vistula, had been summoned to situation meetings in the capital to report on the status of defensive preparations. Like all the other participants, he had to submit to being physically searched by SS officers before being allowed to enter the Führer's bunker. He later recalled not believing his eyes when he saw Hitler, hardly capable of lifting his feet, shuffling towards him for the first time. "His left arm jerked up and down, twitching," Heinrici remembered. "The skin around his eyes was a harried red, otherwise it was white as chalk. My first impression was that this was a man with less than twenty-four hours to live." Yet he soon noticed that he was thoroughly mistaken. After he had concluded his report, Hitler asked several precise questions, showing "no trace of weakness or lack of clarity." On the contrary, the dictator projected renewed optimism. As long as everyone was convinced that it not only must but could be won, he said, the battle on the Oder would go down as "the greatest defensive victory of this war and the bloodiest defeat for the enemy."[163]

In a proclamation to the "Soldiers on the German Eastern Front!" of 15 April, Hitler called upon his followers one final time to meet their "Jewish-Bolshevik mortal enemy" with extreme fanaticism and to drown its attack in blood. "Berlin remains German," Hitler declared. "Vienna will be German again, and Europe will never be Russian."[164]

17

The Final Days in the Bunker

"I do not want to be anything but the first soldier of the German Reich!" Hitler had proclaimed in his speech to the Reichstag at the start of the Second World War on 1 September 1939. "For that I have donned the uniform that was always most holy and valuable to me. I will only take it off after our victory—otherwise I will never see the end of this war!"[1] By mid-April 1945, with Germany's inescapable defeat only a few weeks away, the time had come for Hitler to keep his word. Although the dictator had always feared dying young, and this anxiety had motivated him to force his domestic and foreign agendas in the late 1930s, he had always kept open the option of suicide. It was clear early on that Hitler was willing to risk everything, and his own life was no exception. Even as his star was rising, in critical situations, for instance after the failed 1923 putsch or at the height of the Strasser crisis in early December 1932, he had repeatedly threatened to kill himself.[2] This latent willingness to do himself in would never leave Hitler. In his book *Germany: Jekyll & Hyde*, published from British exile in 1940, the perspicacious Sebastian Haffner predicted: "Hitler is the potential suicide par excellence."[3]

Over the course of the war as well, Hitler made no secret of the fact that he would take his life if Germany were defeated. As we have seen, in early February 1943, after learning that the 6th Army had surrendered at Stalingrad, he declared that it would be "child's play" to turn a pistol on oneself and launched into a scathing criticism of General Paulus for lacking the courage to shoot himself. As far as Hitler was concerned, his military commander should have followed the example of Roman generals who fell on their swords if they lost a battle. On numerous occasions, he remarked that he failed to under-stand how people could shy back from suicide since it only took "a fraction of a second," after which one was "released from everything" and would attain "calm and eternal peace."[4] But the distance between words and deeds was great. And the dictator by no means found it as easy to pull the trigger as he had pretended in the presence of others. Hitler would wait until almost the very last moment before finally deciding to take his own life.

On 16 April 1945, the Red Army launched its final offensive. Stalin was in a hurry to conquer Berlin before the Western powers got there. Three Soviet fronts, the 1st and 2nd Belorussian Front and the 1st Ukrainian Front—encompassing 2.5 million soldiers and more than 6,000 tanks—participated in the operation. The main assault was carried out by the 1st Belorussian Front under Marshal Zhukov. His men were charged with destroying German defensive lines from their bridgehead at Küstrin on the western bank of the Oder and then advancing directly on Berlin down Reich Motorway 1. "There has not been a day at the front yet like today," wrote one Soviet sapper. "At four o'clock in the morning thousands of Katyushas and machine guns opened fire, and the sky was as bright as day from horizon to horizon . . . Then came the tanks. In front of the whole column, floodlights shone, which was to dazzle the Germans. And then people everywhere started shouting, 'To Berlin! To Berlin!'"[5]

The 1st Belorussian Front was met by the German 9th Army, part of Army Group Vistula, under General Busse. With their 190,000 men and 512 operational tanks and assault guns, the Germans were at a massive disadvantage not just in terms of numbers, but also in equipment and battle-readiness. However, in the preceding weeks they had managed to establish a deeply layered system of defences, adapted to the landscape and difficult to overcome. The German military leadership had also anticipated that the assault would commence on 16 April, allowing them to pull back their troops from the foremost front line and rendering the initial Soviet artillery barrage largely ineffective. Moreover, the searchlights Zhukov had installed to blind the enemy backfired since the morning fog and the smoke created by the Soviet artillery reflected the light.[6] German defenders had no problem seeing the advancing Red Army infantrymen, and Soviet losses in the early hours of fighting were enormous. At the end of the first day, Zhukov was still far from achieving his operational goal, and on the second day of battle the 9th Army continued its dogged resistance. But by that evening the situation had become critical for the German defenders, who by now lacked reserves to offset the losses they had sustained. The battle reached its peak on 18 April when the attackers finally succeeded in ripping apart German defensive positions and took the Seelow Heights. The final German line of defence was overcome the following day. On 20 April, Soviet tanks reached Bernau, fifteen kilometres east of Berlin.[7]

The assault of the 1st Ukrainian Front under Marshal Konev met far less resistance and broke through German lines at the river Neisse in Lusatia the very first day. Vanguard tank units pressed west towards the Elbe and northwest in the direction of Berlin. The German High Command had to evacuate its command centre at Zossen in a panic. It was initially moved to Eiche, near Potsdam, and later to Rheinsberg, west of Berlin. On 20 April, Konev's troops entered Zossen, and the following day they reached the southern outskirts of Berlin near the village of Stahnsdorf.[8]

"The artillery fire from the eastern front can already be heard," wrote Eva Braun to Herta Schneider on 19 April. She and Hitler's secretaries practised firing pistols every day in the Chancellery garden and "achieved such mastery that no man dares to take us on." But despite the dire situation around Berlin, Braun assured her friend that she was "convinced everything will take a turn for the positive again" and that Hitler was "as full of hope as seldom before."[9]

"Unfortunately not exactly a festive birthday occasion," noted Bormann in his pocket calendar on 20 April, Hitler's fifty-sixth birthday.[10] The previous day, reports had arrived that Allied advances in the west were continuing apace and Nuremberg, the city of the Nazi Party rallies, was now surrounded.[11] Yet even in this hopeless situation, there were still Germans eager to extend their best wishes to Hitler. Countess Elisabeth Fugger zu Wellenburg sent a telegram wishing "God's protection and blessing for you, my Führer, and our beloved fatherland." The justice official Willibald von Zezschwitz, who had defended General Erich Ludendorff at the trial following the Beer Hall Putsch, expressed his hope from the Bavarian town of Mittenwald an der Isar that Hitler would be able "in the best of health to bid halt to the enemy who has forced his way deep into German territory in east and west" and shape the future of Greater Germany and Europe "fundamentally differently" from how the "excessively arrogant world Jewry with its impertinent delusions imagines it."[12]

On the eve of 20 April, Goebbels held his traditional radio address. He praised Hitler as a "man of truly historical greatness, with a courage beyond compare, and a steadfastness that lifts and moves hearts." Never, Goebbels vowed, would "history say of these days that a people deserted their Führer or a Führer his people."[13] Listening to this speech, the journalist Ursula von Kardorff wondered whether it was "insanity or genius." Party functionaries were committing suicide and the front was drawing closer every day, she noted in her diary, but Goebbels talked "as though we were poised for victory."[14]

As was customary, Hitler's staff members congregated around midnight to congratulate the dictator. But Hitler refused to receive them, telling Linge to inform them that he had nothing to be congratulated for. Only when Braun pleaded with him did he consent to appear in the antechamber of his bunker. He hastily shook everyone's hand, then immediately retreated. After the nighttime situation meeting, he had tea with Braun alone in his office. Hardly had he gone to bed when, at 9 a.m., his head Wehrmacht adjutant, Wilhelm Burgdorf, woke him with the news that the Red Army had advanced to the southern edge of Berlin. Hitler told his valet: "Linge, I still have not slept. Wake me in an hour."[15]

At 3 p.m., Hitler laboriously dragged himself up the stairs to the bunker entrance, where he was awaited by a delegation of Hitler Youth and men from the SS Division *Frundsberg* and the Courland Army. Hunched over, with the collar of his coat turned up, he shuffled through their ranks. "The battle for Berlin must be won," he proclaimed, ending his appeal: "Hail to you!" But none of the boys or men answered. "All that could be heard," Reich youth leader Axmann wrote, "was the thunder of the front, scarcely 60 kilometres away."[16] It was the final time Hitler would see daylight.

That afternoon, the leading representatives of the Third Reich— Göring, Himmler, Goebbels, Speer, Ribbentrop, Ley, Bormann, Kaltenbrunner and, from the military, Keitel, Jodl, Dönitz, Burgdorf and Krebs—lined up in the situation room of the bunker to pay their respects. Speer remembered Hitler accepting their congratulations "as befitting the circumstances[:] coolly, almost as though warding them off." Nearly everyone in attendance urged the Führer to relocate his headquarters from Berlin to Berchtesgaden, pointing out that it was only a matter of hours until the final road connections south would be cut off. The dictator brushed off such suggestions: "How can I motivate the troops to fight the decisive battle for Berlin if at the very same moment I spirit myself to safety?"[17] Hitler's minions anxiously awaited the end of the situation meeting, after which a great exodus immediately commenced. The first to slip away was Göring. He had already brought his wife and daughter to safety on the Obersalzberg and had arranged for whole truckloads of looted art to be taken away from his country estate at Carinhall. He bade farewell to Hitler, saying that he had "urgent matters" to attend to in southern Germany. The dictator registered the departure of his designated successor without any show of emotion, indeed with near indifference.[18]

Dönitz, charged with taking command in northern Germany, also took his leave, and Himmler, Kaltenbrunner, Speer and Ribbentrop did the same, followed the next day by the majority of Reich ministers. If Hitler was disappointed by his paladins' hasty exits, he did not show it. Wordlessly, he allowed the men he had made so powerful and who had competed for years for his favour simply to go on their way.[19] On the evening of 20 April, he had a drink with Braun, his secretaries, his cook Constanze Manziarly and his adjutants Schaub and Below, during which he re-emphasised his determination not to leave the Reich capital, declaring: "I must either bring about a decision here in Berlin or perish!"[20] Earlier he had announced that the military situation had dramatically worsened in the past few days and that he wanted to "thin out" his personal staff. As an initial measure, the older two of his secretaries, Johanna Wolf and Christa Schroeder, were to head south. On the morning of 21 April, they flew from Berlin's Tempelhof Airport to Salzburg, from where they were taken to the Obersalzberg by bus.[21]

The previous night, after Hitler had gone to bed, Braun held a small party in her apartment on the first floor of the Old Reich Chancellery. The young woman wanted to escape the oppressive atmosphere of the Führer's bunker one last time and have fun. Someone got hold of a gramophone, and guests danced to the popular ditty "Blood Red Roses Should Surround You." Eva Braun sucked "everyone into a desperate delirium," recalled Traudl Junge. "Champagne was drunk, shrill laughter abounded and I laughed along because I did not want to cry."²²

On 21 April, Hitler was woken up at 9:30 a.m., with Linge telling him that Russian artillery was shelling Berlin. A few minutes later, the groggy, unshaven dictator entered the antechamber of the situation room, where Burgdorf was waiting. "What has happened?" Hitler asked. "What is this shooting, and where does it come from?" Hitler's chief Wehrmacht adjutant answered that the centre of Berlin was under fire from a powerful Soviet battery that had taken position north of Zossen. Hitler went pale. "The Russians are already that close?" he asked.²³ The Führer had a connection established with Luftwaffe chief of staff Karl Koller, demanding to know where exactly the Soviet battery was located. The answer came from a German observation post on the tall flak tower atop the bunker near the city zoo: Russian artillery was firing from the Marzahn district, only around 12 kilometres from the city centre. Hitler received this information with "disbelief," Koller wrote in his diary.²⁴

At the situation meeting that afternoon, Chief of the General Staff Krebs suggested withdrawing the forces of the 9th Army, who were still deployed south of Berlin, and using them to defend the capital. But Hitler refused, instead ordering a counter-offensive from the Eberswalde region towards the south, with the aim of cutting off vanguard Soviet tanks and re-establishing a coherent line of defence. A tank corps under the command of SS-Obergruppenführer Felix Steiner was charged with the assault. Any forces still available should be united under his leadership. "The fate of the German capital depends on the success of your mission," Hitler stressed to the SS officer.²⁵ But the Führer's order was already obsolete. The remnants of Busse's 9th Army were barely able to fight on and were desperately trying to avoid being surrounded. Right from the beginning, it was delusional to think that the tank corps and the remnants of this army group, some of whom only existed on paper, could strike a liberating blow. Nonetheless, that evening Hitler projected confidence, telling Koller: "You will see: the Russians will suffer the biggest and bloodiest defeat in their history before the gates of Berlin."²⁶

That same day, Goebbels held his final ministerial conference, in his house on Hermann-Göring-Strasse because the Propaganda

Ministry on Wilhelmplatz had been destroyed in an air raid on 13 March. If we believe the account of ministerial director and radio commentator Hans Fritzsche, the propaganda minister now announced that he considered the situation hopeless, adding: "The German people have deserved the fate that now awaits them." After all, Goebbels argued, they had decided to leave the League of Nations in a "free vote" in October 1933 in order to embark on a politics of risk, and this gambit had "simply failed." He himself had never forced anyone to work for him, so no one should be surprised if "his little throat were slit." As he left the room, Goebbels cried out bathetically: "But if we do go down, let the globe tremble!"[27] It seems that Goebbels was determined to commit suicide, thereby both sharing Hitler's fate and avoiding being held responsible for his deeds.

Meanwhile the exodus from Berlin continued. A motorcade advanced towards the Gatow airstrip, where chief government pilot Hans Baur had a squadron of planes ready and waiting. Hitler's navy adjutant Karl-Jesko von Puttkamer, adjutant Albert Bormann, dentist Hugo Blaschke, cameraman Walter Frentz and two stenographers took off for the Obersalzberg.[28] One plane, with Hitler's valet Wilhelm Arndt on board, never reached its destination, crashing near Börnersdorf, south of Dresden, on the night of 23 April.[29] Almost four decades later, in April 1983, *Stern* magazine in West Germany would claim that more than sixty volumes of Hitler's diaries had been recovered from the wreckage of that crash. But it soon emerged that the magazine was the victim of a grotesque act of forgery.[30]

On the evening of 21 April 1945, Hitler abruptly broke with his personal physician, Theo Morell. The exact reasons remain unclear. Morell had been "too shaken" to administer Hitler's pick-me-up injection on his birthday and the Führer's back-up physician, Stumpfegger, had taken over.[31] It is also possible that Hitler feared Morell might administer such powerful drugs that he could be brought to the Obersalzberg against his will.[32] In any case, Morell told Schroeder when he arrived at the Berghof on 24 April that the Führer had simply "dismissed" him.[33]

On the morning of 22 April, Berlin city centre came under heavy Soviet artillery fire from several locations. More and more shells landed in the Tiergarten and the courtyards of the ministries on

Wilhelmstrasse.[34] The 3 p.m. situation meeting was dominated by dismal reports. The 2nd Belorussian Front under Marshal Konstantin Rokossovsky had established a number of bridgeheads across the Oder and was about to break through to West Pomerania.[35] Soviet troops had breached the outermost German defensive lines to the north and east of Berlin, and street battles were being fought in the suburbs. At first Hitler took this bad news well, but suddenly a tempest erupted, the like of which situation meeting participants had never previously experienced.

It started when the dictator asked about Steiner's operations, and Krebs was forced to admit that no counter-offensive had taken place. That was too much for Hitler. His face went red, and he threw a handful of coloured pens across the table, ordering everyone but Keitel, Jodl, Krebs, Bormann and Burgdorf to leave the room. For the next fifteen minutes, those five were subjected to a tirade in which Hitler vented all his disappointment, rage and hatred. In repeated cascades of invective, he complained about disloyalty, cowardice and betrayal in his own ranks. Even the SS was abandoning him, he fumed. Since his orders were no longer being carried out, there was no point continuing the fight any more. In one fell swoop, his laboriously maintained façade of unshakable optimism collapsed. Falling back in his chair exhausted, Hitler conceded for the first time: "The war is lost!" He immediately added: "But if you believe I am leaving Berlin, gentlemen, you are sadly mistaken. I would rather put a bullet in my head!"[36]

The officers in the antechamber eavesdropped on Hitler's tantrum. A short time later, the door of the situation room opened, and the dictator dragged himself back into his private quarters. "His face had no expression, and his eyes were blank," Traudl Junge recalled. With unusual brusqueness, Hitler ordered his two younger secretaries to ready themselves to leave for southern Germany. "Everything is lost, hopelessly lost," he announced. Gerda Christian and Junge declared that they wanted to stay, as did Manziarly. Hitler was moved: "I wish my generals were as brave as you are."[37]

Keitel, Jodl and Bormann sought in vain to change Hitler's mind and get him to flee. Himmler and Dönitz also tried to convince him by telephone, but the Führer stuck to his decision. He was going to stay in Berlin, he repeatedly insisted, and personally direct the defence of the city. If he was no longer physically able to fight with a weapon in his hands, he would shoot himself at the last possible moment to avoid capture by the enemy. His successor, Göring, would have to take care of everything else. In response to objections that German soldiers would never fight under the Reich marshal, Hitler snapped back: "Fighting—what does that mean? There is not much left to fight for any more. And if negotiations are necessary, the Reich marshal can do that better than I can."[38]

Around 5 p.m., Hitler summoned Goebbels. We do not know what the two men talked about, but it is likely that the propaganda minister declared his support for the dictator in his plans and promised that he and his family would follow him to the grave. Directly afterwards, Goebbels informed Junge that his wife and six children would soon be arriving and would from now on, at the Führer's request, reside in the bunker.[39] The propaganda minister moved into the room vacated by Morell, while Magda Goebbels and her children were quartered in the "ante-bunker."

On the evening of 22 April, Braun wrote a letter of farewell to her friend Herta Schneider, saying that this would be her "final sign of life" since the end was drawing "perilously nearer and nearer." She could not describe how much she was "personally suffering because of the Führer," she wrote, adding: "Maybe everything will turn out all right, but he has lost faith, and we, I fear, are hoping without reason." Braun apologised for her "somewhat confused" lines, blaming the Goebbels children around her, who were "anything but still."[40]

It was a testament to Hitler's state of mind that he ordered his adjutant Schaub to remove his personal papers from the safe in his bedroom and the two vaults on the first floor of the Old Reich Chancellery and burn them in the building's courtyard. Three days later, on the night of 25–26 April, Schaub caught the final plane from Gatow and flew to Munich. There, he cleared out the vault in Hitler's Prinzregentenstrasse apartment and drove to the Obersalzberg to complete the task of destroying Hitler's personal documents. The Berghof had been badly bombed by British planes the previous day but the vault in Hitler's office had not been damaged. Schaub emptied and burned its contents, together with the documents he had brought from Munich, on the Berghof's terrace.[41] By then at the latest, it was clear to everyone in Hitler's Alpine retreat that he was not coming back.

On the evening of 22 April, the mood in the Führer's bunker had lifted somewhat after a report by the supreme commander of Army Group Centre, Ferdinand Schörner, who had been promoted to field marshal. "We can only change our fate if we apply ourselves with the most extreme fanaticism in this critical hour, clearly display this expression of our National Socialist fighting spirit and thus convince all our officers that this is the only way," Schörner had told his commanding generals in late February in an appeal to their sense of duty.[42] Indeed, Schörner's armies were still putting up stiff resistance in Silesia and the Protectorate of Bohemia and Moravia, and his presence alone was enough to buck up Hitler's spirits. "If I had my way I would draw and quarter you, so that I had four Schörners," he remarked when he greeted the field marshal.[43] The military delegation tried to cheer up the completely exhausted and demoralised Führer and convince him that the situation was not entirely without hope.

New plans were hastily drawn up for the reconstituted 12th Army under General Wenck, currently deployed southwest of Berlin on the Elbe with the task of slowing down the advancing Americans, to turn around, unite with the remnants of the 9th Army and make a joint push for the Reich capital. "You see, there still are some military options we need to seize," Hitler told Schörner. If the planned operation were a success, there would be hope of "stopping the Russian assault" and "stabilising the situation around Berlin."[44] Keitel and Jodl were tasked with directing a relief attack on Berlin from outside the city. While Jodl went to the Wehrmacht Supreme Command's new headquarters in Krampnitz, a district of Potsdam, on the night of 22–23 April Keitel travelled to Wenck's command post, a hunting lodge in the Wiesenburg forest near Beelitz, southwest of Berlin. There he beseeched the general to "free the Führer from his captivity," arguing: "His destiny is Germany's destiny, and it is in your hands, Wenck, to save Germany."[45]

On 22 April, Hitler named SS-Brigadeführer Wilhelm Mohnke battle commander of the "citadel," the interior defensive ring around Berlin's government district. He took command of the final remaining Waffen-SS forces, some small army, Luftwaffe and navy units, and Hitler Youth formations. All told they numbered around four thousand men and boys.[46]

★

Russian artillery continued to blast away at the government district on 23 April, with several shells landing in the "Memorial Courtyard" of the New Chancellery building. Metro trains and trams in the capital were forced to suspend operations, and the city was now largely without electricity, gas and water. In districts such as Frohnau, Friedrichshain, Tegel, Pankow and Köpernick, fierce street-to-street fighting was already underway.[47] In an appeal to the German people, Goebbels announced that the Führer had remained in the city and assumed ultimate command of "all forces mustered in defence of Berlin." The propaganda minister asserted: "All the defenders of the Reich capital are suffused with the single will to beat back and destroy the Bolshevik arch-enemy, wherever he should appear."[48]

Depending on how much news there was, meetings were by now held several times a day at varying hours in the Führer's bunker. As a rule they did not last longer than thirty minutes to an hour, and the number of participants had been reduced to Krebs and his general staff officers Freytag von Loringhoven and Gerhard Boldt; Wehrmacht adjutant Burgdorf and his associates; adjutants Below, Lieutenant Rudolf Weiss and Major Willi Johannmeyer; navy liaison officer Vice-Admiral Hans-Erich Voss; Himmler and Ribbentrop's representatives Fegelein and Hewel; press spokesman Heinz Lorenz; "citadel" commander Mohnke; Hitler's valet Otto Günsche; Bormann; and—now that he had moved into the bunker—Goebbels.[49] Instead of the ten large-scale maps of the eastern and western fronts that had been usually unfolded on the table, there were only two smaller ones: one of Berlin and its surroundings and another of all of Germany.[50]

By 23 April, Hitler had collected himself following his meltdown the previous day. In a postscript to a letter of farewell to her sister Gretl, Braun wrote that the Führer was once again looking to the future "somewhat more brightly" than yesterday.[51] All hopes were now pinned on Wenck's 12th Army. At midday, Keitel returned and told the Führer that "Wenck sends you his respectful greetings and hopes to shake your hand soon in the Chancellery."[52] Hitler demanded that all available reserves be devoted to the general, remarking that following Goebbels' appeal enemy troops now knew that the Führer was still in Berlin and would do everything to get their hands on the government district as quickly as possible. This was the perfect opportunity, Hitler claimed, to "lure them into a trap." But it required "that all of us are finally clear about the significance of the hour and obey the plans ordered from above." Krebs opined that Germany only had four more days, to which Hitler replied, "Then the matter must be decided in four days."[53] At the end of the meeting, Keitel requested permission to rejoin Wenck's army to ensure that Hitler's commands were being carried out. He would not return from this journey. The head of the Wehrmacht Supreme Command, who had served Hitler for years with dog-like obedience, turned his back on him like so many of the Führer's underlings.[54]

By contrast, on the afternoon of 23 April, Speer unexpectedly arrived in the bunker. A few days before, after congratulating Hitler on his birthday, the armaments minister had travelled to Hamburg without personally taking his leave of Hitler. Now he seemed to want to see the man who had promoted him and with whom he had worked for twelve years for a final time. Speer had taken a plane from the test airstrip in Rechlin in Mecklenburg to Gatow, from where he flew in on a light Fieseler Fi-156, landing on the broad Ost-West-Achse in front of the Brandenburg Gate. Hitler had not been "moved at all" by their reunion and had worn his "business face," Speer later recalled. Like Goebbels before him, Hitler's former favourite Speer supported the Führer's decision to remain in Berlin instead of fleeing to Berchtesgaden. In a tired voice and with seeming composure, the dictator spoke of his imminent demise, repeating his statement from the day before that he would not fight because the risk was too great of being captured by the Soviets and held as a prisoner of war. Because he wanted to avoid "mischief being made" with his remains, he had ordered his body to be burned. Death, he said, would come as a relief: "One short moment, and then I shall be free of everything." Speer later claimed to have confessed to Hitler that he had systematically undermined his "scorched earth" orders in the preceding weeks, whereupon the dictator stared at him "absently," without any discernible reaction.[55] But we should be sceptical about this account—as we should be about much of what Speer wrote in his memoirs—since even in the final days of the Third Reich such an open confession of disobedience could have had drastic consequences. After all, the armaments minister was determined to survive Hitler and had already begun to consider his post-war career.

Over the course of 23 April, the Führer's bunker was thrown into turmoil by a pair of telegrams from Göring on the Obersalzberg, who had heard from Koller about Hitler's explosion of rage the previous day and specifically about his remark that the Reich marshal might be in a better position to negotiate with the Western Allies. Göring, who had been named Hitler's successor in the Führer's secret decree of 29 June 1941, now asked in cagey language whether the conditions that applied for that edict had come into force. If he did not receive an answer by 10 p.m., the Reich marshal wrote, he would assume that Hitler had been "robbed of his freedom to act" and that the conditions of the succession decree had been fulfilled.[56] Koller seems to have urged Göring to take this risk, arguing that Hitler had *de facto* abdicated the leadership of the state and the Wehrmacht. Göring was initially hesitant, fearing that his arch-enemy Bormann would accuse him of disloyalty: "He is just waiting to shoot me down." But the head of the Reich Chancellery, Hans Heinrich Lammers, who was hastily summoned from Berchtesgaden, convinced Göring that, legally, the decree from 1941 had to be enacted. Nonetheless, Göring was careful to maintain a tone of loyalty in his telegram, concluding with the statement: "I cannot express in words what I feel for you in this, the hardest hour of my life. May God protect you and allow you to travel here despite everything as soon as possible."[57]

In Speer's account, when shown the telegram on the afternoon of 23 April, Hitler took it "pretty much in his stride." That was to change at 6 p.m. when Hitler learned of a second telegram sent by Göring to Ribbentrop, in which he instructed the foreign minister to travel to the Obersalzberg "immediately" or as soon as the succession had taken effect.[58] It was child's play for Bormann to portray Göring's initiative as a blatant grab for power. Hitler's anger at his Reich marshal, which had been building for quite some time, discharged itself in a cascade of invective: "He let the Luftwaffe go to pot . . . His example enabled the corruption in our state. And what is more, he is a morphine addict. I have known that for some time."[59]

Responding in a terse telegram on the evening of 23 April, Hitler declared that he himself would decide when the edict of 29 June 1941 came into force. There could be no talk of him having been robbed of his capacity to act, he added, and he expressly forbade "any step in the direction you have indicated."[60] At the same time, the commandant of the Obersalzberg, SS-Obersturmbannführer Bernhard Frank, was instructed to arrest Göring and his staff. On the morning of 24 April, Frank brought the Reich marshal a second telegram that classified his behaviour as "high treason," a capital crime. In view of previous services, the telegram continued, this punishment would not be enforced if Göring voluntarily stepped down from all his posts under the pretence of grave illness. Göring quickly agreed, and on 25 April, these developments were reported on the radio.[61]

Lammers, who had advised Göring, was also taken into custody on the evening of 23 April in Berchtesgaden. In a telegram signed "Hail to my Führer!" the head of the Chancellery tried to justify his actions: "In my more than twelve years in office, I have been loyal to you and have not done anything now, either, that would call for my arrest. Please appoint an investigating judge and give me the chance to defend myself."[62] It is unclear whether Hitler ever read this telegram.

Late in the evening on 23 April, Eva Braun got Speer to come to her tiny room in the bunker and told him that she and Hitler were going to commit suicide. The day before, she explained, the Führer had stressed that the situation was hopeless and told her to get ready. It had taken some persuasion to get him to put off the act.[63] In the early morning of 24 April, Speer took his final leave. Again the dictator showed no emotion, merely saying: "So you are off. Good. Farewell." The two men's former familiarity was gone. For a final time, Speer walked through the New Reich Chancellery building, which he had completed in record time in 1938 and which was now badly damaged by fires and shelling. From the East–West Axis, he flew his Fieseler light aircraft back to the Rechlin airstrip. Berlin from the air was a terrible sight. Major fires blazed everywhere, the mouths of Soviet artillery pieces flashed constantly, and flares lit up the night sky. Only the darkness over the northwest of the city showed that a narrow corridor of escape was still open.[64] Over the course of the day, however, Soviet tanks cut off the final land bridge at Nauen. Tempelhof and Gatow airports were subjected to artillery barrages, and the East–West Axis between the Victory Column and the Brandenburg Gate had to be hastily adapted into a landing strip.[65]

At noon on 24 April, Hitler named artillery general Helmuth Weidling commandant of "Fortress Berlin"—only one day after contemplating having the general executed for allegedly transferring his tank corps command post to Döberitz, west of Berlin, without permission. Weidling had hurried to the Chancellery bunker to explain himself. "I saw a swollen face with the eyes of someone ill with a fever," he would later write of his encounter with Hitler. "The Führer tried to stand up. I noticed to my horror that his hands and one of his legs trembled constantly. With great effort, he finally succeeded in raising himself. With a crooked smile, he shook my hand and asked in a scarcely audible voice if we had ever met." The dictator was so impressed by Weidling's report that he promoted him a few hours later. "It would have been better if you had ordered me shot," Weidling told Krebs, who announced the promotion. "Then I would not be put through this."[66] Weidling replaced Colonel Ernst Kaether, who had held the post for only two days, while Kaether's predecessor, Colonel-General Hellmuth Reymann, had managed to last several weeks, from 7 March to 21 April. Berlin's new city commandant was charged with defending the capital with patchwork units of Wehrmacht soldiers, Volkssturm militiamen, Hitler Youths and members of the Organisation Todt—all in all around ninety-four thousand men—against the strongest divisions in the Red Army. From the very start, it was an impossible task.[67]

Meanwhile, the atmosphere in the subterranean world of Hitler's bunker was growing more and more surreal. Like an uncanny, restless shadow, Hitler shuffled through the rooms. His mood changed throughout the day, so that his underlings had no idea what they would have to deal with next. Some of the few people who remained loyal to the Führer asked themselves what he was waiting for: he might as well kill himself now that everything seemed lost.[68] Discipline was dissolving even in the circles closest to him. As Speer noted of his visit on 23 April: "Formerly, when [Hitler] entered a room, everyone stood up until he had taken a seat. Now seated conversations were continued, and his valets spoke with guests in his presence."[69] There was a lot of smoking and drinking, even with Hitler present. The stocks of wine and schnapps that the long-time director of the Führer's household, Arthur Kannenberg, had horded in the Chancellery cellar were plundered, and empty bottles were strewn everywhere.[70] The favourite topic of bunker conversation was the easiest way to kill oneself. Was it better to put a bullet in your head or swallow a cyanide pill? "I want to be a nice-looking corpse," Eva Braun declared. "I am taking poison."[71]

Hitler's consort was the only one to maintain countenance amid the general chaos. Always neatly dressed and made up, she continued to display "the same calm ease, almost cheerfulness," various members of Hitler's entourage unanimously reported.[72] She had made up her mind early on to follow Hitler into the grave. "I am going to die as I lived," she wrote to her friend Hertha Schneider in her farewell letter of 22 April. "I do not find it difficult." One day later she asked her sister to destroy all her private correspondence except letters from the Führer and the drafts of her replies. These were to be "packed up watertight and perhaps buried."[73] But perhaps Greta Fegelein ignored her sister's wish, or Schaub destroyed this correspondence along with the rest of the Führer's private papers, for no letters between Hitler and Braun have ever been discovered.[74]

A constant feature of the spectral world of Hitler's catacombs was the six Goebbels children. "They played, laughed, sang and acted boisterously and carefree just as children do," recalled the switchboard operator, Rochus Misch.[75] Magda Goebbels, Braun and Hitler's secretaries tried to make bunker life as bearable as possible for them. The Goebbelses had already decided to take their children with them when they committed suicide. On 28 April, in her final letter to her son from her first marriage, Harald Quandt, now a British POW in northern Africa, Magda Goebbels wrote that the family had been in the bunker for six days to "give their National Socialist lives the only possible honourable end": "The world to come after the Führer and National Socialism is not worth living in, and for that reason I have brought the children here. They are too good for the life to come after us, and a merciful God will understand when I give them salvation myself."[76]

Around noon on 25 April, the vanguards of Konev's and Zhukov's armies linked up in Ketzin, 12 kilometres northwest of Potsdam. The noose around the Reich capital had closed. Moreover, that afternoon, reports came that American and Soviet troops had met in Torgau, on the Elbe. With that, the remnants of non-occupied Germany were split into northern and southern halves.[77] There was no hope any more that the enemy coalition would fall apart before Germany's final defeat.

But Hitler refused to accept the situation. If Berlin could be defended and a blow struck against the Soviets, he declared that day at a situation meeting, the Americans and the British would realise that "there is only one man who can halt the Bolshevik colossus. And I am that man." Hitler spent most of the meeting justifying his decision to stay in Berlin and lead the fight from there. As an "inglorious refugee"— a phrase that he liked so much he repeated it four times—he would have "no authority, neither in northern Germany nor in southern Germany, and especially not in Berchtesgaden." His purpose in this world was not to defend the Berghof, he added. Only a "heroic bearing" could help in this "most difficult time." It was entirely possible that he would end his life in Berlin, but at least he would have "fallen honourably." Goebbels offered his support: "If things turn out well, that will be good. If they do not, and the Führer finds an honourable death in Berlin, and Europe should become Bolshevik, in five years at the latest the Führer will be a legendary figure and National Socialism a mythology, having been sanctified by the ultimate sacrifice—and anything human that people criticise about him today will be wiped away in one fell swoop."[78]

Those holding out in the Führer's bunker were anxiously awaiting news from Wenck's army. That morning, Keitel had reported that the army was marching on Berlin, and its vanguards had advanced to within 40 kilometres of Potsdam. But then there was no more good news. Hitler mostly sat around slumped in his chair. "It had gone deathly quiet in the room, and everyone stared silently at the map," recalled one of those present.[79] In a radio message after the evening situation meeting, the dictator called upon Jodl and Wenck to push through the relief attack on the Reich capital with "severity and determination." That was the only way to "re-establish the connection between the 9th Army and Berlin and destroy powerful parts of the enemy forces."[80]

For all of 26 April, Soviet artillery continuously shelled the government district and the Chancellery. For a time, the fans that supplied the bunker with fresh air had to be turned off because, despite their filters, they were sucking in smoke, dust and sulphurous fumes. In several places the roof of the underground passage to the New Reich Chancellery caved in. The night before, Red Army soldiers had severed the subterranean cable connecting the bunker switchboard with the military commands outside Berlin. All that was left were radio communications, which were repeatedly disrupted. As a result, the occupants of the bunker received no news for hours at a time. Hitler constantly asked what was keeping Wenck's troops, but Krebs had nothing new to tell him. Instead, word arrived in the afternoon that the Oder front between Stettin and Gartz had completely collapsed and that Rokossovsky's tanks were rolling towards Neustrelitz and Neubrandenburg. In northeast Berlin, Soviet soldiers had fought their way along the Frankfurter Allee to Alexanderplatz.[81]

That evening, Luftwaffe colonel-general Robert Ritter von Greim arrived at the bunker. Hitler had summoned him to appoint him Göring's successor as the head of the Luftwaffe. Accompanied by the well-known test pilot and fervent Hitler admirer Hanna Reitsch, Greim had flown from Munich to Rechlin and then on to Gatow. There, like Speer before him, he had got into a Fieseler light aircraft, injuring his right foot as they landed on the Ost–West Achse, when the floor of his plane was ripped open by artillery fire. Reitsch had taken over the joystick and managed to land the machine safely in front of the Brandenburg Gate. Greim was treated by doctors before being brought to Hitler on a stretcher. "His posture was severely hunched, both arms trembled incessantly, and his eyes had something glassy and faraway," Reitsch later described the Führer. "He welcomed us in an almost toneless voice." Only then did Greim learn why he had been told to make the dangerous journey. Hitler let him read Göring's telegrams and told him the Reich marshal had been dismissed and arrested. He then promoted Greim to field marshal and named him supreme commander of the Luftwaffe. "I am spared nothing in the world," Hitler complained, proceeding to his familiar litany of gripes. "No disappointment, no violation of trust, no dishonour and no betrayal."[82]

On 27 April, Soviet troops took control of Tempelhof and Gatow airports and pushed even further towards the centre of the city. Fighting was fierce around Alexanderplatz, and the Chancellery remained under heavy barrage. Every time a shell hit the building above, the walls of the bunker shook as though rocked by an earthquake. When the enemy fire relented somewhat, Hitler asked his valet Linge to accompany him into the courtyard so that he could see with his own eyes what it looked like. But hardly had Linge opened the reinforced door to the emergency exit than a shell landed next to the bunker. Hitler immediately turned round on the stairs and dragged himself back down to his quarters.[83]

That morning at around 10:30 news finally arrived from Wenck, who reported that the vanguards of his army had reached the village of Ferch on Lake Schwielow, some 12 kilometres southwest of Potsdam. The news quickly spread throughout the bunker, causing a temporary euphoria. "Joyful voices and laughter were heard every-where," reported one occupant. "Maps of Berlin and beyond were produced to determine the distance from Potsdam to Berlin. People were enthusiastically patting each other on the back."[84] His eyes feverishly glimmering, Hitler studied a map brought to him by Freytag von Loringhoven, which had been freshly marked. With a triumphant expression, he turned to Krebs: "I always told you . . . We will make it."[85]

The day's first situation meeting was dominated by speculations about Wenck's army. Hitler projected confidence that if Berlin could be held for "two or three or four days," Wenck would be able to reach the capital. "Imagine that," Hitler said. "It will spread through Berlin like wildfire, if news arrives that a German army has broken in from the west and established contact with the fortress . . . It will be a focal point of the highest order." At the same time, Hitler was aware that Wenck, with his three divisions, would not be able to turn the tide on his own but would require help from Busse's 9th Army and an army group under Lieutenant-General Rudolf Holste in the northwest of Berlin. Hitler and his military advisers in the bunker no longer had reliable information about the fighting strength of these formations. In reality, these divisions had already been decimated or ceased to exist altogether. Nonetheless, Hitler told those around him that he would "go to bed a tiny bit more calmly" that night, adding sarcas-tically that he only wanted to be woken up "if a Russian tank turned up outside my bedroom."[86]

Hopes for a turnaround dissipated as quickly as they had coalesced. Over the course of the day, Mohnke reported that the first Soviet tanks had been sighted near Wilhelmplatz and a handful of Red Army snipers had set up at Potsdamer Platz, both very close to the bunker. By the evening, it became clear that the assault by Wenck's men had been halted before Potsdam. There was little prospect any more of relief arriving for the capital. Hitler raged against the leadership of the 9th Army, who had moved most of their forces west instead of northwest towards Berlin, as they had been ordered. It was impossible to lead, Hitler fumed, "if every commander or corps general did whatever he thought was right with no regard for the larger plan." Realistically appraising the situation, Busse had decided to break out of the cauldron near Halbe with the rest of his army towards the west and allow himself to be taken prisoner by the Americans. In light of the catastrophic circumstances, Weidling suggested attempting a break-out from Berlin to Potsdam, promising that he could get Hitler out of the capital unharmed, but the dictator refused. The point now, the Führer said, was to wage "a heroic fight for one final little island." In the day's last situation meeting, Hitler returned to what had become his favourite topic, remarking that it "was no bad end to a life to fall in battle for the capital of the Reich."[87] The mood in the bunker had turned positively apocalyptic. While most of the occupants sought to numb their fear with alcohol, Bormann noted in his pocket calendar: "We will stand and fall with the Führer, true unto death."[88]

By 28 April, the artillery barrage of the government district had become a veritable hurricane. Shells pounded the Chancellery without interruption. Mohnke reported that in places Soviet troops had breached the inner defensive ring around the "citadel," and Red Army soldiers were advancing threateningly close to Wilhelmstrasse from Hallesches Tor and Belle-Alliance-Platz a few kilometres to the south. Small agitated groups congregated throughout the bunker, with everyone talking at the same time.[89] That morning Krebs issued another urgent appeal to Keitel: "The Führer expects the swiftest help. We only have forty-eight hours at the most. If assistance does not arrive by then, it will be too late." Keitel promised to spur Wenck and Busse on "with the utmost energy."[90] But then the connection went dead, and no more news was forthcoming from Wenck's army. Those close to Hitler suspected another instance of treachery. "Loyalty seems to be retreating before disloyalty," Bormann wrote in a telegram to Puttkammer. "We are staying put. The Reich Chancellery is already a pile of rubble."[91] In his calendar he quoted, slightly wrongly, a line from Schiller's play *Wallenstein's Camp*: "On the point of a spear the world now stands."[92]

That evening, a frenetic Heinz Lorenz, the regime's deputy press secretary, arrived in the bunker with a report from Reuters, via Radio Stockholm, that had initially not been taken seriously but had now been confirmed by a reliable second source. Heinrich Himmler had tried to use the Swedish diplomat and vice-president of the Swedish Red Cross, Count Folke Bernadotte, to initiate negotiations with the Western Allies, offering Germany's unconditional surrender.[93]

The SS leader had been in contact with Bernadotte since February. Originally the topic of their discussions was the release of concentration camp inmates, specifically those from Scandinavia, but Walter Schellenberg, head of foreign espionage in the Reich Security Main Office, had pressured his boss to negotiate on his own with the Western powers about a partial German capitulation. Himmler was initially uncertain, torn between his loyalty to Hitler and his conviction that the war was lost. After hearing Fegelein's descriptions of the dramatic situation meeting on 22 April, he now believed like Göring that the Führer was no longer capable of making decisions and that action would have to be taken without his approval. During the night of 23–24 April, Himmler met with Bernadotte in the Swedish consulate in Lübeck and asked him to convince the Swedish government to set up a meeting with Eisenhower so that he could make his surrender offer. As could have been expected, the Western powers rejected the idea and publicised Himmler's act of betrayal by broadcasting the Reuters report on the BBC.[94]

Hitler was apoplectic when he received the news. "He raged like a lunatic," Hanna Reitsch recalled. "His skin went purplish red, and his face was almost unrecognisable."[95] Himmler, of all people, whose SS men were ordered to live by the motto "Our honour is loyalty," had gone behind his back and was acting as though he were Hitler's successor. Bormann, Goebbels and Hitler's entire entourage shared the Führer's outrage. The bunker echoed with them cursing "faithless Heinrich."

The affair would have fatal consequences for one man, Himmler's liaison Hermann Fegelein, who had left the bunker on 25 April and whose absence had only been noticed two days later. Hitler ordered a search for him, and he was located in civilian clothing, completely drunk and in the company of a young woman, in his apartment on Bleibtreustrasse. Apparently, he had called from there to convince his sister-in-law Eva Braun to flee the bunker. A suitcase full of jewellery and cash in foreign denominations confiscated in the apartment suggested that he wanted to flee west. Fegelein was arrested on the evening of 27 April, demoted on the spot and detained in the Führer's bunker. He was being interrogated the next day when news of Himmler's betrayal came in. His fate was sealed when a search of Fegelein's office turned up a briefcase full of documents evincing his knowledge of Himmler's negotiations with Bernadotte. Hitler, thirsting for revenge, ordered him to be executed, and a hastily convened court-martial chaired by Mohnke handed down that punishment. Fegelein was shot around midnight, and his remains were buried in the Chancellery courtyard.[96]

A short time later, Hitler ordered his new Luftwaffe head, Greim, to meet with Dönitz in Plön in northern Germany and get him to arrest Himmler. Never should a traitor be allowed to succeed him, he explained. Greim and Reitsch asked to be allowed to stay in the bunker but Hitler insisted they go. An Arado Ar-96 aircraft was readied for them at the Brandenburg Gate. Fighting was going on at nearby Potsdamer Platz, so an armoured vehicle brought the two pilots to the makeshift runway. In taking his leave, Hitler—whom Reitsch described as "a shade paler, more sunken into himself, with the wan fallen face of a geriatric"—presented her with two vials of poison so that she would have, in his words, "the freedom to decide at all times." He would voluntarily depart from this life with Eva Braun, he added, if there was no longer any hope of General Wenck relieving Berlin. Reitsch managed to pilot the plane out of the inferno that was Berlin,[97] but their mission at Dönitz's headquarters in Plön was to be a failure. Although the admiral summoned Himmler, who had quartered himself in a police barracks in Lübeck, for questioning on 30 April, the head of the SS flatly denied having negotiated with the Western powers behind Hitler's back, and Dönitz was satisfied with that explanation.[98]

On the night of 28–29 April, soon after Greim and Reitsch had flown off, Hitler married Eva Braun. There is considerable evidence that the marriage was an off-the-cuff decision by the dictator: even those closest to him were informed about the wedding only a few hours beforehand.[99] Hitler had always told his underlings that marriage was out of the question because as Führer he could not enter into such a close union with one woman. From early on, he had depicted himself as a politician who had renounced all personal happiness to completely dedicate himself to his historical mission in the service of the German people. For that reason, he had taken various measures to conceal the existence of his lover from the German public.[100] But now that his aura as Führer was gone and he had decided to commit suicide with Braun, there was no longer any need for this role-playing. Marrying Braun in their final hours was apparently his way of thanking the woman who had always been unconditionally loyal and true to him. That was all the more important to Hitler after the actions of his paladins Göring and Himmler. And perhaps Wagnerian motifs also played a part: during evenings at the Berghof, Hitler had often said that he wanted the "Liebestod" from *Tristan and Isolde* played at his deathbed.[101]

Whatever Hitler's motivations, Linge was required to prepare the situation room for the civil ceremony. A notary coincidentally named Walter Wagner from Goebbels' staff as Berlin Gauleiter was fetched to perform the wedding. Hitler wore his usual military jacket with his Iron Cross First Class and the First World War Wounded Badge. Braun had donned a long, high-necked, dark silk dress. Bormann and Goebbels served as witnesses. When signing the marriage certificate, the freshly wedded bride began to sign with her maiden name, before quickly crossing out the "B" and writing "Eva Hitler née Braun." The whole ceremony was over within ten minutes. Then the newly betrothed couple and their witnesses withdrew to Hitler's office to drink a glass of champagne and reminisce about days gone by.[102]

Just before midnight, ahead of the wedding, Hitler had asked Traudl Junge to follow him into the situation room. "Take a notepad," he ordered and began to dictate, with a fixed stare and his hands braced on the table top, what he called "my political will." Her own hands trembled at those words, the secretary later recalled, adding that she had felt "curious to the extreme." Was she about to witness what many of the bunker's occupants had been awaiting for days—"the explanation for what had happened, a confession, perhaps even an admission of guilt?"[103] But Junge was to be disappointed. Hitler's will amounted to further evidence, in the words of the historian Hans-Ulrich Thamer, of "his unbroken ideological dogmatism and unrepentant self-justification."[104]

It was untrue, Hitler said, that he had wanted war in 1939. It had been provoked "exclusively by those international statesmen who either were of Jewish origin or worked for Jewish interests." Once again, Hitler's fanatical anti-Semitism emerged as the core of his ideological obsessions. He had never left any doubt, he continued, that he would "hold that people accountable which is truly to blame for this murderous battle: Jewry!" He went on to gloat in barely concealed form about the destruction of European Jews: "Furthermore I have never left anyone in any doubt that this time around . . . millions of adult men would not die, and hundreds of thousands of women and children would not be immolated and bombed to death in cities, without those who are actually to blame being made to atone for their guilt, albeit through more humane means."

Hitler justified his decision to stay in Berlin and go to his death "of his own free will" by saying that he did "not want to fall into the hands of the enemy, who need a new spectacle, arranged by Jews, to entertain their incited masses." The dictator called upon the leaders of the German army, navy and air force to "strengthen the spirit of resistance of our soldiers in the National Socialist sense by the most extreme means"—that is, by pointing out that the Führer himself had "preferred death to cowardly flights or, even worse, surrender."

The second half of Hitler's will dealt with his succession. Göring and Himmler were expelled from the party and all state offices for having "inflicted incalculable damages" on the Reich with their secret negotiations and attempts to grab power. Dönitz was named Hitler's successor as political leader and Wehrmacht supreme commander. He was given the title Reich president, which Hitler himself had abolished after Hindenburg's death in August 1934. Goebbels and Bormann were rewarded for their loyalty, being named Reich chancellor and "party minister," respectively. Ribbentrop was no longer part of the new Reich cabinet, fulfilling Goebbels' long-term aim. The Reich's new foreign minister was Arthur Seyss-Inquart, previously Reich commissar for the Netherlands. Speer too received his comeuppance for his manoeuvring during the final weeks of the war, as his old rival, Karl-Otto Saur, was named armaments minister.[105] Himmler was replaced as interior minister by Munich Gauleiter Paul Giesler and as the head of the SS and the police by Breslau Gauleiter Karl Hanke. Funk (economics), Backe (agriculture), Thierack (justice) and Schwerin von

Krosigk (finance) retained their ministries, making Schwerin von Krosigk the only man to survive all the governmental shake-ups since Papen's "cabinet of barons" in 1932.[106] Goebbels' deputy Werner Naumann was to take over the propaganda ministry, and Schörner was made the new supreme commander of the army. In conclusion, Hitler exhorted "the leadership of the nations and their followers to scrupulously abide by the racial laws and to remorselessly resist the global poisoner of all peoples, international Jewry."[107]

As she listened to the list of members of the new government, Junge looked up questioningly. "If everything was lost . . . if the Führer himself saw no way out other than suicide, what were the men he named to do?" she asked in her memoirs.[108] But Hitler simply continued after a brief pause, moving on to his "private will." Junge now learned that her boss intended to marry. He had decided, Hitler said, "to take as my wife the girl who after long years of faithful friendship volun- tarily came to this almost besieged city to share my fate: she will go to death at her own wish as my wife." Hitler bequeathed his assets to the party and, should the NSDAP no longer exist, to the German state, adding: "Should the state too be destroyed, no further decision will be required of me." He willed his collection of paintings, as long planned, to a gallery in Linz. As the executor of his will, Hitler named Bormann, calling him his "truest party comrade." Bormann was to see to it that enough funds as were "necessary to maintain a modest middle-class existence" were diverted from his estate to his sister Paula, his half-sister Angela Hammitzsch, Eva Braun's mother and his closest employees, especially his secretaries and his housekeeper Anni Winter. Hitler's private will concluded in the florid, bathetic tone of a Wagnerian opera: "In order to escape the shame of flight and surrender, I myself and my spouse choose death. It is our will that we should be immediately burned on the spot where I performed the largest part of my daily work in my twelve years of service to my people."[109]

No sooner had Hitler ended his dictation than he let go of the table top against which he had propped himself up the entire time and ordered Junge to type out both documents in triplicate. While the wedding party was still celebrating, he repeatedly came over to check how she was getting on with her work. At 4 a.m. on 29 April, every- thing was finally done. Goebbels and Bormann witnessed Hitler's political will as representatives of the state and party, while Krebs and

Burgdorf were present for the military. The private will was witnessed by Goebbels, Bormann and Hitler's adjutant Below, who regarded his master's gesture as an honour.[110]

Hitler then retreated, but for his secretary, work was not over yet. Suddenly, Goebbels limped into the room and asked her to take down an "addendum" to the Führer's political will. Hitler had ordered him to leave Berlin and take over the leading position in the Reich government, Goebbels said. But for the first time in his life, he was forced to refuse a command from the Führer. Within this "delirium of betrayal," Goebbels dictated, there had to be at least a handful of men "who stuck by him unconditionally and until death." For this reason, Goebbels and his wife had reached the "unshakable decision" to remain in the Reich capital and end their lives at Hitler's side.[111]

At 8:00 on the morning of 29 April, couriers were appointed to take these documents out of Berlin. Hitler's army adjutant Major Willi Johannmeyer, Bormann's adjutant SS-Standartenführer Wilhelm Zander and deputy press secretary Lorenz were to bring one copy each of the will to the new army supreme commander, Schörner; Hitler's designated successor, Dönitz; and to Nazi Party headquarters, the "Brown House" in Munich. The trio left the bunker around midday and set off, trying to escape to the West by any means possible. None of them made it to his destination, but Hugh Trevor-Roper, a member of the British Secret Intelligence Service and later a historian, succeeded in tracking down all three couriers in the winter of 1945–46 and securing the three copies of Hitler's wills as well as his marriage certificate. In his book *The Last Days of Hitler*, published in March 1947, Trevor-Roper detailed his detective-like search for the missing men and documents.[112]

"Once again artillery barrage," noted Bormann in his pocket calendar on 29 April.[113] Shells of all calibres fell on the Chancellery in short intervals. The Wehrmacht report that day described "the fanatic house-to-house fighting for the centre of Berlin" as going on "day and night."[114] Soviet troops were preparing to storm the government district from Alexanderplatz to the south and the Tiergarten and Potsdamer Platz to the west.[115] At around 1:30 p.m., after the noon situation meeting, officers Freytag von Loringhoven, Boldt and Weiss took their leave. They were trying to break through to the 12th Army, they announced, to inform Wenck about the situation in Berlin. In reality, they wanted to flee the mausoleum of the bunker and escape Berlin with their lives. Hitler shook their hands before they left, saying: "Pay my regards to Wenck—he should hurry or it will be too late."[116] Freytag von Loringhoven and Boldt succeeded in escaping to the West, while Weiss was captured by the Soviets. Below too left the Chancellery shortly after midnight as the last of Hitler's adjutants. As a British POW in 1946, he told his interrogator, Trevor-Roper, that he was supposed to bring Keitel a secret message from Hitler, but that turns out to have been a fairy tale, which was passed on in *The Last Days of Hitler* and afterwards uncritically accepted by many other historians.[117]

That afternoon, Hitler had ordered his German shepherd Blondi poisoned. The dog-loving Hitler had been given the animal in the spring of 1942, and as previously described, he had spent considerable time training her.[118] Now he did not want his dog to survive him. Moreover, since Himmler's act of betrayal, he had come to doubt whether the vials of prussic acid supplied by the SS really did lead to a quick death, and he wanted to test the poison's effectiveness on his pet. The attending physician, Professor Werner Haase, was summoned from the operations bunker under the New Reich Chancellery, and he crushed the vial of poison with a pair of pliers while a sergeant held the dog's mouth open. Hitler came to see the animal die. "His face looked like his own death mask," Junge recalled.[119]

That evening, Hitler received word that Mussolini was dead. On 27 April, the fleeing Duce and his lover Claretta Petacci had been identified and arrested by communist partisans on Lake Como. The two had been executed the following afternoon on the outskirts of the village of Giulino di Mezzegra. The next morning their bodies were brought by removal van to Milan and strung up by their feet at a petrol station on Piazzale Loreto after being badly mutilated by the crowd.[120] It is improbable that Hitler would have learned of the grisly details, but the news of corpses being publicly displayed alone would have strengthened him in his decision to have his own remains and those of Braun burned.[121]

Around 11 p.m., Hitler sent a final radio message to Jodl in Dobbin in northern Germany, where the Wehrmacht Supreme Command had moved its headquarters, demanding answers to five questions: "1. Where are the vanguards of Wenck? 2. When are they attacking again?

3. Where is the 9th Army? 4. Where is it going to break through? 5. Where are the vanguards of Holste?"[122] It was an hour after midnight before Keitel's answer arrived: "1. Wenck's vanguard is stuck south of Lake Schwielow. 2. For that reason the 12th Army cannot continue attack on Berlin. 3. Most of 9th Army surrounded. Armoured units broke out westwards. Whereabouts not reported. 4. Holste Corps . . . forced on the defensive."[123] With that, it was definitely clear that all was lost.

Hitler began preparing himself for his personal end. In the night of 29–30 April, he took his leave of his valets, his guards and the medical personnel in the bunker's field hospital. The physician Günther Schenck, who saw him for the first time on this occasion, felt a "sensation of almost unbearable disappointment." The man standing in front of him did not resemble the Führer of the old days in the slightest. "He may have been wearing a grey field jacket with the golden national emblem and the Iron Cross on its left breast, as well as the long, dark trousers, but the human being inside these vestments had collapsed back unimaginably upon himself. I looked down on a bent back with protruding shoulder blades from which he raised his head almost torturously."[124] Hitler shook everyone's hand and thanked them for their service. He had decided to take his life, he told them, and thereby released them from their oath of loyalty. They should try to make their way to American or British lines to avoid being taken prisoner by the Soviets.[125]

By 5:00 the next morning, the Chancellery was again being shelled heavily. An hour later, Hitler summoned Mohnke and asked how long his troops could hold out. "One to two days" was the answer. Soviet troops had taken Potsdamer Platz and most of the Tiergarten and were now only 400 metres from the Chancellery. Around noon a final situation meeting was held. Weidling confirmed Mohnke's gloomy prognosis, saying that "in all probability the battle for Berlin will be ended on the evening of 30 April," since the defenders would have run out of ammunition and no further supplies could be expected by air. After conferring with Krebs, Hitler authorised the defenders of the capital, in case no more reserves arrived, to attempt to break out in small groups and link up with units still fighting in the west. But he once again explicitly forbade any surrender.[126]

At 1 p.m., Hitler ate lunch with his two secretaries and his cook. They talked about trivialities, avoiding the topic of his imminent suicide. Junge later characterised the scene as a "feast of death under the mask of cheerful relaxation and composure."[127] In the meantime, Bormann had informed Otto Günsche that Hitler intended to commit suicide together with his wife that afternoon and had ordered their bodies to be burned. Günsche was to procure the necessary quantity of petrol. A short time later Hitler made his personal adjutants promise that his orders would be strictly carried out. He said he did not want his body to be taken to Moscow and "put on display in a panopticon." Günsche immediately called Hitler's chauffeur and head of the regime's car fleet, Erich Kempka, and instructed him to get ten cans of petrol and place them outside the emergency exit to the Chancellery courtyard.[128]

It was now time for Hitler to say goodbye to his entourage. As a farewell present, he gave his chief pilot, Baur, the portrait of Friedrich the Great by Anton Graff. He said he knew that "by tomorrow . . . millions of people would already curse him," but that was what destiny had intended.[129] At 3:15 p.m., Hitler's closest associates—Goebbels, Bormann, Hewel, Krebs, Burgdorf and his secretaries—gathered in the corridor. Hitler appeared together with his wife, shook their hands, murmured a few words of thanks and withdrew to his rooms.[130] Immediately afterwards, a weeping Magda Goebbels appeared and asked to be allowed to speak with Hitler. It seems that she wanted to make one last attempt to convince him to leave Berlin. A terse Hitler refused to admit her.[131] Everyone was now waiting for the end.

After around ten minutes, shortly after 3:30 p.m., Linge opened the door to Hitler's office, cast a glance inside and reported to Bormann: "Reichsleiter, it has happened." Followed by Günsche, they both entered the room, where they saw Hitler on the left of his floral sofa, his head bent slightly forward. There was a penny-sized wound to his right temple from which blood dripped down his face. The wall and the couch were splashed with blood, and a pool of blood about the size of a plate had formed on the floor. Next to Hitler's right foot was his Walther 7.65mm pistol. On the right of the sofa sat Eva Hitler with her legs drawn up and her lips pressed together. The bitter almond scent that emanated from her body indicated that she had poisoned herself with cyanide.[132]

Günsche went to the situation room and announced: "The Führer is dead!" Goebbels, Krebs, Burgdorf, Axmann and SS-General Hans Rattenhuber hurried to the antechamber of Hitler's quarters. At that moment, Linge, followed by two SS men, emerged with Hitler's body from his office. The corpse was wrapped in a blanket, with only the black trouser cuffs, socks and shoes showing. The bodies of Hitler and his wife were carried up the stairs to the courtyard of the Chancellery, where they were placed three or four metres from the entrance of the bunker. Bormann approached for a final time, lifted the blanket back from Hitler's face and stood in silence for a few seconds. Then, with shells continuing to detonate nearby and overhead, he quickly withdrew. During a break in the shelling, Günsche, Kempka and Linge poured the canisters of petrol over the bodies. At first they were unable to light a match because of the strong wind unleashed by the fires all around. In the end, Linge made a torch of some paper, lit it and tossed it on the corpses. A tongue of flame leaped up immediately. Those who had congregated on the site raised their arms in a Hitler salute and then retreated into the bunker.[133]

The remains of Adolf and Eva Hitler were buried in a crater in the Chancellery courtyard that evening. One of the Reich Security Service guards who was charged with the burial later testified that he had found only a heap of ashes that had fallen apart when he touched it with his foot. Several days later, when the Soviets went looking for Hitler's remains after capturing the Chancellery, they discovered gold upper-jaw bridgework with porcelain inlays and a lower jawbone with teeth and bridgework among carbonised body parts. A dental technician and a dental assistant from Hugo Blaschke's practice identified these remains beyond question as Hitler's.[134] There was hardly anything else left of the man who at the height of his career had fancied himself the ruler of the world.

At 5:40 p.m. on 30 April, while Hitler's corpse was still burning, Bormann sent a radio message to Dönitz informing him that the admiral had been named the Führer's successor and that written authorisation was on its way. Bormann did not mention the fact that Hitler was dead, and in a follow-up telegram that arrived on 1 May in Plön, he merely stated that Hitler's testament, which had not got to Dönitz, was now in force and he, Bormann, wanted to come to

Plön as soon as possible. It was only in a third telegram, arriving shortly before 3 p.m., that Goebbels explicitly wrote of Hitler's death—the Führer "passed at 3:30 p.m. yesterday"—and the constitution of a new government. The admiral himself, he added, was to determine when the news should be made public.[135] Thus it took another seven hours before, at 10:26 p.m., the state radio station in Hamburg announced that Hitler was dead. The Führer, the report claimed, had "fallen for Germany this afternoon in his operational headquarters in the Chancellery, fighting Bolshevism down to his final breath." The report thus consciously falsified not just the time but the circumstances of Hitler's death in order to conceal from the public the fact that Hitler had evaded responsibility by committing suicide. Dönitz supported this lie in his subsequent radio address when he spoke of Hitler having "died a hero's death in the capital of the German Reich."[136]

On the evening of 30 April, Goebbels and Bormann had sent an emissary to the Soviet lines to ask whether General Chuikov would receive a representative of the German regime. The Soviets agreed, and that night Krebs, who as a former military attaché in Moscow spoke Russian, set off with a missive from Goebbels, announcing Hitler's death and offering to open talks about an armistice. Around noon the following day, Krebs returned to the bunker and reported that the Soviet Supreme Command insisted that Germany surrender unconditionally.[137] For Joseph and Magda Goebbels, it was time to make their final preparations. That evening, they had their six children drugged with morphine and poisoned. Then they themselves took cyanide capsules. There was no longer enough petrol available to completely burn their bodies, and Soviet officers found their scorched corpses the following day in the Chancellery courtyard.[138]

Krebs, Burgdorf and the commander of Hitler's SS bodyguard, Franz Schädle, also chose to end their own lives. Late that evening, the remaining members of the Führer's entourage tried to break out of the bunker in several groups and make it to the West. Only a few of them—Axmann and the secretaries Junge and Christian—succeeded; most, including Baur, Linge, Günsche and Misch, were captured by the Russians. Others, like Hewel, Bormann and the physician Ludwig Stumpfegger, committed suicide to avoid being taken captive. It would not be until December 1972, during construction work at Berlin's

Lehrter train station, that Bormann's remains would be discovered. The final entry in his pocket calendar from 1 May 1945 simply read: "Escape attempt."[139]

On the morning of 2 May, the commandant of "Fortress Berlin," General Weidling, signed an order stopping the fighting. Five days later, Germany unconditionally surrendered at Eisenhower's headquarters in Reims. At Stalin's request, that ceremony was repeated shortly after midnight on 9 May at Zhukov's headquarters in the Karlshorst district of Berlin. Japan was only willing to end hostilities after American atomic bombs were dropped on Hiroshima on 6 August and on Nagasaki three days later. On 2 September, the Japanese signed their surrender on the battleship USS *Missouri*. The Second World War, the most destructive conflict in human history, which had been started by Hitler's Germany, was over.

18

Hitler's Place in History

"The day is ours. The bloody dog is dead." With these words from Shakespeare's *Richard III*, the BBC announced Hitler's death on 1 May 1945. Thomas Mann, who repeated the quotation in a diary entry the following day, was immediately sceptical about Dönitz's tale of the dictator having "fallen in the fight against Bolshevism." Most probably Hitler had committed suicide, wrote Mann, adding that it was also possible he had suffered a stroke, since he had supposedly "shaken like aspen leaves for some time."[1]

The CBS correspondent William Shirer heard of Hitler's death on 1 May 1945 in San Francisco, where the founding conference of the United Nations had been meeting since 24 April. "It never seemed to me possible that a man who incarnated all that was evil and bestial and degrading in our human life . . . would get away with it in the end," Shirer wrote. Considering the destruction Hitler and National Socialism had left behind, he continued: "I do not think man has ever witnessed such a debacle on this planet—at least on such a scale."[2]

On 2 May, conversations among German generals in British captivity, interned in Trent Park near London, were dominated by Hitler's death. The Führer, most of them agreed, was a man who had rendered "great services" to the German people and a "historical personality" to whom only posterity could give his true due. But he had tragically failed because he had surrounded himself with "inadequate, criminal people."[3] The idea that Hitler had become a victim of his advisers was not shared by all the officers. Several, among them Major-General Johannes Bruhn, had come to the realisation that they had served a system that had violated "all ethical laws." Under surveillance, Bruhn was recorded as saying: "We can only shake our heads at how all of us followed this lunatic."[4] Similar scruples soon began to plague

Colonel-General Hans-Georg Reinhardt, whom Hitler had dismissed in late January 1945 from his post as head of Army Group Centre and who had been in an American POW camp since early June. His "faith in the person of Hitler" had been shaken, he confided to his diary. "Or were, as we thought until now, those around him to blame? How terrible if you are beginning to doubt everything you previously believed in and served."[5] The process of disillusionment had commenced several weeks earlier for the society hostess and former Hitler patroness Elsa Bruckmann. She had written to her sister in mid-April: "Our home destroyed, Munich annihilated, what we believed in—disappointed, betrayed and our Germany at an end!"[6]

When the news of the Führer's death was made public on 1 May 1945, Albert Speer was quartered with Hitler's successor, Dönitz, in Plön. As he opened his travelling trunk, a leather case fell out, containing the portrait Hitler had dedicated to him in March, proclaiming his friendship in handwriting that was barely legible any more. Propping up the photo, a "fit of weeping" had overcome him, Speer later recalled: "That was the end of my relationship with Hitler. Only now was the spell broken, the magic extinguished . . . I fell into a deep, exhausted sleep."[7] But Speer's relationship with the Führer he had so admired was by no means concluded. He hardly mourned his deceased patron. On the contrary, after he was arrested together with the other members of the Dönitz government on 23 May, he continued his efforts, begun before the end of the war, to cover up his status as one of Hitler's most powerful protégés and his culpability in the genocidal crimes of National Socialism.[8]

To the fanatical Hitler followers who had believed in his promises of miracle weapons and ultimate victory down to the very last, news of Hitler's demise came as a massive shock. It was to these people that the editor-in-chief of the *Hamburger Zeitung*, Hermann Okrass, addressed his obituary, entitled "Taking Leave of Hitler," on 2 May— only a few hours before Hamburg would be declared an "open city" and occupied without a fight by the British. "A great man has passed from this world," Okrass wrote, who "only wanted the best for the people" and for that reason had been "so very deeply loved." Hitler, his eulogist continued, had united "the best virtues, the most passionate wishes, the noblest desires, and the entire fine longing of our people." His image would never be darkened by the fact that "traitors and bad advisers" had abandoned him, and he had only succumbed to "the massive superior forces of steel and gold." The ultimate judgement over Hitler, Okrass concluded, could "be left in good conscience to posterity."[9]

In the diary of the twenty-six-year-old German literature student Lore Walb, sadness at the loss of her beloved Führer alternated with self-pity. "He is now at peace," she noted on 2 May. "That is no doubt best for him. But what about us? We are abandoned, exposed to everything and can never rebuild in our lifetimes what this war has destroyed." Originally, Hitler had wanted to realise some "positive ideas," Walb wrote, and domestically "much good" had been done, but Hitler had "completely failed" in foreign policy and particularly as supreme commander in war: "And now the people will have to pay!" A few days later she noted: "Hitler is now dead. But we and those coming after us will carry the burden he put on us for our entire lives . . . It seems God no longer loves us."[10] Walb was not alone in such lamentations. On the contrary, her reaction was typical of the emotional ambivalence with which many of Hitler's former devotees reacted to the news of his death. The credulous trust shown towards him for so many years changed into utter disillusionment, even hatred. The man once worshipped as saviour was made into the sole bearer of blame for the entire German catastrophe.

Friedrich Kellner spoke for the much smaller group of Hitler opponents who had seen disaster coming, when he reminded his fellow Germans: "Every party comrade is responsible for the deeds and actions of the party. It is not right to ascribe the entire blame to Hitler and his leadership staff." On 1 May, the court official, who a few weeks later would be named deputy mayor of his hometown of Laubach, wrote: "The most ignominious of all political systems, this one-of-a-kind Führer state, has found the end it deserved. History will record for all eternity that the German people were incapable of shaking off the National Socialist yoke on their own."[11]

It seems that most Germans greeted the news of Hitler's death not with sadness but with apathy, even relief. The Führer myth had lost nearly all its power in the final months of the war, and with that, National Socialism was robbed of its major appeal. The spell had indeed been broken. On 2 May in Berlin, Ursula von Kardorff reported: "People here are utterly indifferent to whether the once so deified, beloved Führer is still alive or already dead. He has played his role to its end."[12]

Most Germans were in any case far more concerned with their own survival to worry about the end of their dictator. On the morning of 2 May, an eighteen-year-old schoolgirl from a Social Democratic household in a working-class neighbourhood of Hamburg noted on her way to school: "It is strange that no one was crying or looked sad, although their beloved, revered Führer, whom these idiots had treated almost like a god, was no longer alive . . . So this was the dedicated ethnic-popular community that had sworn an oath to give *everything* for him, their Führer . . . Now that drill camp was over, everyone was breathing easier."[13]

German disavowal of National Socialism proceeded at breathtaking speed. Everywhere symbols of Nazi rule—Hitler portraits, party insignia, swastika flags and uniforms—were disposed of. The writer Erich Kästner, who in March had moved with his colleagues at the state film studio UFA from Berlin to Mayrhofen in the Zillertal Valley in Tyrol, made an interesting observation in early May: "We looked into people's homes and in every window saw the almost identical scene. People were removing the swastikas from their Hitler flags. They were cutting up white bedsheets . . . Darker-coloured patches on the walls revealed how quickly wallpaper tends to fade and how large the portraits of Hitler had been. In one or the other domicile, the paterfamilias stood in front of his shaving mirror, pulling faces, as he impiously scraped his little Führer moustache from his upper lip."[14]

National Socialism disappeared like a ghost, almost overnight. Loyal supporters of the regime swiftly transformed into equally committed opponents of the same. The Berlin diarist Martha Hillers, whose anonymously published diaries created a stir in the 1950s for their descriptions of mass rapes of German women by Soviet soldiers, summarised what people were saying to one another while queuing outside shops in mid-May 1945: "Everyone is trying to get away from Adolf now, and no one was ever part of it. Everyone was persecuted, and no one denounced anyone else."[15] Victor Klemperer, who had escaped the February inferno in Dresden with his wife by fleeing to Bavaria, noted: "Now everyone here was *always* an enemy of the party.

If only they really had *always* been that . . . The Third Reich has been practically forgotten."[16] Twelve years previously, the opposite had been the case, as Friedrich Kellner recalled all too well. When Hitler had come to power in early 1933, he wrote, many Germans had tried to prove "with the most threadbare arguments" that they had "always been National Socialists."[17]

Journalists from Allied countries who reported on the destroyed Germany in the spring and summer of 1945 often asked themselves how the Nazi regime had been able to wage five and a half years of war when no Germans seemed to have supported it. The American war reporter Martha Gellhorn did not believe the stories many forlorn-looking and bitter Germans were telling her. On the contrary, she was revolted by the spectacle of "a whole nation passing the buck."[18]

Because their connection with Hitler had remained intact deep into the second half of the war, the vast majority of the German population saw 8 May 1945 as a day not of liberation but of collapse and defeat. In the initial weeks following Germany's surrender, radio and newspapers constantly reported on the horrors of the concentration and death camps. These revelations shocked victors and vanquished alike, uncovering with painful clarity what Germans had repressed in the preceding years. There was no denying the truth given the sheer amount of material documenting the Holocaust. "It is our just deserts that we are confronted every day with the horrors of the concentration camps," wrote Mathilde Wolff-Mönckeberg, the wife of Emil Wolff, the first post-war rector of Hamburg University. "We all have to bear the responsibility for these monstrous crimes, and no one should be allowed to escape it."[19]

But few Germans were truly willing to confront the horrific images and acknowledge their own complicity. Most reflexively looked the other way, just as they had during the Third Reich when faced with the suffering of their Jewish neighbours or other persecuted people. "'We didn't know anything,'" wrote *Life* magazine photographer Margaret Bourke-White in the spring of 1945. "We all got to hear these words so often and so monotonously that they seemed to us like a German national anthem."[20] Of course, any German who had wanted to find out about the Nazi crimes could have done so.[21]

At the end of October, William Shirer returned to Berlin, the city he had left as a foreign correspondent in December 1940. The immense destruction was evident from the plane as he flew in. "The great city demolished almost beyond recognition," Shirer wrote. "The center of the capital around the Leipziger Strasse and the Friedrichstrasse a vast acreage of rubble." But the journalist would soon conclude that far worse than such physical destruction was the damage National Socialism had left behind in people's minds: "They had no sense of guilt or even remorse for Germany's crime in making war and regretted merely having lost it." Most Germans defiantly protested their own innocence and sought to blame Hitler alone for Germany's defeat, as one woman Shirer met at Berlin's Press Club did. "If only Hitler had let the generals run the war," she told the journalist. "If only we had not attacked Russia, or, if after we had, you Americans had not come in to help them, we might have won and been spared this."[22]

After 1945, the myth of the Führer as saviour flipped into its absolute negative. Hitler was declared a monster, a demon in human guise whose infernal powers of seduction the German people had been helpless to resist.[23] It was a convenient way of evading accountability or having to take stock of one's own complicity in National Socialism. Even the defendants at the main war crimes trial in Nuremberg in 1945 and 1946, without exception, denied any involvement or even knowledge of the Nazi regime's crimes against humanity and tried to pass themselves off as innocent.[24]

Germans' general aversion to confronting their own history undermined all of the Allies' well-intentioned re-education programmes. The de-Nazification initiative devolved into a large-scale process of rehabilitation, in which even former regime functionaries accused of committing grave crimes got off with light sentences or no punishment at all.[25] The academic elites, who as a group had disproportionately served the Nazi regime, clamoured for the de-Nazification certificates that became known as "Persil tickets" after the brand of laundry detergent. "Almost every day I see the same thing: people coming to be rehabilitated," Klemperer wrote in a letter from Dresden in June 1946. "And all of them swear that they themselves knew nothing, nothing whatsoever, about all the horrors . . . all of them, literally all of them, have Jewish friends, if not a Jewish grandmother they risked their lives to help. It is such a pathetic bit of theatre, a miserable farce."[26]

Increasingly, Germans began to portray themselves as victims who had suffered terribly from Allied bombardments or displacement in the east. There was little interest in, to say nothing of empathy for, the suffering they had inflicted on other people. In August 1949, when Hannah Arendt returned to Germany, to the newly founded Federal Republic, for the first time since she had fled the country, she was appalled by the emotional paralysis of her former compatriots, which she saw as "only the most conspicuous outward symptom of a deep-rooted, stubborn and at times vicious refusal to face and come to terms with what really happened." "Watching the Germans busily stumble through the ruins of a thousand years of their own history," Arendt wrote, "shrugging their shoulders at the destroyed landmarks or resentful when reminded of the deeds of horror that haunt the entire world, one comes to realise that busyness has become their chief defence against reality."[27] The "inability to mourn" was how the psychoanalysts Alexander and Margarete Mitscherlich described the process of collective repression in a widely read book in 1967.[28] It was in that year that German university students began to rebel against the silence of their parents' generation and call for a re-examination of the past.

In an article for *Stars and Stripes* in early May 1945, the writer Klaus Mann, son of Thomas, asked how it had been possible that a "neurotic clown" like Hitler had obtained control over the lives of millions of people. What enabled him to do this? What was the secret of Hitler's terrible career?[29] These questions have lost none of their urgency seventy-five years later. How was it possible for a politician of Hitler's ilk to gain power in Germany, establish an unfettered dictatorship and plunge the world into an unparalleled crisis of civilisation?

Answers to such questions will always have to address the issue of Adolf Hitler as a person. What happened is unthinkable without him, and his life is a particularly vivid example of how a single individual can influence the course of history. For precisely this reason, we must keep our eyes on the personality of the man, with all his characteristic proclivities and behavioural traits yet without losing sight of the historical circumstances and conditions that allowed for his mercurial rise.

In *Mein Kampf*, that avowal of faith he published in 1925 and 1926, Hitler stylised his years in Vienna and Munich before 1914 into a prelude, a school of hard knocks which his historical calling required him, an unfairly neglected artistic genius, to complete.[30] The reality is that absolutely nothing in the first thirty years of Hitler's life suggested that he was destined for an extraordinary career. On the contrary, the man who returned to Munich as a humble private from the First World War in November 1918 was a failure in many respects— a shy eccentric without a degree or a trained career and without any social contacts. In short, he was a nobody who seemed headed for anything but a glorious future.[31]

But while Hitler's entry onto the political stage following the First World War was inauspicious, within four years, he succeeded in becoming the undisputed leader of the nationalist, ethnically chauvinist right wing in Bavaria—someone who dared grasp for power in November 1923 at the side of former general Erich Ludendorff, Germany's *de facto* dictator in the final years of the First World War. This phenomenal rise would have been impossible had Hitler not possessed some extraordinary talents other populist agitators in the early 1920s lacked. First and foremost, there was his speaking ability. Hitler's discovery of his power as an orator in the autumn of 1919 can be considered his central "breakthrough" as a politician.[32] He was incomparably skilled at pulling the strings of his listeners' emotions and successful at playing on not only their fears and resentments, but also their hopes and desires. For the historian Ludolf Herbst he was a "virtuoso at reeling people in."[33]

Hitler hit a nerve not only with *what* he said, but *how* he said it. The agitated state into which he regularly worked himself seemed genuine and authentic, and his audience overlooked his tendency to play loose with the facts and interpret them in extremely idiosyncratic ways. He was interested not in the truth of his statements, but in whether they produced the maximum effect. Right from the beginning Hitler was a master of lies and deceit. The Foreign Ministry official Ernst von Weizsäcker was correct of both the later and the early Hitler when he wrote in retrospect: "He had no relationship to the truth of what had been. It seemed that, to suit his needs, he could forget some facts while convincing himself of others."[34]

Hitler combined his speaking talent with a sophisticated sense of effective staging, for magical settings and light effects. The historian Wolfram Pyta has convincingly shown how well Hitler was served by his detailed knowledge of the overwhelming spectacle of Wagner's musical dramas from his time in Vienna.[35] It helped that Hitler himself was gifted with considerable talent as an actor. Early on, he trained himself to switch from one role to another and adapt flexibly to differing environments.[36] This made him better able to cope with the demands of the media than his political competitors. He was a modern type of politician who had mastered different roles and could coolly calculate how to use them towards his ends. Thus he was able to entrance not just his supporters but his detractors too. The more intoxicating the enthusiasm he unleashed in the major public halls of Munich, the greater became his confidence and sense of being chosen for a special historic mission.

Hitler, however, was not only a persuasive mass orator and a chameleon-like actor. He also possessed an often underappreciated talent for organisation. There can be no doubt that without him the NSDAP would have remained one of many small sects in the racist subculture of Germany after the First World War. After its reconstitution in 1925, the party was very much his work and oriented itself around him as its sacrosanct Führer. He alone possessed the authority to hold together the heterogeneous ideological elements within National Socialism and form the NSDAP and its ancillary organisations into a cohesive movement. His term of imprisonment in Landsberg after the failed Beer Hall Putsch, during which the party quickly fell apart into rival factions, made it abundantly clear how crucial he was as a figure of integration. After his release from prison, with great tactical skill and persuasive power, he was able to best all potential competitors for the party leadership and completely subjugate the NSDAP to his will.

In his second bid for power too, from 1930 to 1933, Hitler was the one pulling all the strings. It was he who decided that the party would pursue a strategy of seeming to obey the law and who did not shy back from taking on rebellious forces in the SA to push through his ideas. Nevertheless, as we saw in the first volume of this biography, the path to 30 January 1933 was no simple victory parade. There were many miscalculations and setbacks. By insisting that he be appointed chancellor by the president, Hitler had steered the party into a seeming dead end by November 1932. The fact that Hitler ultimately achieved his goal, despite his missteps, was down less to his allegedly infallible political intuition than to nefarious manoeuvring behind the scenes, with Hindenburg's protégé Franz von Papen playing a lead role.

While Hitler's conservative coalition partners in the "Cabinet of National Concentration" believed that they could harness Hitler and his movement for their reactionary ends, after only a few weeks the Nazi leader shook off all attempts at "taming" him and began removing, one by one, all barriers to his dictatorial ambitions. In the tempestuous process of seizing and consolidating power, Hitler remained in charge, unscrupulously exploiting unforeseen events like the Reichstag fire of late February 1933. Moreover, just as he did with his conservative coalition partners, in his foreign policy Hitler successfully played a game of deceit and catching his opponents unawares. All in all, it is difficult not to agree with the historian Hans-Ulrich Wehler, who ascribed to Hitler a "standout ability" that made him one of Europe's "most cold-blooded, cunning and single-minded professional politicians."[37] This assessment contradicts many scholars' tendency to dismiss Hitler as a mediocre figure of limited intellectual gifts. In so doing, they make the same mistake that led many of Hitler's contemporaries to fatally underestimate him.

The system of rule Hitler established was also inseparable from himself as a person. Under an extreme monocratic summit in the form of the Führer, a polycracy of various ruling cliques competed for influence and power. "It is part and parcel of authoritarian regimes," Ernst von Weizsäcker wrote in December 1940, "that everything presses toward the *one* peak, causing a free-for-all, in which everyone steps on others' toes."[38] By feeding rivalries according to the divide-and-conquer principle and encouraging the creation of special regime agencies parallel to traditional government departments, Hitler was able to play potential competitors against one another and secure unlimited power. "We suffer from a complete lack of hierarchies of responsibility," Goebbels was still complaining in June 1943. "If only the Führer would take a few decisions!"[39] The propaganda minister failed to recognise that he was criticising something Hitler deliberately intended. The impenetrable tangle of competing responsibilities and jurisdictions in the Third Reich did not reflect weakness at the top: it was the product of a consciously chosen strategy for maintaining power. It kept Hitler out of the wrangling between his paladins, meaning he only had to intervene when a decision from him became absolutely necessary.

All that increased rather than limited the regime's efficiency because it created constant competition below the level of the Führer and encouraged functionaries to anticipate the supreme leader's will, start their own initiatives and in some cases trump one another with greater radicalism. "You know that it is not presumptuousness or vanity if I say there is hardly anyone else in Germany who has so constantly acted in the interests of the Führer," the state secretary in the Agriculture Ministry, Herbert Backe, wrote to his wife in April 1941.[40] Backe was one of those responsible for the murderous "hunger plan" that foresaw the deaths of millions of people in the occupied parts of the Soviet Union.

Germany's path into the Second World War also completely followed Hitler's ideas. It was the Führer who forced through the transition from a policy of revising the Treaty of Versailles to one of expansionism in 1937. Part of his rationale was personal. He feared that like his parents he would not live to old age, and he was determined to lead the planned war for "living space" himself. Hitler's obsessive worry with running out of time accelerated the belligerence of the Third Reich.[41] It is entirely possible that an authoritarian military regime—seemingly the only possible alternative to Hitler's dictatorship in 1933—would also have eventually engaged in an armed conflict with Poland. After all, the desire to regain the eastern territories Germany had lost in the Treaty of Versailles also ran strong among the country's generals. But Hitler was the one who ordered an unprecedented radicalisation of warfare the moment he authorised the attack on Poland. And the brutality was only increased with Operation Barbarossa, which in keeping with the dictator's wishes was run as a unique racist-ideological campaign of annihilation. Hitler's plans, of course, elicited no significant resistance from his military leadership. On the contrary, his generals fell over themselves trying to translate his directives into military orders that would conform ideologically to the dictator's world view.

It was also Hitler who ultimately determined the tempo and direction of the regime's anti-Semitic policies—from the first anti-Jewish measures in the spring of 1933 to the final homicidal quantum leap of the systematic destruction of Europe's Jews that commenced in 1941. Without Hitler, this much is certain, there would have been no Holocaust. His fanatical anti-Semitism was the engine driving genocide.

While it may have been difficult to tell sometimes when Hitler was play-acting, the Führer was always deadly serious when he vented his maniacal hatred of Jews. From his Spandau Prison cell, Albert Speer remembered one characteristic scene. On a walk together to the teahouse on the Obersalzberg in the second half of November 1942, by which point the Holocaust was well underway, Hitler suddenly began yelling: "We will get our hands on them! Then we will settle accounts! Then they will find out who I really am! This time none of them will escape! I have always been too kind-hearted! Not any more! Now it is time to settle accounts!" He had never realised, Speer commented, "how much Hitler needed the figure of the Jew—it was both an object of hatred and a vanishing point."[42]

All the way back in his first written ideological statement as a Munich rabble-rouser in September 1919, Hitler had insisted on "the complete removal of the Jews" as essential, and he never gave up this goal as long as he lived. In 1939 "removal" still meant social exclusion and displacement, not physical annihilation. Only after Germany's occupation of Poland and its invasion of the Soviet Union did geno- cide become an option. The search for a written command by Hitler ordering the Holocaust is a pointless exercise. As we have seen, it was his style of leadership to express decisions of fundamental scope in terms of general wishes, which were then to be translated into concrete instructions by the executors of his policies. We should not forget that this abominable crime against humanity could not have been carried out without the participation of hundreds of thousands of ready helpers.

That fact underlines an important point. The "Hitler phenomenon" is not merely the sum of his thoughts and deeds: it can only be under- stood by simultaneously examining the social pathology of German society at the time. Only the reciprocal influence between individual and collective sensitivities and neuroses can explain Hitler's otherwise baffling rise and his undeniably massive appeal. That is already true for the beginning of his political career. In his prophetic book *Germany: Jekyll & Hyde*, Sebastian Haffner wrote in 1940 that it was a tragic coincidence that Hitler's "personal plight coincided so much with the German plight in 1919."[43] Indeed, the frustration of the young failed individual dovetailed with the traumas of the wartime and post-war generations, and when they came together they released tremendous destructive energy, without which it is impossible to understand the later crimes of National Socialism.

In the first volume of this biography we saw how important the far-right scene in Munich was to Hitler's political beginnings in 1919. The tumultuous weeks of counter-revolution against the Bavarian Soviet Republic offered a perfect platform for the no-holds-barred demagoguery of this instinctive populist. There was an extensive network of counter-revolutionary military men, racist writers and publishers, and far-right associations. In this unique biotope, National Socialism quickly blossomed into a movement, benevolently tolerated by the Bavarian police and courts. In the upper-class salons of the Bruckmanns and Hanfstaengls, the rising star of the Munich political scene soon found influential patrons who introduced him to respectable society and supported him financially.[44] From the very start, Hitler had no qualms about using violence as a means of political struggle. The paramilitary units under him included not only frontline veterans who had become accustomed to killing in the war and had continued their homicidal activities in Freikorps militias, but also members of a younger generation who as teenagers had been brutalised by the war and were now willing to attack political adversaries in the most vicious ways.[45]

The reciprocal influence between Hitler and German society was even more evident in the years of his breakthrough to power. As Max Weber knew, one of the preconditions for the rise of a charismatic politician is an existential crisis that disrupts conventional thinking. The onset of the Great Depression in 1929 and 1930 created precisely such a situation. The depression hit Germany particularly hard, and the consequences were more severe because it coincided with the political crisis of the Weimar Republic and the collapse of democratic institutions. Hitler was the main beneficiary of this dual economic and political emergency. Conversely, he was better able than any of his contemporaries to portray himself as a messiah and mobilise the German public's manifold hopes for salvation. He was capable of tapping into mass psychological and psychosocial dispositions and needs like the desire for a strong leader—a "second Bismarck" who promised to overcome the crisis and lead Germany to new greatness—that were deeply anchored in post-war German political culture. At the same time, however, he exploited the longing for a synthesis of nationalism and socialism, expressed in the attractive slogan of an "ethnic-popular community" that promised to put an end to the class conflicts and party squabbling of the Weimar Republic.[46]

Hitler would not have been able to sell himself so effectively if there had not been social demand for someone of his ilk and if a broad swathe of the population had not been receptive to his message and promises. At the same time, we should remember that the NSDAP never received an absolute majority in free elections. Its best showing of 37.3 per cent of the vote came in the Reichstag elections of late July 1932. The following November, for the first time in party history when running on its own, it suffered significant losses. Hitler's nimbus as the German people's coming saviour seemed to be paling. It is a bitter irony of German history that the leader of the NSDAP came to power at a point when the worst of the economic crisis was over and his movement was in decline. What sealed Germany's fate was a camarilla around Hindenburg that believed Hitler was so "cosseted" in the Cabinet of National Concentration as to tame his ambitions to power and control the dynamic of his movement. This was an enormous mistake, as would soon become apparent.

By comparison, the influence of powerful interest groups on Hitler being named chancellor has sometimes been overestimated. The chairman of the Nazi Party was not the painstakingly built-up candidate of big money, as Marxist historians liked to depict him, and the NSDAP's breakthrough as a mass movement cannot be explained by financial assistance from big industry. The party financed most of its campaigns on its own. Before 1933, the majority of business leaders in the Rhine and Ruhr valleys took a reserved, wait-and-see attitude towards Hitler, not least because there was great uncertainty as to what Nazi economic policies actually entailed. Only after 30 January of that year did they quickly change course and began to curry favour with the new chancellor.[47] More significant in the final act of the drama of how Hitler was enthroned was the influence of the large landowners in eastern Germany via their lobby organisation, the Agricultural League. Exploiting their privileged access to President Hindenburg, they undermined the position of the last chancellor of the Weimar Republic, Kurt von Schleicher, paving the way for Hitler to take over that office.

One of the most astonishing aspects of Hitler's biography is the rapidity with which he was able to establish a dictatorship once he was in control of the levers of power. It only took him one and a half years to get rid of or neutralise all rival sources of power. Intimidation and terror, above all against the left, of course played a role. But Germany could not have been so quickly and easily Nazified had there not been widespread willingness to be brought into line among almost all German institutions. Moreover, the cultish worship of Hitler, already extreme in 1933, was not solely the work of the master propagandist Joseph Goebbels, who ensured that the Führer was continually featured in the state-directed media. On the contrary, Hitler voters and followers themselves contributed to the pseudo-religious elevation of the dictator by projecting all their expectations and desires onto him. Many Germans would have agreed with the hysterical raptures of Hans Frank, later governor-general of Poland, who in 1937 wrote in his diary about visiting a Berlin Philharmonic concert directed by Wilhelm Furtwängler, at which Hitler had been in the spotlight. "Oh, God! How happy you have made us that we can call the single greatest man in world history our *own!*" Frank gushed. "Generations will come and envy us for having been his contemporaries."[48] The myth of the Führer fulfilled an important integrating function within the Nazi system and would prove the strongest point of adhesion deep into the war years.[49] People believed that the chancellor of the "new Germany" was capable of performing miracles. Criticism of the regime's negative aspects, particularly rampant corruption, was reserved for subordinate leaders, the so-called brown bigwigs. As a rule, Hitler was exempted from expressions of discontent.

The question of how much support Hitler and his regime enjoyed cannot be easily answered. There were no independent opinion polls, and results of 90 per cent and more regularly achieved in plebiscites are of course no reliable indication of the actual public mood. At the same time, after getting rid of mass unemployment with unexpected speed through rearmament and racking up some sensational foreign policy victories, Hitler doubtlessly succeeded in uniting a large majority behind him. Even in traditionally Social Democratic and communist parts of society, which had not embraced the Nazis before 1933 and had often battled in the streets against them, Hitler's popularity grew. The reports of the Social Democratic Party leadership-in-exile, based on information from observers within the Third Reich, are a reliable source in this regard. Sebastian Haffner too recalled that "anyone in 1938 who said a critical word about Hitler in circles where such criticism used to be possible would inevitably be told, sooner or later: 'But think of everything he has accomplished!'"[50]

Yet to characterise the Third Reich, with Götz Aly, as a "dictatorship of pleasing the people" is to underestimate the extent of coercion and oppression characteristic of the regime from its very inception. Given the great consensus between Hitler and large segments of German society, at least between 1933 and 1939, it seems more accurate to call it a "dictatorship of consent."[51] The Führer and his paladins were at pains to enlist popular feelings and moods, and to this end they offered a cornucopia of populist measures: tax relief for families, loans for newly-weds, child support, raising the tax threshold and so on.[52] Spouting slogans such as "Full steam ahead for hardworking people," the Nazis claimed to promote mass upward social mobility. Of course, the much-touted "ethnic-popular community" in the Third Reich was more a promise than a social reality, but one of the main attractions of National Socialism remained the idea of greater equality of opportunity and social justice. The price, of course, was the exclusion of all "ethnically foreign elements."

Into the first years of war, Hitler and the Nazi regime tried to keep the burdens they placed on the population as light as possible. This was inspired by the trauma of the revolution of November 1918, a repetition of which had to be avoided at all costs. But popular support for the regime began to crumble with military setbacks, especially the Stalingrad debacle, and the increasingly tangible effects of the Allied bombing raids. Even Hitler's popularity gradually began to decay, although the myth of the Führer never fully lost its integrative force and even surged briefly after the failed assassination attempt of 20 July 1944.[53] People did not distance themselves from Nazism in spectacular protest actions, but rather silently by internally renouncing their bonds of loyalty with the regime.[54] It helped that after the turn in Germany's military fortunes, the dictator appeared increasingly rarely in public. For most Germans, the once omnipresent Führer became a phantom.

Thus, by the time the Allies occupied Germany in the spring of 1945, a process of social "self-de-Nazification" had already commenced.

Even glowing Hitler followers turned away from the regime. "It seems calamitous to me that criticism now no longer stops before the Führer, the National Socialist idea or the National Socialist movement. Even many comrades are now starting to waver," Goebbels had to admit in late March 1945.[55]

Nonetheless, there was an astonishing amount of perseverance in the Wehrmacht and among the population throughout the final death agonies of the Third Reich.[56] The main reason was apparently the sheer fear that the crimes of war, genocide and occupation would rebound on the German people themselves. But Germans also continued to be fixated on their Führer. That is the only explanation for why the dictator, who ended his days as a limping wreck in an underground bunker complex, still exerted a magnetic force on those around him and could get others, even in his final hours, to follow his orders. "A geriatric figure, hunched and speaking in a dull voice, but still at the centre of everything that happened" was how Albert Speer remembered Hitler twenty years on from the final days in the bunker.[57]

Did Hitler's dictatorship represent a continuity or a radical break in German history? This question has been the subject of heated debate. Allied propaganda before and after 1945 tended to depict the Third Reich as the logical extension of an essentially flawed German *Sonderweg*, or abnormal path, through history. "Hitler is no accident," concluded Sir Robert Vansittart, chief diplomatic adviser to the British government, in 1941. "He is the natural and continuous product of a breed which from the dawn of history has been predatory and belli-cose."[58] The historian A. J. P. Taylor's *The Course of German History*, which was published immediately after the war and soon became a kind of Bible for the first generation of occupation officers, also treated the German national character as fundamentally rapacious and war-loving.[59] Long lines of continuity between Martin Luther, Friedrich the Great and Hitler became a popular trope, and when he published *The Rise and Fall of the Third Reich* in 1960, William Shirer could not resist constructing another such genealogy. That book's fourth chapter, "The Mind of Hitler and the Roots of the Third Reich," also reached back into history to identify the allegedly formative influence of Luther and Prussian militarism and concluded: "The mind and the passion of

Hitler—all the aberrations that possessed his feverish brain—had roots that lay deep in German experience and thought. Nazism and the Third Reich, in fact, were but a logical continuation of German history."[60]

Conversely, a great many German historians and writers after 1945 were eager to present Hitler as an invasive element from a foreign culture that had overwhelmed German society seemingly out of nowhere. "This person is not actually part of our race," the historian Otto Hintze told his colleague Friedrich Meinecke. "There is something foreign about him, like an extinct prehistoric race of people that was completely amoral."[61] In his much-praised 1958 book, *The History of Germany since 1789*, Golo Mann also treated Hitler as an entity foreign to Germany, describing him as an "alien" and a "vagabond," and going so far as to refuse to write out his name, instead referring to him merely as "H."[62] In later years, Mann would continue such efforts to symbolically expatriate the dictator. In a letter to the editor of the *Frankfurter Allgemeine Zeitung*, Joachim Fest, in November 1986, the seventy-seven-year-old was still proposing that Hitler was "not at all a typical German" but rather someone "essentially without a homeland who came from no man's land."[63] By contrast, with his far keener eye, Thomas Mann had characterised Hitler as "a truly German phenomenon" as long ago as October 1937.[64]

If Hitler had arrived like an extraterrestrial to conquer the German people, so the logic ran, then his dictatorship was not anchored in German social history, and his rise to power in 1933 would have to be seen as a kind of unfortunate accident. Such apologetic interpretations remained in vogue for an astonishingly long time. As recently as 1999, the former mayor of Hamburg, Klaus von Dohnanyi, the son of resistance figure Hans von Dohnanyi, dismissed Hitler as an "Austrian accident on Prussian soil."[65] In a similar vein, in 1996 the historian Eberhard Jäckel compared Hitler's ascent to power to a "maximum credible accident" in a nuclear power station.[66]

Today's historical profession has disabused itself of dubious explanatory paradigms of both sorts. Hitler was neither the inevitable outcome of a baneful German historical destiny nor a regrettable accident suddenly visited upon Germans like a natural disaster.[67] In many areas, Hitler was able to adopt what others had thought and done during Germany's imperial era, but he always radicalised what he inherited and took it to extremes. Good examples are the German aspirations for hegemony in continental Europe that had led the Imperial German government to risk world war in 1914 or the anti-democratic, anti-Western resentment that engendered among many German elites a hateful enmity to the Weimar Republic as a form of state allegedly foreign to the German nature and imposed by the victors of the First World War. Most prominently, such influences applied to the two core elements of Hitler's world view: his anti-Semitism and his demand for German "living space" in eastern Europe.

In his post-war historical rumination *The German Catastrophe*, Friedrich Meinecke identified the rise of anti-Semitic movements in the 1880s as a "first warning sign" and a "minor prelude to Hitler's later successes."[68] Although the influence of anti-Semitic parties had diminished by 1914 in Wilhelmine Germany, anti-Jewish sentiment continued to spread in large sections of the old *Mittelstand*, Germany's rural population and, more surprisingly, among educated people. It was also far more virulent in aristocratic Wilhelmine society than historians long thought. The writings of racist hate-mongers such as Paul de Lagarde, Theodor Fritsch or Houston Stewart Chamberlain stigmatised Germany's Jewish minority as a dangerous "foreign entity" that needed to be surgically removed from Imperial Germany's economy and society. Particularly significant in spreading racist anti-Semitism was the influence of the Pan-German League, the most radical nationalist organisation in Wilhelmine Germany. In his widely read pamphlet of 1912, "If I Were the Kaiser," league chairman Heinrich Class demanded that Germany close its borders to further Jewish immigration, that Jews living in Germany who did not yet possess German citizenship be deported, and that those who were German citizens be stripped of their right to vote and subjected to special laws governing foreigners.[69]

Anti-Jewish resentment became more radical during the First World War and began to affect government policy. In October 1916, the Prussian Ministry of War ordered a "Jewish census" in the army after anti-Semites spread the completely unjustified accusation that Jews were shirking military service in large numbers. The founding in 1917 of the German Fatherland Party, the first pre-fascist mass movement in Germany, gave radical anti-Semites an extended platform for increas-ingly no-holds-barred agitation.[70] By the end of the war, the situation was becoming directly threatening for Germany's Jewish minority, with the Pan-German League and far-right circles determined to make Jews into scapegoats for the country's military defeat. He would "not shy back from any means" to advance his ends, Class declared, employing a phrase by the Romantic writer Heinrich von Kleist, originally referring to Napoleon's soldiers 100 years earlier: "Smite them dead! The Last Judgement will not ask you the reasons why."[71]

Jews and the radical left were now conflated into the single *bête noire* of "Jewish Bolshevism." Hitler did not need to invent this hybrid enemy, which was already firmly anchored in the minds of conservative counter-revolutionaries in 1918–19. On 11 November 1918 in Berlin, the navy officer Bogislav von Selchow wrote in his diary: "This morning I went to the Reich Navy Office, which was flying a red flag. In front of the building, a Jewish Bolshevik in civilian dress was standing guard with a rifle." Four days later he noted: "Jews and deserters, a mob that is nothing other than the gutter in the worst sense of the word, now rule Germany. But the hour of retribution will come to the Jews, and then woe unto them!"[72] With Germany stunned by military defeat and revolution, pre-war anti-Semitism was augmented with fantasies of revenge and annihilation, which in turn gave birth to the wish to expel Jews from German society using whatever means necessary.

In September 1919, Victor Klemperer complained about "the horrible anti-Jewish hate-mongering that is being practised in shameless and threatening fashion all over Germany." Such "insane incitements to hatred" were influencing even educated circles. "It is terrible," Klemperer wrote. "Jews are to blame for everything: the war, the revolution, Bolshevism, capitalism, everything."[73] The anti-Semitic hothouse of the reactionary counter-revolution in Munich was where Hitler began his political career in 1919, and like a sponge he soaked up the anti-Jewish sentiments circulating there. He also availed himself of the arsenal of clichés and stereotypes provided by jingoistic and racist authors like Ernst Moritz Arndt and Julius Langbehn from the early nineteenth century onwards. What distinguished Hitler from his predecessors and contemporaries was less the radicalism with which he insisted on his stated goal of "removing" Jews from Germany than his iron will to make this goal a reality once he had obtained power. After 1933, one by one, the constraints that had protected German Jews from social marginalisation and persecution disappeared. Hitler was serious about doing what others had mentally thought out—right down to the ultimate homicidal stage of physically destroying European Jews.

Hitler's demand for the conquest of "living space" in eastern Europe was equally unoriginal. The idea that the German people, given the size of their population, had too little room to live and would need to settle territories in Russia was common among pre-1914 pan-German and racist ideologues. During the First World War, this perspective also gained influence on government policy. In the notorious war aims programme of early September 1914, Chancellor Theobald von Bethmann Hollweg insisted that Russia had to be "pushed back from its border with Germany and its rule over non-Russian vassal peoples broken."[74] After Germany's victories on the eastern front the following summer, plans to carve up the "eastern realm" anew commenced in practice. Lithuania and Courland were placed under direct German military administration as "land of the supreme commander east." Here, Erich Ludendorff—who together with Hindenburg would become the head of the Army Supreme Command and the most powerful figure in the military leadership from August 1916—was allowed to subjugate an occupied territory in line with his Pan-German, racist ideas of long-term German domination. "Here we have won breeding grounds for people who we need for further battles in the east," Ludendorff wrote in late December 1915 to the historian Hans Delbrück. "And such battles will come, unavoidably."[75]

After the October Revolution in Russia in 1917, which Germany had supported as much as it could, the military and political leadership of the Wilhelmine Reich thought they had achieved their ends and concluded a separate peace with the new Soviet government at Brest-Litovsk on 3 March 1918. "It was a peace of conquest and violence unparalleled in recent history," the historian Heinrich August Winkler has written.[76] The great eastern European power, the former Romanov Empire, saw its borders pushed back to where they had been before Peter the Great. It lost a third of its population—around fifty million people—as well as much of its natural resources and industrial capacity. As if that were not enough, German troops exploited the beginnings of the Russian Civil War to continue their advance, pushing forward into Ukraine and on to the Donets basin, conquering Crimea and reaching the Caucasus. In other words, they got almost as far as Hitler's soldiers did in the Second World War.[77] With Germany's defeat on the western front in 1918, the dream of a gigantic "eastern empire" burst like a bubble, but this episode made a deep mark on the imagination of Germany's military leaders as well as Private Hitler. They were convinced that Bolshevik Russia was a colossus with feet of clay that only needed a slight push to collapse. There is a direct line from Ludendorff's plans for ruling occupied territories in eastern Europe to Hitler's "living space" project. The difference was Hitler's infinite hunger for territory and the criminal energy with which he pursued his racist goals. The war of annihilation Hitler waged on the Soviet Union exploded the framework of Wilhelmine imperial power politics and entailed a new dimension of violence.

The historian Fritz Fischer's words marking the centenary of Hitler's birth on 20 April 1989 remain true today: "Hitler came from neither heaven nor hell and was not an 'avoidable accident.' In terms of the conditions that enabled him to have the effect he had, he should be seen as deeply connected to nineteenth- and twentieth-century German history."[78] On the other hand, Hitler went far beyond the cultural universe from where he came. The genocidal ideological fanaticism that drove him and the monstrous crimes that resulted were without precedent. Hitler's dictatorship thus represented both a continuity in German history and a fundamental caesura.

"If ever a person grew thanks to success but also possessed the gift of growing with that success, it is Hitler," wrote Konrad Heiden in the second volume of his Hitler biography, published in Zurich in 1937. "The rising pillar of fortune lifted him along with it, expanding his vision and the reach of his voice. Only when he had success did his personality gain full momentum."[79] At that point, the dictator could in fact look back on a remarkable record. He had taken over the NSDAP at the humblest of beginnings, formed it into a powerful mass organisation and led it to power despite a variety of resistance. By forcing through Germany's rearmament, he had eradicated mass unemployment and brought about a kind of "economic miracle." And one by one he got rid of the restrictions imposed on Germany by the Treaty of Versailles and re-established the country as a major power. With the amalgamation of Austria and the annexation of the Czech border region in 1938, Hitler's winning streak continued. "There is no end to the amazement," gushed Marianne von

Weizsäcker, the wife of the state secretary in the Foreign Office, in March 1939 after the break-up of the remaining Czech parts of Czechoslovakia. "Our historical atlas lies permanently open, and you can see how the great German Reich of Charles IV is suddenly springing back to life." A few days later, she found herself "deeply happy" about the return of the Memel region: "It constantly astonishes how non-violently and smoothly everything is proceeding. Success breeds success."[80]

Certainly, Hitler benefited from the circumstances of his day. Weimar democracy was on its last legs, undermined by presidentially appointed governments from Brüning to Schleicher, and was ripe for the National Socialists to put it out of its misery. By the end of 1932, the worst of the depression was over so that the rapid economic recovery that followed under the Nazis was in truth anything but a miracle. Moreover, the system created by the Treaty of Versailles was already crumbling before Hitler buried it once and for all. At the same time, Hitler profited from being perennially underestimated—and not only by his conservative coalition partners. Western statesmen comforted themselves with the illusion that Nazi Germany could be bound by treaties into a system of collective European security and that Hitler's aggression could be curbed. In addition, more than a few representatives of the British aristocracy felt great affinities with the "strongman" of the Third Reich and fell over themselves to pay their respects to him.[81]

Some not insignificant reasons for Hitler's successes resided in his own personality. The dictator had a keen nose for his enemies' weak spots and had no scruples about exploiting them. He also had a deft sense of the right moment, which he seized in lightning-like strikes. In the process he showed an enormous willingness to take risks, such as ordering German troops to march into the demilitarised Rhineland in March 1936. His proclivity for going for broke was an integral feature of his political career from its very inception, and he would not change even after a series of impressive triumphs gave him something to lose. But by violating the Munich Agreement in March 1939 he crossed a line. Anyone in London who wishfully believed an arrangement could be reached with the German dictator found themselves rudely awakened. Appeasement was at an end, replaced by a British readiness to go to war with Hitler's Germany if necessary.

Hitler's luck continued with his initial military endeavours. After the conquest of Poland, the occupation of Denmark and Norway and the defeat of France, he seemed unstoppable. But for the first time he also faced a serious adversary in Winston Churchill. The new British prime minister clearly recognised that it was impossible to negotiate in any form with Hitler. He believed that the only way to deal with this "monster of wickedness, insatiable in his lust for blood and plunder" was to put him down like a rabid dog.[82] Britain's decision in the summer of 1940 to fight on alone was the end of Hitler's winning streak. The zenith of his career had been reached.

In *Defying Hitler*, Sebastian Haffner proposed an interesting thought experiment. What would have happened, he asked, if after his victory in the west, Hitler had been content with what he had achieved, offered France a mild peace settlement and convened a congress that could have led to a European league of nations?[83] Yet such a scenario, Haffner admitted, was utterly implausible. Hitler could not begin to conceive of a Europe, even under German hegemony, that was united in fairness and partnership. In December 1942, when the "Führer" of the National Socialist movement in the Netherlands, Anton Mussert, proposed a "league of Germanic nations," Hitler brushed off the idea, saying that it would not provide the necessary stability. Instead, he said, he was striving for a "secure, completely solid structure to withstand the future storms from the east."[84] For Hitler, the occupied countries were only means to the end of increasing his own potential for power and war. Accordingly, they were subjected to unfettered economic exploitation and, wherever people refused to cooperate, brutal political terror.[85]

The concept of a peaceful European order also contradicted Hitler's unwritten law of keeping things in flux and avoiding fixed commitments. Just as he refused domestically to write a new German constitution or clearly define areas of responsibility, there could be no stop to Germany's external expansion. The Greater German Reich he had created by 1938 was nothing more than a springboard for a still larger "Greater Germanic Reich," which was in turn just a preliminary step towards world domination. In early July 1940, after his triumphant return to Berlin following Germany's western victory, he expounded to Goebbels upon his idea for the future reordering of Europe. "It will be a Germanic Reich without borders," he told the propaganda minister.[86] For this reason, Hitler also left open where the war for "living space" in the east, which he began preparing later that month, would actually end. In a speech to the Reichsleiters and Gauleiters in early October 1942, he told his audience that the war was "about the expansion of our living space in the broadest sense." Germany had set itself a goal, he added, "whose significance will extend over centuries."[87]

For a short moment—in late June and early July 1941, when the first great cauldron battles seemed to have brought the Soviet Union to the verge of collapse—Hitler believed he was close to achieving his goals. "Our successes so far in this theatre have been enormous," Munich historian Karl Alexander von Müller wrote to his Königsberg colleague Theodor Schieder. "What you hear about our plans for a reordering are of a dimension that can make you dizzy."[88] In his monologues in his headquarters, Hitler left no doubt that this reordering of eastern Europe involved the enslavement, displacement and liquidation of millions of civilians. But just as he had been underestimated by his adversaries for so long, now he and the German military command failed to appreciate the Soviet capacity for resistance. It remains a unique historical achievement of the Red Army that it struck the decisive blows against the seemingly invincible Wehrmacht. With the failure of Operation Barbarossa and the United States' entry into the war in December 1941, the basis was removed from Hitler's entire strategy. By the summer and autumn of 1942, with the failure of the second attempt to force a decision in the east before the full might of the American war potential could be brought to bear, Germany's ultimate defeat was sealed.

All the factors that worked in Hitler's favour for so long and helped him achieve his unexpected triumphs now swung round to his detriment. In the very moment when he overplayed his hand and lost the game, his instinctive sense for his enemies' weak spots also disappeared. Whereas earlier, despite his intense fixation on his ultimate goals, he had always shown a remarkable tactical flexibility, his war strategy now ossified into an unimaginative holding of territory at all costs, which drew criticism from his military commanders. "Tactics is not an art that consists solely of ordering 'Stay put and let yourself be killed,'" Field Marshal von Kluge wrote in a private letter in December 1942.[89] Nonetheless it would be false, as many former Wehrmacht generals did in their post-1945 memoirs, to reduce Hitler's role as military commander to the rigid defensive strategy of the final years of the war, thus portraying the Führer as a hopeless military dilettante. The historian Bernd Wegner has rightly stressed that, compared to Germany's professional military leaders, Hitler possessed a "much more modern and complex understanding of war and a keener sense of the demands of war on all of society."[90] The dictator was forever complaining that his generals understood nothing of the economy of war. Precisely because Hitler thought in larger contexts, he realised earlier than his military advisers, who were fixated on the operational side, that after the failures of 1942 the war could no longer be won. He was unable, however, to draw the logical conclusions from this insight. His rigid orders to hold territory and the nonsensical attempts to turn the tide with the Battle of Kursk in 1943 and the Battle of the Bulge the following year reflected the mentality of the all-or-nothing gambler who had always played for high stakes and could never imagine folding. Unable to change himself, he constantly sought to blame others for setbacks, which caused the personnel carousel at the top of the Wehrmacht to spin ever faster.

Hitler displayed the same inflexibility in the field of diplomacy. Whereas during the 1930s, the dictator had always come up with manoeuvres to extract himself from diplomatic dead ends, he developed no initiatives whatsoever for a negotiated end to the war. No doubt most of the Nazi leadership realised that with the war in the east, which violated all the norms of international law, and the parallel genocide of Jews, the Third Reich had burned its bridges. "[We are] so committed . . . on the Jewish question that there is no escape for us," Göring and Goebbels agreed in early March 1943.[91] Germany's options were thus reduced to total victory or total demise. "Everyone in Germany must understand that this war is a battle for existence or non-existence," Hitler stressed to the Reichsleiters and Gauleiters in April 1944. "In certain situations, the creed has to be 'Exterminate, so that you yourself will not be exterminated!' "[92]

An inveterate high-stakes gambler, Hitler knew that for himself the only option would be suicide should the war be lost. The more hopeless Germany's situation became, the more his thoughts focused on how to stage his downfall most effectively, in the style of Wagner's *Twilight of the Gods*.[93] Hitler was obsessed with the choreography of "glorious defeat" right down to his final days while at the same time maintaining a façade of unshakable faith in victory towards those around him. Speer recalled Hitler talking himself into a state of "self-hypnotic euphoria" in situation meetings in the spring of 1945, invoking the precedent of Friedrich the Great, whom he increasingly sought to imitate. Speer quoted the dictator as saying: "He did not earn the sobriquet 'Great' because he achieved victory in the end but because he remained courageous in the face of adversity. In exactly the same fashion, posterity will see my significance not primarily in the triumphs of the first years of war, but in the resolve I have shown after the grave setbacks of the past months. The will, gentlemen, always triumphs."[94]

In February 1945, Hitler's chief propagandist and most fervent disciple, Joseph Goebbels, could still write: "I am convinced that the Führer will go down in history as the man of the century."[95] The Hitler opponent Klaus Mann, however, opened his post-mortem analysis of Hitler in May 1945 by asserting that the dictator was "not great in any respect" despite the great power he had achieved. "Although he lacked stature and genius," Mann wrote, "he was able to terrorise a whole continent and challenge the entire civilised world."[96]

Historians have always struggled with the question of Hitler's "greatness." For Alan Bullock in the early 1950s, the catastrophe that ended the Third Reich did not itself negate Hitler's claims to greatness as much as the fact that he was motivated by base emotions like "hatred, resentment, the lust to dominate, and, where he could not dominate, destroy." Hitler's reign, Bullock argued, was about nothing other than increasing his own power, which is what had made him "so repellent and so barren a figure." Bullock wrote: "Hitler will have his place in history, but it will be alongside Attila the Hun, the barbarian king who was surnamed, not 'the Great,' but 'the Scourge of God.'"[97]

"History as we know it contains no figure like him—should we call him 'great'?" asked Joachim Fest in 1973 at the opening of his Hitler biography, and he was inclined to give a preliminary answer of "yes." Fest cited Jacob Burckhardt's dictum: "History loves to condense itself into one person whom the world obeys. These great individuals are the coincidence of the general and the particular, the abiding and the fluid in one person."[98] Indeed, as Fest emphasised, Hitler's phenomenal

career was only possible thanks to "the coming together of individual
and general preconditions, the inscrutable correspondence between
the man and his time and the times with this man." But in the end
Fest also hesitated to ascribe "historical greatness" to Hitler. His scruples were primarily aesthetic. Hitler's "dark, instinctual characteristics"
and his "unmistakably crude traits" represented "an element of repulsive baseness that is incommensurate with the conventional meaning
of greatness."[99]

By contrast, in the first volume of his Hitler biography, published
in 1998, Ian Kershaw encouraged readers not to ask questions of
"greatness" at all. "It is a red herring: misconstrued, pointless, irrelevant, and potentially apologetic . . . apologetic, because even to pose
the question cannot conceal a certain admiration for Hitler, however
grudging and whatever his faults," Kershaw wrote.[100] This is a sober
and reasonable perspective. If the concept must be used at all in
conjunction with Hitler, then let it be at most in the form of "negative" or "worthless" greatness, as Heiden did in 1936.[101] Hitler was
"great" only in the destructive sense of tearing down and annihilating
things and people—that is, in his monstrous crimes. In fact, Burckhardt
had ruled out the use of the attribute "great" for those who achieved
nothing productive. "Mere strongmen who ruin things are not great
at all," the Swiss historian wrote.[102]

That is the difference between Hitler and Napoleon. The French
dictator did not just destroy; he created things that outlived his reign,
above all the *code civil*, the body of laws that enshrined the fundamental
achievements of the French Revolution. Hitler, who made a special
point of visiting the emperor's tomb in the Dôme des Invalides in
occupied Paris in June 1940, respected Napoleon primarily as a field
commander, while criticising his "sense of family" as corrupt. All his
brothers and sisters, whom Napoleon had provided with sinecures,
were "incompetent and morally inferior," Hitler proclaimed over dinner
in March 1942. But Napoleon's greatest failing in the Führer's eyes was
his marriage to the Austrian princess Marie Louise. Hitler never tired
of repeating that a leader was not allowed to have a family since he
was dedicated to serving his country, and those around him bought
into this mantra. Napoleon had also been wrong, in Hitler's eyes, to
make himself emperor since he would never have been acknowledged
as such by Europe's other monarchs. He himself, Hitler asserted,

"would always remain just the Führer" and never become "a duke or something like that," which would be a "ridiculous masquerade."[103]

Nevertheless, there were many similarities between Napoleon and Hitler. The Corsican general too was a parvenu who had presented himself as a saviour during the crisis of 1799, promising to impose order on a situation of post-revolutionary chaos. Napoleon too was extraordinarily popular for a long time and subjugated large parts of the European continent. But here is where the parallels end, since as much suffering as Napoleon's constant wars caused and as oppressive as the French occupation might have been, they pale in comparison to the annihilative conquests of the Nazis and their genocidal occupation policies, particularly in eastern Europe. Napoleon may have also invaded Russia with his Grande Armée as an indirect way of bringing Britain to its knees, of swiping its "Continental sword" out of its hands, and the end result was his demise just as it was Hitler's. But the strategic calculations behind Operation Barbarossa were connected with racist ideology and Hitler's obsession with conquering "living space." That turned the German campaign into a war of annihilation whose criminal intent exceeded that of everything that had come before it.

There were also commonalities between Hitler and Stalin. Both dictators had overcome major obstacles in bitter struggles for power; both saw violence as a key means for exercising their authority; and both knew no scruples in pursuing their allegedly higher goals. Both were characterised by a lack of human empathy and extreme vengefulness and cruelty. But unlike Hitler, Stalin was no gambler. The Soviet leader remained acutely aware of foreign policy realities and acted with extreme caution in this arena. It was precisely because he believed Hitler to be guided by the same rationality as he was that he was unable to imagine that the German dictator would attack the Soviet Union in June 1941 and ignored the many warning signs.[104]

In early 1940 Hitler had mocked Stalin as a "modern Ivan the Terrible."[105] But over the course of the war, his respect for the Soviet leader grew. Whereas Hitler rarely missed an opportunity to heap scorn on the democratic statesmen of the West, Churchill and Roosevelt, the Führer privately expressed his admiration for his rival in Moscow. "In Stalin, he recognised a man of stature who towers over the democratic figures of the Anglo-Saxon powers," Goebbels wrote of a speech Hitler gave to the Reichsleiters and Gauleiters in May

1942.[106] The Führer was particularly impressed by the brutality with which Stalin had purged the Red Army officer corps in 1937, getting rid of its leaders. The more friction developed between himself and his military commanders after the setbacks on the eastern front, the more the German dictator regretted not having done something similar. "Our most tragic mistake was to see it as a sign of weakness when Stalin had Tukhachevsky and his lot shot," Hitler told Goebbels in October 1943. "Thus he got rid of all opposition from his generals. It is a shame we did not do likewise. We would not have so many difficulties today."[107] Even during one of his final situation meetings in the Chancellery bunker, on 27 April 1945, Hitler was still expressing his regret that he had not created a *tabula rasa* in 1933 and swept out the "whole clique of this scum": "Afterwards, you regret that you were so good-hearted," he concluded.[108]

Hitler's tyranny lasted only twelve years, but it fundamentally changed the face of the world—albeit in a way completely different from what the dictator had intended. Hitler had wanted to lead the Third Reich from hegemony in Europe to global domination. In the end, the Reich lay in ruins, and the German national state Bismarck had forged in three wars in the nineteenth century perished in an orgy of violence and criminal atrocities. As agreed at Tehran and Yalta, Germany was divided into four occupation zones and was forced to cede its territory east of the Oder and Neisse rivers to Poland. Prussia, which the victors considered a hotbed of aggressive militarism, was dissolved on the orders of the Allied Control Council in February 1947.

But the moral trauma Hitler left behind lasted far longer than Germany's temporary loss of its status as a sovereign nation. After visiting the ruins of Munich in mid-May 1945, Klaus Mann advised his father, Thomas, against returning to his homeland. "It will take years and maybe decades to rebuild these cities," he wrote. "This pitiful, terrible nation will remain physically and morally crippled for generations."[109]

Hitler's tyranny also wrought fundamental changes to the international order. Western Europe's tenure as the gravitational centre of world politics was over. It was replaced by a bipolar order between the two superpowers, the United States and the Soviet Union. "In the long run, it is impossible that the capitalist interests of the Western states coincide with the communist interests of Bolshevism," Hitler had predicted to his field marshals and generals on 27 January 1944. "Every day you can see the ulcer grow stronger."[110] And indeed, after the common goal of defeating Hitler had been achieved, these deep conflicts of interest came to the fore. The breakdown of the anti-Hitler coalition on which the Nazi leadership had always speculated right until the end became reality once Hitler was no more, and the incipient Cold War would keep the world holding its breath for decades. The border between the democratic West and the communist East ran straight through Germany, and the two states that emerged from the rubble of the Third Reich—the democratic Federal Republic of Germany and the communist German Democratic Republic—were part and parcel of this competition between these political systems. It was an open question whether there would ever again be a unified German national state. Many contemporaries considered the division of Germany to be a just consequence of the world war the Third Reich had unleashed, a kind of penance for the crimes of the past. Never again would Germany be able to strive for hegemony in central Europe; never again would it subjugate its neighbours.

It would be four and a half decades before the Cold War ended and the post-1945 European order dissolved. As the Soviet Union collapsed, the peoples of central and eastern Europe were able to liberate themselves from Moscow's dominance and determine their own fates again. Against all expectations, Germans too were given the chance to unify their nation—not through "blood and iron" but as the outcome of peaceful negotiations with the victors of the Second World War. The Federal Republic as it has existed since 1990 is firmly anchored in the European Union and NATO. The danger of Germany "going it alone" seems to be over once and for all.

Whether this second experiment with a German nation-state will prove better in the long term than the catastrophic first will depend largely on whether those in power realise that a unified Germany at the heart of Europe is only tolerable to other nations if it exercises self-restraint and renounces all hegemonic aspirations. But the tendency of many politicians and journalists for some years now to assume that Germany is entitled to play a leading international role should give cause for concern as to whether the lessons of history have been learned as thoroughly as they should be.

Another crucial factor will be whether the German culture of self-critically examining the past, which established itself after much trial and tribulation in the historical profession and public sphere of the Federal Republic, will continue to define the culture of memory in the united Germany. It is no accident that the far-right populists in Germany, although part of a renaissance of nationalism and racism throughout Europe, have made the culture of remembrance one of their central issues. The far right in Germany wants to return to a narrative in which the twelve years of Hitler's dictatorship were an unhappy but minor episode in an otherwise normal, in parts glorious, national history. Those who whitewash history in this way need to realise that they are attacking the very foundations of the Federal Republic.

"We are not and cannot be done with confronting Adolf Hitler," wrote the Catholic author Reinhold Schneider in 1946. "In a certain sense, we will be bound to him for all eternity."[111] Schneider's words remain pertinent today. Hitler will remain a cautionary example for all time. If his life and career teaches us anything, it is how quickly democracy can be prised from its hinges when political institutions fail and civilising forces in society are too weak to combat the lure of authoritarianism; how thin the mantle separating civilisation and barbarism actually is; and what human beings are capable of when the rule of law and ethical norms are suspended and some people are granted unlimited power over the lives of others.

Maps

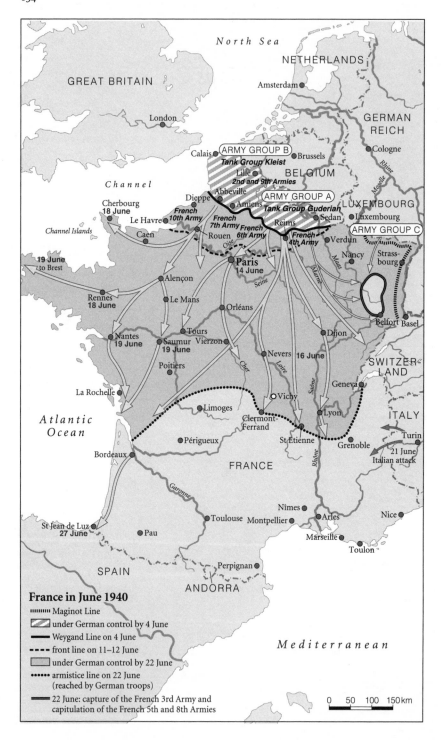

France in June 1940

- ⫶⫶⫶⫶⫶ Maginot Line
- ▨ under German control by 4 June
- ▬▬ Weygand Line on 4 June
- ▬ ▬ ▬ front line on 11–12 June
- ▨ under German control by 22 June
- •••••• armistice line on 22 June
  (reached by German troops)
- ▬▬ 22 June: capture of the French 3rd Army and
  capitulation of the French 5th and 8th Armies

0 50 100 150km

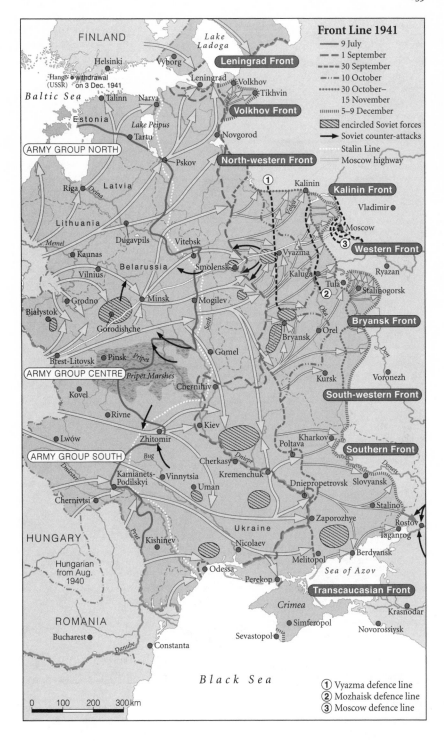

Front Line 1941

- —— 9 July
- – – 1 September
- – – – 30 September
- –·–·– 10 October
- ·········· 30 October–
  15 November
- ⅲⅲⅲ 5–9 December

▨ encircled Soviet forces
➤ Soviet counter-attacks
········· Stalin Line
—— Moscow highway

FINLAND

Lake Ladoga

Helsinki
Vyborg

Hango (USSR) withdrawal on 3 Dec. 1941

Baltic Sea

Talinn
Narva

Leningrad
Volkhov
Tikhvin

Leningrad Front

Volkhov Front

Estonia

Lake Peipus

Tartu

Novgorod

ARMY GROUP NORTH

Pskov

North-western Front

Riga
Dvina
Latvia

Kalinin

Vladimir

Kalinin Front

Lithuania

Moscow

Memel

Dugavpils

Vitebsk

Vyazma

③

Western Front

Kaunas

Volga

Vilnius

Belarussia

Smolensk

Kaluga

Ryazan

Grodno

Minsk

Mogilev

Tula

Stalinogorsk

Białystok

Gorodishche

Sozh

②

Orel

Bryansk Front

Brest-Litovsk
Pinsk
Pripet

Bryansk

Gomel

Oka

Kursk

Voronezh

ARMY GROUP CENTRE
Pripet Marshes

Chernihiv

South-western Front

Kovel

Rivne

Kiev

Kharkov
Poltava

Southern Front

Lwów

Zhitomir

Bug

Cherkasy
Dnepr

Kremenchuk

Donets

ARMY GROUP SOUTH

Kamianets-
Podilskyi
Vinnytsia
Uman

Dniepropetrovsk

Slovyansk

Dniester

Chernivtsi

Ukraine

Zaporozhye

Stalino

Rostov

HUNGARY

Kishinev

Nicolaev

Melitopol

Berdyansk

Taganrog

Hungarian
from Aug.
1940

Odessa

Perekop

Sea of Azov

Transcaucasian Front

ROMANIA

Crimea

Simferopol

Krasnodar

Bucharest

Sevastopol

Novorossiysk

Danube
Constanta

Black Sea

① Vyazma defence line
② Mozhaisk defence line
③ Moscow defence line

0   100   200   300 km

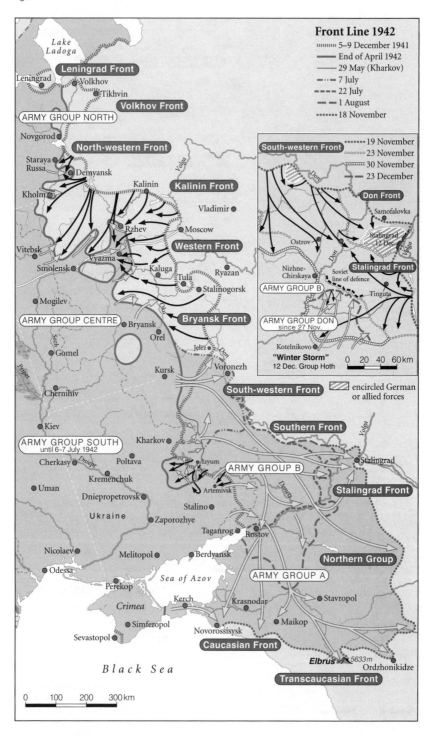

Front Line 1942

⫲⫲⫲⫲⫲ 5–9 December 1941
━━━━━ End of April 1942
───── 29 May (Kharkov)
─·─·─ 7 July
━ ━ ━ 22 July
── ── 1 August
•••••••• 18 November

Lake Ladoga

Leningrad Front

Leningrad · Volkhov · Tikhvin

Volkhov Front

(ARMY GROUP NORTH)

Novgorod

North-western Front

Staraya Russa · Demyansk · Kholm · Kalinin

Kalinin Front

Vladimir · Moscow · Rzhev

Vitebsk · Vyazma · Kaluga · Ryazan

Western Front

Smolensk · Tula · Stalinogorsk

Mogilev

(ARMY GROUP CENTRE) · Bryansk · Orel

Bryansk Front

Gomel · Jelez · Don

Chernihiv · Kursk · Voronezh

Kiev

(ARMY GROUP SOUTH until 6–7 July 1942)

Kharkov

South-western Front

Southern Front

Cherkasy · Poltava · Izyum · (ARMY GROUP B) · Stalingrad

Uman · Kremenchuk · Artemivsk

Dniepropetrovsk · Stalino

Stalingrad Front

Ukraine · Zaporozhye

Taganrog · Rostov

Nicolaev · Melitopol · Berdyansk

Northern Group

Odessa

Perekop

(ARMY GROUP A)

Sea of Azov

Krasnodar · Stavropol

Crimea · Kerch

Simferopol · Novorossisysk · Maikop

Sevastopol

Caucasian Front

Black Sea

Elbrus 5633m · Ordzhonikidze

Transcaucasian Front

0   100   200   300 km

Inset (top right):

South-western Front

•••••• 19 November
○○○○○○ 23 November
⫲⫲⫲⫲⫲ 30 November
━━━━━ 23 December

Don

Don Front

Samofalovka

Ostrov · Stalingrad 12 Dec.

Nizhne-Chirskaya · Don · **Stalingrad Front**

Soviet line of defence

(ARMY GROUP B) · Tinguta

(ARMY GROUP DON since 27 Nov.)

Kotelnikovo

"Winter Storm"
12 Dec. Group Hoth

0   20   40   60 km

⧄ encircled German or allied forces

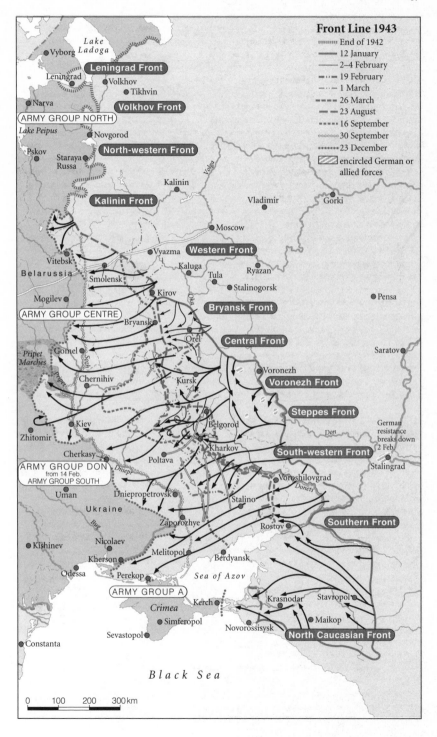

Front Line 1943

‖‖‖‖‖‖	End of 1942
——	12 January
——	2–4 February
—·—·—	19 February
—··—··—	1 March
– – – –	26 March
▬ ▬ ▬	23 August
▪▪▪▪▪▪	16 September
∘∘∘∘∘∘	30 September
••••••	23 December
▨	encircled German or allied forces

Lake Ladoga
Vyborg
Leningrad
Volkhov
Tikhvin
Leningrad Front
Narva
Volkhov Front
ARMY GROUP NORTH
Lake Peipus
Novgorod
North-western Front
Pskov
Staraya Russa
Kalinin
Volga
Vladimir
Gorki
Kalinin Front
Moscow
Vitebsk
Belarussia
Vyazma
Western Front
Kaluga
Ryazan
Smolensk
Tula
Stalinogorsk
Pensa
Mogilev
Oka
Kirov
Bryansk Front
ARMY GROUP CENTRE
Bryansk
Orel
Central Front
Pripet Marches
Gomel
Sozh
Saratov
Chernihiv
Kursk
Voronezh
Voronezh Front
Pripet
Kiev
Belgorod
Steppes Front
Zhitomir
Don
German resistance breaks down 2 Feb.
Cherkasy
Kharkov
South-western Front
ARMY GROUP DON
from 14 Feb.
ARMY GROUP SOUTH
Dniepr
Poltava
Stalingrad
Uman
Dniepropetrovsk
Voroshilovgrad
Donets
Stalino
Ukraine
Bug
Zaporozhye
Rostov
Southern Front
Kishinev
Nicolaev
Melitopol
Berdyansk
Kherson
Odessa
Perekop
Sea of Azov
ARMY GROUP A
Kerch
Krasnodar
Stavropol
Crimea
Simferopol
Maikop
Sevastopol
Novorossisysk
North Caucasian Front
Constanta

Black Sea

0   100   200   300 km

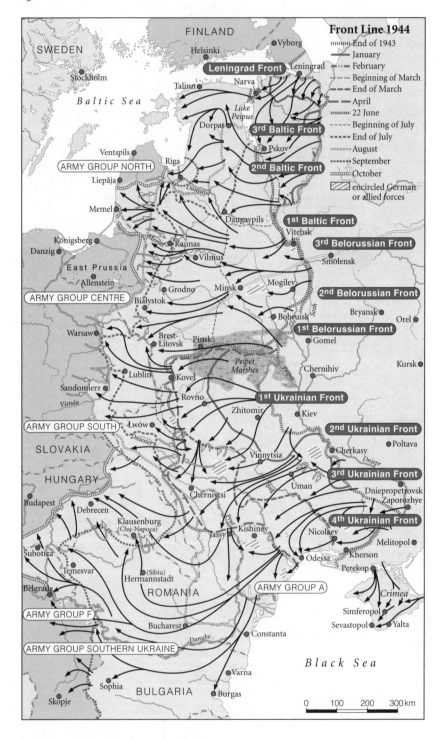

Front Line 1944

Legend:
- End of 1943
- January
- February
- Beginning of March
- End of March
- April
- 22 June
- Beginning of July
- End of July
- August
- September
- October
- encircled German or allied forces

SWEDEN

FINLAND

Baltic Sea

Stockholm

Helsinki · Vyborg

Leningrad Front

Talinn · Narva · Leningrad

Lake Peipus

Dorpat

3rd Baltic Front

Ventspils · Riga

ARMY GROUP NORTH

Pskov

2nd Baltic Front

Liepāja

Daugava

Memel · Daugavpils

1st Baltic Front

Vitebsk

Königsberg · Kaunas

3rd Belorussian Front

Danzig

Memel · Vilnius · Smolensk

East Prussia

Allenstein

ARMY GROUP CENTRE

Grodno · Minsk · Mogilev

Białystok

2nd Belorussian Front

Sozh

Bryansk · Orel

Warsaw

Brest-Litovsk · Pinsk · Bobruisk

1st Belorussian Front

Gomel

Pripyat

Pripet Marshes

Chernihiv · Kursk

Lublin · Kovel

Sandomierz · Rovno

Zhitomir · Kiev

Vistula

ARMY GROUP SOUTH

Lwów

1st Ukrainian Front

Dniester

Vinnytsia · Cherkasy · Poltava

2nd Ukrainian Front

SLOVAKIA

Dniepr

HUNGARY

Chernivtsi · Uman · Dnieptopetrovsk · Zaporozhye

3rd Ukrainian Front

Budapest · Debrecen

Klausenburg (Cluj-Napoca)

4th Ukrainian Front

Nicolaev · Melitopol

Subotica

Prut

Jassy · Kishinev · Kherson

Temesvar

(Sibiu)

Hermannstadt

Odessa · Perekop

Belgrade

ROMANIA

ARMY GROUP A

Crimea

ARMY GROUP F

Bucharest · Constanta · Simferopol

Danube · Sevastopol · Yalta

ARMY GROUP SOUTHERN UKRAINE

Black Sea

Sophia · Varna

Skopje · BULGARIA · Burgas

0   100   200   300 km

Normandy Landings

Allied bridgeheads at the end of D-Day

original targets for D-Day

flooded areas

Supreme Allied Commander
(General Dwight D. Eisenhower)

Eastern Naval Task Force,
Rear-Admiral Sir Philip Vian

21st Army Group
(Lt Gen Bernard Montgomery)
LAND FORCES

2nd BRITISH ARMY
(Maj Gen Miles Dempsey)

Western Naval Task Force,
Rear-Admiral Alan G. Kirk

1st US ARMY
(Lt Gen Omar N. Bradley)

Le Havre

British 6th Airborne Division

711th Infantry Division

Pegasus-Bridge

Merville

Sword

British 3rd Infantry Division

Units of 21st Tank Division

Juno

Canadian 3rd Infantry Division

Gold

British 50th Infantry Division

716th Infantry Division

Bénouville

Caen

Orne

Bayeux

Omaha

US 1st and 29th Infantry Divisions

WN62

Colleville

St Laurent

352nd Infantry Division

Rangers

Pointe du Hoc

Isigny

St Lô

Vire

Utah

US 4th Infantry Division

Ste-Mère-Église

US 82nd Airborne Division

US 101st Airborne Division

91st Airborne Division

Carentan

709th Infantry Division

Cherbourg

243rd Infantry Division

0   5   10   15 km

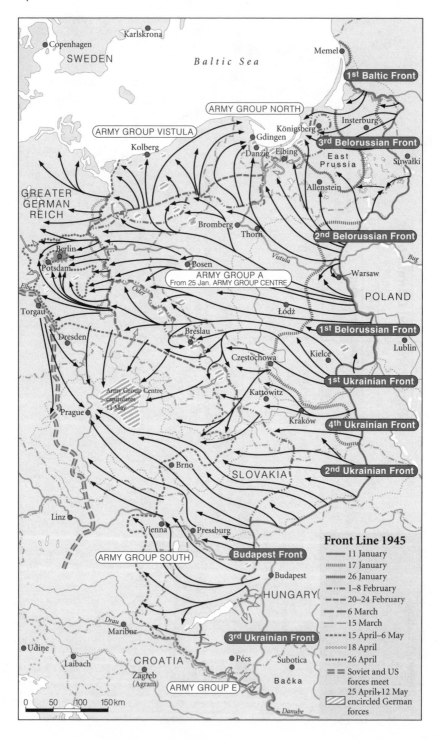

Copenhagen

Karlskrona

SWEDEN

Baltic Sea

Memel

1st Baltic Front

ARMY GROUP NORTH

ARMY GROUP VISTULA

Königsberg

Insterburg

3rd Belorussian Front

Gdingen

Kolberg

Danzig Elbing

East Prussia

Suwałki

GREATER GERMAN REICH

Allenstein

Bromberg

Thorn

2nd Belorussian Front

Berlin

Posen

Vistula

Bug

Potsdam

Warsaw

Elbe

Oder

ARMY GROUP A
From 25 Jan. ARMY GROUP CENTRE

POLAND

Torgau

Łódź

Dresden

Breslau

1st Belorussian Front

Kielce

Lublin

Częstochowa

1st Ukrainian Front

Army Group Centre capitulates 11 May

Kattowitz

Prague

Kraków

4th Ukrainian Front

Brno

SLOVAKIA

2nd Ukrainian Front

Linz

Vienna

Pressburg

Budapest Front

ARMY GROUP SOUTH

Budapest

HUNGARY

Drau

Maribor

3rd Ukrainian Front

Udine

CROATIA

Pécs

Subotica

Laibach

Zagreb (Agram)

Bačka

ARMY GROUP E

Danube

0   50   100   150 km

Front Line 1945

— 11 January
⋯⋯ 17 January
⋙⋙ 26 January
—·— 1–8 February
— — 20–24 February
━ ━ 6 March
— — 15 March
⋯⋯⋯ 15 April–6 May
∘∘∘∘ 18 April
•••••• 26 April
═ ═ Soviet and US forces meet
25 April–12 May
▨ encircled German forces

Notes

Introduction

1   Hans-Ulrich Thamer, *Verführung und Gewalt: Deutschland 1933–1945*, Berlin, 1986, p. 627.

2   Bernd Wegner, "Wozu Operationsgeschichte?," in Thomas Kühne and Benjamin Ziemann (eds), *Was ist Militärgeschichte?*, Paderborn, 2000, pp. 105–13 (at p. 110).

3   One of the indispensable sources used here is the ten-volume *The German Reich and the Second World War* published by the Military Historical Research Office in Freiburg: *Das Deutsche Reich und der Zweite Weltkrieg*, ed. Militärgeschichtliches Forschungsamt, 10 vols, Stuttgart and Munich, 1979–2008.

4   Franz Halder, *Hitler als Feldherr*, Munich, 1949 (at p. 63). See also Christian Hartmann, *Halder: Generalstabschef Hitlers 1938–1942*, 2nd edition, Paderborn, 2010, pp. 18–21; Henrik Eberle, *Hitlers Weltkriege: Wie der Gefreite zum Feldherrn wurde*, Hamburg, 2014, pp. 13–17.

5   See the two exhibition catalogues of the Hamburg Institute for Social Research: *Verbrechen der Wehrmacht 1941 bis 1944*, Hamburg, 1996; *Verbrechen der Wehrmacht: Dimensionen des Vernichtungskrieges 1941 bis 1944*, Hamburg, 2002.

6   See also in particular Johannes Hürter, *Hitlers Heerführer: Die deutschen Oberbefehlshaber im Krieg gegen die Sowjetunion 1941/42*, Munich, 2007, pp. 509ff.; Christian Hartmann, *Wehrmacht im Ostkrieg: Front und militärisches Hinterland*, Munich, 2009, pp. 635ff.

7   Eberhard Jäckel, "Die elende Praxis der Untersteller," in *"Historikerstreit": Die Dokumentation der Kontroverse um die Einzigartigkeit der nationalsozialistischen Judenvernichtung*, Munich and Zurich, 1987, pp. 115–22 (at p. 118). For a more recent discussion, see also Sybille Steinbacher (ed.), *Holocaust und Völkermorde: Die Reichweite des Vergleichs*, Frankfurt am Main and New York, 2012.

8   Joachim Fest, *Hitler: Eine Biographie*, Frankfurt am Main, Berlin and Vienna, 1973, pp. 929–33.

9   See also the following: Frank Bajohr and Andrea Löw (eds), *Der Holocaust: Ergebnisse und neue Fragen der Forschung*, Frankfurt am Main, 2015, pp. 9ff. Hilberg's book initially appeared in the early 1990s in German translation with the small Berlin publisher Olle & Wolter and remained widely unread. It was not until 1990 that S. Fischer published it in three volumes, making it more widely available. See Raul Hilberg, *Unerbetene Erinnerung: Der Weg eines Holocaust-Forschers*, Frankfurt am Main, 1994; idem, *Anatomie des Holocaust: Essays und Erinnerungen*, ed. Walter H. Pehle and René Schlott, Frankfurt am Main, 2016.

10 *Die Verfolgung und Ermordung der europäischen Juden durch das nationalsozialistische Deutschland 1933–1945*, commissioned by the Federal Archives, the Institute for

Contemporary History and the Department of History at the Albert-Ludwigs-Universität Freiburg, edited by Götz Aly, Wolf Gruner, Susanne Heim, Ulrich Herbert, Hans-Dieter Kreikamp, Horst Möller, Dieter Pohl und Hartmut Weber, Munich, 2008ff.

11 Heinz Boberach (ed.), *Meldungen aus dem Reich 1938–1945: Die geheimen Lageberichte des Sicherheitsdienstes der SS*, 17 vols, Herrsching, 1984. See also the introduction by Heinz Boberach, vol. 1, pp. 22–4.

12 *Die Tagebücher von Joseph Goebbels*, commissioned by the Institute for Contemporary History, with support from the State Archive of Russia, ed. Elke Fröhlich, *Part I: Aufzeichnungen 1923–1941*, 9 vols in 14 parts, Munich, 1998–2008; *Part II: Diktate 1941–1945*, 15 vols, Munich, 1993–6.

13 Lore Walb, *Ich, die Alte—ich, die Junge: Konfrontation mit meinen Tagebüchern 1933–1945*, Berlin, 1997.

14 Thomas Mann, *Tagebücher 1940–1943*, ed. Peter de Mendelssohn, Frankfurt am Main, 1982; *idem*, *Tagebücher 1944–1. 4. 1946*, ed. Inge Jens, Frankfurt am Main, 1986; *idem*, *An die gesittete Welt: Schriften und Reden im Exil*, Frankfurt am Main, 1986; Victor Klemperer, *Ich will Zeugnis ablegen bis zum letzten: Tagebücher*, vol. 1: 1933–1941, vol. 2: 1942–1945, ed. Walter Nowojski with Hadwig Klemperer, Berlin, 1995; Wilhelm Muehlon, *Tagebuch der Kriegsjahre 1940–1944*, ed. Jens Heisterkamp, Dornach, 1992.

15 Friedrich Kellner, *"Vernebelt, verdunkelt sind alle Hirne": Tagebücher 1939–1945*, 2 vols, ed. Sascha Feuchert, Robert Martin Scott Kellner, Erwin Leibfried, Jörg Riecke and Markus Roth, Göttingen, 2011.

16 Frank Bajohr and Christoph Strupp (eds), *Fremde Blicke auf das "Dritte Reich": Berichte ausländischer Diplomaten über Herrschaft und Gesellschaft in Deutschland 1933–1945*, Göttingen, 2011.

17 Gabriel Gorodetsky (ed.), *Die Maiski-Tagebücher: Ein Diplomat im Kampf gegen Hitler 1932–1943*, Munich, 2016.

18 Hugh R. Trevor-Roper, *The Last Days of Hitler*, 7th edition, London, 2012, first published in 1947; Joachim Fest, *Der Untergang: Hitler und das Ende des Dritten Reiches. Eine historische Skizze*, Berlin, 2002. Fest's book acted as the source material for producer and screenwriter Bernd Eichinger's film *Downfall* in 2004.

19 Kellner, *Tagebücher 1939–1945*, vol. 1, p. 366 (entry for 17 Dec. 1942)

20 Since the publication of the first volume of this work, there have been some publications we should consider more closely.

Peter Longerich's *Hitler: Biographie* (Munich, 2015) returns the Führer more to the centre of an analysis of the National Socialist regime. Longerich depicts Hitler as a strong, extraordinarily insistent politician. In an explicit refutation of the interpretations advanced by Ian Kershaw, Hans-Ulrich Wehler and Ludolf Herbst, Longerich does not relate Hitler's unique position back to his charisma-based popularity but to the dictatorial instruments of power, which gave him an unprecedented autonomy of political action. In Longerich's view, Hitler kept a firm grip on the reins in all areas of politics and took an intense interest in the daily running of things.

Two objections can be made to this interpretation. First, while the dictator no doubt wielded immense power after disabling all constraints to his authority in 1933 and 1934, the importance of his underlings "working towards" the Führer—to use Kershaw's phrase—should never be underestimated. As we saw in the first volume, Hitler's characteristic "oral" style of leadership often consisted of hastily made remarks, which his underlings snapped up and turned into "orders from the Führer." Hitler rarely had any desire to get involved in details, nor did he usually need to. Second, Longerich's depiction of society in the Third Reich remains strangely fuzzy amid his presentation of an omnipotent dictator who could act upon his every whim. For by no means did Hitler's power rest solely on the repressive instruments of his dictatorship: equally important was the fact that large parts of the German population were prepared to follow a messiah who seemed to fulfil their wishes and desires. Longerich dismisses the "ethnic-popular community" (*Volksgemeinschaft*) as a mere propaganda myth and underestimates the appeal of the solidarity that this idea promised. Indeed, generally, Longerich tends to acknowledge less popular support for the Nazi regime and the Führer than there actually was.

With *Hitler: Der Künstler als Politiker und Feldherr. Eine Herrschaftsanalyse* (Munich, 2015) Wolfram Pyta has published an often original and innovative study that interprets Hitler the politician and military commander in terms of his artistic aspirations. Pyta's interdisciplinary approach, drawing on aesthetic categories, goes a long way towards explaining the unprecedented resonance of Hitler's public appearances. But Pyta overgeneralises his conclusions when he applies them to the entire political sphere and deems Hitler a "performance artist-politician." Hitler may have seen himself in this role, and staging himself as such was part of his carefully maintained image. But in reality he did not practise the business of politics in the style of an artist but rather as a robust, tactically astute, unscrupulously brutal Machiavellian. We risk falling into the trap, being hoodwinked by Hitler's own self-mythologising, if we place too much emphasis on how he saw himself and fail to distinguish it from what he actually did. This also applies to Hitler's role as a military commander. He gleefully integrated the idea of his "genius," which his entourage ascribed to him after Germany's initial military victories, into his own self-image, using it to legitimise his monopoly on military leadership. But it had little to do with the way he actually ran the war.

At the end of 2015, the copyright to Hitler's *Mein Kampf*, which had rested with the state of Bavaria, expired. The Institute for Contemporary History in Munich used the occasion to publish a historical-critical edition of this hateful screed—an ambitious and largely successful project: Christian Hartmann, Thomas Vordermayer, Othmar Plöckinger and Roman Töppel (eds), *Hitler, Mein Kampf: Eine kritische Edition*, 2 vols (Munich and Berlin, 2016). Today, we can more clearly recognise the intellectual roots of Hitler's ideological obsessions and the dubious sources— primarily jingoistic and racist pamphlets from the nineteenth and early twentieth centuries—he drew upon. Our knowledge has also been increased by the revelation of the many lies, half-truths and omissions in the autobiographical passages of Hitler's dilettantish book. In more than 3,500 footnotes, the editors of this critical edition have exposed Hitler's factual errors and deliberately misleading statements, rendering a huge pool of information available to future scholars.

Surprisingly, although it is commonly assumed that nothing new can be said about Hitler and all the relevant facts about him have been uncovered, new sources continually turn up. One example is the private diaries of Alfred Rosenberg, the chief ideologue of the NSDAP and later Reich minister for the occupied eastern territories. One of the US prosecutors at the Nuremberg trials, Robert M. W. Kempner, took the diaries back with him to America, where they disappeared after his death and were only rediscovered in 2013. Two years later they were published as *Alfred Rosenberg: Die Tagebücher von 1934 bis 1944*, edited and annotated by Jürgen Matthäus and Frank Bajohr (Frankfurt am Main, 2015). Their significance is evident from the fact alone that no other high-ranking Nazi functionary apart from Goebbels kept a diary. Even if Rosenberg's journals were neither as voluminous nor as informative as those of Goebbels—he sometimes went weeks and months without writing a line—they still give us valuable insight into the Nazi system of rule and the permanent struggles for power at the top of the party.

In June 2010, an auction house in the German town of Fürth offered for sale Hitler's prison file from his term in Landsberg in 1923 and 1924, which had long been believed lost. These documents were seized by the state of Bavaria and published, in an exemplary edition, as *Hitler als Häftling in Landsberg am Lech 1923/24:*

Der Gefangenen-Personalakt aus der Schutzhaft-, Untersuchungshaft- und Festungshaftanstalt Landsberg am Lech, edited and annotated by Peter Fleischmann (Neustadt an der Aisch, 2015). They included correspondence about the famous prisoner, confiscated letters to Hitler and comprehensive information about the more than 300 people who paid visits to the failed putschist. But the biggest revelation came in a short entry in the prison's "registry book." A few hours after Hitler was brought there on 11 November 1923, prison doctor Josef Brinsteiner examined Hitler and diagnosed a "right-sided cryptorchidism," a non-descended testicle that he had since birth or early infancy. That spelled the end of rumours that Hitler had lost a testicle in 1916 when he was wounded in the First World War. The discovery also means that my assumption in the first volume of this biography that Hitler had normally developed sexual organs must be corrected. We can only speculate about the effects this physical anomaly may have had. Perhaps it explains Hitler's reluctance to appear naked before others and was one cause of his difficult relations with women. It is very likely that the abnormality strengthened the feelings of inferiority Hitler carried from his failures at secondary school in Linz and the Vienna Academy of Fine Art.

1 Unleashing the War

1   Max Domarus, *Hitler: Reden und Proklamationen 1932–1945,* vol. 2, part 1, Munich, 1965, p. 1178.

2   Sebastian Haffner, *Anmerkungen zu Hitler,* 21st edition, Munich, 1978, p. 46. Haffner offers a more differentiated picture in his book *Germany: Jekyll & Hyde* (Berlin, 1996, pp. 65–7), which he wrote from exile in 1940. In his estimation, roughly 60 per cent of the German population were loyal followers of the regime, compared to 40 per cent that were not.

3   Joachim Fest, *Hitler: Eine Biographie,* Frankfurt am Main, Berlin and Vienna, 1973, p. 25.

4   Otto Dietrich, *12 Jahre mit Hitler,* Munich, 1955, p. 58.

5   *Heeresadjutant bei Hitler 1938–1943: Aufzeichnungen des Majors Engel,* ed. and annotated by Hildegard von Kotze, Stuttgart, 1974, p. 40 (entry for 1 Oct. 1938).

6   *Akten zur deutschen Auswärtigen Politik 1918–1945 (ADAP) (The Political Archives of the Federal Foreign Office),* Series D, *1937–1941,* vols 1–13, Frankfurt am Main, 1956–70, vol. 5, no. 81, pp. 87–9. See also Joachim von Ribbentrop, *Zwischen London und Moskau: Erinnerungen und letzte Aufzeichnungen,* ed. Annelies von Ribbentrop, Leoni am Starnberger See, 1961, pp. 154–6; Hermann Graml, *Europas Weg in den Krieg: Hitler und die Mächte 1939,* Munich, 1990, pp. 129–32; Stefan Kley, *Hitler, Ribbentrop und die Entfesselung des Zweiten Weltkriegs,* Paderborn, 1996, pp. 204f.

7   *ADAP,* Series D, vol. 5, no. 101, pp. 106–8; see also Ribbentrop, *Zwischen London und Moskau,* pp. 156–8; Graml, *Europas Weg in den Krieg,* p. 133; Kley, *Hitler, Ribbentrop und die Entfesselung des Zweiten Weltkriegs,* p. 205f.

8   Quotation in Dieter Schenk, *Hitlers Mann in Danzig: Gauleiter Forster und die NS-Verbrechen in Danzig-Westpreussen,* Bonn, 2000, p. 96.

9   *ADAP,* Series D, vol. 5, no. 119, pp. 127–32; no. 120, pp. 132–4; no. 126, pp. 139f. See also Graml, *Europas Weg in den Krieg,* pp. 137–9; Kley, *Hitler, Ribbentrop und die Entfesselung des Zweiten Weltkriegs,* pp. 207–9, 213; Rolf-Dieter Müller, *Der Feind steht im Osten: Hitlers geheime Pläne für einen Krieg gegen die Sowjetunion im Jahr 1939,* Berlin, 2011, pp. 108–12.

10   Domarus, *Hitler,* vol. 2, part 1, p. 1065.

11   *Die Tagebücher von Joseph Goebbels,* commissioned by the Institue for Contemporary History, with support from the State Archive of Russia, ed. Elke Fröhlich, *Part I: Aufzeichnungen 1923–1941,* 9 vols in 14 parts, Munich, 1998–2008, vol. 6, p. 247 (entry for 3 Feb. 1939).

12   Feliks Chiczewski to Jozef Lipski, 23 March 1939; Frank Bajohr and Christoph Strupp (eds), *Fremde Blicke auf das "Dritte Reich": Berichte ausländischer Diplomaten über Herrschaft und Gesellschaft in Deutschland 1933–1945,* Göttingen, 2011, p. 528.

13   *ADAP*, Series D, vol. 6, no. 61, pp. 58–60; see also Kley, *Hitler, Ribbentrop und die Entfesselung des Zweiten Weltkriegs*, p. 216.

14   See Richard Overy, *1939: Countdown to War*, London, 2009, p.9.

15   Quotation in Graml, *Europas Weg in den Krieg*, p. 185.

16   *ADAP*, Series D, vol. 6, no. 101, pp. 101–4; see also Graml, *Europas Weg in den Krieg*, pp. 189–92; Kley, *Hitler, Ribbentrop und die Entfesselung des Zweiten Weltkriegs*, pp. 218f.

17   *ADAP*, Series D, vol. 6, no. 118, pp. 122f.; see also Graml, *Europas Weg in den Krieg*, pp. 194f.

18   Goebbels, *Tagebücher*, part I, vol. 6, pp. 300 (entry for 25 March 1939), 301 (entry for 26 March 1939).

19   *ADAP*, Series D, vol. 6, no. 99, pp. 98f.; see also Christian Hartmann, *Halder: Generalstabschef Hitlers 1938–1942*, 2nd edition, Paderborn, 2010, pp. 122f.; Nicolaus von Below, *Als Hitlers Adjutant 1937–45*, Mainz, 1980, p. 157; Horst Rohde, "Hitlers erster 'Blitzkrieg' und seine Auswirkungen auf Nordosteuropa," in *Das Deutsche Reich und der Zweite Weltkrieg, Vol. 2: Die Errichtung der Hegemonie auf dem europäischen Kontinent*, Stuttgart, 1979, pp. 81f.

20   Goebbels, *Tagebücher*, part I, vol. 6, p. 302 (entry for 28 March 1939).

21   Below, *Als Hitlers Adjutant*, p. 157.

22   Quotation in Graml, *Europas Weg in den Krieg*, p. 183. See also Gottfried Niethardt, "Die britisch-französischen Garantieerklärungen für Polen vom 31. März 1939," in *Francia* 2 (1974), pp. 597–618; Rainer F. Schmidt, *Die Aussenpolitik des Dritten Reiches 1933–1939*, Stuttgart, 2002, p. 322–8.

23   William Shirer, *Berlin Diary 1934–41: The Rise of the Third Reich*, London, 1997, p. 87 (entry for 6 April 1939).

24   Domarus, *Hitler*, vol. 2, part 1, pp. 1119–27 (at pp. 1120, 1122). On Hitler's journey to Wilhelmshaven see Below, *Als Hitlers Adjutant*, pp. 157f.; on the Wilhelmshaven speech see also Shirer, *Berlin Diary*, pp. 86–7 (entry for 1 April 1939).

25   See Goebbels, *Tagebücher*, part I, vol. 6, pp. 316 (entry for 14 April 1939), 317 (entry for 15 April 1939), 378 (entry for 14 June 1939).

26   See Below, *Als Hitlers Adjutant*, pp. 158f.; Domarus, *Hitler*, vol. 2, part 1, pp. 1127f.

27   *ADAP*, Series D, vol. 6, no. 149, p. 154. Keitel immediately informed the deputy head of the Wehrmacht leadership staff, Walter Warlimont, "that the Führer has issued instructions to the supreme commanders of the branches of the Wehrmacht to prepare themselves by the end of August for an increasingly inevitable-looking military confrontation with Poland." Recorded in Walter Warlimont's "Polen 1939" (dated 24 Sept. 1945); BA Koblenz, N 1033/24.

28   *ADAP*, Series D, vol. 6, no. 185, pp. 186–90; Walther Hubatsch (ed.), *Hitlers Weisungen für die Kriegsführung*, Munich, 1965, pp. 19–22 (at pp. 19f.).

29   Christian Hartmann and Sergej Slutsch, "Franz Halder und die Kriegsvorbereitungen im Frühjahr 1939: Eine Ansprache des Generalstabschefs des Heeres," in *Vierteljahrshefte für Zeitgeschichte*, 45 (1997), pp. 467–95 (at pp. 480, 483, 488, 489, 495). See also, Hartmann, *Halder*, pp. 398f.

30   Quoted in Domarus, *Hitler*, vol. 2, part 1, pp. 1142f.

31   See Goebbels, *Tagebücher*, part I, vol. 6, pp. 326 (entry for 24 April 1939), 327 (entry for 25 April 1939), 329 (entry for 26 April 1939), 331 (entry for 28 Apr 1939).

32   *ADAP*, Series D, vol. 6, no. 200, pp. 202–4. See also Günter Moltmann, "Franklin D. Roosevelts Friedensappell vom 14. April 1939: Ein fehlgeschlagener Versuch zur Friedenssicherung," in *Jahrbuch für Amerikastudien*, 9 (1964), pp. 91–109.

33   Goebbels, *Tagebücher*, part I, vol. 6, p. 319 (entry for 17 April 1939).

34   Domarus, *Hitler*, vol. 2, part 1, pp. 1148–79 (at p. 1173). On the reactions of various countries to the German request, see Moltmann, "Franklin D. Roosevelts Friedensappell," pp. 98–107.

35   Letter from Marianne von Weizsäcker to her mother, 29 April 1939; BA Koblenz, N 1273/29.

36   Shirer, *Berlin Diary*, p. 89 (entry for 28 April 1939). See Goebbels, *Tagebücher*, part I, vol. 6, p. 332: "And then the fierce whipping of Roosevelt. He is being slapped silly. The house bends over in laughter. It is a pleasure to listen to."

37   Quotation from Graml, *Europas Weg in den Krieg*, p. 212.

38   Goebbels, *Tagebücher*, part I, vol. 6, p. 339 (entry for 6 May 1939).

39   Ibid., pp. 333 (entry for 30 April 1939), 335 (entry for 2 May 1939).

40   Engel, *Heeresadjutant bei Hitler*, p. 45 (entry for 8 April 1939).

41   *ADAP*, Series D, vol. 6, no. 205, pp. 207–11, no. 211, pp. 215–20. See also Paul Schmidt, *Statist auf diplomatischer Bühne 1923–45*, Bonn, 1950, p. 434; Alfred Kube, *Pour le mérite und Hakenkreuz: Hermann Göring im Dritten Reich*, Munich, 1986, pp. 308f.; Galeazzo Ciano, *Tagebücher, 1939–1943*, Bern, 1946, p. 76 (entry for 16 April 1939).

42   Attolico to Ciano, 18 April 1939; quoted in Graml, *Europas Weg in den Krieg*, p. 199.

43   *ADAP*, Series D, vol. 6, no. 340, p. 366, no. 341, p. 372; see Ciano, *Tagebücher, 1939–1943*, p. 86 (entries for 6 and 7 May 1939); Graml, *Europas Weg in den Krieg*, p. 216; Schmidt, *Statist auf diplomatischer Bühne*, p. 437; Gianluca Falanga, *Mussolinis Vorposten in Hitlers Reich: Italiens Politik in Berlin 1933–1945*, Berlin, 2008, pp. 121f. On Mussolini's motives, see Hans Woller, *Mussolini: Der erste Faschist. Eine Biografie*, Munich, 2016, pp. 185–8.

44   *ADAP*, Series D, vol. 6, no. 426, pp. 466–9; Domarus, *Hitler*, vol. 2, part 1, pp. 1192f.

45   Ciano, *Tagebücher, 1939–1943*, p. 92 (entry for 22 May 1939).

46   Ibid., p. 89 (entry for 13 May 1939); Goebbels, *Tagebücher*, part I, vol. 6, p. 356 (entry for 23 May 1939). See also Below, *Als Hitlers Adjutant*, p. 165: "Behind the scenes of the splendid signing ceremony, people were already murmuring that the treaty would result in a very one-sided alliance."

47   *ADAP*, Series D, vol. 6, no. 433, pp. 477–83; Domarus, *Hitler*, vol. 2, part 1, pp. 1198–1201. See Below, *Als Hitlers Adjutant*, pp. 164f.; Kley, *Hitler, Ribbentrop und die Entfesselung des Zweiten Weltkriegs*, pp. 258f.; Schmidt, *Die Aussenpolitik des Dritten Reiches*, pp. 329f.; Bernd-Jürgen Wendt, *Grossdeutschland, Aussenpolitik und Kriegs-vorbereitung des Hitler-Regimes*, Munich, 1987, pp. 175f.

48   See Below, *Als Hitlers Adjutant*, pp. 165f.; Goebbels, *Tagebücher*, part I, vol. 6, pp. 365 (entry for 2 May 1939), 366 (entry for 3 June 1939), 367f. (entry for 4 June 1939), 371 (entry for 8 June 1939); Domarus, *Hitler*, vol. 2, part 1, pp. 1203f., 1208–11.

49   Goebbels, *Tagebücher*, part I, vol. 6, p. 375 (entry for 12 June 1939).

50   See Below, *Als Hitlers Adjutant*, pp. 166–9.

51   Goebbels, *Tagebücher*, part I, vol. 6, p. 387 (entry for 21 June 1939); see also Below, *Als Hitlers Adjutant*, pp. 169f.: "Hitler did not believe England would actively inter-vene because he assumed that the English would need at least two years to arm themselves for war."

52   Goebbels, *Tagebücher*, part I, vol. 7, pp. 33f. (entry for 5 July 1939).

53   See Below, *Als Hitlers Adjutant*, pp. 175f.; on plans for the campaign, see *Das Deutsche Reich und der Zweite Weltkrieg*, vol. 2, pp. 92–9 (Rohde's essay).

54   See Domarus, *Hitler*, vol. 2, part 1, p. 1217.

55   Goebbels, *Tagebücher*, part I, vol. 7, p. 43 (entry for 15 July 1939).

56   Domarus, *Hitler*, vol. 2, part 1, p. 1218.

57   Ulrich von Hassell, *Vom andern Deutschland: Aus den nachgelassenen Tagebüchern 1938–1944*, Frankfurt am Main, 1964, p. 58 (entry for 22 July 1939).

58   See Dietrich, *12 Jahre mit Hitler*, pp. 59f.; Brigitte Hamann, *Winifred Wagner oder Hitlers Bayreuth*, Munich and Zurich, 2002, pp. 388f.

59   Engel, *Heeresadjutant bei Hitler*, p. 56 (entry for 28 July 1939).

60   Goebbels, *Tagebücher*, part I, vol. 6, p. 373 (entry for 11 June 1939).

61   Ibid., p. 346 (entry for 13 May 1939). On the German smear campaign against Poland see Richard J. Evans, *The Third Reich in Power, 1933–1939*, London, 2005, pp. 695–6; Graml, *Europas Weg in den Krieg*, pp. 200f.; Schenk, *Hitlers Mann in Danzig*, pp. 110f.

62   Carl J. Burckhardt, *Meine Danziger Mission 1937–1939*, 3rd rev. edition, Munich, 1980, p. 331; Schenk, *Hitlers Mann in Danzig*, pp. 117f. Forster sent a telegram to Hitler on

10 August 1939 that read: "Many thousands of German Danzigers . . . look to you with the greatest of trust and welcome you as their Führer with reverence and unshakable loyalty." BA Berlin-Lichterfelde, NS 10/17.

63 Burckhardt, *Meine Danziger Mission*, pp. 341, 345. On the authenticity of Burckhardt's account, see Ian Kershaw, *Hitler 1936–1945: Nemesis*, London, 2001, pp. 898-9n118.

64 Goebbels, *Tagebücher*, part I, vol. 7, p. 64 (entry for 12 Aug. 1939).

65 Generaloberst Halder, *Kriegstagebuch: Tägliche Aufzeichnungen des Chefs des Generalstabs des Heeres 1939–1942*, vol. 1, ed. Hans-Adolf Jacobsen, Stuttgart, 1962, pp. 8–15 (at pp. 11, 14). Hitler also boasted to Keitel in August 1939 that "Those coffee-swilling old ladies in London and Paris will keep their mouths shut this time as well!" Bernhard von Lossberg, *Im Wehrmachtführungsstab: Bericht eines Generalstabsoffiziers*, Hamburg, 1950, p. 32.

66 Below, *Als Hitlers Adjutant*, p. 179.

67 Attolico to Ciano, 7 July 1939; quoted in Graml, *Europas Weg in den Krieg*, p. 227.

68 See Graml, *Europas Weg in den Krieg*, pp. 227–31; Falanga, *Mussolinis Vorposten in Hitlers Reich*, pp. 126f.; Ciano, *Tagebücher, 1939–1943*, pp. 115–19 (entries for 19 July, 22 July, 26 July, 28 Juy, 31 July 1939). On 20 July 1939, Goebbels noted: "The Führer will soon meet Mussolini on the Brenner [Pass]." Goebbels, *Tagebücher*, part I, vol. 7, p. 46.

69 Ciano, *Tagebücher, 1939–1943*, p. 122 (entry for 10 Aug. 1939). See ibid., p. 121 (entry for 9 Aug. 1939): "The Duce insists I prove to the Germans, based on documents, that it would be insanity to unleash a war."

70 Ibid., p. 122 (entry for 11 Aug. 1939). See Graml, *Europas Weg in den Krieg*, pp. 231–3; Schmidt, *Die Aussenpolitik des Dritten Reiches 1933–1939*, pp. 332f.; Kley, *Hitler, Ribbentrop und die Entfesselung des Zweiten Weltkriegs*, pp. 283f.

71 Schmidt, *Statist auf diplomatischer Bühne*, p. 438.

72 Ciano, *Tagebücher, 1939–1943*, pp. 122f. (entry for 12 Aug. 1939). See Graml, *Europas Weg in den Krieg*, pp. 233f.; Kley, *Hitler, Ribbentrop und die Entfesselung des Zweiten Weltkriegs*, pp. 284f.

73 Schmidt, *Statist auf diplomatischer Bühne*, p. 440.

74 Ciano, *Tagebücher, 1939–1943*, p. 123 (entry for 13 Aug. 1939).

75 *ADAP*, Series D, vol. 6, no. 1, pp. 1–3. See Graml, *Europas Weg in den Krieg*, p. 253; Dietmar Neutatz, *Träume und Alpträume: Eine Geschichte Russlands im 20. Jahrhundert*, Munich, 2013, pp. 281f.

76 On Stalin's motives see Graml, *Europas Weg in den Krieg*, p. 255; Neutatz, *Träume und Alpträume*, pp. 280f.

77 Goebbels, *Tagebücher*, part I, vol. 6, p. 339 (entry for 6 May 1939). On Litvinov's dismissal see Gabriel Gorodetsky (ed.), *Die Maiski-Tagebücher: Ein Diplomat im Kampf gegen Hitler*, Munich, 2016, pp. 296-9 (entry for 3 May 1939).

78 *ADAP*, Series D, vol. 6, no. 332, p. 355; see Graml, *Europas Weg in den Krieg*, p. 257.

79 *ADAP*, Series D, vol. 6, no. 446, pp. 497f.; see Graml, *Europas Weg in den Krieg*, p. 261.

80 Diary entry by Weizsäcker for 18 June 1939; Leonidas Hill (ed.), *Die Weizsäcker-Papiere 1933–1950*, Frankfurt am Main, Berlin and Vienna, 1974, p. 154. See also Weizsäcker's diaries from February to September 1939 in BA Koblenz, N 1273/42.

81 Goebbels, *Tagebücher*, part I, vol. 6, p. 365 (entry for 2 June 1939); see ibid., p. 373 (entry for 11 June 1939): "[Hitler] does not know what Moscow wants: whether it hopes to extract as high a price as possible from London or whether it does not want to participate at all. This will have to become clear shortly."

82 Ibid., vol. 7, p. 38 (entry for 9 July 1939).

83 *ADAP*, Series D, vol. 6, no. 729, pp. 846–9. See also Hill (ed.), *Die Weizsäcker-Papiere 1933–1950*, p. 157: "We will become more insistent with Moscow."

84 *ADAP*, Series D, vol. 6, no. 758, p. 882, no. 760, pp. 883f.; see Graml, *Europas Weg in den Krieg*, p. 272; Kley, *Hitler, Ribbentrop und die Entfesselung des Zweiten Weltkriegs*, pp. 277f.

85 *ADAP*, Series D, vol. 7, no. 56, pp. 51f.

86 *ADAP*, Series D, vol. 7, no. 73, p. 67, no. 75, p. 70.

87   See Hill (ed.), *Die Weizsäcker-Papiere 1933–1950*, p. 159 (entry for 18 Aug. 1939): "Ribbentrop is offering to fly to Moscow . . . We are doing this very urgently because in eight days the blow is to be struck against Poland."

88   Goebbels, *Tagebücher*, part I, vol. 7, pp. 67f. (entry for 17 Aug. 1939), 70 (entry for 20 Aug. 1939), 71f. (entry for 22 Aug. 1939).

89   *ADAP*, Series D, vol. 7, no. 142, p. 131; see Graml, *Europas Weg in den Krieg*, pp. 275f.; Kley, *Hitler, Ribbentrop und die Entfesselung des Zweiten Weltkriegs*, pp. 296f.

90   Albert Speer, *Erinnerungen: Mit einem Essay von Jochen Thies*, Frankfurt am Main and Berlin, 1993, p. 176. See also *idem, "Alles was ich weiss": Aus unbekannten Geheimdienst-protokollen vom Sommer 1945*, ed. Ulrich Schlie, Munich, 1999, p. 181. Heinrich Hoffmann recalled Ribbentrop's message being passed along to Hitler by phone (*Hitler wie ich ihn sah: Aufzeichnungen seines Leibfotografen*, Munich and Berlin, 1974, pp. 101f.). In Otto Dietrich's account (*12 Jahre mit Hitler*, p. 79), Hitler jumped up from the dinner table with a spontaneous cry of "We won!"

91   *ADAP*, Series D, vol. 7, no. 159, pp. 140f.

92   Goebbels, *Tagebücher*, part I, vol. 7, p. 72 (dated 22 Aug. 1939). See Shirer, *Berlin Diary*, p. 95 (entry for 24 Aug. 1939): "The announcement was as much of a bomb-shell for most of the big Nazis as for the rest of the world." Eduard Wagner, *Der Generalquartiermeister: Briefe und Tagebuchaufzeichnungen*, ed. Elisabeth Wagner, Munich and Vienna, 1963, p. 90 (dated 22 Aug. 1939): "Everybody strongly impressed by pact with Russia. Complete turnaround in foreign policy possible." On the reaction in London see Gorodetsky (ed.), *Die Maiski-Tagebücher*, pp. 341f. (entry for 22 Aug. 1939).

93   *ADAP*, Series D, vol. 7, no. 192, pp. 167–72; Domarus, *Hitler*, vol. 2, part 1, pp. 1234–8; Helmuth Greiner's memoirs dated 22 Aug. 1939; BA Koblenz, N 1033/13; Halder, *Kriegstagebuch*, vol. 1, pp. 23–6 (entry for 22 Aug. 1939). For a comparison of the various surviving versions see Winfried Baumgart, "Zur Ansprache Hitlers vor den Führern der Wehrmacht am 22. August 1939: Eine quellenkritische Untersuchung," in *Vierteljahrshefte für Zeitgeschichte*, 16 (1968), pp. 120–49; Hermann Böhm, "Zur Ansprache Hitlers vor den Führern der Wehrmacht am 22. August 1939," in *Vierteljahrshefte für Zeitgeschichte*, 19 (1971), pp. 294–300; Winfried Baumgart, "Erwiderung," in ibid., pp. 301–4. Colonel-General Fedor von Bock seemed impressed by Hitler's "excellent speech." Fedor von Bock, *Zwischen Pflicht und Verweigerung: Das Kriegstagebuch*, ed. Klaus Gerbet, Munich, 1995, p. 33 (entry for 22 Aug. 1939). See also Michael Mueller, *Canaris: Hitlers Abwehrchef*, Berlin, 2006, pp. 259–61.

94   Engel, *Heeresadjutant bei Hitler*, p. 58 (entry for 22 Aug. 1939). In 1945, Warlimont remembered that Hitler was only able to dispel worries "among part of his audience" of military leaders: "The only description for the general mood was subdued." Appendix to Walter Warlimont's notes on "Polen 1939" (dated 24 Sept. 1945); BA Koblenz, N 1033/24.

95   *ADAP*, Series D, vol. 7, no. 200, pp. 180f.; also published in Nevile Henderson, *Failure of a Mission: Berlin 1937-1939*, London, 1940, p. 302.

96   *ADAP*, Series D, vol. 7, no. 200, pp. 176–80. See Henderson, *Failure of a Mission*, pp. 256–7.

97   *ADAP*, Series D, vol. 7, no. 201, pp. 181–3. See Henderson, *Failure of a Mission*, pp. 303–5.

98   Ernst von Weizsäcker, *Erinnerungen*, Munich, 1950, p. 252; see Hill (ed.), *Die Weizsäcker-Papiere 1933–1945*, p. 159 (entry for 23 Aug. 1939): "The Führer's intention was to use brutality to force the British away from keeping their guarantees to Poland."

99   Goebbels, *Tagebücher*, part I, vol. 7, pp. 74f. (entry for 24 Aug. 1939).

100   See Hoffmann, *Hitler wie ich ihn sah*, p. 103.

101   See Schmidt, *Statist auf diplomatischer Bühne*, p. 442.

102   Ibid., p. 444; see Kley, *Hitler, Ribbentrop und die Entfesselung des Zweiten Weltkriegs*, pp. 300f.

103 Below, *Als Adjutant Hitlers*, p. 183. Speer, *Erinnerungen*, p. 177, has Below putting these words in Hitler's mouth.

104 See Below, *Als Adjutant Hitlers*, p. 183.

105 Goebbels, *Tagebücher*, part I, vol. 7, p. 75 (entry for 24 Aug. 1939).

106 See Heike B. Görtemaker, *Eva Braun: Leben mit Hitler*, Munich, 2010, p. 229. The snapshots are reproduced in Nerin E. Gun, *Eva Braun-Hitler: Leben und Schicksal*, Velbert and Kettwig, 1968, between pp. 176 and 177. Gun incorrectly asserts that the images were made in the chancellery (p. 146).

107 Goebbels, *Tagebücher*, part I, vol. 7, p. 75 (entry for 24 Aug. 1939).

108 *ADAP*, Series D, vol. 7, no. 228, 229, pp. 205–7. Facsimiles in Erwin Oberländer (ed.), *Hitler-Stalin-Pakt 1939: Das Ende Ostmitteleuropas?*, Frankfurt am Main, 1989.

109 Shirer, Berlin Diary, p. 94 (entry for 24 Aug. 1939). See also Shirer, *This is Berlin: Reporting from Nazi Germany 1938–40*, London, 1999, p. 56 (broadcast of 22 Aug. 1939): "Well, even in Berlin where as a foreign correspondent I've seen many surprises since Adolf Hitler came to power in 1933—even here in Berlin people are still rubbing their eyes."

110 Friedrich Kellner, "*Vernebelt, verdunkelt sind alle Hirne": Tagebücher, 1939–1945*, ed. Sascha Feuchert et al., Göttingen, 2011, vol. 1, p. 17 (Aug. 1939).

111 Baldur von Schirach, *Ich glaubte an Hitler*, Hamburg, 1967, p. 249.

112 Goebbels, *Tagebücher*, part I, vol. 7, p. 73 (entry for 23 Aug. 1939).

113 Jürgen Matthäus and Frank Bajohr (eds), *Alfred Rosenberg: Die Tagebücher von 1934 bis 1944*, Frankfurt am Main, 2015, pp. 284f. (entry for 25 Aug. 1939).

114 Burckhardt, *Meine Danziger Mission*, p. 348.

115 Halder, *Kriegstagebuch*, vol. 1, p. 38 (entry for 28 Aug.1939).

116 See Overy, *1939: Countdown to War*, p. 25.

117 Goebbels, *Tagebücher*, part I, vol. 7, p. 76 (dated 25 Aug. 1939).

118 Speer, *Erinnerungen*, p. 178.

119 See Shirer, *This is Berlin*, p. 59 (broadcast of 24–25 Aug. 1939).

120 Below, *Als Hitlers Adjutant*, p. 184; see Kley, *Hitler, Ribbentrop und die Entfesselung des Zweiten Weltkriegs*, p. 302.

121 Weizsäcker, *Erinnerungen*, p. 254.

122 *Das Hitler-Bild: Die Erinnerungen des Fotografen Heinrich Hoffmann*, ed. Joe J. Heydecker, St. Pölten and Salzburg, 2008, pp. 118–22; see Hoffmann, *Hitler wie ich ihn sah*, pp. 110f. Goebbels teased Hoffmann by saying he had found "a good drinking buddy in Stalin." Below, *Als Hitlers Adjutant*, p. 186.

123 Hans Baur, *Ich flog Mächtige dieser Erde*, Kempten (Allgäu), 1956, pp. 178f.

124 *ADAP*, Series D, vol. 7, no. 266, pp. 235f.; Domarus, *Hitler*, vol. 2, part 1, pp. 1254f.

125 *ADAP*, Series D, vol. 7, no. 265, pp. 233–5; Domarus, *Hitler*, vol. 2, part 1, pp. 1256f.; see Henderson, *Failure of a Mission*, pp. 259; 306–308; Schmidt, *Statist auf diplomatischer Bühne*, pp. 449f.

126 Goebbels, *Tagebücher*, part I, vol. 7, pp. 77f. (entry for 26 Aug. 1939).

127 See Hill (ed.), *Die Weizsäcker-Papiere 1933–1950*, p. 161 (entry for 25 Aug. 1939); Nikolaus von Vormann, *So begann der Zweite Weltkrieg: Zeitzeuge der Entscheidungen. Als Offizier bei Hitler 22. August 1939–1. Oktober 1939*, Leoni, 1988, p. 37.

128 Goebbels, *Tagebücher*, part I, vol. 7, p. 77 (entry for 26 Aug. 1939).

129 Coulondre to the French foreign secretary, Georges Bonnet, 25 Aug. 1939; Walter Hofer, *Die Entfesselung des Zweiten Weltkriegs*, Frankfurt am Main, 1960, no. 52, pp. 218–21; see Robert Coulondre, *Von Moskau nach Berlin 1936–1939: Erinnerungen des französischen Botschafters*, Bonn, 1950, pp. 421–4; Goebbels, *Tagebücher*, part I, vol. 7, p. 78 (entry for 26 Aug. 1939).

130 Overy, *1939: Countdown to War*, p. 37. The interpreter Paul Schmidt reported that Hitler, once he had been given the news, "remained seated at the table for quite some time, brooding." Schmidt, *Statist auf diplomatischer Bühne*, pp. 450f.

131 Note by Schwerin von Krosigk about his state visit to Italy in August 1939 (dated 28 Feb. 1945); BA Koblenz, N 276/45; see also Schwerin von Krosigk's telegram to Ribbentrop, 23 Aug. 1939; ibid.

132   *ADAP*, Series D, vol. 7, no. 271, pp. 238f.; see Ciano, *Tagebücher, 1939–1943*, p. 131 (entry for 25 Aug. 1939); Woller, *Mussolini*, p. 192.

133   Engel, *Heeresadjutant bei Hitler*, p. 59 (entry for 25 Aug. 1939). Engel mistakenly dates Mussolini's answer to the morning of 25 Aug. 1939.

134   Schmidt, *Statist auf diplomatischer Bühne*, p. 453.

135   Goebbels, *Tagebücher*, part I, vol. 7, p. 78 (entry for 26 Aug. 1939); see Halder, *Kriegstagebuch*, vol. 1, p. 34 (entry for 26 Aug. 1939): "The Führer extremely broken down."

136   See Generalfeldmarschall Keitel, *Verbrecher oder Offizier? Erinnerungen, Briefe, Dokumente des Chefs des OKW*, ed. Walter Görlitz, Berlin and Frankfurt am Main, 1961, pp. 211f.; Halder, *Kriegstagebuch*, vol. 1, p. 31 (entry for 25 Aug. 1939); Engel, *Heeresadjutant bei Hitler*, p. 59 (entry for 25 Aug. 1939). On Hitler's relief after his conversation with Brauchitsch see the letters from Karl-Jesko von Puttkamer to Heinrich Uhlig dated 27 March und 16 April 1952; IfZ München, ZS 285.

137   Helmuth Groscurth, *Tagebücher eines Abwehroffiziers 1938–1940*, ed. Helmuth Krausnick and Harold C. Deutsch with Hildegard von Kotze, Stuttgart, 1970, p. 185 (entry for 25 Aug. 1939). Fedor von Bock noted: "It's like being hit by a thunderbolt"; *Das Kriegstagebuch*, p. 34 (entry for 25 Aug. 1939). See also the letter by Günther von Kluge, supreme commander of the 4th Army, of 27 August 1939: "You can imagine the mood we are in. If the Führer does not receive major concessions, there is no way to understand this delay." BA-MA Freiburg, MSg 2/11185.

138   See Mueller, *Canaris*, pp. 279f.

139   Marianne von Weizsäcker to her mother, 25 Aug. 1939; BA Koblenz, N 1273/29.

140   Hassell, *Vom andern Deutschland*, pp. 68f. (entry for 26 Aug. 1939).

141   Shirer, *This is Berlin*, p. 60 (broadcast of 26–27 Aug. 1939).

142   Quoted in Kershaw, *Hitler 1936–1945*, p. 215.

143   Birger Dahlerus, *Der letzte Versuch: London-Berlin Sommer 1939*, Munich, 1973, pp. 54–130. In addition, see Kube, *Pour le mérite und Hakenkreuz*, pp. 319–22; Overy, *1939: Countdown to War*, pp. 51–3.

144   Goebbels, *Tagebücher*, part I, vol. 7, pp. 78f. (entry for 27 Aug. 1939).

145   On 20 August in Carinhall, Göring revealed to Economics Minister Funk, Agriculture Minister Darré and their closest associates Hitler's plan to attack Poland and informed them about the state of preparations for war. It was decided to introduce rationing for all food except bread and potatoes at the start of the conflict. See Herbert Backe, Secretary of State in the Ministry for Food and Agriculture, to his wife, 31 Aug. 1939; BA Koblenz, N 1075/25.

146   See Domarus, *Hitler*, vol. 2, part 1, p. 1263; Shirer, *This is Berlin*, pp. 61–2 (broadcast of 26–7 Aug. 1939).

147   Engel, *Heeresadjutant bei Hitler*, p. 60 (entry for 27 Aug. 1939). In an interview with Harold Deutsch on 5 April 1971, Gerhard Engel quoted Hewel as saying: "My Führer, do not be led astray. I know the English . . . And this time they will march." IfZ München, ZS 222, vol. 1.

148   Schmidt, *Statist auf diplomatischer Bühne*, p. 454; see *ADAP*, Series D, vol. 7, no. 277, p. 242, no. 301, pp. 258f.; Ciano, *Tagebücher, 1939–1943*, pp. 131f. (entry for 26 Aug. 1939).

149   *ADAP*, Series D, vol. 7, no. 307, pp. 262f.

150   *ADAP*, Series D, vol. 7, no. 324, pp. 276f.

151   Coulondre. *Von Moskau nach Berlin*, pp. 425–7; see Goebbels, *Tagebücher*, part I, vol. 7, p. 79 (entry for 27 Aug. 1939): "Coulondre was with the Führer carrying a letter from Daladier. It contained nothing of interest, though, and only concerned responsibility for the war."

152   Goebbels, *Tagebücher*, part I, vol. 7, pp. 80f. (entry for 28 Aug. 1939).

153   *ADAP*, Series D, vol. 7, no. 354, pp. 297–300; see Coulondre, *Von Moskau nach Berlin*, pp. 428f.

154 Halder, *Kriegstagebuch*, vol. 1, p. 38 (entry for 28 Aug. 1939); see Groscurth, *Tagebücher eines Abwehroffiziers*, p. 190 (entry for 28 Aug. 1939). Nikolaus von Vormann, the newly appointed army liaison officer with Hitler, found him to be "a visibly exhausted, hyper-nervous man with flickering, deep-lying eyes and crooked, sagging shoulders." (*So begann der Zweite Weltkrieg*, p. 32).

155 Engel, *Heeresadjutant bei Hitler*, p. 60 (entry for 29 Aug. 1939).

156 Goebbels, *Tagebücher*, part I, vol. 7, pp. 82f. (entry for 29 Aug. 1939).

157 See Halder, *Kriegstagebuch*, vol. 1, p. 40 (entry for 28 Aug. 1939).

158 Shirer, *This is Berlin*, p. 62 (broadcast of 28 Aug. 1939). See Goebbels, *Tagebücher*, part I, vol. 7, p. 83 (dated 29 Aug. 1939): "In the city some small trouble in front of shops."

159 Shirer, *This is Berlin*, p. 63 (broadcast of 28 Aug. 1939).

160 Henderson, *Failure of a Mission*, p. 262.

161 *ADAP*, Series D, vol. 7, no. 384, pp. 318–21 (with appendix); Henderson, *Failure of a Mission*, pp. 308–311.

162 Hill (ed.), *Die Weizsäcker-Papiere 1933–1950*, p. 162 (entry for 29 Aug. 1939). See Groscurth, *Tagebücher eines Abwehroffiziers*, p. 193 (entry for 29 Aug. 1939): "Göring is said to have been the voice of reason, telling the Führer, 'This time you cannot go all in.'" On Dahlerus's view of Göring, see Dahlerus, *Der letzte Versuch*, pp. 85f., 93f. On Göring's approach see Kube, *Pour le mérite und Hakenkreuz*, pp. 318f.

163 Groscurth, *Tagebücher eines Abwehroffiziers*, p. 190 (entry for 28 Aug. 1939).

164 Goebbels, *Tagebücher*, part I, vol. 7, p. 83 (entry for 29 Aug. 1939).

165 Engel, *Heeresadjutant bei Hitler*, pp. 60f. (entry for 29 Aug. 1939). Engel commented: "We parted ways in a thoroughly subdued mood."

166 *ADAP*, Series D, vol. 7, no. 421, pp. 345–7.

167 Henderson, *Failure of a Mission*, pp. 264–6; see Schmidt, *Statist auf diplomatischer Bühne*, pp. 455f.; Ribbentrop, *Zwischen London und Moskau*, p. 191.

168 Schmidt, *Statist auf diplomatischer Bühne*, p. 456; see Ciano, *Tagebücher, 1939–1943*, p. 135 (entry for 29 Aug. 1939); *ADAP*, Series D, vol. 7, no. 411, pp. 338–40.

169 See Graml, *Europas Weg in den Krieg*, p. 299.

170 Goebbels, *Tagebücher*, part I, vol. 7, p. 86 (entry for 31 Aug. 1939). See Shirer, *This is Berlin*, pp. 66–7 (broadcast of 30 Aug. 1939).

171 See Below, *Als Hitlers Adjutant*, p. 191; Domarus, *Hitler*, vol. 2, part 1, pp. 1289f.

172 *ADAP*, Series D, vol. 7, no. 458, pp. 372–5; Domarus, *Hitler*, vol. 2, part 1, pp. 1291f.

173 Schmidt, *Statist auf diplomatischer Bühne*, p. 460. See Goebbels, *Tagebücher*, part I, vol. 7, p. 86 (entry for 31 Aug. 1939): "The Führer intends to toss out this document to the global public at the most opportune moment." The Soviet ambassador in London, Ivan Maisky, saw through Hitler's game, writing, "This can only be a manoeuvre." Gorodetsky (ed.), *Die Maiski-Tagebücher*, p. 345 (entry for 31 Aug. 1939).

174 *ADAP*, Series D, vol. 7, no. 461, pp. 376–8 (with appendix).

175 Schmidt, *Statist auf diplomatischer Bühne*, pp. 456–60; see also Henderson, *Failure of a Mission*, pp. 270–1; Hill (ed.), *Die Weizsäcker-Papiere 1933–1950*, p. 162 (entry for 30 Aug. 1939): Weizsäcker wrote of Ribbentrop treating Henderson "en canaille."

176 Henderson, *Failure of a Mission*, pp. 273.

177 Below, *Als Hitlers Adjutant*, pp. 191f.

178 Ibid., p. 194.

179 Hubatsch (ed.), *Hitlers Weisungen für die Kriegführung 1939–1945*, p. 23; Domarus, *Hitler*, vol. 2, part 1, pp. 1299f. On the reaction among military officers see Wagner, *Der Generalquartiermeister*, p. 109 (entry for 31 Aug. 1939): "We believe we will be done with Poland quickly, and honestly, we are looking forward to it. The situation must be cleaned up." General Erich Hoepner wrote to his wife one hour before the attack: "The Polish question simply *must* be solved." BA-MA Freiburg, N 51/9.

180 Goebbels, *Tagebücher*, part I, vol. 7, p. 87 (entry for 1 Sept. 1939).

181 Schmidt, *Statist auf diplomatischer Bühne*, p. 460; see Hill (ed.), *Die Weizsäcker-Papiere 1933–1950*, p. 163 (entry for 31 Aug. 1939).

182 Domarus, *Hitler*, vol. 2, part 1, pp. 1305f.; see Goebbels, *Tagebücher*, part I, vol. 7, p. 88 (entry for 1 Sept. 1939): "Then we fire out the Führer's memorandum. It will attract massive attention all over the world."

183 Goebbels, *Tagebücher*, part I, vol. 7, pp. 87f. (entry for 1 Sept. 1939). See Jürgen Runzheimer, "Der Überfall auf den Sender Gleiwitz im Jahr 1939," in *Vierteljahrshefte für Zeitgeschichte*, 10 (1962), pp. 408–26; Evans, *The Third Reich in Power*, pp. 699–700; Robert Gerwarth, *Reinhard Heydrich: Eine Biographie*, Munich, 2011, p. 173; Mueller, *Canaris*, pp. 270f.

184 Goebbels, *Tagebücher*, part I, vol. 7, p. 88 (entry for 1 Sept. 1939); Henrik Eberle and Matthias Uhl (eds), *Das Buch Hitler*, Bergisch Gladbach, 2005, p. 103.

185 See Schenk, *Hitlers Mann in Danzig*, pp. 125–33; Dieter Schenk, *Die Post von Danzig: Geschichte eines deutschen Justizmords*, Reinbek bei Hamburg, 1995, pp. 57ff.; Overy, *1939: Countdown to War*, pp. 69f.; Evans, *The Third Reich in Power*, p. 700. On Wieluń see the contribution from Joachim Trenkner in Richard Overy (ed.), *Ein Volk von Opfern? Die neue Debatte um den Bombenkrieg 1940–45*, Berlin, 2003, pp. 15–23.

186 See Eberle and Uhl (eds), *Das Buch Hitler*, p. 104.

187 Rudolf Buttmann's diary entry for 1 Sept. 1939; BayHStA München, Nl Buttmann 89. For an extensive account of Hitler's appearance, see Christoph Raichle, *Hitler als Symbolpolitiker*, Stuttgart, 2014, pp. 160–9.

188 Domarus, *Hitler*, vol. 2, part 1, pp. 1312–17.

189 See Shirer, *Berlin Diary*, p. 100 (entry for 1 Sept. 1939); Below, *Als Hitlers Adjutant*, p. 195.

190 See Gun, *Eva Braun*, p. 147; Görtemaker, *Eva Braun*, pp. 231f. Navy adjutant Karl-Jesko von Puttkamer noted Eva Braun's presence in the chancellery on 1 September 1939. See David Irving's notes on a conversation with Puttkamer and Mrs. Schmundt, 2 Apr. 1967; IfZ München, ZS 285.

191 Quotation in Henric L. Wuermeling, *August 1939—11 Tage zwischen Krieg und Frieden*, Munich, 1984, p. 181.

192 Shirer, *Berlin Diary*, p. 100 (entry for 1 Sept. 1939).

193 See the report of the Polish consul general in Hamburg, Władysław Ryzanek, to the Polish embassy in Berlin on 6 July 1939: "People believe in Hitler's genius and think that he will solve this problem too in the near future—and without a war." Bajohr and Strupp (eds), *Fremde Blicke auf das "Dritte Reich,"* p. 535.

194 Ibid., p. 536. See Willy Cohn, *Kein Recht, nirgends: Tagebuch vom Untergang des Breslauer Judentums 1933–1941*, ed. Norbert Conrads, vol. 2, Cologne, Weimar and Vienna, 2006, p. 683 (entry for 1 Sept. 1939): "No patriotic enthusiasm on the streets. Silent brooding."

195 Goebbels, *Tagebücher*, part I, vol. 7, p. 89 (entry for 2 Sept. 1939). See Speer, *Erinnerungen*, p. 181.

196 See Shirer, *Berlin Diary*, p. 100 (entry for 1 Sept. 1939); *idem, This is Berlin*, p. 70 (broadcast of 1 Sept. 1939).

197 Klemperer, *Tagebücher, 1933–1941*, p. 482 (entry for 3 Sept. 1939). In comparison, see Cohn, *Kein Recht, nirgends*, vol. 2, p. 682 (entry for 1 Sept. 1939): "With that, destiny is taking its course. The others will now intervene as well, and that means world war."

198 See Overy, *1939: Countdown to War*, pp. 74–6; Henderson, *Failure of a Mission*, p. 279; Coulondre, *Von Moskau nach Berlin*, p. 453.

199 Eberle and Uhl (eds), *Das Buch Hitler*, p. 105; Below, *Als Hitlers Adjutant*, p. 196. See also Goebbels, *Tagebücher*, part I, vol. 7, p. 87 (entry for 1 Sept. 1939): "The Führer does not believe that England will intervene. At the moment no one knows."

200 Goebbels, *Tagebücher*, part I, vol. 7, p. 90 (entry for 3 Sept. 1939).

201 See Overy, *1939: Countdown to War*, pp. 78–82; Schmidt, *Statist auf diplomatischer Bühne*, p. 462; Ciano, *Tagebücher, 1939–1943*, pp. 138f. (entry for 2 Sept. 1939).

202 See Overy, *1939: Countdown to War*, pp. 87, 92; Henderson, *Failure of a Mission*, pp. 283f.

203 Schmidt, *Statist auf diplomatischer Bühne*, p. 464.

204 For arguments against the thesis that Hitler mistakenly reckoned with British neutrality, see Adam Tooze, *The Wages of Destruction: The Making and Breaking of the Nazi Economy*, London, 2007, pp. 247f.; Kley, *Hitler, Ribbentrop und die Entfesselung des Zweiten Weltkriegs*, p. 318. On the other hand, Otto Dietrich (*12 Jahre mit Hitler*, p. 62) remarked: "Hitler had not expected England and France to go to war for Poland. You could clearly see how shocked he was." Manny von Neurath, the wife of Reich Protector of Bohemia and Moravia and former German foreign minister Konstantin von Neurath, also noted in her diary that Hitler, "led astray by von Ribbentrop," had not believed that England would enter into war because of Poland and was now "unpleasantly surprised." Lars Lüdicke, *Konstantin von Neurath: Eine politische Biographie*, Paderborn, 2014, p. 527. Adjutant Gerhard Engel recalled that Hitler had suffered a "full nervous breakdown." Memorandum by Helmut Heiber on a conversation with Engel on 20 March 1959; IfZ München, ZS 222, vol. 1. In an interview with Heinrich Uhlig on 17 November 1951, Engel spoke of a "total shock effect" and a "day of depression in the chancellery" (ibid.). See also Vormann, *So begann der Zweite Weltkrieg*, p. 75.

205 See Overy, *1939: Countdown to War*, pp. 100f.; Coulondre, *Von Moskau nach Berlin*, pp. 460–3.

206 Domarus, *Hitler*, vol. 2, part 1, pp. 1339–41 (at p. 1340); see Below, *Als Hitlers Adjutant*, p. 197. Hitler subsequently dictated his appeals to the eastern and western armies and the NSDAP to his secretaries. See Domarus, *Hitler*, vol. 2, part 1, pp. 1341–3; Vormann, *So begann der Zweite Weltkrieg*, p. 76.

207 Shirer, *Berlin Diary*, p. 101 (entry for 3 Sept. 1939); see also *idem, This is Berlin*, p. 75 (broadcast of 3 Sept. 1939).

208 See *Deutschland-Berichte der Sopade*, 6 (1939), pp. 980–3. For a summary see Marlies Steinert, *Hitlers Krieg und die Deutschen: Stimmung und Haltung der deutschen Bevölkerung im Zweiten Weltkrieg*, Düsseldorf and Vienna, 1970, pp. 91–3; Nicholas Stargardt, *The German War: A Nation Under Arms, 1939–45*, London, 2015, pp. 30–4.

209 Helmuth James von Moltke, *Briefe an Freya 1939–1945*, ed. Beate Ruhm von Oppen, Munich, 1988, p. 61 (entry for 3 Sept. 1939), p. 63 (entry for 5 Sept. 1939).

210 Speer, *Erinnerungen*, p. 179.

211 Goebbels, *Tagebücher*, part I, vol. 7, p. 92 (dated 4 Sept. 1939).

212 Christopher Clark, *The Sleepwalkers: How Europe Went to War in 1914*, London, 2012. For a critical view, see Volker Ullrich, "Zündschnur und Pulverdampf," in *Die Zeit*, no. 38, 12 Sept. 2013, p. 53; *idem*, "Nun schlittern sie wieder," in *Die Zeit*, no. 4, 16 Jan. 2014, p. 17. A concise overview of the historical research is provided by Annika Mombauer, *Die Julikrise: Europas Weg in den Ersten Weltkrieg*, Munich, 2014.

213 See Hans-Ulrich Wehler, *Deutsche Gesellschaftsgeschichte*, vol. 4, Munich, 2003, p. 842.

214 Thomas Mann, *Tagebücher, 1937–1939*, ed. Peter de Mendelssohn, Frankfurt am Main, 1980, p. 461 (see also entry for 28 Aug. 1939). See also Thomas Mann's radio address to German listeners of 15 January 1943, in which he said that "from the very beginning everything pointed and ran towards war." Thomas Mann, *An die gesittete Welt: Politische Schriften und Reden im Exil*, Frankfurt am Main, 1986, p. 551.

215 Kellner, *Tagebücher, 1939–1945*, vol. 2, p. 905 (entry for 12 Dec. 1944).

216 Hitler's speech to the commanders, 23 November 1939; Groscurth, *Tagebücher eines Abwehroffiziers*, p. 415. A different account had Hitler saying, "The decision to strike out always existed within me." Domarus, *Hitler*, vol. 2, part 1, p. 1423.

217 Goebbels, *Tagebücher*, part I, vol. 8, pp. 332f. (entry for 18 Sept. 1940). In March 1939 in San Francisco, Hitler's former adjutant Fritz Wiedemann recalled the dictator frequently saying in the summer of 1938: "Every generation needs to have gone through a war." BA Koblenz, N 1720/4.

218 Quoted in Hans Otto Eglau, *Fritz Thyssen: Hitlers Gönner und Geisel*, Berlin, 2003, pp. 226f. See Goebbels, *Tagebücher*, part I, vol. 7, p. 258 (entry for 4 Jan. 1940):

"Thyssen has sent the Führer a treasonous letter threatening to publish it ... A dirty trick!"

2 Poland 1939–1940: Prelude to a War of Annihilation

1   Max Domarus, *Hitler: Reden und Proklamationen 1932–1945*, vol. 2, part 1, Munich, 1965, p. 1238; See also Helmuth Greiner's notes of 22 August 1939: "[Hitler said] there could be no pity, no human emotions. He was duty-bound to the German people, which were unable to live in their present space." BA Koblenz, N 1033/13.

2   See Richard J. Evans, *The Third Reich at War, 1939–1945*, London, 2008, p. 13; on the preceding quotes, see the first volume of this biography, *Hitler: Ascent 1889–1939*, London, 2016, pp. 416, 749.

3   *Die Tagebücher von Joseph Goebbels*, commissioned by the Institute for Contemporary History, with support from the State Archive of Russia, ed. Elke Fröhlich, *Part I: Aufzeichnungen 1923–1941*, 9 vols in 14 parts, Munich, 1998–2008, vol. 7, p. 98 (entry for 9 Sept. 1939). On 9 September 1939, Erich Hoepner, commanding general of the 16th Army Corps, wrote to his wife: "To a large extent, the Poles are already demoralised. Huge columns of soldiers who have thrown away their weapons arrive without any German accompaniment." BA-MA Freiburg, N 51/9.

4   On the course of the operation, see Horst Rohde, "Hitlers erster 'Blitzkrieg' und seine Auswirkungen auf Nordosteuropa," in *Das Deutsche Reich und der Zweite Weltkrieg, Vol. 2: Die Errichtung der Hegemonie auf dem europäischen Kontinent*, Stuttgart, 1979, pp. 111ff.

5   William L. Shirer, *This is Berlin: Reporting from Nazi Germany, 1938–40*, London, 1999, p. 92 (broadcast of 24 Sept. 1939).

6   See *Das Deutsche Reich und der Zweite Weltkrieg*, vol. 2, p. 134 (Rohde's essay).

7   Goebbels, *Tagebücher*, part I, vol. 7, p. 96 (entry for 7 Sept. 1939). See ibid., p. 99 (dated 10 Sept. 1939): "All quiet on the western front." See Eduard Wagner, *Der Generalquartiermeister: Briefe und Tagebuchaufzeichnungen*, ed. Elisabeth Wagner, Munich and Vienna, 1963, p. 123 (entry for 4 Sept. 1939): "And still not a shot has been fired in the west, a strange beginning to a war."

8   Shirer, *This is Berlin*, p. 78 (broadcast of 5–6 Sept. 1939); William L. Shirer, *Berlin Diary 1934–41: The Rise of the Third Reich*, London, 1997, p. 103 (entry for 9 Sept. 1939).

9   Generaloberst Halder, *Kriegstagebuch: Tägliche Aufzeichnungen des Chefs des Generalstabs des Heeres 1939–1942*, vol. 1, ed. Hans-Adolf Jacobsen, Stuttgart, 1962, vol. 1, p. 89 (entry for 20 Sept. 1939). In a letter of 23 September 1939, General Günther von Kluge remarked: "The Russians are following quite quickly, and we cannot take away everything important (even the loot)." BA-MA Freiburg, MSg 2/11185.

10 See *Das Deutsche Reich und der Zweite Weltkrieg*, vol. 2, pp. 131–3 (Rohde's essay). In conversation with tank general Heinz Guderian, Hitler said he was "quite amazed" at the small number of losses the general's corps had suffered and compared them with casualty statistics for his own "List Regiment" on the first day alone of his frontline service in 1914. See Heinz Guderian, *Erinnerungen eines Soldaten*, Heidelberg, 1951, p. 65.

11 BA Koblenz, N 1310/74.

12 See Franz W. Seidler and Dieter Zeigert, *Die Führerhauptquartiere: Anlagen und Planungen im Zweiten Weltkrieg*, Munich, 2000, pp. 124–8; Uwe Neumärker, Robert Conrad and Cord Woywodt, *Wolfsschanze: Hitlers Machtzentrale im Zweiten Weltkrieg*, 3rd edition, Berlin, 2007, pp. 20f.

13 See Geheime Kommandosache, *Führerzug*; BA Koblenz, N 1340/288; Nicolaus von Below, *Als Hitlers Adjutant 1937–45*, Mainz, 1980, p. 204; Neumärker *et al.*, *Wolfsschanze*, p. 20; Stefan Krings, *Hitlers Pressechef: Otto Dietrich 1897–1952. Eine Biographie*,

Göttingen, 2010, pp. 404ff.; Jochen von Lang, *Der Sekretär: Martin Bormann. Der Mann, der Hitler beherrschte*, Stuttgart, 1977, pp. 149f; Nikolaus von Vormann, *So begann der Zweite Weltkrieg: Zeitzeuge der Entscheidungen. Als Offizier bei Hitler 22. August 1939–1. Oktober 1939*, Leoni, 1988, pp. 78f.

14 Christa Schroeder to Johanna Nusser, 11 Sept. 1939; IfZ München, ED 524; published in Schroeder, *Er war mein Chef: Aus dem Nachlass der Sekretärin von Adolf Hitler*, ed. Anton Joachimsthaler, 3rd edition, Munich and Vienna, 1985, pp. 98–100 (at p. 99). There was always a "veritable jostling" about the order of vehicles in the motorcade; Bernhard von Lossberg, *Im Wehrmachtführungsstab: Bericht eines Generalstabsoffiziers*, Hamburg, 1950, p. 40; Vormann, *So begann der Zweite Weltkrieg*, p. 87. On the visits to the front, see also Christoph Raichle, *Hitler als Symbolpolitiker*, Stuttgart, 2014, pp. 177–92.

15 See Jürgen Löffler, *Walther von Brauchitsch (1981–1948): Eine politische Biographie*, Frankfurt am Main, 2001, p. 165; Geoffrey P. Megargee, *Hitler und die Generäle: Das Ringen um die Führung der Wehrmacht 1939–1945*, Paderborn, 2006, p. 86; Walter Warlimont, *Im Hauptquartier der deutschen Wehrmacht 1939–1945: Grundlagen— Formen—Gestalten*, Frankfurt am Main and Bonn, 1964, p. 46; Generalfeldmarschall Keitel, *Verbrecher oder Offizier? Erinnerungen, Briefe, Dokumente des Chefs des OKW*, ed. Walter Görlitz, Berlin and Frankfurt am Main, 1961, pp. 216f.; Christian Hartmann, *Halder: Generalstabschef Hitlers 1938–1942*, 2nd edition, Paderborn, 2010, p. 146; Seidler and Zeigert, *Die Führerhauptquartiere*, pp. 126f.

16 See Rudolf Herz, *Hoffmann & Hitler: Fotografie als Medium des Führer-Mythos*, Munich, 1994, pp. 302–5; Wolfram Pyta, *Hitler: Der Künstler als Politiker und Feldherr*, Munich, 2015, pp. 275f.

17 Otto Dietrich, *Auf den Strassen des Sieges: Erlebnisse mit dem Führer in Polen*, Munich, 1940; see Krings, *Hitlers Pressechef*, pp. 403f.; Raichle. *Hitler als Symbolpolitiker*, pp. 173–7; Pyta, *Hitler*, p. 276.

18 Vormann, *So begann der Zweite Weltkrieg*, p. 141.

19 Domarus, *Hitler*, vol. 2, part 1, pp. 1354–66 (at pp. 1359, 1364).

20 Thomas Mann, *Tagebücher, 1937–1939*, ed. Peter de Mendelssohn, Frankfurt am Main, 1980, p. 474 (entry for 19 Sept. 1939).

21 See Below, *Als Hitlers Adjutant*, pp. 207, 210.

22 BA-MA Freiburg, MSg 2/11185.

23 See Keitel, *Verbrecher oder Offizier?*, p. 219; Hans Baur, *Ich flog Mächtige dieser Erde*, Kempten (Allgäu), 1956, p. 180. On Frisch's death and Hitler's reaction, see Karl-Heinz Janssen and Fritz Tobias, *Der Sturz der Generäle: Hitler und die Blomberg-Fritsch-Krise 1938*, Munich, 1994, pp. 248–51; Raichle, *Hitler als Symbolpolitiker*, pp. 206–13.

24 Galeazzo Ciano, *Tagebücher, 1939–1943*, Bern, 1946, p. 155 (entry for 1 Oct. 1939); see Schmidt, *Statist auf diplomatischer Bühne*, p. 471; Andreas Hillgruber (ed.), *Staatsmänner und Diplomaten bei Hitler: Vertrauliche Aufzeichnungen über Unterredungen mit Vertretern des Auslandes 1939–1941*, Frankfurt am Main, 1967, pp. 34–47.

25 See Keitel, *Verbrecher oder Offizier?*, p. 219; Erich von Manstein, *Verlorene Siege*, Bonn, 1955, p. 55; Pyta, *Hitler*, p. 276. On the victory parade in Warsaw, see Below, *Als Hitlers Adjutant*, p. 211.

26 Shirer, *Berlin Diary*, pp. 103 (entry for 8 Sept. 1939), 194 (entries for 10 Sept. and 11 Sept. 1939); see also idem, *This is Berlin*, p. 80 (broadcast of 8 Sept. 1939).

27 Friedrich Kellner, *"Vernebelt, verdunkelt sind alle Hirne": Tagebücher, 1939–1945*, ed. Sascha Feuchert et al., Göttingen, 2011, vol. 1, p. 24 (entry for 16 Sept. 1939).

28 Shirer, *Berlin Diary*, pp. 108 (entry for 20 Sept. 1939).

29 Victor Klemperer, *Ich will Zeugnis ablegen bis zum letzten: Tagebücher*, vol. 1: 1933–1941, vol. 2: 1942–1945, ed. Walter Nowojski with Hadwig Klemperer, Berlin, 1995, p. 493 (entry for 29 Sept. 1939). In late September 1939, the 20-year-old German literature student Lore Walb wrote in her diary: "The world has never seen such a campaign, with the total destruction of the enemy in barely four weeks. It is wonderful to

be German." Lore Walb, *Ich, die Alte—ich, die Junge: Konfrontation mit meinen Tagebüchern 1933–1945*, Berlin, 1997, p. 141.

30   Goebbels, *Tagebücher*, part I, vol. 7, p. 119 (entry for 24 Sept. 1939). See *Deutschland-Berichte der Sozialdemokratischen Partei Deutschlands (Sopade) 1934–1940*, ed. Klaus Behnken, Frankfurt am Main, 1980, 6 (1939), p. 980. The reports of the Social Democratic Party in exile spoke of a "widespread naïve belief that peace could follow quickly upon the Polish campaign." See also Generalfeldmarschall Wilhelm Ritter von Leeb, *Tagebuchaufzeichnungen und Lagebeurteilungen aus zwei Weltkriegen*, ed. Georg Meyer, Stuttgart, 1976, p. 184 (entry for 3 Oct. 1939): "Everyone is waiting for peace. The people sense that war is unnecessary."

31   Goebbels, *Tagebücher*, part I, vol. 7, p. 106 (entry for 15 Sept. 1939).

32   Ibid., p. 120 (entry for 24 Sept. 1939).

33   Halder, *Kriegstagebuch*, vol. 1, pp. 86–9 (at pp. 86, 88); memorandum by Helmuth Greiner of 27 Sept. 1939 (removed from the war diary on Warlimont's orders); BA Koblenz, N 1033/2. After his speech, Hitler tore up his handwritten notes of bullet points and burned them in his office fireplace. See Walter Warlimont's memorandum "Militärpolitische Vorgänge um den Westfeldzug" 1939/40, dated 25 Sept. 1945; IfZ München, ZS 312. Hitler also told the leaders of the army groups and armies two days later that, "if diplomatic efforts to end the war did not succeed, he would have to force a decision. Compromise was out of the question." Fedor von Bock, *Zwischen Pflicht und Verweigerung: Das Kriegstagebuch*, ed. Klaus Gerbet, Munich, 1995, p. 61 (entry for 30 Sept. 1939). For further context, see Hans Umbreit, "Der Kampf um die Vormachtstellung im Westen," in *Das Deutsche Reich und der Zweite Weltkrieg*, vol. 2, p. 238.

34   Goebbels, *Tagebücher*, part I, vol. 7, p. 132 (entry for 1 Oct. 1939).

35   Ibid., p. 139 (entry for 6 Oct. 1939).

36   See Shirer, *This is Berlin*, p. 106 (broadcast of 6 Oct. 1939); Wagner, *Der Generalquartiermeister*, p. 139 (entry for 6 Oct. 1939): "The speech lost much of its effect because he read through it at breakneck speed."

37   Domarus, *Hitler*, vol. 2, part 1, pp. 1377–93 (at pp. 1389, 1393). See Leeb, *Tagebuchaufzeichnungen*, p. 187 (entry for 6 Oct. 1939): "Hitler's speech in the Reichstag, talked about peace but made no concrete suggestions—weak! ... I fear he will be rebuffed by England and France with derisive laughter."

38   Thomas Mann, *Tagebücher, 1937–1939*, p. 483 (entry for 6 Oct. 1939).

39   Heinz Boberach (ed.), *Meldungen aus dem Reich: Die geheimen Lageberichte des Sicherheitsdienstes der SS 1938–1945*, Herrsching, 1984, vol. 2, p. 339. See Ruth Andreas-Friedrich, *Der Schattenmann: Tagebuchaufzeichnungen 1938–1945*, Frankfurt am Main, 1983, p. 64 (entry for 10 Oct. 1939); Goebbels, *Tagebücher*, part I, vol. 7, p. 148 (entry for 11 Oct. 1939); Nicholas Stargardt, *The German War: A Nation Under Arms, 1939–45*, London, 2015, pp. 48–9.

40   Domarus, *Hitler*, vol. 2, part 1, p. 1398.

41   Gabriel Gorodetsky (ed.), *Die Maiski-Tagebücher: Ein Diplomat im Kampf gegen Hitler*, Munich, 2016, p. 359 (entry for 6 Oct. 1939).

42   Published in Hans-Adolf Jacobsen (ed.), *Dokumente zur Vorgeschichte des Westfeldzuges 1939–1940*, Göttingen, 1956, pp. 4–21 (at p. 6). See Halder, *Kriegstagebuch*, vol. 1, pp. 101–3. See also the extensive account in Hans-Adolf Jacobsen, *Fall Gelb: Der Kampf um den deutschen Operationsplan zur Westoffensive 1940*, Wiesbaden, 1957, pp. 15–18.

43   Walther Hubatsch (ed.), *Hitlers Weisungen für die Kriegsführung*, Munich, 1965, p. 37.

44   Goebbels, *Tagebücher*, part I, vol. 7, p. 153 (entry for 14 Oct. 1939). See ibid., p. 166 (entry for 24 Oct. 1939): "[The Führer] no longer thinks at all about peace. He would like to put England to the sword."

45   Ibid., p. 158 (entry for 18 Oct. 1939). See ibid., p. 164 (entry for 23 Oct. 1939): "I am stubbornly working on this man's fall. He is the cause of war and the extension of war."

46 Domarus, *Hitler*, vol. 2, part 1, p. 1382.

47 Notes about a confidential speech by Hitler to the Reichsleiter and Gauleiter in the chancellery on 21 Oct. 1939; Helmuth Groscurth, *Tagebücher eines Abwehroffiziers 1938–1940*, ed. Helmuth Krausnick and Harold C. Deutsch with Hildegard von Kotze, Stuttgart, 1970, appendix I, no. 26, p. 385; Goebbels, *Tagebücher*, part I, vol. 7, p. 164 (entry for 22 Oct. 1939). See ibid., p. 198 (entry for 17 Nov. 1939): "He is thinking about completely liquidating the Peace of Westphalia, which was concluded in Münster and which he wants to eradicate in Münster. That would be our very great goal. If that is achieved, we could sleep peacefully at night." Hitler also told former German chancellor Franz von Papen in October 1939: "The opportunity will never come again to revise the Peace of Westphalia." Franz von Papen, *Der Wahrheit eine Gasse*, Munich, 1952, p. 518.

48 *ADAP*, Series D, vol. 7, no. 229, p. 207.

49 Quotation from Martin Broszat, *Nationalsozialistische Polenpolitik 1939–1945*, Frankfurt am Main, 1965, p. 15. See also Halder, *Kriegstagebuch*, vol. 1, p. 65 (dated 7 Sept. 1939).

50 Domarus, *Hitler*, vol. 2, part 1, p. 1362.

51 See Broszat, *Nationalsozialistische Polenpolitik*, pp. 16–18.

52 Domarus, *Hitler*, vol. 2, part 1, p. 1383.

53 Jürgen Matthäus and Frank Bajohr (eds), *Alfred Rosenberg: Die Tagebücher von 1934 bis 1944*, Frankfurt am Main, 2015, p. 290 (entry for 29 Sept. 1939). See also Ciano's account of Hitler's statement on 1 October 1939: "When visiting the front, he found Poland so decrepit and run-down that he wanted to have as little to do with it as possible." Hillgruber (ed.), *Staatsmänner und Diplomaten bei Hitler 1939–1941*, p. 40.

54 Goebbels, *Tagebücher*, part I, vol. 7, p. 147 (entry for 10 Oct. 1939); see ibid., p. 141 (entry for 7 Oct. 1939).

55 See Broszat, *Nationalsozialistische Polenpolitik*, p. 18.

56 See ibid., pp. 36–41. For more on Greiser see Catherine Epstein, *Model Nazi: Arthur Greiser and the Occupation of Western Poland*, Oxford and New York, 2010.

57 See Dieter Schenk, *Hans Frank: Hitlers Kronjurist und Generalgouverneur*, Frankfurt am Main, 2006, pp. 146f., 153f. See Goebbels, *Tagebücher*, part I, vol. 7, p. 286 (entry for 28 Jan. 1940): "Frank feels somewhat like a frustrated tzar."

58 "Führer's meeting with the chief of the High Command of the Wehrmacht about Germany's intentions for Poland," 17 Oct. 1939; *Der Prozess gegen die Hauptkriegsverbrecher vor dem internationalen Militärtribunal in Nürnberg*, 42 vols, Nuremberg, 1947–9 (hereafter *IMT*), vol. 26, pp. 377–83; see Schenk, *Hans Frank*, p. 148; Michael Wildt, *Generation des Unbedingten: Das Führungskorps des Reichssicherheitshauptamtes*, Hamburg, 2002, p. 474. Halder learned from General Quartermaster Wagner about the meeting and summarised Hitler's intentions: "Prevent Polish intelligentsia from rising into a new leadership class. Low standard of living should be preserved. Cheap slaves. The rabble must entirely disappear from German territory." Halder, *Kriegstagebuch*, vol. 1, p. 107 (entry for 18 Oct. 1939).

59 See Helmut Krausnick, *Hitlers Einsatzgruppen: Die Truppen des Weltanschauungskrieges 1938–1942*, Frankfurt am Main, 1985, pp. 71f.; Wildt, *Generation des Unbedingten*, pp. 477f.

60 Cited in Krausnick, *Hitlers Einsatzgruppen*, p. 29; see Robert Gerwarth, *Reinhard Heydrich: Eine Biographie*, Munich, 2011, pp. 170–2; Wildt, *Generation des Unbedingten*, pp. 422–8; Evans, *The Third Reich at War*, pp. 16–18. On the whole organisation, see Klaus-Michael Mallmann, Jochen Böhler and Jürgen Matthäus (eds), *Einsatzgruppen in Polen: Darstellung und Dokumentation*, Darmstadt, 2008.

61 Quoted in Krausnick, *Hitlers Einsatzgruppen*, p. 36; Wildt, *Generation des Unbedingten*, p. 449.

62 See Gerwarth, *Reinhard Heydrich*, pp. 169, 177.

63 Quotation in Broszat, *Nationalsozialistische Polenpolitik*, p. 21; see Wildt, *Generation des Unbedingten*, p. 458. Goebbels noted on 25 October 1939: "There's not much left of the intelligentsia." *Tagebücher*, part I, vol. 7, p. 167.

64 See Gerwarth, *Reinhard Heydrich*, pp. 177, 185. For an overview of the mass executions in Poland from the autumn of 1939 to the spring of 1940, see Peter Longerich, *Politik der Vernichtung: Eine Gesamtdarstellung der nationalsozialistischen Judenverfolgung*, Munich and Zurich, 1998, pp. 243–8.

65 See Christian Jansen and Arno Weckbecker, *Der "Volksdeutsche Selbstschutz" in Polen 1939/40*, Munich, 1992, pp. 27f.; Wildt, *Generation des Unbedingten*, pp. 439f.n71). On the current state of research, see Markus Krzoska, "Der 'Bromberger Blutsonntag' 1939: Kontroversen und Forschungsergebnisse," in *Vierteljahrshefte für Zeitgeschichte*, 60 (2012), pp. 237–48.

66 Christian Jansen and Arno Weckbecker, "Eine Miliz im 'Weltanschauungskrieg,' " in Wolfgang Michalka (ed.), *Der Zweite Weltkrieg: Analysen—Grundzüge—Forschungsbilanz*, Munich, 1989, pp. 482–500 (at p. 490). See also Evans, *The Third Reich at War*, p. 14.

67 See Wildt, *Generation des Unbedingten*, pp. 480f.

68 Erich Hoepner to his wife, 9 Sept. 1939; BA-MA Freiburg, N 51/9.

69 See Jochen Böhler, *Auftakt zum Vernichtungskrieg: Die Wehrmacht in Polen*, Frankfurt am Main, 2006, pp. 42ff., 54ff.; Michaela Kipp, *"Grossreinemachen im Osten": Feindbilder in deutschen Feldpostbriefen im Zweiten Weltkrieg*, Frankfurt am Main, 2014, pp. 386–93. On the 1914 massacres in Belgium, see John Horne and Alan Kramer, *German Atrocities 1914: A History of Denial*, Yale, 2001.

70 Wagner, *Der Generalquartiermeister*, p. 127 (entry for 5 Sept. 1939).

71 See Böhler, *Auftakt zum Vernichtungskrieg*, in particular pp. 169ff., 188ff.; Saul Friedländer, *The Years of Extermination: Nazi Germany and the Jews 1939–1945*, London, 2007, pp. 27f.

72 On the parallels and differences between 1939 and 1941, see Dieter Pohl, *Die Herrschaft der Wehrmacht: Deutsche Militärbesatzung und einheimische Bevölkerung in der Sowjetunion 1941–1944*, Munich, 2008, pp. 53–6.

73 Halder, *Kriegstagebuch*, vol. 1, p. 68 (entry for 10 Sept. 1939).

74 Groscurth, *Tagebücher eines Abwehroffiziers*, pp. 201 (entry for 8 Sept. 1939), 202 (entry for 9 Sept. 1939).

75 Note for the file by Lieutenant von Lahousen about the discussion in the Führer's train, 12 Sept. 1939; ibid., no. 12, p. 358. See Michael Mueller, *Canaris: Hitlers Abwehrchef*, Berlin, 2006, p. 297.

76 Cited in Gerwarth, *Reinhard Heydrich*, p. 184; see Böhler, *Auftakt zum Vernichtungskrieg*, p. 237.

77 Hellmuth Stieff, *Briefe*, ed. Horst Mühleisen, Berlin, 1991, p. 108 (dated 21 Nov. 1939).

78 Quotation in Krausnick, *Hitlers Einsatzgruppen*, pp. 79, 84. See Broszat, *Nationalsozialistische Polenpolitik*, pp. 44f.; Bock, *Das Kriegstagebuch*, p. 78 (entry for 20 Nov. 1939): "I am hearing a lot about the 'colonisation' of the east that has deeply shocked me."

79 *Heeresadjutant bei Hitler 1938–1943: Aufzeichnungen des Majors Engel*, ed. Hildegard von Kotze, Stuttgart, 1974, pp. 66 (entry for 15 Oct. 1939), 68 (entry for 18 Nov. 1939). See Evans, *The Third Reich at War*, pp. 25f.

80 Quoted in Krausnick, *Hitlers Einsatzgruppen*, p. 67; see Böhler, *Auftakt zum Vernichtungskrieg*, p. 153; Wildt, *Generation des Unbedingten*, p. 473.

81 *Die Verfolgung und Ermordung der europäischen Juden durch das nationalsozialistische Deutschland 1933–1945*, vol. 3, ed. Andrea Löw, Munich, 2012, doc. 18, pp. 115–17. See Peter Longerich, *Heinrich Himmler: Biographie*, Munich, 2008, pp. 449, 453; Wildt, *Generation des Unbedingten*, p. 462.

82 Engel, *Heeresadjutant bei Hitler*, pp. 62f. (entries for 26 Sept. and 28 Sept. 1939).

83 Goebbels, *Tagebücher*, part I, vol. 7, p. 130 (entry for 30 Sept. 1939).

84 See Broszat, *Nationalsozialistische Polenpolitik*, pp. 64f., 84–6; Longerich, *Heinrich Himmler*, pp. 451f.; Gerwarth, *Reinhard Heydrich*, pp. 189f.

85   See Broszat, *Nationalsozialistische Polenpolitik*, p. 89.

86   Wilm Hosenfeld, *"Ich versuche jeden zu retten": Das Leben eines deutschen Offiziers in Briefen und Tagebüchern*, ed. Thomas Vogel, Munich, 2004, pp. 301f. (entry for 14 Dec. 1939). See Evans, *The Third Reich at War*, p. 30f; Longerich, *Politik der Vernichtung*, pp. 264f.

87   See Broszat, *Nationalsozialistische Polenpolitik*, pp. 91–7; Longerich, *Heinrich Himmler*, pp. 460f.; Gerwarth, *Reinhard Heydrich*, pp. 199f.; Schenk, *Hans Frank*, pp. 206f.

88   Quoted in Schenk, *Hans Frank*, p. 144.

89   Cited in ibid., p. 158.

90   Quoted in Markus Roth, *Herrenmenschen: Die deutschen Kreishauptleute im besetzten Polen. Karrierewege, Herrschaftspraxis und Nachgeschichte*, Göttingen, 2009, p. 11. On the lifestyles of the district leaders, see ibid. pp. 50ff; on recruiting, pp. 87ff.; and on their scope of action, pp. 72ff.

91   Quoted in ibid., pp. 177; see Schenk, *Hans Frank*, p. 223.

92   See Roth, *Herrenmenschen*, pp. 178ff.

93   See Broszat, *Nationalsozialistische Polenpolitik*, pp. 99–102; Schenk, *Hans Frank*, pp. 208–10; Roth, *Herrenmenschen*, pp. 121–31.

94   Note for the file by Bormann dated 2 Oct. 1940; BA Berlin-Lichterfelde NS 6/772. See Goebbels, *Tagebücher*, part I, vol. 8, p. 406 (entry for 5 Nov. 1940): "The Führer has decided that Poland will be a huge reservoir of labour for us, from which he can draw the people we need for menial jobs. We have to get them from somewhere."

95   Leeb, *Tagebuchaufzeichnungen*, p. 207 (entry for 3 Jan. 1940). This was preceded by a message from Leeb to Halder on 19 December 1939, in which he, on the basis of information provided by Groscurth, described the "behaviour of the police in Poland" as "unworthy of a cultured nation." Ibid., appendix VII, p. 473. See also the diary entry of 19 Dec. 1939, ibid., p. 206.

96   Quoted in Krausnick, *Hitlers Einsatzgruppen*, p. 85.

97   *Heinrich Himmlers Taschenkalender 1940: Kommentierte Edition*, ed. Markus Moors and Moritz Pfeiffer, Paderborn, 2013, pp. 216f. For context see Klaus-Jürgen Müller, "Zur Vorgeschichte und Inhalt der Rede Himmlers vor der höheren Generalität am 13. März 1940 in Koblenz," in *Vierteljahrshefte für Zeitgeschichte*, 18 (1970), pp. 95–122; Krausnick, *Hitlers Einsatzgruppen*, pp. 86f.; Löffler, *Walther von Brauchitsch*, p. 178.

98   IfZ München, ZS 627 (memorandum by Wilhelm Ulex from 1953). See Krausnick, *Hitlers Einsatzgruppen*, p. 87.

99   See Johannes Hürter, *Hitlers Heerführer: Die deutschen Oberbefehlshaber im Krieg gegen die Sowjetunion 1941/42*, Munich, 2007, p. 188: "People are increasingly and knowingly arranging themselves with a criminal system."

3 Decision in the West?

1   Hans-Adolf Jacobsen (ed.), *Dokumente zur Vorgeschichte des Westfeldzuges 1939–1940*, Göttingen, 1956, pp. 6f. See Generaloberst Halder, *Kriegstagebuch: Tägliche Aufzeichnungen des Chefs des Generalstabs des Heeres 1939–1942*, vol. 1, ed. Hans-Adolf Jacobsen, Stuttgart, 1962, p. 101 (entry for 10 Oct. 1939): "Change in the Russian stance not to be expected in the foreseeable future. Questionable whether later."

2   Jacobsen, *Dokumente zur Vorgeschichte des Westfeldzugs*, p. 9. See Andreas Hillgruber, "Der Faktor Amerika in Hitlers Strategie 1938–1941," in idem, *Deutsche Grossmacht- und Weltpolitik im 19. und 20. Jahrhundert*, Düsseldorf, 1977, pp. 197–222 (at pp. 205f.).

3   *Die Tagebücher von Joseph Goebbels*, commissioned by the Institute for Contemporary History, with support from the State Archive of Russia, ed. Elke Fröhlich, *Part I: Aufzeichnungen 1923–1941*, 9 vols in 14 parts, Munich, 1998–2008, vol. 7, p. 166 (entry for 24 Oct. 1939). See also Jürgen Matthäus and Frank Bajohr (eds), *Alfred Rosenberg:*

Die Tagebücher von 1934 bis 1944, Frankfurt am Main, 2015, p. 296 (entry for 1 Nov. 1939): "[The English] will not see the light until they absorb a terrible blow."

4   See Christian Hartmann, *Halder: Generalstabschef Hitlers 1938–1942*, 2nd edition, Paderborn, 2010, p. 160; *Das Deutsche Reich und der Zweite Weltkrieg, Vol. 2: Die Errichtung der Hegemonie auf dem europäischen Kontinent*, Stuttgart, 1979, p. 240 (Umbreit's essay).

5   Memorandum from Leeb to Brauchitsch, 11 Oct. 1939; Generalfeldmarschall Wilhelm Ritter von Leeb, *Tagebuchaufzeichnungen und Lagebeurteilungen aus zwei Weltkriegen*, ed. Georg Meyer, Stuttgart, 1976, appendix V, pp. 468–71. General Günther von Kluge also concluded in a letter of 13 October 1939 that "there is no thinking about a definitive defeat of England and France . . . because we simply lack the strength." The result would be "a bleeding out on a very grand scale." For that reason, Kluge found it advisable to hold the Siegfried Line, which "will become stronger and stronger month by month." BA-MA Freiburg, MSg 2/11185.

6   Halder, *Kriegstagebuch*, vol. 1, p. 107 (entry for 17 Oct. 1939).

7   Helmuth Groscurth, *Tagebücher eines Abwehroffiziers 1938–1940*, ed. Helmuth Krausnick and Harold C. Deutsch with Hildegard von Kotze, Stuttgart, 1970, p. 218 (entry for 16 Oct. 1939). The supreme commander of Army Group B, General von Bock, also found Halder "visibly subdued" one day later. Fedor von Bock, *Zwischen Pflicht und Verweigerung: Das Kriegstagebuch*, ed. Klaus Gerbet, Munich, 1995, p. 65 (entry for 17 Oct. 1939). See Hartmann, *Halder*, p. 165.

8   See Generalfeldmarschall Keitel, *Verbrecher oder Offizier? Erinnerungen, Briefe, Dokumente des Chefs des OKW*, ed. Walter Görlitz, Berlin and Frankfurt am Main, 1961, pp. 223f.

9   See Halder, *Kriegstagebuch*, vol. 1, pp. 114f. (entry for 27 Oct. 1939); Hartmann, *Halder*, pp. 166f.

10 Leeb, *Tagebuchaufzeichnungen*, pp. 194f. (entries for 30 Oct. and 31 Oct. 1939).

11 Halder, *Kriegstagebuch*, vol. 1, p. 105 (entry for 14 Oct. 1939).

12 See Elisabeth Chowaniec, *Der "Fall Dohnanyi" 1943–1945: Widerstand, Militärjustiz, SS-Willkür*, Munich, 1991, p. 15; Elisabeth Sifton and Fritz Stern, *Keine gewöhnlichen Männer: Dietrich Bonhoeffer und Hans von Dohnanyi im Widerstand gegen Hitler*, Munich, 2013, pp. 88f.

13 Hasso von Etzdorf, "Erinnerungen an den bei Stalingrad gefallenen Oberst i. G. Helmuth Groscurth," 14. Nov. 1947: "In the Army High Command, [Groscurth] was the soul of the resistance." IfZ München, ZS 322, vol. 1. See Joachim Fest, *Staatsstreich: Der lange Weg zum 20. Juli*, Berlin, 1994, pp. 125–7; Klaus-Jürgen Müller, *Generaloberst Ludwig Beck: Eine Biographie*, Paderborn, 2008, pp. 389, 395f., 400. For a general account of the plans for a coup, see Peter Hoffmann, *Widerstand, Staatsstreich, Attentat: Der Kampf der Opposition gegen Hitler*, 4th edition, Munich and Zurich, 1985, pp. 146–86.

14 Ulrich von Hassell, *Vom andern Deutschland: Aus den nachgelassenen Tagebüchern 1938–1944*, Frankfurt am Main, 1964, pp. 78f. (entry for 11 Oct. 1939).

15 Ibid., pp. 84 (entry for 19 Oct. 1939), p. 86 (entry for 29 Oct. 1939). See Groscurth, *Tagebücher eines Abwehroffiziers*, p. 220 (dated 23 Oct. 1939): "Everything now depends on moving v. B[rauchitsch] and H[alder] to take immediate action."

16 See Hartmann, *Halder*, p. 166.

17 Groscurth, *Tagebücher eines Abwehroffiziers*, pp. 222f. (entry for 1 Nov. 1939).

18 Müller, *Generaloberst Ludwig Beck*, p. 402.

19 Leeb, *Tagebuchaufzeichnungen*, p. 199 (entry for 9 Nov. 1939).

20 Ibid., appendix VI, p. 472.

21 Keitel, *Verbrecher oder Offizier?*, p. 225. Keitel was summoned by Hitler during the meeting. See file note by Helmuth Greiner of 5 Nov. 1939 ("by order of Warlimont stricken from the war diary"), BA Koblenz, N 1033/2; Walter Warlimont's memorandum "Militärpolitische Vorgänge um den Westfeldzug" 1939/40, dated 25 Sept. 1945; IfZ München, ZS 312. See also Jürgen Löffler, *Walther von Brauchitsch*

(1981–1948): Eine politische Biographie, Frankfurt am Main, 2001, pp. 193–5; Halder, *Kriegstagebuch*, vol. 1, pp. 120 (entry for 5 Nov. 1939), 132 (entry for 23 Nov. 1939). Karl Jasko von Puttkamer recalled Hitler exploding, after being told of "troop indiscipline verging on mutiny": "Which regiment was that? I am going there immediately!" Interview by Heinrich Uhlig with Puttkamer dated 12 March 1952; IfZ München, ZS 285.

22 *Heeresadjutant bei Hitler 1938–1943: Aufzeichnungen des Majors Engel*, ed. Hildegard von Kotze, Stuttgart, 1974, p. 67 (entry for 7 Nov./10 Nov. 1939). See also the testimony of Gerhard Engel on 3 May 1966, "betr. Aussprache Hitler–Oberbefehlshaber des Heeres am 5. November 1939 im grossen Kongresssaal der alten Reichskanzlei"; IfZ München, ZS 222, vol. 1. On Hitler's continuing mistrust of Brauchitsch, see Leeb, *Tagebuchaufzeichnungen*, p. 207 (entry for 3 Jan. 1940); file note by Greiner dated 5 Nov. 1939; BA Koblenz, N 1033/2.

23 Testimony of Gerhard Engel dated 3 May 1966; IfZ München, ZS 222, vol. 1. See Groscurth, *Tagebücher eines Abwehroffiziers*, p. 224 (entry for 5 Nov. 1939): "Br[auchitsch] has completely broken down."

24 See Hartmann, *Halder*, p. 170.

25 Groscurth, *Tagebücher eines Abwehroffiziers*, p. 225 (entry for 5–6 Nov. 1939). See the testimony of Groscurth's secretary, Inge Haag, on 4 April 1948; IfZ München, ZS 2093. Decades later Halder still insisted that while Groscurth had intended "the best . . . he lost sight of the limits of what was possible." Franz Halder to Helmut Krausnick, 7 July 1967; IfZ München, ZS 240, vol. 5.

26 Erich Hoepner to his wife, 7 Nov. 1939; BA-MA Freiburg, N 51/9.

27 Goebbels, *Tagebücher*, part I, vol. 7, pp. 184 (entry for 7 Nov. 1939), 187 (entry for 9 Nov. 1939).

28 See Helmut G. Haasis, *Den Hitler jag ich in die Luft: Der Attentäter Georg Elser*, Hamburg, 2009, pp. 112f. According to Max Wünsche's appointment diary, Hitler went from his private apartment to the Bürgerbräukeller at 7:55 p.m. At 8:15 p.m., after being introduced by Christian Weber, he began his speech, which lasted until 9:05. At 9:15, he and his entourage left for the train station. At 9:30 p.m., his train departed, not arriving in Berlin until 10:23 a.m. the following day. BA Berlin-Lichterfelde, NS 10/591. See also Harald Sandner, *Hitler: Das Itinerar. Aufenthaltsorte und Reisen von 1889–1945*, Berlin, 2016, vol. 3, pp. 1758–60.

29 Goebbels, *Tagebücher*, part I, vol. 7, pp. 187f. (entry for 9 Nov. 1939).

30 Max Domarus, *Hitler: Reden und Proklamationen 1932–1945*, vol. 2, part 1, Munich, 1965, pp. 1404–14 (at pp. 1406, 1412f.). For a comprehensive analysis of the speech, see Haasis, *Den Hitler jag ich in die Luft*, pp. 114–20.

31 Testimony of Julius Schaub, "Der 8. November 1939"; IfZ München, ED 100, vol. 203. See Rosenberg, *Die Tagebücher von 1934 bis 1944*, p. 300 (entry for 11 Nov. 1939).

32 See Haasis, *Den Hitler jag ich in die Luft*, pp. 133–45; Nerin E. Gun, *Eva Braun-Hitler: Leben und Schicksal*, Velbert and Kettwig, 1968, pp. 159f.; Heike B. Görtemaker, *Eva Braun: Leben mit Hitler*, Munich, 2010, p. 236.

33 Reich Transport Ministry to the Head of the Reich Press Office, Dietrich, 2 Dec. 1939; BA Berlin-Lichterfelde, NS 10/38.

34 Goebbels, *Tagebücher*, part I, vol. 7, p. 188 (entry for 9 Oct. 1939). Hans Frank was also convinced that "good fortune has saved the Führer" and suspected that British agents were behind the attack. Hans Frank to Brigitte Frank, 9 Nov. 1939; BA Koblenz, N 1110/50. In late January 1940 Hitler spoke of having had "constant premonitions of death" before the Munich assassination attempt. Now, he added, he was overwhelmed "by a joyful feeling of absolute security." Goebbels, *Tagebücher*, part I, vol. 7, p. 291 (entry for 1 Feb. 1940).

35 Nicolaus von Below, *Als Hitlers Adjutant 1937–45*, Mainz, 1980, p. 214.

36 Haasis, *Den Hitler jag ich in die Luft*, p. 156.

37 See Domarus, *Hitler*, vol. 2, part 1, p. 1417; Below, *Als Hitlers Adjutant*, p. 214.

38 Goebbels, *Tagebücher*, part I, vol. 7, pp. 190 (entry for 11 Nov. 1939), 195 (entry for 15 Nov. 1939). See also Weizsäcker's letter to his mother of 12 November 1939: "I don't know whether a genuine trail will ever be found to the perpetrator. I believe it was a professional, someone who was paid and put up to it by others." BA Koblenz, N 1273/29.

39 See Haasis' nuanced depiction, *Den Hitler jag ich in die Luft*, pp. 11–107, 120–31, 180–6, 211–13 (at pp. 51, 68). The Gestapo interrogation transcript was first published in Lothar Gruchmann (ed.), *Autobiographie eines Attentäters: Johann Georg Elser. Aussage zum Sprengstoffanschlag im Bürgerbräukeller München am 8. November 1939*, Stuttgart, 1970.

40 Goebbels, *Tagebücher*, part I, vol. 7, pp. 196 (entry for 16 Nov. 1939), 197f. (entry for 17 Nov. 1939). See ibid., p. 201 (entry for 19 Nov. 1939): "Otto Strasser and the Secret Service are behind it all."

41 See Volker Ullrich, *Hitler: Ascent 1889–1939*, London, 2016, pp. 227–9; Haasis, *Den Hitler jag ich in die Luft*, pp. 245–7.

42 Goebbels, *Tagebücher*, part I, vol. 7, p. 205 (entry for 22 Nov. 1939).

43 See Haasis, *Den Hitler jag ich in die Luft*, pp. 218–28.

44 Quoted in ibid., p. 215. See William L. Shirer, *Berlin Diary 1934–1941: The Rise of the Third Reich*, London, 1997, p. 120 (entry for 21 Sept. 1939): "Himmler's account of how Elser did it sounds fishy indeed."

45 See Haasis, *Den Hitler jag ich in die Luft*, pp. 178f., 242.

46 Ibid., p. 264.

47 Goebbels, *Tagebücher*, part I, vol. 9, p. 237 (entry for 9 April 1941).

48 See Haasis, *Den Hitler jag ich in die Luft*, pp. 279, 288f., 297–314.

49 Gerhard Ritter to Lutz Graf Schwerin von Krosigk, 1 March 1955; BA Koblenz, N 276/45.

50 *Deutschland-Berichte der Sozialdemokratischen Partei Deutschlands (Sopade) 1934–1940*, ed. Klaus Behnken, Frankfurt am Main, 1980, 6 (1939), pp. 1023f. See Heinz Boberach (ed.), *Meldungen aus dem Reich: Die geheimen Lageberichte des Sicherheitsdienstes der SS 1938–1945*, Herrsching, 1984, vol. 2, p. 441 (entry for 10 Nov. 1939): "Among all sections of society, people speak about what has happened with deep emotion . . . Rumours are emerging everywhere."

51 *Deutschland-Berichte der Sopade*, 6 (1939), p. 1024. See Danish consul Herluf Zahle's report dated 11 Nov. 1939; Frank Bajohr and Christoph Strupp (eds), *Fremde Blicke auf das "Dritte Reich": Berichte ausländischer Diplomaten über Herrschaft und Gesellschaft in Deutschland 1933–1945*, Göttingen, 2011, p. 545.

52 Balck's diary, 9 Nov. 1939; BA-MA Freiburg, N 647/7.

53 Friedrich Kellner, *"Vernebelt, verdunkelt sind alle Hirne": Tagebücher, 1939–1945*, ed. Sascha Feuchert et al., Göttingen, 2011, vol. 1, p. 46 (entry for 10 Nov. 1939). William Shirer (*Berlin Diary*, p. 118, entry for 9 Nov. 1939) also suspected that this was a "another Reichstag fire," i.e. a faked attack. See Ruth Andreas-Friedrich, *Der Schattenmann: Tagebuchaufzeichnungen 1938–1945*, Frankfurt am Main, 1983, p. 65 (entry for 9 Nov. 1939).

54 Groscurth, *Tagebücher eines Abwehroffiziers*, p. 227 (entry for 9 Nov. 1939). See also Galeazzo Ciano, *Tagebücher, 1939–1943*, Bern, 1946, p. 166 (entry for 9 Nov. 1939), where he speculates that "this could be a family affair among people who are part of the innermost circle."

55 *Meldungen aus dem Reich*, vol. 3, p. 449 (entry for 13 Nov. 1939).

56 Hassell, *Vom andern Deutschland*, p. 90 (entry for 16 Nov. 1939).

57 See *Deutschland-Berichte der Sopade*, 6 (1939), p. 1025: "Some go so far as to say: 'Twenty minutes too late.' But, of course, only in their most trusted circles." The journalist Ruth Andreas-Friedrich quoted a colleague saying, "Look, if [the bomb] had been on the money, we would all be rolling around drunk under the table." *Der Schattenmann*, p. 64 (entry for 9 Nov. 1939).

58   Herluf Zahle's report dated 18 Nov. 1939; Bajohr / Strupp (eds), *Fremde Blicke auf das "Dritte Reich,"* p. 546. See also the report by US deputy consul Ralf C. Getsinger of 10 November 1939: "The citizen of Hamburg dislikes the war and its attendant hardships but morale is higher today than it was in the first week of the war." Ibid., p. 544.

59   *Deutschland-Berichte der Sopade,* 6 (1939), p. 1025.

60   Domarus, *Hitler,* vol. 2, part 1, pp. 1421–7. A summary of the speech is in Groscurth, *Tagebücher eines Abwehroffiziers,* appendix I, no. 40, pp. 414–18; note by Ritter von Leeb in Leeb, *Tagebuchaufzeichnungen,* pp. 202f. (entry for 23 Nov. 1939). According to a handwritten note by General Walter von Reichenau, commander of the 6th Army, Hitler declared at the end that he would "fight on as long as I have a host of brave men around me." BA-MA Freiburg, N 372/22.

61   Hassell, *Vom andern Deutschland,* p. 94 (entry for 5 Dec. 1939).

62   Groscurth, *Tagebücher eines Abwehroffiziers,* p. 234 (entry for 10 Dec. 1939).

63   Leeb, *Tagebuchaufzeichnungen,* p. 203 (entry for 23 Nov. 1939).

64   Engel, *Heeresadjutant bei Hitler,* p. 69 (entry for 23 Nov. 1939).

65   *Der Prozess gegen die Hauptkriegsverbrecher vor dem internationalen Militärtribunal in Nürnberg,* 42 vols, Nuremberg, 1947–9 (hereafter *IMT*), vol. 20, p. 628 (statement by Brauchitsch dated 9 Aug. 1946); Domarus, *Hitler,* vol. 2, part 1, p. 1427. See Halder, *Kriegstagebuch,* vol. 1, p. 132 (entry for 23 Nov. 1939). To Guderian, who asked for an audience a few days later because of the accusations levelled against military commanders, Hitler declared that the only one he distrusted was Brauchitsch. But he also rejected all of Guderian's suggestions for a successor as army supreme commander. Heinz Guderian, *Erinnerungen eines Soldaten,* Heidelberg, 1951, pp. 77f.

66   See Engel, *Heeresadjutant bei Hitler,* p. 69 (entry for 23 Nov. 1939); Goebbels, *Tagebücher,* part I, vol. 7, p. 207 (entry for 23 Nov. 1939).

67   Goebbels, *Tagebücher,* part I, vol. 7, p. 225 (entry for 9 Dec. 1939).

68   Ibid., p. 228 (entry for 12 Nov. 1939).

69   Ibid., pp. 236f. (entry for 19 Dec. 1939).

70   Hassell, *Vom andern Deutschland,* p. 98 (entry for 22 Dec. 1939). See Wolfgang Martynkewicz, *Salon Deutschland: Geist und Macht 1900–1945,* Berlin, 2009, pp. 512f.

71   Goebbels, *Tagebücher,* part I, vol. 7, pp. 247f. (entry for 28 Dec. 1939). On the 1939 "Christmas visit to the front," see Christoph Raichle, *Hitler als Symbolpolitiker,* Stuttgart, 2014, pp. 244–50.

72   Shirer, *Berlin Diary,* p. 130 (entry for 11 Jan. 1940). On the "coal crisis" in the winter of 1939–40, see Marlies Steinert, *Hitlers Krieg und die Deutschen: Stimmung und Haltung der deutschen Bevölkerung im Zweiten Weltkrieg,* Düsseldorf and Vienna, 1970, pp. 119–21.

73   Goebbels, *Tagebücher,* part I, vol. 7, p. 266 (entry for 11 Jan. 1940). See ibid., pp. 267 (entry for 12 Jan. 1940), 269 (entry for 13 Jan. 1940), 274 (entry for 17 Jan. 1940).

74   *Meldungen aus dem Reich,* vol. 3, p. 687 (entry for 26 Jan. 1940); see ibid., p. 635 (entry for 12 Jan. 1940).

75   Groscurth's notes on a conversation with Count Helldorf, 5 Jan. 1940; Groscurth, *Tagebücher eines Abwehroffiziers,* appendix I, no. 58, p. 467.

76   See Goebbels, *Tagebücher,* part I, vol. 7, p. 261 (entry for 7 Jan. 1940).

77   Halder, *Kriegstagebuch,* p. 154 (entry for 10 Jan. 1940).

78   On the so-called Mechelen incident, see Hans-Adolf Jacobsen, *Fall Gelb: Der Kampf um den deutschen Operationsplan zur Westoffensive 1940,* Wiesbaden, 1957, pp. 93–9.

79   Domarus, *Hitler,* vol. 2, part 1, p. 1446. See Below, *Als Hitlers Adjutant,* p. 220.

80   See Jacobsen, *Der Fall Gelb,* p. 93.

81   Goebbels, *Tagebücher,* part I, vol. 7, p. 273 (entry for 16 Jan. 1940).

82   Ibid., p. 280 (entry for 22 Jan. 1940).

83   Domarus, *Hitler,* vol. 2, part 1, pp. 1449, 1459f.

84   See Jacobsen, *Der Fall Gelb,* pp. 25–31; *Das Deutsche Reich und der Zweite Weltkrieg,* vol. 2, pp. 244f. (Umbreit's essay).

85   Keitel, *Verbrecher oder Offizier?*, p. 226. See also Engel, *Heeresadjutant bei Hitler*, p. 69 (entry for 6 Dec. 1939): "The F[ührer] rejects that 'tired old Schlieffen stuff.'" Otto Dietrich recalled Hitler speaking "very derisively about the 'general staff's ossified strategy' and the 'Schlieffen worshippers.'" (Otto Dietrich, *12 Jahre mit Hitler*, Munich, 1955, p. 96).

86   See Below, *Als Hitlers Adjutant*, pp. 214f. Conversation between Heinrich Uhlig and Karl-Jesko von Puttkamer on 13 March 1952: "In February 1940, Hitler spent whole nights brooding over a relief map of the Ardennes." IfZ München, ZS 285. On Hitler's intensive "reading" of maps, see Wolfram Pyta, *Hitler: Der Künstler als Politiker und Feldherr*, Munich, 2015, pp. 284f.

87   Bock, *Das Kriegstagebuch*, p. 69 (entry for 25 Oct. 1939). See Jacobsen, *Der Fall Gelb*, pp. 39f.; *Das Deutsche Reich und der Zweite Weltkrieg*, vol. 2, pp. 246f. (Umbreit's essay).

88   Helmuth Greiner's subsequent notes in his war diary, 18 Oct. 1940; BA Koblenz, N 1033/13.

89   See Erich von Manstein, *Verlorene Siege*, Bonn, 1955, pp. 100–3; Jacobsen, *Der Fall Gelb*, pp. 68–82; *Das Deutsche Reich und der Zweite Weltkrieg*, vol. 2, pp. 249f. (Umbreit's essay); Karl-Heinz Frieser, *Blitzkrieg-Legende: Der Westfeldzug 1940*, Munich, 1995, pp. 78f.; Oliver von Wrochem, *Erich von Manstein: Vernichtungskrieg und Geschichtspolitik*, Paderborn, 2006, pp. 49f.

90   See Manstein, *Verlorene Siege*, p. 118; Frieser, *Blitzkrieg-Legende*, pp. 79f.

91   See Engel, *Heeresadjutant bei Hitler*, p. 74 (entry for 4 Feb. 1940). In a conversation with Heinrich Uhlig on 18 March 1953, Gerhard Engel also emphasised that "Manstein and Hitler arrived independently of one another at similar conclusions that previous plans for the western offensive would have to be revised." IfZ München, ZS 222, vol. 1.

92   Engel, *Heeresadjutant bei Hitler*, pp. 74f. (entries for 3 Feb. and 19 Feb. 1940). See Manstein's diary entry for 17 Feb. 1940 in Pyta, *Hitler*, p. 282. See also Manstein, *Verlorene Siege*, pp. 118–20; Jacobsen, *Der Fall Gelb*, pp. 115f.; Frieser, *Blitzkrieg-Legende*, pp. 80f.

93   Bock, *Das Kriegstagebuch*, p. 101 (entry for 24 Feb. 1940).

94   See Jacobsen, *Der Fall Gelb*, p. 118; Frieser, *Blitzkrieg-Legende*, p. 82; *Das Deutsche Reich und der Zweite Weltkrieg*, vol. 2, pp. 254f. (Umbreit's essay).

95   Domarus, *Hitler*, vol. 2, part 1, pp. 1464–9. See Goebbels, *Tagebücher*, part I, vol. 7, p. 324 (entry for 26 Feb. 1940): "Once again the Führer has really socked it to the English."

96   Goebbels, *Tagebücher*, part I, vol. 7, p. 329 (entry for 1 March 1940). Aside from Goebbels' diary entry, there is no record of Hitler's three-hour-long speech.

97   Ibid., p. 298 (entry for 6 Feb. 1940).

98   See Albert Speer, *Erinnerungen: Mit einem Essay von Jochen Thies*, Frankfurt am Main and Berlin, 1993, pp. 182f.

99   Goebbels, *Tagebücher*, part I, vol. 7, p. 326 (entry for 28 Feb. 1940).

100   Hitler's instructions for Sumner Welles's visit, 29 Feb. 1940; *Akten zur deutschen Auswärtigen Politik 1918–1945 (ADAP) (The Political Archives of the Federal Foreign Office)*, Series D, 1937–1941, vols 1–13, Frankfurt am Main, 1956–70, vol. 8, no. 637, pp. 644f. See Domarus, *Hitler*, vol. 2, part 1, pp. 1470f.

101   Minutes of the conversations with Sumner Welles of 2 March 1940; Hillgruber (ed.), *Staatsmänner und Diplomaten bei Hitler 1939–1941*, pp. 68–76 (at p. 76).

102   Goebbels, *Tagebücher*, part I, vol. 7, pp. 333 (entry for 5 March 1940), 331 (entry for 3 March 1940).

103   Mussolini to Hitler, 3 Jan. 1940; *ADAP*, Series D, vol. 8, part 1, no. 504, pp. 474–7. Italian Foreign Minister Ciano was of the opinion that the letter would be to no avail: "Hitler only listens to Mussolini's suggestions when they completely conform to his own ideas." *Tagebücher, 1939–1943*, p. 184 (entry for 5 Jan. 1940).

104 Hitler to Mussolini, 8 March 1940; *ADAP, Series D*, vol. 8, part 1, no. 663, pp. 685–93; See Domarus, *Hitler*, vol. 2, part 1, pp. 1475f.

105 *ADAP, Series D*, vol. 8, part 1, no. 667, pp. 703f.; no. 670, p. 714. See Paul Schmidt, *Statist auf diplomatischer Bühne 1923–45*, Bonn, 1950, p. 477; Gianluca Falanga, *Mussolinis Vorposten in Hitlers Reich: Italiens Politik in Berlin 1933–1945*, Berlin, 2008, p. 143.

106 See Ciano, *Tagebücher, 1939–1943*, p. 211 (entry for 18 March 1940); Schmidt, *Statist auf diplomatischer Bühne*, pp. 479f.; Hillgruber (ed.), *Staatsmänner und Diplomaten bei Hitler 1939–1941*, pp. 87–106.

107 Ciano, *Tagebücher, 1939–1943*, p. 212 (entry for 19 March 1940). See Leonidas Hill (ed.), *Die Weizsäcker-Papiere 1933–1950*, Frankfurt am Main, Berlin and Vienna,1974, p. 195 (dated 19 March 1940): "The Duce, who was mostly relegated to listening at the Brenner, can hardly have returned to Rome with swelled sails."

108 Jodl's diary entry for 19 March 1940; BA-MA Freiburg, N 69/10.

109 Goebbels, *Tagebücher*, part I, vol. 7, p. 356 (entry for 19 March 1940). See ibid., pp. 357f. (entry for 20 March 1940): "Mussolini will march by our side until the end . . . In him, we have an honest and great friend."

110 On Attolico's recall, see Falanga, *Mussolinis Vorposten in Hitlers Reich*, pp. 143–51; Goebbels, *Tagebücher*, part I, vol. 8, p. 85 (entry for 30 April 1940): "With Alfiere, we are getting a true fascist."

111 See Adam Tooze, *The Wages of Destruction: The Making and Breaking of the Nazi Economy*, London, 2006, pp. 349–51; Rolf-Dieter Müller, "Die Mobilisierung der deutschen Wirtschaft für Hitlers Kriegführung," in *Das Deutsche Reich und der Zweite Weltkrieg*, vol. 5/1, Stuttgart, 1988, pp. 474f.

112 Goebbels, *Tagebücher*, part I, vol. 7, p. 359 (dated 21 March 1940).

113 See Tooze, *The Wages of Destruction*, pp. 351–3; Richard J. Evans, *The Third Reich at War, 1939–1945*, London, 2008, pp. 114f.

114 See Klaus A. Maier and Bernd Stegemann, "Die Sicherung der europäischen Nordflanke," in *Das Deutsche Reich und der Zweite Weltkrieg*, vol. 2, pp. 196f. On Quisling's meeting with Hitler, see Rosenberg, *Die Tagebücher von 1934 bis 1944*, pp. 306f. (entry for 19 Dec. 1939).

115 Goebbels, *Tagebücher*, part I, vol. 7, p. 317 (entry for 20 Feb. 1940). Weizsäcker too found that the *Altmark* incident was an "instance of the worst sort of piracy"; Ernst von Weizsäcker to his mother, 18 Feb. 1940; BA Koblenz, N 1273/29. Jodl noted on 19 Feb. 1940: "Führer urgently insists on preparations for Operation Weserübung." BA-MA Freiburg, N 69/10.

116 Walther Hubatsch (ed.), *Hitlers Weisungen für die Kriegführung*, Munich, 1965, pp. 54–7 (at p. 54).

117 Halder, *Kriegstagebuch*, vol. 1, p. 204 (entry for 21 Feb. 1940). See Jodl's diary entry for 5 March 1940: "3 p.m.: major meeting about Weserübung with the three supreme commanders. Field m[arshal] vents anger because not previously informed." BA-MA Freiburg, N 69/10.

118 See Walter Warlimont, *Im Hauptquartier der deutschen Wehrmacht 1939–1945: Grundlagen—Formen—Gestalten*, Frankfurt am Main and Bonn, 1964, pp. 58f.

119 Below, *Als Hitlers Adjutant*, pp. 224f. On Hitler's return to Berlin on 26 March 1940, see Goebbels, *Tagebücher*, part I, vol. 7, p. 367 (entry for 27 March 1940).

120 See Jodl's diary entry for 2 April 1940; BA-MA Freiburg, N 69/10.

121 Goebbels, *Tagebücher*, part I, vol. 8, pp. 41f. (entry for 9 April 1940).

122 On 9 April 1940, Hitler told Alfred Rosenberg: "Just as Bismarck's Reich arose from the year 1866, the Greater Germanic Reich will arise from this day." Rosenberg, *Die Tagebücher von 1934 bis 1944*, p. 321. See also Goebbels, *Tagebücher*, part I, vol. 8, p. 45 (entry for 10 April 1940): "At the end of the war in 1870, we had the German Reich. At the end of this war, we will have the Germanic Reich."

123 Goebbels, *Tagebücher*, part I, vol. 8, p. 46 (entry for 10 April 1940).

124 See *Das Deutsche Reich und der Zweite Weltkrieg*, pp. 212–25 (Maier and Stegemann's essay); Gerhard L. Weinberg, *Eine Welt in Waffen: Die globale Geschichte des Zweiten Weltkriegs*, Stuttgart, 1995, pp. 133–6.

125 Goebbels, *Tagebücher*, part I, vol. 8, p. 53 (entry for 14 April 1940).

126 Lossberg's notes on a report to Keitel and Jodl in the Chancellery on 15 April 1940; BA Koblenz, N 1033/13.

127 Jodl's diary entries for 14 Jan. and 17 April 1940; BA-MA Freiburg, N 69/10. See Jodl's notes on "Mein Verhältnis zu Hitler," 18 Jan. 1946; BA-MA Freiburg, N 69/48; Bernhard von Lossberg, *Im Wehrmachtführungsstab: Bericht eines Generalstabsoffiziers*, Hamburg, 1950, pp. 66–9. At lunch Goebbels found Hitler "very serious": *Tagebücher*, part I, vol. 8, p. 58 (entry for 17 April 1940).

128 Jodl's diary dated 19 April 1940; BA-MA Freiburg, N 69/10. See Lossberg, *Im Wehrmachtführungsstab*, pp. 69–72.

129 See Albert Bormann to the Bavarian prime minister, Ludwig Siebert, 16 April 1940; BA Berlin-Lichterfelde NS 10/38.

130 Goebbels, *Tagebücher*, part I, vol. 8, p. 65 (entry for 21 April 1940); Shirer, *Berlin Diary*, p. 148 (entry for 19 April 1940).

131 Jodl's diary dated 30 April 1940; BA-MA Freiburg, N 69/10. See Goebbels, *Tagebücher*, part I, vol. 8, p. 87 (entry for 1 May 1940). Rosenberg recorded Hitler as saying, "This is more than a battle won—it is a campaign won." Rosenberg, *Die Tagebücher von 1934 bis 1944*, p. 329 (entry for 30 April 1940). Halder too attributed Jodl's rise to *von* become Hitler's most important operational advisor to his firm stance during the Norwegian campaign, which Hitler had "never forgotten." Franz Halder to Prof. Walter Baum, 29 March 1955; IfZ München, ZS 240, vol. 5.

132 Helmuth Greiner's subsequent notes in his war diary dated 18 Oct. 1940; BA Koblenz, N 1033/13.

133 Lossberg, *Im Wehrmachtführungsstab*, p. 69.

134 Goebbels, *Tagebücher*, part I, vol. 8, p. 96 (entry for 7 May 1940). On the setting of the date for the attack, see Jacobsen, *Der Fall Gelb*, p. 140.

135 See Eduard Wagner, *Der Generalquartiermeister: Briefe und Tagebuchaufzeichnungen*, ed. Elisabeth Wagner, Munich and Vienna, 1963, p. 167 (entry for 9 May 1940).

136 See Below, *Als Hitlers Adjutant*, pp. 228f.

137 Christa Schroeder, *Er war mein Chef: Aus dem Nachlass der Sekretärin von Adolf Hitler*, ed. Anton Joachimsthaler, 3rd edition, Munich and Vienna, 1985, pp. 101f. See Jodl's diary entry for 10 May 1940, BA-MA Freiburg, N 69/10; Below, *Als Hitlers Adjutant*, pp. 222f.; Heinrich Hoffmann, *Hitler wie ich ihn sah: Aufzeichnungen seines Leibfotografen*, Munich and Berlin, 1974, pp. 113–15; Franz W. Seidler and Dieter Zeigert, *Die Führerhauptquartiere: Anlagen und Planungen im Zweiten Weltkrieg*, Munich, 2000, p. 167.

138 See Seidler and Zeigert, *Die Führerhauptquartiere*, pp. 163, 166f.; Uwe Neumärker, Robert Conrad and Cord Woywodt, *Wolfsschanze: Hitlers Machtzentrale im Zweiten Weltkrieg*, 3rd edition, Berlin, 2007, pp. 23f.; Below, *Als Hitlers Adjutant*, p. 230; Schroeder, *Er war mein Chef*, p. 102; Keitel, *Verbrecher oder Offizier?*, p. 231; Henrik Eberle and Matthias Uhl (eds), *Das Buch Hitler*, Bergisch Gladbach, 2005, p. 120.

139 Adolf Hitler, *Monologe im Führerhauptquartier 1941–1944: Die Aufzeichnungen Heinrich Heims*, ed. Werner Jochmann, Hamburg, 1980, p. 300 (dated 26–27 Feb. 1942); see ibid., p. 92 (dated 17–18 Oct. 1941).

140 Domarus, *Hitler*, vol. 2, part 1, p. 1503. See Goebbels, *Tagebücher*, part I, vol. 8, p. 107 (entry for 11 May 1940).

141 Kellner, *Tagebücher, 1939–1945*, vol. 1, p. 70 (entry for 10 May 1940).

142 Wilhelm Muehlon, *Tagebuch der Kriegsjahre 1940–1944*, ed. Jens Heisterkamp, Dornach, 1992, p. 87 (entry for 10 May 1940).

143 Marianne von Weizsäcker to her mother, 11 May 1940; BA Koblenz, N 1273/29.

144 Figures taken from *Das Deutsche Reich und der Zweite Weltkrieg*, vol. 2, p. 282 (Umbreit's essay). Alternative figures, particularly concerning German air superiority, from

Rolf-Dieter Müller, *Der letzte deutsche Krieg 1939–1945*, Stuttgart, 2005, p. 46. On the relative strengths of the two sides, see also Hartmann, *Halder*, p. 192; Evans, *The Third Reich at War*, p. 124.

145 Goebbels, *Tagebücher*, part I, vol. 8, p. 158 (entry for 5 June 1940).

146 See Olaf Groehler, *Bombenkrieg gegen Deutschland*, Berlin, 1990, pp. 12–14; Richard Overy, *The Bombing War: Europe 1939–1945*, London, 2013, pp. 64f.

147 Halder, *Kriegstagebuch*, vol. 1, p. 297 (entry for 16 May 1940). See also Halder's letter to his wife dated 13 May 1940: "My operation is flowing like a well-cut film. It is an undeserved gift from God." Hartmann, *Halder*, p. 193.

148 Goebbels, *Tagebücher*, part I, vol. 8, p. 115 (entry for 15 May 1940). When the Allies had advanced into Belgium and fallen into the trap he had set, he could have "wept with joy," Hitler remarked in October 1941. *Monologe*, p. 92 (dated 17–18 Oct. 1941).

149 Shirer, *Berlin Diary*, p. 155 (entry for 15 May 1940).

150 See Geoffrey P. Megargee, *Hitler und die Generäle: Das Ringen um die Führung der Wehrmacht 1939–1945*, Paderborn, 2006, pp. 98f; Keitel, *Verbrecher oder Offizier?*, pp. 232f.

151 Halder, *Kriegstagebuch*, vol. 1, pp. 302 (entry for 17 May 1940), 302f. (entry for 18 May 1940). On Hitler's "panic" concerning German troops' flanks, see Frieser, *Blitzkrieg-Legende*, pp. 319–22; Warlimont, *Im Hauptquartier der Wehrmacht*, pp. 101–11; Hartmann, *Halder*, pp. 194f.; Guderian, *Erinnerungen eines Soldaten*, p. 98: Hitler was "scared of his own daring."

152 Goebbels, *Tagebücher*, part I, vol. 8, pp. 124f. (entry for 20 May 1940).

153 Jodl's diary entry for 20 May 1940; BA-MA Freiburg, N 69/10.

154 Goebbels, *Tagebücher*, part I, vol. 8, p. 128 (entry for 22 May 1940).

155 Wagner, *Der Generalquartiermeister*, pp. 171 (entry for 18 May 1940), 172 (entry for 23 May 1940). See Ernst von Weizsäcker to his mother, 23 May 1940: "In short, the world looks different than it did fourteen days ago. I repeat: 'how wonderful things are facts.'" BA Koblenz, N 1273/29.

156 Muehlon, *Tagebuch der Kriegsjahre*, p. 93 (entry for 21 May 1940).

157 Halder, *Kriegstagebuch*, vol. 1, p. 320 (entry for 26 May 1940). See Bock, *Das Kriegstagebuch*, p. 134 (entry for 24 May 1940): "That can have very unpleasant effects on the outcome of my battle, which is still raging."

158 See Helmuth Greiner's subsequent notes in his war diary entry for 18 Oct. 1940; BA Koblenz, N 1033/13; Frieser, *Blitzkrieg-Legende*, pp. 363–73.

159 Schroeder, *Er war mein Chef*, p. 105.

160 For an extensive discussion of Hitler's motives, see Frieser, *Blitzkrieg-Legende*, pp. 382–93. In a letter to Heinrich Uhlig of 3 February 1954, Halder wrote that it was "completely wrongheaded" to think that Hitler had wanted to build a "golden bridge" to the English in order to bring about peace talks: "Even this mysterious person cannot possibly have believed that." The true reasons, Halder noted, lay in "Göring's own personality and the concern, typical of the usurper, about his own position vis-à-vis an all-too-successful military leadership." BA-MA Freiburg, N 220/88.

161 Bock, *Das Kriegstagebuch*, p. 140 (entry for 30 May 1940). See Frieser, *Blitzkrieg-Legende*, pp. 374–9.

162 Müller, *Der letzte deutsche Krieg 1939–1945*, p. 49.

163 See Seidler and Zeigert, *Die Führerhauptquartiere*, pp. 173–6; Neumärker et al., *Wolfsschanze*, pp. 25f. On the improvised nature of Hitler's new headquarters, see Schroeder, *Er war mein Chef*, p. 103.

164 Lossberg, *Im Wehrmachtführungsstab*, p. 85; *Monologe*, p. 300 (entry for 26–27 Feb. 1942).

165 Goebbels, *Tagebücher*, part I, vol. 8, p. 159 (entry for 6 June 1940).

166 Wagner, *Der Generalquartiermeister*, p. 182 (entry for 11 June 1940).

167 Shirer, *Berlin Diary*, p. 181 (entry for 17 June 1940).

168   See Hans Georg Hiller von Gaertringen (ed.), *Das Auge des Dritten Reiches: Hitlers Kameramann und Fotograf Walter Frentz*, Berlin, 2006, p. 92. See Heinz Linge, *Bis zum Untergang: Als Chef des Persönlichen Dienstes bei Hitler*, Munich, 1982, p. 204: "Never again did I see Hitler so elated as on that day."

169   Schroeder, *Er war mein Chef*, p. 106.

170   Wilhelm II to Hitler, 19 June 1940; Willibald Gutsche, *Ein Kaiser im Exil: Der letzte deutsche Kaiser Wilhelm II. in Holland*, Marburg, 1991, p. 204 (which also contains Hitler's answer of 26 June 1940). See John C. G. Röhl, *Wilhelm II: Der Weg in den Abgrund 1900–1941*, Munich, 2008, p. 1320.

171   Crown Prince Wilhelm to Hitler, 17 June 1940, and Hitler's response; BA Berlin-Lichterfelde NS 10/18.

172   All telegrams cited in BA Berlin-Lichterfelde, NS 10/18.

173   Goebbels, *Tagebücher*, part I, vol. 8, p. 179 (entry for 18 June 1940).

174   Theodor Morell to Hanni Morell, 26 May 1940; BA Koblenz, N 1348/6.

175   See Falanga, *Mussolinis Vorposten in Hitlers Reich*, pp. 153–5; Hans Woller, *Mussolini: Der erste Faschist. Eine Biografie*, Munich, 2016, pp. 199f.

176   See Eberle and Uhl (eds), *Das Buch Hitler*, pp. 123–6; Hill (ed.), *Die Weizsäcker-Papiere 1933–1950*, p. 212 (dated 10 July 1940).

177   Ciano, *Tagebücher, 1939–1943*, p. 249 (entry for 18–19 June 1940). On the negotiations of 18 June 1940, see Schmidt, *Statist auf diplomatischer Bühne*, pp. 484f.; Falanga, *Mussolinis Vorposten in Hitlers Reich*, p. 159; Hillgruber (ed.), *Staatsmänner und Diplomaten bei Hitler 1939–1941*, pp. 139–43.

178   See Schmidt, *Statist auf diplomatischer Bühne*, pp. 485–7.

179   See Seidler and Zeigert, *Die Führerhauptquartiere*, p. 177; Eberle and Uhl (eds), *Das Buch Hitler*, p. 131. Goebbels, *Tagebücher*, part I, vol. 8, p. 176 (entry for 16 June 1940): "[Hitler] carefully studied the ceremony of the armistice and the Treaty of Versailles. That was to be the model."

180   See Pyta, *Hitler*, pp. 302f.; in more detail, Raichle, *Hitler als Symbolpolitiker*, pp. 287–311.

181   Domarus, *Hitler*, vol. 2, part 1, p. 1529.

182   Shirer, *Berlin Diary*, p. 186 (entry for 21 June 1940). The broadcast of 21 June 1940 is reproduced in William L. Shirer, *This is Berlin: Reporting from Nazi Germany 1938–40*, London, 1999, pp. 328–33. Two years later, Hitler remembered the "powerful emotions that came over him when he saw Foch's salon car for the first time in Compiègne, and the hour was at hand when he could . . . pay back France for the humiliation of November 1918"; *Die Tagebücher von Joseph Goebbels*, commissioned by the Institute for Contemporary History, with support from the State Archive of Russia, ed. Elke Fröhlich, *Part II: Diktate 1941–1945*, 15 vols, Munich, 1993–6, vol. 4, p. 491 (entry for 10 June 1942).

183   Domarus, *Hitler*, vol. 2, part 1, p. 1529.

184   Schmidt, *Statist auf diplomatischer Bühne*, p. 489.

185   Goebbels, *Tagebücher*, part I, vol. 8, p. 186 (entry for 22 June 1940).

186   Karl Haushofer to Rudolf Hess, 21 June 1940 ("before the solstice sunrise"); BA Koblenz, N 1122/15.

187   Hill (ed.), *Die Weizsäcker-Papiere 1933–1950*, p. 207 (dated 21 June 1940). On the Franco-German ceasefire agreement, see Eberhard Jäckel, *Frankreich in Hitlers Europa: Die deutsche Frankreichpolitik im Zweiten Weltkrieg*, Stuttgart, 1966, pp. 43f.

188   Speer, *Erinnerungen*, p. 185. See Raichle, *Hitler als Symbolpolitiker*, pp. 324–30. On the radio broadcast, see Goebbels, *Tagebücher*, part I, vol. 8, p. 193 (entry for 25 June 1940).

189   *Monologe*, p. 116 (dated 29 Oct. 1941). On the dating, see Sandner, *Hitler: Das Itinerar*, vol. 4, pp. 1836–41.

190   See Speer, *Erinnerungen*, pp. 185–7; Arno Breker, *Im Strahlungsfeld der Ereignisse: Leben und Wirken eines Künstlers. Porträts, Begegnungen, Schicksale*, Preussisch Oldendorf,

1972, pp. 151–65; Hermann Giesler, *Ein anderer Hitler: Berichte, Gespräche, Reflexionen,* Leoni, 1977, pp. 387–93; Baur, *Ich flog Mächtige dieser Erde,* pp. 192f.; Below, *Als Hitlers Adjutant,* p. 235. Days later, Hitler still returned "again and again to the trip to Paris, which had made a powerful impression on him"; Engel, *Heeresadjutant bei Hitler,* p. 83 (entry for 26 Jun. 1940).

191 Speer, *Erinnerungen,* pp. 187f. (on p. 193 see the facsimile of Hitler's decree of 25 June 1940). See Goebbels on Speer's plan for a remodeling of Berlin: "The programme is to be carried out as quickly as possible. Ten years maximum." *Tagebücher,* part I, vol. 8, p. 258 (entry for 7 Aug. 1940).

192 Halder, *Kriegstagebuch,* vol. 1, p. 375 (entry for 30 June 1940). Hitler's adjutant Engel recorded him as saying that the British would "back down one way or the other." Engel, *Heeresadjutant bei Hitler,* p. 83 (entry for 20 June 1940). On 2 June, at a meeting in Army Group A's headquarters in Charleville, Hitler was already said to have expressed his expectation that, if England were "ready for a sensible peace agreement," he would "finally have his hands free for his actual great mission: confronting Bolshevism." Karl Klee, *Das Unternehmen "Seelöwe": Die geplante deutsche Landung in England 1940,* Göttingen, 1958, p. 189 (based on reports by Infantry General Georg von Sodenstern in 1954 and 1955).

193 See Eberle and Uhl (eds), *Das Buch Hitler,* p. 127; Linge, *Bis zum Untergang,* pp. 198f. For an extensive account of Hitler's visits to all his stations in the First World War, see Raichle, *Hitler als Symbolpolitiker,* pp. 353–79. On the relocation of Hitler's headquarters, see Seidler and Zeigert, *Die Führerhauptquartiere,* pp. 180f.; Neumärker et al., *Wolfsschanze,* pp. 26f.

194 Goebbels, *Tagebücher,* part I, vol. 8, p. 202 (entry for 3 July 1940). On 20 June 1940 Christa Schroeder wrote to her friend Johanna Nusser: "The boss wants to speak to the Reichstag soon. Probably it will be his final appeal to the English. If they do not respond, he will proceed pitilessly." IfZ München, ED 524; reprinted with slight variations in Schroeder, *Er war mein Chef,* p. 105.

195 Goebbels, *Tagebücher,* part I, vol. 8, p. 210 (entry for 7 July 1940). See also the report by Danish consul Herluf Zahle of 8 July 1940: "Mr. Hitler is now being celebrated not just as the leader of his people but as a great military commander." Bajohr and Strupp (eds). *Fremde Blicke auf das "Dritte Reich,"* p. 550.

196 Shirer, *This is Berlin,* p. 309 (broadcast of 2 June 1940). See Victor Klemperer, *Ich will Zeugnis ablegen bis zum letzten: Tagebücher,* vol. 1: 1933–1941, ed. Walter Nowojski with Hadwig Klemperer, Berlin, 1995, p. 535 (entry for 29 June 1940): "Among the people there is absolute certainty of a rapid, conclusive victory before the autumn."

197 Ian Kershaw, *The Hitler Myth: Image and Reality in the Third Reich,* Oxford, 1987, p. 155.

198 Lore Walb, *Ich, die Alte—ich, die Junge: Konfrontation mit meinen Tagebüchern 1933–1945,* Berlin, 1997, pp. 177, 179 (entry for 21 May 1940).

199 Quoted in Pyta, *Hitler,* p. 289; see Raichle, *Hitler als Symbolpolitiker,* pp. 267–71.

200 *Meldungen aus dem Reich,* vol. 4, p. 1293 (dated 24 June 1940). On the reaction of the German population, see Steinert, *Hitlers Krieg und die Deutschen,* pp. 132–6.

201 W. Hellpach to K. Haushofer, 2 June 1940; BA Koblenz N 1122/15. The letter is signed off with "Heil Hitler!"

202 Friedrich Meinecke, *Werke, vol. VI: Ausgewählter Briefwechsel,* Stuttgart, 1962, p. 364 (dated 4 July 1940).

203 Hill (ed.), *Die Weizsäcker-Papiere 1933–1950,* p. 207 (dated 21 June 1940).

204 Goebbels, *Tagebücher,* part I, vol. 8, p. 158 (entry for 6 June 1940).

205 Wagner, *Der Generalquartiermeister,* p. 183 (entry for 15 June 1940).

206 Heinrici's diary entry of 24 June 1940; cited in Johannes Hürter, *Hitlers Heerführer: Die deutschen Oberbefehlshaber im Krieg gegen die Sowjetunion 1941/42,* Munich, 2007, p. 173.

207 *Monologe*, p. 101 (dated 21–22 Oct. 1941).

208 Hassell, *Vom andern Deutschland*, p. 140 (entry for 27 June 1940).

209 Helmuth James von Moltke, *Briefe an Freya 1939–1945*, ed. Beate Ruhm von Oppen, Munich, 1988, pp. 142f. (dated 1 June 1940). See Volker Ullrich, *Der Kreisauer Kreis*, Reinbek bei Hamburg, 2008, p. 59.

210 Thomas Mann, *Tagebücher, 1940–1943*, pp. 80 (entry for 22 May 1940), 111 (entry for 4 July 1940). Wilhelm Muehlon was of a similar opinion, writing that everything now depended on whether "England can stand its ground on its island and at sea." *Tagebuch der Kriegsjahre 1940–1944*, pp. 128f. (entry for 8 July 1940).

211 Sebastian Haffner, *Churchill: Eine Biographie*, Berlin, 2001, p. 131. See John Lukacs, *Churchill und Hitler: Der Zweikampf. 10. Mai—31. Juli 1940*, Stuttgart, 1992, pp. 12ff. On Churchill's determination to continue the war, see Andreas Hillgruber, *Hitlers Strategie: Politik und Kriegführung 1940–1941*, Frankfurt am Main, 1965, pp. 79–90.

212 Winston Churchill, *Never Give In! The Best of Winston Churchill's Speeches*, ed. by Winston S. Churchill, London, 2003, p. 206.

213 See Ian Kershaw, *Fateful Choices: Ten Decisions that Changed the World 1940–1941*, London, 2007, pp. 28–53; John Lukacs, *Fünf Tage in London: England und Deutschland im Mai 1940*, Berlin, 2000, pp. 70ff.

214 Domarus, *Hitler*, vol. 2, part 1, pp. 1524f.; see Lukacs, *Churchill und Hitler*, pp. 174–6; Hillgruber, *Hitlers Strategie*, p. 146; Goebbels, *Tagebücher*, part I, vol. 8, pp. 172 (entry for 14 June 1940), 177 (entry for 17 June 1940).

215 Churchill, *Never Give In!*, pp. 218, 229.

216 Gabriel Gorodetsky (ed.), *Die Maiski-Tagebücher: Ein Diplomat im Kampf gegen Hitler*, Munich, 2016, p. 434 (entry for 23 June 1940).

217 See Lukacs, *Churchill und Hitler*, pp. 232f.

218 See Goebbels, *Tagebücher*, part I, vol. 8, p. 210 (entry for 7 July 1940).

219 Ernst von Weizsäcker to his mother, 7 July 1940; BA Koblenz, N 1273/29.

220 Ciano, *Tagebücher, 1939–1943*, p. 257 (entry for 7 July 1940). See Goebbels, *Tagebücher*, part I, vol. 8, p. 213 (entry for 9 July 1940): "He is not yet prepared for the decisive blow. He wants to think over his speech once more in peace and will travel to that end to the Obersalzberg."

221 Franz Halder, *Kriegstagebuch, vol. II: Von der geplanten Landung in England bis zum Beginn des Ostfeldzugs (1. Juli 1940–21. Juni 1941)*, ed. Hans-Adolf Jacobsen, Stuttgart, 1963, p. 21 (entry for 13 July 1940). Jodl's memorandum of 30 June 1940 is in Karl Klee (ed.), *Dokumente zum Unternehmen "Seelöwe": Die geplante deutsche Landung in England 1940*, Göttingen, 1959, pp. 298–300. See Below, *Als Hitlers Adjutant*, pp. 239f.; Lukacs, *Churchill und Hitler*, pp. 239–41.

222 Hubatsch (ed.), *Hitlers Weisungen für die Kriegführung*, pp. 71–5 (at p. 71). See Klee, *Das Unternehmen "Seelöwe"*, pp. 75–7.

223 See Franz von Papen, *Der Wahrheit eine Gasse*, Munich, 1952, pp. 522f.

224 Goebbels, *Tagebücher*, part I, vol. 8, p. 229 (entry for 20 July 1940). The purpose of his speech was "to make it clear to England how its government was leading it around by the nose," wrote Weizsäcker on 14 July 1940 to his mother; BA Koblenz, N 1273/29.

225 See Below, *Als Hitlers Adjutant*, p. 241.

226 Shirer, *Berlin Diary*, p. 197 (entry for 19 July 1940).

227 Engel, *Heeresadjutant bei Hitler*, pp. 85f. (entry for 22 July 1940). On the "compensation payments," see Gerd R. Ueberschär and Winfried Vogel, *Dienen und Verdienen: Hitlers Geschenke an seine Eliten*, Frankfurt am Main, 1999, pp. 101–4.

228 For a transcript of the speech see Domarus, *Hitler*, vol. 2, part 1, pp. 1540–59. Wilhelm Muehlon accurately commented: "The insults he heaps upon the leaders of England demonstrate that no matter who might appear in England's name before him, he would necessarily have a noose around his neck." *Tagebuch der Kriegsjahre*, p. 142 (entry for 20 July 1940).

229 Goebbels, *Tagebücher*, part I, vol. 8, p. 231 (entry for 21 July 1940). Hitler's speech had not made "the slightest impression" in London, Ivan Maiski noted. Gorodetsky (ed.), *Die Maiski-Tagebücher*, p. 449 (entry for 22 July 1940).

230 Goebbels, *Tagebücher*, part I, vol. 8, pp. 234f. (entry for 24 July 1940).

4 Strategic Stalemate

1 On the following, see also Generaloberst Halder, *Kriegstagebuch: Tägliche Aufzeichnungen des Chefs des Generalstabs des Heeres 1939–1942*, vol. 2, ed. Hans-Adolf Jacobsen, Stuttgart, 1962, pp. 30–3 (entry for 22 July 1940); based on Brauchitsch's reports to Halder.

2 *Akten zur deutschen Auswärtigen Politik 1918–1945 (ADAP) (The Political Archives of the Federal Foreign Office)*, Series D, 1937–1941, vols 1–13, Frankfurt am Main, 1956–70, vol. 10, no. 199, pp. 213f. See Andreas Hillgruber, *Hitlers Strategie: Politik und Kriegführung 1940–1941*, Frankfurt am Main, 1965, pp. 199, 217; idem, "Der Faktor Amerika in Hitlers Strategie 1938–1941," in idem, *Deutsche Grossmacht- und Weltpolitik im 19. und 20. Jahrhundert*, Düsseldorf, 1977, pp. 197–222 (at p. 210).

3 Halder, *Kriegstagebuch*, vol. 2, pp. 31–33 (entry for 22 July 1940).

4 Ibid., p. 6 (entry for 3 July 1940).

5 Klaus Hildebrand, *Das vergangene Reich: Deutsche Aussenpolitik von Bismarck bis Hitler*, Stuttgart, 1995, pp. 734f. See Hillgruber, *Hitlers Strategie*, p. 225; Jürgen Förster, "Hitlers Entscheidung für den Krieg gegen die Sowjetunion," in *Das Deutsche Reich und der Zweite Weltkrieg*, ed. Militärgeschichtliches Forschungsamt (Military Historical Research Office), 10 vols, Stuttgart and Munich, 1979–2008, vol. 4, Stuttgart 1983, p. 16; Gerd R. Ueberschär, "Hitlers Entschluss zum 'Lebensraum'-Krieg im Osten," in idem and Wolfram Wette, *Der deutsche Überfall auf die Sowjetunion: "Unternehmen Barbarossa" 1941*, revised edition, Frankfurt am Main, 2011, pp. 13–43.

6 Telegram of 17 July 1940 from Winifred Wagner to Hitler and Hitler's telegram in reply; BA Berlin-Lichterfelde, NS 10/20.

7 See Brigitte Hamann, *Winifred Wagner oder Hitlers Bayreuth*, Munich and Zurich, 2002, pp. 408–10; Bernd Buchner, *Wagners Welttheater: Die Geschichte der Bayreuther Festspiele zwischen Kunst und Politik*, Darmstadt, 2013, pp. 156f. Theatre programme for *Götterdämmerung* as staged by Heinz Tietjen with Max Lorenz as Siegfried in IfZ München, ED 100, vol. 79.

8 See Hamann, *Winifred Wagner oder Hitlers Bayreuth*, pp. 394 ff.; Eva Rieger, *Friedelind Wagner: Die rebellische Enkelin Richard Wagners*, Munich and Zurich 2012, pp. 107ff.

9 *Die Tagebücher von Joseph Goebbels*, commissioned by the Institute for Contemporary History, with support from the State Archive of Russia, ed. Elke Fröhlich, *Part I: Aufzeichnungen 1923–1941*, 9 vols in 14 parts, Munich, 1998–2008; *Part II: Diktate 1941–1945*, 15 vols, Munich, 1993–6; part I, vol. 8, p. 104 (entry for 10 May 1940). See ibid., pp. 92 (entry for 4 May 1940), 94 (entry for 5 May 1940), 109 (entry for 12 May 1940).

10 Ibid., p. 159 (entry for 6 June 1940).

11 Hamann, *Winifred Wagner oder Hitlers Bayreuth*, p. 415.

12 Adolf Hitler, *Monologe im Führerhauptquartier 1941–1944: Die Aufzeichnungen Heinrich Heims*, ed. Werner Jochmann, Hamburg, 1980, p. 308 (dated 28 Feb.–1 March 1942). Winifred Wagner later said that she saw Hitler for the last time in June or July 1944, when he stopped briefly in Bayreuth. Interview of Wagner by David Irving, 13 March 1971; IfZ München, ZS 2242.

13 Goebbels, *Tagebücher*, part I, vol. 8, p. 236 (entry for 25 July 1940).

14 Walter Warlimont, *Im Hauptquartier der deutschen Wehrmacht 1939–1945: Grundlagen— Formen—Gestalten*, Frankfurt am Main and Bonn, 1964, pp. 126f.; Walter Warlimont's testimony, "Militärpolitische Vorgänge um den Feldzug gegen Sowjetrussland,"

dated 5 Oct. 1945; IfZ München, ZS 312. See Bernhard von Lossberg, *Im Wehrmachtführungsstab: Bericht eines Generalstabsoffiziers*, Hamburg, 1950, p. 105.

15   Raeder's memorandum on a meeting with the Führer, 31 July 1940; Karl Klee (ed.), *Dokumente zum Unternehmen "Seelöwe": Die geplante deutsche Landung in England 1940*, Göttingen, 1959, pp. 253–6 (at pp. 253, 256); Halder, *Kriegstagebuch*, vol. 2, pp. 46–9 (entry for 31 July 1940). See *Kriegstagebuch des Oberkommandos der Wehrmacht (Wehrmachtführungsstab)* (hereafter *KTB OKW*), *vol. I: 1. August 1940–31. Dezember 1941*, ed. Percy Ernst Schramm, Munich, 1982, pp. 3f. (entry for 1 Aug. 1940). A memo from the naval war command of 29 July 1940 argued that it would be "irresponsible" to attempt a landing that year and that in any case a successful attempt was "highly unlikely." Klee, *Dokumente zum Unternehmen "Seelöwe*," pp. 315–23 (at p. 323).

16   Halder, *Kriegstagebuch*, vol. 2, p. 46 (entry for 30 July 1940).

17   Ibid., pp. 49f. (entry for 31 July 1940). On the meeting of 31 July 1940, see Hillgruber, *Hitlers Strategie*, pp. 223–6; *Das Deutsche Reich und der Zweite Weltkrieg*, vol. 2, pp. 13–16 (Förster's essay); Rolf-Dieter Müller, *Der letzte deutsche Krieg 1939–1945*, Stuttgart, 2005, pp. 78–81.

18   See Nicolaus von Below, *Als Hitlers Adjutant 1937–45*, Mainz, 1980, p. 242. Goebbels too concluded from the Soviets' war in Finland: "Russia's army is not worth much. Badly led and even worse equipped." *Tagebücher*, part I, vol. 7, p. 190 (entry for 11 Nov. 1939). See ibid., pp. 219 (entry for 4 Dec. 1939), 259 (entry for 5 Jan. 1940).

19   *Heeresadjutant bei Hitler 1938–1943: Aufzeichnungen des Majors Engel*, ed. Hildegard von Kotze, Stuttgart, 1974, p. 86 (entry for 10 Aug. 1940). Walter Warlimont recalled Hitler asserting that the Soviet armed forces would "prove to be a soap bubble that would burst when pricked." Walter Warlimont's testimony "Militärpolitische Vorgänge um den Feldzug gegen Sowjetrussland," dated 5 Oct. 1945; IfZ München, ZS 312.

20   Cited in Hillgruber, *Hitlers Strategie*, p. 229. On the Marcks study, see also Ernst Klink, "Die militärische Konzeption des Krieges gegen die Sowjetunion," in *Das Deutsche Reich und der Zweite Weltkrieg*, vol. 4, pp. 219–25. On the larger context, see also Andreas Hillgruber, "Das Russland-Bild der führenden deutschen Militärs vor dem Angriff auf die Sowjetunion," in Hans-Erich Volkmann (ed.), *Das Russlandbild im Dritten Reich*, Cologne, Weimar and Vienna, 1994, pp. 125–40.

21   See *KTB OKW*, vol. I, pp. 5 (entry for 1 Aug. 1940), 16 (entry for 8 Aug. 1940).

22   Walter Frick to Wilhelm Frick, 9 Sept. 1940; BA Koblenz, N 1241/3.

23   Fedor von Bock, *Zwischen Pflicht und Verweigerung: Das Kriegstagebuch*, ed. Klaus Gerbet, Munich, 1995, p. 166 (entry for 1 Sept. 1940). See Johannes Hürter, *Hitlers Heerführer: Die deutschen Oberbefehlshaber im Krieg gegen die Sowjetunion 1941/42*, Munich, 2007, p. 207. On the redeployment of troops to the east, see Klink's essay in *Das Deutsche Reich und der Zweite Weltkrieg*, vol. 4, pp. 216–19.

24   Telegram of 21 Dec. 1939 from Hitler to Stalin; Max Domarus, *Hitler: Reden und Proklamationen 1932–1945*, Munich, 1965, vol. 2, part 1, p. 1434; Stalin's telegram of 25 Dec. 1939 in reply; BA Berlin-Lichterfelde, NS 10/11; Rolf-Dieter Müller, "Von der Wirtschaftsallianz zum kolonialen Ausbeutungskrieg," in *Das Deutsche Reich und der Zweite Weltkrieg*, vol. 4, pp. 104–6.

25   See Neutatz, *Träume und Alpträume*, p. 283; Manfred Hildermeier, *Geschichte der Sowjetunion 1917–1991: Entstehung und Niedergang des ersten sozialistischen Staates*, Munich, 1998, pp. 595f.

26   Goebbels, *Tagebücher*, part I, vol. 8, p. 197 (entry for 29 July 1940).

27   Ibid., pp. 240 (entry for 27 July 1940), 262 (entry for 9 Aug. 1940).

28   Generalfeldmarschall Wilhelm Ritter von Leeb, *Tagebuchaufzeichnungen und Lagebeurteilungen aus zwei Weltkriegen*, ed. Georg Meyer, Stuttgart, 1976, p. 252 (entry for 14 Aug. 1940); Bock, *Das Kriegstagebuch*, p. 165 (entry for 14 Aug. 1940): "Should [Russia] make a move to subdue Finland or attack Romania, we would be forced

to intervene. Russia cannot be allowed to establish sole dominance over the eastern Baltic Sea, and we need Romanian oil."

29 Leeb, *Tagebuchaufzeichnungen*, p. 251 (entry for 14 Aug. 1940).

30 See Adam Tooze, *The Wages of Destruction: The Making and Breaking of the Nazi Economy*, London, 2006, pp. 381f., 411.

31 Goebbels, *Tagebücher*, part I, vol. 8, p. 298 (entry for 31 Aug. 1940): "Because of the oil issue, [Hitler] wants calm in the Balkans." See *KTB OKW*, vol. 1, p. 36 (entry for 15 Aug. 1940).

32 Paul Schmidt, *Statist auf diplomatischer Bühne 1923–45*, Bonn, 1950, p. 495. See Galeazzo Ciano, *Tagebücher, 1939–1943*, Bern, 1946, p. 268 (entry for 28 Aug. 1940): "The only thing he cares about is that peace be preserved in the Balkans and that Romanian petroleum continue to flow into his reservoirs."

33 Domarus, *Hitler*, vol. 2, part I, p. 1572. See Hillgruber, *Hitlers Strategie*, p. 234; Leonidas Hill (ed.), *Die Weizsäcker-Papiere 1933–1950*, Frankfurt am Main, Berlin and Vienna, 1974, p. 216 (dated 1 Sept. 1940): "Of course it is the guarantee to Romania that Russia perceives as a barrier and objects to."

34 See Domarus, *Hitler*, vol. 2, part I, p. 1583. On Antonescu's biography, see Dennis Deletant, *Hitler's Forgotten Ally: Ion Antonescu and his Regime. Romania 1940–44*, London, 2006.

35 Heinz Boberach (ed.), *Meldungen aus dem Reich: Die geheimen Lageberichte des Sicherheitsdienstes der SS 1938–1945*, Herrsching, 1984, vol. 5, p. 1362 (dated 11 July 1940). See ibid., pp. 1333 (dated 4 July 1940), 1352 (dated 8 July 1940), 1388f. (dated 18 July 1940), 1424 (dated 29 July 1940).

36 William L. Shirer, *This is Berlin: Reporting from Nazi Germany 1938–40*, London 1999, p. 360 (broadcast of 27 July 1940). See also William L. Shirer, *Berlin Diary 1934–41: The Rise of the Third Reich*, London, 1997, pp. 199 (entry for 23 July 1940), 201 (entry for 1 Aug. 1940); Victor Klemperer, *Ich will Zeugnis ablegen bis zum letzten: Tagebücher*, vol. 1: 1933–1941, ed. Walter Nowojski with Hadwig Klemperer, Berlin, 1995, p. 535 (entry for 29 June 1940): "Among the population absolute certainty about rapid final victory before the autumn."

37 Walter Frick to Wilhelm Frick, 12 July 1940; BA Koblenz N 1241/3.

38 Goebbels, *Tagebücher*, part I, vol. 8, pp. 238f. (entry for 26 July 1940), 243 (entry for 29 July 1940). See the despatch of the Danish consul, Herluf Zahle, from Berlin, 2 Aug. 1940: "You can sense a certain apprehension because of the stagnation that predominates at the moment." Frank Bajohr and Christoph Strupp (eds), *Fremde Blicke auf das "Dritte Reich": Berichte ausländischer Diplomaten über Herrschaft und Gesellschaft in Deutschland 1933–1945*, Göttingen, 2011, p. 550. Weizsäcker noted: "The glory of the German victory in France has begun to fade." Hill (ed.), *Die Weizsäcker-Papiere 1933–1950*, p. 215 (dated 4 Aug. 1940).

39 Walther Hubatsch (ed.), *Hitlers Weisungen für die Kriegsführung*, Munich, 1965, pp. 75f.; see Klee, *Das Unternehmen "Seelöwe,"* pp. 170f.

40 Goebbels, *Tagebücher*, part I, vol. 8, pp. 270 (entry for 14 Aug. 1940), 273 (entry for 15 Aug. 1940).

41 *KTB OKW*, vol. 1, pp. 26f. (entry for 13 Aug. 1940). Jodl said much the same the following day: "The planned landing operation cannot be allowed to fail under any circumstances, because failure might have political consequences that go further than the military ones." Ibid., p. 31 (entry for 14 Aug. 1940).

42 Leeb, *Tagebuchaufzeichnungen*, p. 251 (entry for 14 Aug. 1940). See Bock, *Das Kriegstagebuch*, p. 165 (entry for 14 Aug. 1940): "A landing in England can only be considered as a last resort, when all other means of exerting pressure have failed."

43 See Klaus A. Maier and Hans Umbreit, "Direkte Strategie gegen England," in *Das Deutsche Reich und der Zweite Weltkrieg*, vol. 2, pp. 382f.; Richard Overy, *The Bombing War: Europe 1939–1945*, London, 2013, pp. 73–89.

44   See Richard J. Evans, *The Third Reich at War, 1939–1945*, London, 2008, pp. 140f.; Müller, *Der letzte deutsche Krieg*, p. 58.

45   Shirer, *Berlin Diary*, p. 208 (entry for 17 Aug. 1940).

46   Shirer, *This is Berlin*, p. 384 (broadcast of 24 Aug. 1940).

47   Goebbels, *Tagebücher*, part I, vol. 8, p. 287 (entry for 24 Aug. 1940).

48   Shirer, *Berlin Diary*, pp. 209 (entry for 26 Aug. 1940), 211 (entry for 29 Aug. 1940). See Overy, *The Bombing War*, pp. 82f.

49   *Meldungen aus dem Reich*, vol. 5, p. 1525 (dated 2 Sept. 1940).

50   Goebbels, *Tagebücher*, part I, vol. 8, p. 297 (entry for 30 Aug. 1940).

51   Domarus, *Hitler*, vol. 2, part 1, pp. 1575–83 (at pp. 1580, 1577).

52   Shirer, *Berlin Diary*, p. 209 (entry for 4–5 Sept. 1940). See also *idem, This is Berlin*, pp. 394f. (broadcast of 4 Sept. 1940); Goebbels, *Tagebücher*, part I, vol. 8, p. 307 (entry for 5 Sept. 1940): "The Führer is in top form, and the audience is going crazy."

53   *Meldungen aus dem Reich*, vol. 5, p. 1549 (dated 9 Sept. 1940).

54   *KTB OKW*, vol. 1, p. 53 (entry for 30 Aug. 1940). On 28 August, Ciano already got the impression that Hitler had "now finally postponed the operation"; *Tagebücher, 1939–1943*, p. 268 (entry for 28 Aug. 1940).

55   *KTB OKW*, vol. 1, p. 70 (entry for 10 Sept. 1940).

56   Halder, *Kriegstagebuch*, vol. 2, pp. 98f. See Raeder's notes on Hitler's meeting with the supreme commanders on 14 Sept. 1940; Klee, *Dokumente zum Unternehmen "Seelöwe,"* pp. 263f.; *KTB OKW*, vol. 1, p. 76 (entry for 14 Sept. 1940); Below, *Als Hitlers Adjutant*, p. 246: "I had the impression from this talk that Hitler had given up hopes for a successful invasion of England the following spring."

57   Directive from the Wehrmacht Supreme Command dated 12 Oct. 1940; Klee, *Dokumente zum Unternehmen "Seelöwe,"* p. 441; *Das Deutsche Reich und der Zweite Weltkrieg*, vol. 2, p. 374 (Maier and Umbreit's essay).

58   Goebbels, *Tagebücher*, part I, vol. 8, p. 344 (entry for 25 Sept. 1940). See Ilse Hess to Rudolf Hess, 24 Sept. 1940: "The English are a stubborn lot, and it seems to be taking a little longer with our air supremacy, which you said would be established within ten days." BA Bern, Nl R. Hess, J1. 211–1989/148, 63.

59   See Frederick Taylor, *Coventry: Thursday, 14 November 1940*, London, 2015.

60   Ruth Andreas-Friedrich, *Der Schattenmann: Tagebuchaufzeichnungen 1938–1945*, Frankfurt am Main, 1983, p. 75 (entry for 16 Dec. 1940).

61   Walter Frick to Wilhelm Frick, 2 Dec. 1940; BA Koblenz N 1241/3.

62   Shirer, *Berlin Diary*, p. 232 (entry for 31 Oct. 1940). See also Gabriel Gorodetsky (ed.), *Die Maiski-Tagebücher: Ein Diplomat im Kampf gegen Hitler*, Munich, 2016, p. 474 (entry for 4 Nov. 1940).

63   Hans-Ulrich Wehler, *Deutsche Gesellschaftsgeschichte*, vol. 4, Munich, 2003, p. 855.

64   Goebbels, *Tagebücher*, part I, vol. 8, p. 378 (entry for 15 Oct. 1940).

65   See Ronald Gerste, *Roosevelt und Hitler: Todfeindschaft und totaler Krieg*, Paderborn, 2011, pp. 156f.; Dietmar Süss, *Tod aus der Luft: Kriegsgesellschaft und Luftkrieg in Deutschland und England*, Munich, 2011, pp. 98f.

66   See Ian Kershaw, *Fateful Choices: Ten Decisions that Changed the World 1940–1941*, London, 2007, pp. 208–220; Gerste, *Roosevelt und Hitler*, pp. 164f.

67   Goebbels, *Tagebücher*, part I, vol. 8, p. 306 (entry for 5 Sept. 1940). See Ciano, *Tagebücher, 1939–1943*, p. 269 (entry for 4 Sept. 1940): "The United States are letting Britain have fifty destroyers. Great outrage and fuss in Berlin."

68   *Meldungen aus dem Reich*, vol. 5, p. 1677 (dated 17 Oct. 1940); See ibid., pp. 1595 (dated 23 Sept. 1940), 1654 (dated 10 Oct. 1940), 1665 (dated 14 Oct. 1940).

69   Goebbels, *Tagebücher*, part I, vol. 8, pp. 362f. (entry for 6 Oct. 1940), 392 (entry for 26 Oct. 1940).

70   Engel, *Heeresadjutant bei Hitler*, p. 90 (entry for 4 Nov. 1940).

71   Goebbels, *Tagebücher*, part I, vol. 8, p. 377 (entry for 15 Oct. 1940).

72 Memorandum by Jodl dated 30 June 1940; Klee, *Dokumente zum Unternehmen "Seelöwe,"* pp. 298–300; *KTB OKW* vol. 1, p. 17 (entry for 9 Aug. 1940). See Hillgruber, *Hitlers Strategie*, pp. 178f.; idem, "Politik und Strategie Hitlers im Mittelmeerraum," in idem, *Deutsche Grossmacht- und Weltpolitik im 19. und 20. Jahrhundert*, pp. 276–95 (at pp. 277f.).

73 See Hillgruber, *Hitlers Strategie*, pp. 188–90; Kershaw, *Fateful Choices*, pp. 78–80; *Das Deutsche Reich und der Zweite Weltkrieg*, pp. 409f. (Maier and Umbreit's essay).

74 *KTB OKW*, vol. 1, pp. 63f. (entry for 5 Sept. 1940).

75 See Erich Raeder, *Mein Leben. Vol. 2: Von 1935 bis Spandau 1955*, Tübingen, 1957, pp. 246–9.

76 See Hillgruber, *Hitlers Strategie*, pp. 238f.; *Das Deutsche Reich und der Zweite Weltkrieg*, vol. 2, p. 412 (Maier and Umbreit's essay).

77 Domarus, *Hitler*, vol. 2, part 1, p. 1589; telegram of 28 Sept. 1940 from Mussolini and Kaiser Hirohito to Hitler in BA Berlin-Lichterfelde, NS 10/15.

78 Hill (ed.), *Die Weizsäcker-Papiere 1933–1950*, p. 219 (dated 28 Sept. 1940). See Goebbels, *Tagebücher*, part I, vol. 8, p. 349 (entry for 28 Sept. 1940): "Directed at the US, and Roosevelt will think twice about getting involved."

79 Ibid., p. 351 (entry for 29 Sept. 1940). The Security Service too reported: "The admiring population sees that the Führer has again chosen the correct point in time to keep America out of the war." *Meldungen aus dem Reich*, vol. 5, p. 1620 (dated 30 Sept. 1940).

80 Ciano, *Tagebücher, 1939–1943*, p. 274 (entry for 27 Sept. 1940). See Gianluca Falanga, *Mussolinis Vorposten in Hitlers Reich: Italiens Politik in Berlin 1933–1945*, Berlin, 2008, pp. 164f.

81 See Hillgruber, *Hitlers Strategie*, pp. 137f.

82 Halder, *Kriegstagebuch*, vol. 2, p. 100 (entry for 14 Sept. 1940).

83 Hillgruber, *Hitlers Strategie*, pp. 185f. On the plans for a German colonial realm in central Africa, see ibid., pp. 242 ff.; Klaus Hildebrand, *Vom Reich zum Weltreich: Hitler, NSDAP und koloniale Frage 1919–1945*, Munich, 1969.

84 Ramon Serrano Suñer, *Zwischen Hendaye und Gibraltar*, Zurich, 1948; cited in Ernst Deuerlein, *Hitler: Eine politische Biographie*, Munich, 1969, p. 149.

85 Minutes of talks between Hitler and Serrano, 17 Sept. 1940, in Andreas Hillgruber (ed.), *Staatsmänner und Diplomaten bei Hitler: Vertrauliche Aufzeichnungen über Unterredungen mit Vertretern des Auslandes 1939–1941*, Frankfurt am Main, 1967, pp. 210, 212.

86 See Hillgruber, *Hitlers Strategie*, pp. 286f.

87 Minutes of talks between Hitler and Ciano, 28 Sept. 1940, in Hillgruber (ed.), *Staatsmänner und Diplomaten bei Hitler 1939–1941*, pp. 221–4 (at p. 223).

88 Minutes of talks between Hitler and Mussolini, 4 Oct. 1940, in Hillgruber (ed.), *Staatsmänner und Diplomaten bei Hitler 1939–1941*, pp. 230–47 (at pp. 238, 241).

89 *KTB OKW*, vol. 1, p. 111 (entry for 5 Nov. 1940).

90 See Hillgruber, *Hitlers Strategie*, pp. 143, 279; Malte König, *Kooperation als Machtkampf: Das faschistische Achsenbündnis Berlin–Rom im Krieg 1940/41*, Cologne, 2007, p. 31.

91 Minutes of talks between Hitler and Laval, 2 Oct. 1940, in Hillgruber (ed.), *Staatsmänner und Diplomaten bei Hitler 1939–1941*, pp. 258–63 (at pp. 258f., 263). See Eberhard Jäckel, *Frankreich in Hitlers Europa: Die deutsche Frankreichpolitik im Zweiten Weltkrieg*, Stuttgart, 1966, pp. 115–17.

92 Schmidt, *Statist auf diplomatischer Bühne*, pp. 500f.

93 Minutes of talks between Hitler and Franco, 23 Oct. 1940, in Hillgruber (ed.), *Staatsmänner und Diplomaten bei Hitler 1939–1941*, pp. 266–71 (at pp. 270). Because these notes have only been preserved in fragmentary form, the following analysis is based on Schmidt's recollections; Schmidt, *Statist auf diplomatischer Bühne*, pp. 501–3.

94   Engel, *Heeresadjutant bei Hitler*, p. 88 (entry for 24 Oct. 1940). See Below, *Als Hitlers Adjutant*, p. 249; Generalfeldmarschall Keitel, *Verbrecher oder Offizier? Erinnerungen, Briefe, Dokumente des Chefs des OKW*, ed. Walter Görlitz, Berlin and Frankfurt am Main, 1961, p. 247.

95   Halder, *Kriegstagebuch*, vol. 2, p. 158 (entry for 1 Nov. 1940); Domarus, *Hitler*, vol. 2, part 1, p. 1596. Months later Hitler still called Franco a "vain peacock" and a "fool" who, even after he had worked on him for hours, "could not bring himself to take a bold decision"; Goebbels, *Tagebücher*, part I, vol. 9, pp. 217 (entry for 1 April 1941), 300 (entry for 9 May 1941). Walter Warlimont recalled Hitler saying: "A man like that would not even have become a district leader under me." Entry for 22 Sept. 1945; IfZ München, ZS 312. Albert Speer quoted Hitler as saying "He is no leader. Nothing but a fat little sergeant." Speer's testimony, "Hitler als Politiker"; BA Koblenz, N 1340/496.

96   Paul Preston, "Franco and Hitler: The Myth of Hendaye 1940," in *Contemporary European History*, 1 (1992), pp. 1–16 (at p. 12). See Ian Kershaw, *Hitler 1936–1945: Nemesis*, London, 2001, pp. 330.

97   Goebbels, *Tagebücher*, part I, vol. 8, p. 390 (entry for 25 Oct. 1940).

98   See Below, *Als Hitlers Adjutant*, p. 249; Henrik Eberle and Matthias Uhl (eds), *Das Buch Hitler*, Bergisch Gladbach, 2005, p. 140.

99   Minutes of talks between Hitler, Pétain and Laval, 24 Oct. 1940, in Hillgruber (ed.), *Staatsmänner und Diplomaten bei Hitler 1939–1941*, pp. 272–80 (at pp. 274, 276, 277, 280). See also the handwritten notes by Hasso von Etzdorf, the Foreign Ministry's liaison with the Army High Command, dated 28 Oct. 1940; IfZ München, ED 100, vol. 63. For a summary, see Jäckel, *Frankreich in Hitlers Europa*, pp. 118, 120.

100   *KTB OKW*, vol. 1, p. 135 (entry for 29 Oct. 1940). See Goebbels, *Tagebücher*, part I, vol. 8, pp. 399f. (entry for 1 Nov. 1940): "Pétain still a clear and clever mind . . . made a deep impression on the Führer"

101   Hill (ed.), *Die Weizsäcker-Papiere 1933–1950*, p. 221 (dated 25 Oct. 1940). See Halder, *Kriegstagebuch*, vol. 2, p. 158 (entry for 1 Nov. 1940).

102   Engel, *Heeresadjutant bei Hitler*, p. 88 (entry for 28 Oct. 1940).

103   Ciano, *Tagebücher, 1939–1943*, p. 278 (entry for 12 Oct. 1940). See Hans Woller, *Mussolini: Der erste Faschist. Eine Biografie*, Munich, 2016, pp. 211f.; Falanga, *Mussolinis Vorposten in Hitlers Reich*, pp. 166f.

104   Keitel, *Verbrecher oder Offizier?*, p. 248. See Schmidt, *Statist auf diplomatischer Bühne*, p. 506.

105   Protocol on talks between Hitler and Mussolini, 28 Oct. 1940; Hillgruber (ed.), *Staatsmänner und Diplomaten bei Hitler 1939–1941*, pp. 281–94 (at p. 288). See Woller, *Mussolini*, pp. 212f.

106   *KTW OKW*, vol. 1, p. 144 (entry for 1 Nov. 1940); Bock, *Das Kriegstagebuch*, p. 169 (entry for 11 Nov. 1940).

107   See König, *Kooperation als Machtkampf*, pp. 35–7; Müller, *Der letzte deutsche Krieg*, pp. 61–3; Kershaw, *Fateful Choices*, pp. 176f.; Woller, *Mussolini*, pp. 214–16.

108   Goebbels, *Tagebücher*, part I, vol. 8, p. 423 (entry for 16 Nov. 1940). See ibid., pp. 432 (entry for 23 Nov. 1940), 436 (entry for 26 Nov. 1940); vol. 9, pp. 33 (entry for 4 Dec. 1940), 35 (entry for 5 Dec. 1940), 37 (entry for 6 Dec. 1940), 42 (entry for 10 Dec. 1940), 63 (entry for 22 Dec. 1940).

109   Ciano, *Tagebücher, 1939–1943*, p. 288 (entry for 18 Nov. 1940).

110   Hitler to Mussolini, 20 Nov. 1940; *ADAP*, Series D, vol. 11, part 2, no. 369, pp. 535–9. See König, *Kooperation als Machtkampf*, p. 39.

111   Ciano, *Tagebücher, 1939–1943*, p. 290 (entry for 21 Nov. 1940).

112   Goebbels, *Tagebücher*, part I, vol. 8, p. 409 (entry for 7 Nov. 1940). On Roosevelt's re-election, see Gerste, *Roosevelt und Hitler*, pp. 259–62; Kershaw, *Fateful Choices*, p. 221.

113   Ernst von Weizsäcker to his mother, 10 Nov. 1940; BA Koblenz, N 1273/29.

114 Thomas Mann, *Tagebücher, 1940–1943*, ed. Peter de Mendelssohn, Frankfurt am Main, 1982, p. 175 (entry for 6 Nov. 1940).

115 Halder, *Kriegstagebuch*, vol. 2, p. 165 (entry for 4 Nov. 1940).

116 See ibid., p. 101 (entry for 16 Sept. 1940); Goebbels, *Tagebücher*, part I, vol. 8, pp. 322 (entry for 13 Sept. 1940), 381 (entry for 17 Oct. 1940); Ernst von Weizsäcker to his mother, 22 Sept. 1940: "We are having some trouble with the Russians." BA Koblenz, N 1273/29.

117 Ribbentrop to Stalin, 13 Oct. 1940; *ADAP*, Series D, vol. 11, part 1, no. 176, pp. 291f. See Joachim von Ribbentrop, *Zwischen London und Moskau: Erinnerungen und letzte Aufzeichnungen*, ed. Annelies von Ribbentrop, Leoni am Starnberger See, 1961, pp. 230f.

118 See Hill (ed.), *Die Weizsäcker-Papiere 1933–1950*, p. 220 (dated 15 Oct. 1940): Weizsäcker was of the opinion that the Soviets would not let themselves "be included . . . in the front of the Tripartite Pact powers."

119 Bock, *Das Kriegstagebuch*, p. 169 (entry for 11 Nov. 1940).

120 Hubatsch (ed.), *Hitlers Weisungen für die Kriegführung*, pp. 77–82 (at p. 81).

121 Goebbels, *Tagebücher*, part I, vol. 8, p. 414 (entry for 12 Nov. 1940).

122 Minutes of talks between Hitler and Molotov, 12 Nov. 1940, in Hillgruber (ed.), *Staatsmänner und Diplomaten bei Hitler 1939–1941*, pp. 295–304 (at pp. 299, 298, 302, 303). See Schmidt, *Statist auf diplomatischer Bühne*, pp. 520–2. For a Russian perspective on Molotov's visit, see Lew A. Besymenski, "Wjatscheslaw Molotows Berlin-Besuch vom November 1940 im Licht neuer Dokumente," in Bianka Pietrow-Ennker (ed.), *Präventivkrieg? Der deutsche Angriff auf die Sowjetunion*, expanded new edition, Frankfurt am Main, 2011, pp. 118–32.

123 Goebbels, *Tagebücher*, part I, vol. 8, pp. 417f. (entry for 14 Nov. 1940).

124 Hill (ed.), *Die Weizsäcker-Papiere 1933–1950*, p. 225 (dated 15 Nov. 1940).

125 Minutes of talks between Hitler and Molotov, 13 Nov. 1940, in Hillgruber (ed.), *Staatsmänner und Diplomaten bei Hitler 1939–1941*, pp. 304–19 (at pp. 309, 314, 316). See Schmidt, *Als Statist auf diplomatischer Bühne*, pp. 522–4.

126 Minutes of talks between Ribbentrop and Molotov, 13 Nov. 1940; *ADAP*, Series D, vol. 11, part 1, no. 325, pp. 448–55. See Ribbentrop, *Zwischen London und Moskau*, pp. 234f.

127 Engel, *Heeresadjutant bei Hitler*, p. 91 (entry for 15 Nov. 1940), also for the subsequent quotation. In conversation with Heinrich Uhlig on 17 November 1951, Gerhard Engel stressed that Hitler had only made his final "decision to take on Russia" after Molotov's visit. IfZ München, ZS 222, vol. 1

128 See Engel, *Heeresadjutant bei Hitler*, p. 92 (entry for 19 Dec. 1940); Below, *Als Hitlers Adjutant*, p. 253; Franz W. Seidler and Dieter Zeigert, *Die Führerhauptquartiere: Anlagen und Planungen im Zweiten Weltkrieg*, Munich, 2000, pp. 193f.; Uwe Neumärker, Robert Conrad and Cord Woywodt, *Wolfsschanze: Hitlers Machtzentrale im Zweiten Weltkrieg*, 3rd edition, Berlin, 2007, pp. 37f.

129 Karl-Jesko von Puttkamer to Friedrich Hossbach, 21 Nov. 1940; BA-MA Freiburg, N 24/13.

130 Ernst von Weizsäcker to his mother, 24 Nov. 1940; BA Koblenz, N 1273/29.

131 See Domarus, *Hitler*, vol. 2, part 1, pp. 1619, 1623f.; Below, *Als Hitlers Adjutant*, pp. 252f.; Schmidt, *Statist auf diplomatischer Bühne*, pp. 511f.; Goebbels, *Tagebücher*, part I, vol. 8, p. 437 (entry for 26 Nov. 1940): "The Führer has found words of the highest recognition for Antonescu, who defended his people with passion."

132 Minutes of talks between Hitler and Antonescu, 22 Nov. 1940, in Hillgruber (ed.), *Staatsmänner und Diplomaten bei Hitler 1939–1941*, pp. 352–62 (at pp. 361f.). Goebbels told others that over lunch in the chancellery Hitler had said: "Neither Romania nor Hungary recognise the Vienna award. That is not so bad. A little hostility in the Balkans is always a good bit of protection. But now they should keep quiet." *Tagebücher*, part I, vol. 8, p. 437 (entry for 26 Nov. 1940).

133 Bock, *Das Kriegstagebuch*, p. 170 (entry for 3 Dec. 1940).

134 Halder, *Kriegstagebuch*, vol. 2, pp. 211–14; *KTB OKW*, vol. 1, p. 205 (entry for 5 Dec. 1940).

135 Halder's notes for the briefing of 13 Dec. 1940; Halder, *Kriegstagebuch*, vol. 2, pp. 224–31 (at p. 227).

136 Hubatsch (ed.), *Hitlers Weisungen für die Kriegführung*, pp. 96–101 (at pp. 96f., 100).

137 Engel, *Heeresadjutant bei Hitler*, p. 92 (entry for 18 Dec. 1940), also for the subsequent quotation.

138 See *KTB OKW*, vol. 1, pp. 219 (entry for 8 Dec. 1940), 222 (entry for 10 Dec. 1940); Halder, *Kriegstagebuch*, vol. 2, pp. 218 (entry for 8 Dec. 1940), 219 (entry for 9 Dec. 1940); Hillgruber, *Hitlers Strategie*, p. 330; Michael Mueller, *Canaris: Hitlers Abwehrchef*, Berlin, 2006, pp. 342f.

139 Hubatsch (ed.), *Hitlers Weisungen für die Kriegführung*, pp. 91–3.

140 See Jäckel, *Frankreich in Hitlers Europa*, pp. 140–8.

141 Notes on the conversation between Hitler and Darlan, 25 Dec. 1940, in Hillgruber (ed.), *Staatsmänner und Diplomaten bei Hitler 1939–1941*, pp. 409–14 (at pp. 411, 412). See Schmidt, *Statist auf diplomatischer Bühne*, p. 513.

142 Shirer, *Berlin Diary*, p. 246 (entry for 1 Dec. 1940).

143 Domarus, *Hitler*, vol. 2, part 1, pp. 1602–8 (at p. 1605). See Goebbels, *Tagebücher*, part I, vol. 8, p. 411 (entry for 9 Nov. 1940): "A bold, proud and rousing speech."

144 Domarus, *Hitler*, vol. 2, part 1, pp. 1627–34 (at pp. 1632, 1633).

145 Goebbels, *Tagebücher*, part I, vol. 9, p. 48 (entry for 12 Dec. 1940): "The Führer speaks with a powerful faith that is transferred to his listeners."

146 Domarus, *Hitler*, vol. 2, part 1, pp. 1639f.

147 New Year's address by Goebbels 1940/41 (with Hitler's handwritten corrections); BA Berlin-Lichterfelde, NS 10/37.

148 Friedrich Kellner, *"Vernebelt, verdunkelt sind alle Hirne": Tagebücher, 1939–1945*, ed. Sascha Feuchert et al., Göttingen, 2011, vol. 1, p. 109 (entry for 31 Dec. 1940).

5 Operation Barbarossa

1 Max Domarus, *Hitler: Reden und Proklamationen 1932–1945*, vol. 2, part 2, Munich, 1965, p. 1649.

2 See Heinz Boberach (ed.), *Meldungen aus dem Reich: Die geheimen Lageberichte des Sicherheitsdienstes der SS 1938–1945*, Herrsching, 1984, vol. 6, p. 1886 (dated 9 Jan. 1941).

3 Report by the US Consul Sydney B. Redecker, 16 Jan. 1941; Frank Bajohr and Christoph Strupp (eds), *Fremde Blicke auf das "Dritte Reich": Berichte ausländischer Diplomaten über Herrschaft und Gesellschaft in Deutschland 1933–1945*, Göttingen, 2011, p. 554.

4 See Nicolaus von Below, *Als Hitlers Adjutant 1937–45*, Mainz, 1980, pp. 258, 262; Christa Schroeder to Johanna Nusser, 7 March 1941: "It is time for us to be returning to Berlin. We have been here long enough." IfZ München, ED 524; Christa Schroeder, *Er war mein Chef: Aus dem Nachlass der Sekretärin von Adolf Hitler*, ed. Anton Joachimsthaler, 3rd edition, Munich and Vienna, 1985, p. 108.

5 *Kriegstagebuch des Oberkommandos der Wehrmacht (Wehrmachtführungsstab)* (hereafter *KTB OKW*), *vol. 1: 1. August 1940–31. Dezember 1941*, ed. Percy Ernst Schramm, Munich, 1982, pp. 257f. (entry for 9 Jan. 1941). See also Generaloberst Halder, *Kriegstagebuch: Tägliche Aufzeichnungen des Chefs des Generalstabs des Heeres 1939–1942*, vol. 2, ed. Hans-Adolf Jacobsen, Stuttgart, 1962, pp. 243f. (entry for 16 Jan. 1941). General Friedrich Paulus had represented Halder at the meeting, and the latter was relating what the former had told him. See Thorsten Diedrich, *Paulus: Das Trauma von Stalingrad. Eine Biographie*, Paderborn, 2008, pp. 166f.

6 Below, *Als Hitlers Adjutant*, p. 259.

7 Halder, *Kriegstagebuch*, vol. 2, p. 261 (entry for 28 Jan. 1941).

8 Leonidas Hill (ed.), *Die Weizsäcker-Papiere 1933–1950*, Frankfurt am Main, Berlin and Vienna, 1974, pp. 229 (entry for 22 Dec. 1940), 233 (entry for 19 Jan. 1941).

9 Fedor von Bock, *Zwischen Pflicht und Verweigerung: Das Kriegstagebuch*, ed. Klaus Gerbet, Munich, 1995, pp. 172f. (entry for 31 Jan. 1941). See Halder, *Kriegstagebuch*, vol. 2, p. 264 (entry for 31 Jan. 1941); Generalfeldmarschall Wilhelm Ritter von Leeb, *Tagebuchaufzeichnungen und Lagebeurteilungen aus zwei Weltkriegen*, ed. Georg Meyer, Stuttgart, 1976, p. 267 (entry for 31 Jan. 1941). See also Andreas Hillgruber, *Hitlers Strategie: Politik und Kriegführung 1940–1941*, Frankfurt am Main, 1965, p. 373.

10 Bock, *Das Kriegstagebuch*, pp. 173f. (entry for 1 Feb. 1941).

11 According to a report by Lieutenant Fritz von Lossberg to Paulus, who was at the time superior quartermaster I in the army general staff; Friedrich Paulus to the USSR government, 8 Jan. 1946; IfZ München, ZS 652.

12 Mobilisation plan "Barbarossa," 31 Jan. 1941; Halder, *Kriegstagebuch*, vol. 2, pp. 463–9 (at pp. 464, 465). See ibid., pp. 266–70 for Halder's notes on his presentation to Hitler on 3 Feb. 1941; see also *KTB OKW*, vol. 1, pp. 297f. (entry for 3 Feb. 1941). At a meeting with the commander of the Replacement Army and head of army weaponry, Friedrich Fromm, and other generals on 28 January, Halder had stressed that there could be "no stumbles" and that "this alone will ensure success." Halder, *Kriegstagebuch*, vol. 2, p. 258 (entry for 28 Jan. 1941).

13 *KTB OKW*, vol. 1, p. 298 (entry for 3 Feb. 1941).

14 See Franz Halder to Heinrich Uhlig, 21 Dec. 1955; BA-MA Freiburg, N 220/88; Johannes Hürter, *Hitlers Heerführer: Die deutschen Oberbefehlshaber im Krieg gegen die Sowjetunion 1941/42*, Munich, 2007, pp. 223f.

15 *KTB OKW*, vol. 1, p. 328 (entry for 17 Feb. 1941). See Halder, *Kriegstagebuch*, vol. 2, p. 292 (entry for 251 Feb. 1941): "Operation against Afghanistan."

16 *KTB OKW*, vol. 1, p. 244 (entry for 28 Dec. 1941).

17 *Die Tagebücher von Joseph Goebbels*, commissioned by the Institute for Contemporary History, with support from the State Archive of Russia, ed. Elke Fröhlich, *Part I: Aufzeichnungen 1923–1941*, 9 vols in 14 parts, Munich, 1998–2008; *Part II: Diktate 1941–1945*, 15 vols, Munich, 1993–6; part I, vol. 9, p. 83 (entry for 7 Jan. 1941).

18 *KTB OKW*, vol. 1, p. 253 (entry for 9 Jan. 1941). See Halder, *Kriegstagebuch*, vol. 2, p. 244 (entry for 16 Jan. 1941): "[We] cannot risk Italy collapsing . . . We have to help."

19 Walther Hubatsch (ed.), *Hitlers Weisungen für die Kriegsführung*, Munich, 1965, pp. 107–109 (at pp. 107f.).

20 See Galeazzo Ciano, *Tagebücher, 1939–1943*, Bern, 1946, p. 309 (entry for 19 Jan. 1941): "The encounter is emotional, indeed very directly emotional, which surprises me a lot." On the meeting at the Berghof on 19–20 January 1941, see Malte König, *Kooperation als Machtkampf: Das faschistische Achsenbündnis Berlin–Rom im Krieg 1940/41*, Cologne, 2007, pp. 49–62.

21 Minutes of talks between Hitler and Mussolini, 20 Jan. 1941, in Andreas Hillgruber (ed.), *Staatsmänner und Diplomaten bei Hitler: Vertrauliche Aufzeichnungen über Unterredungen mit Vertretern des Auslandes 1939–1941*, Frankfurt am Main, 1967, pp. 443–52 (at p. 448); *KTB OKW*, vol. 1, pp. 274–7 (at p. 275); Ciano, *Tagebücher, 1939–1943*, p. 310 (entry for 20 Jan. 1941).

22 Ciano, *Tagebücher, 1939–1943*, p. 310 (entry for 21 Jan. 1941). See Goebbels, *Tagebücher*, part I, vol. 9, p. 103 (entry for 21 Jan. 1941): "Mussolini was on the [Obersalzberg] for almost three days. Exhaustive exchange of thoughts . . . Complete consensus."

23 Goebbels, *Tagebücher*, part I, vol. 9, p. 111 (entry for 27 Jan. 1941).

24 *Meldungen aus dem Reich*, vol. 6, p. 1938 (dated 27 Jan. 1941).

25 Hubatsch (ed.), *Hitlers Weisungen für die Kriegsführung*, pp. 116f.

26 *Heeresadjutant bei Hitler 1938–1943: Aufzeichnungen des Majors Engel*, ed. Hildegard von Kotze, Stuttgart, 1974, p. 94 (entry for 1 Feb. 1941).

27 *KTB OKW*, vol. 1, pp. 300f. (entry for 3 Feb. 1941).

28   Hitler to Mussolini, 5 Feb. 1941; *Akten zur deutschen Auswärtigen Politik 1918–1945* (*ADAP*) (*The Political Archives of the Federal Foreign Office*), Series D, 1937–1941, vols 1–13, vol. 12, doc. 17, p. 25.

29   Ralf Georg Reuth, *Rommel: Das Ende einer Legende*, Munich and Zurich, 2004, p. 55.

30   Rommel to Friedrich Paulus, deputy chief of the general staff, 26 Feb. 1941; BA-MA Freiburg, N 372/22. On the above see also *KTB OKW*, vol. 1, p. 321 (entry for 13 Feb. 1941); König, *Kooperation als Machtkampf*, pp. 63f.

31   See Richard Overy, *The Bombing War: Europe 1939–1945*, London, 2013, p. 502.

32   Goebbels, *Tagebücher*, part I, vol. 9, p. 198 (entry for 21 March 1941). See Below, *Als Hitlers Adjutant*, p. 264.

33   Goebbels, *Tagebücher*, part I, vol. 9, p. 363 (entry for 11 June 1941). See Reuth, *Rommel*, pp. 64f.; Geoffrey P. Megargee, *Hitler und die Generäle: Das Ringen um die Führung der Wehrmacht 1939–1945*, Paderborn, 2006, pp. 16f.; Rolf-Dieter Müller, *Der letzte deutsche Krieg 1939–1945*, Stuttgart, 2005, p. 73: Diedrich, *Friedrich Paulus*, pp. 172–5.

34   Minutes of talks between Hitler and Mussolini, 19 Jan. 1941; Hillgruber (ed.), *Staatsmänner und Diplomaten bei Hitler 1939–1941*, pp. 435–43 (at p. 442).

35   Hewel's diary entry for 14 Feb. 1941; IfZ München, ED 100/78. A transcription of the diary is kept in the IfZ archive and was used for the first time by David Irving in his book *Hitler und seine Feldherren* (Frankfurt am Main, Berlin and Vienna, 1975).

36   Notes on Kurusu's leaving ceremony, 3 Feb. 1941, in Hillgruber (ed.), *Staatsmänner und Diplomaten bei Hitler 1939–1941*, pp. 453–5 (at p. 453).

37   Telegram from Oshima to Foreign Minister Matsuoka, 2 March 1941; printed in Andreas Hillgruber, "Japan und der Fall 'Barbarossa,'" in idem, *Deutsche Grossmacht- und Weltpolitik im 19. und 20. Jahrhundert*, Düsseldorf, 1977, pp. 235–9 (at pp. 238f.).

38   Hubatsch (ed.), *Hitlers Weisungen für die Kriegführung*, pp. 121–3.

39   Goebbels, *Tagebücher*, part I, vol. 9, p. 207 (entry for 27 March 1941). On Matsuoka's reception, see Paul Schmidt, *Statist auf diplomatischer Bühne 1923–45*, Bonn, 1950, pp. 526–8.

40   Friedrich Kellner, *"Vernebelt, verdunkelt sind alle Hirne": Tagebücher, 1939–1945*, ed. Sascha Feuchert et al., Göttingen, 2011, vol. 1, p. 128 (entry for 8 April 1941).

41   Minutes of talks between Hitler and Matsuoka, 27 March 1941, in Hillgruber (ed.), *Staatsmänner und Diplomaten bei Hitler 1939–1941*, pp. 503–14 (at pp. 507f., 510, 514). See Schmidt, *Statist auf diplomatischer Bühne*, pp. 532f.

42   Telegram from Oshima to the Japanese prime minister Konoye, 1 April 1941, in Hillgruber, "Japan und der Fall 'Barbarossa,'" in idem, *Deutsche Grossmacht- und Weltpolitik*, pp. 239f.

43   Minutes of talks between Hitler and Matsuoka, 4 April 1941, in Hillgruber (ed.), *Staatsmänner und Diplomaten bei Hitler 1939–1941*, pp. 518–24 (at p. 522).

44   See Goebbels, *Tagebücher*, part I, vol. 9, p. 247 (entry for 14 April 1941): "Great sensation: Russian–Japanese friendship and no-aggression pact." See ibid., p. 248 (entry for 15 April 1941): "With regard to what we know of his further plans, that does not suit the Führer at all."

45   See telegram from Oshima to Konoye, 16 April 1941, in Hillgruber, "Japan und der Fall 'Barbarossa,'" in idem, *Deutsche Grossmacht- und Weltpolitik*, pp. 240–4.

46   Telegram from Schulenburg to the Foreign Office, 13 April 1941; *ADAP*, Series D, vol. 12, doc. 333, p. 537.

47   Goebbels, *Tagebücher*, part I, vol. 9, p. 279 (entry for 29 April 1941). The first reference to the "great operation . . . against R[ussia]" can be found in the entry of 29 March 1941; ibid., p. 221. On Stalin's stance, Dietmar Neutatz, *Träume und Alpträume: Eine Geschichte Russlands im 20. Jahrhundert*, Munich, 2013, p. 283; Manfred Hildermeier, *Geschichte der Sowjetunion 1917–1991: Entstehung und Niedergang des ersten sozialistischen Staates*, Munich, 1998, p. 597.

48   See *Meldungen aus dem Reich*, vol. 6, p. 1965 (dated 3 Feb. 1941): "Very often in the reports, there was talk about why the Führer did not mention Russia."

49 *KTB OKW*, vol. 1, p. 341 (entry for 3 March 1941).

50 Hubatsch (ed.), *Hitlers Weisungen für die Kriegführung*, pp. 101–5. See Jürgen Förster, "Das Unternehmen 'Barbarossa' als Eroberungs- und Vernichtungskrieg," in *Das Deutsche Reich und der Zweite Weltkrieg*, ed. Militärgeschichtliches Forschungsamt (Military Historical Research Office), 10 vols, Stuttgart and Munich, 1979–2008, vol. 4, pp. 415f.; Hürter, *Hitlers Heerführer*, p. 238.

51 Halder, *Kriegstagebuch*, vol. 2, p. 320 (entry for 17 March 1941).

52 Testimony of the First General Staff Officer of the Army High Command 18, Baron Mauritz von Strachwitz; cited in *Das Deutsche Reich und der Zweite Weltkrieg*, vol. 4, pp. 416f. (Förster's essay). See Hürter, *Hitlers Heerführer*, pp. 231, 238.

53 Hürter, *Hitlers Heerführer*, p. 1.

54 Warlimont estimated the number of participants as "around 200–250," which is clearly too high. See Walter Warlimont, *Im Hauptquartier der deutschen Wehrmacht 1939–1945: Grundlagen—Formen—Gestalten*, Frankfurt am Main and Bonn, 1964, p. 175. See Hürter, *Hitlers Heerführer*, p. 3 (n. 8).

55 Halder, *Kriegstagebuch*, vol. 2; pp. 335–7 (entry for 30 March 1941); Hoth's notes on a "discussion by the Führer on 30 March 41 in the chancellery" are reproduced and interpreted in Hürter, *Hitlers Heerführer*, pp. 5–8. For a short summary of the content of the speech see Bock, *Das Kriegstagebuch*, pp. 180f. (entry for 30 March 1941).

56 Hoth's notes; Hürter, *Hitlers Heerführer*, p. 5n 21.

57 Ibid., p. 6n 23; See Halder, *Kriegstagebuch*, vol. 2, p. 325: "Advantage for England's situation because of Italy's defeats."

58 Hoth's notes; Hürter, *Hitlers Heerführer*, p. 7. See Halder, *Kriegstagebuch*, vol. 2, p. 335 (entry for 30 March 1941): "Only if we resolve the land question comprehensively and finally, will we be capable of mastering our materiel and personnel challenges in the air and on the world's seas in two years."

59 Bock, *Das Kriegstagebuch*, p. 181 (entry for 30 March 1941).

60 Halder, *Kriegstagebuch*, vol. 2, p. 336 (entry for 30 March 1941).

61 Ibid., pp. 336f. (entry for 30 March 1941). See Hoth's notes: "Crimes by the Russian commissars . . . Do not deserve to be gone easy on. To be removed not by court martial, but by the troops. Not to be sent to the rear." Hürter, *Hitlers Heerführer*, p. 7.

62 Hoth's notes; Hürter, *Hitlers Heerführer*, p. 8.

63 Warlimont, *Im Hauptquartier der Wehrmacht*, p. 176.

64 Halder's statement to the Munich de-Nazification tribunal, 20 Sept. 1948; IfZ München, ZS 240, vol. 6. See Hürter, *Hitlers Heerführer*, p. 10.

65 Bock, *Das Kriegstagebuch*, p. 181 (entry for 30 March 1941).

66 See Hürter, *Hitlers Heerführer*, pp. 213–17.

67 Cited in Hürter, *Hitlers Heerführer*, p. 218.

68 Cited in Gerd R. Ueberschär and Wolfram Wette (ed.), *Der deutsche Überfall auf die Sowjetunion: "Unternehmen Barbarossa" 1941*, expanded edition, Frankfurt am Main, 2011, p. 251.

69 Ernst von Weizsäcker to his mother, 2 March 1941; BA Koblenz, N 1273/30.

70 Minutes of talks between Hitler and Filoff, 4 Jan. 1941, in Hillgruber (ed.), *Staatsmänner und Diplomaten bei Hitler 1939–1941*, pp. 415–25 (at p. 420).

71 Goebbels, *Tagebücher*, part I, vol. 9, pp. 169 (entry for 4 March 1941), 171 (entry for 5 March 1941). See Balck's diary entry for 3 March 1941: "Bulgaria has entered the Tripartite Pact. Since 2 March we have been on the march in Bulgaria." BA-MA Freiburg, N 647/8.

72 Hitler to Inönü, 1 March 1941; *ADAP*, Series D, vol. 12, part 1, no. 113, pp. 166f. See Franz von Papen, *Der Wahrheit eine Gasse*, Munich, 1952, p. 535; Halder, *Kriegstagebuch*, vol. 2, p. 300 (entry for 3 March 1941).

73 Minutes of talks between Hitler and Cvetković, 14 Feb. 1941, in Hillgruber (ed.), *Staatsmänner und Diplomaten bei Hitler 1939–1941*, pp. 456–64 (at p. 463).

74   Hewel's diary entry for 14 Feb. 1941; IfZ München, ED 100/78. See Below, *Als Hitlers Adjutant*, p. 263; Halder, *Kriegstagebuch*, vol. 2, p. 282 (entry for 17 Feb. 1941).

75   Goebbels, *Tagebücher*, part I, vol. 9, p. 205 (entry for 26 March 1941).

76   Generalfeldmarschall Keitel, *Verbrecher oder Offizier? Erinnerungen, Briefe, Dokumente des Chefs des OKW*, ed. Walter Görlitz, Berlin and Frankfurt am Main, 1961, p. 261. See Hewel's diary, 27 March 1941; IfZ München, ED 100/78.

77   *KTB OKW*, vol. 1, p. 368 (entry for 27 March 1941); see Halder, *Kriegstagebuch*, vol. 2, p. 330 (entry for 27 March 1941).

78   Minutes of talks between Hitler and Döme Sztojay, 27 March 1941, in Hillgruber (ed.), *Diplomaten und Staatsmänner bei Hitler 1939–1941*, pp. 498–501 (at pp. 498, 500).

79   Minutes of talks between Hitler and Parvan Draganoff, 27 March 1941; ibid., pp. 501f.

80   *Der Prozess gegen die Hauptkriegsverbrecher vor dem internationalen Militärtribunal in Nürnberg*, 42 vols, Nuremberg, 1947–9 (hereafter *IMT*), vol. 28, p. 23; Domarus, *Hitler*, vol. 2, part 2, pp. 1677f.

81   Hubatsch (ed.), *Hitlers Weisungen für die Kriegführung*, pp. 124–6 (at p. 124).

82   See Christian Hartmann, *Halder: Generalstabschef Hitlers 1938–1942*, 2nd edition, Paderborn, 2010, p. 256.

83   Goebbels, *Tagebücher*, part I, vol. 9, p. 230 (entry for 6 April 1941).

84   Hewel's diary, 9 April 1941; IfZ München, ED 100/78. See Goebbels, *Tagebücher*, part I, vol. 9, p. 239 (entry for 10 April 1941). Goebbels wrote that Hitler had "great concern . . . that there would be no breakthrough" and "had not slept at all that night," but was now "beaming with glee."

85   See Goebbels, *Tagebücher*, part I, vol. 9, p. 241 (entry for 11 April 1941); Below, *Als Hitlers Adjutant*, p. 268. In retribution, the Luftwaffe launched a devastating attack on London on 16 April 1941; see Overy, *The Bombing War*, pp.107f.

86   See Below, *Als Hitlers Adjutant*, pp. 268f.; Franz W. Seidler and Dieter Zeigert, *Die Führerhauptquartiere: Anlagen und Planungen im Zweiten Weltkrieg*, Munich, 2000, pp. 130–3.

87   On the course of the Balkans campaign, see Detlef Vogel, "Das Eingreifen Deutschlands auf dem Balkan," in *Das Deutsche Reich und der Zweite Weltkrieg*, vol. 3, Stuttgart, 1984, pp. 417–511; Müller, *Der letzte deutsche Krieg*, pp. 69–71; Gerhard L. Weinberg, *Eine Welt in Waffen: Die globale Geschichte des Zweiten Weltkriegs*, Stuttgart, 1995, pp. 247–9.

88   Hewel's diary entry for 21 April 1941; IfZ München, ED 100/78. See also the entry for 25 April 1941: "Great irritation at the Italians . . . Führer used the strongest language." Ibid. Goebbels, *Tagebücher*, part I, vol. 9, p. 278: "The Italians are acting insolently, arrogantly and almost shamelessly." On the conflict over Greece's surrender, see König, *Kooperation als Machtkampf*, pp. 69–71; Mark Mazower, *Griechenland unter Hitler: Das Leben während der deutschen Besatzung*, Frankfurt am Main, 2016, pp. 39–41.

89   See German News Bureau, no. 110, dated 20 April 1941: "Führer-Geburtstag im Hauptquartier"; BA Berlin-Lichterfelde, R 43 II/957. See Goebbels, *Tagebücher*, part I, vol. 9, p. 261 (entry for 21 April 1941); Hewel's diary entry for 20 Apr. 1941; IfZ München, ED 100/78; Ministerial Counsel Helmuth Greiner to his wife, 22 April 1941; IfZ München, ED 100, vol. 76.

90   Hewel's diary entry for 27 April 1941; IfZ München, ED 100/78; Seidler and Zeigert, *Die Führerhauptquartiere*, pp. 133f.

91   Goebbels, *Tagebücher*, part I, vol. 9, p. 279 (entry for 29 April 1941).

92   *Meldungen aus dem Reich*, vol. 6, p. 2193 (dated 10 April 1941), vol. 7, pp. 2227f. (dated 25 April 1941).

93   Schulenburg's notes on his conversation with Hitler on 28 April 1941; *ADAP*, Series D, vol. 12, part 2, no. 423, p. 666. See Ingeborg Fleischhauer, *Diplomatischer Widerstand gegen das "Unternehmen Barbarossa": Die Friedensbemühungen der deutschen Botschaft Moskau 1939–1941*, Frankfurt am Main, 1991, pp. 307–9.

94   Gustav Hilger, *Wir und der Kreml: Deutsch-sowjetische Beziehungen 1918–1941*, Frankfurt am Main, 1959, p. 306. See Fleischhauer, *Diplomatischer Widerstand*, p. 310.

95   Hill (ed.), *Die Weizsäcker-Papiere 1933–1950*, pp. 249f. (dated 28 April 1941).

96   Ibid., p. 252 (entry for 1 May 1941).

97   Domarus, *Hitler*, vol. 2, part 2, p. 1696.

98   Ibid., pp. 1697–1709 (at pp. 1704, 1708).

99   Goebbels, *Tagebücher*, part I, vol. 9, p. 293 (entry for 6 May 1941). See *Meldungen aus dem Reich*, vol. 7, p. 2271 (dated 8 May 1941): "The Führer's words . . . strengthened fears that have recently re-emerged among the population that the war will not end in 1941 either."

100   Goebbels, *Tagebücher*, part I, vol. 9, p. 235 (entry for 8 July 1941).

101   On the detail, see Klaus Olshausen, *Zwischenspiel auf dem Balkan: Die deutsche Politik gegenüber Jugoslawien und Griechenland März bis Juli 1941*, Stuttgart, 1973, pp. 153–233; Marie-Janine Calic, *Geschichte Jugoslawiens im 20. Jahrhundert*, Munich, 2010, pp. 137f. For a summary, see Richard J. Evans, *The Third Reich at War, 1939-1945*, London, 2008, p. 157; Heinrich August Winkler, *Geschichte des Westens: Die Zeit der Weltkriege 1914–1945*, Munich, 2011, pp. 936f.

102   Olshausen, *Zwischenspiel auf dem Balkan*, pp. 222–33, 308–10 (at p. 233).

103   Albert Speer, *Erinnerungen: Mit einem Essay von Jochen Thies*, Frankfurt am Main and Berlin, 1993, p. 190. On Hess's loss of influence, Rainer F. Schmidt, *Rudolf Hess: "Botengang eines Toren"? Der Flug nach Großbritannien vom 10. Mai 1941*, Düsseldorf, 1997, pp. 61–90; Kurt Pätzold and Manfred Weissbecker, *Rudolf Hess: Der Mann an Hitlers Seite*, Leipzig, 1999, pp. 207–41.

104   Karl Haushofer to Albrecht Haushofer, 3 Sept. 1940; Hans-Adolf Jacobsen (ed.), *Karl Haushofer: Leben und Werk. Vol. 2: Ausgewählter Schriftwechsel 1917–1946*, Boppard am Rhein, 1979, p. 453.

105   See Schmidt, *"Botengang eines Toren"?*, pp. 91–125.

106   See Rudolf Hess to Ilse Hess, 4 Dec. 1928; Rudolf Hess to his father, 24 Oct. 1930; BA Bern, Nl R. Hess, J1. 211–1989/148, vols 41, 45.

107   See Armin Nolzen, "Der Hess-Flug vom 10. Mai 1941 und die öffentliche Meinung im NS-Staat," in Martin Sabrow (ed.), *Skandal und Diktatur: Öffentliche Empörung im NS-Staat und in der DDR*, Göttingen, 2004, pp. 130–56 (at pp. 135–7).

108   See Hans Frank's diary entry for 5 May 1941: "Gauleiter and Reichsleiter conference. Hess failed to attend." BA Koblenz, N 1110/10.

109   See transcript of Bohle's interrogation by Lt. Col. O. J. Hale, 26–27 July 1945; IfZ München, ZS 209. On the morning of 10 May 1941, Alfred Rosenberg had spoken with Hess in the latter's private apartment without Hess giving any indication about what he was about to do. See Jürgen Matthäus and Frank Bajohr (eds), *Alfred Rosenberg: Die Tagebücher von 1934 bis 1944*, Frankfurt am Main, 2015, pp. 384–6 (entry for 14 May 1941).

110   See Schmidt, *"Botengang eines Toren"?*, pp. 175–82 (at p. 182); Ian Kershaw, *Hitler 1936–1945: Nemesis*, London, 2001, pp. 370f.; Peter Padfield, *Hess: The Führer's Disciple*, London, 1993, pp. 192–201.

111   Cited in Schmidt, *"Botengang eines Toren"?*, p. 206; see also Rainer F. Schmidt, "Der Hess-Flug und das Kabinett Churchill: Hitlers Stellvertreter im Kalkül der britischen Kriegsdiplomatie Mai–Juni 1941," in *Vierteljahrshefte für Zeitgeschichte*, 42 (1994), pp. 1–38 (at pp. 13f.).

112   Engel, *Heeresadjutant bei Hitler*, p. 103 (entry for 11 May 1941). According to Engel, the letter was delivered at 11 a.m. during his military report. This is unlikely since Hitler was usually still asleep at that hour. More plausible is Linge's account that he woke Hitler and told him what had happened; Henrik Eberle and Matthias Uhl (eds), *Das Buch Hitler*, Bergisch Gladbach, 2005, p. 142. On the sequence of events, see also Below, *Als Hitlers Adjutant*, p. 273.

113   Hewel's diary entry for 11 May 1941; IfZ München, ED 100/78. See also Otto Dietrich, *12 Jahre mit Hitler*, Munich, 1955, p. 76. Three days later, Hitler told Rosenberg that he had felt "literally nauseous" upon reading the letter. Rosenberg, *Die Tagebücher von 1934 bis 1944*, p. 387 (entry for 14 May 1941).

114   Speer, *Erinnerungen*, p. 189. See Albert Speer, *"Alles was ich weiss": Aus unbekannten Geheimdienstprotokollen vom Sommer 1945*, ed. Ulrich Schlie, Munich, 1999, p. 102. A member of the SS bodyguard commando, Rochus Misch, remembered Hitler crying out: "Hess?! Hess? Hess of all people is supposed to have done this? ... Why is he inflicting this on me?" See Rochus Misch, *Der letzte Zeuge: "Ich war Hitlers Telefonist, Kurier und Leibwächter,"* Zurich and Munich, 2008, p. 123.

115   Interview by David Irving with Karl Bodenschatz, 30 Nov. 1970; IfZ München, ZS 10.

116   Ilse Hess later claimed that she had kept a copy of her husband's farewell letter to Hitler in a small safe in her house in Munich-Harlaching, but that she had destroyed it shortly before the end of the war. She recalled the letter concluding with the words: "And, my Führer, should my attempt, which I must admit has only a very small chance of success, fail, and should destiny be against me, it cannot have any negative consequences for either you or Germany: you can always distance yourself from me by declaring me insane." Ilse Hess to Albert Speer, 3 Oct. 1967; BA Koblenz, N 1340/27.

117   Dietrich, *12 Jahre mit Hitler*, p. 77. Goebbels also read Hess's testament on the Berghof on 13 May and commented: "A confused jumbled, schoolboy dilettantism: he was going to England to convince the country of the hopelessness of its situation, to overthrow the Churchill government with Lord Hamilton in Scotland and then to conclude a face-saving peace for London. He unfortunately overlooked the fact that Churchill would immediately have him arrested." Goebbels, *Tagebücher*, part I, vol. 9, p. 311 (entry for 14 May 1941).

118   Rudolf Hess to Adolf Hitler, 14 June 1941; copy in BA Bern, Nl R. Hess, J1. 211–1989/148, vol. 67. The letter was signed: "Hail, my Führer! Your devoted Rudolf Hess." See also Hess's farewell letter to his family, in which he wrote: "I have completely committed myself to a great idea! I am convinced that my efforts will bear fruit regardless of what happens. Perhaps despite my death, or maybe precisely because of it, peace will be the outcome of my flight."

119   Engel, *Heeresadjutant bei Hitler*, pp. 103f. (entry for 11 May 1941); Hermann Göring's appointment diary under 11 May 1941: "2 p.m. Call from Führer (come immediately)." See Hewel's diary entry for 11 May 1941: "F[oreign] M[inister] and Göring need to come immediately." IfZ München, ED 100/78; interview by David Irving with Karl Bodenschatz, 30 Nov. 1970; IfZ München, ZS 10.

120   Engel, *Heeresadjutant bei Hitler*, p. 104 (entry for 10 May 1941). See Hewel's diary entry for 11 May 1941: "Führer very absent-minded. Conversation slow." IfZ München, ED 100/78.

121   Notes by Julius Schaub, "Der Flug von Rudolf Hess nach England am 11 Mai 1941"; IfZ München, ED 100, vol. 203; see also, in slightly varied form, Olaf Rose (ed.), *Julius Schaub—In Hitlers Schatten: Erinnerungen und Aufzeichnungen des Chefadjutanten 1925–1945*, Stegen am Ammersee, 2005, p. 253.

122   Hewel's diary, 12 May 1941; IfZ München, ED 100/78. See Hermann Göring's appointment dairy under 11 and 12 May 1941; IfZ München, ED 180/5; Dietrich, *12 Jahre mit Hitler*, pp. 77f.; Engel, *Heeresadjutant bei Hitler*, p. 105 (entry for 12 May 1941): "The whole night was spent wondering whether he could have made it over there or not."

123   Domarus, *Hitler*, vol. 2, part 2, p. 1714. Christa Schroeder reported that Hitler had never struggled so much with dictation as he did with the communiqué of 12 May 1941; Schroeder, *Er war mein Chef*, p. 192.

124   Goebbels, *Tagebücher*, part I, vol. 9, p. 309 (entry for 13 May 1941).

125   Ibid., p. 311 (entry for 14 May 1941).

126   See ibid., p. 310 (entry for 14 Sept. 1941). Wilhelm Muehlon commented: "Sometimes you experience unexpected joys . . . My mood lifts when I hear the details of his flight into the camp of the mortal enemy." *Tagebuch der Kriegsjahre 1940–1944*, ed. Jens Heisterkamp, Dornach, 1992, pp. 450f. (entry for 13 May 1941).

127   Domarus, *Hitler*, vol. 2, part 2, pp. 1715f.

128   *Meldungen aus dem Reich*, vol. 7, p. 2302 (dated 15 May 1941). On the effects of the Hess affair on the mood of the population, see Nolzen, *Der Hess-Flug*, pp. 143–5; Ian Kershaw, *The Hitler Myth: Image and Reality in the Third Reich*, Oxford, 1987, pp. 166f.; Marlies Steinert, *Hitlers Krieg und die Deutschen: Stimmung und Haltung der deutschen Bevölkerung im Zweiten Weltkrieg*, Düsseldorf and Vienna, 1970, pp. 193–5.

129   Goebbels, *Tagebücher*, part I, vol. 9, p. 310 (entry for 13 May 1941).

130   Dispatch from Danish diplomat Vincens Steensen-Leth, 24 May 1941; Bajohr and Strupp (eds), *Fremde Blicke auf das "Dritte Reich,"* p. 559. Hess's flight was also the topic of the day among military men. "It seems impossible . . . ," noted Hermann Balck on 14 May 1941. "The consequences are regrettable and capable of temporarily paralysing the will to victory." BA-MA Freiburg, N 647/8.

131   Kellner, *Tagebücher, 1939–1945*, vol. 1, p. 135 (entry for 13 May 1941). See Willy Cohn, *Kein Recht, nirgends: Tagebuch vom Untergang des Breslauer Judentums 1933–1941*, ed. Norbert Conrads, vol. 2, Cologne, Weimar and Vienna, 2006, p. 935 (entry for 13 May 1941): "The Führer's deputy has flown off to the enemy. This could be the beginning of the end."

132   Ulrich von Hassell, *Vom andern Deutschland: Aus den nachgelassenen Tagebüchern 1938–1944*, Frankfurt am Main, 1964, p. 182 (entry for 18 May 1941). See Kellner, *Tagebücher, 1939–1945*, vol. 1, p. 136 (entry for 14 May 1941): "No one believes that he is deranged. There is no way a lunatic could fly from Augsburg to Scotland."

133   Ruth Andreas-Friedrich, *Der Schattenmann: Tagebuchaufzeichnungen 1938–1945*, Frankfurt am Main, 1983, p. 79 (entry for 16 May 1941).

134   Victor Klemperer, *Ich will Zeugnis ablegen bis zum letzten: Tagebücher*, vol. 1: 1933–1941, ed. Walter Nowojski with Hadwig Klemperer, Berlin, 1995, p. 594 (entry for 24 May 1941). For other jokes, see Hassell, *Vom andern Deutschland*, p. 185 (entry for 29 May 1941); Evans, *The Third Reich at War*, p. 170.

135   See Jochen von Lang, *Der Sekretär: Martin Bormann, der Mann, der Hitler beherrschte*, Stuttgart, 1977, pp. 164–6; Volker Koop, *Martin Bormann: Hitlers Vollstrecker*, Cologne and Weimar, 2012, pp. 37f., 45, 57f.

136   Engel, *Heeresadjutant bei Hitler*, p. 105 (entry for 12 May 1941). See Eberle and Uhl (eds), *Das Buch Hitler*, p. 144: "People who knew Bormann well sensed behind his façade of sadness a deep satisfaction that his hour was at hand."

137   Goebbels, *Tagebücher*, part I, vol. 9, p. 324 (entry for 20 May 1941).

138   Heydrich to Himmler, 15 May 1941 (with a copy of a telegram to Bormann); BA Berlin-Lichterfelde, NS 19/3872.

139   See Schmidt, *"Botengang eines Toren?,"* pp. 199–202; Nolzen, *Der Hess-Flug*, p. 140. See also the testimony of Leitgen in 1952 and Schulte-Strathaus in 1963; IfZ München ZS 262, 2089.

140   Ilse Hess to Elsa Bruckmann, 10 June 1941; partially reproduced in Anton Joachimsthaler, *Hitlers Liste: Ein Dokument persönlicher Beziehungen*, Munich, 2003, p. 129.

141   Ilse Hess to Hans Grimm, 1 Nov. 1943; BA Bern, J1. 211–1993/300, vol. 6. Ilse Hess added: "Our common friend, Mrs. Elsa Bruckmann, once told me that see saw him [Rudolf Hess] and his action as comparable to the mythic deeds the Valkyrie rendered to Wotan. You know our friend and her indomitably romantic and enthusiastic heart, but there is some truth in this." On 3 December 1966 Ilse Hess wrote to Albert Speer that since 1941 she had been "an object and no longer a subject." Once, during the Nuremberg Trials, she had turned and fled when she encountered Mrs. von Ribbentrop and Mrs. Göring "because I did not know how they, who pretended that I did not exist for 4 ½ years, would react"; BA Koblenz, N 1340/27.

142   See Bormann's telegram to Gauleiter Fritz Sauckel of 12 May 1941, asking him not to appear at the Berghof until shortly before 4 p.m.; BA Koblenz, N 1582/3.

143   Baldur von Schirach, *Ich glaubte an Hitler*, Hamburg, 1967, p. 278. See also the notes written from memory by Hans Frank on 21 May 1941: "The Führer had . . . only

made that sort of impression on him once before, when his niece died." Cited in Schmidt, *"Botengang eines Toren?,"* p. 192. On the timing, see Göring's appointment diary under 13 May 1941; IfZ München, ED 180/5; Frank's pocket calendar of 13 May 1941; BA Koblenz, N 1110/10.

144   On the subject of Hitler's speech, see the testimony of Gauleiter Ernst Wilhelm Bohle, head of the NSDAP Foreign Organisation, at the Nuremberg Trials in Robert W. Kempner, *Das Dritte Reich im Kreuzverhör: Aus den unveröffentlichten Vernehmungsprotokollen des Anklägers in den Nürnberger Prozessen*, Munich, 2005, p. 129. See Kershaw, *Hitler 1936–1945*, pp. 375f.; Schmidt, *"Botengang eines Toren?,"* pp. 192f., who refers to a report by Gauleiter Rudolf Jordan (*Erlebt und erlitten: Weg eines Gauleiters von München nach Moskau*, Leoni am Starnberger See, 1971, pp. 210–14).

145   Hewel's diary entry for 13 May 1941; IfZ München ED 100/78.

146   Goebbels, *Tagebücher*, part I, vol. 9, p. 312 (entry for 14 May 1941).

147   See Ciano, *Tagebücher, 1939–1943*, pp. 320f. (entry for 13– 14 May 1941).

148   For a detailed discussion, see Schmidt, *"Botengang eines Toren?,"* pp. 186–9, 280–2; Kershaw, *Hitler 1936–1945*, pp. 376–9. See also the transcription of a conversation with Alfred Leitgen on 1 April 1952: "I am convinced Hess did not fly to England with Hitler's permission." IfZ München, ZS 262.

149   Goebbels, *Tagebücher*, part I, vol. 9, pp. 314 (entry for 15 May 1941), 316 (entry for 16 May 1941).

150   On the word-of-mouth propaganda, see Nolzen, *Der Hess-Flug*, pp. 149–53.

151   Goebbels, *Tagebücher*, part I, vol. 9, p. 319 (entry for 18 May 1941). See ibid., p. 327 (entry for 22 May 1941): "The Hess affair almost forgotten"; Hill (ed.), *Die Weizsäcker-Papiere 1933–1950*, p. 255 (dated 18 May 1941): "Soon the name Hess will disappear from conversations just as it will disappear from the cinemas and propaganda books."

152   Hewel's diary entry for 12 May 1941; IfZ München, ED 100/78.

153   Goebbels, *Tagebücher*, part I, vol. 9, p. 315 (entry for 16 May 1941).

154   See Schmidt, *"Der Hess-Flug und das Kabinett Churchill,"* pp. 16ff.; idem, *"Botengang eines Toren?,"* pp. 203ff., 282ff.

155   Ian Kershaw, *Fateful Choices: Ten Decisions that Changed the World 1940–1941*, London, 2007, p. 231. On the genesis of the Lend-Lease Act, see ibid., pp. 226–31; Ronald Gerste, *Roosevelt und Hitler: Todfeindschaft und totaler Krieg*, Paderborn, 2011, pp. 166–9.

156   *Kriegstagebuch des Oberkommandos der Wehrmacht (Wehrmachtführungsstab)* (hereafter *KTB OKW*), vol. 1: 1. *August 1940–31. Dezember 1941*, ed. Percy Ernst Schramm, Munich, 1982, p. 363 (entry for 18 March 1941). See Goebbels, *Tagebücher*, part I, vol. 9, p. 186 (entry for 14 March 1941).

157   Engel, *Heeresadjutant bei Hitler*, p. 99 (entry for 24 March 1941).

158   See Kershaw, *Fateful Choices*, p. 235; Gerste, *Roosevelt und Hitler*, p. 172.

159   See Hillgruber, *Hitlers Strategie*, pp. 402f.

160   Hewel's diary entry for 22 May 1941; IfZ München, ED 100/78.

161   Minutes of talks between Hitler and Cudahy, 23 May 1941, in Hillgruber (ed.), *Staatsmänner und Diplomaten bei Hitler 1939–1941*, pp. 550–8 (at pp. 551f.). See Goebbels, *Tagebücher*, part I, vol. 9, p. 334 (entry for 25 May 1951). The interview was published in *Life* on 7 June 1941; ibid., p. 356 (entry for 7 June 1941). On 27 June 1941, Germany's chargé d'affaires in Washington, Hans Thomsen, passed along a second article by Cudahy, in which he described the hostile reception he had been given at the Berghof; IfZ München, ED 100, vol. 36.

162   Kershaw, *Fateful Choices*, pp. 236f.

163   Goebbels, *Tagebücher*, part I, vol. 9, p. 340 (entry for 29 May 1941).

164   Hewel's diary, entry for 27 May 1941; IfZ München, ED 100/78.

165   See Below, *Als Hitlers Adjutant*, p. 276.

166   Hubatsch (ed.), *Hitlers Weisungen für die Kriegführung*, pp. 134f.

167 Hewel's diary entry for 31 May 1941; IfZ München, ED 100/78. On the casualty figures, see Heinz A. Richter, *Operation Merkur: Die Eroberung der Insel Kreta im Mai 1941*, Mainz and Ruhpolding, 2011, pp. 241f.

168 Hubatsch (ed.), *Hitlers Weisungen für die Kriegführung*, pp. 139–41 (at p. 140). According to Engel, Hitler opined that only after a successful campaign in the Soviet Union could "a gate from there to the Orient be established." Engel, *Heeresadjutant bei Hitler*, p. 102 (entry for 24 April 1941).

169 Army High Command order on the "Regelung des Einsatzes der Sicherheitspolizei und des SD im Verbande des Heeres," 28 April 1941; Ueberschär and Wette (eds), *Der deutsche Überfall auf die Sowjetunion*, pp. 249f.; on the Wagner–Heydrich negotiations, see Robert Gerwarth, *Reinhard Heydrich: Eine Biographie*, Munich, 2011, pp. 229–31.

170 Ueberschär and Wette (eds), *Der deutsche Überfall auf die Sowjetunion*, pp. 251–3. On the army's lack of accountability, see Hürter, *Hitlers Heerführer*, pp. 248–50; *Das Deutsche Reich und der Zweite Weltkrieg*, vol. 4, pp. 428–32 (Förster's essay).

171 Ueberschär and Wette (eds), *Der deutsche Überfall auf die Sowjetunion*, pp. 253f. See Hürter, *Hitlers Heerführer*, pp. 250f.; *Das Deutsche Reich und der Zweite Weltkrieg*, vol. 4, pp. 432f. (Förster's essay).

172 Bock, *Das Kriegstagebuch*, p. 190 (entry for 4 June 1941).

173 See Hürter, *Hitlers Heerführer*, p. 250.

174 Ueberschär and Wette (eds), *Der deutsche Überfall auf die Sowjetunion*, pp. 259f. See Hürter, *Hitlers Heerführer*, pp. 258f.; *Das Deutsche Reich und der Zweite Weltkrieg*, vol. 4, pp. 435–40 (Förster's essay); Felix Römer, *Der Kommissarbefehl: Wehrmacht und NS-Verbrechen an der Ostfront*, Paderborn, 2008, pp. 75–81.

175 Römer, *Der Kommissarbefehl*, p. 553. On the transmission of the order, see ibid., pp. 89–159.

176 Habicht's diary entry for 20 June 1941; Felix Römer, *Die narzisstische Volksgemeinschaft: Theodor Habichts Kampf 1914 bis 1944*, Frankfurt am Main, 2017, pp. 303–5 (at p. 305).

177 Römer, *Der Kommissarbefehl*, p. 555. On the leeway people had between conformist and deviating behaviour, see ibid., pp. 159–201. See also Hürter, *Hitlers Heerführer*, pp. 259f.

178 Ueberschär and Wette (eds), *Der deutsche Überfall auf die Sowjetunion*, p. 258. See Römer, *Der Kommissarbefehl*, pp. 85f.

179 Ueberschär and Wette (eds), *Der deutsche Überfall auf die Sowjetunion*, p. 261; See Hürter, *Hitlers Heerführer*, pp. 261–3.

180 Rosenberg, *Die Tagebücher von 1934 bis 1944*, p. 372 (entry for 2 April 1941).

181 See ibid., pp. 375 (entry for 9 April 1941), 376f. (entry for 11 April 1941), 379f. (entry for 20 April 1941). See also Ernst Piper, *Alfred Rosenberg: Hitlers Chefideologe*, Munich, 2005, pp. 509–16.

182 See Rolf-Dieter Müller, "Von der Wirtschaftsallianz zum kolonialen Ausbeutungskrieg," in *Das Deutsche Reich und der Zweite Weltkrieg*, vol. 4, pp. 129–35.

183 Ueberschär and Wette (eds), *Der deutsche Überfall auf die Sowjetunion*, p. 323. In a letter to his wife of 8 April 1941, Herbert Backe reported extensively on his preparations for Operation Barbarossa, writing that he was "at times very grateful and happy for his enormous new task"; BA Koblenz, N 1075/25. On the "Hunger Plan," see Christian Gerlach, *Kalkulierte Morde: Die deutsche Wirtschafts- und Vernichtungspolitik in Weissrussland 1941 bis 1944*, Hamburg, 1999, pp. 46–59; Adam Tooze, *The Wages of Destruction: The Making and Breaking of the Nazi Economy*, London, 2006, pp. 476–80.

184 Johannes Hürter, *Ein deutscher General an der Ostfront: Die Briefe und Tagebücher des Gotthard Heinrici 1941/42*, Erfurt, 2001, p. 61 (entry for 13 June 1941).

185 *Meldungen aus dem Reich*, vol. 7, pp. 2286f. (dated 12 May 1941).

186 Walter Frick to Wilhelm Frick, 29 May 1941; BA Koblenz, N 1241/3. According to one of the rumours that circulated, Ukraine was to be leased to Germany for

ninety-nine years. See the letter from Erich Hoepner to his wife, 26 May 1941; BA-MA Koblenz, N 51/9.

187   Goebbels, *Tagebücher*, part I, vol. 9, p. 286 (entry for 2 May 1941). See Wolfram Wette, "Die propagandistische Begleitmusik zum deutschen Überfall auf die Sowjetunion am 22. Juni 1941," in Ueberschär and Wette (eds), *Der deutsche Überfall auf die Sowjetunion*, pp. 46–8.

188   See Goebbels, *Tagebücher*, part I, vol. 9, pp. 329 (entry for 23 May 1941), 332 (entry for 24 May 1941), 335 (entry for 25 May 1941).

189   See ibid., pp. 332 (entry for 24 May 1941), 336 (entry for 26 May 1941), 343 (entry for 30 May 1941), 345 (entry for 31 May 1941), 368 (entry for 13 June 1941); part II, vol. 2, p. 143 (entry for 19 Oct. 1941).

190   Ibid., p. 365 (entry for 11 June 1941). See ibid., p. 357 (entry for 7 June 1941).

191   Ibid., p. 371 (entry for 14 June 1941).

192   Hewel's diary entry for 8 June 1941; IfZ München, ED 100/78. Hitler had already said something similar in late May: "Like everything else Barbarossa is a gamble. If it fails, everything will be lost anyway." Hewel's diary entry for 29 May 1941; ibid.

193   Minutes of talks between Hitler and Mussolini, 2 June 1941, in Hillgruber (ed.), *Staatsmänner und Diplomaten bei Hitler 1939–1941*, pp. 559–74 (at p. 570). See Schmidt, *Statist auf diplomatischer Bühne*, pp. 538f.; Hans Woller, *Mussolini: Der erste Faschist. Eine Biografie*, Munich, 2016, p. 222.

194   Ciano, *Tagebücher, 1939–1943*, p. 330 (entry for 2 June 1941).

195   Telegram of 5 June 1941 from Oshima to Matsuoka; Hillgruber, "Japan und der Fall 'Barbarossa,'" in idem, *Deutsche Grossmacht- und Weltpolitik*, pp. 249–52.

196   Telegram of 5 June 1941 from Oshima to Matsuoka, on the talks with Ribbentrop on 4 June; ibid., pp. 245–8.

197   Minutes of talks between Hitler and Antonescu, 12 June 1941, in Hillgruber (ed.), *Staatsmänner und Diplomaten bei Hitler 1939–1941*, pp. 581–94 (at pp. 581, 583).

198   See Alwin Broder Albrecht (adjutant in the Reich Chancellery) to his wife, 13 June 1941: "A bit more life has returned because the boss is back in the country since this morning." IfZ München, ED 100/33.

199   See Warlimont, *Im Hauptquartier der Wehrmacht*, p. 162.

200   Below, *Als Hitlers Adjutant*, p. 277.

201   Halder, *Kriegstagebuch*, vol. 2, p. 455 (entry for 14 June 1941).

202   Bock, *Das Kriegstagebuch*, pp. 193f. (entry for 14 June 1941). See also the notes taken by one of the other participants, Luftwaffe General Otto Hoffmann von Waldau, in David Irving, *Hitler und seine Feldherren*, Frankfurt am Main, Berlin and Vienna, 1975, pp. 273f. According to Göring's appointment diary under 14 June 1941, the meeting lasted from 11 a.m. to 6 p.m. with a one-hour lunch break from 3 to 4 p.m. IfZ München, ED 180/5.

203   Below, *Als Hitlers Adjutant*, p. 277.

204   Schroeder, *Er war mein Chef*, p. 113 (letter of 28 June 1941). See Below, *Als Hitlers Adjutant*, p. 279: "[Hitler] talked a lot, paced up and down and seemed to be urgently awaiting something."

205   Hewel's diary entry for 20 June 1941; IfZ München, ED 100/78. Otto Dietrich quoted Hitler saying on the night of the attack: "It feels as if I have pushed open a door to a dark, never-before-seen room—without knowing what is behind that door." Dietrich, *12 Jahre mit Hitler*, p. 82. See also Adolf Hitler, *Monologe im Führerhauptquartier 1941–1944: Die Aufzeichnungen Heinrich Heims*, ed. Werner Jochmann, Hamburg, 1980, p. 83 (dated 17–18 Oct. 1941): "On 22 June [1941] a gate opened without us knowing what lay behind it."

206   Goebbels, *Tagebücher*, part I, vol. 9, pp. 377–80 (entry for 16 June 1941).

207   Ueberschär and Wette (eds), *Der deutsche Überfall auf die Sowjetunion*, pp. 265–9.

208   Goebbels, *Tagebücher*, part I, vol. 9, p. 387 (entry for 19 June 1941). See ibid., pp. 389 (entry for 20 June 1941), 391 (entry for 21 June 1941).

209 See *KTB OKW*, vol. 1, pp. 408 (entry for 21 June 1941), 417 (entry for 21 June 1941).

210 Hitler to Mussolini, 21 June 1941; *ADAP*, Series D, vol. 12,part 2, doc. 660, pp. 889–92 (at p. 892). On handing over the letter, see Ciano, *Tagebücher, 1939–1943*, p. 337 (entry for 22 June 1941).

211 See Fleischhauer, *Diplomatischer Widerstand gegen Unternehmen "Barbarossa,"* pp. 334–43 (at p. 337).

212 Goebbels, *Tagebücher*, part I, vol. 9, p. 372 (entry for 14 June 1941).

213 Ibid., p. 373 (entry for 14 June 1941).

214 See *Meldungen aus dem Reich*, vol. 7, p. 2408 (dated 16 June 1941); Andreas-Friedrich, *Der Schattenmann*, pp. 79f. (entry for 15 June 1941); Kellner, *Tagebücher, 1939–1945*, vol. 1, p. 151 (entry for 16 June 1941).

215 Jörg Baberowski, *Verbrannte Erde: Stalins Herrschaft der Gewalt*, Munich, 2012, pp. 397f. See Simon Sebag Montefiore, *Stalin: The Court of the Red Tsar*, London, 2003, pp. 361–6; Oleg Chlewnjuk, *Stalin: Eine Biographie*, Munich, 2015, pp. 317–19. The Soviet ambassador in London, Ivan Maisky, was also of the opinion that the concentration of German troops on the Soviet border was "a strategic move by Hitler in the 'war of nerves'" since, in Maisky's eyes, attacking the Soviet Union would "ultimately be the equivalent of suicide." Gabriel Gorodetsky (ed.), *Die Maiski-Tagebücher: Ein Diplomat im Kampf gegen Hitler*, Munich, 2016, pp. 533f. (entry for 18 June 1941).

216 Hewel's diary entry for 18 June 1941; IfZ München, ED 100/78.

217 Hill (ed.), *Die Weizsäcker-Papiere 1933–1950*, p. 260 (dated 18 June 1941).

218 Weizsäcker's notes, 21 June 1941; *ADAP*, Series D, vol. 12, part 2, no. 658, p. 885. See Hill (ed.), *Die Weizsäcker-Papiere 1933–1950*, pp. 260f. (dated 23 June 1941). On Molotov's parallel complaint to German Ambassador Schulenburg on the evening of 21 June 1941, see Fleischhauer, *Diplomatischer Widerstand gegen das Unternehmen "Barbarossa,"* pp. 344–6.

219 See Schmidt, *Statist auf diplomatischer Bühne*, pp. 539f.; on the timing, see Hill (ed.), *Die Weizsäcker-Papiere 1933–1950*, p. 261 (dated 23 June 1941).

220 Goebbels, *Tagebücher*, part I, vol. 9, p. 396 (entry for 22 June 1941). The exact wording of the proclamation can be found in Domarus, *Hitler*, vol. 2, part 2, pp. 1726–32.

221 On the press conference, see Howard K. Smith, *Feind schreibt mit: Ein amerikanischer Korrespondent erlebt Nazi-Deutschland*, Berlin, 1982, pp. 62–5. On the timing, see Hewel's diary entry for 22 June 1941; IfZ München, ED 100/78.

222 See the introduction by Bianka Pietrow-Ennker in *idem* (ed.), *Präventivkrieg? Der deutsche Angriff auf die Sowjetunion*, expanded new edition, Frankfurt am Main, 2011, pp. 9–19.

223 Goebbels, *Tagebücher*, part I, vol. 9, p. 377 (entry for 16 June 1941). Hitler remarked during the first months of the campaign: "A lot of lucky things have happened: for instance, the Russians confronting us at the border and not luring us deep into the country." Schroeder, *Er war mein Chef*, p. 120 (letter of 28 June 1941).

224 Hill (ed.), *Die Weizsäcker-Papiere 1933–1950*, p. 260 (dated 18 June 1941).

225 Goebbels, *Tagebücher*, part I, vol. 9, pp. 395f. (entry for 22 June 1941).

226 *Meldungen aus dem Reich*, vol. 7, p. 2426 (dated 23 June 1941).

227 Walter Kempowski, *Das Echolot: Barbarossa '41. Ein kollektives Tagebuch*, Munich, 2002, p. 46. On the reaction to Barbarossa, see also Evans, *The Third Reich at War*, pp. 189f.; Ulrich Herbert, *Geschichte Deutschlands im 20. Jahrhundert*, Munich, 2014, pp. 435f.; Hans Mommsen, "Der Krieg gegen die Sowjetunion und die deutsche Gesellschaft," in Pietrow-Ennker (ed.), *Präventivkrieg?*, pp. 59f.; Steinert, *Hitlers Krieg und die Deutschen*, pp. 206f.; Nicholas Stargardt, *The German War: A Nation Under Arms, 1939–45*, London, 2015, pp. 159–62.

228 Goebbels, *Tagebücher*, part I, vol. 9, p. 398 (entry for 23 June 1941). See the report of Danish legation councillor Vincens Steesen-Leth from Berlin of 24 June 1941, in which he wrote that the Nazi leadership could "hardly have counted on any sort

of enthusiasm for a new crusade"; Bajohr and Strupp (eds), *Fremde Blicke auf das "Dritte Reich,"* p. 560.

229   Gianluca Falanga, *Mussolinis Vorposten in Hitlers Reich: Italiens Politik in Berlin 1933–1945*, Berlin, 2008, p. 183.

230   Klemperer, *Tagebücher, 1933–1941*, p. 601 (entry for 22 June 1941).

231   Hewel's diary, entry for 23 June 1941; IfZ München, ED 100/78.

232   Hürter, *Ein deutscher General*, p. 62 (entry for 21 June 1941). Hans Frank noted in his pocket calendar: "Invasion of Soviet Russia. May God be with our forces!" BA Koblenz, N 1110/10.

6 The War Turns, 1941–42

1   *Die Tagebücher von Joseph Goebbels*, commissioned by the Institute for Contemporary History, with support from the State Archive of Russia, ed. Elke Fröhlich, *Part I: Aufzeichnungen 1923–1941*, 9 vols in 14 parts, Munich, 1998–2008; *Part II: Diktate 1941–1945*, 15 vols, Munich, 1993–6; part I, vol. 9, p. 377 (entry for 16 June 1941).

2   Ibid., part II, vol. 1, pp. 36f. (entry for 9 July 1941).

3   Ibid., part I, vol. 9, p. 399 (entry for 23 June 1941).

4   Letter by Günther von Kluge, dated 12 July 1941; BA-MA Freiburg, MSg 2/11185.

5   Erich Hoepner to his wife, 12 Dec. 1941; BA-MA Freiburg, N 51/9.

6   Helmuth James von Moltke, *Briefe an Freya 1939–1945*, ed. Beate Ruhm von Oppen, Munich, 1988, p. 343 (dated 11 Jan. 1942).

7   On the details, see Franz W. Seidler and Dieter Zeigert, *Die Führerhauptquartiere: Anlagen und Planungen im Zweiten Weltkrieg*, Munich, 2000, pp. 193–205; Uwe Neumärker, Robert Conrad and Cord Woywodt, *Wolfsschanze: Hitlers Machtzentrale im Zweiten Weltkrieg*, 3rd edition, Berlin, 2007, pp. 37–69.

8   Goebbels, *Tagebücher*, part II, vol. 1, p. 30 (entry for 9 July 1941).

9   Christa Schroeder to Johanna Nusser, 28 June 1941; Schroeder, *Er war mein Chef: Aus dem Nachlass der Sekretärin von Adolf Hitler*, ed. Anton Joachimsthaler, 3rd edition, Munich and Vienna, 1985, pp. 111f. See Traudl Junge, *Bis zur letzten Stunde: Hitlers Sekretärin erzählt ihr Leben*, Munich, 2002, p. 47; Rochus Misch, *Der letzte Zeuge: "Ich war Hitlers Telefonist, Kurier und Leibwächter,"* Zurich and Munich, 2008, p. 131. Ministerial Counsel Helmuth Greiner, the keeper of the daily war journal of the Wehrmacht leadership staff, wrote to his wife on 27 June 1941: "We continue to be afflicted by a terrible mosquito plague. We could hardly have chosen a more stupid location. Deciduous forest with brackish ponds, sandy ground and standing lake— an ideal habitat for these revolting creatures." IfZ München, ED 100, vol. 76. On the "gloomy atmosphere" in the Führer's headquarters, see Paul Schmidt, *Statist auf diplomatischer Bühne 1923–45*, Bonn, 1950, p. 545.

10   See Neumärker *et al.*, *Wolfsschanze*, pp. 59, 66.

11   Christa Schroeder to Johanna Nusser, 30 Aug. 1941; Schroeder, *Er war mein Chef*, p. 125.

12   See Nicolaus von Below, *Als Hitlers Adjutant 1937–45*, Mainz, 1980, p. 248; Schroeder, *Er war mein Chef*, pp. 38f.

13   Christa Schroeder to Johanna Nusser, 13 July 1941; Schroeder, *Er war mein Chef*, p. 121. On the above, see ibid., pp. 114–16; Below, *Als Hitlers Adjutant*, pp. 282f.; Bernhard von Lossberg, *Im Wehrmachtführungsstab: Bericht eines Generalstabsoffiziers*, Hamburg, 1950, pp. 121f.; Seidler and Zeigert, *Die Führerhauptquartiere*, pp. 203f.; Neumärker *et al.*, *Wolfsschanze*, pp. 74–6; *Herbst 1941 im "Führerhauptquartier": Berichte Werner Koeppens an seinen Minister Rosenberg*, ed. Martin Vogt, Koblenz, 2002, introduction, p. vii; Werner Jochmann's introduction to Adolf Hitler, *Monologe im Führerhauptquartier 1941–1944: Die Aufzeichnungen Heinrich Heims*, ed. Werner Jochmann, Hamburg, 1980, p. 13. Hewel noted in his diary after one

nocturnal session: "Until 4 a.m. Down." Entry for 19 June 1941; IfZ München, ED 100/76.

14 See Schroeder, *Er war mein Chef*, p. 112. Otto Dietrich told Goebbels by telephone on 25 June 1941: "The Führer has high hopes." Goebbels, *Tagebücher*, part I, vol. 9, p. 405 (entry for 26 June 1941).

15 On the German army's early successes, see *Das Deutsche Reich und der Zweite Weltkrieg*, ed. Militärgeschichtliches Forschungsamt (Armed Forces Historical Research Office), 10 vols, Stuttgart and Munich, 1979–2008, vol. 4, pp. 451–86 (Klink's essay); Christian Hartmann, *Wehrmacht im Ostkrieg: Front und militärisches Hinterland 1941/42*, Munich, 2009, pp. 250–5; Gerhard L. Weinberg, *Eine Welt in Waffen: Die globale Geschichte des Zweiten Weltkriegs*, Stuttgart, 1995, pp. 294f.

16 Ernst von Weizsäcker to his mother, 29 June 1941; BA Koblenz, N 1273/30.

17 Georg Meyer, *Adolf Heusinger: Dienst eines deutschen Soldaten*, Hamburg, Berlin and Bonn, 2001, p. 151.

18 Heinz Boberach (ed.), *Meldungen aus dem Reich: Die geheimen Lageberichte des Sicherheitsdienstes der SS 1938–1945*, Herrsching, 1984, vol. 7, p. 2440. See also Goebbels, *Tagebücher*, part I, vol. 9, p. 411 (entry for 29 June 1941): "The initial shock has been entirely overcome."

19 Goebbels, *Tagebücher*, part I, vol. 9, p. 412 (entry for 30 June 1941).

20 Otto Dietrich, *12 Jahre mit Hitler*, Munich, 1955, p. 104.

21 Ruth Andreas-Friedrich, *Der Schattenmann: Tagebuchaufzeichnungen 1938–1945*, Frankfurt am Main, 1983, pp. 81f. (entry for 29 June 1941). See Friedrich Kellner, *"Vernebelt, verdunkelt sind alle Hirne": Tagebücher, 1939–1945*, ed. Sascha Feuchert et al., Göttingen, 2011, vol. 1, p. 163 (entry for 30 June 1941): "Like a carnival ride."

22 *Meldungen aus dem Reich*, vol. 7, p. 2458 (dated 30 June 1941).

23 Kellner, *Tagebücher, 1939–1945*, vol. 1, pp. 165 (entry for 1 July 1941), 167 (entry for 4 July 1941). See Lore Walb, *Ich, die Alte—ich, die Junge: Konfrontation mit meinen Tagebüchern 1933–1945*, Berlin, 1997, p. 225 (entry for 30 June 1941): "The battle is gigantic, but it is already clear, after seven days, that our victory is assured and will soon be confirmed . . . You just have to believe that our soldiers are the best in the world."

24 Franz Halder, *Kriegstagebuch, vol. 3: Der Russlandfeldzug bis zum Marsch auf Stalingrad*, ed. Hans-Adolf Jacobsen, Stuttgart, 1964, p. 38 (entry for 3 July 1941). See also Halder's private letter to Luise von Benda, later to become Jodl's wife, of 3 July 1941: "The Russians lost the war in the first eight days. Their losses in terms of casualties and materiel are unimaginable. Russia's vastness will allow them to battle on for some time, but they will not be able to change their destiny." IfZ München, ZS 240, vol. 7.

25 Schroeder, *Er war mein Chef*, pp. 120 (entry for 28 June 1941), p. 114. See also David Irving's interview with Christa Schroeder, 2 Dec. 1970; IfZ München, ZS 2240.

26 *Kriegstagebuch des Oberkommandos der Wehrmacht (Wehrmachtführungsstab)* (hereafter *KTB OKW*), *vol. I: 1. August 1940–31. Dezember 1941*, ed. Percy Ernst Schramm, Munich, 1982, vol. 1, p. 1020 (entry for 4 July 1941). See Helmuth Greiner's letter to his wife, 4 July 1941: "We already advanced two-thirds of the way to Leningrad and one half of the way to Moscow. I think we will arrive there in fourteen days. The Russians seem to be softening up. There are reports of their forces disintegrating in many places." IfZ München, ED 100, vol. 76.

27 Goebbels, *Tagebücher*, part II, vol. 1, pp. 30–7 (entry for 9 July 1941).

28 Hewel's diary entry for 11 July 1941; IfZ München, ED 100/78.

29 Minutes of talks between Hitler and Oshima, 15 July 1941, in Andreas Hillgruber (ed.), *Staatsmänner und Diplomaten bei Hitler: Vertrauliche Aufzeichnungen über Unterredungen mit Vertretern des Auslandes 1939–1941*, Frankfurt am Main, 1967, pp. 598–608 (at pp. 600, 605). See also the minutes of Hitler's conversation with Croatia's Marshal Sladko Kvaternik on 21 July 1941: "The Soviet armies have been basically

destroyed, and [Hitler] does not believe that there will be any serious resistance in six weeks' time." Ibid. pp. 609-15. In mid-July, during a visit to Berlin, Otto Dietrich told Goebbels that Hitler was of "the view that the eastern campaign is as good as won." Goebbels, *Tagebücher*, part II, vol. 1, p. 72 (entry for 15 July 1941).

30   Ernst von Weizsäcker to his mother, 13 July 1941; BA Koblenz, N 1273/30.

31   Walther Hubatsch (ed.), *Hitlers Weisungen für die Kriegsführung*, Munich, 1965, pp. 159f.

32   *KTB OKW*, vol. 1, pp. 1022–5.

33   Werner Jochmannn's introduction to *Monologe*, pp. 7f.; see Wolfram Pyta, *Hitler: Der Künstler als Politiker und Feldherr*, Munich, 2015, pp. 32–6. Heim's minutes run from 5 July 1941 to 7 September 1942. During Heim's absence from 21 March 1942 to 31 July 1942, his deputy, senior civil servant Dr. Henry Picker, took over the minutes of the conversations. See Jochmann, introduction to *Monologe*, pp. 8f.; *Hitlers Tischgespräche im Führerhauptquartier*, ed. Henry Picker, Stuttgart, 1976, pp. 128ff.

34   See protocol of the conversation with Heinrich Heim on 1 July 1952 and 17 July 1952; IfZ München, ZS 243, vol. 1; Jochmann, introduction to *Monologe*, p. 16.

35   See Martin Vogt's introduction to Koeppen, pp. vii–xi.

36   *Monologe*, pp. 39 (dated 5–6 July 1941), 68 (dated 25 Sept. 1941). See Koeppen, p. 44 (entry for 24 Sept. 1941): "Our task is to push back the border as far east as possible, if necessary, across the Urals."

37   *Monologe*, p. 48 (dated 27 Sept. 1941). See Hewel's diary entry for 27 July 1941: "Soldier-farmers sworn to defend themselves and equipped with weapons including machine guns." IfZ München, ED 100/78.

38   *Monologe*, pp. 54f. (dated 8–9, 9–10, 10–11 Aug. 1941).

39   Ibid., pp. 58 (dated 19–20 Aug. 1941), 62f. (dated 17–18 Sept. 1941).

40   Ibid., pp. 62f. (dated 17–18 Sept. 1941). See ibid., p. 48 (dated 27 July 1941): "Just look at the English, who rule over 400 million Indians . . . with 250,000 men."

41   Ibid., p. 66 (dated 23 Sept. 1941). See Koeppen, p. 44 (entry for 24 Sept. 1941): "It is the eternal law of nature of [survival of] the fittest that gives Germany the historical right to subjugate, rule over and force these racially inferior people to do productive labour."

42   Bormann's notes of the meeting of 16 July 1941 in *Der Prozess gegen die Hauptkriegs-verbrecher vor dem internationalen Militärtribunal in Nürnberg*, 42 vols, Nuremberg, 1947–9 (hereafter *IMT*), vol. 38, pp. 86–94; partially reproduced in Gerd R. Ueberschär and Wolfram Wette (ed.), *Der deutsche Überfall auf die Sowjetunion: "Unternehmen Barbarossa" 1941*, expanded edition, Frankfurt am Main, 2011, pp. 276f. See Jürgen Matthäus and Frank Bajohr (eds), Alfred Rosenberg, *Die Tagebücher von 1934 bis 1944*, Frankfurt am Main, 2015, pp. 393–9 (entry for 20 July 1941).

43   *KTB OKW*, vol. 1, pp. 1027f. See Sebastian Lehmann, Robert Bohn and Uwe Danker (eds), *Reichskommissariat Ostland: Tatort und Erinnerungsobjekt*, Paderborn, 2012.

44   *KTB OKW*, vol. 1, pp. 1019, 1028f.

45   See Ernst Piper, *Alfred Rosenberg: Hitlers Chefideologe*, Munich, 2005, pp. 527–31; Ian Kershaw, *Hitler 1936–1945: Nemesis*, London, 2001, pp. 405f.; Mark Mazower, *Hitler's Empire: Nazi Rule in Occupied Europe*, London 2008, pp. 144–51.

46   Richard J. Evans, *The Third Reich at War, 1939–1945*, London, 2008, pp. 173f. (at p. 174). See Peter Longerich, *Heinrich Himmler: Biographie*, Munich, 2008, pp. 597f.; Michael Wildt, *Generation des Unbedingten: Das Führungskorps des Reichssicherheitshauptamtes*, Hamburg, 2002, pp. 663–9; Mazower, *Hitler's Empire*, pp. 204–211; Karl Heinz Roth, "'Generalplan Ost'—'Gesamtplan Ost': Forschungsstand, Quellenprobleme, neue Ergebnisse," in Mechthild Rössler and Sabine Schleiermacher (eds), *Der "Generalplan Ost*," Berlin, 1993, pp. 25–95 (at pp. 59f.).

47   Koeppen, pp. 24f. (entry for 19 Sept. 1941).

48   Reproduced in Ueberschär and Wette (eds), *Der deutsche Überfall auf die Sowjetunion*, pp. 271f. See Jörg Baberowski, *Verbrannte Erde: Stalins Herrschaft der Gewalt*, Munich,

2012, pp. 399f., 417; Simon Sebag Montefiore, *Stalin: The Court of the Red Tsar,* London, 2008, p. 374; Oleg Chlewnjuk, *Stalin: Eine Biographie,* Munich, 2015, pp. 324–9.

49 Stalin's speech of 3 July 1941, reproduced in Ueberschär and Wette (eds), *Der deutsche Überfall auf die Sowjetunion,* pp. 272–5. See Chlewnjuk, *Stalin,* pp. 330f. On its effects, see Catherine Merridale, *Ivan's War: The Red Army 1939–45,* London, 2005, pp. 84–7; Dietmar Neutatz, *Träume und Alpträume: Eine Geschichte Russlands im 20. Jahrhundert,* Munich, 2013, p. 289.

50 See Felix Römer, *Der Kommissarbefehl: Wehrmacht und NS-Verbrechen an der Ostfront,* Paderborn, 2008, pp. 358f., 398–400, 561. See also *idem,* "Die Wehrmacht und der Kommissarbefehl: Neue Forschungsergebnisse," in *Militärgeschichtliche Zeitschrift,* 69 (2010), pp. 243–74 (particularly pp. 249–52); *idem, Kameraden: Die Wehrmacht von innen,* Munich and Zurich, 2012, pp. 415–17; *idem,* "Der Kommissarbefehl in den Frontdivisionen des Ostheeres 1941/42," in Babette Quinkert and Jörg Morré (eds), *Deutsche Besatzung in der Sowjetunion 1941–1944: Vernichtungskrieg—Reaktionen— Erinnerung,* Paderborn, 2014, pp. 95–112.

51 Cited in Johannes Hürter, *Hitlers Heerführer: Die deutschen Oberbefehlshaber im Krieg gegen die Sowjetunion 1941/42,* Munich, 2007, p. 397. On the implementation of the commissar order on a divisional level, see Hartmann, *Wehrmacht im Ostkrieg,* pp. 492–501; on a regimental level, see Felix Römer, *Die narzisstische Volksgemeinschaft: Theodor Habichts Kampf 1914 bis 1944,* Frankfurt am Main, 2017, pp. 247f. On the execution of Soviet commissars in German concentration camps, see Nikolaus Wachsmann, *KL: Die Geschichte der nationalsozialistischen Konzentrationslager,* Munich, 2016, pp. 304ff.

52 Johannes Hürter, *Ein deutscher General an der Ostfront: Die Briefe und Tagebücher des Gotthard Heinrici 1941/42,* Erfurt, 2001, p. 65 (entry for 6 July 1941). On the shooting of Soviet prisoners of war, see Christian Streit, *Keine Kameraden: Die Wehrmacht und die sowjetischen Kriegsgefangenen 1941–1945,* new edition, Bonn, 1991, pp. 106–8; Christian Gerlach, *Kalkulierte Morde: Die deutsche Wirtschafts- und Vernichtungspolitik in Weissrussland 1941 bis 1944,* Hamburg, 1999, pp. 774–81; Hartmann, *Wehrmacht im Ostkrieg,* pp. 516–26; Sönke Neitzel and Harald Welzer, *Soldaten: Protokolle vom Sterben, Töten und Kämpfen,* Frankfurt am Main, 2011, pp. 134–8; Römer, *Kameraden,* pp. 417–22 (based on the surveillance transcripts of German POWs in Fort Hunt).

53 Fedor von Bock, *Zwischen Pflicht und Verweigerung: Das Kriegstagebuch,* ed. Klaus Gerbet, Munich, 1995, p. 204 (entry for 30 June 1941). See Habicht's diary entry for 12 July 1941; Römer, *Die narzisstische Volksgemeinschaft,* pp. 305–8; Goebbels, *Tagebücher,* part II, vol. 1, p. 77 (entry for 16 July 1941): "Letters from the front show that . . . such rage predominates among our soldiers that mercy is almost unknown."

54 Sönke Neitzel, *Abgehört: Deutsche Generäle in britischer Kriegsgefangenschaft 1942–1945,* Berlin, 2005, p. 254. See Streit, *Keine Kameraden,* pp. 162–4; Hartmann, *Wehrmacht im Ostkrieg,* pp. 553–7; Timothy Snyder, *Bloodlands: Europe between Hitler and Stalin,* London, 2010, p. 176.

55 Cited in Streit, *Keine Kameraden,* p. 131.

56 Ulrich Herbert, *Geschichte Deutschlands im 20. Jahrhundert,* Munich, 2014, p. 445. On the mass deaths of Soviet prisoners of war, see Hartmann, *Wehrmacht im Ostkrieg,* pp. 586–608; Dieter Pohl, *Die Herrschaft der Wehrmacht: Deutsche Militärbesatzung und einheimische Bevölkerung in der Sowjetunion 1941–1944,* Munich, 2008, pp. 217–30; Gerlach, *Kalkulierte Morde,* pp. 788–830; Snyder, *Bloodlands,* pp. 175–82; Mazower, *Hitler's Empire,* pp. 160–3; Römer, *Kameraden,* pp. 436–41.

57 See Ortwin Buchbender and Reinhold Storz, *Das andere Gesicht: Deutsche Feldpostbriefe 1939–1945,* Munich, 1983, pp. 78 (dated 20 Aug. 1941), 81 (dated 21 Sept. 1941), 84 (dated 15 Oct. 1941), 85 (dated 29 Oct. 1941); Neitzel and Welzer, *Soldaten,* pp. 140–3; Michaela Kipp, *"Grossreinemachen im Osten": Feindbilder in deutschen Feldpostbriefen im Zweiten*

Weltkrieg, Frankfurt am Main, 2014, pp. 92ff. Goebbels noted on 4 October 1941: "Here and there prisoners killed and ate their own comrades to avoid starving. Different standards need to be applied to Russians than to other European peoples. They are half-savages, comparable only with animals." Goebbels, *Tagebücher*, part II, vol. 2, p. 48.

58   See Pohl, *Die Herrschaft der Wehrmacht*, pp. 183–8; Evans, *The Third Reich at War*, pp. 192–5; Heinrici to his wife, 19 Nov. 1941: "Soon the stretch of land we are in will be eaten bare." Johannes Hürter, *Ein deutscher General an der Ostfront*, p. 112 (entry for 19 Nov. 1941).

59   See Pohl, *Die Herrschaft der Wehrmacht*, pp. 158–70; Hürter, *Hitlers Heerführer*, pp. 404–18.

60   Bormann's file notes on the meeting of 16 July 1941; *IMT*, vol. 38, p. 88; Hubatsch (ed.), *Hitlers Weisungen für die Kriegführung*, p. 167.

61   Walter Frick to Wilhelm Frick, 17 July 1941, as well as the death notification from the staff doctor dated 30 July 1941; BA Koblenz, N 1241/3. See Bock, *Das Kriegstagebuch*, p. 202 (entry for 26 June 1941): "Despite the heaviest fire and the employment of all means, defenders will not surrender. Every man has to be killed individually."

62   Erich Hoepner to his wife, 16 July 1941; BA-MA Freiburg, N 51/9. See also Hans-Georg Reinhardt to his wife, 16 July 1941: "The Russians are making it somewhat more difficult for us than [our enemies] in previous campaigns." BA-MA Freiburg, N 245/2. Reinhardt has often been referred to as Georg-Hans Reinhardt: this book follows Hürter as to his first name.

63   Goebbels, *Tagebücher*, part II, vol. 1, pp. 115f., 118 (entry for 24 July 1941), 161 (entry for 1 Aug. 1941). See ibid., p. 209 (entry for 10 Aug. 1941): "There still need to be very tough and bloody confrontations before the Soviet Union lies broken in pieces on the ground."

64   *Meldungen aus dem Reich*, vol. 7, p. 2608 (dated beginning of Aug. 1941). See Kellner, *Tagebücher, 1939–1945*, vol. 1, pp. 174 (entry for 27 July 1941), 178 (entry for 2 Aug. 1941); Victor Klemperer, *Ich will Zeugnis ablegen bis zum letzten: Tagebücher*, vol. 1: *1933–1941*, ed. Walter Nowojski with Hadwig Klemperer, Berlin, 1995, p. 655 (entry for 27 July 1941): "Advances in Russia seem to be faltering. Everyone knows or gossips about heavy German losses."

65   Bock, *Das Kriegstagebuch*, p. 229 (entry for 24 July 1941); Hürter, *Ein deutscher General an der Ostfront*, pp. 69 (entry for 20 July 1941), 71f. (entries for 30 July and 1 Aug. 1941). See also Rundstedt's letters to his wife, 10 and 12 Aug. 1941: "I shudder to think of winter in this country. Who knows where we will be . . . Russia's vastness is devouring us." BA-MA Freiburg, MSg 2/12538.

66   Halder, *Kriegstagebuch*, vol. 3, p. 170 (entry for 11 Aug. 1941). On 10 August 1941, Weizsäcker wrote in a letter to his mother that military leaders would now "admit without hesitation that they had underestimated the Russians'; BA Koblenz, N 1273/30.

67   Hellmuth Stieff, *Briefe*, ed. Horst Mühleisen, Berlin, 1991, p. 119 (dated 12 Aug. 1941). See Rosenberg, *Die Tagebücher von 1934 bis 1944*, p. 405 (entry for 1 Sept. 1941): "The Russians' tenacious resistance is something we all talk about."

68   See Helmuth Greiner to his wife, 21 July 1941; IfZ München, ED 100, vol. 76.

69   Morell's daily notes from 7 to 13 Aug. 1941; BA Koblenz, N 1348/4. See Hans-Joachim Neumann and Henrik Eberle, *War Hitler krank? Ein abschliessender Befund*, Bergisch Gladbach, 2009, pp. 226–34; Norman Ohler, *Der totale Rausch: Drogen im Dritten Reich*, Cologne, 2015, pp. 155–7; Ernst Günther Schenck, *Patient Hitler: Eine medizinische Biographie*, Düsseldorf, 1989, pp. 133–5, 346–8.

70   Below, *Als Hitlers Adjutant*, p. 286. Morell allegedly hinted to Below that Hitler had suffered a "mild stroke," but there is no indication of such in Morell's records. See Neumann and Eberle, *War Hitler krank?*, p. 228. On 31 Aug. 1941, Himmler wrote

to his wife: "With the Führer this morning and afternoon and took a walk with him. He is doing quite well again." Katrin Himmler and Michael Wildt (eds), *Himmler privat: Briefe eines Massenmörders*, Munich, 2014, p. 260.

71 Goebbels, *Tagebücher*, part II, vol. 1, pp. 257–62 (entry for 19 Aug. 1941).

72 *KTB OKW*, vol. 1, pp. 1041–3. On the conflicts between Hitler and the Army High Command about how to continue operations, see Christian Hartmann, *Halder: Generalstabschef Hitlers 1938–1942*, 2nd edition, Paderborn, 2010, pp. 276–82; *Das Deutsche Reich und der Zweite Weltkrieg*, vol. 4, pp. 486–503 (Klink's essay); Ian Kershaw, *Hitler 1936–1945: Nemesis*, pp. 407–411.

73 *Heeresadjutant bei Hitler 1938–1943: Aufzeichnungen des Majors Engel*, ed. Hildegard von Kotze, Stuttgart, 1974, p. 108 (entry for 8 Aug. 1941). Hitler had said much the same to Antonescu on 6 Aug. 1941; see Hillgruber (ed.), *Staatsmänner und Diplomaten bei Hitler*, vol. 1, pp. 618f.

74 *KTB OKW*, vol. 1, pp. 1055–9 (at p. 1056).

75 Ibid., pp. 1062f.

76 Ibid., pp. 1063–8.

77 Engel, *Heeresadjutant bei Hitler*, p. 110 (entry for 21 Aug. 1941); Stieff, *Briefe*, p. 122 (dated 23 Aug. 1941).

78 Halder, *Kriegstagebuch*, vol. 3, p. 193 (entry for 22 Aug. 1941). See Hartmann, *Halder*, p. 283.

79 On Hitler's conversation with Guderian on 23 Aug. 1941, see Heinz Guderian, *Erinnerungen eines Soldaten*, Heidelberg, 1951, pp. 179–83; Halder, *Kriegstagbuch*, vol. 3, pp. 194f. (entry for 24 Aug. 1941); Bock, *Das Kriegstagebuch*, p. 257 (entry for 24 Aug. 1941). Jodl told Halder that Hitler's "intuition" had decided otherwise, and "the Führer happens to have a sixth sense"; letter from Halder to Heinrich Uhlig, 26 June 1953; BA-MA Freiburg, N 220/88.

80 Cited in Gianluca Falanga, *Mussolinis Vorposten in Hitlers Reich: Italiens Politik in Berlin 1933–1945*, Berlin, 2008, p. 184. On Mussolini's arrival, see Hewel's diary entry for 25 Aug. 1941; IfZ München, ED 100/78.

81 See Schmidt, *Statist auf diplomatischer Bühne*, p. 547; Falanga, *Mussolinis Vorposten in Hitlers Reich*, p. 185.

82 Max Domarus, *Hitler: Reden und Proklamationen 1932–1945*, vol. 2, part 2, Munich, 1965, p. 1749f. See Reuth, *Hitler*, p. 536f.; Rolf-Dieter Müller, *An der Seite der Wehrmacht. Hitlers ausländische Helfer beim "Kreuzzug gegen den Bolschewismus" 1941–1945*, Frankfurt am Main, 2010, p. 23 ff.

83 Domarus, *Hitler*, vol. 2, part 2, p. 1751.

84 Hewel's diary entry for 8 Sept. 1941: IfZ München, ED 100/78. On the above, see Below, *Als Hitlers Adjutant*, p. 289.

85 *Meldungen aus dem Reich*, vol. 8, pp. 2724 (dated 4 Sept. 1941), 2746 (dated 11 Sept. 1941).

86 Klemperer, *Tagebücher, 1935–1941*, p. 661 (entry for 2 Sept. 1941).

87 Goebbels, *Tagebücher*, part II, vol. 1, pp. 375 (entry for 8 Sept. 1941), 392 (entry for 10 Sept. 1941).

88 Schroeder, *Er war mein Chef*, p. 124 (entry for 30 Aug. 1941).

89 See *Das Deutsche Reich und der Zweite Weltkrieg*, vol. 4, pp. 508–59 (Klink's essay); Hartmann, *Wehrmacht im Ostkrieg*, pp. 288–303.

90 See Koeppen, pp. 29 (entry for 20 Sept. 1941), 37 (entry for 22 Sept. 1941), 42 (entry for 23 Sept. 1941).

91 Goebbels, *Tagebücher*, part II, vol. 1, p. 508 (entry for 28 Sept. 1941). See ibid., pp. 460 (entry for 20 Sept. 1941), 463 (entry for 21 Sept. 1941); *Meldungen aus dem Reich*, vol. 8, p. 2787 (dated 22 Sept. 1941).

92 Letter from Hans-Georg Reinhardt to his wife, 22 Sept. 1941; BA-MA Freiburg, N 245/2; see also the letter from Erich Hoepner to his wife, 12 Sept. 1941; BA-MA Freiburg, N 51/9.

93   Koeppen, p. 16 (entry for 10 Sept. 1941). Hitler had said something similar as early as the beginning of July 1941. See Halder, *Kriegstagebuch*, vol. 3, p. 53 (entry for 8 July 1941); *KTB OKW*, vol. 2, p. 1021 (entry for 8 July 1941).

94   Goebbels, *Tagebücher*, part II, vol. 1, p. 377 (entry for 8 Sept. 1941). See ibid., p. 451 (entry for 19 Sept. 1941).

95   See Johannes Hürter, "Die Wehrmacht vor Leningrad," in *Vierteljahrshefte für Zeitgeschichte*, 49 (2001), pp. 377–440 (at pp. 399ff.); Jörg Ganzenmüller, *Das belagerte Leningrad 1941–1944*, 2nd revised edition, Paderborn, 2007, pp. 32ff., 64ff.; idem, "Hungerpolitik als Problemlösungsstrategie: Der Entscheidungsprozess zur Blockade Leningrads und zur Vernichtung seiner Zivilbevölkerung," in Quinkert and Morré (eds), *Deutsche Besatzung in der Sowjetunion 1941–1944*, pp. 34–53.

96   Goebbels, *Tagebücher*, part II, vol. 1, pp. 481–7.

97   Hubatsch (ed.), *Hitlers Weisungen für die Kriegführung*, pp. 174–7; see Halder, *Kriegstagebuch*, vol. 3, p. 215 (entry for 5 Sept. 1941).

98   Cited in Hartmann, *Halder*, p. 289.

99   Domarus, *Hitler*, vol. 2, part 2, pp. 1756–8 (at p. 1757).

100 Goebbels, *Tagebücher*, part II, vol. 1, p. 520 (entry for 30 Sept. 1941), vol. 2, p. 39 (entry for 2 Oct. 1941).

101 See Koeppen, p. 51 (entry for 3 Oct. 1941).

102 See Goebbels, *Tagebücher*, part II, vol. 1, pp. 265 (entry for 19 Aug. 1941), 292 (entry for 22 Aug. 1941), 398 (entry for 11 Sept. 1941), 429 (entry for 16 Sept. 1941), 484 (entry for 24 Sept. 1941).

103 Ibid., vol. 2, p. 50 (entry for 4 Oct. 1941).

104 Domarus, *Hitler*, vol. 2, part 2, pp. 1756–67 (at pp. 1760, 1762f.). See Goebbels, *Tagebücher*, part II, vol. 2, pp. 55f. (entry for 4 Oct. 1941).

105 Koeppen, p. 54 (entry for 5 Oct. 1941).

106 Goebbels, *Tagebücher*, part II, vol. 2, p. 61 (entry for 5 Oct. 1941). See ibid., p. 82 (entry for 9 Oct. 1941); *Meldungen aus dem Reich*, vol. 8, p. 2835 (dated 6 Oct. 1941). General Walther von Seydlitz wrote to his wife on 13 Oct. 1941: "The Führer spoke extremely well again, and for many these were words of relief after such a long silence." Torsten Diedrich and Jens Ebert (eds), *Nach Stalingrad: Walther von Seydlitz. Feldpostbriefe und Kriegsgefangenenpost 1939–1955*, Göttingen, 2018, p. 187.

107 Hewel's diary entry for 7 Oct. 1941; IfZ München, ED 100/78. See Koeppen, p. 69 (entry for 8 Oct. 1941). According to this source, Jodl remarked at dinner that the war was "finally and without exaggeration" won. On the course of Operation Typhoon, see *Das Deutsche Reich und der Zweite Weltkrieg*, vol. 4, pp. 575–85 (Klink's essay).

108 Hürter, *Ein deutscher General an der Ostfront*, p. 93 (entry for 8 Oct. 1941). Hoepner also wrote to his wife on 11 Oct. 1941: "Serious deficits in the Russians' fighting morale are already recognisable." BA-MA Freiburg, N 51/9. In a letter of 11 Oct. 1941 to Paulus, Walter von Reichenau, the commander of the 6th Army, wrote that he had got the impression the Russians were "no longer quite as determined and proud" as they had been in June and July. BA-MA Freiburg, N 372/22.

109 Guderian to his wife, 11 Oct. 1941; IfZ München, ED 100/77.

110 Hewel's diary entry for 10 Oct. 1941; IfZ München, ED 100/78. See ibid., 13 Oct. 1941: "Führer at ease and in the best of moods."

111 Operational briefing on 13 Oct. 1941; cited in Hartmann, *Halder*, p. 290.

112 *KTB OKW*, vol. 1, pp. 1070f.

113 *Monologe*, p. 90f. (dated 17–18 Oct. 1971). See Koeppen, p. 80 (entry for 18 Oct. 1941): "He said that, as the Führer, he would create a new administration with cold, hard rationality. It did not matter at all to him what the Slavs thought about it."

114 *Monologe*, p. 110 (dated 26–27 Oct. 1941).

115 Cited in Stefan Krings, *Hitlers Pressechef: Otto Dietrich 1897–1952. Eine Biographie*, Göttingen, 2010, p. 414. On Hitler's instructions, see Dietrich, *12 Jahre mit Hitler*, pp.

101f.; Helmut Sündermann, *Hier stehe ich . . . Deutsche Erinnerungen 1914/45*, Leoni, 1975, p. 192.

116 Howard K. Smith, *Feind schreibt mit: Ein amerikanischer Korrespondent erlebt Nazi-Deutschland*, London, 2000, p. 77.

117 Kellner, *Tagebücher, 1939–1945*, vol. 1, p. 187 (entry for 11 Oct. 1941).

118 Goebbels, *Tagebücher*, part II, vol. 2, pp. 87 (entry for 10 Oct. 1941), 94 (entry for 11 Oct. 1941).

119 Kellner, *Tagebücher, 1939–1945*, vol. 1, p. 188 (entry for 19 Oct. 1941).

120 *Meldungen aus dem Reich*, vol. 8, pp. 2916 (dated 27 Oct. 1941), 2927f. (dated 30 Oct. 1941). See Goebbels, *Tagebücher*, part II, vol. 2, p. 230 (entry for 4 Nov. 1941). Weizsäcker remarked that "a certain wave of doubt" was rolling through the country; Leonidas Hill (ed.), *Die Weizsäcker-Papiere 1933–1950*, Frankfurt am Main, Berlin and Vienna, 1974, p. 275 (dated 2 Nov. 1941).

121 Goebbels, *Tagebücher*, part II, vol. 3, p. 93 (entry for 11 Jan. 1942). See ibid., vol. 2, pp. 444 (entry for 2 Dec. 1941), 483 (entry for 12 Dec. 1941), 555 (entry for 21 Dec. 1941), vol. 3, p. 45 (entry for 3 Jan. 1942).

122 Hürter, *Ein deutscher General an der Ostfront*, pp. 101 (entry for 27 Oct. 1941), 102 (entry for 30 Oct. 1941). See Eduard Wagner, *Der Generalquartiermeister: Briefe und Tagebuchaufzeichnungen*, ed. Elisabeth Wagner, Munich and Vienna, 1963, pp. 207 (entry for 20 Oct. 1941), 211 (entry for 29 Oct. 1941), 212 (entry for 2 Nov. 1941); Bock, *Das Kriegstagebuch*, pp. 297 (entry for 19 Oct. 1941), 309 (entry for 3 Nov. 1941); Guderian to his wife, 15 Oct. and 31 Oct. 1941; IfZ München, ED 100/77; Hoepner to his wife, 19 Oct. and 30 Oct. 1941; BA-MA Freiburg, N 51/9; Reinhardt to his wife, 23 Oct. 1941; BA-MA Freiburg, N 245/2.

123 Minutes of talks between Hitler and Ciano, 25 Oct. 1941, in Hillgruber (ed.), *Staatsmänner und Diplomaten bei Hitler 1939–1941*, pp. 626–38 (at pp. 626, 628). See Galeazzo Ciano, *Tagebücher, 1939–1943*, Bern, 1946, p. 361 (entry for 25 Oct. 1941). In the Foreign Ministry too people reckoned that "in about a fortnight we will declare, at least unilaterally and without allowing any weakness, that the Russian campaign is virtual complete." Ernst von Weizsäcker to his mother, 26 Nov. 1941; BA Koblenz, N 1273/30.

124 See Sebag Montefiore, *Stalin*, pp. 401–16; Baberowski, *Verbrannte Erde*, pp. 409f.; Neutatz, *Träume und Alpträume*, p. 290; Chlewnjuk, *Stalin*, pp. 340–8.

125 See Hewel's diary entry for 7 Nov. 1941: IfZ München, ED 100/78; Koeppen, p. 115 (entry for 6 Nov. 1941).

126 Domarus, *Hitler*, vol. 2, part 2, pp. 1771–81 (at p. 1776).

127 Goebbels, *Tagebücher*, part II, vol. 2, pp. 262f. (entry for 10 Nov. 1941).

128 Stieff, *Briefe*, p. 133 (dated 11 Nov. 1941). On the above, see Hartmann, *Halder*, pp. 293f.; Hürter, *Hitlers Heerführer*, pp. 303–7.

129 Bock, *Das Kriegstagebuch*, pp. 327 (entry for 23 Nov. 1941), 331f. (entry for 29 Nov. 1941). See also Balck's diary for 25 Nov. 1941 about a visit to Guderian's tank army: "The picture here is the same as everywhere. The troops are at the end of their strength. They cannot go on." BA-MA Freiburg, N 647/8.

130 See Adam Tooze, *The Wages of Destruction: The Making and Breaking of the Nazi Economy*, London, 2006, p. 506.

131 Goebbels, *Tagebücher*, part II, vol. 2, pp. 336–47 (at pp. 337, 340).

132 Engel, *Heeresadjutant bei Hitler*, p. 116 (entry for 25 Nov. 1941).

133 See for instance Hitler's talks with Finnish Foreign Minister Rolf Witting and Hungarian Minister President László Bárdossy on 27 Nov. 1941, and with Ciano on 29 Nov. 1941, in Hillgruber (ed.), *Staatsmänner und Diplomaten bei Hitler 1939–1941*, pp. 643, 647f., 675 (quotation), 677. Hitler's adjutants Schmundt and Engel were "somewhat taken aback at the emphatic, overly optimistic description of the war situation" by Hitler. Engel, *Heeresadjutant bei Hitler*, p. 117 (entry for 30 Nov. 1941).

134 Goebbels, *Tagebücher*, part II, vol. 2, pp. 398–404 (at p. 403).

135   See Hartmann, *Halder*, p. 297; Hürter, *Hitlers Heerführer*, p. 309.

136   Lammers to Schmundt, 11 Dec. 1941 and Lammers to Rundstedt, 28 Feb. 1942; BA Berlin-Lichterfelde, R 43 II/985a.

137   Kellner, *Tagebücher*, 1939–1945, vol. 1, p. 203 (entry for 1–2 Dec. 1941). See *Meldungen aus dem Reich*, vol. 8, p. 3059 (dated 4 Dec. 1941): according to this source, the withdrawal from Rostov caused "great astonishment" since, "after the serious blows dealt to the enemy in the south, most ethnic comrades had reckoned that operations there would be continued swiftly."

138   Hürter, *Ein deutscher General an der Ostfront*, pp. 116f. (entry for 4 Dec. 1941), 120 (entry for 5 Dec. 1941).

139   See Hoepner's letter to his wife, 4 Dec. 1941: "Their strength is no longer sufficient. The troops on the whole are at an end." BA-MA Freiburg, N 51/9.

140   See *Das Deutsche Reich und der Zweite Weltkrieg*, vol. 4, pp. 599f. (Klink's essay); Hartmann, *Halder*, pp. 297f.; idem, *Wehrmacht im Ostkrieg*, p. 354; Hürter, *Hitlers Heerführer*, pp. 314f.

141   Guderian to his wife, 8 Dec. 1941; IfZ München, ED 100/77; slightly amended and abridged in Guderian, *Erinnerungen eines Soldaten*, pp. 236f. See Reinhardt's war diary entries for 5–9 Dec. 1941; BA-MA Freiburg, N 245/3; Reinhardt's letter to his wife, 9 Dec. 1941. BA-MA Freiburg, N 245/2.

142   Stieff, *Briefe*, pp. 139f. (dated 7 Dec. 1941). See Heinrici's diary entry for 6 Dec. 1941: "Complaint upon complaint can be heard against the uppermost leadership, which did not recognise the point at which an end had to be found." Hürter, *Ein deutscher General an der Ostfront*, p. 121.

143   Engel, *Heeresadjutant bei Hitler*, p. 120 (entry for 8. Dec. 1941).

144   Hubatsch (ed.), *Hitlers Weisungen für die Kriegführung*, pp. 199–203 (at p. 199).

145   *Generalfeldmarschall Keitel, Verbrecher oder Offizier? Erinnerungen, Briefe, Dokumente des Chefs des OKW*, ed. Walter Görlitz, Berlin and Frankfurt am Main, 1961, p. 285. See Dietrich, *12 Jahre mit Hitler*, p. 85. Hitler remarked over lunch in January 1942 that with the news that Japan had entered the war a "millstone" had fallen from his heart; *Monologe*, p. 179 (dated 5 Jan. 1942).

146   Walter Warlimont, *Im Hauptquartier der deutschen Wehrmacht 1939–1945: Grundlagen— Formen—Gestalten*, Frankfurt am Main and Bonn, 1964, p. 221. See Lossberg, *Im Wehrmachtführungsstab*, p. 147; Goebbels, *Tagebücher*, part II, vol. 2, p. 453 (entry for 8 Dec. 1941): "The Führer and his entire headquarters were overjoyed at this development."

147   Goebbels, *Tagebücher*, part II, vol. 2, p. 458 (entry for 9 Dec. 1941).

148   Ibid., p. 453 (entry for 8 Dec. 1941).

149   Hewel's diary entry for 8 Dec. 1941; IfZ München, ED 100/78.

150   Gerhard Wagner (ed.), *Lagevorträge des Oberbefehlshabers der Kriegsmarine vor Hitler 1939–1945*, Munich, 1972, p. 264 (entry for 9 July 1941). See Ian Kershaw, *Fateful Choices: Ten Decisions that Changed the World 1940–1941*, London, 2007, p. 404.

151   Hitler articulated this obsessive idea with particular clarity in his speech to the Reichstag on 11 Dec. 1941: "We know what force is backing Roosevelt. It is the eternal Jew who thinks the time has come to do to us what we had to witness and experience to our horror in Russia." Domarus, *Hitler*, vol. 2, part 2, p. 1808.

152   Goebbels, *Tagebücher*, part II, vol. 1, pp. 236f. (entry for 15 Aug. 1941).

153   Ibid., p. 263 (entry for 19 Aug. 1941).

154   On the Greer affair and the reaction, see Ronald Gerste, *Roosevelt und Hitler: Todfeindschaft und totaler Krieg*, Paderborn, 2011, pp. 176–8.

155   Goebbels, *Tagebücher*, part II, vol. 1, pp. 408 (entry for 13 Sept. 1941), 417 (entry for 14 Sept. 1941). See ibid., p. 420 (entry for 15 Sept. 1941): "We do not want to make it any easier for Roosevelt to go down his desired path to war."

156   Domarus, *Hitler*, vol. 2, part 2, p. 1778.

157   See Kershaw, *Fareful Choices*, pp. 405f., 410f.

158   Goebbels, *Tagebücher*, part II, vol. 2, pp. 299 (entry for 16 Nov. 1941), 308 (entry for 18 Nov. 1941). See ibid., pp. 149 (entry for 21 Oct. 1941), 189 (entry for 26 Oct. 1941), 239f. (entry for 6 Nov. 1941).

159   On Japan's decision to enter the war, see Kershaw, *Fateful Choices*, pp. 331–81.

160   *Akten zur deutschen Auswärtigen Politik 1918–1945 (ADAP) (The Political Archives of the Federal Foreign Office)*, Series D, 1937–1941, vols 1–13, Frankfurt am Main, 1956–70, vol. 13, part 2, doc. 512, p. 709; See Kershaw, *Fateful Choices*, pp. 412–14.

161   See Kershaw, *Fateful Choices*, p. 415.

162   Goebbels, *Tagebücher*, part II, vol. 2, p. 452 (entry for 8 Dec. 1942). On 25 Nov. 1941, Goebbels noted: "The conflict between the US and Japan is rushing with gigantic steps towards its dramatic peak." Ibid., p. 362.

163   Ibid., p. 339 (entry for 22 Nov. 1941).

164   See Kershaw, *Fateful Choices*, p. 418.

165   See Hill (ed.), *Die Weizsäcker-Papiere 1933–1950*, p. 280 (dated 10 Dec. 1941).

166   Ernst von Weizsäcker, *Erinnerungen*, Munich, 1950, p. 328.

167   See Hans-Ulrich Wehler, *Deutsche Gesellschaftsgeschichte*, vol. 4, Munich, 2003, p. 862; Kurt Pätzold and Manfred Weissbecker, *Adolf Hitler: Eine politische Biographie*, Leipzig, 1995, p. 471; Andreas Hillgruber, *Hitlers Strategie: Politik und Kriegführung 1940–1941*, Frankfurt am Main, 1965, p. 553.

168   Goebbels, *Tagebücher*, part II, vol. 2, pp. 463–9 (entry for 10 Dec. 1941). After a further conversation the following noon, Goebbels was forced to admit that the Führer too was "of the opinion that things are not all that good in the east right now." Above all, there was unfortunately a "complete lack of winter equipment." Ibid., p. 475 (entry for 11 Dec. 1941).

169   Schmidt, *Statist auf diplomatischer Bühne*, pp. 542f.; for the wording of the declaration of war, see *ADAP*, Series D, vol. 13, part 2, doc. 577, p. 817.

170   Domarus, *Hitler*, vol. 2, part 2, pp. 1794–811 (at pp. 1794, 1800, 1804, 1807, 1809).

171   *Meldungen aus dem Reich*, vol. 8, p. 3089 (dated 15 Dec. 1941).

172   Friedrich Kellner recorded people around him saying things like, "Now the German victory will be achieved all the sooner." *Tagebücher, 1939–1945*, vol. 1, p. 207 (entry for 12 Dec. 1941). It is doubtful, however, whether such sentiments were representative of the population as a whole.

173   Goebbels, *Tagebücher*, part II, vol. 2, pp. 494–7 (entry for 13 Dec. 1941).

174   Hillgruber (ed.), *Staatsmänner und Diplomaten bei Hitler*, vol. 1, pp. 682–8 (at pp. 683, 684).

175   See Goebbels, *Tagebücher*, part II, vol. 2, p. 506 (entry for 14 Dec. 1941).

176   See Below, *Als Hitlers Adjutant*, p. 298; Hewel's diary entry for 16 Dec. 1941; IfZ München, ED 100/78.

177   Hoepner to his wife, 12 Dec. 1941; BA-MA Freiburg, N 51/9. See Reinhardt's letter to his wife, 15 Feb. 1941; BA-MA Freiburg, N 245/2.

178   Stieff, *Briefe*, p. 142 (dated 9 Dec. 1941). See Hürter, *Ein deutscher General an der Ostfront*, p. 128 (entry for 16 Dec. 1941); Generalfeldmarschall Wilhelm Ritter von Leeb, *Tagebuchaufzeichnungen und Lagebeurteilungen aus zwei Weltkriegen*, ed. Georg Meyer, Stuttgart, 1976, p. 418 (entry for 16 Dec. 1941). The head of the operations division, Adolf Heusinger, remarked on 5 December 1941 that the cautionary example of Napoleon was standing "directly in front of our soul"; see Meyer, *Georg Heusinger*, p. 165. The memoirs of the early nineteenth-century French general Armand-Augustin-Louis de Caulaincourt, *With Napoleon in Russia*, were popular reading material among German officers in late 1941 and early 1942. See Hoepner's letter to his wife, 23 Dec. 1941; BA-MA Freiburg, N 51/9.

179   Halder, *Kriegstagebuch*, vol. 3, p. 336 (entry for 9 Dec. 1941). See also the notes of General Kurt von Liebenstein, Guderian's chief of staff in the 2nd Tank Army, on 9 Dec. 1941; IfZ München, ED 100/77.

180   Halder, *Kriegstagebuch*, vol. 3, p. 348 (entry for 15 Dec. 1941).

181   See Bernhard R. Kroener, *Generaloberst Friedrich Fromm: Eine Biographie*, Paderborn, 2005, pp. 422f.
182   *KTB OKW*, vol. 1, p. 1083.
183   Bock, *Das Kriegstagebuch*, p. 354 (entry for 16 Dec. 1941). Hoepner wrote to his wife on 17 Dec. 1941: "H[itler] has ruled out all evasive action. That may mean my death sentence!"; BA-MA Freiburg, N 51/9.
184   *KTB OKW*, vol. 1, p. 1084. On Hitler's order to hold territory at all costs, see Hürter, *Hitlers Heerführer*, pp. 326f.
185   Halder to Heinrich Uhlig, 17 June 1953; BA-MA Freiburg, N 220/88.
186   Halder, *Kriegstagebuch*, vol. 3, p. 285 (entry for 10 Nov. 1941); Jürgen Löffler, *Walther von Brauchitsch (1981–1948): Eine politische Biographie*, Frankfurt am Main, 2001, p. 254. On the relationship between Brauchitsch and Hitler, see the recollections of Charlotte von Brauchitsch (3–4 April 1952), Helmuth Greiner (21 Feb. 1952), Adolf Heusinger (25 Jan. and 20 Feb. 1952) and Heinz von Gyldenfeldt (2 March 1952); IfZ München, ZS 18, ZS 238, ZS 69, ZS 239.
187   Halder, *Kriegstagebuch*, vol. 3, p. 332 (entry for 7 Dec. 1941). See Engel, *Heeresadjutant bei Hitler*, p. 117 (entry for 6 Dec. 1941): "[Loss of] trust between the Führer and the Supreme Commander irreparable."
188   Goebbels, *Tagebücher*, part II, vol. 2, p. 538 (entry for 18 Dec. 1941); see Below, *Als Hitlers Adjutant*, p. 298.
189   Goebbels, *Tagebücher*, part II, vol. 3, p. 510 (entry for 20 March 1942).
190   Guderian to his wife, 16 Dec. 1941; IfZ München, ED 100/77; Hürter, *Ein deutscher General an der Ostfront*, p. 130 (entry for 20 Dec. 1941).
191   Cited in Hartmann, *Halder*, p. 303. Hermann Balck, who reported back to Halder on 31 Dec. 1941, found Hitler "fresh and confident" and said that "he has gained decisive energy." BA-MA Freiburg, N 647/3.
192   Christa Schroeder to Johanna Nusser, 15 Jan. 1942; Schroeder, *Er war mein Chef*, p. 127. See Warlimont, *Im Hauptquartier der Wehrmacht*, pp. 231f.
193   *KTB OKW*, vol. 1, pp. 1085 (entry for 21 Dec. 1941), 1086 (entry for 26 Dec. 1941).
194   Guderian, *Erinnerungen eines Soldaten*, pp. 240–3 (at pp. 241f.).
195   As in Hürter, *Hitlers Heerführer*, p. 332.
196   Goebbels, *Tagebücher*, part II, vol. 2, p. 539 (entry for 18 Dec. 1941). See *Monologe*, p. 210 (dated 17–18 Jan. 1942): "The generals have to be cold, hard dogs."
197   See Hoepner's report dated 13 Feb. 1942; BA-MA Freiburg, N 51/3. On the background, see also Hoepner's letter to his wife, 4 Jan. 1942; BA-MA Freiburg, N 51/9. After a few months, thanks to Schmundt, Hoepner's expulsion from the Wehrmacht was changed to an honorable discharge so that the general could claim his pension. Below, *Als Hitlers Adjutant*, p. 304.
198   Domarus, *Hitler* vol. 2, part 2, p. 1815; Goebbels, *Tagebücher*, part II, vol. 2, p. 556 (entry for 21 Dec. 1941).
199   Goebbels, *Tagebücher*, part II., vol. 3, p. 39 (entry for 2 Jan. 1942).
200   See *Meldungen aus dem Reich*, vol. 9, p. 3120 (dated 5 Jan. 1942).
201   Hewel's diary entry for 24 Dec. 1941; IfZ München, ED 100/78.
202   See Hewel's diary entry for 31 Dec. 1941; IfZ München, ED 100/78.; Dietrich, *12 Jahre mit Hitler*, pp. 107f.; Below, *Als Hitlers Adjutant*, p. 297; Halder, *Kriegstagebuch*, vol. 3, p. 371 (entry for 2 Jan. 1941).
203   Hewel's diary entry for 31 Dec. 1941; IfZ München, ED 100/78. See Schroeder, *Er war mein Chef*, p. 127; David Irving, *Hitler und seine Feldherren*, Frankfurt am Main, Berlin and Vienna, 1975, p. 367.
204   Domarus, *Hitler*, vol. 2, part 2, pp. 1820f.
205   Goebbels, *Tagebücher*, part II, vol. 3, p. 35 (entry for 1 Jan. 1942).
206   Kellner, *Tagebücher*, *1939–1945*, vol. 1, p. 223 (entry for 1 Jan. 1942).
207   Hürter, *Ein deutscher General an der Ostfront*, p. 139 (entry for 11 Jan. 1942).

208 Halder, *Kriegstagebuch*, vol. 3, pp. 372 (entry for 2 Jan. 1941), 373 (entry for 3 Jan. 1942); see Meyer, *Adolf Heusinger*, p. 171.

209 *Monologe*, p. 171 (dated 3–4 Jan. 1942).

210 Ibid., pp. 195 (dated 12–13 Jan. 1942), 210 (dated 17–18 Jan. 1942).

211 *KTB OKW*, vol. 2, pp. 1268f.; see Hürter, *Hitlers Heerführer*, p. 339.

212 Goebbels, *Tagebücher*, part II, vol. 3, pp. 143f. (entry for 20 Jan. 1942).

213 Ibid., p. 146 (entry for 20 Jan. 1942). See also ibid., p. 500 (entry for 20 March 1942): "The Führer alone saved the front last winter."

214 Karl-Jesko von Puttkamer to Friedrich Hossbach, 2 March 1942; BA-MA Freiburg, N 24/13.

215 Keitel, *Verbrecher oder Offizier?*, p. 293. See also Jodl's testimony on his relationship with Hitler of 18 Jan. 1946, in which he said that he had never "admired Hitler more" than in the winter of 1941–42 when he "alone stabilised the shaky eastern front." BA-MA Freiburg, N 69/48.

216 Franz Halder, *Hitler als Feldherr*, Munich, 1949, pp. 46f.

217 Hürter, *Ein deutscher General an der Ostfront*, p. 147 (entry for 28 Feb. 1942). On the significance of Hitler's order to hold territory at all costs, see Hürter, *Hitlers Heerführer*, pp. 327, 344f.

218 See Richard Overy, *Russia's War 1941–1945*, London, 1998, pp. 119–22; Hartmann, *Wehrmacht im Ostkrieg*, p. 380.

219 Goebbels, *Tagebücher*, part II, vol. 3, pp. 221f.

220 See Below, *Als Hitlers Adjutant*, p. 305.

221 Domarus, *Hitler*, vol. 2, part 2, pp. 1826–34 (at pp. 1827, 1832f.). On the incendiary mood at the event, see Goebbels, *Tagebücher*, part II, vol. 3, pp. 227f. (entry for 31 Jan. 1942).

222 Goebbels, *Tagebücher*, part II, vol. 3, p. 229 (entry for 31 Jan. 1942).

223 See *Meldungen aus dem Reich*, vol. 3, pp. 3233–6 (dated 2 Feb. 1942). By contrast, Kellner commented that the Soviets had "already been destroyed and conquered so often that announcements of this kind make no impression on me at all." *Tagebücher, 1939–1945*, vol. 1, p. 234 (entry for 4 Feb. 1942).

224 Domarus, *Hitler*, vol. 2, part 2, p. 1833.

225 Goebbels, *Tagebücher*, part II, vol. 3, p. 207 (entry for 28 Jan. 1942).

226 See ibid., pp. 187 (entry for 25 Jan. 1942), 340 (entry for 29 Feb. 1942), 412f. (entry for 5 March 1942), 499 (entry for 20 March 1942).

227 Major König to Friedrich Hossbach, 5 Feb. 1943; BA-MA Freiburg, N 24/17.

228 See Volker Ullrich, "Alles oder nichts," in *ZEIT-Geschichte* 4 (2011), pp. 90–3; Pyta, *Hitler*, pp. 336, 623 ff.

229 See Tooze, *The Wages of Destruction*, p. 507.

230 See Albert Speer to Karl Thieme, 20 Dec. 1975; BA Koblenz, N 1340/64; Albert Speer, *Erinnerungen: Mit einem Essay von Jochen Thies*, Frankfurt am Main and Berlin, 1993, pp. 207f.

231 See the final report of the military court for the commanding general of Air Gau I, Königsberg, 8 March 1943; BA Koblenz, N 1340/518; Franz W. Seidler, *Fritz Todt: Baumeister des Dritten Reiches*, Munich and Berlin, 1986, pp. 367ff.; Joachim Fest, *Speer: Eine Biographie*, Berlin, 1999, pp. 179–82.

232 Below, *Als Adjutant Hitlers*, pp. 305f. See Goebbels, *Tagebücher*, part II, vol. 3, p. 277 (entry for 9 Feb. 1942): "The Führer has been hurt most deeply by this loss."

233 See Speer's testimony on his responsibilities as minister, 8 Feb. 1942–23 May 1945, Nuremberg, 10 Aug. 1946, p. 6; BA Koblenz N 1340/84. This account is consistent with the one in Speer's memoirs. Speer, *Erinnerungen*, p. 210.

234 Rudolf Wolters, *Kurzer Lebensabriss*, p. 18; BA Koblenz, N 1340/76.

235 See Magnus Brechtken, *Albert Speer: Eine deutsche Karriere*, Munich, 2017, pp. 157ff., 205ff.; Tooze, *The Wages of Destruction*, pp. 553–7; Martin Kitchen, *Speer: Hitler's*

Architect, New Haven and London, 2015, pp. 120ff. Speer's insistence that he assumed his ministerial post unwilling, as a "kind of war service," is not credible; see *Erinnerungen*, p. 213. Speer also claimed to have been "quite unhappy" about this ministerial appointment in a letter to his wife of 8 Nov. 1950; BA Koblenz, N 1340/133.

236 Goebbels, *Tagebücher*, part II, vol. 3, p. 391 (entry for 13 Feb. 1942). The speech is reproduced in Domarus, *Hitler*, vol. 2, part 2, pp. 1836–40. Fritz Sauckel's estate contains an invitation to the state funeral for Fritz Todt; BA Koblenz, N 1582/3. The Security Service report on the occasion contained statements that never before had the Führer "shown his human side to this extent." *Meldungen aus dem Reich*, vol. 9, p. 3314 (dated 16 Feb. 1942).

237 *KTB OKW*, vol. 1, pp. 1093–8 (at p. 1093).

238 See Goebbels, *Tagebücher*, part II, vol. 3, pp. 300 (entry for 13 Feb. 1942), 318f. (entry for 15 Feb. 1942). Hitler said much the same to Antonescu on 11 Feb. 1942; see Hillgruber (ed.), *Staatsmänner und Diplomaten bei Hitler 1942–1944*, pp. 44f.

239 Noted by Walter Scherff, who would in May 1942 become the "Führer's commissioner for military history writing," on 13 Feb. 1942, reprinted in Marianne Feuersenger, *Im Vorzimmer der Macht: Aufzeichnungen aus dem Wehrmachtführungsstab und Führerhauptquartier 1940–1945*, 4th edition, Munich, 2001, pp. 106–10 (at pp. 108, 107).

240 Hitler's speech to officer candidates in Berlin's Sportpalast on 14 Feb. 1942; BA Berlin-Lichterfelde, NS 51/28.

241 Goebbels, *Tagebücher*, part II, vol. 3, p. 314 (entry for 15 Feb. 1942); see *Meldungen aus dem Reich*, vol. 9, pp. 3314f. (dated 16 Feb. 1942).

242 See the statistics in Halder, *Kriegstagebuch*, vol. 3, p. 418 (entry for 25 March 1942). Rüdiger Overmans put the number of German casualties on the eastern front by late March 1942 at 438,891. See *Deutsche militärische Verluste im Zweiten Weltkrieg*, Munich, 2000, p. 279. By February 1942, the Soviets had almost 3 million soldiers taken captive and 2,663,000 killed; Catherine Merridale, *Ivan's War: The Red Army 1939–45*, London 2005, p. 128.

243 See Rolf-Dieter Müller, *Der letzte deutsche Krieg 1939–1945*, Stuttgart, 2005, pp. 115f.

244 Christa Schroeder to Johanna Nusser, 27 Feb. 1942; Schroeder, *Er war mein Chef*, p. 129. The Führer had "been through a lot this winter," wrote Karl-Jesko Puttkamer to Friedrich Hossbach on 2 March 1941; BA-MA Freiburg, N 24/13.

245 Goebbels, *Tagebücher*, part II, vol. 3, pp. 501–15 (at pp. 512, 509, 501, 510).

246 *Monologe*, p. 300 (dated 26–27 Feb. 1942).

247 Goebbels, *Tagebücher*, part II, vol. 3, p. 506 (entry for 20 March 1942).

248 *KTB OKW*, vol. 4, p. 1503 (entry for 15 May 1945).

249 Ulrich von Hassell, *Vom andern Deutschland: Aus den nachgelassenen Tagebüchern 1938–1944*, Frankfurt am Main, 1964, p. 242 (entry for 11 July 1942), according to Elsa Bruckmann.

250 Hillgruber (ed.), *Staatsmänner und Diplomaten bei Hitler 1939–1941*, p. 657. See similar in *Monologe*, p. 239 (dated 27 Jan. 1942): "This matter too leaves me completely cold. If the German people are not prepared to devote themselves to their self-preservation, so be it. Then they should disappear!"

7 The Road to the Holocaust

1 Max Domarus, *Hitler: Reden und Proklamationen 1932–1945*, Munich, 1965, vol. 2, part 2, p. 1829. Hitler had already said something very similar in his Reichstag speech of 30 January 1941. See ibid., p. 1663.

2 See Volker Ullrich, *Hitler: Ascent 1889–1939*, London, 2016, pp. 680f.

3 See Ian Kershaw, *Fateful Choices: Ten Decisions that Changed the World 1940–1941*, London, 2007, p. 434; Ludolf Herbst, *Das nationalsozialistische Deutschland 1933–1945*, Frankfurt am Main, 1996 p. 384.

4　See Hans Mommsen, "Die Realisierung des Utopischen: Die 'Endlösung' der Judenfrage im Dritten Reich," in *Geschichte und Gesellschaft*, 9 (1983), pp. 381–420; also in *idem, Der Nationalsozialismus und die deutsche Gesellschaft: Ausgewählte Aufsätze*, Reinbek bei Hamburg, 1991, pp. 184–232.

5　Hans-Ulrich Wehler, *Deutsche Gesellschaftsgeschichte*, Munich, 2003, vol. 4, p. 885.

6　Friedrich Kellner, *"Vernebelt, verdunkelt sind alle Hirne": Tagebücher, 1939–1945*, ed. Sascha Feuchert et al., Göttingen, 2011, vol. 1, p. 48 (entry for 14 Nov. 1939). On the intensification of anti-Jewish repression with the start of the war, see Saul Friedländer, *The Years of Extermination: Nazi Germany and the Jews, 1939–1945*, London, 2007, pp. 48–51; Christopher Browning, *The Origins of the Final Solution: The Evolution of Nazi Jewish Policy September 1939–March 1942*, London, 2004, pp. 169–78; Hans Mommsen, *Das NS-Regime und die Auslöschung des Judentums in Europa*, Göttingen, 2014, p. 113f.; Markus Roth, *"Ihr wisst, wollt es aber nicht wissen": Verfolgung, Terror und Widerstand im Dritten Reich*, Munich, 2015, pp. 220–6; David Cesarani, *Final Solution: The Fate of the Jews 1933–1949*, London, 2016, pp. 278–81.

7　Victor Klemperer, *Ich will Zeugnis ablegen bis zum letzten: Tagebücher*, vol. 1: 1933–1941, ed. Walter Nowojski with Hadwig Klemperer, Berlin, 1995, p. 529 (entry for 26 May 1940).

8　Willy Cohn, *Kein Recht, nirgends: Tagebuch vom Untergang des Breslauer Judentums 1933–1941*, ed. Norbert Conrads, Cologne, Weimar and Vienna, 2006, vol. 2, p. 745 (entry for 26 Jan. 1940); Klemperer, *Tagebücher, 1933–1941*, p. 537 (entry for 6 July 1940).

9　Otto Dov Kulka and Eberhard Jäckel (eds), *Die Juden in den geheimen NS-Stimmungsberichten 1939–1945*, Düsseldorf, 2004, doc. 514, p. 431. On emigration after the start of the war, see Friedländer, *Die The Years of Extermination*, pp. 82–9; Peter Longerich, *Politik der Vernichtung: Eine Gesamtdarstellung der nationalsozialistischen Judenverfolgung*, Munich and Zurich, 1998, pp. 232f.; Roth, *Verfolgung, Terror und Widerstand im Dritten Reich*, pp. 222f.

10　Cohn, *Kein Recht, nirgends*, vol. 2, p. 685 (entry for 4 Sept. 1939).

11　See Wolfgang Benz, *Der Holocaust*, Munich, 1995, p. 33; Dieter Pohl, *Holocaust: Die Ursachen, das Geschehen, die Folgen*, Freiburg, Basel and Vienna, 2000, p. 42.

12　Domarus, *Hitler*, vol. 2, part 1, p. 1342.

13　Kulka and Jäckel (eds), *Die Juden in den geheimen NS-Stimmungsberichten 1939–1945*, doc. 471, p. 412.

14　Domarus, *Hitler*, vol. 2, part 1, pp. 1442, 1468.

15　Klemperer, *Tagebücher 1933–1941*, p. 536 (entry for 29 June 1941).

16　*Die Tagebücher von Joseph Goebbels*, commissioned by the Institute for Contemporary History, with support from the State Archive of Russia, ed. Elke Fröhlich, *Part I: Aufzeichnungen 1923–1941*, 9 vols in 14 parts, Munich, 1998–2008; *Part II: Diktate 1941–1945*, 15 vols, Munich, 1993–6; part I, vol. 7, pp. 293 (entry for 3 Feb. 1940), 367 (entry for 27 March 1940).

17　Ibid., vol. 9, pp. 399f. (entry for 24 June 1941).

18　Ibid., vol. 7, p. 138 (entry for 5 Oct. 1939). See also Friedländer, *The Years of Extermination*, pp. 19–22, 98–102.

19　See Goebbels, *Tagebücher*, part I, vol. 7, pp. 173 (entry for 29 Oct. 1939), 202 (entry for 19 Nov. 1939), 214 (entry for 28 Nov. 1939), 235 (entry for 18 Dec. 1939).

20　Ibid., vol. 8, p. 35 (entry for 4 April 1940).

21　Ibid., vol. 8, p. 372 (entry for 11 Oct. 1940). See also ibid., pp. 103 (entry for 9 May 1940), 165 (entry for 9 June 1940), 304 (entry for 3 Sept. 1940).

22　See Alexandra Przyrembel and Jörg Schönert (eds), *"Jud Süss": Hofjude, literarische Figur, antisemitisches Zerrbild*, Frankfurt am Main, 2006.

23　Goebbels, *Tagebücher*, vol. 8, p. 279 (entry for 18 Aug. 1940). See also ibid., vol. 7, pp. 208 (entry for 23 Nov. 1939), 220 (entry for 5 Dec. 1939); vol. 8, p. 77 (entry for 26 April 1940).

24　Ibid., vol. 8, pp. 345 (entry for 25 Sept. 1940), 346 (entry for 26 Sept. 1940).

25 Heinz Boberach (ed.), *Meldungen aus dem Reich: Die geheimen Lageberichte des Sicherheitsdienstes der SS 1938–1945*, Herrsching, 1984, vol. 6, pp. 1811f. (dated 28 Nov. 1940).

26 Kulka and Jäckel (eds), *Die Juden in den geheimen NS-Stimmungsberichten 1933–1945*, doc. 524, p. 435.

27 *Meldungen aus dem Reich*, vol. 6, pp. 1918f (dated 20 Jan. 1941). See also the report by the Security Service branch office in Höxter of 7 Feb. 1941; Kulka and Jäckel (eds), *Die Juden in den geheimen NS-Stimmungsberichten 1933–1945*, doc. 536, p. 441. In Dresden, the film's run in cinemas ended after a week. See Klemperer, *Tagebücher, 1933–1941*, p. 564 (entry for 10 Dec. 1940).

28 Cited in Friedländer, *The Years of Extermination*, p. 101.

29 *Meldungen aus dem Reich*, vol. 6, p. 1918 (dated 20 Jan. 1941).

30 Wiedemann's statement of 9 June 1961 cited in Ernst Klee, *"Euthanasie" im Dritten Reich: Die "Vernichtung lebensunwerten Lebens,"* fully revised edition, Frankfurt am Main, 2010, p. 78.

31 On the details, see Ulf Schmidt, *Hitlers Arzt Karl Brandt: Medizin und Macht im Dritten Reich*, Berlin, 2009, pp. 177–84.

32 See Klee, *"Euthanasie" im Dritten Reich*, pp. 333–40; Schmidt, *Hitlers Arzt Karl Brandt*, pp. 185–9; Michael Burleigh, *The Third Reich: A New History*, London, 2000, pp. 382–4.

33 Sworn testimony by Lammers in Nuremberg of 30 Jan. 1947, cited in Burleigh, *The Third Reich*, p. 383. On the dates, see Henry Friedlander, *Der Weg zum NS-Genozid: Von der Euthanasie zur Endlösung*, Berlin, 1997, pp. 119f.; Schmidt, *Hitlers Arzt Karl Brandt*, p. 645, n. 41.

34 On the struggle for control of the homicidal programme, see Schmidt, *Hitlers Arzt Karl Brandt*, pp. 191–6.

35 See Klee, *"Euthanasie" im Dritten Reich*, pp. 87f., 90–2.

36 For an extensive discussion of the meeting of 9 Oct. 1940, see Götz Aly, *Die Belasteten: "Euthanasie" 1939–1945. Eine Gesellschaftsgeschichte*, Frankfurt am Main, 2013, pp. 44–6.

37 Ernst Klee, *Dokumente zur "Euthanasie,"* Frankfurt am Main, 1985, p. 85.

38 See Aly, *Die Belasteten*, p. 42; Schmidt, *Hitlers Arzt Karl Brandt*, pp. 197–9; Ian Kershaw, *Hitler 1936–1945: Nemesis*, London, 2001, pp. 260f .

39 See Klee, *"Euthanasie" im Dritten Reich*, pp. 94–111; Longerich, *Politik der Vernichtung*, pp. 236f.; Götz Aly, *"Endlösung": Völkerverschiebung und der Mord an den europäischen Juden*, Frankfurt am Main, 1995, pp. 114–26.

40 See Klee, *"Euthanasie" im Dritten Reich*, pp. 134–65; for a summary, see Longerich, *Politik der Vernichtung*, pp. 238f. One the location, see Annette Hinz-Wessels, *Tiergartenstrasse 4: Schaltstelle der nationalsozialistischen "Euthanasie" Morde*, Berlin, 2015. On the statistics, see Aly, *Die Belasteten*, p. 48.

41 Goebbels, *Tagebücher*, part I, vol. 8, p. 87 (entry for 1 May 1940). On the formation of rumours, see Klee, *"Euthanasie" im Dritten Reich*, pp. 136–8, 172–8.

42 Goebbels, *Tagebücher*, part I, vol. 8, p. 336 (entry for 20 Sept. 1940); see Klee, *"Euthanasie" im Dritten Reich*, pp. 213–15.

43 William L. Shirer, *Berlin Diary 1934–1941: The Rise of the Third Reich*, London, 1997, pp. 219 (entry for 21 Sept. 1940), 239f., 242 (entry for 25 Nov. 1940).

44 See Sara Berger, *Experten der Vernichtung: Das T 4-Reinhardt-Netzwerk in den Lagern Belzec, Sobibor, Treblinka*, Hamburg, 2013, pp. 9, 31–3.

45 Raul Hilberg, *Die Vernichtung der europäischen Juden*, vol. 2, Frankfurt am Main, 1990, p. 937.

46 See Browning, *The Origins of the Final Solution*, pp. 12–14; Longerich, *Politik der Vernichtung*, pp. 250–2.

47 *Die Verfolgung und Ermordung der europäischen Juden durch das nationalsozialistische Deutschland*, vol. 4, ed. Klaus-Peter Friedrich, Munich, 2011, doc. 12, pp. 88–82. See Longerich, *Politik der Vernichtung*, pp. 253f.; Robert Gerwarth, *Reinhard Heydrich:*

Eine Biographie, Munich, 2011, pp. 194f.; Mommsen, *Das NS-Regime und die Auslöschung des Judentums*, pp. 114f.; Cesarani, *Final Solution*, pp. 255–8.

48 Goebbels, *Tagebücher*, part I, vol. 7, p. 130 (entry for 30 Sept. 1939). The corresponding passage in Rosenberg's diary reads: "Between the Vistula and Bug: the entirety of Jewry (also from the Reich) as well as all unreliable elements of any sort." Jürgen Matthäus and Frank Bajohr (eds), *Alfred Rosenberg: Die Tagebücher von 1934 bis 1944*, Frankfurt am Main, 2015, pp. 290f. (entry for 29 Sept. 1939).

49 Goebbels, *Tagebücher*, part I, vol. 7, p. 141 (entry for 7 Oct. 1939).

50 *Heeresadjutant bei Hitler 1938–1943: Aufzeichnungen des Majors Engel*, ed. Hildegard von Kotze, Stuttgart, 1974, p. 65 (entry for 8 Oct. 1939).

51 Goebbels, *Tagebücher*, part I, vol. 7, pp. 177 (entry for 2 Nov. 1939), 179f. (entry for 3 Nov. 1939). Himmler's wife Marga wrote something similar in her diary on 7 March 1940 after visiting Posen, Łodz and Warsaw: "This pack of Jews and the Polacks, most of whom do not even look like human beings, and the indescribable filth. It is an unprecedented task to create order there." Katrin Himmler and Michael Wildt (eds), *Himmler privat: Briefe eines Massenmörders*, Munich, 2014, p. 226.

52 Goebbels, *Tagebücher*, part I, vol. 7, pp. 220f. (entry for 5 Dec. 1939).

53 *Die Verfolgung und Ermordung der europäischen Juden*, vol. 4, doc. 18, p. 102.

54 On the Nisko project, see Longerich, *Politik der Vernichtung*, pp. 256–8; Browning, *The Origins of the Final Solution*, pp. 36–43; Mommsen, *Das NS-Regime und die Auslöschung des Judentums in Europa*, pp. 115–17; Gerwarth, *Reinhard Heydrich*, pp. 196f.; Michael Wildt, *Generation des Unbedingten: Das Führungskorps des Reichssicherheitshauptamtes*, Hamburg, 2002, pp. 468–70; David Cesarani, *Eichmann: His Life and Crimes*, London, 2005, pp. 77–81; *idem, Final Solution*, pp. 258–60.

55 Kulka and Jäckel (eds), *Die Juden in den geheimen NS-Stimmungsberichten 1933–1945*, doc. 480, p. 416 (dated 27 Nov. 1939).

56 See Wildt, *Generation des Unbedingten*, pp. 472f.; Cesarani, *Adolf Eichmann*, pp. 81f.

57 On the halting of the Nisko project, see Longerich, *Politik der Vernichtung*, pp. 258f.; Browning, *The Origins of the Final Solution*, pp. 42f.; Mommsen, *Das NS-Regime und die Auslöschung des Judentums in Europa*, pp. 118f.

58 Goebbels, *Tagebücher*, part I, vol. 7, p. 281 (entry for 23 Jan. 1940).

59 See Longerich, *Politik der Vernichtung*, pp. 267–9; Browning, *The Origins of the Final Solution*, pp. 96–101. On the deportation of the Jews of Stettin, see *Die Verfolgung und Ermordung der europäischen Juden*, vol. 3, doc. 52 and 53, pp. 169–73; Aly, *"Endlösung,"* p. 97f.

60 Notes by Walther Hewel about Hitler's conversation with Colin Ross on 13 March 1940; *Akten zur deutschen Auswärtigen Politik 1918–1945 (ADAP) (The Political Archives of the Federal Foreign Office)*, Series D, 1937–1941, vols 1–13, Frankfurt am Main, 1956–70, vol. 8, part 1, no. 671, pp. 714–17 (at p. 716); See Browning, *The Origins of the Final Solution*, p. 68. On Ross's audience with Hitler, see also Goebbels, *Tagebücher*, part I, vol. 7, pp. 349f. (entry for 15 March 1940).

61 See Friedländer, *The Years of Extermination*, 38, 104, 144–6; Browning, *The Origins of the Final Solution*, pp. 114–20; Cesarani, *Final Solution*, pp. 270–3; Andrea Löw, *Juden im Ghetto Litzmannstadt: Lebensbedingungen, Selbstwahrnehmung, Verhalten*, Göttingen, 2006.

62 Ullrich, *Hitler: Ascent 1889–1939*, p. 667. See Hans Jansen, *Der Madagaskar-Plan: Die beabsichtigte Deportation der europäischen Juden nach Madagaskar*, Munich, 1997; Magnus Brechtken, *"Madagaskar für die Juden": Antisemitische Idee und politische Praxis 1885–1945*, Munich, 1998.

63 Helmut Krausnick, "Denkschrift Himmlers über die Behandlung der Fremdvölkischen im Osten (Mai 1940)," in *Vierteljahrshefte für Zeitgeschichte*, 5 (1957), pp. 194–8 (at p. 197).

64 See Himmler's pocket calendar for 25 May 1940, p. 261. In a file note on Hitler's reaction, Himmler wrote on 28 May 1940: "The Führer read through the six pages and voiced his approval." Krausnick, "Denkschrift Himmlers," p. 194.

65   Franz Rademacher, "Gedanken über die Arbeit und Aufgaben des Ref. D III," 3 June 1940; cited in Browning, *The Origins of the Final Solution*, pp. 82f. See Hans-Jürgen Döscher, *Das Auswärtige Amt im Dritten Reich: Diplomatie im Schatten der "Endlösung,"* Berlin, 1987, p. 215; Eckart Conze, Norbert Frei, Peter Hayes and Moshe Zimmermann, *Das Amt und die Vergangenheit: Deutsche Diplomaten im Dritten Reich und in der Bundesrepublik*, Munich, 2010, pp. 183f.

66   Franz Rademacher, "Plan zur Lösung der Judenfrage," 2 July 1940; cited in Longerich, *Politik der Vernichtung*, p. 275; idem, "Die Judenfrage im Friedensvertrage," 3 July 1940; *Die Verfolgung und Ermordung der europäischen Juden*, vol. 3, doc. 92, pp. 251–3. See Browning, *The Origins of the Final Solution*, pp. 85f.

67   See Galeazzo Ciano, *Tagebücher, 1939–1943*, Bern, 1946, p. 249 (entry for 18–19 June 1940); Paul Schmidt, *Statist auf diplomatischer Bühne 1923–45*, Bonn, 1950, p. 485.

68   See Gerhard Wagner (ed.), *Lagevorträge des Oberbefehlshabers der Kriegsmarine vor Hitler 1939–1945*, Munich, 1972, p. 107 (dated 20 June 1940).

69   Werner Präg and Wolfgang Jacobmeyer (eds), *Das Diensttagebuch des deutschen Generalgouverneurs in Polen 1939–1945*, Stuttgart, 1975, p. 252 (entry for 12 July 1940).

70   Goebbels, *Tagebücher*, part I, vol. 8, p. 238 (entry for 26 July 1940).

71   Ibid., p. 276 (entry for 17 Aug. 1940). On 15 August 1940, Rademacher learned from Luther about a conversation that had taken place between Hitler and the German ambassador in Paris, Otto Abetz, on 3 August, in which Hitler said he intended after the war "to evacuate all Jews from Europe." *ADAP*, Series D, vol. 10, no. 345, p. 399.

72   *Im Warschauer Ghetto: Das Tagebuch des Adam Czerniaków 1939–1942*, Munich, 1986, p. 88 (entry for 1 July 1940).

73   Klemperer, *Tagebücher, 1933–1941*, p. 538 (entry for 7 July 1940).

74   *Die Verfolgung und Ermordung der europäischen Juden*, vol. 3, doc. 89, pp. 246f. See Gerwarth, *Reinhard Heydrich*, p. 223.

75   *Die Verfolgung und Ermordung der europäischen Juden*, vol. 3, doc. 99, pp. 266–73 (at pp. 267, 271); see Wildt, *Generation des Unbedingten*, pp. 502f.; Cesarani, *Final Solution*, p. 300.

76   Engel, *Heeresadjutant bei Hitler*, pp. 94f. (entry for 2 Feb. 1941).

77   Andreas Hillgruber (ed.), *Staatsmänner und Diplomaten bei Hitler: Vertrauliche Aufzeichnungen über Unterredungen mit Vertretern des Auslandes 1939–1941*, Frankfurt am Main, 1967, pp. 573f.

78   See Rademacher's letter to envoy Bielfeld of 10 February 1942, in which he wrote of Hitler's decision that "the Jews shall be deported not to Madagascar but to the east." Cited in Conze et al., *Das Amt und die Vergangenheit*, p. 185.

79   See Browning, *The Origins of the Final Solution*, pp. 88f; Wildt, *Generation des Unbedingten*, p. 596.

80   Czerniaków, *Im Warschauer Ghetto*, p. 125 (entry for 25 Oct. 1940). See Friedländer, *The Years of Extermination*, pp. 105f.; Roth, *Herrenmenschen*, pp. 183f.; Cesarani, *Final Solution*, pp. 331–4.

81   Heinrici to his family, 17 June 1941; BA-MA Freiburg, N 265/35. See also Johannes Hürter, *Ein deutscher General an der Ostfront: Die Briefe und Tagebücher des Gotthard Heinrici 1941/42*, Erfurt, 2001, pp. 58–61.

82   See Ullrich, *Hitler: Ascent 1889–1939*, pp. 657f.

83   Cohn, *Kein Recht, nirgends*, vol. 2, pp. 864 (entry for 30 Oct. 1940), 865 (entry for 2 Nov. 1940). On the deportation of Jews from Baden and Saarpfalz, see Friedländer, *The Years of Extermination*, p. 93; Gerwarth, *Reinhard Heydrich*, pp. 225f.; Longerich, *Politik der Vernichtung*, pp. 282f.

84   File note by Bormann, 2 Oct. 1940; BA Berlin-Lichterfelde, NS 6/772. See also Longerich, *Politik der Vernichtung*, pp. 283–5; Aly, *"Endlösung,"* pp. 181–3; Wildt, *Generation des Unbedingten*, pp. 533f.

85   Lammers to Schirach, 3 Dec. 1940; *Die Verfolgung und Ermordung der europäischen Juden*, vol. 3, doc. 123, pp. 332f.; see Browning, *The Origins of the Final Solution*, pp. 98f.

86 *Die Verfolgung und Ermordung der europäischen Juden*, vol. 3, doc. 125, p. 336. See Aly, "Endlösung," pp. 195–200; Longerich, *Politik der Vernichtung*, pp. 285f.; Browning, *The Origins of the Final Solution*, p. 102f.

87 *Die Verfolgung und Ermordung der europäischen Juden*, vol. 3, doc. 138, pp. 373–5 (at p. 373). See Aly, "Endlösung," p. 269; Longerich, *Politik der Vernichtung*, p. 287; Browning, *The Origins of the Final Solution*, pp. 103f.

88 *Die Verfolgung und Ermordung der europäischen Juden durch das nationalsozialistische Deutschland*, vol. 7, ed. Bert Hoppe and Hildrun Glass, Munich, 2011, doc. 1, pp. 113–17 (at p. 116). See Aly, "Endlösung," pp. 270–2; Longerich, *Politik der Vernichtung*, p. 290; Gerwarth, *Reinhard Heydrich*, p. 228.

89 Präg and Jacobmeyer (eds), *Das Diensttagebuch des deutschen Generalgouverneurs in Polen*, pp. 335 (entry for 25 March 1941), 386 (entry for 19 July 1941). See *Die Verfolgung und Ermordung der europäischen Juden*, vol. 4, doc. 260, p. 561, doc. 316, p. 683. In his pocket calendar, Frank wrote under the date 17 March 1941: '12:15 p.m. with the Führer in his apartment. He took me into his confidence about everything he is planning." Under 19 June 1941 Frank wrote: "With the Führer at noon. First meal . . . then a detailed extensive discussion." BA Koblenz, N 1110/10.

90 Reproduced in Gerd R. Ueberschär and Wolfram Wette (ed.), *Der deutsche Überfall auf die Sowjetunion: "Unternehmen Barbarossa" 1941*, expanded edition, Frankfurt am Main, 2011, pp. 249f. On the Heydrich–Wagner negotiations, see Gerwarth, *Reinhard Heydrich*, pp. 229–31; Wildt, *Generation des Unbedingten*, pp. 540–4. See above pp. 177f.

91 See Krausnick, *Hitlers Einsatzgruppen*, pp. 118f.; Longerich, *Politik der Vernichtung*, pp. 302–4.

92 For an overview, see Peter Klein (ed.), *Die Einsatzgruppen in der besetzten Sowjetunion 1941/42*, Berlin, 1997.

93 See Wildt, *Generation des Unbedingten*, pp. 546–53; Hilberg, *Die Vernichtung der europäischen Juden*, vol. 2, pp. 300–3; Klaus-Michael Mallmann, Andrej Angrick, Jürgen Matthäus and Martin Cüppers (eds), *Die "Ereignismeldungen UdSSR" 1941: Dokumente der Einsatzgruppen in der Sowjetunion*, vol. 1, Darmstadt, 2011, pp. 21–3 (introduction).

94 See Longerich, *Politik der Vernichtung*, pp. 310–12; Browning, *The Origins of the Final Solution*, pp. 226f.; Wildt, *Generation des Unbedingten*, pp. 553–8; *Die "Ereignismeldungen UdSSR" 1941*, pp. 23f.; Andrej Angrick, *Besatzungspolitik und Massenmord: Die Einsatzgruppe D in der südlichen Sowjetunion 1941–1943*, Hamburg, 2003, pp. 98–104.

95 Heydrich's instructions of 29 June and 2 July 1941 reproduced in Klein (ed.), *Einsatzgruppen*, pp. 318f., 323–8; *Die Verfolgung und Ermordung der europäischen Juden*, vol. 7, doc. 11, pp. 137f.; doc. 15, pp. 145–8.

96 See Longerich, *Politik der Vernichtung*, pp. 315f.; Wildt, *Generation des Unbedingten*, pp. 558–61; Klaus-Michael Mallmann, "Die Türöffner der 'Endlösung': Zur Genesis des Genozids," in Gerhard Paul and Klaus-Michael Mallmann (eds), *Die Gestapo im Zweiten Weltkrieg: "Heimatfront" und besetztes Europa*, Darmstadt, 2000, pp. 442, 449f.

97 So Browning, *The Origins of the Final Solution*, p. 245.

98 For more detail, see Christoph Dieckmann, *Deutsche Besatzungspolitik in Litauen 1941–1944*, Göttingen, 2011, vol. 1, pp. 299–391. On the pogroms and mass shootings in Lithuania, see also Ernst Klee, Willi Dressen and Volker Riess (eds), *"Schöne Zeiten": Judenmord aus der Sicht der Täter und Gaffer*, Frankfurt am Main, 1988, pp. 32–51; Cesarani, *Final Solution*, pp. 364–9.

99 See Thomas Sandkühler, *"Endlösung" in Galizien: Der Judenmord in Ostpolen und die Rettungsinitiativen von Berthold Beitz 1941–1944*, Bonn, 1996, pp. 113–22; Dieter Pohl, *Nationalsozialistische Judenverfolgung in Ostgalizien 1941–1944: Organisation und Durchführung eines staatlichen Massenverbrechens*, Munich, 1997, pp. 43–74. On the NKWD murders, see Bogdan Musial, *"Konterrevolutionäre Elemente sind zu erschiessen": Die Brutalisierung des deutsch-sowjetischen Krieges im Sommer 1941*, Munich, 2000.

100   See Frank Bajohr and Andrea Löw, "Tendenzen und Probleme der neueren Holocaust-Forschung: Eine Einführung," in idem, (eds), Der Holocaust: Ergebnisse und neue Fragen der Forschung, Frankfurt am Main, 2015, p. 18; Vincas Bartusevicius, Joachim Tauber and Wolfram Wette (eds), Holocaust in Litauen: Krieg, Judenmorde und Kollaboration, Cologne, Weimar and Vienna, 2003, pp. 7f.; Götz Aly, Europa gegen die Juden 1880–1945, Frankfurt am Main, 2017, pp. 10, 318f.

101   Goebbels, Tagebücher, part I, vol. 9, pp. 428 (entry for 6 July 1941), 433 (entry for 8 July 1941).

102   Meldungen aus dem Reich, vol. 7, p. 2536 (dated 17 July 1941). See Peter Longerich, "Davon haben wir nichts gewusst!" Die Deutschen und die Judenverfolgung 1933–1945, Munich, 2006, pp. 161f.

103   See Die "Ereignismeldungen UdSSR" 1941, pp. 7–17; Mallmann, "Die Türöffner der 'Endlösung,'" p. 449; Conze et al., Das Auswärtige Amt und die Vergangenheit, pp. 186–8.

104   See Die "Ereignismeldungen UdSSR" 1941, pp. 17f.

105   Peter Longerich, Heinrich Himmler: Biographie, Munich, 2008, p. 543. See Der Dienstkalender Heinrich Himmlers 1941/42, ed. Peter Witte et al., Hamburg, 1999, p. 181 (entry for 30 June 1941).

106   See Christopher Browning, Ordinary Men: Reserve Police Battalion 101 and the Final Solution in Poland, revised edition, London, 2017, pp. 11–15; Daniel Jonah Goldhagen, Hitler's Willing Executioners: Ordinary Germans and the Holocaust, New York, 1996, pp. 188–91.

107   See Longerich, Heinrich Himmler, p. 544; Gerwarth, Reinhard Heydrich, p. 238; Browning, The Origins of the Final Solution, p. 257.

108   Die "Ereignismeldungen UdSSR" 1941, p. 642 (dated 7. Oct. 1941). See Klee et al., (eds), "Schöne Zeiten," pp. 66–70; Longerich, Politik der Vernichtung, pp. 377–9; Pohl, Die Herrschaft der Wehrmacht, pp. 259–61; Wolfram Wette, Die Wehrmacht: Feindbilder, Vernichtungskrieg, Legenden, Frankfurt am Main, 2002, pp. 115–28.

109   Die "Ereignismeldungen UdSSR" 1941, p. 75 (dated 4 July 1941). See also the summary report by Stahlecker of 15 October 1941, in which he stressed "that the work with the Wehrmacht is generally good and in individual cases, for example with Tank Group 4 under General Hoepner, very close, almost heartfelt." See Klee et al., (eds), "Schöne Zeiten," p. 32.

110   Progress report from Nebe for the period between 23 June and 13 July 1941, 14 July 1941; reproduced in Klein (ed.), Die Einsatzgruppen, pp. 375–86 (at p. 380).

111   Die "Ereignismeldungen UdSSR" 1941, pp. 321f. (dated 20 Aug. 1941).

112   See Johannes Hürter, Hitlers Heerführer: Die deutschen Oberbefehlshaber im Krieg gegen die Sowjetunion 1941/42, Munich, 2007, pp. 517–35; Pohl, Die Herrschaft der Wehrmacht, pp. 243–54, 256–71; Christian Hartmann, Wehrmacht im Ostkrieg: Front und militärisches Hinterland 1941/42, Munich, 2009, pp. 653–61, 695–8.

113   Reproduced in Ueberschär and Wette (eds), Der deutsche Überfall auf die Sowjetunion, pp. 285f. See Hürter, Hitlers Heerführer, pp. 380–2. On the role of the 6th army, see Bernd Boll and Hans Safrian, "Auf dem Weg nach Stalingrad: Die 6. Armee 1941/42," in Hannes Heer and Klaus Naumann (eds), Vernichtungskrieg: Verbrechen der Wehrmacht, Hamburg, 1995, pp. 266–96.

114   Order by Rundstedt of 12 Oct. 1941; order by the Army High Command of 28 Oct. 1941; reproduced in Ueberschär and Wette (eds), Der deutsche Überfall auf die Sowjetunion, pp. 286f.; see Hürter, Hitlers Heerführer, pp. 583f.

115   Order by Hoth of 17 Nov. 1941; reproduced in Ueberschär and Wette (eds), Der deutsche Überfall auf die Sowjetunion, pp. 287–9 (at p. 288).

116   Walter Manoschek (ed.), "Es gibt nur eines für das Judentum: Vernichtung": Das Judenbild in deutschen Soldatenbriefen 1939–1944, Hamburg, 1995, pp. 41, 43, 49. See also Omer Bartov, Hitlers Wehrmacht: Soldaten, Fanatismus und die Brutalisierung des Krieges, Reinbek, 1995, pp. 239–49; Klaus Latzel, "Tourismus und Gewalt:

Kriegswahrnehmungen in Feldpostbriefen," in Heer and Naumann (eds), *Vernichtungskrieg*, pp. 447–59.

117 See Klee et al., (eds), *"Schöne Zeiten,"* pp. 7, 112; Hürter, *Hitlers Heerführer*, p. 530; Richard J. Evans, *The Third Reich at War, 1939–1945*, London, 2008, p. 224.
118 See Hürter, *Hitlers Heerführer*, p. 559; Hartmann, *Wehrmacht im Ostkrieg*, p. 659.
119 See Walter Manoschek, *"Serbien ist judenfrei": Militärische Besatzungspolitik und Judenvernichtung in Serbien 1941/42*, Munich, 1993.
120 See Longerich, *Politik der Vernichtung*, p. 418; Evans, *The Third Reich at War*, p. 239.
121 The so-called Jäger report of 1 Dec. 1941, reproduced in Klee et al., (eds), *"Schöne Zeiten,"* pp. 52–62 (at p. 59). On Jäger's actions in Lithuania, see Wolfram Wette, *Karl Jäger: Mörder der litauischen Juden*, Frankfurt am Main, 2011, pp. 87–154.
122 *Die "Ereignismeldungen UdSSR" 1941*, p. 744 (dated 3 Nov. 1941).
123 Cited in Aly, *"Endlösung,"* p. 329. See Wildt, *Generation des Unbedingten*, p. 613.
124 *Der Dienstkalender Heinrich Himmlers 1941/42*, p. 195 (entry for 15 Aug. 1941).
125 See *Das Auge des Dritten Reiches: Hitlers Kameramann und Fotograf Walter Frentz*, ed. Hans Georg Hiller von Gaertringen, Berlin, 2007, pp. 179–94 (Klaus Hesse's essay). Gerlach, on the other hand, suggests that Hitler saw the film. Christian Gerlach, *Kalkulierte Morde: Die deutsche Wirtschafts- und Vernichtungspolitik in Weissrussland 1941 bis 1944*, Hamburg, 1999, pp. 537f.
126 See Wildt, *Politik des Unbedingten*, pp. 576f.; Longerich, *Heinrich Himmler*, p. 552; Berger, *Experten der Vernichtung*, pp. 26f.
127 Kellner, *Tagebücher, 1939–1945*, vol. 1, p. 176 (entry for 28 July 1941). See also Klemperer, *Tagebücher, 1933–1941*, p. 660 (entry for 22 Aug. 1941): "There is general talk now about the killing of the mentally ill in institutions."
128 Reproduced in Klee (ed.), *Dokumente zur "Euthanasie,"* pp. 194–8 (at p. 197).
129 Kellner, *Tagebücher, 1939–1945*, vol. 1, p. 190 (entry for 20 Oct. 1941). See Ulrich von Hassell, *Vom andern Deutschland: Aus den nachgelassenen Tagebüchern 1938–1944*, Frankfurt am Main, 1964, p. 197 (entry for 20 Aug. 1941).
130 Goebbels, *Tagebücher*, part II, vol. 1, pp. 232 (entry for 14 Aug. 1941), 239 (entry for 15 Aug. 1941), 258 (entry for 19 Aug. 1941). See ibid., p. 397 (entry for 30 Nov. 1941): "The Führer is keeping a beady eye on the activities of Bishop Galen and does not miss a thing. If possible he wants to avoid an open confrontation with the Church during the war. He is waiting for the right time. But then he is determined to act severely."
131 See Klee, *"Euthanasie" im Dritten Reich*, pp. 386ff. On the end of the T4 action, see Winfried Süss, *Der "Volkskörper" im Krieg: Gesundheitspolitik, Gesundheitsverhältnisse und Krankenmord im nationalsozialistischen Deutschland 1939–1945*, Munich, 2003, pp. 127–51.
132 See Berger, *Die Experten der Vernichtung*, p. 34.
133 See Heinz Schneppen, *Walther Rauff: Organisator der Gaswagenmorde*, Berlin, 2011, pp. 21–5.
134 See Longerich, *Politik der Vernichtung*, pp. 442f., 451; Friedländer, *The Years of Extermination*, pp. 314–18.
135 See Longerich, *Heinrich Himmler*, pp. 565f.; Berger, *Experten der Vernichtung*, pp. 35f., 38 ff.; Johannes Sachslehner, *Zwei Millionen ham" ma erledigt: Odilo Globocnik—Hitlers Manager des Todes*, Vienna, Graz and Klagenfurt, 2014, pp. 186–93.
136 Browning, *The Origins of the Final Solution*, p. 314.
137 *Die Verfolgung und Ermordung der europäischen Juden*, vol. 3, doc. 196, pp. 496f. Under 31 July 1941 Göring's appointment diary read: "Carinhall . . . 6.15 Heydrich." IfZ München, ED 180/5.
138 See Longerich, *Politik der Vernichtung*, pp. 441f.; Friedländer, *The Years of Extermination*, pp. 237f.; Aly, *"Endlösung,"* p. 307; Ian Kershaw, *Fateful Choices: Ten Decisions that Changed the World 1940–1941*, London, 2007, p. 460.
139 Notes of Hitler's conversation with Kvaternik, 22 July 1941; *ADAP*, Series D, vol. 13, part 2, appendix III, p. 838; see Longerich, *Politik der Vernichtung*, p. 427.

140   See Kershaw, *Fateful Choices*, p. 460; Aly, *"Endlösung,"* pp. 308f.; Cesarani, *Final Solution*, p. 416.

141   Klemperer, *Tagebücher, 1933–1941*, p. 654 (entry for 23 July 1941). See also Goebbels' hate-mongering article in *Das Reich* on 20 July 1941 in which he threatened Jews with a "terrible reckoning": "The blow shall be struck pitilessly and mercilessly. Our global enemy will fall, and Europe will have peace." *Die Verfolgung und Ermordung der europäischen Juden*, vol. 3, doc. 193, pp. 486–9 (at p. 489).

142   Goebbels, *Tagebücher*, part II, vol. 1, p. 35 (entry for 9 July 1941). See ibid., pp. 50 (entry for 11 July 1941), 76f. (entry for 16 July 1941).

143   Friedländer, *The Years of Extermination*, pp. 205f. See Evans, *The Third Reich at War*, pp. 245f.; Jeffrey Herf, *The Jewish Enemy: Nazi Propaganda during World War II and the Holocaust*, Cambridge, MA, 2006, pp. 282ff.; Wolfgang Benz, "Judenvernichtung aus Notwehr? Die Legenden um Theodore N. Kaufman," in *Vierteljahrshefte für Zeitgeschichte*, 29 (1981), pp. 615–30.

144   Goebbels, *Tagebücher*, part II, vol. 1, pp. 168f. (entry for 3 Aug. 1941).

145   See ibid., pp. 271 (entry for 19 Aug. 1941), 328 (entry for 29 Aug. 1941), vol. 2, p. 155 (entry for 22 Oct. 1941).

146   *Meldungen aus dem Reich*, vol. 7, p. 2593 (dated 31 July 1941).

147   See the reports of the Bielefeld and Minden Security Service local offices dated 5 Aug., 25 Aug., 28 Aug. 1941; Kulka and Jäckel (eds), *Die Juden in den geheimen NS-Stimmungsberichten 1933–1945*, docs 561–563, pp. 452–4.

148   Goebbels, *Tagebücher*, part II, vol. 1, p. 218 (entry for 12 Aug. 1941). See the Propaganda Ministry's draft for Goebbels' report to the Führer on 17 Aug. 1941; *Die Verfolgung und Ermordung der europäischen Juden*, vol. 3, doc. 204, pp. 504–8.

149   Goebbels, *Tagebücher*, part II, vol. 1, pp. 265, 269 (entry for 19 Aug. 1941).

150   *Die Verfolgung und Ermordung der europäischen Juden*, vol. 3, doc. 212, pp. 522f. See Hilberg, *Die Vernichtung der europäischen Juden*, vol. 1, pp. 187f.; Friedländer, *The Years of Extermination*, pp. 251f.

151   Klemperer, *Tagebücher, 1933–1941*, pp. 663 (entry for 15 Sept. 1941), 671 (entry for 20 Sept. 1941).

152   Cohn, *Kein Recht, nirgends*, vol. 2, p. 978 (entry for 8 Sept. 1941).

153   Report from the Bielefeld Security Services local office, 13 Sept. 1941; Kulka and Jäckel (eds), *Die Juden in den geheimen NS-Stimmungsberichten 1933–1945*, doc. 566, p. 456. See ibid., docs 567, 568, 569, 571, pp. 456–60. On the reaction of the German people, see Marlies Steinert, *Hitlers Krieg und die Deutschen: Stimmung und Haltung der deutschen Bevölkerung im Zweiten Weltkrieg*, Düsseldorf and Vienna, 1970, pp. 239f.; Cesarani, *Final Solution*, pp. 421f.

154   Ruth Andreas-Friedrich, *Der Schattenmann: Tagebuchaufzeichnungen 1938–1945*, Frankfurt am Main, 1983, p. 82 (entry for 19 Sept. 1941). See also the telegrams of US diplomat Leland B. Morris, sent from Berlin on 30 September and 14 Octobr 1941; Frank Bajohr and Christoph Strupp (eds), *Fremde Blicke auf das "Dritte Reich": Berichte ausländischer Diplomaten über Herrschaft und Gesellschaft in Deutschland 1933–1945*, Göttingen, 2011, pp. 561f.; Mark Mazower, *Hitler's Empire: Nazi Rule in Occupied Europe*, London, 2008, pp. 372.

155   Cohn, *Kein Recht, nirgends*, vol. 2, p. 982 (entry for 19 Sept. 1941).

156   Hassell, *Vom andern Deutschland*, p. 211 (entry for 30 Nov. 1941). For further evidence, see Friedländer, *The Years of Extermination*, pp. 251–5. Longerich, *"Davon haben wir nichts gewusst!,"* pp. 175–9.

157   See Friedländer, *The Years of Extermination*, pp. 254f. David Bankier, *Die öffentliche Meinung im Hitler-Staat: Die "Endlösung" und die Deutschen. Eine Berichtigung*, Berlin, 1995, pp. 170–9.

158   Goebbels, *Tagebücher*, par II, vol. 2, p. 194 (entry for 28 Oct. 1941). See ibid., p. 188 (entry for 27 Oct. 1941).

159   Ibid., vol. 1, p. 278 (entry for 20 Aug. 1941). See Gerwarth, *Reinhard Heydrich*, p. 249.

160 See Goebbels, *Tagebücher*, part II, vol. 1, pp. 384 (entry for 9 Sept. 1941), 380f. (entry for 10 Sept. 1941); Rosenberg, *Die Tagebücher von 1934 bis 1944*, p. 408 (entry for 12 Sept. 1941). For a summary of Hitler's reasons for the decision, see Peter Longerich, *Hitler: Biographie*, Munich, 2015, pp. 812–14; Cesarani, *Final Solution*, pp. 422f.

161 Ernst Piper, *Alfred Rosenberg: Hitlers Chefideologe*, Munich, 2005, p. 583. See Kershaw, *Hitler 1936–1945: Nemesis*, pp. 478.

162 See Longerich, *Politik der Vernichtung*, pp. 431f.; Friedländer, *The Years of Extermination*, pp. 265f.

163 Frank Bajohr, "Hamburgs 'Führer': Zur Person und Tätigkeit des Hamburger NSDAP-Gauleiters Karl Kaufmann (1900–1969)," in *idem* and Joachim Szodrzynski (eds), *Hamburg in der NS-Zeit*, Hamburg, 1995, p. 81; see Götz Aly, *Hitlers Volksstaat: Raub, Rassenkrieg und nationaler Sozialismus*, Frankfurt am Main, 2005, pp. 139f.

164 *Der Dienstkalender Heinrich Himmlers 1941/42*, pp. 211 (entry for 16 Sept. 1941), 213 (entry for 17 Sept. 1941). See Kershaw, *Hitler 1936–1945: Nemesis*, pp. 479.

165 Peter Longerich (ed.), *Die Ermordung der europäischen Juden: Eine umfassende Dokumentation des Holocaust 1941–1945*, Munich, 1989, p. 157; *Die Verfolgung und Ermordung der europäischen Juden*, vol. 3, doc. 223, p. 542.

166 Goebbels, *Tagebücher*, part II, vol. 1, p. 485 (entry for 24 Sept. 1941).

167 See Browning, *The Origins of the Final Solution*, pp. 375–7.

168 Goebbels, *Tagebücher*, part II, vol. 2, pp. 194f. (entry for 28 Oct. 1941).

169 Ibid., p. 309 (entry for 18 Nov. 1941).

170 Ibid., p. 341 (entry for 22 Nov. 1941).

171 See Friedländer, *The Years of Extermination*, pp. 306f.; Hilberg, *Die Vernichtung der europäischen Juden*, vol. 2, pp. 476f., 494f.; Browning, *Die Entfesselung der "Endlösung,"* pp. 378–88; Benz, *Der Holocaust*, pp. 69f.

172 Klemperer, *Tagebücher, 1933–1941*, p. 680 (entry for 25 Oct. 1941); see ibid., p. 685 (entry for 9 Nov. 1941): "The deportations to Poland are continuing. Everywhere among Jews the deepest depression."

173 See Friedländer, *The Years of Extermination*, p. 308. On Cologne, see the report by the Swiss consul Franz-Rudolf von Weiss on 28 Nov. 1941; Bajohr and Strupp (eds), *Fremde Blicke auf das Dritte Reich,"* pp. 562f.

174 Helmuth James von Moltke, *Briefe an Freya 1939–1945*, ed. Beate Ruhm von Oppen, Munich, 1988, pp. 318 (dated 13 Nov. 1941), 308 (dated 21 Oct. 1941). See Ursula von Kardorff, *Berliner Aufzeichnungen 1942–1945*, new edition, ed. Peter Hartl, Munich, 1992, p. 44 (letter of 17 Oct. 1941): "All Jews up to the age of eighty are being transported to Poland. Tear-stained faces are all you see on the street. It is beyond all bounds, and it all cuts your heart. Especially because you can only helplessly watch and do so little."

175 On reactions to the deportations, see Frank Bajohr and Dieter Pohl, *Der Holocaust als offenes Geheimnis: Die Deutschen, die NS-Führung und die Alliierten*, Munich, 2006, pp. 47–50.

176 Kulka and Jäckel, *Die Juden in den geheimen NS-Stimmungsberichten 1933–1945*, doc. 604, p. 477. See also the report of the Security Service branch office in Bielefeld of 16 Dec. 1941; ibid., doc. 605, pp. 478f.

177 See Wette, *Karl Jäger*, pp. 124–6; Cohn, *Kein Recht, nirgends*, vol. 2, p. 1009 (editor's afterword).

178 *Der Dienstkalender Heinrich Himmlers*, p. 278 (entry for 30 Nov. 1941).

179 See Dieckmann, *Deutsche Besatzungspolitik in Litauen 1941–1944*, vol. 2, pp. 961–3 (at p. 962).

180 See Gerlach, *Kalkulierte Morde*, pp. 624f., 751–4.

181 Friedländer, *The Years of Extermination*, p. 272. For the following, see also ibid., pp. 272–6.

182 Domarus, *Hitler*, vol. 2, part 2, p. 1756.

183   *Monologe*, p. 99 (dated 21 Oct. 1941).

184   Ibid., p. 106 (dated 25 Oct. 1941).

185   Ibid., pp. 130f. (dated 5 Nov. 1941). In conversation with Goebbels in May 1943 Hitler reiterated: "World Jewry thinks it is standing before a global victory. But this global victory will not come. Instead there will be a global downfall." Goebbels, *Tagebücher*, part II, vol. 8, p. 290 (entry for 13 May 1943).

186   Domarus, *Hitler*, vol. 2, part 2, pp. 1771–81 (at pp. 1772f., 1774, 1779). For a transcript of the audio recordings of the speech, see *Die Verfolgung und Ermordung der europäischen Juden*, vol. 7, doc. 112, pp. 357–69.

187   Cited in Friedländer, *The Years of Extermination*, p. 276; see Herf, *The Jewish Enemy*, pp. 122ff.

188   Goebbels, *Tagebücher*, part II, vol. 2, pp. 304 (entry for 17 Nov. 1941), 352 (entry for 23 Nov. 1941).

189   Speech by Alfred Rosenberg on 18 Nov. 1941; reproduced in Rosenberg, *Die Tagebücher von 1934 bis 1941*, doc. 13, pp. 574–8 (at pp. 576f.). See Browning, *The Origins of the Final Solution*, p. 408; Piper, *Alfred Rosenberg*, pp. 545–7.

190   See *Der Dienstkalender Heinrich Himmlers 1941/42*, pp. 262 (entry for 15 Nov. 1941), 265 (entry for 16 Nov. 1942).

191   *ADAP*, Series D, vol. 13, part 2, no. 515, pp. 718–21 (at p. 720); see Browning, *The Origins of the Final Solution*, p. 406. On al-Husseini's reception, see David Motadel, *Für Prophet und Führer: Die Islamische Welt und das Dritte Reich*, Stuttgart, 2017, pp. 55ff.

192   For a reproduction of Heydrich's letter of invitation of 29 November 1941 and Göring's authorisation of 31 July 1941, see Norbert Kampe and Peter Klein (eds), *Die Wannsee-Konferenz am 20. Januar 1942: Dokumente, Forschungsstand, Kontroversen*, Cologne, Weimar and Vienna, 2013, pp. 32–4. See in addition Eichmann's note of 1 December 1941 in *Die Verfolgung und Ermordung der europäischen Juden durch das nationalsozialistische Deutschland*, vol. 9, ed. Klaus-Peter Friedrich, Munich, 2014, doc. 22, pp. 144f. See also Mark Roseman, *The Villa, the Lake, the Meeting: Wannsee and the Final Solution*, London, 2002, pp. 55–60; Peter Longerich, *Wannseekonferenz: Der Weg zur "Endlösung,"* Munich, 2016; pp. 18–20, 57–61.

193   For a reproduction of the second letter of invitation of 8 January 1942, see Kampe and Klein (eds), *Die Wannsee-Konferenz*, p. 38; see Roseman, *The Villa, the Lake, the Meeting*, pp. 63f.

194   Goebbels, *Tagebücher*, part II, vol. 2, pp. 498f. (entry for 13 Dec. 1941). The meeting with the Reichsleiter and Gauleiter took place between 4 and 7 p.m. in Hitler's apartment in the Old Chancellery building. See *Der Dienstkalender Heinrich Himmlers 1941/42*, p. 289 (entry for 12 Dec. 1941).

195   Goebbels, *Tagebücher*, part II, vol. 2, pp. 533f. (entry for 18 Dec. 1941).

196   *Der Dienstkalender Heinrich Himmlers 1941/42*, p. 294 (entry for 18 Dec. 1941).

197   Himmler to Gottlob Berger, chief of the SS head office, 28 July 1942; *Die Verfolgung und Ermordung der europäischen Juden*, vol. 7, doc. 242, p. 628.

198   Christian Gerlach, *Krieg, Ernährung, Völkermord: Forschungen zur deutschen Vernichtungspolitik im Zweiten Weltkrieg*, Hamburg, 1998, pp. 87, 123, 135, 160; idem, *Der Mord an den europäischen Juden: Tatsachen, Ereignisse, Dimensionen*, Munich, 2017, pp. 88–92. For a critique, see Longerich, *Politik der Vernichtung*, p. 467; Mommsen, *Das NS-Regime und die Auslöschung des Judentums in Europa*, pp. 185f.; Hermann Graml, "Ist Hitlers 'Anweisung' zur Ausrottung der europäischen Judenheit endlich gefunden? Zu den Thesen von Christian Gerlach," in *Jahrbuch für Antisemitismus-forschung*, 7 (1998), pp. 352–62.

199   Friedländer, *The Years of Extermination*, p. 287.

200   Präg and Jacobmeyer (eds), *Das Diensttagebuch des deutschen Generalgouverneurs in Polen*, pp. 457f. (entry for 16 Dec. 1941); *Die Verfolgung und Ermordung der europäischen Juden*, vol. 9, doc. 26, pp. 159f. See Longerich, *Politik der Vernichtung*, pp. 467f.; Dieter

Schenk, *Hans Frank: Hitlers Kronjurist und Generalgouverneur*, Frankfurt am Main, 2006, pp. 232–4; Mazower, *Hitler's Empire*, pp. 376f.; Roth, *Herrenmenschen*, pp. 203f.

201   Peter Klein, "Die Wannsee-Konferenz als Echo auf die gefallene Entscheidung zur Ermordung der europäischen Juden," in Kampe and Klein (eds), *Die Wannsee-Konferenz*, pp. 182–201 (at p. 198). After the war, like so many other functionaries in the Third Reich, Stuckart tried to shift all the blame for the Holocaust to Hitler: "There was something demonic inside this man." Stuckart's notes on Hitler's personality, *c.*1948; BA Koblenz, N 1292/6. On Stuckart see Christian Jasch, *Staatssekretär Wilhelm Stuckart und die Judenpolitik: Der Mythos von der sauberen Verwaltung*, Munich, 2012.

202   See Roseman, *The Villa, the Lake, the Meeting*, pp. 65–7; Longerich, *Wannseekonferenz*, pp. 62–91.

203   See Christian Mentel, "Das Protokoll der Wannsee-Konferenz: Überlieferung, Veröffentlichung und revisionistische Infragestellung," in Kampe and Klein (eds), *Die Wannsee-Konferenz*, pp. 116–38.

204   Reproduction of the protocol in Kampe and Klein (eds), *Die Wannsee-Konferenz*, pp. 40–54. On Heydrich's remarks, see Roseman, *The Villa, the Lake, the Meeting*, pp. 68–72; Cesarani, *Final Solution*, pp. 455–7; Longerich, *Wannseekonferenz*, pp. 93–115.

205   For an extensive discussion on this topic, see Gerwarth, *Reinhard Heydrich*, pp. 263–5; Roseman, *The Villa, the Lake, the Meeting*, pp. 79–83; Longerich, *Wannseekonferenz*, pp. 117–25; Beate Meyer, *"Jüdische Mischlinge": Rassenpolitik und Verfolgungserfahrung 1933–1945*, Hamburg, 1999, pp. 51f.

206   See Cesarani, *Eichmann*, p. 114; Gerwarth, *Reinhard Heydrich*, pp. 265f.; protocol of the 79th session of the Eichmann trial, 26 June 1961; Kampe and Klein (eds), *Die Wannsee-Konferenz*, pp. 95–100 (at p. 96).

207   Telegram from Eichmann to the state police leadership offices of 31 January 1942; Longerich (ed.), *Die Ermordung der europäischen Juden*, pp. 165–7.

208   Report on the meeting in the Reich Security Services headquarters, 9 March 1942; ibid., pp. 167–9.

209   See Longerich, *Politik der Vernichtung*, pp. 484–6.

210   Goebbels, *Tagebücher*, part II, vol. 3, p. 576 (entry for 29 March 1942).

211   See Gerlach, *Krieg, Ernährung, Völkermord*, p. 147. Goebbels was only informed on 6 March 1942 about the minutes of the Wannsee Conference; see Goebbels, *Tagebücher*, part II, vol. 3, p. 431 (entry for 7 March 1942).

212   *Monologe*, pp. 228f. (dated 25 Jan. 1942). See ibid., pp. 241 (dated 27 Jan. 1942), 245 (dated 31 Jan. 1942), 263 (dated 3–4 Feb. 1942), 293 (dated 22 Feb. 1942).

213   *Meldungen aus dem Reich*, vol. 9, p. 3235 (dated 2 Feb. 1942).

214   Goebbels, *Tagebücher*, part II, vol. 3, pp. 320f. (entry for 15 Feb. 1942). The propaganda minister emphasised: "This rabble must be completely uprooted; otherwise it will not be possible to bring peace to the world." Ibid., p. 335 (entry for 18 Feb. 1942). See ibid., pp. 425f. (entry for 6 March 1942): "The Jews are Europe's misfortune. They have to be removed in some fashion."

215   Ibid., p. 513 (entry for 20 March 1942).

216   See Berger, *Experten der Vernichtung*, pp. 51–5, 81–4; Dieter Pohl, *Von der "Judenpolitik" zum Judenmord: Der Distrikt Lublin des Generalgouvernements 1939–1944*, Frankfurt am Main, 1993, pp. 113f.

217   See *Der Dienstkalender Heinrich Himmlers 1941/42*, p. 380 (entry for 14 March 1942); Longerich, *Heinrich Himmler*, pp. 580f.

218   Goebbels, *Tagebücher*, part II, vol. 3, p. 561 (entry for 27 March 1942).

219   See Berger, *Experten der Vernichtung*, pp. 56, 64–72, 85.

220   See Conze et al., *Das Amt und die Vergangenheit*, pp. 189f.

221   See Longerich, *Politik der Vernichtung*, pp. 491–505; Evans, *The Third Reich at War*, pp. 273f.

222   Goebbels, *Tagebücher*, part II, vol. 4, p. 184 (entry for 27 April 1942). Two days later Goebbels commented on the "police report from the east," which the Security Service had sent him: "Swift work is being made of the Jews in all the occupied eastern territories. Tens of thousands are being dealt with, fulfilling the Führer's prophecy that Jewry would have to pay with the extermination of their race if they started a new world war." Ibid., p. 201 (entry for 29 April 1942).

223   See Regina Scheer, *Im Schatten der Sterne: Eine jüdische Widerstandsgruppe*, Berlin, 2004.

224   Goebbels, *Tagebücher*, part II, vol. 4, pp. 350f. (entry for 24 May 1942). See ibid., p. 405 (entry for 30 May 1942).

225   See Gerwarth, *Reinhard Heydrich*, pp. 251f., 275ff.; Lars Lüdicke, *Konstantin von Neurath: Eine politische Biographie*, Paderborn, 2014, pp. 538f.

226   See Gerwarth, *Reinhard Heydrich*, pp. 339–45; Evans, *The Third Reich at War*, pp. 277f.

227   Domarus, *Hitler*, vol. 2, part 2, p. 1891; see Goebbels, *Tagebücher*, part II, vol. 4, p. 488 (entry for 10 June 1942); Gerwarth, *Reinhard Heydrich*, pp. 337f.

228   Cited in Gerwarth, *Reinhard Heydrich*, p. 346.

229   Heinz Doering to his mother, 1 June 1942; Roth, *Herrenmenschen*, p. 227.

230   Longerich (ed.), *Die Ermordung der europäischen Juden*, pp. 201f.; *Die Verfolgung und Ermordung der europäischen Juden*, vol. 9, doc. 96, p. 337.

231   Czerniakow, *Im Warschauer Ghetto*, pp. 284f. (entries for 22 and 23 July 1942). After visiting Warsaw on 20 August 1942, Goebbels reported: "Here the Jewish question is being tackled in the right place, without sentimentality and any great scruples. That is the only way to solve the Jewish problem." *Tagebücher*, part II, vol. 5, p. 378 (entry for 21 Aug. 1942). On the deportations from the Warsaw ghetto to Treblinka, see Cesarani, *Final Solution*, pp. 484–503.

232   Heydrich spelled his Christian name both with and without a "t." See Gerwarth, *Reinhard Heydrich*, pp. 346f. and 431, n. 43.

233   See Evans, *The Third Reich at War*, p. 294. On the larger context, ibid., pp. 282–94; Yitzhak Arad, *Belzec, Sobibor, Treblinka: The Operation Reinhard Death Camps*, Bloomington, Indiana, 1999; Stephan Lehnstaedt, *Der Kern des Holocaust: Belzec, Sobibor, Treblinka und die Aktion Reinhardt*, Munich, 2017.

234   See Berger, *Experten der Vernichtung*, p. 9.

235   Among the extensive literature, see the overview by Sybille Steinbacher, *Auschwitz: Geschichte und Nachgeschichte*, Munich, 2004, pp. 15–18, 21–6, 70–6; see also Robert-Jan van Pelt and Deborah Dwork, *Auschwitz: Von 1270 bis heute*, Zurich and Munich, 1998, pp. 179ff.; Nikolaus Wachsmann, *KL: Die Geschichte der nationalsozialistischen Konzentrationslager*, Munich, 2016, pp. 239–41, 314–16, 348–72, 393–417, 528–34; Cesarani, *Final Solution*, pp. 520–33, 651–62.

236   *Rudolf Höss: Kommandant in Auschwitz: Autobiographische Aufzeichnungen*, ed. Martin Broszat, 4th edition, Munich, 1978, pp. 182f.; on the Himmler visit, see Wachsmann, *KL*, pp. 339–41.

237   Steinbacher, *Auschwitz*, pp. 77–81, 84–7, 105f. (figures). See Wolfgang Benz (ed.), *Dimensionen des Völkermords: Die Zahl der jüdischen Opfer des Nationalsozialismus*, Munich, 1991, pp. 15–17.

238   See, most recently, Andreas Engwerth and Susanne Kill (eds), *Sonderzüge in den Tod: Die Deportationen mit der Deutschen Reichsbahn*, Cologne, 2009.

239   In addition to the aforementioned study by Conze et al., *Das Auswärtige Amt und die Vergangenheit*, see Sebastian Weitkamp, *Braune Diplomaten: Horst Wagner und Eberhard von Thadden als Funktionäre der "Endlösung,"* Bonn, 2008; Christopher Browning, *The Final Solution and the German Foreign Office: A Study of Referat D III of Abteilung Deutschland, 1940–43*, New York, 1978.

240 Annegret Schüle, *Industrie und Holocaust: Topf & Söhne—Die Ofenbauer von Auschwitz*, Göttingen, 2010; Jürgen Kalthoff and Martin Werner, *Die Händler des Zyklon B. Tesch & Stabenow: Eine Firmengeschichte zwischen Hamburg und Auschwitz*, Hamburg, 1998.

241 See, most recently, Diarmuid Jeffreys, *Weltkonzern und Kriegskartell: Das zerstörerische Werk der IG-Farben*, Munich, 2011, pp. 411ff.

242 See Ernst Klee, *Auschwitz, die NS-Medizin und ihre Opfer*, Frankfurt am Main, 1997.

243 See Götz Aly, *Hitlers Volksstaat: Raub, Rassenkrieg und nationaler Sozialismus*, Frankfurt am Main, 2005.

244 Richard Walter Darré, Aufzeichnungen "Drehbühne," p. 157, BA Koblenz, N 1094 I/28.

245 Goebbels, *Tagebücher*, part II, vol. 5, p. 551 (entry for 22 Sept. 1942).

246 See Browning, *The Origins of the Final Solution*, p. 425; Aly, ;Endlösung," p. 396.

247 Bajohr and Löw, *Der Holocaust*, p. 18; see also Steinbacher, *Auschwitz*, p. 66.

248 See Ian Kershaw, "Hitler's Role in the 'Final Solution,'" in idem, *Hitler, the Germans, and the Final Solution*, New Haven and London, 2008, pp. 89–116 (at pp. 105f.).

249 Goebbels, *Tagebücher*, part II, vol. 3, p. 561 (entry for 27 March 1942). See Kershaw, "Hitler's Role in the 'Final Solution,'" p. 111. Longerich also repeatedly stresses Hitler's central role in the radicalisation of anti-Jewish policy up to the Holocaust (*Hitler*, pp. 705, 817f., 849f.).

250 Goebbels, *Tagebücher*, part II, vol. 7, p. 595 (entry for 20 March 1943).

251 Ibid., vol. 11, p. 403 (entry for 4 March 1944).

252 Hilberg, *Die Vernichtung der europäischen Juden*, vol. 3, p. 1081. See also Longerich, "Davon haben wir nichts gewusst!"; Bajohr and Pohl, *Der Holocaust als offenes Geheimnis*; Bernward Dörner, *Die Deutschen und der Holocaust: Was niemand wissen wollte, aber jeder wissen konnte*, Berlin, 2007; Nicholas Stargardt, *The German War: A Nation under Arms, 1939–45*, London, 2015, pp. 233–67 (Ch. 8: "The Shared Secret"). For a summary, see Herbert, *Geschichte Deutschlands im 20. Jahrhundert*, pp. 482–7.

253 See Felix Römer, *Kameraden: Die Wehrmacht von innen*, Munich and Zurich, 2012, pp. 442–62; Sönke Neitzel and Harald Welzer, *Soldaten: Protokolle vom Sterben, Töten und Kämpfen*, Frankfurt am Main, 2011, pp. 145–57.

254 Sophie Scholl and Fritz Hartnagel, *Damit wir uns nicht verlieren: Briefwechsel 1937–1943*, ed. Thomas Hartnagel, Frankfurt am Main, 2005, p. 368 (dated 26 June 1942).

255 Wilm Hosenfeld, *"Ich versuche jeden zu retten": Das Leben eines deutschen Offiziers in Briefen und Tagebüchern*, ed. Thomas Vogel, Munich, 2004, p. 630 (entry for 25 July 1942). See Roth, *Herrenmenschen*, pp. 227–30.

256 Balck's diary, entry for 16 Feb. 1944; BA-MA Freiburg, N 647/12.

257 Kellner, *Tagebücher, 1939–1945*, vol. 1, pp. 191f. (entry for 28 Oct. 1941). See the report of the Security Service main branch office in Erfurt of 30 April 1942 about rumours within the population: "Jews in their thousands were herded together and shot to death after they had first dug their own graves." Kulka and Jäckel (eds), *Die Juden in den geheimen NS-Stimmungsberichten 1933–1945*, doc. 628, p. 491. See also Longerich, "Davon haben wir nichts gewusst!," pp. 224–6.

258 Ursula Büttner, "Die deutsche Bevölkerung und die Judenverfolgung im Dritten Reich," in idem, (ed.), *Die Deutschen und die Judenverfolgung im Dritten Reich*, Hamburg, 1992, p. 78. Further evidence in Bajohr and Pohl, *Der Holocaust als offenes Geheimnis*, pp. 61f.; Dörner, *Die Deutschen und der Holocaust*, pp. 433–7.

259 Kellner, *Tagebücher, 1939–1945*, vol. 1, p. 311 (entry for 16 Sept. 1942). On 3 October 1943, Swiss consul Franz Rudolf von Weiss reported from Cologne: "It is increasingly emerging that, without exception, evacuated Jews are being killed." Bajohr and Strupp (eds), *Fremde Blicke auf das "Dritte Reich,"* p. 577.

260 See Volker Ullrich, "'Wir haben nichts gewusst'—Ein deutsches Trauma," in *1999: Zeitschrift für Sozialgeschichte des 20. und 21. Jahrhunderts*, 6 (1991), pp. 11–46 (at p. 31).

261   Herbert and Sibylle Obenaus (eds), *"Schreiben wie es wirklich war!": Aufzeichnungen Karl Dürkefäldens aus den Jahren 1933–1945*, Hanover, 1985, pp. 107, 109f., 117, 125, 126f. For an example of how regularly listening to the BBC could educate people, see also Wilhelm Muehlon, *Tagebuch der Kriegsjahre 1940–1944*, ed. Jens Heisterkamp, Dornach, 1992, pp. 590 (entry for 5 Oct. 1941), 646 (entry for 6 Dec. 1941), 786 (entry for 27 June 1942), 787 (entry for 29 June 1941). On the BBC's reporting of the "Final Solution," see Eric A. Johnson, *Terror: Gestapo, Juden und gewöhnliche Deutsche*, Berlin, 2001, pp. 472ff.

262   See Bernd C. Wagner, "Gerüchte, Wissen, Verdrängung: Die IG-Auschwitz und das Vernichtungslager Birkenau," in Norbert Frei, Sybille Steinbacher and Bernd C. Wagner (eds), *Ausbeutung, Vernichtung, Öffentlichkeit: Neue Studien zur nationalsozialistischen Lagerpolitik*, Munich, 2000, pp. 236ff.; on the spread of knowledge about Auschwitz, see Wachsmann, *KL*, p. 554.

263   Cited in Norbert Frei and Sybille Steinbacher, "Auschwitz: Die Stadt, das Lager und die Wahrnehmung der Deutschen," in Klaus-Dietmar Henke (ed.), *Auschwitz: Sechs Essays zu Geschehen und Vergegenwärtigung*, Dresden, 2001, p. 51.

264   Klemperer, *Tagebücher, 1942–1945*, pp. 47 (entry for 16 March 1942), 259 (entry for 16 Oct. 1942), 335 (entry for 27 Feb. 1943), 606 (entry for 24 Oct. 1944).

265   Erich Kuby, *Mein Krieg: Aufzeichnungen 1939–1944*, Munich, 1989, p. 164.

266   Kardorff, *Berliner Aufzeichnungen 1942 bis 1945*, p. 272 (entry for 27 Dec. 1944).

267   Peter Brückner, *Das Abseits als sicherer Ort: Kindheit und Jugend zwischen 1933 und 1945*, Berlin, 1980, p. 147.

8 Stalingrad and the Battle for Oil

1   Max Domarus, *Hitler: Reden und Proklamationen 1932–1945*, Munich, 1965, vol. 2, part 2, pp. 1848–51 (at p. 1850).

2   *Hitlers Tischgespräche im Führerhauptquartier*, ed. Henry Picker, Stuttgart, 1976, p. 323 (dated 21 May 1942).

3   Adolf Heusinger, *Befehl im Widerstreit: Schicksalsstunden der deutschen Armee 1923–1945*, Tübingen and Stuttgart, 1950, p. 186.

4   *Die Tagebücher, von Joseph Goebbels*, commissioned by the Institute for Contemporary History, with support from the State Archive of Russia, ed. Elke Fröhlich, *Part II: Diktate 1941–1945*, 15 vols, Munich, 1993–6; vol. 3, p. 577 (entry for 29 March 1942), vol. 4, p. 169 (entry for 25 April 1942).

5   Johannes Hürter, *Ein deutscher General an der Ostfront: Die Briefe und Tagebücher des Gotthard Heinrici 1941/42*, Erfurt, 2001, p. 152 (entry for 12 March 1942). On the figures, see Christian Hartmann, *Halder: Generalstabschef Hitlers 1938–1942*, 2nd edition, Paderborn, 2010, p. 313; Bernd Wegner, "Der Krieg gegen die Sowjetunion 1942/43," in: *Das Deutsche Reich und der Zweite Weltkrieg*, ed. Militärgeschichtliches Forschungsamt (Military Historical Research Office), vol. 6, Stuttgart, 1990, pp. 778f.

6   Franz Halder, *Kriegstagebuch, vol. 3: Der Russlandfeldzug bis zum Marsch auf Stalingrad*, ed. Hans-Adolf Jacobsen, Stuttgart, 1964, pp. 431f. (entry for 21 April 1942).

7   Goebbels, *Tagebücher*, part II, vol. 3, p. 511 (entry for 20 March 1942).

8   *Tischgespräche*, p. 452 (dated 22 July 1942); Adolf Hitler, *Monologe im Führerhauptquartier 1941–1944: Die Aufzeichnungen Heinrich Heims*, ed. Werner Jochmann, Hamburg, 1980, p. 366 (dated 22 Aug. 1942). See ibid., pp. 336 (dated 9 Aug. 1942), 363 (dated 24 Aug. 1942).

9   Franz Halder, *Hitler als Feldherr*, Munich, 1949, p. 49. See *Kriegstagebuch des Oberkommandos der Wehrmacht (Wehrmachtführungsstab)* (hereafter *KTB OKW*), *ed.* Percy Ernst Schramm, Munich, 1982, vol. 2, p. 314 (entry for 2 April 1942): "Given their industrial capacity, [the Führer] considers it unlikely that the Russians can raise any new armies worthy of the name."

10 Hartmann, *Halder*, p. 316. See also Ernst von Weizsäcker to his mother, 22 Feb. 1942: "The Russians are no longer considered capable of very much." BA Koblenz, N 1273/30. In a letter to Gauleiter Fritz Sauckel of 1 April 1942, the commander of the 2nd Tank Army, Rudolf Schmidt, evaluated the situation differently: "In general the Russians have not displayed any weakness. There will be many hard nuts to crack. But crack them we must." BA Koblenz, N 1582/3.

11 Adam Tooze, *The Wages of Destruction: The Making and Breaking of the Nazi Economy*, London, 2006, p. 588.

12 Gianluca Falanga, *Mussolinis Vorposten in Hitlers Reich: Italiens Politik in Berlin 1933–1945*, Berlin, 2008, p. 197.

13 See Halder, *Kriegstagebuch*, vol. 2, pp. 420f. (entry for 28 March 1942); *KTB OKW*, vol. 2, pp. 315f. (entry for 5 April 1942). See Helmuth Greiner's pocket calendar under 29 March 1942: "Führer issued directives for summer offensive yesterday." IfZ München, ED 100, vol. 76.

14 Walther Hubatsch (ed.), *Hitlers Weisungen für die Kriegsführung*, Munich, 1965, pp. 213–18 (at pp. 213f.).

15 *Der Prozess gegen die Hauptkriegsverbrecher vor dem internationalen Militärtribunal in Nürnberg*, 42 vols, Nuremberg, 1947–9 (hereafter *IMT*), vol. 7, p. 290 (Paulus' statement). See Thorsten Diedrich, *Paulus: Das Trauma von Stalingrad. Eine Biographie*, Paderborn, 2008, p. 214. In his table talk, Hitler also repeatedly stressed the importance of petroleum. See *Tischgespräche*, p. 274 (dated 9 May 1942); *Monologe*, p. 328 (dated 5 Aug. 1942): "Without oil we have no chance!"

16 Cited in *Das Deutsche Reich und der Zweite Weltkrieg*, vol. 6, p. 774 (Wegner's essay). In an interrogation on 17 June 1945, Keitel stated that the goals of the offensive were to "rip out the Donets Basin from Russia's arms-economic potential, interrupt the flow of oil transported on the Volga and seize the most important sources of oil." Wassili S. Christoforow, Wladimir G. Makarow and Matthias Uhl (eds), *Verhört: Die Befragungen deutscher Generale und Offiziere durch die sowjetischen Geheimdienste 1945–1952*, Berlin and Boston, 2015, p. 108.

17 See Olaf Groehler, *Bombenkrieg gegen Deutschland*, Berlin, 1990, pp. 32–6; Richard Overy, *The Bombing War: Europe 1939–1945*, London, 2013, pp. 286–9.

18 See Groehler, *Bombenkrieg gegen Deutschland*, pp. 37–42.

19 *Tischgespräche*, p. 173 (dated 1 April 1942); see ibid., p. 156 (dated 29 March 1942).

20 Goebbels, *Tagebücher*, part II, vol. 3, pp. 582f. (entry for 30 March 1942).

21 Ibid., vol. 4, p. 47 (entry for 4 Apr. 1942).

22 See Groehler, *Bombenkrieg gegen Deutschland*, pp. 48–59.

23 See ibid., pp. 65–7; Overy, *The Bombing War*, pp. 292f.

24 Goebbels, *Tagebücher*, part II, vol. 4, p. 183 (entry for 27 April 1942).

25 Friedrich Kellner, *"Vernebelt, verdunkelt sind alle Hirne": Tagebücher, 1939–1945*, ed. Sascha Feuchert et al., Göttingen, 2011, vol. 1, p. 267 (entry for 2 June 1942).

26 Thomas Mann, *An die gesittete Welt: Politische Schriften und Reden im Exil*, Frankfurt am Main, 1986, p. 525 (dated April 1942). See Thomas Mann, *Tagebücher, 1940–1943*, ed. Peter de Mendelssohn, Frankfurt am Main, 1982, p. 413 (entry for 4 April 1942).

27 See Overy, *The Bombing War*, p. 118; Richard J. Evans, *The Third Reich at War, 1939–1945*, London, 2008, p. 439. The phrase "Baedecker blitz" came from a statement by the deputy press spokesman of the German Foreign Ministry, Gustaf Braun von Stumm, who had told foreign journalists that all buildings given three stars by the famous guidebook would be attacked. Goebbels was furious that, "in the clumsiest fashion, the English have been handed an extremely useful catchphrase." Goebbels, *Tagebücher*, part II, vol. 4, p. 227 (entry for 3 May 1942).

28 Heinz Boberach (ed.), *Meldungen aus dem Reich: Die geheimen Lageberichte des Sicherheitsdienstes der SS 1938–1945*, Herrsching, 1984, vol. 10, p. 3567 (dated 2 April 1942); see ibid., p. 3787 (dated 4 June 1942).

29 Frank Bajohr and Christoph Strupp (eds), *Fremde Blicke auf das "Dritte Reich": Berichte ausländischer Diplomaten über Herrschaft und Gesellschaft in Deutschland 1933–1945*, Göttingen, 2011, pp. 564, 567.

30   *Meldungen aus dem Reich*, vol. 9, p. 3505 (entry for 23 March 1942).
31   Goebbels, *Tagebücher*, part II, vol. 4, p. 192 (entry for 28 April 1942).
32   Ibid., vol. 3, pp. 504f. (entry for 20 March 1942).
33   *Heeresadjutant bei Hitler 1938–1943: Aufzeichnungen des Majors Engel*, ed. Hildegard von Kotze, Stuttgart, 1974, p. 120 (entry for 21 April 1942). See *Tischgespräche*, p. 161 (dated 29 March 1942): "Today Hitler states clearly and unambiguously that everyone who was a lawyer was in his eyes either born defective or would become so."
34   Goebbels, *Tagebücher*, part II, vol. 4, pp. 174, 176 (entry for 26 April 1942).
35   Ibid., p. 186 (entry for 27 April 1942).
36   Domarus, *Hitler*, vol. 2, part 2, pp. 1865–77 (at p. 1877). At Hitler's behest, the head of the Reich chancellery, Lammers, had composed the directive and then given it to Göring. Lammers' notes of 1 May 1942 on the Reichsstag resolution of 26 April 1942; BA Berlin-Lichterfelde, R 43 II/958.
37   Goebbels, *Tagebücher*, part II, vol. 4, p. 188 (entry for 27 April 1942).
38   *Meldungen aus dem Reich*, vol. 10, pp. 3673 (dated 27 April 1942), 3686 (dated 30 April 1942).
39   Kellner, *Tagebücher, 1939–1945*, vol. 1, p. 242 (entry for 27 April 1942).
40   Goebbels, *Tagebücher*, part II, vol. 4, p. 188 (entry for 27 April 1942).
41   Galeazzo Ciano, *Tagebücher, 1939–1943*, Bern, 1946, p. 431 (entry for 29 April 1942).
42   Andreas Hillgruber (ed.), *Staatsmänner und Diplomaten bei Hitler: Vertrauliche Aufzeichnungen über Unterredungen mit Vertretern des Auslandes 1939–1941*, Frankfurt am Main, 1967, part 2, pp. 65–78 (at p. 70).
43   Ciano, *Tagebücher, 1939–1943*, p. 431 (entry for 30 April 1942).
44   Hillgruber (ed.), *Staatsmänner und Diplomaten bei Hitler*, part 2, pp. 79f.
45   Ciano, *Tagebücher, 1939–1943*, p. 432 (entry for 30 April 1942).
46   Goebbels, *Tagebücher*, part II, vol. 4, p. 223 (entry for 2 May 1942).
47   See ibid., p. 212 (entry for 30 April 1942); *Tischgespräche*, p. 248 (dated 29 April 1942).
48   Goebbels, *Tagebücher*, part II, vol. 4, p. 320 (entry for 20 May 1942). On 14 May 1942, Hans Frank noted in his diary: "A sublime start to the most decisive phase of Adolf Hitler's global struggle for the final liberation of the continent of culture." BA Koblenz, N 1110/2. See *Das Deutsche Reich und der Zweite Weltkrieg*, vol. 6, pp. 842f. (Wegner's essay).
49   *Tischgespräche*, p. 406 (dated 8 Aug. 1942); *Monologe*, p. 334 (dated 8 Aug. 1942). On the battle for Sevastopol, see *Das Deutsche Reich und der Zweite Weltkrieg*, vol. 6, pp. 845–50 (Wegner's essay).
50   See ibid., pp. 852–60 (Wegner's essay).
51   See Diedrich, *Paulus*, pp. 217–19. In a handwritten note of 25 May 1942, Halder congratulated Paulus on his "great triumph of arms"; BA-MA Freiburg, N 372/20. Five days earlier, Hitler's chief adjutant, Schmundt, had told Paulus that the Führer "appreciated the success of the 6th Army against an enemy far superior in numbers," BA-MA Freiburg, N 372/22.
52   Kellner, *Tagebücher, 1939–1945*, vol. 1, p. 262 (entry for 28 May 1942).
53   *Meldungen aus dem Reich*, vol. 10, pp. 3746 (dated 18 May 1942), 3752f. (dated 28 May 1942).
54   *Tischgespräche*, p. 345 (dated 1 June 1942).
55   See Walter Warlimont, *Im Hauptquartier der deutschen Wehrmacht 1939–1945: Grundlagen—Formen—Gestalten*, Frankfurt am Main and Bonn, 1964, p. 254; *KTB OKW*, vol. 2, p. 380 (entry for 24 May 1942).
56   Goebbels, *Tagebücher*, part II, vol. 4, pp. 354–64 (entry for 24 May 1942). Under 23 May 1942, Hans Frank noted in his pocket calendar: "Major speech by the Führer." BA Koblenz, N 1110/10.
57   The complete text of Hitler's speech of 30 May 1942 is reproduced in the appendix to *Tischgespräche*, pp. 491–502 (at pp. 491, 493).

58 Goebbels, *Tagebücher*, part II, vol. 4, pp. 401f. (entry for 30 May 1942), 418 (entry for 31 May 1942).

59 See Bernd Wegner, "Hitlers Besuch in Finnland: Das geheime Tonprotokoll seiner Unterredung mit Mannerheim am 4. Juni 1942," in *Vierteljahrshefte für Zeitgeschichte*, 41 (1993), pp. 117–38.

60 Goebbels, *Tagebücher*, part II, vol. 4, p. 489 (entry for 10 June 1942). See *Tischgespräche*, p. 356 (dated 5 June 1942): "[He said that] the Finns were really a heroic people."

61 See Nicolaus von Below, *Als Hitlers Adjutant 1937–45*, Mainz, 1980, p. 312; Domarus, *Hitler*, vol. 2, art 2, p. 1892.

62 Radio messages from Hitler to Rommel of 22 June 1942 and from Rommel to Hitler of 23 June 1942; BA-MA Freiburg, N 117/3.

63 See Ralf Georg Reuth, *Rommel: Das Ende einer Legende*, Munich and Zurich, 2004, p. 183.

64 Goebbels, *Tagebücher*, part II, vol. 4, pp. 582, 580 (entry for 23 June 1942).

65 Ibid., p. 580 (entry for 23 June 1942).

66 Cited in Reuth, *Rommel*, p. 186.

67 Goebbels, *Tagebücher*, part II, p. 590 (entry for 23 June 1942). See also *Tischgespräche*, pp. 372f. (dated 22 June 1942).

68 *Tischgespräche*, p. 391 (dated 28 June 1942).

69 See *Meldungen aus dem Reich*, vol. 10, p. 3923 (dated 9 July 1942). On the battle of El-Alamein, see Reinhard Stumpf, "Der Krieg im Mittelmeerraum 1942/43," in *Das Deutsche Reich und der Zweite Weltkrieg*, vol. 6, pp. 595–647; Gerhard L. Weinberg, *Eine Welt in Waffen: Die globale Geschichte des Zweiten Weltkriegs*, Stuttgart, 1995, pp. 386f.

70 Goebbels, *Tagebücher*, part II, vol. 4, pp. 482 (entry for 10 June 1942), 606f. (entry for 24 June 1942).

71 See *Das Deutsche Reich und der Zweite Weltkrieg*, vol. 6, pp. 868f. (Wegner's essay); Diedrich, *Paulus*, pp. 220–2; Rolf-Dieter Müller, *Der letzte deutsche Krieg 1939–1945*, Stuttgart, 2005, p. 166.

72 Hillgruber (ed.), *Staatsmänner und Diplomaten bei Hitler*, part 2, p. 89.

73 Gabriel Gorodetsky (ed.), *Die Maiski-Tagebücher: Ein Diplomat im Kampf gegen Hitler*, Munich, 2016, p. 653 (entry for 19 July 1942).

74 Halder, *Kriegstagebuch*, vol. 3, p. 472 (entry for 3 July 1942).

75 Fedor von Bock, *Zwischen Pflicht und Verweigerung: Das Kriegstagebuch*, ed. Klaus Gerbet, Munich, 1995, p. 470 (entry for 13 July 1942). See the pocket calendar of Ewald von Kleist, 15 July 1942; BA-MA Freiburg, N 354/21; *Das Deutsche Reich und der Zweite Weltkrieg*, vol. 6, pp. 878, 884f. (Wegner's essay); Diedrich, *Paulus*, p. 223.

76 Weichs, *Erinnerungen*, part 4, Bl. 4f.; BA-MA Freiburg, N 19/10.

77 See Franz W. Seidler and Dieter Zeigert, *Die Führerhauptquartiere: Anlagen und Planungen im Zweiten Weltkrieg*, Munich, 2000, pp. 221–5; Uwe Neumärker, Robert Conrad and Cord Woywodt, *Wolfsschanze: Hitlers Machtzentrale im Zweiten Weltkrieg*, 3rd edition, Berlin, 2007, p. 101.

78 See Albert Speer, *Erinnerungen: Mit einem Essay von Jochen Thies*, Frankfurt am Main and Berlin, 1993, p. 250; Paul Schmidt, *Statist auf diplomatischer Bühne 1923–45*, Bonn, 1950, p. 553; Goebbels, *Tagebücher*, part II, vol. 5, p. 348 (entry for 20 Aug. 1942). On the atmosphere in and around Hitler's headquarters in Vinnitsa, see Felix Hartlaub, *Im Sperrkreis: Aufzeichnungen aus dem Zweiten Weltkrieg*, ed. Geno Hartlaub, Reinbek bei Hamburg, 1955, pp. 113–26.

79 *Monologe*, p. 336 (dated 9 Aug. 1942). See Helmuth Greiner to his wife, 31 Aug. 1942: "The Führer is not handling the climate and the heat well. He very much wants to return to his bunker." IfZ München, ED 100, vol. 76. See also, Warlimont, *Im Hauptquartier*, p. 258; Hans-Joachim Neumann and Henrik Eberle, *War Hitler krank? Ein abschliessender Befund*, Bergisch Gladbach, 2009, p. 240.

80   Christa Schroeder to Johanna Nusser, 14 Aug. 1942; Schroeder, *Er war mein Chef: Aus dem Nachlass der Sekretärin von Adolf Hitler*, ed. Anton Joachimsthaler, 3rd edition, Munich and Vienna, 1985, p. 137.

81   See *Generalfeldmarschall Keitel, Verbrecher oder Offizier? Erinnerungen, Briefe, Dokumente des Chefs des OKW*, ed. Walter Görlitz, Berlin and Frankfurt am Main, 1961, p. 308; Henrik Eberle and Matthias Uhl (eds), *Das Buch Hitler*, Bergisch Gladbach, 2005, p. 171.

82   *KTB OKW*, vol. 2, p. 624 (entry for 22 Aug. 1942); see Warlimont, *Im Hauptquartier*, p. 260; Georg Meyer, *Adolf Heusinger: Dienst eines deutschen Soldaten*, Hamburg, Berlin and Bonn, 2001, pp. 187f.

83   Halder, *Kriegstagebuch*, vol. 3, p. 489 (entry for 23 July 1942).

84   Hubatsch (ed.), *Hitlers Weisungen für die Kriegführung*, pp. 227–30 (at p. 227).

85   See *Das Deutsche Reich und der Zweite Weltkrieg*, vol. 6, pp. 891f. (Wegner's essay); Diedrich, *Paulus*, pp. 224f.

86   See Halder, *Hitler als Feldherr*, p. 50.

87   *KTB OKW*, vol. 2, p. 449 (entry for 25 June 1942).

88   Ibid., p. 56. See *Das Deutsche Reich und der Zweite Weltkrieg*, vol. 6, p. 895 (Wegner's essay).

89   See Weinberg, *Eine Welt in Waffen*, pp. 453f.; Overy, *The Bombing War*, pp. 296f. Oleg Chlewnjuk, *Stalin: Eine Biographie*, Munich, 2015, pp. 355f.

90   Transcript of Hitler's meeting in the Reich Chancellery on 29 Sept. 1942; BA Koblenz, N 1340/496. See *KTB OKW*, vol. 2, pp. 609f. (entry for 19 Aug. 1942); *Das Deutsche Reich und der Zweite Weltkrieg*, vol. 6, pp. 895f. (Wegner's essay).

91   See Tooze, *The Wages of Destruction*, p. 585; *Das Deutsche Reich und der Zweite Weltkrieg*, vol. 6, pp. 942f. (Wegner's essay).

92   Goebbels, *Tagebücher*, part II, vol. 5, p. 354 (entry for 20 Aug. 1942). See Albert Speer, *Spandauer Tagebücher: Mit einem Vorwort von Joachim Fest*, Munich, 2002, pp. 85f. (entry for 26 March 1947), According to Speer, in August 1942 Hitler said that a further advance would be launched along the Caspian Sea towards Afghanistan and India: "Then the English will run out of oil. In two years we will have reached the Indian border. Twenty to thirty elite German divisions will be enough. Then the British Empire will collapse."

93   Goebbels, *Tagebücher*, part II, vol. 5, p. 372 (entry for 20 Aug. 1942).

94   Speer, *Erinnerungen*, p. 253; see Below, *Als Hitlers Adjutant*, p. 313.

95   See *KTB OKW*, vol. 2, p. 654 (entry for 29 Aug. 1942); Hartmann, *Halder*, p. 329; *Das Deutsche Reich und der Zweite Weltkrieg*, vol. 6, p. 940 (Wegner's essay).

96   Paulus to Gauleiter Florin, Düsseldorf, 5 Aug. 1942; BA-MA Freiburg, N 372/19. See also Paulus to General Ludz on 5 Aug. 1942: "What matters is to defeat the Russians in such a way that they will not be able to recover any time soon." BA-MA Freiburg, N 372/21.

97   See Diedrich, *Paulus*, pp. 228–31; *Das Deutsche Reich und der Zweite Weltkrieg*, vol. 6, pp. 964–6 (Wegner's essay).

98   Weichs, *Erinnerungen*, part 4, Bl. 13; BA-MA Freiburg, N 19/10.

99   See Catherine Merridale, *Ivan's War: The Red Army 1939–45*, London, 2005, pp. 134f.; Richard Overy, *Why the Allies Won*, 2nd edition, London, 2006, pp. 83.

100   See *Das Deutsche Reich und der Zweite Weltkrieg*, vol. 6, pp. 898–910 (Wegner's essay); Weinberg, *Eine Welt in Waffen*, pp. 461–3.

101   Goebbels, *Tagebücher*, part II, vol. 5, p. 361 (entry for 20 Aug. 1942).

102   Heusinger, *Befehl im Widerstreit*, pp. 200f. See Engel, *Heeresadjutant bei Hitler*, p. 125 (entry for 4 Sept. 1942). According to Engel, Hitler bellowed: "Mr. Halder, what do think you can tell me about the troops, you who also did nothing in the First World War but sit on your revolving chair, you who did not even earn a Wounded Badge Third Class?" In Halder's diary there is only the brief entry: "Major collision over the evaluation of the situation in Rshev, in which I pointed out the possibility of the troops deployed there burning out." *Kriegstagebuch*, vol. 3, p. 510 (entry for 24

Aug. 1942). On the clash between Hitler and Halder on 24 Aug. 1942, see Hartmann, *Halder*, pp. 330–2; Warlimont, *Im Hauptquartier*, p. 263.

103 Minutes of a conversation with A. Heusinger, 25 Jan. 1952; IfZ München ZS 69. On 29 Aug. 1942, Heusinger wrote to his wife that Halder had "really got into it" with Hitler but had "become afraid and backed off like a schoolboy hit by a blow." Meyer, *Adolf Heusinger*, p. 188.

104 See Engel, *Heeresadjutant bei Hitler*, p. 125 (entry for 4 Sept. 1942).

105 Halder, *Kriegstagebuch*, vol. 3, p. 513 (entry for 30 Aug. 1942).

106 See *KTB OKW*, vol. 2, pp. 658 (entry for 30 Aug. 1942), 662 (entry for 31 Aug. 1942); Below, *Als Hitlers Adjutant*, p. 314; Halder, *Kriegstagebuch*, vol. 3, pp. 513f. (entry for 31 Aug. 1942).

107 Keitel, *Verbrecher oder Offizier?*, p. 306; Luise Jodl, *Jenseits des Endes: Der Weg des Generaloberst Alfred Jodl*, Stuttgart, 1987, p. 66. See *KTB OKW*, vol. 2, pp. 690 (entry for 7 Sept. 1942), 695–7 (entry for 8 Sept. 1942); Warlimont, *Im Hauptquartier*, pp. 267f.; *Das Deutsche Reich und der Zweite Weltkrieg*, vol. 6, pp. 941f., 951 (Wegner's essay). During an interrogation on 17 June 1945, Jodl stated: "It came to a row between us such as had never before been seen in [Hitler's] headquarters." Christoforow, *el al.* (eds), *Verhört*, p. 122.

108 Engel, *Heeresadjutant bei Hitler*, p. 126 (entry for 8 Sept. 1942). See Halder, *Kriegstagebuch*, vol. 3, p. 519 (entry for 8 Sept. 1942): "Seriously foul mood." Pocket calendar of Helmuth Greiner, under 9 Sept. 1942: "Serious crisis of trust." IfZ München, ED 100/76.

109 Letter from Kluge dated 15 Sept. 1942; BA-MA Freiburg, MSg 2/11185.

110 *KTB OKW*, vol. 2, pp. 704f. (entry for 9 Sept. 1942). See Halder, *Kriegstagebuch*, vol. 3, p. 519 (entry for 9 Sept. 1942).

111 Johannes Hürter and Matthias Uhl, "Hitler in Vinnica: Ein neues Dokument zur Krise im September 1942," in *Vierteljahrshefte für Zeitgeschichte*, 63 (2015), pp. 581–639 (at p. 623). The stenographic minutes of Hitler's meeting with Keitel on 18 September 1942 (pp. 601–38) were discovered in the files of the Wehrmacht Supreme Command and is preserved in the central archive of the Defence Ministry of the Russian Federation.

112 See ibid., pp. 615, 617f.

113 Engel, *Heeresadjutant bei Hitler*, p. 127 (entry for 14 Sept. 1942).

114 See Warlimont, *Im Hauptquartier*, p. 268; Below, *Als Hitlers Adjutant*, p. 315; Speer, *Erinnerungen*, p. 253; Helmuth Greiner to his wife, 21 Sept. 1942: "Meals with the Führer . . . will for the time being be discontinued because the gentleman at the top has withdrawn into isolation." IfZ München, ED 100, vol. 76.

115 Halder, *Kriegstagebuch*, vol. 3, p. 520 (entry for 11 Sept. 1942); see Engel, *Heeresadjutant bei Hitler*, p. 127 (entry for 18 Sept. 1942).

116 *KTB OKW*, vol. 2, p. 697 (Warlimont's explications of Greiner's testimony of 8 Sept. 1942). According to Jodl's statement of 17 June 1945, the "state of alienation" persisted until late January 1943. Christoforow et al. (eds), *Verhört*, p. 122. See also Jodl's testimony of December 1945, "Streiflichter aus dem Führerhauptquartier," BA-MA Freiburg, N 69/44.

117 See Helmut Heiber (ed.), *Hitlers Lagebesprechungen: Die Protokollfragmente seiner militärischen Konferenzen 1942–1945*, Stuttgart, 1962, pp. 14–19 (introduction); Wolfram Pyta, *Hitler: Der Künstler als Politiker und Feldherr*, Munich, 2015, pp. 38–41, 332–4; Hürter and Uhl, *Hitler in Vinnica*, p. 588.

118 Engel, *Heeresadjutant bei Hitler*, pp. 126f. (entry for 8 Sept. 1942).

119 Ibid., p. 128 (entry for 18 Sept. 1942); see ibid., p. 125 (entry for 27 Aug. 1942).

120 Warlimont, *Im Hauptquartier*, p. 269; see *KTB OKW*, vol. 2, p. 702 (Warlimont's explications of Greiner's notes from 12 Aug. to 8 Sept. 1942). See also Warlimont's testimony of 5 October 1945: "Back then and later, I could not help but feel that Hitler, whose behaviour and appearance changed noticeably at the same time,

recognised for the first time at this juncture the possibility that he could lose the war." IfZ München, ZS 312.

121 Halder, *Kriegstagebuch*, vol. 3, p. 528 (entry for 24 Sept. 1942). See Halder, *Hitler als Feldherr*, pp. 52f.; Engel, *Heeresadjutant bei Hitler*, pp. 128 (entry for 24 Sept. 1942), 131 (entry for 19 Oct. 1942).

122 Kurt Zeitzler, "Zwei Jahre Generalstabschef des Heeres im Zweiten Weltkrieg," book 2, pp. 26–8; BA-MA Freiburg, N 63/19. See Helmuth Greiner to his wife, 27 Sept. 1942: "We will have to wait and see how [Zeitzler] gets on with his job. For the time being, he is the sort of man the Führer appreciates." IfZ München, ED 100, vol. 76.

123 Heusinger, *Befehl im Widerstreit*, p. 212; see Hartmann, *Halder*, pp. 337–9; Geoffrey P. Megargee, *Hitler und die Generäle: Das Ringen um die Führung der Wehrmacht 1939–1945*, Paderborn, 2006, pp. 222f.

124 Karl-Jesko von Puttkamer to Friedrich Hossbach, 21 Nov. 1942; BA-MA Freiburg, N 24/15.

125 Zeitzler, "Zwei Jahre Generalstabschef," book 2, p. 43; BA-MA Freiburg, N 63/19.

126 See Schmundt to Friedrich Paulus, 1 Oct. 1942; BA-MA Freiburg, N 372/22.

127 Engel, *Heeresadjutant bei Hitler*, p. 129 (entry for 30 Sept. 1942). See Megargee, *Hitler und die Generäle*, pp. 224–7; Hartmann, *Halder*, pp. 340f.; Hürter and Uhl, *Hitler in Vinnica*, pp. 598f.

128 The figure of 40,000 casualties most often cited in the literature is probably exaggerated. See Overy, *The Bombing War*, pp. 209–12.

129 *KTB OKW*, vol. 2, p. 669 (entry for 2 Sept. 1942). See Halder, *Kriegstagebuch*, vol. 3, p. 514 (entry for 31 Aug. 1942): "Stalingrad: male population to be destroyed, female to be transported away."

130 Goebbels, *Tagebücher*, part II, vol. 5, p. 463 (entry for 9 Sept. 1942); see ibid., pp. 482f. (entry for 12 Sept. 1942), 488f. (entry for 13 Sept. 1942).

131 See Halder, *Kriegstagebuch*, vol. 3, p. 521 (entry for 11 Sept. 1942).

132 Führer Directive of 13 Sept. 1942; *KTB OKW*, vol. 2, p. 1298. See Diedrich, *Paulus*, pp. 235f.; *Das Deutsche Reich und der Zweite Weltkrieg*, vol. 6, pp. 981–3 (Wegner's essay).

133 Jochen Hellbeck, *Die Stalingrad-Protokolle: Sowjetische Augenzeugen berichten aus der Schlacht*, Frankfurt am Main, 2012, p. 361.

134 See Diedrich, *Paulus*, pp. 238f.; Overy, *Why the Allies Won*, pp. 90–2; *Das Deutsche Reich und der Zweite Weltkrieg*, vol. 6, pp. 984–7 (Wegner's essay). For a comprehensive description of the battle of Stalingrad, see Manfred Kehrig, *Stalingrad: Analyse und Dokumentation einer Schlacht*, 3rd edition, Stuttgart, 1979; Antony Beevor, *Stalingrad*, London, 1998. For a critique of Beevor's account, see Hellbeck, *Die Stalingrad-Protokolle*, pp. 24f.

135 Goebbels, *Tagebücher*, part II, vol. 5, p. 555 (entry for 23 Sept. 1942).

136 *Meldungen aus dem Reich*, vol. 11, p. 4244 (dated 28 Sept. 1942).

137 Wilhelm Muehlon, *Tagebuch der Kriegsjahre 1940–1944*, ed. Jens Heisterkamp, Dornach, 1992, pp. 817 (entry for 4 Sept. 1942), 826 (entry for 26 Sept. 1942).

138 See Goebbels, *Tagebücher*, part II, p. 370 (entry for 20 Aug. 1942).

139 Ibid., pp. 594–7 (entry for 29 Sept. 1942).

140 See Bernhard R. Kroener, *Generaloberst Friedrich Fromm: Eine Biographie*, Paderborn, 2005, pp. 457–68.

141 Goebbels, *Tagebücher*, part II, vol. 6, p. 36 (entry for 1 Oct. 1942).

142 Domarus, *Hitler*, vol. 2, part 2, pp. 1913–24 (at pp. 1915, 1920, 1916). Ulrich von Hassell commented: "Unprecedentedly empty, rather halting speech by Hitler, lacking in moral depth, and probably aesthetically lower than ever before. Street urchin tone directed at the enemy." *Vom andern Deutschland: Aus den nachgelassenen Tagebüchern 1938–1944*, Frankfurt am Main, 1964, p. 254 (entry for 4 Oct. 1942).

143 Engel, *Heeresadjutant bei Hitler*, p. 129 (entry for 2 Oct. 1942). See Kurt Zeitzler, "Das Ringen um die grossen Entscheidungen im Zweiten Weltkrieg, vol. 1: Stalingrad— der Wendepunkt des Krieges," p. 18; BA-MA Freiburg, N 63/79.

144 Goebbels, *Tagebücher*, part II. vol. 6, pp. 42–53 (entry for 2 Oct. 1942) (at pp. 47, 49, 53).

145 *KTB OKW*, vol. 2, p. 67.

146 Hillgruber (ed.), *Staatsmänner und Diplomaten bei Hitler*, part 2, pp. 127–30 (at pp. 129, 128).

147 *KTB OKW*, vol. 2, p. 864 (entry for 26 Oct. 1942). See Diedrich, *Paulus*, pp. 242f.; *Das Deutsche Reich und der Zweite Weltkrieg*, vol. 6, pp. 994f. (Wegner's essay).

148 *Meldungen aus dem Reich*, vol. 11, p. 4366 (dated 26 Oct. 1942).

149 Ibid., pp. 4366f. (dated 26 Oct. 1942). See Kellner, *Tagebücher, 1939–1945*, vol. 1, p. 320 (entry for 22 Oct. 1942).

150 See Werner Rahn, "Der Krieg im Pazifik," in *Das Deutsche Reich und der Zweite Weltkrieg*, vol. 6, pp. 251–71.

151 Goebbels, *Tagebücher*, part II, vol. 6, pp. 35f. (entry for 1 Oct. 1942).

152 Ibid., p. 65 (entry for 4 Oct. 1942).

153 Domarus, *Hitler*, vol. 2, part 2, p. 1925. See Kellner, *Tagebücher, 1939–1945*, vol. 1, p. 337 (entry for 4 Nov. 1942); Reuth, *Rommel*, pp. 186f.

154 Quoted in David Irving, *Hitler und seine Feldherren* Frankfurt am Main, Berlin and Vienna, 1975, p. 431. On the British counter-offensive at El Alamein, see *Das Deutsche Reich und der Zweite Weltkrieg*, vol. 6, op. 688–709 (Stumpf's essay).

155 Goebbels, *Tagebücher*, part II, vol. 6, pp. 230f. (entry for 4 Nov. 1942).

156 Domarus, *Hitler*, vol. 2, part 2, p. 1931. The telegram reached Rommel at 1:30 p.m. on 3 November.

157 See *KTB OKW*, vol. 2, pp. 111, 894–8 (entry for 3 Nov. 1942 with explications from Warlimont); Warlimont, *Im Hauptquartier*, pp. 280f.; Helmuth Greiner's pocket calendar, under 3 Nov. and 5 Nov. 1942; IfZ München, ED 100, vol. 76.

158 See Below, *Als Hitlers Adjutant*, p. 321; Neumärker et al., *Wolfsschanze*, p. 104.

159 See Below, *Als Hitlers Adjutant*, p. 321; *KTB OKW*, vol. 2, pp. 916 (entry for 7 Nov. 1942), 921f. (entry for 8 Nov. 1942). On the Allied landing in French north Africa, Operation Torch, see *Das Deutsche Reich und der Zweite Weltkrieg*, vol. 6, pp. 710–20 (Stumpf's essay).

160 Speer's testimony about his activities as minister, Nuremberg, 12 Aug. 1946, p. 5; BA Koblenz, N 1340/84.

161 Engel, *Heeresadjutant bei Hitler*, p. 134 (entry for 8 Nov. 1942). See Below, *Als Hitlers Adjutant*, p. 322.

162 See Goebbels, *Tagebücher*, part II, vol. 6, pp. 257f. On Himmler's participation, see *Der Dienstkalender Heinrich Himmlers 1941/42*, ed. Peter Witte et al., Hamburg, 1999, p. 608 (entry for 8 Nov. 1942).

163 Goebbels, *Tagebücher*, part II, p. 259 (entry for 9 Nov. 1942).

164 Muehlon, *Tagebuch der Kriegsjahre 1940–1944*, p. 853 (entry for 8 Nov. 1942).

165 Domarus, *Hitler*, vol. 2, part 2, pp. 1933–44 (at pp. 1943, 1935, 1938).

166 Engel, *Heeresadjutant bei Hitler*, p. 134 (entry for 10 Nov. 1942).

167 *Meldungen aus dem Reich*, vol. 12, p. 4453 (dated 12 Nov. 1942).

168 Ciano, *Tagebücher, 1939–1943*, p. 487 (entry for 9 Nov. 1942). See Hillgruber (ed.), *Staatsmänner und Diplomaten bei Hitler*, part 2, pp. 131–5.

169 Hillgruber (ed.), *Staatsmänner und Diplomaten bei Hitler*, part 2, pp. 137–47 (at p. 137). See Ciano, *Tagebücher, 1939–1943*, p. 487 (entry for 10 Nov. 1942); Schmidt, *Statist auf diplomatischer Bühne*, p. 564: "This conference was purely about receiving orders."

170 Domarus, *Hitler*, vol. 2, part 2, pp. 1945–7 (at p. 1946).

171 Goebbels, *Tagebücher*, part II, vol. 6, p. 318 (entry for 23 Nov. 1942).

172 Rommel's diaries, entry for 28 Nov. 1942; BA-MA Freiburg, N 117/74. See *KTB OKW*, vol. 2, pp. 112f. In January 1943, Hitler again communicated to Rommel's emissary,

Lieutenant Alfred-Ingmar Berndt, "the significance he attached to the Africa bridge-head and how important he considered it that [the bridgehead] be held as long and as fully as possible." Rommel's diaries, entry for 12 Jan. 1943; BA-MA Freiburg, N 117/74.

173 Goebbels, *Tagebücher*, part II, vol. 6, p. 303 (entry for 16 Nov. 1942).

174 See Below, *Als Hitlers Adjutant*, pp. 322f.; Speer, *Erinnerungen*, p. 261; *KTB OKW*, vol. 2, p. 988 (entry for 19 Nov. 1942). In his memoirs (Bl. 31) Weichs called 19 November 1942 "the blackest day of the war" for the Wehrmacht, "because on that day the enemy seized the initiative." BA-MA Freiburg, N 19/10.

175 See Overy, *Why the Allies Won*, pp. 87, 96; Weinberg, *Eine Welt in Waffen*, p. 460.

176 See Diedrich, *Paulus*, pp. 247–9, 251f.; Overy, *Why the Allies Won*, pp. 96–7.

177 Goebbels, *Tagebücher*, part II, vol. 6, p. 317 (entry for 23 Nov. 1942).

178 Engel, *Heeresadjutant bei Hitler*, p. 138 (entry for 21 Nov. 1942). See Diedrich, *Paulus*, pp. 249–51; *Das Deutsche Reich und der Zweite Weltkrieg*, vol. 6, pp. 1024f. (Wegner's essay).

179 See Below, *Als Hitlers Adjutant*, pp. 323f.

180 Zeitzler, "Das Ringen um die grossen Entscheidungen," vol. 1, pp. 35–9; BA-MA Freiburg, N 63/79.

181 Diedrich, *Paulus*, p. 254; Kehrig, *Stalingrad*, p. 560 (doc. 10).

182 Engel, *Heeresadjutant bei Hitler*, p. 139 (entry for 25 Nov. 1942). See also Speer, *Erinnerungen*, p. 262; Diedrich, *Paulus*, p. 254; Kehrig, *Stalingrad*, p. 220.

183 Kehrig, *Stalingrad*, p. 564 (doc. 14). See Diedrich, *Paulus*, pp. 257f.; *Das Deutsche Reich und der Zweite Weltkrieg*, vol. 6, pp. 1031f. (Wegner's essay).

184 Kehrig, *Stalingrad*, p. 570 (doc. 18).

185 Kehrig, *Stalingrad*, p. 572 (doc. 20). See Diedrich, *Paulus*, p. 259; *Das Deutsche Reich und der Zweite Weltkrieg*, vol. 6, p. 1035 (Wegner's essay).

186 Kehrig, *Stalingrad*, p. 277.

187 See Jens Ebert (ed.), *Feldpostbriefe aus Stalingrad*, Göttingen, 2003, pp. 81 (dated 28 Nov. 1942), 88 (dated 29 Nov. 1942), 116 (dated 7 Dec. 1942), 125 (dated 9 Dec. 1942), 130 (dated 10 Dec. 1942).

188 Helmuth Greiner's pocket calendar, under 9 Dec., 14 Dec., 16 Dec. 1942; IfZ München, ED 100, vol. 76.

189 See *Das Deutsche Reich und der Zweite Weltkrieg*, vol. 6, pp. 1040–2 (Wegner's essay); Diedrich, *Paulus*, pp. 264f.

190 See Zeitzler, "Das Ringen um die grossen Entscheidungen," vol. 1, pp. 63–5; BA-MA Freiburg, N 63/79; Engel, *Heeresadjutant bei Hitler*, pp. 140f. (entries for 18 and 19 Dec. 1942); Diedrich, *Paulus*, pp. 266f.

191 Engel, *Heeresadjutant bei Hitler*, p. 142 (entry for 22 Dec. 1942). In a letter of 22 December 1942, Heusinger wrote of a "crisis the scope of which we haven't previously experienced"; Meyer, *Adolf Heusinger*, p. 200. See Speer, *Erinnerungen*, p. 263: "The mood is becoming ever gloomier, people's faces are frozen like masks, and we often stand together in silence."

192 See Ciano, *Tagebücher, 1939–1943*, p. 500 (entry for 18 Dec. 1942).

193 Hillgruber (ed.), *Staatsmänner und Diplomaten bei Hitler*, vol. 2, pp. 160–81, 192–6 (at pp. 163, 165, 169f., 171, 193).

194 Schmidt, *Statist auf diplomatischer Bühne*, p. 566.

195 Ebert (ed.), *Feldpostbriefe aus Stalingrad*, p. 163 (dated 17 Dec. 1942). See also Paulus to his wife, 8 Jan. 1943: "There is a soldiers' song that runs: 'Everything goes by, everything does pass / After every December, another May comes at last.'" BA-MA Freiburg, N 372/35.

196 Ebert (ed.), *Feldpostbriefe aus Stalingrad*, pp. 178 (dated 21 Dec. 1942), 241f. (dated 31 Dec. 1942).

197 *Meldungen aus dem Reich*, vol. 12, p. 4576 (dated 17 Dec. 1942).

198 See Wolfram Wette, "Das Massensterben als 'Heldenepos': Stalingrad in der NS-Propaganda," in *idem*, and Gerd R. Ueberschär (eds), *Stalingrad: Mythos und Wirklichkeit einer Schlacht*, Frankfurt am Main, 1992, pp. 45–7.

199 See Ebert (ed.), *Feldpostbriefe aus Stalingrad*, pp. 103 (dated 4 Dec. 1942), 107 (dated 4 Dec. 1942), 118 (dated 7 Dec. 1942).

200 Goebbels, *Tagebücher*, part II. vol. 6, pp. 341f. (dated 27 Nov. 1942).

201 Domarus, *Hitler*, vol. 2, part 2, pp. 1967–71 (at pp. 1967, 1968, 1970). One Gauleiter reported: "Thanks to the open, clear and confident language, the Führer's New Year's greetings to the Wehrmacht and the German people did not fail to have their intended effect." Extracts from reports from the Gaue, 20 Dec. 1942–9 Jan. 1943; BA Berlin-Lichterfelde, NS 6/414.

202 Diedrich, *Paulus*, pp. 274f.

203 See ibid., pp. 275f. Facsimile of the leaflets in Wette and Ueberschär (eds), *Stalingrad*, pp. 30f.

204 Diedrich, *Paulus*, p. 279.

205 See ibid., pp. 279–81; *Das Deutsche Reich und der Zweite Weltkrieg*, vol. 6, pp. 1056f. (Wegner's essay).

206 Hillgruber (ed.), *Staatsmänner und Diplomaten bei Hitler*, part 2, pp. 197–208 (at p. 200).

207 See Diedrich, *Paulus*, pp. 282f.

208 Zeitzler, "Das Ringen um die grossen Entscheidungen," vol. 1, pp. 86f.; BA-MA Freiburg, N 63/79.

209 Wette, "Das Massensterben als 'Heldenepos,'" in *idem* and Ueberschär (eds), *Stalingrad*, p. 47.

210 *Meldungen aus dem Reich*, vol. 12, pp. 4694 (dated 18 Jan. 1943), 4707 (dated 21 Jan. 1943).

211 Goebbels, *Tagebücher*, part II, vol. 7, pp. 153f. (entry for 21 Jan. 1943).

212 Ibid., pp. 162, 175 (entry for 23 Jan. 1943).

213 Paulus to his wife, 16 Jan. 1943; BA-MA Freiburg, N 372/35.

214 Diedrich, *Paulus*, p. 285. See also Helmuth Greiner's pocket calendar under 23 January 1943: "Order to the 6th Army to hold out. Paulus's answer: Command will be obeyed. God bless Germany." IfZ München, ED 100, vol. 76.

215 Diedrich, *Paulus*, p. 289.

216 Goebbels, *Tagebücher*, part II, vol. 7, p. 152 (entry for 21 Jan. 1943); see ibid., p. 173 (entry for 23 Jan. 1943).

217 Helmut Heiber (ed.), *Goebbels-Reden. Vol. 2: 1939–1945*, Düsseldorf, 1972, pp. 158–71 (at p. 170).

218 Domarus, *Hitler*, vol. 2, part 2, pp. 1976–80 (at p. 1979).

219 See Pyta's analysis of Göring's speech; *Hitler*, pp. 433–5; Nicholas Stargardt, *The German War: A Nation under Arms, 1939–45*, London, 2015, pp. 329f.

220 Habicht's diary, entry for 31 Jan. 1943; Felix Römer, *Die narzisstische Volksgemeinschaft: Theodor Habichts Kampf 1914 bis 1944*, Frankfurt am Main, 2017, p. 315.

221 Diedrich, *Paulus*, p. 289.

222 See ibid., p. 290; Wette, "Das Massensterben als 'Heldenepos,'" in *idem* and Ueberschär (eds), *Stalingrad*, pp. 58f. On Paulus's promotion to colonel-general on 30 Nov. 1942, see Paulus to his wife, 7 Dec. 1942; BA-MA Freiburg, N 372/35.

223 On the details, see Hellbeck, *Die Stalingrad-Protokolle*, pp. 272–316; Diedrich, *Paulus*, pp. 290–2.

224 See ibid., pp. 293f.

225 Heiber (ed.), *Hitlers Lagebesprechungen*, pp. 120–36 (at p. 135). See Engel, *Heeresadjutant bei Hitler*, p. 143 (entry for 1 Feb. 1943).

226 Heiber (ed.), *Hitlers Lagebesprechungen*, p. 126.

227 Reproduced in Wette, "Das Massensterben als 'Heldenepos,'" in *idem* and Ueberschär (eds), *Stalingrad*, p. 54.

228 Goebbels, *Tagebücher*, part II, vol. 7, pp. 253f. (entry for 3 Feb. 1943), 255 (entry for 4 Feb. 1943). See Wette, "Das Massensterben als 'Heldenepos,'" in *idem* and Ueberschär (eds), *Stalingrad*, p. 55.

229 Goebbels, *Tagebücher*, part II, vol. 7, p. 256 (entry for 4 Feb. 1943).

230   Lore Walb, *Ich, die Alte—ich, die Junge: Konfrontation mit meinen Tagebüchern 1933–1945*, Berlin, 1997, pp. 260f. (entry for 3 Feb. 1943).

231   *Meldungen aus dem Reich*, vol. 12, pp. 475of. (dated 4 Feb. 1943). On the reactions, see Evans, *The Third Reich at War*, pp. 420–3 ; Stargardt, *Der deutsche Krieg*, pp. 332f.

232   Extracts from reports from the Gaue, 31 Jan.–12. Feb. 1943; BA Berlin-Lichterfelde, NS 6/414.

233   See extracts from the reports from the Gaue, 14– 20 Feb. 1943: 'People find it bitter and embarrassing that the Führer's prophesies concerning Stalingrad bore so little resemblance to the real events that followed." BA Berlin-Lichterfelde, NS 6/414.

234   Hassell, *Vom andern Deutschland*, p. 260 (entry for 14 Feb. 1943).

235   Goebbels, *Tagebücher*, part II, vol. 7, p. 326 (entry for 12 Feb. 1943). See ibid., p. 228 (entry for 31 Jan. 1943). For further examples of remarks critical of Hitler, see Ian Kershaw, *The "Hitler Myth": Image and Reality in the Third Reich*, Oxford, 1987, pp. 193f.

236   Speer, *Erinnerungen*, p. 271.

237   Cited in Evans, *The Third Reich at War*, p. 424.

238   Muehlon, *Tagebuch der Kriegsjahre 1940–1944*, p. 926 (entry for 1 Feb. 1943).

239   Mann, *Tagebücher, 1940–1943*, p. 533 (entry for 5 Feb. 1943). For the text of his congratulations, see ibid., p. 1082.

240   Victor Klemperer, *Ich will Zeugnis ablegen bis zum letzten: Tagebücher*, vol. 2: 1942–1945, ed. Walter Nowojski with Hadwig Klemperer, Berlin, 1995, p. 326 (entry for 5 Feb. 1943).

241   See Barbara Beuys, *Sophie Scholl: Biographie*, Munich, 2010, pp. 425ff.; Barbara Ellermeier, *Hans Scholl: Biographie*, Hamburg, 2012, pp. 342ff.; Detlef Bald, *Die Weisse Rose: Von der Front in den Widerstand*, Berlin, 2003, pp. 146ff.; Miriam Gebhardt, *Die Weisse Rose: Wie aus ganz normalen Deutschen Widerstandskämpfer wurden*, Munich, 2017. The text of the sixth leaflet is reproduced in Ulrich Chaussy and Gerd R. Ueberschär, *"Es lebe die Freiheit!" Die Geschichte der "Weissen Rose" und ihrer Mitglieder in Dokumenten und Berichten*, Frankfurt am Main, 2013, pp. 42–4.

242   Kershaw, *The "Hitler Myth,"* p. 195.

243   Hans Zurlinden, Munich, to Minister Pierre Bonna, Bern, 22 Apr. 1943; Bajohr and Strupp (eds), *Fremde Blicke auf das "Dritte Reich,"* p. 571.

244   Kellner, *Tagebücher, 1939–1945*, vol. 1, p. 395 (entry for 4 Feb. 1943).

245   Goebbels, *Tagebücher*, part II, vol. 7, pp. 285–97 (at pp. 285, 291, 293, 296).

246   See Below, *Als Hitlers Adjutant*, pp. 329f.

247   See Kurt Zeitzler, "Das Ringen um die grossen Entscheidungen im Zweiten Weltkrieg, vol. 2: Abwehrschlachten in Russland nach dem Wendepunkt des Krieges," pp. 26–8; BA-MA Freiburg, N 63/80.

248   See *Das Deutsche Reich und der Zweite Weltkrieg*, vol. 6, pp. 1064–8 (Wegner's essay).

249   See the daily notes by Generaloberst von Weichs, 18 Jan.–10 Feb. 1943; BA-MA Freiburg, N 19/5.

250   See *Das Deutsche Reich und der Zweite Weltkrieg*, vol. 6, pp. 1089–91 (Wegner's essay).

251   See Erich von Manstein, *Verlorene Siege*, Bonn, 1955, pp. 437–44; Engel, *Heeresadjutant bei Hitler*, p. 144 (entry for 7 Feb. 1943); Below, *Als Hitlers Adjutant*, p. 329; Pyta, *Hitler*, pp. 444f.

252   See *Das Deutsche Reich und der Zweite Weltkrieg*, vol. 6, pp. 1073–5 (Wegner's essay); Weinberg, *Eine Welt in Waffen*, p. 494.

253   *Meldungen aus dem Reich*, vol. 12, p. 4821 (dated 18 Feb. 1943).

254   Zeitzler, "Das Ringen um die grossen Entscheidungen," vol. 2, pp. 13–15; BA-MA Freiburg, N 63/80.

255   Manstein, *Verlorene Siege*, pp. 454–9 (at p. 457). See Below, *Als Hitlers Adjutant*, p. 330; Engel, *Heeresadjutant bei Hitler*, p. 144 (entry for 18 Feb. 1943). On the timing of Hitler's departure by plane, see Ewald von Kleist's pocket calendar under 19 Feb. 1943; BA-MA Freiburg, N 354/22. According to a statement by Luftwaffe General

Rainer Stahel on 21 November 1951, Soviet tanks were only 5 kilometres away from the airstrip. Christoforow, *et al.* (eds), *Verhört*, p. 212.

256 See Seidler and Zeigert, *Die Führerhauptquartiere*, pp. 233f.; Goebbels, *Tagebücher*, part II, vol. 7, p. 388 (entry for 21 Feb. 1943).

257 Goebbels, *Tagebücher*, part II, vol. 7, p. 557 (entry for 15 March 1943). See extracts from the reports from the Gaue, 7–20 March 1943: "The recapture of Kharkov has been welcomed with cheerful satisfaction." BA Berlin-Lichterfelde, NS 6/414.

258 See Eberhard Schwarz, *Die Stabilisierung der Ostfront nach Stalingrad: Mansteins Gegenschlag zwischen Donez und Dnjepr im Frühjahr 1943*, Göttingen and Zurich, 1986; Weinberg, *Eine Welt in Waffen*, pp. 496f.

259 Mathilde Wolff-Mönckeberg, *Briefe, die sie nicht erreichten: Briefe einer Mutter an ihre fernen Kinder in den Jahren 1940–1946*, Hamburg, 1980, p. 80. See also Norbert Frei, "Mythos Stalingrad: Die 'Kriegswende' in der Wahrnehmung der Deutschen," in *idem, 1945 und wir: Das Dritte Reich im Bewusstsein der Deutschen*, Munich, 2005, p. 97.

260 Cited in Merridale, *Ivan's War*, p. 162. Maisky noted: "The moral and psychological significance of Stalingrad is colossal." Gorodetsky (ed.), *Die Maiski-Tagebücher*, p. 689 (entry for 7 Feb. 1943).

261 See *Das Deutsche Reich und der Zweite Weltkrieg*, vol. 6, p. 1082 (Wegner's essay).

262 Goebbels, *Tagebücher*, part II, vol. 7, p. 275 (entry for 7 Feb. 1943). See Weinberg, *Eine Welt in Waffen*, pp. 499–501; Falanga, *Mussolinis Vorposten in Hitlers Reich*, pp. 203f.

263 Goebbels, *Tagebücher*, part II, vol. 7, pp. 171 (entry for 23 Jan. 1943), 512 (entry for 9 March 1943). See ibid., pp. 230 (entry for 31 Jan. 1943), 595 (entry for 20 March 1943).

264 See Ernst Günther Schenck, *Patient Hitler: Eine medizinische Biographie*, Düsseldorf, 1989, p. 388; Neumann and Eberle, *War Hitler krank?*, pp. 243f.; Eberle and Uhl (eds), *Das Buch Hitler*, p. 187. On Goebbels' 45th birthday in late October 1942, Hitler had sent him a handwritten letter in which he remarked that he hoped the propaganda minister could read his writing since his hands had "gradually begun to tremble." Goebbels, *Tagebücher*, part II, vol. 6, p. 209 (entry for 30 Oct. 1942).

265 Heinz Guderian, *Erinnerungen eines Soldaten*, Heidelberg, 1951, p. 402. On Guderian's appointment as general inspector of tank troops, see ibid., pp. 258ff.

266 Goebbels, *Tagebücher*, part II, vol. 7, p. 454 (entry for 2 March 1943).

267 Schroeder, *Er war mein Chef*, p. 130. See Goebbels, *Tagebücher*, part II, vol. 7, p. 171 (entry for 23 Jan. 1943).

268 Ibid., vol. 6, p. 156 (entry for 20 Oct. 1942). See ibid., pp. 81 (entry for 6 Oct. 1942), 92 (entry for 8 Oct. 1942).

269 See Speer, *Erinnerungen*, p. 312.

270 Ibid., p. 259; see Evans, *The Third Reich at War*, p. 506.

271 Goebbels, *Tagebücher*, part II, vol. 7, pp. 504 (entry for 9 March 1943), 532 (entry for 12 March 1943), 556 (entry for 15 March 1943).

272 Ibid., p. 594 (entry for 20 March 1943).

273 Mann, *An die gesittete Welt*, pp. 558f. (entry for 28 March 1943). For the text of the speech, see Domarus, *Hitler*, vol. 2, part 2, pp. 1999–2002.

274 On the rumours, see extracts from the reports from the Gaue, 21–27 March 1943; BA Berlin-Lichterfelde, NS 6/414; Kershaw, *The "Hitler Myth,"* p. 196.

275 *Meldungen aus dem Reich*, vol. 13, p. 5038 (dated 1 April 1943).

9 Total War and Ethnic-Popular Community

1 *Die Tagebücher, von Joseph Goebbels*, commissioned by the Institute for Contemporary History, with support from the State Archive of Russia, ed. Elke Fröhlich, *Part II: Diktate 1941–1945*, 15 vols, Munich, 1993–6, vol. 7, p. 32 (entry for 1 Jan. 1943).

2   Quotations in the following order: ibid., vol. 5, p. 581 (entry for 27 Sept. 1942), vol. 6, pp. 336 (entry for 26 Nov. 1942), 496 (entry for 24 Dec. 1942), 113 (entry for 12 Oct. 1942).

3   Ludolf Herbst, *Der totale Krieg und die Ordnung der Wirtschaft: Die Kriegswirtschaft im Spannungsfeld von Politik, Ideologie und Propaganda 1939–1945*, Stuttgart, 1982, pp. 198f. See Dieter Rebentisch, *Führerstaat und Verwaltung im Zweiten Weltkrieg: Verfassungsentwicklung und Verwaltungspolitik 1939–1945*, Stuttgart, 1989, pp. 470–2.

4   Cited in Rebentisch, *Führerstaat und Verwaltung*, p. 475.

5   Goebbels, *Tagebücher*, part II, vol. 7, p. 267 (entry for 5 Feb. 1943). See Albert Speer, *Erinnerungen: Mit einem Essay von Jochen Thies*, Frankfurt am Main and Berlin, 1993, p. 267; Ralf Georg Reuth, *Goebbels*, Munich and Zurich, 1990, p. 510.

6   Entry in Bormann's notebook on 27 Dec. 1942; Jochen von Lang, *Der Sekretär: Martin Bormann—Der Mann, der Hitler beherrschte*, Stuttgart, 1977, p. 236; see Rebentisch, *Führerstaat und Verwaltung*, p. 475; Reuth, *Goebbels*, p. 511.

7   Goebbels, *Tagebücher*, part II, vol. 6, p. 518 (entry for 29 Dec. 1942).

8   Herbst, *Der totale Krieg*, pp. 199f.; see Rebentisch, *Führerstaat und Verwaltung*, pp. 475f.

9   Goebbels, *Tagebücher*, part II, vol. 7, p. 39 (entry for 3 Jan. 1943).

10   Ibid., p. 51 (entry for 5 Jan. 1943).

11   Ibid., pp. 74–6 (entry for 9 Jan. 1943).

12   See Herbst, *Der totale Krieg*, pp. 207–9; Rebentisch, *Führerstaat und Verwaltung*, pp. 476–9.

13   Goebbels, *Tagebücher*, part II, vol. 7, p. 120 (entry for 15 Jan. 1943); see Herbst, *Der totale Krieg*, p. 209; Reuth, *Goebbels*, p. 513.

14   See Herbst, *Der totale Krieg*, p. 209.

15   Goebbels, *Tagebücher*, part II, vol. 7, pp. 169f. (entry for 23 Jan. 1943).

16   Goebbels, "Der totale Krieg," in *Das Reich*, 17 Jan. 1943; "Die Optik des Krieges," in *Das Reich*, 24 Jan. 1943; Peter Longerich, *Joseph Goebbels*, Munich, 2010, p. 544; Herbst, *Der totale Krieg*, pp. 200f.

17   Goebbels, *Tagebücher*, part II, vol. 7, p. 229 (entry for 31 Jan. 1943). On the reception of the speech, see also Heinz Boberach (ed.), *Meldungen aus dem Reich: Die geheimen Lageberichte des Sicherheitsdienstes der SS 1938–1945*, Herrsching, 1984, vol. 12, p. 4733 (dated 1 Feb. 1943).

18   Goebbels, *Tagebücher*, part II, vol. 7, pp. 356 (entry for 16 Feb. 1943), 336 (entry for 13 Feb. 1943). See ibid., pp. 345 (entry for 14 Feb. 1943), 351 (entry for 15 Feb. 1943).

19   Ibid., pp. 336 (entry for 13 Feb. 1943), 373 (entry for 19 Feb. 1943). See Speer, *Erinnerungen*, p. 269; Reuth, *Goebbels*, p. 518.

20   Text of the speech in Iring Fetscher, *Joseph Goebbels im Berliner Sportpalast 1943: "Wollt ihr den totalen Krieg,"* Hamburg, 1998, pp. 63–98 (quotations in the following order at pp. 65, 63, 65, 69, 68, 73, 76, 78, 94, 95, 98). For an analysis of the speech, see ibid., pp. 107–18; Günter Moltmann, "Goebbels' Rede zum Totalen Krieg am 18. Februar 1943," in *Vierteljahrshefte für Zeitgeschichte*, 12 (1964), pp. 13–43. For a summary, Longerich, *Goebbels*, pp. 551–4; Reuth, *Goebbels*, pp. 518–21. On Goebbels' "slip of the tongue," see Saul Friedländer, *The Years of Extermination: Nazi Germany and the Jews, 1939–1945*, London, 2007, pp. 472f.

21   Goebbels, *Tagebücher*, part II, vol. 7, pp. 373f. (entry for 19 Feb. 1943), 378 (entry for 20 Feb. 1943), 385 (entry for 21 Feb. 1943). On the "extraordinarily strong echo," see extracts from the reports from the Gaue, 21–27 Feb. 1943; BA Berlin-Lichterfelde, NS 6/414; *Meldungen aus dem Reich*, vol. 12, p. 483 (dated 22 Feb. 1943).

22   Goebbels, *Tagebücher*, part II, vol. 7, p. 408 (entry for 24 Feb. 1943). See ibid., pp. 389 (entry for 21 Feb. 1943), 401 (entry for 23 Feb. 1943).

23   See ibid., p. 412 (entry for 25 Feb. 1943). The text of the proclamation of 24 Feb. 1943 is reproduced in Max Domarus, *Hitler: Reden und Proklamationen 1932–1945*, Munich, 1965, vol. 2, part 2, pp. 1990–3.

24 Goebbels, *Tagebücher*, part II, vol. 7, p. 374 (entry for 19 Feb. 1943). See also Speer, *Erinnerungen*, pp. 270–4.

25 Goebbels, *Tagebücher*, part II, vol. 7, pp. 430f. (entry for 27 Feb. 1943).

26 Ibid., pp. 438f. (entry for 28 Feb. 1943), 444f. (entry for 1 March 1943).

27 Ibid, pp. 450–8 (entry for 2 March 1943).

28 See ibid., pp. 478 (entry for 5 March 1943), 502 (entry for 9 March 1943).

29 Ibid., pp. 502, 505, 507 (entry for 9 March 1943); Speer, *Erinnerungen*, pp. 274–6.

30 Goebbels, *Tagebücher*, part II, vol. 7, pp. 576–9 (entry for 18 March 1943).

31 See Hitler's edict of 12 April 1943 and Lammers' explanatory memorandum to the higher Reich offices of 8 May 1943; BA Berlin-Lichterfelde, NS 6/159.

32 See Bormann's conversation with Ley, 23 Aug. 1943; BA Berlin Lichterfelde, NS 6/156; Ley said that Bormann had succeeded in "putting up a cordon around the Führer that was impenetrable for many people." Ley's testimony, "Gedanken um den Führer," 1945; BA Koblenz, N 1468/4.

33 See Lang, *Der Sekretär*, p. 233; Volker Koop, *Martin Bormann: Hitlers Vollstrecker*, Cologne and Weimar, 2012, pp. 58–60, 77f. On 1 January 1945 Lammers complained to Bormann that he had been "completely 'hung out to dry' by the Führer and his headquarters"; BA Berlin-Lichterfelde, R 43 II/1641.

34 Goebbels, *Tagebücher*, part II, vol. 8, p. 251 (entry for 9 May 1943).

35 See ibid., pp. 346f. (entry for 22 May 1943), 392 (entry for 30 May 1943), 495 (entry for 19 June 1943).

36 See ibid., vol. 9, p. 267 (entry for 10 Aug. 1943): "The Führer works excellently with Bormann. He is very satisfied with him." On Goebbels turn towards Bormann, see Speer's testimony about his activities as minister, Nuremberg, 10 Aug. 1946, p. 23; BA Koblenz, N 1340/84.

37 *Meldungen aus dem Reich*, vol. 13, p. 4945 (dated 15 March 1943).

38 See Herbst, *Der totale Krieg*, p. 214.

39 Goebbels, *Tagebücher*, part II, vol. 7, p. 616 (entry for 22 March 1943). See ibid., vol. 8, p. 262 (entry for 10 May 1943): "Above all, no war must be waged against women in total war. Never has such a war been won by a government."

40 See ibid., vol. 7, p. 245 (entry for 2 Feb. 1943).

41 See Herbst, *Der totale Krieg*, p. 212.

42 *Meldungen aus dem Reich*, vol. 12, pp. 4746, 4752 (dated 4 Feb. 1943).

43 Ibid., vol. 13, p. 4903 (dated 8 March 1943).

44 See Herbst, *Der totale Krieg*, pp. 226f.; Goebbels, *Tagebücher*, part II, vol. 8, p. 524 (entry for 25 June 1943).

45 See the seminal study by Ulrich Herbert, *Fremdarbeiter: Politik und Praxis des "Ausländer-Einsatzes" in der Kriegswirtschaft des Dritten Reiches*, Berlin and Bonn, 1985; idem, *Geschichte der Ausländerpolitik in Deutschland: Saisonarbeiter, Zwangsarbeiter, Gastarbeiter, Flüchtlinge*, Munich, 2001, pp. 129–66. For a summary, see idem, *Geschichte Deutschlands im 20. Jahrhundert*, pp. 487–93. See also Mark Spoerer, *Zwangsarbeit unter dem Hakenkreuz: Ausländische Zivilarbeiter, Kriegsgefangene und Häftlinge im Dritten Reich und im besetzten Europa 1939–1945*, Stuttgart, 2001; Adam Tooze, *The Wages of Destruction: The Making and Breaking of the Nazi Economy*, London, 2006, pp. 517–23; Richard J. Evans, *The Third Reich at War, 1939–1945*, London, 2008, pp. 346–72 438–70; Tim Schanetzky, *"Kanonen statt Butter": Wirtschaft und Konsum im Dritten Reich*, Munich, 2015, pp. 223–36; Dietmar Süss, *"Ein Volk, ein Reich, ein Führer": Die deutsche Gesellschaft im Dritten Reich*, Munich, 2017, pp. 201–8.

46 Herbert, *Fremdarbeiter*, p. 160.

47 Goebbels, *Tagebücher*, part II, vol. 4, p. 567 (entry for 21 June 1942); see ibid., pp. 34f. (entry for 1 April 1942), 516 (entry for 23 June 1942), vol. 5, p. 239 (entry for 3 Aug. 1942).

48 Frank Bajohr and Christoph Strupp (eds), *Fremde Blicke auf das "Dritte Reich": Berichte ausländischer Diplomaten über Herrschaft und Gesellschaft in Deutschland 1933–1945*,

Göttingen, 2011, p. 571. See Winfried Nerdinger (ed.), *München und der Nationalsozialismus: Katalog des NS-Dokumentationszentrums München*, Munich, 2015, pp. 259f.

49 *Hitlers Tischgespräche im Führerhauptquartier*, ed. Henry Picker, Stuttgart, 1976, pp. 315 (dated 21 May 1942), 354 (dated 4 June 1942).

50 Goebbels, *Tagebücher*, part II, vol. 4, pp. 516f. (entry for 13 June 1942).

51 Herbert, *Fremdarbeiter*, p. 142.

52 See Michael Schneider, *In der Kriegsgesellschaft: Arbeiter und Arbeiterbewegung 1939 bis 1945*, Bonn, 2014, pp. 520f., 621–9.

53 Bajohr and Strupp (eds), *Fremde Blicke auf das "Dritte Reich,"* p. 573.

54 Speer, *Erinnerungen*, p. 229.

55 Götz Aly, *Hitlers Volksstaat: Raub, Rassenkrieg und nationaler Sozialismus*, Frankfurt am Main, 2005, p. 30.

56 Goebbels, *Tagebücher*, part II, vol. 4, p. 526 (entry for 14 June 1942); see ibid., p. 406 (entry for 30 May 1942).

57 See Aly, *Hitlers Volksstaat*, pp. 67f.; Marie-Luise Recker, *Nationalsozialistische Sozialpolitik im Zweiten Weltkrieg*, Munich, 1985, pp. 33f.

58 Cited in Recker, *Nationalsozialistische Sozialpolitik im Zweiten Weltkrieg*, p. 44.

59 See Aly, *Hitlers Volksstaat*, pp. 69f.

60 See ibid., pp. 71f.

61 On the growth of wages see Schneider, *In der Kriegsgesellschaft*, pp. 541–54.

62 See the reactions to the "Iron Savings" initiative in the reports of the Gau economic consultants, 5 Jan. 1942; BA Berlin-Lichterfelde, NS 6/289.

63 Philipp Kratz, "Sparen für das kleine Glück," in Götz Aly (ed.), *Volkes Stimme: Skepsis und Führervertrauen im Nationalsozialismus*, Frankfurt am Main, 2006, pp. 59–79 (at p. 79); See also Aly, *Hitlers Volksstaat*, pp. 334–6.

64 Goebbels, *Tagebücher*, part II, vol. 9, p. 58 (entry for 7 July 1943). See also ibid., vol. 8, p. 263 (entry for 10 May 1943), vol. 9, p. 29 (entry for 1 July 1943), vol. 10, p. 313 (entry for 18 Nov. 1943). On the spring 1943 tax proposals, see Recker, *Nationalsozialistische Sozialpolitik*, p. 217–23; Aly, *Hitlers Volksstaat*, pp. 74f. Hitler initially signed off on proposals in the autumn of 1944 that would have raised direct and indirect taxes and instituted a wealth tax but made his definitive approval contingent upon military victory. Because that did not happen, the tax reforms never came into force. See Lutz Schwerin von Krosigk to Albert Speer, 29 April 1970; BA Koblenz, N 1340/60.

65 See Aly, *Hitlers Volksstaat*, pp. 86–9; Schanetzky, *Wirtschaft und Konsum im Dritten Reich*, p. 195; Birthe Kundrus, *Kriegerfrauen: Familienpolitik und Geschlechterverhältnisse im Ersten und Zweiten Weltkrieg*, Hamburg, 1995, pp. 247–55, 264–6, 433f.

66 Domarus, *Hitler*, vol. 2, part 2, p. 1664.

67 See Nicole Kramer, *Volksgenossinnen an der Heimatfront: Mobilisierung, Verhalten, Erinnerung*, Göttingen, 2011, pp. 181–93, 206–18.

68 See ibid., pp. 252–70; Dietmar Süss, *Tod aus der Luft: Kriegsgesellschaft und Luftkrieg in Deutschland und England*, Munich, 2011, pp. 227f.; Richard Overy, *The Bombing War: Europe 1939–1945*, London, 2013, pp. 427–30; Armin Nolzen, "Die NSDAP, der Krieg und die deutsche Gesellschaft," in *Das Deutsche Reich und der Zweite Weltkrieg*, ed. Militärgeschichtliches Forschungsamt (Military Historical Research Office), vol. 9, part 1, Munich, 2004, pp. 99–193 (at pp. 151–9).

69 Cited in Süss, *Tod aus der Luft*, p. 228.

70 See Goebbels, *Tagebücher*, part II, vol. 7, p. 125 (entry for 16 Jan. 1943).

71 Ibid., vol. 8, p. 494 (entry for 16 June 1943).

72 Frank Bajohr, *"Arisierung" in Hamburg: Die Verdrängung der jüdischen Unternehmer 1933–1945*, Hamburg, 1997, pp. 333–5 (at p. 335). See Aly, *Hitlers Volksstaat*, pp. 139–55; Schanetzky, *Wirtschaft und Konsum im Dritten Reich*, pp. 203f.

73 Goebbels, *Tagebücher*, part II, vol. 10, p. 192 (entry for 27 Oct. 1943). A facsimile of the Führer directive of 11 Oct. 1843 is contained in Domarus, *Hitler*, vol. 2, part 2,

p. 2046. On Speer's plans for post-war reconstruction, see Sebastian Tesch, *Albert Speer (1905–1981)*, Vienna, Cologne and Weimar, 2016, pp. 207–9.

74 Goebbels, *Tagebücher*, part II., vol. 8, p. 528 (entry for 25 June 1943); see ibid., vol. 5, p. 358 (entry for 20 Aug. 1942), vol. 11, p. 472 (entry for 14 March 1944).

75 See Christoph Buchheim, "Der Mythos vom 'Wohlleben': Der Lebensstandard der deutschen Zivilbevölkerung im Zweiten Weltkrieg," in *Vierteljahrshefte für Zeitgeschichte*, 58 (2010), pp. 299–328 (at pp. 304–9); Schanetzky, *Wirtschaft und Konsum im Dritten Reich*, pp. 197f.

76 Cited in Nicholas Stargardt, *The German War: A Nation under Arms, 1939–45*, London, 2015, p. 282.

77 Goebbels, *Tagebücher*, part II, vol. 4, pp. 294 (entry for 15 May 1942), 394 (entry for 29 May 1942), 616 (entry for 25 June 1942). See ibid., vol. 5, pp. 48 (entry for 3 July 1942), 106 (entry for 12 July 1942).

78 Ibid., vol. 5, p. 362 (entry for 20 Aug. 1942). See ibid., vol. 8, p. 260 (entry for 10 May 1943); *Tischgespräche*, p. 214 (dated 11 April 1942): efforts had to be made "to get everything that could be got economically, using any and all means, out of the occupied Russian territories."

79 Text of Göring's speech of 4 Oct. 1942 in Aly (ed), *Volkes Stimme*, pp. 149–94 (at pp. 163, 154, 162, 155).

80 *Meldungen aus dem Reich*, vol. 11, p. 4309 (dated 12 Oct. 1942).

81 Victor Klemperer, *Ich will Zeugnis ablegen bis zum letzten: Tagebücher*, vol. 2: 1942–1945, ed. Walter Nowojski with Hadwig Klemperer, Berlin, 1995, p. 245 (entry for 16 Sept. 1942).

82 Aly, *Hitlers Volksstaat*, p. 125.

83 Heinrich Böll, *Briefe aus dem Krieg 1939–1945*, ed. Jochen Schubert, Cologne, 2001, vol. 1, p. 108 (dated 4 Sept. 1940), vol. 2, p. 903 (dated 24 Sept. 1943). For an overview, see Aly, *Hitlers Volksstaat*, pp. 114–32 (Chapter: "Hitlers zufriedene Räuber"); Schanetzky, *Wirtschaft und Konsum im Dritten Reich*, pp. 199–201; Stargardt, *The German War*, pp. 132f., 289.

84 Adolf Hitler, *Monologe im Führerhauptquartier 1941–1944: Die Aufzeichnungen Heinrich Heims*, ed. Werner Jochmann, Hamburg, 1980, p. 346 (dated 16 Aug. 1942); see *Tischgespräche*, p. 438 (dated 17 July 1942): "Soldiers on leave [are] the ideal and simplest means of transport and should be given as much food as they are able to carry for their family members."

85 Goebbels, *Tagebücher*, part II, vol. 6, p. 209 (entry for 30 Oct. 1942).

86 Aly, *Hitlers Volksstaat*, p. 326. For a critical perspective, see Buchheim, "Der Mythos vom 'Wohlleben,'" pp. 300ff.

87 Herbert Backe to his wife, 14 Nov. 1943; BA Koblenz, N 1075/26.

88 See Goebbels, *Tagebücher*, part II, vol. 8, pp. 298 (entry for 14 May 1943), 320 (entry for 19 May 1943).

89 Ibid., vol. 10, p. 222 (entry for 2 Nov. 1943).

90 Friedrich Kellner, *"Vernebelt, verdunkelt sind alle Hirne": Tagebücher, 1939–1945*, ed. Sascha Feuchert et al., Göttingen, 2011, vol. 1, pp. 452f. (entry for 6 July 1943). For a case study of this, see Malte Zierenberg, *Stadt der Schieber: Der Berliner Schwarzmarkt 1939–1950*, Göttingen, 2008, pp. 85–151. For a summary, see Schanetzky, *Wirtschaft und Konsum im Dritten Reich*, pp. 204–8; Stargardt, *The German War*, pp. 284–90.

91 Goebbels, *Tagebücher*, part II, vol. 4, p. 601 (entry for 24 June 1942). On the stereotype of the fence, see Zierenberg, *Stadt der Schieber*, pp. 163–76.

92 Memorandum by Martin Bormann dated 15 July 1943; BA Berlin-Lichterfelde, NS 6/342.

93 *Meldungen aus dem Reich*, vol. 9, p. 3505 (dated 23 March 1942). See extracts from reports from the Gaue, 6–12 June 1943: depressing the general mood was the fact that "the increasing restrictions on food every month are obviously by no means being borne equally by all classes within the ethnic community." BA Berlin–Lichterfelde, NS 6/415.

94   Cited in Frank Bajohr, *Parvenüs und Profiteure: Korruption in der NS-Zeit*, Frankfurt am Main, 2001, p. 165.

95   Goebbels, *Tagebücher*, part II, vol. 6, p. 52 (entry for 2 Oct. 1942), vol. 7, p. 284 (entry for 8 Feb. 1943).

96   See ibid., vol. 4, p. 630 (entry for 27 June 1942): "There is outspoken criticism of the lifestyles of a series of prominent state and party figures—and not without reason, as I sometimes unfortunately have to admit."

97   See the investigation report of 17 December 1941 by SS judge Reinecke to the Reichsführer SS, and Himmler's file notes on the meeting with Frank on 5 March 1942; BA Berlin-Lichterfelde, NS 19/3899. On the wider context, see Dieter Schenk, *Hans Frank: Hitlers Kronjurist und Generalgouverneur*, Frankfurt am Main, 2006, pp. 243–53.

98   Goebbels, *Tagebücher*, part II, vol. 7, p. 284 (entry for 8 Feb. 1943).

99   Memorandum by Bormann dated 1 March 1943; cited in Marlies Steinert, *Hitlers Krieg und die Deutschen: Stimmung und Haltung der deutschen Bevölkerung im Zweiten Weltkrieg*, Düsseldorf and Vienna, 1970, p. 346. See also Martin Bormann's announcement of 6 May 1944 concerning the fight against corruption; BA Berlin-Lichterfelde, NS 6/350.

100   See Henrik Eberle and Matthias Uhl (eds), *Das Buch Hitler*, Bergisch Gladbach, 2005, p. 205.

101   See Gerd R. Ueberschär and Winfried Vogel, *Dienen und Verdienen: Hitlers Geschenke an seine Eliten*, Frankfurt am Main, 1999, pp. 111–86; Albert Speer, *Spandauer Tagebücher: Mit einem Vorwort von Joachim Fest*, Munich, 2002, p. 171 (entry for 28 Dec. 1948).

102   *Monologe*, p. 200 (dated 15–16 Jan. 1942); see Bajohr, *Parvenüs und Profiteure*, p. 161.

103   See Daniel Roos, *Julius Streicher und "Der Stürmer" 1923–1945*, Paderborn, 2014, pp. 350–7, 389–96.

104   See Lothar Gruchmann, "Korruption im Dritten Reich: Zur 'Lebensmittelversorgung' der NS-Führerschaft," in *Vierteljahrshefte für Zeitgeschichte*, 42 (1994), pp. 571–93 (at pp. 572–6). For a summary, see Bajohr, *Parvenüs und Profiteure*, pp. 171–3; Stargardt, *The German War*, pp. 300f.

105   Goebbels, *Tagebücher*, part II, vol. 7, p. 572 (entry for 17 March 1943).

106   Ibid., p. 618 (entry for 22 March 1943).

107   Gruchmann, "Korruption im Dritten Reich," pp. 580, 582. In late June 1943, Hitler decided once and for all that "in the case of Nöthling nothing shall be done against the prominent figures." Goebbels was "not entirely in agreement" with this. He would have liked to see the persons concerned "at least receive a moral warning." Goebbels, *Tagebücher*, part II, vol. 9, p. 149 (entry for 23 July 1943).

108   Gruchmann, "Korruption im Dritten Reich," p. 581.

109   Goebbels, *Tagebücher*, part II, vol. 3, p. 377 (entry for 26 Feb. 1942).

110   In addition, see Bernd Sösemann, "Propaganda und Öffentlichkeit in der 'Volksgemeinschaft,'" in *idem* (ed.), *Der Nationalsozialismus und die deutsche Gesellschaft*, Stuttgart and Munich, 2002, pp. 114–54; Birthe Kundrus, "Totale Unterhaltung? Die kulturelle Kriegführung 1939 bis 1945 in Film, Rundfunk und Theater," in *Das Deutsche Reich und der Zweite Weltkrieg*, vol. 9, part 2, pp. 93–157; Erwin Leiser, *"Deutschland erwache!" Propaganda im Film des Dritten Reiches*, Reinbek bei Hamburg, 1968, pp. 59–63. For an overview, see Evans, *The Third Reich at War*, pp. 567–73; 574–6; Herbert, *Deutsche Geschichte im 20. Jahrhundert*, pp. 504–8; Stargardt, *The German War*, p. 335; Moritz Föllmer, *"Ein Leben wie im Traum": Kultur im Dritten Reich*, Munich, 2016, pp. 167–70.

111   Goebbels, *Tagebücher*, part II, vol. 7, p. 298 (entry for 8 Feb. 1943); see ibid., pp. 177 (entry for 23 Jan. 1943), 320 (entry for 11 Feb. 1943).

112 Decree by Hitler of 15 Feb. 1940; Recker, *Nationalsozialistische Sozialpolitik im Zweiten Weltkrieg*, pp. 115f.

113 Ibid., p. 98. On the "Social Works of German People," see ibid., pp. 82–154; Schneider, *In der Kriegsgesellschaft*, pp. 380–410; Schanetzky, *Wirtschaft und Konsum im Dritten Reich*, pp. 187–90.

114 Domarus, *Hitler*, vol. 2, part 1, p. 1617 (dated 14 Nov. 1940).

115 Goebbels, *Tagebücher*, part II, vol. 7, p. 621 (entry for 22 March 1943); see ibid., vol. 4, p. 217 (entry for 1 May 1942), vol. 10, p. 517 (entry for 20 Dec. 1943).

116 *Tischgespräche*, p. 315 (dated 20 May 1942).

117 Goebbels, *Tagebücher*, part II, vol. 4, pp. 263 (entry for 9 May 1942), 327 (entry for 21 May 1942). On the awarding of medals to armaments workers, see Tooze, *The Wages of Destruction*, pp. 554f.; Schneider, *In der Kriegsgesellschaft*, pp. 177f.; Schanetzky, *Wirtschaft und Konsum im Dritten Reich*, pp. 216f.

118 Goebbels, *Tagebücher*, part II, vol. 10, p. 131 (entry for 19 Oct. 1943).

119 *Meldungen aus dem Reich*, vol. 11, p. 4164 (dated 3 Sept. 1942). See Goebbels, *Tagebücher*, part II, vol. 5, p. 516 (entry for 17 Sept. 1942): "The people are afraid that the war will exceed all limits, especially as at the moment there is no end in sight."

120 *Meldungen aus dem Reich*, vol. 13, p. 5063 (dated 5 April 1943).

121 Kellner, *Tagebücher, 1939–1945*, vol. 1, p. 451 (entry for 28 June 1943).

122 Otto Dov Kulka and Eberhard Jäckel (eds), *Die Juden in den geheimen NS-Stimmungsberichten 1939–1945*, Düsseldorf, 2004, no. 725, p. 537. For further examples see also nos 699, 706, 709, 711 and Stargardt, *The German War*, pp. 376–9.

123 See Peter Longerich, *"Davon haben wir nichts gewusst!" Die Deutschen und die Judenverfolgung 1933–1945*, Munich, 2006, pp. 266f.

124 *Meldungen aus dem Reich*, vol. 14, pp. 5445, 5447 (dated 8 July 1943).

125 See also Nikolaus Wachsmann, *Gefangen unter Hitler: Justizterror und Strafverfolgung im NS-Staat*, Munich, 2004, pp. 195–239; Evans, *The Third Reich at War*, pp. 513–17 643–7.

126 See Robert Gellately, *Backing Hitler: Consent and Coercion in Nazi Germany*, Oxford, 2001, pp. 183–203; Süss, *Die deutsche Gesellschaft im Dritten Reich*, pp. 187–9.

127 Goebbels, *Tagebücher*, part II, vol. 4, p. 361 (entry for 24 May 1942).

128 *Monologe*, p. 448 (dated 20 Aug. 1942); *Tischgespräche*, pp. 200f. (dated 7 April 1942).

129 Goebbels, *Tagebücher*, part II, vol. 10, p. 279 (entry for 12 Nov. 1943).

130 See Volker Ullrich, *Hitler: Ascent 1889–1939*, London, 2016, pp. 534f.

131 See Hans-Ulrich Thamer, "Die Widersprüche der 'Volksgemeinschaft' in den späten Kriegsjahren," in Detlef Schmiechen-Ackermann (ed.), *"Volksgemeinschaft": Mythos, wirkungsmächtige soziale Verheissung oder soziale Realität im "Dritten Reich"?*, Paderborn, 2012, pp. 289–300 (at pp. 289f.).

132 Domarus, *Hitler*, vol. 2, part 2, p. 1922 (dated 30 Sept. 1942); see ibid., pp. 1941 (dated 8 Nov. 1942), 2002 (dated 21 March 1943), 2085 (dated 30 Jan. 1944).

133 See Norbert Frei, "'Volksgemeinschaft': Erfahrungsgeschichte und Lebenswirklichkeit der Hitler-Zeit," in *idem, 1945 und wir: Das Dritte Reich im Bewusstsein der Deutschen*, Munich, 2005, pp. 107–28 (at p. 126); Hans-Ulrich Wehler, *Deutsche Gesellschaftsgeschichte*, vol. 4, Munich, 2003, p. 929; Herbert, *Deutsche Geschichte im 20. Jahrhundert*, pp. 509f.; Jörg Echternkamp, "Im Kampf an der inneren und äusseren Front: Grundzüge der deutschen Gesellschaft im Zweiten Weltkrieg," in *Das Deutsche Reich und der Zweite Weltkrieg*, vol 9, part 1, pp. 1–98 (at pp. 14f.).

134 See Frei, "Volksgemeinschaft," p. 127.

135 *Meldungen aus dem Reich*, vol. 13, p. 5157 (dated 22 April 1943). See ibid., vol. 15, p. 6064 (dated 29 Nov. 1943): "While a disappearance of trust in individual leading personalities or offices can be identified relatively often, trust in the Führer remains almost untouched."

10 *On the Defensive*

1   Albert Speer, *Spandauer Tagebücher: Mit einem Vorwort von Joachim Fest*, Munich, 2002, p. 33 (entry for 8 Nov. 1946).

2   *Die Tagebücher von Joseph Goebbels*, commissioned by the Institute for Contemporary History, with support from the State Archive of Russia, ed. Elke Fröhlich, *Part II: Diktate 1941–1945*, 15 vols, Munich, 1993–6, vol. 7, p. 293 (entry for 8 Feb. 1943).

3   Cited in Bernd Wegner, "Von Stalingrad nach Kursk," in *Das Deutsche Reich und der Zweite Weltkrieg. Vol. 8: Die Ostfront 1943/44*, Munich, 2007, p. 61. Hitler made similar remarks at a meeting with commanders of Army Group Centre on 13 March 1943. Colonel-General Reinhardt commented: "All of us can only hope that the Führer does not get too ambitious and that we remain within the unalterable limits of our strength." Letter from Reinhardt to his wife, 14 March 1943; BA-MA Freiburg, N 245/2.

4   See Roman Töppel, "Kursk—Mythen und Wirklichkeit einer Schlacht," in *Vierteljahrshefte für Zeitgeschichte*, 57 (2009), pp. 349–84 (at pp. 350–2). See also *idem, Kursk 1943: Die grösste Schlacht des Zweiten Weltkriegs*, Paderborn, 2017, pp. 23–9.

5   Text in *Kriegstagebuch des Oberkommandos der Wehrmacht (Wehrmachtführungsstab)* (hereafter *KTB OKW*), ed. Percy Ernst Schramm, Munich, 1982, vol. 3, part 2, pp. 1420–2 (at p. 1420). See *Das Deutsche Reich und der Zweite Weltkrieg*, vol. 8, p. 68 (Wegner's essay).

6   Text in *KTB OKW*, vol. 3, part 2, pp. 1425–7 (at p. 1425).

7   See Kurt Zeitzler, "Das Ringen um die grossen Entscheidungen im Zweiten Weltkrieg, vol. 2: Abwehrschlachten in Russland nach dem Wendepunkt des Krieges," pp. 56–9; BA-MA Freiburg, N 63/80

8   Goebbels, *Tagebücher*, part II, vol. 7, p. 593 (entry for 20 March 1943). See ibid., p. 510 (entry for 9 March 1943): "The Führer believes that it cannot be ruled out that [the Bolsheviks] will collapse sooner or later."

9   See Zeitzler, "Das Ringen um die grossen Entscheidungen," vol. 2, pp. 61–4; BA-MA Freiburg, N 63/80.

10   See Hitler's appointment diary, kept by Heinz Linge, under 29 April 1943; IfZ München, F 19/4.

11   Goebbels, *Tagebücher*, part II, vol. 7, p. 622 (entry for 22 March 1943).

12   Ibid., p. 348 (entry for 15 Feb. 1943).

13   See Heinz Linge's appointment diary under 21 March to 29 April; IfZ München, F 19/4; Max Domarus, *Hitler: Reden und Proklamationen 1932–1945*, vol. 2, part 2, Munich, 1965, pp. 2003–8 (with the incorrect date for the visit by the Bulgarian king).

14   See Nicolaus von Below, *Als Hitlers Adjutant 1937–45*, Mainz, 1980, p. 335: "What you can say generally about all the visits this month is that the guests were mistrustful when they arrived and they were mistrustful when they left."

15   See Hans Woller, *Geschichte Italiens im 20. Jahrhundert*, Munich, 2010, pp. 184–6.

16   See Galeazzo Ciano, *Tagebücher, 1939–1943*, Bern, 1946, pp. 529f. (entries for 5, 6, 8 Feb. 1943); Gianluca Falanga, *Mussolinis Vorposten in Hitlers Reich: Italiens Politik in Berlin 1933–1945*, Berlin, 2008, p. 204; Woller, *Mussolini*, p. 255.

17   Hitler to Mussolini, 16 Feb. 1943; *Akten zur deutschen Auswärtigen Politik 1918–1945 (ADAP) (The Political Archives of the Federal Foreign Office), Series E, 1941–1945*, vols 1–8 Göttingen, 1975, vol. 5, no. 135, pp. 227ff.

18   Goebbels, *Tagebücher*, part II, vol. 7, p. 464 (entry for 3 March 1943). Leonidas Hill (ed.), *Die Weizsäcker-Papiere 1933–1950*, Frankfurt am Main, Berlin and Vienna, 1974, p. 327 (dated 5 March 1943).

19   See Below, *Als Hitlers Adjutant*, pp. 333f.; Walter Warlimont, *Im Hauptquartier der deutschen Wehrmacht 1939–1945: Grundlagen—Formen—Gestalten*, Frankfurt am Main and Bonn, 1964, pp. 325–8.

20   See Rommel's diary entry for 11 March 1943; BA-MA Freiburg, N 117/74; Ralf Georg Reuth, *Rommel: Das Ende einer Legende*, Munich and Zurich, 2004, pp. 79f.

21   See Wolfram Pyta, *Hitler: Der Künstler als Politiker und Feldherr*, Munich, 2015, pp. 461f.

22   Traudl Junge, *Bis zur letzten Stunde: Hitlers Sekretärin erzählt ihr Leben*, Munich, 2002, pp. 101f. On the Italian visit of 1938, see Volker Ullrich, *Hitler: Ascent 1889–1939*, London, 2016, pp. 723–6.

23   Goebbels, *Tagebücher*, part II, vol. 8, p. 225 (entry for 7 May 1943); see ibid., p. 139 (entry for 20 Apr. 1943). On Mussolini and Hitler's talks, see Falanga, *Mussolinis Vorposten in Hitlers Reich*, pp. 205f.; Alan Bullock, *Hitler: A Study in Tyranny*, London, 1990, p. 705.

24   Goebbels, *Tagebücher*, part II, vol. 8, p. 89 (entry for 11 April 1943). See Gerhard L. Weinberg, *Eine Welt in Waffen: Die globale Geschichte des Zweiten Weltkriegs*, Stuttgart, 1995, p. 482; Gerhard Schreiber, "Das Ende des nordafrikanischen Feldzugs und der Krieg in Italien 1943 bis 1945," in *Das Deutsche Reich und der Zweite Weltkrieg*, vol. 8, p. 1107.

25   See Manstein, "Entstehung, Durchführung und Abschluss des Unternehmens 'Zitadelle,'" dated 4 May 1943; BA-MA Freiburg, N 597/121; Erich von Manstein, *Verlorene Siege*, Bonn, 1955, pp. 488–92; Heinz Guderian, *Erinnerungen eines Soldaten*, Heidelberg, 1951, pp. 276–8; *Das Deutsche Reich und der Zweite Weltkrieg*, vol. 8, pp. 75f. (Wegner's essay). On the postponement of the date of the attack, see Zeitzler, "Das Ringen um die grossen Entscheidungen," vol. 2, pp. 64–6; BA-MA Freiburg, N 63/80; *KTB OKW*, vol. 3, part 2, pp. 749f. (entry for 5 July 1943).

26   Goebbels, *Tagebücher*, part II, vol. 8, pp. 223f. (entry for 7 May 1943).

27   Ibid., pp. 233–40.

28   *Das Deutsche Reich und der Zweite Weltkrieg*, vol. 8, p. 39 (Wegner's essay).

29   Goebbels, *Tagebücher*, part II, vol. 8, pp. 265, 274 (entries for 10 and 11 May 1943). See ibid., p. 407 (entry for 2 June 1943): "He is the essential factor in our faith in ultimate victory. As long as he remains at the head of the Reich, I am firmly convinced that no lasting ill can befall the nation."

30   See Heinz Linge's appointment diary under 12 May 1943; IfZ München, F 19/4.

31   See *Das Deutsche Reich und der Zweite Weltkrieg*, vol. 8, pp. 1108f. (Schreiber's essay); Rolf-Dieter Müller, *Der letzte deutsche Krieg 1939–1945*, Stuttgart, 2005, p. 183.

32   Goebbels, *Tagebücher*, part II, p. 266 (entry for 10 May 1943). See Reuth, *Rommel*, pp. 193f. For the text of the Wehrmacht Supreme Command announcement of 11 May 1943, see Domarus, *Hitler*, vol. 2, part 2, p. 2014.

33   See extracts from the reports from the Gaue, 11–17 April, 9–15 May 1943; BA Berlin-Lichterfelde, NS 6/414 und NS 6/415; Heinz Boberach (ed.), *Meldungen aus dem Reich: Die geheimen Lageberichte des Sicherheitsdienstes der SS 1938–1945*, Herrsching, 1984, vol. 13, pp. 5061 (dated 5 April 1943), 5104 (dated 12 April 1943), 5124 (dated 15 April 1943).

34   Goebbels, *Tagebücher*, part II, vol. 8, p. 297 (entry for 14 May 1943).

35   Friedrich Kellner, *"Vernebelt, verdunkelt sind alle Hirne": Tagebücher, 1939–1945*, ed. Sascha Feuchert et al., Göttingen, 2011, vol. 1, p. 415 (entry for 11 May 1943). See Ulrich von Hassell, *Vom andern Deutschland: Aus den nachgelassenen Tagebüchern 1938–1944*, Frankfurt am Main, 1964, p. 275 (entry for 15 May 1943): "Senseless propaganda that tries to pass off our serious defeat in Tunis as a triumph will not strew sand in anyone's eyes."

36   Cited in *Das Deutsche Reich und der Zweite Weltkrieg*, vol. 8, p. 35 (Wegner's essay). See *KTB OKW*, vol. 3, part 2, p. 832; Ralf Georg Reuth, *Hitler: Eine Biographie*, Munich and Zurich, 2003, pp. 592f.

37   Helmut Heiber (ed.), *Hitlers Lagebesprechungen: Die Protokollfragmente seiner militärischen Konferenzen 1942–1945*, Stuttgart, 1962, pp. 220–38 (at pp. 226, 232). See Goebbels, *Tagebücher*, part II, vol. 8, p. 348 (entry for 22 May 1943): "Hitler is most concerned at the moment with how Italy is holding up. He fears that one fine day, under certain circumstances, Italy might collapse."

38   See Werner Rahn, "Der Seekrieg im Atlantik und Nordmeer," in *Das Deutsche Reich und der Zweite Weltkrieg*, ed. Militärgeschichtliches Forschungsamt (Military Historical Research Office), vol. 6, Stuttgart, 1990, pp. 347–66; Richard J. Evans, *The Third Reich at War, 1939–1945*, London, 2008, pp. 479–82; Adam Tooze, *The Wages of Destruction: The Making and Breaking of the Nazi Economy*, London, 2006, pp. 592f. On Raeder's replacement by Dönitz, see Erich Raeder, *Mein Leben. Vol. 2: Von 1935 bis Spandau 1955*, Tübingen, 1957, pp. 286–90; Karl Dönitz, *Zehn Jahre und zwanzig Tage*, Frankfurt am Main, 1967, pp. 292f.

39   Goebbels, *Tagebücher*, part II, vol. 8, pp. 306f. (entry for 16 May 1943).

40   See Victor Zaslavsky, *Klassensäuberung: Das Massaker von Katyn*, Berlin, 2007; Thomas Urban, *Katyn: Geschichte eines Verbrechens*, Munich, 2015. For a summary, see Jörg Baberowski, *Verbrannte Erde: Stalins Herrschaft der Gewalt*, Munich, 2012, pp. 390–3.

41   Goebbels, *Tagebücher*, part II, vol. 8, p. 104 (entry for 14 April 1943).

42   Ibid., p. 135 (entry for 20 April 1943); see ibid., p. 159 (entry for 24 April 1943): "We will continue to work on the Katyn story with all the elan we have."

43   Ibid., p. 119 (entry for 17 April 1943); see ibid., pp. 260f. (entry for 10 May 1943).

44   Gabriel Gorodetsky (ed.), *Die Maiski-Tagebücher: Ein Diplomat im Kampf gegen Hitler*, Munich, 2016, pp. 732f. (entry for 23 April 1943).

45   *Meldungen aus dem Reich*, vol. 13, p. 5145 (dated 19 April 1943). Further examples in Otto Dov Kulka and Eberhard Jäckel (eds), *Die Juden in den geheimen NS-Stimmungsberichten 1939–1945*, Düsseldorf, 2004, pp. 518–25. On Goebbels' campaign and the reactions of the German population, see Peter Longerich, *"Davon haben wir nichts gewusst!" Die Deutschen und die Judenverfolgung 1933–1945*, Munich, 2006, pp. 267–89.

46   *Die Verfolgung und Ermordung der europäischen Juden durch das nationalsozialistische Deutschland*, vol. 9, ed. Klaus-Peter Friedrich, Munich, 2014, doc. 243, p. 648.

47   Goebbels, *Tagebücher*, part II, vol. 8, p. 351 (entry for 23 May 1943). Hitler's plane left Rastenburg at 1 p.m., landing at 3:40 p.m. at the airstrip near Salzburg. He arrived at around 4:30 p.m. at the Berghof. See Heinz Linge's appointment diary under 21 May 1943; IfZ München, F 19/4.

48   Goebbels, *Tagebücher*, part II, vol. 8, p. 359 (entry for 25 May 1943).

49   Extracts from the reports from the Gaue, 16–21 May 1943; BA Berlin-Lichterfelde, NS 6/415.

50   Goebbels, *Tagebücher*, part II, vol. 8, pp. 493–9 (entry for 16 June 1943; at p. 497). On the air battle over the Ruhr Valley, see Horst Boog, "Strategischer Luftkrieg in Europa und Reichsluftverteidigung 1943–1944," in *Das Deutsche Reich und der Zweite Weltkrieg. Vol. 7: Das Deutsche Reich in der Defensive*, Stuttgart and Munich, 2001, p. 16–21; Richard Overy, *The Bombing War: Europe 1939–1945*, London, 2013, pp. 445–8; Nicholas Stargardt, *The German War: A Nation under Arms, 1939–45*, London, 2015, pp. 347–52.

51   Goebbels, *Tagebücher*, part II, vol. 8, p. 527 (entry for 25 June 1943).

52   Ibid., vol. 11, p. 332 (entry for 23 Feb. 1944).

53   See Zeitzler, "Das Ringen um die grossen Entscheidungen," vol. 2, p. 68; BA-MA Freiburg, N 63/80; Warlimont, *Im Hauptquartier der Wehrmacht*, p. 347. Manstein had also come to share such doubts: see Manstein, "Entstehung, Durchführung und Abschluss des Unternehmens 'Zitadelle'"(dated 1–2 June 1943); BA-MA Freiburg, N 507/121.

54   Guderian, *Erinnerungen eines Soldaten*, pp. 280f.; see *KTB OKW*, vol. 3, part 2, p. 750 (entry for 5 July 1943); *Das Deutsche Reich und der Zweite Weltkrieg*, vol. 8, p. 77 (Wegner's essay).

55   Cited in Töppel, "Kursk," p. 352.

56   Goebbels, *Tagebücher*, part II, vol. 8, pp. 531f. (entry for 25 June 1943).

57 See Manstein, *Verlorene Siege*, p. 496. On 1 July 1943, Manstein wrote in his diary: "Necessity of a military triumph with an eye towards allies, neutrals and mood of own population." Pyta, *Hitler*, p. 467.

58 Domarus, *Hitler*, vol. 2, part 2, pp. 2021f.

59 Gehlen's statement of 4 July 1943; cited in *Das Deutsche Reich und der Zweite Weltkrieg*, vol. 8, p. 77 (Wegner's essay).

60 See Richard Overy, *Why the Allies Won*, London, 2006, pp. 108–11.

61 See Karl-Heinz Frieser, "Die Schlacht im Kursker Bogen," in *Das Deutsche Reich und der Zweite Weltkrieg*, vol. 8, p. 101. Frieser's numbers were slightly revised by Töppel ("Kursk," pp. 356–62; *Kursk 1943*, p. 98–101). According to Töppel, German forces had about 2,900 deployable armoured vehicles.

62 Friedrich Hossbach, "Erinnerungen," chapter 8, appendix to p. 13; BA-MA Freiburg, N 24/39.

63 See *Das Deutsche Reich und der Zweite Weltkrieg*, vol. 8, pp. 107–35 (Frieser's essay); Töppel, "Kursk," pp. 367–78; *idem, Kursk 1943*, pp. 159–69, 230–5.

64 Zeitzler, "Das Ringen um die grossen Entscheidungen," vol. 2, p. 70; BA-MA Freiburg, N 63/80.

65 Goebbels, *Tagebücher*, part II, vol. 9, pp. 58 (entry for 7 July 1943), 70 (entry for 9 July 1943), 92 (entry for 13 July1943).

66 Zeitzler, "Das Ringen um die grossen Entscheidungen," vol. 2, p. 88; BA-MA Freiburg, N 63/80; Manstein, *Verlorene Siege*, pp. 501–3. On Hitler's motives for the decision, see Töppel, "Kursk," pp. 378–84; *idem, Kursk 1943*, pp. 170–3.

67 Cited in Catherine Merridale, *Ivan's War: The Red Army 1939–45*, London, 2005, p. 194.

68 See *Das Deutsche Reich und der Zweite Weltkrieg*, vol. 8, pp. 1111–14 (Schreiber's essay); Warlimont, *Im Hauptquartier der Wehrmacht*, pp. 350–2.

69 Goebbels, *Tagebücher*, part II, vol. 9, p. 108 (entry for 16 July 1943); see ibid., p. 114 (entry for 17 July 1943).

70 See Norman Ohler, *Der totale Rausch: Drogen im Dritten Reich*, Cologne, 2015, pp. 185–8; Hans-Joachim Neumann and Henrik Eberle, *War Hitler krank? Ein abschliessender Befund*, Bergisch Gladbach, 2009, p. 251; Ernst Günther Schenck, *Patient Hitler: Eine medizinische Biographie*, Düsseldorf, 1989, p. 142.

71 See Junge, *Bis zur letzten Stunde*, pp. 126–8; Henrik Eberle and Matthias Uhl (eds), *Das Buch Hitler*, Bergisch Gladbach, 2005, pp. 222f.

72 Notes on the conversation between Hitler and Mussolini, 19 July 1943, in Andreas Hillgruber (ed.), *Staatsmänner und Diplomaten bei Hitler: Vertrauliche Aufzeichnungen über Unterredungen mit Vertretern des Auslandes 1939–1941*, Frankfurt am Main, 1967, part 2, pp. 287–300 (at pp. 289, 296). A summary can be found in *KTB OKW*, vol. 2, part 2, pp. 805–8.

73 Paul Schmidt, *Statist auf diplomatischer Bühne 1923–45*, Bonn, 1950, p. 568.

74 Cited in David Irving, *Hitler und seine Feldherren*, Frankfurt am Main, Berlin and Vienna, 1975, p. 498.

75 See Woller, *Geschichte Italiens im 20. Jahrhundert*, pp. 186f.; *idem, Mussolini: Der erste Faschist. Eine Biografie*, Munich, 2016, pp. 267–70; *idem, Die Abrechnung mit dem Faschismus in Italien 1943 bis 1948*, Munich, 1996, pp. 9f.; Falanga, *Mussolinis Vorposten in Hitlers Reich*, pp. 209–11.

76 BA Koblenz, N 1273/32; see Hill (ed.), *Die Weizsäcker-Papiere 1933–1950*, pp. 343f. (dated 26 July 1943).

77 Evening briefing of 25 July 1943; Heiber (ed.), *Hitlers Lagebesprechungen*, pp. 309–25 (at pp. 312, 315); second evening briefing of 25 July 1943; ibid., pp. 325–31 (at p. 329).

78 Goebbels, *Tagebücher*, part II, vol. 9, p. 169 (entry for 27 July 1943). See Rommel's diary, entry for 26 July 1943; BA-MA Freiburg, N 117/77.

79 Hitler's meeting with Kluge, 26 July 1943; Heiber (ed.), *Hitlers Lagebesprechungen*, pp. 369–84 (at pp. 370, 373).

80 See Goebbels, *Tagebücher*, part II, vol. 9, pp. 179f. (entry for 27 July 1943).

81 See *KTB OKW*, vol. 3, part 2, pp. 837 (entry for 26 July 1943), 850 (entry for 28 July 1943), 855f. (entry for 29 July 1943), 860 (entry for 30 July 1943), 868 (entry for 1 Aug. 1943).

82 See Ursula von Kardorff, *Berliner Aufzeichnungen 1942–1945*, new edition, ed. Peter Hartl, Munich, 1992, p. 97 (entry for 30 July 1943).

83 Report from the head of the provincial government of Upper Bavaria, 9 Aug. 1943; cited in Marlies Steinert, *Hitlers Krieg und die Deutschen: Stimmung und Haltung der deutschen Bevölkerung im Zweiten Weltkrieg*, Düsseldorf and Vienna, 1970, p. 394.

84 *Meldungen aus dem Reich*, vol. 14, pp. 5540f. (dated 29 July 1943).

85 Goebbels, *Tagebücher*, part II, vol. 9, p. 190 (entry for 29 July 1943). On Operation Gomorrah, see Overy, *The Bombing War*, pp. 327–38; Olaf Groehler, *Bombenkrieg gegen Deutschland*, Berlin, 1990, pp. 106–21; Stargardt, *The German War*, pp. 366–70.

86 Mathilde Wolff-Mönckeberg, *Briefe, die sie nicht erreichten: Briefe einer Mutter an ihre fernen Kinder in den Jahren 1940–1946*, Hamburg, 1980, p. 92; *Meldungen aus dem Reich*, vol. 14, p. 5563 (dated 2 Aug. 1943). See Ursula Büttner, " 'Gomorrha' und die Folgen: Der Bombenkrieg," in Forschungsstelle für Zeitgeschichte in Hamburg (ed.), *Hamburg im "Dritten Reich,"* Göttingen, 2005, pp. 613–32 (at pp. 622f.).

87 See Martin Bormann's memorandum of 26 July 1943; BA Berlin-Lichterfelde, NS 19/1880; Goebbels, *Tagebücher*, part II, vol. 9, p. 173 (entry for 27 July 1943).

88 Ibid., p. 265 (entry for 10 Aug. 1943). See Marga Himmler's diary entry for 3 Sept. 1943: "H[einrich] has been made interior minister. The people of Germany believe that he can save them. May God let it be so." Katrin Himmler and Michael Wildt (eds), *Himmler privat: Briefe eines Massenmörders*, Munich, 2014, p. 312.

89 Victor Klemperer, *Ich will Zeugnis ablegen bis zum letzten: Tagebücher*, vol. 2: 1942–1945, ed. Walter Nowojski with Hadwig Klemperer, Berlin, 1995, p. 423 (entry for 26 Aug. 1943). See also Kellner, *Tagebücher 1939–1945*, vol. 1, p. 507 (entry for 26 Aug. 1943): "That is the utmost . . . Now the most radical men occupy all the posts."

90 Goebbels, *Tagebücher*, part II, vol. 9, p. 324 (entry for 21 Aug. 1943).

91 Ibid., vol. 11, p. 152 (entry for 25 Jan. 1944).

92 Ibid., vol. 9, pp. 250f. (entry for 10 Aug. 1943). See also Rommel's diary entry for 11 Aug. 1943: "The Führer points out that the Italians are only trying to gain time so that they can get out." BA-MA Freiburg, N 117/77.

93 See *Das Deutsche Reich und der Zweite Weltkrieg*, vol. 8, p. 1114 (Schreiber's essay).

94 Balck's diary entry for 10 Sept. 1943; BA-MA Freiburg, N 647/10.

95 See *KTB OKW*, vol. 3, part 2, pp. 1076f. (entry for 8 Sept. 1943).

96 According to Heinz Linge's appointment diary under 8 Sept. 1943, the dictator went to bed at 5 a.m.; IfZ München, F 19/4.

97 Goebbels, *Tagebücher*, part II, vol. 9, pp. 457–60 (entry for 10 Sept. 1943).

98 Speer to Himmler, 9 Oct. 1943; BA Berlin-Lichterfelde, NS 19/1880.

99 See Woller, *Geschichte Italiens im 20. Jahrhundert*, pp. 190f., 196–8; Falanga, *Mussolinis Vorposten in Hitlers Reich*, pp. 224f., 238f.; Gerhard Schreiber, *Die italienischen Militärinternierten im deutschen Machtbereich 1943 bis 1945: Verraten—verachtet—vergessen*, Munich, 1990; idem, *Deutsche Kriegsverbrechen in Italien: Täter—Opfer—Strafverfolgung*, Munich, 1996, pp. 76–85; 95ff.

100 Goebbels, *Tagebücher*, part II, vol. 9, pp. 206 (entry for 2 Aug. 1943), 229 (entry for 6 Aug. 1943), 252 (entry for 10 Aug. 1943).

101 See ibid., pp. 475 (entry for 10 Sept. 1943), 486f. (entry for 11 Sept. 1943).

102 Text in Domarus, *Hitler*, vol. 2, part 2, pp. 2035–9 (at pp. 2036, 2038).

103 *Meldungen aus dem Reich*, vol. 15, p. 5753 (dated 13 Sept. 1943). See Gerda to Martin Bormann, 11 Sept. 1943; Hugh Trevor-Roper (ed.), *The Bormann Letters*, London, 1954 p. 26.

104 *Meldungen aus dem Reich*, p. 5770 (dated 16 Sept. 1943).

105 Goebbels, *Tagebücher*, part II, vol. 9, p. 489 (entry for 12 Sept. 1943).

106 Ibid., pp. 500f. (entry for 13 Sept. 1943). See Woller, *Mussolini*, pp. 276f.

107 Eberle and Uhl (eds), *Das Buch Hitler*, p. 233. Ernst von Weizsäcker, who saw Mussolini when the latter's plane stopped in Munich, reported after returning to Rome, on 15 September 1943, that the Duce "in his blue suit looked haggard and tired but excited at the occasion." BA Koblenz, N 1273/32.

108 Goebbels, *Tagebücher*, part II, vol. 9, p. 567 (entry for 23 Sept. 1943).

109 See Woller, *Geschichte Italiens im 20. Jahrhundert*, pp. 191f., 194f.; idem, *Mussolini*, p. 291; Falanga, *Mussolinis Vorposten in Hitlers Reich*, pp. 250f.

110 Goebbels, *Tagebücher*, vol. 11, p. 158 (entry for 25 Jan. 1944).

111 See also *Das Deutsche Reich und der Zweite Weltkrieg*, vol. 8, pp. 173ff., 277ff. (Frieser's essay). For a summary, see Müller, *Der letzte deutsche Krieg*, pp. 191–5.

112 Goebbels; *Tagebücher*, part II, vol. 9, p. 333 (entry for 21 Aug. 1943).

113 Cited in Merridale, *Ivan's War*, p. 198. On the scorched-earth strategy at the battalion and company level, see Felix Römer, *Die narzisstische Volksgemeinschaft: Theodor Habichts Kampf 1914 bis 1944*, Frankfurt am Main, 2017, pp. 279–82.

114 Goebbels, *Tagebücher*, part II, vol. 9, p. 567 (entry for 23 Sept. 1943). The commander of the 4th Tank Army, Hermann Hoth, was likewise optimistic in a letter to Gauleiter Fritz Sauckel on 2 October 1943: "The army is in entirely good shape despite their lengthy evasive actions." BA Koblenz, N 1582/5.

115 Hossbach, "Erinnerungen," chapter 8, appendix to p. 36; BA-MA Freiburg, N 24/39.

116 Zeitzler, "Das Ringen um die grossen Entscheidungen," vol. 2, p. 129; BA-MA Freiburg, N 63/80. See Manstein, *Verlorene Siege*, p. 554; *Das Deutsche Reich und der Zweite Weltkrieg*, vol. 8, p. 373 (Frieser's essay).

117 Goebbels, *Tagebücher*, part II, vol. 10, p. 195 (entry for 27 Oct. 1943). See also the statement by Field Marshal Schörner on 20 August 1945 about a conversation with Hitler on 14 October 1943 in the Wolf's Lair; Wassili S. Christoforow, Wladimir G. Makarow and Matthias Uhl (eds), *Verhört: Die Befragungen deutscher Generale und Offiziere durch die sowjetischen Geheimdienste 1945–1952*, Berlin and Boston, 2015, pp. 171–3.

118 See Heinz Linge's appointment diary for 8 Nov. 1943; IfZ München, F 19/4.

119 Goebbels, *Tagebücher*, part II, vol. 10, p. 262 (entry for 9 Nov. 1943).

120 Domarus, *Hitler*, vol. 2, part 2, pp. 2050–9 (at pp. 2052, 2051, 2058, 2056).

121 Goebbels, *Tagebücher*, part II, vol. 10, p. 262 (entry for 9 Nov. 1943).

122 *Meldungen aus dem Reich*, vol. 15, p. 5988 (dated 11 Nov. 1943).

123 Ibid., p. 6034 (dated 18 Nov. 1943).

124 Ruth Andreas-Friedrich, *Der Schattenmann: Tagebuchaufzeichnungen 1938–1945*, Frankfurt am Main, 1983, p. 116 (entry for 10 Sept. 1943). See Kellner, *Tagebücher 1939–1945*, vol. 1, pp. 529 (entry for 21 Sept. 1943), 610 (entry for 26 Jan. 1944).

125 Domarus, *Hitler*, vol. 2, part 2, p. 2061. At 10:30 p.m. on 19 November 1943, Hitler departed from the train station in Görlitz, arriving at Breslau at 11:50 a.m. the following day. The speech began at 12 noon. At 2:45 p.m. Hitler left Breslau, arriving at 1:55 a.m. back in Görlitz. See Linge's appointment diary under 19 and 20 Nov. 1943. IfZ München, F 19/4. See Harald Sandner, *Hitler: Das Itinerar. Aufenthaltsorte und Reisen von 1889–1945*, Berlin, 2016, vol. 4, p. 2177.

126 Hassell, *Vom andern Deutschland*, p. 282 (entry for 18 July 1943).

127 See *Das Deutsche Reich und der Zweite Weltkrieg*, vol. 8, pp. 52–5 (Wegner's essay); Pyta, *Hitler*, pp. 501–3; Woller, *Mussolini*, pp. 249f.

128 Goebbels, *Tagebücher*, part II, vol. 9, p. 464 (entry for 10 Sept. 1943).

129 Ibid., pp. 566, 582f. (entry for 23 Sept. 1943).

130 Ibid., vol. 10, pp. 183f. (entry for 27 Oct. 1943).

131 In his memoirs, Speer claimed that from the autumn of 1943, Hitler had increasingly remarked at situation meetings: "Do not fool yourself. There is no turning back. We can only move forward. We have burned our bridges." Albert Speer, *Erinnerungen: Mit einem Essay von Jochen Thies*, Frankfurt am Main and Berlin, 1993. p. 306.

132 On this topic, see Ingeborg Fleischhauer, *Die Chance des Sonderfriedens: Deutsch-sowjetische Geheimgespräche 1941–1945*, Berlin, 1986. For the Soviet side, see Jochen Laufer, *Pax Sovietica: Stalin, die Westmächte und die deutsche Frage 1941–1945*, Cologne, Weimar and Vienna, 2009, pp. 203–28.

133 See Robin Edmonds, *Die Grossen Drei: Churchill, Roosevelt und Stalin in Frieden und Krieg*, Berlin, 1992, pp. 323–39; Laufer, *Pax Sovietica*, pp. 364–78.

134 Goebbels, *Tagebücher*, part II, vol. 10, p. 432 (entry for 7 Dec. 1943); see ibid., pp. 402f. (entry for 2 Dec. 1943), 427 (entry for 6 Feb. 1943).

135 See Below, *Als Hitlers Adjutant*, pp. 355f.; Walter Schellenberg, *Aufzeichnungen: Die Memoiren des letzten Geheimdienstchefs unter Hitler*, Munich, 1979, pp. 315–24; Franz von Papen, *Der Wahrheit eine Gasse*, Munich, 1952, pp. 578–90; Reuth, *Hitler*, p. 601.

136 Herbert Backe to his wife, 26 Nov. 1943; BA Koblenz, N 1075/26.

137 Goebbels, *Tagebücher*, part II, vol. 10, pp. 340f. (entry for 23 Nov. 1943). On the Battle of Berlin, see Groehler, *Bombenkrieg über Deutschland*, pp. 182ff.; *Das Deutsche Reich und der Zweite Weltkrieg*, vol. 7, pp. 75ff. (Boog's essay).

138 See Goebbels, *Tagebücher*, part II, vol. 10, pp. 369 (entry for 27 Nov. 1943), 382 (entry for 29 Nov. 1943).

139 *Meldungen aus dem Reich*, vol. 15, p. 6187 (dated 27 Dec. 1943).

140 Goebbels, *Tagebücher*, part II, vol. 10, p. 457 (entry for 11 Dec. 1943).

141 Ibid., pp. 513–16 (entry for 20 Dec. 1943).

142 Balck's diary, entry for 26 Dec. 1943; BA-MA Freiburg, N 647/11. See also Reinhardt's letters to his wife, 15 Dec. and 22 Dec. 1943; BA-MA Freiburg, N 245/2.

143 Hitler's meeting with Zeitzler, 27 Dec. 1943; Heiber (ed.), *Hitlers Lagebesprechungen*, pp. 469–85 (at pp. 477f.).

144 Meeting between Hitler and Küchler, 30 Dec. 1943; ibid., pp. 516–25.

145 See *Das Deutsche Reich und der Zweite Weltkrieg*, vol. 8, pp. 284–91 (Frieser's essay).

146 See Below, *Als Hitlers Adjutant*, p. 357.

147 Goebbels, *Tagebücher*, part II, vol. 11, p. 35 (entry for 1 Jan. 1944).

148 Domarus, *Hitler*, vol. 2, part 2, pp. 2071–6 (at p. 2075).

149 See Goebbels, *Tagebücher*, part II, vol. 9, pp. 575 (entry for 23 Sept. 1943), 137 (entry for 21 July 1943).

150 Ibid., vol. 10, pp. 178f. (entry for 27 Oct. 1943).

151 Ibid., vol. 11, p. 240 (entry for 3 Feb. 1944); see ibid., vol. 10, pp. 298f. (entry for 16 Nov. 1943), 349 (entry for 24 Nov. 1943). In this context, see also *Das Deutsche Reich und der Zweite Weltkrieg*, vol. 8, pp. 225f. (Wegner's essay); Pyta, *Hitler*, pp. 506–10. See also the portrait by Torsten Diedrich, "Walther von Seydlitz-Kurzbach—der lange verkannte deutsche Patriot," in Torsten Diedrich and Jens Ebert (eds), *Nach Stalingrad: Walther von Seydlitz" Feldpostbriefe und Kriegsgefangenenpost 1939–1955*, Göttingen, 2018, pp. 319–412.

152 See Sönke Neitzel, *Abgehört: Deutsche Generäle in britischer Kriegsgefangenschaft 1942–1945*, Berlin, 2005, doc. 178, pp. 392f.

153 Meeting between Hitler and General Reinecke, 7 Jan. 1944; Gerhard L. Weinberg, "Adolf Hitler und der NS-Führungsoffizier (NSFO): Dokumentation," in *Vierteljahrshefte für Zeitgeschichte*, 12 (1964), pp. 443–56 (at pp. 454, 446). On the Führer's decree of 22 Dec. 1943, see Jürgen Förster, "Geistige Kriegführung in Deutschland 1919 bis 1945," in *Das Deutsche Reich und der Zweite Weltkrieg*, ed. Militärgeschichtliches Forschungsamt (Military Historical Research Office), vol. 9, part 1, Munich, 2004, pp. 590–601.

154 Goebbels, *Tagebücher*, part II, vol. 10, p. 177 (entry for 27 Oct. 1943).

155 Manstein's diary entry for 4 Jan. 1944; Pyta, *Hitler*, p. 478.

156 Manstein, *Verlorene Siege*, pp. 569–73 (at pp. 572f.).

157 Goebbels, *Tagebücher*, part II, vol. 11, p. 168 (entry for 25 Jan. 1944).

158 BA Berlin-Lichterfelde, NS 6/777. Further transcripts of the speech in BA-MA Freiburg, N 745, no. 38 und IfZ München, F 19/3. Subsequently cited in Pyta, *Hitler*, pp. 481, 512f.; Ian Kershaw, *Hitler 1936–1945: Nemesis*, London, 2001, p. 619. For a slightly different wording, see Manstein, *Verlorene Siege*, p. 580. In August 1944, a participant at the meeting, General Dietrich von Choltitz, told his fellow officer POWs about the incident. See Neitzel, *Abgehört*, doc. 32, pp. 130f.

159 See Pyta's extensive interpretation in *Hitler*, pp. 214f., 481–3, 512–14.

160 Manstein, *Verlorene Siege*, p. 580.

161 Marianne Feuersenger, *Im Vorzimmer der Macht: Aufzeichnungen aus dem Wehrmachtführungsstab und Führerhauptquartier 1940–1945*, 4th edition, Munich, 2001, p. 198 (entry for 9 Feb. 1944). See Eberle and Uhl (eds), *Das Buch Hitler*, p. 239: "Hitler berated Manstein for ten minutes. At the end the latter looked like a schoolboy who had done something wrong and been punished accordingly." Even courageous generals like Manstein, wrote Speer to Rudolf Wolters on 12 December 1952, had "all knelt down before Hitler." BA Koblenz, N 1318/20.

162 See Goebbels, *Tagebücher*, part II, vol. 11, p. 169 (entry for 25 Jan. 1944).

163 Text in Domarus, *Hitler*, vol. 2, part 2, pp. 2082–6 (at p. 2083).

164 *Meldungen aus dem Reich*, vol. 16, p. 6298 (dated 4 Feb. 1944); see ibid., p. 6311 (dated 10 Feb. 1944.)

165 Goebbels, *Tagebücher*, part II, vol. 11, pp. 273f. (entry for 10 Feb. 1944).

166 Ibid., p. 208 (entry for 31 Jan. 1944).

167 "Führer Directive No. 11," dated 8 March 1944; Walther Hubatsch (ed.), *Hitlers Weisungen für die Kriegsführung*, Munich, 1965, pp. 281–3. See *Das Deutsche Reich und der Zweite Weltkrieg*, vol. 8, pp. 424–31 (Frieser's essay).

168 Junge, *Bis zur letzten Stunde*, p. 131; see Eberle and Uhl (eds), *Das Buch Hitler*, p. 243.

169 See Uwe Neumärker, Robert Conrad and Cord Woywodt, *Wolfsschanze: Hitlers Machtzentrale im Zweiten Weltkrieg*, 3rd edition, Berlin, 2007, pp. 132f.

170 See Morell's notes of 11–15 Feb. 1944; BA Koblenz, N 1348/4; Schenck, *Patient Hitler*, pp. 144f. On Hitler's illness, see Goebbels, *Tagebücher*, part II, vol. 11, p. 300 (entry for 17 Feb. 1944). During their final conversation in the Wolf's Lair on 6 February 1944, Hitler reminded General Governor Hans Frank of "a tired, spent man." Hans Frank, *Im Angesicht des Galgens: Deutung Hitlers und seiner Zeit auf Grund eigener Erlebnisse und Erkenntnisse*, Munich and Gräfelfing, 1953, p. 422.

171 Goebbels, *Tagebücher*, part II, vol. 11, pp. 347 (entry for 25 Feb. 1944), 361 (entry for 28 Feb. 1944).

172 *Meldungen aus dem Reich*, vol. 16, p. 6412 (dated 16 March 1944); see ibid., p. 6432 (dated 23 March 1944).

173 Minutes of talks between Hitler and Antonescu on 26–27 Feb. 1944; Hillgruber (ed.), *Staatsmänner und Diplomaten bei Hitler*, part II, pp. 348–63 (at p. 362). Hitler said much the same to members of the Bulgarian Governing Council on 16 March 1944; ibid., pp. 370–84 (at pp. 373f.).

174 Goebbels, *Tagebücher*, part II, vol. 11, p. 367 (entry for 29 Feb. 1944).

175 See ibid., p. 455 (entry for 11 March 1944).

176 Reproduced in Henrik Eberle (ed.), *Briefe an Hitler: Ein Volk schreibt seinem Führer. Unbekannte Dokumente aus Moskauer Archiven—zum ersten Mal veröffentlicht*, Bergisch Gladbach, 2007, pp. 418f.

177 See Manstein, *Verlorene Siege*, p. 603. Goebbels learned that Hitler had been "deeply moved and impressed by this"; *Tagebücher*, part II, vol. 11, p. 515 (entry for 20 March 1944). See ibid., vol. 12, p. 60 (entry for 6 April 1944); Manstein's report for the Führer's briefing at the Berghof on 19 March 1944 in BA-MA Freiburg, N 507/113.

178 Manstein, *Verlorene Siege*, pp. 615f.; see Balck's diary for 1 April 1944: "Thus far his successor Model has mastered every difficult defensive situation." BA-MA Freiburg. N 647/12; see also Below, *Als Hitlers Adjutant*, p. 361; *Das Deutsche Reich und der Zweite Weltkrieg*, vol. 8, pp. 448f. (Frieser's essay).

179   Zeitzler, "Das Ringen um die grossen Entscheidungen," vol. 2, pp. 138f.; BA-MA Freiburg, N 63/80.

180   Goebbels, *Tagebücher*, part II, vol. 11, p. 397 (entry for 4 June 1944); see ibid., p. 435 (entry for 8 March 1944).

181   Ibid., p. 462 (entry for 13 March 1944).

182   See Ullrich, *Hitler: Ascent 1889–1945*, pp. 710–12, 750f.

183   Schmidt, *Statist auf diplomatischer Bühne*, pp. 577f. On 17 April 1944, Hitler described his meeting with Horthy to the Reichsleiter and Gauleiter. Goebbels summarised: "He used quite an extortionate method here since the old gentleman had not wanted to accept the necessary measures." Goebbels, *Tagebücher*, part II, vol. 12, p. 137 (entry for 18 April 1944).

184   See Eckart Conze, Norbert Frei, Peter Hayes and Moshe Zimmermann, *Das Amt und die Vergangenheit: Deutsche Diplomaten im Dritten Reich und in der Bundesrepublik*, Munich, 2010, pp. 261–3.

185   This account is based on Christian Gerlach and Götz Aly, *Das letzte Kapitel: Der Mord an den ungarischen Juden*, Stuttgart and Munich, 2002. For a summary of the fate of Hungarian Jews, see David Cesarani, *Final Solution: The Fate of the Jews 1933–1949*, London, 2016, pp. 702–11.

186   Minutes of the talks between Hitler and Antonescu, 23–24 March 1944, in Hillgruber (ed.), *Staatsmänner und Diplomaten bei Hitler*, part II, pp. 389–406 (at pp. 391, 401f., 403).

187   Zeitzler, "Das Ringen um die grossen Entscheidungen," vol. 2, p. 147; BA-MA Freiburg, N 63/80.

188   See Norbert Kunz, *Die Krim unter deutscher Herrschaft 1941–1944*, Darmstadt, 2005; Karl Heinz Roth and Jan Peter Abraham, *Reemtsma auf der Krim: Tabakproduktion und Zwangsarbeit unter der deutschen Besatzungsherrschaft 1941–1944*, Hamburg, 2011, pp. 337–45.

189   Balck's diary entry for 22 April 1944; BA-MA Freiburg, N 647/12. See Reinhardt's letter to his wife of 20 April 1944: "All continues to be calm here. I think great things are brewing among the Russians for the time when the mud is gone. We have to be prepared for anything—and we are!" BA-MA Freiburg, N 245/2.

11   *Operations Overlord and Bagration*

1   Walther Hubatsch (ed.), *Hitlers Weisungen für die Kriegsführung*, Munich, 1965, pp. 270–4 (at pp. 270f.). See Dieter Ose, *Entscheidung im Westen 1944: Der Oberbefehlshaber West und die Abwehr der alliierten Invasion*, Stuttgart, 1982, pp. 33–5.

2   Helmut Heiber (ed.), *Hitlers Lagebesprechungen: Die Protokollfragmente seiner militärischen Konferenzen 1942–1945*, Stuttgart, 1962, pp. 440–55 (at pp. 444, 452).

3   Friedrich Hossbach to his wife, 23 Feb. 1944; "Erinnerungen," chapter 8, footnote to p. 17; BA-MA Freiburg, N 24/39.

4   See Karl-Heinz Frieser, "Der Zusammenbruch im Osten" in *Das Deutsche Reich und der Zweite Weltkrieg. Vol. 8: Die Ostfront 1943/44*, Munich, 2007, p. 501.

5   Jodl's briefing to the Reichsleiter and Gauleiter, 7 Nov. 1943; *Kriegstagebuch des Oberkommandos der Wehrmacht (Wehrmachtführungsstab)* (hereafter *KTB OKW*), ed. Percy Ernst Schramm, Munich, 1982, vol. 4, pp. 1534–62 (at pp. 1560, 1557, 1561f.). See *Die Tagebücher von Joseph Goebbels*, commissioned by the Institute for Contemporary History, with support from the State Archive of Russia, ed. Elke Fröhlich, *Part II: Diktate 1941–1945*, 15 vols, Munich, 1993–6, vol. 10, p. 254 (entry for 8 Nov. 1943): "As such, Jodl's analyses tell me nothing new, but for the Gauleiter they are a kind of sensation."

6   Heinz Guderian, *Erinnerungen eines Soldaten*, Heidelberg, 1951, p. 295. See Albert Speer, *Erinnerungen: Mit einem Essay von Jochen Thies*, Frankfurt am Main and Berlin,

1993, p. 363. On the Atlantic Wall, see Detlev Vogel, "Deutsche und alliierte Kriegführung im Westen," in *Das Deutsche Reich und der Zweite Weltkrieg. Vol. 7: Das Deutsche Reich in der Defensive*, Stuttgart and Munich, 2001, pp. 465–71.

7   Ralf Georg Reuth, *Rommel: Das Ende einer Legende*, Munich and Zurich, 2004, pp. 85–8 (at p. 87). Rommel's reports on his daily inspections in April and May 1944 in BA-MA Freiburg, N 117/78. See Friedrich Ruge, *Rommel und die Invasion: Erinnerungen*, Stuttgart, 1959, pp. 95–101; Hans Speidel, *Invasion 1944: Ein Beitrag zu Rommels und des Reiches Schicksal*, Tübingen and Stuttgart, 1949, pp. 46–8.

8   See Guderian, *Erinnerungen eines Soldaten*, pp. 298–301; Ose, *Entscheidung im Westen*, pp. 47–57; Richard Overy, *Why the Allies Won*, London, 2006, pp. 189–91; Paul Kennedy, *Engineers of Victory: The Problem Solvers who Turned the Tide in the Second World War*, London, 2013, pp. 261–3

9   Goebbels, *Tagebücher*, part II, vol. 11, p. 160 (entry for 25 Jan. 1944).

10   Ibid., p. 400 (entry for 4 March 1944).

11   Ibid., p. 482 (entry for 15 March 1944). At the situation meeting on 6 April 1944, Hitler also voiced doubts as to whether the Western Allies were serious about a landing, saying that he could not help but get the "impression that the whole thing may turn out to be a piece of impudent theatre." Heiber (ed.), *Hitlers Lagebesprechungen*, p. 556.

12   Goebbels, *Tagebücher*, part II, vol. 12, pp. 126–30, 134–40 (entry for 18 April 1944).

13   Ibid., p. 160 (entry for 21 April 1944).

14   Ibid., p. 92 (entry for 12 April 1944); see ibid., p. 155 (entry for 20 April 1944).

15   Thomas Mann, *Tagebücher, 1944–1. April 1946*, ed. Inge Jens, Frankfurt am Main, 1986, p. 46 (entry for 19 April 1944).

16   See Goebbels, *Tagebücher*, part II, vol. 12, p. 168 (entry for 22 April 1944). Nicolaus von Below, *Als Hitlers Adjutant 1937–45*, Mainz, 1980, pp. 367f. In late August 1943, Hitler had given Hube 50,000 reichsmarks as a wedding present. Schmundt to Lammers, 31 Aug. 1943; BA Berlin-Lichterfelde, R 43 II/986.

17   See Goebbels, *Tagebücher*, part II, vol. 12, p. 542 (entry for 24 June 1944); Below, *Als Hitlers Adjutant*, p. 376.

18   Goebbels, *Tagebücher*, part II, vol. 12, pp. 195–205 (entry for 27 April 1944).

19   Ibid., p. 201 (entry for 27 April 1944).

20   Notes on Hitler's conversation with Mussolini, 22–23 April 1944, in Andreas Hillgruber (ed.), *Staatsmänner und Diplomaten bei Hitler: Vertrauliche Aufzeichnungen über Unterredungen mit Vertretern des Auslandes 1939–1941*, Frankfurt am Main, 1967, part 2, pp. 406–38 (at pp. 410, 417, 418, 419, 421).

21   See Ernst von Weizsäcker's circular from Rome of 23 Jan. and 8 June 1944; BA Koblenz, N 1273/32; Leonidas Hill (ed.), *Die Weizsäcker-Papiere 1933–1950*, Frankfurt am Main, Berlin and Vienna, 1974, pp. 366, 378; see also *Das Deutsche Reich und der Zweite Weltkrieg*, vol. 8, pp. 1147–52 (Schreiber's essay); Gerhard L. Weinberg, *Eine Welt in Waffen: Die globale Geschichte des Zweiten Weltkriegs*, Stuttgart, 1995, pp. 699, 714.

22   Goebbels, *Tagebücher*, part II, vol. 12, p. 283 (entry for 13 May 1944); see ibid., pp. 277 (entry for 12 May 1944), 319 (entry for 19 May 1944), 357 (entry for 25 May 1944).

23   Heinz Boberach (ed.), *Meldungen aus dem Reich: Die geheimen Lageberichte des Sicherheitsdienstes der SS 1938–1945*, Herrsching, 1984, vol. 17, pp. 6510f. (dated 4 May 1944); see ibid., pp. 6521f. (dated 11 May 1944), 6535 (dated 18 May 1944), 6551 (dated 25 May 1944).

24   Jodl, "Die strategische Lage im Frühjahr 1944: Vortragsmanuskript," pp. 8, 50; BA-MA Freiburg, N 69/18. See Herbert Backe to his wife, 7 May 1944: "Everything well, severely and firmly delivered." BA Koblenz, N 1075/27.

25   Reuth, *Rommel*, pp. 89f. See also Rommel's daily reports of 25 April, 13 May and 18 May 1944; BA-MA Freiburg, N 117/78. On 16 May 1944 Tank General Hermann

Balck wrote in his diary: "It feels uncanny to stand before the decisive battle not just in this war, but in German history itself. Everything will likely depend on the invasion in the west." BA-MA Freiburg, N 647/12.

26   Notes on the conversation between Hitler and Tiso, 12 May 1944, in Hillgruber (ed.), *Staatsmänner und Diplomaten bei Hitler*, part 2, pp. 438–54 (at p. 444).

27   Notes on the conversation between Hitler and Oshima, 20 May 1944, in ibid., pp. 454–60 (at p. 457). At a meeting with Antonescu on 23 March 1944, Hitler had already speculated that "the area south of the Gironde estuary or the peninsulas of Brittany and Normandy may be considered as landing points for the invasion." Ibid., p. 390.

28   See Ulrich Chaussy and Christoph Püschner, *Nachbar Hitler: Führerkult und Heimatzerstörung am Obersalzberg*, Berlin, 1995, p. 146.

29   Hans-Wilhelm Heinrich, "Hitlers Ansprache vor Generalen und Offizieren am 26. May 1944", in *Militärgeschichtliche Mitteilungen*, 2 (1976), pp. 123–70 (at pp. 155f.).

30   Goebbels, *Tagebücher*, part II, vol. 12, pp. 405–15 (entry for 6 June 1944).

31   See Peter Lieb, *Unternehmen Overlord: Die Invasion in der Normandie und die Befreiung Westeuropas*, Munich, 2014, pp. 57–61; Overy, *Why the Allies Won*, pp. 167–78.

32   See Richard Overy, *The Bombing War: Europe 1939–1945*, London, 2013, pp. 370f., 589–92.

33   See ibid., pp. 572–8 ; Lieb, *Unternehmen Overlord*, pp. 64f.

34   See Kennedy, *Engineers of Victory*, pp. 257f. Weinberg, *Eine Welt in Waffen*, pp. 717f.; Overy, *Why the Allies Won*, pp. 183–7; Lieb, *Unternehmen Overlord*, pp. 65–7.

35   See Lieb, *Unternehmen Overlord*, pp. 68–89; Overy, *Why the Allies Won*, pp. 193–8; Kennedy, *Engineers of Victory*, pp. 263–75.

36   See Speidel, *Invasion 1944*, pp. 97–9; Ruge, *Rommel und die Invasion*, pp. 165–7; Reuth, *Rommel*, p. 90.

37   See Ose, *Entscheidung im Westen*, pp. 103f.; Walter Warlimont, *Im Hauptquartier der deutschen Wehrmacht 1939–1945: Grundlagen—Formen—Gestalten*, Frankfurt am Main and Bonn, 1964, pp. 454f.

38   See Speer's testimony on his activities as minister, Nuremberg, 14 Aug. 1946, pp. 25f.; BA Koblenz, N 1340/84; Speer, *Erinnerungen*, p. 364.

39   Warlimont, *Im Hauptquartier der Wehrmacht*, p. 457. See Below, *Als Hitlers Adjutant*, p. 374.

40   Goebbels, *Tagebücher*, part II, vol. 12, p. 418 (entry for 7 June 1944).

41   Hillgruber (ed.), *Staatsmänner und Diplomaten bei Hitler*, part 2, pp. 460–8 (at p. 468).

42   Cited in Ose, *Entscheidung im Westen*, p. 101.

43   *Meldungen aus dem Reich*, vol. 17, pp. 6572 (dated 8 June 1944), 6576 (dated 8 June 1944). See Alwin-Broder Albrecht, the adjutant in the Führer's chancellery, to his wife, 9 June 1944: "A general sigh of relief could be sensed here." IfZ München, ED 100, vol. 33.

44   On the various reactions, see Friedrich Kellner, *"Vernebelt, verdunkelt sind alle Hirne": Tagebücher, 1939–1945*, ed. Sascha Feuchert et al., Göttingen, 2011, vol. 2, p. 716 (entry for 6 June 1944); Ulrich von Hassell, *Vom andern Deutschland: Aus den nachgelassenen Tagebüchern 1938–1944*, Frankfurt am Main, 1964, p. 314 (entry for 12 June 1944); Ruth Andreas-Friedrich, *Der Schattenmann: Tagebuchaufzeichnungen 1938–1945*, Frankfurt am Main, 1983, p. 140 (entry for 7 July 1944).

45   See Lieb, *Unternehmen Overlord*, pp. 91ff.; *Das Deutsche Reich und der Zweite Weltkrieg*, vol. 7, pp. 545f. (Vogel's essay).

46   Andreas-Friedrich, *Der Schattenmann*, p. 141 (entry for 8 June 1944).

47   See Speer, *Erinnerungen*, p. 365. On the German countermeasures, see Lieb, *Unternehmen Overlord*, pp. 112–15; Overy, *Why the Allies Won*, pp. 199–201.

48   Hubatsch (ed.), *Hitlers Weisungen für die Kriegführung*, pp. 291f.

49   Traudl Junge, *Bis zur letzten Stunde: Hitlers Sekretärin erzählt ihr Leben*, Munich, 2002, p. 136. For Hitler's views on "miracle weapons," see Heinz Dieter Hölsken, *Die V-Waffen: Entstehung—Propaganda—Kriegseinsatz*, Stuttgart, 1984, pp. 87–93.

50   Goebbels, *Tagebücher*, part II, vol. 12, pp. 407f. (entry for 6 June 1944).

51 See Hölsken, *Die V-Waffen*, pp. 131–3.

52 *Meldungen aus dem Reich*, vol. 17, p. 6596 (dated 19 June 1944). See also Marlies Steinert, *Hitlers Krieg und die Deutschen: Stimmung und Haltung der deutschen Bevölkerung im Zweiten Weltkrieg*, Düsseldorf and Vienna, 1970, p. 459.

53 See Goebbels, *Tagebücher*, part II, vol. 12, p. 544 (entry for 25 June 1944).

54 See ibid., pp. 488f., 491 (entry for 18 June 1944), 503 (entry for 20 June 1944). See Helmut Sündermann, *Hier stehe ich . . . Deutsche Erinnerungen 1914/45*, Leoni, 1975, p. 269 (entry for 17 June 1944).

55 See Overy, *The Bombing War*, pp. 192f.

56 Andreas-Friedrich, *Der Schattenmann*, pp. 143f. (entry for 18 June 1944). See Victor Klemperer, *Ich will Zeugnis ablegen bis zum letzten: Tagebücher*, vol. 2: 1942–1945, ed. Walter Nowojski with Hadwig Klemperer, Berlin, 1995, p. 532 (entry for 19 June 1944): "Perhaps this whole thing has been cooked up to distract and reassure the German public."

57 Rundstedt to Keitel, 11 June 1944; reproduced in Ose, *Entscheidung im Westen*, pp. 319–21.

58 *KTB OKW*, vol. 4, pp. 1593f.

59 Junge, *Bis zur letzten Stunde*, p. 140.

60 See Franz W. Seidler and Dieter Zeigert, *Die Führerhauptquartiere: Anlagen und Planungen im Zweiten Weltkrieg*, Munich, 2000, pp. 184–90.

61 Speidel, *Invasion 1944*, pp. 113f.

62 Ibid., pp. 114–18. On the meeting in Margival on 17 June 1944, see the report by the chief of staff of the Supreme Commander West, Günter Blumentritt, who had taken part. "Der 20. Juli 1944 (Januar 1946)"; IfZ München, ZS 208/1; see also, Below, *Als Hitlers Adjutant*, p. 375; Ose, *Entscheidung im Westen*, pp. 132–6.

63 Ruge, *Rommel und die Invasion*, p. 184.

64 Cited in Reuth, *Rommel*, pp. 92f.

65 Cited in Ose, *Entscheidung im Westen*, p. 143.

66 See Erwin Leiser, *"Deutschland erwache!" Propaganda im Film des Dritten Reiches*, Reinbek bei Hamburg, 1968, pp. 110–20; Moritz Föllmer, *"Ein Leben wie im Traum": Kultur im Dritten Reich*, Munich, 2016, pp. 252f. In June 1943 Goebbels discussed the film script with Harlan. Afterwards he noted that he expected the Kolberg film to do "a lot for our inner fortitude"; *Tagebücher*, part II, vol. 8, p. 425 (entry for 5 June 1943).

67 Goebbels, *Tagebücher*, part II, vol. 12, pp. 518–28 (entry for 22 June 1944). See also Elke Fröhlich, "Hitler und Goebbels im Krisenjahr 1944," in *Vierteljahrshefte für Zeitgeschichte*, 38 (1990), pp. 195–224 (at pp. 200–5).

68 Hitler's speech to generals and officers on 22 June 1944 in the Platterhof Hotel; BA Berlin-Lichterfelde, NS 6/777.

69 Heiber (ed.), *Hitlers Lagebesprechungen*, pp. 600f. (dated 31 July 1944).

70 See Lieb, *Unternehmen Overlord*, pp. 106, 96.

71 *KTB OKW*, vol. 4, p. 1594.

72 See Reuth, *Rommel*, pp. 93f. On the meeting of 29 June 1944, see Speidel, *Invasion 1944*, pp. 127f.; Guderian, *Erinnerungen eines Soldaten*, p. 302; Blumentritt, "Der 20. Juli 1944"; IfZ München, ZS 208/1.

73 Goebbels, *Tagebücher*, part II, vol. 12, p. 567 (entry for 29 June 1944). On the change in personnel, see Speidel, *Invasion 1944*, pp. 129–31; Wolfram Pyta, *Hitler: Der Künstler als Politiker und Feldherr*, Munich, 2015, pp. 553–5.

74 *Meldungen aus dem Reich*, vol. 17, p. 6618 (dated 29 June 1944). See also the summary report of the Reich propaganda offices of 4 July 1944; BA Berlin-Lichterfelde, R 55/601.

75 Summary report of the Reich propaganda offices of 17 July 1944; BA Berlin-Lichterfelde, R 55/601. See *Meldungen aus dem Reich*, vol. 17, p. 6636 (dated 13 July 1944).

76   Goebbels, *Tagebücher*, part II, vol. 12, p. 504 (entry for 20 June 1944).

77   Ibid., p. 524 (entry for 22 June 1944).

78   See *Das Deutsche Reich und der Zweite Weltkrieg*, vol. 8, pp. 506f., 527f. (Frieser's essay).

79   See Balck's diary entries for 25 June and 27 June 1944; BA-MA Freiburg, N 647/12. Statement by Jodl of 17 June 1945; Wassili S. Christoforow, Wladimir G. Makarow and Matthias Uhl (eds), *Verhört: Die Befragungen deutscher Generale und Offiziere durch die sowjetischen Geheimdienste 1945–1952*, Berlin and Boston, 2015, p. 130.

80   See *Das Deutsche Reich und der Zweite Weltkrieg*, vol. 8, p. 535 (Frieser's essay).

81   Reinhardt to his wife, 23 June 1944; BA-MA Freiburg, N 245/2. The same day, Reinhardt noted in his diary: "Terrible day. Collapses and breaches everywhere, no more reserves, hardly any air assistance." BA-MA Freiburg, N 245/3.

82   See *Das Deutsche Reich und der Zweite Weltkrieg*, vol. 8 (Frieser's essay), pp. 539–43; Weinberg, *Eine Welt in Waffen*, p. 744.

83   Goebbels, *Tagebücher*, part II, vol. 12, p. 557 (entry for 27 June 1944). See the summary report of the Reich propaganda offices of 10 July 1944: many "failed to understand how the Soviets could succeed with the first attack in taking in a system of positions which Germans troops had defended for the entire winter." BA Berlin-Lichterfelde, R 55/601.

84   Such were Hitler's words in a conversation with Friedrich Hossbach on 19 July 1944; "Erinnerungen," ch. 9: Ostpreussen, p. 4; BA-MA Freiburg, N 24/39. On Busch's dismissal, see *Das Deutsche Reich und der Zweite Weltkrieg*, vol. 8, pp. 544f., 548 (Frieser's essay).

85   Goebbels, *Tagebücher*, part II, vol. 12, p. 579 (entry for 30 June 1944).

86   See *Das Deutsche Reich und der Zweite Weltkrieg*, vol. 8, pp. 548f. (Frieser's essay).

87   See ibid., pp. 552f.

88   Cited in Catherine Merridale, *Ivan's War: The Red Army 1939–45*, London, 2005, p. 240.

89   See Kurt Zeitzler, "Das Ringen um die grossen Entscheidungen im Zweiten Weltkrieg, vol. 2: Abwehrschlachten in Russland nach dem Wendepunkt des Krieges," pp. 161–5; BA-MA Freiburg, N63/80.

90   See *Das Deutsche Reich und der Zweite Weltkrieg*, vol. 8, pp. 563f. (Frieser's essay).

91   Goebbels, *Tagebücher*, part II, vol. 13, p. 77 (entry for 10 July 1944).

92   See Below, *Als Hitlers Adjutant*, p. 378.

93   See *Das Deutsche Reich und der Zweite Weltkrieg*, vol. 8, pp. 566f. (Frieser's essay).

94   Goebbels, *Tagebücher*, part.II, vol. 13, p. 90 (entry for 12 July 1944). See also *Das Deutsche Reich und der Zweite Weltkrieg*, vol. 8, p. 556 (Frieser's essay).

95   See Junge, *Bis zur letzten Stunde*, p. 141; Henrik Eberle and Matthias Uhl (eds), *Das Buch Hitler*, Bergisch Gladbach, 2005, pp. 269f.; Uwe Neumärker, Robert Conrad and Cord Woywodt, *Wolfsschanze: Hitlers Machtzentrale im Zweiten Weltkrieg*, 3rd edition, Berlin, 2007, p. 139.

96   Rommel to Kluge, to be forwarded to Hitler, 15 July 1944; *KTB OKW*, vol. 4, pp. 1572f.

97   See Ruge, *Rommel und die Invasion*, pp. 221f.; Speidel, *Invasion 1944*, p. 140; Reuth, *Rommel*, pp. 95–7.

98   See Merridale, *Ivan's War*, p. 241. Chlewnjuk puts the figure at 70,000 German soldiers; Oleg Chlewnjuk, *Stalin: Eine Biographie*, Munich, 2015, p. 366.

12 The Berghof during the War

1   *Die Tagebücher von Joseph Goebbels*, commissioned by the Institute for Contemporary History, with support from the State Archive of Russia, ed. Elke Fröhlich; *Part II: Diktate 1941–1945*, 15 vols, Munich, 1993–6, vol. 13, p. 116 (entry for 14 July 1944).

2   Interview with Nicolaus von Below by David Irving, 18 April 1971; IfZ München, ZS 7. Nicolaus von Below, *Als Hitlers Adjutant 1937–45*, Mainz, 1980, p. 380. Below stated that Hitler set off for the Wolf's Lair on the morning of 16 July, but in fact he was already back in his East Prussian headquarters on 14 July. See Martin Bormann to his wife, Gerda, 15 July 1944; Hugh Trevor-Roper (ed.), *The Bormann Letters*, London, 1954, p. 56; Morell's daily notes of 14 July 1944; BA Koblenz, N 1348/2; Harald Sandner, *Hitler: Das Itinerar. Aufenthaltsorte und Reisen von 1889–1945*, Berlin, 2016, vol. 4, p. 2233.

3   See Heike B. Görtemaker, *Eva Braun: Leben mit Hitler*, Munich, 2010, pp. 232f.; Franz W. Seidler and Dieter Zeigert, *Die Führerhauptquartiere: Anlagen und Planungen im Zweiten Weltkrieg*, Munich, 2000, p. 271.

4   Gerhard Engel to Gauleiter Albert Forster, 29 Dec. 1940: "At the moment I am on the [Obersalzberg] with the Führer, with a pleasant trip to the front behind us." BA-MA Freiburg, N 118/5; see Below, *Als Hitlers Adjutant*, p. 219.

5   Ibid., pp. 224f. See Albert Speer, *Erinnerungen: Mit einem Essay von Jochen Thies*, Frankfurt am Main and Berlin, 1993, p. 105; Otto Dietrich, *12 Jahre mit Hitler*, Munich, 1955, p. 229.

6   Hitler was at the Berghof 10–14 July 1940 (four days), 26 July–3 Aug. 1940 (eight days), 8–12 Aug. 1940 (four days), 17–29 Aug. 1940 (eleven days), 4–8 Oct. 1940 (four days), 16–20 Oct. 1940 (four days), 16–19 Nov. 1940 (three days), 27 Nov.–2 Dec. 1940 (five days), 13–16 Dec. 1940 (three days). See Seidler and Zeigert, *Die Führerhauptquartiere*, p. 260.

7   See Dietrich, *12 Jahre mit Hitler*, p. 223.

8   *Die Tagebücher von Joseph Goebbels*, commissioned by the Institute for Contemporary History, with support from the State Archive of Russia, ed. Elke Fröhlich, *Part I: Aufzeichnungen 1923–1941*, 9 vols in 14 parts, Munich, 1998–2008, vol. 9, p. 308 (entry for 13 May 1941). See also Below, *Als Hitlers Adjutant*, pp. 258f., 261–4. Hitler was at the Obersalzberg 28 Dec. 1940–27 Jan. 1941 (thirty-one days), 7 Feb.–14 March 1941 (thirty-four days), 9 May–11 June 1941 (thirty-three days). See Seidler and Zeigert, *Die Führerhauptquartiere*, p. 260.

9   See the extensive documents in BA Berlin-Lichterfelde, NS 6/115 und NS 6/116.

10   See Ulrich Chaussy and Christoph Püschner, *Nachbar Hitler: Führerkult und Heimatzerstörung am Obersalzberg*, Berlin, 1995, pp. 116, 142–6; Albert A. Feiber, "'Filiale von Berlin': Der Obersalzberg im Dritten Reich", in Volker Dahm, Albert A. Feiber, Hartmut Mehringer and Horst Möller, *Die tödliche Utopie: Bilder, Texte, Dokumente. Daten zum Dritten Reich*, Munich, 2010, pp. 79f.; Lioba Schmitt-Imkamp, *Roderich Fick (1886–1955)*, Vienna, Cologne and Weimar, 2014, pp. 96f.

11   Karl-Jesko von Puttkamer to Friedrich Hossbach, 21 Nov. 1942; BA-MA Freiburg, N 24/15.

12   See Below, *Als Hitlers Adjutant*, pp. 312, 322f.; Goebbels, *Tagebücher*, part II, vol. 6, pp. 286 (entry for 13 Nov. 1942), 324 (entry for 24 Nov. 1942).

13   Traudl Junge, *Bis zur letzten Stunde: Hitlers Sekretärin erzählt ihr Leben*, Munich, 2002, p. 59.

14   Hitler stayed at the Berghof 22 March–2 May 1943 (forty-one days) and 31 May–30 Jun. 1943 (thirty days). See Seidler and Zeigert, *Die Führerhauptquartiere*, p. 260.

15   See Goebbels, *Tagebücher*, part II, vol. 7, p. 664 (entry for 29 March 1943), vol. 8, p. 105 (entry for 14 Apr. 1943), 351 (entry for 23 May 1943), 407 (entry for 2 Jun. 1943).

16   Albert Speer, *Spandauer Tagebücher: Mit einem Vorwort von Joachim Fest*, Munich, 2002, p. 325 (entry for 20 Nov. 1952).

17   See Richard Overy, *The Bombing War: Europe 1939–1945*, London, 2013, pp. 472f.

18   Goebbels, *Tagebücher*, part II, vol. 8, p. 523 (entry for 25 June 1943).

19   Ibid., vol. 10, p. 516 (entry for 20 Dec. 1943). See also Martin Bormann to Gerda Bormann, 26 July 1943; Trevor-Roper (ed.), *The Bormann Letters*, p. 15.

20 Henrik Eberle and Matthias Uhl (eds), *Das Buch Hitler*, Bergisch Gladbach, 2005, p. 246. See also Chaussy and Püschner, *Nachbar Hitler*, pp. 147–51; Seidler and Zeigert, *Die Führerhauptquartiere*, pp. 265–7; Dahm et al. (eds), *Die tödliche Utopie*, pp. 655–62; Florian M. Beierl, *Hitlers Berg: Licht ins Dunkel der Geschichte. Geschichte des Obersalzbergs und seiner geheimen Bunkeranlagen*, Berchtesgaden, 2004, pp. 47–84.

21 From 24 Feb. to 14 July 1944 (139 days). See Seidler and Zeigert, *Die Führerhauptquartiere*, p. 260.

22 See Karl-Jesko von Puttkamer to Friedrich Hossbach, 13 March 1944: "Metres of snow, and there is more every day. Unfortunately no sun." BA-MA Freiburg, N 24/19; Junge, *Bis zur letzten Stunde*, p. 134; Goebbels, *Tagebücher*, part II, vol. 11, p. 471 (entry for 14 March 1944).

23 Speer, *Erinnerungen*, pp. 369f. The speech is reproduced in Hildegard von Kotze and Helmut Krausnick (eds), *"Es spricht der Führer": 7 exemplarische Hitler-Reden*, Gütersloh, 1966, pp. 335–68.

24 See Junge, *Bis zur letzten Stunde*, p. 140.

25 On what follows see Linge's appointment diary under 23 March to 20 June 1943; IfZ München, F 19/4; Junge, *Bis zur letzten Stunde*, pp. 72–94; Eberle and Uhl (eds), *Das Buch Hitler*, pp. 200–4, 244f.; Dietrich, *12 Jahre mit Hitler*, p. 223. On the daily routine in peacetime, see Volker Ullrich, *Hitler: Ascent 1889–1939*, London, 2016, pp. 628–32; Feiber, "Filiale von Berlin," in Dahm *et al.* (eds), *Die tödliche Utopie*, pp. 88f.

26 Junge, *Bis zur letzten Stunde*, p. 74.

27 See Speer, *Spandauer Tagebücher*, pp. 325–7 (entry for 20 Nov. 1952); Goebbels, *Tagebücher*, part II, vol. 8, p. 536 (entry for 25 June 1943), vol. 12, p. 410 (entry for 6 June 1944).

28 See Eberle and Uhl (eds), *Das Buch Hitler*, pp. 207f.

29 See Dietrich, *12 Jahre mit Hitler*, p. 230.

30 Goebbels, *Tagebücher*, part II, vol. 11, p. 408 (entry for 4 March 1944). See Junge, *Bis zur letzten Stunde*, pp. 134–6; Eberle and Uhl (eds), *Das Buch Hitler*, pp. 245–7.

31 Junge, *Bis zur letzten Stunde*, pp. 136f.

32 Max Domarus, *Hitler: Reden und Proklamationen 1932–1945*, Munich, 1965, vol. 2, part 2, p. 2206.

33 See Christa Schroeder, *Er war mein Chef: Aus dem Nachlass der Sekretärin von Adolf Hitler*, ed. Anton Joachimsthaler, 3rd edition, Munich and Vienna, 1985, pp. 211f.; Chaussy and Püschner, *Nachbar Hitler*, pp. 160–3; Beierl, *Hitlers Berg*, pp. 123–9; Dahm et al. (eds), *Die tödliche Utopie*, p. 663.

34 Klaus Mann, *Der Wendepunkt: Ein Lebensbericht*, Frankfurt am Main, 1963, p. 429.

35 See Enrico Syring, "Walter Hewel—Ribbentrops Mann beim 'Führer,'" in Ronald Smelser, Enrico Syring and Rainer Zitelmann (eds), *Die braune Elite II: 21 weitere biographische Skizzen*, Darmstadt, 1993, p. 160.

36 See Brandt's testimony of 20 Sept. 1945: "It was perceived by all the gentlemen in Hitler's circle as enormously cruel that Hitler simply dimissed Brückner, whom he had known for so long and who was highly regarded, from one day to the next." BA Koblenz, N 1128/33; Schroeder, *Er war mein Chef*, pp. 39, 45, 57.

37 Birthday telegram from Speer to Schaub, 21 Aug. 1942; BA Berlin-Lichterfelde, NS 51/39.

38 See Karl Krause, *Zehn Jahre Kammerdiener bei Hitler*, Hamburg, 1949, pp. 62–5.

39 See Junge, *Bis zur letzten Stunde*, pp. 110f., 116.

40 See Schaub to Lammers, 21 Nov. 1942; Lammers to Speer, 15 Dec. 1942 and 21 Aug. 1943; BA Berlin-Lichterfelde, R 43 II/986.

41 Schroeder, *Er war mein Chef*, pp. 132f. Heinrich Hoffmann was "drunk almost every night," Hitler's physician Morell wrote to his wife from Hitler's headquarters in May 1940; BA Koblenz, N 1346/6.

42 Junge, *Bis zur letzten Stunde*, p. 108.

43 See Hans Georg Hiller von Gaertringen (ed.), *Das Auge des Dritten Reiches: Hitlers Kameramann und Fotograf Walter Frentz*, Berlin, 2006, pp. 110–25; Boris von Brauchitsch, *Der Schatten des Führers: Der Fotograf Walter Frentz zwischen Avantgarde und Obersalzberg*, Berlin, 2017, pp. 118, 121, 123–5; interview with Walter Frentz by David Irving, 8 Dec. 1971; IfZ München, ZS 2260.

44 See Görtemaker, *Eva Braun*, pp. 244–6.

45 Goebbels, *Tagebücher*, part II, vol. 11, p. 472 (entry for 14 March 1944).

46 Conversation with Anni Winter conducted by Georg Franz (no date); IfZ München, ZS 194.

47 See Julius Schaub's testimony about Eva Braun; IfZ München, ED 100, vol. 203; also in Olaf Rose (ed.), *Julius Schaub—In Hitlers Schatten: Erinnerungen und Aufzeichnungen des Chefadjutanten 1925–1945*, Stegen am Ammersee, 2005, pp. 317, 325; Junge, *Bis zur letzten Stunde*, p. 64; Görtemaker, *Eva Braun*, p. 246.

48 Junge, *Bis zur letzten Stunde*, pp. 73f.

49 See ibid., p. 74; Rochus Misch, *Der letzte Zeuge: "Ich war Hitlers Telefonist, Kurier und Leibwächter,"* Zurich and Munich, 2008, p. 110; Nerin E. Gun, *Eva Braun-Hitler: Leben und Schicksal*, Velbert and Kettwig, 1968, p. 160.

50 See Schaub's testimony on Eva Braun; IfZ München, ED 100, vol. 203; also in Rose (ed.), *Julius Schaub*, pp. 317f.

51 Schroeder, *Er war mein Chef*, p. 182; See Görtemaker, *Eva Braun*, p. 247.

52 Junge, *Bis zur letzten Stunde*, p. 134.

53 See Speer, *Erinnerungen*, p. 320; Misch, *Der letzte Zeuge*, p. 110; Eberle and Uhl (eds), *Das Buch Hitler*, p. 188.

54 Junge, *Bis zur letzten Stunde*, p. 120.

55 See Misch, *Der letzte Zeuge*, p. 111; Trevor-Roper (ed.), *The Bormann Letters*, p. 19 (Gerda to Martin Bormann, 13 Aug. 1943); Schroeder, *Er war mein Chef*, p. 196; Gun, *Eva Braun-Hitler*, p. 162 (also see p. 160 for the passport issued on 3 April 1942). Braun embarked on the trip on 21 June and returned on 17 July 1942.

56 Goebbels, *Tagebücher*, part II, vol. 8, p. 537 (entry for 25 June 1943). See Görtemaker, *Eva Braun*, p. 251.

57 Goebbels, *Tagebücher*, part II, vol. 9, p. 267 (entry for 10 Aug. 1943).

58 Ibid., vol. 12, p. 414 (entry for 6 June 1944).

59 Albert Speer, *"Alles was ich weiss": Aus unbekannten Geheimdienstprotokollen vom Sommer 1945*, ed. Ulrich Schlie, Munich, 1999, p. 60.

60 See Junge, *Bis zur letzten Stunde*, p. 141; Misch, *Der letzte Zeuge*, p. 113; Goebbels, *Tagebücher*, part II, vol. 11, pp. 395 (entry for 4 March 1944), 474 (entry for 14 March 1944).

61 Eberle and Uhl (eds), *Das Buch Hitler*, p. 248. See Rolf Aurich, *Kalanag: Die kontrollierten Illusionen des Helmut Schreiber*, Berlin, 2016, pp. 137f., 150f.

62 See Junge, *Bis zur letzten Stunde*, pp. 77f.; Gitta Sereny, *Albert Speer: His Battle with Truth*, new edition, London, 1996, p. 435; Below, *Als Hitlers Adjutant*, p. 370.

63 See Gaertringen (ed.), *Das Auge des Dritten Reiches*, pp. 111–13. Three photos by Frentz show Hitler and Himmler taking a walk to the tea house on 3 April 1944.

64 Hans-Wilhelm Heinrich, "Hitlers Ansprache vor Generalen und Offizieren am 26. May 1944", in *Militärgeschichtliche Mitteilungen*, 2 (1976), p. 156.

65 See Dietrich, *12 Jahre mit Hitler*, p. 172. Dietrich claimed that in late 1944 he presented Hitler with reports about the genocide of Jews in Poland in the foreign press and asked if he should issue a denial. Hitler rejected the idea, acting "offended" and calling the reports "the same old 'enemy propaganda lies and distortions.'" Ibid.

66 Henriette von Schirach, *Der Preis der Herrlichkeit: Erlebte Zeitgeschichte*, Munich and Berlin, 1975, pp. 214f. Baldur von Schirach gave a similar description: "The last thing I need is for you to come with this sentimental nonsense," Hitler is supposed to have shouted. "What business of yours are these Jew women?" (*Ich glaubte an Hitler,*

Hamburg, 1967, pp. 292f.) In somewhat different form Henriette von Schirach told this story in an interview with David Irving on 27 Nov. 1970; IfZ München, ZS 2238.

67   See Schroeder, *Er war mein Chef*, pp. 194f.; Junge, *Bis zur letzten Stunde*, pp. 100f. The Schirachs' description of events is used, without critical examination, in John Toland, *Adolf Hitler*, vol. 2, Bergisch-Gladbach, 1981, p. 922; Ian Kershaw, *Hitler 1936–1945: Nemesis*, London, 2001, p. 590; Feiber, "Filiale von Berlin," in Dahm et al. (eds), *Die tödliche Utopie*, pp. 101f. For a critical perspective, see Anton Joachimsthaler, *Hitlers Liste: Ein Dokument persönlicher Beziehungen*, Munich, 2003, pp. 262–5.

68   Goebbels, *Tagebücher*, part II, vol. 8, pp. 538–41 (entry for 25 June 1943; at pp. 539, 541).

69   See ibid., vol. 9, p. 267 (entry for 10 Aug. 1943).

70   Even after the war, individual members of the Berghof society maintained a "connection to the old circle of fate," Gerhard Engel told Speer after the latter's release from Spandau Prison. Gerhard Engel to Albert Speer, 28 June 1968; BA Koblenz, N 1340/14. See also Johanna Wolf to Albert Speer, 18 March 1967; BA Koblenz, N 1340/75. On the network of Hitler's court after 1945, see Heike Görtemaker, *Hitlers Hofstaat: Der innere Kreis im Dritten Reich und danach*, Munich, 2019, pp. 361ff.

71   Goebbels, *Tagebücher*, part II, vol. 8, pp. 521 (entry for 24 June 1943), 553 (entry for 27 June 1943).

72   See the detailed description of Hitler's 54th birthday on 20 April 1943 in Junge, *Bis zur letzten Stunde*, pp. 104–9. For a photo by Frentz of the birthday party guests, see Gaertringen (ed.), *Das Auge des Dritten Reiches*, p. 28. On the children's birthday wishes, see Speer, *Spandauer Tagebücher*, p. 99 (entry for 20 April 1947). For a photo of Hitler surrounded by the children, see Margret Nissen, *Sind Sie die Tochter von Speer?*, Munich, 2005, p. 20. On Hitler's 55th birthday on 20 April 1944, see Below, *Als Hitlers Adjutant*, p. 367; Goebbels, *Tagebücher*, part II, vol. 12, p. 160 (entry for 21 April 1944). For a photo by Frentz of the weapons demonstration on the afternoon of 20 April 1944, see Gaertringen (ed.), *Das Auge des Dritten Reiches*, p. 106.

73   Eberle and Uhl (eds), *Das Buch Hitler*, pp. 258–61 (at pp. 260f.). See Junge, *Bis zur letzten Stunde*, pp. 138f.; Schroeder, *Er war mein Chef*, pp. 167f.; Dietrich, *12 Jahre mit Hitler*, pp. 233f. For a group photo of the wedding, taken in the Great Hall, see Joachimsthaler, *Hitlers Liste*, p. 477. See also Anton Joachimsthaler, *Hitlers Ende: Legenden und Dokumente*, Munich and Berlin, 1995, pp. 451–9.

13 *The Stauffenberg Assassination Attempt and its Aftermath*

1   Christa Schroeder, *Er war mein Chef: Aus dem Nachlass der Sekretärin von Adolf Hitler*, ed. Anton Joachimsthaler, 3rd edition, Munich and Vienna, 1985, pp. 147f.; see Traudl Junge, *Bis zur letzten Stunde: Hitlers Sekretärin erzählt ihr Leben*, Munich, 2002, p. 151.

2   See Reich Security Service to the Führer's adjutants (Obergruppenführer Brückner) on 5 May 1939 and Reich Transport Ministry to the Führer's adjutants (Obergruppenführer Brückner) on 10 Sept. 1940; BA Berlin-Lichterfelde, NS 10/37 und NS 10/38.

3   Order of Albert Bormann and Rudolf Schmundt on 20 Sept. 1943; BA Berlin-Lichterfelde, NS 6/130.

4   *Die Tagebücher von Joseph Goebbels*, commissioned by the Institute for Contemporary History, with support from the State Archive of Russia, ed. Elke Fröhlich, *Part II: Diktate 1941–1945*, 15 vols, Munich, 1993–6, vol. 9, p. 575 (entry for 23 Sept. 1943).

5   See Theo Morell's memorandum of 21 Aug. 1943; BA Koblenz, N 1348/4.

6   See Nicolaus von Below, *Als Hitlers Adjutant 1937–45*, Mainz, 1980, p. 363. For an overview, see Peter Hoffmann, *Die Sicherheit des Diktators: Hitlers Leibwachen, Schutzmassnahmen, Residenzen, Hauptquartiere*, Munich, 1975, pp. 215–27.

7 Andreas Hillgruber (ed.), *Staatsmänner und Diplomaten bei Hitler: Vertrauliche Aufzeichnungen über Unterredungen mit Vertretern des Auslandes 1939–1941*, Frankfurt am Main, 1967, part 2, p. 469.

8 Goebbels, *Tagebücher*, part II, vol. 13, p. 306 (entry for 24 Aug. 1944). Hitler told a similar story to his personal physician, Morell, in early November 1944. See Morell's daily notes for 9 Nov. 1944; BA Koblenz, N 1348/4.

9 On the details, see Peter Hoffmann, *Widerstand, Staatsstreich, Attentat: Der Kampf der Opposition gegen Hitler*, 4th edition, Munich and Zurich, 1985, pp. 74–186; Joachim Fest, *Staatsstreich: Der lange Weg zum 20. Juli*, Berlin, 1994, pp. 76–139; weighing the evidence, Klaus-Jürgen Müller, *Generaloberst Ludwig Beck: Eine Biographie*, Paderborn, 2008, pp. 366–8, 396–402.

10 See above pp. 78–84.

11 See the summary by Ger van Roon, *Widerstand im Dritten Reich*, 6th edition, Munich, 1994, pp. 123–39; Fest, *Staatsstreich*, pp. 148–59. For an overview, see the study by Theodore S. Hamerow, *Die Attentäter: Der 20. Juli—von der Kollaboration zum Widerstand*, Munich, 1999.

12 Sabine Gillmann and Hans Mommsen (eds), *Politische Schriften und Briefe Carl Friedrich Goerdelers*, Munich, 2003, vol. 2, pp. 896, 1185. For an apologist account, see Peter Hoffmann, *Carl Goerdeler gegen die Judenverfolgung*, Cologne, Weimar and Vienna, 2013.

13 See the summary in Volker Ullrich, *Der Kreisauer Kreis*, Reinbek bei Hamburg, 2008, pp. 34–81.

14 See Johannes Hürter, "Auf dem Weg zur Militäropposition: Tresckow, Gersdorff, der Vernichtungskrieg und der Judenmord," in *Vierteljahrshefte für Zeitgeschichte*, 52 (2004), pp. 527–62.

15 See letters by Kluge dated 3 Dec., 15 Dec., 20 Dec. 1942; BA-MA Freiburg, MSg 2/11185.

16 See Fest, *Staatsstreich*, p. 192; Müller, *Generaloberst Ludwig Beck*, pp. 452, 454, 457f.

17 See Roon, *Widerstand in Deutschland*, p. 174; Fest, *Staatsstreich*, p. 194.

18 See Bernhard R. Kroener, *Generaloberst Friedrich Fromm: Eine Biographie*, Paderborn, 2005, pp. 600f. On Schulenburg, see the biography by Ulrich Heinemann, *Ein konservativer Rebell: Fritz-Dietlof Graf von der Schulenburg und der 20. Juli*, Berlin, 1990, particularly pp. 132ff.

19 See Fabian von Schlabrendorff, *Offiziere gegen Hitler*, fully revised edition, ed. Walter Bussmann, Berlin, 1984, pp. 67–78. Based on this, see Hoffmann, *Widerstand, Staatsstreich, Attentat*, pp. 351–3; Fest, *Staatsstreich*, pp. 195–7; Ian Kershaw, *Hitler 1936–1945: Nemesis*, London, 2001, pp. 661f.

20 See Rudolf-Christoph Freiherr von Gersdorff, *Soldat im Untergang*, Frankfurt am Main, Berlin and Vienna, 1977, pp. 128–32. Based on this, see Hoffmann, *Widerstand, Staatsstreich, Attentat*, pp. 353–60; Fest, *Staatsstreich*, pp. 198f.; Kershaw, *Hitler*, pp. 662f.

21 See Müller, *Generaloberst Ludwig Beck*, p. 470.

22 See Michael Mueller, *Canaris: Hitlers Abwehrchef*, Berlin, 2006, pp. 390–2; Elisabeth Sifton and Fritz Stern, *Keine gewöhnlichen Männer: Dietrich Bonhoeffer und Hans von Dohnanyi im Widerstand gegen Hitler*, Munich, 2013, pp. 117f.; Elisabeth Chowaniec, *Der "Fall Dohnanyi" 1943–1945: Widerstand, Militärjustiz, SS-Willkür*, Munich, 1991, pp. 43–50.

23 See Bodo Scheurig, *Henning von Tresckow: Ein Preusse gegen Hitler*, Frankfurt am Main and Berlin, 1987, pp. 195–7.

24 Goebbels, *Tagebücher*, part II, vol. 10, p. 255 (entry for 8 Nov. 1943).

25 See Fest, *Staatsstreich*, pp. 232f.; Anne C. Nagel, *Johannes Popitz (1884–1945): Görings Finanzminister und Verschwörer gegen Hitler. Eine Biogaphie*, Cologne, Weimar and Vienna, 2015, pp. 178–80.

26 Goebbels, *Tagebücher*, part II, vol. 9, p. 577 (entry for 23 Sept. 1943). See Albert Speer, *Erinnerungen: Mit einem Essay von Jochen Thies*, Frankfurt am Main and Berlin, 1993, p. 390.

27 Cited in Peter Longerich, *Heinrich Himmler: Biographie*, Munich, 2008, p. 717.

28 See Ullrich, *Der Kreisauer Kreis*, pp. 93, 109–11.

29 See Mueller, *Canaris*, pp. 416f.; Fest, *Staatsstreich*, pp. 231f.

30 Helmuth James von Moltke, *Briefe an Freya 1939–1945*, ed. Beate Ruhm von Oppen, Munich, 1988, p. 282 (dated 6 Sept. 1941).

31 See Ullrich, *Der Kreisauer Kreis*, p. 112.

32 On this topic, see Klemens von Klemperer, *Die verlassenen Verschwörer: Der deutsche Widerstand auf der Suche nach Verbündeten 1938–1945*, Berlin, 1994.

33 Handwritten letter from Stauffenberg to Paulus, 12 June 1942; BA-MA Freiburg, N 372/22.

34 Peter Hoffmann, *Claus Schenk Graf von Stauffenberg und seine Brüder*, Stuttgart, 1992, p. 268. On Stauffenberg's turning against Hitler, see ibid., pp. 251ff.

35 See Fest, *Staatsstreich*, pp. 222f.; Müller, *Generaloberst Ludwig Beck*, pp. 483f.; Peter Hoffmann, "Henning von Tresckow und die Staatsstreichpläne im Jahr 1943," in *Vierteljahrshefte für Zeitgeschichte*, 55 (2007), pp. 331–64.

36 See Hoffmann, *Widerstand, Staatsstreich, Attentat*, pp. 396–410; Fest, *Staastreich*, pp. 226–30.

37 Cited in Scheurig, *Henning von Tresckow*, p. 210; with slightly altered wording in Schlabrendorff, *Offiziere gegen Hitler*, p. 109.

38 Ursula von Kardorff, *Berliner Aufzeichnungen 1942–1945*, new edition, ed. Peter Hartl, Munich, 1992, p. 209 (entry for 18 July 1944). See also Ullrich, *Der Kreisauer Kreis*, pp. 114f.; Fest, *Staatsstreich*, pp. 245f.

39 See Roon, *Widerstand im Dritten Reich*, p. 187; Kershaw, *Hitler 1936–1945* , p. 670.

40 See Hoffmann, *Claus Schenk Graf von Stauffenberg und seine Brüder*, pp. 407–9; Müller, *Generaloberst Ludwig Beck*, pp. 505f.

41 For a comprehensive discussion of 15 July 1944, see Kroener, *Generaloberst Friedrich Fromm*, pp. 669–78; Hoffmann, *Claus Schenk Graf von Stauffenberg und seine Brüder*, pp. 416–19; Müller, *Generaloberst Ludwig Beck*, pp. 598–610.

42 Cited in Ullrich, *Der Kreisauer Kreis*, p. 116.

43 See Fest, *Staatsstreich*, pp. 258f.; Hoffmann, *Widerstand, Staatsstreich, Attentat*, pp. 486–8; Gerd R. Ueberschär, *Stauffenberg: Der 20. Juli 1944*, Frankfurt am Main, 2004, pp. 14f.; Ulrich Schlie, *"Es lebe das heilige Deutschland": Ein Tag im Leben des Claus Schenk Graf von Stauffenberg. Ein biographisches Porträt*, Freiburg, Basel and Vienna, 2009, pp. 11–14.

44 See Adolf Heusinger, *Befehl im Widerstreit: Schicksalsstunden der deutschen Armee 1923–1945*, Tübingen and Stuttgart, 1950, pp. 352f; Walter Warlimont, *Im Hauptquartier der deutschen Wehrmacht 1939–1945: Grundlagen—Formen—Gestalten*, Frankfurt am Main and Bonn, 1964, p. 472; Fest, *Staatsstreich*, pp. 260f.; Hoffmann, *Widerstand, Staatsstreich, Attentat*, pp. 489f.; Schlie, *"Es lebe das heilige Deutschland,"* pp. 15f.

45 See Heusinger, *Befehl im Widerstreit*, p. 355; Walter Warlimont, *Im Hauptquartier der Wehrmacht*, p. 471; Fest, *Staatsstreich*, pp. 261f.; Schlie, *"Es lebe das heilige Deutschland,"* pp. 16f.

46 Goebbels, *Tagebücher*, part II, p. 139 (entry for 23 July 1944); Speer, *Erinnerungen*, p. 399.

47 Below, *Als Hitlers Adjutant*, p. 381; See Henrik Eberle and Matthias Uhl (eds), *Das Buch Hitler*, Bergisch Gladbach, 2005, p. 274.

48 See Karl-Jesko von Puttkamer to Friedrich Hossbach, 28 Aug. 1944; BA-MA Freiburg, N 24/19; Nicolaus von Below to Julius Schaub, 10 Sept. 1944; Henrik Eberle (ed.), *Briefe an Hitler: Ein Volk schreibt seinem Führer. Unbekannte Dokumente aus Moskauer Archiven—zum ersten Mal veröffentlicht*, Bergisch Gladbach, 2007, pp. 422f.; Below, *Als Hitlers Adjutant*, pp. 386f., 391. See also statements made by General Karl Bodenschatz

on 15 May 1945 and naval Captain Heinz Assmann on 23 May 1945; IfZ München, ZS 10 und ZS 2015.

49 Karl Fischer, *Ich fuhr Stauffenberg: Erinnerungen an die Kriegsjahre 1939–1945*, ed. Ursula and Ulrich Fischer, Angermünde, 2008, p. 93; see Schlie, *"Es lebe das heilige Deutschland,"* p. 18.

50 Erwin Giesing, "Bericht über meine Behandlung bei Hitler," p. 10; IfZ München, ED 100, vol. 70. On Hitler's injuries, see Morell's daily notes dated 20 July 1944; BA Koblenz N 1348/4; notes on a conversation with Hanskarl von Hasselbach, 6 Sept. 1952; IfZ München, ZS 242; Hans-Joachim Neumann and Henrik Eberle, *War Hitler krank? Ein abschliessender Befund*, Bergisch Gladbach, 2009, pp. 262f.

51 Junge, *Bis zur letzten Stunde*, p. 146. See Below, *Als Hitlers Adjutant*, p. 382: Below wrote that Hitler had "the lively, almost joyous expression of a person who had been expecting a serious misfortune which he luckily survived."

52 Schroeder, *Er war mein Chef*, p. 148. Traudl Junge recalled that on hearing of the assassination attempt, Eva Braun had written a "concerned and despairing letter" and that Hitler had been "very moved" by her "devotion." (*Bis zur letzten Stunde*, p. 151).

53 See Jodl's account "Der 20. Juli 1944 im Führerhauptquartier"; BA-MA Freiburg, N 69/3.

54 Goebbels, *Tagebücher*, part II, vol. 13, p. 140 (entry for 23 July 1944). See also Junge, *Bis zur letzten Stunde*, pp. 146–8; Olaf Rose (ed.), *Julius Schaub—In Hitlers Schatten: Erinnerungen und Aufzeichnungen des Chefadjutanten 1925–1945*, Stegen am Ammersee, 2005, p. 299; Eberle and Uhl (eds), *Das Buch Hitler*, p. 275.

55 Paul Schmidt, *Statist auf diplomatischer Bühne 1923–45*, Bonn, 1950, pp. 582f.; see also the notes on Hitler's discussion with Mussolini of 20 July 1944, in Hillgruber (ed.), *Staatsmänner und Diplomaten bei Hitler*, part II, pp. 468–75.

56 See Fest, *Staatsstreich*, pp. 265f.; Müller, *Generaloberst Ludwig Beck*, pp. 514f.

57 See Kroener, *Generaloberst Friedrich Fromm*, pp. 682–4; Müller, *Generaloberst Ludwig Beck*, pp. 515f. Goebbels was not mistaken when he surmised that Fromm was trying to "get himself out of the matter." Goebbels, *Tagebücher*, part II, vol. 13, p. 140 (entry for 23 July 1944).

58 See Kroener, *Generaloberst Friedrich Fromm*, pp. 684–92 (at p. 688); Müller, *Generaloberst Ludwig Beck*, p. 516.

59 See Müller, *Generaloberst Ludwig Beck*, pp. 516–18 (at pp. 517f.).

60 See Hoffmann, *Widerstand, Staatsstreich, Attentat*, pp. 532f.; Müller, *Generaloberst Ludwig Beck*, p. 520. Text of the official announcement in Max Domarus, *Hitler: Reden und Proklamationen 1932–1945*, Munich, 1965, vol. 2, part 2, p. 2127.

61 See Rose, *Julius Schaub*, p. 305; Rochus Misch, *Der letzte Zeuge: "Ich war Hitlers Telefonist, Kurier und Leibwächter,"* Zurich and Munich, 2008, pp. 171f.

62 The first telegram was sent at 8:30 p.m. Four more followed between then and 10:45 p.m.; BA Berlin-Lichterfelde, NS 6/1; excerpts reproduced in Volker Koop, *Martin Bormann: Hitlers Vollstrecker*, Cologne and Weimar, 2012, pp. 249–52.

63 This theory is discussed by Kershaw, *Hitler 1936–1945*, p. 644f.

64 Rose, *Julius Schaub*, p. 306; David Irving, *Hitler und seine Feldherren*, Frankfurt am Main, Berlin and Vienna, 1975, p. 616. See also Wilfred von Oven, *Finale Furioso: Mit Goebbels bis zum Ende*, Tübingen, 1974, pp. 401f. (entry for 23 July 1944): Goebbels justified his refusal to bring out the news of the assassination uncommented by citing the need to cushion the psychological shock.

65 See Remer's written account of the course of events of 22 July 1944; BA Berlin-Lichterfelde, NS 6/2; reproduced in Hans-Adolf Jacobsen (ed.), *"Spiegelbild einer Verschwörung": Die Opposition gegen Hitler und der Staatsstreich vom 20. Juli 1944 in der SD-Berichterstattung*, Stuttgart, 1984, vol. 2, pp. 637–42 (at p. 637).

66 Speer, *Erinnerungen*, pp. 392f. After the war, Speer tried to insinuate that he was among the conspirators, although he was never involved in the assassination plans

at any stage. See Magnus Brechtken, *Albert Speer: Eine deutsche Karriere*, Munich, 2017, pp. 267f.

67 See the report by Captain Hans Hagen of 26 Oct. 1944; BA Berlin-Lichterfelde, NS 6/2.

68 It was not until hours later that the employees of the Ministry of Nutrition and Agriculture learned that the conspirators had cordoned off the government district. "Unbeknownst to us, we were prisoners," Agriculture Minister Backe wrote to his wife on 21 July 1944; BA Koblenz, N 1075/27.

69 See Remer's report, 22 July 1944; Jacobsen (ed.), *"Spiegelbild einer Verschwörung,"* pp. 639f.; Speer, *Erinnerungen*, pp. 394–6.

70 See Hoffmann, *Claus Schenk Graf von Stauffenberg und seine Brüder*, pp. 430f.; Fest, *Staatsstreich*, p. 274.

71 See Müller, *Generaloberst Ludwig Beck*, pp. 524f.

72 See Kroener, *Generaloberst Friedrich Fromm*, pp. 697f.; Müller, *Generaloberst Ludwig Beck*, pp. 525f.

73 See Kroener, *Generaloberst Friedrich Fromm*, pp. 699–708 (at p. 700); Müller, *Generaloberst Ludwig Beck*, pp. 527–30; Fest, *Staatsstreich*, pp. 279–81.

74 Junge, *Bis zur letzten Stunde*, p. 149; see Schroeder, *Er war mein Chef*, p. 149.

75 See Rose, *Julius Schaub*, pp. 306f.

76 Domarus, *Hitler*, vol. 2, part 2, pp. 2127–9. Because so few Germans were still awake to hear the speech, it was broadcast again at 12:30 p.m. on 21 July.

77 See Speer, *Erinnerungen*, pp. 397f.; Kroener, *Generaloberst Friedrich Fromm*, pp. 710f.

78 Irving, *Hitler und seine Feldherren*, p. 619; see Below, *Als Hitlers Adjutant*, p. 384; Rose, *Julius Schaub*, p. 306

79 BA Berlin-Lichterfelde, NS 6/1. See Koop, *Martin Bormann*, p. 252.

80 Herbert Backe to his wife, 21 July 1944; BA Koblenz, N 1075/27. See Alwin-Broder Albrecht to his wife, 22 July 1944: "The Führer of the Reich will soon deal with the remaining cowards in uniform, and what was an attempt to weaken our capacity for self-defence will strengthen us significantly." IfZ München, ED 100, vol. 33.

81 On the course of events in Paris, see the detailed recollections of Günter Blumentritt, the chief of staff of the Supreme Commander West: "Der 20. Juli 1944," pp. 26–42; IfZ München, ZS 208/1; Fest, *Staatsstreich*, pp. 282–7; Ueberschär, *Stauffenberg: Der 20. Juli 1944*, pp. 50–62.

82 On 30 December 1944, Ursula von Kardorff described the events retrospectively in her diary as an "utterly stupid revolution of dilettantes." *Berliner Aufzeichnungen 1942 bis 1945*, p. 215n3.

83 See Fest, *Staatsstreich*, pp. 288–90; Richard J. Evans, *The Third Reich at War, 1939–1945*, London, 2008, pp. 644f.; Winfried Heinemann, "Der militärische Widerstand und der Krieg," in *Das Deutsche Reich und der Zweite Weltkrieg*, ed. Militärgeschichtliches Forschungsamt (Military Historical Historical Research Office), vol. 9, part 1, Munich, 2004, pp. 840f.; Eberhard Jäckel, "Wenn der Anschlag gelungen wäre . . . ," in *idem*, *Umgang mit der Vergangenheit: Beiträge zur Geschichte*, Stuttgart, 1989, pp. 195–206 (at pp. 198f.).

84 Schlabrendorff, *Offiziere gegen Hitler*, p. 129.

85 First report by the chief of the Security Police and the SD, Kaltenbrunner, 21 July 1944; BA Berlin-Lichterfelde, NS 6/2. For an extended analysis of the reactions, see Ian Kershaw, *The "Hitler Myth": Image and Reality in the Third Reich*, Oxford, 1987, pp. 215–19.

86 Second report by Kaltenbrunner, 21 July 1944; BA Berlin-Lichterfelde, NS 6/2.

87 Ronald Smelser, *Robert Ley: Hitlers Mann an der "Arbeitsfront." Eine Biographie*, Paderborn, 1989, p. 285. See also Ian Kershaw: *The End: The Defiance and Destruction of Hitler's Germany, 1944–45*, London, 2011, p. 51; Evans, *The Third Reich at War*, pp. 650f.; Wolfram Pyta, *Hitler: Der Künstler als Politiker und Feldherr*, Munich, 2015, p. 584; Nicholas Stargardt, *The German War: A Nation under Arms, 1939–45*, London, 2015, p. 453.

88 Bormann to the Reichsleiter and Gauleiter, 24 July 1944; BA Berlin-Lichterfelde, NS 6/1.

89 Heinz Boberach (ed.), *Meldungen aus dem Reich: Die geheimen Lageberichte des Sicherheitsdienstes der SS 1938–1945*, Herrsching, 1984, vol. 17, p. 6684 (dated 28 July 1944). See also the summary report of the Reich propaganda offices of 24 July 1944: "Loyalty to the Führer has once again become a force among all ethnic comrades and provides a powerful motivation." BA Berlin-Lichterfelde, R 55/601.

90 Goebbels, *Tagebücher*, part II, vol. 13, p. 173 (entry for 26 July 1944). On the wave of pro-Hitler demonstrations, see ibid., p. 145 (entry for 23 July 1944).

91 Kardorff, *Berliner Aufzeichnungen 1942 bis 1945*, p. 213 (entry for 23 July 1944).

92 Heinrich Breloer (ed.), *Mein Tagebuch: Geschichten vom Überleben 1939–1947*, Cologne, 1984, p. 133; see Kershaw, *Hitler 1936–1945*, pp. 700f.

93 Reproduced in Ortwin Buchbender and Reinhold Storz, *Das andere Gesicht: Deutsche Feldpostbriefe 1939–1945*, Munich, 1983, pp. 20–4 (at p. 21).

94 Ibid., pp. 142 (dated 21 July 1944), 147 (dated 8 Aug. 1944).

95 See Marlies Steinert, *Hitlers Krieg und die Deutschen: Stimmung und Haltung der deutschen Bevölkerung im Zweiten Weltkrieg*, Düsseldorf and Vienna, 1970, p. 479.

96 Balck's diary entry for 5 Aug. 1944; BA-MA Freiburg, N 647/12.

97 Reinhardt to his wife, 21 July 1944; BA-MA Freiburg, N 245/2.

98 Reinhardt's diary entry for 21 July 1944; BA-MA Freiburg, N 245/3.

99 Sönke Neitzel, *Abgehört: Deutsche Generäle in britischer Kriegsgefangenschaft 1942–1945*, Berlin, 2005, doc. 146, p. 327, doc. 147, p. 332, doc. 152, p. 345.

100 Friedrich Kellner, *"Vernebelt, verdunkelt sind alle Hirne": Tagebücher, 1939–1945*, ed. Sascha Feuchert et al., Göttingen, 2011, vol. 2, pp. 762f. (entry for 27 July 1944).

101 Thomas Mann, *Tagebücher, 1944–1. April 1946*, ed. Inge Jens, Frankfurt am Main, 1986, p. 79 (entry for 21 July 1944).

102 Victor Klemperer, *Ich will Zeugnis ablegen bis zum letzten: Tagebücher*, vol. 2: 1942–1945, ed. Walter Nowojski with Hadwig Klemperer, Berlin, 1995, pp. 550 (entry for 22 July 1944), 553 (entry for 23 July 1944).

103 Cited in Evans, *The Third Reich at War*, p. 652.

104 Goebbels, *Tagebücher*, part II, vol. 13, p. 322 (entry for 25 Aug. 1944).

105 Giesing, "Bericht über meine Behandlung bei Hitler"; IfZ München, ED 100, vol. 71.

106 See Goebbels, *Tagebücher*, part II, vol. 13, p. 152 (entry for 24 July 1944). Giesing's account put Eicken's arrival on 25 July 1944 and is generally not always reliable. See Neumann and Eberle, *War Hitler krank?*, pp. 77f.

107 Heinz Guderian, *Erinnerungen eines Soldaten*, Heidelberg, 1951, p. 309.

108 Bernd Freytag von Loringhoven, *Mit Hitler im Bunker: Die letzten Monate im Führerhauptquartier Juli 1944–April 1945*, Berlin, 2006, p. 10. See also the transcript of Bernd Freytag von Loringhoven's interrogation in 1949: "I was completely taken aback by his appearance. I thought, 'This is an aged man!'" IfZ München, ZS 38. Two days after the assassination attempt, Goebbels wrote "that the Führer has grown very old . . . he makes a positively fragile impression." *Tagebücher*, part II, vol. 13, p. 142 (entry for 23 July 1944).

109 Helmut Heiber (ed.), *Hitlers Lagebesprechungen: Die Protokollfragmente seiner militärischen Konferenzen 1942–1945*, Stuttgart, 1962, p. 608 (dated 31 July 1944). In early October 1944, Hitler told Morell that in the weeks following the assassination attempt he had needed to "summon all his energy" to stay on his feet. See Morell's daily notes of 4 Oct. 1944; BA Koblenz, N 1348/4.

110 See Morell's daily notes of 29 July and 15 Sept. 1944; BA Koblenz, N 1348/2; Ernst Günther Schenck, *Patient Hitler: Eine medizinische Biographie*, Düsseldorf, 1989, pp. 147f.; Heiber (ed.), *Hitlers Lagebesprechungen*, pp. 608f.; Below recalled that Hitler's trembling returned "after a few days." Below, *Als Hitlers Adjutant*, p. 384,

111 Goebbels, *Tagebücher*, part II, vol. 13, p. 305 (entry for 24 Aug. 1944). See ibid., pp. 209f. (entry for 3 Aug. 1944), 231f. (entry for 5 Aug. 1944).

112   Hermann Jung, *Die Ardennenoffensive 1944/45: Ein Beispiel für die Kriegführung Hitlers*, Göttingen, 1971, p. 209. See Junge, *Bis zur letzten Stunde*, p. 156. Junge recalled that Hitler was "very concerned . . . lest anyone notice his constant trembling." For that reason he tended to keep his left hand behind his back.

113   Schroeder, *Er war mein Chef*, pp. 148f.

114   See Jodl's testimony "Der 20. Juli 1944 im Führerhauptquartier"; BA-MA Freiburg, N 69/3; Speer, *Erinnerungen*, p. 399; Below, *Als Hitlers Adjutant*, p. 353. In a letter of 8 Sept. 1944 to the Gauleiter of Halle/Merseburg, Joachim Eggeling, Bormann also blamed the collapse of Army Group Centre on Henning von Tresckow; BA Berlin-Lichterfelde, NS 6/153.

115   Goebbels, *Tagebücher*, part II, vol. 13, p. 152 (entry for 24 July 1944).

116   Excerpt of a speech by Hitler in the morning situation meeting on 24 July 1944; BA Berlin-Lichterfelde, NS 6/24.

117   Goebbels, *Tagebücher*, part II, vol. 14, p. 350 (entry for 4 Dec. 1944).

118   Ibid., vol. 13, p. 138 (entry for 23 July 1944).

119   Ibid., p. 303 (entry for 24 Aug. 1944).

120   Order of the Wehrmacht adjutants to the Führer of 14 Sept. 1944; IfZ München, ED 9; Goebbels, *Tagebücher*, part II, vol. 13, p. 210 (entry for 3 Aug. 1944); Eberle and Uhl (eds), *Das Buch Hitler*, p. 284.

121   See Hitler's order of 7 Sept. 1944; BA Berlin-Lichterfelde, NS 6/130.

122   Warlimont, *Im Hauptquartier*, p. 473; see Domarus, *Hitler*, vol. 2, part 2, p. 2131.

123   Goebbels, *Tagebücher*, part II, vol. 13, pp. 141f. (entry for 23 July 1944); see ibid., p. 210 (entry for 3 Aug. 1944).

124   Marianne Feuersenger, *Im Vorzimmer der Macht: Aufzeichnungen aus dem Wehrmacht-führungsstab und Führerhauptquartier 1940–1945*, 4th edition, Munich, 2001, p. 247 (based on reports by Scherff's deputy Wilhelm Heinrich Scheidt of late December 1944).

125   See Arnim Ramm, *Der 20. Juli vor dem Volksgerichtshof*, Berlin, 2007, pp. 161–7.

126   Guderian's adjutant reported that SS-Gruppenführer Fegelein had thrown a pile of photos on the card table, whereupon the dictator had inspected the death throes of the condemned men "avariciously" and "with almost lustful glee" (Freytag von Loringhoven, *Mit Hitler im Bunker*, pp. 65f.). By contrast, Below recalled that neither he nor Hitler had viewed the photos (Below, *Als Hitlers Adjutant*, p. 385). Speer wrote that he had seen a large pile of photos of the hanged men on the situation-room card table and that they included an image of Field Marshal von Witzleben in prisoner's clothing. Speer claimed that he had excused himself from viewing the film in the cinema room, claiming that he was "overworked," but that those present at the screening of the footage had said Hitler had been among them. See Speer to Erich Fromm, 1 July 1973; BA Koblenz, N 1340/21. Speer wrote to Peter Hoffmann on 14 Dec. 1970 that "It can be safely assumed that Hitler watched the film"; Speer, *Erinnerungen*, p. 404.

127   See Jacobsen (ed.), *"Spiegelbild einer Verschwörung,"* vol. 1, pp. 1 ff.

128   Goebbels, *Tagebücher*, part II, vol. 13, p. 167 (entry for 25 July 1944).

129   Ibid., pp. 165 (entry for 25 July 1944), 210 (entry for 3 Aug. 1944), 245 (entry for 16 Aug. 1944).

130   See the overview in Ramm, *Der 20. Juli vor dem Volksgerichtshof*, pp. 449–64.

131   See ibid., pp. 67f.; Longerich, *Heinrich Himmler*, pp. 718f.

132   Cited in Peter Lieb, "Erwin Rommel: Widerstandskämpfer oder Nationalsozialist?," in *Vierteljahrshefte für Zeitgeschichte*, 61 (2013), pp. 303–43 (at p. 334).

133   Jodl's diary, 1 Aug. 1944; Ralf Georg Reuth, *Rommel: Das Ende einer Legende*, Munich and Zurich, 2004, p. 227.

134   Goebbels, *Tagebücher*, part II, vol. 13, p. 210 (entry for 3 Aug. 1944).

135   Report by Kronmüller to Martin Bormann concerning Field Marshal Rommel on 19 Sept. 1944; BA-MA Freiburg, N 117/29.

136   Bormann to Himmler, 27 Sept. 1944, and file note by Bormann for Friedrichs (Party Chancellery Munich) of 28 Sept. 1944; BA-MA Freiburg, N 117/29. See also Reuth, *Rommel*, pp. 237f.

137   Rommel to Hitler, 1 Oct. 1944; BA-MA Freiburg, N 117/32.

138   See Reuth, *Rommel*, pp. 242–55 (at p. 254).

139   See minutes of meeting with Hitler on 22 July 1944; BA Berlin-Lichterfelde, R 43 II/664 a.

140   Goebbels, *Tagebücher*, part II, vol. 13, p. 137 (entry for 23 July 1944).

141   Ibid., pp. 154, 157.

142   Ibid., p. 174 (entry for 26 July 1944). The draft and final version of the directive in BA Berlin-Lichterfelde, R 43 II/664; Domarus, *Hitler*, vol. 2, part 2, p. 2132.

143   That was how the Gauleiter of Hamburg, Karl Kaufmann, referred to the Führer's secretary in conversation with Speer in 1943. See Speer's testimony on his activities as minister, Nuremberg, 10 Aug. 1946, p. 21; BA Koblenz, N 1340/84.

144   See Kershaw, *The End*, pp. 41f; Albert Speer to John M. Tray, 19 Nov. 1973: "Without doubt, in the final period of the war, Bormann was the most powerful figure after Hitler." BA Koblenz, N 1340/60.

145   See Bormann's telegram to the Reichsleiter and Gauleiter of 1 Aug.1944; BA Berlin-Lichterfelde, NS 6/1.

146   See Hitler's directive on the concentration of the war economy, 2 Sept. 1943; BA Berlin-Lichterfelde, NS 6/342. See Speer, *Erinnerungen*, pp. 288–90; Goebbels, *Tagebücher*, part II, vol. 8, p. 537 (entry for 25 June 1943), vol. 9, p. 267 (entry for 10 Aug. 1943), vol. 11, pp. 114f. (entry for 18 Jan. 1944).

147   Rudolf Wolters to Albert Speer, 1 Nov. 1969; BA Koblenz, N 1340/76.

148   See Speer's testimony on his activity as minister, Nuremberg, 12 Aug. 1946, pp. 17f.; BA Koblenz, N 1340/84. Numerous files on Speer's illness are kept in BA Koblenz, N 1340/291.

149   See Speer, *Erinnerungen*, pp. 339–60; Fest, *Speer*, pp. 268–94; Martin Kitchen, *Speer: Hitler's Architect*, New Haven and London, 2015, pp. 188–97, 214; Brechtken, *Albert Speer*, pp. 240–51. On 6 June 1944, Goebbels wrote that Speer once more stood "high in the Führer's estimation": "Because of his long illness, he had lost some of his reputation with the Führer, but with his most recent achievements, he has effortlessly regained it." *Tagebücher*, part II, vol. 12, p. 407.

150   Albert Speer to Rudolf Wolters, 6 July 1975; BA Koblenz, N 1340/76.

151   See Kershaw, *The End*, p. 35; Longerich, *Heinrich Himmler*, p. 721; Stargardt, *The German War*, pp. 455f.

152   See Goebbels, *Tagebücher*, part II, vol. 13, pp. 221–3 (entry for 4 Aug. 1944).

153   Domarus, *Hitler*, vol. 2, part 2, pp. 2138f.; see Speer, *Erinnerungen*, pp. 402f. Contrary to his usual habit, Hitler gave the speech sitting down; see Helmut Sündermann, *Hier stehe ich . . . Deutsche Erinnerungen 1914/45*, Leoni, 1975, p. 278 (entry for 5 Aug. 1944).

154   Goebbels to Lammers, 1 Aug. 1944 (includes memorandum entitled "Way of life during Total War"); BA Berlin-Lichterfelde, R 43 II/665.

155   Goebbels, *Tagebücher*, part II, vol. 13, p. 526 (entry for 20 Sept. 1944).

156   See Speer, *Erinnerungen*, pp. 400f.; Kershaw, *The End*, pp. 42–4, 77–9.

157   Bormann to Goebbels, 14 Aug. 1944; BA Berlin-Lichterfelde, R 43 II/665.

158   Goebbels, *Tagebücher*, part II, vol. 13, pp. 308f. (entry for 24 Aug. 1944).

159   See Kershaw, *Hitler 1936–1945*, p. 712f.; Evans, *The Third Reich at War*, p. 656.

160   Kardorff, *Berliner Aufzeichnungen 1942 bis 1945*, p. 273 (entry for 31 Dec. 1944).

14 Final Rally

1   Helmut Heiber (ed.), *Hitlers Lagebesprechungen. Die Protokollfragmente seiner militärischen Konferenzen 1942–1945*, Stuttgart, 1962, pp. 609–21 (at pp. 620, 616). In early September 1944, Hitler also expressed to Goebbels his "unshakable certainty

that we will succeed in mastering this crisis and his limitless confidence in his lucky star." *Die Tagebücher von Joseph Goebbels*, commissioned by the Institute for Contemporary History, with support from the State Archive of Russia, ed. Elke Fröhlich; *Part II: Diktate 1941–1945*, 15 vols, Munich, 1993–6, vol. 13, p. 406 (entry for 3 Sept. 1944).

2   Heiber (ed.), *Hitlers Lagebesprechungen*, p. 615.

3   Goebbels, *Tagebücher*, part II, vol. 13, p. 401 (entry for 3 Sept. 1944).

4   Wolfram Pyta, *Hitler: Der Künstler als Politiker und Feldherr*, Munich, 2015, p. 633.

5   Walter Warlimont, *Im Hauptquartier der deutschen Wehrmacht 1939–1945: Grundlagen— Formen—Gestalten*, Frankfurt am Main and Bonn, 1964, p. 492.

6   Letter from Kluge dated 6 Aug. 1944; BA-MA Freiburg, MSg 2/11185. See *Das Deutsche Reich und der Zweite Weltkrieg. Vol. 7: Das Deutsche Reich in der Defensive*, Stuttgart and Munich, 2001, pp. 556f. (Vogel's essay); Gerhard L. Weinberg, *Eine Welt in Waffen: Die globale Geschichte des Zweiten Weltkriegs*, Stuttgart, 1995, pp. 731f.

7   Heiber (ed.), *Hitlers Lagebesprechungen*, pp. 584–609 (at pp. 585, 594).

8   See Martin Bormann's notes on the letters of the Gauleiter of Magdeburg-Anhalt, Rudolf Jordan, of 28 and 30 Aug. 1944; BA Berlin-Lichterfelde, NS 6/785.

9   Kluge to Hitler, 18 Aug. 1944; *Kriegstagebuch des Oberkommandos der Wehrmacht (Wehrmachtführungsstab)* (hereafter *KTB OKW*), ed. Percy Ernst Schramm, Munich, 1982, vol. 4, part 2, pp. 1574–6 (at p. 1576). On 19 August 1944, in his private suicide note ("Valmy, midday"), Kluge wrote that being replaced by Model had made him decide to take his own life; BA-MA Freiburg, MSg 2/11185. See also *Das Deutsche Reich und der Zweite Weltkrieg*, vol. 7, pp. 558–60 (Vogel's essay); Peter Lieb, *Unternehmen Overlord: Die Invasion in der Normandie und die Befreiung Westeuropas*, Munich, 2014, pp. 155–7.

10 See *Das Deutsche Reich und der Zweite Weltkrieg*, vol. 7, pp. 597–602 (Vogel's essay); Lieb, *Unternehmen Overlord*, pp. 165–70.

11 See Eberhard Jäckel, *Frankreich in Hitlers Europa: Die deutsche Frankreichpolitik im Zweiten Weltkrieg*, Stuttgart, 1966, pp. 349ff.

12 Cited in Lieb, *Unternehmen Overlord*, p. 160.

13 Letter from Private Albin Greiner to his parents, 27 Aug. 1944; BA Berlin-Lichterfelde, R 55/575.

14 Goebbels, *Tagebücher*, part II, vol. 13, p. 336 (entry for 27 Aug. 1944).

15 For Kluge's 60th birthday on 30 October 1942 Hitler gave him a cheque for 250,000 reichsmarks. BA Berlin-Lichterfelde, R 43 II/ 985b. See Gerd R. Ueberschär and Winfried Vogel, *Dienen und Verdienen: Hitlers Geschenke an seine Eliten*, Frankfurt am Main, 1999, p. 222.

16 Goebbels, *Tagebücher*, part II, vol. 13, p. 402 (entry for 3 Sept. 1944). In conversation with General Hermann Balck, Guderian also blamed Germany's collapse in the west on Kluge's "betrayal." See Balck's diary entry for 10 Sept. 1944; BA-MA Freiburg, N 647/12.

17 See *Das Deutsche Reich und der Zweite Weltkrieg*, vol. 7, pp. 573f. (Vogel's essay).

18 See Ian Kershaw, *The End: The Defiance and Destruction of Hitler's Germany, 1944–45*, London, 2011, pp. 59, 62–4. Dietmar Henke, *Die amerikanische Besetzung Deutschlands*, Munich, 1995, pp. 154f.

19 Cited in Kershaw, *The End*, pp. 69–70. In late November 1944, at Hitler's behest, the Reich organisational director of the Nazi Party, Robert Ley, travelled to the western Gaue to remind the Gauleiter of the Führer's directive that "every square metre of territory and every house, village and city be defended down to the very last drop of blood." Ley to Hitler, 30 Nov. 1944; BA Berlin-Lichterfelde, NS 6/135.

20 Goebbels, *Tagebücher*, part II, vol. 13, pp. 491f. (entry for 16 Sept. 1944), 501 (entry for 17 Sept. 1944). See Albert Speer, *Erinnerungen: Mit einem Essay von Jochen Thies*, Frankfurt am Main and Berlin, 1993, pp. 409f.

21 See *Das Deutsche Reich und der Zweite Weltkrieg*, vol. 7, pp. 606–11 (Vogel's essay); Lieb, *Unternehmen Overlord*, pp. 193–8.

22 Goebbels, *Tagebücher*, part II, vol. 13, p. 545 (entry for 23 Sept. 1944); see ibid., vol. 14, p. 30 (entry for 1 Oct. 1944).

23 Heiber (ed.), *Hitlers Lagebesprechungen*, p. 615 (dated 31 Aug. 1944).

24 See *Das Deutsche Reich und der Zweite Weltkrieg. Vol. 8: Die Ostfront 1943/44*, Munich, 2007, vol. 8, pp. 570–84 (Frieser's essay).

25 Hans Frank to Brigitte Frank, 14 Aug. 1944; BA Koblenz, N 1110/50.

26 On 6 September 1944, the commander of Army Group Centre, Hans-Georg Reinhardt, noted in his diary: "In Warsaw. Terrible scenes. Thank God I did not have to order this action." BA-MA Freiburg, N 245/3.

27 See Wlodzimierz Borodziej, *Der Warschauer Aufstand 1944*, Frankfurt am Main, 2001; Norman Davies, *Rising '44: "The Battle for Warsaw,"* London, 2003. For a summary, see Mark Mazower, *Hitler's Empire: Nazi Rule in Occupied Europe*, London, 2008, pp. 512—14; Richard J. Evans, *The Third Reich at War, 1939–1945*, London, 2008, pp. 621–3.

28 See *Das Deutsche Reich und der Zweite Weltkrieg*, vol. 8, pp. 587–91 (Frieser's essay).

29 See Hans Friessner, *Verratene Schlachten: Die Tragödie der deutschen Wehrmacht in Rumänien und Ungarn*, Hamburg, 1956, pp. 65ff.; Klaus Schönherr, "Die Rückzugskämpfe in Rumänien und Siebenbürgen im Sommer/Herbst 1944," in *Das Deutsche Reich und der Zweite Weltkrieg*, vol. 8, pp. 747–72.

30 Goebbels, *Tagebücher*, part II, vol. 13, p. 301 (entry for 24 Aug. 1944).

31 Notes on Hitler's meeting with Antonescu on 5 Aug. 1944; Andreas Hillgruber (ed.), *Staatsmänner und Diplomaten bei Hitler: Vertrauliche Aufzeichnungen über Unterredungen mit Vertretern des Auslandes 1939–1941*, Frankfurt am Main, 1967, part 2, pp. 481–501 (at pp. 494, 495, 496). See also Antonescu's notes from memory of the meeting in *Das Deutsche Reich und der Zweite Weltkrieg*, vol. 8, pp. 740f. (Schönherr's essay).

32 Goebbels, *Tagebücher*, part II, vol. 13, p. 313 (entry for 24 Aug. 1944).

33 See Friessner, *Verratene Schlachten*, pp. 92ff.; *Das Deutsche Reich und der Zweite Weltkrieg*, vol. 8, pp. 779–819 (Schönherr's essay).

34 See ibid., pp. 816f.

35 See Klaus Schönherr, "Der Rückzug aus Griechenland," in *Das Deutsche Reich und der Zweite Weltkrieg*, vol. 8, pp. 1089–94.

36 Goebbels, *Tagebücher*, part II, vol. 13, p. 574 (entry for 27 Sept. 1944).

37 See Bernd Wegner, "Das Kriegsende in Skandinavien," in *Das Deutsche Reich und der Zweite Weltkrieg*, vol. 8, pp. 963–1000.

38 Goebbels, *Tagebücher*, part II, vol. 13, p. 412 (entry for 4 Sept. 1944).

39 See *Das Deutsche Reich und der Zweite Weltkrieg*, vol. 8, pp. 961–3 (Wegner's essay); Wilhelm M. Carlgreen, *Swedish Foreign Policy during the Second World War*, London, 1977, pp. 199 ff.

40 See Martin Zückert, Jürgen Zarusky and Volker Zimmermann (eds), *Partisanen im Zweiten Weltkrieg: Der Slowakische Nationalaufstand im Kontext der europäischen Widerstandsbewegungen*, Göttingen, 2017; for a summary, see Weinberg, *Eine Welt in Waffen*, pp. 751f.; Evans, *The Third Reich at War*, p. 654.

41 Goebbels, *Tagebücher*, part II, vol. 13, pp. 489f. (entry for 16 Sept. 1944).

42 See the summary reports of the Reich propaganda offices of 21 Aug. and 4 Sept. 1944; BA Berlin-Lichterfelde, R 55/601.

43 Goebbels, *Tagebücher*, part II, vol. 13, p. 478 (entry for 14 Sept. 1944); see ibid., pp. 465 (entry for 12 Sept. 1944), 519 (entry for 19 Sept. 1944); vol. 14, p. 72 (entry for 10 Oct. 1944).

44 Reproduced in Friedrich Kellner, *"Vernebelt, verdunkelt sind alle Hirne": Tagebücher, 1939–1945*, ed. Sascha Feuchert et al., Göttingen, 2011, vol. 2, p. 821 (entry for 3 Sept. 1944). See Nicholas Stargardt, *The German War: A Nation under Arms, 1939–45*, London, 2015, pp. 464.

45   Goebbels, *Tagebücher*, part II, vol. 13, p. 493 (entry for 16 Sept. 1944). After travelling to the western front, Speer reported that "the belief in the imminent deployment of weapons to decide the war" was "widespread" among German troops. Speer asked whether "this propaganda was appropriate." See "Bericht über die Reise nach den Westgebieten vom 10.–14. September 1944"; BA Koblenz, N 1340/219.

46   Victor Klemperer, *Ich will Zeugnis ablegen bis zum letzten: Tagebücher*, vol. 2: 1942–1945, ed. Walter Nowojski with Hadwig Klemperer, Berlin, 1995, p. 574 (entry for 1 Sept. 1944).

47   Goebbels, *Tagebücher*, part II, vol. 3, pp. 542f. (entry for 25 March 1942).

48   Hillgruber (ed.), *Staatsmänner und Diplomaten bei Hitler*, part 2, p. 484.

49   See Mark Walker, *Die Uranmaschine: Mythos und Wirklichkeit der deutschen Atombombe*, Berlin, 1990; *idem*, "Legenden um die deutsche Atombombe," in *Vierteljahrshefte für Zeitgeschichte*, 38 (1990), pp. 45–74; Speer, *Erinnerungen*, pp. 239–43; for a summary, Evans, *The Third Reich at War*, pp. 667–9; Weinberg, *Eine Welt in Waffen*, pp. 609–12; *Das Deutsche Reich und der Zweite Weltkrieg*, vol. 5, part 2, pp. 727–43 (Müller's essay). The historian of science Rainer Karlsch has put forward the thesis that German scientists carried out initial tests of atomic weapons on the island of Rügen and in the town of Ohrdruf in Thuringia in October 1944 and March 1945, but he has never presented any convincing evidence for this contention. Rainer Karlsch, *Hitlers Bombe: Die geheime Geschichte der deutschen Kernwaffenversuche*, Munich, 2005.

50   See Gerhard Krebs, "Der Krieg im Pazifik 1943–1945," in *Das Deutsche Reich und der Zweite Weltkrieg*, vol. 7, pp. 691–714.

51   See Goebbels, *Tagebücher*, part II, vol. 13, p. 419 (entry for 6 Sept. 1944).

52   Ibid., pp. 524f. (entry for 20 Sept. 1944).

53   Ibid., p. 478 (entry for 14 Sept. 1944).

54   See ibid., pp. 461 (entry for 12 Sept. 1944), 507 (entry for 18 Sept. 1944).

55   Ibid., p. 512 (entry for 18 Sept. 1944).

56   Ibid., pp. 536–42. In the view of his press spokesman, Goebbels was trying to do "nothing less than knock Ribbentrop from his saddle and take his place." Wilfred von Oven, *Finale Furioso: Mit Goebbels bis zum Ende*, Tübingen, 1974, p. 480 (entry for 22 Sept. 1944). On Goebbels' memorandum of 20 Sept. 1944 see also Peter Longerich, *Joseph Goebbels*, Munich, 2010, pp. 664f.; Ralf Georg Reuth, *Goebbels*, Munich and Zurich, 1990, pp. 565–7.

57   Goebbels, *Tagebücher*, part II, vol. 13, p. 562 (entry for 25 Sept. 1944).

58   See ibid., vol. 14, p. 194 (entry for 10 Nov. 1944): "I cannot understand why the Führer sticks by [Ribbentrop] and expects him to achieve anything special in wartime politics in future."

59   Heiber (ed.), *Hitlers Lagebesprechungen*, p. 614.

60   Traudl Junge, *Bis zur letzten Stunde: Hitlers Sekretärin erzählt ihr Leben*, Munich, 2002, p. 161; see Christa Schroeder, *Er war mein Chef: Aus dem Nachlass der Sekretärin von Adolf Hitler*, ed. Anton Joachimsthaler, 3rd edition, Munich and Vienna, 1985, p. 149. Albert Speer, who had seen Hitler while the latter was bedridden, found him "a completely changed man ready to listen to all arguments." However, Speer added that the situation immediately turned around again once Hitler was able to leave his sickbed. Albert Speer to Rudolf Wolters, 10 July 1955; BA Koblenz, N 1318/23.

61   See Morell's notes of 28 Sept.–13 Oct. 1944; BA Koblenz, N 1348/4; Ernst Günther Schenck, *Patient Hitler: Eine medizinische Biographie*, Düsseldorf, 1989, pp. 148–53; Hans-Joachim Neumann and Henrik Eberle, *War Hitler krank? Ein abschliessender Befund*, Bergisch Gladbach, 2009, pp. 266–9; See Bormann's letters to his wife of 30 Sept., 1 and 4 Oct. 1944 in Hugh Trevor-Roper (ed.), *The Bormann Letters*, London, 1954, pp. 127, 129, 130.

62   See Ulf Schmidt, *Hitlers Arzt Karl Brandt: Medizin und Macht im Dritten Reich*, Berlin, 2009, pp. 494f.; Neumann and Eberle, *War Hitler krank?*, pp. 181f.

63　Goebbels, *Tagebücher*, part II, vol. 13, p. 297 (entry for 23 Aug. 1944). See Martin Bormann to his wife, 14 Aug. 1944; Trevor-Roper (ed.), *The Bormann Letters*, pp. 78–80; Schmidt, *Hitlers Arzt Karl Brandt*, pp. 482–9.

64　Morell's daily notes of 3. Oct. 1944; BA Koblenz, N 1348/4. See Neumann and Eberle, *War Hitler krank?*, p. 182.

65　Morell's daily notes of 3 Oct. 1944; BA Koblenz N 1348/4. See Neumann and Eberle, *War Hitler krank?*, pp. 184f.; Schmidt, *Hitlers Arzt Karl Brandt*, pp. 496f.

66　Junge, *Bis zur letzten Stunde*, pp. 156f.; see Martin Bormann to his wife, 4 Oct. 1944; Trevor-Roper (ed.), *The Bormann Letters*, p. 130. In notes on Theo Morrell of 19 Sept. 1945, Karl Brandt wrote it was "incomprehensible" that Morell not only had been able to remain Hitler's personal physician for ten years but had enjoyed "increasingly close contact" to the dictator. BA Koblenz, N 1128/33.

67　See Morell's daily notes of 8 Oct. 1944 and Bormann's letter to Reich press chief Dietrich of 10 Oct. 1944; BA Koblenz, N 1348/4; see Neumann and Eberle, *War Hitler krank?*, pp. 186f.; Martin Bormann to his wife, 10 Oct. 1944; Trevor-Roper (ed.), *The Bormann Letters*, p. 137.

68　Goebbels, *Tagebücher*, part II, vol. 14, pp. 79f. (entry for 11 Oct. 1944). On Brandt's loss of influence, see also Speer's letter to Paul Hoedeman, 8 Nov. 1976; BA Koblenz, N 1340/28.

69　Morell's daily notes of 8 Nov. 1944; BA Koblenz, N 1348/4; see Schenck, *Patient Hitler*, p. 259; Neumann and Eberle, *War Hitler krank?*, p. 187.

70　See *Das Deutsche Reich und der Zweite Weltkrieg*, vol. 8, pp. 643–64 (Frieser's essay); Weinberg, *Eine Welt in Waffen*, pp. 757f.; Heinz Guderian, *Erinnerungen eines Soldaten*, Heidelberg, 1951, p. 337.

71　See Kershaw, *Das Ende*, pp. 101–105. Stargardt, *The German War*, pp. 467f.

72　See *Das Deutsche Reich und der Zweite Weltkrieg*, vol. 8, pp. 614–19 (Frieser's essay).

73　See Catherine Merridale, *Ivan's War: The Red Army 1939–45*, London, 2005, pp. 260, 264f, 267–9; Kershaw, *The End*, p. 112; Werner Zeidler, *Kriegsende im Osten: Die Rolle der Roten Armee und die Besetzung Deutschlands östlich von Oder und Neisse 1944/45*, Munich, 1996, pp. 135ff.

74　Kreipe's diary entry for 13 Oct. 1945; Hermann Jung, *Die Ardennenoffensive 1944/45: Ein Beispiel für die Kriegführung Hitlers*, Göttingen, 1971, appendix 1, p. 227.

75　See Bernhard Fisch, *Nemmersdorf, Oktober 1944: Was in Ostpreussen tatsächlich geschah*, Berlin, 1997. For a summary, see Kershaw, *The End*, pp. 111–14; Stargardt, *The German War*, pp. 470f. After visiting the recaptured territory south of Gumbinnen, the commander of Army Group Centre, Hans-Georg Reinhardt, reported that German soldiers had taken revenge on Russian POWs by "beating whole regiments to death." See Reinhardt to his wife, 26 Oct. 1944; BA-MA Freiburg, N 245/2.

76　Goebbels, *Tagebücher*, part II, vol. 14, p. 110 (entry for 26 Oct. 1944).

77　Kershaw, *The End*, p. 115; see Oven, *Finale furioso*, p. 505 (entry for 27 Oct. 1944)

78　Otto Dov Kulka and Eberhard Jäckel (eds), *Die Juden in den geheimen NS-Stimmungsberichten 1939–1945*, Düsseldorf, 2004, doc. 749, p. 546.

79　Goebbels, *Tagebücher*, part II, vol. 14, p. 145 (entry for 3 Nov. 1944); see ibid., pp. 192f. (entry for 10 Nov. 1944).

80　Junge, *Bis zur letzten Stunde*, p. 162.

81　Goebbels, *Tagebücher*, part II, vol. 14, p. 31 (entry for 1 Oct. 1944).

82　See Krisztián Ungváry, "Kriegsschauplatz Ungarn," in *Das Deutsche Reich und der Zweite Weltkrieg*, vol. 8, pp. 876–8; Margit Szöllösi-Janze, *Die Pfeilkreuzlerbewegung in Ungarn: Historischer Kontext, Entwicklung und Herrschaft*, Munich, 1989, pp. 314ff.

83　See Szöllösi-Janze, *Die Pfeilkreuzlerbewegung in Ungarn*, pp. 426–30; Christian Gerlach and Götz Aly, *Das letzte Kapitel: Der Mord an den ungarischen Juden*, Stuttgart and Munich, 2002, pp. 357–61; *Das Deutsche Reich und der Zweite Weltkrieg*, vol. 8, pp. 881f. (Ungváry's essay).

84 Hitler's decree of 25 Sept. 1944 und regulatory statutes of 27 Sept. 1944; BA Berlin-Lichterfelde, NS 51/29; Max Domarus, *Hitler: Reden und Proklamationen 1932–1945*, Munich, 1965, vol. 2, part 2, pp. 2151f.

85 See Andreas Kunz, *Wehrmacht und Niederlage: Die bewaffnete Macht in der Endphase der nationalsozialistischen Herrschaft 1944 bis 1945*, Munich, 2005, pp. 133–41; Kershaw, *The End*, pp. 86–9, 106–8.

86 Summary report of the Reich propaganda office dated 23 Oct. 1944; BA Berlin-Lichterfelde, R 55/601.

87 See Richard Overy, *The Bombing War: Europe 1939–1945*, London, 2013, pp. 467–85.

88 Goebbels, *Tagebücher*, part II, vol. 14, p. 238 (entry for 19 Nov. 1944).

89 On the "1944 Autumn Inferno," see Olaf Groehler, *Bombenkrieg gegen Deutschland*, Berlin, 1990, pp. 342ff.

90 Goebbels, *Tagebücher*, part II, vol. 14, pp. 67 (entry for 10 Oct. 1944), 309 (entry for 1 Dec. 1944), 139 (entry for 2 Nov. 1944). On the demoralising effects of the bombing war, see Ian Kershaw, *The "Hitler Myth": Image and Reality in the Third Reich*, Oxford, 1987, pp. 206f.

91 See Kreipe's diary entries of 5 Sept. and 18 Sept. 1944; Jung, *Die Ardennen-Offensive 1944/45*, appendix 1, pp. 215f., 219; Nicolaus von Below, *Als Hitlers Adjutant 1937–45*, Mainz, 1980, pp. 387, 392, 394; Ian Kershaw, *Hitler 1936–1945: Nemesis*, London, 2001, pp. 738f.

92 See Speer, *Erinnerungen*, pp. 372–4; Adam Tooze, *The Wages of Destruction: The Making and Breaking of the Nazi Economy*, London, 2006, pp. 620f; Overy, *The Bombing War*, p. 388; Evans, *The Third Reich at War*, p. 671f.

93 Martin Bormann to his wife, 25 Oct. and 26 Oct. 1944; Trevor-Roper (ed.), *The Bormann Letters*, pp. 139, 141f.; see Schroeder, *Er war mein Chef*, p. 150; Goebbels, *Tagebücher*, part II, vol. 14, pp. 88 (entry for 23 Oct. 1944), 97 (entry for 24 Oct. 1944).

94 See Martin Bormann to his wife, 26 Oct. 1944; Trevor-Roper (ed.), *The Bormann Letters*, p. 142; Goebbels, *Tagebücher*, part II, vol. 14, p. 93 (entry for 24 Oct. 1944). On the "mood of departure" in the Wolf's Lair, see also Helmut Sündermann, *Hier stehe ich . . . Deutsche Erinnerungen 1914/45*, Leoni, 1975, p. 283 (entry for 22 Oct. 1944).

95 Domarus, *Hitler*, vol. 2, part 2, pp. 2160–87 (at pp. 2162, 2165, 2167). The Morgenthau Plan was made public in Germany in late September 1944 and was depicted, according to Goebbels' instructions, as evidence for the "threat of extermination coming from international financial Jewry." See Longerich, *Goebbels*, p. 642. President Roosevelt scrapped the plan shortly after the Quebec Conference. See Bernd Greiner, *Die Morgenthau-Legende: Zur Geschichte eines umstrittenen Plans*, Hamburg, 1995.

96 Goebbels, *Tagebücher*, part II, vol. 14, p. 210 (entry for 13 Nov. 1944).

97 Kellner, *Tagebücher, 1939–1945*, vol. 2, p. 885 (entry for 19 Nov. 1944).

98 Goebbels, *Tagebücher*, part II, vol. 13, p. 396 (entry for 3 Sept. 1944); see ibid., pp. 363 (entry for 30 Aug. 1944), 417 (entry for 5 Sept. 1944), 458 (entry for 11 Sept. 1944).

99 Ibid., vol. 13, pp. 503f. (entry for 17 Sept. 1944); see ibid., pp. 463f. (entry for 12 Sept. 1944).

100 See *Das letzte halbe Jahr: Stimmungsberichte der Wehrmachtpropaganda 1944/45*, ed. Wolfram Wette, Ricarda Brenner and Detlef Vogel, Essen, 2001, doc. 63, p. 153 (dated 21 Nov. 1944). See Goebbels, *Tagebücher*, part II, vol. 14, p. 214 (entry for 16 Nov. 1944).

101 Thomas Mann, *Tagebücher, 1944–1. Apr. 1946*, ed. Inge Jens, Frankfurt am Main, 1986, p. 123 (entry for 15 Nov. 1944). See Klemperer, *Tagebücher, 1942–1945*, p. 613 (entry for 16 Nov. 1944): "Rumours everywhere about Hitler and Himmler."

102 Goebbels, *Tagebücher*, part II, vol. 14, p. 310 (entry for 1 Dec. 1944). See *Das letzte halbe Jahr*, doc. 66, p. 167 (dated 9 Dec. 1944).

103 Kershaw, *The Hitler Myth*, p. 221.

104 See Alan Bullock, *Hitler: A Study in Tyranny*, London, 1990, p. 460; Kershaw, *The End*, p. 127.

105 Jodl's diary entry for 19 Aug. 1944; Warlimont, *Im Hauptquartier der Wehrmacht*, p. 487; see Jung, *Die Ardennen-Offensive 1944/45*, p. 101.

106 Goebbels, *Tagebücher*, part II, vol. 13, p. 403 (entry for 3 Sept. 1944).

107 Balck's diary entry for 10 Sept. 1944; BA-MA Freiburg, N 647/12. Balck found Hitler "hardy and confident" but recognised that "events are taking their toll on him nonetheless."

108 Kreipe's diary entry for 16 Sept. 1944; Jung, *Die Ardennen-Offensive 1944/45*, appendix 1, p. 218; see ibid., pp. 101f.; David Irving, *Hitler und seine Feldherren*, Frankfurt am Main, Berlin and Vienna, 1975, pp. 644f.

109 Hitler's order of 10 Nov. 1944; Jung, *Die Ardennen-Offensive 1944/45*, appendix 16, pp. 306–11. See also ibid., pp. 105–17; *Das Deutsche Reich und der Zweite Weltkrieg*, vol. 7, pp. 619–21 (Vogel's essay).

110 See Morell's daily notes of 8 Nov. 1944; BA Koblenz, N 1348/4.

111 Speer, *Erinnerungen*, p. 423.

112 See Lieb, *Unternehmen Overlord*, p. 206.

113 See Jodl's testimony on Hitler as a military leader, May–July 1946; IfZ München, ZS 678.

114 See Morell's daily notes of 27 Oct. 1944: "F[ührer] in a bad mood. He said his voice was too weak to speak into a microphone to the German people"; BA Koblenz, N 1348/4.

115 See Morell's daily notes of 17 and 18 Nov. 1944; BA Koblenz, N 1348/4; see Neumann and Eberle, *War Hitler krank?*, p. 173.

116 See Heinz Linge's appointment diary under 20 Nov. and 21 Nov. 1944; IfZ München, F 19/4; Morell's appointment diary under 20 and 21 Nov. 1944; BA Koblenz, N 1348/2; Harald Sandner, *Hitler: Das Itinerar. Aufenthaltsorte und Reisen von 1889–1945*, Berlin, 2016, vol. 4, p. 2273.

117 Junge, *Bis zur letzten Stunde*, p. 164.

118 See Uwe Neumärker, Robert Conrad and Cord Woywodt, *Wolfsschanze: Hitlers Machtzentrale im Zweiten Weltkrieg*, 3rd edition, Berlin, 2007, pp. 162–4; Goebbels, *Tagebücher*, part II, vol. 15, pp. 208 (entry for 24 Jan. 1945), 242 (entry for 27 Jan. 1945).

119 See Morell's daily notes of 22 Nov. 1944 and the evaluation by Professor Roessle from the Pathological Institute of Berlin's Charité Hospital for Professor von Eicken on 25 Nov. 1944; BA Koblenz, N 1348/4; see Neumann and Eberle, *War Hitler krank?*, p. 173.

120 See Goebbels, *Tagebücher*, part II, vol. 14, p. 269 (entry for 24 Nov. 1944); Bernd Freytag von Loringhoven, *Mit Hitler im Bunker: Die letzten Monate im Führerhauptquartier Juli 1944–April 1945*, Berlin, 2006, p. 68.

121 Junge, *Bis zur letzten Stunde*, pp. 167f.

122 See Gerda Bormann to Martin Bormann, 24 Oct. 1944; Trevor-Roper (ed.), *The Bormann Letters*, p. 138.

123 For the wording of the will, see Nerin E. Gun, *Eva Braun-Hitler: Leben und Schicksal*, Velbert and Kettwig, 1968, pp. 175–8. See also Heike B. Görtemaker, *Eva Braun: Leben mit Hitler*, Munich, 2010, pp. 261–3.

124 See Heinz Linge's appointment diary under 21 Nov.–9 Dec. 1944; IfZ München, F19/4. This source contradicts Heike Görtemaker's contention that Eva Braun "left after a few days" (*Eva Braun*, p. 264).

125 See Freytag von Loringhoven, *Mit Hitler im Bunker*, pp. 72f.

126 Goebbels, *Tagebücher*, part II, vol. 14, pp. 317–34 (entry for 2 Dec. 1944).

127 Ibid., pp. 350f. (entry for 4 Dec. 1944).

128 See notes on Hitler's meeting with Szálasi on 4 Dec. 1944, in Hillgruber (ed.), *Staatsmänner und Diplomaten bei Hitler*, part 2, pp. 520–36 (at pp. 521, 530).

129 See Goebbels, *Tagebücher*, part II, vol. 14, pp. 344 (entry for 3 Dec. 1944), 357 (entry for 5 Dec. 1944), 376 (entry for 8 Dec. 1944).

130 Brigitte Hamann, *Winifred Wagner oder Hitlers Bayreuth*, Munich and Zurich, 2002, pp. 486–8. See also the statements made by Winifred Wagner in her interview with David Irving on 13 March 1971; IfZ München, ZS 2242. Dinner was served thirty minutes past midnight on the night of 7–8 December; see Linge's appointment diary, IfZ München, F 19/4. On the night of 6–7 April 1945, Wieland Wagner travelled together with his brother-in-law Bodo Lafferentz to Berlin to see Hitler. They wanted to convince him to send some Wagner manuscripts— including the original score of *Rienzi* and the original fair copies of the scores to *The Rheingold* and *The Valkyrie*, which wealthy industrialists had purchased for 800,000 reichsmarks and given to Hitler as a present for his fiftieth birthday— back to Bayreuth for safe keeping. Hitler refused with the words, "Where I have put them is much safer than with you." The manuscripts have not been seen since the end of the war. See Winifred Wagner to Albert Speer, 1 Dec. 1966, 17 Sept. 1973; BA Koblenz, N 1340/70; Hamann, *Winifred Wagner oder Hitlers Bayreuth*, p. 502.

131 See Morell's daily notes of 11 Dec. 1944; BA Koblenz, N 1348/5; see Schenck, *Patient Hitler*, p. 157.

132 See Heinz Linge's appointment diary under 10–11 Dec. 1944; IfZ München, F 19/4; Martin Bormann to his wife, 11 Dec. 1944; Trevor-Roper (ed.), *The Bormann Letters*, p. 148; Sandner, *Hitler: Das Itinerar*, vol. 4, p. 2281.

133 See Franz W. Seidler and Dieter Zeigert, *Die Führerhauptquartiere: Anlagen und Planungen im Zweiten Weltkrieg*, Munich, 2000, pp. 143ff.

134 See ibid., p. 156; Heinz Linge's appointment diary under 12 Dec. 1944–14 Jan. 1945; IfZ München, F 19/4.

135 See Morell's notes in his desk diary for 13–21 Dec. 1944; BA Koblenz, N 1348/3; Martin Bormann to his wife, 26 Dec. 1944; Trevor-Roper (ed.), *The Bormann Letters*, p. 152; Neumann and Eberle, *War Hitler krank?*, p. 274. Traudl Junge, who arrived after a stay in Munich at the Eagle's Nest on 12 January 1944, found that Hitler looked "rejuvenated and fresher than in Berlin." Junge, *Bis zur letzten Stunde*, p. 171. That same day, when Morell asked him how he was feeling, Hitler knocked on wood and said "Quite well." Morell's daily notes of 12 Jan. 1945; BA Koblenz, N 1348/4; see Schenck, *Patient Hitler*, p. 158.

136 Heiber (ed.), *Hitlers Lagebesprechungen*, pp. 713–24 (at pp. 721, 722). Morell noted: "The Führer was said to be very fresh and lively, impulsive and contagiously enthusiastic. Entirely without complaints." BA Koblenz, N 1348/5; see Schenck, *Patient Hitler*, p. 157.

137 Jung, *Die Ardennen-Offensive 1944/45*, appendix 31, p. 350.

138 Ibid., appendix 32, p. 351.

139 On the Malmedy massacre, see Henke, *Die amerikanische Besetzung Deutschlands*, pp. 324–8.

140 On the course of the Ardennes Offensive, see *Das Deutsche Reich und der Zweite Weltkrieg*, vol. 7, pp. 625–9 (Vogel's essay); Jung, *Die Ardennen-Offensive 1944/45*, pp. 142ff. On the supply problems, see Albert Speer's report on his travels in the west, 15–31 Dec. 1944; BA Koblenz, N 1340/219.

141 Goebbels, *Tagebücher*, part II, vol. 14, p. 452 (entry for 20 Dec. 1944).

142 See ibid., p. 429 (entry for 17 Dec. 1944); Oven, *Finale furioso*, p. 527 (entry for 17 Dec. 1944).

143 See the summary report of the Reich propaganda offices of 19 Dec. 1944; BA Berlin-Lichterfelde, R 55/601.

144 Goebbels, *Tagebücher*, part II, vol. 14, pp. 449f. (entry for 20 Dec. 1944).

145 See *Das Deutsche Reich und der Zweite Weltkrieg*, vol. 7, p. 629 (Vogel's essay); Jung, *Die Ardennen-Offensive 1944/45*, pp. 166ff.

146 Goebbels, *Tagebücher*, part II, vol. 14, p. 487 (entry for 29 Dec. 1944). See Martin Bormann to his wife, 28 Dec. 1944; Trevor-Roper (ed.), *The Bormann Letters*, p. 154.

147 Guderian, *Erinnerungen eines Soldaten*, pp. 347–9. See Freytag von Loringhoven, *Mit Hitler im Bunker*, p. 128.

148 See *Das Deutsche Reich und der Zweite Weltkrieg*, vol. 7, p. 631 (Vogel's essay).

149 Heiber (ed.), *Hitlers Lagebesprechungen*, pp. 738–58 (at pp. 742, 743). See Jung, *Die Ardennen-Offensive 1944/45*, pp. 179f.

150 See Goebbels, *Die Tagebücher*, part II, vol. 15, p. 33 (entry for 1 Jan. 1945); Oven, *Finale furioso*, p. 537 (New Year 1945).

151 Domarus, *Hitler*, vol. 2, part 2, pp. 2179–85 (at pp. 2180, 2182, 2185).

152 See the reports by the Reich propaganda offices in Oldenburg and Danzig of 1 Jan. 1945; BA Berlin-Lichterfelde, R 55/612; see Goebbels, *Tagebücher*, part II, vol. 15, pp. 36 (entry for 2 Jan. 1945), 43 (entry for 3 Jan. 1945), 70f. (entry for 5 Jan. 1945); *Das letzte halbe Jahr*, doc. 71, p. 198 (entry for 9 Jan. 1945).

153 Joseph Goebbels, "Der Führer," in *Das Reich*, 31 Dec. 1944; Kershaw, *The Hitler Myth*, p. 221. Victor Klemperer wrote that the article was "so excessively glorifying that the headline might as well have been 'The Saviour.'" Klemperer, *Tagebücher, 1942–1945*, p. 635 (entry for 1 Jan. 1945).

154 Speer, *Erinnerungen*, p. 426; see Joachim Fest, *Speer: Eine Biographie*, Berlin, 1999, pp. 327f.

155 See *Das Deutsche Reich und der Zweite Weltkrieg*, vol. 7, pp. 631f. (Vogel's essay); Weinberg, *Eine Welt in Waffen*, pp. 807f.; Lieb, *Unternehmen Overlord*, pp. 208–10.

156 Goebbels, *Tagebücher*, part II, vol. 15, pp. 52–7, 59–65 (entry for 4 Jan. 1945) (at pp. 55, 56, 60). On the meeting of 3 Jan. 1945, see Speer, *Erinnerungen*, pp. 426f.; Fest, *Speer*, pp. 328f.; Martin Kitchen, *Speer: Hitler's Architect*, New Haven and London, 2015, p. 258.

157 See Weinberg, *Eine Welt in Waffen*, p. 808.

158 See *KTB OKW*, vol. 4, part 2, p. 1346; Jung, *Die Ardennen-Offensive 1944/45*, pp. 190–4.

159 See Richard Lakowski, "Der Zusammenbruch der deutschen Verteidigung zwischen Ostsee und Karpaten," in *Das Deutsche Reich und der Zweite Weltkrieg*, vol. 10, part 1, Munich, 2008, pp. 516f.

160 Heinz Linge's appointment diary for 15–16 Jan. 1945; IfZ München, F 14/9; Rochus Misch, *Der letzte Zeuge: "Ich war Hitlers Telefonist, Kurier und Leibwächter,"* Zurich and Munich, 2008, pp. 178f.; Junge, *Bis zur letzten Stunde*, pp. 173f.

15 Decline of a Dictator

1 Lutz Graf Schwerin von Krosigk, "Niederschrift zur Persönlichkeit Hitlers" (c.1945); IfZ München, ZS 145, vol. 5. See also *idem, Es geschah in Deutschland: Menschenbilder unseres Jahrhunderts*, Tübingen and Stuttgart, 1951, p. 220.

2 Joachim Fest, *Hitler: Eine Biographie*, Frankfurt am Main, Berlin and Vienna, 1973, p. 913.

3 Sebastian Haffner, "Der Hitler von 1943," in *idem, Schreiben für die Freiheit. 1942–1949: Als Journalist im Sturm der Ereignisse*, Berlin, 2001, pp. 23–6 (at pp. 24f.).

4 Reinhardt's report of 30 Oct. 1939; BA-MA Freiburg, N 245/21. On the awarding of medals, see also Wolfram Pyta, *Hitler: Der Künstler als Politiker und Feldherr*, Munich, 2015, pp. 336–8.

5 Torsten Diedrich and Jens Ebert (eds), *Nach Stalingrad: Walther von Seydlitz" Feldpostbriefe und Kriegsgefangenenpost 1939–1955*, Göttingen, 2018, p. 101 (dated 21 May 1940).

6 See Jodl's notes on his relationship with Hitler, 18 Jan. 1946; BA-MA Freiburg, N 69/48.

7 See *Die Tagebücher von Joseph Goebbels*, commissioned by the Institute for Contemporary History, with support from the State Archive of Russia, ed. Elke Fröhlich, *Part II: Diktate 1941–1945*, 15 vols, Munich, 1993–6; vol. 2, pp. 538f. (entry for

18 Dec. 1941), vol. 3, p. 506 (entry for 20 March 1942); Albert Speer, *"Alles was ich weiss": Aus unbekannten Geheimdienstprotokollen vom Sommer 1945*, ed. Ulrich Schlie, Munich, 1999, pp. 61f.

8   See Nicolaus von Below, *Als Hitlers Adjutant 1937–45*, Mainz, 1980, p. 300.

9   See Jodl's notes, "Streiflichter aus dem Führerhauptquartier," Dec. 1945; BA-MA Freiburg, N 69/47.

10   Kurt Zeitzler, "Zwei Jahre Generalstabschef des Heeres," book 2, pp. 29f.; BA-MA Freiburg, N 63/19; See *idem*, "Das Ringen um die grossen Entscheidungen," vol. 1, p. 10; BA-MA Freiburg, N 63/79.

11   Albert Speer, *Erinnerungen: Mit einem Essay von Jochen Thies*, Frankfurt am Main and Berlin, 1993, p. 319.

12   Hermann Giesler, *Ein anderer Hitler: Berichte, Gespräche, Reflexionen*, Leoni, 1977, pp. 402f.

13   Letter from Kluge of 13 Sept. 1942; BA-MA Freiburg, MSg 2/11185. See Helmuth Greiner to his wife, 27 Sept. 1942: "Yes, we produce a great many field marshals, but we also use them up quite swiftly." IfZ München, ED 100, vol. 76.

14   See Goebbels, *Tagebücher*, part II, vol. 7, pp. 503, 506 (entry for 9 March 1943); vol. 12, p. 521 (entry for 22 June 1944).

15   Zeitzler, "Zwei Jahre Generalstabschef des Heeres," book 2, pp. 44f.; BA-MA Freiburg, N 63/19.

16   Helmuth Greiner complained about the "terrible brown-nosing" and "sycophancy" within the circles around Hitler. See Greiner's pocket calendar under 15 and 17 Oct. 1942; IfZ München, ED 100, vol. 76. On the occasion of Keitel's 60th birthday in September 1942, Hitler thanked him for his "loyalty and obedience" and presented him with a cheque for 250,000 reichsmarks. BA Berlin-Lichterfelde, R 43 II/985b. See Gerd R. Ueberschär and Winfried Vogel, *Dienen und Verdienen: Hitlers Geschenke an seine Eliten*, Frankfurt am Main, 1999, p. 221.

17   Schlie (ed.), *Albert Speer*, pp. 68f.

18   Goebbels, *Tagebücher*, part II, vol. 9, p. 333 (entry for 21 Aug. 1943).

19   Ibid., vol. 6, p. 53 (entry for 2 Oct. 1942).

20   See ibid., vol. 13, p. 305 (entry for 24 Aug. 1944).

21   See Albert Speer, *Spandauer Tagebücher: Mit einem Vorwort von Joachim Fest*, Munich, 2002, p. 521 (entry for 24 March 1960).

22   Heinz Guderian, *Erinnerungen eines Soldaten*, Heidelberg, 1951, p. 310.

23   Marianne Feuersenger, *Im Vorzimmer der Macht: Aufzeichnungen aus dem Wehrmachtführungsstab und Führerhauptquartier 1940–1945*, 4th edition, Munich, 2001, p. 245 (entry for 27 Dec. 1944).

24   Goebbels, *Tagebücher*, part II, vol. 14, p. 333 (entry for 2 Dec. 1944).

25   See Jodl's testimony on his relationship with Hitler, 18 Jan. 1946; BA-MA Freiburg, N 69/48.

26   Bernd Freytag von Loringhoven, *Mit Hitler im Bunker: Die letzten Monate im Führerhauptquartier Juli 1944–April 1945*, Berlin, 2006, p. 77.

27   See Fest, *Hitler*, pp. 925f.; *Das Deutsche Reich und der Zweite Weltkrieg. Vol. 8: Die Ostfront 1943/44*, Munich, 2007, vol. 8, p. 493 (Frieser's essay). On Hitler's obsession with maps, see Pyta, *Hitler*, pp. 346–50.

28   Speer, *Erinnerungen*, p. 312.

29   Freytag von Loringhoven, *Mit Hitler im Bunker*, p. 85.

30   Otto Dietrich, *12 Jahre mit Hitler*, Munich, 1955, p. 121.

31   Heinrich Hoffmann, "Mein Beruf—Meine Arbeit für die Kunst—Mein Verhältnis zu Adolf Hitler," notes composed after the trial in Jan. 1947, p. 61; IfZ München, MS 2049.

32   Speer, *Spandauer Tagebücher*, p. 309 (entry for 4 July 1952).

33   *Die Tagebücher von Joseph Goebbels*, commissioned by the Institute for Contemporary History, with support from the State Archive of Russia, ed. Elke Fröhlich, *Part I:*

Aufzeichnungen 1923–1941, 9 vols in 14 parts, Munich, 1998–2008; vol. 9, p. 45 (entry for 11 Dec. 1940).

34 Ibid., part II, vol. 9, p. 206 (entry for 2 Aug. 1943). On the decrease in Hitler's public appearances, see also Ian Kershaw, *Hitler 1936–1945: Nemesis*, London, 2001, pp. 565f; Richard J. Evans, *The Third Reich at War, 1939–1945*, London, 2008, pp. 508f.

35 See Kershaw, *Hitler 1936–1945*, p. 598.

36 See Traudl Junge, *Bis zur letzten Stunde: Hitlers Sekretärin erzählt ihr Leben*, Munich, 2002, p. 96.

37 See Hans Rudolf Schreyer to Goebbels, 10 Aug. 1944; BA Berlin-Lichterfelde, R 55/574.

38 Goebbels, *Tagebücher*, part II, vol. 13, p. 363 (entry for 30 Aug. 1944).

39 Ibid., vol. 10, p. 325 (entry for 20 Nov. 1943).

40 Ibid., part I, vol. 8, p. 415 (entry for 12 Nov. 1940). See ibid., vol. 7, pp. 172 (entry for 15 Jan. 1940), 291 (entry for 1 Feb. 1940); vol. 8, pp. 211 (entry for 8 July 1940), 316 (entry for 9 Sept. 1940).

41 Speer, *Erinnerungen*, pp. 313f.; see Schlie (ed.), *Albert Speer*, p. 45.

42 Hoffmann, "Mein Beruf—Meine Arbeit—Mein Verhältnis zu Hitler," p. 61; IfZ München, MS 2049.

43 See Junge, *Bis zur letzten Stunde*, pp. 120–2.

44 Goebbels, *Tagebücher*, part II, vol. 7, p. 171 (entry for 23 Jan. 1943).

45 Helmut Heiber (ed.), *Hitlers Lagebesprechungen. Die Protokollfragmente seiner militärischen Konferenzen 1942–1945*, Stuttgart, 1962, pp. 616f. (dated 31 Aug. 1944).

46 Goebbels, *Tagebücher*, part II, vol. 8, pp. 265f. (entry for 10 May 1943).

47 Ibid., vol. 7, p. 454 (entry for 2 March 1943).

48 Zeitzler, "Das Ringen um die grossen Entscheidungen," vol. 1, p. 36; BA-MA Freiburg, N 63/79. See also Hitler's speech to the field marshals and generals on 27 January 1944 in the Wolf's Lair: "If [Friedrich the Great] had given in back then, the Seven Years War would have ended with the annihilation of Prussia. It was only because the man remained stubborn that the war was ultimately decided in Prussia's favour." BA Berlin-Lichterfelde, NS 6/777.

49 Goebbels, *Tagebücher*, part II, vol. 4, p. 410 (entry for 30 May 1942); see ibid., pp. 493 (entry for 10 June 1942), 604 (entry for 10 June 1942); vol. 5, p. 366 (entry for 21 Aug. 1942); vol. 9, p. 477 (entry for 11 Sept. 1943).

50 See Junge, *Bis zur letzten Stunde*, p. 47; Christa Schroeder, *Er war mein Chef: Aus dem Nachlass der Sekretärin von Adolf Hitler*, ed. Anton Joachimsthaler, 3rd edition, Munich and Vienna, 1985, pp. 130f.

51 Speer, *Erinnerungen*, p. 315.

52 Ibid., pp. 306, 309.

53 Speer, *Spandauer Tagebücher*, p. 100 (entry for 20 April 1947).

54 See Lammers' draft and the note about Hitler's rejection of it on 16 Jan. 1942; BA Berlin-Lichterfelde, R 43 II/958.

55 Hans Kehrl, *Krisenmanager im Dritten Reich, 6 Jahre Frieden—6 Jahre Krieg: Erinnerungen*, 2nd revised edition, Düsseldorf, 1973, pp. 395f.

56 Goebbels, *Tagebücher*, part II, vol. 8, p. 265 (entry for 10 May 1943); see ibid., vol. 10, p. 191 (entry for 27 Oct. 1943).

57 Ibid., vol. 12, p. 204 (entry for 27 April 1944); see ibid., vol. 4, p. 407 (entry for 30 May 1942); vol. 5, pp. 62 (entry for 5 July 1942) 377 (entry for 20 Aug. 1942). Giesler, *Ein anderer Hitler*, pp. 213–15. For an extensive account of Hitler's detour to Linz in April 1943, see Speer, *Spandauer Tagebücher*, pp. 255–60 (entries for 13–14 Jan. 1951). See also, Hanns C. Löhr, *Hitlers Linz: Der "Heimatgau des Führers,"* Berlin, 2013.

58 See Birgit Schwarz, *Auf Befehl des Führers: Hitler und der NS-Kunstraub*, Darmstadt, 2014, pp. 39ff., 235ff.; Meike Hoffmann and Nicola Kuhn, *Hitlers Kunsthändler: Hildebrand Gurlitt 1895–1956. Die Biographie*, Munich, 2016, pp. 213ff.

59 Junge, *Bis zur letzten Stunde*, p. 95; see Schroeder, *Er war mein Chef*, p. 150.

60   Percy Ernst Schramm, *Hitler als militärischer Führer: Erkenntnisse und Erfahrungen aus dem Kriegstagebuch des Oberkommandos der Wehrmacht*, Frankfurt am Main, 1962, p. 67.

61   See Jodl's notes on "Hitler's influence on the waging of the war"; BA-MA Freiburg N 69/50; reproduced in Schramm, *Hitler als militärischer Führer*, pp. 147–54 (at p. 154).

62   See *Das Deutsche Reich und der Zweite Weltkrieg*, vol. 8, p. 36 (Wegner's essay).

63   Goebbels, *Tagebücher*, part II, vol. 10, p. 193 (entry for 27 Oct. 1943); see ibid., vol. 8, p. 534 (entry for 25 June 1943); vol. 9, p. 337 (entry for 21 Aug. 1943).

64   Ibid., vol. 12, p. 421 (entry for 7 June 1944).

65   Dietrich, *12 Jahre mit Hitler*, p. 139. Albert Speer recalled that even in times of defeat Hitler was able to "force headstrong frontline generals to obey his commands." Speer wrote that he had seen "men go to Hitler determined to oppose him and ready to accept any and all consequences—only to return defeated, having given in against their better judgement and agreed to decisions which any external observer would have considered mistakes and which indeed proved to be mistakes only a short time later." Speer: "Erinnerungen," manuscript, 2nd corrected version, chapter 1, p. 4; BA Koblenz, N 1340/384.

66   Goebbels, *Tagebücher*, part II, vol. 2, p. 539 (entry for 18 Dec. 1941).

67   Ibid., vol. 8, p. 238 (entry for 8 May 1943); see ibid., vol. 7, p. 173 (entry for 23 Jan. 1943); vol. 10, pp. 194f. (entry for 27 Oct. 1943); vol. 13, p. 213 (entry for 3 Aug. 1944).

68   Henrik Eberle and Matthias Uhl (eds), *Das Buch Hitler*, Bergisch Gladbach, 2005, p. 171.

69   See Theodor Morell to Hanni Morell, 26 May 1940; BA Koblenz, N 1348/6.

70   Goebbels, *Tagebücher*, part II, vol. 3, p. 501 (entry for 20 March 1942).

71   Letter from Kluge, 15 Sept. 1942; BA-MA Freiburg, MSg 2/11185.

72   Goebbels, *Tagebücher*, part II, vol. 8, p. 526 (entry for 25 June 1943).

73   Hossbach memoirs, chapter 7, p. 44; BA-MA Freiburg, N 24/39. See ibid., chapter 8, p.4, which concerns an encounter with Hitler on 19 July 1944: "A hunched, prematurely aged man stood before me—not the battlefield commander!"

74   See Ellen Gibbels, *Hitlers Parkinson-Krankheit: Zur Frage eines hirnorganischen Psychosyndroms*, Berlin and Heidelberg, 1990; *idem*, "Hitlers Nervenkrankheit: Eine neurologisch-psychiatrische Studie," in *Vierteljahrshefte für Zeitgeschichte*, 42 (1994), pp. 155–220. See also Ernst Günther Schenck, *Patient Hitler: Eine medizinische Biographie*, Düsseldorf, 1989, pp. 426–38; Hans-Joachim Neumann and Henrik Eberle, *War Hitler krank? Ein abschliessender Befund*, Bergisch Gladbach, 2009, pp. 215–18.

75   In early January, Hitler asked his personal physician how he could get rid of the trembling in his left hand. Morell responded that this would require a sedative, which he could not administer because of the constant pressure Hitler was under. Morell's daily notes of 2 Jan. c1945; BA Koblenz, N 1348/4.

76   On Hitler's medication, see the extensive account in Neumann and Eberle, *War Hitler krank?*, pp. 125–49. On Eukodal, ibid., pp. 163f. Morell was paid handsomely for his services as a physician. As of October 1941, in addition to an annual taxed stipend of 36,000 reichsmarks, he received tax-free compensation of 24,000 reichsmarks a year. For the six previous years he received a "compensation payment" of 360,000 reichsmarks and a tax-free stipend of 250,000 reichsmarks. See Lammers to Morell, 24 Oct. 1941, IfZ München, F 123. On the tenth anniversary of Hitler taking power in 1943, the Führer also approved another tax-free stipend of 100,000 reichsmarks as a gesture of thanks for keeping him "in top health for the current time and all the work it entails." See note by Lammers of 26 Jan. 1943, BA Berlin-Lichterfelde, R 43 II/985c.

77   Goebbels, *Tagebücher*, part II, vol. 12, p. 413 (entry for 6 June 1944).

78   See Leonard L. and Renate Heston, *The Medical Casebook of Adolf Hitler*, London, 1980. Like Ohler, Heston, an American psychiatrist at the University of Minnesota,

relies on notes by Morell. He corresponded extensively with Speer about his hypothesis. See the detailed correspondence, 1974–9, BA Koblenz, N 1340/27. See also the German Press Agency (dpa) report of 15 June 1979; BA Koblenz, N 1340/9.

79   Norman Ohler, *Der totale Rausch: Drogen im Dritten Reich*, Cologne, 2015, pp. 231, 233, 242.

80   Neumann and Eberle, *War Hitler krank?*, pp. 149, 291f.; see also Schenck, *Patient Hitler*, pp. 446–50.

81   See Morell's daily notes of 27 Oct. 1944, in which he wrote that Hitler "is constantly in his bunker without daylight" and got "at most ten to fifteen minutes of fresh air" a day; BA Koblenz, N 1348/4.

82   Giesler, *Ein anderer Hitler*, p. 456.

16 *Staged Exit*

1   Nicolaus von Below, *Als Hitlers Adjutant 1937–45*, Mainz, 1980, p. 398.

2   *Die Tagebücher von Joseph Goebbels*, commissioned by the Institute for Contemporary History, with support from the State Archive of Russia, ed. Elke Fröhlich, *Part II: Diktate 1941–1945*, 15 vols, Munich, 1993–6; vol. 15, p. 264 (entry for 29 Jan. 1945). See Jodl's statement at Nuremberg in 1946: "What [Hitler] had in mind was a heroic downfall from which coming generations would perhaps derive the strength to rise again." IfZ München, ZS 678. For context, see Bernd Wegner, "Hitler, der Zweite Weltkrieg und die Choreographie des Untergangs," in *Geschichte und Gesellschaft*, 26 (2000), pp. 493–518.

3   Goebbels, *Tagebücher*, part II, vol. 15, p. 298 (entry for 1 Feb. 1945).

4   See Herfried Münkler, *Die Deutschen und ihre Mythen*, Berlin, 2009, pp. 69–107.

5   Martin Bormann to his wife, 2 April 1945; Hugh Trevor-Roper (ed.), *The Bormann Letters*, London, 1954, p. 196.

6   See Münkler, *Die Deutschen und ihre Mythen*, pp. 106f.; Sebastian Werr, *Heroische Weltsicht: Hitler und die Musik*, Cologne, Weimar and Vienna, 2014, p. 239.

7   Cited in Bernd Wegner, "Deutschland am Abgrund," *Das Deutsche Reich und der Zweite Weltkrieg. Vol. 8: Die Ostfront 1943/44*, Munich, 2007, p. 1205. On the appeal of Clausewitz, see also Wolfram Pyta, *Hitler: Der Künstler als Politiker und Feldherr*, Munich, 2015, pp. 649–52.

8   Hitler's political will, dated 29 April 1945; *Kriegstagebuch des Oberkommandos der Wehrmacht (Wehrmachtführungsstab)* (hereafter *KTB OKW*), ed. Percy Ernst Schramm, Munich, 1982, vol. 4, part 2, pp. 1666–9 (at p. 1668). In his final statement to the court in Munich during the Beer Hall Putsch trial on 27 March 1924, Hitler had invoked Clausewitz, declaring: "It is better when a people goes down struggling honorably, since after such a collapse it can be resurrected." *Der Hitler-Prozess 1924*, ed. Lothar Gruchmann and Reinhard Weber, part 4, Munich, 1999, p. 1577. Hitler also took up this idea in the second volume of *Mein Kampf* (pp. 759f.).

9   Thomas Mann, *An die gesittete Welt: Politische Schriften und Reden im Exil*, Frankfurt am Main, 1986, p. 597. See also Mann's address on 20 March 1945: "Germany's continuation of the fight beyond defeat up to the brink of extinction has nothing to do with heroism. It is in fact a crime committed against the German people by its leaders." Ibid., p. 609.

10   Hans Frank to Brigitte Frank, 12 Jan. 1945; BA Koblenz, N 1110/50.

11   See Dieter Schenk, *Hans Frank: Hitlers Kronjurist und Generalgouverneur*, Frankfurt am Main, 2006, pp. 360f.

12   See *Das Deutsche Reich und der Zweite Weltkrieg*, vol. 10, part 1, pp. 516ff. (Lakowski's essay). For a summary, see Ian Kershaw, *The End: The Defiance and Destruction of Hitler's Germany, 1944–45*, London, 2011, pp. 172–6.

13   Cited in Werner Zeidler, *Kriegsende im Osten: Die Rolle der Roten Armee und die Besetzung Deutschlands östlich von Oder und Neisse 1944/45*, Munich, 1996, p. 138. On

the Red Army's treatment of the civilian population, see ibid., pp. 135–54; Catherine Merridale, *Ivan's War: The Red Army 1939–45*, London, 2005, pp. 259–89.

14   See Kershaw, *The End*, pp. 178–80, 183. The casualty figures vary: see ibid., pp. 445–6n49.

15   See summary report of the Reich propaganda offices of 24 Jan. 1945; BA Berlin-Lichterfelde, R 55/601.

16   Ruth Andreas-Friedrich, *Der Schattenmann: Tagebuchaufzeichnungen 1938–1945*, Frankfurt am Main, 1983, p. 193 (entry for 31 Jan. 1945).

17   Goebbels, *Tagebücher*, part II, vol. 15, p. 338 (entry for 8 Feb. 1945). See also ibid., pp. 216 (entry for 25 Jan. 1945), 327 (entry for 7 Feb. 1945).

18   See Kershaw, *The End*, pp. 187f., 191, 195.

19   Wilfred von Oven, *Finale Furioso: Mit Goebbels bis zum Ende*, Tübingen, 1974, p. 564 (entry for 31 Jan. 1945). See Martin Bormann to his wife, 31 Jan. 1945; Trevor-Roper (ed.), *The Bormann Letters*, p. 165.

20   Goebbels, *Tagebücher*, part II, vol. 15, p. 277 (entry for 30 Jan. 1945); see ibid., pp. 288f. (entry for 31 Jan. 1945).

21   Memorandum from Martin Bormann dated 15 Feb. 1945; BA Berlin-Lichterfelde, NS 6/354.

22   See Heinz Guderian, *Erinnerungen eines Soldaten*, Heidelberg, 1951, pp. 359–61; Bernd Freytag von Loringhoven, *Mit Hitler im Bunker: Die letzten Monate im Führerhauptquartier Juli 1944–April 1945*, Berlin, 2006, pp. 135–8.

23   See Guderian, *Erinnerungen eines Soldaten*, pp. 358, 363f.; Reinhardt's war diary entry for 27 Jan. 1945; BA-MA Freiburg, N 245/3; Hossbach, "Erinnerungen," chapter 9, p. 48; BA-MA Freiburg, N24/39; *Das Deutsche Reich und der Zweite Weltkrieg*, vol. 10, part 1, p. 541 (Lakowski's essay).

24   See Hitler's order of 21 Jan. 1945, attached to Martin Bormann's memorandum of 23 Jan. 1945; BA Berlin-Lichterfelde, NS 6/354. See *Das Deutsche Reich und der Zweite Weltkrieg*, vol. 10, part 1, pp. 524f. (Lakowski's essay).

25   Goebbels, *Tagebücher*, part II, vol. 15, p. 165 (entry for 20 Jan. 1945); see ibid., p. 338 (entry for 8 Feb. 1945): "I think the Führer made a good move entrusting Army Group Vistula to [Himmler]."

26   Hans-Georg Eismann, "Das Kriegstagebuch der Heeresgruppe Weichsel (Januar 1945 bis zur Kapitulation)," pp. 14f.; IfZ München, ZS 3095. Himmler wrote to his wife on 20 January 1945: "This will be the most difficult task I have yet been given. But I think I will master it, and I continue to believe in our ultimate victory despite all the difficulty weighing down upon us." Katrin Himmler and Michael Wildt (eds), *Himmler privat: Briefe eines Massenmörders*, Munich, 2014, p. 337.

27   Hitler's order of 21 Jan. 1945; Max Domarus, *Hitler: Reden und Proklamationen 1932–1945*, Munich, 1965, vol. 2, part 2, pp. 2190f.

28   Guderian, *Erinnerungen eines Soldaten*, p. 357.

29   Goebbels, *Tagebücher*, part II, vol. 15, p. 193 (entry for 23 Jan. 1945); see ibid., p. 218 (entry for 25 Jan. 1945).

30   Ibid., p. 231 (entry for 26 Jan. 1945); see ibid., p. 275 (entry for 30 Jan. 1945): "The trains of thought the Führer presented are entirely logical and correct but they contain a series of uncertain factors that cannot be calculated in advance."

31   *KTB OKW*, vol. 4, part 2, p. 1700. See also the description of a situation meeting in early February 1945 in Gerhard Boldt, *Hitler: Die letzten zehn Tage in der Reichskanzlei*, Munich, 1976, pp. 12–28. Boldt was a cavalry captain and ordinance officer who occasionally filled in for Freytag von Loringhoven at situation meetings.

32   See Guderian, *Erinnerungen eines Soldaten*, pp. 374f.; Freytag von Loringhoven, *Mit Hitler im Bunker*, p. 132f.; Albert Speer, *Erinnerungen: Mit einem Essay von Jochen Thies*, Frankfurt am Main and Berlin, 1993, p. 428.

33   Guderian, *Erinnerungen eines Soldaten*, pp. 376f.; Freytag von Loringhoven, *Mit Hitler im Bunker*, p. 133. Zeitzler was also convinced that Hitler's fits of anger were often

far show, writing: "No statement—even in private conversation!—without calculation . . . What seem outbursts of emotion are mostly calculation! Enormous achievement." BA-MA Freiburg, N 153/42; see *Das Deutsche Reich und der Zweite Weltkrieg*,
vol. 8, p. 38n157 (Wegner's essay).

34 Goebbels, *Tagebücher*, part II, vol. 15, p. 295 (entry for 1 Feb. 1945); see ibid., p. 262
(entry for 29 Jan. 1945): "Guderian has also failed to live up to expectations."

35 Ibid., p. 256 (entry for 28 Jan. 1945).

36 Domarus, *Hitler*, vol. 2, part 2, pp. 2195–8.

37 Goebbels, *Tagebücher*, part II, vol. 15, p. 285 (entry for 31 Jan. 1945). On the reaction
in Hitler's circles, see Alwin-Broder Albrecht's letter to his wife of 31 January 1945:
"The response from all sides to Hitler's speech is unprecedentedly positive despite
the somewhat negative harbingers of the times." IfZ München, ED 100, Bd. 33. An
admirer of Hitler, Friede Nögler from Düsseldorf, wrote in a letter to the Führer
on 27 February 1945: "How elated I was when I was able to hear your voice in its
old freshness on 30 January." BA Berlin-Lichterfelde, NS 6/770.

38 *Das letzte halbe Jahr: Stimmungsberichte der Wehrmachtpropaganda 1944/45*, ed. Wolfram
Wette, Ricarda Brenner and Detlef Vogel, Essen, 2001, p. 228 (dated 1 Feb. 1945).

39 Goebbels, *Tagebücher*, part II, vol. 15. p. 352 (entry for 10 Feb. 1945).

40 Susanne Wiborg and Jan Peter Wiborg, *Glaube, Führer, Hoffnung: Der Untergang der
Clara S.*, Munich, 2015, pp. 151f., 157.

41 See Richard Overy, *The Bombing War: Europe 1939–1945*, London, 2013, p. 394; Olaf
Groehler, *Bombenkrieg gegen Deutschland*, Berlin, 1990, pp. 398–400; Sven Felix
Kellerhoff, *Hitlers Ende: Der Untergang im Führerbunker*, Berlin, 2015, pp. 22–30.

42 See Goebbels, *Tagebücher*, part II, vol. 15, pp. 309 (entry for 5 Feb. 1945), 320 (entry
for 6 Feb. 1945); Martin Bormann to his wife, 4 Feb. 1945; Trevor-Roper (ed.), *The
Bormann Letters*, p. 168. In a memorandum on 1 February 1945, Bormann stressed
that "no one is allowed to enter the Führer's apartment in Berlin without express
permission and special notification." BA Berlin-Lichterfelde, R 43 II/957a.

43 See Joachim Fest, "Der Führerbunker," in Étienne François and Hagen Schulze
(eds), *Deutsche Erinnerungsorte*, vol. 1, Munich, 2001, pp. 128f.; *idem, Der Untergang:
Hitler und das Ende des Dritten Reiches. Eine historische Skizze*, Berlin, 2002, p. 27f.;
Kellerhoff, *Hitlers Ende*, pp. 75–94; Dietmar Arnold, *Neue Reichskanzlei und
"Führerbunker": Legenden und Wirklichkeit*, Berlin, 2005, pp. 126–8.

44 See Fest, *Der Untergang*, pp. 31–3; Kellerhoff, *Hitlers Ende*, pp. 94–104; Arnold, *Neue
Reichskanzlei und "Führerbunker,"* pp. 129f.; Henrik Eberle and Matthias Uhl (eds),
Das Buch Hitler, Bergisch Gladbach, 2005, pp. 321–3; Traudl Junge, *Bis zur letzten
Stunde: Hitlers Sekretärin erzählt ihr Leben*, Munich, 2002, pp. 174f.; Rochus Misch,
Der letzte Zeuge: "Ich war Hitlers Telefonist, Kurier und Leibwächter," Zurich and
Munich, 2008, pp. 183–9; Christa Schroeder, *Er war mein Chef: Aus dem Nachlass der
Sekretärin von Adolf Hitler*, ed. Anton Joachimsthaler, 3rd edition, Munich and Vienna,
1985, pp. 197f. The quotation is from Guderian, *Erinnerungen eines Soldaten*, p. 378.

45 See Heinz Linge's appointment diary under 19 Jan. 1945; IfZ München, F 19/4; Lew
Besymenski, *Die letzten Notizen von Martin Bormann: Ein Dokument und sein Verfasser*,
Stuttgart, 1974, p. 64 (entries for 18 and 19 Jan. 1945).

46 Goebbels, *Tagebücher*, part II, vol. 15, p. 296 (entry for 1 Feb. 1945); see Heike B.
Görtemaker, *Eva Braun: Leben mit Hitler*, Munich, 2010, pp. 265f. Christa Schroeder
recalled Eva Braun saying: "I owe him everything nice in my life, and the only
thing I can do for him is to stay by his side." Interview by David Irving with
Schroeder on 10 Sept. 1971; IfZ München, ZS 2240.

47 See Linge's appointment diary under 19 Jan–9 Feb. 1945; IfZ München, F 19/4.

48 See Martin Bormann to his wife, 6 Feb. 1945; Trevor-Roper (ed.), *The Bormann Letters*,
pp. 174f.; Görtemaker, *Eva Braun*, pp. 267f. The fact that Speer participated in the
meeting is indicated by a passing remark by Bormann in a letter to his wife of 4
February 1945. See Trevor-Roper (ed.), *The Bormann Letters*, p. 172.

49   See Ulf Schmidt, *Hitlers Arzt Karl Brandt: Medizin und Macht im Dritten Reich*, Berlin, 2009, pp. 501–5.

50   See Besymenski, *Die letzten Notizen von Martin Bormann*, p. 107 (entry for 9 Feb. 1945); Martin Bormann to his wife, 18 Feb. 1945; Trevor-Roper (ed.), *The Bormann Letters*, p. 183; Görtemaker, *Eva Braun*, pp. 269f.

51   See *Das Hitler-Bild: Die Erinnerungen des Fotografen Heinrich Hoffmann*, ed. Joe J. Heydecker, St. Pölten and Salzburg, 2008, pp. 207f.; Heinrich Hoffmann, *Hitler wie ich ihn sah: Aufzeichnungen seines Leibfotografen*, Munich and Berlin, 1974, pp. 230f.; Below, *Als Hitlers Adjutant*, p. 407; Misch, *Der letzte Zeuge*, p. 190.

52   See Morell's daily notes of 9 April 1945; BA Koblenz, N 1348/3; notes of ophthalmologist Dr. Löhlein of 7 April 1945; BA Koblenz, N 1348/4.

53   Goebbels, *Tagebücher*, part II, vol. 15, p. 323 (entry for 6 Feb. 1945); see ibid., p. 371 (entry for 12 Feb. 1945).

54   Boldt, *Hitler: Die letzten zehn Tage in der Reichskanzlei*, p. 13.

55   *KTB OKW*, vol. 4, part 2, pp. 1701f.

56   Albert Speer, *"Alles was ich weiss": Aus unbekannten Geheimdienstprotokollen vom Sommer 1945*, ed. Ulrich Schlie, Munich, 1999, p. 44.

57   Schroeder, *Er war mein Chef*, p. 198.

58   Balck's diary entry for 19 Feb. 1945; BA-MA Freiburg, N 647/13.

59   See Alan Bullock, *Hitler: A Study in Tyranny*, London, 1990, p. 776f.; Dieter Schenk, *Hitlers Mann in Danzig: Gauleiter Forster und die NS-Verbrechen in Danzig-Westpreussen*, Bonn, 2000, pp. 261f.

60   Schroeder, *Er war mein Chef*, p. 198. On the daily routine, see ibid., pp. 198f.; Eberle and Uhl (eds), *Das Buch Hitler*, p. 349; Anton Joachimsthaler, *Hitlers Ende: Legenden und Dokumente*, Munich and Berlin, 1995, pp. 122f.

61   Hermann Giesler, *Ein anderer Hitler: Berichte, Gespräche, Reflexionen*, Leoni, 1977, pp. 478–80 (at p. 479). Frentz's shots are reproduced in Hans Georg Hiller von Gaertringen (ed.), *Das Auge des Dritten Reiches: Hitlers Kameramann und Fotograf Walter Frentz*, Berlin, 2006, pp. 86f.

62   Goebbels, *Tagebücher*, part I, vol. 15, p. 379 (entry for 13 Feb. 1945).

63   On Hitler's "warfare as make-believe," see *Das Deutsche Reich und der Zweite Weltkrieg*, vol. 8, pp. 1165ff. (Wegner's essay).

64   See Frederick Taylor, *Dresden: Tuesday, 13 February 1945*, London, 2004; Overy, *The Bombing War*, pp. 391–5; Nicholas Stargardt, *The German War: A Nation under Arms, 1939–45*, London, 2015, pp. 500f.

65   See Victor Klemperer, *Ich will Zeugnis ablegen bis zum letzten: Tagebücher*, vol. 2: *1942–1945*, ed. Walter Nowojski with Hadwig Klemperer, Berlin, 1995, pp. 661ff.; Richard J. Evans, *The Third Reich at War, 1939–1945*, London, 2008, pp. 700–702.

66   See Overy, *The Bombing War*, pp. 396f.

67   Giesler, *Ein anderer Hitler*, p. 482.

68   See Joachim von Ribbentrop, *Zwischen London und Moskau: Erinnerungen und letzte Aufzeichnungen*, ed. Annelies von Ribbentrop, Leoni am Starnberger See, 1961, pp. 266f.; Ralf Georg Reuth, *Goebbels*, Munich and Zurich, 1990, pp. 581f.; David Irving, *Hitler und seine Feldherren*, Frankfurt am Main, Berlin and Vienna, 1975, p. 693.

69   Domarus, *Hitler*, vol. 2, part 2, pp. 2203–6 (at pp. 2203, 2205, 2206). Similar in tone was an appeal by Bormann to the Nazi Party on 24 February 1945; BA Berlin-Lichterfelde, NS 6/353.

70   Heinz Boberach (ed.), *Meldungen aus dem Reich: Die geheimen Lageberichte des Sicherheitsdienstes der SS 1938–1945*, Herrsching, 1984, vol. 17, pp. 6733f.; Ian Kershaw, *Hitler 1936–1945: Nemesis*, London, 2000, p. 781.

71   See Below, *Als Hitlers Adjutant*, p. 402.

72   Baldur von Schirach, *Ich glaubte an Hitler*, Hamburg, 1967, p. 307. On the date, see Linge's appointment diary under 24 Feb. 1945; IfZ München, F 19/4.

73 Karl Wahl, "... *es ist das deutsche Herz": Erlebnisse und Erkenntnisse eines ehemaligen Gauleiters*, Augsburg, 1954, pp. 385f.; see also Rudolf Jordan, *Erlebt und erlitten: Weg eines Gauleiters von München nach Moskau*, Leoni am Starnberger See, 1971, pp. 253f.

74 Wahl, "... *es ist das deutsche Herz,"* p. 391. Hitler told his valet Linge: "Only now can I appreciate how Friedrich the Great felt when his teeth fell out from worry during the Seven Years War. With me, it is my left hand and right eye that suffer from the burden of war." Eberle and Uhl (eds), *Das Buch Hitler*, pp. 349f.

75 Reich press chief Otto Dietrich told his deputy about this statement by Hitler; Helmut Sündermann, *Deutsche Notizen: 1945/65*, Leoni, 1966, p. 284 (entry for 25 Feb. 1945). For something similar, see the Gauleiter of Kärnten, Friedrich Rainer, cited in *KTB OKW*, vol. 4, part 1, p. 66n4. Irving passes on the following version of the statement: "I used to have a trembling leg. Now my arm trembles. Maybe one day my head will shake. But of one thing I can assure you: my heart will never tremble." *Hitler und seine Feldherren*, p. 695.

76 See Ewald von Kleist's pocket calendar under 19 Feb. 1943; BA-MA Freiburg, N 354/22.

77 Pyta, *Hitler*, pp. 637f.; see also Birgit Schwarz, *Geniewahn: Hitler und die Kunst*, Vienna, Cologne and Weimar, 2009, pp. 301–6 ("Mit Friedrich im Bunker").

78 Goebbels, *Tagebücher*, part II, vol. 15, pp. 220f.; see ibid., p. 366 (entry for 12 Feb. 1945): "He can indeed be compared with Friedrich the Great. In fact, in view of the gigantic catastrophe this war has brought upon our people recently, he sometimes even exceeds that man's greatness."

79 Ibid., p. 264 (entry for 29 Jan. 1945).

80 Junge, *Bis zur letzten Stunde*, p. 183. Albert Speer also noted that Hitler's uniform, "usually clean beyond reproach," was often "shabby and food-stained" during the final weeks of his life; *Erinnerungen*, p. 474.

81 Goebbels, *Tagebücher*, part II, vol. 15, pp. 383f. (entry for 28 Feb. 1945). Goebbels used almost exactly the same words in a conversation with Hitler on 11 March 1945; ibid. p. 479 (entry for 12 March 1945). On Hitler's reading of Carlyle's biography of Friedrich the Great, see Timothy W. Ryback, *Hitler's Private Library: The Books That Shaped His Life*, London, 2009, pp. 206–11.

82 Goebbels, *Tagebücher*, part II, vol. 15, p. 479 (entry for 12 March 1945).

83 Ibid., pp. 587f. (entry for 24 March 1943).

84 See Schwerin von Krosigk's diary entry of 15 April 1945; cited in Hugh R. Trevor-Roper, *The Last Days of Hitler*, 6th edition, London, 2012, p. 87

85 See Goebbels, *Tagebücher*, part II, vol. 15, pp. 196 (entry for 23 Jan. 1945), 232 (entry for 26 Jan. 1945) 273 (entry for 30 Jan. 1945), 368 (entry for 12 Feb. 1945) 485 (entry for 12 Mar. 1945).

86 On the conference at Yalta, see Robin Edmonds, *Die Grossen Drei: Churchill, Roosevelt und Stalin in Frieden und Krieg*, Berlin, 1992, pp. 393–7; Jochen Laufer, *Pax Sovietica: Stalin, die Westmächte und die deutsche Frage 1941–1945*, Cologne, Weimar and Vienna, 2009, pp. 477–90.

87 Below, *Als Hitlers Adjutant*, p. 402.

88 Goebbels, *Tagebücher*, part II, vol. 15, p. 382 (entry for 13 Feb. 1945). In a letter to Goebbels of 21 Februaruy 1945, Finance Minister von Krosigk also demanded that "every thread possible must be spun" to arrive at a diplomatic settlement. BA Koblenz, N 276/45.

89 On the inquiries, see Fritz Hesse's testimony on the feelers for peace extended on behalf of Ribbentrop in 1945 (BA Koblenz, N 1332/2) and the sworn statement of the former ministerial director of the Foreign Ministry, Bruno Peter Kleist, of 4 May 1948; BA Koblenz, N 1332/4. See also Reimar Hansen, "Ribbentrops Friedensfühler im Frühjahr 1945," in *Geschichte in Wissenschaft und Unterricht*, 18 (1967), pp. 716–30; Ingeborg Fleischhauer, *Die Chance des Sonderfriedens: Deutsch-sowjetische Geheimgespräche 1941–1945*, Berlin, 1986, pp. 273–5.

90 Goebbels, *Tagebücher*, part II, vol. 15, p. 377 (entry for 13 Feb. 1945).

91   Ibid., p. 486 (entry for 12 March 1945).

92   See Hans-Georg Eismann, "Das Kriegstagebuch der Heeresgruppe Weichsel (Januar 1945 bis zur Kapitulation)," p. 78; IfZ München, ZS 3095; Peter Longerich, *Heinrich Himmler: Biographie*, Munich, 2008, p. 739.

93   Goebbels, *Tagebücher*, part II, vol. 15, p. 480 (entry for 12 March 1945).

94   Eberle and Uhl (eds), *Das Buch Hitler*, pp. 340f.

95   Goebbels, *Tagebücher*, part II, vol. 15, p. 522 (entry for 16 March 1945). See also the report by an officer with the 9th Army: "Was this still the same man we experienced a long time ago, before 20 July? Horror and pity went through the ranks." Cited in Peter Gosztony (ed.), *Der Kampf um Berlin 1945 in Augenzeugenberichten*, Düsseldorf, 1970, p. 91.

96   See Gaertringen (ed.), *Das Auge des Dritten Reiches*, p. 107 (contains a photo of Hitler's visit); Domarus, *Hitler*, vol. 2, part 2, p. 2211.

97   Goebbels, *Tagebücher*, part II, vol. 15, p. 495 (entry for 13 March 1945).

98   Balck's diary entry for 10 March 1945; BA-MA Freiburg, N 647/13.

99   See *Das Deutsche Reich und der Zweite Weltkrieg*, vol. 8, pp. 930–51 (Ungváry's essay).

100   See Eberle and Uhl (eds), *Das Buch Hitler*, pp. 332–4. Goebbels noted: "That will naturally be the worst sort of humiliation imaginable for Sepp Dietrich." *Tagebücher*, part II, vol. 15, p. 614 (entry for 28 March 1945).

101   Ibid., pp. 521 (entry for 16 March 1945), 564 (entry for 22 March 1945).

102   Gotthard Heinrici, "Der Endkampf des Dritten Reiches," pp. 1f.; IfZ München, ZS 66/1.

103   Domarus, *Hitler*, vol. 2, part 2, p. 2215. See Goebbels, *Tagebücher*, part II, vol. 15, p. 551 (entry for 21 March 1945).

104   Goebbels, *Tagebücher*, part II, vol. 15, p. 432 (entry for 6 March 1945); see ibid., p. 422 (entry for 5 March 1945). On the taking of territory on the left bank of the Rhine, see Dietmar Henke, *Die amerikanische Besetzung Deutschlands*, Munich, 1995, pp. 343–7; John Zimmermann, "Die deutsche militärische Kriegführung im Westen 1944/45," in *Das Deutsche Reich und der Zweite Weltkrieg*, vol. 10, part 1, pp. 409 ff.

105   See Henke, *Die amerikanische Besetzung Deutschlands*, pp. 347f.

106   See Eberle and Uhl (eds), *Das Buch Hitler*, pp. 343–5; Goebbels, *Tagebücher*, part II, vol. 15, p. 538 (entry for 19 March 1945).

107   Ibid., p. 465 (entry for 10 March 1945).

108   See Albert Kesselring, *Soldat bis zum letzten Tag*, Bonn, 1953, p. 339.

109   Goebbels, *Tagebücher*, part II, vol. 15, p. 576 (entry for 23 March 1945). See Henke, *Die amerikanische Besetzung Deutschlands*, pp. 348–50.

110   Goebbels, *Tagebücher*, part II, vol. 15, p. 589 (entry for 25 March 1945).

111   Speer to Schwerin von Krosigk, 14 Feb. 1945; BA Koblenz, N 276/45.

112   See Heinrich Schwendemann, "'Verbrannte Erde'? Hitlers 'Nero-Befehl' vom 19. März 1945," in *Kriegsende in Deutschland*, Hamburg, 2005, pp. 161f.

113   Goebbels, *Tagebücher*, part II, vol. 15, pp. 511 (entry for 15 March 1945), 501 (entry for 14 March 1945).

114   Memorandum from Speer to Hitler, 15 March 1945; *Der Prozess gegen die Hauptkriegsverbrecher vor dem Internationalen Militärtribunal in Nürnberg*, 42 vols, Nuremberg, 1947–9 (hereafter *IMT*), vol. 41, pp. 420–5. See Schwendemann, "'Verbrannte Erde'?," pp. 161f.; Kershaw, *The End*, pp. 287f.

115   See Speer, *Erinnerungen*, p. 443; Below, *Als Hitlers Adjutant*, p. 404.

116   Heinrich Schwendemann, "'Drastische Massnahmen zur Verteidigung des Reiches an der Oder und am Rhein . . .' Eine vergessene Denkschrift Albert Speers vom 18. März 1945," in *Studia Historica Slavo-Germanica*, 25 (2003), pp. 179–98 (text of the memorandum on pp. 189f.). See Heinrich Breloer, *Die Akte Speer: Spuren eines Kriegsverbrechers*, Berlin, 2006, p. 301.

117   These statements are contained in a letter from Speer to Hitler of 29 March 1945; *IMT*, vol. 41, pp. 425–9 (at p. 428); reprinted in *KTB OKW*, vol. 4, part 2, pp. 1581–4 (at p. 1583). See Speer, *Erinnerungen*, pp. 445f.

118   *IMT*, vol. 41, pp. 430f., reprinted in Walther Hubatsch (ed.), *Hitlers Weisungen für die Kriegsführung*, Munich, 1965, pp. 348f.

119   See Schwendemann, "'Verbrannte Erde'?," p. 164.

120   See Speer, *Erinnerungen*, pp. 451–6; Martin Kitchen, *Speer: Hitler's Architect*, New Haven and London, 2015, pp. 266–8.

121   Goebbels, *Tagebücher*, part II, vol. 15, pp. 619f. (entry for 28 March 1945).

122   See, albeit with a tendency towards dramatisation, Speer, *Erinnerungen*, pp. 457–9.

123   Speer to Hitler, 29 March 1945; *IMT*, vol. 41, pp. 425–9; *KTB OKW*, vol. 4, part 2, pp. 1581–4 (at pp. 1581, 1583). Hitler apparently never saw the letter, and it is conceivable that Speer wrote it with a view to what was to come after the war. Breloer, *Die Akte Speer*, pp. 303, 308; Magnus Brechtken, *Albert Speer: Eine deutsche Karriere*, Munich, 2017, pp. 280f.

124   Speer, *Erinnerungen*, p. 460.

125   Goebbels, *Tagebücher*, part II, vol. 15, p. 643 (entry for 31 March 1945).

126   See Hitler's directive and Speer's orders on how to implement the measures of laming and destruction of 30 March 1945.; *IMT*, vol. 41, pp. 435–7.

127   Henke, *Die amerikanische Besetzung Deutschlands*, pp. 452f.; See Schwendemann, "'Verbrannte Erde'?," pp. 165f. On Fest's role in manufacturing the Speer legend, see Volker Ullrich, "Die Speer-Legende," in *Die Zeit*, no. 39, 23 Sept. 1999; *idem*, "Speers Erfindung," in *Die Zeit*, no. 19, 4 May 2005; *idem*, "Zum Dank ein Bild vom Führer," in *Die Zeit*, no. 22, 19 May 2016; Brechtken, *Albert Speer*, pp. 387ff., 556–76.

128   Guderian, *Erinnerungen eines Soldaten*, p. 389.

129   Goebbels, *Tagebücher*, part II, vol. 15, p. 645 (entry for 31 March 1945); see ibid., p. 338 (entry for 8 Feb. 1945).

130   Cited in Stefan Krings, *Hitlers Pressechef: Otto Dietrich 1897–1952. Eine Biographie*, Göttingen, 2010, p. 439. See Helmut Sündermann, *Hier stehe ich . . . Deutsche Erinnerungen 1914/45*, Leoni, 1975, pp. 303f. Goebbels noted: "Finally I have the path cleared for my work." *Tagebücher*, part II, vol. 15, p. 651 (entry for 31 March 1945).

131   See *Das Deutsche Reich und der Zweite Weltkrieg*, vol. 10, part 1, pp. 435ff. (Zimmermann's essay); Henke, *Die amerikanische Besetzung Deutschlands*, pp. 359f.

132   Herfried Münkler, *Machtzerfall: Die letzten Tage des Dritten Reiches am Beispiel der hessischen Kreisstadt Friedberg*, Berlin, 1985, p. 93; on the disintegration of the western army, see Henke, *Die amerikanische Besetzung Deutschlands*, pp. 958–64.

133   Friedrich Kellner, *"Vernebelt, verdunkelt sind alle Hirne": Tagebücher, 1939–1945*, ed. Sascha Feuchert et al., Göttingen, 2011, vol. 2, pp. 922f. (entry for 28 March 1945).

134   See Münkler, *Machtzerfall*, p. 121; Kershaw, *The End*, p. 261.

135   Goebbels, *Tagebücher*, part II, p. 606 (entry for 27 March 1945).

136   Ibid., pp. 429 (entry for 6 March 1945), 471f. (entry for 11 March 1945), 482 (entry for 12 March 1945).

137   See the report by the directors of the Gau Magdeburg-Anhalt of 16 February 1945; BA Berlin-Lichterfelde, NS 6/135.

138   See Elisabeth Kohlhaas, "'Aus einem Haus, aus dem eine weisse Fahne erscheint, sind alle männlichen Personen zu erschiessen': Durchhalteterror und Gewalt gegen Zivilisten am Ende des Krieges," in Cord Arendes, Edgar Wolfrum and Jörg Zedler (eds), *Terror nach innen: Verbrechen am Ende des Zweiten Weltkriegs*, Göttingen, 2006, pp. 51–65. For an essential overview, see Sven Keller, *Volksgemeinschaft am Ende: Gesellschaft und Gewalt 1944/45*, Munich, 2013.

139   See Bormann's memorandums to the Reichsleiter and Gauleiter of 17 March and 1 April 1945; BA Berlin-Lichterfelde, NS 6/353 und NS 6/352.

140   Goebbels, *Tagebücher*, part II, vol. 15, p. 672 (entry for 4 April 1945); see ibid., p. 659 (entry for 1 April 1945). On the behaviour of party functionaries, see Henke, *Die amerikanische Besetzung Deutschlands*, pp. 825–34; Keller, *Volksgemeinschaft am Ende*, pp. 119–23.

141   Goebbels, *Tagebücher*, part II, vol. 15, p. 514 (entry for 15 March 1945).

142   Ibid., p. 613 (entry for 28 March 1945); see ibid., p. 603 (entry for 27 March 1945).

143 Ibid., pp. 615, 617f. (entry for 28 March 1945), 648 (entry for 31 March 1945), 678 (entry for 4 April 1945).

144 *Meldungen aus dem Reich*, vol. 17, p. 6734 (dated end of March 1945).

145 *Das letzte halbe Jahr*, pp. 309f. (dated 31 March 1945), 334 (dated 10 April 1945).

146 Goebbels, *Tagebücher*, part II, vol. 15, pp. 586 (entry for 24 March 1945), 659 (entry for 1 April 1945). See *Meldungen aus dem Reich*, vol. 17, p. 6737 (dated end of March 1945): "A lot of people are getting used to the idea of putting an end to it all. The demand for poison, pistols and other ways of ending one's life is great everywhere."

147 See Christian Goeschel, *Selbstmord im Dritten Reich*, Berlin, 2011, pp. 241–53; Hans Liebrandt, *"Das Recht mich zu richten, das spreche ich Ihnen ab!" Der Selbstmord der nationalsozialistischen Elite 1944/45*, Paderborn, 2017; Evans, *The Third Reich at War*, pp. 731–3; Keller, *Volksgemeinschaft am Ende*, pp. 203–8.

148 See Ulrich Herbert, *Fremdarbeiter: Politik und Praxis des "Ausländer-Einsatzes" in der Kriegswirtschaft des Dritten Reiches*, Berlin and Bonn, 1985, pp. 336–8; idem, *Geschichte der Ausländerpolitik in Deutschland: Saisonarbeiter, Zwangsarbeiter, Gastarbeiter, Flüchtlinge*, Munich, 2001, pp. 181f.; Andreas Heusler, "Die Eskalation des Terrors: Gewalt gegen ausländische Zwangsarbeiter in der Endphase des Zweiten Weltkriegs," in *Terror nach innen*, pp. 172–82; Keller, *Volksgemeinschaft am Ende*, pp. 218–27, 291–8.

149 On this topic, see Daniel Blatman's excellent study, *Die Todesmärsche 1944/45: Das letzte Kapitel des nationalsozialistischen Massenmords*, Reinbek bei Hamburg, 2011. See also Gabriele Hauenstein, "Die Todesmärsche aus den Konzentrationslagern 1944/45," in *Terror nach innen*, pp. 122–48; Katrin Greiser, *Die Todesmärsche von Buchenwald: Räumung, Befreiung und Spuren der Erinnerung*, Göttingen, 2008; Keller, *Volksgemeinschaft am Ende*, pp. 299–305.

150 Henke, *Die amerikanische Besetzung Deutschlands*, p. 943.

151 See Goebbels, *Tagebücher*, part II, vol. 15, p. 666 (entry for 2 April 1945).

152 Ibid., p. 623 (entry for 28 March 1945).

153 Ibid., pp. 637 (entry for 30 March 1945), 647 (entry for 31 March 1945).

154 See Perry Biddiscombe, *Werwolf! The History of the National Socialist Guerrilla Movement, 1944–1946*, Cardiff, 1998; Cord Arendes, "Schrecken aus dem Untergrund: Endphaseverbrechen des 'Werwolf,'" in *Terror nach innen*, pp. 149–71; Henke, *Die amerikanische Besetzung Deutschlands*, pp. 943–54; Kershaw, *The End*, pp. 279f.; Keller, *Volksgemeinschaft am Ende*, pp. 168–83.

155 Mann, *An die gesittete Welt*, p. 613 (dated 19 April 1945). See idem, *Tagebücher, 1944–1. April 1946*, ed. Inge Jens, Frankfurt am Main, 1986, p. 187 (dated 12. Apri 1945): "Heard this afternoon with great sorrow the news of Roosevelt's death." For the background, see Joseph Lelyveld, *The Final Battle: The Last Months of Franklin Roosevelt*, New York, 2016.

156 Trevor-Roper, *The Last Days of Hitler*, pp. 89f. (based on a statement by Goebbels' secretary Inge Haberzettel).

157 Speer, *Erinnerungen*, p. 467. See also Schlie (ed.), *Albert Speer*, p. 48. This account of Hitler's reaction is supported by a statement by stenographer Gerhard Hergesell from April 1948: "Suddenly Hitler went . . . wild. He jumped up, took a few steps with great joy and said: 'I always said that I had a premonition.'" Cited in Joachimsthaler, *Hitlers Ende*, p. 133. By contrast Below recalled Hitler receiving the news "soberly without any great optimism." *Als Hitlers Adjutant*, p. 408. See also Misch, *Der letzte Zeuge*, p. 191.

158 Schwerin von Krosigk to Goebbels, 14 April 1945; BA Koblenz, N 276/45.

159 See Henke, *Die amerikanische Besetzung Deutschlands*, pp. 402–4.

160 Goebbels, *Tagebücher*, part II, vol. 15, p. 692 (entry for 9 April 1945).

161 Hubatsch (ed.), *Weisungen für die Kriegführung*, pp. 355–7.

162 Goebbels, *Tagebücher*, part II, vol. 15, pp. 310f. (entry for 5 Feb. 1945); see ibid., pp. 321 (entry for 6 Feb. 1945), 370 (entry for 12 Feb. 1945), 614 (entry for 28 March 1945).

163 Heinrici, "Der Endkampf des Dritten Reiches," pp. 12, 16, 42; IfZ München ZS 66/1; *idem*, "Bericht über die Erlebnisse bei der Heeresgruppe Weichsel im April 1945 vom 12. May 1945," p. 9; BA-MA Freiburg, N 265/108. See Hans-Georg Eismann, "Das Kriegstagebuch der Heeresgruppe Weichsel (Januar 1945 bis zur Kapitulation)," pp. 103, 108f.; IfZ München, ZS 3095. Albert Kesselring, who after being named supreme commander met with Hitler four times between 10 March and 12 April 1945, also concluded: "His mental vigour stood in marked contrast to his physical disposition." *Soldat bis zum letzten Tag*, p. 386.

164 Domarus, *Hitler*, vol. 2, part 2, pp. 2223f.

17 The Final Days in the Bunker

1 Max Domarus, *Hitler: Reden und Proklamationen 1932–1945*, Munich, 1965, vol. 2, part 1, p. 1316. See also Christian Goeschel, *Selbstmord im Dritten Reich*, Berlin, 2011, pp. 231–4,

2 See Volker Ullrich, *Hitler: Ascent 1889–1939*, London, 2016, pp. 163, 344.

3 Sebastian Haffner, *Germany: Jekyll & Hyde. Deutschland von innen betrachtet*, Berlin, 1996, p. 21.

4 Helmut Heiber (ed.), *Hitlers Lagebesprechungen: Die Protokollfragmente seiner militärischen Konferenzen 1942–1945*, Stuttgart, 1962, pp. 126 (dated 1 Feb. 1943), 620 (dated 31 Aug. 1944). See Albert Speer to Erich Fromm, 15 Feb. 1973: "Hitler stressed often enough, and with increasingly frequency towards the end of the war, that he was not afraid of death." BA Koblenz, N 1340/21.

5 Catherine Merridale, *Ivan's War: The Red Army 1939–45*, London, 2006, p. 283. On the final offensive against Berlin, see *Das Deutsche Reich und der Zweite Weltkrieg*, ed. Militärgeschichtliches Forschungsamt (Military Historical Research Office), 10 vols, Stuttgart and Munich, 1979–2008, vol. 10, part 1, pp. 588–679 (Lakowski's essay).

6 See Merridale, *Ivan's War*, pp. 283f.

7 See *Das Deutsche Reich und der Zweite Weltkrieg*, vol. 10, part 1, pp. 633–42 (Lakowski's essay).

8 See ibid., pp. 646–9.

9 Nerin E. Gun, *Eva Braun-Hitler: Leben und Schicksal*, Velbert and Kettwig, 1968, p. 186 (reproduction of the letter on p. 192). On the women shooting pistols in the Chancellery courtyard, see also Traudl Junge, *Bis zur letzten Stunde: Hitlers Sekretärin erzählt ihr Leben*, Munich, 2002, p. 182.

10 Lew Besymenski, *Die letzten Notizen von Martin Bormann: Ein Dokument und sein Verfasser*, Stuttgart, 1974, p. 188.

11 Situation reports from the Gaue to Martin Bormann on 19 April 1945; BA Berlin-Lichterfelde, NS 6/277.

12 BA Berlin-Lichterfelde, NS 6/770.

13 Cited in Ralf Georg Reuth, *Goebbels*, Munich and Zurich, 1990, p. 597; Peter Longerich, *Joseph Goebbels*, Munich, 2010, p. 671.

14 Ursula von Kardorff, *Berliner Aufzeichnungen 1942–1945*, new edition, ed. Peter Hartl, Munich, 1992, pp. 307f. (entry for 20 April 1945).

15 Henrik Eberle and Matthias Uhl (eds), *Das Buch Hitler*, Bergisch Gladbach, 2005, pp. 375f.; see Heinz Linge, *Bis zum Untergang: Als Chef des Persönlichen Dienstes bei Hitler*, Munich, 1982, pp. 271f.

16 Cited in Peter Gosztony (ed.), *Der Kampf um Berlin 1945 in Augenzeugenberichten*, Düsseldorf, 1970, p. 202; see Eberle and Uhl (eds), *Das Buch Hitler*, pp. 376f.; Linge, *Bis zum Untergang*, pp. 273f.

17 Albert Speer, *Erinnerungen: Mit einem Essay von Jochen Thies*, Frankfurt am Main and Berlin, 1993, p. 477. Hitler told Keitel: "I will do battle before, in or behind Berlin." Generalfeldmarschall Keitel, *Verbrecher oder Offizier? Erinnerungen, Briefe, Dokumente*

des Chefs des OKW, ed. Walter Görlitz, Berlin and Frankfurt am Main, 1961, p. 343. On the reception, see also Hugh R. Trevor-Roper, *The Last Days of Hitler*, 6th edition, London, 2012, pp. 98f.; Joachim Fest, *Der Untergang: Hitler und das Ende des Dritten Reiches. Eine historische Skizze*, Berlin, 2002, pp. 59–61.

18   See Speer, *Erinnerungen*, pp. 477f.; Nicolaus von Below, *Als Hitlers Adjutant 1937–45*, Mainz, 1980, p. 410: "I had the impression that Hitler no longer took any note of Göring. It was an unpleasant moment."

19   See Olaf Rose (ed.), *Julius Schaub—In Hitlers Schatten: Erinnerungen und Aufzeichnungen des Chefadjutanten 1925–1945*, Stegen am Ammersee, 2005, p. 327; Anton Joachimsthaler, *Hitlers Ende: Legenden und Dokumente*, Munich and Berlin, 1995, p. 140. Finance Minister Schwerin von Krosigk left Berlin by car on 21 April 1945 and arrived the following day in Eutin in northwestern Germany, where the ministers had agreed to meet. See the detailed description of events in the letter from Krosigk (as an American POW) to his wife, 18 Dec. 1945; BA Koblenz N 276/113.

20   Junge, *Bis zur letzten Stunde*, pp. 176f.; see Below, *Als Hitlers Adjutant*, p. 411.

21   See Christa Schroeder, *Er war mein Chef: Aus dem Nachlass der Sekretärin von Adolf Hitler*, ed. Anton Joachimsthaler, 3rd edition, Munich and Vienna, 1985, pp. 200–204. According to a post-war letter, before her departure Christa Schroeder asked Speer to intervene on behalf of her friend Karl Brandt, who had been sentenced to death. Speer replied: "I will get him out, and if he is no longer alive, I will shoot Martin Bormann dead with my own two hands." Christa Schroeder to Albert Speer, 14 Sept. 1975; BA Koblenz, N 1340/58. But in her memoirs Schroeder writes only of Speer promising to "illegally free" Brandt. Schroeder, *Er war mein Chef*, p. 202.

22   Junge, *Bis zur letzten Stunde*, pp. 177f.; see Heike B. Görtemaker, *Eva Braun: Leben mit Hitler*, Munich, 2010, p. 275.

23   Eberle and Uhl (eds), *Das Buch Hitler*, pp. 379f.; see Fest, *Der Untergang*, pp. 66f.

24   Karl Koller, *Der letzte Monat: Die Tagebuchaufzeichnungen des ehemaligen Chefs des Generalstabs der deutschen Luftwaffe vom 14. April bis zum 27. Mai 1945*, Mannheim, 1949, pp. 20f. (entry for 21 April 1945).

25   Joachimsthaler, *Hitlers Ende*, p. 146; see *Das Deutsche Reich und der Zweite Weltkrieg*, vol. 10, part 1, pp. 661f. (Lakowski's essay).

26   Koller, *Der letzte Monat*, p. 25 (entry for 21 April 1945).

27   Hildegard Springer, *Es sprach Hans Fritzsche: Nach Gesprächen, Briefen und Dokumenten*, Stuttgart, 1949, pp. 28–31; see Max Bonacker, *Goebbels' Mann beim Radio: Der NS-Propagandist Hans Fritzsche (1900–1953)*, Munich, 2007, p. 213; Fest, *Der Untergang*, pp. 69–71.

28   See Eberle and Uhl (eds), *Das Buch Hitler*, p. 383. On 21 April, Bormann noted: "Morning: Puttkamer + crowd fly off." Besymenski, *Die letzten Notizen von Martin Bormann*, p. 188.

29   See Hans Baur, *Ich flog Mächtige dieser Erde*, Kempten im Allgäu, 1956, p. 267. See also Baur's lecture "Die letzten Tage in der Reichskanzlei," undated, pp. 12f.; IfZ München, ZS 638.

30   See Michael Seufert, *Der Skandal um die Hitler-Tagebücher*, Frankfurt am Main, 2008, as well as the *Zeit* dossier no. 15, 4 April 2013 (with contributions from the former editor-in-chief of *Stern*, Felix Schmidt, as well as Volker Ullrich and Harald Welzer).

31   Morell's daily notes of 20–21 April 1944; BA Koblenz, N 1348/5; see Hans-Joachim Neumann and Henrik Eberle, *War Hitler krank? Ein abschliessender Befund*, Bergisch Gladbach, 2009, p. 283. On 17 February 1945, Morell had noted that Hitler had behaved "somewhat oddly" towards him. BA Koblenz, N 1348/3.

32   See Junge, *Bis zur letzten Stunde*, p. 189.

33   Schroeder, *Er war mein Chef*, p. 205. In a letter to his wife of 24 April 1945, Morell wrote: "I have some adventurous days behind me, which I will never forget." Ernst Günther Schenck, *Patient Hitler: Eine medizinische Biographie*, Düsseldorf, 1989, p.

502. Eva Braun gave Morell jewellery for her sister Gretl, who was at the Berghof in an advanced state of pregnancy. In her final letter on 23 April 1945, she wrote: "Hopefully Morell has arrived with my jewellery. It would be horrible if something had happened. 'Gun, *Eva Braun-Hitler*, p. 191 (copy of the letter on p. 192).

34   See Eberle and Uhl (eds), *Das Buch Hitler*, p. 385.

35   See *Das Deutsche Reich und der Zweite Weltkrieg*, vol. 10, part 1, pp. 649–53 (Lakowski's essay).

36   Eberle and Uhl (eds), *Das Buch Hitler*, p. 386. On the situation meeting of 22 April 1945, see the interrogation transcript of Freytag von Loringhoven (1949); IfZ München, ZS 38; Trevor-Roper, *The Last Days of Hitler*, pp. 105f; Joachimsthaler, *Hitlers Ende*, pp. 147–52; Fest, *Der Untergang*, pp. 77–9.

37   Junge, *Bis zur letzten Stunde*, pp. 180, 184.

38   This was how Jodl summarised to Karl Koller what Hitler had said on the night of 22–23 April; Koller, *Der letzte Monat*, p. 31 (entry for 23 April 1945); see also Keitel, *Verbrecher oder Offizier?*, pp. 346–8; Junge, *Bis zur letzten Stunde*, p. 186.

39   Junge, *Bis zur letzten Stunde*, p. 186. After their conversation, Goebbels told Hitler's entourage: "Hitler is completely deflated . . . I have never seen him in such a state." Eberle and Uhl (eds), *Das Buch Hitler*, p. 387.

40   Gun, *Eva Braun-Hitler*, pp. 189f. Braun wrote to her sister Gretl on 23 April 1945: "The Führer himself has lost all faith in a positive outcome. Everyone here, including me, maintains hope as long as we still breathe . . . But it goes without saying that we will not let us be taken alive." Ibid., p. 190 (copy of the letter on p. 192).

41   See Rose, *Julius Schaub*, pp. 329–45; Schroeder, *Er war mein Chef*, p. 213: "Schaub's act of destruction under an overcast sky was a desolate sight."

42   See Bormann's memorandum of 19 March 1945 (included with Schörner's correspondence to the supreme commanders of the armies and commanding generals of 27 February 1945); BA Berlin-Lichterfelde, NS 6/354. On Schörner's outlook, see also his letter to Colonel von Trotha in the general staff of the army of 22 February 1945: "Either we will succeed in having truly fanatic and uncompromising followers of the Führer in high places, or things will go south again." BA-MA Freiburg, N 60/17.

43   Eberle and Uhl (eds), *Das Buch Hitler*, p. 390. On the date of his visit, see Bormann's calendar under 22 April 1945: "Evening: Schörner in Berlin." Besymenski, *Die letzten Notizen von Martin Bormann*, p. 189.

44   Testimony of Field Marshal Schörner about the "report to the Führer," Moscow, 20 Aug. 1945 (wrongly dated 21–22 April 1945); Wassili S. Christoforow, Wladimir G. Makarow and Matthias Uhl (eds), *Verhört: Die Befragungen deutscher Generale und Offiziere durch die sowjetischen Geheimdienste 1945–1952*, Berlin and Boston, 2015, p. 175.

45   Walter Wenck, "Berlin war nicht zu retten," in *Stern*, 18 April 1965; cited in Reuth, *Goebbels*, p. 600. See Joachimsthaler, *Hitlers Ende*, p. 160; Fest, *Der Untergang*, pp. 83–5.

46   See Joachimsthaler, *Hitlers Ende*, pp. 158f.

47   See Eberle and Uhl (eds), *Das Buch Hitler*, pp. 392f.; Joachimsthaler, *Hitlers Ende*, p. 160.

48   *Kriegstagebuch des Oberkommandos der Wehrmacht (Wehrmachtführungsstab)* (hereafter *KTB OKW*), ed. Percy Ernst Schramm, Munich, 1982, vol. 4, part 2, p. 1262.

49   See Eberle and Uhl (eds), *Das Buch Hitler*, pp. 393f.; Below, *Als Hitlers Adjutant*, p. 412.

50   See Eberle and Uhl (eds), *Das Buch Hitler*, p. 394; Speer, *Erinnerungen*, p. 483.

51   Gun, *Eva Braun-Hitler*, p. 191 (copy on p. 192).

52   Eberle and Uhl (eds), *Das Buch Hitler*, p. 395; see Keitel, *Verbrecher oder Offizier?*, p. 350.

53   "'. . . warum dann überhaupt noch leben!' Hitlers Lagebesprechungen am 23., 25. und 27. April 1945," in *Der Spiegel*, no. 3, 10 Jan. 1966, pp. 32–46 (at pp. 32f., dated 23 April 1945).

54   See Eberle and Uhl (eds), *Das Buch Hitler*, p. 395; Keitel, *Offizier oder Verbrecher?*, pp. 352ff.

55 Speer, *Erinnerungen*, pp. 479–83 (at pp. 482f.). Joachim Fest, *Speer: Eine Biographie*, Berlin, 1999, pp. 361–5, uncritically follows Speer. In contrast, see Magnus Brechtken, *Albert Speer: Eine deutsche Karriere*, Munich, 2017, pp. 285–8.

56 Domarus, *Hitler*, vol. 2, part 2, p. 2228n165).

57 Koller, *Der letzte Monat*, pp. 35–8 (entry for 23 April 1945). See Trevor-Roper, *The Last Days of Hitler*, pp. 114–16; Fest, *Der Untergang*, pp. 101–3.

58 Transcript of the telegram in BA Koblenz, N 1340/496.

59 Speer, *Erinnerungen*, pp. 485f.; see Below, *Als Hitlers Adjutant*, pp. 412f.; Junge, *Bis zur letzten Stunde*, p. 190.

60 Koller, *Der letzte Monat*, p. 42. The French researcher Bruno Ledoux discovered the original telegrams between Hitler and Göring in July 2013 and published them in the newspaper *Le Figaro*. See Joseph Hanimann, "Obersalzberg an Führerbunker," in *Süddeutsche Zeitung*, 29 July 2013.

61 Transcript of Soviet interrogation of Göring, Mondorf, 17 June 1945; Christoforow et al. (eds), *Verhört*, p. 82. See Domarus, *Hitler*, vol. 2, part 2, p. 2229. Bormann noted on 25 April: "Göring has been expelled from the party!" Besymenski, *Die letzten Notizen von Martin Bormann*, p. 230.

62 See Lammers' notes of 24 April 1945 and his telegram to Hitler of 25 April 1945; BA Berlin-Lichterfelde, R 43 II/1641.

63 See Speer's testimony about his activities as minister, Nuremberg, 28 Sept. 1946, p. 4; BA Koblenz, N 1340/84; see Speer, *Erinnerungen*, p. 487f.

64 According to Speer, he left the Chancellery at 3 a.m. and took his return flight an hour later. Albert Speer to David Irving, 10 Oct. 1974; BA Koblenz, N 1340/30. See Speer, *Erinnerungen*, p. 488; Fest, *Speer*, pp. 367–9.

65 See Joachimsthaler, *Hitlers Ende*, p. 164.

66 Helmuth Weidling, "Der Endkampf in Berlin," in *Wehrwissenschaftliche Rundschau*, 12 (1962), pp. 42ff.; cited in Gosztony (ed.), *Der Kampf um Berlin 1945*, pp. 234–8 (at pp. 235, 238). See Joachimsthaler, *Hitlers Ende*, pp. 163f.; Fest, *Der Untergang*, pp. 74f.

67 See Joachimsthaler, *Hitlers Ende*, p. 164; *Das Deutsche Reich und der Zweite Weltkrieg*, vol. 10, part 1, p. 658 (Lakowski's essay).

68 See Junge, *Bis zur letzten Stunde*, p. 196; Below, *Als Hitlers Adjutant*, p. 416.

69 Speer, *Erinnerungen*, pp. 475f.

70 See Junge, *Bis zur letzten Stunde*, p. 195; Bernd Freytag von Loringhoven, *Mit Hitler im Bunker: Die letzten Monate im Führerhauptquartier Juli 1944–April 1945*, Berlin, 2006, pp. 157f.

71 Junge, *Bis zur letzten Stunde*, pp. 195f.; see Eberle and Uhl (eds), *Das Buch Hitler*, p. 421; Freytag von Loringhoven, *Mit Hitler im Bunker*, p. 157.

72 Junge, *Bis zur letzten Stunde*, p. 197; see Albert Speer to Jeremy Granat, 5 Jan. 1970; BA Koblenz, N 1340/24; Speer, *Erinnerungen*, p. 487; Albert Speer, *"Alles was ich weiss": Aus unbekannten Geheimdienstprotokollen vom Sommer 1945*, ed. Ulrich Schlie, Munich, 1999, pp. 58f.; Schroeder, *Er war mein Chef*, p. 169; Below, *Als Hitlers Adjutant*, p. 408; Rochus Misch, *Der letzte Zeuge: "Ich war Hitlers Telefonist, Kurier und Leibwächter,"* Zurich and Munich, 2008, pp. 208, 220. See also Baur's statement: "I was not the only one in the final days before their double suicide who admired her ease and almost cheerful inner calm. She was a woman of stature." James P. O'Donnell and Uwe Bahnsen, *Die Katakombe: Das Ende in der Reichskanzlei*, Stuttgart 1975, p. 130.

73 Gun, *Eva Braun-Hitler*, pp. 189, 191 (copy of the letter on. 192).

74 See Görtemaker, *Eva Braun*, p. 101; Ullrich, *Hitler: Ascent 1889–1939*, p. 614.

75 Misch, *Der letzte Zeuge*, p. 205.

76 Cited in Reuth, *Goebbels*, p. 604.

77 See Joachimsthaler, *Hitlers Ende*, pp. 165, 167; Eberle and Uhl (eds), *Das Buch Hitler*, p. 407. On the meeting in Torgau, see Henke, *Die amerikanische Besetzung Deutschlands*, pp. 657f.

78   "Hitlers Lagebesprechung vom 25. April 1945"; *Der Spiegel*, no. 3, 10 Jan. 1966, pp. 34–9.

79   Eberle and Uhl (eds), *Das Buch Hitler*, pp. 405f.

80   Joachimsthaler, *Hitlers Ende*, p. 167.

81   See Gerhard Boldt, *Hitler: Die letzten zehn Tage in der Reichskanzlei*, Munich, 1976, p. 107; Eberle and Uhl (eds), *Das Buch Hitler*, pp. 412f.; Joachimsthaler, *Hitlers Ende*, pp. 168, 176.

82   Hanna Reitsch, *Fliegen: Mein Leben*, Stuttgart, 1951, pp. 292–301. See Trevor-Roper, *The Last Days of Hitler*, pp. 131–4; Alan Bullock, *Hitler: A Study in Tyranny*, London, 1990, pp. 789f., 792; Fest, *Der Untergang*, pp. 104f.

83   See Joachimsthaler, *Hitlers Ende*, p. 171; Boldt, *Hitler: Die letzten Tage in der Reichskanzlei*, p. 117; Eberle and Uhl (eds), *Das Buch Hitler*, p. 422.

84   Eberle and Uhl (eds), *Das Buch Hitler*, p. 423. See also Bernd Freytag von Loringhoven, "Die Schlacht um Berlin (1949)," p. 5: "Such good news unleashed paroxysms of joy among the occupants of the Führer's bunker, who had been torn between fear and hope." IfZ München, ZS 38.

85   Freytag von Loringhoven, *Mit Hitler im Bunker*, p. 164.

86   "1. Lagebesprechung vom 27. April 1945"; *Der Spiegel*, no. 3, 10 Jan. 1966, pp. 39–42.

87   "2. und 3. Lagebesprechung am 27. April 1945"; ibid., pp. 42–6; Eberle and Uhl (eds), *Das Buch Hitler*, pp. 426f.; Gosztony (ed.), *Der Kampf um Berlin 1945*, pp. 313–15 (Weidling's report).

88   Besymenski, *Die letzten Notizen von Martin Bormann*, p. 230 (entry for 27 April 1945).

89   See Joachimsthaler, *Hitlers Ende*, p. 181; Eberle and Uhl (eds), *Das Buch Hitler*, pp. 432f.

90   *KTB OKW*, vol. 4, part 2, p. 1462.

91   Trevor-Roper, *The Last Days of Hitler*, pp. 144f.; see Jochen von Lang, *Der Sekretär: Martin Bormann, Der Mann, der Hitler beherrschte*, Stuttgart, 1977, p. 334

92   Besymenski, *Die letzten Notizen von Martin Bormann*, p. 230 (entry for 28 April 1945).

93   See Joachimsthaler, *Hitlers Ende*, pp. 182f.; Fest, *Der Untergang*, pp. 113f.

94   See Bullock, *Hitler*, pp. 791; Ian Kershaw, *Hitler 1936–1945: Nemesis*, London, 2000, pp. 816–19; Peter Longerich, *Heinrich Himmler: Biographie*, Munich, 2008, pp. 745–50.

95   Trevor-Roper, *The Last Days of Hitler*, p. 149; see Eberle and Uhl (eds), *Das Buch Hitler*, p. 429; Misch, *Der letzte Zeuge*, p. 215; Freytag von Loringhoven, *Mit Hitler im Bunker*, p. 166.

96   See Trevor-Roper, *The Last Days of Hitler*, pp. 150f.; Joachimsthaler, *Hitlers Ende*, pp. 183f., 463–5; Fest, *Der Untergang*, pp. 116–20.

97   Reitsch, *Fliegen: Mein Leben*, pp. 302–4; see Trevor-Roper, *The Last Days of Hitler*, pp. 151–3; Fest, *Der Untergang*, pp. 114f.

98   See Karl Dönitz, *Zehn Jahre und zwanzig Tage*, Frankfurt am Main, 1967, p. 433; Longerich, *Heinrich Himmler*, p. 754.

99   Hitler's adjutant Schaub said that in all the time he spent in the bunker, there was never any talk of Hitler and Braun marrying. Julius Schaub's testimony "Eva Braun"; IfZ München, ED 100, vol. 203.

100 See Ullrich, *Hitler: Ascent 1889–1939*, pp. 284, 287f., 380f., 618–21.

101 See ibid., p. 632. Fest also surmises that the marriage was meant to echo Wagner's *Liebestod*. Joachim Fest, *Hitler: Eine Biographie*, Frankfurt am Main, Berlin and Vienna, 1973, p. 1016.

102 A copy of the marriage certificate is reproduced in Joachimsthaler, *Hitlers Ende*, pp. 186f. On the wedding ceremony, see Trevor-Roper, *The Last Days of Hitler*, p. 154; Bullock, *Hitler*, p. 793; Fest, *Der Untergang*, pp. 120f.; Eberle and Uhl (eds), *Das Buch Hitler*, pp. 435f.; Below, *Als Hitlers Adjutant*, pp. 413f.

103 Junge, *Bis zur letzten Stunde*, p. 202.

104 Hans-Ulrich Thamer, "Der tote Hitler: Das Ende des Diktators und die Wandlungen eines Mythos," in Thomas Grossbölting and Rüdiger Scheidt (eds), *Der Tod des*

Diktators: Ereignis und Erinnerung im 20. Jahrhundert, Göttingen, 2011, pp. 81–93 (at p. 88).

105   Speer himself blamed his dismissal on the fact that he had "failed to execute Hitler's destructive plans" and on backbiting by Saur, "with whom Hitler had been in close contact for quite some time behind my back." Albert Speer to Jeremy Granat, 29 Oct. 1976; BA Koblenz, N 1340/24.

106   In September 1944, Krosigk had offered to resign because his brother-in-law, Friedrich Karl von Zitzewitz, had known about Goerdeler's plans for the coup and had been hauled up in front of the People's Court. Hitler refused the offer after his finance minister convinced him that he had never spoken with his brother-in-law about any plans to overthrow him. Krosigk to Hitler, 19 Sept. 1944 (the letter was signed "Heil Hitler! In immutable loyalty"); BA Koblenz, N 276/45.

107   For the text of Hitler's political will, see *KTB OKW*, vol. 4, part 2, pp. 1666–9; Domarus, *Hitler*, vol. 2, part 2, pp. 2236–9 (with minor variations). A facsimile is included in Joachimsthaler, *Hitlers Ende*, pp. 190–2, from which the quotes are taken.

108   Junge, *Bis zur letzten Stunde*, pp. 202f.

109   Domarus, *Hitler*, vol. 2, part 2 pp. 2240f.; facsimile in Joachimsthaler, *Hitlers Ende*, p. 192.

110   Junge, *Bis zur letzten Stunde*, p. 203; Below, *Als Hitlers Adjutant*, p. 416.

111   Reproduced in Trevor-Roper, *The Last Days of Hitler*, pp. 164f.; Domarus, *Hitler*, vol. 2, part 2, p. 2241.

112   See Trevor-Roper, *The Last Days of Hitler*, pp. 165–8, 194–7, xxx–xxxiv; Edward D. R. Harrison, "Hugh Trevor-Roper und 'Hitlers letzte Tage,'" in *Vierteljahrshefte für Zeitgeschichte*, 57 (2009), pp. 33–60 (at pp. 41–3).

113   Besymenski, *Die letzten Notizen von Martin Bormann*, p. 233.

114   *KTB OKW*, vol. 4, part 2, p. 1271.

115   Joachimsthaler, *Hitlers Ende*, pp. 193f.

116   Boldt, *Hitler: Die letzten zehn Tage in der Reichskanzlei*, pp. 133–5; see Freytag von Loringhoven, *Mit Hitler im Bunker*, pp. 170–2.

117   See Below, *Als Hitlers Adjutant*, pp. 418, 424f.; Trevor-Roper, *The Last Days of Hitler*, pp. 170–2; Kershaw, *Hitler 1936–45*, pp. 825f.

118   See above p. 529

119   Junge, *Bis zur letzten Stunde*, p. 200; see Eberle and Uhl (eds), *Das Buch Hitler*, p. 441; Joachimsthaler, *Hitlers Ende*, pp. 194–7.

120   See Hans Woller, *Mussolini: Der erste Faschist. Eine Biografie*, Munich, 2016, pp. 313–16.

121   See Junge, *Bis zur letzten Stunde*, p. 195; Misch, *Der letzte Zeuge*, pp. 219, 221.

122   *KTB OKW*, vol. 4, part 2, p. 1466.

123   Ibid., p. 1467; facsimile in Joachimsthaler, *Hitlers Ende*, p. 202.

124   Schenck, *Patient Hitler*, p. 400; see O'Donnell and Bahnsen, *Die Katakombe*, pp. 187f.

125   See Joachimsthaler, *Hitlers Ende*, pp. 203f.

126   Joachimsthaler, *Hitlers Ende*, pp. 206–8; Fest, *Der Untergang*, pp. 129–31.

127   Junge, *Bis zur letzten Stunde*, p. 205.

128   Eberle and Uhl (eds), *Das Buch Hitler*, pp. 444f.; see Joachimsthaler, *Hitlers Ende*, pp. 210–13.

129   Baur, *Ich flog Mächtige der Erde*, p. 275f. See Hans Baur's lecture, "Die letzten Tage in der Reichskanzlei," undated, pp. 22–5; IfZ München, ZS 638.

130   See Joachimsthaler, *Hitlers Ende*, p. 220; Fest, *Der Untergang*, p. 133; Junge, *Bis zur letzten Stunde*, p. 206.

131   See Joachimsthaler, *Hitlers Ende*, pp. 221f.; Fest, *Der Untergang*, pp. 135f.

132   See Joachimsthaler, *Hitlers Ende*, pp. 230–73 (with a critical evaluation of all witness accounts); Fest, *Der Untergang*, pp. 136–8; Eberle and Uhl (eds), *Das Buch Hitler*, pp. 447f. To leave nothing to chance, Hitler presumably also took a cyanide capsule before he shot himself in the head. See Ulrich Völklein (ed.), *Hitlers Tod: Die letzten Tage im Führerbunker*, Göttingen, 1999, pp. 123, 158ff.

133 See Joachimsthaler, *Hitlers Ende*, pp. 288–332; Fest, *Der Untergang*, pp. 138–40; Eberle and Uhl (ed.), *Das Buch Hitler*, pp. 448f.

134 See Joachimsthaler, *Hitlers Ende*, pp. 333–83; Völklein, *Hitlers Tod*, pp. 146 f.

135 The three telegrams are reproduced in Joachimsthaler, *Hitlers Ende*, pp. 227, 280, 281f.; see Lang, *Der Sekretär*, pp. 337f.; Dönitz, *Zehn Jahre und ein Tag*, pp. 433–8; transcript of the Soviet interrogation of Admiral Karl Dönitz, Mohndorf, 17 June 1945; Christoforow, *et al.* (eds), *Verhört*, pp. 63f.

136 Domarus, *Hitler*, vol. 2, part 2, p. 2250; Joachimsthaler, *Hitlers Ende*, p. 283.

137 See Reuth, *Goebbels*, pp. 610f.

138 See ibid., pp. 613–15.

139 Besymenski, *Die letzten Notizen von Martin Bormann*, p. 272. See Lang, *Der Sekretär*, pp. 340–2, 402 ff.; Junge, *Bis zur letzten Stunde*, pp. 213–15; Misch, *Der letzte Zeuge*, pp. 233–8; Eberle and Uhl (eds), *Das Buch Hitler*, pp. 456–60.

18 Hitler's Place in History

1 Thomas Mann, *Tagebücher, 1944–1. April 1946*, ed. Inge Jens, Frankfurt am Main, 1986, p. 197 (entry for 2 May 1945). See ibid., p. 627 (n. 3 to 2 May 1945).

2 William L. Shirer, *Berliner Tagebuch: Das Ende 1944–1946*, ed. Jürgen Schebera, Leipzig, 1994 pp. 65 (entry for 1 May 1945), 74 (entry for 6 May 1945).

3 Sönke Neitzel, *Abgehört: Deutsche Generäle in britischer Kriegsgefangenschaft 1942–1945*, Berlin, 2005, doc. 79, pp. 210–12.

4 Ibid., doc. 72, p. 195, doc. 73, p. 197.

5 Reinhardt's diary entry for 9 June 1945; BA-MA Freiburg, N 245/3.

6 Elsa Bruckmann to Marie von Hellingrath, 14 April 1945; cited in Wolfgang Martynkewicz, *Salon Deutschland: Geist und Macht 1900–1945*, Berlin, 2009, p. 523.

7 Albert Speer, *Erinnerungen: Mit einem Essay von Jochen Thies*, Frankfurt am Main and Berlin, 1993, p. 491.

8 See Martin Kitchen, *Speer: Hitler's Architect*, New Haven and London, 2015, pp. 283ff.; Magnus Brechtken, *Albert Speer: Eine deutsche Karriere*, Munich, 2017, pp. 295ff.; Isabell Trommer, *Rechtfertigung und Entlastung: Albert Speer in der Bundesrepublik*, Frankfurt am Main, 2016.

9 Hermann Okrass, "Abschied von Hitler," in *Hamburger Zeitung*, 2 May 1945; reproduced in *Die Zeit*, no. 17, 23 Apr. 2015, p. 19. See ibid. for a nuanced interpretation. from Benedikt Erenz.

10 Lore Walb, *Ich, die Alte—ich, die Junge: Konfrontation mit meinen Tagebüchern 1933–1945*, Berlin, 1997, pp. 338 (entry for 2 May 1945), 345 (entry for 8 May 1945).

11 Friedrich Kellner, *"Vernebelt, verdunkelt sind alle Hirne": Tagebücher, 1939–1945*, ed. Sascha Feuchert et al., Göttingen, 2011, vol. 2, pp. 931 (entry for 6 May 1943), 930 (entry for 1 May 1945).

12 Ursula von Kardorff, *Berliner Aufzeichnungen 1942–1945*, new edition, ed. Peter Hartl, Munich, 1992, p. 320 (entry for 2 May 1945).

13 Heinrich Breloer (ed.), *Mein Tagebuch: Geschichten vom Überleben 1939–1947*, Cologne, 1984, p. 182.

14 Erich Kästner, *Notabene 45: Ein Tagebuch*, Munich, 1993, pp. 114f. (entry for 4 May 1945).

15 Anonyma, *Eine Frau in Berlin: Tagebuchaufzeichnungen vom 20. April bis 22. Juni 1945*, Frankfurt am Main, 2003, p. 186 (entry for 11 May 1945).

16 Victor Klemperer, *Ich will Zeugnis ablegen bis zum letzten: Tagebücher*, vol. 2: 1942–1945, ed. Walter Nowojski with Hadwig Klemperer, Berlin, 1995, pp. 761 (entry for 1 May 1945), 773 (entry for 11 May 1945).

17 Kellner, *Tagebücher, 1939–1945*, vol. 2, p. 932 (entry for 6 May 1945).

18 Martha Gellhorn, *The Face of War*, London, 1998, p. 177

19 Mathilde Wolff-Mönckeberg, *Briefe, die sie nicht erreichten: Briefe einer Mutter an ihre fernen Kinder in den Jahren 1940–1946*, Hamburg, 1980, p. 171 (dated 1 June 1945).

20 Margaret Bourke-White, *Deutschland—April 1945: "Dear Fatherland Rest Quietly,"* Munich, 1979, p. 90.

21 See above pp. 292–6; Volker Ullrich, "Das offene Geheimnis," in *Zeit-Geschichte*, 1 (2017), pp. 92–7.

22 Shirer, *Berliner Tagebuch*, pp. 162 (entry for 30 Oct. 1945), 161 (entry for 3 Nov. 1945).

23 See Norbert Frei, "Führerbilderwechsel: Hitler und die Deutschen nach 1945," in Hans-Ulrich Thamer and Simone Erpel (eds), *Hitler und die Deutschen: Volksgemeinschaft und Verbrechen*, Dresden, 2011, pp. 142–7 (at p. 144).

24 See Gustave M. Gilbert, *Nürnberger Tagebuch*, Frankfurt am Main, 1962; Leon Goldensohn, *Die Nürnberger Interviews: Gespräche mit Angeklagten und Zeugen*, Düsseldorf and Zurich, 2005.

25 See Lutz Niethammer, *Die Mitläuferfabrik: Die Entnazifizierung am Beispiel Bayerns*, Bonn, 1982.

26 Victor Klemperer, *Warum soll man nicht auf bessere Zeiten hoffen: Ein Leben in Briefen*, ed. Walter Nowojski and Nele Holdack with Christian Löser, Berlin, 2017, p. 335 (dated 20 June 1946).

27 Hannah Arendt, *Besuch in Deutschland*, Berlin, 1993, pp. 25, 35.

28 Alexander und Margarete Mitscherlich, *Die Unfähigkeit zu trauern: Grundlagen kollektiven Verhaltens*, Munich, 1967, in particular pp. 27ff., 71ff.

29 Klaus Mann, "Hitler ist tot," in *idem, Auf verlorenem Posten: Aufsätze, Reden, Kritiken 1942–1949*, ed. Uwe Naumann and Michael Töteberg, Reinbek bei Hamburg, 1994, pp. 211–15 (at p. 211).

30 See Hartmann et al., (eds), *Hitler, Mein Kampf: Eine kritische Edition*, Munich and Berlin, 2016, vol. 1 (Introduction), pp. 30–4; Andreas Wirsching, "Hitlers Authentizität: Eine funktionalistische Deutung," in *Vierteljahrshefte für Zeitgeschichte*, 64 (2016), pp. 387–417 (at pp. 396–8).

31 See Peter Longerich, *Hitler: Biographie*, Munich, 2015, pp. 14f., 997f.

32 Sebastian Haffner, *Anmerkungen zu Hitler*, 21st edition, Munich, 1978, p. 22. See Schwerin von Krosigk to Fred L. Casmir, 27 July 1960: "In the demagogy, which he was able to fully unfold as a speaker, he was an unrivalled master. Without his oratorical gift, he would have remained an obscure bohemian." BA Koblenz, N 1276/40.

33 Ludolf Herbst, *Hitlers Charisma: Die Erfindung eines deutschen Messias*, Frankfurt am Main, 2010, p. 128. See Richard Walter Darré, "Drehbühne," notes written at Nuremberg, p. 139: Hitler knew how "to bundle the psychological currents of the mass event like a reflecting mirror and represent them in simple, succinct words" so that everyone present felt personally addressed. BA Koblenz, N 1094 I/28.

34 Ernst von Weizsäcker, *Erinnerungen*, handwritten manuscript, composed in August 1944 in the Vatican, p. 253; BA Koblenz, N 1273/47.

35 See Wolfram Pyta, *Hitler: Der Künstler als Politiker und Feldherr*, Munich, 2015, p. 10–14. On the influence of the stage works of Richard Wagner on Hitler, see Hans Rudolf Vaget: *"Wehvolles Erbe": Richard Wagner in Deutschland. Hitler, Knappertsbusch, Mann*, Frankfurt am Main, 2017, pp. 110ff., 135ff.

36 In 1973 Speer wrote that one of Hitler's "great gifts" was the ability to "adapt his behaviour, diction and tone of voice" to every situation and audience. Albert Speer to Erich Fromm, 15 Feb. 1973; BA Koblenz, N 1340/21.

37 Hans-Ulrich Wehler, *Deutsche Gesellschaftsgeschichte*, vol. 4, Munich, 2003, p. 560.

38 Ernst von Weizsäcker to his mother, 8 Dec. 1940; BA Koblenz, N 1273/30. For a summary of the Nazi system of rule, see Hans-Ulrich Thamer, *Adolf Hitler: Biographie eines Diktators*, Munich, 2018, pp. 192–8.

39 *Die Tagebücher von Joseph Goebbels*, commissioned by the Institute for Contemporary History, with support from the State Archive of Russia, ed. Elke Fröhlich, *Part II: Diktate 1941–1945*, 15 vols, Munich, 1993–6; vol. 8, p. 510 (entry for 22 June 1943). Alfred Rosenberg also complained in July 1943 about the lack of leadership, saying that there was "no government" or "war cabinet" but only "various cliques . . . groups of unworthy followers." Jürgen Matthäus and Frank Bajohr (eds), *Alfred Rosenberg: Die Tagebücher von 1934 bis 1944*, Frankfurt am Main, 2015, p. 481 (entry for 30 July 1943).

40 Herbert Backe to his wife, 27 April 1941; BA Koblenz, N 1075/25.

41 See testimony of Richard Walter Darré, vol. 1, p. 34. Darré said that Hitler had been obsessed with the idea of "having to take care of everything fate had given him to do on his own before his death . . . For that reason he succumbed to a kind of frenzy that of course took hold of his surroundings and his subordinates." IfZ München, ED 110, vol. 1.

42 Albert Speer, *Spandauer Tagebücher: Mit einem Vorwort von Joachim Fest*, Munich, 2002, p. 327 (entry for 20 Nov. 1952).

43 Sebastian Haffner, *Germany: Jekyll & Hyde. Deutschland von innen betrachtet*, Berlin, 1996, p. 31.

44 See also Peter Longerich, "Warum München? Wie Bayerns Metropole die 'Hauptstadt der Bewegung' wurde," in Winfried Nerdinger (ed.), *München und der Nationalsozialismus: Katalog des NS-Dokumentationszentrums München*, Munich, 2015, pp. 387–407.

45 See Mark Jones, *Am Anfang war Gewalt: Die deutsche Revolution 1918/19 und der Beginn der Weimarer Republik*, Berlin, 2017, pp. 340f.

46 See Wehler, *Deutsche Gesellschaftsgeschichte*, vol. 4, pp. 547ff.; idem, "Hitler als historische Figur," in idem, *Land ohne Unterschichten? Neue Essays zur deutschen Geschichte*, Munich, 2010, pp. 92–105 (at pp. 100–3).

47 See Harold James, *Krupp: Deutsche Legende und globales Unternehmen*, Munich, 2011, pp. 196–201; Christian Marx, *Paul Reusch und die Gutehoffnungshütte: Leitung eines deutschen Grossunternehmens*, Göttingen, 2013, pp. 196–201; Werner Plumpe, *Carl Duisberg 1861–1935: Anatomie eines Industriellen*, Munich, 2016, pp. 784–93.

48 Hans Frank's diary entry for 10 Feb. 1937; BA Koblenz, N 1110/2.

49 See Ian Kershaw, *The "Hitler Myth": Image and Reality in the Third Reich*, Oxford, 1987, pp. 48–82

50 Haffner, *Anmerkungen zu Hitler*, p. 47.

51 See Frank Bajohr, "Die Zustimmungsdiktatur: Grundzüge nationalsozialistischer Herrschaft in Hamburg," in idem and Joachim Szodrzynski (eds), *Hamburg in der NS-Zeit*, Hamburg, 1995, pp. 69–120. On the formation of a pro-Nazi consensus, see also Robert Gellately, *Backing Hitler: Consent and Coercion in Nazi Germany*, Oxford, 2001, pp. 15–16.

52 See Götz Aly, *Hitlers Volksstaat: Raub, Rassenkrieg und nationaler Sozialismus*, Frankfurt am Main, 2005, pp. 36, 51.

53 See Kershaw, *The Hitler Myth*, pp. 169–99.

54 See Hans Mommsen, "Die Rückkehr zu den Ursprüngen: Betrachtungen zur inneren Auflösung des Dritten Reiches nach der Niederlage von Stalingrad," in idem, *Von Weimar nach Auschwitz: Zur Geschichte Deutschlands in der Weltkriegsepoche*, Stuttgart, 1999, pp. 309–24.

55 Goebbels, *Tagebücher*, part II, vol. 15, p. 586 (entry for 24 March 1945).

56 See the summary report of the Reich propaganda offices on 21 March 1945: "Despite all the cursing and gloom, the vast majority of the population continues to be determined and prepared to do everything imaginable and bear all burdens, indeed to make great sacrifices." BA Berlin-Lichterfelde, R 55/601.

57 Speer, *Spandauer Tagebücher*, p. 632 (entry for 28 April 1965).

58   Cited in Sebastian Ullrich, *Der Weimar-Komplex: Das Scheitern der ersten deutschen Demokratie und die politische Kultur der frühen Bundesrepublik 1945–1959*, Göttingen, 2009, pp. 62f. See Jörg Später, *Vansittart: Britische Debatten über Deutsche und Nazis 1902–1945*, Göttingen, 2003.

59   See Ullrich, *Der Weimar-Komplex*, p. 77; Kathleen Burk, *Troublemaker: The Life and History of A. J. P. Taylor*, New Haven and London, 2000.

60   William L. Shirer, *The Rise and Fall of the Third Reich*, London, 1998, p. 82.

61   Friedrich Meinecke, *Die deutsche Katastrophe*, Wiesbaden, 1946, p. 89.

62   Golo Mann, *Deutsche Geschichte des 19. und 20. Jahrhunderts*, new edition, Frankfurt am Main, 1992, p. 812. A strange contrast was the esteem Golo Mann had for Albert Speer. Shortly before the latter's death in 1981, Mann wrote to him: "You may . . . consider your fate strange enough: having been part of this past world, and at the same time not having been a part of it, and today being the final one left and being enough in the present to bear witness to the past, with an authority you alone possess. We must be grateful to you that you do this and never tire of doing so." Golo Mann to Albert Speer, 27 July 1981; BA Koblenz, N 1340/37.

63   Golo Mann to Joachim Fest, 25 Nov. 1986; Golo Mann, *Briefe 1932–1992*, ed. Tilmann Lahme and Katrin Lüssi, Göttingen, 2006, p. 304.

64   Thomas Mann, *Tagebücher, 1937–1939*, ed. Peter de Mendelssohn, Frankfurt am Main, 1980, p. 119 (entry for 19 Oct. 1937).

65   Klaus von Dohnanyi, "Im Land der Verlorenen," in *Frankfurter Allgemeine Zeitung* no. 160, 14 July 1999, p. 53.

66   Eberhard Jäckel, *Das deutsche Jahrhundert: Eine historische Bilanz*, Stuttgart, 1996, p. 154. In conclusion Ralf Georg Reuth also describes Hitler as "the result of historical accident"; *Hitler: Eine Biographie*, Munich and Zurich, 2003, p. 642.

67   See Thomas Nipperdey's illuminating thoughts, "1933 und die Kontinuität der deutschen Geschichte," in *idem, Kann Geschichte objektiv sein? Historische Essays*, ed. Paul Nolte, Munich, 2013, pp. 253–78; Helmut Walser Smith, *Fluchtpunkt 1941: Kontinuitäten der deutschen Geschichte*, Stuttgart, 2010, in particular pp. 189ff.

68   Meinecke, *Die deutsche Katastrophe*, pp. 29f.

69   See the summary in Volker Ullrich, *Die nervöse Grossmacht: Aufstieg und Untergang des deutschen Kaiserreichs*, expanded new edition, Frankfurt am Main, 2013, pp. 383–97. On "If I were the Kaiser," see also Johannes Leicht, *Heinrich Class 1868–1953: Die politische Biographie eines Alldeutschen*, Paderborn, 2012, pp. 152–64.

70   See Ullrich, *Die nervöse Grossmacht*, pp. 485–92; Heinz Hagenlücke, *Deutsche Vaterlandspartei: Die nationale Rechte am Ende des Kaiserreichs*, Düsseldorf, 1997, pp. 143ff.

71   Cited in Uwe Lohalm, *Völkischer Radikalismus: Die Geschichte des Deutsch-Völkischen Schutz- und Trutzbundes 1919–1923*, Hamburg, 1970, p. 42.

72   Michael Epkenhans, "'Wir als deutsches Volk sind doch nicht kleinzukriegen . . .': Aus den Tagebüchern des Fregattenkapitäns Bogislav von Selchow 1918/19," in *Militärgeschichtliche Mitteilungen*, 55 (1996), pp. 199f.

73   Victor Klemperer, *Leben sammeln, nicht fragen wozu und warum: Tagebücher, 1918–1924*, ed. Walter Nowojski, Berlin, 1996, p. 183 (entry for 21 Sept. 1919).

74   Fritz Fischer, *Griff nach der Weltmacht: Die Kriegszielpolitik des kaiserlichen Deutschland 1914/18*, Düsseldorf, 1961, p. 111.

75   Egmont Zechlin, "Ludendorff im Jahre 1915: Unveröffentlichte Briefe," in *Historische Zeitschrift*, 211 (1970), p. 352.

76   Heinrich August Winkler, *Der lange Weg nach Westen*, vol. 1, Munich, 2000, p. 358.

77   See Sebastian Haffner, *Von Bismarck zu Hitler: Ein Rückblick*, Munich, 1987, p. 141.

78   Fritz Fischer, *Hitler war kein Betriebsunfall: Aufsätze*, Munich, 1992, pp. 174–81 (at p. 181).

79　Konrad Heiden, *Adolf Hitler: Ein Mann gegen Europa. Eine Biographie*, Zurich, 1937, p. 209.

80　Marianne von Weizsäcker to her mother, 17 March and 24 March 1939; BA Koblenz, N 1273/39.

81　See Ian Kershaw, *Making Friends with Hitler: Lord Londonderry, the Nazis, and the Road to War*, London, 2004; Volker Ullrich, "The Führer's Best Friends," in *ZeitGeschichte*, 3 (2013), pp. 56–61.

82　Churchill's radio broadcast of 22 June 1941, after the German invasion of the Soviet Union; Winston Churchill, *Never Give In! The Best of Winston Churchill's Speeches*, ed. Winston S. Churchill, London, 2003 p. 290.

83　See Haffner, *Anmerkungen zu Hitler*, pp. 138f.

84　Notes by Martin Bormann on the conversation between Hitler and Mussert on 10 Dec. 1942; BA Berlin-Lichterfelde, NS 6/161.

85　See Mark Mazower, *Hitler's Empire: Nazi Rule in Occupied Europe*, London, 2008, pp. 259ff.

86　Goebbels, *Tagebücher*, part I, vol. 8, p. 214 (entry for 9 July 1940).

87　Ibid., part II, vol. 6, p. 52 (entry for 2 Oct. 1942). Hitler also told Rosenberg that "the mission in the east is the challenge of the century." Rosenberg, *Die Tagebücher von 1934 bis 1944*, p. 400 (entry for 20 July 1941).

88　Karl Alexander von Müller to Theodor Schieder, 17 Sept. 1941; cited in Matthias Berg, *Karl Alexander von Müller: Historiker für den Nationalsozialismus*, Göttingen, 2014, p. 332.

89　Letter by Günther von Kluge, 3 Dec. 1942; BA-MA Freiburg, MSg 2/11185.

90　*Das Deutsche Reich und der Zweite Weltkrieg. Vol. 8: Die Ostfront 1943/44*, Munich, 2007, p. 1193 (Wegner's essay).

91　Goebbels, *Tagebücher*, part II, vol. 7, p. 454 (entry for 2 March 1943).

92　Ibid., vol. 12, p. 140 (entry for 18 April 1944).

93　See Walther Funk's statement to the court psychiatrist Leon Goldensohn on 12 May 1946; Goldensohn, *Die Nürnberger Interviews*, p. 158.

94　Speer, *Spandauer Tagebücher*, p. 35 (entry for 8 Nov. 1946). See also Hanskarl von Hasselbach's testimony on Hitler's "understanding of people" of 27 September 1945, in which he said that in the final phase of the war, Hitler had "talked himself, despite knowing better, into believing unshakably that he would ultimately be victorious." BA Koblenz, N 1128/33.

95　Goebbels, *Tagebücher*, part II, vol. 15, p. 371 (entry for 12 Feb. 1945).

96　Klaus Mann, *Auf verlorenem Posten*, p. 211.

97　Alan Bullock, *Hitler: A Study in Tyranny*, London, 1990, p. 805

98　Jacob Burckhardt, *Weltgeschichtliche Betrachtungen: Historisch-kritische Gesamtausgabe*, Pfullingen, 1949, p. 278.

99　Joachim Fest, *Hitler: Eine Biographie*, Frankfurt am Main, Berlin and Vienna, 1973, pp. 17, 22, 20.

100　Ian Kershaw, *Hitler 1889–1936: Hubris*, London, 2001, p. xxiv.

101　Konrad Heiden, *Adolf Hitler: Das Zeitalter der Verantwortungslosigkeit. Eine Biographie*, Zurich, 1936, p. 6.

102　Burckhardt, *Weltgeschichtliche Betrachtungen*, p. 278.

103　Handwritten statement by Helmuth Greiner, 31 March 1942; BA Koblenz, N 1033/13.

104　See Horst Möller's foreword to Henrik Eberle and Matthias Uhl (eds), *Das Buch Hitler*, Bergisch Gladbach, 2005, p. 6. On Stalin's rise to power and his relationship to violence, see Jörg Baberowski, *Verbrannte Erde: Stalins Herrschaft der Gewalt*, Munich, 2012, pp. 109ff., 131ff., 212ff. For an overview, see Alan Bullock, *Hitler and Stalin: Parallel Lives*, London, 1991.

105　Goebbels, *Tagebücher*, part I, vol. 7, p. 269 (entry for 13 Jan. 1940).

106　Ibid., part II, vol. 4, p. 355 (entry for 24 May 1942).

107　Ibid., vol. 10, pp. 178f. (entry for 27 Oct. 1943). See ibid., vol. 8, p. 233 (entry for 8 May 1943), vol. 11, pp. 162 (entry for 25 Jan. 1944), 403 (entry for 4 March 1944).

108   *Der Spiegel*, no. 3, 10 Jan. 1966, p. 42.
109   Klaus Mann to Thomas Mann, 16 May 1945; Tilmann Lahme, Holger Pils and Kerstin Klein (eds), *Die Briefe der Manns: Ein Familienporträt*, Frankfurt am Main, 2016, p. 314.
110   BA Berlin-Lichterfelde, NS 6/777.
111   Cited in Ernst Deuerlein, *Hitler: Eine politische Biographie*, Munich, 1969, p. 158.

Bibliography

1. Primary Sources

1.1 Unpublished Sources

Bundesarchiv (BA) Berlin-Lichterfelde

Bestand NS 6 (NSDAP party office) 1, 2, 17, 23, 24, 115, 116, 130, 135, 140, 142, 153, 156, 159, 161, 162, 166, 277, 289, 342, 343, 350, 353, 354, 414, 415, 518, 770, 772, 777, 785, 793; Bestand 10 (personal adjutancy of the Führer and Reich Chancellor) 11, 12, 14, 15, 17, 18, 19, 20, 37, 38, 591; Bestand NS 19 (personal staff of the Reichsführer SS) 650, 1205, 1880, 3872, 3899; Bestand NS 51 (office of the Führer/Bouhler's department) 28, 29, 39; Bestand R 43 (New Reich Chancellery) II/615c, 664a, 665, 957, 957a, 958, 615c, 985a, 985b, 985c, 986, 1641; Bestand R 55 (Propaganda Ministry) 570, 571, 572, 573, 574, 575, 601, 602, 603, 612

Bundesarchiv (BA) Koblenz

N 1110 (Nachlass Hans Frank) 2, 10, 18, 50; N 1122 (Nachlass Karl Haushofer) 15; N 1033 (Nachlass Helmuth Greiner) 2, 13, 20, 21, 24; N 1075 (Nachlass Herbert Backe) 25, 26, 27; N 1094 (Nachlass Walter Darré) I/23, 24, 28, II/9b; N 1128 (Nachlass Adolf Hitler) 33; N 1241 (Nachlass Wilhelm Frick) 3, 4; N 1273 (Nachlass Ernst von Weizsäcker) 29, 30, 32, 42, 47, 48, 49, 50; N 1276 (Nachlass Lutz Graf Schwerin von Krosigk) 40, 45, 113; N 1292 (Nachlass Wilhelm Stuckart) 6; N 1310 (Nachlass Konstantin Freiherr von Neurath) 74; N 1318 (Nachlass Rudolf Wolters) 21, 23; N 1322 (Nachlass Fritz Hesse) 2, 4; N 1340 (Nachlass Albert Speer) 9, 14, 21, 24, 27, 28, 30, 37, 58, 60, 64, 70, 75, 76, 84, 133, 183, 219, 288, 291, 384, 518, 596; N 1348 (Nachlass Theodor Morell) 1, 2, 3, 4, 5, 6, 8; N 1720 (Nachlass Fritz Wiedemann) 4; N 1582 (Nachlass Fritz Sauckel) 3, 4, 5

Bundesarchiv-Militärarchiv (BA-MA) Freiburg

N 19 (Nachlass Maximilian Freiherr von und zu Weichs) 10, 15; N 24 (Nachlass Friedrich Hossbach) 6, 13, 14, 15, 16, 17, 18, 19, 38, 39; N 51 (Nachlass Erich Hoepner) 2, 3, 9; N 54 (Nachlass Wilhelm Keitel) 12, 46; N 60 (Nachlass Ferdinand Schörner) 17; N 63 (Nachlass Kurt Zeitzler) 15, 19, 79, 80, 83; N 69 (Nachlass Alfred Jodl) 3, 10, 18, 22, 27, 47, 48, 50; N 117 (Nachlass Erwin Rommel) 1, 2, 3, 4, 29, 32, 72, 73, 74, 75, 76, 77, 78, 79; N 118 (Nachlass Gerhard Engel) 5; N 220 (Nachlass Franz Halder) 72, 88, 124; N 245 (Nachlass Hans Georg Reinhardt) 2, 3, 21; N 265 (Nachlass Gotthard Heinrici) 35, 108, 117, 118; N 354 (Nachlass Ewald von Kleist) 21, 22; N 372 (Nachlass Friedrich Paulus) 9, 19, 20, 21, 22, 35; N 507 (Nachlass Erich von Manstein) 113, 121; N 647 (Nachlass Hermann Balck) 7, 8, 9, 10, 11, 12, 13; MSg 2/11185 (extracts from letters by Günther von Kluge); MSg 2/12583 (extracts from letters by Gerd von Rundstedt)

Institut für Zeitgeschichte (IfZ) Munich

Bestand ED 100 (David Irving collecton) Bd. 33 (letters of Alwin Broder Albrecht, 1941–1945), Bd. 63/64 (Hasso von Etzdorf's file notes), Bd. 70/71 (reports by Erwin Giesing about the medicical treatment of Hitler, 1944), Bd. 76 (pocket calendar and letters of Helmuth Greiner, 1941–1943), Bd. 77 (letters of Heinz Guderian, June to December 1941), Bd. 78 (diary of Walther Hewel), Bd. 79 (personal papers of Walther Hewel), Bd. 203 (notes by Julius Schaub); 110 (notes by Richard Walter Darré, 1945–1948); 180/5 (appointment diary of Hermann Göring); 524 (correspondence between Christa Schroeder and Johanna Nusser, 1939–1942)

Bestand MS 2049 (Heinrich Hoffmann's report, 1947)

Bestand F 19/4 (appointment diary of Heinz Linge März, 1943–Februar 1945; 123 (Theodor Morell collection)

Bestand ZS 7 (Nicolaus von Below), 10 (Karl Bodenschatz), 18 (Charlotte von Brauchitsch), 19 (Walther von Brauchitsch), 38 (Bernd Freytag von Loringhoven), 57 (Heinz Guderian), 66 (Gotthard Heinrici), 69 (Adolf Heusinger), 145 (Lutz Graf Schwerin von Krosigk), 194 (Anni Winter), 208 (Günther Blumentritt), 209 (Ernst Wilhelm Bohle), 222 (Gerhard Engel), 238 (Helmuth Greiner), 239 (Heinz von Gyldenfeldt), 240 (Franz Halder), 242 (Hanskarl von Hasselbach), 243 (Heinrich Heim), 262 (Alfred Leitgen), 266 (Heinz Lorenz), 285 (Karl-Jesko von Puttkamer), 312 (Walter Warlimont), 322 (Hasso von Etzdorf), 627 (Wilhelm Ulex), 652 (Friedrich Paulus), 638 (Hans Baur), 678 (Alfred Jodl), 917 (Fritz Hesse), 1786 (Hans Erich Voss), 2015 (Heinz Assmann), 2089 (Ernst Schulte-Strathaus), 2093 (Inga Haag), 2235 (Traudl Junge), 2238 (Henriette von Schirach), 2240 (Christa Schroeder), 2242 (Winifred Wagner), 2250 (Max Wünsche), 2260 (Walter Frentz), 3095 (Hans-Georg Eismann)

Bayerisches Hauptstaatsarchiv (BayHStA) Munich

Nachlass Rudolf Buttmann 89

Schweizerisches Bundesarchiv (BA) Bern

Nachlass Rudolf Hess, Bestand J1. 211: 1989/148 (private correspondence of Rudolf Hess), Bd. 41, 45, 63, 67; 1993/300 (private correspondence of the Hess family), Bd. 6.

1.2 Published Sources

Akten zur deutschen Auswärtigen Politik 1918–1945 (ADAP), Series D: 1937–1941, vols 5–13, Frankfurt am Main, 1956–1970

Bajohr, Frank and Christoph Strupp (eds), *Fremde Blicke auf das "Dritte Reich": Berichte ausländischer Diplomaten über Herrschaft und Gesellschaft in Deutschland 1933–1945*, Göttingen, 2011

Boberach, Heinz (ed.), *Meldungen aus dem Reich: Die geheimen Lageberichte des Sicherheitsdienstes der SS*, 18 vols, Herrsching 1984

Boelcke, Willi A. (ed.), *Deutschlands Rüstung im Zweiten Weltkrieg: Hitlers Konferenzen mit Albert Speer 1942–1945*, Frankfurt am Main, 1969

Breloer, Heinrich (with Rainer Zimmer), *Die Akte Speer: Spuren eines Kriegsverbrechers*, Berlin, 2006

Christoforow, Wassili S., Wladimir G. Makarow and Matthias Uhl (eds), *Verhört: Die Befragungen deutscher Generale und Offiziere durch die sowjetischen Geheimdienste 1945–1952*, Berlin and Boston, 2015

Churchill, Winston, *Never Give In! The Best of Winston Churchill's Speeches*, ed. Winston S. Churchill, London, 2003

Das letzte halbe Jahr: Stimmungsberichte der Wehrmachtpropaganda 1944/45, ed. Wolfram Wette, Ricarda Brenner und Detlev Vogel, Essen, 2001

Der Prozess gegen die Hauptkriegsverbrecher vor dem Internationalen Militärtribunal in Nürnberg (IMT), 42 vols, Nuremberg, 1947–1949

Deutschland-Berichte der Sozialdemokratischen Partei Deutschlands (Sopade), ed. Klaus Behnken, vol. 6 (1939), vol. 7 (1940), Berlin, 1997

Die Verfolgung und Ermordung der europäischen Juden durch das nationalsozialistische Deutschland 1933–1945, vol. 3, ed. Andrea Löw, Munich, 2012; vol. 4, ed. Klaus-Peter Friedrich, Munich, 2013; vol. 7, ed. Bert Hoppe and Hildrun Glass, Munich, 2011; vol. 9, ed. Klaus-Peter Friedrich, Munich, 2014

Domarus, Max, *Hitler: Reden und Proklamationen. Vol. 2: Untergang. Part 1: 1939–1940. Part 2: 1941–1945*, Munich, 1965

Enzensberger, Hans Magnus (ed.), *Europa in Ruinen: Augenzeugenberichte aus den Jahren 1944–1948*, Frankfurt am Main, 2001

Gellhorn, Martha, *The Face of War*, London, 1998

Gillmann, Sabine and Hans Mommsen (eds), *Politische Schriften und Briefe Carl Friedrich Goerdelers*, 2 vols, Munich, 2003

Goldensohn, Leon, *Die Nürnberger Interviews: Gespräche mit Angeklagten und Zeugen*, Düsseldorf and Zürich, 2005

Gosztony, Peter (ed.), *Der Kampf um Berlin 1945 in Augenzeugenberichten*, Düsseldorf, 1970

Gruchmann, Lothar (ed.), *Autobiographie eines Attentäters: Johann Georg Elser. Aussage zum Sprengstoffattentat im Bürgerbräukeller in München am 8. November 1939*, Stuttgart, 1970

Haffner, Sebastian, *Schreiben für die Freiheit 1942–1949: Journalist im Sturm der Ereignisse*, Berlin, 2001

Hartmann, Christian, Thomas Vordermayer, Othmar Plöckinger and Roman Töppel (eds), *Hitler: Mein Kampf. Eine kritische Edition*, 2 vols, Munich and Berlin, 2016

Hartmann, Christian and Sergej Slutsch, "Franz Halder und die Kriegsvorbereitungen im Frühjahr 1939: Eine Ansprache des Generalstabschefs des Heeres," in *Vierteljahrshefte für Zeitgeschichte*, 45 (1997), pp. 467–95

Heiber, Helmut (ed.), *Hitlers Lagebesprechungen: Die Protokollfragmente seiner militärischen Konferenzen 1942–1945*, Stuttgart, 1962

Heinrich, Hans-Wilhelm, "Hitlers Ansprache vor Generalen und Offizieren am 26. 5. 1944," in *Militärgeschichtliche Mitteilungen*, 2 (1976), pp. 123–70

Hellbeck, Jochen, *Die Stalingrad-Protokolle: Sowjetische Augenzeugen berichten aus der Schlacht*, Frankfurt am Main, 2012

Hillgruber, Andreas (ed.), *Staatsmänner und Diplomaten bei Hitler: Aufzeichnungen über Unterredungen mit Vertretern des Auslandes. Vol 1: 1939–1941. Vol. 2: 1942–1944*, Frankfurt am Main, 1967/1970

Hitler, Adolf, *Monologe im Führerhauptquartier 1941–44: Die Aufzeichnungen Heinrich Heims*, ed. Werner Jochmann, Hamburg, 1980

Hofer, Walther, *Die Entfesselung des Zweiten Weltkriegs*, Frankfurt am Main, 1960

Hubatsch, Walther (ed.), *Hitlers Weisungen für die Kriegführung*, Munich, 1965

Hürter, Johannes and Matthias Uhl, "Hitler in Vinnica: Ein neues Dokument zur Krise im September 1942," in *Vierteljahrshefte für Zeitgeschichte*, 63 (2015), pp. 581–639

Jacobsen, Hans-Adolf (ed.), *Dokumente zur Vorgeschichte des Westfeldzuges 1939–1940*, Göttingen, 1956

Jacobsen, Hans-Adolf (ed.), *Karl Haushofer: Leben und Werk. Vol. 2: Ausgewählter Schriftwechsel 1917–1946*, Boppard am Rhein, 1979

Jacobsen, Hans-Adolf (ed.), *"Spiegelbild einer Verschwörung": Die Opposition gegen Hitler und der Staatsstreich vom 20. Juli in der SD-Berichterstattung*, 2 vols, Stuttgart, 1984

Kempner, Robert W., *Das Dritte Reich im Kreuzverhör: Aus den unveröffentlichten Vernehmungsprotokollen des Anklägers in den Nürnberger Prozessen*, Munich, 2005

Klee, Ernst, Willi Dressen and Volker Riess (eds), *"Schöne Zeiten": Judenmord aus der Sicht der Täter und Gaffer*, Frankfurt am Main, 1988

Klee, Karl (ed.), *Dokumente zum Unternehmen "Seelöwe": Die geplante deutsche Landung in England 1940*, Göttingen, 1959

Klein, Peter (ed.), *Die Einsatzgruppen in der besetzten Sowjetunion 1941/42*, Berlin, 1997

(Koeppen, Werner) *Herbst 1941 im "Führerhauptquartier": Berichte Werner Koeppens an seinen Minister Rosenberg*, ed. Martin Vogt, Koblenz, 2002

Kotze, Hildegard von and Helmut Krausnick (eds), *"Es spricht der Führer": 7 exemplarische Hitler-Reden*, Gütersloh, 1966

Kriegstagebuch des Oberkommandos der Wehrmacht (Wehrmachtführungsstab) (KTB OKW) 1940–1945, ed. Percy Ernst Schramm, vols 1–4, Munich, 1982

Krausnick, Helmut, "Denkschrift Himmlers über die Behandlung der Fremdvölkischen im Osten (Mai 1940)," in *Vierteljahrshefte für Zeitgeschichte*, 5 (1957), pp. 194–8

Kulka, Otto Dov and Eberhard Jäckel (eds), *Die Juden in den geheimen NS-Stimmungsberichten 1939–1945*, Düsseldorf, 2004

Lehnstaedt, Stephan and Jochen Böhler, *Die Berichte der Einsatzgruppen aus Polen 1939: Vollständige Edition*, Berlin, 2013

Longerich, Peter (ed.) *Die Ermordung der europäischen Juden: Eine umfassende Dokumentation des Holocaust 1941–1945*, Munich, 1989

Mallmann, Klaus-Michael, Jochen Böhler and Jürgen Matthäus (eds), *Einsatzgruppen in Polen: Darstellung und Dokumentation*, Darmstadt, 2008

Mallmann, Klaus-Michael, Andrej Angrick, Jürgen Matthäus and Martin Cüppers (eds), *Dokumente der Einsatzgruppen in der Sowjetunion*, vols 1–2, Darmstadt, 2011–2014

Mann, Klaus, *Auf verlorenem Posten: Aufsätze, Reden, Kritiken 1942–1949*, ed. Uwe Naumann and Michael Töteberg, Reinbek bei Hamburg, 1994

Mann, Thomas, *An die gesittete Welt: Politische Schriften und Reden im Exil*, Frankfurt am Main, 1986

Manoschek, Walter (ed.): *"Es gibt nur eines für das Judentum: Vernichtung": Das Judenbild in deutschen Soldatenbriefen 1939–1944*, Hamburg, 1995

Neitzel, Sönke (ed.), *Abgehört: Deutsche Generäle in britischer Gefangenschaft 1942–1945*, Berlin, 2005

Picker, Henry, *Hitlers Tischgespräche im Führerhauptquartier*, 3rd revised edition, Stuttgart, 1976

Pölking, Hermann, *Wer war Hitler? Ansichten und Berichte von Zeitgenossen*, Berlin-Brandenburg, 2017

Sandner, Harald, *Hitler: Das Itinerar. Aufenthaltsorte und Reisen von 1889 bis 1945*, vols 3–4, Berlin, 2016

Schwendemann, Heinrich, " 'Drastische Massnahmen zur Verteidigung des Reiches an der Oder und am Rhein . . .': Eine vergessene Denkschrift Albert Speers vom 18. März 1945," in *Studia Historica Slavo-Germanica*, T. XXV (2003), pp. 179–98

Shirer, William L., *This is Berlin: Reporting from Nazi Germany 1938–40*, London, 1999

Wagner, Gerhard (ed.), *Lagevorträge des Oberbefehlshabers der Kriegsmarine vor Hitler 1939–1945*, Munich, 1972

Weinberg, Gerhard L., "Adolf Hitler und der NS-Führungsoffizier (NSFO): Dokumentation," in *Vierteljahrshefte für Zeitgeschichte*, 12 (1964), pp. 443–56

2. Diaries, Letters, Memoirs

Andreas-Friedrich, Ruth, *Der Schattenmann: Tagebuchaufzeichnungen 1938–1945*, Frankfurt am Main, 1983

Anonyma, *Eine Frau in Berlin: Tagebuchaufzeichnungen vom 20. April bis 22. Juni 1945*, Frankfurt am Main, 2003

Arendt, Hannah, *Besuch in Deutschland*, Berlin, 1993

Baur, Hans, *Ich flog Mächtige dieser Erde*, Kempten im Allgäu, 1956

Below, Nicolaus von, *Als Hitlers Adjutant 1937–45*, Mainz, 1980

Besymenski, Lew, *Die letzten Notizen von Martin Bormann: Ein Dokument und sein Verfasser*, Stuttgart, 1974

Böll, Heinrich, *Briefe aus dem Krieg 1939–1945*, ed. Jochen Schubert, Cologne, 2001

Boldt, Gerhard, *Hitler: Die letzten Tage in der Reichskanzlei*, Munich, 1976

Bourke-White, Margaret, *Deutschland—April 1945: "Dear Fatherland Rest Quietly,"* Munich, 1979

Breker, Arno, *Im Strahlungsfeld der Ereignisse: Leben und Wirken eines Künstlers. Porträts, Begegnungen, Schicksale*, Preussisch Oldendorf, 1972

Breloer, Heinrich, *Mein Tagebuch: Geschichten vom Überleben 1939–1947*, Cologne, 1984

Brückner, Peter, *Das Abseits als sicherer Ort: Kindheit und Jugend zwischen 1933 und 1945*, Berlin, 1980

Buchbender, Ortwin and Reinhold Sterz, *Das andere Gesicht: Deutsche Feldpostbriefe 1939–1945*, Munich, 1983

Burckhardt, Carl J. *Meine Danziger Mission 1937–1939*, 3rd revised edition, Munich, 1980

Bock, Fedor von, *Zwischen Pflicht und Verweigerung: Das Kriegstagebuch*, ed. Klaus Gerbet, Munich, 1995

Ciano, Galeazzo, *Tagebücher 1939–1943*, Bern, 1946

Cohn, Willy, *Kein Recht, nirgends: Tagebuch vom Untergang des Breslauer Judentums 1933–1941*, 2 vols, ed. Norbert Conrads, Cologne, Weimar and Vienna, 2006

Coulondre, Robert, *Von Moskau nach Berlin 1936–1939: Erinnerungen des französischen Botschafters*, Bonn, 1950

(Czerniakow, Adam) *Im Warschauer Ghetto: Das Tagebuch des Adam Czerniakow 1939–1942*, Munich, 1986

Dahlerus, Birger, *Der letzte Versuch: London–Berlin, Sommer 1939*, Munich, 1973

Das Hitler-Bild: Die Erinnerungen des Fotografen Heinrich Hoffmann, ed. Joe J. Heydecker, St Pölten-Salzburg, 2008

Dietrich, Otto, *Auf den Strassen des Sieges: Erlebnisse mit dem Führer in Polen*, Munich, 1940

Dietrich, Otto, *Zwölf Jahre mit Hitler*, Munich, 1955

Dönitz, Karl, *Zehn Jahre und zwanzig Tage*, Frankfurt am Main, 1967

Eberle, Henrik and Matthias Uhl (eds), *Das Buch Hitler: Geheimdossier des NKWD für Josef W. Stalin aufgrund der Verhörprotokolle des Persönlichen Adjutanten Hitlers, Otto Günsche, und des Kammerdieners Heinz Linge, Moskau 1946/49*, Bergisch Gladbach, 2005

Eberle, Henrik (ed.), *Briefe an Hitler: Ein Volk schreibt seinem Führer. Unbekannte Dokumente aus Moskauer Archiven—zum erstenmal veröffentlicht*, Bergisch Gladbach, 2007

Ebert, Jens (ed.) *Feldpostbriefe aus Stalingrad*, Göttingen, 2003

(Engel, Gerhard) *Heeresadjutant bei Hitler 1938–1943: Aufzeichnungen des Majors Engel*, ed. Hildegard von Kotze, Stuttgart, 1974

Feuersenger, Marianne, *Im Vorzimmer der Macht: Aufzeichnungen aus dem Wehrmachtführungsstab und Führerhauptquartier 1940–1945*, 4th edition, Munich, 2001

Fischer, Karl, *Ich fuhr Stauffenberg: Einnerungen an die Kriegsjahre 1939–1945*, ed. Ursula and Ulrich Fischer, Angermünde, 2008

Frank, Hans, *Im Angesicht des Galgens: Deutung Hitlers und seiner Zeit auf Grund eigener Erlebnisse und Erkenntnisse*, Munich-Gräfelding, 1953

Freytag von Loringhoven, Bernd, *Mit Hitler im Bunker: Die letzten Monate im Führerhauptquarter Juli 1944–April 1945*, Berlin, 2006

Friessner, Hans, *Verratene Schlachten: Die Tragödie der deutschen Wehrmacht in Rumänien und Ungarn*, Hamburg, 1956

Gersdorff, Rudolf-Christoph Freiherr von, *Soldat im Untergang*, Frankfurt am Main, Berlin and Vienna, 1977

Giesler, Hermann, *Ein anderer Hitler: Berichte, Gespräche, Reflexionen*, Leoni, 1977

Gilbert, Gustave M., *Nürnberger Tagebuch*, Frankfurt am Main, 1962

(Goebbels, Joseph) *Die Tagebücher von Joseph Goebbels*, commissioned by the Institute for Contemporary History with support from the State Archive of Russia, ed. Elke Fröhlich, *Part 1: Aufzeichnungen 1923–1941*, vols 6–9, Munich, 1998; *Part 2: Diktate 1941–1945*, vols 1–15, Munich, 1993–1998

Gorodetsky, Gabriel (ed.), *Die Maiski-Tagebücher: Ein Diplomat im Kampf gegen Hitler*, Munich, 2016

Groscurth, Helmuth, *Tagebücher eines Abwehroffiziers 1938–1940*, ed. Helmut Krausnick and Harold C. Deutsch with Hildegard von Kotze, Stuttgart, 1970

Guderian, Heinz, *Erinnerungen eines Soldaten*, Heidelberg, 1951

Halder, Franz, *Hitler als Feldherr*, Munich, 1949

Halder, Franz, *Kriegstagebuch: Tägliche Aufzeichnungen des Chefs des Generalstabs*, ed. Hans-Adolf Jacobsen, 3 vols, Stuttgart, 1962–64

Hartlaub, Felix, *Im Sperrkreis: Aufzeichnungen aus dem Zweiten Weltkrieg*, ed. Geno Hartlaub, Reinbek bei Hamburg, 1955

Hassell, Ulrich von, *Vom andern Deutschland: Aus den nachgelassenen Tagebüchern 1938–1944*, Frankfurt am Main, 1964

Henderson, Nevile, *Failure of a Mission*, London, 1940

Heusinger, Adolf, *Befehl im Widerstreit: Schicksalsstunden der deutschen Armee 1923–1945*, Tübingen and Stuttgart, 1950

Hilger, Gustav, *Wir und der Kreml: Deutsch-sowjetische Beziehungen 1918–1941*, Frankfurt am Main, 1959

Hill, Leonidas (ed.), *Die Weizsäcker-Papiere 1933–1950*, Frankfurt am Main, Berlin and Vienna, 1974

(Himmler, Heinrich) *Der Dienstkalender Heinrich Himmlers 1941/42*, ed. Peter Witte, Michael Wildt, Martina Vogt, Dieter Pohl, Peter Klein, Christian Gerlach, Christoph Dieckmann und Andrej Angrick, Hamburg, 1999

(Himmler, Heinrich) *Heinrich Himmlers Taschenkalender 1940. Kommentierte Edition*, ed. Markus Moors and Moritz Pfeiffer, Paderborn, 2013

Himmler, Katrin and Michael Wildt (eds), *Himmler privat: Briefe eines Massenmörders*, Munich, 2014

Höss, Rudolf, *Kommandant in Auschwitz: Autobiographische Aufzeichnungen*, 4th edition, Munich, 1978

Hoffmann, Heinrich, *Hitler wie ich ihn sah: Aufzeichnungen seines Leibfotografen*, Munich and Berlin, 1974

Hosenfeld, Wilm, *"Ich versuche jeden zu retten": Das Leben eines deutschen Offiziers in Briefen und Tagebüchern*, ed. Thomas Vogel, Munich, 2004

Hürter, Johannes, *Ein deutscher General an der Ostfront: Die Briefe und Tagebücher des Gotthard Heinrici 1941/42*, Erfurt, 2001

Jordan, Rudolf, *Erlebt und erlitten: Weg eines Gauleiters von Munich nach Moskau*, Leoni, 1971

Junge, Traudl (with Melissa Müller), *Bis zur letzten Stunde: Hitlers Sekretärin erzählt ihr Leben*, Munich, 2002

Kästner, Erich, *Notabene 45: Ein Tagebuch*, Munich, 1993

Kardorff, Ursula von, *Berliner Aufzeichnungen 1942–1945*, new edition, ed. Peter Hartl, Munich, 1992

Keitel, Wilhelm, *Verbrecher oder Offizier? Erinnerungen, Briefe, Dokumente des Chefs des OKW*, ed. Walter Görlitz, Berlin and Frankfurt am Main, 1961

Kehrl, Hans, *Krisenmanager im Dritten Reich: 6 Jahre Frieden—6 Jahre Krieg. Erinnerungen*, 2nd edition, Düsseldorf, 1973

Kellner, Friedrich, *"Vernebelt, verdunkelt sind alle Hirne": Tagebücher 1939–1945*, 2 vols, ed. Sacha Feuchert, Robert Martin Scott Kellner, Erwin Leibfried, Jörg Riecke und Markus Roth, Götttingen, 2011

Kempowski, Walter, *Das Echolot: Barbarossa 41. Ein kollektives Tagebuch*, Munich, 2002

Kesselring, Albert, *Soldat bis zum letzten Tag*, Bonn, 1953

Klemperer, Victor, *Ich will Zeugnis ablegen bis zum letzten: Tagebücher 1939–1945*, 2 vols, ed. Walter Nowojski with Hadwig Klemperer, Berlin, 1995

Klemperer, Victor, *Leben sammeln, nicht fragen wozu und warum: Tagebücher 1918–1924*, ed. Walter Nowojski with Christian Löser, Berlin, 1996

Klemperer, Victor, *Warum soll man nicht auf bessere Zeiten hoffen? Ein Leben in Briefen*, ed. Walter Nowojski und Nele Holdack with Christian Löser, Berlin, 2017

Koller, Karl, *Der letzte Monat: 14. April bis 27. Mai 1945. Tagebuchaufzeichnungen des ehemaligen Chefs des Generalstabs der deutschen Luftwaffe*, Mannheim, 1949

Krause, Karl, *Zehn Jahre Kammerdiener bei Hitler*, Hamburg, 1949

Kuby, Erich, *Mein Krieg: Aufzeichnungen 1939–1944*, Munich, 1989

Lahme, Tilmann, Holger Pils and Kerstin Klein (eds), *Die Briefe der Manns: Ein Familienporträt*, Frankfurt am Main, 2016

Leeb, Wilhelm Ritter von, *Tagebuchaufzeichnungen und Lagebeurteilungen aus zwei Weltkriegen*, ed. Georg Meyer, Stuttgart, 1976

Lossberg, Bernhard von, *Im Wehrmachtführungsstab: Bericht eines Generalstabsoffiziers*, Hamburg, 1950

Linge, Heinz, *Bis zum Untergang: Als Chef des Persönlichen Dienstes bei Hitler*, Munich, 1982

Mann, Golo, *Briefe 1932–1992*, ed. Tilmann Lahme and Katrin Lüssi, Göttingen, 2006

Mann, Klaus, *Der Wendepunkt: Ein Lebensbericht*, Frankfurt am Main, 1963

Mann, Thomas, *Tagebücher 1937–1939*, ed. Peter de Mendelssohn, Frankfurt am Main, 1980

Mann, Thomas, *Tagebücher 1940–1943*, ed. Peter de Mendelssohn, Frankfurt am Main, 1982

Mann, Thomas, *Tagebücher 1944–1. 4. 1946*, ed. Inge Jens, Frankfurt am Main, 1986

Manstein, Erich, *Verlorene Siege*, Bonn, 1955

Meinecke, Friedrich, *Werke. Vol. 6: Ausgewählter Briefwechsel*, Stuttgart, 1982

Misch, Rochus, *Der letzte Zeuge: "Ich war Hitlers Telefonist, Kurier und Leibwächter,"* Zurich and Munich, 2008

Moltke, Helmuth James von, *Briefe an Freya 1939–1945*, ed. Beate Ruhm von Oppen, Munich, 1988

Muehlon, Wilhelm, *Tagebuch der Kriegsjahre 1940–1944*, ed. Jens Heisterkamp, Dornach, 1992

Nissen, Margret, *Sind Sie die Tochter von Speer?*, Munich, 2005

Obenaus, Herbert und Sibylle (eds), *"Schreiben wie es wirklich war": Aufzeichnungen Karl Dürkefäldens aus den Jahren 1933–1945*, Hannover, 1985

Oven, Wilfred von, *Finale furioso: Mit Goebbels bis zum Ende*, Tübingen, 1974

Papen, Franz von, *Der Wahrheit eine Gasse*, Munich, 1952

Präg, Werner and Wolfgang Jacobmeyer (ed.), *Das Diensttagebuch des deutschen Generalgouverneurs in Polen 1939–1945*, Stuttgart, 1975

Raeder, Erich, *Mein Leben. Vol. 2: Von 1935 bis Spandau 1955*, Tübingen, 1957

Reitsch, Hanna, *Fliegen: Mein Leben*, Stuttgart, 1951

Rosenberg, Alfred, *Die Tagebücher 1934–1944*, ed. Jürgen Matthäus and Frank Bajohr, Frankfurt am Main, 2015

Ribbentrop, Joachim von, *Zwischen London und Moskau: Erinnerungen und letzte Aufzeichnungen*, ed. Annelies von Ribbentrop, Leoni, 1961

Ruge, Friedrich, *Rommel und die Invasion: Erinnerungen*, Stuttgart, 1959

Schellenberg, Walter, *Aufzeichnungen: Die Memoiren des letzten Geheimdienstchefs unter Hitler*, Munich, 1979

Schirach, Baldur von, *Ich glaubte an Hitler*, Hamburg, 1967

Schirach, Henriette von, *Der Preis der Herrlichkeit: Erlebte Zeitgeschichte*, Munich and Berlin, 1975

Schlabrendorff, Fabian von, *Offiziere gegen Hitler*, revised edition, ed. Walter Bussmann, Berlin, 1984

Schmidt, Paul, *Statist auf diplomatischer Bühne 1923–45*, Bonn, 1950

Scholl, Sophie and Fritz Hartnagel, *Damit wir uns nicht verlieren: Briefwechsel 1937–1943*, ed. Thomas Hartnagel, Frankfurt am Main, 2005

Schroeder, Christa, *Er war mein Chef: Aus dem Nachlass der Sekretärin von Adolf Hitler*, 3rd edition, ed. Anton Joachimsthaler, Munich and Vienna, 1985

Schwerin von Krosigk, Lutz Graf, *Es geschah in Deutschland: Menschenbilder unseres Jahrhunderts*, Tübingen and Stuttgart, 1951

(Seydlitz, Walther) Diedrich, Torsten and Jens Ebert (ed.), *Nach Stalingrad: Walther von Seydlitz" Feldpostbriefe und Kriegsgefangenenpost 1939–1955*, Göttingen, 2018

Shirer, William L., *Berlin Diary 1934–1941: The Rise of the Third Reich*, London, 1997

Shirer, William L., *Berliner Tagebuch: Das Ende 1944–1946*, ed. Jürgen Schebera, Leipzig, 1994

Smith, Howard K., *Feind schreibt mit: Ein amerikanischer Korespondent erlebt Nazi-Deutschland*, Berlin, 1982

Speer, Albert, *Erinnerungen. Mit einem Essay von Jochen Thies*, Frankfurt am Main and Berlin, 1993

Speer, Albert, *Spandauer Tagebücher: Mit einem Vorwort von Joachim Fest*, Munich, 2002

Speer, Albert, *"Alles was ich weiss": Aus unbekannten Geheimdienstprotokollen vom Sommer 1945*, ed. Ulrich Schlie, Munich, 1999

Speidel, Hans, *Invasion 1944: Ein Beitrag zu Rommels und des Reiches Schicksal*, Tübingen and Stuttgart, 1949

Springer, Hildegard, *Es sprach Hans Fritzsche: Nach Gesprächen, Briefen und Dokumenten*, Stuttgart, 1949

Stieff, Hellmuth, *Briefe*, ed. Horst Mühleisen, Berlin, 1991

Sündermann, Helmut, *Deutsche Notizen 1945–65*, Leoni 1966

Sündermann, Helmut, *Hier stehe ich . . . Deutsche Erinnerungen 1914–45*, Leoni, 1975

Suner, Ramon Serrano, *Zwischen Hendaye und Gibraltar*, Zurich, 1948

Trevor-Roper, Hugh R. (ed.), *The Bormann Letters*, London, 1954

Vormann, Nikolaus von, *So begann der Zweite Weltkrieg: Zeitzeuge der Entscheidungen. Als Offizier bei Hitler 22. 8. 1939–1. 10. 1939*, Leoni, 1988

Wagner, Eduard, *Der Generalquartiermeister: Briefe und Tagebuchaufzeichnungen*, ed. Elisabeth Wagner, Munich and Vienna, 1963

Wahl, Karl, *". . . es ist ein deutsches Herz": Erlebnisse und Erkenntnisse eines ehemaligen Gauleiters*, Augsburg, 1954

Walb, Lore: *Ich, die Alte—ich, die Junge: Konfrontation mit meinen Tagebüchern 1933–1945*, Berlin, 1997

Warlimont, Walter, *Im Hauptquartier der deutschen Wehrmacht 1939–1945: Grundlagen— Formen—Gestalten*, Frankfurt am Main and Bonn, 1964

"'. . . warum dann überhaupt noch leben!': Hitlers Lagebesprechungen am 23., 25. und 27. April 1945," in *Der Spiegel*, no 3, 10 Jan. 1966, pp. 32–46

Weizsäcker, Ernst von, *Erinnerungen*, Munich, 1950

Wolff-Mönckeberg, Mathilde, *Briefe, die sie nie erreichten: Briefe einer Mutter an ihre fernen Kinder in den Jahren 1940–1946*, Hamburg, 1980

3. Secondary Sources

Aly, Götz, *"Endlösung": Völkerverschiebung und der Mord an den europäischen Juden*, Frankfurt am Main, 1995

Aly, Götz, *Hitlers Volksstaat: Raub, Rassenkrieg und nationaler Sozialismus*, Frankfurt am Main, 2005

Aly, Götz (ed.), *Volkes Stimme: Skepsis und Führervertrauen im Nationalsozialismus*, Frankfurt am Main, 2006

Aly, Götz, *Die Belasteten: "Euthanasie" 1939–1945. Eine Gesellschaftsgeschichte*, Frankfurt am Main, 2013

Aly, Götz, *Europa gegen die Juden 1880–1945*, Frankfurt am Main, 2017

Angrick, Andrej, *Besatzungspolitik und Massenmord: Die Einsatzgruppe D in der südlichen Sowjet- union 1941–1943*, Hamburg, 2003

Arad, Yitzak, *Belzec, Sobibor, Treblinka: The Operation Reinhard Death Camp*, Bloomington, Indiana, 1999

Arendes, Cord, Edgar Wolfrum and Jörg Zedler (eds), *Terror nach innen: Verbrechen am Ende des Zweiten Weltkriegs*, Göttingen, 2006

Arnold, Dietmar, *Neue Reichskanzlei und "Führerbunker": Legenden und Wirklichkeit*, Berlin, 2005

Aurich, Rolf, *Kalanag: Die kontrollierten Illusionen des Helmut Schreiber*, Berlin, 2016

Baberowski, Jörg, *Verbrannte Erde: Stalins Herrschaft der Gewalt*, Munich, 2012

Bajohr, Frank, *"Arisierung" in Hamburg: Die Verdrängung der jüdischen Unternehmer 1933–1945*, Hamburg, 1997

Bajohr, Frank and Joachim Szodrzynski (eds), *Hamburg in der NS-Zeit*, Hamburg, 1995

Bajohr, Frank, *Parvenüs und Profiteure: Korruption in der NS-Zeit*, Frankfurt am Main, 2001

Bajohr, Frank and Dieter Pohl, *Der Holocaust als offenes Geheimnis: Die Deutschen, die NS-Führung und die Alliierten*, Munich, 2006

Bajohr, Frank and Andrea Löw (eds), *Der Holocaust: Ergebnisse und neue Fragen der Forschung*, Frankfurt am Main, 2015

Bankier, David, *Die öffentliche Meinung im NS-Staat: Die "Endlösung" und die Deutschen. Eine Berichtigung*, Berlin, 1995

Baumgart, Winfried, "Zur Ansprache Hitlers vor den Führern der Wehrmacht am 22. August 1939: Eine quellenkritische Untersuchung," in *Vierteljahrshefte für Zeitgeschichte*, 16 (1968), pp. 120–49

Beevor, Antony, *Stalingrad*, London, 1998

Beevor, Antony, *Berlin: The Downfall 1945*, London, 2002

Beierl, Florian, *Hitlers Berg: Licht ins Dunkel der Geschichte. Geschichte des Obersalzbergs und seiner geheimen Bunkeranlagen*, Berchtesgaden, 2004

Benz, Wolfgang (ed.), *Dimensionen des Völkermords: Die Zahl der jüdischen Opfer des Nationalsozialismus*, Munich, 1991

Benz, Wolfgang, *Der Holocaust*, Munich, 1995

Benz, Wolfgang, "Judenvernichtung aus Notwehr? Die Legenden um Theodore N. Kaufman," in *Vierteljahrshefte für Zeitgeschichte*, 29 (1981), pp. 615–30

Berg, Matthias, *Karl Alexander von Müller: Historiker für den Nationalsozialismus*, Göttingen, 2014

Berger, Sara, *Experten der Vernichtung: Das T4-Reinhardt-Netzwerk in den Lagern Belzec, Sobibor, Treblinka*, Hamburg, 2013

Beuys, Barbara, *Sophie Scholl: Biographie*, Munich, 2010

Besymenski, Lew A., "Wjatschelaw Molotows Berlin-Besuch vom November 1940 im Licht neuer Dokumente," in Pietrow-Ennker (ed.), *Präventivkrieg?*, pp. 118–32

Biddiscombe, Perry, *Werwolf! The History of the National Socialist Guerilla Movement, 1944–1946*, Cardiff, 1998

Blatman, Daniel, *Die Todesmärsche 1944/45: Das letzte Kapitel des nationalsozialistischen Massenmords*, Reinbek bei Hamburg, 2011

Böhler, Jochen, *Auftakt zum Vernichtungskrieg: Die Wehrmacht in Polen*, Frankfurt am Main, 2006

Böhm, Hermann, "Zur Ansprache Hitlers vor den Führern der Wehrmacht am 22. August 1939," in *Vierteljahrshefte für Zeitgeschichte*, 19 (1971), pp. 294–500

Boog, Horst, "Der angloamerikanische strategische Luftkrieg über Europa und die deutsche Luftverteidigung," in *Das Deutsche Reich und der Zweite Weltkrieg*, vol. 6, Stuttgart, 1990, pp. 429–565

Boog, Horst, "Strategischer Luftkrieg in Europa und Reichsluftverteidigung 1943–1944," in *Das Deutsche Reich und der Zweite Weltkrieg*, vol. 7, Stuttgart and Munich, 2001, pp. 3–415

Borodziej, Wlodzimierz, *Der Warschauer Aufstand 1944*, Frankfurt am Main, 2001

Brauchitsch, Boris von, *Der Schatten des Führers: Der Fotograf Walter Frentz zwischen Avantgarde und Obersalzberg*, Berlin, 2017

Brechtken, Magnus, *"Madagaskar für die Juden": Antisemitische Idee und politische Praxis 1805–1945*, Munich, 1998

Brechtken, Magnus, *Albert Speer: Eine deutsche Karriere*, Munich, 2017

Brewing, Daniel, *Im Schatten von Auschwitz: Deutsche Massaker an polnischen Zivilisten 1939–1945*, Darmstadt, 2016

Broszat, Martin, *Nationalsozialistische Polenpolitik 1939–1945*, Frankfurt am Main, 1965

Browning, Christopher, *Ordinary Men: Reserve Police Battalion 101 and the Final Solution in Poland*, revised edition, London, 2017

Browning, Christopher, *The Origins of the Final Solution: The Evolution of Nazi Jewish Policy, September 1939–March 1942*, London, 2004

Browning, Christopher, *Die "Endlösung" und das Auswärtige Amt: Das Referat D III der Abteilung Deutschland 1940–1943*, Darmstadt, 2010

Buchheim, Christoph, "Der Mythos vom 'Wohlleben': Der Lebensstandard der deutschen Zivilbevölkerung im Zweiten Weltkrieg," in *Vierteljahrshefte für Zeitgeschichte*, 56 (2010), pp. 299–328

Buchner, Bernd, *Wagners Welttheater: Die Geschichte der Bayreuther Festspiele zwischen Kunst und Politik*, Darmstadt, 2013

Büttner, Ursula (ed.), *Die Deutschen und die Judenverfolgung im Dritten Reich*, Hamburg, 1992

Bullock, Alan, *Hitler: A Study in Tyranny*, revised edition, London, 1990

Bullock, Alan, *Hitler and Stalin: Parallel Lives*, London, 1991

Burleigh, Michael, *The Third Reich: A New History*, London, 2000

Calic, Marie-Janine, *Geschichte Jugoslawiens im 20. Jahrhundert*, Munich, 2010

Cesarani, David, *Eichmann: His Life and Crimes*, London, 2004

Cesarani, David, *Final Solution: The Fate of the Jews 1933–1949*, London, 2016

Chaussy, Ulrich and Christoph Püschner, *Nachbar Hitler: Führerkult und Heimatzerstörung am Obersalzberg*, Berlin, 1995

Chlewnjuk, Oleg, *Stalin: Eine Biographie*, Munich, 2015

Chowaniec, Elisabeth, *Der "Fall Dohnanyi" 1943–1945: Widerstand, Militärjustiz, SS-Willkür*, Munich, 1991

Conze, Eckart, Norbert Frei, Peter Hayes and Moshe Zimmermann, *Das Amt und die Vergangenheit: Deutsche Diplomaten im Dritten Reich und in der Bundesrepublik*, Munich, 2010

Dahm, Volker, Albert A. Feiber, Hartmut Mehringer and Horst Möller, *Die tödliche Utopie: Bilder, Texte, Dokumente. Daten zum Dritten Reich*, Munich 2010

Das Deutsche Reich und der Zweite Weltkrieg, ed. Militärgeschichtliches Forschungsamt, vols 1–10, Stuttgart and Munich, 1979–2008

Davies, Norman, *Rising '44: 'The Battle for Warsaw,"* London, 2003

Deletant, Dennis, *Hitler's Forgotten Ally: Ion Antonescu and his Regime. Romania 1940–1944*, London, 2006

Deuerlein, Ernst, *Hitler: Eine politische Biographie*, Munich, 1969

Dieckmann, Christoph, *Deutsche Besatzungspolitik in Litauen 1941–1944*, 2 vols, Göttingen, 2011

Diedrich, Thorsten, *Paulus: Das Trauma von Stalingrad. Eine Biographie*, Paderborn, 2008

Dörner, Bernward, *Die Deutschen und der Holocaust: Was niemand wissen wollte, aber jeder wissen konnte*, Berlin, 2007

Döscher, Hans-Jürgen, *Das Auswärtige Amt im Dritten Reich: Diplomatie im Schatten der "Endlösung,"* Berlin, 1987

Eberle, Henrik, *Hitlers Weltkriege: Wie der Gefreite zum Feldherrn wurde*, Hamburg, 2014

Echternkamp, Jörg, "Im Kampf an der inneren und äußeren Front: Grundzüge der deutschen Gesellschaft im Zweiten Weltkrieg," in *Das Deutsche Reich und der Zweite Weltkrieg*, vol. 9/1, Stuttgart, 2004, pp. 1–98

Edmonds, Robin, *Die Grossen Drei: Churchill, Roosevelt und Stalin in Frieden und Krieg*, Berlin, 1992

Eglau, Hans Otto, *Fritz Thyssen: Hitlers Gönner und Geisel*, Berlin, 2003

Epstein, Catherine, *Model Nazi: Arthur Greiser and the Occupation of Western Poland*, Oxford and New York, 2010

Evans, Richard J., *The Third Reich in Power, 1933–1939*, London, 2005

Evans, Richard J., *The Third Reich at War, 1939–1945*, London, 2008

Falanga, Gianluca, *Mussolinis Vorposten in Hitlers Reich: Italiens Politik in Berlin 1933–1945*, Berlin, 2008

Fest, Joachim, *Hitler: Eine Biographie*, Frankfurt am Main, Berlin and Vienna, 1973

Fest, Joachim, *Staatsstreich: Der lange Weg zum 20. Juli*, Berlin, 1994

Fest, Joachim, *Speer: Eine Biographie*, Berlin, 1999

Fest, Joachim, *Der Untergang: Hitler und das Ende des Dritten Reiches. Eine historische Skizze*, Berlin, 2002

Fest, Joachim, "Der Führerbunker," in Étienne François and Hagen Schulze (eds), *Deutsche Erinnerungsorte*, vol. 1, Munich, 2001, pp. 122–37

Fetscher, Iring, *Joseph Goebbels im Berliner Sportpalast 1943: "Wollt ihr den totalen Krieg?,"* Hamburg, 1998

Fisch, Bernhard, *Nemmersdorf, Oktober 1944: Was in Ostpreussen tatsächlich geschah*, Berlin, 1997

Fischer, Fritz, *Bündnis der Eliten: Zur Kontinuität der Machtstrukturen in Deutschland 1871–1945*, 2nd edition, Düsseldorf, 1985

Fischer, Fritz, *Hitler war kein Betriebsunfall: Aufsätze*, Munich, 1992

Fleischhauer, Ingeborg, *Die Chance des Sonderfriedens: Deutsch-sowjetische Geheimgespräche 1941–1945*, Berlin, 1986

Fleischhauer, Ingeborg, *Diplomatischer Widerstand gegen das "Unternehmen Barbarossa": Die Friedensbemühungen der deutschen Botschaft Moskau 1939–1941*, Frankfurt am Main, 1991

Föllmer, Moritz, *"Ein Leben wie im Traum": Kultur im Dritten Reich*, Munich, 2016

Förster, Jürgen, "Hitlers Entscheidung für den Krieg gegen die Sowjetunion," in *Das Deutsche Reich und der Zweite Weltkrieg*, vol. 4, Stuttgart, 1983, pp. 3–37

Förster, Jürgen, "Das Unternehmen 'Barbarossa' als Eroberungs- und Vernichtungskrieg," in *Das Deutsche Reich und der Zweite Weltkrieg*, vol. 4, Stuttgart, 1983, pp. 413–47

Forschungsstelle für Zeitgeschichte Hamburg (ed.), *Hamburg im "Dritten Reich,"* Göttingen, 2005

Frei, Norbert, Sybille Steinbacher, Bernd C. Wagner (eds), *Ausbeutung, Vernichtung, Öffentlichkeit: Neue Studien zur nationalsozialistischen Lagerpolitik*, Munich, 2000

Frei, Norbert, *1945 und wir: Das Dritte Reich im Bewusstsein der Deutschen*, Munich, 2005

Friedländer, Saul, *The Years of Extermination: Nazi Germany and the Jews 1939–1945*, London, 2007

Friedlander, Henry, *Der Weg zum NS-Genozid: Von der Euthanasie zur Endlösung*, Berlin, 1997

Frieser, Karl-Heinz, *Blitzkrieg-Legende: Der Westfeldzug 1940*, Munich, 1995

Frieser, Karl-Heinz, "Die Schlacht im Kursker Bogen," in *Das Deutsche Reich und der Zweite Weltkrieg*, vol. 8, Munich, 2001, pp. 83–208

Frieser, Karl-Heinz, "Der Rückschlag des Pendels: Das Zurückweichen der Ostfront von Sommer 1943 bis Sommer 1944," in *Das Deutsche Reich und der Zweite Weltkrieg*, vol. 8, Munich, 2001, pp. 277–450

Frieser, Karl-Heinz, "Der Zusammenbruch im Osten: Die Rückzugskämpfe seit Sommer 1944," in *Das Deutsche Reich und der Zweite Weltkrieg*, vol. 8, Munich, 2001, pp. 493–678

Fröhlich, Elke, "Hitler und Goebbels im Krisenjahr 1944," in *Vierteljahrshefte für Zeitgeschichte*, 38 (1990), pp. 195–224

Gaertringen, Hans Georg Hiller von (ed.), *Das Auge des Dritten Reiches: Hitlers Kameramann und Fotograf Walter Frentz*, Berlin n. d. (2006)

Ganzenmüller, Jörg, *Das belagerte Leningrad 1941–1944*, 2nd edition, Paderborn, 2007

Ganzenmüller, Jörg, "Hungerpolitik als Problemlösungsstrategie: Der Entscheidungsprozess zur Blockade Leningrads und zur Vernichtung seiner Zivilbevölkerung," in Qinkerta and Morré, *Deutsche Besatzung in der Sowjetunion 1941–1944*, pp. 34–53

Gebhardt, Miriam, *Die Weisse Rose: Wie aus ganz normalen Deutschen Widerstandskämpfer wurden*, Munich, 2017

Gellately, Robert, *Backing Hitler: Consent and Coercion in Nazi Germany*, Oxford, 2001

Gellately, Robert, *Lenin, Stalin and Hitler: The Age of Social Catastrophe*, London, 2007

Gerlach, Christian, *Kalkulierte Morde: Die deutsche Wirtschafts- und Vernichtungspolitik in Weissrussland 1941 bis 1944*, Hamburg, 1999

Gerlach, Christian, *Krieg, Ernährung, Völkermord: Forschungen zur deutschen Vernichtungspolitik im Zweiten Weltkrieg*, Hamburg, 1998

Gerlach, Christian and Götz Aly, *Das letzte Kapitel: Der Mord an den ungarischen Juden*, Stuttgart and Munich, 2002

Gerlach, Christian, *Der Mord an den europäischen Juden: Ursachen, Ereignisse, Dimensionen*, Munich, 2017

Gerste, Ronald, *Roosevelt und Hitler: Todfeindschaft und totaler Krieg*, Paderborn, 2011

Gerwarth, Robert, *Reinhard Heydrich: Eine Biographie*, Munich, 2011

Gibbels, Ellen, *Hitlers Parkinson-Krankheit: Zur Frage eines hirnorganischen Psychosyndroms*, Berlin and Heidelberg, 1990

Gibbels, Ellen, "Hitlers Nervenkrankheit: Eine neurologisch-psychiatrische Studie," in *Vierteljahrshefte für Zeitgeschichte*, 42 (1994), pp. 155–220

Goeschel, Christian, *Selbstmord im Dritten Reich*, Berlin, 2011

Görtemaker, Heike B., *Eva Braun: Leben mit Hitler*, Munich, 2010

Goldhagen, Daniel Jonah, *Hitler's Willing Executioners: Ordinary Germans and the Holocaust*, New York, 1996

Graml, Hermann, *Europas Weg in den Krieg: Hitler und die Mächte 1939*, Munich, 1990

Graml, Hermann, "Ist Hitlers 'Anweisung' zur Ausrottung der europäischen Judenheit endlich gefunden? Zu den Thesen von Christian Gerlach," in *Jahrbuch für Antisemitismusforschung*, 7 (1998), pp. 352–62

Greiner, Bernd, *Die Morgenthau-Legende: Zur Geschichte eines umstrittenen Plans*, Hamburg, 1995
Greiser, Katrin, *Die Todesmärsche von Buchenwald: Räumung, Befreiung und Spuren der Erinnerung*, Göttingen, 2008
Groehler, Olaf, *Bombenkrieg gegen Deutschland*, Berlin, 1990
Gruchmann, Lothar, "Korruption im Dritten Reich: Zur 'Lebensmittelversorgung' der NS-Führerschaft," in *Vierteljahrshefte für Zeitgeschichte*, 42 (1994), pp. 571–93
Gun, Nerin E., *Eva Braun-Hitler: Leben und Schicksal*, Velbert and Kettwig, 1968
Gutsche, Willibald, *Ein Kaiser im Exil: Der letzte deutsche Kaiser Wilhelm II. in Holland*, Marburg, 1991
Haasis, Helmut G., *Den Hitler jag ich in die Luft: Der Attentäter Georg Elser*, Hamburg, 2009
Haffner, Sebastian, *Anmerkungen zu Hitler*, 21st edition, Munich, 1978
Haffner, Sebastian, *Von Bismarck zu Hitler: Ein Rückblick*, Munich, 1987
Haffner, Sebastian, *Churchill: Eine Biographie*, new edition, Berlin, 2001
Haffner, Sebastian, *Germany: Jekyll & Hyde. Deutschland von innen betrachtet*, Berlin, 1996
Hamann, Brigitte, *Winifred Wagner oder Hitlers Bayreuth*, Munich and Zurich, 2002
Hamerow, Theodore S., *Die Attentäter: Der 20. Juli—von der Kollaboration zum Widerstand*, Munich, 1999
Hansen, Reimar, "Ribbentrops Friedensfühler im Frühjahr 1945," in *Geschichte in Wissenschaft und Unterricht*, 18 (1967), pp. 716–30
Harrison, Edward D. R., "Hugh Trevor-Roper und 'Hitlers letzte Tage,'" in *Vierteljahrshefte für Zeitgeschichte*, 57 (2009), pp. 33–60
Hartmann, Christian, *Wehrmacht im Ostkrieg: Front und militärisches Hinterland 1941/42*, Munich, 2009
Hartmann, Christian, *Halder: Generalstabschef Hitlers 1938–1942*, 2nd edition, Paderborn, 2010
Hartmann, Christian, *Unternehmen Barbarossa: Der deutsche Krieg im Osten 1941–1945*, Munich, 2011
Heer, Hannes and Klaus Naumann (eds), *Vernichtungskrieg: Verbrechen der Wehrmacht*, Hamburg, 1995
Heiden, Konrad, *Adolf Hitler: Eine Biographie*, 2 vols, Zurich, 1936/37
Heinemann, Ulrich, *Ein konservativer Rebell: Fritz-Dietlof Graf von der Schulenburg und der 20. Juli*, Berlin, 1984
Henke, Klaus-Dietmar, *Die amerikanische Besetzung Deutschlands*, Munich, 1995
Herbert, Ulrich, *Fremdarbeiter: Politik und Praxis des "Ausländer-Einsatzes" in der Kriegswirtschaft des Dritten Reiches*, Berlin and Bonn, 1985
Herbert, Ulrich, *Geschichte der Ausländerpolitik in Deutschland: Saisonarbeiter, Zwangsarbeiter, Gastarbeiter, Flüchtlinge*, Munich, 2001
Herbert, Ulrich, *Geschichte Deutschlands im 20. Jahrhundert*, Munich, 2014
Herbst, Ludolf, *Der totale Krieg und die Ordnung der Wirtschaft: Die Kriegswirtschaft im Spannungsfeld von Politik, Ideologie und Propaganda 1939–1945*, Stuttgart, 1982
Herbst, Ludolf, *Das nationalsozialistische Deutschland 1933–1945*, Frankfurt am Main, 1996
Herbst, Ludolf, *Hitlers Charisma: Die Erfindung eines deutschen Messias*, Frankfurt am Main, 2010
Herf, Jeffrey, *The Jewish Enemy: Nazi Propaganda during World War II and the Holocaust*, Cambridge, MA, 2006
Herz, Rudolf, *Hoffmann & Hitler: Fotografie als Medium des Führer-Mythos*, Munich, 1994
Hilberg, Raul, *Die Vernichtung der europäischen Juden*, 3 vols, Frankfurt am Main, 1990
Hilberg, Raul, *Anatomie des Holocaust: Essays und Erinnerungen*, ed. Walter H. Pehle und René Schlott, Frankfurt am Main, 2016
Hildebrand, Klaus, *Vom Reich zum Weltreich: NSDAP und koloniale Frage 1919–1945*, Munich, 1969
Hildebrand, Klaus, *Das vergangene Reich: Deutsche Aussenpolitik von Bismarck bis Hitler*, Stuttgart, 1995
Hildermeier, Manfred, *Geschichte der Sowjetunion 1917–1991: Entstehung und Niedergang des ersten sozialistischen Staates*, Munich, 1998
Hillgruber, Andreas, *Hitlers Strategie: Politik und Kriegführung 1940–1941*, Frankfurt am Main, 1965
Hillgruber, Andreas, *Deutsche Grossmacht- und Weltpolitik im 19. und 20. Jahrhundert*, Düsseldorf, 1977

Hillgruber, Andreas, "Das Russland-Bild der führenden deutschen Militärs vor dem Angriff auf die Sowjetunion," in Hans-Erich Volkmann (eds), *Das Russlandbild im Dritten Reich*, Cologne, Weimar and Vienna, 1994, pp. 125–40

Hinz-Wessels, Annette, *Tiergartenstraße 4: Schaltstelle der nationalsozialistischen "Euthanasie"-Morde*, Berlin, 2015

Hölsken, Hans-Dieter, *Die V-Waffen: Entstehung—Propaganda—Kriegseinsatz*, Stuttgart, 1984

Hoffmann, Meike and Nicola Kuhn, *Hitlers Kunsthändler: Hildebrand Gurlitt 1895–1956. Die Biographie*, Munich, 2016

Hoffmann, Peter, *Die Sicherheit des Diktators: Hitlers Leibwachen, Schutzmassnahmen, Residenzen, Hauptquartiere*, Munich, 1975

Hoffmann, Peter, *Widerstand, Staatsstreich, Attentat: Der Kampf der Opposition gegen Hitler*, 4th edition, Munich and Zurich, 1985

Hoffmann, Peter, *Claus Schenk Graf von Stauffenberg und seine Brüder*, Stuttgart, 1992

Hoffmann, Peter, *Carl Goerdeler gegen die Judenverfolgung*, Cologne, Weimar and Vienna, 2013

Hoffmann, Peter, "Henning von Tresckow und die Staatsstreichpläne im Jahr 1943," in *Vierteljahrshefte für Zeitgeschichte*, 55 (2007), pp. 331–64

Hürter, Johannes, *Hitlers Heerführer: Die deutschen Oberbefehlshaber im Krieg gegen die Sowjetunion 1941/42*, Munich, 2007

Hürter, Johannes, "Die Wehrmacht vor Leningrad," in *Vierteljahrshefte für Zeitgeschichte*, 49 (2001), pp. 377–440

Hürter, Johannes, "Auf dem Weg zur Militäropposition: Tresckow, Gersdorff, der Vernichtungskrieg und der Judenmord," in *Vierteljahrshefte für Zeitgeschichte*, 52 (2004), pp. 527–62

Irving, David, *Hitler und seine Feldherren*, Frankfurt am Main, Berlin and Vienna, 1975

Jacobsen, Hans-Adolf, *Fall Gelb: Der Kampf um den deutschen Operationsplan zur Westoffensive 1940*, Wiesbaden, 1957

Jäckel, Eberhard, *Frankreich in Hitlers Europa: Die deutsche Frankreichpolitik im Zweiten Weltkrieg*, Stuttgart, 1966

Jäckel, Eberhard, *Das deutsche Jahrhundert: Eine historische Bilanz*, Stuttgart, 1996

Jansen, Christian and Arno Weckbecker, *Der "Volksdeutsche Selbstschutz" in Polen 1939/40*, Munich, 1992

Jansen, Hans, *Der Madagaskar-Plan: Die beabsichtigte Deportation der europäischen Juden nach Madagaskar*, Munich, 1997

Janssen, Karl-Heinz and Fritz Tobias, *Der Sturz der Generäle: Hitler und die Blomberg-Fritsch-Krise 1938*, Munich, 1994

Jasch, Christian, *Staatssekretär Wilhelm Stuckart und die Judenpolitik: Der Mythos von der sauberen Verwaltung*, Munich, 2012

Jeffreys, Diarmuid, *Weltkonzern und Kriegskartell: Das zerstörerische Werk der IG-Farben*, Munich, 2011

Jenkins, Roy, *Churchill*, London, Basingstone and Oxford, 2001

Joachimsthaler, Anton, *Hitlers Ende: Legenden und Dokumente*, Munich and Berlin, 1995

Johnson, Eric A., *Terror: Gestapo, Juden und gewöhnliche Deutsche*, Berlin, 2001

Jones, Mark, *Am Anfang war Gewalt: Die deutsche Revolution 1918/19 und der Beginn der Weimarer Republik*, Berlin, 2017

Jung, Hermann, *Die Ardennenoffensive 1944/45: Ein Beispiel für die Kriegführung Hitlers*, Göttingen, 1971

Käppner, Joachim, *1941: Als der Zweite Weltkrieg wirklich begann*, Berlin, 2016

Kampe, Norbert and Peter Klein (eds), *Die Wannsee-Konferenz vom 20. Januar 1942: Dokumente, Foschungsstand, Kontroversen*, Cologne, Weimar and Vienna, 2013

Karlsch, Rainer, *Hitlers Bombe: Die geheime Geschichte der deutschen Kernwaffenversuche*, Munich, 2005

Kehrig, Manfred, *Stalingrad: Analyse und Dokumentation einer Schlacht*, 3rd edition, Stuttgart, 1979

Keller, Sven, *Volksgemeinschaft am Ende: Gesellschaft und Gewalt 1944/45*, Munich, 2013

Kellerhoff, Sven Felix, *Hitlers Ende: Der Untergang im Führerbunker*, Berlin, 2015

Kellerhoff, Sven Felix, *Die NSDAP: Eine Partei und ihre Mitglieder*, Stuttgart, 2017

Kennedy, Paul, *Engineers of Victory: The Problem Solvers who Turned the Tide in the Second World War*, London, 2014

Kershaw, Ian, *The "Hitler Myth": Image and Reality in the Third Reich*, Oxford, 1987

Kershaw, Ian, *Hitler 1889–1936: Hubris*, London, 1998

Kershaw, Ian, *Hitler 1936–1945: Nemesis*, London, 2000

Kershaw, Ian, *Fateful Choices: Ten Decisions that Changed the World 1940–1941*, London, 2007

Kershaw, Ian, *The End: The Defiance and Destruction of Hitler's Germany, 1944–45*, London, 2011

Kipp, Michaela, *"Grossreinemachen im Osten": Feindbilder in deutschen Feldpostbriefen im Zweiten Weltkrieg*, Frankfurt am Main, 2014

Kitchen, Martin, *Speer: Hitler's Architect*, New Haven and London, 2015

Klee, Ernst, *Auschwitz, die NS-Medizin und ihre Opfer*, Frankfurt am Main, 1997

Klee, Ernst, *"Euthanasie" im Dritten Reich: Die "Vernichtung lebensunwerten Lebens,"* fully revised edition, Frankfurt am Main, 2010

Klee, Karl, *Das Unternehmen "Seelöwe": Die geplante deutsche Landung in England*, Göttingen, 1958

Klemperer, Klemens von, *Die verlassenen Verschwörer: Der deutsche Widerstand auf der Suche nach Verbündeten 1938–1945*, Berlin 1994

Kley, Stefan, *Hitler, Ribbentrop und die Entfesselung des Zweiten Weltkriegs*, Paderborn, 1996

Klink, Ernst, "Die militärische Konzeption des Krieges gegen die Sowjetunion," in *Das Deutsche Reich und der Zweite Weltkrieg*, vol. 4, Stuttgart, 1983, pp. 190–277

Klink, Ernst, "Der Krieg gegen die Sowjetunion bis zur Jahreswende 1941/42," in *Das Deutsche Reich und der Zweite Weltkrieg*, vol. 4, Stuttgart, 1983, pp. 451–652

König, Malte, *Kooperation als Machtkampf: Das faschistische Achsenbündnis Berlin–Rom im Krieg 1940/41*, Cologne, 2007

Koop, Volker, *Martin Bormann: Hitlers Vollstrecker*, Cologne and Weimar, 2012

Koop, Volker, *Hans Heinrich Lammers: Der Chef von Hitlers Reichskanzlei*, Bonn, 2017

Kramer, Nicole, *Volksgenossinnen an der Heimatfront: Mobilisierung, Verhalten, Erinnerung*, Göttingen, 2011

Krausnick, Helmut, *Hitlers Einsatzgruppen: Die Truppen des Weltanschauungskrieges*, Frankfurt am Main, 1985

Krebs, Gerhard, "Der Krieg im Pazifik 1943–1945," in *Das Deutsche Reich und der Zweite Weltkrieg*, vol. 7, Stuttgart and Munich, 2001, pp. 643–771

Krings, Stefan, *Hitlers Pressechef: Otto Dietrich 1897–1952. Eine Biographie*, Göttingen, 2010

Kröner, Bernhard R., *Generaloberst Friedrich Fromm: Eine Biographie*, Paderborn, 2005

Krzoska, Markus, "Der 'Bromberger Blutsonntag' 1939: Kontroversen und Forschungsergebnisse," in *Vierteljahrshefte für Zeitgeschichte*, 60 (2012), pp. 237–48

Kube, Alfred, *Pour le mérite und Hakenkreuz: Hermann Göring im Dritten Reich*, Munich, 1986

Kundrus, Birthe, *Kriegerfrauen: Familienpolitik und Geschlechterverhältnisse im Ersten und Zweiten Weltkrieg*, Hamburg, 1995

Kundrus, Birthe, "Totale Unterhaltung? Die kulturelle Kriegführung 1939 bis 1945 in Film, Rundfunk und Theater," in *Das Deutsche Reich und der Zweite Weltkrieg*, vol. 9/2, Stuttgart 2005, pp. 93–157

Kunz, Andreas, *Wehrmacht und Niederlage: Die bewaffnete Macht in der Endphase der nationalsozialistischen Herrschaft 1944 bis 1945*, Munich, 2005

Kunz, Norbert, *Die Krim unter deutscher Herrschaft 1941–1944*, Darmstadt, 2005

Lakowski, Richard, "Der Zusammenbruch der deutschen Verteidigung zwischen Ostsee und Karpaten," in *Das Deutsche Reich und der Zweite Weltkrieg*, vol. 10/1, Munich, 2008, pp. 491–679

Lang, Jochen von, *Der Sekretär Martin Bormann: Der Mann, der Hitler beherrschte*, Stuttgart, 1977

Laufer, Jochen, *Pax Sovietica: Stalin, die Westmächte und die deutsche Frage 1941–1945*, Cologne, Weimar and Vienna, 2009

Lehmann, Sebastian, Robert Bohn and Uwe Danker (eds), *Reichskommissariat Ostland: Tatort und Erinnerungsobjekt*, Paderborn, 2012

Lehnstaedt, Stephan, *Der Kern des Holocaust: Belzec, Sobibor, Treblinka und die Aktion Reinhardt*, Munich, 2017

Leiser, Erwin, *"Deutschland erwache!" Propaganda im Film des Dritten Reiches*, Reinbek bei Hamburg, 1968

Lelyveld, Joseph, *The Final Battle: The Last Months of Franklin Roosevelt*, New York, 2016

Lieb, Peter, *Unternehmen Overlord: Die Invasion in der Normandie und die Befreiung Westeuropas*, Munich, 2014

Lieb, Peter, "Erwin Rommel: Widerstandskämpfer oder Nationalsozialist?," in *Vierteljahrshefte für Zeitgeschichte*, 61 (2013), pp. 303–43

Liebrandt, Hans, *"Das Recht mich zu richten, das spreche ich Ihnen ab!": Der Selbstmord der nationalsozialistischen Elite 1944/45*, Paderborn, 2017

Löffler, Jürgen, *Walther von Brauchitsch: Eine politische Biographie*, Frankfurt am Main, 2001

Löhr, Hanns C., *Hitlers Linz: Der "Heimatgau des Führers,"* Berlin, 2013

Löw, Andrea, *Juden im Ghetto Litzmannstadt: Lebensbedingungen, Selbstwahrnehmung, Verhalten*, Göttingen, 2006

Longerich, Peter, *Politik der Vernichtung: Eine Gesamtdarstellung der nationalsozialistischen Judenverfolgung*, Munich and Zurich, 1998

Longerich, Peter, *"Davon haben wir nichts gewusst!" Die Deutschen und die Judenverfolgung 1933–1945*, Munich, 2006

Longerich, Peter, *Heinrich Himmler: Biographie*, Munich, 2008

Longerich, Peter, *Joseph Goebbels*, Munich, 2010

Longerich, Peter, *Hitler: Biographie*, Munich, 2015

Longerich, Peter, *Wannseekonferenz: Der Weg zur "Endlösung,"* Munich, 2016

Lüdicke, Lars, *Konstantin von Neurath: Eine politische Biographie*, Paderborn, 2014

Lukacs, John, *Churchill und Hitler. Der Zweikampf: 10. Mai–31. Juli 1940*, Stuttgart, 1992

Lukacs, John, *Hitler: Geschichte und Geschichtsschreibung*, Munich, 1997

Lukacs, John, *Fünf Tage in London: England und Deutschland im Mai 1940*, Berlin, 2000

Maier, Klaus A. and Hans Umbreit, "Direkte Strategie gegen England," in *Das Deutsche Reich und der Zweite Weltkrieg*, vol. 2, Stuttgart, 1979, pp. 365–416

Maier, Klaus A. and Bernd Stegemann, "Die Sicherung der europäischen Nordflanke," in *Das Deutsche Reich und der Zweite Weltkrieg*, vol. 2, Stuttgart, 1979, pp. 189–231

Mallmann, Klaus-Michael, "Die Türöffner der 'Endlösung': Zur Genesis des Genozids," in Gerhard Paul and Klaus-Michael Mallmann (eds), *Die Gestapo im Zweiten Weltkrieg: "Heimatfront" und besetztes Europa*, Darmstadt 2000, pp. 437–63

Mann, Golo, *Deutsche Geschichte des 19. und 20. Jahrhunderts*, new edition, Frankfurt am Main, 1992

Manoschek, Walter, *"Serbien ist judenfrei": Militärische Besatzungspolitik und Judenvernichtung in Serbien 1941/42*, Munich 1993

Martynkewicz, Wolfgang, *Salon Deutschland: Geist und Macht 1900–1945*, Berlin, 2009

Mazower, Mark, *Hitler's Empire: Nazi Rule in Occupied Europe*, London, 2008

Mazower, Mark, *Griechenland unter Hitler: Das Leben während der deutschen Besatzung*, Frankfurt am Main, 2016

Megargee, Geoffrey P., *Hitler und die Generäle: Das Ringen um die Führung der Wehrmacht 1939–1945*, Paderborn, 2006

Meinecke, Friedrich, *Die deutsche Katastrophe*, Wiesbaden, 1946

Merridale, Catherine, *Ivan's War: The Red Army 1939–45*, London, 2005

Meyer, Beate, *"Jüdische Mischlinge": Rassenpolitik und Verfolgungserfahrung 1933–1945*, Hamburg, 1999

Meyer, Georg, *Adolf Heusinger: Dienst eines deutschen Soldaten*, Hamburg, Berlin and Bonn, 2001

Michalka, Wolfgang (ed.), *Der Zweite Weltkrieg: Analysen—Grundzüge—Forschungsbilanz*, Munich, 1989

Mitscherlich, Alexander und Margarete, *Die Unfähigkeit zu trauern: Grundlagen kollektiven Verhaltens*, Munich, 1967

Moltmann, Günter, "Franklin D. Roosevelts Friedensappell vom 14. April 1939: Ein fehlgeschlagener Versuch zur Friedenssicherung," in *Jahrbuch für Amerikastudien*, 9 (1964), pp. 91–109

Mommsen, Hans, *Von Weimar nach Auschwitz: Zur Geschichte Deutschlands in der Weltkriegsepoche*, Stuttgart, 1999

Mommsen, Hans, *Das NS-Regime und die Auslöschung des Judentums in Europa*, Göttingen, 2014

Mommsen, Hans, "Die Realisierung des Utopischen: Die 'Endlösung der Judenfrage' im Dritten Reich," in *Geschichte und Gesellschaft*, 9 (1983), pp. 381–420

Mommsen, Hans, "Der Krieg gegen die Sowjetunion und die deutsche Gesellschaft," in Pietrow-Ennker (ed.), *Präventivkrieg?*, pp. 59–77

Montefiore, Simon Sebag, *Stalin: The Court of the Red Tsar*, London, 2008

Moorhouse, Roger, *The Devils' Alliance: Hitler's Pact with Stalin*, London, 2014

Motadel, David, *Für Prophet und Führer: Die islamische Welt und das Dritte Reich*, Stuttgart, 2017

Mueller, Michael, *Canaris: Hitlers Abwehrchef*, Berlin, 2006

Müller, Klaus-Jürgen, *Generaloberst Ludwig Beck: Eine Biographie*, Paderborn, 2008

Müller, Klaus-Jürgen, "Zur Vorgeschichte und Inhalt der Rede Himmlers vor der höheren Generalität am 13. Mai 1940 in Koblenz," in *Vierteljahrshefte für Zeitgeschichte*, 18 (1970), pp. 95–122

Müller, Rolf-Dieter, "Von der Wirtschaftsallianz zum kolonialen Ausbeutungskrieg," in *Das Deutsche Reich und der Zweite Weltkrieg*, vol. 4, Stuttgart, 1983, pp. 98–189

Müller, Rolf-Dieter, "Die Mobilisierung der deutschen Wirtschaft für Hitlers Kriegführung," in *Das Deutsche Reich und der Zweite Weltkrieg*, vol. 5/1, Stuttgart, 1988, pp. 349–689

Müller, Rolf-Dieter and Erich Volkmann (eds), *Die Wehrmacht: Mythos und Realität*, Munich, 1999

Müller, Rolf-Dieter, *Der letzte deutsche Krieg 1939–1945*, Stuttgart, 2005

Müller, Rolf-Dieter, *An der Seite der Wehrmacht: Hitlers ausländische Helfer beim "Kreuzzug gegen den Bolschewismus" 1941–1945*, Frankfurt am Main, 2010

Müller, Rolf-Dieter, *Der Feind steht im Osten: Hitlers geheime Pläne für einen Krieg gegen die Sowjetunion im Jahr 1939*, Berlin, 2011

Münkler, Herfried, *Machtzerfall: Die letzten Tage des Dritten Reiches am Beispiel der hessischen Kleinstadt Friedberg*, Berlin, 1985

Münkler, Herfried, *Die Deutschen und ihre Mythen*, Berlin, 2009

Musial, Bogdan, *"Konterrevolutionäre Elemente sind zu erschiessen": Die Brutalisierung des deutsch-sowjetischen Krieges im Sommer 1941*, Munich, 2000

Nagel, Anne C., *Johannes Popitz (1884–1945): Görings Finanzminister und Verschwörer gegen Hitler. Eine Biographie*, Cologne, Weimar and Vienna, 2015

Neitzel, Sönke and Harald Welzer, *Soldaten: Protokolle vom Sterben, Töten und Kämpfen*, Frankfurt am Main, 2011

Nerdinger, Winfried (ed.), *Munich und der Nationalsozialismus: Katalog des Dokumentationszentrums München*, Munich, 2015

Neumärker, Uwe, Robert Conrad and Cord Woywodt, *Wolfsschanze: Hitlers Machtzentrale im Zweiten Weltkrieg*, 3rd edition, Berlin, 2007

Neumann, Hansjoachim and Henrik Eberle, *War Hitler krank? Ein abschliessender Befund*, Bergisch Gladbach, 2009

Neutatz, Dietmar, *Träume und Alpträume: Eine Geschichte Russlands im 20. Jahrhundert*, Munich, 2013

Niedhart, Gottfried, "Die britisch-französischen Garantieerklärungen für Polen am 31. 3. 1939," in *Francia*, 2 (1974), pp. 597–618

Nolzen, Armin, "Die NSDAP, der Krieg und die deutsche Gesellschaft," in *Das Deutsche Reich und der Zweite Weltkrieg*, vol. 9/1, Munich, 2004, pp. 99–159

Nolzen, Armin, "Der Hess-Flug vom 10. Mai 1941 und die öffentliche Meinung im NS-Staat," in Martin Sabrow (ed.), *Skandal und Diktatur: Öffentliche Empörung im NS-Staat und in der DDR*, Göttingen 2004, pp. 130–56

O'Donnell, James and Uwe Bahnsen, *Die Katakombe: Das Ende in der Reichskanzlei*, Stuttgart, 1975

Oberländer, Erwin (ed.), *Hitler-Stalin-Pakt 1939: Das Ende Ostmitteleuropas?*, Frankfurt am Main, 1989

Ohler, Norman, *Der totale Rausch: Drogen im Dritten Reich*, Cologne, 2015

Olshausen, Klaus, *Zwischenspiel auf dem Balkan: Die deutsche Politik gegenüber Jugoslawien und Griechenland März bis Juli 1941*, Stuttgart, 1973

Ose, Dieter, *Entscheidung im Westen 1944: Der Oberbefehlshaber West und die Abwehr der alliierten Invasion*, Stuttgart, 1982

Overmans, Rüdiger, *Deutsche militärische Verluste im Zweiten Weltkrieg*, Munich, 2000

Overy, Richard, *Russia's War 1941–1945*, London, 1998

Overy, Richard, *Interrogations: The Nazi Elite in Allied Hands*, London, 2001

Overy, Richard (ed.), *Ein Volk von Opfern? Die neue Debatte um den Bombenkrieg 1940–1945*, Berlin, 2003

Overy, Richard, *Why the Allies Won*, 2nd edition, London, 2006

Overy, Richard, *1939: Countdown to War*, London, 2009

Overy, Richard, *The Bombing War: Europe 1939–1945*, London, 2013

Padfield, Peter, *Hess: The Führer's Disciple*, London, 1993

Pätzold, Kurt and Manfred Weissbecker, *Adolf Hitler: Eine politische Biographie*, Leipzig, 1995

Pätzold, Kurt and Manfred Weissbecker, *Rudolf Hess: Der Mann an Hitlers Seite*, Leipzig, 1999

Pelt, Robert-Jan van and Deborah Dwork, *Auschwitz: Von 1270 bis heute*, Zurich and Munich, 1998

Pietrow-Ennker, Bianca (ed.), *Präventivkrieg? Der deutsche Angriff auf die Sowjetunion*, new and expanded edition, Frankfurt am Main, 2011

Piper, Ernst, *Alfred Rosenberg: Hitlers Chefideologe*, Munich, 2005

Pötzl, Norbert F., *Casablanca 1943: Das geheime Treffen, der Film und die Wende des Krieges*, Munich, 2017

Pohl, Dieter, *Nationalsozialistische Judenverfolgung in Ostgalizien 1941–1944: Organisation und Durchführung eines staatlichen Massenverbrechens*, Munich, 1997

Pohl, Dieter, *Holocaust: Die Ursachen, das Geschehen, die Folgen*, Freiburg, Basel and Vienna, 2000

Pohl, Dieter, *Die Herrschaft der Wehrmacht: Deutsche Militärbesatzung und einheimische Bevölkerung in der Sowjetunion 1941–1944*, Munich, 2008

Preston, Paul, "Franco and Hitler: The Myth of Hendaye 1940," in *Contemporary European History*, 1 (1992), pp. 1–16

Przyrembel, Alexandra and Jörg Schönert (ed.), *"Jud Süss": Hofjude, literarische Figur, antisemitisches Zerrbild*, Frankfurt am Main, 2006

Pyta, Wolfram, *Hitler: Der Künstler als Politiker und Feldherr*, Munich, 2015

Quinkert, Babette and Jörg Morré (ed.), *Deutsche Besatzung in der Sowjetunion 1941–1944: Vernichtungskrieg—Reaktionen—Erinnerung*, Paderborn, 2014

Rahn, Werner, "Der Krieg im Pazifik," in *Das Deutsche Reich und der Zweite Weltkrieg*, vol. 6, Stuttgart, 1990, pp. 173–271

Rahn, Werner, "Der Seekrieg im Atlantik und Nordmeer," in *Das Deutsche Reich und der Zweite Weltkrieg*, vol. 6, Stuttgart, 1990, pp. 275–425

Rahn, Werner, "Die deutsche Seekriegführung 1943 bis 1945," in *Das Deutsche Reich und der Zweite Weltkrieg*, vol. 10/1, Munich, 2008, pp. 3–273

Raichle, Christoph, *Hitler als Symbolpolitiker*, Stuttgart, 2014

Ramm, Arnim, *Der 20. Juli vor dem Volksgerichtshof*, Berlin, 2007

Rebentisch, Dieter, *Führerstaat und Verwaltung im Zweiten Weltkrieg: Verfassungsentwicklung und Verwaltungspolitik 1939–1945*, Stuttgart, 1989

Recker, Marie-Luise, *Nationalsozialistische Sozialpolitik im Zweiten Weltkrieg*, Munich, 1985

Reuth, Ralf Georg, *Goebbels*, Munich and Zurich, 1990

Reuth, Ralf Georg, *Hitler: Eine Biographie*, Munich and Zurich, 2003

Reuth, Ralf Georg, *Rommel: Das Ende einer Legende*, Munich and Zurich, 2004

Richter, Heinz A., *Operation Merkur: Die Eroberung der Insel Kreta im Mai 1941*, Mainz und Ruhpolding, 2011

Rieger, Eva, *Friedelind Wagner: Die rebellische Enkelin Richard Wagners*, Munich and Zurich, 2012

Röhl, John C. G., *Wilhelm II.: Der Weg in den Abgrund 1900–1941*, Munich, 2008

Römer, Felix, *Der Kommissarbefehl: Wehrmacht und NS-Verbrechen an der Ostfront*, Paderborn, 2008

Römer, Felix, *Kameraden: Die Wehrmacht von innen*, Munich and Zurich, 2012

Römer, Felix, *Die narzisstische Volksgemeinschaft: Theodor Habichts Kampf 1914–1944*, Frankfurt am Main, 2017

Römer, Felix, "Die Wehrmacht und der Kommissarbefehl: Neue Forschungsergebnisse," in *Militärgeschichtliche Zeitschrift*, 69/2 (2010), pp. 243–74

Rohde, Horst, "Hitlers erster 'Blitzkrieg' und seine Auswirkungen auf Nordosteuropa," in *Das Deutsche Reich und der Zweite Weltkrieg*, vol. 2, Suttgart, 1979, pp. 79–156

Roon, Ger van, *Widerstand im Dritten Reich*, 6th edition, Munich, 1994

Roos, Daniel, *Julius Streicher und Der Stürmer 1923–1945*, Paderborn, 2014

Roseman, Mark, *The Villa, the Lake, the Meeting: Wannsee and the Final Solution*, London, 2002

Roth, Karl-Heinz and Jan Peter Abraham, *Reemtsma auf der Krim: Tabakproduktion und Zwangsarbeit unter der deutschen Besatzungsherschaft 1941–1944*, Hamburg, 2011

Roth, Karl-Heinz, "'Generalplan Ost'—'Gesamtplan Ost': Forschungsstand, Quellenprobleme, neue Ergebnisse," in Mechthild Rössler and Sabine Schleiermacher (eds), *Der "Generalplan Ost,"* Berlin, 1993, pp. 25–117

Roth, Markus, *Herrenmenschen: Die deutschen Kreishauptleute im besetzten Polen. Karrierewege, Herrschaftspraxis und Nachgeschichte*, Göttingen, 2009

Roth, Markus, *"Ihr wisst, wollt es aber nicht wissen": Verfolgung, Terror und Widerstand im Dritten Reich*, Munich, 2015

Runzheimer, Jürgen, "Der Überfall auf den Sender Gleiwitz im Jahr 1939," in *Vierteljahrshefte für Zeitgeschichte*, 10 (1962), pp. 408–422

Ryback, Timothy W., *Hitler's Private Library: The Books that Shaped his Life*, London, 2009

Sachslehner, Johannes, *Zwei Millionen ham'ma erledigt: Odilo Globocnik, Hitlers Manager des Todes*, Vienna, Graz and Klagenfurt, 2014

Sandkühler, Thomas, *"Endlösung" in Galizien: Der Judenmord in Ostpolen und die Rettungsinitiativen von Berthold Beitz 1941–1944*, Bonn, 1996

Schanetzky, Tim, *"Kanonen statt Butter": Wirtschaft und Konsum im Dritten Reich*, Munich, 2015

Scheer, Regina, *Im Schatten der Sterne: Eine jüdische Widerstandsgruppe*, Berlin, 2004

Schenck, Ernst Günther, *Patient Hitler: Eine medizinische Biographie*, Düsseldorf, 1989

Schenk, Dieter, *Die Post von Danzig: Geschichte eines deutschen Justizmords*, Reinbek bei Hamburg, 1995

Schenk, Dieter, *Hitlers Mann in Danzig: Gauleiter Forster und die NS-Verbrechen in Danzig-Westpreussen*, Bonn, 2000

Schenk, Dieter, *Hans Frank: Hitlers Kronjurist und Generalgouverneur*, Frankfurt am Main, 2006

Scheurig, Bodo, *Henning von Tresckow: Ein Preusse gegen Hitler*, Frankfurt am Main and Berlin, 1987

Schieder, Wolfgang, *Faschistische Diktaturen: Studien zu Italien und Deutschland*, Göttingen, 2008

Schieder, Wolfgang, *Benito Mussolini*, Munich, 2014

Schlie, Ulrich, *"Es lebe das heilige Deutschland": Ein Tag im Leben des Claus Schenk von Stauffenberg. Ein biographisches Porträt*, Freiburg, Basel and Vienna, 2009

Schmidt, Ulf, *Hitlers Arzt Karl Brandt: Medizin und Macht im Dritten Reich*, Berlin, 2009

Schmidt, Rainer F., *Rudolf Hess: "Botengang eines Toren"? Der Flug nach Grossbritannien vom 10. Mai 1941*, Düsseldorf, 1997

Schmidt, Rainer F., *Die Aussenpolitik des Dritten Reiches 1933–1939*, Stuttgart, 2002

Schmidt, Rainer F., "Der Hess-Flug und das Kabinett Churchill: Hitlers Stellvertreter im Kalkül der britischen Kriegsdiplomatie Mai–Juni 1941," in *Vierteljahrshefte für Zeitgeschichte*, 42 (1994), pp. 1–38

Schmiechen-Ackermann, Detlef (ed.), *"Volksgemeinschaft": Mythos, wirkungsmächtige soziale Verheissung oder soziale Realität im "Dritten Reich"?*, Paderborn, 2012

Schmitt-Imkamp, Lioba, *Roderich Fick (1886–1955)*, Vienna, Cologne and Weimar, 2014

Schneider, Michael, *In der Kriegsgesellschaft: Arbeiter und Arbeiterbewegung 1939 bis 1945*, Bonn, 2014

Schneppen, Heinz, *Walther Rauff: Organisator der Gaswagenmorde*, Berlin, 2011

Schönherr, Klaus, "Die Rückzugskämpfe in Rumänien und Siebenbürgen im Sommer/ Herbst 1944," in *Das Deutsche Reich und der Zweite Weltkrieg*, vol. 8, Munich, 2001, pp. 731–848

Schönherr, Klaus, "Der Rückzug aus Griechenland," in *Das Deutsche Reich und der Zweite Weltkrieg*, vol. 8, Munich, 2001, pp. 1089–99

Schramm, Percy Ernst, *Hitler als militärischer Führer: Erkenntnisse und Erfahrungen aus dem Kriegstagebuch des Oberkommandos der Wehrmacht*, Frankfurt am Main, 1962

Schreiber, Gerhard, *Die italienischen Militärinternierten im deutschen Machtbereich 1943 bis 1945: Verraten—verachtet—vergessen*, Munich, 1990

Schreiber, Gerhard, *Deutsche Kriegsverbrechen in Italien: Täter—Opfer—Strafverfolgung*, Munich, 1996

Schreiber, Gerhard, "Das Ende des nordafrikanischen Feldzugs und der Krieg in Italien 1943 bis 1945," in *Das Deutsche Reich und der Zweite Weltkrieg*, vol. 8, Munich, 2001, pp. 1100–62

Schüle, Annegret, *Industrie und Holocaust: Topf & Söhne—Die Ofenbauer von Auschwitz*, Göttingen, 2010

Schwarz, Birgit, *Geniewahn: Hitler und die Kunst*, Vienna, Cologne and Weimar, 2009

Schwarz, Birgit, *Auf Befehl des Führers: Hitler und der NS-Kunstraub*, Darmstadt, 2014

Schwarz, Eberhard, *Die Stabilisierung der Ostfront nach Stalingrad: Mansteins Gegenschlag zwischen Donez und Dnepr im Frühjahr 1943*, Göttingen and Zurich, 1986

Schwendemann, Heinrich, "'Verbrannte Erde'? Hitlers 'Nero-Befehl' vom 19. März 1945," in *Kriegsende in Deutschland*, Hamburg, 2005, pp. 158–67

Seidler, Franz W., *Fritz Todt: Baumeister des Dritten Reiches*, Munich and Berlin, 1986

Seidler, Franz W. and Dieter Zeigert, *Die Führerhauptquartiere: Anlagen und Planungen im Zweiten Weltkrieg*, Munich, 2000

Sereny, Gitta, *Albert Speer: His Battle with Truth*, new edition, London, 1998

Shirer, William L., *The Rise and Fall of the Third Reich*, London, 1998

Sifton, Elisabeth and Fritz Stern, *Keine gewöhnlichen Männer: Dietrich Bonhoeffer und Hans von Dohnanyi im Widerstand gegen Hitler*, Munich, 2013

Smelser, Ronald, *Robert Ley: Hitlers Mann an der "Arbeitsfront." Eine Biographie*, Paderborn, 1989

Smelser, Ronald and Rainer Zitelmann (eds), *Die braune Elite: 22 biographische Skizzen*, Darmstadt, 1989

Smelser, Ronald, Enrico Syring and Rainer Zitelmann (eds), *Die braune Elite II: 21 weitere biographische Skizzen*, Darmstadt, 1993

Smith, Helmut Walser, *Fluchtpunkt 1941: Kontinuitäten der deutschen Geschichte*, Stuttgart, 2010

Snyder, Timothy, *Bloodlands: Europe between Hitler and Stalin*, London, 2010

Snyder, Timothy, *Black Earth: The Holocaust as History and Warning*, London, 2015

Sösemann, Bernd (ed.), *Der Nationalsozialismus und die deutsche Gesellschaft*, Stuttgart and Munich, 2002

Spoerer, Mark, *Zwangsarbeit unter dem Hakenkreuz: Ausländische Zivilarbeiter, Kriegsgefangene und Häftlinge im Dritten Reich und im besetzten Europa 193–1945*, Stuttgart, 2001

Stargardt, Nicholas, *The German War: A Nation under Arms, 1939–1945*, London, 2015

Steinbacher, Sybille, *Auschwitz: Geschichte und Nachgeschichte*, Munich, 2004

Steinbacher, Sybille (ed.), *Holocaust und Völkermorde: Die Reichweite des Vergleichs*, Frankfurt am Main and New York, 2012

Steinert, Marlies, *Hitlers Krieg und die Deutschen: Stimmung und Haltung der deutschen Bevölkerung im Zweiten Weltkrieg*, Düsseldorf and Vienna, 1970

Streit, Christian, *Keine Kameraden: Die Wehrmacht und die sowjetischen Kriegsgefangenen 1941–1945*, new edition, Bonn, 1991

Stumpf, Reinhard, "Der Krieg im Mittelmeerraum 1942/43," in *Das Deutsche Reich und der Zweite Weltkrieg*, vol. 6, Stuttgart, 1990, pp. 595–647

Süss, Dietmar, *Tod aus der Luft: Kriegsgesellschaft und Luftkrieg in Deutschland und England*, Munich, 2011

Süss, Dietmar, *'Ein Volk, ein Reich, ein Führer": Die deutsche Gesellschaft im Dritten Reich*, Munich, 2017

Süss, Winfried, *Der "Volkskörper" im Krieg: Gesundheitspolitik, Gesundheitsverhältnisse und Krankenmord im nationalsozialistischen Deutschland 1939–1945*, Munich, 2003

Taylor, Frederick, *Coventry: Thursday, 14 November 1940*, London, 2015

Tesch, Sebastian, *Albert Speer (1905–1981)*, Vienna, Cologne and Weimar, 2016

Thamer, Hans-Ulrich, *Verführung und Gewalt: Deutschland 1933–1945*, Berlin, 1986

Thamer, Hans-Ulrich and Simone Erpel (eds.), *Hitler und die Deutschen: Volksgemeinschaft und Verbrechen*, Dresden, 2011

Thamer, Hans-Ulrich, "Der tote Hitler: Das Ende des Diktators und die Wandlungen eines Mythos," in Thomas Grossböltig and Rüdiger Scheidt (ed.), *Der Tod des Diktators: Ereignis und Erinnerung im 20. Jahrhundert*, Göttingen, 2011, pp. 81–93

Töppel, Roman, *Kursk 1943: Die grösste Schlacht des Zweiten Weltkriegs*, Paderborn, 2017

Töppel, Roman, "Kursk—Mythen und Wirklichkeit einer Schlacht," in *Vierteljahrshefte für Zeitgeschichte*, 57 (2009), pp. 349–84

Toland, John, *Adolf Hitler*, 2 vols, Bergisch Gladbach, 1981

Tooze, Adam, *The Wages of Destruction: The Making and Breaking of the Nazi Economy*, London, 2006

Trevor-Roper, Hugh R., *The Last Days of Hitler*, 7th edition, London, 2012

Trommer, Isabell, *Rechtfertigung und Entlastung: Albert Speer in der Bundesrepublik*, Frankfurt am Main and New York, 2016

Ueberschär, Gerd R. (ed.), *Hitlers militärische Elite*, 2 vols, Darmstadt, 1998

Ueberschär, Gerd R. and Winfried Vogel, *Dienen und Verdienen: Hitlers Geschenke an seine Eliten*, Frankfurt am Main, 1999

Ueberschär, Gerd R., *Der 20. Juli 1944*, Frankfurt am Main, 2004

Ueberschär, Gerd R. and Wolfram Wette, *Der deutsche Überfall auf die Sowjetunion: "Unternehmen Barbarossa" 1941*, new and expanded edition, Frankfurt am Main, 2011

Ullrich, Sebastian, *Der Weimar-Komplex: Das Scheitern der ersten deutschen Demokratie und die politische Kultur der frühen Bundesrepublik 1945–1959*, Göttingen, 2009

Ullrich, Volker, *Der Kreisauer Kreis*, Reinbek bei Hamburg, 2008

Ullrich, Volker, *Die nervöse Grossmacht: Aufstieg und Untergang des deutschen Kaiserreichs*, new edition, Frankfurt am Main, 2013

Ullrich, Volker, *Hitler: Ascent 1889–1939*, London, 2016

Ullrich, Volker, " 'Wir haben nichts gewusst': Ein deutsches Trauma," in *1999. Zeitschrift für Sozialgeschichte des 20. und 21. Jahrhunderts*, 6 (1991), pp. 11–46

Umbreit, Hans, "Der Kampf um die Vormachtstellung im Westen," in *Das Deutsche Reich und der Zweite Weltkrieg*, vol. 2, Stuttgart, 1979, pp. 235–327

Ungváry, Krisztián, "Kriegsschauplatz Ungarn," in *Das Deutsche Reich und der Zweite Weltkrieg*, vol. 8, Munich, 2001, pp. 849–958

Urban, Thomas, *Katyn: Geschichte eines Verbrechens*, Munich, 2015

Vaget, Hans Rudolf, *"Wehvolles Erbe": Richard Wagner in Deutschland. Hitler, Knappertsbusch, Mann*, Frankfurt am Main, 2017

Valentin, Sonja, *"Steine in Hitlers Fenster": Thomas Manns Radiosendungen* Deutsche Hörer! *1940–1945*, Göttingen, 2015

Völklein, Ulrich (ed.), *Hitlers Tod: Die letzten Tage im Führerbunker*, Göttingen, 1999

Vogel, Detlef, "Das Eingreifen Deutschlands auf dem Balkan," in *Das Deutsche Reich und der Zweite Weltkrieg*, vol. 3, Stuttgart, 1984, pp. 417–511

Vogel, Detlev, "Deutsche und alliierte Kriegführung im Westen," in *Das Deutsche Reich und der Zweite Weltkrieg*, vol. 7, Stuttgart and Munich, 2001, pp. 419–639

Walker, Mark, *Die Uranmaschine: Mythos und Wirklichkeit der deutschen Atombombe*, Berlin, 1990

Wachsmann, Nikolaus, *Gefangen unter Hitler: Justizterror und Strafverfolgung im NS-Staat*, Munich, 2004

Wachsmann, Nikolaus, *KL: Die Geschichte der nationalsozialistischen Konzentrationslager*, Munich, 2016

Wegner, Bernd, "Der Krieg gegen die Sowjetunion 1942/43," in *Das Deutsche Reich und der Zweite Weltkrieg*, vol. 6, Stuttgart 1990, pp. 761–1102

Wegner, Bernd, "Von Stalingrad nach Kursk," in *Das Deutsche Reich und der Zweite Weltkrieg*, vol. 8, Munich, 2007, pp. 3–79

Wegner, Bernd, "Das Kriegsende in Skandinavien," in *Das Deutsche Reich und der Zweite Weltkrieg*, vol. 8, Munich, 2007, pp. 961–1005

Wegner, Bernd, "Deutschland am Abgrund," in *Das Deutsche Reich und der Zweite Weltkrieg*, vol. 8, Munich, 2007, pp. 1165–1209

Wegner, Bernd, "Hitlers Besuch in Finnland: Das geheime Tonprotokoll seiner Unterredung mit Mannerheim am 4. Juni 1942," in *Vierteljahrshefte für Zeitgeschichte*, 41 (1993), pp. 117–38

Wegner, Bernd, "Hitler, der Zweite Weltkrieg und die Choreographie des Untergangs," in *Geschichte und Gesellschaft*, 26 (2000), pp. 493–518

Wehler, Hans-Ulrich, *Deutsche Gesellschaftsgeschichte*, vol. 4, Munich, 2003

Wehler, Hans-Ulrich, "Hitler als historische Figur," in *idem, Land ohne Unterschichten? Neue Essays zur deutschen Geschichte*, Munich, 2010, pp. 92–105

Weinberg, Gerhard L., *Eine Welt in Waffen: Die globale Geschichte des Zweiten Weltkriegs*, Stuttgart, 1995

Wendt, Bernd-Jürgen, *Grossdeutschland: Aussenpolitik und Kriegsvorbereitung des Hitler-Regimes*, Munich, 1987

Werr, Sebastian, *Heroische Weltsicht: Hitler und die Musik*, Cologne, Weimar and Vienna, 2014

Wette, Wolfram and Gerd R. Ueberschär, *Stalingrad: Mythos und Wirklichkeit einer Schlacht*, Frankfurt am Main, 1992

Wette, Wolfram, *Die Wehrmacht: Feindbilder, Vernichtungskrieg, Legenden*, Frankfurt am Main, 2002

Wette, Wolfram, *Karl Jäger: Mörder der litauischen Juden*, Frankfurt am Main, 2011

Wette, Wolfram, "Die propagandistische Begleitmusik zum deutschen Überfall auf die Sowjetunion am 22. Juni 1941," in Ueberschär and Wette (eds), *Der deutsche Überfall auf die Sowjetunion*, pp. 45–65

Wiborg, Susanne and Jan Peter Wiborg, *Glaube, Führer, Hoffnung: Der Untergang der Clara S.*, Munich, 2015

Winik, Jay, *1944: Roosevelt und das Jahr der Entscheidung*, Darmstadt, 2017

Wildt, Michael, *Generation des Unbedingten: Das Führungskorps des Reichssicherheitshauptamtes*, Hamburg, 2002

Winkler, Heinrich August, *Der lange Weg nach Westen*, 2 vols, Munich, 2000

Winkler, Heinrich August, *Geschichte des Westens. Vol 2: Die Zeit der Weltkriege 1914–1945*, Munich, 2011

Wirsching, Andreas, "Hitlers Authentizität: Eine funktionalistische Deutung," in *Vierteljahrshefte für Zeitgeschichte*, 64 (2016), pp. 387–417

Woller, Hans, *Die Abrechnung mit dem Faschismus in Italien 1943 bis 1948*, Munich, 1996

Woller, Hans, *Geschichte Italiens im 20. Jahrhundert*, Munich, 2010

Woller, Hans, *Mussolini: Der erste Faschist. Eine Biographie*, Munich, 2016

Wrochem, Oliver von, *Erich von Manstein: Vernichtungskrieg und Geschichtspolitik*, Paderborn, 2006

Wuermeling, Henric L., *August 1939—11 Tage zwischen Krieg und Frieden*, Munich, 1984

Zaslavsky, Victor, *Klassensäuberung: Das Massaker von Katyn*, Berlin, 2007

Zeidler, Werner, *Kriegsende im Osten: Die Rolle der Roten Armee und die Besetzung Deutschlands östlich der Oder und Neisse 1944/45*, Munich, 1996

Zeidler, Werner, "Die Rote Armee auf deutschem Boden," in *Das Deutsche Reich und der Zweite Weltkrieg*, vol. 10/1, Munich, 2008, pp. 681–775

Zierenberg, Malte, *Stadt der Schieber: Der Berliner Schwarzmarkt 1939–1950*, Göttingen, 2008

Zimmermann, John, "Die deutsche militärische Kriegführung im Westen 1944/45," in *Das Deutsche Reich und der Zweite Weltkrieg*, vol. 10/1, Munich, 2008, pp. 277–489

Acknowledgements

I have many people to thank for the fact that the concluding volume of this biography could appear in Germany in the autumn of 2018 and is now also available in English translation. My gratitude begins with the staff of the archives who offered their friendly assistance during my research: Beatrix Diestel at the Bundesarchiv-Militärarchiv in Freiburg, Annegret Neupert at the Bundesarchiv in Koblenz, Torsten Zarwel at the Bundesarchiv in Berlin-Lichterfelde, Klaus A. Lankheit at the Institute for Contemporary History in Munich and Marlies Hertig at the Schweizerisches Bundesarchiv in Bern.

Once again I must thank Mirjam Zimmer and Kerstin Wilhelms at the documentation department of *Die Zeit* newspaper and Karl-Otto Schütt, the librarian at the Forschungsstelle für Zeitgeschichte in Hamburg, who were very helpful to me in procuring literature.

In addition, I am grateful to Walter H. Pehle, editor of many years at S. Fischer, who saw the project he originally suggested through to its conclusion with constant friendly attention, reading the manuscript and selecting the pictures. Thanks are also due to his successor Tanja Hommen for her thorough editing.

I owe particular thanks to my colleague at *Die Zeit*, Benedikt Erenz, who went over the page proofs with the practiced eyes of an editor and whose critical suggestions greatly benefitted the text.

My greatest thanks, however, go to my wife, Gudrun, and my son, Sebastian, with whom I had many long conversations during my eight-year engagement with this terrible figure. Without their constant encouragement, questions and suggestions, this second volume would also never have been written.

Last but not least, I would like to thank Jefferson Chase for another very dedicated translation and Jörg Hensgen for seeing this volume through with great care to publication with The Bodley Head.

Volker Ullrich
Hamburg
November 2019

Index

STALIN

The Court of the Red Tsar

by Simon Sebag Montefiore

This widely acclaimed biography of Stalin and his entourage during the terrifying decades of his supreme power transforms our understanding of Stalin as Soviet dictator, Marxist leader, and Russian tsar. Based on groundbreaking research, Simon Sebag Montefiore reveals the fear and betrayal, privilege and debauchery, family life and murderous cruelty of this secret world. Written with bracing narrative verve, this feat of scholarly research has become a classic of modern history writing. Showing how Stalin's triumphs and crimes were the products of his fanatical Marxism and his gifted but flawed character, this is an intimate portrait of a man as complicated and human as he was brutal and chilling.

History

LENIN

The Man, the Dictator, and the Master of Terror

by Victor Sebestyen

Victor Sebestyen's riveting biography of Vladimir Ilyich Lenin—the first major biography in English in nearly two decades—is not only a political examination of one of the most important historical figures of the twentieth century but also a fascinating portrait of Lenin the man. Brought up in comfort and with a passion for hunting and fishing, chess, and the English classics, Lenin was radicalized after the execution of his brother in 1887. Sebestyen traces the story from Lenin's early years to his long exile in Europe and return to Petrograd in 1917 to lead the first Communist revolution in history. Uniquely, Sebestyen has discovered that throughout Lenin's life his closest relationships were with his mother, his sisters, his wife, and his mistress. The long-suppressed story told here of the love triangle that Lenin had with his wife, Nadezhda Krupskaya, and his beautiful, married mistress and comrade, Inessa Armand, reveals a more complicated character than that of the coldly one-dimensional leader of the Bolshevik Revolution. With Lenin's personal papers and those of other leading political figures now available, Sebestyen gives new details that bring to life the dramatic and gripping story of how Lenin seized power in a coup and ran his revolutionary state. In *Lenin*, Victor Sebestyen has written a brilliant portrait of this dictator as a complex and ruthless figure, and he also brings to light important new revelations about the Russian Revolution, a pivotal point in modern history.

Biography

AMERICAN PROMETHEUS
The Triumph and Tragedy of J. Robert Oppenheimer
by Kai Bird and Martin J. Sherwin

J. Robert Oppenheimer is one of the iconic figures of the twentieth century, a brilliant physicist who led the effort to build the atomic bomb for his country in a time of war, and who later found himself confronting the moral consequences of scientific progress. In this magisterial, acclaimed biography twenty-five years in the making, Kai Bird and Martin J. Sherwin capture Oppenheimer's life and times, from his early career to his central role in the Cold War. This is biography and history at its finest, riveting and deeply informative.

Biography

ONE MINUTE TO MIDNIGHT
Kennedy, Khrushchev, and Castro on the Brink of Nuclear War
by Michael Dobbs

In October 1962, at the height of the Cold War, the United States and the Soviet Union came to the brink of nuclear conflict over the placement of Soviet missiles in Cuba. In this hour-by-hour chronicle of those tense days, veteran *Washington Post* reporter Michael Dobbs reveals just how close we came to Armageddon. Here, for the first time, are gripping accounts of Khrushchev's plan to destroy the U.S. naval base at Guantánamo; the handling of Soviet nuclear warheads on Cuba; and the extraordinary story of a U-2 spy plane that got lost over Russia at the peak of the crisis. Written like a thriller, *One Minute to Midnight* is an exhaustively researched account of what Arthur Schlesinger Jr. called "the most dangerous moment in human history," and the definitive book on the Cuban missile crisis.

History